# BENSON and HEDGES
# Cricket Year
THIRD EDITION

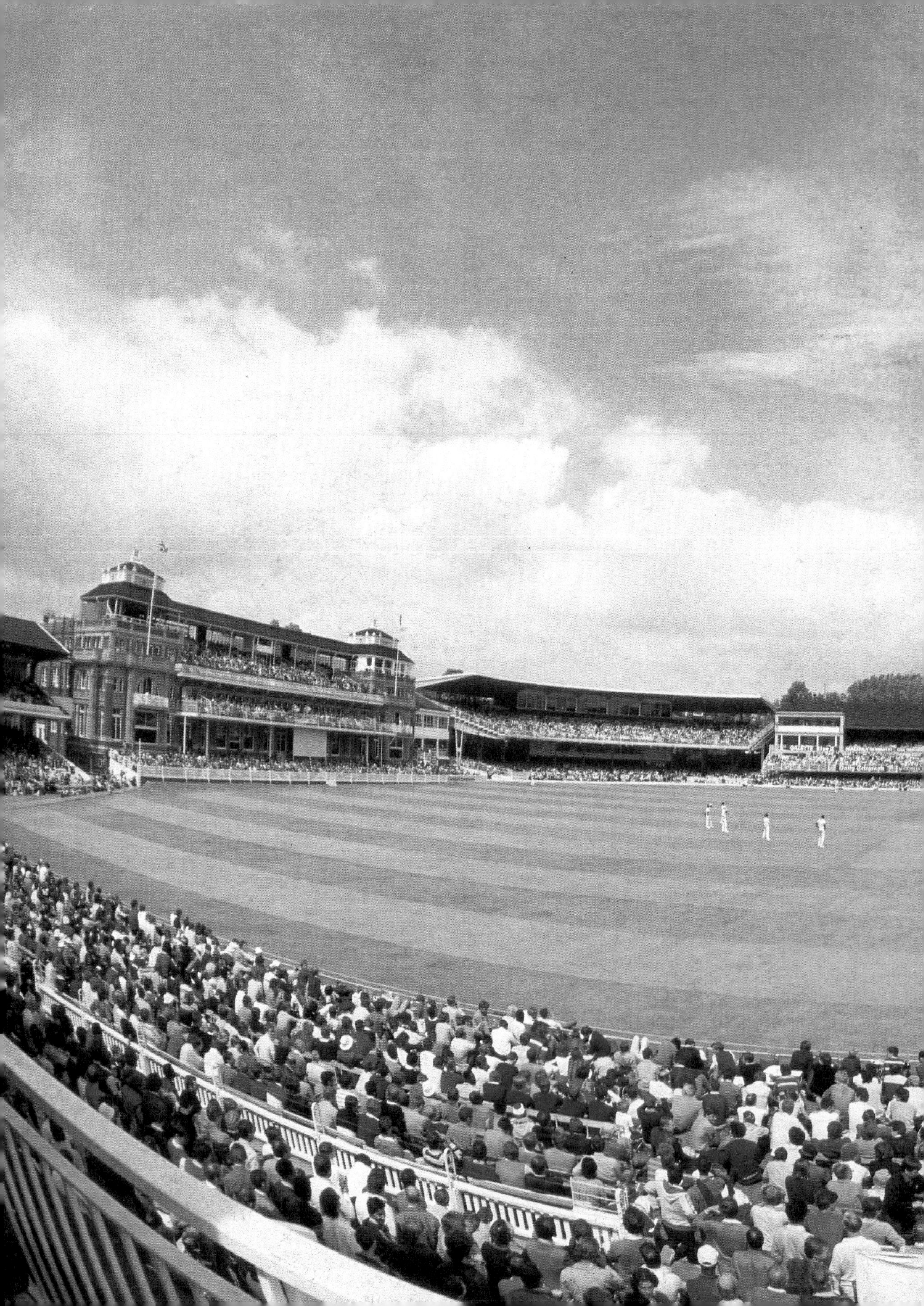

# BENSON and HEDGES
# Cricket Year

**THIRD EDITION**

*October 1983 to September 1984*

Editor David Lemmon
Associate Editor Tony Lewis

PELHAM BOOKS

First published in Great Britain by
Pelham Books Ltd
44 Bedford Square
London WC1B 3DP
1984



British Library Cataloguing in Publication Data
Benson and Hedges cricket year. – 3rd ed.
1. Cricket – Periodicals
796.35′8′05 GV911

ISBN 0-7207-1546-6

Filmset in Times and Univers by MS Filmsetting Limited, Frome, Somerset
Printed and bound in Great Britain by Blantyre Printing and Binding Company Limited, Glasgow

## Editor's Note

The aim of *Benson and Hedges Cricket Year* is that the cricket enthusiast shall be able to read through the happenings in world cricket, from each October until the following September (the end of the English season). Form charts are printed and a player's every appearance will be given on these charts, and date and place allow those appearances to be readily found in the text.

The symbol * indicates 'not out' or 'wicket-keeper' according to the context and the symbol † indicates captain.

The editor wishes to express his deepest thanks to Victor Isaacs, the Hampshire C.C.C. scorer, for his corrections and advice in the preparation of the English Counties form charts which appear at the end of this book.

Mr Isaacs is one of the country's leading statisticians, with particular reference to limited-over cricket. His research and pursuit of accuracy are renowned and we are deeply indebted to him.

Thanks are also due to Brian Croudy, Brian Heald, Barry MacAuley and Qamar Ahmed.

Unless otherwise stated, all the comments and written material in the book are the work of the editor who also compiles the statistics.

Julian Knight

## Sponsor's message

The *Benson and Hedges Cricket Year* has now established itself as an authoritative report on first class cricket played around the world during the previous year. As with the first two editions, this Third Edition is available just two months after the close of the English season – providing a winter reminder of past triumphs and tragedies for all enthusiasts and those professionally involved in the game.

Paul Rutherford

PAUL RUTHERFORD
Director, Benson and Hedges

# Comment

## Are the West Indies Legal?

### Tony Lewis

The past year proved again that there are two types of cricket, the one played by the West Indies, the other by everyone else. The West Indies won series against India, Australia and England, never losing a match.

They did it mainly by fast bowling which was often pitched short and directed well above the stumps to the batsman's head. By including so many fast bowlers who relentlessly through a day's play base their attack on intimidation as much as skill, they have distorted the very nature of the game. No longer is the object to bowl at wickets in order to knock them over, it is to shock batsmen into a rushed defensive jumble of gloves, helmets and bat-handlers.

Andy Roberts, Colin Croft, Michael Holding, Malcolm Marshall, Wayne Daniel, Winston Davis, Joel Garner, unwittingly, by their high speed and by an eye for the maximum effect, have turned batting into an attritious war of self-defence.

Illegal? The Cricket Law, Law 42, is clear. It comes under the heading Unfair Play no 8.

'The bowling of fast, short-pitched balls is unfair if, in the opinion of the umpire at the bowler's end, it constitutes an attempt to intimidate the striker. Umpires shall consider intimidation to be the deliberate bowling of fast short-pitched balls which by their length, height and direction are intended or likely to inflict physical injury on the striker. The relative skill of the striker shall also be taken into consideration.'

There follows the system of progressive warnings which leads to the umpire removing an offending bowler from the attack.

Defenders of the West Indies will argue that their world superiority comes from team-work, and they will be right, Clive Lloyd's is a splendid side. They will put forward Vivian Richard's genius; point out that Lloyd himself headed the batting averages in India, that Desmond Haynes averaged 93.60 against Australia, Richie Richardson 81.75 and Gordon Greenidge 78.60.

We can all follow that up with glorious descriptions of the two double centuries scored by Greenidge in the series against England, and of the quiet dedication of Larry Gomes.

Nor must one forget the all-round skills of Jeffrey Dujon or the considerable performances of the young off-spinner Roger Harper. Yet, we come back to the brutal, irresistible force which denies hope to any opponent – the high ingredient of physical intimidation in their bowling.

Now, wait a minute, I hear you say. How often have we heard short-pitched fast bowling praised? Alongside me in the BBC Radio Commentary box I hear Trevor Bailey congratulate Malcolm Marshall on sending down a 'beautiful bouncer' – and Trevor would have his own memories of Lindwall and Miller bouncers hitting him or flying past his temple.

In my playing days I have ducked under bouncers from Fred Trueman, Frank Tyson, Wesley Hall, Charlie Griffith, Brian Statham, John Snow and a host of others.

Batsmanship has always been to do with personal courage as well as skill. The bouncer was the legitimate surprise weapon in the fast bowler's armoury. Ah! Surprise. That is the difference.

What went wrong? Why do batsmen now walk to the crease, helmeted, padded with foam chest-protectors, forearm protectors and batting gloves like boxing gloves?

As far as England were concerned it began with Dennis Lillee and Jeff Thomson in 1974–75 on the tour to Australia led by Mike Denness. With Max Walker a third, lively fast-medium bowler, there was a day-long rotation of fast short-pitched bowling. Experienced and talented batsmen like John Edrich, Dennis Amiss, David Lloyd, Denness himself, Keith Fletcher, were never quite the same again. They were shell-shocked.

Lillee boasted that he aimed for the ribcage and he did. That was intimidation in speech and in action.

The Australians, however, would tell you that Ray Illingworth started the planned attacks on the body by instructing John Snow to greatly increase the number of short-pitched balls in Australia in 1971. We could go back to Douglas Jardine with Larwood and Voce in the 1930s.

The truth is that top class fast bowling is usually decisive and the more of it you have in your side, the more decisive your victories.

Back to Law 42, no 8. Why do the umpires not uphold it? There were warnings of West Indians during the summer in England, but the truth is probably that the strictest application of the law would be sensational, a volte-face, and the umpires rightly fear that their stand would not be supported by the Boards of Control.

The West Indies barrage of bowling aimed at the man not the stumps has become habit. The West Indies themselves would be the last to appreciate how they have eroded the pleasurable side of cricket.

It is time for the International Cricket Conference, which meets annually in London each summer, to argue the issue and pledge universal support for umpires by instructing them to eliminate intimidation from cricket.

The game has always been richest when bowlers are trying to hit wickets not batsmen, and as soon as they begin to do so again, the old skills will return of swing, flight, spin and seam, and batsmen will stop shuffling in defensive parries under suits of armour. They will all have the confidence to move to the ball again.

# Contents

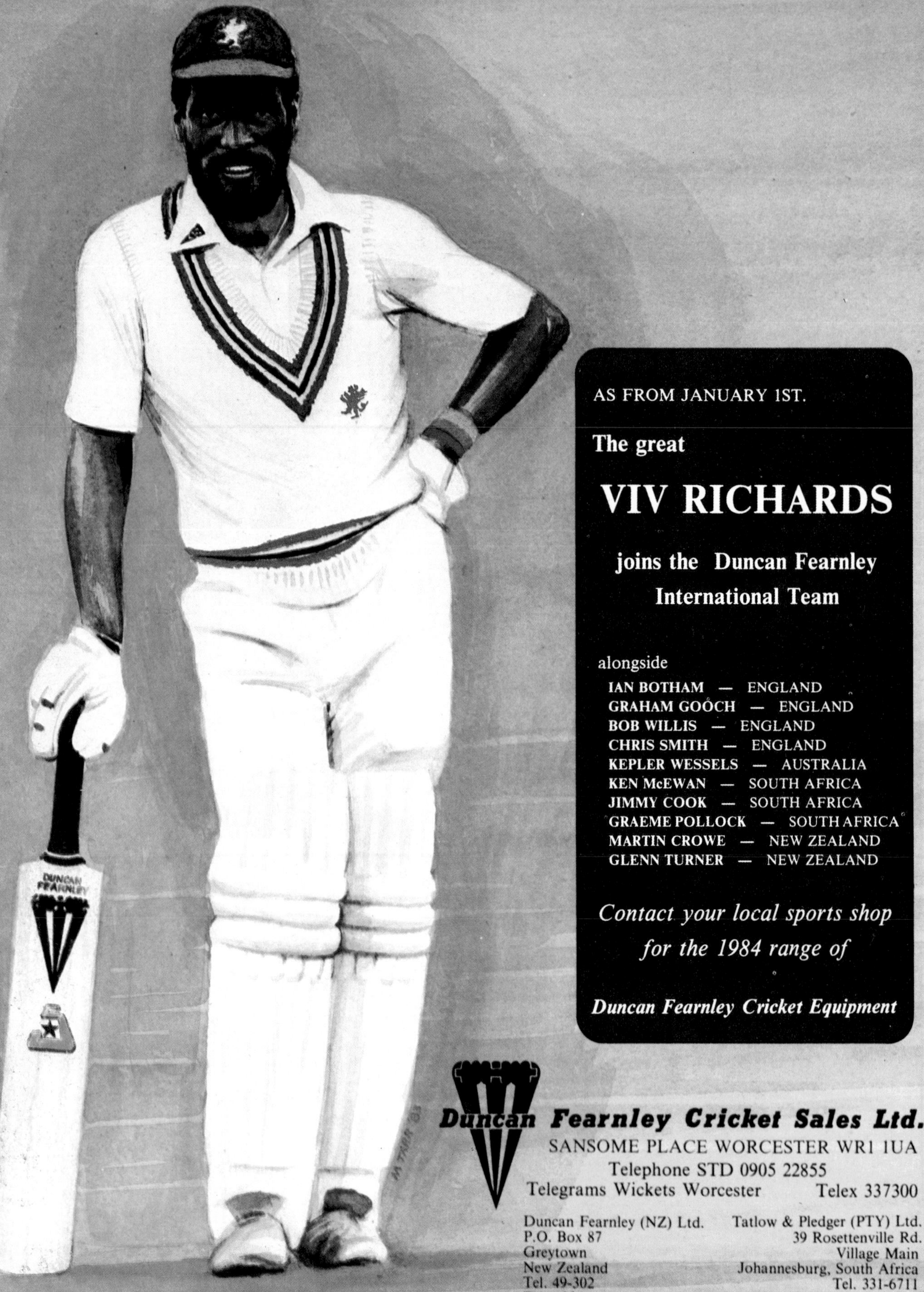
AS FROM JANUARY 1ST.
The great
VIV RICHARDS
joins the Duncan Fearnley
International Team
alongside
IAN BOTHAM — ENGLAND
GRAHAM GOOCH — ENGLAND
BOB WILLIS — ENGLAND
CHRIS SMITH — ENGLAND
KEPLER WESSELS — AUSTRALIA
KEN McEWAN — SOUTH AFRICA
JIMMY COOK — SOUTH AFRICA
GRAEME POLLOCK — SOUTH AFRICA
MARTIN CROWE — NEW ZEALAND
GLENN TURNER — NEW ZEALAND
Contact your local sports shop
for the 1984 range of
Duncan Fearnley Cricket Equipment
Duncan Fearnley Cricket Sales Ltd.
SANSOME PLACE WORCESTER WR1 1UA
Telephone STD 0905 22855
Telegrams Wickets Worcester
Telex 337300
Duncan Fearnley (NZ) Ltd.
P.O. Box 87
Greytown
New Zealand
Tel. 49-302
Telex 3316
Tatlow & Pledger (PTY) Ltd.
39 Rosettenville Rd.
Village Main
Johannesburg, South Africa
Tel. 331-6711
Telex 8-0840
DUNCAN FEARNLEY

# Bear essentials for every supporter.

**For Great Lager... Follow the Bear.**

# Idem Carbonless Paper. First for speed.

IDEM* is the quick answer to copies. Fast-moving business machines and their operators can both go the pace with Idem, because there are no extra interleaves to slow either of them down. Use Idem with Idem in manual, typewritten or computer-produced forms–ply after ply, with nothing added–for a speedy demonstration of why it's Europe's No. 1 carbonless paper, with the widest range available.

*IDEM is a trade mark of Wiggins Teape (UK) plc.

SECTION A

# The Decline and Fall of the World Champions

Cricket in India.
Test series and one-day international series *v.* Pakistan and West Indies.
Duleep and Ranji Trophy matches. Irani Cup.

The editor is greatly indebted to Sudhir Vaidya, the renowned statistician and chronicler of Indian cricket, for his help in compiling this section.

*Rolling the wicket at Bombay.*
*(Adrian Murrell)*

It took India fourteen years to play her first nine Test matches. In three and a half months at the end of 1983 she engaged in the same number. It took India four years and a World Cup tournament to play her first eight one-day internationals, the same number that she played between September and December, 1983. Such has been the growth of international cricket in the past decade.

The proliferation of international matches is something upon which the controllers of the game need to reflect with great soberness. Imran Khan, even before his injury, had said that he would not be available for the series against India as he needed a rest from international cricket before the arduous tour of Australia, and by the end of the six Test series against West Indies, Gavaskar, with records behind him, was talking of retirement and the need to enjoy his cricket away from the strain of continuous Test matches.

We are in grave danger of destroying what is, economically, the most lucrative part of the game by a surfeit. In excess most things cease to delight, and both players and spectators will be wearied by an unending diet of international cricket. There seemed to be little joy for Pakistan in their contests with India and the series was doomed to stalemate before it began.

The season began with the Irani Cup match in which Karnataka, holders of the Ranji Trophy, took on the Rest of India who were without both Gavaskar and Kapil Dev.

The champions began uneasily, losing the Viswanath brothers and Binny for 31, but Srinavas Prasad batted

*Roger Binny. His innings of 158 for Karnataka was the highlight of the Irani Cup Final. (Adrian Murrell)*

## IRANI CUP: KARNATAKA *v.* REST OF INDIA

1, 2, 3 and 4 September, 1983 at Race Course Stadium, Rajkot

**KARNATAKA**

| | FIRST INNINGS | | SECOND INNINGS | |
|---|---|---|---|---|
| R.M.H. Binny | b Valson | 17 | (5) c Vengsarkar, b Yadav | 158 |
| M. Srinivas Prasad | c Shastri, b Kulkarni | 117 | (1) c Amarnath, b Shastri | 20 |
| S. Viswanath* | c More, b Valson | 2 | (2) c Kulkarni, b Shastri | 14 |
| G.R. Viswanath | c. More, b Kulkarni | 2 | c Srikkanth, b Shastri | 15 |
| A.V. Jayaprakash | b Yadav | 40 | (3) c Srikkanth, b Yadav | 12 |
| B.P. Patel† | c Kulkarni, b Shastri | 25 | c Shastri, b Yashpal | 39 |
| B. Sudhakar Rao | c Khandkar, b Valson | 67 | c Khandkar, b Kulkarni | 62 |
| J. Abhiram | b Yadav | 7 | b Yadav | 50 |
| R. Khanvilkar | lbw, b Kulkarni | 29 | b Shastri | 17 |
| B. Vijaykrishna | c Valson, b Yadav | 1 | | |
| A.R.B. Bhat | not out | 23 | (10) not out | 0 |
| Extras | | 20 | | 18 |
| | | 350 | (for 9 wkts dec) | 405 |

| | O | M | R | W | O | M | R | W |
|---|---|---|---|---|---|---|---|---|
| Valson | 14 | 5 | 50 | 3 | 11 | 2 | 41 | — |
| Kulkarni | 17.4 | 2 | 57 | 3 | 18 | 2 | 73 | 1 |
| Yadav | 37 | 13 | 91 | 3 | 46 | 9 | 117 | 3 |
| Amarnath | 3 | 1 | 5 | — | | | | |
| Shastri | 39 | 9 | 111 | 1 | 22.2 | 5 | 101 | 4 |
| Yashpal Sharma | 3 | — | 7 | — | 21 | 4 | 41 | 1 |
| Patil | 2 | 1 | 9 | — | 3 | — | 10 | — |
| Srikkanth | | | | | 1 | — | 4 | — |

FALL OF WICKETS
1- 20, 2- 26, 3- 31, 4- 111, 5- 166, 6- 273, 7- 285, 8- 301, 9- 305
1- 36, 2- 39, 3- 53, 4- 69, 5- 143, 6- 283, 7- 361, 8- 400, 9- 405

**REST OF INDIA**

| | FIRST INNINGS | | SECOND INNINGS | |
|---|---|---|---|---|
| K. Srikkanth | c Jayaprakash, b Vijay | 34 | b Khanvilkar | 22 |
| S. Khandkar | c G. Viswanath, b Bhat | 19 | c Vijay, b Bhat | 37 |
| D.B. Vengsarkar | c Rao, b Vijay | 25 | c and b Bhat | 7 |
| M.B. Amarnath† | c Abhiram, b Vijay | 5 | not out | 66 |
| Yashpal Sharma | c S. Viswanath b Vijay | 76 | not out | 53 |
| S.M. Patil | c and b Bhat | 6 | | |
| R.J. Shastri | c and b Bhat | 0 | | |
| K. More* | c G. Viswanath, b Bhat | 3 | | |
| S.N. Yadav | c Abhiram, b Vijay | 5 | | |
| R. Kulkarni | c S. Viswanath, b Bhat | 2 | | |
| S. Valson | not out | 5 | | |
| Extras | | 5 | | 1 |
| | | 185 | (for 3 wkts) | 186 |

| | O | M | R | W | O | M | R | W |
|---|---|---|---|---|---|---|---|---|
| Binny | 9 | 2 | 21 | — | | | | |
| Khanvilkar | 4 | — | 17 | — | 9 | — | 48 | 1 |
| Bhat | 30.4 | 10 | 65 | 5 | 23 | 8 | 63 | 2 |
| Vijaykrishna | 29.1 | 9 | 63 | 5 | 8 | 4 | 21 | — |
| Sudhakar Rao | 5.2 | 1 | 14 | — | 3 | 2 | 4 | — |
| G.R. Viswanath | | | | | 9 | 1 | 31 | — |
| Srinivas Prasad | | | | | 4 | 1 | 12 | — |
| Abhiram | | | | | 1 | — | 6 | — |

FALL OF WICKETS
1- 42, 2- 56, 3- 64, 4- 94, 5- 101, 6- 101, 7- 119, 8- 124, 9- 132
1- 46, 2- 55, 3- 88

**Match drawn – Karnataka won on first innings**

**FIRST ONE-DAY INTERNATIONAL: INDIA v. PAKISTAN**
10 September 1983 at Hyderabad

| PAKISTAN | | |
|---|---|---|
| Mohsin Khan | b Sandhu | 6 |
| Mudassar Nazar | c Kirmani, b Kapil Dev | 0 |
| Zaheer Abbas† | c Kirmani, b Sandhu | 20 |
| Javed Miandad | not out | 66 |
| Wasim Raja | c Kapil Dev, b Sandhu | 0 |
| Qasim Umar | c Kirmani, b Binny | 5 |
| Wasim Bari* | run out | 18 |
| Tahir Naqqash | c Amarnath, b Binny | 1 |
| Jalal-ud-Din | run out | 5 |
| Azeem Hafeez | not out | 5 |
| Mohammad Nazir | | |
| Extras | b 1, lb 2, w 18, nb 4 | 25 |
| (46 overs) | (for 8 wickets) | 151 |

| | O | M | R | W |
|---|---|---|---|---|
| Kapil Dev | 9 | 3 | 16 | 1 |
| Sandhu | 9 | 2 | 27 | 3 |
| Madan Lal | 10 | 2 | 22 | — |
| Binny | 8 | 1 | 34 | 2 |
| Amarnath | 10 | — | 27 | — |

FALL OF WICKETS
1- 0, 2- 23, 3- 35, 4- 36, 5- 62, 6- 123, 7- 129, 8- 136

| INDIA | | |
|---|---|---|
| S.M. Gavaskar | c Wasim Bari, b Mudassar | 33 |
| K. Srikkanth | lbw, b Jalal-ud-Din | 16 |
| M.B. Amarnath | not out | 60 |
| Yashpal Sharma | b Mudassar | 2 |
| S.M. Patil | c Javed Miandad, b Mudassar | 1 |
| Kirti Azad | c Wasim Raja, b Nazir | 7 |
| R.N. Kapil Dev† | c Mohsin Khan, b Azeem | 18 |
| R.M.H. Binny | not out | 0 |
| S. Madan Lal | | |
| S.M.H. Kirmani* | | |
| B.S. Sandhu | | |
| Extras | b 1, lb 3, w 10, nb 1 | 15 |
| (43 overs) | (for 6 wickets) | 152 |

| | O | M | R | W |
|---|---|---|---|---|
| Jalal-ud-Din | 8 | — | 34 | 1 |
| Tahir Naqqash | 5 | 1 | 16 | — |
| Mudassar Nazar | 10 | 4 | 17 | 3 |
| Azeem Hafeez | 10 | — | 43 | 1 |
| Mohammad Nazir | 10 | 1 | 27 | 1 |

FALL OF WICKETS
1- 30, 2- 69, 3- 77, 4- 81, 5- 113, 6- 151

**India won by 4 wickets**

steadily to score 117 out of 285 and, with solid contributions from the middle order, help Karnataka to a reasonable score.

It was the Karnataka bowlers who took the honours, however, as Raguram Bhat's slow left-arm and the medium pace of Vijaykrishna troubled all batsmen and took Karnataka to a first innings lead of 165 which would have been greater had not Yashpal Sharma, who batted splendidly, and Valson added 53 for the last wicket. Bhat's bowling performance was all the more meritorious in that he was forced to leave the field with nausea in the middle of one over but returned to take four more wickets.

Gundappa Viswanath became the first batsman to reach 1000 runs in Irani Cup matches, but the main honours went to Roger Binny who hit seventeen fours in a fine innings of 158. Sadly, Patel delayed his declaration until after lunch on the last day so that a draw became inevitable, Karnataka taking the cup on the first innings.

The Rest of India again had some problems before Amarnath and Yashpal Sharma restored sanity and Bhat reached 100 wickets in first-class cricket when he caught and bowled Vengsarkar.

### First One-Day International
### INDIA v. PAKISTAN

India played their first match in their own country since their triumph in the World Cup and fielded the same side that had won at Lord's. Their celebrations continued as they beat Pakistan with three overs and four wickets to spare.

Pakistan never totally recovered from losing Mudassar in Kapil Dev's second over and, although Javed batted sensibly, the Pakistan score of 151 did not seem likely to trouble India unduly.

Gavaskar and Srikkanth founded the Indian innings well and Mohinder Amarnath played with the same authority that he had shown in the World Cup in England. There was a

*Mohinder Amarnath's fine all-round cricket in the first one-day international against Pakistan was, sadly, the prelude to a miserable season. (Adrian Murrell)*

## FIRST TEST MATCH: INDIA *v.* PAKISTAN
14, 15, 17, 18 and 19 September 1983 at Bangalore

### INDIA

| | FIRST INNINGS | | SECOND INNINGS | |
|---|---|---|---|---|
| S.M. Gavaskar | lbw, b Tahir | 42 | not out | 103 |
| A.D. Gaekwad | b Mudassar | 11 | not out | 66 |
| M.B. Amarnath | b Mudassar | 4 | | |
| Yashpal Sharma | c Bari, b Mudassar | 16 | | |
| S.M. Patil | c Miandad, b Tahir | 6 | | |
| R.N. Kapil Dev† | c Mohsin, b Azeem | 0 | | |
| R.M.H. Binny | not out | 83 | | |
| S. Madan Lal | c Bari, b Azeem | 74 | | |
| S.M.H. Kirmani* | c Bari, b Tahir | 14 | | |
| S. Venkataraghavan | c Saleem, b Tahir | 5 | | |
| D.R. Doshi | lbw, b Tahir | 0 | | |
| Extras | b 1, lb 8, w 6, nb 5 | 20 | lb 4, w 1, nb 2 | 7 |
| | | 275 | (for no wkt) | 176 |

| | O | M | R | W | O | M | R | W |
|---|---|---|---|---|---|---|---|---|
| Tahir Naqqash | 34.5 | 11 | 76 | 5 | 17 | 2 | 54 | — |
| Azeem Hafeez | 39 | 11 | 102 | 2 | 8 | 2 | 20 | — |
| Mohammad Nazir | 10 | 2 | 26 | — | 21 | 4 | 47 | — |
| Mudassar Nazar | 23 | 6 | 44 | 3 | 2.1 | — | 19 | — |
| Iqbal Qasim | 13 | 7 | 18 | — | 12 | 2 | 29 | — |
| Zaheer Abbas | | | | | 1 | — | 3 | — |

FALL OF WICKETS
1- 38, 2- 42, 3- 72, 4-, 80, 5- 81, 6- 85, 7- 240, 8- 269, 9- 275

*Umpires:* Swaroop Kishen and M.V. Gothaskar

### PAKISTAN

| | FIRST INNINGS | |
|---|---|---|
| Mohsin Khan | c Kirmani, b Madan Lal | 17 |
| Mudassar Nazar | c Kirmani, b Kapil Dev | 25 |
| Saleem Malik | c Amarnath, b Kapil Dev | 5 |
| Javed Miandad | c sub (Srikkanth), b Madan Lal | 99 |
| Zaheer Abbas† | c Kapil Dev, b Madan Lal | 22 |
| Wasim Raja | b Doshi | 39 |
| Wasim Bari* | b Kapil Dev | 64 |
| Tahir Naqqash | b Kapil Dev | 1 |
| Iqbal Qasim | c Gaekwad, b Venkataraghavan | 9 |
| Azeem Hafeez | b Kapil Dev | 0 |
| Mohammad Nazir | not out | 0 |
| Extras | b 1, lb 4, nb 2 | 7 |
| | | 288 |

| | O | M | R | W |
|---|---|---|---|---|
| Kapil Dev | 29 | 6 | 68 | 5 |
| Madan Lal | 24 | 5 | 72 | 3 |
| Binny | 18 | 2 | 42 | — |
| Venkataraghavan | 21.1 | 4 | 49 | 1 |
| Doshi | 20 | 5 | 52 | 1 |

FALL OF WICKETS
1- 32, 2- 37, 3- 58, 4- 99, 5- 187, 6- 243, 7- 244, 8- 288, 9- 288

**Match drawn**

*Anshuman Gaekwad. The slowest double century maker in first-class cricket. (Adrian Murrell)*

minor crisis when Yashpal Sharma, Patil and Gavaskar fell for 12 runs, but Amarnath's determination and a brief flourish from Kapil Dev gave India a comfortable victory.

### First Test Match
### INDIA *v.* PAKISTAN

On winning the toss, Kapil Dev elected to bat, but rain and bad light restricted play on the first day to 117 minutes and from thereon a draw always seemed likely. India fielded the veteran spin pair, Doshi and Venkataraghavan, but it was the seam bowlers who took most of the honours with 18 of the 20 wickets that fell in the match.

India closed the shortened first day at 57 for 2, and in the last over before lunch on the second morning, Yashpal Sharma was magnificently caught down the leg-side by Wasim Bari to give Mudassar his third wicket of the innings. Tahir Naqqash bowled finely in the afternoon session and when Kapil Dev fell to Test debutant Azeem Hafeez for nought India were 81 for 5. Patil fell to Tahir five runs later as he slashed wildly and Pakistan were very much on top, but Binny and Madan Lal joined in a record seventh wicket stand for India–Pakistan matches of 155. They were not separated until Madan Lal played loosely at Azeem Hafeez ten minutes before lunch on the third day. Madan Lal had escaped early in his innings when Wasim Bari missed an easy chance. Roger Binny was left unbeaten on 83, his highest Test score.

Javed Miandad batted splendidly for Pakistan, but he detracted from his fine cricket with his constant taunting of Doshi. The bickering reached its climax when Javed stood out of his ground inviting Doshi to run him out. As the batsman had covered all three stumps, Doshi's only recourse was to throw the ball over his head to the wicket-keeper. Javed swatted at the ball as it passed above him and was severely reprimanded by the umpires. It is one of the great regrets of the modern game that Javed Miandad, one of its most accomplished players, finds it necessary to indulge in antics which bring credit neither to himself nor to cricket.

Wasim Bari batted as well as he has done in a Test for several years and Pakistan took a lead of 13, but the game had long since been set for a draw.

Gavaskar and Gaekwad began a somewhat meaningless second Indian innings and at 147 for 0 with 14 of the last 20 overs bowled, Zaheer led his team from the field believing that the game was over as 77 overs, the required number, had been bowled during the day. The umpires remained in the middle and insisted that the final 20 overs should be completed. The Pakistanis returned and Gavaskar reached his twenty-eighth Test century so drawing closer to Don Bradman's record, but the players left the field as soon as Gavaskar had reached his hundred, the umpires not insisting on the last over being completed.

## Second One-Day International
## INDIA *v.* PAKISTAN

The first floodlit international match to be played in India had a most fitting dramatic finale when Kirti Azad hit the third ball of the last over for four to give India victory by one wicket and to complete a personal triumph in the match.

There was a crowd of approximately 60,000 and a 24-minute disruption caused by a floodlight failure reduced the match from a sixty to a fifty over contest. Zaheer chose to bat first and Mohsin and Mudassar gave their side a fine start. It was only the off-spin of Kirti Azad which troubled the Pakistanis and stemmed the flow of runs.

Both Indian openers were run out with the score at 28 and wickets fell regularly so that with 35 overs gone, the home side were 101 for 7 and sliding quickly to defeat. It was then that Kirti Azad cut loose. He found an able partner in Madan Lal and the pair added 86 before Zaheer, who had bowled himself as a last resort, dismissed Madan Lal. Shastri fell with the scores level, but Kirti Azad, unquestionably the Man of the Match, stroked India to victory amid great excitement shortly after midnight.

Kirti Azad hit four sixes and six fours in his fine innings.

## Second Test Match
## INDIA *v.* PAKISTAN

For the first time Burlton Park, Jullundur was the venue for a Test match, but it was a match that will quickly be forgotten. There was no play possible on the third day and Zaheer refused to count that day as the rest day so that the match was doomed to a draw. Shoaib Mohammad, son of the great Hanif, and Qasim Umar, who had done so splendidly in the Quaid-e-Azam Trophy for Muslim Commercial Bank in 1982–3, came in the Pakistan side to make their Test debuts, and Shastri replaced Doshi in the Indian side.

Kapil Dev won the toss and asked Pakistan to bat on a grassy pitch. He had immediate reward when he trapped Mohsin lbw with the first ball of the match. In his second over the Indian captain accounted for Shoaib.

Qasim Umar looked solid, but when he was caught behind off Roger Binny Pakistan were 55 for 3. Zaheer now found a good partner in Javed Miandad who was still recovering from influenza and the pair added 46 before Zaheer was bowled as he charged at Shastri. Pakistan closed the day on a modest 185 for 7, but on the second day they moved into a strong position. They owed most to Wasim Raja who made his highest Test score and shared a Pakistani eighth wicket record against India of 95 with Tahir Naqqash.

Wasim Raja began circumspectly, but played some savage

**SECOND ONE-DAY INTERNATIONAL: INDIA *v.* PAKISTAN**
21 September 1983 at Jawaharlal Nehru Stadium, New Delhi

| PAKISTAN | | | |
|---|---|---|---|
| | Mohsin Khan | c Kapil Dev, b Azad | 50 |
| | Mudassar Nazar | c and b Azad | 65 |
| | Zaheer Abbas† | st Yashpal Sharma, b Azad | 11 |
| | Wasim Raja | not out | 38 |
| | Qasim Umar | not out | 19 |
| | Wasim Bari* | | |
| | Jalal-ud-Din | | |
| | Azeem Hafeez | | |
| | Mohammad Nazir | | |
| | Atiq-ur-Rehman | | |
| | Iqbal Qasim | | |
| | Extras | b 2, lb 6, w 6 | 14 |
| | (50 overs) | (for 3 wkts) | 197 |

| | O | M | R | W |
|---|---|---|---|---|
| Kapil Dev | 10 | 2 | 49 | — |
| Sandhu | 10 | 1 | 33 | — |
| Madan Lal | 8 | 1 | 22 | — |
| Binny | 10 | — | 39 | — |
| Kirti Azad | 10 | 1 | 28 | 3 |
| Amarnath | 2 | — | 12 | — |

FALL OF WICKETS
1- 108, 2- 130, 3- 145

| INDIA | | | |
|---|---|---|---|
| | K. Srikkanth | run out | 13 |
| | S.M. Gavaskar | run out | 2 |
| | M.B. Amarnath | c Wasim Bari b Jalal-ud-Din | 11 |
| | S.M. Patil | c Iqbal Qasim, b Nazir | 12 |
| | Yashpal Sharma* | b Mudassar | 12 |
| | R.N. Kapil Dev† | c Wasim Bari, b Mudassar | 6 |
| | Kirti Azad | not out | 71 |
| | R.M.H. Binny | st Wasim Bari, b Iqbal Qasim | 9 |
| | S. Madan Lal | c Nazir, b Zaheer Abbas | 35 |
| | R.J. Shastri | c Azeem Hafeez, b Zaheer Abbas | 2 |
| | B.S. Sandhu | not out | 0 |
| | Extras | b 1, lb 7, w 13, nb 7 | 28 |
| | (49.3 overs) | (for 9 wkts) | 201 |

| | O | M | R | W |
|---|---|---|---|---|
| Azeem Hafeez | 10 | 1 | 43 | — |
| Atiq-ur-Rehman | 2 | — | 4 | — |
| Jalal-ud-Din | 9 | 2 | 33 | 1 |
| Mudassar Nazar | 10 | 3 | 18 | 2 |
| Mohammad Nazir | 10 | 1 | 24 | 1 |
| Iqbal Qasim | 6 | — | 37 | 1 |
| Zaheer Abbas | 3.3 | — | 14 | 2 |

FALL OF WICKETS
1- 15, 2- 28, 3- 44, 4- 62, 5- 75, 6- 80, 7- 101, 8- 187, 9- 197

**India won by 1 wicket**

## SECOND TEST MATCH: INDIA *v.* PAKISTAN

24, 25, 26, 28 and 29 September, 1983 at Jullundur

**PAKISTAN**

| | FIRST INNINGS | | SECOND INNINGS | |
|---|---|---|---|---|
| Mohsin Khan | lbw, b Kapil Dev | 0 | not out | 7 |
| Shoaib Mohammad | c Kirmani, b Kapil Dev | 6 | not out | 6 |
| Qasim Umar | c Kirmani, b Binny | 15 | | |
| Zaheer Abbas† | b Shastri | 49 | | |
| Javed Miandad | c Shastri, b Kapil Dev | 66 | | |
| Mudassar Nazar | c sub, b Shastri | 24 | | |
| Wasim Raja | c Kirmani, b Shastri | 125 | | |
| Wasim Bari* | c Kirmani, b Kapil Dev | 0 | | |
| Tahir Naqqash | b Binny | 37 | | |
| Mohammad Nazir | run out | 2 | | |
| Azeem Hafeez | not out | 2 | | |
| Extras | b 3, lb 6, w 1, nb 1 | 11 | nb 3 | 3 |
| | | 337 | (for no wkt) | 16 |

| | O | M | R | W | O | M | R | W |
|---|---|---|---|---|---|---|---|---|
| Kapil Dev | 32 | 8 | 80 | 4 | 2 | — | 9 | — |
| Madan Lal | 20 | 4 | 61 | — | 1 | — | 1 | — |
| Binny | 16 | 1 | 69 | 2 | | | | |
| Shastri | 37.2 | 12 | 63 | 3 | 3 | 2 | 1 | — |
| Venkataraghavan | 28 | 5 | 55 | — | | | | |
| Patil | | | | | 2 | 1 | 2 | — |
| Gavaskar | | | | | 1 | — | 3 | — |

FALL OF WICKETS
1- 0, 2- 7, 3- 55, 4- 101, 5- 154, 6- 169, 7- 169, 8- 264, 9- 309

**INDIA**

| | FIRST INNINGS | |
|---|---|---|
| S.M. Gavaskar | b Azeem | 5 |
| A.D. Gaekwad | c and b Wasim Raja | 201 |
| M.B. Amarnath | c Bari, b Azeem | 7 |
| Yashpal Sharma | lbw, b Tahir | 7 |
| S.M. Patil | c Bari, b Tahir | 26 |
| R.J. Shastri | c Bari, b Azeem | 26 |
| R.M.H. Binny | b Zaheer | 54 |
| R.N. Kapil Dev† | lbw, b Wasim Raja | 4 |
| S. Madan Lal | c Bari, b Wasim Raja | 11 |
| S.M.H. Kirmani* | not out | 8 |
| S. Venkataraghavan | b Wasim Raja | 6 |
| Extras | b 2, lb 4, w 9, nb 4 | 19 |
| | | 374 |

| | O | M | R | W |
|---|---|---|---|---|
| Tahir Naqqash | 27 | 3 | 74 | 2 |
| Azeem Hafeez | 23 | 3 | 65 | 3 |
| Mudassar Nazar | 28 | 6 | 80 | — |
| Mohammad Nazir | 52 | 16 | 76 | — |
| Wasim Raja | 28 | 5 | 50 | 4 |
| Mohsin Khan | 5 | 2 | 9 | — |
| Zaheer Abbas | 6 | 1 | 14 | 1 |

FALL OF WICKETS
1- 5, 2- 20, 3- 73, 4- 137, 5- 209, 6- 330, 7- 345, 8- 353, 9- 368

*Umpires:* D.N. Dotiwala and B. Ganguli

**Match drawn**

shots later in his innings, particularly as he and Azeem Hafeez added 28 for the last wicket.

Azeem completed a good day when he dismissed both Gavaskar and Amarnath before the close with his fast-medium left-arm. As already stated, the third day was lost to rain and Zaheer's decision not to press for a result when the opportunity was offered to him was inexplicable. In Pakistan, Sarfraz Nawaz gave his reasons for the decision when, in an attack on the selectors, he stated that the reason that he had been omitted from the party to tour Australia was that he refused to agree to Pakistan's plan to play for three draws in the series with India.

The fourth day's play was dreadful. India moved from 37 for 2 to 201 for 4 in the 85 overs bowled. The fifth day was as bad as Anshuman Gaekwad reached 201 off 426 deliveries in 652 minutes, the slowest ever double century in first-class cricket. Pakistan dropped catches liberally and a dismal Test crawled to its end.

Wasim Raja followed his fine century with four wickets, the last of them being Venkataraghavan who was almost certainly playing his last Test match.

### Third One-Day International INDIA *v.* PAKISTAN

India completed their triumph over Pakistan in the one-day series with their third victory in as many matches.

Sandeep Patil, who had just been dropped from the Test side, responded to his rejection by the selectors with an innings of 51 off 28 deliveries which earned him the Man of the Match award.

Pakistan had begun well with Mohsin and Mudassar putting on 55 in 20 overs, but both openers and Javed Miandad fell as five runs were added. Zaheer rallied the innings with a hard-hit 48, but the final total of 166 was disappointing.

Gavaskar and Patil added 57 in just over eight overs for India's third wicket and the home side were able to cruise to victory with more than five overs to spare.

The experiment of counting wides and no-balls against the bowler's analysis which had been introduced in the Test series was extended to a limited-over international for the first time.

### Third Test Match INDIA *v.* PAKISTAN

Sandeep Patil earned a late recall to the Indian side when Mohinder Amarnath reported unfit on the first morning. Patil was flown from his home in Bombay and did not arrive at Nagpur until the evening of the first day of the match, but rain delayed the start until 50 minutes before tea and Kapil Dev won the toss for the third time in the series.

Resuming on the second day at 92 for 2, India went for quick runs in an attempt to force a result, but, although Pakistan seized the initiative when 3 wickets fell for 7 runs early in the day, Zaheer failed to press the advantage. He supported Mohammad Nazir, who was turning the ball appreciably, with defensive fields and medium pace support when Wasim Raja, successful in the previous Test with his leg-breaks, was not used.

The Pakistan innings began unpromisingly, but Javed,

## THIRD ONE-DAY INTERNATIONAL: INDIA *v.* PAKISTAN
2 October 1983 at Sawai Mansingh Stadium, Jaipur

**PAKISTAN**

| | | |
|---|---|---|
| Mohsin Khan | c Patil, b Madan Lal | 22 |
| Mudassar Nazar | b Binny | 27 |
| Zaheer Abbas† | lbw, b Kapil Dev | 48 |
| Javed Miandad | lbw, b Madan Lal | 1 |
| Wasim Raja | run out | 17 |
| Saleem Malik | c Azad, b Kapil Dev | 27 |
| Wasim Bari* | not out | 5 |
| Tahir Naqqash | run out | 0 |
| Jalal-ud-Din | c and b Madan Lal | 0 |
| Azeem Hafeez | run out | 7 |
| Mohammad Nazir | not out | 0 |
| Extras | lb 6, w 4, nb 2 | 12 |
| (46 overs) | (for 9 wickets) | 166 |

| | O | M | R | W |
|---|---|---|---|---|
| Kapil Dev | 10 | 2 | 33 | 2 |
| Sandhu | 10 | 1 | 36 | — |
| Madan Lal | 10 | 1 | 27 | 3 |
| Binny | 10 | — | 38 | 1 |
| Amarnath | 6 | — | 26 | — |

FALL OF WICKETS
1- 55, 2- 57, 3- 60, 4- 100, 5- 153, 6- 155, 7- 155, 8- 155, 9- 165

**INDIA**

| | | |
|---|---|---|
| S.M. Gavaskar | b Nazir | 41 |
| K. Srikkanth | b Jalal-ud-Din | 17 |
| M.B. Amarnath | b Tahir | 1 |
| S.M. Patil | c Mohsin, b Nazir | 51 |
| R.N. Kapil Dev† | c Wasim Bari, b Jalal-ud-Din | 9 |
| Kirti Azad | b Mudassar | 4 |
| Yashpal Sharma | not out | 23 |
| R.M.H. Binny | not out | 11 |
| S. Madan Lal | | |
| S.M.H. Kirmani* | | |
| B.S. Sandhu | | |
| Extras | b 4, lb 3, w 4, nb 1 | 12 |
| (40.4 overs) | (for 6 wickets) | 169 |

| | O | M | R | W |
|---|---|---|---|---|
| Azeem Hafeez | 6.4 | 2 | 24 | — |
| Jalal-ud-Din | 10 | 2 | 41 | 2 |
| Tahir Naqqash | 4 | — | 19 | 1 |
| Mudassar Nazar | 10 | — | 41 | 1 |
| Mohammad Nazir | 10 | 2 | 37 | 2 |

FALL OF WICKETS
1- 30, 2- 52, 3- 109, 4- 120, 5- 129, 6- 134

**India won by 4 wickets**

Zaheer and Mudassar provided stability in the middle order and the visitors took a first innings lead of 77. Once more India showed a willingness to attack and on the last afternoon came close to disaster as they slipped from 172 for 3 to 207 for 8. Madan Lal and Kirmani saved the match with an unbeaten stand of 55, but Zaheer's unwillingness to encourage his bowlers to attack and his defensive field-settings revealed that he had no thoughts other than drawing the match and the series 0–0. One must ponder on the wisdom of an annual Test series between the two countries if the leader

## THIRD TEST MATCH: INDIA *v.* PAKISTAN
5, 6, 8, 9 and 10 October 1983 at Nagpur

**INDIA**

| | FIRST INNINGS | | SECOND INNINGS | |
|---|---|---|---|---|
| S.M. Gavaskar | c Mudassar, b Azeem | 50 | c Mudassar, b Nazir | 64 |
| A.D. Gaekwad | c Bari, b Tahir | 6 | c Raja, b Nazir | 29 |
| D.B. Vengsarkar | c Bari, b Malik | 21 | c Mohsin, b Nazir | 40 |
| Yashpal Sharma | lbw, b Nazir | 13 | c Bari, b Azeem | 15 |
| S.M. Patil | c Raja, b Azeem | 6 | lbw, b Raja | 26 |
| R.N. Kapil Dev† | c Bari, b Mudassar | 32 | (8) st Bari, b Raja | 10 |
| R.J. Shastri | c Mudassar, b Azeem | 52 | (6) c Mudassar, b Nazir | 0 |
| Kirti Azad | c Mohsin, b Azeem | 11 | (7) c Zaheer, b Nazir | 0 |
| S. Madan Lal | c Malik, b Nazir | 5 | not out | 32 |
| S.M.H. Kirmani* | run out | 30 | not out | 31 |
| A.R.B. Bhat | not out | 0 | | |
| Extras | b 9, lb 6, w 1, nb 3 | 19 | b 7, lb 7, nb 1 | 15 |
| | | 245 | (for 8 wkts dec) | 262 |

| | O | M | R | W | O | M | R | W |
|---|---|---|---|---|---|---|---|---|
| Azeem Hafeez | 27 | 10 | 58 | 4 | 19 | 1 | 67 | 1 |
| Tahir Naqqash | 19.2 | 3 | 72 | 1 | 23 | 7 | 55 | — |
| Mudassar Nazar | 14 | 2 | 43 | 1 | | | | |
| Saleem Malik | 3 | — | 7 | 1 | | | | |
| Mohammad Nazir | 22 | 5 | 50 | 2 | 50 | 19 | 72 | 5 |
| Zaheer Abbas | | | | | 1 | 1 | 0 | — |
| Wasim Raja | | | | | 10 | 1 | 46 | 2 |
| Mohsin Khan | | | | | 3 | 1 | 7 | — |
| Javed Miandad | | | | | 1 | — | 1 | — |

FALL OF WICKETS
1- 27, 2- 66, 3- 96, 4- 103, 5- 103, 6- 171, 7- 190, 8- 205, 9- 242
1- 78, 2- 125, 3- 148, 4- 172, 5- 172, 6- 188, 7- 188, 8- 207

*Umpires:* S.R. Bose and M.G. Subramaniam

**Match drawn**

**PAKISTAN**

| | FIRST INNINGS | | SECOND INNINGS | |
|---|---|---|---|---|
| Mohsin Khan | c Kirmani, b Shastri | 44 | | |
| Shoaib Mohammad | c Yashpal, b Kapil Dev | 9 | | |
| Saleem Malik | lbw, b Kapil Dev | 0 | (3) not out | 0 |
| Javed Miandad | lbw, b Bhat | 60 | | |
| Zaheer Abbas† | c Kirmani, b Kapil Dev | 85 | | |
| Mudassar Nazar | st Kirmani, b Bhat | 78 | | |
| Wasim Raja | c Yashpal, b Shastri | 16 | | |
| Wasim Bari* | c Patil, b Shastri | 1 | | |
| Tahir Naqqash | c Gaekwad, b Shastri | 6 | (1) not out | 18 |
| Mohammad Nazir | not out | 13 | | |
| Azeem Hafeez | c Patil, b Shastri | 4 | (2) b Kirmani | 18 |
| Extras | b 1, lb 1, nb 4 | 6 | b 4, lb 1, nb 1 | 6 |
| | | 322 | (for 1 wkt) | 42 |

| | O | M | R | W | O | M | R | W |
|---|---|---|---|---|---|---|---|---|
| Kapil Dev | 27 | 8 | 68 | 3 | 1 | 1 | 0 | — |
| Madan Lal | 13 | 2 | 44 | — | | | | |
| Bhat | 39 | 16 | 65 | 2 | | | | |
| Kirti Azad | 25 | 7 | 68 | — | | | | |
| Shastri | 30.3 | 7 | 75 | 5 | | | | |
| Vengsarkar | | | | | 2 | — | 15 | — |
| Yashpal Sharma | | | | | 1 | — | 10 | — |
| Kirmani | | | | | 2 | — | 9 | 1 |
| Gaekwad | | | | | 1 | — | 3 | — |
| Gavaskar | | | | | 1 | 1 | 0 | — |

FALL OF WICKETS
1- 20, 2- 26, 3- 83, 4- 153, 5- 254, 6- 287, 7- 289, 8- 305, 9- 309
1- 42

*Mohammad Nazir of Pakistan. He took 5 for 72 in India's second innings in the third Test, but his international career was drawing to a close. (Adrian Murrell)*

of one side, either by his own judgement or by instructions given to him, adopts such a negative approach to the game. One must ponder too on the feelings of Iqbal Sikander who, although a member of the Pakistan party, did not play in a single match on the tour.

### *4, 5 and 6 October*

***at Jaipur***

**West Indians** 373 (C.H. Lloyd 85, R.A. Harper 70, P.J. Dujon 56, Gopal Sharma 8 for 155) and 104 for 1 (D.L. Haynes 67 not out)
**Central Zone** 204 (H.A. Gomes 4 for 30)
*Match drawn*

The West Indians began their tour indifferently when, having been put in to bat, their early batsmen struggled. There was, however, much substance from the middle order and Roger Harper suggested his all-round potential. The highlight of the West Indian innings was the bowling of off-spinner Gopal Sharma who had a career best 8 for 155. Lloyd decided not to enforce the follow-on and Haynes hit a six and seven fours in what was little more than batting practice.

### *8, 9 and 10 October*

***at Hyderabad***

**West Indians** 367 for 4 dec (I.V.A. Richards 109, C.G. Greenidge 66, H.A. Gomes 65 not out, D.L. Haynes 64) and 170 for 6 (M.D. Marshall 61)
**South Zone** 176 (L. Sivaramakrishnan 52)
*Match drawn*

## India *v.* Pakistan – Test Match Averages

**INDIA BATTING**

| | M | Inns | NOs | Runs | HS | Av | 100s | 50s |
|---|---|---|---|---|---|---|---|---|
| R.M.H. Binny | 2 | 2 | 1 | 137 | 83* | 137.00 | | 2 |
| A.D. Gaekwad | 3 | 5 | 1 | 313 | 201 | 78.25 | 1 | 1 |
| S.M. Gavaskar | 3 | 5 | 1 | 264 | 103* | 66.00 | 1 | 2 |
| S.M.H. Kirmani | 3 | 4 | 2 | 83 | 31* | 41.50 | | |
| S. Madan Lal | 3 | 4 | 1 | 122 | 74 | 40.66 | | 1 |
| R.J. Shastri | 2 | 3 | | 78 | 52 | 26.00 | | 1 |
| S.M. Patil | 3 | 4 | | 64 | 26 | 16.00 | | |
| Yashpal Sharma | 3 | 4 | | 51 | 16 | 12.75 | | |
| R.N. Kapil Dev | 3 | 4 | | 46 | 32 | 11.50 | | |
| M.B. Amarnath | 2 | 2 | | 11 | 7 | 5.50 | | |
| S. Venkataraghavan | 2 | 2 | | 11 | 6 | 5.50 | | |

Played in one Test: D.R. Doshi 0; D.B. Vengsarkar 21 and 40; Kirti Azad 11 and 0; A.R.B. Bhat 0*

**INDIA BOWLING**

| | Overs | Mds | Runs | Wkts | Av | Best | 5/inn |
|---|---|---|---|---|---|---|---|
| R.J. Shastri | 70.5 | 21 | 139 | 8 | 17.37 | 5/75 | 1 |
| R.N. Kapil Dev | 91 | 23 | 225 | 12 | 18.75 | 5/68 | 1 |
| R.M.H. Binny | 34 | 3 | 111 | 2 | 55.50 | 2/69 | |
| S. Madan Lal | 58 | 11 | 178 | 3 | 59.33 | 3/72 | |
| S. Venkataraghavan | 49.1 | 9 | 104 | 1 | 104.00 | 1/49 | |
| S.M. Gavaskar | 2 | 1 | 3 | 0 | — | | |

Bowled in one innings: D.R. Doshi 20–5–52–1; S.M. Patil 2–1–2–0; Kirti Azad 25–7–68–0; A.D. Gaekwad 1–0–3–0; D.B. Vengsarkar 2–0–15–0; A.R.B. Bhat 39–16–65–2; Yashpal Sharma 1–0–10–0; S.M.H. Kirmani 2–0–9–1
No-balls and wides were counted against the bowler. India bowled one wide and eleven no-balls.

**INDIA CATCHES**

9–S.M.H. Kirmani (ct 8/st 1); 2–A.D. Gaekwad, Yashpal Sharma, S.M. Patil and subs; 1–M.B. Amarnath, R.N. Kapil Dev and R.J. Shastri

**PAKISTAN BATTING**

| | M | Inns | NOs | Runs | HS | Av | 100s | 50s |
|---|---|---|---|---|---|---|---|---|
| Javed Miandad | 3 | 3 | | 225 | 99 | 75.00 | | 3 |
| Wasim Raja | 3 | 3 | | 180 | 125 | 60.00 | 1 | |
| Zaheer Abbas | 3 | 3 | | 156 | 85 | 52.00 | | 1 |
| Mudassar Nazar | 3 | 3 | | 127 | 78 | 42.33 | | 1 |
| Mohsin Khan | 3 | 4 | 1 | 68 | 44 | 22.66 | | |
| Wasim Bari | 3 | 3 | | 65 | 64 | 21.66 | | 1 |
| Tahir Naqqash | 3 | 4 | 1 | 62 | 37 | 20.66 | | |
| Mohammad Nazir | 3 | 3 | 2 | 15 | 13* | 15.00 | | |
| Shoaib Mohammad | 2 | 3 | 1 | 21 | 9 | 10.50 | | |
| Azeem Hafeez | 3 | 4 | 1 | 24 | 18 | 8.00 | | |
| Saleem Malik | 2 | 3 | 1 | 5 | 5 | 2.50 | | |

Played in one Test: Iqbal Qasim 9; Qasim Umar 15

**PAKISTAN BOWLING**

| | Overs | Mds | Runs | Wkts | Av | Best | 5/inn |
|---|---|---|---|---|---|---|---|
| Wasim Raja | 38 | 6 | 96 | 6 | 16.00 | 4/50 | |
| Zaheer Abbas | 8 | 2 | 17 | 1 | 17.00 | 1/14 | |
| Azeem Hafeez | 116 | 27 | 312 | 10 | 31.20 | 4/58 | |
| Mohammad Nazir | 155 | 46 | 271 | 7 | 38.71 | 5/72 | 1 |
| Tahir Naqqash | 121.1 | 26 | 331 | 8 | 41.37 | 5/76 | 1 |
| Mudassar Nazar | 67.1 | 14 | 186 | 4 | 46.50 | 3/44 | |
| Mohsin Khan | 8 | 3 | 16 | 0 | — | | |
| Iqbal Qasim | 25 | 9 | 47 | 0 | — | | |

Bowled in one innings: Saleem Malik 3–0–7–1; Javed Miandad 1–0–1–0

**PAKISTAN CATCHES**

12–Wasim Bari (ct 11/st 1); 4–Mudassar Nazar; 3–Mohsin Khan and Wasim Raja; 2–Saleem Malik; 1–Javed Miandad and Zaheer Abbas

No-balls and wides were counted against the bowler. Pakistan bowled 17 wides and 15 no-balls.

**FIRST ONE-DAY INTERNATIONAL: INDIA *v.* WEST INDIES**
13 October 1983 at Srinagar Stadium, Srinagar

| INDIA | | |
|---|---|---|
| S.M. Gavaskar | c Richards, b Marshall | 11 |
| K. Srikkanth | c Greenidge, b Harper | 40 |
| D.B. Vengsarkar | c Marshall, b Baptiste | 28 |
| Yashpal Sharma | c Haynes, b Harper | 7 |
| S.M. Patil | b Baptiste | 0 |
| R.N. Kapil Dev† | c Dujon, b Holding | 17 |
| Kirti Azad | c and b Harper | 21 |
| R.M.H. Binny | c Dujon, b Roberts | 10 |
| S. Madan Lal | run out | 13 |
| S.M.H. Kirmani* | not out | 8 |
| B.S. Sandhu | c Richards, b Marshall | 0 |
| Extras | | 21 |
| (41.2 overs) | | 176 |

| | O | M | R | W |
|---|---|---|---|---|
| Roberts | 9 | — | 26 | 1 |
| Marshall | 7.2 | 2 | 13 | 2 |
| Holding | 7 | — | 32 | 1 |
| Baptiste | 9 | 1 | 50 | 2 |
| Harper | 9 | 1 | 34 | 3 |

FALL OF WICKETS
1-19, 2-65, 3-80, 4-90, 5-114, 6-143, 7-151, 8-155, 9-176

| WEST INDIES | | |
|---|---|---|
| C.G. Greenidge | not out | 44 |
| D.L. Haynes | not out | 55 |
| I.V.A. Richards | | |
| H.A. Gomes | | |
| C.H. Lloyd† | | |
| P.J. Dujon* | | |
| E.A.E. Baptiste | | |
| R.A. Harper | | |
| M.D. Marshall | | |
| A.M.E. Roberts | | |
| M.A. Holding | | |
| Extras | lb 4, w 2, nb 3 | 9 |
| (22.4 overs) | (for no wicket) | 108 |

| | O | M | R | W |
|---|---|---|---|---|
| Kapil Dev | 5 | 1 | 12 | — |
| Sandhu | 7 | — | 10 | — |
| Madan Lal | 6.4 | — | 51 | — |
| Binny | 4 | — | 26 | — |

**West Indies won on faster scoring rate**

After the West Indian batsmen, led by the dashing Viv Richards, had imposed themselves upon the game, South Zone, with seven Test players in their side, wilted badly against the pace of Roberts and Baptiste and closed the second day at 58 for 5. Young Sivarakrishnan provoked a mild recovery on the last morning and with West Indies once more declining to enforce the follow-on, the match limped to a draw with Marshall taking the opportunity to hit some lusty blows after his colleagues had failed.

### First One-Day International
### INDIA *v.* WEST INDIES

In the first meeting of the sides since the Prudential World Cup Final at Lord's, West Indies totally outplayed India and gained some semblance of revenge.

Lloyd won the toss and asked India to bat first on a fast wicket in misty weather. Both Gavaskar and Srikkanth struggled painfully against the West Indian pace-men and Gavaskar was taken at slip off Marshall. Srikkanth survived with some luck and was fifth out at 114. He was the second of Harper's victims and the off-spinner once more revealed that he was a worthwhile addition to the West Indian side.

All out in the forty-second over, India had to endure some bad behaviour from a crowd of 25,000 who chose to abuse and pelt the national side with fruit after their batting failure. The spectators become more unruly as Greenidge and Haynes completely dominated the Indian attack to score at nearly five an over. Eventually, the match was abandoned in the twenty-third over of the West Indian innings because of bad light and the visitors were declared winners on a scoring rate of 4.76 as opposed to the Indian rate of 3.52.

RIGHT: *Roger Harper. An international debut at Srinagar and an impressive all-rounder throughout the tour. (Adrian Murrell)*

*15, 16 and 17 October*

***at Amritsar***

**North Zone** 291 for 5 dec (Navjot Singh 122, Yashpal Sharma 55) and 175 for 5 dec (A. Malhotra 52 not out)
**West Indians** 217 for 7 dec (P.J. Dujon 55 not out) and 122 for 5 (I.V.A. Richards 61)
*Match drawn*

Although lacking some of their leading players, notably Kapil Dev, North Zone, the Duleep Trophy holders, caused the West Indians great misgivings in the match at Amritsar. Twenty-year-old student Navjot Singh batted splendidly as he combined sound defence with a willingness to hit the ball when the opportunity presented itself. He shared century stands with Gursharan Singh and skipper Yashpal Sharma before being stumped off Harper. Dujon had five dismissals in the match and kept wicket well.

The West Indians received more shocks when sixteen-year-old Chetan Sharma, already bowling at a fast medium pace, bowled both Greenidge and Richards. Maninder Singh also bowled well and, Dujon and Richardson apart, the visitors struggled.

North Zone batted briskly in their second innings and Yashpal Sharma hit five sixes, four of them in succession off the bowling of Richards. Set to make to 250, West Indies were inspired by a dashing innings from Richards, but Chetan Sharma again shocked them, dismissing Richardson, Gomes and Greenidge in his 7 overs at a cost of 33 runs so that he finished with match figures of 5 for 94.

## First Test Match
## INDIA *v.* WEST INDIES

The West Indians suffered a blow on the eve of the match when Roberts injured his back during net practice and was forced to withdraw from the side. It was decided to include Eldine Baptiste as his replacement rather than Harper as the wicket was fast and green. Baptiste won his first Test cap, but Harper could consider himself rather unlucky for he had played well in the matches leading up to the first Test.

Lloyd won the toss and somewhat surprisingly decided to bat first. It was apparent from Kapil Dev's first delivery which left Greenidge beaten that the pitch would aid the quick bowlers and that the batsmen needed to play with care and patience. Greenidge was willing to do this, but Haynes drove loosely at Kapil Dev and was caught in the gully. Richards batted with an arrogance similar to the style he had adopted in the World Cup final and in 42 minutes he hit five fours before edging to Kirmani at the end of Kapil Dev's opening spell. Gomes batted for over an hour without ever looking settled and although Lloyd batted with caution, he fell to a splendid delivery from Bhat and with Logie also falling before tea, West Indies were struggling at 157 for 5.

Greenidge had now achieved mastery over the attack, however, and Dujon batted with ease and grace that mocked the earlier struggles. They continued their stand into the second day and Greenidge, in an innings which lasted 522 minutes, made his highest score in Test cricket. The pair added 152 before Dujon was bowled by Binny and then Marshall came in to play a blistering innings. Marshall was to cause India even greater distress when he took the ball at

**FIRST TEST MATCH: INDIA *v.* WEST INDIES**
**21, 22, 23 and 25 October 1983 at Kanpur**

**WEST INDIES**

| | FIRST INNINGS | |
|---|---|---|
| C.G. Greenidge | c Kirmani, b Amarnath | 194 |
| D.L. Haynes | c Madan Lal, b Kapil Dev | 6 |
| I.V.A. Richards | c Kirmani, b Kapil Dev | 24 |
| H.A. Gomes | c Gaekwad, b Shastri | 21 |
| C.H. Lloyd† | c Kirmani, b Bhat | 23 |
| A.L. Logie | lbw, b Bhat | 0 |
| P.J. Dujon* | b Binny | 81 |
| M.D. Marshall | c and b Kapil Dev | 92 |
| E.A.E. Baptiste | run out | 6 |
| M.A. Holding | lbw, b Kapil Dev | 0 |
| W.W. Davis | not out | 0 |
| Extras | b 4, lb 2, nb 1 | 7 |
| | | 454 |

| | O | M | R | W |
|---|---|---|---|---|
| Kapil Dev | 25.2 | 3 | 99 | 4 |
| Madan Lal | 17 | 5 | 50 | — |
| Binny | 17 | 2 | 74 | 1 |
| Bhat | 34 | 6 | 86 | 2 |
| Shastri | 38 | 7 | 103 | 1 |
| Gaekwad | 1 | — | 6 | — |
| Amarnath | 7 | 1 | 30 | 1 |

FALL OF WICKETS
1- 9, 2- 58, 3- 102, 4- 157, 5- 157, 6- 309, 7- 439, 8- 449, 9- 450

**INDIA**

| | FIRST INNINGS | | SECOND INNINGS | |
|---|---|---|---|---|
| S.M. Gavaskar | c Dujon, b Marshall | 0 | c Davis, b Marshall | 7 |
| A.D. Gaekwad | c Dujon, b Marshall | 4 | c Richards, b Marshall | 5 |
| M.B. Amarnath | lbw, b Marshall | 0 | (6) b Davis | 0 |
| D.B. Vengsarkar | b Marshall | 14 | c Davis, b Marshall | 65 |
| S.M. Patil | c Richards, b Davis | 19 | b Davis | 3 |
| R.J. Shastri | c Dujon, b Davis | 0 | (7) not out | 46 |
| S.M.H. Kirmani* | b Holding | 20 | (9) b Holding | 14 |
| R.N. Kapil Dev† | c Gomes, b Baptiste | 27 | c Dujon, b Holding | 3 |
| R.M.H. Binny | c Richards, b Holding | 39 | (3) c Dujon, b Marshall | 7 |
| S. Madan Lal | not out | 63 | (10) b Holding | 0 |
| A.R.B. Bhat | b Holding | 0 | b Davis | 6 |
| Extras | b 6, lb 6, w 6, nb 3 | 21 | b 2, lb 2, w 1, nb 3 | 8 |
| | | 207 | | 164 |

| | O | M | R | W | O | M | R | W |
|---|---|---|---|---|---|---|---|---|
| Marshall | 15 | 7 | 19 | 4 | 17 | 7 | 47 | 4 |
| Holding | 14.4 | 6 | 37 | 3 | 19 | 2 | 59 | 3 |
| Davis | 13 | 2 | 57 | 2 | 16.3 | 3 | 46 | 3 |
| Baptiste | 11 | — | 58 | 1 | 6 | 1 | 8 | — |
| Gomes | 6 | — | 24 | — | | | | |

FALL OF WICKETS
1- 0, 2- 0, 3- 9, 4- 18, 5- 29, 6- 49, 7- 90, 8- 90, 9- 207
1- 8, 2- 13, 3- 38, 4- 43, 5- 43, 6- 105, 7- 109, 8- 135, 9- 143

*Umpires:* Swaroop Kishen and B. Ganguli

**West Indies won by an innings and 83 runs**

the beginning of the Indian innings. In his first five overs he took 4 wickets for 5 runs. The first to fall was Gavaskar, caught behind when he played well inside the line and from that point the innings disintegrated against Marshall's pace for India to end the second day at 34 for 5.

There was little sign of recovery on the third morning as Davis, Holding and Baptiste exerted pressure, but Binny and Madan Lal displayed a sense, courage and application lacking in the earlier batsmen with a ninth wicket stand of 117. It could not save the follow-on and Marshall again devastated the Indian openers so that the world champions ended the third day at 73 for 5 with Vengsarkar, 41 not out, looking to be the only batsman capable of withstanding the ferocity of the West Indian attack.

Predictably, West Indies achieved victory shortly after lunch on the fourth day. Marshall removed the elegant Vengsarkar who had looked a class above his colleagues and Holding accounted for the pockets of resistance as Baptiste was unable to bowl because of a stomach upset. Bhat and Shastri added 21 for the last wicket in 45 minutes which suggested that earlier batsmen could have achieved more.

*Malcolm Marshall. 92 and match figures of 8 for 66 at Kanpur and the scourge of India throughout the series. (Adrian Murrell)*

*Gordon Greenidge – 194, his highest score in Test cricket at Kanpur. (Adrian Murrell)*

### Second Test Match
### INDIA *v.* WEST INDIES

In his ninety-fifth Test match, Sunil Gavaskar scored his twenty-ninth Test century and so equalled Don Bradman's record which had been achieved in 52 Tests. Gavaskar batted with great panache on a placid pitch. He lost Gaekwad early, caught at third slip, but he never allowed the bowlers to dominate him. His fifty came off 37 balls and his hundred came when he on-drove Marshall for his thirteenth four. He also hit two sixes. It was exhilarating stuff.

Vengsarkar joined Gavaskar in a stand of 178 before the opener was bowled by Gomes when playing a casual shot. In all he hit fifteen fours. India closed the first day at 299 for 3 and Vengsarkar reached his highest Test score the next day in an innings which lasted 6 hours and 10 minutes. It seemed that India would fritter away the advantage given them by Gavaskar and Vengsarkar, but Binny played well after Amarnath, out of form and far from fit, had again failed.

Greenidge fell to Azad's quicker ball and West Indies slipped to 173 for 5 in spite of a violent assault by Viv Richards who hit a six and eight fours. Lloyd and Logie joined in a watchful stand of 131 which virtually made West Indies immune from defeat. Lloyd reached his sedate century on the fourth morning and the Indian lead was cut to 80. Kapil Dev bowled finely to record his best figures against the West Indies.

## SECOND TEST MATCH: INDIA *v.* WEST INDIES

29 and 30 October, 1, 2 and 3 November 1983 at New Delhi

### INDIA

| | FIRST INNINGS | | SECOND INNINGS | |
|---|---|---|---|---|
| S.M. Gavaskar | b Gomes | 121 | lbw, b Holding | 15 |
| A.D. Gaekwad | c Richards, b Holding | 8 | b Daniel | 32 |
| D.B. Vengsarkar | c Richards, b Holding | 159 | b Marshall | 63 |
| Yashpal Sharma | b Holding | 5 | lbw, b Daniel | 0 |
| R.J. Shastri | lbw, b Davis | 49 | lbw, b Holding | 26 |
| R.M.H. Binny | lbw, b Holding | 52 | b Daniel | 32 |
| M.B. Amarnath | c Dujon, b Daniel | 1 | c Davis, b Marshall | 0 |
| R.N. Kapil Dev† | c Lloyd, b Marshall | 18 | c Gomes, b Marshall | 0 |
| Kirti Azad | lbw, b Daniel | 5 | run out | 9 |
| S. Madan Lal | c sub, b Daniel | 3 | not out | 24 |
| S.M.H. Kirmani* | not out | 1 | c Logie, b Gomes | 3 |
| Extras | b 4, lb 9, w 2, nb 27 | 42 | b 5, lb 10, w 2, nb 12 | 29 |
| | | 464 | | 233 |

| | O | M | R | W | O | M | R | W |
|---|---|---|---|---|---|---|---|---|
| Marshall | 24 | 1 | 105 | 1 | 18 | 3 | 52 | 3 |
| Holding | 28.2 | — | 107 | 4 | 12 | 4 | 36 | 2 |
| Davis | 25 | 2 | 87 | 1 | 12 | 1 | 45 | — |
| Daniel | 21 | 1 | 86 | 3 | 15 | 3 | 38 | 3 |
| Gomes | 21 | 2 | 58 | 1 | 20.1 | 1 | 47 | 1 |
| Richards | 3 | 1 | 8 | — | | | | |

FALL OF WICKETS
1- 28, 2- 206, 3- 221, 4- 366, 5- 382, 6- 383, 7- 422, 8- 452, 9- 462
1- 20, 2- 73, 3- 73, 4- 133, 5- 151, 6- 152, 7- 153, 8- 166, 9- 218

### WEST INDIES

| | FIRST INNINGS | | SECOND INNINGS | |
|---|---|---|---|---|
| C.G. Greenidge | lbw, b Azad | 33 | not out | 72 |
| D.L. Haynes | c Sharma, b Kapil Dev | 12 | b Shastri | 17 |
| W.W. Davis | b Azad | 19 | | |
| I.V.A. Richards | lbw, b Kapil Dev | 67 | (3) c Gaekwad, b Shastri | 22 |
| H.A. Gomes | c Kirmani, b Shastri | 19 | (4) not out | 1 |
| C.H. Lloyd† | lbw, b Kapil Dev | 103 | | |
| A.L. Logie | c and b Kapil Dev | 63 | | |
| P.J. Dujon* | lbw, b Kapil Dev | 22 | | |
| M.D. Marshall | b Kapil Dev | 17 | | |
| M.A. Holding | b Shastri | 14 | | |
| W.W. Daniel | not out | 1 | | |
| Extras | b 5, lb 7, nb 2 | 14 | lb 4, w 1, nb 3 | 8 |
| | | 384 | (for 2 wickets) | 120 |

| | O | M | R | W | O | M | R | W |
|---|---|---|---|---|---|---|---|---|
| Kapil Dev | 31 | 2 | 77 | 6 | 7 | 2 | 26 | — |
| Madan Lal | 15 | 2 | 59 | — | 7 | — | 15 | — |
| Binny | 15 | 3 | 35 | — | 3 | — | 16 | — |
| Shastri | 38 | 7 | 106 | 2 | 17 | 3 | 36 | 2 |
| Kirti Azad | 26 | 5 | 84 | 2 | 14 | 4 | 22 | — |
| Gaekwad | 3 | 1 | 11 | — | 1 | 1 | 0 | — |
| Gavaskar | | | | | 1 | — | 1 | — |

FALL OF WICKETS
1- 44, 2- 45, 3- 112, 4- 153, 5- 173, 6- 304, 7- 331, 8- 357, 9- 370
1- 50, 2- 107

*Umpires:* M.V. Gothaskar and D.N. Dotiwala

**Match drawn**

India suffered a shock in their second innings when Gaekwad and Yashpal Sharma fell in the same over to Daniel who was making his return to Test cricket after an absence of seven years. At 73 for 3, India were in danger, but Vengsarkar again batted well and they closed at 145 for 4.

Malcolm Marshall struck severe blows against India on the last morning when he took 3 wickets in 11 balls and in 32 minutes the home side had slumped to 166 for 8 so that West Indies had a real chance of victory. Once more it was Binny and Madan Lal who saved the day for India with a stand of 52. Kirmani batted tenaciously to prolong the innings after the interval and West Indies were left an impossible task.

### *5, 6 and 7 November 1983*

#### *at Nagpur*

**West Indians** 257 (C.H. Lloyd 71, Maninder Singh 5 for 79) and 254 for 9 dec (M.R. Pydanna 59)
**President's XI** 214 (Navjot Singh 58, E.A. Baptiste 5 for 55) and 52 for 4

*Match drawn*

Some good spin bowling by Maninder Singh, Shivlal Yadav and, in the second innings, Sivaramakrishnan forced the West Indians into some introspective batting in a match which ended lamely. Dujon, Lloyd and Pydanna rescued the West Indian innings on the first day, and it was only Pydanna who brightened a dull second innings.

Navjot Singh faced 165 deliveries to reach a dour half-century for the President's XI who withstood the early attack of Roberts and Daniel, but fell to Baptiste who gave his best display of the tour as he achieved both pace and movement.

### Second One-Day International
### INDIA *v.* WEST INDIES

India, who were without Vengsarkar and Gavaskar, elected to bat on winning the toss, and, after an uncertain start, gave a solid display to reach 214 at more than four an over.

Greenidge, Man of the Match, and Haynes made a very brisk start, scoring 69 at over five an over. The spinners, Shastri and Azad, halted the flow of runs and accounted for both Greenidge and Richards so that, at 180 for 4, West Indies needed 35 off 46 deliveries. Clive Lloyd was in a ferocious mood, however, and his 31, including four fours and a six, came off 17 balls. After his dismissal 12 runs were needed from 5 overs and West Indies struggled to victory with 7 balls to spare.

### Third Test Match
### INDIA *v.* WEST INDIES

With Vengsarkar unfit and Mohinder Amarnath neither fully fit nor in any sort of form, India gave a first Test cap to Navjot Singh who had played two good innings against the tourists.

Kapil Dev won the toss and after much soul-searching and debate, he asked West Indies to bat first on a grassy wicket. He and Sandhu moved the ball appreciably and rendered the batsmen strokeless, but it was Roger Binny who captured the wickets. In the space of 14 deliveries he dismissed Haynes, Greenidge and Richards and left West Indies at 27 for 3. Well as Binny bowled, it was once more a case of lack of discipline on an uncertain wicket that brought about the West Indian decline. Unfortunately, Binny hurt his back during his devastating spell and did not bowl again in the match, a fact which had no small influence on the eventual outcome.

Lloyd and Gomes provided the West Indian innings with the discipline it had needed. They added 107 watchful runs before Gomes was taken at slip off the slow left-arm of Maninder Singh. Tea was then taken, but Logie went first ball on the resumption and, at 158, Lloyd's 168-minute innings ended when he was taken at short-leg, the first of four fine catches that substitute Gursharan Singh was to take in the match. Young Maninder Singh also accounted for Marshall, but Dujon rallied West Indies and the next day took his score to 90 before being last out. He batted for 192 minutes and faced 154 deliveries from which he hit fourteen fours. As both batsman and wicket-keeper, he matured considerably on this tour and now looks a player of Test class, realising the potential which he had shown when first appearing in the Benson and Hedges series in Australia. He was helped by some sensible batting from Winston Davis who stayed for 75 minutes and faced 75 balls while 51 runs were added for the last wicket. In the context of the match this was a vital contribution.

India responded majestically with an innings of great authority from Gavaskar. He and Gaekwad put on 127 for the first wicket before Gaekwad's off stump was knocked back by Holding and Gavaskar was taken at slip off the same bowler. Gavaskar's 90 was made in 182 minutes and included thirteen fours. It was made off only 120 deliveries. Most importantly, when he reached 83 he became the most prolific scorer in Test cricket beating Boycott's aggregate of 8114 made in 12 more Tests.

India finished the second day happily on 173 for 2. The joy did not last into the third day. As the pitch increased in

RIGHT: *Jeff Dujon. No West Indian player showed a greater advance on the tour. (Adrian Murrell)*

**SECOND ONE-DAY INTERNATIONAL: INDIA *v.* WEST INDIES**
9 November 1983 at Baroda

| WEST INDIES | | | |
|---|---|---|---|
| C.G. Greenidge | st Kirmani, b Azad | 63 |
| D.L. Haynes | b Madan Lal | 38 |
| I.V.A. Richards | c Gaekwad, b Shastri | 18 |
| H.A. Gomes | lbw, b Kapil Dev | 26 |
| C.H. Lloyd† | c Sandhu, b Kapil Dev | 31 |
| P.J. Dujon* | not out | 15 |
| M.D. Marshall | b Madan Lal | 3 |
| E.A.E. Baptiste | not out | 4 |
| R.A. Harper | | |
| A.M.E. Roberts | | |
| W.W. Daniel | | |
| Extras | b 7, lb 8, w 4 | 19 |
| (47.5 overs) | (for 6 wickets) | 217 |

| | O | M | R | W |
|---|---|---|---|---|
| Kapil Dev | 8.5 | 1 | 38 | 2 |
| Sandhu | 8 | — | 53 | — |
| Madan Lal | 9 | — | 39 | 2 |
| Binny | 2 | — | 16 | — |
| Shastri | 10 | 2 | 23 | 1 |
| Kirti Azad | 10 | 1 | 29 | 1 |

FALL OF WICKETS
1- 69, 2- 101, 3- 156, 4- 180, 5- 203, 6- 212

| INDIA | | |
|---|---|---|
| A.D. Gaekwad | c Dujon, b Daniel | 0 |
| K. Srikkanth | b Harper | 19 |
| R.J. Shastri | c Richards, b Gomes | 65 |
| S.M. Patil | c Gomes, b Baptiste | 31 |
| A.O. Malhotra | c Haynes, b Gomes | 29 |
| R.M.H. Binny | not out | 22 |
| R.N. Kapil Dev† | b Marshall | 15 |
| Kirti Azad | not out | 9 |
| S. Madan Lal | | |
| S.M.H. Kirmani* | | |
| B.S. Sandhu | | |
| Extras | b 5, lb 12, w 3, nb 4 | 24 |
| (49 overs) | (for 6 wickets) | 214 |

| | O | M | R | W |
|---|---|---|---|---|
| Roberts | 3 | 2 | 30 | — |
| Daniel | 8 | 1 | 23 | 1 |
| Marshall | 9 | — | 34 | 1 |
| Baptiste | 10 | 2 | 39 | 1 |
| Harper | 10 | — | 47 | 1 |
| Gomes | 3 | — | 17 | 2 |

FALL OF WICKETS
1- 7, 2- 47, 3- 116, 4- 157, 5- 167, 6- 189

**West Indies won by 4 wickets**

malevolence, as had been prophesied, so the bowlers dominated. Wayne Daniel destroyed any hope India had of taking a first innings lead and they were out half an hour after lunch.

Kapil Dev threw himself into the task of bowling India back into the match with a furious attack which exploited the unpredictability of the wicket and, had he had the necessary support, may well have won the game for India, but Binny was unable to bowl and Sandhu, in spite of dismissing Haynes, could neither stem the flow of runs from his end nor sustain a persistent attack on the batsmen. Lloyd and Dujon both batted well, but the disappointment for India was that, with West Indies at 114 for 7, Holding and Marshall batted through the last 40 minutes of a day in which 15 wickets had fallen to add 38 runs.

Kapil Dev, operating from the same end from which Daniel had had his best figures in Test cricket, took the last three wickets to fall in the West Indian innings and, having bowled unchanged, finished with his best figures of 9 for 83. He is only the third Indian to have taken 9 wickets in a Test match and the eleventh in the history of Test cricket. West Indies added 49 runs on the fourth morning, Marshall and Holding extending their eighth wicket stand to 74, a mighty contribution.

From the start of their second innings India batted like a

LEFT: *Kapil Dev – a magnificent 9 for 83 in the second innings of the third Test but still his side was beaten. (Adrian Murrell)*

## THIRD TEST MATCH: INDIA *v.* WEST INDIES

12, 13, 14 and 16 November 1983 at Motera Stadium, Ahmedabad

**WEST INDIES**

| | FIRST INNINGS | | SECOND INNINGS | |
|---|---|---|---|---|
| C.G. Greenidge | c Maninder, b Binny | 7 | b Kapil Dev | 3 |
| D.L. Haynes | lbw, b Binny | 9 | c Patil, b Sandhu | 1 |
| I.V.A. Richards | c Azad, b Binny | 8 | c sub (Gursharan) b Kapil Dev | 20 |
| H.A. Gomes | c Gavaskar b Maninder | 38 | lbw, b Kapil Dev | 25 |
| C.H. Lloyd† | c sub (Gursharan), b Maninder | 68 | c Gavaskar, b Kapil Dev | 33 |
| A.L. Logie | c Kirmani, b Maninder | 0 | lbw, b Kapil Dev | 0 |
| P.J. Dujon* | c Kapil Dev, b Shastri | 98 | c sub (Gursharan), b Kapil Dev | 20 |
| M.D. Marshall | b Maninder | 10 | c sub (Gursharan), b Kapil Dev | 29 |
| W.W. Daniel | run out | 6 | (10) b Kapil Dev | 0 |
| M.A. Holding | b Kapil Dev | 16 | (9) lbw, b Kapil Dev | 58 |
| W.W. Davis | not out | 3 | not out | 1 |
| Extras | b 8, lb 6, nb 4 | 18 | lb 9, nb 2 | 11 |
| | | 281 | | 201 |

| | O | M | R | W | O | M | R | W |
|---|---|---|---|---|---|---|---|---|
| Kapil Dev | 27 | 5 | 52 | 1 | 30.3 | 6 | 83 | 9 |
| Sandhu | 14 | 6 | 33 | — | 10 | 1 | 45 | 1 |
| Binny | 6 | — | 18 | 3 | | | | |
| Maninder Singh | 34 | 6 | 85 | 4 | 14 | 1 | 48 | — |
| Kirti Azad | 7 | — | 34 | — | 4 | 2 | 7 | — |
| Shastri | 16.3 | 2 | 45 | 1 | 2 | — | 9 | — |

FALL OF WICKETS
1- 16, 2- 22, 3- 27, 4- 134, 5- 134, 6- 158, 7- 168, 8- 190, 9- 230
1- 4, 2- 8, 3- 43, 4- 74, 5- 74, 6- 107, 7- 114, 8- 188, 9- 188

**INDIA**

| | FIRST INNINGS | | SECOND INNINGS | |
|---|---|---|---|---|
| S.M. Gavaskar | c Lloyd, b Holding | 90 | lbw, b Holding | 1 |
| A.D. Gaekwad | b Holding | 39 | b Davis | 29 |
| Navjot Singh | run out | 15 | c Dujon, b Holding | 4 |
| S.M. Patil | c Dujon, b Marshall | 22 | c Daniel, b Marshall | 1 |
| R.J. Shastri | c Lloyd, b Daniel | 13 | c Dujon, b Holding | 1 |
| R.M.H. Binny | c Haynes, b Davis | 5 | (8) c Greenidge, b Holding | 1 |
| R.N. Kapil Dev† | lbw, b Daniel | 31 | b Davis | 1 |
| Kirti Azad | b Daniel | 0 | (6) b Marshall | 3 |
| S.M.H. Kirmani* | c Haynes, b Daniel | 5 | not out | 24 |
| B.S. Sandhu | not out | 7 | lbw, b Davis | 1 |
| Maninder Singh | lbw, b Daniel | 0 | lbw, b Daniel | 15 |
| Extras | b 7, lb 4, nb 3 | 14 | b 6, lb 12, nb 4 | 22 |
| | | 241 | | 103 |

| | O | M | R | W | O | M | R | W |
|---|---|---|---|---|---|---|---|---|
| Marshall | 26 | 9 | 66 | 1 | 13 | 3 | 23 | 2 |
| Holding | 26 | 5 | 80 | 2 | 17 | 5 | 30 | 4 |
| Daniel | 11.5 | — | 39 | 5 | 6.1 | 2 | 11 | 1 |
| Davis | 11 | 3 | 23 | 1 | 11 | 2 | 21 | 3 |
| Gomes | 6 | — | 22 | — | | | | |

FALL OF WICKETS
1- 127, 2- 148, 3- 174, 4- 186, 5- 197, 6- 213, 7- 214, 8- 222, 9- 241
1- 1, 2- 7, 3- 8, 4- 24, 5- 27, 6- 38, 7- 39, 8- 61, 9- 63

*Umpires:* K.B. Ramaswamy and S.N. Hanumantha Rao

**West Indies won by 138 runs**

team without hope. The West Indian pace attack, often exploiting the vicious pitch by bowling short from round the wicket, demoralised them and but for a brave last wicket stand of 40 between Maninder Singh and the ever-courageous Kirmani, the humiliation would have been total.

Kapil Dev's magnificent bowling was overshadowed by his error in asking West Indies to bat first. Clive Lloyd complained about both the pitch and the umpires.

***19, 20 and 21 November 1983***

***at Kolhapur***

**West Indians** 417 for 9 dec (R.B. Richardson 77, D.L. Haynes 67, E.A. Baptiste 64 not out, A.L. Logie 56) and 205 for 7 (R.B. Richardson 61, S. Hazare 5 for 51)
**West Zone** 235 (G.A.M.H. Parkar 77, R.A. Harper 5 for 62)

*Match drawn*

When Viv Richards chose not to enforce the follow-on the West Indians' match against West Zone was doomed to a draw. The tourists took little benefit from the chance of batting practice offered to them as they squandered wickets to the leg-breaks of Sunjay Hazare. Richardson alone batted with sense in both innings and won his place in the West Indian Test side for the first time. Roger Harper, also pressing for a Test place, gave another good account of himself as an all-rounder.

West Zone were without Gavaskar who had been summoned to New Delhi to meet H.M. The Queen, but they began well with a stand of 109 between Parkar and Prasad Pradhan. The rest of the batsmen failed to cope with Harper's off-breaks after Winston Davis had made the initial break-through.

*Richie Richardson, who played himself into the Test side with two fine knocks, is caught bat and pad by Gunjal off Borde. More is the wicket-keeper. (Adrian Murrell)*

## Fourth Test Match
## INDIA *v.* WEST INDIES

India recalled Yadav and Malhotra to Test cricket and West Indies gave a first cap to Richardson.

India began excitingly in spite of Gavaskar being judged lbw somewhat harshly and Gaekwad and Vengsarkar added 133 in 28 overs with Vengsarkar in fluent form. Gaekwad was out half an hour after lunch, but Vengsarkar went on to reach his eighth Test century off 135 deliveries with thirteen fours. Immediately after reaching his hundred he aimed to square cut and was caught in the gully. The Indian innings now lost momentum. The end of the first day saw them at 259 for 4 and a laborious pace was continued into the second day, but Shastri and Binny provided a solidity which had previously been absent from the Indian middle order.

With the wicket turning, albeit slowly, the Indian score began to take on great proportions, particularly when Shivlal Yadav bowled Greenidge and had Richardson lbw second ball with his off-spin.

Richards defended until lunch and then after the interval launched a fierce attack on Yadav. Richards reached his hundred off 130 balls and hit a six and thirteen fours on the way, but he was twice missed. The only other success that India had on the third day was when Haynes, who had struggled for $3\frac{3}{4}$ hours, got an inside edge to a ball from Kapil Dev and brushed it away with his hand as it rolled towards his stumps so becoming the fourth batsman in the history of Test cricket to be dismissed 'handled ball'. West Indies closed at 204 for 3 and now seemed immune from defeat.

Kapil Dev bowled Gomes in the first over of the fourth morning and Indian hopes soared again, but dropped catches again dominated and Dujon and Lloyd again prospered, both batsmen showing the concentration and discipline necessary on the uncertain pitch. It must be emphasised though that Dujon, in particular, benefitted from some dreadful lapses by the Indian fielders.

*Desmond Haynes is run out by More for 67. (Adrian Murrell)*

*Vengsarkar turns Daniel past the diving Dujon on his way to his 100. (Adrian Murrell)*

*Viv Richards on his way to 120. (Adrian Murrell)*

West Indies trailed by 70 on the first innings and Gavaskar and Gaekwad fell before the close to suggest an interesting final day.

Malhotra and Shastri batted very well on the final morning and Kapil Dev declared leaving West Indies 156 minutes to make 244 to win on a worn wicket. Greenidge went in the first over. Richardson promised survival, but he was eager for runs and succumbed in pursuit of them. Richards, too, found the context not to his taste and West Indies were 48 for 3 with more than an hour to play. Haynes fell with 13 overs remaining, but there were to be no more signs of hope for India whose lapses in the field in the first innings had cost them dearly.

*Binny offers no shot at a ball from Marshall and is lbw. (Adrian Murrell)*

*Yadav has Richardson lbw for 0, one of the off-break bowler's five victims. (Adrian Murrell)*

## FOURTH TEST MATCH: INDIA v. WEST INDIES

24, 25, 26, 28 and 29 November 1983 at Bombay

**INDIA**

| | FIRST INNINGS | | SECOND INNINGS | |
|---|---|---|---|---|
| S.M. Gavaskar | lbw, b Marshall | 12 | c Davis, b Marshall | 3 |
| A.D. Gaekwad | b Holding | 48 | c Richards, b Holding | 3 |
| D.B. Vengsarkar | c Richards, b Davis | 100 | | |
| A.O. Malhotra | c Dujon, b Holding | 32 | (3) not out | 72 |
| R.J. Shastri | b Holding | 77 | (4) run out | 38 |
| R.M.H. Binny | lbw, b Marshall | 65 | (5) lbw, b Davis | 18 |
| R.N. Kapil Dev† | b Holding | 8 | (6) c Dujon, b Daniel | 1 |
| S. Madan Lal | lbw, b Marshall | 0 | (7) not out | 26 |
| S.M.H. Kirmani* | not out | 43 | | |
| S.N. Yadav | b Daniel | 12 | | |
| Maninder Singh | c Lloyd, b Holding | 9 | | |
| Extras | b 16, lb 14, w 1, nb 26 | 57 | b 1, lb 6, nb 5 | 12 |
| | | 463 | (for 5 wkts dec) | 173 |

| | O | M | R | W | O | M | R | W |
|---|---|---|---|---|---|---|---|---|
| Marshall | 32 | 6 | 88 | 3 | 13 | 3 | 47 | 1 |
| Holding | 40.5 | 10 | 102 | 5 | 11 | 1 | 39 | 1 |
| Davis | 36 | 3 | 127 | 1 | 8 | — | 35 | 1 |
| Daniel | 30 | 3 | 113 | 1 | 14 | 3 | 45 | 1 |
| Gomes | 4 | 1 | 3 | — | | | | |

FALL OF WICKETS
1- 12, 2- 145, 3- 190, 4- 234, 5- 361, 6- 372, 7- 373, 8- 385, 9- 433
1- 3, 2- 6, 3- 91, 4- 118, 5- 121

*Umpires:* M.V. Gothaskar and Swaroop Kishen

**WEST INDIES**

| | FIRST INNINGS | | SECOND INNINGS | |
|---|---|---|---|---|
| C.G. Greenidge | b Yadav | 13 | b Kapil Dev | 4 |
| D.L. Haynes | handled ball | 55 | b Maninder Singh | 24 |
| R.B. Richardson | lbw, b Yadav | 0 | b Shastri | 26 |
| I.V.A. Richards | st Kirmani, b Shastri | 120 | c Kirmani, b Shastri | 4 |
| H.A. Gomes | b Kapil Dev | 26 | not out | 37 |
| P.J. Dujon* | c Kirmani, b Yadav | 84 | | |
| C.H. Lloyd† | run out | 67 | (6) not out | 9 |
| M.D. Marshall | c Gavaskar, b Yadav | 4 | | |
| M.A. Holding | c and b Yadav | 2 | | |
| W.W. Daniel | c Gavaskar, b Shastri | 0 | | |
| W.W. Davis | not out | 4 | | |
| Extras | b 4, lb 8, nb 6 | 18 | | 0 |
| | | 393 | (for 4 wickets) | 104 |

| | O | M | R | W | O | M | R | W |
|---|---|---|---|---|---|---|---|---|
| Kapil Dev | 23 | 10 | 41 | 1 | 5 | 1 | 13 | 1 |
| Shastri | 35 | 8 | 98 | 2 | 13 | 4 | 32 | 2 |
| Maninder Singh | 27 | 7 | 71 | — | 15 | 7 | 25 | 1 |
| Madan Lal | 13 | 6 | 29 | — | 3 | 1 | 8 | — |
| Binny | 4 | 1 | 11 | — | | | | |
| Yadav | 44.1 | 8 | 131 | 5 | 12 | 5 | 22 | — |
| Gaekwad | | | | | 1 | — | 4 | — |
| Gavaskar | | | | | 1 | 1 | 0 | — |
| Malhotra | | | | | 1 | 1 | 0 | — |

FALL OF WICKETS
1- 47, 2- 47, 3- 128, 4- 205, 5- 238, 6- 357, 7- 377, 8- 383, 9- 384
1- 4, 2- 40, 3- 48, 4- 68

**Match drawn**

### Third One-Day International
### INDIA v. WEST INDIES

West Indies gained total revenge for their defeat in the Prudential World Cup Final when they beat India with 10 balls to spare to win the series 3–0.

India began badly. Srikkanth ran himself out, Gavaskar fell to a ball that lifted sharply and touched his glove and Arun Lal, returning to the international arena, mistimed a pull to make them 39 for 3.

## THIRD ONE-DAY INTERNATIONAL: INDIA v. WEST INDIES

1 December 1983 at Indore

**WEST INDIES**

| | | |
|---|---|---|
| C.G. Greenidge | lbw, b Kapil Dev | 96 |
| D.L. Haynes | st Kirmani, b Shastri | 54 |
| I.V.A. Richards | not out | 49 |
| C.H. Lloyd† | not out | 27 |
| H.A. Gomes | | |
| P.J. Dujon* | | |
| E.A. Baptiste | | |
| R.A. Harper | | |
| M.D. Marshall | | |
| A.M.E. Roberts | | |
| M.A. Holding | | |
| Extras | b 1, lb 12, nb 2 | 15 |
| (45.2 overs) | (for 2 wickets) | 241 |

| | O | M | R | W |
|---|---|---|---|---|
| Kapil Dev | 9.2 | 1 | 41 | 1 |
| Sandhu | 7 | — | 26 | — |
| Madan Lal | 9 | — | 36 | — |
| Binny | 3 | — | 26 | — |
| Shastri | 8 | 1 | 53 | 1 |
| Amarnath | 9 | — | 44 | — |

FALL OF WICKETS
1- 149, 2- 193

**INDIA**

| | | |
|---|---|---|
| S.M. Gavaskar | c Dujon, b Roberts | 15 |
| K. Srikkanth | run out | 0 |
| M.B. Amarnath | run out | 55 |
| J. Arun Lal | c Haynes, b Holding | 0 |
| A.O. Malhotra | c Harper, b Baptiste | 40 |
| R.N. Kapil Dev† | c Holding, b Harper | 28 |
| R.M.H. Binny | c and b Harper | 12 |
| R.J. Shastri | not out | 41 |
| S. Madan Lal | not out | 19 |
| S.M.H. Kirmani* | | |
| B.S. Sandhu | | |
| Extras | b 6, lb 8, w 11, nb 5 | 30 |
| (47 overs) | (for 7 wickets) | 240 |

| | O | M | R | W |
|---|---|---|---|---|
| Marshall | 9 | 1 | 27 | — |
| Roberts | 8 | — | 35 | 1 |
| Holding | 7 | 2 | 19 | 1 |
| Baptiste | 10 | — | 44 | 1 |
| Harper | 10 | — | 55 | 2 |
| Gomes | 2 | — | 30 | — |

FALL OF WICKETS
1- 3, 2- 32, 3- 39, 4- 123, 5- 153, 6- 172, 7- 180

**West Indies won by 8 wickets**

Amarnath, in a welcome show of return to form, batted fluently and he and Malhotra added 84 in 17 overs. Kapil Dev, Shastri and Madan Lal did not allow the run rate to slacken, and they were aided by a miscalculation from Lloyd who found that Gomes was left bowling an over more than was necessary, an over that cost 18 runs.

West Indies faced a daunting 240, but Greenidge and Haynes began with a fine stand of 149. Greenidge was in exhilarating form and hit a six and ten fours off the 127 balls that he faced. Richards and Lloyd, building on the solid base that the openers had given them, continued at a brisk pace, each hitting three fours and a six. When the rate threatened to slacken Lloyd hit Amarnath for a four and a six in the forty-first over which, in all, yielded 15 runs.

From that point West Indies swept to victory and defeat must have been bitterly disappointing to India after their encouraging batting.

***3, 4 and 5 December 1983***

***at Cuttack***

**West Indians** 420 (C.G. Greenidge 190 not out, D.R. Doshi 5 for 126)
**East Zone** 98 and 198 (R.A. Harper 5 for 66)
*West Indians won by an innings and 124 runs*

In the absence of Lloyd and Richards, Gordon Greenidge led the West Indians against East Zone and, batting at number five, battered the East Zone bowling as the tourists recovered from the uncertain start of 95 for 4, four wickets, including the completely out-of-form Logie, having fallen for 26 runs.

Doshi had used the wicket well in the West Indian innings and when the home side batted Harper and Gomes exploited the turning pitch as the last seven wickets fell for 34 runs. Following-on, East Zone fared better and reached 152 for 3, but once more the off-spin of Harper brought about a decline and they slumped to 198 all out although Arun Lal had to retire hurt and Nandy was unable to bat through illness.

In winning their first first-class match outside the Tests, West Indies owed much to Harper who, with match figures of 8 for 89, once again demonstrated his right to be considered for a Test place.

## Fourth One-Day International
## INDIA *v.* WEST INDIES

In one of the most powerful displays of batting ever seen in a limited-over international, Gordon Greenidge and Viv Richards added 221 for the second West Indian wicket and led their side to 333 for 8 off 45 overs. This score has been equalled once and beaten twice in limited-over internationals, but on each occasion a sixty-over World Cup match was being played. Greenidge was first out when he attempted to reverse sweep Shastri. He had faced 94 balls and had hit five sixes and ten fours. Richards was out at 304 after a ferocious assault which had brought him three sixes and twenty fours off 99 deliveries.

Dujon also batted aggressively, but six West Indian wickets tumbled for 29 in a wild pursuit of runs. Gavaskar and Malhotra added 105 for India's third wicket, but the task of scoring at 7.5 runs an over was always too much for the home side.

## Fifth Test Match
## INDIA *v.* WEST INDIES

Roberts returned to the West Indian side to take his place in the attack for the first time in the series and another change saw Harper make his debut in Test cricket. The inclusion of Harper suggested that the visitors believed that the wicket would take spin and the Indian attack was based almost exclusively on the spin of Yadav, Shastri and Maninder as support to the untiring efforts of Kapil Dev.

India won the toss and batted first on a slow pitch. No

### FOURTH ONE-DAY INTERNATIONAL: INDIA *v.* WEST INDIES
7 December 1983 at Jamshedpur

| WEST INDIES | | |
|---|---|---|
| C.G. Greenidge | b Shastri | 115 |
| D.L. Haynes | b Sharma | 1 |
| I.V.A. Richards | c Amarnath, b Kapil Dev | 149 |
| P.J. Dujon* | lbw, b Sharma | 49 |
| C.H. Lloyd† | c Amarnath, b Kapil Dev | 3 |
| E.A.E. Baptiste | st Kirmani, b Madan Lal | 1 |
| M.D. Marshall | b Kapil Dev | 5 |
| A.M.E. Roberts | not out | 1 |
| R.A. Harper | b Sharma | 0 |
| M.A. Holding | not out | 0 |
| H.A. Gomes | | |
| Extras | lb 4, w 4, nb 1 | 9 |
| (45 overs) | (for 8 wickets) | 333 |

| | O | M | R | W |
|---|---|---|---|---|
| Kapil Dev | 9 | 1 | 44 | 3 |
| Sharma | 9 | — | 60 | 3 |
| Binny | 1.5 | — | 17 | — |
| Madan Lal | 9 | — | 47 | 1 |
| Amarnath | 9.1 | — | 79 | — |
| Shastri | 7 | — | 77 | 1 |

FALL OF WICKETS
1-27, 2-248, 3-303, 4-320, 5-324, 6-331, 7-333, 8-333

| INDIA | | |
|---|---|---|
| S.M. Gavaskar | c Dujon, b Roberts | 83 |
| K. Srikkanth | c Dujon, b Roberts | 3 |
| M.B. Amarnath | b Holding | 16 |
| A.O. Malhotra | st Dujon, b Harper | 65 |
| R.N. Kapil Dev† | not out | 44 |
| J. Arun Lal | lbw, b Roberts | 0 |
| R.M.H. Binny | not out | 12 |
| R.J. Shastri | | |
| S. Madan Lal | | |
| S.M.H. Kirmani* | | |
| C. Sharma | | |
| Extras | lb 3, w 2, nb 1 | 6 |
| (45 overs) | (for 5 wickets) | 229 |

| | O | M | R | W |
|---|---|---|---|---|
| Marshall | 6 | — | 18 | — |
| Roberts | 10 | 1 | 54 | 3 |
| Holding | 6 | 1 | 15 | 1 |
| Baptiste | 10 | — | 51 | — |
| Harper | 10 | — | 52 | 1 |
| Gomes | 2 | — | 25 | — |
| Richards | 1 | — | 8 | — |

FALL OF WICKETS
1-23, 2-50, 3-155, 4-181, 5-181

**West Indies won by 104 runs**

*Gaekwad bowled Marshall 2. (Adrian Murrell)*

*Clive Lloyd in his magnificent innings of 161 not out. (Adrian Murrell)*

pitch, however, is too slow for Malcolm Marshall with the new ball. His first delivery climbed steeply, took Gavaskar on the glove and was caught down the leg-side by Dujon. Gaekwad was yorked as he reacted clumsily and slowly and Amarnath, bereft of all confidence, played with unwise aggression at a ball that held back. India were 13 for 3 and once more faced humiliation.

Vengsarkar and Malhotra suggested exciting recovery, but Holding came into the attack and Vengsarkar played on as he attempted to square cut. Malhotra mistimed a ball from Davis and was taken at cover and Shastri was yorked by Holding. India were 63 for 6 and a deep depression gripped them once again.

Kapil Dev should have been caught at slip by Richards shortly after he came in, but he survived that chance and another when he was 48 to hit 69 off 73 deliveries and share a

*Clive Lloyd survives an lbw appeal from Ravi Shastri. (Adrian Murrell)*

*Shastri bowled Marshall 2 in the second innings and India face defeat. (Adrian Murrell)*

stand of 82 with Roger Binny who prospered when Holding lost direction. Binny was out to Roberts and Kapil Dev fell when he played across the line, but Kirmani batted with courage and good sense and India closed the day at 231 for 8.

Only ten more runs were added the next morning before Roberts finished the innings and so became the third West Indian to reach 200 Test wickets. Greenidge began with a flourish, three fours and a six, but became a victim of his own excesses when he was caught at cover. In a magnificent spell of bowling Kapil Dev took the wickets of Richards, Haynes and Dujon for the addition of one run and gave India an advantage for the first time in the series. His control was exemplary and he deceived all batsmen with late movement as he moved into second place behind Bedi as India's leading wicket-taker in Test cricket. At the age of twenty-four Kapil Dev was playing in his sixty-first Test.

Gomes batted grimly before being beaten by Yadav's off-spin, always difficult for the left-hander for whom the stock ball becomes a leg-break. Lloyd, however, showed no signs of difficulty and batted with great care. Marshall was more adventurous and hit a fierce 54 in a stand of 87 which restored West Indies to parity in the match.

The next day they climbed into the ascendancy. Clive Lloyd played an innings of great control. His stamina was remarkable as he batted for 496 minutes with unrelenting concentration. He came to the wicket when West Indies were 42 for 4 and remained 161 not out when the innings closed for 377. He hit only twelve fours.

Neither Holding nor Harper lasted long on the third morning, but Roberts, first with only survival in mind and then with a sense of aggression, helped Lloyd in a record ninth wicket stand of 161. Roberts reached his highest score in Test cricket before being caught on the long-off boundary in attempting to hit his fourth six. The stand had taken West Indies from a point where they trailed India by 28 runs to a first innings lead of 136 runs.

This was a formidable advantage and by the end of the day it had become a winning one as Holding and Marshall generated a furious pace that had India devastated at 36 for 5. Gaekwad was bowled off stump before he could get his bat down, poor Amarnath had his middle stump laid flat by a ball of full length, Vengsarkar was lbw to an inswinger and Gavaskar, with much depending on him, played a totally irresponsible shot that gave the wanton waste of his wicket. Night-watchmen Yadav survived ten minutes before being bowled in the last over of the day.

There was no miracle for India after the rest day. Malhotra played some elegant drives, Harper showed his brilliance as a fielder and catcher and Marshall returned his best figures in Test cricket. India were bowled out before lunch for 90 and the temper of the crowd which had been ugly at the end of the one-day international in Jamshedpur became positively menacing. There were cries of 'shameless batting' as the Indian players left the ground. Many of the players were those who had received a hero's welcome four months earlier.

### Fifth One-Day International
### INDIA *v.* WEST INDIES

With Kapil Dev asking to be rested because of wear on his injured knee and Gavaskar asking to be omitted without giving a reason, India were led by Kirmani. Parkar returned

## FIFTH TEST MATCH: INDIA *v.* WEST INDIES
10, 11, 12 and 14 December 1983 at Calcutta

**INDIA**

| | FIRST INNINGS | | SECOND INNINGS | |
|---|---|---|---|---|
| S.M. Gavaskar | c Dujon, b Marshall | 0 | c Dujon, b Holding | 20 |
| A.D. Gaekwad | b Marshall | 2 | b Holding | 4 |
| D.B. Vengsarkar | b Holding | 23 | lbw, b Marshall | 1 |
| M.B. Amarnath | c and b Marshall | 0 | b Holding | 0 |
| A.O. Malhotra | c Gomes, b Davis | 20 | (6) c Dujon, b Marshall | 30 |
| R.J. Shastri | b Holding | 12 | (7) b Marshall | 2 |
| R.M.H. Binny | lbw, b Roberts | 44 | (8) c Harper, b Marshall | 6 |
| R.N. Kapil Dev† | b Holding | 69 | (9) c Dujon, b Marshall | 0 |
| S.M.H. Kirmani* | b Roberts | 49 | (10) b Roberts | 13 |
| S.N. Yadav | c Greenidge, b Roberts | 10 | (5) b Marshall | 4 |
| Maninder Singh | not out | 0 | not out | 0 |
| Extras | lb 6, nb 6 | 12 | b 1, lb 5, nb 4 | 10 |
| | | 241 | | 90 |

| | O | M | R | W | O | M | R | W |
|---|---|---|---|---|---|---|---|---|
| Marshall | 22 | 7 | 65 | 3 | 15 | 4 | 37 | 6 |
| Roberts | 23.4 | 9 | 56 | 3 | 4 | 1 | 11 | 1 |
| Davis | 14 | 1 | 39 | 1 | 2 | — | 7 | — |
| Holding | 20 | 4 | 59 | 3 | 9 | 3 | 29 | 3 |
| Harper | 8 | 2 | 16 | — | | | | |

FALL OF WICKETS
1- 0, 2- 9, 3- 13, 4- 41, 5- 63, 6- 63, 7- 145, 8- 212, 9- 240
1- 14, 2- 29, 3- 29, 4- 33, 5- 36, 6- 50, 7- 77, 8- 77, 9- 80

**WEST INDIES**

| | FIRST INNINGS | |
|---|---|---|
| C.G. Greenidge | c Yadav, b Binny | 25 |
| D.L. Haynes | lbw, b Kapil Dev | 5 |
| I.V.A. Richards | c Kirmani, b Kapil Dev | 9 |
| H.A. Gomes | b Yadav | 18 |
| P.J. Dujon* | c Gaekwad, b Kapil Dev | 0 |
| C.H. Lloyd† | not out | 161 |
| M.D. Marshall | lbw, b Maninder | 54 |
| M.A. Holding | c Shastri, b Maninder | 17 |
| R.A. Harper | lbw, b Kapil Dev | 0 |
| A.M.E. Roberts | c Amarnath, b Yadav | 68 |
| W.W. Davis | lbw, b Yadav | 0 |
| Extras | b 8, lb 7, w 1, nb 4 | 20 |
| | | 377 |

| | O | M | R | W |
|---|---|---|---|---|
| Kapil Dev | 35 | 5 | 91 | 4 |
| Binny | 13 | 2 | 62 | 1 |
| Amarnath | 7 | 1 | 19 | — |
| Yadav | 27 | 1 | 80 | 3 |
| Shastri | 18 | 2 | 56 | — |
| Maninder Singh | 28 | 7 | 54 | 2 |

FALL OF WICKETS
1- 32, 2- 41, 3- 42, 4- 42, 5- 88, 6- 175, 7- 213, 8- 213, 9- 374

*Umpires:* M.V. Gothoskar and Swaroop Krishnan

**West Indies won by an innings and 46 runs**

**FIFTH ONE-DAY INTERNATIONAL: INDIA v. WEST INDIES**
17 December 1983 at Gauhati

| INDIA | | | |
|---|---|---|---|
| K. Srikkanth | b Daniel | 11 |
| G.A.M.H. Parkar | c Daniel, b Baptiste | 42 |
| D.B. Vengsarkar | c Pydanna, b Baptiste | 2 |
| A.O. Malhotra | run out | 26 |
| M.B. Amarnath | c Holding, b Richards | 23 |
| R.M.H. Binny | c Haynes, b Richards | 33 |
| R.J. Shastri | run out | 18 |
| S.M.H. Kirmani†* | not out | 6 |
| R. Kulkarni | not out | 1 |
| C. Sharma | | |
| Randhir Singh | | |
| Extras | b 5, lb 6, w 1, nb 4 | 16 |
| (44 overs) | (for 7 wickets) | 178 |

| | O | M | R | W |
|---|---|---|---|---|
| Marshall | 5 | 2 | 8 | — |
| Holding | 7 | 1 | 28 | — |
| Baptiste | 9 | — | 31 | 2 |
| Daniel | 4 | 1 | 9 | 1 |
| Harper | 9 | — | 39 | — |
| Richards | 8 | — | 33 | 2 |
| Gomes | 2 | — | 14 | — |

FALL OF WICKETS
1- 54, 2- 62, 3- 67, 4- 113, 5- 117, 6- 162, 7- 172

| WEST INDIES | | |
|---|---|---|
| C.G. Greenidge | c Parkar, b Randhir Singh | 35 |
| D.L. Haynes | run out | 14 |
| R.B. Richardson | st Kirmani, b Shastri | 46 |
| I.V.A. Richards† | c Kirmani, b Shastri | 23 |
| H.A. Gomes | not out | 33 |
| M.D. Marshall | not out | 10 |
| E.A.E. Baptiste | | |
| R.A. Harper | | |
| M.R. Pydanna* | | |
| M.A. Holding | | |
| W.W. Daniel | | |
| Extras | b 4, lb 8, w 4, nb 5 | 21 |
| (41.4 overs) | (for 4 wickets) | 182 |

| | O | M | R | W |
|---|---|---|---|---|
| Sharma | 9 | — | 31 | — |
| Kulkarni | 9 | 1 | 26 | — |
| Binny | 6 | — | 35 | — |
| Randhir Singh | 6 | — | 30 | 1 |
| Shastri | 9 | 2 | 19 | 2 |
| Amarnath | 2.4 | — | 20 | — |

FALL OF WICKETS
1- 99, 2- 119, 3- 157, 4- 163

**West Indies won by 6 wickets**

to international cricket and young Sharma was joined in attack by Kulkarni and Randhir Singh. Lloyd stood down from the West Indies side as did Dujon so allowing Pydanna an international appearance.

Richards won the toss and asked India to bat. Srikkanath and Parkar began cautiously and the first run did not come until the fourth over, but they did give their side a solid start and put on 54 before Srikkanth was out in the fourteenth over. India failed to build on this good start even though Marshall left the field unwell. The West Indies attack was mainly in the hands of the spinners, but India could never maintain a brisk run rate on a pitch which was always difficult for the batsmen.

Greenidge, Richardson, Richards and Gomes made light of the task that they had been set and West Indies won with 2.2 overs to spare and so took the one-day series 5–0. India's victory in the World Cup seemed a long way in the past.

***20 and 21 December 1983***

***at Trivandrum***

**Indian Under-22 XI** 239 for 8 dec (J. Sanghani 104, Y.A. Khan 52)
**West Indians** 321 for 9 (R.B. Richardson 53, H.A. Gomes 51, W.V. Raman 5 for 80)
*Match drawn*

Not unexpectedly, the two-day match between the tourists and the Indian Under-22 side ended in a tame draw. The one highlight of the match was a stylish century by Jignesh Sanghani on the first day.

**Sixth Test Match**
**INDIA v. WEST INDIES**

With rain washing out the first day's play and severely curtailing other days, a draw was inevitable in the final Test of the series.

West Indies batted solidly and without hurry when their innings began and closed on 207 for 5. Lloyd again played well and Dujon confirmed his form of the tour which had seen him move to number five in the batting order and combine his rich array of strokes with sound defence.

The innings received an injection on the third day when Holding hit four sixes in his stand of 71 with Marshall for the eighth wicket. Marshall then gave his side an opportunity to win the match when, in his second over, he dismissed Gaekwad and Vengsarkar with successive balls. Both were brilliantly taken at third slip by Roger Harper whose exciting fielding was again much in evidence.

Harper took his maiden Test wicket when he had Malhotra taken at short-leg. By then Navjot Singh had also fallen after helping Gavaskar, batting at number four to strengthen India's weak middle order, to effect a recovery with a stand of 54. Concentration had been broken when the players left the field for half an hour after Davis had been hit by a stone thrown from the crowd. India closed at 69 for 4.

Next day, following night-watchman Yadav's dismissal at 92, Shastri and Gavaskar added 170, an Indian sixth wicket record against West Indies. Shastri was out to the last ball of a shortened day, but by then all honours had gone to his partner. When Gavaskar reached his century after 271 minutes of concentration he passed Don Bradman's record of twenty-nine Test hundreds. Gavaskar was playing his 174th innings in his 99th Test match. He received a standing ovation from the crowd of 35,000 and there was rejoicing throughout India, which welcomed the opportunity to celebrate after a most unhappy series in terms of results.

On the last day of mostly meaningless cricket, Gavaskar reached 236 not out off 425 deliveries in 644 minutes. He hit twenty-three fours and his innings was the highest score ever made by an Indian in a Test match. He and Kirmani also set a ninth wicket record of 143 for India against the West Indies.

Marshall again bowled splendidly to reach 33 wickets for

## West Indies in India 1983
First Class Matches

| BATTING | v. Central Zone (Jaipur) 4–6 October 1983 | | v. South Zone (Hyderabad) 8–10 October 1983 | | v. North Zone (Amritsar) 15–17 October 1983 | | First Test Match (Kanpur) 21–25 October 1983 | | Second Test Match (New Delhi) 20 Oct–3 Nov. 1983 | | v. Presidents XI (Nagpur) 5–7 November 1983 | | Third Test Match (Ahmedabad) 12–16 November 1983 | | v. West Zone (Kolhapur) 19–21 Nov. 1983 | | Fourth Test Match (Bombay) 24–29 Nov. 1983 | | v. East Zone (Cuttack) 3–5 December 1983 | | Fifth Test Match (Calcutta) 10–14 December 1983 | |
|---|---|---|---|---|---|---|---|---|---|---|---|---|---|---|---|---|---|---|---|---|---|---|
| D.L. Haynes | 45 | 67* | 64 | 38 | | | 6 | — | 12 | 17 | 24 | 26 | 9 | 1 | 67 | 20 | 55 | 24 | 33 | — | 5 | — |
| R.B. Richardson | 21 | 32 | 23 | — | 47 | 26 | | | | | 0 | 24 | | | 77 | 61 | 0 | 26 | 43 | — | | |
| H.A. Gomes | 0 | 3* | 65* | 20* | 32 | 1 | 21 | — | 19 | 1* | 4 | 39 | 38 | 25 | 41 | 2 | 26 | 37* | 11 | — | 18 | — |
| I.V.A. Richards | 16 | — | 109 | — | 24 | 61 | 24 | — | 67 | 22 | | | 8 | 20 | 11 | — | 120 | 4 | | | 9 | — |
| C.H. Lloyd | 85 | — | | | 1 | 18* | 23 | — | 103 | — | 71 | — | 68 | 33 | | | 67 | 9* | | | 161* | — |
| A.L. Logie | 26 | — | 28* | 17 | 18 | 4 | 0 | — | 63 | — | | | 0 | 0 | 56 | 1 | | | 1 | — | | |
| P.J. Dujon | 56 | — | | | 55* | 2* | 81 | — | 22 | — | 42 | 15 | 98 | 20 | | | 84 | — | 45 | — | 0 | — |
| W.W. Daniel | 27 | — | | | — | — | | | 1* | — | 7* | 28* | 6 | 0 | | | 0 | — | | | | |
| R.A. Harper | 70 | — | — | 0 | 10 | — | | | | | 19 | 4 | | | 30 | 34 | | | 37 | — | 0 | — |
| M.A. Holding | 5 | — | | | | | 0 | — | 14 | — | | | 16 | 58 | | | 2 | — | 25 | — | 17 | — |
| W.W. Davis | 0* | — | | | — | — | 0* | — | 19 | — | 4 | 16 | 3* | 1* | 1* | 1 | 4* | — | | | 0 | — |
| C.G. Greenidge | | | 66 | 0 | 1 | 6 | 194 | — | 33 | 72* | | | 7 | 3 | 35 | 6* | 13 | 4 | 190* | — | 25 | — |
| M.R. Pydanna | | | — | 0 | | | | | | | 30 | 59 | | | 3 | 34 | | | 0 | — | | |
| M.D. Marshall | | | — | 61 | | | 92 | — | 17 | — | | | 10 | 29 | | | 4 | — | | | 54 | — |
| E.A. Baptiste | | | — | 34* | | | 6 | — | | | 18 | 5 | | | 64* | 32* | | | 22 | — | | |
| A.M.E. Roberts | | | — | — | 15* | — | | | | | 12 | 29 | | | 7— | | | | 0 | — | 68 | — |
| Byes | 2 | | 1 | | 6 | 1 | 4 | | 5 | | 8 | | 8 | | 1 | 12 | 4 | | | | 8 | |
| Leg-byes | 15 | 1 | 6 | | 6 | 1 | 2 | | 7 | 4 | 11 | 4 | 6 | 9 | 14 | 1 | 8 | | 4 | | 7 | |
| Wides | | | | | 1 | | | | | 1 | | | | | 1 | | | | 2 | | 1 | |
| No-balls | 5 | 1 | 5 | | 1 | 2 | 1 | | 2 | 3 | 7 | 5 | 4 | 2 | 9 | 1 | 6 | | 7 | | 4 | |
| Total | 373 | 104 | 367 | 170 | 217 | 122 | 454 | | 384 | 120 | 257 | 254 | 281 | 201 | 417 | 205 | 393 | 104 | 420 | | 377 | |
| Wickets | 10 | 1 | 4 | 6 | 7 | 5 | 10 | | 10 | 2 | 10 | 9 | 10 | 10 | 9 | 7 | 10 | 4 | 10 | | 10 | |
| Result | D | | D | | D | | W | | D | | D | | W | | D | | D | | W | | W | |

*Catches* 26 – P.J. Dujon (ct 23/st 3)
10 – I.V.A. Richards
8 – R.A. Harper
6 – C.H. Lloyd and W.W. Davis
5 – D.L. Haynes, R.B. Richardson, M.R. Pydanna (ct 4/st 1) and subs
4 – H.A. Gomes and C.G. Greenidge
3 – E.A. Baptiste
2 – A.L. Logie and M.A. Holding
1 – M.D. Marshal and W.W. Daniel

| BOWLING | M.A. Holding | W.W. Davis | R.A. Harper | W.W. Daniel | H.A. Gomes | M.D. Marshall | A.M.E. Roberts | E.A. Baptiste | I.V.A. Richards |
|---|---|---|---|---|---|---|---|---|---|
| v. Central Zone (Jaipur) | 15–5–23–2 | 18–1–58–1 | 23–2–48–2 | 13–1–36–1 | 19–7–30–4 | | | | |
| 4–6 October | | | | | | | | | |
| v. South Zone (Hyderabad) | | | 25–5–59–2 | | 5–2–9–0 | 13–5–20–1 | 8–1–22–2 | 12–3–21–2 | 4.3–0–25–2 |
| 8–10 October | | | | | | | | | |
| v. North Zone (Amritsar) | | 19–4–74–2 | 30–11–64–2 | 14–4–38–0 | 13–1–40–1 | | 18–7–38–0 | | 4–0–13–0 |
| 15–17 October | | 5–1–19–1 | 16–0–45–1 | 6–0–21–1 | 12–4–48–1 | | | | 5–0–37–1 |
| First Test Match | 14.4–6–37–3 | 13–2–57–2 | | | 6–0–24–0 | 15–7–19–4 | | 11–0–58–1 | |
| (Kanpur) 21–25 October | 19–2–59–3 | 16.3–3–46–3 | | | | 17–7–47–4 | | 6–1–8–0 | |
| Second Test Match (New Delhi) | 28.2–0–107–4 | 25–2–87–1 | | 21–1–86–3 | 21–2–58–1 | 24–1–105–1 | | | 3–1–8–0 |
| 29 October–3 November | 12–4–36–2 | 12–1–45–0 | | 15–3–38–3 | 20.1–1–47–1 | 18–3–52–3 | | | |
| v. President's XI (Nagpur) | | 7–2–19–0 | 19–4–59–2 | 14–2–47–1 | | | 20–8–29–2 | 16.5–1–55–5 | |
| 5–7 November | | 5–1–9–0 | 10.3–2–21–2 | | 4–3–2–1 | | 5–4–2–0 | 7–1–14–1 | |
| Third Test Match (Ahmedabad) | 26–5–80–2 | 11–3–23–1 | | 11.5–0–39–5 | 6–0–22–0 | 26–9–66–1 | | | |
| 12–16 November | 17–5–30–4 | 11–2–21–3 | | 6.1–2–11–1 | | 13–3–23–2 | | | |
| v. West Zone (Kolhapur) | | 19–7–50–3 | 29.3–11–62–5 | | 3–0–28–1 | | 21–6–62–1 | 7–0–26–0 | 5–4–5–0 |
| 19–21 November | | | | | | | | | |
| Fourth Test Match (Bombay) | 40.5–10–102–5 | 36–3–127–1 | | 30–3–113–1 | 4–1–3–0 | 32–6–88–3 | | | |
| 24–29 November | 11–1–39–1 | 8–0–35–1 | | 14–3–45–1 | | 13–3–47–1 | | | |
| v. East Zone (Cuttack) | 10–5–11–1 | | 12–3–23–3 | | 3–1–7–2 | | 13–3–25–1 | 17–5–23–2 | |
| 3–5 December | 8–0–29–1 | | 25–6–66–5 | | 9–0–26–0 | | 7–0–29–0 | 15–3–40–1 | |
| Fifth Test Match (Calcutta) | 20–4–59–3 | 14–1–39–1 | 8–2–16–0 | | | 22–7–65–3 | 23.4–9–56–3 | | |
| 10–14 December | 9–3–29–3 | 2–0–7–0 | | | | 15–4–37–6 | 4–1–11–1 | | |
| Sixth Test Match (Madras) | 26–2–85–0 | 30–4–75–1 | 42–7–108–1 | | 8–0–24–0 | 26–8–72–5 | 28–4–81–1 | | |
| 24–29 December | | | | | | | | | |
| | 256.5–52–726–34 *av.* 21.35 | 251.3–37–791–21 *av.* 37.66 | 240–53–571–25 *av.* 22.84 | 145–19–474–17 *av.* 27.88 | 133.1–22–368–12 *av.* 30.66 | 224–63–641–34 *av.* 18.85 | 147.4–43–355–11 *av.* 32.27 | 91.5–14–245–12 *av.* 20.41 | 21.3–5–88–3 *av.* 29.33 |

†J. Arun Lal retired hurt, P. Nandy absent ill

| Sixth Test Match (Madras) 24–29 December 1983 | | M | Inns | NOs | Runs | HS | Av |
|---|---|---|---|---|---|---|---|
| 23 | 24 | 11 | 19 | 1 | 560 | 67* | 31.11 |
| | | 7 | 12 | — | 380 | 77 | 31.66 |
| 28 | 10* | 12 | 21 | 6 | 441 | 65* | 29.40 |
| 32 | — | 10 | 14 | — | 527 | 120 | 37.64 |
| 32 | — | 9 | 12 | 3 | 671 | 161* | 74.55 |
| | | 8 | 12 | 1 | 214 | 63 | 19.45 |
| 62 | — | 10 | 13 | 2 | 582 | 98 | 52.90 |
| | | 6 | 7 | 3 | 69 | 28* | 17.25 |
| 0 | — | 8 | 10 | — | 204 | 70 | 20.40 |
| 34 | — | 8 | 9 | — | 171 | 58 | 19.00 |
| 12 | — | 10 | 12 | 6 | 61 | 19 | 10.16 |
| 34 | 26* | 10 | 17 | 4 | 715 | 194 | 55.00 |
| | | 4 | 6 | — | 126 | 59 | 21.00 |
| 38 | — | 7 | 8 | — | 305 | 92 | 38.12 |
| | | 5 | 7 | 3 | 181 | 64* | 45.25 |
| 0* | — | 7 | 7 | 2 | 131 | 68 | 26.20 |
| 12 | 2 | | | | | | |
| 6 | 2 | | | | | | |
| 313 | 64 | | | | | | |
| 10 | 1 | | | | | | |
| D | | | | | | | |

| D.L. Haynes | Byes | Leg-byes | Wides | No-balls | Total | Wkts |
|---|---|---|---|---|---|---|
| | 7 | 3 | | 17 | 205 | 10 |
| | 10 | 9 | | 6 | 175 | 10 |
| | 22 | 2 | | 15 | 291 | 5 |
| | 4 | 1 | | 4 | 175 | 5 |
| | 6 | 6 | 6 | 3 | 207 | 10 |
| | 2 | 2 | 1 | 3 | 164 | 10 |
| | 4 | 9 | 2 | 27 | 464 | 10 |
| | 5 | 10 | 2 | 12 | 233 | 10 |
| | 1 | 4 | 1 | 13 | 214 | 10 |
| | | 4 | | 1 | 52 | 4 |
| | 7 | 4 | | 3 | 241 | 10 |
| | 6 | 12 | | 4 | 103 | 10 |
| | 1 | 1 | | 16 | 235 | 10 |
| | 16 | 14 | 1 | 26 | 463 | 10 |
| | 1 | 6 | | 5 | 173 | 5 |
| | 6 | 3 | 1 | 6 | 98 | 10 |
| 0.4–0–6–1 | | 2 | 1 | 2 | 198 | 8† |
| | | 6 | | 6 | 241 | 10 |
| | 1 | 5 | | 4 | 90 | 10 |
| | 1 | 5 | 9 | 6 | 451 | 8 |
| 0.4–0–6–1 *av.* 6.00 | | | | | | |

ABOVE: *Sunil Gavaskar, 236 not out in the sixth Test match and Bradman's record is beaten.* BELOW: *Andy Roberts – the end of a great international career. (Adrian Murrell)*

## SIXTH TEST MATCH: INDIA *v.* WEST INDIES
24, 26, 27, 28 and 29 December 1983 at Madras

### WEST INDIES

| | FIRST INNINGS | | SECOND INNINGS | |
|---|---|---|---|---|
| C.G. Greenidge | c Gavaskar, b Shastri | 34 | not out | 26 |
| D.L. Haynes | b Maninder | 23 | c Vengsarkar, b Shastri | 24 |
| I.V.A. Richards | c Kirmani, b Maninder | 32 | | |
| H.A. Gomes | b Yadav | 28 | (3) not out | 10 |
| P.J. Dujon* | c Kapil Dev, b Binny | 62 | | |
| C.H. Lloyd† | lbw, b Kapil Dev | 32 | | |
| W.W. Davis | c Navjot, b Binny | 12 | | |
| M.D. Marshall | lbw, b Kapil Dev | 38 | | |
| M.A. Holding | lbw, b Kapil Dev | 34 | | |
| A.M.E. Roberts | not out | 0 | | |
| R.A. Harper | c and b Maninder | 0 | | |
| Extras | lb 12, nb 6 | 18 | lb 2, nb 2 | 4 |
| | | 313 | (for 1 wicket) | 64 |

| | O | M | R | W | O | M | R | W |
|---|---|---|---|---|---|---|---|---|
| Kapil Dev | 15 | 3 | 44 | 3 | 6 | 2 | 11 | — |
| Binny | 12 | 1 | 48 | 2 | 2 | — | 14 | — |
| Shastri | 28 | 6 | 72 | 1 | 6 | 3 | 10 | 1 |
| Yadav | 28 | 4 | 96 | 1 | 1 | — | 9 | — |
| Maninder Singh | 29.3 | 9 | 41 | 3 | 6 | 2 | 10 | — |
| Kirmani | | | | | 1 | — | 4 | — |
| Vengsarkar | | | | | 1 | — | 4 | — |

FALL OF WICKETS
1- 47, 2- 91, 3- 100, 4- 136, 5- 200, 6- 226, 7- 232, 8- 303, 9- 312 1- 38

### INDIA

| | FIRST INNINGS | |
|---|---|---|
| A.D. Gaekwad | c Harper, b Marshall | 0 |
| Navjot Singh | c Richards, b Roberts | 20 |
| D.B. Vengsarkar | c Harper, b Marshall | 0 |
| S.M. Gavaskar | not out | 236 |
| A.O. Malhotra | c sub, b Harper | 9 |
| S.N. Yadav | c Dujon, b Marshall | 3 |
| R.J. Shastri | lbw, b Davis | 72 |
| R.M.H. Binny | c sub, b Marshall | 1 |
| R.N. Kapil Dev† | c sub, b Marshall | 26 |
| S.M.H. Kirmani* | not out | 63 |
| Maninder Singh | | |
| Extras | b 1, lb 5, w 9, nb 6 | 21 |
| | (for 8 wkts dec) | 451 |

| | O | M | R | W |
|---|---|---|---|---|
| Marshall | 26 | 8 | 72 | 5 |
| Roberts | 28 | 4 | 81 | 1 |
| Davis | 30 | 4 | 75 | 1 |
| Holding | 26 | 2 | 85 | — |
| Harper | 42 | 7 | 108 | 1 |
| Gomes | 8 | — | 24 | — |

FALL OF WICKETS
1- 0, 2- 0, 3- 54, 4- 67, 5- 92, 6- 262, 7- 269, 8- 308

*Umpires:* Swaroop Krishnan and M.G. Subramanium
**Match drawn**

## India *v.* West Indies – Test Match Averages

### INDIA BATTING

| | M | Inns | NOs | Runs | HS | Av | 100s | 50s |
|---|---|---|---|---|---|---|---|---|
| D.B. Vengsarkar | 5 | 8 | | 425 | 159 | 53.15 | 2 | 2 |
| S.M. Gavaskar | 6 | 11 | 1 | 505 | 236* | 50.50 | 2 | 1 |
| A.O. Malhotra | 3 | 5 | 1 | 163 | 72* | 40.75 | | 1 |
| S.M.H. Kirmani | 6 | 10 | 4 | 235 | 63* | 39.16 | | 1 |
| S. Madan Lal | 3 | 6 | 3 | 116 | 63* | 38.66 | | 1 |
| R.J. Shastri | 6 | 11 | 1 | 336 | 77 | 33.60 | | 2 |
| R.M.H. Binny | 6 | 11 | | 270 | 65 | 24.54 | | 2 |
| R.N. Kapil Dev | 6 | 11 | | 184 | 69 | 16.72 | | 1 |
| A.D. Gaekwad | 6 | 11 | | 174 | 48 | 15.81 | | |
| Navjot Singh | 2 | 3 | | 39 | 20 | 13.00 | | |
| S.M. Patil | 2 | 4 | | 45 | 22 | 11.25 | | |
| Maninder Singh | 4 | 5 | 2 | 24 | 15 | 8.00 | | |
| S.N. Yadav | 3 | 4 | | 29 | 12 | 7.25 | | |
| Kirti Azad | 2 | 4 | | 17 | 9 | 4.25 | | |
| M.B. Amarnath | 3 | 6 | | 1 | 1 | 0.16 | | |

Played in one Test: A.R.B. Bhat 0 and 6; Yashpal Sharma 5 and 0; B.S. Sandhu 7* and 1.

### INDIA BOWLING

| | Overs | Mds | Runs | Wkts | Av | Best | 5/inn | 10/m |
|---|---|---|---|---|---|---|---|---|
| R.N. Kapil Dev | 204.5 | 39 | 537 | 29 | 18.51 | 9/83 | 2 | 1 |
| Maninder Singh | 153.3 | 39 | 334 | 10 | 33.40 | 4/85 | | |
| S.N. Yadav | 112.1 | 18 | 338 | 9 | 37.55 | 5/131 | 1 | |
| R.M.H. Binny | 72 | 9 | 278 | 7 | 39.71 | 3/18 | | |
| R.J. Shastri | 211.3 | 42 | 567 | 12 | 47.25 | 2/32 | | |
| M.B. Amarnath | 14 | 2 | 49 | 1 | 49.00 | 1/30 | | |
| Kirti Azad | 51 | 11 | 147 | 2 | 73.50 | 2/84 | | |
| A.D. Gaekwad | 6 | 2 | 21 | 0 | — | 0/0 | | |
| S. Madan Lal | 55 | 14 | 161 | 0 | — | 0/8 | | |

Also bowled: A.R.B. Bhat 34–6–86–2; S.M. Gavaskar 2–1–1–0; S.M.H. Kirmani 1–0–4–0; D.B. Vengsarkar 1–0–4–0; B.S. Sandhu 24–7–78–1; A.O. Malhotra 1–1–0–0.

### INDIA CATCHES

10–S.M.H. Kirmani (ct 9/st 1); 5–S.M. Gavaskar; 4–R.N. Kapil Dev and subs; 3–A.D. Gaekwad; 2–S.N. Yadav and Maninder Singh; 1–Kirti Azad, S. Madan Lal, Yashpal Sharma, D.B. Vengsarkar, Navjot Singh, M.B. Amarnath, R.J. Shastri and S.M. Patil.

### WEST INDIES BATTING

| | M | Inns | NOs | Runs | HS | Av | 100s | 50s |
|---|---|---|---|---|---|---|---|---|
| C.H. Lloyd | 6 | 8 | 2 | 496 | 161* | 82.66 | 2 | 2 |
| P.J. Dujon | 6 | 7 | | 367 | 98 | 52.42 | | 4 |
| C.G. Greenidge | 6 | 10 | 2 | 411 | 194 | 51.37 | 1 | 1 |
| M.D. Marshall | 6 | 7 | | 244 | 92 | 34.85 | | 2 |
| I.V.A. Richards | 6 | 9 | | 306 | 120 | 34.00 | 1 | 1 |
| H.A. Gomes | 6 | 10 | 3 | 223 | 38 | 31.85 | | |
| M.A. Holding | 6 | 7 | | 141 | 58 | 20.14 | | 1 |
| D.L. Haynes | 6 | 10 | | 176 | 55 | 17.60 | | 1 |
| A.L. Logie | 3 | 4 | | 63 | 63 | 15.75 | | 1 |
| W.W. Davis | 6 | 7 | 4 | 39 | 19 | 13.00 | | |
| W.W. Daniel | 3 | 4 | 1 | 7 | 6 | 2.33 | | |

Played in two Tests: R.A. Harper 0 and 0; A.M.E. Roberts 68 and 0*.
Played in one Test: R.B. Richardson 26 and 0; E.A.E. Baptiste 6.

### WEST INDIES BOWLING

| | Overs | Mds | Runs | Wkts | Av | Best | 5/inn |
|---|---|---|---|---|---|---|---|
| M.D. Marshall | 221 | 58 | 621 | 33 | 18.81 | 6/37 | 2 |
| M.A. Holding | 223.5 | 42 | 663 | 30 | 22.10 | 5/102 | 1 |
| W.W. Daniel | 98 | 12 | 332 | 14 | 23.71 | 5/39 | 1 |
| A.M.E. Roberts | 55.4 | 14 | 148 | 5 | 29.60 | 3/56 | |
| W.W. Davis | 178.3 | 21 | 562 | 14 | 40.14 | 3/21 | |
| H.A. Gomes | 65.1 | 4 | 178 | 2 | 89.00 | 1/47 | |
| R.A. Harper | 50 | 9 | 124 | 1 | 124.00 | 1/108 | |

Also bowled: E.A.E. Baptiste 17–1–66–1; I.V.A. Richards 3–1–8–0.

### WEST INDIES CATCHES

16–P.J. Dujon; 8–I.V.A. Richards; 4–C.H. Lloyd, W.W. Davis and subs; 3–R.A. Harper and H.A. Gomes; 2–C.G. Greenidge and D.L. Haynes; 1–M.D. Marshall, W.W. Daniel and A.L. Logie.

the series and equal Valentine's record. After all the celebrations, however, India could only reflect that they had been overwhelmed 3–0 in the Test series and humiliated 5–0 in the limited-over series. West Indian supremacy had been restored.

***31 December 1983***

***at Bangalore***

**Indian XI** 208 for 6 (D.B. Vengsarkar 62)
**West Indians** 211 for 7 (I.V.A. Richards 54)

*West Indians won by 3 wickets*

In their final match of the tour, a forty-five over match played for the benefit of former Indian Test player Ghulam Ahmed, West Indies won in festival spirit, reaching their target in 34.2 overs.

It had been a highly successful tour for the West Indies who now set off for Australia and the Benson and Hedges World Series, but their side was in a transitional stage and about their batting questions remained.

## Duleep Trophy

### Quarter-Final

***6, 7, 8 and 9 January 1984***

***at Dhanbad***

**Central Zone** 375 (Padam Shastri 71, S. Mudkavi 62 not out) and 320 for 6 (S. Chaturvedi 115, S. Phadkar 59, S. Mudkavi 50 not out)
**South Zone** 623 (Azharauddin 226, Abdul Jabbar 105, K.A. Qayyum 77, K. Srikkanth 54, L. Sivaramakrishnan 50, P. Sundaram 5 for 168, S. Mudkavi 4 for 147)

*Match drawn*
*South Zone won on first innings and qualified for the semi-finals*

The decision to play the Duleep Trophy in the midst of the Ranji Trophy competition did not please many people, but once again a domestic tournament had become the victim of the proliferation of Test matches. The quarter final was a triumph for players making their debut in the competition. On the first day Padam Shastri of Rajasthan hit 71, but he was totally overshadowed by Hyderabad's Azharuddin who hit a career best 226 and shared stands of 232 for the third wicket with Abdul Jabbar and 148 for the fourth with Khalid Abdul Qayyum. Another newcomer, Sundaram of Rajasthan, bowled manfully for 38 overs to earn some late reward when Kirmani decided to bat on, thereby ensuring South Zone of a place in the semi-final but destroying the match.

Central Zone hit freely on the last day with Chaturvedi completing a good century and Mudkavi ending a fine all-round match with his second fifty.

### Semi-Finals

***12, 13, 14 and 15 January 1984***

***at Jamshedpur***

**South Zone** 224 (R.R. Kulkarni 6 for 58) and 235 (Azharuddin 72, S. Viswanath 53)
**West Zone** 473 for 9 dec (A.D. Gaekwad 131, S.M. Patil 108, R. Khanwilkar 5 for 94)

*West Zone won by an innings and 14 runs*

***at Cuttack***

**East Zone** 251 (K. Dubey 105, A. Mitra 57, Chetan Sharma 5 for 65) and 164
**North Zone** 392 (Yashpal Sharma 123, Randhir Singh 5 for 122) and 26 for 0

*North Zone won by 10 wickets*

Both of these matches, scheduled for four days, were over on the third. Kulkarni, the young Bombay pace bowler, made a most impressive debut in the competition when he routed South Zone on the opening day at Jamshedpur, taking 6 of the first 7 wickets. Skipper Gaekwad and Sandeep Patil batted West Zone into an impregnable position with a third wicket stand of 165. Azharuddin and Sadanand Viswanath held up West with a second wicket partnership of 132, but Kulkarni returned to bowl Azharuddin and Viswanath was run out. Kulkarni finished with match figures of 9 for 143.

There was an equally impressive debut by the exciting young pace bowler Chetan Sharma at Cuttack. Only Dubey and Mitra withstood him in the first innings and then Yashpal Sharma led North Zone to a comfortable lead. East Zone again collapsed to Chetan Sharma and Maninder Singh, Sharma finishing with 8 for 111.

### Duleep Trophy Final
### NORTH ZONE *v.* WEST ZONE

North Zone retained the trophy by virtue of their lead on the first innings. Gaekwad won the toss and asked North Zone to bat. The champions' innings was founded on a fine knock by Surinder Khanna, the Delhi wicket-keeper opening batsman, who hit his second Duleep Trophy hundred. He shared a stand of 134 for the third wicket with Ashok Malhotra and there was some good late hitting from Shukla and Madan Lal, who was leading the side in the absence of Kapil Dev.

Thanks to a stand of 146 between Gaekwad, his sixth century in the Duleep Trophy, and Gunjal of Maharashtra for the fourth wicket, West Zone recovered, but they could never match North Zone's score, and the second innings served only to help Amarnath in his search for lost form.

## Ranji Trophy

### West Zone

***18, 19 and 20 December 1983***

***at Karad***

**Baroda** 313 (K.S. More 153 not out, G. D'Monte 5 for 102) and 187 for 4 dec (A.D. Gaekwad 66, N.Y. Satham 55 not out)
**Maharashtra** 335 (R. Poonawala 93, M.D. Gunjal 78, R.B. Bhalekar 56, A. Petiwale 4 for 86, H.A. Pandya 4 for 111) and 26 for 0

*Match drawn*
*Baroda 9 pts, Maharashtra 8 pts*

***at Baikot***

**Saurashtra** 398 for 6 dec (B. Jadeja 113 not out, K. Chauhan 99, S. Keshwala 54) and 235 for 8 dec (R. Badiyani 69, J. Pandya 4 for 63)
**Gujarat** 357 (K. Bramhabhatt 114, B. Mistry 77, A. Patel 5 for 71) and 132 for 4

*Match drawn*
*Saurashtra 14 pts, Gujarat 11 pts*

## DULEEP TROPHY FINAL – NORTH ZONE *v.* WEST ZONE
17, 18, 19 and 20 January 1984 at Cuttack

**NORTH ZONE**

| | FIRST INNINGS | | SECOND INNINGS | |
|---|---|---|---|---|
| S.C. Khanna* | c Patil, b Patel | 146 | c Patil, b D'Monte | 14 |
| Navjot Singh | c Gaekwad, b D'Monte | 11 | c More, b Kulkani | 0 |
| Gursharan Singh | c More, b Shastri | 30 | run out | 69 |
| A.O. Malhotra | lbw, b D'Monte | 70 | lbw, b Patel | 28 |
| Yashpal Sharma | lbw, b Patel | 2 | c Patil, b Patel | 11 |
| M.B. Amarnath | b D'Monte | 16 | st More, b Gunjal | 79 |
| Kirti Azad | run out | 13 | c D'Monte, b Patel | 19 |
| R.S. Shukla | c Gunjal, b Patel | 34 | not out | 43 |
| S. Madan Lal† | not out | 40 | | |
| Chetan Sharma | c Patil, b Patel | 7 | | |
| Maninder Singh | c and b Shastri | 0 | | |
| Extras | b 9, lb 4, w 2, nb 17 | 32 | b 3, lb 6, w 2, nb 9 | 20 |
| | | 401 | (for 7 wickets) | 283 |

| | O | M | R | W | O | M | R | W |
|---|---|---|---|---|---|---|---|---|
| Kulkarni | 24 | 2 | 76 | — | 14 | 3 | 52 | 1 |
| D'Monte | 23 | 9 | 64 | 3 | 12 | — | 37 | 1 |
| Keshwala | 19 | 3 | 74 | — | 17 | 2 | 69 | — |
| Shastri | 36 | 5 | 83 | 2 | | | | |
| Patel | 34 | 9 | 87 | 4 | 28 | 5 | 74 | 3 |
| Gaekwad | 1 | — | 2 | — | | | | |
| Patil | 3 | 1 | 2 | — | 3 | — | 12 | — |
| Gunjal | | | | | 7.2 | — | 12 | 1 |
| Parkar | | | | | 4 | — | 18 | — |

FALL OF WICKETS
1- 30, 2- 115, 3- 249, 4- 255, 5- 288, 6- 297, 7- 328, 8-381, 9- 393
1- 5, 2- 21, 3- 102, 4- 134, 5- 137, 6- 163, 7- 283

**WEST ZONE**

| | FIRST INNINGS | |
|---|---|---|
| J. Sanghani | c Khanna, b Chetan Sharma | 0 |
| G.A.H.M. Parkar | lbw, b Chetan Sharma | 4 |
| A.D. Gaekwad† | b Chetan Sharma | 143 |
| S.M. Patil | c Gursharan, b Chetan Sharma | 47 |
| M.D. Gunjal | c Khanna, b Maninder | 59 |
| R.J. Shastri | b Maninder | 0 |
| K.S. More* | lbw, b Chetan Sharma | 4 |
| A. Patel | c Khanna, b Kirti Azad | 16 |
| S. Keshwala | not out | 35 |
| R.R. Kulkarni | b Chetan Sharma | 5 |
| G. D'Monte | b Chetan Sharma | 0 |
| Extras | b 13, lb 4, nb 13 | 30 |
| | | 343 |

| | O | M | R | W |
|---|---|---|---|---|
| Chetan Sharma | 27.5 | 5 | 83 | 7 |
| Madan Lal | 19 | 5 | 68 | — |
| Maninder Singh | 34 | 5 | 82 | 2 |
| Shukla | 13 | 3 | 35 | — |
| Kirti Azad | 22 | 5 | 49 | 1 |
| Amarnath | 6 | 1 | 9 | — |

FALL OF WICKETS
1- 0, 2- 33, 3- 88, 4- 234, 5- 238, 6- 271, 7- 283, 8- 336, 9- 343

*Umpires:* S.K. Ghosh and P.G. Pandit

**Match drawn – North Zone won trophy on first innings**

*Raju Kulkarni – splendid bowling for West Zone and Bombay brought him to the verge of international honours. (Adrian Murrell)*

Scoring was heavy on the matting at Baikot and a draw always looked likely after Bramhabhatt and Desai had established Gujarat's reply to Saurashtra's 398 for 6 with a fourth wicket stand of 108. Then Bramhabhatt and Mistry put on 123 for the sixth wicket and the home side's expected lead shrank.

On the first day an even batting performance had taken Saurashtra to a commanding position and they were never troubled in their second innings after which it was a jostle for bonus points between the sides who had finished in the bottom places in the previous season.

There was an equally even balance at Karad where Gaekwad won the toss and the visitors took first innings. They were in desperate straits when D'Monte reduced them to 69 for 6. Then Kiran More played a magnificent innings, scoring a career best 153 not out from the last 257 runs. He received support from Vadkar in a seventh wicket stand of 93. Solid batting took Maharashtra to a first innings lead, but a draw became inevitable.

***1, 2 and 3 January 1984***

***at Nanded***

**Maharashtra** 335 for 5 dec (R. Poonawala 133)
**Saurashtra** 164 for 5 (B. Jadeja 56 not out, G. D'Monte 4 for 58)

*Match drawn*
*Maharashtra 6 pts, Saurashtra 3 pts*

This match was completely ruined by rain. Poonawala and P. Pradhan began the home side's innings with a stand of 123, but no play was possible on the second day and bonus points were the only spoils to be won.

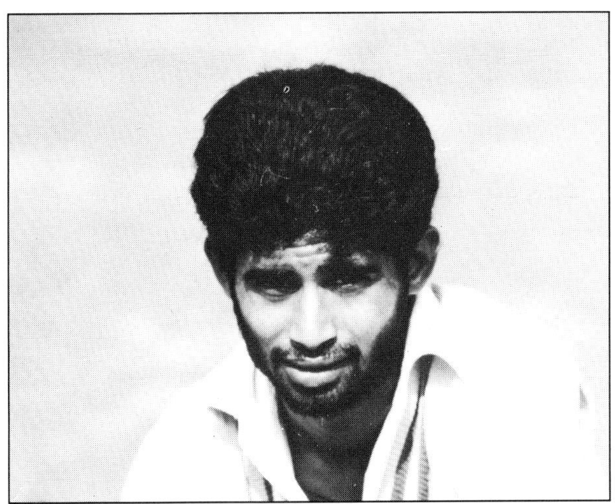

*Chetan Sharma – an outstanding season for Haryana and North Zone marked him as a future partner for Kapil Dev. (Adrian Murrell)*

***3, 4 and 5 January 1984***

***at Bulsar***

**Gujarat** 301 for 8 dec (K. Bramhabhatt 136, B. Mistry 61, S. Talati 57, R.C. Thakkar 4 for 90) and 193
**Bombay** 317 for 7 dec (R.J. Shastri 161 not out) and 129 for 4

*Match drawn*
*Bombay 11 pts, Gujarat 10 pts*

Some more splendid batting by Bramhabhatt and Mistry gave the home side a good opening day. They had been 6 for 2 before Talati and Bramhabhatt added 129, and although P. Desai went for 1, Bramhabhatt and Mistry added 122 to raise Gujarat's confidence. That confidence soared as Bombay lost both openers for 15 and had half their side out for 148, but Ravi Shastri played a mighty innings to put the visitors in the lead. His career best 161 not out was scored out of 244 and made at more than 4 an over. Shastri then took 2 wickets as Gujarat were bowled out for 193, but Bombay had only 20 overs in which to score 178 to win, a task which they attempted but found too difficult.

***7, 8 and 9 January 1984***

***at Ahmedabad***

**Gujarat** 235 and 169 (K. Bramhabhatt 70)
**Baroda** 200 for 8 dec (A.D. Gaekwad 53, J. Pandya 5 for 56) and 24 for 2

*Match drawn*
*Gujarat 7 pts, Baroda 7 pts*

***at Bombay***

**Saurashtra** 349 (S. Keshwala 117, D. Nanavati 81, R.R. Kulkarni 5 for 90) and 172 (B.S. Sandhu 6 for 64)
**Bombay** 365 for 4 dec (S.M. Patil 178, G.A.M.H. Parkar 104) and 159 for 3 (R.J. Shastri 81 not out, S.M. Gavaskar 57 not out)

*Bombay won by 7 wickets*
*Bombay 30 pts, Saurashtra 9 pts*

An uneasy wicket at Ahmedabad made batting difficult, but Gujarat showed consistent application and then Gaekwad demonstrated his rich skill and experience before declaring 35 runs in arrears. Bramhabhatt alone showed the necessary technical ability in Gujarat's dour second innings, but weather interruptions had left Baroda too little time in which to get the 205 needed for victory and they limped through 20 overs.

When Gavaskar asked Saurashtra to bat he was quickly rewarded with wickets from young pace man Kulkarni, but wicket-keeper Nanavati and Keshwala dominated the opening day with a brilliant fourth wicket stand of 199. Even this was overshadowed on the second day when Test players Parkar and Patil added 226 for Bombay's third wicket at six and a half runs an over. It was breathtaking batting and a jaded Saurashtra crumpled when they batted again. Chauhan was forced to retire hurt and with skipper Ghavri absent injured, they were out for 172, Sandhu's pace and movement proving decisive.

Time was against Bombay as they sought the 153 needed for victory. They were in deep trouble at 14 for 3, but Shastri joined Gavaskar and out-scored his captain in a brilliant match-winning stand of 145 at more than 5 an over.

***23, 24 and 25 January 1984***

***at Bombay***

**Maharashtra** 319 (R. Poonawalla 82, S. Jadhav 75, R.R. Kulkarni 4 for 85) and 226 for 9 dec (S. Kalyani 90)
**Bombay** 329 for 6 dec (S.M. Gavaskar 110, G.A.M.H. Parkar 108) and 219 for 2 (L.S. Rajput 103 not out, S.M. Patil 64)

*Bombay won by 6 wickets*
*Bombay 29 pts, Maharashtra 9 pts*

*More – a fine wicket-keeper and commanding batsman who helped Baroda to success. (Adrian Murrell)*

***at Porbandar***

**Baroda** 336 (S.B. Amarnath 75, N.Y. Satham 67, Ashok Patel 5 for 71, S. Keshwala 5 for 106) and 184 for 4 dec
**Saurashtra** 253 (K. Chauhan 59, B. Jadeja 57, N.Y. Satham 4 for 43) and 135 for 6 (V. Wadkar 4 for 50)

*Match drawn*
*Baroda 14 pts, Saurashtra 10 pts*

The power of Bombay was shown to great effect in their match with Maharashtra. Gavaskar put the visitors in and must have been a little disappointed with the stubborn resistance his bowlers faced after reducing Maharashtra to 56 for 3.

Bombay responded by claiming a lead of 10, scoring their runs at 4 an over. The highlight of their innings was a fourth wicket partnership of 159 between Parkar and Gavaskar, who batted at number 5.

Maharashtra effected another recovery in their second innings after losing both openers for 8. They went for brisk runs in an effort to give themselves some chance of victory and Shetty declared, leaving Bombay the daunting task of scoring 217 at 6 an over.

*Ashok Patel – an excellent all-round season for Saurashtra. (Adrian Murrell)*

Pandit opened with Rajput and there was an immediate attack on the bowling. Pandit fell to D'Monte at 48, but Rajput and the brilliant Sandeep Patil added 110 for the second wicket. Patil was caught off Azim Khan, but Vengsarkar helped Rajput to accomplish a fine victory and the opener concluded with a boundary to bring him his century.

Put in to bat on the matting wicket at Porbandar, Baroda founded their innings on a second wicket stand of 111 between R.Y. Deshmukh and Surinder Amarnath who was by far the dominant partner. Seven wickets fell for 68 runs, but Satham found a good partner in Hazare, and Pardeshi hit well so that 300 was passed.

Saurashtra batted soberly and bowled even more soberly when Baroda batted for a second time, being penalised 24 runs for failing by 6 overs to deliver their quota. The game ended with Saurashtra hitting well, but with no hope of victory.

***28, 29 and 30 January 1984***

***at Surat***

**Gujarat** 383 for 6 dec (S. Talati 127, K. Bramhabhatt 80, P. Desai 76 not out) and 298 for 5 dec (K. Bramhabhatt 120 not out, J. Bakrania 57, S. Pathak 52)
**Maharashtra** 368 (R.B. Bhalekar 81, M.D. Gunjal 61, V.B. Shetty 58, N. Patel 7 for 122) and 151 for 3

*Match drawn*
*Gujarat 12 pts, Maharashtra 11 pts*

***29, 30 and 31 January 1984***

***at Baroda***

**Baroda** 309 for 8 dec (A.D. Gaekwad 135, N.Y. Satham 61, B.S. Sandhu 4 for 61) and 217 for 9 dec (A. Bhansali 77 not out, R.Y. Deshmukh 50)
**Bombay** 350 for 9 dec (C.S. Pandit 82, S.M. Patil 73, L.S. Rajput 71, D.B. Vengsarkar 58) and 179 for 3 (D.B. Vengsarkar 96 not out, L.S. Rajput 60)

*Bombay won by 7 wickets*
*Bombay 30 pts, Baroda 12 pts*

The match on the matting at Surat was for the benefit of E.S. Maka. Gujarat's big first innings score was built on a third wicket partnership of 185 between Talati and the prolific Bramhabhatt. Maharashtra batted consistently well after losing 3 wickets for 30. Bhalekar and Gunjal added 124 for the fourth wicket and there was a last wicket stand of 74 between Oak and Daniel. Bramhabhatt hit his third century in four matches in the second innings as he and Pathak put on 139 for the fifth wicket. Bramhabhatt's 8 innings for Gujarat had produced 619 runs at an average of 103.16. All that was left was for Maharashtra to plunder three more bonus points in their second innings.

With Bombay already assured of a place in the quarter finals, Baroda needed to score 11 points in their home game with the champions to oust Gujarat from second place. Gaekwad won the toss and led by example, Baroda were 65 for 4 when he and Satham came together in a stand of 151 and Baroda took 4 batting points. Bombay gained a lead through consistent batting, and a third wicket stand of 109 between Rajput and Patil, but Baroda took 9 wickets by the ninetieth over and 4 points. More purposeful batting brought Baroda the 3 points that they required and Gaekwad declared and set Bombay 177 to win at nearly 5 an over.

*Ravi Shastri's success was as batsman rather than bowler for Bombay. (Adrian Murrell)*

*Sandeep Patil, brisk and elegant for Bombay. (Adrian Murrell)*

Parkar left at 14, but Vengsarkar joined Rajput in a thrilling stand of 113 and Bombay achieved their third victory in the tournament while no other side in the West Zone had managed a win.

**West Zone Final Table**

| | *P* | *W* | *L* | *D* | *Pts* |
|---|---|---|---|---|---|
| Bombay | 4 | 3 | — | 1 | 100 |
| Baroda | 4 | — | 1 | 3 | 42 |
| Gujarat | 4 | — | — | 4 | 40 |
| Saurashtra | 4 | — | 1 | 3 | 36 |
| Maharashtra | 4 | — | 1 | 3 | 34 |

## North Zone

***24, 25 and 26 November 1983***

***at Chandigarh***

**Haryana** 337 for 9 dec (Salim Ahmed 72, Saad Bin Jung 54)
**Services** 105 (C. Sharma 6 for 64) and 132 (R. Goel 5 for 46)

*Haryana won by an innings and 100 runs*
*Haryana 28 pts, Services 3 pts*

Put in to bat by Services, Haryana were in trouble with both openers out for 40, but Jung and Kumar added 75. Six wickets were lost before 200 was reached and it was left to Salim Ahmed and the later order to effect a revival.

Services batted limply in both innings as they struggled against the pace of young Chetan Sharma and the spin of veteran left-armer Rajinder Goel. Sudhakar Rao was the only Services' batsman to show the necessary application with innings of 26 and 48, top score each time, but his determination could not stop reigning North Zone champions, Haryana, beginning the season with an easy win.

***3, 4 and 5 December 1983***

***at Chandigarh***

**Services** 337 for 9 dec (B. Ghosh 110, C. Vijay 109) and 139 for 1 dec (N. Gadkari 62 not out, C. Vijay 50 not out)
**Punjab** 302 for 4 dec (A. Kaypee 112 not out, D. Chopra 55 not out) and 51 for 0

*Match drawn*
*Punjab 5 pts, Services 4 pts*

***4, 5 and 6 December 1983***

***at Delhi***

**Delhi** 293 for 7 dec (Gursharan Singh 103, S.C. Khanna 56, R. Goel 4 for 103) and 205 for 6 dec (R. Lamba 64)
**Haryana** 306 (R. Chaddha 126, Ashwini Kumar 50, Maninder Singh 5 for 115) and 110 for 2 (Ashwini Kumar 50 not out)

*Match drawn*
*Delhi 9 pts, Haryana 6 pts*

There was a run feast at Chadigarh but most attention focussed on Delhi and the meeting of the two top teams of the previous season. Gursharan Singh displayed the form which had brought him close to the Test side. In an innings lasting 182 minutes, he faced 183 balls and hit ten fours. He was particularly strong on the front foot and reached his second century in the Ranji Trophy. Surinder Khanna hit a four and two sixes, but most batsmen were tied down by the spin of Goel and Talwar who bowled 90 overs between them and Delhi failed to reach 300 on the first day.

After 25 uninterrupted years in the Ranji Trophy Goel, who first played for Patiala at the age of 17, showed his customary command of flight and length as he bowled unchanged for 50 overs and brought his total of wickets in the competition to 567.

Haryana were 117 for 5, but skipper Chaddha completed his hundred on the last morning to revive his side whose innings was brought to a close when Sarkar Talwar was hit by a bouncer from Valson and retired hurt. Spin had again dominated with Maninder and Shukla capturing 8 of the 9 wickets in the 81 overs they bowled.

When Delhi batted again Lamba ran out Sethi first ball, but then added 109 with Gursharan Singh in the feverish dash for bonus points.

### *8 and 9 December 1983*

***at Amritsar***

**Punjab** 372 for 7 dec (D. Chopra 101 not out, Yashpal Sharma 97, A. Kaypee 61)
**Jammu and Kashmir** 130 (Satish Kumar 5 for 31) and 79 (Umesh Kumar 5 for 9)

*Punjab won by an innings and 163 runs*
*Punjab 32 pts, Jammu and Kashmir 3 pts*

### *10, 11 and 12 December 1983*

***at Delhi***

**Services** 160 (Bhaskar Ghosh 51, Kirti Azad 4 for 23) and 163 (S. Valson 4 for 37)
**Delhi** 211 (Rajesh Peter 50, A. Jha 5 for 112) and 114 for 1

*Delhi won by 9 wickets*
*Delhi 25 pts, Services 6 pts*

Having tasted victory for the first time in 1982–83, Jammu and Kashmir had hopes of beginning the new season successfully, but they were quickly dashed when they were overwhelmed and beaten in two days in Amritsar.

In Delhi, Services had the better of an interesting opening day's play on the Air Force Ground, for, although bowled out for 160, they had the strong Delhi side unhappily placed at 134 for 7 at the close. Bhaskar Ghosh was the stalwart of the Services' innings, prompting some revival after seeing his side at 49 for 4. He batted for 77 minutes and hit eight fours. Gohil flourished well at the end with six fours in his 28 not out. Ajay Jha was the player who seized the initiative for Services when he bowled an opening stint of 19 overs and captured 5 wickets as Delhi slumped to 87 for 6, but Jha had to rest and on the second day he could not break through. Shukla and Peter took their stand to 50, and then Peter who batted 146 minutes and hit four fours, and Valson added 47 for the last wicket to give Delhi an important lead on a pitch of uneven bounce.

Medium-pace left-armer Valson reduced the hosts to 39 for 3 and they never made an effective recovery, being all out half-an-hour before the close. Delhi were 6 for 0 overnight and won shortly after lunch on the final day, Sethi and Lamba laying the foundation with an opening stand of 72.

### *13 and 14 December 1983*

***at Rothak***

**Jammu and Kashmir** 65 (R. Goel 5 for 7, C. Sharma 5 for 49) and 73 (R. Goel 5 for 18)
**Haryana** 200 for 8 dec (Mehboob Iqbal 4 for 80)

*Haryana won by an innings and 62 runs*
*Haryana 30 pts, Jammu and Kashmir 3 pts*

For the second successive match Jammu and Kashmir were overwhelmed in two days. Rajinder Goel continued his record Ranji haul with 10 for 25 in the match, receiving good support from Chetan Sharma and Jolly. Nirmal Singh, with 39 not out, played a lone hand for the visitors in their second innings.

### *17, 18 and 19 December 1983*

***at Delhi***

**Services** 315 for 6 dec (R. Das 129, Sudhakar Rao 122, Ravi Pandit 4 for 62) and 182 for 5 dec (R. Das 96)
**Jammu and Kashmir** 222 (Nirmal Singh 104, Vinod Sharma 58) and 150 for 8 (Ravi Rajan 4 for 39)

Match drawn
Services 14 pts, Jammu and Kashmir 7 pts

### *18, 19 and 20 December 1983*

***at Amritsar***

**Punjab** 147 (Maninder Singh 6 for 34) and 159 (S. Madan Lal 6 for 38, Maninder Singh 4 for 86)
**Delhi** 197 (Rajinder Ghai 4 for 62) and 110 for 2 (S.C. Khanna 60 not out)

*Delhi won by 8 wickets*
*Delhi 24 pts, Punjab 6 pts*

Maninder Singh ran through Punjab on the opening day at Amritsar as the home side were bowled out in 60.2 overs after they had been put in. Delhi did not find batting easy either, with Rajinder Singh Ghai producing a good spell of medium pace, but some aggression from Khanna and Azad led them to 140 for 5 at the close.

Kirti Azad was out-handled ball very early on the second morning. He stopped a ball that was rolling onto his stumps. Shukla showed some spark but had little help from the tail-enders. Their lead of 50 looked to be being eroded as Navjot Singh and Rakesh Rather put on 42 but Madan Lal and Maninder Singh then struck and 3 wickets fell for 2 runs. A rally by Yashpal Sharma and Yogesh Dutta followed, but Punjab were all out for 159 just before the close.

It took Delhi 92 minutes on the last day to win the match, Khanna, Gursharan Singh and Azad hitting vigorously after Lamba had gone for 2.

Jammu and Kashmir could not repeat their triumph of the previous season against Services in Delhi, but at least they avoided defeat for the first time in the season. They were thwarted by two fine innings from Das. He and Sudhakar Rao put on 189 for the third wicket in the first innings. 29 for 4, Jammu and Kashmir recovered through a fighting century from Nirmal Singh who shared a fifth wicket stand of 90 with Vinod Sharma. It was Nirmal Singh who saved the visitors in the second innings after they had been reduced to 48 for 6.

### *22 and 23 December 1983*

***at Delhi***

**Delhi** 412 for 4 dec (R. Lamba 150, S.C. Khanna 126, Rajinder Singh 79 not out)
**Jammu and Kashmir** 74 (S. Madan Lal 5 for 15) and 158

*Delhi won by an innings and 180 runs*
*Delhi 32 pts, Jammu and Kashmir 4 pts*

Having asked Delhi to bat first on a placid wicket in bright sunshine, Jammu and Kashmir could only ponder on their

*Maninder Singh. His slow left-arm bowling was a vital part of Delhi's successful year. (Adrian Murrell)*

error as Lamba and Khanna, 136 by lunch, put on 232 in 193 minutes. Khanna, first out, hit two sixes and sixteen fours in scoring his runs off 139 balls, and Lamba batted for 248 minutes and 186 balls as he hit a six and thirteen fours. It was a welcome return to form after an indifferent season. Rajinder Singh hit seven fours in a pleasing knock which consolidated the work of the openers. The visitors' bowling was weak; their fielding quite dreadful in its apathy.

Ashok Singh fell to the first ball of the second day and from that point Jammu and Kashmir began a period of abject surrender which saw them bowled out twice in just over 4 hours. Delhi took maximum points and moved serenely into the semi-finals.

#### *4, 5 and 6 January 1984*

***at Faridabad***

**Punjab** 135 (R. Goel 7 for 33) and 160 (R. Goel 5 for 49, Chetan Sharma 4 for 49)
**Haryana** 319 (Ashwini Kumar 134, A.O. Malhotra 61, Umesh Kumar 5 for 86)

*Haryana won by an innings and 24 runs*
*Haryana 30 pts, Punjab 1 pt*

Taking 5 wickets or more in an innings for the forty-seventh time, Rajinder Goel routed Punjab on the opening day. Put in to bat on a wicket which encouraged spin, Punjab were bowled out in 72.5 overs. They lost 3 wickets for 2 runs just after lunch when they were 79 for 2 and never recovered. Goel, bowling flat, turned the ball viciously and numbered skipper Yashpal Sharma among his victims, caught at silly point sweeping, a decision which the Test batsman hotly disputed with the umpire.

Ending the day on a commanding 103 for 2, Haryana were well served by Ashwini Kumar who batted fluently until becalmed on 99 for 23 minutes, but on reaching his century, he reasserted himself, hitting a six and fourteen fours in all. Malhotra and Kapil Dev also played well as Haryana took a lead of 184. Punjab ended the day at 84 for 4 and lasted only another 73 minutes on the last morning.

Man of the Match Goel reached 592 Ranji Trophy wickets and Haryana won the North Zone for the second year in succession.

**North Zone Final Table**

| | *P* | *W* | *L* | *D* | *Pts* |
|---|---|---|---|---|---|
| Haryana | 4 | 3 | — | 1 | 94 |
| Delhi | 4 | 3 | — | 1 | 90 |
| Punjab | 4 | 1 | 2 | 1 | 44 |
| Services | 4 | — | 2 | 2 | 27 |
| Jammu and Kashmir | 4 | — | 3 | 1 | 17 |

### South Zone

#### *26, 27 and 28 November 1983*

***at Hyderabad***

**Andhra** 163 (Prasanna Kumar 80, Jyotiprasad 4 for 33) and 174 (D. Meher Baba 73, Arshad Ayub 6 for 47)
**Hyderabad** 390 for 7 dec (Azharuddin 119, K.A. Qayyum 82 not out, V. Mohan Raj 66, K. Hari Prasad 65)

*Hyderabad won by an innings and 53 runs*
*Hyderabad 31 pts, Andhara 6 pts*

Choosing to bat first, Andhra were 77 for 5 to the medium pace of Jyotiprasad before Prasanna Kumar found a partner in Kishore and effected some recovery. In reply, however, Hari Prasad and Mohan Raj began with a stand of 94 and then Mohan Raj and the aggressive Azharuddin put on 116 for the second wicket. Khalid Abdul Qayyum hit well and Hyderabad took a first innings lead of 227.

This proved too much for Andhra who were bowled out in just over three hours, losing their last 6 wickets for 35 runs.

#### *3, 4 and 5 December 1983*

***at Hyderabad***

**Karnataka** 375 for 9 dec (B.P. Patel 114, A.V. Jayaprakash 93, R. Khanwilkar 51 not out, Jyotiprasad 6 for 96) and 70 for 3
**Hyderabad** 410 (K.A. Qayyum 88, V. Mohan Raj 70, Azharuddin 66, Arun Paul 56, A.R.B. Bhat 4 for 113)

*Match drawn*
*Hyderabad 8 pts, Karnataka 5 pts*

Hyderabad enhanced their chances of reaching the quarter finals by having the better of a draw with reigning champions, Karnataka. Led by former Test batsman Brijesh Patel and Jayaprakash, the captain, who added 171 for the fourth wicket, Karnataka reached a good total on the opening day in spite of some more impressive bowling from Jyotiprasad.

Hyderabad's reply was founded on solid batting right down the order; each of the first six wickets realised at least 50. Newcomer Arun Paul hit a fifty and Hyderabad took a lead of 35, but the game was now destined for a draw.

#### *10, 11 and 12 December 1983*

***at Cochin***

**Andhra** 363 for 9 dec (K. Kamaraju 70, S. Kumar 60 not out) and 9 for 1
**Kerala** 195 (S. Rajesh 52) and 176 (J. Kishore 4 for 60)

*Andhra won by 9 wickets*
*Andhra 26 pts, Kerala 5 pts*

On the matting wicket at Cochin, Andhra were 219 for 7 before S. Kumar, making his debut in the Ranji Trophy, and Kamaraju added 139 and lifted their side to a good position. Against a varied attack Kerala, beaten in all four matches in 1982—83, struggled for the best part of two days and were soundly beaten yet again.

### *17, 18 and 19 December 1983*

#### *at Bangalore*

**Tamil Nadu** 489 for 9 dec (A. Jabbar 148, L. Sivaramakrishan 130, R. Madhavan 125, S. Srinivasan 54, Sharad Rao 4 for 101, A.R.B. Bhat 4 for 146) and 6 for 0
**Karnataka** 363 (S. Viswanath 102, R. Khanwilkar 79, T.A. Sekhar 4 for 109)

*Match drawn*
*Tamil Nadu 6 pts, Karnataka 5 pts*

Tamil Nadu lost their first three wickets for 2 runs as each of the first three batsmen was dismissed for 0. Madhavan and S. Srinivasan then added 141. This was followed by a seventh wicket stand of 244 between Jabbar and Laxman Sivaramakrishnan, still days short of his eighteenth birthday, who hit a maiden first-class hundred. Facing a daunting 489, Karnataka batted doggedly with Sadanand Viswanath reaching his maiden hundred.

At 249 for 8, however, the champions were still in danger of having to follow-on, but Khanwilkar and Sharad Rao put on 102 and the game was saved although Karnataka now trailed Hyderabad and Tamil Nadu in the South Zone table.

### *1, 2 and 3 January 1984*

#### *at Waltair*

**Andhra** 292 (J.K. Ghia 94, S. Venkataraghavan 4 for 67, T.A. Sekhar 4 for 83) and 227 (Pratap Kumar 54)
**Tamil Nadu** 330 (C.S. Suresh Kumar 100, K. Srikkanth 63, V. Prasad 4 for 77) and 193 for 5 (V. Sivaramakrishnan 51, A.B. Reddy 50 not out)

*Tamil Nadu won by 5 wickets*
*Tamil Nadu 30 pts, Andhra 12 pts*

Tamil Nadu strengthened their position at the top of the table with a good win at Waltair after struggling to break through solid Andhra batting on the first day. It was the speed at which Tamil Nadu scored their runs which was decisive.

### *22, 23 and 24 January 1984*

#### *at Tirupati*

**Karnataka** 301 for 4 dec (R.M.H. Binny 101 not out, S. Viswanath 86, M.R. Srinivasaprasad 85) and 304 for 6 dec (S. Viswanath 93, A.V. Jayaprakash 53, G.R. Viswanath 52 not out)
**Andhra** 252 (Pratap Kumar 64, K.V.S.D. Kamaraju 52, A.R.B. Bhat 5 for 102) and 212 (Pratap Kumar 50, P. Rathod 4 for 48)

*Karnataka won by 141 runs*
*Karnataka 32 pts, Andhra 10 pts*

#### *at Cochin*

**Kerala** 117 (V. Jyotisprasad 6 for 35) and 118
**Hyderabad** 269 (M.V. Narasimha Rao 73, Faizal Baig 70, S. Santosh 4 for 66)

*Hyderabad won by an innings and 34 runs*
*Hyderabad 30 pts, Kerala 5 pts*

Karnataka swept to victory with some enterprising and exciting batting at Tirupati. Srinivasaprasad and Sadanand Viswanath put on 138 for the first wicket and Viswanath and Binny 102 for the second as Karnataka raced to 301 in 63 overs, only one maiden being bowled in the innings. Andhra recovered well from 17 for 2, both wickets to Binny, and the last 3 wickets added 92. There was more exhilarating batting from the champions before Andhra succumbed in $2\frac{1}{2}$ hours in their second innings.

Kerala chose to bat first on the matting at Cochin, but gave a limp display as Jyotiprasad and Yadav destroyed them twice.

### *27, 28 and 29 January 1984*

#### *at Coimbatore*

**Hyderabad** 171 (V. Mohan Raj 55) and 245 (Azharuddin 59, S. Venkataraghavan 5 for 65)
**Tamil Nadu** 195 (V. Sivaramakrishnan 98 not out, M.V. Narasimha Rao 5 for 81) and 224 for 4 (V. Sivaramakrishnan 86, A. Jabbar 52 not out)

*Tamil Nadu won by 6 wickets*
*Tamil Nadu 25 pts, Hyderabad 10 pts*

### *28, 29 and 30 January 1984*

#### *at Gulbarga*

**Karnataka** 308 for 4 dec (G.R. Viswanath 111 not out, S. Viswanath 83, B.P. Patel 50 not out) and 184 for 1 dec (R.M.H. Binny 108 not out, A.V. Jayaprakash 58 not out)
**Kerala** 122 (A.R.B. Bhat 5 for 40) and 194 (A.R.B. Bhat 8 for 70)

*Karnataka won by 176 runs*
*Karnataka 31 pts, Kerala 4 pts*

The two top teams of the previous season won handsomely, but Hyderabad gained just enough points to thwart Karnataka in their effort to reach the knock-out stage of the competition. V. Sivaramakrishnan played two magnificent innings for Tamil Nadu, carrying his bat in the first knock and making possible an exciting victory in the second.

Karnataka again scored furiously and it was good to see Gundappa Viswanath again in form after such a poor season, but the honours went to Raghuram Bhat who had career best figures of 8 for 70, and career best match figures of 13 for 110.

### *4 and 5 February 1984*

#### *at Madras*

**Kerala** 94 (L. Sivaramakrishnan 5 for 46) and 101
**Tamil Nadu** 390 for 4 dec (C.S. Suresh Kumar 107, R. Madhavan 100 not out, K. Srikkanth 75, S. Srinivasa 53 not out)

*Tamil Nadu won by an innings and 195 runs*
*Tamil Nadu 32 pts, Kerala 2 pts*

Tamil Nadu ended the South Zone matches in the emphatic style of champions. Kerala chose to bat and reached 40 for 1 before the leg-breaks of Laxman Sivaramakrishnan perplexed them to submission in well under 3 hours. Tamil Nadu responded by scoring at nearly 5 an over with Suresh Kumar and Madhavan sharing a third wicket partnership of 138. In their second innings Kerala were bowled out in 2 hours and the match ended with 2 hours of the second day and the whole of the third day to spare.

| South Zone Final Table | P | W | L | D | Pts |
|---|---|---|---|---|---|
| Tamil Nadu | 4 | 3 | — | 1 | 93 |
| Hyderabad | 4 | 2 | 1 | 1 | 79 |
| Karnataka | 4 | 2 | — | 2 | 73 |
| Andhra | 4 | 1 | 3 | — | 54 |
| Kerala | 4 | — | 4 | — | 16 |

## East Zone

### *12, 13 and 14 November 1983*

***at Dhanbad***

**Assam** 84 (M.R. Bhalla 5 for 27) and 202 (R. Bora 51, V. Venkataram 5 for 39)
**Bihar** 366 for 6 dec (S. Das 151, Sandeep Roy 93)

*Bihar won by an innings and 80 runs*
*Bihar 29 pts, Assam 2 pts*

Assam made a depressing start to the season when they were twice spun out and overwhelmed by an innings. Having routed Assam for 84, Bihar began their reply with a stand of 234 between Subrote Das, who hit twenty-two fours, and Sandeep Roy.

### *17, 18 and 19 November 1983*

***at Dhanbad***

**Bihar** 259 for 9 dec (D. Augustus 74 not out, H. Gidwani 57) and 301 for 6 dec (S. Das 77, T.J.S. Lamba 62, D. Augustus 51 not out)
**Bengal** 304 for 3 dec (A. Mitra 137 not out, J. Arun Lal 103 not out) and 55 for 1

*Match drawn*
*Bengal 8 pts, Bihar 6 pts*

***at Baripada***

**Assam** 140 (M. Bhatt 6 for 17) and 112 (M. Bhatt 4 for 25, Paramjit Singh 4 for 32)
**Orissa** 295 for 6 dec (K. Dubey 153, A. Jayakprakash 61, U. Bhattacharjee 5 for 105)

*Orissa won by an innings and 43 runs*
*Orissa 30 pts, Assam 1 pt*

Assam were overwhelmed for the second match in succession as Bhatt returned the remarkable figures of 10 for 42. Well as Bhatt bowled, the reason for his success was as much dreadful batting by Assam as anything else. Dubey hit 153 in 321 minutes with two sixes and eleven fours. He and Jayaprakash added 118 for the second wicket.

At Dhanbad, Bihar won the toss and lost Das without a run on the board. They were 158 for 7 and then Augustus and Randhir Singh added 93. Bengal lost Roy, Nandy and Raja Venkat for 112, but then came a mighty stand of 192 for the fourth wicket. Mitra hit fifteen fours and Arun Lal, the dominant partner, hit a six and nine fours in his aggressive innings. Trailing by 45, Bihar batted solidly in their second innings and a draw became the only result possible.

### *22, 23 and 24 November 1983*

***at Sambalpur***

**Orissa** 222 (R. Panda 67, M.R. Bhalla 4 for 75) and 175 (M.R. Bhalla 5 for 59, N. Venkataram 4 for 74)
**Bihar** 338 (S. Das 107, B.S. Gosain 67, H. Gidwani 66) and 41 for 3

*Match drawn*
*Bihar 7 pts, Orissa 5 pts*

***at Calcutta***

**Bengal** 450 for 1 dec (P.P. Roy 206 not out, P. Nandy 107, J. Arun Lal 103 not out)
**Assam** 155 (A. Bhattacharjee 5 for 29) and 168 (R. Bora 90, D.R. Doshi 7 for 57)

*Bengal won by an innings and 127 runs*
*Bengal 30 pts, Assam 2 pts*

An opening stand of 216 between Pranab Roy, son of the former Test player, and Palash Nandy was followed by a stand of 230 between Roy and Arun Lal. Roy's double century was his first in first-class cricket and it placed Bengal in an impregnable position. Assam twice succumbed to spin with Dilip Doshi having match figures of 9 for 128 and Arup Bhattacharjee 7 for 97. Rajesh Bora and Dutta took Assam's second innings to 105 for 2, but 8 wickets then fell for 63 as the bottom of the table side were beaten by an innings yet again. Arun Lal had recorded a century in each of the three zonal matches.

Bihar failed in their bid to score 60 in 9 overs to beat Orissa and the failure probably cost them a place in the final stages of the competition. The bowling of Bhalla had given them a chance of victory and he was well supported by skipper Venkataram. Having bowled out Orissa for 222, Bihar lost Sandeep Roy at 26, but Das and Gidwani added 168 for the second wicket. There was a collapse and 4 wickets fell for 16 runs, but Balder Singh Gosain steadied the middle order and Bihar took a comfortable lead. At 109 for 7, Orissa faced defeat, but the tail wagged well and, in consequence, saved the match.

### *27, 28 and 29 November 1983*

***at Rourkela***

**Orissa** 262 for 9 dec (D.R. Doshi 6 for 84) and 151 for 8 (K. Dubey 55, D.R. Doshi 5 for 61)
**Bengal** 623 (J. Arun Lal 135, A. Bhattacharjee 123, A. Mitra 59, P. Pandey 53, P. Roy 50)

*Match drawn*
*Bengal 12 pts, Orissa 8 pts*

Solid batting saw Orissa to a reasonable total after Sahu had won the toss. It was his opposing captain, Doshi, who troubled Orissa most. Sahu dismissed Nandy at 45, but Roy and Arun Lal, who hit his third century in three zonal matches, added 5 before Arun Lal shared century partnerships with Mitra and Pandey. A sixth wicket stand of 111 between Arup Bhattacharjee and wicket-keeper Banerjee demoralised Orissa who needed 361 to avoid an innings defeat, but Doshi had left insufficient time to bowl them out. Orissa saved the match and moved into the pre-quarter finals.

| East Zone Final Table | P | W | L | D | Pts |
|---|---|---|---|---|---|
| Bengal | 3 | 1 | — | 2 | 50 |
| Orissa | 3 | 1 | — | 2 | 43 |
| Bihar | 3 | 1 | — | 2 | 42 |
| Assam | 3 | — | 3 | — | 6 |

*Arun Lal hit three centuries in as many matches in the East Zone. (Adrian Murrell)*

## Central Zone

***19, 20 and 21 November 1983***

***at Udaipur***

**Rajasthan** 155 (V. Mathur 60) and 249 for 7 dec
**Vidarbha** 231 (S. Phadkar 62) and 175 for 7

*Vidarbha won by 3 wickets*
*Vidarbha 24 pts, Rajasthan 6 pts*

Vidarbha, who floundered at the bottom of the Central Zone table in 1982–83, created a great surprise when they beat Rajasthan in the opening match. On their own matting, Rajasthan wallowed at 59 for 7 on the first day and owed any semblance of respectability to V. Mathur at number 9 who hit 60 of the last 96 runs.

Vidarbha were indebted to a fine innings from skipper Phadkar who helped them to regain self-belief when it appeared to be waning. Trailing by 76, Rajasthan batted more solidly at the second attempt and, sensing that conditions were moving in his side's favour, P. Sharma declared, leaving the visitors 174 to make to win. Their challenge was a nervous one, but once again Phadkar, with an innings of 45 not out, restored belief and brought victory.

***25, 26 and 27 November 1983***

***at Agra***

**Uttar Pradesh** 358 for 7 dec (S.S. Khandkar 123, A. Bambi 70)
**Vidarbha** 176 (R. Amarnath 65 not out, Gopal Sharma 4 for 35) and 161 (R. Amarnath 72 not out, R.S. Hans 5 for 47)

*Uttar Pradesh won by an innings and 21 runs*
*Uttar Pradesh 31 pts, Vidarbha 3 pts*

***26, 27 and 28 November 1983***

***at Bhilai***

**Railways** 317 (P. Karkera 79, H. Mathur 66, N. Churi 52, N. Bhagtheria 4 for 43) and 221 (Aslam Ali 56, Karan Singh 4 for 18)
**Madhya Pradesh** 303 (S. Ansari 107, Gopal Rao 81, G. Rathod 4 for 71) and 182 for 7 (H. Mathur 4 for 46)

*Match drawn*
*Railways 13 pts, Madhya Pradesh 12 pts*

Shashikant Khandkar, one of India's 'Five Cricketers of the Year' for 1983, began the new season with a fine century which took Uttar Pradesh to a commanding position at Agra. Vidarbha batted disappointingly and only Rajinder Amarnath, with two splendidly defiant innings, showed the necessary application. Rajendrasingh Hans bowled his left-arm spin to great effect and had match figures of 7 for 106 so furthering his claim to be included in the Test side.

Railways batted inconsistently at Bhilai and were lifted by an eighth wicket stand of 89 between Durgaprasad and Mathur. Ansari and Goapal Rao began Madhya Pradesh's reply with a stand of 138, but the later batsmen failed to build on this fine start and Railways gained a narrow first innings lead. Eventually, Madhya Pradesh were asked to make 236 at $5\frac{1}{2}$ runs an over and they were thankful to settle for a draw after they lost 7 wickets for 142.

***2, 3 and 4 December 1983***

***at Nagpur***

**Madhya Pradesh** 373 for 8 dec (Sanjeeva Rao 188, M. Hassan 50, V. Gawate 4 for 96) and 34 for 0
**Vidharba** 91 (Gulrez Ali 7 for 27) and 394 for 6 dec (S. Phadkar 161, S. Hedaoo 88)

*Match drawn*
*Madhya Pradesh 7 pts, Vidharba 3 pts*

***at Delhi***

**Railways** 150 (R.S. Hans 5 for 64, Gopal Sharma 4 for 48) and 173
**Uttar Pradesh** 193 (S. Chaturvedi 58, G.L. Rathore 4 for 57) and 131 for 3

*Uttar Pradesh won by 7 wickets*
*Uttar Pradesh 25 pts, Railways 7 pts*

A remarkable change of fortune saw Vidharba draw a game in which, for most of the time, they had looked to be heading for an innings defeat. Skittled out by Gulrez Ali, who recorded a career best, Vidharba followed-on 282 behind and were 95 for 3 in their second innings. At this point skipper Phadkar and Hedaoo added 232 and saved the match. Opening batsman and captain Sanjeeva Rao had dominated the first day with a magnificent 188, sharing a third wicket stand of 108 with Hassan.

At Delhi runs were hard to come by and Railways collapsed from 42 to 0 to 112 for 8. Only some hard hitting by Durgaprasad and Banerjee lifted them to 150. Uttar Pradesh lost Khandkar for 0, but Chaturvedi and Anil Bhanot added 97. The wickets then tumbled and they gained a meagre lead of 43. Once more Railways middle order failed and although

Uttar Pradesh lost 3 for 37, Vijay Chopra and Ashok Bambi stroked them to victory.

### *9, 10 and 11 December 1983*

***at Bhilwara***

**Madhya Pradesh** 191 (Gulrez Ali 54) and 244 for 7 dec (N. Bhagtheria 71 not out, Sanjeeva Rao 62)
**Rajasthan** 210 (Padam Shastri 54, N. Bhagtheria 4 for 47) and 142 for 6 (Gulrez Ali 4 for 54)

*Match drawn*
*Rajasthan 9 pts, Madhya Pradesh 8 pts*

### *10, 11 and 12 December 1983*

***at Akola***

**Railways** 355 (N. Churi 113, U. Dastane 55, S. Takle 4 for 83) and 163 for 9 dec
**Vidharba** 215 (Prasad Shetty 57) and 254 for 6 (A. Palkar 64)

*Match drawn*
*Vidharba 13 pts, Railways 11 pts*

An innings of 71 not out from Bhagtheria restored hope for Madhya Pradesh when they had looked to be slipping towards defeat. Eventually, it was Rajasthan, troubled by Gulrez Ali, who were happy to settle for a draw.

At Akola, a third wicket stand of 132 between Churi and Dastane helped Railways to a good position on the opening day. Vidharba batted doggedly in reply, but trailed by 140 on the first innings. In an attempt to force victory, Railways went for quick runs and Vidharba took up the challenge to attempt to score 304 at 4 an over, but the game ended in stalemate with Vedraj taking off his pads to become one of nine bowlers used as farce set in.

### *16, 17 and 18 December 1983*

***at Gerakhpur***

**Railways** 286 for 9 dec (U. Dastane 100, P. Sundaram 5 for 98) and 259 for 8 dec (A. Burrows 120, R. Vats 51)
**Rajasthan** 364 for 6 dec (S. Mudkavi 93, Balbir Singh 70, V.B. Singh 69, S. Shastri 54) and 182 for 2 (Padam Shastri 82 not out, S. Mudkavi 52 not out)

*Rajasthan won by 8 wickets*
*Rajasthan 28 pts, Railways 7 pts*

### *17, 18 and 19 December 1983*

***at Rewa***

**Uttar Pradesh** 439 for 6 dec (S. Chaturvedi 157, Rahul Sapru 88, A. Bambi 73 not out)
**Madhya Pradesh** 156 (M. Hassan 50) and 247 for 3 (Gopal Rao 70, M. Hassan 62 not out)

*Match drawn*
*Uttar Pradesh 8 pts, Madhya Pradesh 3 pts*

Coming to the wicket at 59 for 4 on the first day at Gerakhpur, Dastane hit a fierce hundred to lift Railways to 265 before he was eighth out. Balbir Singh and V.B. Singh began Rajasthan's reply with a stand of 157, however, and with Mudkavi plundering the bowling, they took a lead of 78. Railways lost Karkera and Churi for 66 when they batted again, but Alf Burrows and Vats added 115 for the third wicket. The batsmen attacked the bowling, but there seemed little possibility of a result when Ved Raj set Rajasthan 182 to win at $5\frac{1}{2}$ an over. Balbir Singh left at 7 and Deepak Mahan hit fiercely all round the wicket to bring a fine victory.

Put in to bat on the matting wicket at Rewa, Uttar Pradesh were given a splendid start by Chaturvedi and Sapru who put on 182. The impetus was maintained, particularly by the fierce hitting Bambi and Uttar Pradesh took a firm grip on the match. Their dominance continued as the home side were bowled out in 57.3 overs, but some determined batting in the second innings, especially a 106-run third wicket stand by Gopal Rao and Hassan, saved the match.

### *25, 26 and 27 December 1983*

***at Pilbhit***

**Uttar Pradesh** 98 for 2 dec (S. Chaturvedi 50 not out)
**Rajasthan** 12 for 0

*Match abandoned*
*Uttar Pradesh 6 pts, Rajasthan 6 pts*

Only 38 minutes play was possible before lunch on the first day and there was only 85 minutes play on the third when only 8 of the mandatory overs could be bowled by Uttar Pradesh.

**Central Zone Final Table**

| | *P* | *W* | *L* | *D* | *Pts* |
|---|---|---|---|---|---|
| Uttar Pradesh | 4 | 2 | — | 2 | 70 |
| Rajasthan | 4 | 1 | 1 | 2 | 49 |
| Vidarbha | 4 | 1 | 1 | 2 | 43 |
| Railways | 4 | — | 2 | 2 | 38 |
| Madhya Pradesh | 4 | — | — | 4 | 30 |

## Pre-Quarter-Finals

### *22, 23, 24 and 25 February 1984*

***at Rourkela***

**Rajasthan** 502 (P. Sharma 134, Padam Shastri 101, Gajraj Singh 52 not out, H. Praharaj 6 for 149) and 213 for 2 dec (V.B. Singh 101, A. Mudkavi 100 not out)
**Orissa** 438 (A. Jayaprakasham 208 not out. A. Bhardwaj 101, P. Sundaram 5 for 143) and 37 for 4

*Match drawn*
*Rajasthan qualified on first innings lead*

***at Delhi***

**Bengal** 298 (J. Arun Lal 105, S. Valson 5 for 54) and 242 (A. Mitra 93, P. Roy 57, Sushil Kumar 5 for 81)
**Delhi** 400 (S.C. Khanna 126, R.S. Shukla 79, S. Madan Lal 76) and 141 for 2 (R. Lamba 69, S.C. Khanna 54 not out)

*Delhi won by 8 wickets*

With the ruling that in a drawn match the side with first innings lead would pass into the Quarter-Finals, it was inevitable that Rajasthan should attempt to amass a mammoth score when they batted first. At 81 for 4 on the first day, their chances of doing so looked slim. Then Padam Shastri and Parthasarathy Sharma added 210 and the good work of Praharaj and Sahu was nullified. Runs flowed and the last three wickets produced 172, Sundaram and Gajraj Singh adding 91 for the last.

To their credit, the home side batted heroically in reply. At

56 for 4 an innings defeat looked probable, but Jayaprakasham and Bhardwaj put on 149, and Sahu helped the splendid Jayaprakasham to add 112 for the eighth wicket. Jayaprakasham, who came in at 14 for 1, was left unbeaten on 208, the first double century of his career and the highest score made in the Ranji Trophy in 1983–84. What remained was mostly batting practice as V.B. Singh and A. Mudkavi put on 175 for Rajasthan's second wicket.

At Delhi, Arun Lal hit his fourth century in as many matches, but Khanna and Lamba put on 124 for Delhi's first wicket to put their side in a strong position. Then there was a collapse as 4 wickets fell for 45, and Madan Lal and Shukla came together when Khanna was out at 222. They added 107 for the sixth wicket and this stand virtually assured that Delhi would meet Tamil Nadu in the Quarter-Finals. Bengal lost their last 7 second innings wickets for 98 and Lamba and Khanna began the race for victory with a stand of 111, runs coming at 6 an over.

## Quarter-Finals

### *3, 4, 5 and 6 March 1984*

#### *at Baroda*

**Uttar Pradesh** 238 (A. Bambi 66, K.B. Kala 57, V. Patel 4 for 50) and 201 (R. Sapru 61, A. Petiwale 5 for 65)
**Baroda** 483 (K.S. More 181 not out, R.Y. Deshmukh 64, S.B. Amarnath 61, R. Parikh 56, G. Sharma 5 for 147)

*Baroda won by an innings and 44 runs*

#### *at Chandigarh*

**Haryana** 363 (R. Jolly 105, R. Chaddha 71, Chetan Sharma 61, M.V. Narasimha Rao 6 for 102) and 251 (A.O. Malhotra 106, M.V. Narasimha Rao 5 for 110)
**Hyderabad** 240 (K.A. Qayyum 64, V. Jaisimha 54, M.V. Narasimha Rao 53, S. Talwar 5 for 66) and 216 (R. Goel 5 for 68)

*Haryana won by 158 runs*

#### *at Jaipur*

**Rajasthan** 370 (P. Shastri 131, P. Sharma 78) and 276 for 7 dec (P. Shastri 99, P. Sharma 66, Dalbir Singh 53)
**Bombay** 401 (D.B. Vengsarkar 149, C.S. Pandit 56, B.S. Sandhu 52) and 193 for 4 (G.A.H.M. Parkar 57, C.S. Pandit 51 not out)

*Match drawn*
*Bombay qualified on first innings lead*

#### *at Madras*

**Tamil Nadu** 353 (A. Jabbar 88, S. Vasudevan 76, R. Madhavan 56, S. Madan Lal 4 for 69) and 255 for 5 (S. Srinivasan 70, A. Jabbar 62 not out)
**Delhi** 477 (S. Madan Lal 114, B. Pillai 86, R.C. Shukla 80 not out, M.B. Amarnath 60, S.C. Khanna 58, W.V. Raman 4 for 128)

*Match drawn*
*Delhi qualified on first innings lead*

Bowled out for 238 by Patel and Pandya, Uttar Pradesh suffered badly at the hands of the Baroda batsmen. Deshmukh and Parikh put on 118 for the first wicket and although Baroda lost 5 wickets in taking the lead, a remarkable innings by Kiran More, who came in at 221 for 5, put them in an unassailable position. More and Patel added 145 for the last wicket and of these runs Patel scored 34. More hit fiercely all round the wicket to reach a career best. Remarkably he had innings of 153 not out and 181 not out in the competition and had failed to reach double figures on the six other occasions he had been to the wicket. Sharma and Hans sent down 123 overs between them and conceded 279 runs. A somewhat demoralised Uttar Pradesh side collapsed in their second innings.

An eighth wicket stand of 117 between Jolly and Chetan Sharma lifted Haryana to a satisfactory score after they had been struggling at 211 for 7 against the leg-breaks of Narasimha Rao. Narasimha Rao lifted his side in a fifth wicket stand of 107 with Khalid Qayyum, but Hyderabad trailed by 143 on the first innings. Skipper Narasimha Rao again inspired his side with 5 second innings wickets after Ashok Malhotra had hit an attractive century, but Goel and Talwar had the final say and Haryana won easily.

In spite of fine batting in each innings by Padam Shastri and P. Sharma, who shared a fifth wicket stand of 127 in the first innings, Rajasthan could not match the Bombay run machine at Jaipur. It was solid batting throughout the order that took Bombay to their first innings lead and a place in the semi-finals. They owed much to Vengsarkar who batted with his usual elegance, but it was a seventh wicket stand of 72 between Pandit and Sandhu that brought them within 2 runs of Rajasthan's total. In Rajasthan's second innings, Padam Shastri was caught off Sawant one short of his second hundred of the match.

Tamil Nadu were 61 for 4 in Madras, but consistent batting throughout the lower order and a sixth wicket stand of 129 between Jabbar and Vasudevan helped them to a commendable 353. At 109 for 4 Delhi were struggling, but Amarnath and Madan Lal, veterans of many heroic contests, added 123, and Madan Lal then added 99 with Pillai. There was a useful contribution from Shukla and Delhi were now certain of a semi-final place.

## Semi-Finals

### *17, 18, 19 and 20 March 1984*

#### *at Bombay*

**Bombay** 552 (D.B. Vengsarkar 104, R. Baindur 96, S.M. Gavaskar 87, S.V. Nayak 63, C.S. Pandit 57, Chetan Sharma 5 for 150) and 264 for 6 dec (S.M. Patil 101 not out, R. Baindur 86)
**Haryana** 377 (R. Chaddha 168, Aman Kumar 76) and 113 for 1 (S.B. Jung 59 not out)

*Match drawn*
*Bombay qualified on first innings lead*

### *18, 19, 20 and 21 March 1984*

#### *at Delhi (Kotla)*

**Delhi** 349 (S. Madan Lal 157 not out) and 385 for 7 dec (Kirti Azad 64, B. Pillai 64, S. Madan Lal 56, Rajinder Singh 53 not out, M.B. Amarnath 51)
**Baroda** 199 (S. Valson 4 for 65) and 94

*Delhi won by 440 runs*

Once Gavaskar had won the toss it seemed that Bombay would reach the final. Haryana had hopes when Hattangadi, Parkar and Patil fell to Chetan Sharma with 102 scored, but Vengsarkar and Gavaskar added 103 for the fourth wicket and Baindur and Nayak added 108 for the seventh. There was even a stand of 53 for the last wicket between Shetty and

Sawant and Bombay reached a massive 552. Haryana were 30 for 4 in reply, but skipper Chaddha and Aman Kumar put on 149. There were some useful contributions from the late order, but still Haryana finished 175 in arrears. Bombay offered them no second chance. Patil moved to a smooth century. Jung and D. Sharma had an opening stand of 100, but the game had long since been drawn.

At Delhi, Mohinder Amarnath must have wondered what advantage had been squandered as Delhi lost 5 wickets for 96 after he had won the toss and chosen to bat. Then Madan Lal scored his fifteenth century in the Ranji Trophy and, with stubborn assistance from the later batsmen, took his side to a useful, but not invincible, 349. Valson made early inroads into the Baroda batting, however, and Satham was forced to retire hurt before he had scored. Kirti Azad bemused the later batsmen and Delhi led by 150 on the first innings. They gave Baroda no chance of recovery. They scored briskly in their second innings and when Baroda batted again they collapsed dispiritedly and were all out in under 28 overs.

### Ranji Trophy Final
### BOMBAY *v.* DELHI

When Gavaskar won the toss and Bombay batted for over two days it was inevitable that they would win the championship and that the game would lose much of its interest.

Bombay's run-riot started when Vengsarkar and Patil added 108 for the third wicket. Vengsarkar had the distinction of reaching his third century in the knock-out stage of the tournament. Gavaskar then embarked on his innings which lasted 530 minutes and brought him twenty-five fours off 384 deliveries. It was his nineteenth century in the Ranji Trophy and he shared century partnerships for the fifth and sixth wickets with Shastri and Pandit.

Faced by a huge total, Delhi were 47 for 3, but Mohinder Amarnath and Kirti Azad put on 102 and Kirti Azad reached a fine century. In all he batted for 212 minutes and hit fourteen fours off 141 deliveries. Bombay were 95 for 5 in their second innings before Shastri and Patil righted things, but, in spite of centuries from Prabhakar and Amarnath and a stand of 184, Delhi had no hope of victory.

Bombay took the championship on their first innings lead. It was the twenty-ninth time that they had won the Ranji Trophy in thirty-two appearances in the final since 1934–35. They have won the Trophy outright on twenty-five occasions and four times by dint of first innings lead.

It was a triumphant end to the season for Sunil Gavaskar for whom this had been a mighty year.

**RANJI TROPHY FINAL – BOMBAY *v.* DELHI**
30 and 31 March, 1, 2 and 3 April 1984 at Bombay

**BOMBAY**

| | FIRST INNINGS | | SECOND INNINGS | |
|---|---|---|---|---|
| L.S. Rajput | c Khanna, b Maninder | 53 | b Madan Lal | 43 |
| G.A.H.M. Parkar | c Khanna, b Prabhakar | 15 | c Azad, b Prabhakar | 2 |
| D.B. Vengsarkar | c Lamba, b Rajinder | 123 | (6) c Khanna, b Madan Lal | 9 |
| S.M. Patil | c Amarnath, b Rajinder | 31 | (8) b Lamba | 72 |
| S.M. Gavaskar† | not out | 206 | c and b Madan Lal | 19 |
| R.J. Shastri | c Amarnath, b Maninder | 48 | (7) c Madan Lal b Rajinder | 56 |
| C.S. Pandit* | c Khanna, b Azad | 71 | (4) c Amarnath, b Valson | 14 |
| R. Baindur | c Maninder, b Valson | 20 | (3) retired hurt | 1 |
| S.V. Nayak | lbw, b Valson | 0 | c Madan Lal, b Rajinder | 5 |
| B.S. Sandhu | c Azad, b Maninder | 7 | not out | 7 |
| R.R. Kulkarni | c Pillai, b Maninder | 1 | lbw, b Lamba | 3 |
| Extras | b 4, lb 8, w 1, nb 13 | 26 | b 1, lb 1, nb 8 | 10 |
| | penalty runs | 24 | penalty runs | 4 |
| | | 625 | | 245 |

| | O | M | R | W | O | M | R | W |
|---|---|---|---|---|---|---|---|---|
| Valson | 27 | 3 | 108 | 2 | 11 | — | 40 | 1 |
| Prabhakar | 20 | 5 | 56 | 1 | 6 | — | 34 | 1 |
| Madan Lal | 22 | 2 | 74 | — | 15 | 2 | 35 | 3 |
| Maninder Singh | 67.1 | 18 | 172 | 4 | 23 | 6 | 58 | — |
| Amarnath | 10 | 2 | 24 | — | | | | |
| Shukla | 17 | — | 53 | — | | | | |
| Kirti Azad | 20 | 1 | 63 | 1 | 10 | 2 | 37 | — |
| Rajinder Singh | 17 | 2 | 39 | 2 | 9 | 2 | 26 | 2 |
| Lamba | | | | | 4.5 | 2 | 9 | 2 |

FALL OF WICKETS
1- 33, 2- 121, 3- 229, 4- 250, 5- 356, 6- 492, 7- 563, 8- 570, 9- 583
1- 6, 2- 31, 3- 77, 4- 94, 5- 95, 6- 211, 7- 230, 8- 230, 9- 241

**DELHI**

| | FIRST INNINGS | | SECOND INNINGS | |
|---|---|---|---|---|
| M. Prabhakar | c and b Nayak | 27 | lbw, b Pandit | 122 |
| R. Lamba | c Pandit, b Kulkarni | 0 | c Pandit, b Sandhu | 7 |
| B. Pillai | lbw, b Sandhu | 6 | c Pandit, b Kulkarni | 0 |
| M.B. Amarnath† | c Nayak, b Shastri | 49 | not out | 103 |
| Kirti Azad | st Pandit, b Nayak | 106 | run out | 7 |
| S. Madan Lal | c Pandit, b Nayak | 30 | not out | 19 |
| S.C. Khanna* | c Baindur, b Sandhu | 42 | | |
| Rajinder Singh | c and b Shastri | 8 | | |
| R.S. Shukla | not out | 36 | | |
| Maninder Singh | c Pandit, b Kulkarni | 3 | | |
| S. Valson | c Nayak, b Kulkarni | 0 | | |
| Extras | b 1, lb 4, w 1, nb 4 | 10 | b 5, nb 3 | 8 |
| | penalty runs | 16 | | |
| | | 333 | (for 4 wickets) | 266 |

| | O | M | R | W | O | M | R | W |
|---|---|---|---|---|---|---|---|---|
| Kulkarni | 21.4 | 2 | 81 | 3 | 5 | 1 | 18 | 1 |
| Sandhu | 14 | 2 | 55 | 2 | 6 | 3 | 19 | 1 |
| Nayak | 25 | 2 | 98 | 3 | 9 | 1 | 32 | — |
| Shastri | 26 | 2 | 61 | 2 | 9 | 5 | 13 | — |
| Baindur | 6 | 1 | 17 | — | | | | |
| Parkar | | | | | 4 | — | 19 | — |
| Rajput | | | | | 22 | — | 92 | — |
| Gavaskar | | | | | 8 | — | 42 | — |
| Pandit | | | | | 10 | 1 | 26 | 1 |

FALL OF WICKETS
1- 3, 2- 15, 3- 47, 4- 149, 5- 220, 6- 233, 7- 244, 8- 294, 9- 315
1- 27, 2- 32, 3- 216, 4- 243

*Umpires:* M. Banerjee and V.K. Ramaswamy

**Match drawn**
**Bombay won the Ranji Trophy by leading on the first innings**

## First Class Averages

*Surinder Khanna – first-class wicket-keeping and runs galore for Delhi. (Adrian Murrell)*

| BATTING | M | Inns | NOs | Runs | HS | Av | 100s | 50s |
|---|---|---|---|---|---|---|---|---|
| J. Arun Lal | 6 | 9 | 3 | 543 | 135 | 90.50 | 4 | |
| K. Bramhabhatt | 5 | 9 | 2 | 621 | 136 | 88.71 | 3 | 2 |
| S. Das | 3 | 5 | 1 | 347 | 151 | 86.75 | 2 | 1 |
| D. Augustus | 3 | 4 | 2 | 168 | 74* | 84.00 | | 2 |
| N. Gadkari | 3 | 6 | 4 | 164 | 62* | 82.00 | | 1 |
| R. Amarnath | 2 | 4 | 2 | 147 | 72* | 73.50 | | 2 |
| A. Bambi | 5 | 6 | 2 | 289 | 73* | 72.25 | | 3 |
| Azharuddin | 6 | 8 | | 558 | 226 | 69.75 | 2 | 3 |
| S.M. Gavaskar | 15 | 24 | 5 | 1310 | 206* | 68.94 | 5 | 5 |
| S.C. Khanna | 11 | 17 | 4 | 888 | 146 | 68.30 | 3 | 4 |
| R. Baindur | 2 | 4 | 1 | 203 | 96 | 67.66 | | 2 |
| P. Shastri | 7 | 11 | 1 | 674 | 131 | 67.40 | 2 | 4 |
| S. Madan Lal | 14 | 19 | 7 | 800 | 157* | 66.66 | 2 | 4 |
| R. Chaddha | 6 | 7 | | 466 | 168 | 66.57 | 2 | 1 |
| S. Vasudevan | 3 | 4 | 2 | 133 | 76 | 66.50 | | 1 |
| M.D. Gunjal | 6 | 8 | 2 | 371 | 78 | 61.83 | | 3 |
| A. Jabbar | 7 | 11 | 2 | 556 | 148 | 61.77 | 2 | 3 |
| R. Poonawala | 4 | 7 | 1 | 369 | 133 | 61.50 | 1 | 2 |
| D.B. Vengsarkar | 12 | 20 | 2 | 1088 | 159 | 60.44 | 5 | 4 |
| A. Mitra | 6 | 8 | 1 | 419 | 137* | 59.85 | 1 | 3 |
| A. Jayakprakash | 4 | 6 | 1 | 354 | 208* | 59.00 | 1 | 1 |
| R. Das | 2 | 4 | | 235 | 129 | 58.75 | 1 | 1 |
| S. Srinivasan | 5 | 7 | 2 | 289 | 70 | 57.80 | | 2 |
| B. Jadeja | 4 | 7 | 2 | 285 | 113* | 57.00 | 1 | 2 |
| S. Chaturvedi | 7 | 10 | 1 | 494 | 157 | 54.88 | 2 | 2 |
| R.C. Shukla | 10 | 11 | 4 | 374 | 80* | 53.42 | | 2 |
| L.S. Rajput | 4 | 8 | 1 | 372 | 103* | 53.14 | 1 | 3 |
| M. Hassan | 4 | 7 | 1 | 264 | 62* | 52.80 | | 3 |
| R.M.H. Binny | 11 | 19 | 3 | 824 | 158 | 51.50 | 3 | 4 |
| N. Bhagtheria | 4 | 6 | 3 | 153 | 71* | 51.00 | | 1 |
| S.M. Mudkavi | 7 | 12 | 4 | 407 | 93 | 50.87 | | 4 |
| P. Nandy | 4 | 5 | 1 | 203 | 107 | 50.75 | 1 | |
| Rahul Sapru | 3 | 3 | | 151 | 88 | 50.33 | | 2 |
| A. Mudkavi | 3 | 4 | 1 | 151 | 100* | 50.33 | 1 | |
| S. Phadkar | 5 | 10 | 1 | 447 | 161 | 49.66 | 1 | 2 |
| Khalid Abdul Qayyum | 8 | 11 | 2 | 447 | 88 | 49.66 | | 4 |
| R.B. Bhalekar | 4 | 6 | 1 | 248 | 81 | 49.60 | | 2 |
| Sanjeeva Rao | 4 | 8 | 1 | 337 | 188 | 48.14 | 1 | 1 |
| K. Dubey | 5 | 9 | | 426 | 153 | 47.33 | 2 | 1 |
| R. Madhavan | 5 | 8 | 1 | 330 | 125 | 47.14 | 2 | 1 |
| P. Sharma | 5 | 8 | | 373 | 134 | 46.62 | 1 | 2 |
| Amarjeet Kaybee | 4 | 6 | 1 | 231 | 112* | 46.20 | 1 | 1 |
| A.D. Gaekwad | 17 | 27 | 2 | 1153 | 201 | 46.12 | 4 | 3 |
| D. Chopra | 4 | 6 | 2 | 176 | 101* | 44.00 | 1 | 1 |
| B. Ghosh | 4 | 6 | | 263 | 110 | 43.83 | 1 | 1 |
| B.P. Patel | 6 | 9 | 2 | 305 | 114 | 43.57 | 1 | 1 |
| A.O. Malhotra | 10 | 16 | 4 | 521 | 106 | 43.41 | 1 | 4 |
| L. Sivaramakrishnan | 8 | 9 | 1 | 345 | 130 | 43.12 | 1 | 2 |
| R.J. Shastri | 16 | 25 | 4 | 880 | 161* | 41.90 | 1 | 5 |
| P. Roy | 7 | 12 | 2 | 416 | 206* | 41.60 | 1 | 2 |
| V. Sivaramakrishnan | 5 | 9 | 2 | 290 | 98* | 41.42 | | 3 |
| S. Viswanath | 8 | 13 | | 530 | 102 | 40.76 | 1 | 4 |
| M.R. Srinivasaprasad | 6 | 9 | 1 | 326 | 117 | 40.75 | 1 | 1 |
| Ashwini Kumar | 6 | 8 | 1 | 285 | 134 | 40.71 | 1 | 2 |
| S.M. Patil | 14 | 23 | 1 | 879 | 178 | 39.95 | 3 | 3 |
| K. Chauhan | 4 | 7 | 1 | 238 | 99 | 39.66 | | 2 |
| R. Sudhakar Rao | 5 | 9 | | 357 | 122 | 39.66 | 1 | 2 |
| A.V. Jayaprakash | 6 | 10 | 1 | 351 | 93 | 39.00 | | 3 |
| V.B. Singh | 6 | 10 | 3 | 273 | 101 | 39.00 | 1 | 1 |
| P. Desai | 4 | 7 | 2 | 195 | 76* | 39.00 | | 1 |
| Nirmal Singh | 4 | 8 | 2 | 232 | 104 | 38.66 | 1 | |
| U. Dastane | 4 | 8 | 1 | 268 | 100 | 38.28 | 1 | 1 |
| R. Khanwilkar | 7 | 7 | 1 | 228 | 79 | 38.00 | | 2 |
| S. Talati | 4 | 8 | | 302 | 127 | 37.75 | 1 | 1 |
| V. Mathur | 4 | 6 | 2 | 149 | 60 | 37.25 | | 1 |
| G.A.H.M. Parkar | 10 | 15 | | 556 | 108 | 37.06 | 2 | 2 |
| V. Mohan Raj | 5 | 7 | | 259 | 70 | 37.00 | | 3 |
| P. Karkera | 4 | 8 | | 181 | 79 | 36.50 | | 1 |
| S. Keshwala | 6 | 9 | 1 | 291 | 117 | 36.37 | 1 | 1 |
| C.S. Pandit | 9 | 13 | 2 | 398 | 82 | 36.18 | | 5 |
| A. Burrows | 5 | 9 | | 323 | 120 | 35.88 | 1 | |
| Gursharan Singh | 6 | 11 | | 389 | 103 | 35.36 | 1 | 1 |
| S.B. Amarnath | 5 | 9 | 1 | 282 | 75 | 35.25 | | 2 |
| N. Churi | 4 | 8 | | 279 | 113 | 34.87 | 1 | 1 |
| S. Shastri | 5 | 7 | 2 | 174 | 54 | 34.80 | | 1 |
| K.S. More | 10 | 14 | 2 | 415 | 181* | 34.58 | 2 | |
| Pratap Kumar | 4 | 8 | 1 | 242 | 64 | 34.57 | | 2 |
| Yashpal Sharma | 12 | 19 | 1 | 622 | 123 | 34.55 | 1 | 4 |
| N.Y. Satham | 6 | 9 | 2 | 241 | 67 | 34.42 | | 3 |
| Jugal Kishore | 4 | 7 | | 240 | 94 | 34.28 | | 1 |
| Sandeep Roy | 3 | 5 | | 171 | 93 | 34.20 | | 1 |
| Rajinder Singh | 6 | 10 | 3 | 238 | 79* | 34.00 | | 2 |
| B.S. Gosain | 2 | 4 | | 135 | 67 | 33.75 | | 1 |
| V.B. Shetty | 4 | 5 | 1 | 133 | 58 | 33.25 | | 1 |
| R. Bora | 3 | 6 | | 199 | 90 | 33.16 | | 2 |
| S. Hedaoo | 4 | 8 | 1 | 231 | 88 | 33.00 | | 1 |
| M.S. Kumar | 3 | 5 | 1 | 132 | 60* | 33.00 | | 1 |
| S.M.H. Kirmani | 11 | 17 | 6 | 361 | 63* | 32.81 | | 1 |
| Chetan Sharma | 9 | 9 | 2 | 226 | 61 | 32.38 | | 1 |
| S.B. Jung | 6 | 9 | 1 | 256 | 59* | 32.00 | | 2 |
| S. Ansari | 4 | 8 | 1 | 221 | 107 | 31.57 | 1 | |
| C.S. Suresh Kumar | 7 | 12 | 1 | 347 | 107 | 31.54 | 2 | |
| S. Kalyani | 4 | 6 | | 189 | 90 | 31.50 | | 1 |
| Chander Vijay | 4 | 8 | 1 | 217 | 109 | 31.00 | 1 | 1 |
| Salim Ahmed | 6 | 8 | 1 | 217 | 72 | 31.00 | | 1 |
| R. Lamba | 9 | 16 | 1 | 464 | 150 | 30.93 | 1 | 2 |
| B. Mistry | 4 | 8 | | 246 | 77 | 30.75 | | 2 |
| G.R. Viswanath | 6 | 9 | 2 | 215 | 111* | 30.71 | 1 | 1 |
| A.S. Bhansali | 6 | 11 | 4 | 212 | 77* | 30.28 | | 1 |
| A. Patel | 7 | 10 | 2 | 242 | 48 | 30.25 | | |
| Bhaskar Pillay | 7 | 9 | 1 | 241 | 86 | 30.12 | | 2 |
| S. Khandkar | 6 | 9 | | 268 | 123 | 29.77 | 1 | |

| | | | | | | | | |
|---|---|---|---|---|---|---|---|---|
| Sumit Datta | 3 | 6 | | 178 | 42 | 29.66 | | |
| A. Bhattarcharjee | 6 | 7 | | 203 | 123 | 29.00 | 1 | |
| A.B. Reddy | 5 | 5 | 1 | 116 | 50* | 29.00 | | 1 |
| P. Shetty | 3 | 6 | | 174 | 57 | 29.00 | | 1 |
| Gopal Rao | 4 | 7 | | 197 | 81 | 28.14 | | 2 |
| R. Panda | 4 | 7 | 2 | 140 | 67 | 28.00 | | 1 |
| R. Rathore | 4 | 7 | 1 | 167 | 65 | 27.83 | | 1 |
| R. Badiyani | 4 | 7 | | 192 | 69 | 27.42 | | 1 |
| M.B. Amarnath | 12 | 19 | 2 | 464 | 103* | 27.29 | 1 | 4 |
| Durga Prasad | 4 | 8 | 2 | 161 | 35* | 26.83 | | |
| K. Srikkanth | 7 | 11 | | 291 | 75 | 26.45 | | 3 |
| S. Rajesh | 4 | 8 | | 209 | 62 | 26.12 | | 2 |
| R. Jolly | 5 | 6 | | 155 | 105 | 25.83 | 1 | |
| S. Jadhav | 3 | 4 | | 103 | 75 | 25.75 | | 1 |
| D. Meher Baba | 4 | 7 | | 179 | 73 | 25.57 | | 2 |
| R.Y. Deshmukh | 6 | 10 | | 250 | 64 | 25.00 | | 2 |
| P. Hingnikar | 2 | 4 | | 100 | 44 | 25.00 | | |
| K.V.S.D. Kamaraju | 4 | 7 | | 175 | 70 | 25.00 | | 2 |
| Aman Kumar | 5 | 5 | | 124 | 76 | 24.80 | | 1 |
| A. Bhanot | 4 | 5 | | 123 | 44 | 24.60 | | |
| P. Pande | 5 | 5 | | 123 | 53 | 24.60 | | 1 |
| Navjot Singh | 8 | 15 | 1 | 338 | 122 | 24.14 | 1 | 1 |
| Kirti Azad | 14 | 23 | 2 | 506 | 106 | 24.09 | 1 | 1 |
| Abdul Azeem | 4 | 6 | | 141 | 45 | 23.50 | | |
| Faizal Baig | 5 | 7 | 1 | 141 | 70 | 23.50 | | 1 |
| H. Gidwani | 4 | 7 | | 163 | 66 | 23.28 | | 2 |
| J. Bakrania | 4 | 8 | | 182 | 57 | 22.75 | | 1 |
| A. Mathur | 7 | 7 | | 159 | 41 | 22.71 | | |
| H. Praharaj | 4 | 7 | 1 | 136 | 35 | 22.66 | | |
| R. Sudhakar Rao | 6 | 7 | 1 | 135 | 37 | 22.50 | | |
| Dalbir Singh | 6 | 11 | 1 | 222 | 70 | 22.20 | | 2 |
| J. Sanghani | 4 | 6 | 1 | 109 | 39 | 21.80 | | |
| M.N. Ravi Kumar | 4 | 7 | | 151 | 40 | 21.57 | | |
| Gopal Sharma | 7 | 8 | 2 | 129 | 48 | 21.50 | | |
| Deepak Sharma | 6 | 8 | | 170 | 46 | 21.25 | | |
| D. Nanavati | 4 | 7 | 1 | 123 | 81 | 20.50 | | 1 |
| M. Arya | 4 | 5 | | 102 | 36 | 20.40 | | |
| Harsh Mathur | 4 | 8 | 1 | 137 | 66 | 19.57 | | 1 |
| B.S. Sandhu | 9 | 11 | 4 | 131 | 52 | 18.71 | | 1 |
| K.B. Rama Murthy | 4 | 7 | | 131 | 43 | 18.71 | | |
| P. Hazarika | 3 | 6 | | 112 | 41 | 18.66 | | |
| Hans Raj | 4 | 8 | 1 | 127 | 32* | 18.14 | | |
| M.V. Narasimha Rao | 6 | 8 | | 143 | 73 | 17.87 | | 2 |
| Arun Paul | 4 | 6 | | 107 | 56 | 17.83 | | 1 |
| Gulrez Ali | 4 | 6 | | 106 | 54 | 17.66 | | 1 |
| Prasana Kumar | 4 | 8 | | 140 | 80 | 17.50 | | 1 |
| R. Pankule | 4 | 8 | | 138 | 36 | 17.25 | | |
| R.N. Kapil Dev | 11 | 17 | | 288 | 69 | 16.94 | | 1 |
| L. Rajan | 4 | 8 | | 134 | 48 | 16.75 | | |
| S.N. Yadav | 10 | 13 | 1 | 199 | 50 | 16.58 | | 1 |
| P. Ved Raj | 6 | 11 | | 177 | 43 | 16.09 | | |
| S. Sahu | 6 | 11 | 1 | 158 | 47 | 15.80 | | |
| S.S. Hattangadi | 4 | 8 | 1 | 104 | 25 | 14.85 | | |
| Pervez Kaiser | 4 | 8 | 1 | 103 | 39* | 14.71 | | |
| Ranjit Thomas | 4 | 8 | | 110 | 33 | 13.75 | | |
| V. Sharma | 4 | 8 | | 109 | 58 | 13.62 | | 1 |
| P. Banerjee | 5 | 8 | | 104 | 29 | 13.00 | | |
| S. Santosh | 4 | 8 | | 103 | 30 | 12.87 | | |
| V.S. Wadkar | 6 | 8 | | 100 | 43 | 12.50 | | |

(Qualification – 100 runs, average 10.00)
M. Prabhakar 122 and 27 (one match); A. Bhardwaj 101 (one match).

| BOWLING | Overs | Mds | Runs | Wkts | Av | Best | 5/in | 10/m |
|---|---|---|---|---|---|---|---|---|
| R. Goel | 363.3 | 116 | 689 | 48 | 14.35 | 7/33 | 6 | 2 |
| V.B. Singh | 65 | 17 | 160 | 10 | 16.00 | 3/5 | | |
| Jyotiprasad | 137.4 | 31 | 403 | 25 | 16.12 | 6/35 | 2 | |
| M. Bhatt | 80.2 | 19 | 184 | 11 | 16.72 | 6/17 | 1 | 1 |
| M.R. Bhalla | 137.5 | 29 | 288 | 17 | 16.94 | 5/27 | 2 | |
| Umesh Kumar | 109.3 | 38 | 225 | 13 | 17.30 | 5/9 | 2 | |
| Natu Patel | 32.3 | 3 | 173 | 10 | 17.30 | 7/122 | 1 | 1 |
| Arshad Ayub | 139.5 | 24 | 349 | 20 | 17.45 | 6/47 | 1 | |
| R.N. Kapil Dev | 330.1 | 70 | 847 | 46 | 18.41 | 9/83 | 3 | 1 |
| Rajinder Singh | 68 | 7 | 190 | 10 | 19.00 | 3/47 | | |
| Chetan Sharma | 256.5 | 27 | 977 | 51 | 19.15 | 7/83 | 5 | |
| A.D. Gaekwad | 100 | 30 | 234 | 11 | 21.27 | 3/20 | | |
| S. Venkatarag-havan | 221.2 | 54 | 495 | 23 | 21.52 | 5/65 | 1 | |
| N. Venkataram | 124.5 | 22 | 308 | 14 | 22.00 | 5/59 | 1 | |
| N. Bhagtheria | 107.4 | 27 | 243 | 11 | 22.09 | 4/43 | | |
| Gulrez Ali | 169 | 46 | 398 | 18 | 22.11 | 7/27 | 1 | |
| W.V. Raman | 113.5 | 23 | 314 | 14 | 22.42 | 4/128 | | |
| A.R.B. Bhatt | 363.4 | 75 | 976 | 43 | 22.69 | 8/70 | 4 | 1 |
| R.C. Shukla | 171.4 | 29 | 458 | 20 | 22.90 | 3/0 | | |
| P. Rathod | 83.5 | 13 | 279 | 12 | 23.25 | 4/48 | | |
| V. Gawate | 79.3 | 10 | 283 | 12 | 23.58 | 4/96 | | |
| Maninder Singh | 493.5 | 131 | 1237 | 51 | 24.25 | 6/34 | 3 | 1 |
| R.S. Ghai | 82 | 16 | 296 | 12 | 24.66 | 4/69 | | |
| Gopal Sharma | 239.4 | 54 | 644 | 26 | 24.76 | 8/155 | 2 | |
| N.Y. Satham | 109.2 | 28 | 373 | 15 | 24.86 | 4/43 | | |
| D.R. Doshi | 289.5 | 50 | 901 | 36 | 25.02 | 7/57 | 4 | 1 |
| M.V. Narasimha Rao | 153.5 | 9 | 559 | 22 | 25.40 | 6/102 | 3 | 1 |
| R.C. Thakkar | 208.1 | 36 | 565 | 22 | 25.68 | 4/90 | | |
| D.V. Pardeshi | 206.3 | 59 | 388 | 15 | 25.86 | 3/40 | | |
| B.S. Sandhu | 273.4 | 56 | 918 | 35 | 26.22 | 6/64 | 1 | |
| G. D'Monte | 112 | 10 | 394 | 15 | 26.26 | 5/102 | 1 | |
| G.L. Rathore | 149.5 | 27 | 399 | 15 | 26.60 | 4/57 | | |
| H.A. Pandya | 117 | 27 | 360 | 13 | 27.69 | 4/111 | | |
| L. Sivarama-krishnan | 180.3 | 14 | 687 | 25 | 27.48 | 5/446 | 1 | |
| Randhir Singh | 122 | 18 | 390 | 14 | 27.85 | 5/122 | 1 | |
| S. Valson | 232.3 | 38 | 872 | 31 | 28.12 | 5/54 | 1 | |
| D. Chopra | 136.2 | 33 | 366 | 13 | 28.15 | 3/61 | | |
| A. Patel | 234.2 | 46 | 708 | 25 | 28.32 | 5/71 | 2 | |
| B. Mistry | 102.1 | 14 | 341 | 12 | 28.41 | 4/40 | | |
| S.M. Mudkavi | 232 | 49 | 545 | 19 | 28.68 | 4/147 | | |
| R.S. Hans | 280.2 | 70 | 694 | 24 | 28.91 | 5/47 | 2 | |
| A. Petiwale | 118.1 | 25 | 321 | 11 | 29.18 | 5/65 | 1 | |
| P. Sunderam | 222.4 | 38 | 751 | 24 | 31.29 | 5/98 | 3 | |
| S. Madan Lal | 316 | 71 | 887 | 28 | 31.67 | 6/38 | 2 | |
| N. Parsana | 92.2 | 12 | 349 | 11 | 31.72 | 3/47 | | |
| R.R. Kulkarni | 285.4 | 35 | 1117 | 35 | 31.91 | 6/58 | 2 | |
| R. Pankule | 126.4 | 18 | 320 | 10 | 32.00 | 3/35 | | |
| V.S. Wadkar | 119 | 21 | 513 | 16 | 32.06 | 4/50 | | |
| A. Jha | 149 | 23 | 549 | 17 | 32.29 | 5/112 | 1 | |
| Kirti Azad | 285 | 62 | 777 | 24 | 32.27 | 4/23 | | |
| J. Pandya | 103 | 16 | 395 | 12 | 32.91 | 5/56 | 1 | |
| H. Praharaj | 111.4 | 20 | 397 | 12 | 33.08 | 6/149 | 1 | |
| P. Banerjee | 123 | 13 | 498 | 15 | 33.20 | 3/20 | | |
| R.M.H. Binny | 147 | 19 | 504 | 15 | 33.60 | 3/18 | | |
| Harsh Mathur | 101 | 15 | 342 | 10 | 34.20 | 4/46 | | |
| T.A. Sekhar | 175 | 16 | 748 | 21 | 35.61 | 4/83 | | |
| D. Meher Baba | 113.5 | 21 | 392 | 11 | 35.63 | 3/109 | | |
| S. Talwar | 241 | 48 | 656 | 18 | 36.44 | 5/66 | 1 | |
| R.J. Shastri | 531.4 | 117 | 1372 | 36 | 38.11 | 5/75 | 1 | |
| V. Prasad | 135 | 20 | 425 | 11 | 38.63 | 4/77 | | |
| S.N. Yadav | 374.1 | 66 | 1137 | 29 | 39.20 | 5/131 | 1 | |
| A. Bhattarc-garjee | 213 | 37 | 650 | 16 | 40.62 | 5/29 | 1 | |
| S. Sahu | 119.4 | 13 | 511 | 11 | 46.45 | 3/95 | | |
| Mehboob Iqbal | 117 | 9 | 470 | 10 | 47.00 | 4/80 | | |
| S. Keshwala | 151 | 15 | 697 | 11 | 63.36 | 5/106 | 1 | |

(Qualification – 10 wickets)

## FIELDING

42–C.S. Pandit (ct 35/st 7); 28–S.C. Khanna (ct 21/st 7); 27–K.S. More (ct 20/st 7); 21–S.M.H. Kirmani (ct 19/st 2); 18–S. Viswanath (ct 17/st 1); 16–Salim Ahmed (ct 12/st 4); 14–Kirti Azad and A. Wagh (ct 11/st 3); 13—A.D. Gaekwad; 12—R. Lamba; 11–A.B. Reddy (ct 7/st 4); 10–L. Sivaramakrishnan, V. Sivaramakrishnan, P. Roy and S. Kaushik (ct 9/st 1)

SECTION B

# The Season in Australia

McDonald's Cup. Sheffield Shield.
Pakistan and West Indies in Australia.
Review of the season by Frank Tyson.

*Rodney Marsh.*
*(Adrian Murrell)*

Once more Australian cricket fans were confronted by a busy season, a five-match Test series against the Pakistanis, followed by the Benson and Hedges World Series of fifteen one-day internationals and best of three finals between Australia, Pakistan and West Indies, and the full domestic season of Sheffield Shield and McDonald's Cup, both of which would culminate in finals played in March.

Three of the state sides showed changes in captaincy. Ray Bright was appointed to lead Victoria, still in a stage of transition; Dirk Wellham succeeded Rick McCosker as captain of the reigning Sheffield Shield champions, New South Wales; and Allan Border took over from Greg Chappell in Queensland. Brian Davison returned to Tasmania as chief coach, but Tasmania, still led by Roger Woolley, would be without Holding and Roland Butcher. Bruce Yardley and Craig Serjeant retired from first-class cricket so weakening the Western Australian contingent, but as the state welcomed the arrival of Shaun Graf from Victoria and promoted Australian youth captain Mike Veletta, it was unlikely that their powers would be diminished. Victoria lost leg-spinner Jim Higgs as well as Graf and Davis retired so leaving New South Wales with only *nine* Test players in their side. It seemed likely that South Australia would miss Joel Garner who performed so splendidly in 1982–83.

The heavy fixture list had to accommodate an extra match when it was decided to play the 1982–83 McDonald's Cup Final as a curtain-raiser to the new season. The game, originally scheduled for 20 March 1983, in Perth, had been abandoned without a ball being bowled because of rain.

The most disconcerting news before the match was when it was announced that Terry Alderman would not be in the Western Australian side because there were still doubts as to his fitness following the injury to his shoulder sustained in a skirmish with an invading spectator during the Test match at Perth in November, 1982.

New South Wales, led for the first time by Dirk Wellham, batted first and were given a sound start by McCosker and Dyson. Chappell failed, but Wellham held the batting together with some good forcing strokes and New South Wales averaged nearly four runs an over from their fifty overs.

Western Australia lost Laird early, but Wood, Shipperd and Hughes all batted well. Hughes gave the innings its necessary impetus and his fine knock won him the Man of the Match award. There was some panic towards the end of the innings when Macleay was run out, but Western Australia gained revenge for their defeat in the Sheffield Shield final when they won with five balls to spare.

### McDonald's Cup

***15 October 1983***

***at Brisbane***

**Tasmania** 237 for 8 (D.C. Boon 94)
**Queensland** 194 (G.S. Chappell 68)

*Tasmania won by 43 runs*

***at Perth***

**Victoria** 234 for 4 (G.N. Yallop 91, J.M. Wiener 74)
**Western Australia** 235 for 7 (M. Veletta 67, G. Shipperd 60)

*Western Australia won by 3 wickets*

A week after the 1982–83 final the 1983–84 McDonald's Cup competition began. In Brisbane Tasmania gained a splendid and surprising victory over the home side. Boon, jostling for a place in the Australian side, shared stands of 87 for the third wicket with Davison and 80 for the fourth wicket with Roger Woolley. Boon was dismissed by Rackemann for 94, but his innings had placed Tasmania in a strong position and won him the Man of the Match award. Queensland recovered from 41 for 3 when Wessels and Chappell added 84, but they then lost 5 wickets for 38 runs.

**McDONALD'S CUP FINAL 1982–83: WESTERN AUSTRALIA *v.* NEW SOUTH WALES**
8 October 1983 at Perth

| NEW SOUTH WALES | | | |
|---|---|---|---|
| R.B. McCosker | c Marsh, b Boyd | | 21 |
| J. Dyson | c Andrews, b Macleay | | 42 |
| T.M. Chappell | c sub (Veletta), b Boyd | | 0 |
| D.M. Wellham† | not out | | 65 |
| S.B. Smith | c and b Hogan | | 11 |
| P.M. Toohey | c Laird, b Hogan | | 24 |
| S.J. Rixon* | c Marsh, b Clark | | 9 |
| G.F. Lawson | not out | | 5 |
| M.J. Bennett | | | |
| M.R. Whitney | | | |
| G. Spring | | | |
| Extras | b 3, lb 4, w 8, nb 3 | | 18 |
| (50 overs) | (for 6 wickets) | | 195 |

| | O | M | R | W |
|---|---|---|---|---|
| Lillee | 10 | 1 | 38 | — |
| Clark | 10 | — | 36 | 1 |
| Boyd | 10 | 2 | 29 | 2 |
| Macleay | 10 | — | 33 | 1 |
| Hogan | 10 | 1 | 41 | 2 |

FALL OF WICKETS
1- 50, 2- 56, 3- 91, 4- 118, 5- 158, 6- 172

| WESTERN AUSTRALIA | | | |
|---|---|---|---|
| B.M. Laird | c Spring, b Lawson | | 10 |
| G.M. Wood | c Rixon, b Bennett | | 30 |
| G. Shipperd | lbw, b Whitney | | 54 |
| K.J. Hughes† | b Lawson | | 61 |
| W. Andrews | not out | | 22 |
| R.W. Marsh* | b Whitney | | 13 |
| K.H. Macleay | run out | | 0 |
| D.L. Boyd | not out | | 0 |
| T.G. Hogan | | | |
| D.K. Lillee | | | |
| W.M. Clark | | | |
| Extras | lb 3, w 5 | | 8 |
| (49.1 overs) | (for 6 wickets) | | 198 |

| | O | M | R | W |
|---|---|---|---|---|
| Lawson | 10 | 2 | 27 | 2 |
| Spring | 10 | 2 | 26 | — |
| Whitney | 9.1 | — | 35 | 2 |
| Chappell | 10 | — | 39 | — |
| Bennett | 10 | — | 63 | 1 |

FALL OF WICKETS
1- 13, 2- 68, 3- 133, 4- 172, 5- 187, 6- 194

**Western Australia won by 4 wickets**

Wiener and Yallop shared a second wicket stand of 114 in Perth and Victoria seemed well on top when Laird was dismissed in Balcam's first over. Some steady batting from Shipperd followed, but it was a fifth wicket stand of 98 between Mike Veletta and Rodney Marsh that turned the game in the home side's favour and they won a spirited victory with an over to spare, Veletta taking the personal award in his first senior match.

**McDonald's Cup**

***16 October***

***at Brisbane***

**New South Wales** 165 for 8
**Queensland** 166 for 6 (K.C. Wessels 71)

*Queensland won by 4 wickets*

***at Perth***

**South Australia** 136 for 6 (W.B. Phillips 58)
**Western Australia** 112 for 3

*Western Australia won on faster scoring rate*

Rain disrupted the game in Perth, but solid batting ensured the home side of victory and a place in the semi-finals on a faster run rate. Only a hard hit 58 by Wayne Phillips, batting at number 5, and an equally hard hit 39 from Darling at number 7 had saved South Australia from complete rout. No other batsman reached double figures. Lillee bowled with penetration and economy.

Queensland kept alive their hopes of reaching the semi-finals when they beat New South Wales with two balls to spare. Rackemann bowled well and none of the visitors could play a dominant innings. Kerr went for 0, but Wessels batted finely and Henschell played a forceful late innings to clinch victory.

Wessels and Lillee took the individual honours.

***21, 22, 23 and 24 October 1983***

***at Brisbane***

**Queensland** 422 for 6 dec (G.M. Ritchie 196, R.B. Phillips 77 not out, A.R. Border 68, G.K. Whyte 51 not out, Mohammad Nazir 4 for 73) and 227 for 3 dec (K.C. Wessels 127, R.B. Kerr 51)
**Pakistanis** 364 for 6 dec (Mudassar Nazar 104, Mohsin Khan 90, Wasim Raja 52) and 73 for 1

*Match drawn*

***at Perth***

**Western Australia** 439 for 9 dec (K.J. Hughes 129, G. Shipperd 96, B.M. Laird 66)
**New South Wales** 156 (S.B. Smith 56) and 213 (D.K. Lillee 6 for 62)

*Western Australia won by an innings and 70 runs*
*Western Australia 16 pts, New South Wales 0 pts*

***at Adelaide***

**Tasmania** 380 (D.C. Boon 80, I.R. Beven 51, R.M. Hogg 4 for 77) and 362 (B.F. Davison 145, D.C. Boon 70, P.I. Faulkner 57 not out, R.J. Inverarity 6 for 96)
**South Australia** 386 for 5 dec (W.B. Phillips 234, M.D. Haysman 100)

*Match drawn*
*South Australia 4 pts, Tasmania 0 pts*

*Wayne Phillips on his way to 234 against Tasmania, an innings which won him a Test place. (Philip Tyson)*

With Imran Khan unfit, Sarfraz Nawaz suspended and Zaheer Abbas not yet able to join the party because of problems, the Pakistan tour of Australia started in chaos. Javed Miandad led the side in the opening game which saw Queensland recover from 35 for 2 to reach a massive 422 for 6. The home side's hero was Greg Ritchie who hit twenty-four fours in a career best innings of 196. He shared century stands with Border and Phillips for the third and sixth wickets respectively. Mohammad Nazir alone of the Pakistan bowlers bowled with any zest and consistent control.

Mudassar and Mohsin began the Pakistan innings with a

*Haysman began the year with a century for South Australia against Tasmania at Adelaide. (Philip Tyson)*

stand of 208 which virtually determined that the match would be drawn. Kerr and Wessels began the second Queensland innings with a stand of 146 and when Border delayed his declaration until tea-time the game was doomed to end in farce.

Apart from the batting of Wessels and Ritchie, the Australian selectors must have also noted the pace and accuracy of Rackemann who had 3 for 57 in 34 overs in the first innings.

The meeting of last year's Sheffield Shield finalists in Perth was dominated by Western Australia. With Laird, Shipperd and Hughes all in fine form, they reached 290 before the third wicket fell, Hughes and Shipperd sharing a stand of 175.

Facing a total of 439, New South Wales, not helped by the early running out of Dyson, collapsed before Lillee and Graf and were forced to follow-on. McCosker and Dyson began their second innings with a stand of 90, but, with Lillee in splendid form, New South Wales wilted once more and were beaten by an innings.

There were first-class debuts for Veletta and Bensley in this match, and in Adelaide Carmichael and Buckingham made their debuts. Tasmania batted steadily with Boon once again displaying his class and composure, but he was overshadowed when, in the South Australian innings, Wayne Phillips asserted his right to a place in the Australian Test side with a mighty knock of 234, he and Haysman sharing a stand of 227 for the third wicket. Phillips batted for 370 minutes and hit three sixes and twenty-three fours in what was his second double century in two seasons for the state.

Tasmania had problems early in their second innings, but Davison and Boon, again, played well and with over a day's play lost to rain, a draw was inevitable.

### 26 October 1983

#### at Whyalla

**South Australian Country XI** 92 (Abdul Qadir 5 for 15)
**Pakistanis** 95 for 1 (Javed Miandad 61 not out)

*Pakistanis won by 9 wickets*

Abdul Qadir, another who had been at differences with the Pakistan Board and selectors, played his first match of the tour and destroyed the minor eleven who lost 5 wickets for 11 runs in the middle of their innings after reaching 68 for 2. Javed and Qasim Umar opened with a stand of 43 and the tourists reached their target in 26 overs. It was announced that Sarfraz would not be joining the Pakistan side.

### 28, 29, 30 and 31 October 1983

#### at Adelaide

**South Australia** 277 for 5 dec (W.B. Phillips 75, W.M. Darling 58, M.D. Haysman 57, D.W. Hookes 55) and 243 (G.A. Bishop 77, Abdul Qadir 7 for 122)
**Pakistanis** 274 for 7 dec (Mudassar Nazar 93, Wasim Bari 73 not out) and 249 for 3 (Qasim Umar 73 not out, Mudassar Nazar 71)

*Pakistanis won by 7 wickets*

#### at Sydney

**Victoria** 227 (G.N. Yallop 77, G.F. Lawson 6 for 43) and 165 for 3 (D.M.J. Jones 83 not out)
**New South Wales** 409 for 5 dec (J. Dyson 178 not out, S.B. Smith 64, P.M. Toohey 61)

*Match drawn*
*New South Wales 4 pts, Victoria 0 pts*

#### at Brisbane

**Tasmania** 224 (I.R. Beven 57, J.N. Maguire 4 for 44) and 378 (B.F. Davison 156 retired hurt, R.D. Woolley 75, P.I. Faulkner 61 not out)
**Queensland** 470 for 6 dec (G.S. Chappell 93, A.B. Henschell 89 not out, R.B. Kerr 75, A.R. Border 64, G.M. Ritchie 60) and 134 for 3 (G.M. Ritchie 67 not out)

*Queensland won by 7 wickets*
*Queensland 16 pts, Tasmania 0 pts*

With the first four South Australian batsmen scoring 50s and only the bowling of Mudassar Nazar looking as if it could pose problems with its gentle swing, Pakistan seemed in some disarray. Tahir had withdrawn from the match with injury and Abdul Qadir left the field on the first day also with injury. At 25 for 2 Pakistani troubles had deepened, but Mudassar again batted splendidly and found a good partner in Qasim. Then, a late, breezy knock from Wasim Bari brought the tourists to unexpected parity.

South Australia again began soundly and reached 151 for 3, but an unchanged spell of 32.4 overs from Abdul Qadir altered the course of the match. He took 6 of the last 7 wickets to fall while only 92 were added.

Mohsin and Mudassar gave Pakistan a good start with a stand of 89, but the successive batsmen did not fail and Pakistan won by tea-time on the last afternoon.

Rain deprived New South Wales of victory in Sydney where no play was possible on the last day. Yallop batted as firmly as ever for Victoria, but it was only some late blows from Miles and Bright that gave the Victorian score any semblance of respectability. Victoria had lost their first four wickets, all to Lawson, for 52. New South Wales lost McCosker and Chappell for 58, but Dyson played a mighty innings and, after a stand of 82 with Wellham, shared century stands with Smith and Toohey.

Victoria again began badly and lost 3 for 40, but Jones played with great panache before the rain.

Tasmania fared badly in Brisbane never quite coming to terms with the varied Queensland attack. In response the home side built up a first innings lead of 146 with only Wessels (29) and Phillips (39) failing to reach fifty. Tasmania made a brave recovery in their second innings. They were 33 for 3 before Davison and Saunders made a century stand, but Davison was forced to retire hurt at 133 and resumed again at 198 for 6.

Woolley batted well, but a big defeat looked inevitable until Faulkner joined Davison at 258 for 8. They had added 118 when Davison was again forced to retire hurt and 2 runs later the innings was over. Queensland, sparked by the eager Ritchie, scored at $4\frac{1}{2}$ an over to win the match.

### 2 November 1983

#### at Northam

**Pakistanis** 239 for 3 (Zaheer Abbas 117 not out, Qasim Umar 93)
**Western Australian Country XI** 126 (T. Waldron 50)

*Pakistanis won by 113 runs*

Zaheer Abbas played his first innings of the tour, scoring his runs off 94 balls in 101 minutes. Qasim batted 136 minutes before being bowled by Francis, but only the left-handed Waldron, captain of the country side, showed any resistance to the Pakistan attack with 50 off 65 balls.

*4, 5, 6 and 7 November 1983*

*at Perth*

**Pakistanis** 290 (Mudassar Nazar 113, Javed Miandad 94, K.H. Macleay 4 for 50) and 242 (Javed Miandad 52)
**Western Australia** 349 (G.M. Wood 74, S.F. Graf 54, Tahir Naqqash 4 for 80) and 187 for 4 (K.H. Macleay 82)
*Western Australia won by 6 wickets*

A stand of 198 for the third wicket between Mudassar and Javed was Pakistan's one ray of hope on a first day which saw them discomfitted by Lillee and Macleay. Javed survived a torrid time from Lillee to support Mudassar with great determination, but in the last session of the day Pakistan lost 5 wickets for 37 runs.

Western Australia lost Laird at 14, but an even batting display with a late boost from Graf gave them a lead of 59. Tahir and Mohammad Nazir bowled well, but the last 6 state wickets added 166. At the end of the third day Pakistan were precariously placed at 92 for 3, Marsh and Shipperd having made excellent catches and Mudassar having his first failure of the tour. A late revival saw them to 242 all out just before tea on the final day, leaving the home side 140 minutes in which to make 184 to win.

Macleay, with match figures of 7 for 119, was promoted to number 3 and scored 82 off 100 balls. He and Hughes added 108 in 83 minutes. When Mudassar started the last over Western Australia needed 4 to win. Veletta hooked the third ball for 2 and then scored a single. Mudassar brilliantly stopped a fierce straight drive from Marsh, but the home side won off the last ball of the match when Marsh pulled the ball to the mid-wicket boundary.

Disturbing news for Australia on the eve of the first Test match was that David Hookes had entered hospital with a severe infection.

**McDonald's Cup**

*5 November 1983*

*at Launceston*

**New South Wales** 237 for 7 (P.M. Toohey 82, G.R.J. Matthews 61 not out)
**Tasmania** 166 for 9
*New South Wales won by 71 runs*

*at Adelaide*

**Victoria** 205 for 7 (J.M. Wiener 60)
**South Australia** 207 for 2 (M.D. Haysman 92 not out)
*South Australia won by 8 wickets*

Clough and Astley reduced New South Wales to 17 for 3, but Smith and Toohey effected a recovery and a stand of 73 for the seventh wicket between Matthews and Rixon placed the match firmly in the visitors' grip. Matthews bowling (3 for 47) placed him as Man of the Match and New South Wales as easy winners.

There was an equally comfortable win for South Australia in Adelaide. Wiener, Jones and Taylor batted well, but, led by Haysman, the home side romped to victory with 6.3 overs to spare. Haysman and Darling added 98 for the second wicket and Haysman, Man of the Match, and O'Connor joined in an unbeaten stand of 70 for the third wicket.

Tasmania's defeat did not affect their position at the top of group one on a faster striking rate.

**Qualifying Tables**

| Group One | P | W | L | Pts |
|---|---|---|---|---|
| Tasmania | 2 | 1 | 1 | 2 |
| New South Wales | 2 | 1 | 1 | 2 |
| Queensland | 2 | 1 | 1 | 2 |
| **Group Two** | *P* | *W* | *L* | *Pts* |
| Western Australia | 2 | 2 | – | 4 |
| South Australia | 2 | 1 | 1 | 2 |
| Victoria | 2 | – | 2 | – |

*11, 12, 13 and 14 November 1983*

*at Melbourne*

**Victoria** 418 for 5 dec (M.D. Taylor 172 not out, D.M.J. Jones 128, W.G. Whiteside 62) and 294 for 3 (P.A. Hibbert 83, M.D. Taylor 74 not out, D.M.J. Jones 70)
**Tasmania** 450 for 8 dec (D.C. Boon 227, P.I. Faulkner 52) and 145 for 4
*Match drawn*
*Tasmania 4 pts, Victoria 0 pts*

Bowlers continued to suffer in the Sheffield Shield as batsmen plundered runs. Taylor hit his highest score in first-class cricket and he and Dean Jones, who consistently displayed his rich promise, savaged a weak Tasmanian attack. Whiteside scored 62 on his debut and Victoria declared at 418 for 5 which seemed likely to give them a commanding first innings lead.

Tasmania batted doggedly, but at 297 for 6, it seemed that they would fall short of the home side's total. David Boon, still a month short of his twenty-third birthday, was once more in majestic form, however, and furthered his claim for a Test place with a career best 227. He found an eager partner in Peter Faulker whose early season batting form had been a revelation. They added 127 for the seventh wicket and Tasmania took first innings points.

Victoria batted again with a hint of aggression, but the game, inevitably, was drawn after Tasmania had been set 263 to win at six an over.

*David Boon – a career best 227 for Tasmania against Victoria at Melbourne, 11–14 November. (Philip Tyson)*

## First Test Match
## AUSTRALIA *v.* PAKISTAN

Few sides can have been so ill-prepared for a Test match as Pakistan. With Imran captaining the side but unfit to play in a match, dissension and resignation amid selectors, Sarfraz banned and then reinstated after an appeal to the courts of law, it was unlikely that the side would be in the best condition to take on Australia at Perth. The first day realised the Pakistani's worst fears.

A green tinge in the wicket prompted Zaheer to ask Australia to bat when he won the toss, but a pace attack without Imran was somewhat toothless and by the end of the first day Australia were 330 for 3. The Pakistani fielding had been dreadful and the bowling inadequate.

Wessels never looked comfortable and fell to Azeem Hafeez whose left-arm seamers promised most for Pakistan. Tahir was wayward and Mudassar, though steady, did not find this one of the days on which he could break through. Wayne Phillips, playing in his first Test match, was joined by another left-hander, Graham Yallop, in a second wicket stand of 259, a record for Australia against Pakistan.

Phillips was missed by Javed off Abdul Qadir when 39, but he gave a most encouraging display for Australia with some powerful shots and a consistent willingness to hit the ball. He had a quiet period in the early afternoon, but he became the ninth Australian to reach a century in his first Test innings and hit twenty fours in his 159 which came off 247 deliveries. It was a most impressive performance.

Yallop, with his seventh Test century, was equally impressive and savaged the spin of Mohammad Nazir and Abdul Qadir. His hundred came off 170 balls.

Azeem Hafeez gave Pakistan some hope the next day when he took four valuable wickets to restrict Australia to a score far smaller than had seemed likely. Play began $2\frac{1}{2}$ hours late after rain and some minor vandalism of the pitch.

Hughes declared, leaving Pakistan over an hour's batting at the end of the day. By the close they were in total disarray at 28 for 4 and facing defeat. Hogg took three wickets in 10

*Phillips sweeps Abdul Qadir for four on his way to his Test debut hundred. (Philip Tyson)*

*Mohsin Khan caught Border, bowled Rackemann 24. (Philip Tyson)*

balls, and with Lillee removing Mudassar, Pakistan went from 7 for 0 to 15 for 4. There was some very feeble batting, and the lack of application shown by Zaheer and Javed in particular symbolised the disintegration of the Pakistan side. Wayne Phillips added to his triumph of the first day by taking three catches at third slip on the second evening.

On the third morning Hogg and Lillee failed to find the penetration of the previous evening, but Carl Rackemann generated surprising pace and, helped by magnificent slip catching by Greg Chappell, destroyed the Pakistan middle order so that the visitors followed-on 307 runs behind.

Mohsin and Mudassar gave Pakistan a better start in the second innings until both fell to Rackemann but it was Qasim Umar and Javed Miandad who gave Pakistan some hope with 92 runs in the last two hours of the day.

They extended their partnership to 125 in 187 minutes on the fourth morning before Qasim Umar played back to Rackemann and was caught behind. Qasim, who had played so finely in the Quaid-e-Azam trophy in 1982–83 and was unlucky not to have been included in the Pakistan side for the World Cup, played with great courage in both innings of what was only his second Test match. His determination mocked the efforts of some of his colleagues.

Javed was also out to Rackemann only nine runs later, and Pakistan now began to wilt. Wasim Bari was out to a brilliantly acrobatic catch by Marsh. Zaheer who, like Wasim Bari, had not exuded the greatest of confidence against the pace bowling tried to cut Rackemann with the new ball and became another Marsh victim. Tahir provided Marsh with his fifth catch of the day to bring his total in Test cricket to a highly impressive 329.

There was some spirit from the tail, but Rackemann once again proved too quick for most of the Pakistani batsmen and Australia won by an innings with a day to spare.

Rackemann's return to Test cricket was spectacular. In 34 overs he took 11 for 118, a match record for an Australian against Pakistan. He bowled Abdul Qadir in the first innings and had Javed lbw in the second, the rest were taken in the catching cordon behind the wicket as were eight other Pakistani batsmen. Their inability to cope with the pace of the Australian bowlers, particularly Hogg and Rackemann, was at times embarrassing.

## FIRST TEST MATCH – AUSTRALIA *v.* PAKISTAN
11, 12, 13 and 14 November 1983 at Perth

### AUSTRALIA

| | FIRST INNINGS | |
|---|---|---|
| K.C. Wessels | c Wasim Bari, b Azeem Hafeez | 12 |
| W.B. Phillips | c Tahir Naqqash, b Mohammad Nazir | 159 |
| G.N. Yallop | b Azeem Hafeez | 141 |
| K.J. Hughes† | b Abdul Qadir | 16 |
| A.R. Border | c Wasim Raja, b Azeem Hafeez | 32 |
| G.S. Chappell | c Azeem Hafeez, b Abdul Qadir | 17 |
| R.W. Marsh* | c Wasim Bari, b Azeem Hafeez | 24 |
| G.F. Lawson | c Mohammad Nazir, b Abdul Qadir | 9 |
| D.K. Lillee | c Wasim Raja, b Azeem Hafeez | 0 |
| R.M. Hogg | not out | 7 |
| C.G. Rackemann | | |
| Extras | lb 9, w 3, nb 7 | 19 |
| | (for 9 wickets dec) | 436 |

| | O | M | R | W |
|---|---|---|---|---|
| Tahir Naqqash | 22 | 6 | 76 | — |
| Azeem Hafeez | 27.5 | 5 | 100 | 5 |
| Mudassar Nazar | 15 | 1 | 39 | — |
| Mohammad Nazir | 29 | 5 | 91 | 1 |
| Abdul Qadir | 32 | 4 | 121 | 3 |

FALL OF WICKETS
1- 34, 2- 293, 3- 321, 4- 369, 5- 386, 6- 404, 7- 424, 8- 424, 9- 436

### PAKISTAN

| | FIRST INNINGS | | SECOND INNINGS | |
|---|---|---|---|---|
| Mohsin Khan | c Marsh, b Hogg | 8 | c Border, b Rackemann | 24 |
| Mudassar Nazar | c Phillips, b Lillee | 1 | c Chappell, b Rackemann | 27 |
| Qasim Umar | c Yallop, b Rackemann | 48 | c Marsh, b Rackemann | 65 |
| Javed Miandad | c Phillips, b Hogg | 0 | lbw, b Rackemann | 46 |
| Zaheer Abbas† | c Phillips, b Hogg | 0 | c Marsh, b Rackemann | 30 |
| Wasim Raja | c Chappell, b Rackemann | 14 | c Marsh, b Lawson | 4 |
| Wasim Bari* | c Chappell, b Rackemann | 0 | c Marsh, b Lawson | 7 |
| Tahir Naqqash | not out | 29 | c Marsh, b Rackemann | 26 |
| Abdul Qadir | b Rackemann | 5 | run out | 18 |
| Mohammed Nazir | c Chappell b Rackemann | 16 | c Border, b Hogg | 18 |
| Azeem Hafeez | c Border, b Lawson | 1 | not out | 0 |
| Extras | lb 3, nb 4 | 7 | b 4, lb 7, w 2, nb 20 | 33 |
| | | 129 | | 298 |

| | O | M | R | W | O | M | R | W |
|---|---|---|---|---|---|---|---|---|
| Lillee | 13 | 3 | 26 | 1 | 29 | 6 | 56 | — |
| Hogg | 12 | 4 | 20 | 3 | 21.1 | 2 | 72 | 1 |
| Rackemann | 8 | — | 32 | 5 | 26 | 6 | 86 | 6 |
| Lawson | 7.2 | — | 48 | 1 | 13 | 1 | 53 | 2 |
| Chappell | | | | | 9 | 1 | 20 | — |

FALL OF WICKETS
1- 7, 2- 13, 3- 15, 4- 15, 5- 65, 6- 68, 7- 90, 8- 105, 9- 124
1- 62, 2- 63, 3- 188, 4- 197, 5- 206, 6- 218, 7- 257, 8- 267, 9- 281

*Umpires:* M.W. Johnson and P. McConnell

**Australia won by an innings and 9 runs**

### *18, 19, 20 and 21 November 1983*

**_at Sydney_**

**New South Wales** 491 for 8 dec (R.B. McCosker 157, D.M. Wellham 96, G.R.J. Matthews 86, S.B. Smith 67)
**Pakistanis** 194 and 435 for 4 (Mudassar Nazar 139, Qasim Umar 131, Javed Miandad 69 not out, Mohsin Khan 63)
*Match drawn*

**_at Brisbane_**

**South Australia** 406 (P.R. Sleep 144, A.M.J. Hilditch 111)
**Queensland** 380 for 6 (A.R. Border 110, K.C. Wessels 104, G.M. Ritchie 53)
*Match drawn*
*Queensland 2 pts, South Australia 2 pts*

**_at Melbourne_**

**Western Australia** 464 for 4 dec (G. Shipperd 167 not out, R.W Marsh 157 not out, G.M. Wood 82)
**Victoria** 276 (G.N. Yallop 113, P.A. Hibbert 56, D.K. Lillee 4 for 75) and 288 for 3 (G.N. Yallop 145 not out, M.D. Taylor 58 not out)
*Match drawn*
*Western Australia 4 pts, Victoria 0 pts*

The Pakistanis found no respite from their troubles. A weak attack was severely punished on the opening day at Sydney when Rick McCosker hit his twenty-seventh first-class hundred as he and Wellham added 191 for the third wicket. New South Wales ended the day at 300 for 3 and next morning consolidated their position as Matthews led some brisk run-getting. He followed his fine innings with some excellently controlled off-spin which reduced the tourists to 113 for 7 by the close.

Ashraf Ali and Mohammad Nazir had a spirited last wicket stand of 63, but they could not save the follow-on. Mudassar Nazar and Mohsin Khan reduced the deficit by 115 before the close and on the last day Mudassar reached his third century of the tour. Qasim Umar hit his first as he and Mudassar put on 164, and he then shared a stand of 155 with Javed Miandad as the game became batting practice.

In Brisbane, bad weather hampered the match and ruled

*Yallop hits Hogan for four during his first innings century against Western Australia at Melbourne, 18–21 November. Yallop hit another century in the second innings and saved his side. (Philip Tyson)*

out play on the last day. Earlier Hilditch had dominated a second wicket stand of 109 with Haysman. Inverarity retired hurt, but he returned later and with Sleep, who had been showing poor form with his leg-spin, in dominant mood with the bat, the last four wickets realised 135.

Queensland's reply was founded on substantial partnerships between Wessels and Ritchie, 96 for the second wicket; Border and Chappell, 87 for the fourth; and Border and Henschell, 100 for the fifth. Then came the rain.

The limp Victorian attack was savaged once again at Melbourne. Greg Shipperd, such a consistent scorer for Western Australia, emulated Peter Sleep by reaching a career best as he and the ferocious Rodney Marsh added an unbeaten 251 for the fifth wicket. Shipperd had already shared a second wicket stand of 127 with Graeme Wood.

Victoria lost Wiener for 0, but Hibbert and Yallop put on 125 for the second wicket. Thereafter the home side's batting fell away before Lillee and Hogan and they were forced to follow-on. They were in some trouble at 64 for 2, but Yallop once more demonstrated his technique and application with his second century of the match and saved his side from defeat.

## Second Test Match
## AUSTRALIA *v.* PAKISTAN

With so much debate and controversy off the field, it seemed highly unlikely that Pakistan would perform well on it, and, indeed, but for rain which washed out all play after lunch on the fourth day, they would have been crushingly defeated once again.

It was most difficult to keep up with the variety of reports concerning the Pakistan side. One day Imran was deposed as captain and was returning home. The next day he was reinstated and was remaining. One week Sarfraz was banned for remarks he had made, the next week he was flying out to strengthen the side. On the evidence of Pakistan's performance, he was desperately needed as was Saleem Malik who was also reported to be joining the party.

Zaheer chose to bat first on a good wicket and he and Wasim Raja, playing in his fiftieth Test, added 62 for the fifth wicket, the only stand of note in a dreadful batting performance. Once more the Australian pace men shattered the Pakistanis. This time it was Lawson who took the main honours, but Hogg reached a personal landmark with his hundredth Test wicket.

In the field Pakistan were as bad as they had been at the crease. Zaheer's leadership was non-existent, his tactics incomprehensible. By the end of the second day, at 273 for 4, Australia were in total command.

On the third day, Greg Chappell and Allan Border extended their fifth wicket stand to 171. Border reached his tenth Test century, Chappell, the master of elegance, his twenty-third. Chappell hit seventeen fours in his innings which lasted for 334 minutes. He moved within reach of Don Bradman's record aggregate for Australia in Test cricket, and, inevitably, it was all done with grace and charm. He is a man incapable of an ineloquent gesture.

For Pakistan the rain came as a merciful release from further suffering. Had this been a boxing match, the referee might well have stopped the fight early on the third day so outclassed were the Pakistanis.

### SECOND TEST MATCH – AUSTRALIA *v.* PAKISTAN
25, 26, 27, 28 and 29 November 1983 at Brisbane

**PAKISTAN**

| | FIRST INNINGS | | SECOND INNINGS | |
|---|---|---|---|---|
| Mohsin Khan | c Chappell, b Lawson | 2 | b Lawson | 37 |
| Mudassar Nazar | c Marsh, b Lawson | 24 | c Wessels, b Rackemann | 18 |
| Qasim Umar | c Hughes, b Lawson | 17 | not out | 11 |
| Javed Miandad | c Marsh, b Hogg | 6 | c Phillips, b Rackemann | 5 |
| Zaheer Abbas† | c Border, b Lawson | 56 | not out | 3 |
| Wasim Raja | c Hughes, b Rackemann | 27 | | |
| Wasim Bari* | c Border, b Rackemann | 2 | | |
| Abdul Qadir | b Rackemann | 0 | | |
| Rashid Khan | not out | 13 | | |
| Mohammad Nazir | c Marsh, b Hogg | 1 | | |
| Azeem Hafeez | b Lawson | 2 | | |
| Extras | lb 3, w 1, nb 2 | 6 | lb 6, nb 2 | 8 |
| | | 156 | (for 3 wickets) | 82 |

| | O | M | R | W | O | M | R | W |
|---|---|---|---|---|---|---|---|---|
| Lawson | 17.1 | 1 | 49 | 5 | 10 | 3 | 24 | 1 |
| Hogg | 15 | 2 | 43 | 2 | 3 | — | 11 | — |
| Rackemann | 10 | 3 | 28 | 3 | 8 | 1 | 31 | 2 |
| Lillee | 8 | 1 | 33 | — | 2 | — | 10 | — |

FALL OF WICKETS
1- 10, 2- 39, 3- 46, 4- 62, 5- 124, 6- 128, 7- 128, 8- 146, 9- 147
1- 57, 2- 59, 3- 74

**AUSTRALIA**

| | FIRST INNINGS | |
|---|---|---|
| K.C. Wessels | c Qasim Umar, b Azeem Hafeez | 35 |
| W.B. Phillips | b Rashid Khan | 46 |
| G.N. Yallop | c Wasim Bari, b Rashid Khan | 33 |
| K.J. Hughes† | c Mohammad Nazir, b Azeem Hafeez | 53 |
| A.R. Border | c Wasim Bari, b Rashid Khan | 118 |
| G.S. Chappell | not out | 150 |
| R.W. Marsh* | b Azeem Hafeez | 1 |
| G.F. Lawson | b Abdul Qadir | 49 |
| D.K. Lillee | | |
| R.M. Hogg | | |
| C.G. Rackemann | | |
| Extras | b 2, lb 6, w1, nb 15 | 24 |
| | (for 7 wickets dec) | 509 |

| | O | M | R | W |
|---|---|---|---|---|
| Azeem Hafeez | 37 | 7 | 152 | 3 |
| Rashid Khan | 43 | 10 | 129 | 3 |
| Mudassar Nazar | 16 | 2 | 47 | — |
| Abdul Qadir | 32 | 5 | 112 | 1 |
| Mohammad Nazir | 24 | 6 | 50 | — |
| Wasim Raja | 3 | — | 11 | — |

FALL OF WICKETS
1- 56, 2- 120, 3- 124, 4- 232, 5- 403, 6- 406, 7- 509

*Umpires:* M.W. Johnson and R.A. French

**Match drawn**

*Allan Border who shared a 5th wicket stand of 171 with Greg Chappell. (Adrian Murrell)*

***25, 26, 27 and 28 November 1983***

***at Perth***

**Tasmania** 300 (D.C. Boon 55, B.F. Davison 51, T.M. Alderman 4 for 56) and 302 for 6 dec (B.F. Davison 152 not out, P.I. Faulkner 84 not out)

**Western Australia** 284 (G. Shipperd 80, B.M. Laird 57, P.M. Clough 4 for 60, P.A. Blizzard 4 for 84) and 320 for 4 (G.M. Wood 167 not out, S.C. Clements 67)

*Western Australia won by 6 wickets*
*Western Australia 12 pts, Tasmania 4 pts*

***at Adelaide***

**Victoria** 248 (D.M.J. Jones 67, R.J. Bright 64, S.D.H. Parkinson 5 for 41) and 367 for 6 dec (M.D. Taylor 122, W.G. Whiteside 65, D.M.J. Jones 60)

**South Australia** 279 (G.A. Bishop 58, A.I.C. Dodemaide 4 for 63) and 218 for 5 (G.A. Bishop 90, R.J. Inverarity 59 not out)

*Match drawn*
*South Australia 4 pts, Victoria 0 pts*

Tasmania lost Ray, run out for 0, but some steady batting throughout the order took them to a commendable 300 in Perth. From the home side's point of view, the most pleasing aspect of the first day was the evidence of continued improvement from Terry Alderman.

In reply, Western Australia began hesitantly, but Laird, dropped down the order to number 5, joined Shipperd in a stand of 96. There were some important late contributions from Sean Graf and reserve wicket-keeper Hill, 31 not out, who was making his first-class debut, but Western Australia surrendered first innings points by 16 runs. Clough and Blizzard took the honours for Tasmania who collapsed disastrously to 99 for 6 when they batted again. What followed was another remarkable display of batting by Davison and Faulkner. For the third time in four matches, they shared a century partnership. This time their stand was an unbeaten 203, a Tasmanian record for the seventh wicket. Davison's score was the highest made by a Tasmanian against Western Australia and brought his season's average to 122.60. Faulkner was averaging 160.00 at the end of his innings.

Their efforts proved to be of no avail. Set to make 319 at five an over, the home side, inspired by a mighty innings from Graeme Wood, reached their target. A third wicket stand between Wood and Clements of 140 was decisive, but Laird also played well to see Western Australia to victory and to the leadership of the Sheffield Shield table.

With Yallop on Test duty, Victoria found run-getting difficult and were 28 for 4 before Jones, Whiteside, Dodemaide and Bright brought about respectability. Tony Dodemaide, who had come into prominence with the Australian under-19 team in England in 1983 and was making his first-class debut in this match, followed his sound batting with 3 of the first 4 South Australian wickets, but he could not prevent the home side's middle order batting taking the points.

Victoria batted with greater conviction in their second innings, and Jones, Taylor and Whiteside, whose 65 was the best of his short career, made it possible for Bright to declare and set the home side to make 337 at more than five an over. They lost 4 for 71, but Glenn Bishop in a whirlwind display

*Tony Dodemaide – an impressive all-round debut for Victoria against South Australia 25–27 November. (Philip Tyson)*

which brought him a career best added 147 with Inverarity, Bishop's contribution being 90. This draw left Victoria pointless at the bottom of the table.

### *2, 3, 4 and 5 December 1983*

#### *at Melbourne*

**Victoria** 555 for 5 dec (G.N. Yallop 220, M.D. Taylor 101 not out, P.A. Hibbert 83) and 136 for 3 dec
**Pakistanis** 406 for 9 dec (Mudassar Nazar 103, Javed Miandad 85, Qasim Umar 79, Zaheer Abbas 54, R.J. McCurdy 4 for 169) and 288 for 3 (Mudassar Nazar 123, Javed Miandad 106 not out)

*Pakistanis won by 7 wickets*

#### *at Sydney*

**New South Wales** 141 and 297 (D.M. Wellham 108, J.N. Maguire 5 for 108)
**Queensland** 379 (K.C. Wessels 80, G.M. Ritchie 75, A.R. Border 68, R.B. Kerr 55, R.G. Holland 4 for 72) and 62 for 2

*Queensland won by 8 wickets*
*Queensland 16 pts, New South Wales 0 pts*

#### *at Adelaide*

**South Australia** 303 (R.J. Inverarity 69, D.W. Hookes 57) and 182
**Western Australia** 268 (K.J. Hughes 73, R.M. Hogg 5 for 53) and 219 for 5 (G. Shipperd 70 not out, B.M. Laird 64)

*Western Australia won by 5 wickets*
*Western Australia 12 pts, South Australia 4 pts*

With Graeme Yallop hitting his fourth century in five innings, Victoria gave the Pakistani bowlers, strengthened by the arrival of Sarfraz, another gruelling time. Watts and Hibbert began with 94 in 116 minutes, and then runs flowed as Yallop shared century stands with Hibbert, Whiteside and Taylor, who reached an accomplished hundred. Bright declared after tea on the second day and Pakistan closed at 84 for 1.

Next day, Mudassar Nazar extended his stand with Qasim to 147 and reached his fourth hundred of the tour. The tourists were 283 for 2, but lost 3 wickets for 8 runs. Some tenacity from the tail, particularly Wasim Bari and Abdul Qadir, however, saved the follow-on, at which point Zaheer declared.

Victoria hit breezily and Bright declared at lunch on the last day, leaving the visitors 47 overs in which to make 288. Mudassar, in brilliant form again for his second century of the match, and Javed, 100 in 100 minutes off 74 balls, added 109 in 64 minutes, and Pakistan won a thrilling, and improbable victory with an over to spare. Runs had come at more than six an over and no bowler had been spared.

Queensland and Western Australia maintained their lead at the top of the table, twenty points clear of their nearest rivals, when they were both victorious. Once again Western Australia trailed on the first innings, some solid middle order batting, a late flurry by Parkinson and some good bowling by Hogg and Parkinson giving the home side a lead of 35. They collapsed at the second attempt, however, in spite of Hogg's top score of 43, and Western Australia needed only 218 to win. Sensible batting, founded on a second wicket partnership of 76 between Laird, restored to opener, and Shipperd saw them home.

For Queensland at Sydney life was considerably easier. The Queensland seam attack made short work of the home state and relentlessly efficient batting which saw four of the first five men top 50 took the visitors to a first innings lead of 238. At 97 for 4, New South Wales seemed set to lose by an innings, but Wellham played a captain's innings which, if it could not save his side, at least forced Queensland to bat again.

*Wright is caught down the leg side by Marsh off the bowling of Graf, South Australia v Western Australia at Adelaide, 2–5 December. Graf performed consistently, if not spectacularly, for Western Australia throughout the season. (Philip Tyson)*

## Third Test Match
## AUSTRALIA *v.* PAKISTAN

Rackemann withdrew from the Australian side because of injury and left-arm spinner Hogan replaced him. Saleem Malik and Sarfraz Nawaz, who had been flown out to strengthen the Pakistan side, were both included.

Sarfraz and Azeem bowled tightly in the first hour and Azeem had Phillips caught behind, but the left-arm seam bowler also dropped Wessels at deep fine leg when the opener was on 7. It was an unhappy miss for Wessels dominated play for $5\frac{1}{2}$ hours as he reached his highest Test score with a six and twenty-five fours. He shared century stands with Yallop and Border as the Pakistan attack was once again savaged. Throughout the first day runs came at four and a half an over and play was ended when Chappell was out at 376 for 5. Bari's leg-side catch to dismiss Chappell put him third in the list of Test wicket-keepers with only Marsh and Knott having more dismissals.

The second day saw Pakistan play with more confidence than at any other time in the series. The last five Australian wickets went down in 34.5 overs for 89 runs. Azeem once more finished with the best figures, but the steadying influence of Sarfraz was apparent.

Mudassar was dropped by Marsh off Hogg before he had scored and thereafter Pakistan prospered. They finished the day at 184 for 1 and the next morning Mohsin Khan and Qasim Umar both reached centuries. They stayed together until an hour after lunch by which time their stand had realised 233 in 283 minutes. Mohsin, tall and elegant,

*Wessels hits Abdul Qadir for six during his innings of 179. (Philip Tyson)*

*Mohsin Khan turns Hogan to leg during his elegant innings of 149. (Philip Tyson)*

reached his fifth Test century in his twenty-eighth Test and Qasim Umar, short and energetic, reached a maiden Test hundred in his fourth Test match. It was an innings which delighted spectators almost as much as it did the eager little batsman.

Javed Miandad followed Mohsin and Qasim with an innings of patience which took Pakistan to a commanding position. He and Saleem Malik added 186 for Pakistan's fifth wicket and Javed hit his eleventh Test century and moved ahead of Zaheer as Pakistan's leading run-maker in Test cricket. Dennis Lillee finished the Pakistan innings by taking 4 wickets in 18 deliveries, but Pakistan reached a record 624 and took a significant first innings lead of 159. Before the close Wessels had fallen to Sarfraz and Yallop was smartly taken at slip by Javed off Abdul Qadir who spun the ball eagerly as he recognised the opportunity to put Pakistan level in the series and make up for their previous humiliations.

He brought Phillips' fine innings to an end with a googly on the last morning and Australia, still 38 runs in arrears, were in some trouble, but Hughes was joined by Border in a stand which saved the match. Border had scored his second Test century in succession in the first innings and now he

## THIRD TEST MATCH – AUSTRALIA *v.* PAKISTAN

9, 10, 11, 12 and 13 December 1983 at Adelaide

**AUSTRALIA**

| | FIRST INNINGS | | SECOND INNINGS | |
|---|---|---|---|---|
| K.C. Wessels | c Zaheer, b Qadir | 179 | c Bari, b Sarfraz | 2 |
| W.B. Phillips | c Bari, b Azeem | 12 | c Mudassar, b Qadir | 54 |
| G.N. Yallop | c Umar, b Sarfraz | 68 | c Miandad, b Qadir | 14 |
| K.J. Hughes† | c Bari, b Azeem | 30 | c Mudassar, b Azeem | 106 |
| A.R. Border | not out | 117 | lbw, b Azeem | 66 |
| G.S. Chappell | c Bari, b Sarfraz | 6 | run out | 4 |
| R.W. Marsh* | c Mohsin, b Sarfraz | 2 | retired hurt | 33 |
| T.G. Hogan | run out | 2 | c Umar, b Saleem | 8 |
| G.F. Lawson | c Bari, b Azeem | 4 | not out | 7 |
| D.K. Lillee | c Sarfraz, b Azeem | 25 | not out | 4 |
| R.M. Hogg | c Miandad, b Azeem | 5 | | |
| Extras | lb 7, w 4, nb 4 | 15 | b 3, lb 4, w 1, nb 4 | 12 |
| | | 465 | (for 7 wkts) | 310 |

| | O | M | R | W | O | M | R | W |
|---|---|---|---|---|---|---|---|---|
| Azeem Hafeez | 38.2 | 8 | 167 | 5 | 19 | 4 | 50 | 2 |
| Sarfraz Nawaz | 42 | 7 | 105 | 3 | 30 | 8 | 69 | 1 |
| Abdul Qadir | 20 | 1 | 96 | 1 | 47 | 9 | 132 | 2 |
| Mudassar Nazar | 10 | 2 | 45 | — | | | | |
| Mohammad Nazir | 9 | — | 37 | — | 27 | 14 | 39 | — |
| Mohsin Khan | 3 | — | 8 | — | 1 | 1 | 0 | — |
| Javed Miandad | | | | | 3 | — | 10 | — |
| Saleem Malik | | | | | 1 | — | 3 | 1 |
| Qasim Umar | | | | | 1 | 1 | 0 | — |

FALL OF WICKETS

1- 21, 2- 163, 3- 219, 4- 353, 5- 376, 6- 378, 7- 383, 8- 394, 9- 451

1- 3, 2- 44, 3- 121, 4- 216, 5- 228, 6- 293, 7- 305

**PAKISTAN**

| | FIRST INNINGS | |
|---|---|---|
| Mohsin Khan | c Phillips, b Lawson | 149 |
| Mudassar Nazar | c Marsh, b Lillee | 44 |
| Quasim Umar | c Marsh, b Lillee | 113 |
| Javed Miandad | lbw, b Lawson | 131 |
| Zaheer Abbas† | c Yallop, b Hogg | 46 |
| Saleem Malik | c Lawson, b Hogan | 77 |
| Sarfraz Nawaz | c Yallop, b Lillee | 32 |
| Abdul Qadir | b Lillee | 10 |
| Wasim Bari* | c Marsh, b Lillee | 0 |
| Mohammad Nazir | not out | 5 |
| Azeem Hafeez | c Wessels, b Lillee | 5 |
| Extras | b 1, lb 4, nb 7 | 12 |
| | | 624 |

| | O | M | R | W |
|---|---|---|---|---|
| Lawson | 37 | 7 | 127 | 2 |
| Hogg | 34 | 3 | 123 | 1 |
| Lillee | 50.2 | 8 | 171 | 6 |
| Hogan | 37 | 8 | 107 | 1 |
| Chappell | 32 | 6 | 82 | — |
| Border | 1 | — | 9 | — |

FALL OF WICKETS

1- 73, 2- 306, 3- 314, 4- 371, 5- 557, 6- 590, 7- 604, 8- 612, 9- 613

*Umpires:* A.R. Crafter and R.A. French

**Match drawn**

*The end of a splendid innings. Qasim Umar is caught by Marsh, bowled by Lillee for 113. (Philip Tyson)*

played an equally impressive knock, strong in technique against the turning ball and relentless in punishing the loose delivery. Border and Hughes added 95 for the fourth wicket before Hughes was taken at third slip when driving at Azeem. Hughes' innings of 106 was one of the very great Test innings and his duel with Abdul Qadir provided a contest truly fitting to cricket of the highest standard. The Australian captain displayed the utmost discipline and concentration in a stay of $4\frac{1}{2}$ hours. He played each ball on its merits and early on the last morning swept the leg-spinner over square-leg for six. He also played some elegant off-drives, but he tempered all with most watchful defence and produced an innings which was instrumental in saving Australia from defeat.

Marsh gave Border good support late in the day before having a cheek bone fractured, but by that time a fine Test match was already destined to be drawn.

***9, 10, 11 and 12 December 1983***

***at Devonport***

**Tasmania** 389 (S.L. Saunders 138 not out, R.D. Woolley 87, I.R. Carmichael 6 for 105) and 234 for 7 dec (S.M. Small 55, B.F. Davison 53)
**South Australia** 348 (D.W. Hookes 142, P.R. Sleep 51, P.M. Clough 6 for 79) and 228 for 4 (P.R. Sleep 107 not out, A.M.J. Hilditch 52)

*Match drawn*
*Tasmania 4 pts, South Australia 0 pts*

***at Brisbane***

**Victoria** 353 (M.D. Taylor 146, D.M.J. Jones 108, J.R. Thomson 4 for 58, C. McDermott 4 for 75) and 322 for 7 dec (D.M.J. Jones 64, P.A. Hibbert 61)
**Queensland** 354 for 9 dec (G.M. Ritchie 130, G.S. Trimble 84, A.B. Henschell 67, R.J. McCurdy 5 for 81) and 292 (G.M. Ritchie 75, G.K. Whyte 52, D.A. Emerson 4 for 93)

*Victoria won by 29 runs*
*Victoria 12 pts, Queensland 4 pts*

The Tasmanian middle order, led by a career best for Stuart Saunders, put their side in a fine position at Devonport in spite of Ian Carmichael producing the best bowling performance of his short career. Skipper David Hookes replied strongly for the visitors, but Peter Clough showed Tasmania's best bowling of the season to give his side the points. Tasmania went for quick runs and set the visitors to make 276 to win at well over five an over. Peter Sleep hit the fastest hundred of the season, 107 not out in 110 minutes off 99 balls, but the target was always just out of reach.

The sensation of the season came at Brisbane where Victoria recorded their first outright Shield victory for four years. A fourth wicket stand of 225 between Taylor and Jones dominated the earlier stages of the match, but it was not enough to give Victoria first innings points which were snatched by some fine batting by Greg Ritchie and Glenn Trimble with good support from Brett Henschell. Dean Jones again batted well and Bright made a challenging declaration. Ritchie batted purposefully and there was a later flourish from Whyte, but David Emerson's spin prompted some rash shots and Victoria gained a memorable and welcome victory.

***16, 17, 18 and 19 December 1983***

***at Hobart***

**Pakistanis** 354 for 6 dec (Javed Miandad 141 not out, Saleem Malik 80, P.I. Faulkner 4 for 95) and 272 for 6 dec (Wasim Raja 83, Javed Miandad 54)
**Tasmania** 235 (B.F. Davison 62) and 349 (S.M. Small 114, M. Ray 73, S.L. Saunders 59 not out)

*Pakistanis won by 42 runs*

***at Newcastle***

**New South Wales** 245 (P.R. Sleep 4 for 86) and 188 for 6 dec (R.B. McCosker 55)
**South Australia** 101 (M.J. Bennett 5 for 15) and 223 (A.M.J. Hilditch 73, R.G. Holland 7 for 56)

*New South Wales won by 109 runs*
*New South Wales 16 pts, South Australia 0 pts*

***at Perth***

**Queensland** 295 (A.R. Border 90, T.M. Alderman 4 for 74) and 321 for 5 dec (R.B. Kerr 103, A.R. Border 68, K.C. Wessels 58, G.S. Chappell 56 not out)
**Western Australia** 235 (G. Shipperd 67, J.N. Maguire 4 for 60, J.R. Thomson 4 for 64) and 311 for 9 (K.J. Hughes 130, B.M. Laird 75 not out, J.N. Maguire 6 for 62)

*Match drawn*
*Queensland 4 pts, Western Australia 0 pts*

Playing his first match of the tour, Imran Khan scored 13. Qasim Umar and Saleem Malik, who played a capable innings with nine fours, put on 90 for the first wicket and later Javed reached his third hundred in succession in three hours. Richard Soule, a seventeen-year-old wicket-keeper making his first-class debut, took three catches. He also 'bagged a pair'. Tahir bowled well on the second day, and, although Davison hit three sixes in his innings, Tasmania were in danger of following-on, but Williams and Clough averted this with a last wicket stand of 41. Boon was hit on the arm and took no further part in the match. Pakistan went for quick runs in their second innings and after the declaration they dismissed Beven before the close, but on the last day Small hit a six and fifteen fours in a maiden first-class hundred which nearly snatched a surprise victory for Tasmania.

The meeting of the two main contenders for the Sheffield

*John Maguire – match figures of 10 for 122 failed to bring Queensland victory in the vital Sheffield Shield match against Western Australia in Perth, 16–19 December. (Philip Tyson)*

*Mike Valetta – a young player of great promise. His innings of 83 won him the individual honours in the Macdonald's Cup semi-final in Perth. (Philip Tyson)*

Shield saw Laird and Alderman save Western Australia from defeat with a stubborn last wicket stand. Both first innings had been fairly mundane affairs with Queensland just having the edge. Kerr and Wessels gave them a firm grip on the game with an opening partnership of 112 in the second innings. Border was able to declare and set the home side 382 to win. They were 64 for 3, but Hughes, in eloquent form, and Laird took the score to 248 before Hughes was caught behind off Maguire, one of his career best 10 for 22. Wickets fell steadily until 301 for 9, but then the game was saved.

The reigning champions overwhelmed South Australia in a low scoring game at Newcastle. Murray Bennett, slow left-arm, and Bob Holland, leg-break bowler, were the architects of New South Wales' victory with career best bowling performances, but perhaps the hero of the match was the veteran John Inverarity. He square cut a four in the second innings to bring his total of Sheffield Shield runs to 8,929 so passing Don Bradman's record. Inverarity claimed that it was sacrilege to talk of him beating Bradman as he had taken 258 innings to reach his total whereas Bradman had batted only 96 times.

***21 December 1983***

***at Griffith***

**South West New South Wales** 182 for 9
**Pakistanis** 183 for 2 (Mohsin Khan 104 not out, Qasim Umar 64)

*Pakistanis won by 8 wickets*

Mohsin and Qasim put on 155 for the second wicket. Imran bowled three overs in the match.

**McDonald's Cup – Semi-Finals**

***at Perth***

**Western Australia** 230 for 5 (M.R.J. Veletta 83, G. Shipperd 67)
**New South Wales** 184 (D.M. Wellham 64)

*Western Australia won by 46 runs*

***at Adelaide***

**Tasmania** 163 (P. Brinsley 4 for 45)
**South Australia** 167 for 5 (M.D. Haysman 54)

*South Australia won by 5 wickets*

South Australia won with two balls to spare. Earlier Rodney Hogg had bowled ten overs for 10 runs to win the individual award. New South Wales were bowled out with nearly five overs remaining. Only Wellham showed the right approach. Four men were run out. Veletta and Shipperd put on 129 for Western Australia's second wicket.

**Fourth Test Match**
**AUSTRALIA *v.* PAKISTAN**

Australia surprisingly omitted Rackemann from their party even though he was fit again. When Hogg withdrew from the side he was still ignored and Maguire was brought in for his first Test. Greg Matthews also won a first cap and Murray Bennett was made twelfth man. Imran returned to lead Pakistan although still not fit to bowl, and the visitors took the field with only three front line bowlers.

The gamble was partly justified when Imran won the toss, but the early batting was uncertain on a moist wicket and at 112 for 3, there was little cause for confidence, but Mohsin batted with his usual dignity and authority and he and Zaheer added 132. Mohsin was fifth out at 244 after playing a faultless innings. He batted for 354 minutes and hit a six and eighteen fours so that Pakistan ended the day on a commanding 308 for 5.

The position was consolidated the next day when Imran showed a determination and concentration which Pakistan had lacked earlier in the series. He batted for 4 hours and had amirable support from Abdul Qadir with whom he added 108 for the eighth wicket, Qadir reaching his best Test score before becoming off-spinner Matthews' first Test victim. Azeem dismissed both openers before the close and Pakistan had had their best day of the series.

Their joy was ended on the third day when Hughes and Yallop took their third wicket stand to a record 203. Hughes batted with patience and care, but Yallop asserted himself as he reached his highest Test score and his thousand runs for the season. He became only the fifth Australian to achieve this feat before the New Year. As the day drew to its close Qadir produced a biting spell with his leg-spinners which brought him 3 for 12 in 19 balls, but Pakistan's hopes were

*Mudassar Nazar caught Marsh, bowled Lawson 7. (Philip Tyson)*

*Graham Yallop turns the ball to leg during his mighty innings of 268. (Philip Tyson)*

finally dashed the next day when Yallop shared another record stand; this time 185 for the seventh wicket with the left-handed Matthews who, sadly, showed petulance when he was given out after 252 minutes at the crease. He later apologised to umpire Crafter.

Yallop was ninth out after an innings lasting nearly 12 hours and bettered previously by only Bradman, Simpson and Cowper for Australia in a Test match. Since leading Australia's depleted side against Brearley's team in 1978–79, Yallop has had the albatross of failure hung around his neck. Now, as the most prolific run-scorer in Australian cricket, he has lost his burden and the rehabilitation is complete. He had tilted the game Australia's way and Lawson and Lillee disturbed Pakistan more before the close by sending back Mohsin, Qasim and Javed for 38.

At 81 for 5 on the last morning, Pakistan looked to be heading for another defeat, but Zaheer and, in particular, Imran saved the day and they went to the last Test still with a chance of saving the series.

***30 December 1983, 1 and 2 January 1984***

***at Hobart***

**Victoria** 89 (N.F. Williams 4 for 34) and 232

**FOURTH TEST MATCH – AUSTRALIA *v.* PAKISTAN**
26, 27, 28, 29 and 30 December 1983 at Melbourne

**PAKISTAN**

| | FIRST INNINGS | | SECOND INNINGS | |
|---|---|---|---|---|
| Mohsin Khan | lbw, b Lillee | 152 | c Hughes, b Lillee | 3 |
| Mudassar Nazar | c Marsh, b Lawson | 7 | lbw, b Matthews | 35 |
| Qasim Umar | b Maguire | 23 | b Lawson | 9 |
| Javed Miandad | c Marsh, b Maguire | 27 | lbw, b Lillee | 11 |
| Zaheer Abbas | run out | 44 | (6) b Matthews | 50 |
| Saleem Malik | c Maguire, b Lawson | 35 | (8) b Lillee | 14 |
| Imran Khan† | c Marsh, b Lillee | 83 | not out | 72 |
| Sarfraz Nawaz | c Hughes, b Maguire | 22 | (9) not out | 11 |
| Abdul Qadir | c Lawson, b Matthews | 45 | (5) b Lawson | 12 |
| Wasim Bari* | not out | 6 | | |
| Azeem Hafeez | c Maguire, b Matthews | 7 | | |
| Extras | lb 11, nb 8 | 19 | b 10, lb 9, w 2 | 21 |
| | | 470 | (for 7 wkts) | 238 |

| | O | M | R | W | O | M | R | W |
|---|---|---|---|---|---|---|---|---|
| Lawson | 38 | 8 | 125 | 2 | 21 | 8 | 47 | 2 |
| Lillee | 38 | 11 | 113 | 2 | 29 | 7 | 71 | 3 |
| Maguire | 29 | 7 | 111 | 3 | 12 | 3 | 26 | — |
| Matthews | 28.4 | 7 | 95 | 2 | 21 | 8 | 48 | 2 |
| Chappell | 7 | 3 | 15 | — | 8 | 3 | 13 | — |
| Border | | | | | 5 | 3 | 9 | — |
| Marsh | | | | | 2 | — | 3 | — |
| Wessels | | | | | 2 | 1 | 2 | — |

FALL OF WICKETS
1- 13, 2- 64, 3- 112, 4- 244, 5- 294, 6- 321, 7- 349, 8- 457, 9- 459
1- 3, 2- 18, 3- 37, 4- 73, 5- 81, 6- 160, 7- 213

**AUSTRALIA**

| | FIRST INNINGS | |
|---|---|---|
| K.C. Wessels | c Wasim Bari, b Azeem Hafeez | 11 |
| W.B. Phillips | lbw, b Azeem Hafeez | 35 |
| G.N. Yallop | c Wasim Bari, b Sarfraz Nawaz | 268 |
| K.J. Hughes† | lbw, b Azeem Hafeez | 94 |
| A.R. Border | lbw, b Abdul Qadir | 32 |
| G.S. Chappell | c Saleem Malik, b Abdul Qadir | 5 |
| R.W. Marsh* | c Mudassar Nazar, b Abdul Qadir | 0 |
| G.R.J. Matthews | lbw, b Sarfraz Nawaz | 75 |
| G.F. Lawson | c Mudassar Nazar, b Abdul Qadir | 0 |
| J.N. Maguire | c Wasim Bari, b Abdul Qadir | 4 |
| D.K. Lillee | not out | 2 |
| Extras | b 15, lb 9, w 2, nb 3 | 29 |
| | | 555 |

| | O | M | R | W |
|---|---|---|---|---|
| Sharfraz Nawaz | 51 | 12 | 106 | 2 |
| Azeem Hafeez | 35 | 8 | 115 | 3 |
| Abdul Qadir | 54.3 | 12 | 166 | 5 |
| Mudassar Nazar | 20 | — | 76 | — |
| Javed Miandad | 5 | — | 16 | — |
| Zaheer Abbas | 22 | 5 | 42 | — |
| Saleem Malik | 2 | 1 | 10 | — |

FALL OF WICKETS
1- 21, 2- 70, 3- 273, 4- 342, 5- 354, 6- 354, 7- 539, 8- 540, 9- 553

*Umpires:* A.R. Crafter and P. McConnell

**Match drawn**

*Greg Matthews – a promising debut. (Philip Tyson)*

*Greg Chappell – a dignified and record-breaking farewell to Test cricket. (Philip Tyson)*

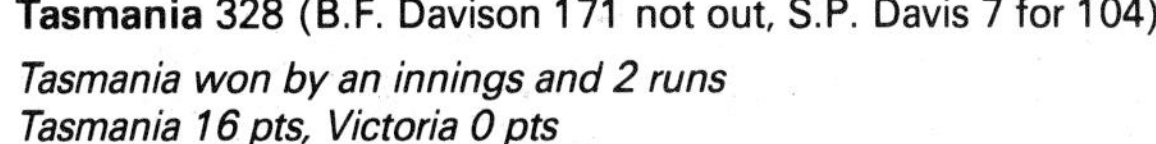

**Tasmania** 328 (B.F. Davison 171 not out, S.P. Davis 7 for 104)
*Tasmania won by an innings and 2 runs*
*Tasmania 16 pts, Victoria 0 pts*

The bowling of left-arm medium pacer Phil Blizzard and Middlesex's Neil Williams shattered a limp Victoria side in both innings. Only Warren Whiteside with a second innings knock of 48 showed any real application. In contrast Brian Davison, surely the world's most underpraised great cricketer, hit with his usual effortless power to reach his fourth century of the season and finish unbeaten on 171 in a match where no other batsman reached fifty. Davison brought his total of runs to 924 for the season in ten completed innings and Tasmania gained their first innings victory since their admission to the Shell Shield. The only consolation for Victoria, bottom of the table, was the determined bowling of medium-paced Simon Davis who has performed well for Durham and Minor Counties in England.

### Fifth Test Match
### AUSTRALIA *v.* PAKISTAN

It was quite remarkable that Pakistan arrived at the final Test in Sydney still able to draw the series. They had been so outplayed for most of the time, appearing unbalanced and disjointed. For the final Test they relied on the side that had played at Melbourne. Australia brought in Hogg for Maguire.

In fact, the Test was dominated by Australia for whom it became a highly emotional affair with the retirements of Greg Chappell and Dennis Lillee from international cricket.

There was rain on the first morning and only 90 minutes play was possible. Pakistan, having been put in, losing Mohsin and Qasim for 62 before the close. Night-watchman Abdul Qadir left early next morning, but Mudassar, playing a solid innings, and Zaheer, showing greater determination than in some previous innings on the tour, were batting soundly until shortly after lunch when Mudassar played loosely at Lawson and was taken at slip by Chappell who thereby equalled Colin Cowdrey's 120 catches in Test cricket.

Zaheer and Saleem batted unhurriedly against Lawson and Lillee who both bowled admirably, sustaining a hostility with their unexpected bounce and movement on a pitch which gave little real help. Zaheer skied an attempted hook, and Saleem became Lawson's fifth victim. Sarfraz was lbw to Lillee, so becoming the great man's 350th Test wicket, and Azeem was caught behind off Lillee, so becoming Rodney Marsh's 350th Test dismissal.

On a cloudy third day, during which Lillee announced that, like Chappell, he was retiring from Test cricket, Australia reached 242 for 3. At five past five, Chappell pushed a ball into the covers where Mohsin picked up and shied at the stumps to give away three over-throws. With these runs Chappell reached 69 and so passed Don Bradman's record as Australia's heaviest scorer in Test cricket.

On the fourth day Hughes was lbw to Sarfraz after having added 171 with Chappell for the fourth wicket. Then Chappell and Border added 153. There was a glorious freedom late in the partnership which ended when Border chased a widish delivery and was caught behind. Twenty-nine runs later Chappell finally fell to Mudassar's nagging accuracy. He had scored his twenty-fourth Test century in his eighty-seventh Test. Batting for nearly 9 hours for his 182 he ended his Test career with 7,110 runs at an average of 53.86. A crowd of nearly 15,000 cheered him long after he had disappeared into the dressing-room. There is a calm in Greg Chappell's batting which is the key to the grace and elegance.

He had not finished his day of glory. Mohsin was caught by him at slip before the close and he now claimed the record number of catches in Test cricket.

The last day belonged to Lillee and to Marsh who, a few weeks later, was to announce that he had played his last Test match. It was his ninety-sixth, an Australian record. Lillee, as aggressive in attitude as ever, and Lawson tore through some feeble Pakistan batting and gave their side an unexpected victory. Rodney Marsh took five catches, two of them spectacular diving efforts, and when Sarfraz steered Lillee to Phillips at slip Pakistan were all out for 210 and Lillee had ended his Test career with a record 355 wickets.

Phillips and Wessels made short work of scoring the 35 needed to win, but that in itself was unimportant. Greg Chappell, Dennis Lillee and Rod Marsh had passed from the Test arena. They left memories of ferocity in competition, elegance in movement and a determination to succeed that will never be erased. An era was at an end.

## Pakistanis in Australia 1983–84
First Class Matches

| BATTING | *v.* Queensland (Brisbane) 21–24 October 1983 | | *v.* South Australia (Adelaide) 28–31 October 1983 | | *v.* Western Australia (Perth) 4–7 November 1983 | | First Test Match (Perth) 11–14 November 1983 | | *v.* New South Wales (Sydney) 18–21 Nov. 1983 | | Second Test Match (Brisbane) 25–29 November 1983 | | *v.* Victoria (Melbourne) 2–5 December 1983 | | Third Test Match (Adelaide) 9–13 December 1983 | | *v.* Tasmania (Hobart) 16–19 Dec. 1983 | | Fourth Test Match (Melbourne) 26–30 December 1983 | | Fifth Test Match (Sydney) 2–6 January 1984 | |
|---|---|---|---|---|---|---|---|---|---|---|---|---|---|---|---|---|---|---|---|---|---|---|---|---|
| Mohsin Khan | 90 | 26 | 0 | 45 | 5 | 36 | 8 | 24 | 12 | 63 | 2 | 37 | 8 | 24 | 149 | — | | | 152 | 3 | 14 | 1 |
| Mudassar Nazar | 104 | 28* | 93 | 71 | 113 | 2 | 1 | 27 | 34 | 139 | 24 | 18 | 103 | 123 | 44 | — | | | 7 | 35 | 84 | 21 |
| Mansoor Akhtar | 20 | 12* | 7 | 25* | | | | | 4 | 0* | | | | | | | | | | | | |
| Javed Miandad | 27 | — | | | 94 | 52 | 0 | 46 | 22 | 69* | 6 | 5 | 85 | 106* | 131 | — | 141* | 54 | 27 | 11 | 16 | 60 |
| Qasim Umar | 16 | — | 39 | 73* | 2 | 23 | 48 | 65 | 25 | 131 | 17 | 11* | 79 | 4 | 113 | — | 21 | 27 | 23 | 9 | 15 | 26 |
| Wasim Raja | 52 | — | 24 | 26 | 11 | 27 | 14 | 4 | | | 27 | — | 0 | — | | | 0 | 83 | | | | |
| Ashraf Ali | 23* | — | | | | | | | 39 | 0 | | | | | | | 4 | 5 | | | | |
| Tahir Naqqash | 5* | — | | | 19 | 7 | 29* | 26 | 0 | — | | | | | | | — | — | | | | |
| Mohammad Nazir | — | — | 2* | — | 1* | 0* | 16 | 18 | 20* | — | 1 | — | | | 5* | — | — | — | | | | |
| Atiq-ur-Rehman | — | — | — | — | | | | | | | | | | | | | | | | | | |
| Azeem Hafeez | — | — | — | — | | | 1 | 0* | | | 2 | — | 1* | — | 5 | — | — | — | 7 | — | 4 | 2* |
| Wasim Bari | | | 73* | — | 11 | 3 | 0 | 7 | | | 2 | — | 25 | — | 0 | — | | | 6* | — | 7* | 20 |
| Abdul Qadir | | | 13 | — | 0 | 37 | 5 | 18 | 5 | — | 0 | — | 18* | — | 10 | — | 31 | 20* | 45 | 12 | 4 | 5 |
| Rashid Khan | | | 16 | — | 7 | 20 | | | 10 | — | 13* | — | 0 | — | | | 45* | 11* | | | | |
| Zaheer Abbas | | | | | 19 | 25 | 0 | 30 | 5 | — | 56 | 3* | 54 | 22* | 46 | — | | | 44 | 50 | 61 | 33 |
| Sarfraz Nawaz | | | | | | | | | | | | | 14 | — | 32 | — | | | 22 | 11* | 5 | 20 |
| Saleem Malik | | | | | | | | | | | | | | | 77 | — | 80 | 39 | 35 | 14 | 54 | 7 |
| Imran Khan | | | | | | | | | | | | | | | | | 13 | 19 | 83 | 72* | 5 | 10 |
| Byes | | | 1 | | | | | 4 | 4 | | | | | 1 | 1 | | 2 | 7 | | 10 | 2 | |
| Leg-byes | 4 | 5 | 2 | 9 | 5 | 4 | 3 | 7 | 3 | 13 | 3 | 6 | 5 | 2 | 4 | | 3 | 3 | 11 | 9 | 7 | 4 |
| Wides | | 1 | | | 3 | 3 | | 2 | | 6 | 1 | | | 2 | | | 1 | | | 2 | | |
| No-balls | 23 | 1 | 4 | | | 3 | 4 | 20 | 11 | 14 | 2 | 2 | 14 | 4 | 7 | | 13 | 4 | 8 | | | 1 |
| Total | 364 | 73 | 274 | 249 | 290 | 242 | 129 | 298 | 194 | 435 | 156 | 82 | 400 | 233 | 624 | | 354 | 272 | 470 | 238 | 278 | 210 |
| Wickets | 6 | 1 | 7 | 3 | 10 | 10 | 10 | 10 | 10 | 4 | 10 | 3 | 9 | 3 | 10 | | 6 | 6 | 10 | 7 | 10 | 10 |
| Result | D | | W | | L | | L | | D | | D | | W | | D | | W | | • D | | L | |

*Catches* 23 – Wasim Bari
10 – Mudassar Nazar
9 – Ashraf Ali (ct 8/st 1)
5 – Mohsin Khan
4 – Qasim Umar and Wasim Raja
3 – Tahir Naqqash, Azeem Hafeez, Mohammad Nazir, Zahir Abbas and Javed Miandad
2 – Sarfraz Nawaz and Saleem Malik
1 – Mansoor Akhtar. Rashid Khan and sub

| BOWLING | Azeem Hafeez | Atiq-Ur-Rehman | Tahir Naqqash | Mudassar Nazar | Mohammad Nazir | Wasim Raja | Rashid Khan | Abdul Qadir | Zaheer Abbas |
|---|---|---|---|---|---|---|---|---|---|
| *v.* Queensland (Brisbane) | 21–2–109–0 | 16–1–115–2 | 18–1–66–0 | 9–2–24–0 | 30–7–73–4 | 12–1–30–0 | | | |
| 21–24 October 1983 | 12–2–50–0 | 9–0–38–0 | 26–7–70–2 | | 24–7–63–1 | 2–0–4–0 | | | |
| *v.* South Australia (Adelaide) | 12.1–2–56–0 | 5–1–24–0 | | 18–4–76–3 | 20–9–26–2 | | 22–8–62–0 | 13–4–31–0 | |
| 28–31 October 1983 | 11–4–32–2 | | | 2–0–12–0 | 28–4–52–1 | | 9–4–16–0 | 32.4–2–122–7 | |
| *v.* Western Australia (Perth) | | | 25.3–3–80–4 | 17–2–53–0 | 16–4–34–3 | | 32–5–77–2 | 29–2–84–1 | |
| 4–7 November 1983 | | | 12–2–62–2 | 7–0–43–1 | 8–0–45–1 | | 10–1–30–0 | | |
| First Test Match (Perth) | 27.3–5–100–5 | | 22–6–76–0 | 15–1–39–0 | 29–5–91–1 | | | 32–4–121–3 | |
| 11–14 November 1983 | | | | | | | | | |
| *v.* New South Wales (Sydney) | | | 26–4–98–1 | 10–3–16–0 | 36.5–3–116–3 | | 39–8–92–2 | 39–4–147–2 | 1–0–5–0 |
| 18–21 November 1983 | | | | | | | | | |
| Second Test Match (Brisbane) | 37–7–152–3 | | | 16–2–47–0 | 24–6–50–0 | 3–0–11–0 | 43–10–129–3 | 32–5–112–1 | |
| 25–29 November 1983 | | | | | | | | | |
| *v.* Victoria (Melbourne) | 22–2–100–0 | | | 6–1–15–1 | | 28–9–70–0 | 22–2–83–1 | 38–3–116–2 | 4–0–16–0 |
| 2–5 December 1983 | 6–1–14–0 | | | 3–0–7–0 | | 9–3–19–0 | 3–0–19–0 | 14–6–28–1 | |
| Third Test Match (Adelaide) | 38.2–8–167–5 | | | 10–2–45–0 | 9–0–37–0 | | | 20–1–96–1 | |
| 9–13 December 1983 | 19–4–50–2 | | | | 27–14–39–0 | | | 47–9–132–2 | |
| *v.* Tasmania (Hobart) | 14.4–6–33–3 | | 16–5–44–3 | | 1–0–1–0 | 8–2–26–0 | 18–4–57–2 | 30–11–65–2 | |
| 16–19 December 1983† | 22–4–90–3 | | 19–3–59–3 | | | | 26–9–68–2 | 26.4–6–88–1 | |
| Fourth Test Match (Melbourne) | 35–8–115–3 | | | 20–0–76–0 | | | | 54.3–12–166–5 | 22–5–42–0 |
| 26–30 December 1983 | | | | | | | | | |
| Fifth Test Match (Sydney) | 36–7–121–1 | | | 31–9–81–3 | | | | 34–9–105–0 | |
| 2–6 January 1984 | 2.4–0–28–0 | | | | | | | | |
| | 316.2–62–1217–27 *av.* 45.07 | 30–2–177–2 *av.* 88.50 | 164.3–31–555–15 *av.* 37.00 | 164–26–534–8 *av.* 66.75 | 252.5–59–627–16 *av.* 39.18 | 62–15–160–0 — | 224–51–633–12 *av.* 52.75 | 441.5–78–1413–28 *av.* 50.46 | 27–5–63–0 — |

†D.C. Boon absent hurt. a Qasim Umar 1–0–10–0 b Qasim Umar 3–0–12–1; Mohsin Khan 4–1–16–0

| M | Inns | NOs | Runs | HS | Av |
|---|---|---|---|---|---|
| 10 | 19 | | 699 | 152 | 36.78 |
| 10 | 19 | 1 | 1071 | 139 | 59.50 |
| 3 | 6 | 3 | 68 | 25* | 22.66 |
| 10 | 18 | 3 | 952 | 141* | 63.46 |
| 11 | 20 | 2 | 767 | 131 | 42.61 |
| 7 | 11 | | 268 | 83 | 24.36 |
| 3 | 5 | 1 | 71 | 39 | 17.75 |
| 5 | 6 | 2 | 86 | 29* | 21.50 |
| 8 | 8 | 5 | 63 | 20* | 21.00 |
| 2 | — | | | | — |
| 9 | 8 | 3 | 22 | 7 | 4.40 |
| 8 | 11 | 3 | 154 | 73* | 19.25 |
| 10 | 15 | 2 | 223 | 45 | 17.15 |
| 6 | 8 | 3 | 122 | 45* | 24.40 |
| 8 | 14 | 2 | 448 | 61 | 37.33 |
| 4 | 6 | 1 | 104 | 32 | 20.80 |
| 4 | 7 | | 306 | 80 | 43.71 |
| 3 | 6 | 1 | 202 | 83 | 40.40 |

| Sarfaz Nawaz | Javed Miandad | Saleem Malik | Byes | Leg-byes | Wides | No-balls | Total | Wkts |
|---|---|---|---|---|---|---|---|---|
| | | | | 5 | 4 | 12 | 422 | 6 |
| | | | | 2 | 1 | 6 | 227 | 3 |
| | | | | 2 | 2 | 3 | 277 | 5 |
| | | | 2 | 7 | | 2 | 243 | 10 |
| | | | 6 | 15 | 8 | 5 | 349 | 10 |
| | | | | 7 | | 1 | 187 | 4 |
| | | | | 9 | 3 | 7 | 436 | 9 |
| | | | 6 | 11 | 1 | 11 | 491 | 8 |
| | | | 2 | 6 | 1 | 15 | 509 | 7 |
| 33–9–81–1 | 13–5–54–0 | | 2 | 8 | 1 | 16 | 555 | 5a |
| 11–5–16–1 | | | 2 | 3 | | 2 | 136 | 3b |
| 42–7–105–3 | | | | 7 | 4 | 4 | 465 | 10c |
| 30–8–69–1 | 3–0–10–0 | 1–0–3–1 | 3 | 4 | 1 | 4 | 310 | 7d |
| | | | 3 | 6 | 2 | 9 | 235 | 10 |
| | | 4–0–26–0 | 14 | 4 | 2 | 5 | 349 | 9† |
| 51–12–106–2 | 5–0–16–0 | 2–1–10–0 | 15 | 9 | 2 | 3 | 555 | 10 |
| 53–13–132–2 | | | | 15 | 1 | 9 | 454 | 6 |
| 3–1–7–0 | | | | | | 2 | 35 | 0 |
| 223–55–516–10 *av.* 51.60 | 21–5–80–0 — | 7–1–39–1 *av.* 39.00 | | | | | | |

c Mohsin Khan 3–0–8–0   d Mohsin Khan 1–1–0–0; Qasim Umar 1–1–0–0

ABOVE: *Dennis Lillee – a memorable farewell to Test cricket.* BELOW: *Kim Hughes led Australia to total triumph in the series. (Philip Tyson)*

## FIFTH TEST MATCH – AUSTRALIA *v.* PAKISTAN

2, 3, 4, 5 and 6 January 1984 at Sydney

### PAKISTAN

| | FIRST INNINGS | | SECOND INNINGS | |
|---|---|---|---|---|
| Mohsin Khan | c Border, b Lillee | 14 | c Chappell, b Lawson | 1 |
| Mudassar Nazar | c Chappell, b Lawson | 84 | b Lawson | 21 |
| Qasim Umar | c Border, b Lillee | 15 | c Marsh, b Lawson | 26 |
| Abdul Qadir | c Hughes, b Lawson | 4 | (9) c Marsh, b Lillee | 5 |
| Javed Miandad | c Lillee, b Matthews | 16 | (4) c Marsh, b Lawson | 60 |
| Zaheer Abbas | c Yallop, b Lawson | 61 | (5) c Marsh, b Hogg | 33 |
| Imran Khan† | c Yallop, b Lawson | 5 | (6) c Marsh, b Hogg | 10 |
| Saleem Malik | c Lillee, b Lawson | 54 | (7) c Chappell, b Lillee | 7 |
| Sarfraz Nawaz | lbw, b Lillee | 5 | (8) c Phillips, b Lillee | 20 |
| Wasim Bari* | not out | 7 | c Phillips, b Lillee | 20 |
| Azeem Hafeez | c Marsh, b Lillee | 4 | not out | 2 |
| Extras | b 2, lb 7 | 9 | lb 4, nb 1 | 5 |
| | | 278 | | 210 |

| | O | M | R | W | O | M | R | W |
|---|---|---|---|---|---|---|---|---|
| Lillee | 31.2 | 10 | 65 | 4 | 29.5 | 5 | 88 | 4 |
| Hogg | 18 | 1 | 61 | — | 14 | 2 | 53 | 2 |
| Chappell | 8 | — | 25 | — | | | | |
| Lawson | 25 | 5 | 59 | 5 | 20 | 7 | 48 | 4 |
| Matthews | 18 | 4 | 59 | 1 | 7 | 4 | 17 | — |

FALL OF WICKETS
1- 18, 2- 57, 3- 67, 4- 131, 5- 150, 6- 158, 7- 254, 8- 267, 9- 267
1- 5, 2- 47, 3- 56, 4- 104, 5- 132, 6- 163, 7- 163, 8- 173, 9- 191

### AUSTRALIA

| | FIRST INNINGS | | SECOND INNINGS | |
|---|---|---|---|---|
| K.C. Wessels | c. Bari, b Azeem | 3 | not out | 14 |
| W.B. Phillips | c Saleem, b Sarfraz | 37 | not out | 19 |
| G.N. Yallop | c Bari, b Mudassar | 30 | | |
| G.S. Chappell | lbw, b Mudassar | 182 | | |
| K.J. Hughes† | lbw, b Sarfraz | 76 | | |
| A.R. Border | c Bari, b Mudassar | 64 | | |
| G.R.J. Matthews | not out | 22 | | |
| R.W. Marsh* | not out | 15 | | |
| G.F. Lawson | | | | |
| D.K. Lillee | | | | |
| R.M. Hogg | | | | |
| Extras | lb 15, w 1, nb 9 | 25 | nb 2 | 2 |
| | (for 6 wkts dec) | 454 | (for no wkt) | 35 |

| | O | M | R | W | O | M | R | W |
|---|---|---|---|---|---|---|---|---|
| Sarfraz Nawaz | 53 | 13 | 132 | 2 | 3 | 1 | 7 | — |
| Azeem Hafeez | 36 | 7 | 121 | 1 | 2.4 | — | 28 | — |
| Mudassar Nazar | 31 | 9 | 81 | 3 | | | | |
| Abdul Qadir | 34 | 9 | 105 | — | | | | |

FALL OF WICKETS
1- 11, 2- 66, 3- 83, 4- 254, 5- 407, 6- 436

**Australia won by 10 wickets**

## Australia *v.* Pakistan – Test Match Averages

### AUSTRALIA BATTING

| | M | Inns | NOs | Runs | HS | Av | 100s | 50s |
|---|---|---|---|---|---|---|---|---|
| G.N. Yallop | 5 | 6 | | 554 | 268 | 92.33 | 2 | 1 |
| A.R. Border | 5 | 6 | 1 | 429 | 118 | 85.80 | 2 | 2 |
| G.S. Chappell | 5 | 6 | 1 | 364 | 182 | 72.80 | 2 | |
| K.J. Hughes | 5 | 6 | | 375 | 106 | 62.50 | 1 | 3 |
| W.B. Phillips | 5 | 7 | 1 | 362 | 159 | 60.33 | 1 | 1 |
| K.C. Wessels | 5 | 7 | 1 | 256 | 179 | 42.66 | 1 | |
| R.W. Marsh | 5 | 6 | 2 | 75 | 33* | 18.75 | | |
| G.F. Lawson | 5 | 5 | 1 | 69 | 49 | 17.25 | | |
| D.K. Lillee | 5 | 4 | 2 | 31 | 25 | 15.50 | | |

Played in four Tests: R.M. Hogg 7* and 5
Played in two Tests: C.G. Rackemann did not bat; G.R.J. Matthews 75 and 22*
Played in one Test: J.N. Maguire 4; T.G. Hogan 2 and 8

### AUSTRALIA BOWLING

| | Overs | Mds | Runs | Wkts | Av | Best | 5/inn | 10/m |
|---|---|---|---|---|---|---|---|---|
| C.G. Rackemann | 52 | 10 | 177 | 16 | 11.06 | 6/86 | 2 | 1 |
| G.F. Lawson | 188.3 | 40 | 580 | 24 | 24.16 | 5/49 | 2 | |
| D.K. Lillee | 280.3 | 51 | 633 | 20 | 31.65 | 6/171 | 1 | |
| R.M. Hogg | 117.1 | 14 | 383 | 9 | 42.55 | 3/20 | | |
| G.R.J. Matthews | 74.4 | 23 | 219 | 5 | 43.80 | 2/48 | | |
| A.R. Border | 6 | 3 | 18 | — | — | 0/9 | | |
| G.S. Chappell | 64 | 13 | 155 | — | — | 0/13 | | |

Bowled in one Test: T.G. Hogan 37–8–107–1; R.W. Marsh 2–0–3–0; K.C. Wessels 2–1–2–0; J.N. Maguire 41–10–137–3

### AUSTRALIA CATCHES

21–R.W. Marsh; 8–G.S. Chappell; 7–W.B. Phillips and A.R. Border; 5–G.N. Yallop and K.J. Hughes; 2–J.N. Maguire, G.F. Lawson, K.C. Wessels and D.K. Lillee

### PAKISTAN BATTING

| | M | Inns | NOs | Runs | HS | Av | 100s | 50s |
|---|---|---|---|---|---|---|---|---|
| Imran Khan | 2 | 4 | 1 | 170 | 83 | 56.66 | | 2 |
| Mohsin Khan | 5 | 9 | | 390 | 152 | 43.33 | 2 | |
| Qasim Umar | 5 | 9 | 1 | 327 | 113 | 40.87 | 1 | 1 |
| Zaheer Abbas | 5 | 9 | 1 | 323 | 61 | 40.37 | | 3 |
| Saleem Malik | 3 | 5 | | 187 | 77 | 37.40 | | 2 |
| Javed Miandad | 5 | 9 | | 302 | 131 | 33.55 | 1 | 1 |
| Mudassar Nazar | 5 | 9 | | 261 | 84 | 29.00 | | 1 |
| Sarfraz Nawaz | 3 | 5 | 1 | 90 | 32 | 22.50 | | |
| Wasim Raja | 2 | 3 | | 45 | 27 | 15.00 | | |
| Mohammad Nazir | 3 | 4 | 1 | 40 | 18 | 13.33 | | |
| Abdul Qadir | 5 | 8 | | 99 | 45 | 12.37 | | |
| Wasim Bari | 5 | 7 | 2 | 42 | 20 | 8.40 | | |
| Azeem Hafeez | 5 | 7 | 2 | 21 | 7 | 4.20 | | |

Played in one Test: Rashid Khan 13*; Tahir Naqqash 29* and 26

### PAKISTAN BOWLING

| | Overs | Mds | Runs | Wkts | Av | Best | 5/inn |
|---|---|---|---|---|---|---|---|
| Saleem Malik | 3 | 1 | 13 | 1 | 13.00 | 1/3 | |
| Azeem Hafeez | 195.3 | 39 | 733 | 19 | 38.57 | 5/100 | 2 |
| Sarfraz Nawaz | 179 | 47 | 419 | 8 | 52.37 | 3/105 | |
| Abdul Qadir | 219.3 | 40 | 732 | 12 | 61.00 | 5/166 | 1 |
| Mudassar Nazar | 92 | 14 | 288 | 3 | 96.00 | 3/81 | |
| Mohammad Nazir | 89 | 25 | 217 | 1 | 217.00 | 1/91 | |
| Javed Miandad | 8 | 0 | 26 | — | — | 0/10 | |

Bowled in one Test: Tahir Naqqash 22–6–76–0; Rashid Khan 43–10–129–3; Wasim Raja 3–0–11–0; Zaheer Abbas 22–5–42–0; Mohsin Khan 4–1–8–0; Qasim Umar 1–1–0–0

### PAKISTAN CATCHES

15–Wasim Bari; 4–Mudassar Nazar; 3–Qasim Umar; 2–Javed Miandad, Wasim Raja, Mohammad Nazir and Saleem Malik; 1–Tahir Naqqash, Azeem Hafeez, Sarfraz Nawaz, Zaheer Abbas and Mohsin Khan

*4 January 1984*

***at Brisbane***

**West Indians** 203 for 9 (C.H. Lloyd 73 not out, C.G. Rackemann 4 for 32)
**Queensland** 204 for 4

*Queensland won by 6 wickets*

In their first match in Australia as a prelude to the Benson and Hedges World Series, West Indies were beaten with 3 balls to spare. Most disturbing for them was that Jeff Dujon, the only wicket-keeper in the party, left the field with torn fibres in a knee.

*6 January 1984*

***at Benalla***

**West Indians** 274 (R.S. Gabriel 100, E.A.E. Baptiste 53)
**Victorian Country XI** 166 for 8

*West Indians won by 108 runs*

Thirty-one-year-old Richard Gabriel, an unexpected addition to the West Indian side following the withdrawal of Greenidge, hit eight fours and a six in a sparkling hundred. Viv Richards kept wicket for the visitors as they moved to an easy victory.

*6, 7, 8 and 9 January 1984*

***at Perth***

**Western Australia** 328 (G. Shipperd 72, K.H. Macleay 67, M.R.J. Veletta 64, I.R. Carmichael 5 for 130) and 290 for 3 dec (M.R.J. Veletta 82, G. Shipperd 78 not out, S.C. Clements 73)
**South Australia** 268 (D.W. Hookes 111) and 140 for 3

*Match drawn*
*Western Australia 4 pts, South Australia 0 pts*

***at Brisbane***

**New South Wales** 229 (S.B. Smith 72, C.J. McDermott 4 for 85) and 173 (D.M. Wellham 65, H. Frei 6 for 55)
**Queensland** 160 (G.M. Ritchie 75, L.S. Pascoe 5 for 53) and 245 for 6 (G.M. Ritchie 129)

*Queensland won by 4 wickets*
*Queensland 12 pts, New South Wales 4 pts*

In Perth, in spite of consistent batting by young Veletta and the ever dependable Greg Shipperd and a hard hit century by David Hookes, the match ambled to a rather meaningless draw. A marathon spell of 55 overs by Ian Carmichael was some consolation for South Australia being left pointless.

In Brisbane, Queensland edged above Western Australia in the Sheffield Shield table with a win of great character over the reigning champions. The New South Wales innings was held together by Steve Smith and with three Queensland wickets falling cheaply before the close, the visitors moved into a strong position. Craig McDermott had bowled well for Queensland on the opening day, showing once more their strength in medium-fast and fast bowling, but it was Greg Ritchie who saved them with the bat. He alone having any answer to a rejuvenated Len Pascoe. Queensland trailed by 69 on the first innings, but 33-year-old Harry Frei, back in the side because of international calls on the leading bowlers, returned a career best with his left-arm fast-medium and gave the home side some hope. They were still required to make the biggest score of the match, however, but with Greg Ritchie in quite magnificent form, they moved to a notable victory and the top of the table.

***Benson and Hedges World Series***

**First One-Day International**
**AUSTRALIA *v.* WEST INDIES**

Australia found West Indies a somewhat stiffer proposition than Pakistan had been and were convincingly beaten in the first of the one-day internationals. Before a crowd of 72,160, West Indies, having won the toss, batted first on a slow wicket. Their innings owed much to a stand of 103 off 112 balls between Richards and Lloyd for the third wicket.

The Australian cause was not helped by some lax fielding, Lloyd being dropped on 31, and by an injury to Yallop, their leading batsman, who tore ligaments in his knee and was not to play again for the rest of the season.

Border batted with the assurance that he had shown in recent weeks, but only Marsh gave him real assistance. There was a spirited knock from Hogg and a courageous one, with the aid of a runner, by Yallop, but the outcome of the match was never in doubt.

Viv Richards took the individual award.

*Gabriel is caught behind by Marsh off Hogg in the first of the one-day internationals. (Philip Tyson)*

***Benson and Hedges World Series***

**Second One-Day International**
**AUSTRALIA *v.* PAKISTAN**

In the first of the day-night matches, Australia were saved by Border and Wessels who came together at 17 for 2 and added 140. Wessels' innings of 92 won him the Man of the Match award and it is interesting to reflect that before the game his place was considered to be in jeopardy.

Sarfraz apart, the Pakistan attack was ragged, and Marsh slashed 66 as he and Hookes added 86 ferocious runs for the fifth wicket.

Pakistan started badly, losing Mohsin, Mudassar and Qasim for 33, but Javed Miandad batted with confidence and zest. He and Imran added 86 quick runs before Javed set off for a short single and then changed his mind to leave Imran stranded and run out. He settled to add another 56 runs with Mansoor, who had replaced Zaheer, before he too was run

**FIRST ONE DAY INTERNATIONAL – AUSTRALIA *v.* WEST INDIES**
8 January 1984 at Melbourne

| WEST INDIES | | | |
|---|---|---|---|
| D.L. Haynes | c Hughes, b Hogg | 17 | |
| R.S. Gabriel | c Marsh, b Hogg | 13 | |
| I.V.A. Richards | c Marsh, b Maguire | 53 | |
| C.H. Lloyd† | c Rackemann, b Matthews | 65 | |
| P.J. Dujon* | c Wessels, b Hogg | 5 | |
| M.D. Marshall | run out | 9 | |
| E.A.E. Baptiste | not out | 28 | |
| H.A. Gomes | b Rackemann | 21 | |
| M.A. Holding | not out | 1 | |
| J. Garner | | | |
| W.W. Daniel | | | |
| Extras | b 1, lb 6, w 1, nb 1 | 9 | |
| (50 overs) | (for 7 wickets) | 221 | |

| | O | M | R | W |
|---|---|---|---|---|
| Lawson | 10 | 1 | 34 | — |
| Rackemann | 10 | 2 | 39 | 1 |
| Hogg | 10 | 1 | 29 | 3 |
| Maguire | 10 | 1 | 47 | 1 |
| Matthews | 10 | — | 65 | 1 |

FALL OF WICKETS
1- 28, 2- 34, 3- 137, 4- 153, 5- 167, 6- 173, 7- 220

| AUSTRALIA | | |
|---|---|---|
| K.C. Wessels | b Garner | 7 |
| W.B. Phillips | c and b Marshall | 10 |
| K.J. Hughes† | run out | 5 |
| A.R. Border | not out | 84 |
| G.R.J. Matthews | c Dujon, b Daniel | 2 |
| R.W. Marsh* | run out | 31 |
| G.F. Lawson | b Baptiste | 2 |
| J.N. Maguire | b Richards | 0 |
| R.M. Hogg | lbw, b Holding | 21 |
| G.N. Yallop | c Lloyd, b Marshall | 13 |
| C.G. Rackemann | run out | 2 |
| Extras | lb 10, w 1, nb 6 | 17 |
| (46 overs) | | 194 |

| | O | M | R | W |
|---|---|---|---|---|
| Garner | 8 | 2 | 28 | 1 |
| Marshall | 9 | 2 | 25 | 2 |
| Daniel | 6 | 1 | 24 | 1 |
| Holding | 10 | — | 42 | 1 |
| Baptiste | 7 | — | 41 | 1 |
| Richards | 6 | 1 | 24 | 1 |

FALL OF WICKETS
1- 12, 2- 28, 3- 31, 4- 44, 5- 108, 6- 114, 7- 115, 8- 153, 9- 191

**West Indies won by 27 runs**

**SECOND ONE-DAY INTERNATIONAL – AUSTRALIA *v.* PAKISTAN**
10 January 1984 at Sydney

| AUSTRALIA | | |
|---|---|---|
| K.C. Wessels | b Sarfraz | 92 |
| W.B. Phillips | c Wasim Bari, b Sarfraz | 2 |
| K.J. Hughes† | c Imran, b Sarfraz | 5 |
| A.R. Border | c Wasim Bari, b Sarfraz | 54 |
| D.W. Hookes | b Azeem | 25 |
| R.W. Marsh* | b Rashid | 66 |
| G.R.J. Matthews | run out | 0 |
| G.F. Lawson | not out | 3 |
| J.N. Maguire | c Wasim Bari, b Azeem | 2 |
| R.M. Hogg | not out | 2 |
| C.G. Rackemann | | |
| Extras | lb 9, w 2, nb 2 | 13 |
| (50 overs) | (for 8 wickets) | 264 |

| | O | M | R | W |
|---|---|---|---|---|
| Sarfraz Nawaz | 10 | 2 | 27 | 4 |
| Rashid Khan | 10 | 1 | 42 | 1 |
| Mohammad Nazir | 9 | — | 67 | — |
| Azeem Hafeez | 10 | — | 60 | 2 |
| Mudassar Nazar | 9 | — | 44 | — |
| Mansoor Akhtar | 2 | — | 15 | — |

FALL OF WICKETS
1- 3, 2- 17, 3- 157, 4- 162, 5- 248, 6- 249, 7- 256, 8- 261

| PAKISTAN | | |
|---|---|---|
| Mohsin Khan | lbw, b Rackemann | 9 |
| Mudassar Nazar | c Marsh, b Lawson | 17 |
| Qasim Umar | lbw, b Rackemann | 1 |
| Javed Miandad | run out | 67 |
| Imran Khan† | run out | 39 |
| Mansoor Akhtar | c Lawson, b Matthews | 33 |
| Sarfraz Nawaz | b Hogg | 6 |
| Wasim Bari* | b Matthews | 13 |
| Rashid Khan | c Marsh, b Rackemann | 10 |
| Mohammad Nazir | not out | 2 |
| Azeem Hafeez | not out | 7 |
| Extras | b 5, lb 16, w 2, nb 3 | 26 |
| (50 overs) | (for 9 wickets) | 230 |

| | O | M | R | W |
|---|---|---|---|---|
| Lawson | 10 | 3 | 26 | 1 |
| Rackemann | 10 | 2 | 35 | 3 |
| Maguire | 10 | — | 49 | — |
| Hogg | 10 | — | 38 | 1 |
| Matthews | 10 | — | 61 | 2 |

FALL OF WICKETS
1- 30, 2- 32, 3- 33, 4- 119, 5- 175, 6- 193, 7- 201, 8- 217, 9- 221

**Australia won by 34 runs**

out in going for a risky second run. Javed clearly disagreed with the umpire's decision.

This second run out was decisive and Pakistan could never muster sufficient substance to threaten Australia.

***Benson and Hedges World Series***

**Third One-Day International**
**WEST INDIES *v.* PAKISTAN**

Qasim Umar was dropped down the Pakistan order to number six after a recent run of indifferent form and responded with an innings of 69 which gained him the Man of the Match award. He came in at 87 for 4 in the twenty-fifth over and he and Javed Miandad, who had earlier been guilty of running out Mansoor, put on 95. It did not seem, however, that Pakistan had scored their runs quickly enough to reach a winning score, but when Gabriel was run out in the first over of the West Indian innings as he unwisely sought an overthrow, they took heart.

Rashid Khan bowled effectively, and with Sarfraz his

## THIRD ONE-DAY INTERNATIONAL – PAKISTAN *v.* WEST INDIES
12 January 1984 at Melbourne

**PAKISTAN**

|  |  |  |
|---|---|---|
| Mudassar Nazar | c Dujon, b Holding | 31 |
| Mohsin Khan | lbw, b Garner | 16 |
| Mansoor Akhtar | run out | 19 |
| Javed Miandad | b Marshall | 41 |
| Imran Khan† | c and b Baptiste | 7 |
| Qasim Umar | b Daniel | 69 |
| Sarfraz Nawaz | c Richards, b Holding | 7 |
| Abdul Qadir | not out | 6 |
| Rashid Khan | run out | 2 |
| Wasim Bari* | | |
| Azeem Hafeez | | |
| Extras | lb 3, w 5, nb 2 | 10 |
| (50 overs) | (for 8 wickets) | 208 |

| | O | M | R | W |
|---|---|---|---|---|
| Garner | 10 | 2 | 21 | 1 |
| Marshall | 6 | — | 27 | 1 |
| Holding | 10 | — | 56 | 2 |
| Daniel | 10 | — | 46 | 1 |
| Richards | 6 | — | 26 | — |
| Baptiste | 8 | — | 29 | 1 |

FALL OF WICKETS
1- 27, 2- 70, 3- 77, 4- 87, 5- 182, 6- 196, 7- 206, 8- 208

**WEST INDIES**

|  |  |  |
|---|---|---|
| D.L. Haynes | b Rashid Khan | 2 |
| R.S. Gabriel | run out | 0 |
| I.V.A. Richards | c Qadir, b Sarfraz Nawaz | 7 |
| H.A. Gomes | c Qadir, b Rashid Khan | 1 |
| C.H. Lloyd† | c Mansoor, b Azeem Hafeez | 12 |
| P.J. Dujon* | c Imran, b Azeem Hafeez | 30 |
| M.D. Marshall | c Azeem Hafeez, b Sarfraz Nawaz | 20 |
| E.A.E. Baptiste | c Mansoor, b Azeem Hafeez | 3 |
| M.A. Holding | c and b Azeem Hafeez | 1 |
| J. Garner | not out | 21 |
| W.W. Daniel | c Sarfraz Nawaz, b Mudassar | 12 |
| Extras | lb 1, nb 1 | 2 |
| (41.4 overs) | | 111 |

| | O | M | R | W |
|---|---|---|---|---|
| Sarfraz Nawaz | 9 | 2 | 24 | 2 |
| Rashid Khan | 6 | 3 | 10 | 2 |
| Azeem Hafeez | 10 | 1 | 22 | 4 |
| Abdul Qadir | 10 | — | 29 | — |
| Mudassar Nazar | 6.4 | — | 25 | 1 |

FALL OF WICKETS
1- 1, 2- 9, 3- 9, 4- 10, 5- 45, 6- 56, 7- 63, 8- 65, 9- 94

**Pakistan won by 97 runs**

usual menacing self, West Indies were reduced to 10 for 4. Abdul Qadir had taken two good catches, but he dropped Clive Lloyd off the first ball of his own bowling. It mattered little. Lloyd and Dujon batted sensibly, but Lloyd drove Azeen to mid-on and, 11 runs later, Dujon mishooked the same bowler to mid-wicket. After this West Indies subsided as the crowd showed their disapproval of an inept performance.

### *13, 14, 15 and 16 January 1984*

***at Perth***

**Western Australia** 184 (A.I.C. Dodemaide 5 for 67) and 284 (S.F. Graf 73, S.C. Clements 64, R.J. McCurdy 5 for 96)
**Victoria** 161 (M. Quinn 54, T.G. Hogan 5 for 31) and 272 (P.A. Hibbert 95, D.M.J. Jones 52, D.K. Lillee 5 for 63, T.M. Alderman 5 for 79)

*Western Australia won by 35 runs*
*Western Australia 16 pts, Victoria 0 pts*

***at Adelaide***

**Queensland** 308 (R.B. Kerr 136, T.V. Hohns 51, P.R. Sleep 4 for 96) and 201 (I.R. Carmichael 5 for 49)
**South Australia** 281 (D. Scott 64, T.V. Hohns 4 for 75) and 229 for 3 (A.M.J. Hilditch 96, D. O'Connor 72)

*South Australia won by 7 wickets*
*South Australia 12 pts, Queensland 4 pts*

***at Devonport***

**New South Wales** 308 (P. Clifford 74, G.R.J. Matthews 72, M.J. Bennett 54, P.I. Faulkner 4 for 68) and 198 for 3 (S.B. Smith 100 not out)
**Tasmania** 394 (R.D. Woolley 79, G.W. Goodman 74)

*Match drawn*
*Tasmania 4 pts, New South Wales 0 pts*

With his side struggling, debutant Peter Clifford joined Greg Matthews in a fifth wicket stand of 149 which helped to take New South Wales to beyond 300. Mark Ray and Gary Goodman began Tasmania's reply with a stand of 102 and some hard hitting by skipper Roger Woolley took the home side into the lead, but rain interfered with the later stages of the match and there was never any chance of a result. Steve Smith took the opportunity of batting practice to reassert his international claims with a fluent century.

Queensland lost ground in the battle at the top of the Sheffield Shield table when, having taken a first innings lead thanks to some tight bowling by Trevor Hohns, they surrendered to Ian Carmichael's medium pace in their second innings. In his first full season, Carmichael brought his total

*Whyte, caught Wright, bowled Carmichael. Carmichael's bowling had much to do with South Australia's surprising success. (Philip Tyson)*

*Winter is caught at short-leg by Kerr off Whyte. (Philip Tyson)*

of wickets to 30. In their first innings Queensland had been indebted to a four-hour innings from Robert Kerr, but South Australia, too, found their batting hero. Andrew Hilditch had shared an opening partnership of 126 with Darryl Scott in the first innings and with his side needing 229 to win, he hit a magnificent 96 to give them a highly commendable victory. He was given excellent support by Don O'Connor, forcing his way into first-class cricket at the age of 25.

Western Australia moved relentlessly towards the Sheffield Shield Final with an exciting win over Victoria who played some good cricket and ended the match pointless. Tony Dodemaide took five wickets in an innings in a first-class match for the first time as the home side were bowled out for 184. Mike Quinn steered Victoria to 102 for 2 and they were seemingly heading for a big lead, but the advent of Tom Hogan caused the last 8 wickets to fall for 59 runs. Now it was the pace of Simon Davis and Rod McCurdy which disconcerted Western Australia, but Clements and Graf effected a recovery and left Victoria with the task of scoring 308 to win. They began well but the old warrior Dennis Lillee and the restored Terry Alderman gave their side a narrow victory.

***Benson and Hedges World Series***

### Fourth One-Day International
### WEST INDIES *v.* PAKISTAN

West Indies gained quick revenge on Pakistan when they won with 9.4 overs to spare. Pakistan collapsed after reaching 97 for 1 when Richards' gentle off-spin accounted for leading scorers Mudassar and Mansoor. The return of Holding cramped the lower order and West Indies were left with a surprisingly easy task of scoring 175 to win.

They reached 102 before the second wicket fell, but with rain threatening, quick runs were necessary and Richards provided them with 37 off 17 balls.

***Benson and Hedges World Series***

### Fifth One-Day International
### AUSTRALIA *v.* PAKISTAN

Hughes asked Pakistan to bat first in damp, overcast conditions and they slumped to 30 for 3, but Qasim and Mansoor added 86. Mansoor and Imran, who hit two tremendous sixes, fell in one over to Hogg, but the umpires reduced the innings to 42 overs because of the weather. In the last 11.1 overs Pakistan hit 76.

After 23 balls of the Australian innings rain returned and, to the disappointment of the crowd of 21,000, the match was abandoned.

Ritchie, after his fine form for Queensland, replaced Phillips in the Australian side.

**FOURTH ONE-DAY INTERNATIONAL – PAKISTAN *v.* WEST INDIES**
14 January 1984 at Brisbane

| PAKISTAN | | |
|---|---|---|
| Mudassar Nazar | c and b Richards | 68 |
| Mohsin Khan | b Daniel | 4 |
| Mansoor Akhtar | b Richards | 32 |
| Javed Miandad | run out | 9 |
| Qasim Umar | c Logie, b Daniel | 18 |
| Imran Khan† | c Dujon, b Holding | 9 |
| Sarfraz Nawaz | c Haynes, b Holding | 0 |
| Abdul Qadir | c Lloyd, b Daniel | 2 |
| Rashid Khan | c Dujon, b Holding | 2 |
| Wasim Bari* | not out | 10 |
| Azeem Hafeez | not out | 3 |
| Extras | b 1, lb 6, w 3, nb 7 | 17 |
| (50 overs) | (for 9 wickets) | 174 |

| | O | M | R | W |
|---|---|---|---|---|
| Holding | 10 | 1 | 46 | 3 |
| Daniel | 10 | 1 | 27 | 3 |
| Davis | 10 | 2 | 29 | — |
| Baptiste | 10 | 2 | 28 | — |
| Richards | 10 | — | 37 | 2 |

FALL OF WICKETS
1- 10, 2- 97, 3- 121, 4- 128, 5- 144, 6- 144, 7- 157, 8- 159, 9- 160

| WEST INDIES | | |
|---|---|---|
| D.L. Haynes | c Wasim Bari, b Mudassar | 53 |
| R.S. Gabriel | b Abdul Qadir | 20 |
| R.B. Richardson | c Wasim Bari, b Rashid Khan | 25 |
| I.V.A. Richards | b Azeem Hafeez | 37 |
| C.H. Lloyd† | c Wasim Bari, b Mudassar | 11 |
| P.J. Dujon* | not out | 10 |
| A.L. Logie | not out | 1 |
| E.A.E. Baptiste | | |
| M.A. Holding | | |
| W.W. Daniel | | |
| W.W. Davis | | |
| Extras | lb 9, w 8, nb 1 | 18 |
| (40.2 overs) | (for 5 wickets) | 175 |

| | O | M | R | W |
|---|---|---|---|---|
| Sarfraz Nawaz | 6 | 2 | 28 | — |
| Rashid Khan | 8 | 3 | 18 | 1 |
| Azeem Hafeez | 9.2 | — | 58 | 1 |
| Abdul Qadir | 7 | 4 | 16 | 1 |
| Mudassar Nazar | 10 | — | 46 | 2 |

FALL OF WICKETS
1- 47, 2- 102, 3- 143, 4- 161, 5- 161

**West Indies won by 5 wickets**

## FIFTH ONE-DAY INTERNATIONAL – AUSTRALIA *v.* PAKISTAN
15 January 1984 at Brisbane

| PAKISTAN | | | |
|---|---|---|---|
| Mudassar Nazar | c Hookes, b Lawson | 2 |
| Mohsin Khan | c Wessels, b Hogg | 14 |
| Mansoor Akhtar | b Hogg | 47 |
| Javed Miandad | c Wessels, b Maguire | 1 |
| Qasim Umar | run out | 40 |
| Imran Khan† | c Marsh, b Hogg | 26 |
| Tahir Naqqash | not out | 13 |
| Rashid Khan | not out | 11 |
| Sarfraz Nawaz | | |
| Wasim Bari* | | |
| Azeem Hafeez | | |
| Extras | lb 23, w 7 | 30 |
| (42 overs) | (for 6 wickets) | 184 |

| | O | M | R | W |
|---|---|---|---|---|
| Lawson | 9 | 3 | 12 | 1 |
| Rackemann | 9 | 3 | 45 | — |
| Hogg | 8 | — | 34 | 3 |
| Maguire | 10 | — | 31 | 1 |
| Macleay | 6 | — | 39 | — |

FALL OF WICKETS
1- 2, 2- 29, 3- 30, 4- 116, 5- 159, 6- 160

| AUSTRALIA | | |
|---|---|---|
| G.M. Ritchie | not out | 6 |
| K.C. Wessels | not out | 5 |
| K.J. Hughes† | | |
| A.R. Border | | |
| D.W. Hookes | | |
| K.H. Macleay | | |
| R.W. Marsh* | | |
| G.F. Lawson | | |
| J.N. Maguire | | |
| R.M. Hogg | | |
| C.G. Rackemann | | |
| Extras | lb 1, w 3 | 4 |
| (3.5 overs) | (for no wicket) | 15 |

| | O | M | R | W |
|---|---|---|---|---|
| Sarfraz Nawaz | 2 | 1 | 8 | — |
| Rashid Khan | 1.5 | — | 6 | — |

**Match abandoned**

***Benson and Hedges World Series***

### Sixth One-Day International AUSTRALIA *v.* WEST INDIES

Australia had a thoroughly miserable match for not only were they beaten but were also fined for not bowling 50 overs in the required time.

The first session of this day-night game had begun well for them when Gabriel was dismissed at 1, and neither Richardson nor Richards stayed long, but Haynes found a good partner in Lloyd who hit two huge sixes as the pair added 80. Haynes carried his bat for a fine century in 210 minutes.

Lloyd had damaged a finger and could not field for West Indies who were troubled by a good opening stand from the Queenslanders Wessels and Ritchie. The partnership ended when Ritchie was brilliantly run out by Daniel from cover and 7 runs later Wessels was lbw. Baptiste bowled tightly, but Marsh and Hookes put on 50 in 23 minutes before Marsh was out at 155 in the fortieth over. Hookes went shortly after, and the impetus and the match were lost.

## SIXTH ONE-DAY INTERNATIONAL – AUSTRALIA *v.* WEST INDIES
17 January 1984 at Sydney

| WEST INDIES | | |
|---|---|---|
| D.L. Haynes | not out | 108 |
| R.S. Gabriel | lbw, b Lawson | 0 |
| R.B. Richardson | c Hughes, b Rackemann | 11 |
| I.V.A. Richards | c Wessels, b Hogg | 19 |
| C.H. Lloyd† | lbw, b Hogg | 40 |
| P.J. Dujon* | c Wessels, b Rackemann | 8 |
| A.L. Logie | b Lawson | 9 |
| E.A.E. Baptiste | b Lawson | 5 |
| M.A. Holding | not out | 6 |
| W.W. Daniel | | |
| W.W. Davis | | |
| Extras | lb 16, w 1 | 17 |
| (49 overs) | (for 7 wickets) | 223 |

| | O | M | R | W |
|---|---|---|---|---|
| Lawson | 10 | 1 | 30 | 3 |
| Rackemann | 10 | — | 33 | 2 |
| Macleay | 10 | — | 47 | — |
| Hogg | 10 | 1 | 59 | 2 |
| Maguire | 9 | 1 | 38 | — |

FALL OF WICKETS
1- 1, 2- 24, 3- 55, 4- 135, 5- 168, 6- 195, 7- 207

| AUSTRALIA | | |
|---|---|---|
| G.M. Ritchie | run out | 30 |
| K.C. Wessels | lbw, b Richards | 27 |
| K.J. Hughes† | b Baptiste | 19 |
| A.R. Border | c Richards, b Baptiste | 1 |
| D.W. Hookes | c Logie, b Daniel | 35 |
| R.W. Marsh* | b Daniel | 27 |
| K.H. Macleay | b Holding | 15 |
| G.F. Lawson | run out | 3 |
| R.M. Hogg | b Holding | 1 |
| C.G. Rackemann | not out | 9 |
| J.N. Maguire | not out | 2 |
| Extras | lb 19, w 4, nb 3 | 26 |
| (49 overs) | (for 9 wickets) | 195 |

| | O | M | R | W |
|---|---|---|---|---|
| Holding | 10 | — | 35 | 2 |
| Daniel | 10 | — | 29 | 2 |
| Davis | 9 | 1 | 39 | — |
| Baptiste | 10 | 1 | 32 | 2 |
| Richards | 10 | — | 41 | 1 |

FALL OF WICKETS
1- 68, 2- 75, 3- 76, 4- 100, 5- 155, 6- 164, 7- 171, 8- 175, 9- 192

**West Indies won by 28 runs**

## SEVENTH ONE-DAY INTERNATIONAL – PAKISTAN *v.* WEST INDIES
19 January 1984 at Sydney

| PAKISTAN | | | |
|---|---|---|---|
| Mudassar Nazar | lbw, b Holding | | 7 |
| Mohsin Khan | c Dujon, b Marshall | | 13 |
| Mansoor Akhtar | c Dujon, b Daniel | | 4 |
| Javed Miandad | b Baptiste | | 31 |
| Qasim Umar | not out | | 67 |
| Imran Khan† | lbw, b Holding | | 17 |
| Rashid Khan | b Holding | | 1 |
| Abdul Qadir | b Holding | | 7 |
| Sarfraz Nawaz | b Daniel | | 0 |
| Wasim Bari* | not out | | 6 |
| Azeem Hafeez | | | |
| Extras | b 1, lb 13, w 7, nb 10 | | 31 |
| (50 overs) | (for 8 wickets) | | 184 |

| | O | M | R | W |
|---|---|---|---|---|
| Holding | 10 | 2 | 26 | 4 |
| Daniel | 10 | 2 | 60 | 2 |
| Davis | 10 | 3 | 30 | — |
| Marshall | 6 | 4 | 5 | 1 |
| Richards | 5 | — | 24 | — |
| Baptiste | 9 | 2 | 25 | 1 |

FALL OF WICKETS
1- 16, 2- 28, 3- 35, 4- 96, 5- 137, 6- 143, 7- 157, 8- 161

| WEST INDIES | | |
|---|---|---|
| D.L. Haynes | c Mudassar, b Qadir | 37 |
| R.S. Gabriel | b Azeem Hafeez | 15 |
| R.B. Richardson | st Wasim Bari, b Qadir | 53 |
| I.V.A. Richards† | c Rashid Khan, b Qadir | 2 |
| P.J. Dujon* | run out | 13 |
| A.L. Logie | not out | 28 |
| M.D. Marshall | not out | 16 |
| E.A.E. Baptiste | | |
| M.A. Holding | | |
| W.W. Daniel | | |
| W.W. Davis | | |
| Extras | b 4, lb 10, w 7 | 21 |
| (48.3 overs) | (for 5 wickets) | 185 |

| | O | M | R | W |
|---|---|---|---|---|
| Sarfraz Nawaz | 9 | 1 | 31 | — |
| Rashid Khan | 9.3 | 3 | 26 | — |
| Azeem Hafeez | 10 | — | 53 | 1 |
| Mudassar Nazar | 10 | 1 | 34 | — |
| Abdul Qadir | 10 | 1 | 27 | 3 |

FALL OF WICKETS
1- 30, 2- 109, 3- 120, 4- 138, 5- 141

**West Indies won by 5 wickets**

***Benson and Hedges World Series***

### Seventh One-Day International
### WEST INDIES *v.* PAKISTAN

Coming in at 35 for 3, Qasim Umar played a fine knock to help Pakistan to some sort of respectability, but their 184 was never likely to give West Indies much trouble.

Haynes and Gabriel started busily enough for West Indies, but it was a stand of 79 between Haynes and Richardson that gave the innings substance. Richardson looked a fine player, the dominant West Indian batsman of the next generation of Test players, until he was stumped off Abdul Qadir who showed his old guile.

It was left to Logie and Marshall to regain the initiative.

***Benson and Hedges World Series***

### Eighth One-Day International
### AUSTRALIA *v.* PAKISTAN

In spite of some splendid bowling by Abdul Qadir, who

## EIGHTH ONE-DAY INTERNATIONAL – AUSTRALIA *v.* PAKISTAN
21 January 1984 at Melbourne

| AUSTRALIA | | |
|---|---|---|
| G.M. Ritchie | c and b Ejaz Faqih | 27 |
| K.C. Wessels | c Imran, b Qadir | 86 |
| K.J. Hughes† | lbw, b Mudassar | 0 |
| A.R. Border | b Azeem Hafeez | 12 |
| D.W. Hookes | st Wasim Bari, b Qadir | 37 |
| S.B. Smith | b Qadir | 0 |
| R.W. Marsh* | c Imran, b Qadir | 11 |
| G.F. Lawson | not out | 14 |
| R.M. Hogg | c and b Qadir | 0 |
| J.N. Maguire | not out | 14 |
| C.G. Rackemann | | |
| Extras | lb 8 | 8 |
| (50 overs) | (for 8 wickets) | 209 |

| | O | M | R | W |
|---|---|---|---|---|
| Azeem Hafeez | 10 | — | 44 | 1 |
| Rashid Khan | 10 | 1 | 32 | — |
| Mudassar Nazar | 10 | 2 | 31 | 1 |
| Ejaz Faqih | 10 | 1 | 41 | 1 |
| Abdul Qadir | 10 | 1 | 53 | 5 |

FALL OF WICKETS
1- 57, 2- 58, 3- 123, 4- 138, 5- 140, 6- 172, 7- 178, 8- 178

| PAKISTAN | | |
|---|---|---|
| Mudassar Nazar | c Wessels, b Hogg | 12 |
| Mohsin Khan | c Marsh, b Border | 22 |
| Mansoor Akhtar | run out | 1 |
| Javed Miandad | b Hogg | 56 |
| Qasim Umar | b Border | 2 |
| Imran Khan† | c Marsh, b Maguire | 17 |
| Ejaz Faqih | b Hogg | 17 |
| Abdul Qadir | b Hogg | 23 |
| Rashid Khan | not out | 2 |
| Wasim Bari* | run out | 2 |
| Azeem Hafeez | b Lawson | 0 |
| Extras | b 1, lb 6, w 4, nb 1 | 12 |
| (45 overs) | | 166 |

| | O | M | R | W |
|---|---|---|---|---|
| Lawson | 8 | 2 | 19 | 1 |
| Rackemann | 7 | — | 23 | — |
| Hogg | 10 | 2 | 33 | 4 |
| Wessels | 7 | — | 28 | — |
| Border | 7 | — | 24 | 2 |
| Maguire | 6 | — | 32 | 1 |

FALL OF WICKETS
1- 33, 2- 35, 3- 56, 4- 61, 5- 89, 6- 124, 7- 161, 8- 162, 9- 164

**Australia won by 43 runs**

*Kim Hughes is lbw to Mudassar for 0 in the 8th one-day international. (Philip Tyson)*

*Viv Richards in blistering form – 106 in the 9th one-day international. (Philip Tyson)*

followed his World Cup feat of June, 1983, with 5 wickets in an innings, Australia beat Pakistan easily enough and edged ahead of them in the qualifying competition.

The Australian innings was given a sound start by Ritchie and Wessels, and Wessels, his confidence and form completely returned, played a steadfast knock of 86 which gave the Australian challenge substance. More surprisingly, Wessels produced an effective spell of bowling when he and Border were used to supplement the successful pace attack. Wessels' gentle off-spin and Border's slow left-arm produced the required economy and with Hogg in fiery form, Australia won with ease.

***Benson and Hedges World Series***

**Ninth One-Day International**
**AUSTRALIA v. WEST INDIES**

Another fine innings by Kepler Wessels, coupled with eight useful overs and the wicket of Gomes, could not disguise the fact that when he missed Richards off a skier behind the wicket-keeper he cost Australia the match. Haynes had gone off with a rare flourish, but he was completely overshadowed by Richards who, enjoying his escape, hit a six and twelve fours off the 94 balls he received. It was thrilling stuff and the record crowd of 86,133 gave him a standing ovation at the close.

His part in the match was not finished, however, for he took the wickets of Wessels and Hookes in his ten overs at a cost of 51. Australia fought hard with Hughes playing a particularly fine innings, but the opening stand had taken too many overs and the task was always too much for the later batsmen.

With each team having played six matches, West Indies had 10 points, Australia 5 and Pakistan 3.

**NINTH ONE-DAY INTERNATIONAL – AUSTRALIA v. WEST INDIES**
22 January 1984 at Melbourne

| WEST INDIES | | |
|---|---|---|
| D.L. Haynes | b Hogg | 64 |
| R.S. Gabriel | c Maguire, b Rackemann | 8 |
| H.A. Gomes | lbw, b Wessels | 7 |
| I.V.A. Richards | c Smith, b Rackemann | 106 |
| C.H. Lloyd† | b Maguire | 27 |
| P.J. Dujon* | not out | 21 |
| M.D. Marshall | b Lawson | 1 |
| A.L. Logie | not out | 9 |
| E.A.E. Baptiste | | |
| M.A. Holding | | |
| W.W. Daniel | | |
| Extras | lb 7, w 2 | 9 |
| (50 overs) | (for 6 wickets) | 252 |

| | O | M | R | W |
|---|---|---|---|---|
| Lawson | 10 | 2 | 28 | 1 |
| Rackemann | 9 | 3 | 43 | 2 |
| Hogg | 10 | — | 56 | 1 |
| Wessels | 8 | — | 32 | 1 |
| Border | 5 | — | 35 | — |
| Maguire | 8 | — | 51 | 1 |

FALL OF WICKETS
1- 24, 2- 50, 3- 140, 4- 199, 5- 230, 6- 238

| AUSTRALIA | | |
|---|---|---|
| G.M. Ritchie | c Holding, b Baptiste | 28 |
| K.C. Wessels | b Richards | 60 |
| A.R. Border | b Baptiste | 0 |
| K.J. Hughes† | b Daniel | 71 |
| D.W. Hookes | c Logie, b Richards | 6 |
| S.B. Smith | c Gomes, b Daniel | 26 |
| W.B. Phillips* | not out | 18 |
| G.F. Lawson | b Holding | 0 |
| J.N. Maguire | b Marshall | 3 |
| C.G. Rackemann | b Holding | 0 |
| R.M. Hogg | b Holding | 2 |
| Extras | b 3, lb 6, w 3 | 12 |
| (49.5 overs) | | 226 |

| | O | M | R | W |
|---|---|---|---|---|
| Holding | 9.5 | — | 35 | 3 |
| Daniel | 10 | — | 38 | 2 |
| Baptiste | 7 | — | 24 | 2 |
| Marshall | 10 | — | 49 | 1 |
| Richards | 10 | — | 51 | 2 |
| Gomes | 3 | — | 20 | — |

FALL OF WICKETS
1- 62, 2- 63, 3- 119, 4- 146, 5- 186, 6- 203, 7- 216, 8- 223, 9- 224

**West Indies won by 26 runs**

*24 January 1984*

***at Manuka Oval, Canberra***

**Prime Minister's XI** 280 for 4 (D.C. Boon 134, K.J. Hughes 53 retired)
**West Indians** 228 for 8

*Prime Minister's XI won by 52 runs*

A crowd of 15,000 saw Lillee and Thomson reunited in attack and David Boon, cruelly omitted by the Australian selectors from the side to tour West Indies, hit eight fours and a six in the 135-minute innings which was his retort. The fixture, resurrected by Prime Minister Bob Hawke after an absence of 19 years, was a great success.

*25 January 1984*

***at Manuka Oval, Canberra***

**West Indians** 243 for 9
**A.C.T.** 184 for 7 (K. Stone 52, R.A. Harper 4 for 24)

*West Indians won by 59 runs*

Pace was used sparingly in this match, Harper, Gomes, Haynes and Logie sending down 33 overs.

***Benson and Hedges World Series***

**Tenth One-Day International**
**AUSTRALIA *v.* PAKISTAN**

Steve Smith, who had passed into the shadows since his remarkable success in the finals of the Benson and Hedges World Series in the previous season, found himself reinstated as Australia's opener and responded with an attractive century, his 106 came off 129 deliveries. He and Ritchie hammered a depleted and sorry looking Pakistan attack for 50 from 10 overs for the second wicket. There were brisk contributions from Marsh and Phillips and Australia reached an impressive 244.

Pakistan started disastrously when Mudassar was run out for 0 and Mohsin was bowled for 1. Javed and Imran steadied the innings until the Pakistan captain became another run out victim, but the game had long since been lost and won.

Australia's victory virtually ensured that they would meet West Indies in the final.

*27, 28, 29 and 30 January 1984*

***at Brisbane***

**Western Australia** 240 (S.F. Graf 74, B.M. Laird 58, J.R. Thomson 4 for 50) and 192 for 4 dec (B.M. Laird 66 not out, G.M. Wood 51)
**Queensland** 229 (T.V. Hohns 58, T.M. Alderman 4 for 51) and 38 for 1

*Match drawn*
*Western Australia 4 pts, Queensland 0 pts*

***at Melbourne***

**Victoria** 203 (P.A. Hibbert 68, M. Quinn 54, D.R. Gilbert 5 for 56) and 396 for 7 (R.J. Bright 100 not out, M.D. Taylor 77, A.I.C. Dodemaide 54 not out)
**New South Wales** 435 for 4 dec (P. Clifford 152 not out, S.J. Rixon 101 not out, G. Giese 77)

*Match drawn*
*New South Wales 4 pts, Victoria 0 pts*

The top of the table clash at Brisbane was suffocated to death by the fear that each side had of giving points to the other. A fifth wicket stand of 120 between Shaun Graf, in the middle of a good spell with the bat, and Bruce Laird helped the visitors to a rather tedious 240. The home side struggled in reply against Lillee and Alderman and it was only a late fifty from Trevor Hohns that helped them near the visitors' score. Once again the innings had moved at a very slow pace, 90 overs for 229 runs. Another crawl then ensued as Western Australia took 77 overs to score 192 for 4 before Lillee

**TENTH ONE-DAY INTERNATIONAL – AUSTRALIA *v.* PAKISTAN**
25 January 1984 at Sydney

| AUSTRALIA | | | |
|---|---|---|---|
| | S.B. Smith | c Qadir, b Rashid Khan | 106 |
| | K.C. Wessels | c Imran, b Tahir | 7 |
| | G.M. Ritchie | st Ashraf, b Qadir | 31 |
| | K.J. Hughes† | b Qadir | 3 |
| | A.R. Border | b Mudassar | 11 |
| | W.B. Phillips | run out | 25 |
| | R.W. Marsh* | c Ashraf, b Tahir | 20 |
| | G.F. Lawson | st Ashraf, b Qadir | 2 |
| | J.N. Maguire | not out | 7 |
| | R.M. Hogg | not out | 8 |
| | C.G. Rackemann | | |
| | Extras | b 8, lb 3, w 10, nb 3 | 24 |
| | (50 overs) | (for 8 wickets) | 244 |

| | O | M | R | W |
|---|---|---|---|---|
| Rashid Khan | 9 | — | 36 | 1 |
| Tahir Naqqash | 10 | 3 | 56 | 2 |
| Abdul Qadir | 9 | 1 | 42 | 3 |
| Mudassar Nazar | 10 | 1 | 33 | 1 |
| Ejaz Faqih | 7 | — | 36 | — |
| Wasim Raja | 5 | — | 30 | — |

FALL OF WICKETS
1-18, 2-85, 3-97, 4-122, 5-196, 6-216, 7-221, 8-234

| PAKISTAN | | | |
|---|---|---|---|
| | Mudassar Nazar | run out | 0 |
| | Mohsin Khan | b Lawson | 1 |
| | Imran Khan† | run out | 41 |
| | Javed Miandad | c Marsh, b Maguire | 26 |
| | Qasim Umar | c Marsh, b Hogg | 0 |
| | Wasim Raja | st Marsh, b Wessels | 32 |
| | Ejaz Faqih | b Hogg | 14 |
| | Tahir Naqqash | b Hogg | 0 |
| | Abdul Qadir | c Marsh, b Hogg | 9 |
| | Rashid Khan | b Border | 17 |
| | Ashraf Ali* | not out | 11 |
| | Extras | b 2, lb 3, w 1 | 6 |
| | (47.2 overs) | | 157 |

| | O | M | R | W |
|---|---|---|---|---|
| Lawson | 6 | 3 | 15 | 1 |
| Rackemann | 10 | 2 | 16 | — |
| Maguire | 9 | 1 | 19 | 1 |
| Hogg | 10 | — | 37 | 4 |
| Wessels | 9 | — | 50 | 1 |
| Border | 3.2 | — | 15 | 1 |

FALL OF WICKETS
1-0, 2-1, 3-45, 4-46, 5-103, 6-103, 7-104, 8-120, 9-129

**Australia won by 87 runs**

*Peter Clifford – a maiden first-class hundred for New South Wales against Victoria, 27–30 January. Hyde is the wicket-keeper. (Philip Tyson)*

declared and left Queensland 90 minutes in which to make 204, the ultimate absurdity.

Mike Quinn and Paul Hibbert added 132 for Victoria's second wicket at Melbourne, but there came the customary collapse as David Gilbert's fast medium brought him a career best 5 for 56. New South Wales then proceeded to savage the Victorian bowling. In his second match Peter Clifford recorded a maiden century and with debutant Greg Giese hitting 77 and Steve Rixon making the fifth century of his career, New South Wales moved into a formidable lead. Needing 232 to make the visitors bat again, Victoria struggled in spite of Mike Taylor's 77, but Ray Bright hit the second century of his career and Tony Dodemaide reached a maiden fifty. The pair added an unbeaten 162 for the eighth wicket and so broke a Victorian record against New South Wales which had stood for 57 years.

### *Benson and Hedges World Series*

### Eleventh One-Day International
### WEST INDIES *v.* PAKISTAN

A very much weakened Pakistan side gave one of their most spirited displays of a miserable tour before losing to West Indies by one wicket and so passing from the competition.

Pakistan were without Imran and Sarfraz, who were injured, and Zaheer who had returned to England to organise his benefit and had taken no part in the one-day internationals. The Pakistan innings never blossomed, mainly because of a relentless spell by Malcolm Marshall who reduced them to 59 for 4, and they owed their score to a fine flourish from Wasim Raja.

It was Raja who bowled Pakistan into the game. He came on after only three overs of the West Indian innings to bowl medium pace and had Haynes caught behind. He sustained an economic six over spell and Abdul Qadir tantalised the batsmen with his leg-spin once more so that West Indies faced defeat at 92 for 7.

Marshall and Baptiste took control and added 53 off 35 deliveries. Wasim Raja then returned to bowl leg-spin and dismissed both Baptiste and Holding so that when last man Wayne Daniel joined Marshall 19 were needed off 4 overs. Marshall reached his fifty off 81 deliveries and then, although 16 had been needed off the last 18 balls, steered his side to victory with 5 balls to spare.

### *Benson and Hedges World Series*

### Twelfth One-Day International
### AUSTRALIA *v.* WEST INDIES

A crowd of 31,424 saw West Indies move to an easy win over

**ELEVENTH ONE-DAY INTERNATIONAL – WEST INDIES *v.* PAKISTAN**
28 January 1984 at Adelaide

| PAKISTAN | | | |
|---|---|---|---|
| | Mudassar Nazar | c Dujon, b Baptiste | 18 |
| | Mansoor Akhtar | c Dujon, b Marshall | 20 |
| | Qasim Umar | run out | 26 |
| | Javed Miandad† | c Dujon, b Marshall | 4 |
| | Saleem Malik | b Marshall | 1 |
| | Wasim Raja | c Richards, b Gomes | 46 |
| | Ejaz Faqih | not out | 23 |
| | Abdul Qadir | c Baptiste, b Gomes | 4 |
| | Tahir Naqqash | run out | 0 |
| | Rashid Khan | not out | 16 |
| | Wasim Bari* | | |
| | Extras | lb 14, w 2, nb 3 | 19 |
| | (50 overs) | (for 8 wickets) | 177 |

| | O | M | R | W |
|---|---|---|---|---|
| Holding | 8 | 1 | 21 | — |
| Daniel | 10 | 3 | 25 | — |
| Marshall | 9 | 1 | 28 | 3 |
| Baptiste | 10 | — | 33 | 1 |
| Richards | 6 | — | 30 | — |
| Gomes | 7 | — | 26 | 2 |

FALL OF WICKETS
1- 40, 2- 42, 3- 54, 4- 59, 5- 127, 6- 127, 7- 135, 8- 136

| WEST INDIES | | | |
|---|---|---|---|
| | D.L. Haynes | c Wasim Bari, b Wasim Raja | 3 |
| | R.S. Gabriel | b Abdul Qadir | 10 |
| | A.L. Logie | c Javed Miandad, b Rashid Khan | 19 |
| | I.V.A. Richards | c Mansoor, b Abdul Qadir | 18 |
| | H.A. Gomes | c Wasim Bari, b Mudassar | 3 |
| | C.H. Lloyd† | run out | 10 |
| | P.J. Dujon* | st Wasim Bari, b Abdul Qadir | 10 |
| | M.D. Marshall | not out | 56 |
| | E.A.E. Baptiste | c Rashid Khan, b Wasim Raja | 24 |
| | M.A. Holding | lbw, b Wasim Raja | 10 |
| | W.W. Daniel | not out | 7 |
| | Extras | b 1, lb 4, w 4, nb 1 | 10 |
| | (49.1 overs) | (for 9 wickets) | 180 |

| | O | M | R | W |
|---|---|---|---|---|
| Rashid Khan | 8.1 | 3 | 29 | 1 |
| Tahir Naqqash | 7 | 1 | 35 | — |
| Wasim Raja | 10 | 1 | 33 | 3 |
| Abdul Qadir | 10 | 1 | 34 | 3 |
| Mudassar Nazar | 10 | — | 32 | 1 |
| Ejaz Faqih | 4 | — | 12 | — |

FALL OF WICKETS
1- 9, 2- 28, 3- 52, 4- 59, 5- 61, 6- 75, 7- 92, 8- 145, 9- 159

**West Indies won by 1 wicket**

## TWELFTH ONE-DAY INTERNATIONAL – AUSTRALIA *v.* WEST INDIES
29 January 1984 at Adelaide

**AUSTRALIA**

|  |  |  |
|---|---|---|
| S.B. Smith | b Marshall | 55 |
| K.C. Wessels | c Dujon, b Daniel | 4 |
| G.M. Ritchie | run out | 0 |
| K.J. Hughes† | c Dujon, b Baptiste | 10 |
| A.R. Border | b Richards | 17 |
| W.B. Phillips | st Dujon, b Richards | 2 |
| R.W. Marsh* | not out | 34 |
| G.F. Lawson | c and b Daniel | 18 |
| J.N. Maguire | not out | 9 |
| R.M. Hogg | | |
| C.G. Rackemann | | |
| Extras | b 7, lb 3, w 2, nb 4 | 16 |
| (50 overs) | (for 7 wickets) | 165 |

| | O | M | R | W |
|---|---|---|---|---|
| Holding | 7 | 2 | 20 | — |
| Daniel | 8 | — | 35 | 2 |
| Marshall | 10 | 3 | 21 | 1 |
| Baptiste | 5 | 2 | 9 | 1 |
| Gomes | 10 | 1 | 42 | — |
| Richards | 10 | — | 28 | 2 |

FALL OF WICKETS
1- 14, 2- 14, 3- 34, 4- 71, 5- 85, 6- 115, 7- 149

**WEST INDIES**

|  |  |  |
|---|---|---|
| D.L. Haynes | c Marsh, b Rackemann | 4 |
| R.S. Gabriel | c Lawson, b Border | 41 |
| H.A. Gomes | run out | 27 |
| I.V.A. Richards | b Border | 0 |
| C.H. Lloyd† | not out | 38 |
| A.L. Logie | not out | 49 |
| P.J. Dujon* | | |
| E.A.E. Baptiste | | |
| M.D. Marshall | | |
| M.A. Holding | | |
| W.W. Daniel | | |
| Extras | lb 7, w 1, nb 2 | 10 |
| (45.1 overs) | (for 4 wickets) | 169 |

| | O | M | R | W |
|---|---|---|---|---|
| Lawson | 6 | 1 | 10 | — |
| Rackemann | 10 | — | 35 | 1 |
| Hogg | 10 | — | 31 | — |
| Maguire | 8 | 1 | 44 | — |
| Wessels | 3 | — | 9 | — |
| Border | 7 | — | 25 | 2 |
| Smith | 1 | — | 4 | — |
| Hughes | 0.1 | — | 4 | — |

FALL OF WICKETS
1- 14, 2- 67, 3- 68, 4- 89

**West Indies won by 6 wickets**

Australia with 4.5 overs to spare. Smith and Marsh, who had had a splendid series with the bat, were the only Australians to show any confidence against the accurate West Indian attack and there seemed little hope that Australia could defend a total so meagre as 165.

Haynes went early, and there was a further boost to Australian morale when Border surprisingly bowled Richards for 0, but Logie and Lloyd hit off the last 80 runs in 63 minutes after the fourth wicket had gone down in the thirtieth over.

***Benson and Hedges World Series***

### Thirteenth One-Day International
### AUSTRALIA *v.* PAKISTAN

The bitter disappointment and frustration of the Pakistani players at their poor performances in Australia was epitomised when, following another big defeat, Mohsin Khan announced that he was retiring from international cricket. He was persuaded to change his mind, but his rash statement indicated the depth of morale in the Pakistan side.

## THIRTEENTH ONE-DAY INTERNATIONAL – AUSTRALIA *v.* PAKISTAN
30 January 1984 at Adelaide

**AUSTRALIA**

|  |  |  |
|---|---|---|
| S.B. Smith | b Ejaz Faqih | 36 |
| K.C. Wessels | b Ejaz Faqih | 61 |
| G.M. Ritchie | b Ejaz Faqih | 12 |
| K.J. Hughes† | st Wasim Bari, b Ejaz Faqih | 11 |
| A.R. Border | run out | 10 |
| W.B. Phillips* | b Mudassar | 17 |
| D.M.J. Jones | not out | 40 |
| T.G. Hogan | c Wasim Raja, b Mudassar | 3 |
| J.N. Maguire | c Mansoor Akhtar, b Rashid Khan | 1 |
| R.M. Hogg | not out | 6 |
| C.G. Rackemann | | |
| Extras | lb 9, w 2, nb 2 | 13 |
| (50 overs) | (for 8 wickets) | 210 |

| | O | M | R | W |
|---|---|---|---|---|
| Rashid Khan | 10 | 1 | 33 | 1 |
| Mudassar Nazar | 10 | — | 50 | 2 |
| Ejaz Faqih | 10 | 1 | 43 | 4 |
| Wasim Raja | 10 | 2 | 23 | — |
| Abdul Qadir | 10 | — | 52 | — |

FALL OF WICKETS
1- 70, 2- 115, 3- 126, 4- 135, 5- 145, 6- 163, 7- 169, 8- 179

**PAKISTAN**

|  |  |  |
|---|---|---|
| Mansoor Akhtar | b Hogg | 22 |
| Javed Miandad† | c Hogg, b Rackemann | 34 |
| Qasim Umar | c Ritchie, b Rackemann | 2 |
| Wasim Raja | c Hughes, b Wessels | 17 |
| Mudassar Nazar | c Phillips, b Rackemann | 1 |
| Mohsin Khan | lbw, b Wessels | 19 |
| Saleem Malik | lbw, b Hogan | 14 |
| Ejaz Faqih | c Phillips, b Rackemann | 13 |
| Abdul Qadir | b Hogg | 3 |
| Rashid Khan | c Hogan, b Rackemann | 1 |
| Wasim Bari* | not out | 2 |
| Extras | b 6, lb 5, w 1 | 12 |
| (45.2 overs) | | 140 |

| | O | M | R | W |
|---|---|---|---|---|
| Hogg | 8 | 2 | 26 | 2 |
| Rackemann | 8.2 | 2 | 16 | 5 |
| Maguire | 10 | 1 | 33 | — |
| Hogan | 10 | 2 | 22 | 1 |
| Wessels | 9 | — | 32 | 2 |

FALL OF WICKETS
1- 56, 2- 56, 3- 58, 4- 60, 5- 98, 6- 115, 7- 123, 8- 137, 9- 137

**Australia won by 70 runs**

The match provided little in the way of contest. Wessels played a sound innings and showed his improvement as a bowler, but it was twenty-two-year-old Dean Jones, in his first international, who made the most significant impression with an innings of 40 not out off 33 balls.

Pakistan moved to 56 without loss and then lost 4 wickets for 4 runs, three of them to Rackemann who finished with outstanding figures, 5 for 16, on a day which belonged entirely to Australia.

***2 February 1984***

***at Bunbury***

**West Indians** 186 for 8 (R.B. Richardson 81, R.S. Gabriel 53)
**Western Australian Country XI** 180 for 4 (T. Waldron 76 not out)

*West Indians won by 6 runs*

Richardson had been handicapped by a thigh injury, but he returned to share a second wicket stand of 119 with Gabriel. Waldron hit five sixes and six fours off 50 deliveries, but he was confronted mainly by irregular bowlers.

***3, 4, 5 and 6 February 1984***

***at Sydney***

**Tasmania** 288 (S.L. Saunders 125) and 319 (R.D. Woolley 102, P.I. Faulkner 76, G.W. Goodman 65, R.G. Holland 4 for 98)
**New South Wales** 289 for 2 dec (J. Dyson 106, P.S. Clifford 94 not out) and 268 (J. Dyson 80, R.B. McCosker 55, P.M. Clough 5 for 60, S.L. Saunders 5 for 114)

*Tasmania won by 50 runs*
*Tasmania 12 pts, New South Wales 4 pts*

In a remarkable turn about of fortune Tasmania achieved a fine victory in Sydney and brought themselves within 14 points of Queensland so raising hopes of winning a place in the Sheffield Shield Final. Woolley won the toss, but he saw his side struggle to 76 for 5 against Gilbert, Matthews and Done. Saunders and Davison added 54 before Davison was bowled by Done, but Saunders then dominated a partnership of 90 with Faulkner. Saunders reached his second century of the season and with the last 3 wickets adding 68, Tasmania reached an unexpected 288. McCosker and Dyson began the home side's reply with a stand of 91 and then Dyson and Clifford added 122 for the second wicket, Dyson reaching his second hundred of the season. McCosker declared as soon as New South Wales had taken first innings points so that Clifford was denied his second century in successive matches.

McCosker, skipper in Wellham's absence, seemed to justify his decision when four Tasmanian wickets fell for 77. Woolley and Goodman added 80 and Woolley, in his final match before leaving for the West Indies, hit his first hundred of the summer. Faulkner again displayed his hitting powers and the last four wickets produced 157 runs. Needing 319 to win, New South Wales were given a splendid start by Dyson and McCosker who put on 122, but then Stuart Saunders effected a break-through with his leg-spin and he and Clough gnawed away regularly at the home side's middle order. The last 4 wickets fell for 4 runs and Tasmania had won a remarkable victory. Saunders' 5 for 114 was his solitary bowling success of the season.

***Benson and Hedges World Series***

**Fourteenth One-Day International**
**PAKISTAN *v.* WEST INDIES**

Pakistan's wretched tour came to an end when West Indies beat them by 7 wickets with 4.5 overs to spare. Mudassar batted well, but Garner conceded only 5 runs from his opening 6 overs.

Already assured of a place in the final, West Indies had problems neither in the field nor with the bat, and Haynes stroked them to comfortable win, even matching the blistering Richards in their 95-run third wicket stand.

**FOURTEENTH ONE-DAY INTERNATIONAL – WEST INDIES *v.* PAKISTAN**
4 February 1984 at Perth

| PAKISTAN | | | |
|---|---|---|---|
| | Mudassar Nazar | c Marshall, b Baptiste | 54 |
| | Mansoor Akhtar | c Garner, b Davis | 3 |
| | Mohsin Khan | b Harper | 32 |
| | Javed Miandad† | b Harper | 26 |
| | Qasim Umar | c Richards, b Davis | 16 |
| | Saleem Malik | b Garner | 14 |
| | Ejaz Faqih | b Garner | 0 |
| | Abdul Qadir | not out | 6 |
| | Rashid Khan | not out | 10 |
| | Azeem Hafeez | | |
| | Ashraf Ali* | | |
| | Extras | b 7, lb 7, w 6, nb 1 | 21 |
| | (50 overs) | (for 7 wickets) | 182 |

| | O | M | R | W |
|---|---|---|---|---|
| Garner | 9 | 3 | 12 | 2 |
| Davis | 10 | — | 34 | 2 |
| Baptiste | 10 | — | 36 | 1 |
| Marshall | 6 | — | 20 | — |
| Harper | 10 | — | 42 | 2 |
| Richards | 5 | — | 24 | — |

FALL OF WICKETS
1- 13, 2- 88, 3- 129, 4- 135, 5- 159, 6- 163, 7- 164

| WEST INDIES | | | |
|---|---|---|---|
| | D.L. Haynes | not out | 78 |
| | R.S. Gabriel | c Ashraf, b Mudassar | 29 |
| | R.B. Richardson | c and b Mudassar | 7 |
| | I.V.A. Richards† | c Saleem Malik, b Ejaz Faqih | 40 |
| | A.L. Logie | not out | 14 |
| | P.J. Dujon* | | |
| | M.D. Marshall | | |
| | E.A.E. Baptiste | | |
| | R.A. Harper | | |
| | W.W. Davis | | |
| | J. Garner | | |
| | Extras | lb 10, w 5 | 15 |
| | (45.1 overs) | (for 3 wickets) | 183 |

| | O | M | R | W |
|---|---|---|---|---|
| Rashid Khan | 10 | 1 | 25 | — |
| Azeem Hafeez | 6 | — | 51 | — |
| Mudassar Nazar | 10 | 1 | 33 | 2 |
| Abdul Qadir | 10 | 3 | 19 | — |
| Ejaz Faqih | 9 | — | 44 | 1 |
| Mansoor Akhtar | 0 | — | 1 | — |

FALL OF WICKETS
1- 38, 2- 58, 3- 153

**West Indies won by 7 wickets**

## FIFTEENTH ONE-DAY INTERNATIONAL – AUSTRALIA *v.* WEST INDIES
5 February 1984 at Perth

| AUSTRALIA | | | |
|---|---|---|---|
| | S.B. Smith | c Dujon, b Daniel | 12 |
| | K.C. Wessels | c Daniel, b Marshall | 50 |
| | G.M. Ritchie | c Gabriel, b Holding | 3 |
| | K.J. Hughes† | c Richardson, b Marshall | 67 |
| | A.R. Border | b Richards | 1 |
| | D.M.J. Jones | b Holding | 23 |
| | R.W. Marsh* | not out | 27 |
| | G.F. Lawson | run out | 3 |
| | R.M. Hogg | run out | 2 |
| | T.M. Alderman | not out | 0 |
| | C.G. Rackemann | | |
| | Extras | b 3, lb 14, w 3, nb 3 | 23 |
| | (50 overs) | (for 8 wickets) | 211 |

| | O | M | R | W |
|---|---|---|---|---|
| Holding | 10 | 1 | 31 | 2 |
| Daniel | 10 | 1 | 43 | 1 |
| Marshall | 10 | 2 | 27 | 2 |
| Baptiste | 10 | — | 46 | — |
| Richards | 10 | — | 47 | 1 |

FALL OF WICKETS
1- 15, 2- 21, 3- 140, 4- 142, 5- 157, 6- 185, 7- 192, 8- 201

| WEST INDIES | | | |
|---|---|---|---|
| | D.L. Haynes | c Marsh, b Wessels | 52 |
| | R.B. Richardson | c Wessels, b Lawson | 2 |
| | A.L. Logie | c Hughes, b Alderman | 3 |
| | I.V.A. Richards | b Alderman | 7 |
| | C.H. Lloyd† | b Hogg | 31 |
| | P.J. Dujon* | b Rackemann | 0 |
| | M.D. Marshall | c Marsh, b Rackemann | 2 |
| | E.A.E. Baptiste | c Marsh, b Lawson | 1 |
| | M.A. Holding | lbw, b Wessels | 64 |
| | R.S. Gabriel | b Rackemann | 12 |
| | W.W. Daniel | not out | 0 |
| | Extras | b 3, lb 11, w 8, nb 1 | 23 |
| | (43.3 overs) | | 197 |

| | O | M | R | W |
|---|---|---|---|---|
| Lawson | 8 | 1 | 32 | 2 |
| Alderman | 10 | 3 | 19 | 2 |
| Hogg | 9 | 2 | 36 | 1 |
| Wessels | 8 | 2 | 50 | 2 |
| Rackemann | 8.3 | — | 46 | 3 |

FALL OF WICKETS
1- 17, 2- 23, 3- 37, 4- 92, 5- 93, 6- 101, 7- 102, 8- 156, 9- 188

**Australia won by 14 runs**

***Benson and Hedges World Series***

### Fifteenth One-Day International
### AUSTRALIA *v.* WEST INDIES

A fine spell of fast bowling from Holding could not prevent Australia from reaching 211 in the last of the qualifying matches. Wessels again batted soundly, but Kim Hughes played as well as he had done for several weeks with some elegant driving in his innings of 67.

Gabriel received a knock and had to retire hurt, but with Alderman showing encouraging form, Australia got on top until Holding hit ten fours and a six while scoring 64 off 38 deliveries in only 52 minutes. It brought him the individual award, but Wessels trapped him lbw and Rackemann bowled Gabriel as he swung wildly and Australia had gained an encouraging victory.

**Benson and Hedges World Series Qualifying Table**

| | *P* | *W* | *L* | *Ab* | *Pts* |
|---|---|---|---|---|---|
| West Indies | 10 | 8 | 2 | — | 16 |
| Australia | 10 | 5 | 4 | 1 | 11 |
| Pakistan | 10 | 1 | 8 | 1 | 3 |

***Benson and Hedges World Series***

### First Final
### AUSTRALIA *v.* WEST INDIES

Bleak weather restricted the crowd to 28,190, and the Australian batting, apart from another compact knock by Steve Smith and some useful blows by Geoff Lawson, did little to cheer them. The relentless speed and accuracy of the West Indian attack made run-getting difficult and even the gentler offerings from Viv Richards allowed few liberties.

Haynes and Richardson began confidently, but Haynes fell to Rackemann in the fifteenth over. That was the last Australian success. Richardson and Gomes had an unbeaten partnership of 132 in two hours. Richardson, who had had a subdued tournament because of injury and was still suffering from hamstring strain, was quite magnificent. Full of style and composure, he hooked Rackemann for 6 early in his innings and faced 137 balls in reaching his 80 not out.

*Richardson square cuts for 4 in his innings of 80 not out. (Match One). (Philip Tyson)*

**FIRST BENSON AND HEDGES WORLD SERIES FINAL – AUSTRALIA *v.* WEST INDIES**
8 February 1984 at Sydney

| AUSTRALIA | | | |
|---|---|---|---|
| | S.B. Smith | c and b Daniel | 50 |
| | K.C. Wessels | c Richards, b Holding | 2 |
| | G.M. Ritchie | lbw, b Garner | 10 |
| | K.J. Hughes† | b Marshall | 0 |
| | A.R. Border | b Daniel | 18 |
| | D.M.J. Jones | b Marshall | 17 |
| | R.W. Marsh* | c Lloyd, b Baptiste | 15 |
| | G.F. Lawson | b Garner | 22 |
| | R.M. Hogg | c Gomes, b Baptiste | 2 |
| | T.M. Alderman | b Holding | 7 |
| | C.G. Rackemann | not out | 4 |
| | Extras | lb 9, w 1, nb 3 | 13 |
| | (44.4 overs) | | 160 |

| | O | M | R | W |
|---|---|---|---|---|
| Holding | 8.4 | — | 27 | 2 |
| Garner | 9 | 2 | 19 | 2 |
| Marshall | 9 | 1 | 24 | 2 |
| Daniel | 9 | — | 42 | 2 |
| Richards | 5 | — | 29 | — |
| Baptiste | 4 | — | 10 | 2 |

FALL OF WICKETS
1- 5, 2- 23, 3- 38, 4- 82, 5- 93, 6- 119, 7- 127, 8- 133, 9- 152

| WEST INDIES | | | |
|---|---|---|---|
| | D.L. Haynes | lbw, b Rackemann | 13 |
| | R.B. Richardson | not out | 80 |
| | H.A. Gomes | not out | 46 |
| | I.V.A. Richards | | |
| | C.H. Lloyd† | | |
| | P.J. Dujon* | | |
| | M.D. Marshall | | |
| | E.A.E. Baptiste | | |
| | M.A. Holding | | |
| | J. Garner | | |
| | W.W. Daniel | | |
| | Extras | b 3, lb 14, w 1, nb 4 | 22 |
| | (43.1 overs) | (for 1 wicket) | 161 |

| | O | M | R | W |
|---|---|---|---|---|
| Lawson | 9 | 1 | 21 | — |
| Alderman | 9 | 2 | 19 | — |
| Rackemann | 9 | — | 31 | 1 |
| Hogg | 7 | — | 40 | — |
| Wessels | 4 | — | 15 | — |
| Border | 5 | — | 17 | — |
| Smith | 0.1 | — | 1 | — |

FALL OF WICKETS
1- 29

**West Indies won by 9 wickets**

*Benson and Hedges World Series*

## Second Final
## AUSTRALIA *v.* WEST INDIES

A crowd of 42,430 saw the most thrilling encounter of the competition, but, like the players, they were left bemused at the end as to what the outcome of the match had been.

The day began disastrously for Australia. Ritchie hurt his right knee when he slipped as he walked on to the field and Smith dislocated his left shoulder when he dived to stop a ball in the covers. Smith was taken to hospital and both players faced fitness tests to determine whether or not they would be able to take their places in the party to tour the West Indies.

Lloyd won the toss and Haynes and Gabriel started briskly although there was something feverish in Gabriel's batting which always encouraged the bowlers. Gabriel fell to Rackemann and Haynes was well taken at mid-on by Hogan, and the Australians would have been well on course for victory had Wessels held a chance offered by Richards when he was 7.

Richardson again batted with an air of purpose and authority, bristling with an eagerness to play shots. Richards made his inevitable contribution, as valuable in terms of the command he appears to assert over his opponents as for the runs themselves. Lloyd was well taken high over his head by Hogg, but Gomes and Dujon plundered runs mercilessly. Richardson, 43 off 69 balls, and Richards, 59 off 70 balls, had scored quickly, but Dujon, 33 off 24 balls, provided the flourish that left Australia wilting.

Without Smith and with Ritchie requiring a runner, Australia were greatly handicapped. Jones went after a few

RIGHT *top: Wessels pulls Marshall for four. (Match Two). (below) Richardson is caught behind on the leg side off Lawson. (Match Two). (Philip Tyson)*

## SECOND BENSON AND HEDGES WORLD SERIES FINAL – AUSTRALIA *v.* WEST INDIES
11 February 1984 at Melbourne

| WEST INDIES | | | |
|---|---|---|---|
| D.L. Haynes | c Hogan, b Border | 18 |
| R.S. Gabriel | c Smith, b Rackemann | 19 |
| R.B. Richardson | c Marsh, b Lawson | 43 |
| I.V.A. Richards | c Hogan, b Wessels | 59 |
| C.H. Lloyd† | c Hogg, b Wessels | 11 |
| H.A. Gomes | not out | 25 |
| P.J. Dujon* | not out | 33 |
| M.D. Marshall | | |
| E.A.E. Baptiste | | |
| M.A. Holding | | |
| J. Garner | | |
| Extras | lb 10, w 3, nb 1 | 14 |
| (50 overs) | (for 5 wickets) | 222 |

| | O | M | R | W |
|---|---|---|---|---|
| Lawson | 10 | 4 | 26 | 1 |
| Rackemann | 10 | 4 | 52 | 1 |
| Hogg | 9 | 1 | 40 | — |
| Hogan | 10 | 2 | 31 | — |
| Border | 6 | — | 34 | 1 |
| Wessels | 5 | — | 29 | 2 |

FALL OF WICKETS
1- 33, 2- 54, 3- 116, 4- 137, 5- 173

| AUSTRALIA | | |
|---|---|---|
| K.C. Wessels | c Marshall, b Holding | 77 |
| D.M.J. Jones | c Dujon, b Holding | 12 |
| K.J. Hughes† | lbw, b Marshall | 53 |
| A.R. Border | c Dujon, b Garner | 14 |
| G.M. Ritchie | c Dujon, b Garner | 4 |
| R.W. Marsh* | b Garner | 16 |
| G.F. Lawson | not out | 21 |
| T.G. Hogan | c sub (Logie), b Holding | 6 |
| R.M. Hogg | run out | 3 |
| C.G. Rackemann | run out | 1 |
| S.B. Smith | | |
| Extras | b 2, lb 8, w 1, nb 4 | 15 |
| (50 overs) | (for 9 wickets) | 222 |

| | O | M | R | W |
|---|---|---|---|---|
| Holding | 10 | — | 39 | 3 |
| Garner | 10 | 1 | 39 | 3 |
| Baptiste | 10 | — | 44 | — |
| Marshall | 10 | 1 | 27 | 1 |
| Richards | 3 | — | 26 | — |
| Gomes | 7 | — | 37 | — |

FALL OF WICKETS
1- 23, 2- 132, 3- 161, 4- 169, 5- 176, 6- 192, 7- 209, 8- 218, 9- 222

**Match tied**

gestures of belligerence and Wessels and Hughes then engaged in a stand of 109. It was an invaluable contribution, but only Hughes, towards the end of his innings, provided the rate of scoring that was required. Wessels' 77 came from 109 deliveries and Hughes' 53 from 88.

Rodney Marsh, making what many believed would be his last appearance for Australia, was given a wonderful reception and struck some lusty blows. Lawson, too, hit mightily and suddenly the Australians had a chance of victory. When the last over began they needed 11 for victory. Lawson slashed a four. Hogg was run out off the third ball. The West Indian fielding was less than composed. As Garner bowled the last ball the scores were level. The ball went through to Dujon and before Rackemann could make his ground and go through for the winning bye the wicket was broken and the game was – tied?

The West Indians ran from the field jubilantly, believing that having lost fewer wickets, they had won the match. After an hour's deliberation it was decided that the match was tied and that a third final was necessary although the logic of the reasoning escaped many.

*Logie during his match-winning innings in the third final. (Philip Tyson)*

***Benson and Hedges World Series***

### Third Final
### AUSTRALIA *v.* WEST INDIES

Inevitably, the third final proved to be an anti-climax. Neither Richards nor Lloyd, who had not fielded on the Saturday, was fit to play and Holding led the West Indies.

Australia included David Boon for his international debut and he and Hughes added 100 after Garner, Man of the Finals, had sent back both openers for 25. Hughes had found form late in the tournament, but it was encouraging to see him and Boon, the Tasmanian who could not find a place in the side to tour West Indies, play so well. Marsh and Phillips increased the scoring rate, but both fell to Garner. Phillips was caught at mid-on and the ebullient Marsh skied to the wicket-keeper. Lawson was bowled on the last ball of the innings to give Garner five wickets.

Lawson, easily the best of the Australian bowlers in the competition, bowled Haynes and had Gomes lbw first ball to make West Indies 3 for 2. Richardson batted positively, but when he was out Logie and Dujon added 124 off 153 balls. Logie, so nearly not in the party, was out for 88, but Dujon, the outstanding success of the long and arduous tour of India and Australia, was unbeaten on 82 as West Indies won the Benson and Hedges World Series with 4.3 overs to spare.

## THIRD BENSON AND HEDGES WORLD SERIES FINAL – AUSTRALIA v. WEST INDIES
12 February 1984 at Melbourne

**AUSTRALIA**

|  |  |  |
|---|---|---|
| K.C. Wessels | b Garner | 17 |
| A.R. Border | b Garner | 4 |
| D.C. Boon | b Davis | 39 |
| K.J. Hughes† | c and b Baptiste | 65 |
| D.M.J. Jones | c Garner, b Holding | 3 |
| W.B. Phillips | c Holding, b Garner | 22 |
| R.W. Marsh* | c Dujon, b Garner | 35 |
| G.F. Lawson | b Garner | 7 |
| T.G. Hogan | not out | 1 |
| R.M. Hogg | | |
| C.G. Rackemann | | |
| Extras | b 1, lb 14, w 2, nb 2 | 19 |
| (50 overs) | (for 8 wickets) | 212 |

| | O | M | R | W |
|---|---|---|---|---|
| Holding | 10 | 1 | 33 | 1 |
| Garner | 10 | 1 | 31 | 5 |
| Marshall | 10 | — | 44 | — |
| Davis | 10 | — | 45 | 1 |
| Baptiste | 10 | — | 44 | 1 |

FALL OF WICKETS
1- 14, 2- 25, 3- 125, 4- 140, 5- 140, 6- 185, 7- 210, 8- 212

**WEST INDIES**

|  |  |  |
|---|---|---|
| D.L. Haynes | b Lawson | 1 |
| R.B. Richardson | lbw, b Hogg | 27 |
| H.A. Gomes | lbw, b Lawson | 0 |
| A.L. Logie | c Rackemann, b Wessels | 88 |
| P.J. Dujon* | not out | 82 |
| M.D. Marshall | not out | 6 |
| R.A. Harper | | |
| M.A. Holding† | | |
| E.A.E. Baptiste | | |
| J. Garner | | |
| W.W. Davis | | |
| Extras | b 4, lb 3, w 2 | 9 |
| (45.3 overs) | (for 4 wickets) | 213 |

| | O | M | R | W |
|---|---|---|---|---|
| Lawson | 9 | 1 | 45 | 2 |
| Rackemann | 9.3 | 2 | 40 | — |
| Hogg | 8 | 1 | 22 | 1 |
| Hogan | 10 | — | 39 | — |
| Border | 3 | — | 13 | — |
| Wessels | 6 | — | 47 | 1 |

FALL OF WICKETS
1- 3, 2- 3, 3- 52, 4- 176

**West Indies won by 6 wickets**

## Benson and Hedges World Series – Averages

### AUSTRALIA BATTING

| | M | Inns | NOs | Runs | HS | Av | 100s | 50s |
|---|---|---|---|---|---|---|---|---|
| K.C. Wessels | 13 | 13 | 1 | 495 | 92 | 41.25 | | 6 |
| S.B. Smith | 8 | 7 | | 285 | 106 | 40.71 | 1 | 2 |
| R.W. Marsh | 11 | 10 | 2 | 282 | 66 | 35.25 | | 1 |
| K.J. Hughes | 13 | 12 | | 309 | 71 | 25.75 | | 4 |
| D.W. Hookes | 5 | 4 | | 103 | 37 | 25.75 | | |
| D.M.J. Jones | 5 | 5 | 1 | 95 | 40* | 23.75 | | |
| A.R. Border | 13 | 12 | 1 | 226 | 84* | 20.54 | | 2 |
| G.M. Ritchie | 10 | 10 | 1 | 151 | 31 | 16.77 | | |
| W.B. Phillips | 7 | 7 | 1 | 96 | 25 | 16.00 | | |
| G.F. Lawson | 12 | 11 | 3 | 95 | 22 | 11.87 | | |
| J.N. Maguire | 9 | 8 | 4 | 38 | 14* | 9.50 | | |
| R.M. Hogg | 13 | 10 | 3 | 47 | 21 | 6.71 | | |
| C.G. Rackemann | 13 | 5 | 2 | 16 | 9* | 5.33 | | |
| T.G. Hogan | 3 | 3 | 1 | 10 | 6 | 5.00 | | |

Played in two matches: T.M. Alderman 7 and 0*; G.R.J. Matthews 2 and 0; K.H. Macleay 15 and 0
Played in one match: D.C. Boon 39; G.N. Yallop 13

### AUSTRALIA BOWLING

| | Overs | Mds | Runs | Wkts | Av | Best | 5/inn |
|---|---|---|---|---|---|---|---|
| T.M. Alderman | 19 | 5 | 38 | 2 | 19.00 | 2/19 | |
| R.M. Hogg | 119 | 10 | 481 | 22 | 21.86 | 4/33 | |
| G.F. Lawson | 105 | 23 | 298 | 13 | 22.92 | 3/30 | |
| C.G. Rackemann | 120.2 | 20 | 454 | 19 | 23.89 | 5/16 | 1 |
| A.R. Border | 36.2 | — | 163 | 6 | 27.16 | 2/24 | |
| K.C. Wessels | 59 | 2 | 292 | 9 | 32.44 | 2/29 | |
| G.R.J. Matthews | 20 | — | 126 | 3 | 42.00 | 2/61 | |
| J.N. Maguire | 80 | 5 | 344 | 5 | 68.80 | 1/19 | |
| T.G. Hogan | 30 | 4 | 92 | 1 | 92.00 | 1/22 | |
| K.H. Macleay | 16 | — | 86 | 0 | — | 0/39 | |

Also bowled: S.B. Smith 1.1–0–5–0; K.J. Hughes 0.1–0–4–0

### AUSTRALIA CATCHES

16–R.W. Marsh (ct 15/st 1); 7–K.C. Wessels; 4–K.J. Hughes; 3–T.G. Hogan; 2–G.F. Lawson, W.B. Phillips, S.B. Smith, R.M. Hogg and C.G. Rackemann; 1–J.N. Maguire, D.W. Hookes and G.M. Ritchie

### WEST INDIES BATTING

| | M | Inns | NOs | Runs | HS | Av | 100s | 50s |
|---|---|---|---|---|---|---|---|---|
| A.L. Logie | 9 | 9 | 5 | 220 | 88 | 55.00 | | 1 |
| D.L. Haynes | 13 | 13 | 2 | 450 | 108* | 40.90 | 1 | 4 |
| R.B. Richardson | 8 | 8 | 1 | 248 | 80* | 35.42 | | 2 |
| P.J. Dujon | 13 | 10 | 4 | 212 | 82* | 35.33 | | 1 |
| I.V.A. Richards | 12 | 11 | | 348 | 106 | 31.63 | 1 | 2 |
| C.H. Lloyd | 10 | 9 | 1 | 245 | 65 | 30.62 | | 1 |
| M.D. Marshall | 11 | 7 | 3 | 110 | 56* | 27.50 | | 1 |
| M.A. Holding | 12 | 5 | 2 | 82 | 64 | 27.33 | | 1 |
| H.A. Gomes | 8 | 8 | 2 | 130 | 46* | 21.66 | | |
| W.W. Daniel | 10 | 3 | 2 | 19 | 12 | 19.00 | | |
| E.A.E. Baptiste | 13 | 5 | 1 | 61 | 28* | 15.25 | | |
| R.S. Gabriel | 11 | 11 | | 167 | 41 | 15.18 | | |

Played in six matches: J. Garner 21*; W.W. Davis played in five matches and R.A. Harper in two but did not bat

### WEST INDIES BOWLING

| | Overs | Mds | Runs | Wkts | Av | Best | 5/inn |
|---|---|---|---|---|---|---|---|
| J. Garner | 56 | 11 | 150 | 14 | 10.71 | 5/31 | 1 |
| M.A. Holding | 113.3 | 8 | 411 | 23 | 17.86 | 4/26 | |
| M.D. Marshall | 95 | 14 | 297 | 14 | 21.21 | 3/28 | |
| W.W. Daniel | 93 | 10 | 369 | 16 | 23.06 | 3/27 | |
| E.A.E. Baptiste | 110 | 7 | 401 | 13 | 30.84 | 2/20 | |
| I.V.A. Richards | 90 | 1 | 387 | 9 | 43.00 | 2/28 | |
| W.W. Davis | 40. | 6 | 177 | 3 | 59.00 | 2/34 | |
| H.A. Gomes | 27 | 1 | 125 | 2 | 62.50 | 2/26 | |

Bowled in one match: R.A. Harper 10–0–42–2

### WEST INDIES CATCHES

17–P.J. Dujon (ct 16/st 1); 5–I.V.A. Richards; 3–W.W. Daniel, E.A.E. Baptiste, C.H. Lloyd, M.D. Marshall and A.L. Logie (including one as sub); 2–H.A. Gomes, J. Garner and M.A. Holding; 1–D.L. Haynes, R.S. Gabriel and R.B. Richardson

### Benson and Hedges World Series – Averages

**PAKISTAN BATTING**

| | M | Inns | NOs | Runs | HS | Av | 100s | 50s |
|---|---|---|---|---|---|---|---|---|
| Wasim Raja | 3 | 3 | | 95 | 46 | 31.66 | | |
| Javed Miandad | 10 | 10 | | 295 | 67 | 29.50 | | 2 |
| Qasim Umar | 10 | 10 | 1 | 241 | 69 | 26.77 | | 2 |
| Imran Khan | 7 | 7 | | 156 | 41 | 22.48 | | |
| Mudassar Nazar | 10 | 10 | | 210 | 68 | 21.10 | | 2 |
| Mansoor Akhtar | 9 | 9 | | 181 | 47 | 20.11 | | |
| Ejaz Faqih | 5 | 5 | 1 | 67 | 23* | 16.75 | | |
| Wasim Bari | 8 | 5 | 3 | 33 | 13 | 16.50 | | |
| Mohsin Khan | 9 | 9 | | 130 | 32 | 14.44 | | |
| Rashid Khan | 10 | 10 | 4 | 72 | 17 | 12.00 | | |
| Abdul Qadir | 8 | 8 | 2 | 60 | 23 | 10.00 | | |
| Azeem Hafeez | 7 | 3 | 2 | 10 | 7* | 10.00 | | |
| Saleem Malik | 3 | 3 | | 29 | 14 | 9.66 | | |
| Tahir Naqqash | 3 | 3 | 1 | 13 | 13* | 6.50 | | |
| Sarfraz Nawaz | 5 | 4 | | 13 | 7 | 3.25 | | |

Played in two matches: Ashraf Ali 11*
Played in one match: Mohammad Nazir 2*

**PAKISTAN BOWLING**

| | Overs | Mds | Runs | Wkts | Av | Best | 5/inn |
|---|---|---|---|---|---|---|---|
| Abdul Qadir | 76 | 11 | 272 | 15 | 18.13 | 5/53 | 1 |
| Sarfraz Nawaz | 36 | 8 | 118 | 6 | 19.66 | 4/27 | |
| Wasim Raja | 25 | 3 | 86 | 3 | 28.66 | 3/33 | |
| Ejaz Faqih | 40 | 2 | 176 | 6 | 29.33 | 4/43 | |
| Azeem Hafeez | 55.2 | 1 | 288 | 9 | 32.00 | 4/22 | |
| Mudassar Nazar | 85.4 | 5 | 328 | 10 | 32.80 | 2/33 | |
| Rashid Khan | 82.3 | 16 | 257 | 7 | 36.71 | 2/10 | |
| Tahir Naqqash | 17 | 4 | 91 | 2 | 45.50 | 2/56 | |

Also bowled: Mohammad Nazir 9–0–67–0; Mansoor Akhtar 2–0–16–0

**PAKISTAN CATCHES**

12–Wasim Bari (ct 8/st 4); 5–Imran Khan; 4–Abdul Qadir, Ashraf Ali (ct 2/st 2) and Mansoor Akhtar; 2–Mudassar Nazar, Rashid Khan and Azeem Hafeez; 1–Javed Miandad, Sarfraz Nawaz, Ejaz Faqih, Wasim Raja and Saleem Malik

*Jeff Dujon in mighty form in the third final. (Philip Tyson)*

*Richardson, 204 not out in his first match of the season for Victoria against Queensland. (Philip Tyson)*

***17, 18, 19 and 20 February 1984***

***at Adelaide***

**New South Wales** 459 for 7 dec (J. Dyson 241, D.M. Wellham 51, G.J. Winter 6 for 113) and 314 for 4 (J. Dyson 92, R.B. McCosker 76, P.S. Clifford 62, G.G. Geise 50 not out)
**South Australia** 395 (A.M.J. Hilditch 121, M.D. Haysman 58, G.A. Bishop 56, D.F. O'Connor 53)

*Match drawn*
*New South Wales 4 pts, South Australia 0 pts*

***at Launceston***

**Tasmania** 297 (M. Ray 94, D.C. Boon 61) and 161 for 6 (G.W. Goodman 61, B.F. Davison 60)
**Western Australia** 324 (S.C. Clements 151, P.M. Clough 8 for 95)

*Match drawn*
*Western Australia 4 pts, Tasmania 0 pts*

***at Melbourne***

**Queensland** 318 (G.S. Trimble 99, B.A. Courtice 53, A.I.C. Dodemaide 4 for 79) and 439 for 5 dec (R.B. Kerr 166, B.A. Courtice 144)
**Victoria** 463 for 5 dec (G.W. Richardson 204 not out, P.A. Hibbert 163) and 99 for 1 (M.B. Quinn 51 not out)

*Match drawn*
*Victoria 4 pts, Queensland 0 pts*

The failure of Tasmania and Queensland to take any points from their matches meant that Tasmania had to beat Queensland in the final match and take first innings points if they were to deprive the northern state of a place in the Shield final. The penultimate round of matches were marked by some outstanding individual performances rather than by any fine team achievements.

At Adelaide, John Dyson hit the first double century of his

fine career and dominated the New South Wales innings. Winter took 6 of the 7 wickets to fall to return a career best bowling performance. Hilditch hit his second century of the season for South Australia.

In Launceston, Ray and Boon took Tasmania from 29 for 1 to 171, but then the home side fell apart. Shane Clements recorded his maiden century in his tenth first-class match and Western Australia took the four points, but there was an outstanding performance from Peter Clough who returned a career best 8 for 95, the best bowling figures of the season.

In his first game of the season, his eighth first-class match, Geoff Richardson reached three figures for the first time. He went on to make 204 not out as he and Hibbert added 277 for Victoria's second wicket, 37 short of their Shield record. Earlier Glenn Trimble had been lbw to McCurdy for 99, a career best. When Queensland batted again Brian Courtice and Rob Kerr both hit career bests as they put on 289 for the first wicket.

***24, 25, 26 and 27 February 1984***

***at Hobart***

**Queensland** 223 (G.S. Trimble 71, N.F. Williams 4 for 45, P.M. Clough 4 for 51) and 333 (G.S. Chappell 129, T.V. Hohns 56, P.A. Blizzard 4 for 79)
**Tasmania** 166 (M. Ray 50, H. Frei 6 for 52) and 304 (M. Ray 76, P.I. Faulkner 70 not out, T.V. Hohns 4 for 90)

*Queensland won by 86 runs*
*Queensland 16 pts, Tasmania 0 pts*

***at Sydney***

**New South Wales** 292 (R.B. McCosker 94, S.J. Rixon 66, J. Dyson 52, K.H. Macleay 4 for 90) and 74 for 1
**Western Australia** 359 for 4 dec (G.M. Wood 173 not out, G.R. Marsh 159)

*Match drawn*
*Western Australia 4 pts, New South Wales 0 pts*

***at Melbourne***

**South Australia** 520 for 7 dec (A.M.J. Hilditch 230, M.D. Haysman 82, P.R. Sleep 68 not out, S.P. O'Donnell 4 for 118) and 101 for 0 (G.A. Bishop 51 not out)
**Victoria** 609 (S.P. O'Donnell 130, W.G. Whiteside 111, P.A. Hibbert 75, M.B. Quinn 73, R.J. McCurdy 55)

*Match drawn*
*Victoria 4 pts, South Australia 0 pts*

When Brian Davison won the toss and asked Queensland to bat he made a positive attempt to gain the points necessary to put Tasmania in the final. His bowlers responded superbly and Queensland were bowled out for a modest 223, boosted only by Trimble's second good innings in successive matches. He had come in at 59 for 3 and saw the score to 200 for 7 before falling to Faulkner. Tasmania, hopes high, had a wretched start to their innings, Goodman, Boon, Small and Saunders falling for 24. Ray and Faulkner added 83, but the last 6 wickets fell for 59 runs and the vital points went to Queensland. Greg Chappell hit his first Shield century of the season when the visitors batted again and Tasmania were left to make 391. They fought bravely with Faulkner hitting 70 not out from number 8, but their season of promise had ended in disappointment.

After Dyson and McCosker had put on 104 for New South Wales first innings, 5 wickets fell for 34. McCosker and Rixon added 92 and when Western Australia lost Clements and Shipperd for 16 it seemed that the visitors might be in trouble, but Graeme Wood and Geoff Marsh put on 330 for the third wicket, a state record for any wicket. Wood's innings was a career best. Marsh was playing his first game of the season.

There were remarkable events at Melbourne, too. Andrew Hilditch hit the first double century of his career as he dominated South Australia's mammoth score. The boost for Victoria was the bowling of debutant O'Donnell who took

ABOVE: *Andrew Hilditch hit his first double century in first-class cricket for South Australia against Victoria at Melbourne, 24–27 February. (Ken Kelly).* BELOW: *Whiteside edges Inverarity to Sleep at slip. The chance was dropped and the batsman went on to record his maiden first-class century. Victoria* v *South Australia, 24–27 February. (Philip Tyson)*

the wickets of Bishop, Haysman, O'Connor and Favell for 118 runs. Hibbert and Quinn began Victoria's reply with a stand of 164, but 4 wickets then fell for 11 runs. At 245 for 5, O'Donnell joined Whiteside and the pair added 215, both young men reaching maiden centuries, O'Donnell on his first-class debut. There was still a career best to come as Rod McCurdy hit a maiden fifty and Victoria took a most improbable, but highly commendable first innings lead to end a miserable season on a note of optimism.

**Sheffield Shield Final Table**

| | P | W | L | D | 1st Inns lead | Pts |
|---|---|---|---|---|---|---|
| Western Australia | 10 | 4 | — | 6 | 7 | 76 |
| Queensland | 10 | 4 | 2 | 4 | 6 | 74 |
| Tasmania | 10 | 2 | 3 | 5 | 5 | 44 |
| New South Wales | 10 | 1 | 4 | 5 | 6 | 36 |
| South Australia | 10 | 1 | 2 | 7 | 3 | 26 |
| Victoria | 10 | 1 | 2 | 7 | 2 | 20 |

(Queensland and South Australia each scored 2 points for an abandoned match where no first innings result was obtained.)

ABOVE: *O'Connor – Man-of-the-Match.* BELOW: *Shipperd is caught behind off Carmichael. (Philip Tyson)*

## McDonald's Cup Final
## SOUTH AUSTRALIA *v.* WESTERN AUSTRALIA

A crowd of nearly 8000 saw South Australia win an exciting victory as Lillee and Graf just failed in their bold bid to win the game for the visitors.

Hilditch and Bishop gave South Australia a solid start, but Haysman and both openers fell in the space of 12 runs. Donald O'Connor celebrated a commendable season in first-class cricket with a match-winning innings of 96 not out

**McDONALD'S CUP FINAL – SOUTH AUSTRALIA *v.* WESTERN AUSTRALIA**
3 March 1984 at Adelaide Oval

**SOUTH AUSTRALIA**

|  |  |  |
|---|---|---|
| A.M.J. Hilditch | lbw, b Macleay | 33 |
| G.A. Bishop | c Marsh, b Macleay | 24 |
| M.D. Haysman | c Wood, b Graf | 3 |
| D.F. O'Connor | not out | 96 |
| P.R. Sleep | run out | 34 |
| P. Brinsley | c Shipperd, b Clements | 38 |
| S. Wundke | run out | 7 |
| K.J. Wright*† | not out | 1 |
| G.J. Winter | | |
| D.A.H. Johnston | | |
| I.R. Carmichael | | |
| Extras | lb 11, w 6, nb 3 | 20 |
| (49 overs) | (for 6 wickets) | 256 |

| | O | M | R | W |
|---|---|---|---|---|
| Lillee | 10 | — | 48 | — |
| Boyd | 9 | — | 52 | — |
| Macleay | 10 | — | 25 | 2 |
| Graf | 6 | — | 30 | 1 |
| Clements | 10 | — | 61 | 1 |
| Mann | 4 | — | 29 | — |

FALL OF WICKETS
1- 63, 2- 65, 3- 75, 4- 142, 5- 240, 6- 252

**WESTERN AUSTRALIA**

|  |  |  |
|---|---|---|
| S.C. Clements | b Brinsley | 9 |
| G.M. Wood | c Bishop, b Wundke | 45 |
| G. Shipperd | c Wright, b Carmichael | 35 |
| G.R. Marsh | c Bishop, b Wundke | 40 |
| D.L. Boyd | b Carmichael | 11 |
| R.W. Marsh* | c Wundke, b Carmichael | 54 |
| B.M. Laird | b Winter | 3 |
| S.F. Graf | not out | 37 |
| K.H. Macleay | c O'Connor, b Carmichael | 0 |
| A.L. Mann | run out | 3 |
| D.K. Lillee† | not out | 1 |
| Extras | b 1, lb 9 | 10 |
| (49 overs) | (for 9 wickets) | 248 |

| | O | M | R | W |
|---|---|---|---|---|
| Johnston | 10 | — | 56 | — |
| Brinsley | 9 | — | 39 | 1 |
| Carmichael | 10 | 1 | 50 | 4 |
| Winter | 10 | — | 46 | 1 |
| Wundke | 10 | — | 47 | 2 |

FALL OF WICKETS
1- 11, 2- 60, 3- 117, 4- 141, 5- 144, 6- 166, 7- 226, 8- 227, 9- 233

**South Australia won by 8 runs**

**SHEFFIELD SHIELD FINAL – WESTERN AUSTRALIA *v.* QUEENSLAND**
9, 10, 11, 12 and 13 March 1984 at Perth

**QUEENSLAND**

| | FIRST INNINGS | | SECOND INNINGS | |
|---|---|---|---|---|
| B.A. Courtice | b Macleay | 77 | (2) c R. Marsh, b Macleay | 22 |
| R.B. Kerr | c R. Marsh, b Macleay | 56 | (1) lbw, b Lillee | 4 |
| C.B. Smart | c R. Marsh, b Graf | 57 | c and b Graf | 62 |
| G.S. Chappell | c Laird, b Lillee | 85 | c Laird, b Macleay | 1 |
| G.S. Trimble | c R. Marsh, b Graf | 0 | c Graf, b Macleay | 6 |
| T.V. Hohns | c Clements, b Milosz | 39 | c Shipperd, b Macleay | 17 |
| R.B. Phillips* | not out | 61 | lbw, b Graf | 10 |
| C.J. McDermott | c R. Marsh, b Graf | 16 | not out | 21 |
| G.K. Whyte | not out | 18 | c Graf, b Milosz | 1 |
| H. Frei | | | run out | 0 |
| J.R. Thomson† | | | b Graf | 0 |
| Extras | b 2, lb 7, w 4, nb 9 | 22 | lb 4, w 1, nb 5 | 10 |
| | (for 7 wkts dec) | 431 | | 154 |

| | O | M | R | W | O | M | R | W |
|---|---|---|---|---|---|---|---|---|
| Lillee | 48 | 8 | 116 | 1 | 12 | 2 | 34 | 1 |
| Macleay | 52 | 13 | 115 | 2 | 21 | 3 | 58 | 4 |
| Graf | 42 | 5 | 111 | 3 | 18.2 | 6 | 34 | 3 |
| Milosz | 26 | 4 | 78 | 1 | 9 | 3 | 24 | 1 |
| Laird | 1 | — | 2 | — | | | | |

FALL OF WICKETS
1- 103, 2- 163, 3- 291, 4- 292, 5- 293, 6- 352, 7- 391
1- 4, 2- 40, 3- 42, 4- 62, 5- 104, 6- 130, 7- 139, 8- 150, 9- 152

*Umpires:* M.W. Johnson and P.J. McConnell

**Western Australia won by 4 wickets**

**WESTERN AUSTRALIA**

| | FIRST INNINGS | | SECOND INNINGS | |
|---|---|---|---|---|
| G.M. Wood | c Kerr, b Thomson | 53 | (2) c Smart, b Thomson | 13 |
| S.C. Clements | c Kerr, b Frei | 6 | (1) b Thomson | 28 |
| G. Shipperd | c Phillips, b Frei | 21 | c Kerr, b Whyte | 41 |
| G.R. Marsh | b Thomson | 107 | c Phillips, b McDermott | 0 |
| B.M. Laird | c Phillips, b Hohns | 63 | not out | 54 |
| M.R.J. Veletta | c Trimble, b Thomson | 12 | c and b Whyte | 0 |
| R.W. Marsh* | b Frei | 7 | c and b Whyte | 45 |
| S.F. Graf | c Chappell, b Hohns | 14 | not out | 17 |
| K.H. Macleay | b Thomson | 21 | | |
| D.K. Lillee† | c Phillips, b Thomson | 18 | | |
| S.J. Milosz | not out | 0 | | |
| Extras | b 5, lb 6, w 4, nb 26 | 41 | b 5, lb 10, w 2, nb 9 | 26 |
| | | 363 | (for 6 wkts) | 224 |

| | O | M | R | W | O | M | R | W |
|---|---|---|---|---|---|---|---|---|
| McDermott | 20 | 5 | 67 | — | 10 | 3 | 20 | 1 |
| Frei | 37 | 10 | 104 | 3 | 12 | 2 | 28 | — |
| Thomson | 25.2 | 6 | 85 | 5 | 19 | — | 96 | 2 |
| Whyte | 14 | 4 | 26 | — | 13 | 6 | 28 | 3 |
| Hohns | 23 | 12 | 35 | 2 | 5.5 | 2 | 22 | — |
| Courtice | 11 | 1 | 35 | — | | | | |
| Chappell | | | | | 11 | 4 | 15 | — |

FALL OF WICKETS
1- 12, 2- 81, 3- 105, 4- 244, 5- 289, 6- 291, 7- 309, 8- 321, 9- 362
1- 34, 2- 52, 3- 53, 4- 134, 5- 138, 6- 199

which took South Australia to a respectable total and won him the individual award.

Western Australia batted consistently in reply, but they could not achieve the required run-rate until a swashbuckling innings from Rod Marsh lifted them into contention. He and Shaun Graf added 60 before Marsh fell to Carmichael who dismissed Macleay one run later. The task now proved too much for the visitors in spite of some desperate running and mighty swipes.

## Sheffield Shield Final
## WESTERN AUSTRALIA *v.* QUEENSLAND

Lillee won the toss and asked Queensland to bat. Courtice and Kerr, who had firmly grasped the opportunities given them by the absence of Wessels and Ritchie, began with a stand of 103. There was no faltering by the Queenslanders who saw the chance to win the Sheffield Shield for the first time in their history. Greg Chappell played with customary charm and authority. Smart batted sensibly and Ray Phillips gave further indication that he should be considered as a successor to Rod Marsh. Thomson was able to declare at 431 for 7 and Frei, who had finished the season strongly, had Clements taken at slip. The Western Australian innings gained its main boost from a stand of 139 between Geoff Marsh and Bruce Laird for the 4th wicket, but Jeff Thomson returned his best figures of the season and Queensland led by 68 on the first innings.

Dreams of glory were quickly shattered. Courtice, Kerr, Chappell and Trimble were out for 62, three of them victims of Macleay, and only Chris Smart, who reached a career best in his sixth first-class game, batted with any assurance. Queensland were out for a miserable 154 and Western

ABOVE: *Smart – two brave innings for Queensland.* BELOW: *Geoff Marsh – a fine hundred. (Philip Tyson)*

Australia needed only 223 to win, a target far shorter of the one that had seemed probable.

Thomson and McDermott raised hopes again as Wood, Clements and Geoff Marsh were shot out for 53, but Shipperd and Laird, who had announced his retirement, stabilised the position. Whyte captured two quick wickets to lift Queensland's hopes again, but Rod Marsh hit lustily and although he became Whyte's third victim, Western Australia were not to be denied. Laird provided the steadiness and Graf the shots and Western Australia regained the Sheffield Shield.

## First Class Averages

| BATTING | M | Inns | NOs | Runs | HS | Av | 100s | 50s |
|---|---|---|---|---|---|---|---|---|
| G.N. Yallop | 8 | 11 | 1 | 1132 | 268 | 113.20 | 5 | 2 |
| G.R. Marsh | 2 | 3 | | 266 | 159 | 88.66 | 2 | |
| P.S. Clifford | 5 | 8 | 3 | 443 | 152* | 88.60 | 1 | 3 |
| G.M. Ritchie | 7 | 12 | 1 | 905 | 196 | 82.27 | 3 | 6 |
| A.R. Border | 10 | 14 | 2 | 929 | 118 | 77.41 | 3 | 7 |
| M.D. Taylor | 11 | 18 | 4 | 1010 | 172* | 72.14 | 4 | 3 |
| B.F. Davison | 11 | 20 | 4 | 1036 | 171* | 64.75 | 4 | 4 |
| J. Dyson | 11 | 19 | 3 | 1015 | 241 | 63.43 | 3 | 3 |
| K.J. Hughes | 10 | 14 | | 867 | 130 | 61.92 | 3 | 4 |
| A.M.J. Hilditch | 10 | 17 | 1 | 937 | 230 | 58.56 | 3 | 3 |
| W.B. Phillips | 10 | 15 | 1 | 763 | 234 | 54.50 | 2 | 2 |
| D.M.J. Jones | 8 | 15 | 1 | 762 | 128 | 54.42 | 2 | 6 |
| P.R. Sleep | 10 | 14 | 5 | 486 | 144 | 54.00 | 2 | 2 |
| G.S. Chappell | 15 | 22 | 4 | 954 | 182 | 53.00 | 3 | 3 |
| M.B. Quinn | 4 | 7 | 1 | 311 | 73 | 51.83 | | 4 |
| K.C. Wessels | 10 | 16 | 1 | 733 | 179 | 48.86 | 3 | 2 |
| G.M. Wood | 12 | 18 | 2 | 778 | 173* | 48.62 | 2 | 4 |
| P.I. Faulkner | 11 | 19 | 6 | 615 | 84* | 47.30 | | 6 |
| D.W. Hookes | 7 | 12 | | 563 | 142 | 46.91 | 2 | 2 |
| G. Shipperd | 12 | 19 | 3 | 811 | 167* | 46.81 | 1 | 6 |
| P.A. Hibbert | 11 | 21 | 1 | 932 | 163 | 46.60 | 1 | 7 |
| R.D. Woolley | 8 | 13 | 1 | 535 | 102 | 44.58 | 1 | 3 |
| B.M. Laird | 12 | 20 | 4 | 706 | 75* | 44.12 | | 8 |
| S.B. Smith | 7 | 12 | 1 | 480 | 100* | 43.63 | 1 | 4 |
| G.R.J. Matthews | 9 | 11 | 2 | 389 | 86 | 43.22 | | 3 |
| R.J. Inverarity | 10 | 15 | 5 | 419 | 69 | 41.90 | | 2 |
| S.J. Rixon | 10 | 14 | 3 | 456 | 101* | 41.45 | 1 | 1 |
| S.C. Clements | 7 | 12 | | 480 | 151 | 40.00 | 1 | 3 |
| R.B. Kerr | 12 | 23 | 1 | 866 | 166 | 39.36 | 3 | 4 |
| G.W. Goodman | 4 | 7 | | 274 | 74 | 39.14 | | 3 |
| R.B. McCosker | 11 | 19 | | 723 | 157 | 38.05 | 1 | 4 |
| T.V. Hohns | 7 | 12 | 1 | 403 | 58 | 36.63 | | 3 |
| W.G. Whiteside | 8 | 14 | 2 | 436 | 111 | 36.33 | 1 | 2 |
| D.F. O'Connor | 4 | 6 | 1 | 180 | 72 | 36.00 | | 2 |
| G.G. Geise | 4 | 5 | 1 | 144 | 77 | 36.00 | | 2 |
| R.W. Marsh | 13 | 17 | 4 | 460 | 157* | 35.38 | 1 | |
| D.C. Boon | 11 | 19 | | 667 | 227 | 35.10 | 1 | 4 |
| S.F. Graf | 11 | 14 | 2 | 420 | 74 | 35.00 | | 3 |
| M.D. Haysman | 11 | 18 | 1 | 594 | 100 | 34.94 | 1 | 3 |
| D.M. Wellham | 10 | 15 | 1 | 486 | 108 | 34.71 | 1 | 3 |
| S.L. Saunders | 11 | 19 | 3 | 550 | 138* | 34.37 | 2 | 1 |
| B.A. Courtice | 7 | 14 | 1 | 445 | 144 | 34.23 | 1 | 2 |
| G.A. Bishop | 9 | 15 | 1 | 472 | 90 | 33.71 | | 5 |
| M. Ray | 11 | 20 | | 654 | 94 | 32.70 | | 4 |
| R.J. Bright | 11 | 12 | 2 | 319 | 100* | 31.90 | 1 | 1 |
| R.B. Phillips | 12 | 20 | 6 | 431 | 77* | 30.78 | | 2 |
| G.S. Trimble | 6 | 11 | | 338 | 99 | 30.72 | | 3 |
| C.B. Smart | 5 | 9 | | 266 | 62 | 29.55 | | 2 |
| P.M. Toohey | 6 | 10 | 1 | 258 | 61 | 28.66 | | 1 |
| K.H. Macleay | 11 | 13 | 2 | 289 | 82 | 26.27 | | 2 |
| S.M. Small | 6 | 10 | | 262 | 114 | 26.10 | 1 | 1 |
| M.J. Bennett | 9 | 9 | 1 | 202 | 54 | 25.25 | | 1 |
| M.J.R. Veletta | 11 | 19 | 1 | 429 | 82 | 23.83 | | 2 |
| R.M. Hogg | 10 | 8 | 3 | 117 | 43 | 23.40 | | |
| A.B. Henschell | 10 | 16 | 3 | 303 | 89* | 23.30 | | 2 |
| A.I.C. Dodemaide | 7 | 11 | 3 | 185 | 54* | 23.12 | | 1 |
| C.J. McDermott | 8 | 13 | 3 | 222 | 38* | 22.20 | | |
| W.S. Andrews | 3 | 6 | 1 | 111 | 27 | 22.20 | | |
| P.A. Hyde | 9 | 14 | 3 | 241 | 43* | 21.90 | | |
| D.A. Emerson | 6 | 10 | 2 | 174 | 50 | 21.75 | | 1 |
| I.R. Beven | 8 | 15 | | 326 | 57 | 21.73 | | 2 |
| W.M. Darling | 4 | 5 | | 108 | 58 | 21.60 | | 1 |
| G.K. Whyte | 9 | 11 | 3 | 163 | 58 | 20.37 | | 2 |
| P.A. Blizzard | 8 | 12 | 2 | 185 | 39* | 18.50 | | |
| G.M. Watts | 5 | 10 | | 178 | 45 | 17.80 | | |
| K.J. Wright | 10 | 12 | 2 | 164 | 48 | 16.40 | | |
| G.F. Lawson | 9 | 10 | 2 | 125 | 49 | 15.62 | | |
| S.D.H. Parkinson | 7 | 8 | 1 | 100 | 49 | 14.28 | | |
| N.F. Williams | 7 | 11 | 1 | 131 | 34 | 13.10 | | |
| D.A. Smith | 4 | 8 | | 104 | 42 | 13.00 | | |
| P.M. Clough | 11 | 15 | 4 | 138 | 27* | 12.54 | | |
| T.M. Chappell | 5 | 8 | | 100 | 32 | 12.50 | | |

(Qualification – 100 runs, average 10.00)
(G.W. Richardson played in two matches, scoring 204* and 0)
(S.P. O'Donnell played in one match, scoring 130)

| BOWLING | Overs | Mds | Runs | Wkts | Av | Best | 5/inn | 10/m |
|---|---|---|---|---|---|---|---|---|
| C.G. Rackemann | 188.4 | 46 | 523 | 28 | 18.67 | 6/86 | 2 | 1 |
| G.F. Lawson | 325 | 78 | 927 | 40 | 23.17 | 6/43 | 3 | |
| H. Frei | 212.2 | 61 | 554 | 23 | 24.08 | 6/52 | 2 | |
| T.M. Alderman | 293.3 | 74 | 758 | 30 | 25.26 | 5/79 | 1 | |
| R.M. Hogg | 281.1 | 50 | 814 | 32 | 25.43 | 5/53 | 1 | |
| D.K. Lillee | 610.5 | 143 | 1513 | 59 | 25.64 | 6/62 | 3 | |
| J.R. Thomson | 373.5 | 64 | 1361 | 48 | 28.35 | 5/85 | 1 | |
| K.H. Macleay | 396.1 | 99 | 1005 | 35 | 28.71 | 4/50 | | |
| J.N. Maguire | 279 | 60 | 870 | 30 | 29.00 | 6/62 | 2 | 1 |
| R.G. Holland | 310.3 | 115 | 718 | 24 | 29.91 | 7/56 | 1 | |
| L.S. Pascoe | 192.3 | 43 | 599 | 20 | 29.95 | 5/53 | 2 | |
| D.R. Gilbert | 276 | 75 | 762 | 25 | 30.48 | 5/56 | 1 | |
| P.M. Clough | 404.5 | 83 | 1320 | 42 | 31.42 | 8/95 | 3 | |
| A.I.C. Dodemaide | 237.3 | 43 | 726 | 23 | 31.56 | 5/67 | 1 | |
| S.F. Graf | 375.1 | 84 | 1048 | 32 | 32.75 | 3/34 | | |
| T.G. Hogan | 366 | 110 | 861 | 26 | 33.11 | 5/31 | 1 | |
| I.R. Carmichael | 508 | 114 | 1446 | 41 | 35.26 | 6/112 | 3 | |
| T.V. Hohns | 229.4 | 64 | 624 | 17 | 36.70 | 4/75 | | |
| P.I. Faulkner | 283.2 | 53 | 850 | 23 | 36.95 | 4/68 | | |
| G.R.J. Matthews | 326.5 | 103 | 821 | 22 | 37.31 | 3/41 | | |
| N.F. Williams | 221.5 | 47 | 840 | 22 | 38.18 | 4/34 | | |
| G.J. Winter | 207.1 | 51 | 544 | 14 | 38.85 | 6/113 | 1 | |
| S.D.H. Parkinson | 193.3 | 37 | 649 | 16 | 40.56 | 5/41 | 1 | |
| M.J. Bennett | 401.5 | 160 | 731 | 18 | 40.61 | 5/15 | 1 | |
| C.J. McDermott | 271.2 | 56 | 816 | 20 | 40.80 | 4/75 | | |
| G.K. Whyte | 309 | 96 | 816 | 20 | 40.80 | 3/28 | | |
| S.P. Davis | 269.3 | 43 | 854 | 20 | 42.70 | 7/104 | 1 | |
| P.A. Blizzard | 233.1 | 52 | 742 | 17 | 43.64 | 4/79 | | |
| M. Ray | 184.4 | 44 | 489 | 11 | 44.45 | 2/34 | | |
| P.R. Sleep | 335.2 | 70 | 1104 | 24 | 46.00 | 4/86 | | |
| R.J. McCurdy | 313.1 | 51 | 1245 | 27 | 46.11 | 5/81 | 2 | |
| R.J. Inverarity | 387.5 | 102 | 891 | 18 | 49.50 | 6/96 | 1 | |
| R.J. Bright | 365 | 81 | 1087 | 20 | 54.35 | 3/100 | | |
| S.L. Saunders | 208.5 | 40 | 683 | 12 | 56.91 | 5/114 | 1 | |

### LEADING FIELDERS

59–R.W. Marsh (ct 54/st 5); 48–R.B. Phillips (ct 45/st 3); 23–K.J. Wright (ct 22/st 1); 22–S.J. Rixon (ct 15/st 7); 21–P.A. Hyde (ct 19/st 2); 19–G.S. Chappell; 16–R.B. Kerr; 15–R.D. Woolley (ct 14/st 1), T.M. Alderman, R.B. McCosker and W.D. Hill; 13–M.D. Haysman; 12–A.R. Border and B.M. Laird; 11–W.B. Phillips; 10–M. Ray, P.R. Sleep, S.F. Graf and M.J. Bennett; 9–R.J. Inverarity; 8–G.K. Whyte, D.C. Boon, A.M.J. Hilditch and G. Shipperd

## THE AUSTRALIAN DOMESTIC SEASON 1983/84
### by Frank Tyson

The word 'Bond' has always suggested connotations of strength and security. After all, Chesty Bond was the hero of the strip cartoons: a sort of Superman in a white vest. He was not as fast as a speeding bullet; nor was he able to leap tall buildings at a single bound; but he was immensely strong and infinitely more credible than the red-suited, quick-change artist of the telephone booth. Bond was something which was the equivalent of an Englishman's word; it was a security which was as solid as the Bank of England. It was not, however, the synonym for sporting success which it has become in modern Australia.

The English immigrant and millionaire, Alan Bond, has brought international athletic éclat to his adopted country. He founded a yachting city at Yanchep, north of the Western Australian capital, Perth. He achieved the impossible by wresting the America Cup from the possessive monopolists of the New York Yacht Club. From a cricketing point of view, he injected a renewed determination into the Western Australian team to reassert the grasp which it had on the Sheffield Shield until 1981, by continuing his sponsorship of the state association. It was therefore appropriate that, in the year that the standard of the Boxing Kangaroo flew proudly at the masthead of the triumphant *Australia II* in Newport harbour, his cricketing protégés should also win the crown of Australian domestic cricket for the ninth time.

This ninth triumph of the occidental state in its thirty-seven year history in Shield competition was not an unexpected event on the sporting calendar. The Perth team is the most efficient unit in the modern Australian game. Its nursery of development squads has, in the past, spawned such outstanding talents as Dennis Lillee, Terry Alderman, Bruce Yardley, Graeme McKenzie and Rod Marsh. Its talent identification and coaching organisation is such that its modern depth of ability is unrivalled since the halcyon days of New South Wales and Surrey in the 1950s. Depleted though it was by the retirement of Test spinner, Bruce Yardley, and former Australian vice-captain, Craig Serjeant, in 1983/84, Western Australia could still call upon the services of nine current or former internationals. The Perth-based team was regularly weakened by the absence of its captain, Kim Hughes, fast-bowling maestro Dennis Lillee, world-champion wicketkeeper Rod Marsh and sometimes, spin-bowler Tom Hogan, who were all called up to the Australian colours at various inopportune times of the domestic season. Medium-pace Test bowler, Terry Alderman struggled to regain full fitness throughout the summer and was seldom at his most potent best for his state; even when he was fit, he was unable to serve Western Australia since he was selected for the final games of the Benson and Hedges/World Series Cup in Perth and Sydney.

Yet, in spite of this periodic blood letting of its ability, Hughes' team still won the Sheffield Shield. It even gained the

*Bruce Laird – a romantic farewell to cricket. (Philip Tyson)*

*Greg Shipperd – 167 not out for Western Australia against Victoria at Melbourne, 18 November. A most consistent and underrated batsman. (Philip Tyson)*

*Brian Davison of Tasmania in action. He scored over 900 runs by the beginning of January. (Philip Tyson)*

home ground advantage for the final of the competition, by vanquishing the title-holders, New South Wales, on the first innings in the last home-and-away game of the season. In the deciding contest and his swan-song in first-class cricket, the nonpareil fast bowler, Dennis Lillee, had the satisfaction of captaining his state to its crowning triumph over its closest rival, Queensland: a side which included one of Lillee's closest collaborators, captain and friend of more than fourteen years standing, Greg Chappell.

A close study of the Western Australian performances in 1983/84 reveals that the Perth side was in reality, a cricketing co-operative. The Sheffield Shield final was decided by a century from Geoff Marsh, 63 from the bat of Bruce Laird, a Grahame Wood half-century and two six-wicket match performances from Shaun Graf and Dennis Lillee. Geoff Marsh was never a regular member of the eleven throughout the summer; Laird was on the verge of being dropped at the beginning of the season and announced his retirement at its conclusion; Wood was initially a West-Indian tour reject, Graf a Victorian import, who departed whence he had come in March, and Lillee was in the twilight of an illustrious career. Yet such was the togetherness of this Western Australian composite eleven, that it fought back from a first-innings deficit of 68 in the final to clinch the game on the fifth afternoon by 4 wickets.

The Western Australian averages were statistical testimony to its esprit de corps.

In 1983/84 Queensland, a virgin in the hardened company of previous Shield winners, had its best opportunity of winning the trophy since it first joined the competition in 1926. Its optimistic expectations were founded on the abilities of Test players, Allan Border, Greg Chappell, Greg Ritchie, Kepler Wessels, Carl Rackemann and John Maguire, all of whom were available for the first two Shield games – and two of whom, Thomson and Chappell – remained in Australia after the departure of the West Indian tourists in February, to help the northern state in its last despairing effort to carry off the Holy Grail of the championship.

The experienced Queenslanders did not let their side down. Chappell's nine appearances for his adopted state yielded 574 runs at an average of 47.83 and produced one century. These were slightly disappointing figures for a player who enjoyed a memorable year which took him past Sir Donald Bradman's Test aggregate of 6996 and the 7000-run mark and saw him become the most prolific non-wicketkeeper catcher in the international game. They were, nonetheless, respectable statistics which, when backed up by Ritchie's average-winning 709 runs and opener Robbie Kerr's tally of 807, suggested that Queensland should have broken its Shield duck in 1983/84.

Kerr's consistency with the bat was extremely pleasing and more than suggested that his 1983 season with the Nottinghamshire Second Eleven had done the elegant right-hander nothing but good. Brett Henschell began the summer well with an unbeaten 89 against Tasmania in Brisbane; he later scored 67 against Victoria, but was struck by a Lillee thunderbolt during the Western Australian game in Brisbane and sustained a broken hand which kept him *hors de combat* for most of the rest of the season. It was therefore gratifying to see the young all-rounder's potential recognised with the award of an Esso Scholarship to play in county second eleven cricket in 1984.

Nor did Jeff Thomson, Allan Border's deputy when the Queensland captain was on Test duty, fail his men. His 47 wickets in Shield games was the largest bag by any bowler, and when one considers that it was boosted by 23 wickets from the left-handed swing bowler, Harry Frei and 25 John Maguire victims, it is all the more surprising that Queensland's rewards were not more substantial. Veteran off-spinner Graeme White and eighteen-year-old pace bowler Craig McDermott were at the opposite extremes of the experience scale but they had one thing in common; they each captured 20 Shield wickets. The Queensland selectors showed much foresight in persevering with McDermott, the Australian Under-19 speedster from Brisbane's satellite city of Ipswich. McDermott was a decisive influence in the victory of Mike Valetta's side over England in the youth Tests of 1983. Although he is slightly open in his delivery stride, McDermott possesses genuine pace: a rare commodity in the modern ranks of up-and-coming bowlers.

If one was asked to identify the main reason behind Queensland's failure to bring home the bacon and the Sheffield Shield in 1983/84, one would be hard pressed to do so. Probably the tall blond pace-bowler, Carl Rackemann, did little to enhance his state's chances of glory when – as he has so often done in the past – he broke down with muscle injury at a crucial juncture of the season. Consequently he was unable to reproduce for his state the form which yielded him 16 Pakistan wickets in two Tests against Imran Khan's tourists. It was impossible, however, to blame Rackemann, in absentia, for the final indignity in Perth. The truth of that match and the season was that Western Australia simply possessed too much experience, too great an all-round ability and too much depth of talent for its opponents.

New South Wales, under the new management of Dirk Wellham declined from its position as market leader in 1982/83 to fourth position in the echelon of successful companies in the following season. It was an inexplicable fall from grace since the directors of the state's fortunes still numbered nine Test players in their ranks. Only one of the side, however, fast bowler Geoff Lawson, commanded a regular place in the Australian eleven – although how the national selectors could consistently ignore the substantial Test claims of opener, John Dyson, was a source of mystification to many astute judges of form. Dyson in 1983/84 was, like Graham Yallop in 1982/83, the forgotten man of first-class cricket. He was the only batsman to top the 1000-run mark in the Shield competition. He notched a double century against South Australia, a near double hundred against Victoria and two three-figure scores in the same game against Tasmania. He shared with the island state's Zimbabwian import, Brian Davison, the distinction of being chosen as the Benson and Hedges Sheffield Shield Player of the Year. Yet in 1983/84, not once did he take the field for his country. One can only surmise that it was Dyson's caution and slow-scoring which militated against him.

It was ironic that the New South Wales opener's sheet-anchor role was, in 1983/84, one of necessity rather than choice. No other Sydney batsman seemed capable of performing consistently. The emergence of the former Australian Under-19 skipper, Peter Clifford, as a senior player of great potential was the one bright spot on the otherwise sombre Sydney scene. Clifford shone briefly towards the end of the season, compiling an aggressive aggregate of 443 runs at an average of 88.6. Yesteryear's skipper, Rick McCosker, reached a laboured total of 566 runs at 31.44 per innings before hanging up his boots for good at the end of the summer. The residual batting was little short of an unmitigated disaster. The inability of the New South Wales batsmen to score heavily compounded the problems created for their side by injuries to their key fast bowlers, Len Pascoe and Gary Whitney, who eventually resigned themselves to the fact that their playing season was over and retired to the Test commentary box. They bequeathed their bowling chores to the young paceman Dave Gilbert and veteran leg-spinner "Dutch" Holland, who both responded nobly to the challenge by harvesting 21 and 24 wickets respectively. New South Wales was in the hunt for Shield honours until early February; but when Tasmania defeated Wellham's men by 50 runs in Sydney, it was obvious that it would not be able to equal the triumph of the previous year.

Without the services of its doyen West Indian fast bowler, Joel Garner, South Australia in 1983/84 had little hope of replicating its Shield glories of two years earlier. There was an oversupply of batting ability in Adelaide; but it was seldom consistent or reliable. Opener Wayne Phillips, a left-handed touch player of hypnotic beauty, ravaged the Tasmanian attack to the tune of 234 – his second double century against the island's bowlers in two years. As a result he ousted Dyson from the opening spot in the Australian side and then consolidated his position by notching 159 on his debut against Pakistan. Then he struggled to glean a miserable 92 runs in his next 6 innings! Skipper David Hookes – arguably one of the most explosive hitters, and captains, in the game – began the season with a string of scores which yielded him a wretched 59 runs in 3 hands. Understandably, therefore, his side scraped up only 10 points from its first three encounters. Former Test batsman, Rick Darling, did little to help South Australia's cause when, in November, he became the authentic reluctant opener, and was relegated firstly to the number 8 position against Victoria and then out of the side.

A few South Australians kept their heads when all around them were losing theirs. The thirty-nine year-old all-rounder, John Inverarity, plodded on in his dogmatic, schoolmasterly fashion and was rewarded in the away game against New South Wales when he equalled – and subsequently surpassed – Sir Donald Bradman's record Sheffield Shield aggregate of 8926 runs. Andrew Hilditch, the former New South Wales' skipper and Australian vice-captain, enjoyed one of his most prolific seasons with the bat. His tally of 921 runs came at the rate of 61.4 per innings and included a patient 230 against Victoria in Melbourne. The South Australian bowling honours were shared between the evergreen Test man, Rodney Hogg and the twenty-three year-old left-handed, medium-paced ingenué from Yorkshire, Ian Carmichael. Hogg's 20 wickets, gathered at a miserly 18.30 each were by far the more economical; but Carmichael's persistence and accuracy yielded him the greater rewards. His 40-wicket return at an average of 34.1 was a fine performance from a bowler in his first season in Shield cricket and deservedly won him an Esso Scholarship and a free trip to England.

Realising at a comparatively early stage of the season that its destiny was to be the fifth position in the Shield ladder, South Australia did not hesitate to give youth its opportunity. Darryl Scott, Donald O'Connor, Craig Bradley, Kim Harris, Glenn Bishop and Andrew Favell – son of the legendary Len – were all given their chances. The result will certainly be a stronger and more vibrant future South Australian challenge for the Sheffield Shield. This year's consolation prize for the South Australia's policy of encouraging youth was a deserved win over the red-hot favourites, Western Australia, in the MacDonald's Cup Final.

Tasmania led the ruck of the also-ran teams in the Shield competition and finished the summer in third position in the ladder. The constant migration of overseas players in and out of the Apple Island continued unabated in 1983/84. West Indian fast bowler Michael Holding, and Middlesex batsman Roland Butcher, departed, to make way for the return of Leicestershire batsman Brian Davison. Davison re-entered Australia as a permanent resident and became Tasmania's Director of Coaching. He also assisted the state's captain and its newest player, Roger Woolley, to direct the

*O'Donnell survives an lbw appeal by Winter and wicket-keeper Wright. O'Donnell went on to score a century on his debut in first-class cricket. (Philip Tyson)*

## New South Wales 1983–84
First Class Matches

| BATTING | *v.* Western Australia (Perth) 21–24 October 1983 | | *v.* Victoria (Sydney) 28–31 October 1983 | | *v.* Pakistanis (Sydney) 18–21 Nov. 1983 | | *v.* Queensland (Sydney) 2–5 December 1983 | | *v.* South Australia (Newcastle) 16–19 Dec. 1983 | | *v.* Queensland (Brisbane) 6–9 January 1983 | | *v.* Tasmania (Devonport) 13–16 January 1984 | | *v.* Victoria (Melbourne) 27–30 January 1984 | | *v.* Tasmania (Sydney) 3–6 February 1984 | | *v.* South Australia (Adelaide) 17–20 February 1984 | | *v.* Western Australia (Sydney) 24–27 February 1984 | |
|---|---|---|---|---|---|---|---|---|---|---|---|---|---|---|---|---|---|---|---|---|---|---|
| R.B. McCosker | 2 | 44 | 32 | — | 157 | — | 8 | 32 | 20 | 55 | 2 | 9 | 16 | 20 | 30 | — | 47 | 55 | 21 | 76 | 94 | 3 |
| J. Dyson | 3 | 46 | 178* | — | 9 | — | 3 | 4 | 40 | 1* | 26 | 19 | 13 | 33 | 28 | — | 106 | 80 | 241 | 92 | 52 | 41* |
| T.M. Chappell | 32 | 7 | 0 | — | 17 | — | 1 | 22 | | | 4 | 17 | | | | | | | | | | |
| D.M. Wellham | 1 | 11 | 33 | — | 96 | — | 12 | 108 | 30 | 1 | 47 | 65 | 1 | 8* | — | — | | | 51 | 12 | 10 | — |
| S.B. Smith | 56 | 3 | 64 | — | 67 | — | 23 | 37 | 0 | 40 | 72 | 0 | 18 | 100* | | | | | | | | |
| P.M. Toohey | 0 | 5 | 61 | — | 25 | — | 29 | 48* | 29 | 38 | 23 | 0 | | | | | | | | | | |
| G.R.J. Matthews | 0 | 26 | 13* | — | 86 | — | | | 15 | 12 | | | 72 | — | 20 | — | — | 48 | | | | |
| M.J. Bennett | | | — | — | 0 | — | | | 46 | 7 | 10 | 20 | 54 | — | — | — | — | 13 | 48* | — | 4 | — |
| G. Dyer | | | | | 5* | — | | | | | | | | | | | | | | | | |
| L.S. Pascoe | | | | | — | — | | | | | 4 | 2 | 23 | — | — | — | | | — | — | 1 | — |
| D.R. Gilbert | | | | | — | — | | | 3* | — | 0* | 0* | 0* | — | — | — | — | 0* | — | — | 0 | — |
| S.J. Rixon | 43* | 18 | — | — | | | 34 | 12 | 22 | 32* | 20 | 3 | 11 | 27 | 101* | — | — | 19 | 48 | — | 66 | — |
| G.R. Bensley | 0 | 3 | | | | | | | | | | | | | | | | | | | | |
| G.F. Lawson | 1 | 37* | — | — | | | 0 | 7 | 11 | — | | | | | | | | | | | | |
| M.R. Whitney | 4 | 0 | — | — | | | 12 | 0 | | | | | | | | | | | | | | |
| R.G. Holland | | | | | | | 3 | 0 | 20 | — | 2 | 18 | 10 | — | — | — | — | 0 | — | — | 37* | — |
| W. Mulherin | | | | | | | 1* | 6 | | | | | | | | | | | | | | |
| P.S. Clifford | | | | | | | | | | | | | 74 | — | 152* | — | 94* | 15 | 17 | 62 | 0 | 29* |
| G.G. Geise | | | | | | | | | | | | | | | 77 | — | — | 4 | 9 | 50* | 4 | — |
| R.J. Bower | | | | | | | | | | | | | | | | | 31* | 21 | | | | |
| R.P. Done | | | | | | | | | | | | | | | | | — | 3 | | | | |
| P.H. Marks | | | | | | | | | | | | | | | | | | | 8 | 19* | 4 | — |
| Byes | | | 7 | | 6 | | | | 4 | | 3 | | | 2 | 2 | | 2 | 1 | 3 | | 3 | |
| Leg-byes | 8 | 8 | 6 | | 11 | | 4 | 7 | 5 | 1 | 5 | 4 | 6 | 3 | 7 | | 6 | 4 | 8 | 3 | 9 | 1 |
| Wides | 2 | | 1 | | 1 | | | | | | 2 | | 3 | 2 | 1 | | | | 1 | | | |
| No-balls | 4 | 5 | 14 | | 11 | | 11 | 14 | | 1 | 9 | 16 | 7 | 3 | 17 | | 3 | 5 | 4 | | 8 | |
| Total | 156 | 213 | 409 | | 491 | | 141 | 297 | 255 | 188 | 229 | 173 | 308 | 198 | 435 | | 289 | 268 | 459 | 314 | 292 | 74 |
| Wickets | 10 | 10 | 5 | | 8 | | 10 | 10 | 10 | 6 | 10 | 10 | 10 | 3 | 4 | | 2 | 10 | 7 | 4 | 10 | 1 |
| Result | L | | D | | D | | L | | W | | L | | D | | D | | L | | D | | D | |
| Points | 0 | | 4 | | — | | 0 | | 16 | | 4 | | 0 | | 4 | | 4 | | 4 | | 0 | |

*Catches* 22 – S.J. Rixon (ct 15/st 7) 15 – R.B. McCosker 10 – M.J. Bennett 6 – P.S. Clifford 5 – J. Dyson, M.R. Whitney and R.G. Holland 4 – G.F. Lawson, D.M. Wellham and S.B. Smith 3 – G. Dyer

| BOWLING | L.S. Pascoe | D.R. Gilbert | M.J. Bennett | G.R.J. Matthews | T.M. Chappell | R.B. McCosker | G.F. Lawson | M.R. Whitney | G.R. Bensley |
|---|---|---|---|---|---|---|---|---|---|
| *v.* Western Australia (Perth) | | | | 43–6–128–3 | 24–5–60–2 | | 31–9–87–1 | 34–7–89–2 | 19–5–62–1 |
| 21–24 October 1983 | | | | | | | | | |
| *v.* Victoria (Sydney) | | | 21–8–46–1 | 22–6–55–2 | 9–1–31–0 | | 19.4–6–43–6 | 15–5–37–1 | |
| 28–31 October 1983 | | | 16–5–43–0 | 6–5–1–0 | 8–0–27–0 | 2–0–12–0 | 13–4–42–2 | 10–3–40–1 | |
| *v.* Pakistanis (Sydney) | 14–2–38–2 | 12–3–62–2 | 16–6–28–2 | 15–4–41–3 | 4–0–18–0 | | | | |
| 18–21 November 1983 | 13–3–43–1 | 32–13–73–2 | 64–27–132–0 | 10.1–3–26–1 | 28–9–73–0 | 16–1–46–0 | | | |
| *v.* Queensland (Sydney) | | | | | 10–1–36–1 | | 30.3–6–89–3 | 24–3–105–1 | |
| 2–5 December 1983 | | | | | 4–0–14–1 | | 11–2–28–1 | | |
| *v.* South Australia (Newcastle) | | 12–3–32–2 | 22–16–15–5 | 14–5–28–1 | | | 17–8–16–1 | | |
| 16–19 December 1983 | | 6–0–30–0 | 23–7–48–0 | 17–4–37–1 | | | 14.2–3–42–2 | | |
| *v.* Queensland (Brisbane) | 17.3–4–53–5 | 10–3–29–1 | 12–3–22–2 | | 11–4–25–2 | | | | |
| 6–9 January 1984 | 25–6–59–1 | 18–3–46–1 | 32.4–13–58–2 | | 10–4–25–0 | | | | |
| *v.* Tasmania (Devonport) | 25–5–78–1 | 25–7–60–2 | 47.3–21–62–3 | 38–13–101–2 | | | | | |
| 13–16 January 1984 | | | | | | | | | |
| *v.* Victoria (Melbourne) | 16–5–43–2 | 21–8–56–5 | 8–3–16–0 | 17–5–37–0 | | | | | |
| 27–30 January 1984 | 30–5–115–5 | 35–7–87–1 | 28–9–55–0 | 21–11–52–0 | | | | | |
| *v.* Tasmania (Sydney) | | 31–7–85–3 | 18–7–40–1 | 28–11–49–3 | | | | | |
| 3–6 February 1984 | | 20–5–58–3 | 32–12–61–1 | 21–7–47–1 | | | | | |
| *v.* South Australia (Adelaide) | 29–10–76–2 | 32–10–70–2 | 23.4–8–45–3 | | | | | | |
| 17–20 February 1984 | | | | | | | | | |
| *v.* Western Australia (Sydney) | 23–3–94–1 | 22–6–74–1 | 38–15–60–0 | | | | | | |
| 24–27 February 1984 | | | | | | | | | |
| | 192.3–43–599–20 *av.* 29.95 | 276–75–762–25 *av.* 30.48 | 401.5–160–731–18 *av.* 40.61 | 252.1–80–602–17 *av.* 35.41 | 108–24–309–6 *av.* 51.50 | 18–1–58–0 — | 136.3–38–347–16 *av.* 21.68 | 83–18–271–5 *av.* 54.20 | 19–5–62–1 *av.* 62.00 |

a J. Dyson 4–0–23–0 P.M. Toohey 0.5–0–0–0 b W. Mulherin 17–1–69–0 c G.G. Geise 1–0–7–0 d G.G. Geise 1–1–0–0

| M | Inns | NOs | Runs | HS | Av |
|---|---|---|---|---|---|
| 11 | 19 | — | 723 | 157 | 38.05 |
| 11 | 19 | 3 | 1015 | 241 | 63.43 |
| 5 | 8 | — | 100 | 32 | 12.50 |
| 10 | 15 | 1 | 486 | 108 | 34.71 |
| 7 | 12 | 1 | 480 | 100* | 43.63 |
| 6 | 10 | 1 | 258 | 61 | 28.66 |
| 7 | 9 | 1 | 292 | 86 | 36.50 |
| 9 | 9 | 1 | 202 | 54 | 25.25 |
| 1 | 1 | 1 | 5 | 5* | — |
| 6 | 4 | — | 30 | 23 | 7.50 |
| 8 | 6 | 5 | 3 | 3* | 3.00 |
| 10 | 14 | 3 | 456 | 101* | 41.45 |
| 1 | 2 | — | 3 | 3 | 1.50 |
| 4 | 5 | 1 | 56 | 37* | 14.00 |
| 3 | 4 | — | 16 | 12 | 4.00 |
| 8 | 8 | 1 | 90 | 37* | 12.85 |
| 1 | 2 | 1 | 7 | 6 | 7.00 |
| 5 | 8 | 3 | 443 | 152* | 88.60 |
| 4 | 5 | 1 | 144 | 77 | 36.00 |
| 1 | 2 | 1 | 52 | 31* | 52.00 |
| 1 | 1 | — | 3 | 3 | 3.00 |
| 2 | 3 | 1 | 31 | 19* | 15.50 |

2 – P.M. Toohey, G.R.J. Matthews and T.M. Chappell (inc. 1 as sub)

1 – D.R. Gilbert, L.S. Pascoe, R.P. Done, R.J. Bower and P.H. Marks

| R.P. Done | P.H. Marks | R.G. Holland | Byes | Leg-byes | Wides | No-balls | Total | Wkts |
|---|---|---|---|---|---|---|---|---|
| | | | 8 | 5 | 5 | 6 | 439 | 10 |
| | | | 7 | 8 | 1 | 3 | 227 | 10 |
| | | | | | 4 | 3 | 165 | 3 |
| | | | 4 | 3 | | 11 | 194 | 10 |
| | | | 13 | 6 | | 14 | 435 | 4a |
| | | 27–8–72–4 | | 8 | 3 | 9 | 379 | 10b |
| | | 7.1–4–19–0 | | 1 | 1 | | 62 | 2 |
| | | 3.4–1–4–0 | 2 | 4 | | 4 | 101 | 10 |
| | | 23–9–56–7 | 5 | 5 | | 1 | 223 | 10 |
| | | 8–4–25–0 | | 6 | 2 | 6 | 160 | 10 |
| | | 24–12–48–1 | 7 | 3 | | 5 | 246 | 5 |
| | | 32–12–81–1 | 2 | 10 | | 10 | 394 | 10 |
| | | 25–12–41–2 | 1 | 2 | 2 | 10 | 203 | 10c |
| | | 35–16–66–1 | 6 | 15 | 3 | 13 | 396 | 7d |
| 22–3–76–2 | | 14.5–4–35–1 | | 3 | | | 288 | 10 |
| 14–2–49–0 | | 32.5–5–98–4 | | 6 | | | 319 | 10 |
| | 31–8–83–0 | 44–13–107–1 | 3 | 11 | 1 | 11 | 395 | 10 |
| | 20–1–56–0 | 34–15–66–2 | 5 | 4 | | 7 | 359 | 4 |
| 36—5—125—2 *av.* 62.50 | 51—9—139—0 — | 310.3—115—718—24 *av.* 29.91 | | | | | | |

fortunes of the Shield side. Tasmania's third place in the national competition was in no small way due to the inspiration and individual achievements of the Zimbabwe-born number 5 batsman. His tally of 955 runs came at the rate of 58.21 runs per innings and was punctuated by four centuries: the most hundreds recorded by an individual player in the Australian domestic season. The West Indian-born, Middlesex pace bowler, Neil Williams, was the second overseas player permitted Tasmania by the Australian Cricket Board. His 21 wickets at 33.14 each was a workmanlike contribution to the rising fortunes of his foster-side. But the professional recruit was far outshone by the home-grown Australian speedster, Peter Clough, whose 40 victims each cost him three runs less. The lively pace of the university graduate from Sydney repeatedly set the best batsmen in the land back on their heels and his 8/95 analysis against Western Australia led to overtures to tempt him to Perth. If his exit visa is granted, Clough's loss will severely deplete the penetration of Tasmania's new-ball attack.

Skipper Roger Woolley's 535 run aggregate in Shield games and his competency behind the wicket were enough to gain him the provisional approval of the Australian selectors as Rodney Marsh's replacement in the touring side to the West Indies in February 1984. Events proved that Marsh's boots were too big for Woolley to fill adequately. It is doubtful, however, whether David Boon would have similarly failed to measure up to the demands of a Caribbean tour. Pound for pound, the nuggety Taswegian was one of the most reliable wielders of the bat in Australia in 1983/84. He began the season in paralysing form, despoiling the Victorian attack to the tune of 227 runs. Further substantial scores eluded him in the ensuing months and he had to content himself with a season's yield of 660 runs. Labour Prime Minister and cricket-lover Bob Hawke, however, publicised his high opinion of the compact Tasmanian batsman, when he put to one side his prejudices against the Liberal-governed island and chose Boon in his team to play the might of the West Indies at Manuka Oval in Canberra. Boon responded to this act of political faith by compiling a faultless century and bringing blushes to the cheeks of the selectors who had already ignored him for the West Indian tour. The rising star amongst Woolley's Taswegians proved to be the fair-haired all-rounder Peter Faulkner, who received no more than his just deserts when he became the second Tasmanian to gain an Esso Scholarship.

Victoria began the 1983/84 Shield season not having won a game outright for 3 seasons and 27 matches! Sadly, the once great eleven were again left clutching the competition's wooden spoon in March 1984. Its only consolation was that it had broken the general drought of victories and an unproductive nineteen-year-old sequence of games in Brisbane by beating Queensland outright on its home ground. The gloomy history of the Victorian summer was not to be wondered at. Captaincy squabbles dominated discussions in the wintery atmosphere of the Melbourne board rooms in 1983. Victoria's future Test star of 1983/84 Graham Yallop, was deemed inadequate in the role of captain, and was already politically discarded before March 1983. Sub-rosa approaches were made to South Australian skipper, David Hookes, to move to Victoria and assume the mantle of leadership; but when open negotiations took place, Hookes' Adelaide connection proved too strong and the Victorian

## Queensland 1983–84
First Class Matches

| BATTING | v. Pakistanis (Brisbane) 21–24 October 1983 | | v. Tasmania (Brisbane) 28–31 October 1983 | | v. South Australia (Brisbane) 18–21 Nov. 1983 | | v. New South Wales (Sydney) 2–5 December 1983 | | v. Victoria (Brisbane) 9–12 Dec. 1983 | | v. Western Australia (Perth) 16–19 Dec. 1983 | | v. New South Wales (Brisbane) 6–9 January 1984 | | v. South Australia (Adelaide) 13–16 January 1984 | | v. Western Australia (Brisbane) 27–30 January 1984 | | v. Victoria (Melbourne) 17–20 February 1984 | | v. Tasmania (Hobart) 24–27 February 1984 | |
|---|---|---|---|---|---|---|---|---|---|---|---|---|---|---|---|---|---|---|---|---|---|---|
| R.B. Kerr | 8 | 51 | 75 | 0 | 14 | — | 55 | 24* | 0 | 37 | 15 | 103 | 0 | 23 | 136 | 10 | 17 | 29 | 3 | 166 | 35 | 5 |
| K.C. Wessels | 0 | 127 | 29 | 46 | 104 | — | 80 | 2 | | | 31 | 58 | | | | | | | | | | |
| G.M. Ritchie | 196 | — | 60 | 67* | 53 | — | 75 | 16 | 130 | 75 | 21 | 8 | 75 | 129 | | | | | | | | |
| A.R. Border | 68 | — | 64 | 14 | 110 | — | 68 | 18* | | | 90 | 68 | | | | | | | | | | |
| G.S. Chappell | 1 | 15* | 93 | 4* | 45 | — | 6 | — | | | 42 | 56* | | | 25 | 27 | 17 | — | 42 | — | 2 | 129 |
| A.B. Henschell | 0 | 6 | 89* | — | 39* | — | 3 | — | 67 | 0 | 8 | 2 | 4 | 1 | 24 | 17 | 21 | — | 8 | 14* | | |
| R.B. Phillips | 77* | — | 39 | — | 0 | — | 19 | — | 8 | 0 | 43 | 17* | 7 | 7* | 20 | 47 | 0 | 3* | 7 | 48* | 10 | 8 |
| J.R. Thomson | — | — | — | — | — | — | 27 | — | 0* | 2* | 4 | — | 8* | — | 1* | 11* | 0* | — | 8 | — | 8 | 5* |
| C.G. Rackemann | — | — | — | — | — | — | 5* | — | | | | | | | | | | | | | | |
| J.N. Maguire | — | 19* | — | — | — | — | 1 | — | 4* | 14 | 23* | — | | | | | | | | | | |
| G.K. Whyte | 51* | — | — | — | 6* | — | 20 | — | 0 | 58 | 1 | — | 7 | — | 0 | 1 | | | | | | |
| C.J. McDermott | | | | | | | | | 5 | 29 | 0 | — | 14 | — | 0 | 29 | 8 | — | 38* | 28 | 10* | 24 |
| B.A. Courtice | | | | | | | | | 11 | 32 | | | 0 | 42 | 7 | 7 | 4 | 3* | 53 | 144 | 20 | 23 |
| G.S. Trimble | | | | | | | | | 84 | 19 | | | 0 | 7 | | | 38 | — | 99 | 1 | 71 | 13 |
| T.V. Hohns | | | | | | | | | 29 | 11 | | | 30 | 22* | 51 | 36 | 58 | — | 20 | — | 34 | 56 |
| H. Frei | | | | | | | | | | | | | 1 | — | 4 | 4 | 2 | — | 0 | — | 4 | 9 |
| C.B. Smart | | | | | | | | | | | | | | | 26 | 11 | 46 | — | 17 | 21 | 20 | 6 |
| A.N. Brown | | | | | | | | | | | | | | | | | | | | | 0 | 32 |
| Byes | | | 1 | 2 | | | | | | 5 | | 1 | | 7 | | | 1 | 1 | 5 | 2 | 2 | 11 |
| Leg-byes | 5 | 2 | 15 | | 8 | | 8 | 1 | 1 | 7 | 11 | 4 | 6 | 3 | 5 | 1 | 7 | | 5 | 14 | 6 | 5 |
| Wides | 4 | 1 | | | | | 3 | 1 | 2 | 1 | 1 | 1 | 2 | | | | 4 | | 1 | | | |
| No-balls | 12 | 6 | 5 | 1 | 1 | | 9 | | 13 | 2 | 5 | 3 | 6 | 5 | 9 | | 6 | 2 | 12 | 1 | 1 | 7 |
| Total | 422 | 227 | 470 | 134 | 380 | | 379 | 62 | 354 | 292 | 295 | 321 | 160 | 246 | 308 | 201 | 229 | 38 | 318 | 439 | 223 | 333 |
| Wickets | 6 | 3 | 6 | 3 | 6 | | 10 | 2 | 9 | 10 | 10 | 5 | 10 | 5 | 10 | 10 | 10 | 1 | 10 | 5 | 10 | 10 |
| Result | D | | W | | D | | W | | L | | D | | W | | L | | D | | D | | W | |
| Points | — | | 16 | | 2 | | 16 | | 4 | | 4 | | 12 | | 4 | | 0 | | 0 | | 16 | |

*Catches* 48 – R.B. Phillips (ct 45/st 3)
16 – R.B. Kerr
11 – G.S. Chappell
9 – G.K. Whyte (inc. 1 as sub)
7 – G.M. Ritchie
6 – A.B. Henschell
5 – A.R. Border and T.V. Hohns (inc. 1 as sub)
4 – B.A. Courtice and H. Frei
3 – G.S. Trimble and J.N. Maguire

| BOWLING | J.R. Thomson | G.C. Rackemann | J.N. Maguire | G.S. Chappell | G.K. Whyte | A.B. Henschell | A.R. Border | C.J. McDermott | H. Frei |
|---|---|---|---|---|---|---|---|---|---|
| v. Pakistanis (Brisbane) | 19–3–98–1 | 34–14–57–3 | 26–2–85–2 | 2–0–16–0 | 29–9–87–0 | 4–1–17–0 | | | |
| 21–24 October 1983 | 5–2–12–0 | | 5–3–4–0 | 2–0–4–0 | | | | | |
| v. Tasmania (Brisbane) | 15–4–50–2 | 19–4–41–1 | 18.4–8–44–4 | 18–4–39–1 | 21–7–38–2 | 1–0–3–0 | | | |
| 28–31 October 1983 | 23–4–102–2 | 22.4–3–83–2 | 21–3–82–1 | 4–1–7–0 | 35–18–89–3 | | 7–3–12–1 | | |
| v. South Australia (Brisbane) | 25.5–4–73–3 | 36–6–97–3 | 31–6–103–2 | 10–0–34–0 | 18–5–66–1 | 4–1–20–1 | | | |
| 18–21 November 1983 | | | | | | | | | |
| v. New South Wales (Sydney) | 8–1–32–3 | 17–8–32–2 | 11–4–28–3 | 13–5–45–2 | | | | | |
| 2–5 December 1983 | 21–4–58–3 | 8–1–36–1 | 34–4–108–5 | 18–7–31–1 | 22–5–47–0 | 2–0–10–0 | | | |
| v. Victoria (Brisbane) | 18–3–58–4 | | 22–4–93–0 | | 16–6–45–2 | 5–1–25–0 | | 25–5–75–4 | |
| 9–12 December 1983 | 13–2–45–2 | | 21–3–64–0 | | 35–10–100–3 | 5–2–14–0 | | 17–6–34–0 | |
| v. Western Australia (Perth) | 16–4–64–4 | | 22.2–7–60–4 | 10–5–19–0 | 7–2–14–1 | | | 20–2–68–1 | |
| 16–19 December 1983 | 23–4–73–1 | | 26–6–62–6 | 10–2–26–0 | 25–6–69–1 | | | 17–3–69–1 | |
| v. New South Wales (Brisbane) | 14–3–40–2 | | | | 17–3–45–1 | | | 19.2–1–85–4 | 16–5–44–2 |
| 6–9 January 1984 | 13–3–38–1 | | | | 6–1–16–0 | | | 19–6–37–3 | 18.3–3–55–6 |
| v. South Australia (Adelaide) | 19–4–51–2 | | | | 34–13–86–3 | | | 14–5–34–0 | 8.5–1–29–1 |
| 13–15 January 1984 | 12–2–43–1 | | | 7–0–10–1 | 17–1–60–0 | 4–1–15–0 | | 9–0–30–0 | 3–1–10–0 |
| v. Western Australia (Brisbane) | 19.2–4–50–4 | | | 14–5–24–0 | | | | 21–8–67–2 | 19–6–41–1 |
| 27–30 January 1984 | 15–4–44–1 | | | 15–3–31–0 | | | | 18–3–48–0 | 14–8–28–2 |
| v. Victoria (Melbourne) | 21–1–105–1 | | | 4–2–6–0 | | 4–0–27–0 | | 22–3–71–0 | 36–9–83–0 |
| 17–20 February 1984 | 4–0–19–0 | | | | | | | 5–0–17–0 | 5–1–21–0 |
| v. Tasmania (Hobart) | 12.4–2–58–2 | | | | | | | 20–4–41–2 | 25–10–52–6 |
| 24–27 February 1984 | 12.4–0–67–2 | | | | | | | 15–2–53–2 | 18–5–59–2 |
| v. Western Australia (Perth) | 25.2–6–85–5 | | | | 14–4–26–0 | | | 20–5–67–0 | 37–10–104–3 |
| 9–13 March 1984 | 19–0–96–2 | | | 11–4–15–0 | 13–6–28–3 | | | 10–3–20–1 | 12–2–28–0 |
| | 373.5–64– 1361–48 *av.* 28.35 | 136.4–36– 346–12 *av.* 28.83 | 238–50– 733–27 *av.* 27.14 | 138–38– 307–5 *av.* 61.40 | 309–96– 816–20 *av.* 40.80 | 29–6– 131–1 *av.* 131.00 | 7–3– 12–1 *av.* 12.00 | 271.2–56– 816–20 *av.* 40.80 | 212.2–61– 554–23 *av.* 24.08 |

a G.M. Ritchie 6–0–27–1
R.B. Phillips 3–0–11–0
K.C. Wessels 6–2–9–0

b G.S. Trimble 1–1–0–0
C.B. Smart 2–0–7–0

c A.N. Brown 10–2–25–0

| v. Western Australia (Perth) 9–13 March 1984 | | M | Inns | NOs | Runs | HS | Av |
|---|---|---|---|---|---|---|---|
| 56 | 4 | 12 | 23 | 1 | 866 | 166 | 39.36 |
| | | 5 | 9 | — | 477 | 127 | 53.00 |
| | | 7 | 12 | 1 | 905 | 196 | 82.27 |
| | | 5 | 8 | 1 | 500 | 110 | 71.42 |
| 85 | 1 | 10 | 16 | 3 | 590 | 129 | 45.38 |
| | | 10 | 16 | 3 | 303 | 89* | 23.30 |
| 61* | 10 | 12 | 20 | 6 | 431 | 77* | 30.78 |
| — | 0 | 12 | 12 | 7 | 74 | 27 | 14.80 |
| | | 4 | 1 | 1 | 5 | 5* | — |
| | | 6 | 5 | 3 | 61 | 23* | 30.50 |
| 18* | 1 | 9 | 11 | 3 | 163 | 58 | 20.37 |
| 16 | 21* | 8 | 13 | 3 | 222 | 38* | 22.20 |
| 77 | 22 | 7 | 14 | 1 | 445 | 144 | 34.23 |
| 0 | 6 | 6 | 11 | — | 338 | 99 | 30.72 |
| 39 | 17 | 7 | 12 | 1 | 403 | 58 | 36.63 |
| — | 0 | 6 | 8 | — | 24 | 9 | 3.00 |
| 57 | 62 | 5 | 9 | — | 266 | 62 | 29.55 |
| | | 1 | 2 | — | 32 | 32 | 16.00 |
| 2 | | | | | | | |
| 7 | 4 | | | | | | |
| 4 | 1 | | | | | | |
| 9 | 5 | | | | | | |
| 431 | 154 | | | | | | |
| 7 | 10 | | | | | | |
| L | | | | | | | |
| — | | | | | | | |

2 – J.R. Thomson
1 – C.B. Smart, A.N. Brown, C.J. McDermott and C.G. Rackemann

| A.B. Courtice | R.B. Kerr | T.V. Hohns | Byes | Leg-byes | Wides | No-balls | Total | Wkts |
|---|---|---|---|---|---|---|---|---|
| | | | | 4 | | 23 | 364 | 6 |
| | 1–0–1–0 | | | 5 | 1 | 1 | 73 | 1a |
| | | | 1 | 8 | | 24 | 224 | 10 |
| | | | 2 | 1 | | 5 | 378 | 9† |
| | | | 4 | 9 | | 6 | 406 | 10 |
| | | | | 4 | | 11 | 141 | 10 |
| | | | | 7 | | 14 | 297 | 10 |
| | | 16–3–52–0 | 1 | 4 | 2 | 10 | 353 | 10 |
| | | 26–10–47–1 | 8 | 10 | | 6 | 322 | 7 |
| | | | 6 | 4 | 1 | 26 | 235 | 10 |
| | | | 3 | 9 | 6 | 18 | 311 | 9 |
| | | 1–0–7–0 | 3 | 5 | 2 | 9 | 229 | 10 |
| | | 11–4–23–0 | | 4 | | 16 | 173 | 10 |
| | | 31–12–75–4 | 1 | 5 | | 17 | 281 | 10 |
| | | 15.5–0–54–1 | 4 | 3 | | 4 | 229 | 3 |
| | | 17–2–48–1 | 1 | 9 | 1 | 8 | 240 | 10 |
| | | 15–6–33–1 | 1 | 7 | 1 | 14 | 192 | 4 |
| 7–0–37–0 | | 35–5–123–3 | 1 | 10 | | 14 | | 5 |
| 4–1–7–0 | 4–1–12–1 | 7–2–14–0 | | 2 | | 3 | 99 | 1b |
| 4–1–6–0 | | 3–2–1–0 | 1 | 7 | 1 | 8 | 166 | 10 |
| | | 23–4–90–4 | 5 | 5 | | 11 | 304 | 10c |
| 11–1–35–0 | | 23–12–35–2 | 5 | 6 | 4 | 26 | 363 | 10 |
| | | 5.5–2–22–0 | 5 | 10 | 2 | 9 | 224 | 6 |
| 26–3–85–0 — | 5–1–13–1 *av.* 13.00 | 229.4–64–624–17 *av.* 36.70 | | | | | | |

†B.F. Davison retired hurt

captaincy devolved by default on to the shoulders of the former Test slow bowler, Ray Bright.

The captaincy transfer was not the only palace revolution within the Victorian camp. Former Test batsmen, Ian Redpath and Keith Stackpole, assumed command of the training of the side, whilst the recently retired players, John Scholes and Jimmy Higgs joined the selection committee. They decided upon radical solutions for the desperate dilemma confronting Victoria. Youth was to be the answer. In spite of their good form in club cricket, the former Test players, Dav Whatmore and Ian Callen, were jettisoned and yet another international batsman, Julien Wiener, was preremptorarily discarded early in the season after he had scored a paltry 84 runs in 8 innings. With both Scholes and Higgs in the ranks of the superannuated and Shaun Graf having transferred his allegiance to Western Australia, the Victorian eleven bore little resemblance to the team of the previous two seasons. Its weakened condition was further debilitated by the unavailability of Test player Yallop for all but two games. The influence which the left-handed batsman might have exerted on his state's fortunes was underlined by the fact that in those two encounters, the number three batsman registered 358 runs at an average of 119.

In spite of Yallop's absence, Bright's side acquitted itself well with the bat. Vice-captain, Mike Taylor, recorded three centuries and 909 runs at an average of 64.93. The ebullient enthusiasm of Dean Jones, produced 751 runs and two hundreds at a mean figure of 57.77: achievements which could have been improved, but for a lack of patience. The left-handed opener and veteran of one Test against India, Paul Hibbert, was the 'old faithful' of the batting order. He scored only one hundred and still accumulated 808 runs at 44.89 runs per innings. To place the batting performances of the young Victorians in their proper perspective, it must be added that all but two of their three-figure scores were notched on the almost moribund Melbourne Cricket Ground wicket: a pitch which in the course of the summer was the setting for eight team innings of more than 400 runs – including one which exceeded 600 and another which surpassed 500.

It was this lack of encouragement in their home wicket which resulted in an unsuccessful and expensive season for the Victorian bowlers. With the former Esso Scholarship winner, fast bowler, Merv Hughes sidelined for the whole of the season by the now endemic speedster's complaint, a bad back, the new ball responsibilities weighed very heavily on the shoulders of Rod McCurdy and newcomers, Simon Davis and Tony Dodemaide. McCurdy and Davis captured 23 and 30 wickets respectively, but at the outrageously expensive rate of 42 runs each. But the star of Australia's Under 19 tour of England in 1983, Tony Dodemaide, began his first-class career auspiciously by claiming 23 victims with his swinging medium-pace at the cheapest Victorian price of 24.96. The end of the season saw the Victorian supporters looking expectantly towards youngsters such as opening batsman Michael Quinn, early order men, Warren Whiteside, Bruce Moir, left-handed wrist-spinner David Emerson and wicketkeeper, Phil Hyde. They hoped that these tyros would alleviate the gloom which has characterised the southern state's performances in the last two years; but until such time as the Victorian selectors can unearth bowlers who move the ball away from the bat and their batsmen can

## South Australia 1983–84
First Class Matches

| BATTING | v. Tasmania (Adelaide) 21–24 October 1983 | | v. Pakistanis (Adelaide) 28–31 October 1983 | | v. Queensland (Brisbane) 18–21 Nov. 1983 | | v. Victoria (Adelaide) 25–28 Nov. 1983 | | v. Western Australia (Adelaide) 2–5 December 1983 | | v. Tasmania (Devonport) 9–12 Dec. 1983 | | v. New South Wales (Newcastle) 16–19 Dec. 1983 | | v. Western Australia (Perth) 6–9 January 1984 | | v. Queensland (Adelaide) 13–16 January 1984 | | v. New South Wales (Adelaide) 17–20 February 1984 | | v. Victoria (Melbourne) 24–27 February 1984 | |
|---|---|---|---|---|---|---|---|---|---|---|---|---|---|---|---|---|---|---|---|---|---|---|
| W.M. Darling | 1 | — | 58 | 1 | 33 | — | 15 | — | | | | | | | | | | | | | | |
| W.B. Phillips | 234 | — | 75 | 15 | 14 | — | | | 1 | 21 | | | 5 | 36 | | | | | | | | |
| M.D. Haysman | 100 | — | 57 | 49 | 28 | — | 6 | 25 | 16 | 24 | 3 | 9 | 20 | 8 | 0 | 49 | 29 | 31* | 58 | — | 82 | — |
| D.W. Hookes | 13 | — | 55 | 35 | | | 41 | 5 | 57 | 22 | 142 | 25 | 15 | 42 | 111 | — | | | | | | |
| G.A. Bishop | | | 3 | 77 | 19 | — | 58 | 90 | 15 | 0 | 13 | 10 | 6 | 10 | | | 33 | — | 56 | — | 31 | 51* |
| A.M.J. Hilditch | | | 16* | 0 | 111 | — | 31 | 24 | 2 | 19 | 45 | 52 | 1 | 73 | 34 | 35 | 47 | 96 | 121 | — | 230 | — |
| P.R. Sleep | 24* | — | 6* | 12 | 144 | — | 4 | — | | | 51 | 107* | 0 | 15 | 47 | — | 2 | 2* | 4 | — | 68* | — |
| K.J. Wright | — | — | — | 11 | 0 | — | 12 | 5 | 48 | 3 | | | 10* | 14 | 0 | — | 20* | — | 3 | — | 38 | — |
| R.E.C. Massey | | | — | 17 | | | | | | | | | | | | | | | | | — | — |
| R.M. Hogg | — | — | — | 15 | 15 | — | | | 14* | 43 | | | 12 | 6* | | | | | | | | |
| I.R. Carmichael | — | — | — | 0* | 0 | — | 1* | — | 1 | 2* | 0 | — | 0 | 0 | 3 | — | 4 | — | 0 | — | — | — |
| K.P. Harris | 9 | — | | | | | | | | | | | | | | | | | | | | |
| R.J. Inverarity | 3* | — | | | 13* | — | 49 | 59* | 69 | 42 | 33 | 19* | 22 | 4 | 18 | 12* | 26 | — | 44 | — | 6 | — |
| S.D.H. Parkinson | — | — | | | 10 | — | 27 | — | 49 | 1 | 0 | — | 0 | 4 | 9* | — | | | | | | |
| A.T. Sincock | | | | | | | 20 | — | | | 12* | — | | | | | | | | | | |
| C.L. Harms | | | | | | | | | 13 | 1 | | | | | | | | | | | | |
| C.E. Bradley | | | | | | | | | | | 3 | — | | | 7 | 15 | | | | | | |
| S.R. Gentle | | | | | | | | | | | 13 | — | | | | | | | | | | |
| D.F. O'Connor | | | | | | | | | | | | | | | 1 | 19* | 5 | 72 | 53 | — | 30 | — |
| G.J. Winter | | | | | | | | | | | | | | | 9 | — | 1 | — | 6 | — | 1* | — |
| D.B. Scott | | | | | | | | | | | | | | | | | 64 | 17 | 14 | — | | |
| R.T. Christensen | | | | | | | | | | | | | | | | | 27 | — | 10* | — | | |
| A.L. Favell | | | | | | | | | | | | | | | | | | | | | 0 | 40* |
| Byes | | | | 2 | 4 | | | 5 | | 1 | 6 | 2 | 2 | 5 | 19 | | 1 | 4 | 3 | | 6 | 1 |
| Leg-byes | 2 | | 2 | 7 | 9 | | 1 | | 3 | 1 | 7 | 2 | 4 | 5 | 3 | 3 | 5 | 3 | 11 | | 10 | 4 |
| Wides | | | 2 | | | | | | 5 | | 2 | | | | | 1 | | | 1 | | 5 | |
| No-balls | | | 3 | 2 | 6 | | 14 | 5 | 10 | 2 | 18 | 2 | 4 | 1 | 7 | 6 | 17 | 4 | 11 | | 13 | 5 |
| Total | 386 | | 277 | 243 | 406 | | 279 | 218 | 303 | 182 | 348 | 228 | 101 | 223 | 268 | 140 | 281 | 229 | 395 | | 520 | 101 |
| Wickets | 5 | | 5 | 10 | 10 | | 10 | 5 | 10 | 10 | 10 | 4 | 10 | 10 | 10 | 3 | 10 | 3 | 10 | | 7 | 0 |
| Result | D | | L | | D | | D | | L | | D | | L | | D | | W | | D | | D | |
| Points | 4 | | — | | 2 | | 4 | | 4 | | 0 | | 0 | | 0 | | 12 | | 0 | | 0 | |

*Catches* 23 – K.J. Wright (ct 22/st 1) 10 – P.R. Sleep 8 – A.M.J. Hilditch 5 – D.W. Hookes and D.B. Scott (inc. 1 as s
13 – M.D. Haysman 9 – R.J. Inverarity 6 – S.R. Gentle 4 – W.B. Phillips, S.D.H. Parkinson 3 – W.M. Darling and C.L. Ha

| BOWLING | R.M. Hogg | I.R. Carmichael | R.E.C. Massey | M.D. Haysman | P.R. Sleep | D.W. Hookes | S.D.H. Parkinson | R.J. Inverarity | A.T. Sincock |
|---|---|---|---|---|---|---|---|---|---|
| *v.* Tasmania (Adelaide) | 29–9–77–4 | 24–8–66–2 | | 3–0–13–0 | 38–12–97–0 | | 22–6–49–2 | 23–3–69–2 | |
| 21–24 October 1983 | 18–4–46–1 | 11–3–32–2 | | 12–4–25–0 | 21–1–71–1 | 11–1–38–0 | 10–1–46–0 | 47.5–18–96–6 | |
| *v.* Pakistanis (Adelaide) | 13–2–40–2 | 21–4–45–0 | 15–1–66–2 | 9–3–43–0 | 12–3–58–1 | 8–3–19–2 | | | |
| 28–31 October 1983 | 11–3–25–1 | 16–4–37–1 | 8–0–36–0 | 1–0–4–0 | 14–1–63–1 | 25–7–62–0 | | | |
| *v.* Queensland (Brisbane) | 29.2–5–91–3 | 21–1–90–1 | | 1–0–4–0 | 12–1–69–1 | | 14–2–52–0 | 26–4–66–1 | |
| 18–21 November 1983 | | | | | | | | | |
| *v.* Victoria (Adelaide) | | 29–5–87–3 | | | 4–0–12–0 | 4–0–15–0 | 14.3–4–41–5 | 19–8–24–0 | 26–7–57–2 |
| 25–28 November 1983 | | 29–3–85–2 | | | 16–5–39–0 | 5–2–8–0 | 24–2–67–2 | 25–6–73–1 | 18–2–80–1 |
| *v.* Western Australia (Adelaide) | 24–6–53–5 | 23–7–66–1 | | | | 7–2–25–1 | 20–4–54–2 | 19–4–40–0 | |
| 2–5 December 1983 | 13–2–30–2 | 14–2–57–0 | | | | 3–1–11–0 | 15.1–2–77–2 | 10–2–42–1 | |
| *v.* Tasmania (Devonport) | | 46–9–112–6 | | | 16–2–61–1 | 4.4–1–14–1 | 27–6–81–1 | 17–2–41–0 | 23–5–76–0 |
| 9–12 December 1983 | | 33–11–61–3 | | | 14–6–21–0 | 21–2–61–1 | 7.5–1–29–1 | 12–5–16–1 | 11–3–37–1 |
| *v.* New South Wales | 16.4–3–45–3 | 4–0–15–0 | | | 25–5–86–4 | 5–0–15–0 | 6–1–20–0 | 26–7–55–2 | |
| (Newcastle) 16–19 Dec. 1983 | 10–2–24–2 | 24–2–77–3 | | | 2–0–8–0 | | 13–2–60–1 | 4–0–18–0 | |
| *v.* Western Australia (Perth) | | 55–17–130–5 | | | 4.3–1–6–3 | 3–2–1–0 | 15–6–43–0 | 18–3–46–0 | |
| 6–9 January 1984 | | 13–2–58–0 | | | 7–0–36–0 | 2–0–13–0 | 5–0–30–0 | 21–3–60–1 | |
| *v.* Queensland (Adelaide) | | 30–7–87–3 | | 3–0–12–0 | 31–6–96–4 | | | 14–5–25–0 | |
| 13–16 January 1984 | | 23–9–49–5 | | 6–0–11–0 | 21.4–4–66–3 | | | 28–5–69–2 | |
| *v.* New South Wales (Adelaide) | | 34–4–125–0 | | 3–0–20–0 | 21–4–76–1 | | | 25–5–61–0 | |
| 17–20 February 1984 | | 14–3–46–1 | | 16–2–42–0 | 14–1–64–1 | | | 16–7–25–0 | |
| *v.* Victoria (Melbourne) | | 44–13–121–3 | 17–4–53–2 | 19–7–33–0 | 62.1–18–175–3 | | | 37–15–65–1 | |
| 24–27 February 1984 | | | | | | | | | |
| | 164–36–431–23 *av.* 18.73 | 508–114–1446–41 *av.* 35.26 | 40–5–155–4 *av.* 38.75 | 73–16–207–0 — | 335.2–70–1104–24 *av.* 46.00 | 98.4–21–282–5 *av.* 56.40 | 193.3–37–649–16 *av.* 40.56 | 387.5–102–891–18 *av.* 49.50 | 78–17–250–4 *av.* 62.50 |

a A.M.J. Hilditch 1–0–5–0, W.B. Phillips 1–0–2–0, G.A. Bishop 0.4–0–6–0
b G.A. Bishop 8–3–21–0, A.M.J. Hilditch 6–3–8–0, D.B. Scott 2–0–9–0, D.F. O'Connor 1.1–0–2–0

| M | Inns | NOs | Runs | HS | Av |
|---|---|---|---|---|---|
| 4 | 5 | — | 108 | 58 | 21.60 |
| 5 | 8 | — | 401 | 234 | 50.12 |
| 11 | 18 | 1 | 594 | 100 | 34.94 |
| 7 | 12 | — | 563 | 142 | 46.91 |
| 9 | 15 | 1 | 472 | 90 | 33.71 |
| 10 | 17 | 1 | 937 | 230 | 58.56 |
| 10 | 14 | 5 | 486 | 144 | 54.00 |
| 10 | 12 | 2 | 164 | 48 | 16.40 |
| 2 | 1 | — | 17 | 17 | 17.00 |
| 5 | 6 | 2 | 105 | 43 | 26.25 |
| 11 | 11 | 3 | 11 | 4 | 1.37 |
| 1 | 1 | — | 9 | 9 | 9.00 |
| 10 | 15 | 5 | 419 | 69 | 41.90 |
| 7 | 8 | 1 | 100 | 49 | 14.28 |
| 2 | 2 | 1 | 32 | 20 | 32.00 |
| 1 | 2 | — | 14 | 13 | 7.00 |
| 2 | 3 | — | 25 | 15 | 8.33 |
| 1 | 1 | — | 13 | 13 | 13.00 |
| 4 | 6 | 1 | 180 | 72 | 36.00 |
| 4 | 4 | 1 | 17 | 9 | 5.66 |
| 2 | 3 | — | 95 | 64 | 31.66 |
| 2 | 2 | 1 | 37 | 27 | 37.00 |
| 1 | 2 | 1 | 40 | 40* | 40.00 |

2 – C.E. Bradley, I.R. Carmichael and G.A. Bishop

1 – R.T. Christensen

| G.J. Winter | C.L. Harms | R.T. Christensen | Byes | Leg-byes | Wides | No-balls | Total | Wkts |
|---|---|---|---|---|---|---|---|---|
| | | | 1 | 8 | 2 | 2 | 380 | 10 |
| | | | 5 | 3 | 1 | | 362 | 10 |
| | | | 1 | 2 | 4 | | 274 | 7 |
| | | | | 9 | | | 249 | 3a |
| | | | | 8 | | 1 | 380 | 6 |
| | | | | 12 | | 6 | 248 | 10 |
| | | | 5 | 10 | 3 | 1 | 367 | 6 |
| | 4–0–21–0 | | | 9 | | 4 | 268 | 10 |
| | | | | 2 | 3 | 1 | 219 | 5 |
| | | | 1 | 3 | 1 | 1 | 389 | 10 |
| | | | 6 | 3 | 8 | 8 | 234 | 7 |
| | | | 4 | 5 | | | 245 | 10 |
| | | | | 1 | | 1 | 188 | 6 |
| 51–16–100–2 | | | | 2 | | 7 | 328 | 10 |
| 23.5–3–88–2 | | | 3 | 2 | 1 | 2 | 290 | 3 |
| 19–5–45–2 | | 17–6–38–1 | | 5 | | 9 | 308 | 10 |
| 3–0–5–0 | | | | 1 | | | 201 | 10 |
| 41.2–11–113–6 | | 15–2–53–0 | 3 | 8 | 1 | 4 | 459 | 7 |
| 20–6–56–2 | | 9–0–38–0 | | 3 | | | 314 | 4b |
| 49–10–137–0 | | | 3 | 17 | 1 | 18 | 609 | 10c |
| 207.1–51–544–14 *av.* 38.85 | 4–0–21–0 — | 41–8–129–1 *av.* 129.00 | | | | | | |

c G.A. Bishop 1–0–5–0

perform consistently away from home, only the most sanguine optimists would anticipate a dramatic upturn in Victoria's recent form.

The Australia Day week-end claimed all the Test stars of Sheffield Shield cricket for the triple-headed, one-day contests between Australia, Pakistan and the West Indies in Adelaide. Having retired from international cricket, however, Dennis Lillee and Greg Chappell were present and correct for the crucial Shield encounter between Queensland and Western Australia in Brisbane. The visitors began in dismal fashion, losing 4/64 before Laird and Graf staged a revival which eventually hoisted their side's total to the semi-respectability of 240. The Queensland camp remained comparatively confident even after losing 2/60; but then a rising Lillee delivery broke Henschell's hand, Graf had Chappell caught by Macleay and the Queensland innings disintegrated to terminate abruptly 11 runs behind its opponents' total. Rain marred the remainder of the game and not even Lillee's second innings declaration of 4/192 could revive the moribund match. Lillee's captaincy in the match was not always cast in the same constructive vein as his second innings declaration. The former Test bowler clashed with the umpires on the question of taking drinks during a session already interrupted by rain. The Western Australian's ignorance of the match conditions and his stubbornness in taking drinks cost him dearly. Reported by the umpires for his transgression, Lillee paid his fourth visit to the A.C.B.'s disciplinary committee. It was a case of fourth time unlucky for the fast bowler-captain. A previously suspended $1,000 fine was reinvoked and the Western Australian skipper was banned from playing in his state's next two, vital Shield games. Lillee appealed against his suspension to the Supreme Court on the grounds that he was being restrained from pursuing his trade as a professional cricketer. He lost his case – and Western Australia lost his services for a month – at a time when it needed every wicket and every point it could glean.

The absence of Lillee could have meant the difference between Western Australia winning or losing the Sheffield Shield. The Perth team's last two games were away fixtures, contested without the assistance of its Test players, who were already on their way to the Caribbean. Moreover, with Queensland winning its final encounter against Tasmania, it was imperative that the westerners should gain first innings points from both clashes if they were to earn the advantage of playing the final on their home ground. Lillee's truancy increased the degree of difficulty of Western Australia's task – especially when one considers that its selectors were once again forced to rely on their third option as skipper – Hughes and Lillee both having disqualified themselves by absence or misbehaviour.

The fact that the men from Perth won 8 points from their games in Launceston and Sydney was a glowing tribute to their reserves. The final day of their sporting dispute with Tasmania was lost to rain; but not before the guests of the Apple Islanders had established a first innings ascendancy of 27 runs, thanks to a brilliant 151 from the bat of Shane Clements. It was no easy job to better the Taswegians. Ray's 94 and Boon's 61 made the life of the Western Australian bowlers difficult, whilst, when the mainland team batted, fast bowler Peter Clough, all but turned the tide of the game in favour of his side with a wholehearted display of fast bowling

## Tasmania 1983–84
First Class Matches

| BATTING | *v.* South Australia (Adelaide) 21–24 October 1983 | | *v.* Queensland (Brisbane) 28–31 October 1983 | | *v.* Victoria (Melbourne) 11–14 Nov. 1983 | | *v.* Western Australia (Perth) 25–28 Nov. 1983 | | *v.* South Australia (Devonport) 9–12 Dec. 1983 | | *v.* Pakistanis (Hobart) 16–19 Dec. 1983 | | *v.* Victoria (Hobart) 30 December 1983–2 January 1984 | | *v.* New South Wales (Devonport) 13–16 Jan. 1984 | | *v.* New South Wales (Sydney) 3–6 February 1984 | | *v.* Western Australia (Launceston) 17–20 Feb. 1984 | | *v.* Queensland (Hobart) 24–27 Feb. 1984 | |
|---|---|---|---|---|---|---|---|---|---|---|---|---|---|---|---|---|---|---|---|---|---|---|
| M. Ray | 15 | 23 | 35 | 10 | 29 | 31 | 0 | 21 | 34 | 15 | 35 | 73 | 46 | — | 49 | — | 2 | 16 | 94 | 0 | 50 | 76 |
| I.R. Beven | 51 | 19 | 57 | 18 | 43 | 7 | 26 | 0 | 41 | 17 | 13 | 10 | 0 | — | | | | | 24 | 0 | | |
| D.C. Boon | 80 | 70 | 12 | 0 | 227 | 35 | 55 | 17 | 9 | 24 | 7 | — | 11 | — | 20 | — | 8 | 4 | 61 | 10 | 2 | 15 |
| S.M. Small | | | | | | | | | 19 | 55 | 2 | 114 | 21 | — | 14 | — | 1 | 25 | | | 1 | 9 |
| B.F. Davison | 40 | 145 | 20 | 156* | 8 | 41* | 51 | 152* | 6 | 53 | 62 | 19 | 171* | — | 0 | — | 21 | 1 | 13 | 60 | 17 | 0 |
| S.L. Saunders | 5 | 0 | 19 | 26 | 30 | — | 0 | 5 | 138* | 33 | 11 | 59* | 7 | — | 45 | — | 125 | 0 | 1 | 5* | 5 | 36 |
| P.I. Faulkner | 18 | 57* | 10* | 61* | 52 | — | 38* | 84* | 5 | 12 | 15 | 2 | 25 | — | 29 | — | 22 | 76 | 0 | 1 | 38 | 70* |
| R. Soule | | | | | | | | | | | 0 | 0 | | | | | | | | | | |
| P.A. Blizzard | 39* | 2 | 1 | 2 | | | 27 | — | 19 | — | 24 | 12 | 5 | — | 28 | — | | | | | 26* | 0 |
| N.F. Williams | | | | | | | | | 2 | 0* | 19 | 22 | 0 | — | 27 | — | 34 | 10 | 0 | — | 6 | 11 |
| P.M. Clough | 13 | 0 | 3 | 5 | — | — | 1 | — | 23 | — | 27* | 13 | 1 | — | 7* | — | 12* | 8* | 14 | — | 3 | 8 |
| D.A. Smith | 42 | 6 | 21 | 5 | 14 | 6 | 10 | 0 | | | | | | | | | | | | | | |
| R.D. Woolley | 45 | 31 | 7 | 75 | 10 | 24* | 46 | 18 | 87 | — | | | 4 | — | 79 | — | 7 | 102 | | | | |
| D.J. Buckingham | 19 | 0 | 6 | 12 | | | | | | | | | | | | | | | | | | |
| R.S. Hyatt | | | | | 10* | — | 11 | — | | | | | | | | | 32 | 6 | 17 | 10* | | |
| G.P. Astley | | | | | 6* | — | | | | | | | | | | | | | | | | |
| G.W. Goodman | | | | | | | | | | | | | | | 74 | — | 21 | 65 | 16 | 61 | 0 | 37 |
| L.G. Allen | | | | | | | | | | | | | | | | | | | 43* | — | 1 | 21 |
| Byes | 1 | 5 | 1 | 2 | 7 | | 2 | 1 | 1 | 6 | 3 | 14 | 9 | | 2 | | | | 5 | 4 | 1 | 5 |
| Leg-byes | 8 | 3 | 8 | 1 | 8 | 1 | 8 | 1 | 3 | 3 | 6 | 4 | 11 | | 10 | | 3 | 6 | 2 | 6 | 7 | 5 |
| Wides | 2 | 1 | | | | | 5 | 1 | 1 | 8 | 2 | 2 | | | | | | | | 1 | 1 | |
| No-balls | 2 | | 24 | 5 | 6 | | 20 | 2 | 1 | 8 | 9 | 5 | 12 | | 10 | | | | 7 | 3 | 8 | 11 |
| Total | 380 | 362 | 224 | 378 | 450 | 145 | 300 | 302 | 389 | 234 | 235 | 349 | 323 | | 394 | | 288 | 319 | 297 | 161 | 166 | 304 |
| Wickets | 10 | 10 | 10 | 9† | 8 | 4 | 10 | 6 | 10 | 7 | 10 | 9‡ | 10 | | 10 | | 10 | 10 | 10 | 6 | 10 | 10 |
| Result | D | | L | | D | | L | | D | | L | | W | | D | | W | | D | | L | |
| Points | 0 | | 0 | | 4 | | 4 | | 4 | | — | | 16 | | 4 | | 12 | | 0 | | 0 | |

*Catches*
15 – R.D. Woolley (ct 14/st 1)
10 – M. Ray
8 – D.C. Boon
7 – S.L. Saunders and I.R. Beven
6 – P.I. Faulkner
5 – P.A. Blizzard (inc. 2 as sub), B.F. Davison and L.G. Allen
4 – R. Soule, N.F. Williams and R.S. Hyatt (inc. 1 as sub)
3 – P.M. Clough and S.M. Small
1 – D.J. Buckingham, G.W. Goodman and D.A. Smith

†B.F. Davison retired hurt  ‡D.C. Boon absent hurt

| BOWLING | P.M. Clough | P.I. Faulkner | P.A. Blizzard | N.F. Williams | S.L. Saunders | M. Ray | I.R. Beven | G.P. Astley | R.S. Hyatt |
|---|---|---|---|---|---|---|---|---|---|
| *v.* South Australia (Adelaide) | 20–4–95–0 | 15–0–43–0 | 16–4–50–2 | | 18–7–48–0 | 27.4–12–56–2 | 32–9–92–1 | | |
| 21–24 October 1983 | | | | | | | | | |
| *v.* Queensland (Brisbane) | 31–4–115–0 | 35.5–5–105–3 | 21–1–88–1 | | 7–1–31–0 | 27–3–67–1 | 22–6–48–0 | | |
| 28–31 October 1983 | 15–2–55–1 | 10–0–30–1 | 5–0–47–0 | | | | | | |
| *v.* Victoria (Melbourne) | 31–5–121–2 | 14–3–39–0 | | | 24–4–74–0 | 11–3–27–1 | 15–1–62–0 | 23–5–66–2 | 7–1–23–0 |
| 11–14 November 1983 | 13–1–62–0 | 11–3–32–0 | | | 25–7–62–1 | 18–3–48–2 | 3–1–10–0 | 8–1–25–0 | 10–1–49–0 |
| *v.* Western Australia (Perth) | 31–11–60–4 | 19.2–7–45–2 | 37–9–84–4 | | 15–3–43–0 | 12–3–32–0 | 4–1–18–0 | | |
| 25–28 November 1983 | 13–1–69–2 | 16–1–82–0 | 12.1–1–57–0 | | | 15–0–67–1 | | | 10–0–36–0 |
| *v.* South Australia (Devonport) | 30–8–79–6 | 23–4–59–0 | 15–2–59–0 | 26–9–93–2 | 7–3–20–1 | 6–1–12–0 | 5–1–13–0 | | |
| 9–12 December 1983 | 9–1–49–1 | | 4–1–23–0 | 7–0–52–2 | 8–0–47–1 | 2–0–15–0 | 12–0–38–0 | | |
| *v.* Pakistanis (Hobart) | 15–4–48–2 | 28–6–95–4 | 12–2–54–0 | 20–3–87–0 | 2–0–19–0 | 4–0–17–0 | 6–0–29–0 | | |
| 16–19 December 1983 | 11–1–33–0 | 11–1–30–3 | 10–1–44–0 | 12–1–57–1 | 14–1–49–1 | | 13–2–49–0 | | |
| *v.* Victoria (Hobart) | 9–2–23–2 | 3.1–1–6–1 | 17–8–21–3 | 12–5–34–4 | | | | | |
| 30 Dec. 1983–2 Jan. 1984 | 23–7–57–2 | 10–3–31–2 | 23–8–48–3 | 17.2–3–81–3 | 4–3–5–0 | | 3–3–0–0 | | |
| *v.* New South Wales | 27.4–6–73–2 | 22–4–68–4 | 11–1–35–0 | 25–5–70–2 | 7–2–22–0 | 14–5–34–2 | | | |
| (Devonport) 13–16 Jan. 1984 | 18–4–56–1 | 14–3–44–0 | 9–2–16–0 | 13–3–50–1 | 2–0–6–0 | 16–8–21–0 | | | |
| *v.* New South Wales (Sydney) | 17–3–54–0 | 9–3–30–0 | | 13–4–52–1 | 17–1–57–0 | 16–3–41–1 | | | 10–3–30–0 |
| 3–6 February 1984 | 19.1–2–60–5 | 3–0–13–0 | | 11–2–43–0 | 35–5–114–5 | 1–0–1–0 | | | 11–2–32–0 |
| *v.* Western Australia | 35–7–95–8 | 10–3–20–0 | | 27–4–75–1 | 11–1–39–0 | 7–1–22–0 | 6–1–16–0 | | 20–9–41–1 |
| (Launceston) 17–20 Feb. 1984 | | | | | | | | | |
| *v.* Queensland (Hobart) | 22–7–51–4 | 19–4–48–2 | 18–5–37–0 | 18.3–6–45–4 | 6–1–13–0 | 6–2–21–0 | | | |
| 24–27 February 1984 | 15–3–65–0 | 10–2–30–1 | 23–7–79–4 | 20–2–101–1 | 6.5–1–34–3 | 2–0–8–1 | | | |
| | 404.5–83–1320–42 *av.* 31.42 | 283.2–53–850–23 *av.* 36.95 | 233.1–52–742–17 *av.* 43.64 | 221.5–47–840–22 *av.* 38.18 | 208.5–40–683–12 *av.* 56.91 | 184.4–44–489–11 *av.* 44.45 | 121–25–375–1 *av.* 375.00 | 31–6–91–2 *av.* 45.50 | 68–16–211–1 *av.* 211.00 |

| M | Inns | NOs | Runs | HS | Av |
|---|---|---|---|---|---|
| 11 | 20 | — | 654 | 94 | 32.70 |
| 8 | 15 | — | 326 | 57 | 21.73 |
| 11 | 19 | — | 667 | 227 | 35.10 |
| 6 | 10 | — | 261 | 114 | 26.10 |
| 11 | 20 | 4 | 1036 | 171* | 64.75 |
| 11 | 19 | 3 | 550 | 138* | 34.37 |
| 11 | 19 | 6 | 615 | 84* | 47.30 |
| 1 | 2 | — | 0 | 0 | 0.00 |
| 8 | 12 | 2 | 185 | 39* | 18.50 |
| 7 | 11 | 1 | 131 | 34 | 13.10 |
| 11 | 15 | 4 | 138 | 27* | 12.54 |
| 4 | 8 | — | 104 | 42 | 13.00 |
| 8 | 13 | 1 | 535 | 102 | 44.58 |
| 2 | 4 | — | 37 | 19 | 9.25 |
| 4 | 6 | 2 | 86 | 32 | 21.50 |
| 1 | 1 | 1 | 6 | 6* | — |
| 4 | 7 | — | 274 | 74 | 39.14 |
| 2 | 3 | 1 | 65 | 43* | 32.50 |

| D.A. Smith | G.W. Goodman | Byes | Leg-byes | Wides | No-balls | Total | Wkts |
|---|---|---|---|---|---|---|---|
| | | | 2 | | | 386 | 5 |
| | | | | | | | |
| | | 1 | 15 | | 5 | 470 | 6 |
| | | 2 | | | 1 | 134 | 3 |
| | | | 6 | 1 | 4 | 418 | 5 |
| 1–0–3–0 | | 1 | 2 | | 7 | 294 | 3 |
| | | | 2 | 2 | 1 | 284 | 10 |
| | | 1 | 8 | 1 | | 320 | 4 |
| | | 6 | 7 | 2 | 18 | 348 | 10 |
| | | 2 | 2 | | 2 | 228 | 4 |
| | | 2 | 3 | 1 | 13 | 354 | 6 |
| | | 7 | 3 | | 4 | 272 | 6 |
| | | 1 | 4 | 2 | 4 | 89 | 10 |
| | | 3 | 7 | 1 | 17 | 232 | 10 |
| | | | 6 | 3 | 7 | 308 | 10 |
| | | 2 | 3 | 2 | 3 | 198 | 3 |
| | 2–0–17–0 | 2 | 6 | | 3 | 289 | 2 |
| | | 1 | 4 | | 5 | 268 | 10 |
| | | 10 | 6 | 1 | 9 | 324 | 10 |
| | | | | | | | |
| | | 2 | 6 | | 1 | 223 | 10 |
| | | 11 | 5 | | 7 | 333 | 10 |
| 1–0–3–0 — | 2–0–17–0 — | | | | | | |

endurance which yielded him the figures of 8/95.

Western Australia ensured that the final of the Sheffield Shield would be played on its own native heath with a slow-but-sure first-innings win over New South Wales in Sydney. Batting first, the home side aggregated 292, with opener McCosker recording 94, Rixon 66 and Dyson 52. Once again, the Western Australian reserve pace spearhead of Macleay and Graf did trojan work, sharing 7 wickets. When its turn to bat arrived, the visiting team made sure of 4 points with a 330-run stand between Graeme Wood and Geoff Marsh for the third wicket. Western Australia declared at 4/359, Marsh having notched 159 and the left-handed Wood remaining unbeaten on 173. New South Wales replied with a token 1/74 in its second innings.

The grand final of the 1983/84 Sheffield Shield competition in Perth was a memorable occasion. It was not only the deciding game of an important national trophy; it was also reputedly the last time that the august names of Greg Chappell, Rod Marsh and and Dennis Lillee would appear on the same first-class scorecard. All three had indicated that they would retire in some degree at the end of the season. Lillee marked his final match with Western Australia by winning the toss and asking Queensland to bat. It was a costly gamble. The northern batsmen exploited Perth's ideal conditions to compile a substantial 7/431 before declaring, Chappell, Courtice, Phillips, Smart and Kerr all exceeding the half-century mark. The home side began its reply late in the second day and never at any stage looked like taking charge of the contest. Slowly and surely, however, through the agency of a Geoff Marsh hundred and fifties from Laird and Wood, the local team edged its way to within 70 runs of the Queensland total. Then, at the psychological moment in Queensland's second innings, Lillee's bowlers struck, tumbling out their opposition in almost unseemly haste for only 154. Only Smart profferred any resistance as Macleay and Graf steamrollered a joint 7 wicket path through the opposition, leaving their side the comparatively simple task of scoring 223 for victory. Queensland skipper, Jeff Thomson – the taker of 5 Western Australian wickets in the first innings – made life as difficult as possible for the home batsmen before victory was achieved. He and off-spinner Graeme Whyte captured 5 of the 6 wickets to fall before the rubicon was crossed. Once again it was its consistency and depth which saw Western Australia past the winning post. Laird recorded a stalwart 54, Shipperd 41 and Marsh 45 in the local team's eventual winning score of 6/224. The greatest satisfaction which the Western Australian players derived from their ninth Sheffield Shield triumph was the realisation that it was an appropriate way in which to mark the end of Dennis Lillee's illustrious career for his state.

At the conclusion of the Sheffield Shield final, it was unclear whether Greg Chappell had retired from first-class cricket or not. Rumour had it that Chappell would retire if his side had won the premiership – and that when they did not, he may decide to make one more attempt on the championship in 1984/85. Rumour, however, is a notoriously unreliable source of information which, over the past year, has speculated on the possibility of Greg Chappell becoming either Lord Mayor of Brisbane or a parliamentarian in the Queensland House of Representatives. There is a far better chance of Chappell resuming the maroon cap of Queensland next summer than assuming public office.

# Victoria 1983–84
First Class Matches

| BATTING | v. New South Wales (Sydney) 28–31 October 1983 | | v. Tasmania (Melbourne) 11–14 Nov. 1983 | | v. Western Australia (Melbourne) 18–21 Nov. 1983 | | v. South Australia (Adelaide) 25–28 Nov. 1983 | | v. Pakistanis (Melbourne) 2–5 December 1983 | | v. Queensland (Brisbane) 9–12 Dec. 1983 | | v. Tasmania (Hobart) 30 December 1983–2 January 1984 | | v. Western Australia (Perth) 13–16 Jan 1984 | | v. New South Wales (Melbourne) 27–20 Jan. 1984 | | v. Queensland (Melbourne) 17–20 February 1984 | | v. South Australia (Melbourne) 24–27 February 1984 | |
|---|---|---|---|---|---|---|---|---|---|---|---|---|---|---|---|---|---|---|---|---|---|---|
| G.M. Watts | 3 | 4 | | | | | | | 45 | 41 | 31 | 40 | 10 | 4 | | | 0 | 0 | | | | |
| P.A. Hibbert | 6 | 46* | 20 | 83 | 56 | 4 | 3 | 25 | 83 | 41 | 13 | 61 | 0 | 26 | 11 | 95 | 68 | 16 | 163 | 37 | 75 | — |
| G.N. Yallop | 77 | 23 | | | 113 | 145* | | | 220 | — | | | | | | | | | | | | |
| D.M.J. Jones | 6 | 83* | 128 | 70 | 21 | 30 | 67 | 60 | 11 | — | 108 | 64 | 11 | 42 | 9 | 52 | | | | | | |
| W.G. Whiteside | | | 62 | 20* | 17 | — | 44 | 65 | 31 | 7* | 0 | 17 | 0 | 48 | 14 | 0 | | | | | 111 | — |
| M.D. Taylor | 14 | — | 172* | 74* | 39 | 58* | 4 | 122 | 101* | — | 146 | 44 | 6 | 12 | 0 | 31 | 29 | 77 | 32 | — | 49 | — |
| D.A. Emerson | | | | | | | | | — | 19* | 14 | 4 | 18 | 0 | 22 | 16 | 10 | 50 | 21* | — | | |
| R.J. Bright | 33 | — | — | — | 2 | — | 64 | — | — | — | 11 | 22* | 3 | 43 | 4 | 1 | 7 | 100* | — | — | 29 | — |
| P.A. Hyde | | | | | 0 | — | 2 | 38* | — | 21 | 5 | 43* | 7 | 24 | 17* | 4 | 9 | 32 | 0 | — | 39 | — |
| R.J. McCurdy | 2 | — | | | 3* | — | 0* | — | — | — | 0* | — | | | 6 | 15* | 0 | — | — | — | 55 | — |
| A.I.C. Dodemaide | | | | | | | 32 | 24* | 37* | — | 3 | 3 | 14 | 3 | 7 | 5 | 3 | 54* | — | — | | |
| J.M. Wiener | 0 | 2 | 8 | 37 | 0 | 23 | 5 | 9 | | | | | | | | | | | | | | |
| G.J. Miles | 42* | — | — | — | | | | | | | | | | | | | | | | | | |
| L.F. Balcam | 10 | — | 10 | — | 6 | — | | | | | | | 7 | 0* | | | | | | | | |
| M.G. Hughes | 15 | — | — | — | | | 8 | — | | | 5 | — | | | | | | | | | | |
| A. Wildsmith | | | 7* | — | | | 1 | 5 | | | | | | | | | | | | | | |
| S.P. Davis | | | — | — | 0 | — | | | | | | | 2* | 2 | 0 | 1 | 0* | — | — | — | 3* | — |
| M.B. Quinn | | | | | | | | | | | | | | | 54 | 37 | 54 | 28 | 14 | 51* | 73 | — |
| B.G. Moire | | | | | | | | | | | | | | | | | 8 | 2 | 4 | 6* | 6 | — |
| G.W. Richardson | | | | | | | | | | | | | | | | | | | 204* | — | 0 | — |
| S.P. O'Donnell | | | | | | | | | | | | | | | | | | | | | 130 | — |
| Byes | 7 | | | 1 | 4 | 12 | | 5 | 2 | 2 | 1 | 8 | 1 | 3 | 4 | 9 | 1 | 6 | 1 | | 3 | |
| Leg-byes | 8 | | 6 | 2 | 5 | 6 | 12 | 10 | 8 | 3 | 4 | 10 | 4 | 7 | 10 | 5 | 2 | 15 | 10 | 2 | 17 | |
| Wides | 1 | 4 | 1 | | | 2 | | 3 | 1 | | 2 | | 2 | 1 | 1 | | 2 | 3 | | | 1 | |
| No-balls | 3 | 3 | 4 | 7 | 10 | 8 | 6 | 1 | 16 | 2 | 10 | 6 | 4 | 17 | 2 | 1 | 10 | 13 | 14 | 3 | 18 | |
| Total | 227 | 165 | 418 | 294 | 276 | 288 | 248 | 367 | 555 | 136 | 353 | 322 | 89 | 232 | 161 | 272 | 203 | 396 | 463 | 99 | 609 | |
| Wickets | 10 | 3 | 5 | 3 | 10 | 3 | 10 | 6 | 5 | 3 | 10 | 7 | 10 | 10 | 10 | 10 | 10 | 7 | 5 | 1 | 10 | |
| Result | D | | D | | D | | D | | L | | W | | L | | L | | D | | D | | D | |
| Points | 0 | | 0 | | 0 | | 0 | | — | | 12 | | 0 | | 0 | | 0 | | 4 | | 4 | |

*Catches* 21 – P.A. Hyde (ct 19/st 2) 7 – D.M.J. Jones and W.G. Whiteside 6 – M.D. Taylor and R.J. Bright (inc. 2 as sub) 5 – D.A. Emerson and M.B. Quinn 4 – P.A. Hibbert and G.J. Miles 3 – R.J. McCurdy and J.M. Wien 2 – M.G. Hughes, G.M. Watts,

| BOWLING | R.J. McCurdy | A.I.C. Dodemaide | D.A. Emerson | R.J. Bright | W.G. Whiteside | L.F. Balcam | M.G. Hughes | J.M. Wiener | S.P. Davis |
|---|---|---|---|---|---|---|---|---|---|
| v. New South Wales (Sydney) | 23–3–102–0 | | | 34–8–100–2 | | 23–3–86–0 | 25–7–77–2 | 10–1–31–1 | |
| 28–31 October 1983 | | | | | | | | | |
| v. Tasmania (Melbourne) | | | | 38–11–98–2 | 13–2–35–2 | 22–3–79–2 | 20–1–92–0 | 9–3–26–1 | 34–5–101–1 |
| 11–14 November 1983 | | | | 11–2–28–1 | 4–1–13–0 | 8–2–32–1 | 5–2–11–0 | 2–1–7–0 | 11–1–46–2 |
| v. Western Australia (Melbourne) | 29–4–99–1 | | | 45–13–87–2 | 10–2–25–0 | 24–5–65–0 | | 18–0–62–0 | 36–6–93–1 |
| 18–21 November 1983 | | | | | | | | | |
| v. South Australia (Adelaide) | 27.3–3–91–3 | 32–9–63–4 | | 20–6–38–2 | 3–1–4–0 | | 21–6–68–1 | 3–0–14–0 | |
| 25–28 November 1983 | 15–6–37–1 | 14–4–47–2 | | 13–2–56–0 | 3–0–15–0 | | 12–2–34–0 | 3–0–10–0 | |
| v. Pakistanis (Melbourne) | 31.2–2–169–4 | 28–2–109–0 | 19–1–63–1 | 20–5–54–2 | 4–0–6–2 | | | | |
| 2–5 December 1983 | 14–0–92–0 | 6–0–43–0 | | 15–1–89–2 | 11–0–61–0 | | | | |
| v. Queensland (Brisbane) | 26–6–81–5 | 22.3–4–65–0 | 20–5–58–1 | 15–4–50–1 | 1–0–4–0 | | 19–2–95–2 | | |
| 9–12 December 1983 | 6–0–48–0 | 4–2–9–1 | 19–2–93–4 | 22–5–100–3 | | | 7–2–30–0 | | |
| v. Tasmania (Hobart) | | 20–5–54–2 | 9–1–22–0 | 9–2–32–0 | 1–1–0–0 | 25–5–91–1 | | | 30.2–7–104–7 |
| 30 Dec 1983–2 Jan. 1984 | | | | | | | | | |
| v. Western Australia (Perth) | 16–5–53–3 | 19–4–67–5 | 1–0–5–0 | | | | | | 20.1–4–57–2 |
| 13–16 January 1984 | 26.4–5–96–5 | 23–4–64–2 | 12–2–54–0 | 15–4–36–0 | | | | | 14–5–28–3 |
| v. New South Wales (Melbourne) | 20–1–114–0 | 34–3–106–3 | 15–4–56–1 | 26–5–62–0 | | | | | 23–2–88–0 |
| 27–30 January 1984 | | | | | | | | | |
| v. Queensland (Melbourne) | 19.4–3–83–3 | 26–4–79–4 | 13–1–43–0 | 18–5–43–1 | | | | | 24–7–60–2 |
| 17–20 February 1984 | 21–4–58–0 | 9–2–20–0 | 25–4–114–0 | 34–4–123–2 | | | | | 30–1–107–2 |
| v. South Australia (Melbourne) | 38–9–122–2 | | | 30–4–91–0 | 8–1–35–1 | | | | 38–4–125–0 |
| 24–27 February 1984 | | | | | 4–0–30–0 | | | | 9–1–45–0 |
| | 313.1–51–1245–27 *av.* 46.11 | 237.3–43–726–23 *av.* 31.56 | 133–20–508–7 *av.* 72.57 | 365–81–1087–20 *av.* 54.35 | 62–8–228–5 *av.* 45.60 | 102–18–353–4 *av.* 88.25 | 109–22–407–5 *av.* 81.40 | 45–5–150–2 *av.* 75.00 | 269.3–43–854–20 *av.* 42.70 |

a G.N. Yallop 1–0–2–0
b P.A. Hibbert 1–0–4–0
c G.W. Richardson 1–0–1–0
d G.W. Richardson 1–0–9–0
M.B. Quinn 1–0–4–0
e M.D. Taylor 2–0–13–0
B.G. Moir 2–0–6–0

| M | Inns | NOs | Runs | HS | Av |
|---|---|---|---|---|---|
| 5 | 10 | — | 178 | 45 | 17.80 |
| 11 | 21 | 1 | 932 | 163 | 46.60 |
| 3 | 5 | 1 | 578 | 220 | 144.50 |
| 8 | 15 | 1 | 762 | 128 | 54.42 |
| 8 | 14 | 2 | 436 | 111 | 36.33 |
| 11 | 18 | 4 | 1010 | 172* | 72.14 |
| 6 | 10 | 2 | 174 | 50 | 21.75 |
| 11 | 12 | 2 | 319 | 100* | 31.90 |
| 9 | 14 | 3 | 241 | 43* | 21.90 |
| 9 | 8 | 4 | 81 | 55 | 20.25 |
| 7 | 11 | 3 | 185 | 54* | 23.12 |
| 4 | 8 | — | 84 | 37 | 10.50 |
| 2 | 1 | 1 | 42 | 42* | — |
| 4 | 5 | 1 | 33 | 10 | 8.25 |
| 4 | 3 | — | 28 | 15 | 9.33 |
| 2 | 3 | 1 | 13 | 7* | 6.50 |
| 7 | 7 | 3 | 8 | 3* | 2.00 |
| 4 | 7 | 1 | 311 | 73 | 51.83 |
| 3 | 5 | 1 | 26 | 8 | 6.50 |
| 2 | 2 | 1 | 204 | 204* | 204.00 |
| 1 | 1 | — | 130 | 130 | 130.00 |

A.I.C. Dodemaide and G.W. Richardson L.F. Balcam and B.G. Moir
1 – G.N. Yallop, A. Wildsmith,

| A. Wildsmith | D.M.J. Jones | S.P. O'Donnell | Byes | Leg-byes | Wides | No-balls | Total | Wkts |
|---|---|---|---|---|---|---|---|---|
| | | | 7 | 6 | 1 | 14 | 409 | 5 |
| 4–2–4–0 | | | 7 | 8 | | 6 | 450 | 8 |
| | 2–0–7–0 | | | 1 | | | 145 | 4 |
| | 3–0–18–0 | | 7 | 6 | | 17 | 464 | 4a |
| | | | | 1 | | 14 | 279 | 10 |
| 4.1–1–10–1 | | | 5 | | | 5 | 218 | 5b |
| | | | | 5 | | 14 | 406 | 9 |
| | | | 1 | 2 | 2 | 4 | 288 | 3 |
| | | | | 1 | 2 | 13 | 354 | 9 |
| | | | 5 | 7 | 1 | 2 | 292 | 10 |
| | | | 9 | 11 | | 12 | 323 | 10 |
| | | | 1 | 1 | | 4 | 184 | 10 |
| | | | | 6 | | 9 | 284 | 10 |
| | | | 2 | 7 | 1 | 17 | 435 | 4 |
| | | | 5 | 5 | 1 | 12 | 318 | 10 |
| | | | 2 | 14 | | 1 | 439 | 5c |
| | | 32–5–118–4 | 6 | 10 | 5 | 13 | 520 | 7d |
| | | 4–3–2–0 | 1 | 4 | | 5 | 101 | 0e |
| 8.1–3–14–1 av. 14.00 | 5–0–25–0 — | 36–8–120–4 av. 30.00 | | | | | | |

## The McDonald's Cup 1983/84

If a limited-over game took place between a side which contained the names of international stars, Rod Marsh, Dennis Lillee, Graeme Wood, Bruce Laird and Ken MacLeay and another team which could not point to one regular Test player in its number, one would expect the latter eleven's chances of victory to be remote. Yet such are the vagaries of cricket that, in the 1983/84 McDonald's Cup Final, the Goliath of Western Australia with 7 international players in its ranks was humbled by the youthful South Australian David: a team with only three fairly irregular Australian representatives in its number.

Drawn in western pool of three teams, the side from Adelaide was extremely fortunate to graduate to the finals. It lost its first-round game in Perth to Western Australia by virtue of an inferior run-rate. The visitors reach 6/136 largely through the efforts of Wayne Phillips who scored 58 – and in spite of the efforts of the Player of the Match, Dennis Lillee. When the contest was prematurely called off, Western Australia were 3/112 in reply.

The redemption of South Australia's aspirations towards the hamburger championship came in the shape of an 8-wicket defeat of Victoria in Adelaide. The Melbourne team batted first and, boosted by a knock of 60 from Wiener, achieved a run-rate of just over 4 per over in its allotted 50 overs. Michael Haysman made light work of scoring the necessary runs. His commanding innings of 92 enabled the home side to pass the Victorian total with only 2 wickets down.

South Australia's triumph over Victoria decided the semi-finalists from the western division – for Victoria had previously been vanquished by Western Australia by 3 wickets in October. Hughes' men had a close call in a high scoring game. Victoria gave the home side 234 runs to chase, with Yallop compiling a quick-fire 91 and Wiener 74. Western Australia overhauled the visitors' total with 3 wickets to spare. Valetta, the Man of the Match, notched 67 and won his title narrowly from Greg Shipperd who contributed 60.

The southern pool of the competition was contested between Queensland, New South Wales and Tasmania and developed into an intriguing struggle. Tasmania upset the apple-cart in the first game by defeating the strongly-fanced Queensland by 8/237 to 194. Boon was Tasmania's hero with a confident innings of 94: a performance which earned him the individual honours in the game on the unanimous verdict of the judges.

Border's Queenslanders set the competition on an even keel by accounting for New South Wales by 1 run: 6/166 to 165. Wessel's knock of 71 proved to be the decisive influence in the Brisbane team's success and was recognised as such by the assessors of individual contributions to the game.

It was New South Wales who put the cat amongst the pigeons, when it scored 7/237 in Launceston and proceeded to dismiss 9 of the locals for 166. The corollary of this Toohey-dominated game was that each of the teams in the southern division had won one game and the semi-finalists were decided on their superior run-rate. Surprisingly, Queensland was eliminated and the penultimate rounds of the competition were fought out between New South Wales, Western Australia, Tasmania and South Australia.

In spite of enjoying a home-ground advantage, New South

## Western Australia 1983–84
First Class Matches

| BATTING | *v.* New South Wales (Perth) 21–24 October 1983 | | *v.* Pakistanis (Perth) 4–7 November 1983 | | *v.* Victoria (Melbourne) 18–21 Nov. 1983 | | *v. Tasmania* (Perth) 25–28 Nov. 1983 | | *v. South Australia* (Adelaide) 2–5 December 1983 | | *v.* Queensland (perth) 16–19 Dec. 1983 | | *v. South Australia* (Perth) 6–9 January 1984 | | *v. Victoria* (Perth) 13–16 January 1984 | | *v.* Queensland (Brisbane) 27–30 January 1984 | | *v.* Tasmania (Launceston) 17–20 February 1984 | | *v. New South Wales* (Sydney) 24–27 February 1984 | | *v.* Queensland (Perth) | |
|---|---|---|---|---|---|---|---|---|---|---|---|---|---|---|---|---|---|---|---|---|---|---|---|---|
| B.M. Laird | 66 | — | 5 | 17 | 15 | — | 57 | 32* | 43 | 64 | 0 | 75* | 19 | 27 | 26 | 16 | 58 | 66* | 0 | — | 3 | — | | |
| G.M. Wood | 23 | — | 74 | 3 | 82 | — | 14 | 167* | 24 | — | 10 | 12 | 35 | — | 0 | 44 | 0 | 51 | 0 | — | 173* | — | | |
| G. Shipperd | 96 | — | 28 | — | 167* | — | 80 | 0 | 8 | 70* | 67 | 4 | 72 | 78* | 4 | 9 | 8 | 8 | 48 | — | 2 | — | | |
| K.J. Hughes | 129 | — | 32 | 47 | 13 | — | | | 73 | 33 | 35 | 130 | | | | | | | | | | | | |
| M.R.J. Veletta | 16 | — | 35 | 9* | 0 | — | 8 | 21 | 12 | 20 | 38 | 24 | 64 | 82 | 25 | 23 | 27 | 3 | 10 | — | | | | |
| R.W. Marsh | 35 | — | 44 | 21* | 157* | — | | | 29 | 18 | 4 | 2 | | | | | | | 23 | — | — | — | | |
| K.H. Macleay | 15 | — | 12 | 82 | — | — | 23 | — | 23 | 5* | 13 | 5 | 67 | — | | | 23 | — | 0 | — | 0* | — | | |
| T.G. Hogan | 3 | — | 19 | — | — | — | | | 0 | — | 6 | 0 | 25 | — | 33* | 0 | | | | | | | | |
| D.K. Lillee | 6* | — | 1 | — | — | — | | | 2* | — | 16 | 4 | | | 3 | 5 | 0 | — | | | | | | |
| S.F. Graf | 17 | — | 54 | — | — | — | 43 | — | 40 | 3 | 1 | 15 | | | 34 | 73 | 74 | 31* | 4 | — | — | — | | |
| W.M. Clark | 9* | — | | | | | | | | | | | | | | | | | | | | | | |
| T.M. Alderman | | | 11* | — | | | 0 | — | 1 | — | 8* | 4* | 0* | — | 0 | 1* | 3* | — | | | | | | |
| S.C. Clements | | | | | | | 18 | 67 | | | | | 2 | 73 | 31 | 64 | 24 | 10 | 151 | — | 6 | — | | |
| W.S. Andrews | | | | | | | 2 | 23 | | | | | 23 | 22* | 14 | 27 | | | | | | | | |
| W.D. Hill | | | | | | | 31* | — | | | | | 10 | — | 8 | 7 | 1 | — | | | | | | |
| B. Mulder | | | | | — | — | 3 | — | | | | | | | | | | | | | | | | |
| D.L. Boyd | | | | | | | | | | | | | 2 | — | | | | | 27 | — | — | — | | |
| A.L. Mann | | | | | | | | | | | | | | | | | 3 | — | 27* | — | — | — | | |
| S.J. Milosz | | | | | | | | | | | | | | | | | | | 8 | — | — | — | | |
| G.R. Marsh | | | | | | | | | | | | | | | | | | | | | 159 | — | | |
| Byes | 8 | | 6 | | 7 | | | 1 | | | 6 | 3 | | 3 | 1 | | 1 | 1 | 10 | | 5 | | | |
| Leg-byes | 5 | | 15 | 7 | 6 | | 2 | 8 | 9 | 2 | 4 | 9 | 2 | 2 | 1 | 6 | 9 | 7 | 6 | | 4 | | | |
| Wides | 5 | | 8 | | | | 2 | 1 | | 3 | 1 | 6 | | 1 | | | 1 | 1 | 1 | | | | | |
| No-balls | 6 | | 5 | 1 | 17 | | 1 | | 4 | 1 | 26 | 18 | 7 | 2 | 4 | 9 | 8 | 14 | 9 | | 7 | | | |
| Total | 439 | | 349 | 187 | 464 | | 284 | 320 | 268 | 219 | 235 | 311 | 328 | 290 | 184 | 284 | 240 | 192 | 324 | | 359 | | | |
| Wickets | 9 | | 10 | 4 | 4 | | 10 | 4 | 10 | 5 | 10 | 9 | 10 | 3 | 10 | 10 | 10 | 4 | 10 | | 4 | | | |
| Result | W | | W | | D | | W | | W | | D | | D | | W | | D | | D | | D | | | |
| Points | 16 | | — | | 4 | | 12 | | 12 | | 0 | | 4 | | 16 | | 4 | | 4 | | 4 | | | |

*Catches* 38 – R.W. Marsh (ct 33/st 5)
15 – T.M. Alderman and W.D. Hill
12 – B.M. Laird
10 – S.F. Graf
8 – G. Shipperd
7 – S.C. Clements
6 – G.M. Wood and K.H. Macleay
3 – T.G. Hogan and D.K. Lillee
2 – K.J. Hughes, A.L. Mann and D.L. Boyd (inc. 1 as sub)
1 – M.R.J. Veletta and S.J. Milosz

| BOWLING | D.K. Lillee | S.F. Graf | K.H. Macleay | T.G. Hogan | W.M. Clark | T.M. Alderman | W.S. Andrews | B. Mulder | S.C. Clements |
|---|---|---|---|---|---|---|---|---|---|
| *v.* New South Wales (Perth) | 16.4–5–39–3 | 16–0–55–3 | 10–2–22–0 | 10–4–17–2 | 6–2–15–0 | | | | |
| 21–24 October 1983 | 30.5–12–62–6 | 4–0–14–0 | 15–6–18–1 | 31–10–62–2 | 18–4–49–0 | | | | |
| *v.* Pakistanis (Perth) | 22–5–55–3 | 16–1–61–2 | 26.3–8–50–4 | 11–2–34–0 | | 23–4–85–1 | | | |
| 4–7 November 1983 | 25–5–58–3 | 15–2–54–2 | 24.4–6–69–3 | 12–5–33–1 | | 6–2–24–0 | | | |
| *v.* Victoria (Melbourne) | 26–5–75–4 | 14.5–3–34–1 | 1–0–3–0 | 38–5–91–3 | | | | 30–10–64–2 | |
| 18–21 November 1983 | 22–6–38–1 | 7–1–32–0 | 18–7–28–1 | 39–11–107–1 | | | | 20–7–56–0 | |
| *v.* Tasmania (Perth) | | 24–7–87–2 | 23–9–55–1 | | | 26.3–10–56–4 | 6–1–18–0 | 20–3–74–1 | |
| 26–28 November 1983 | | 27–5–73–1 | 30–3–95–3 | | | 24–3–82–1 | 3–0–15–0 | 12–3–30–0 | |
| *v.* South Australia (Adelaide) | 27.3–8–58–3 | 12–1–62–0 | 20–8–43–2 | 28–9–67–3 | | 33–6–70–1 | | | |
| 2–5 December 1983 | 26–4–53–2 | 11–2–24–2 | | 34–14–70–2 | | 20.5–6–33–3 | | | |
| *v.* Queensland (Perth) | 26–4–80–2 | 9–1–25–0 | 23–7–62–3 | 15–4–43–1 | | 22.1–6–74–4 | | | |
| 16–19 December 1983 | 21–4–56–1 | 17–2–64–0 | 23–3–86–0 | 18–5–48–1 | | 19–3–62–3 | | | |
| *v.* South Australia (Perth) | | | 20–4–58–2 | 30–12–69–3 | | 29–5–74–3 | 4–4–0–1 | | |
| 6–9 January 1984 | | | 7–3–14–1 | 21–9–30–1 | | 7–2–15–0 | 11–1–40–1 | | |
| *v.* Victoria (Perth) | 19.4–5–46–1 | 24–12–35–3 | | 24–9–31–5 | | 18–6–35–1 | 1–1–0–0 | | |
| 13–16 January 1984 | 28.4–7–63–5 | 31–13–57–0 | | 18–3–52–0 | | 35–12–79–5 | 2–1–7–0 | | |
| *v.* Queensland (Brisbane) | 24–8–46–3 | 16–3–48–2 | 19–2–71–1 | | | 24–8–41–4 | | | |
| 27–30 January 1984 | 5–4–1–0 | | 4–2–3–1 | | | 6–1–28–0 | | | 1–0–4–0 |
| *v.* Tasmania (Launceston) | | 28–10–57–2 | 18–3–38–2 | | | | | | |
| 17–20 February 1984 | | 13–2–36–3 | 5–0–27–0 | | | | | | |
| *v.* New South Wales | | 24–8–70–3 | 36–10–90–4 | | | | | | 4–0–15–0 |
| 24–27 February 1984 | | 6–0–15–0 | | | | | | | |
| *v.* Queensland (Perth) | 48–8–116–1 | 42–5–111–3 | 52–13–115–2 | | | | | | |
| 9–13 March 1984 | 12–2–34–1 | 18.2–6–34–3 | 21–3–58–4 | | | | | | |
| | 380.2–92–880–39 *av.* 22.56 | 375.1–84–1048–32 *av.* 32.75 | 396.1–99–1005–35 *av.* 28.71 | 329–102–754–25 *av.* 30.16 | 24–6–64–0 — | 293.3–74–758–30 *av.* 25.26 | 27–8–80–2 *av.* 40.00 | 82–23–224–3 *av.* 74.66 | 5–0–19–0 — |

a K.J. Hughes 1–0–4–0, B.M. Laird 1–0–4–0, M.R.J. Veletta 1–0–1–0  b G.M. Wood 1–0–5–0
c W.D. Hill 1–1–0–0  d R.W. Marsh 4–0–7–0  e B.M. Laird 1–0–2–0

| | | M | Inns | NOs | Runs | HS | Av |
|---|---|---|---|---|---|---|---|
| 63 | 54* | 12 | 20 | 4 | 706 | 75* | 44.12 |
| 53 | 13 | 12 | 18 | 2 | 778 | 173* | 48.62 |
| 21 | 41 | 12 | 19 | 3 | 811 | 167* | 46.81 |
| | | 5 | 8 | — | 492 | 130 | 61.50 |
| 12 | 0 | 11 | 19 | 1 | 429 | 82 | 23.83 |
| 7 | 45 | 8 | 11 | 2 | 385 | 157* | 42.77 |
| 21 | — | 11 | 13 | 2 | 289 | 82 | 26.27 |
| | | 7 | 8 | 1 | 86 | 33* | 12.28 |
| 18 | — | 8 | 9 | 2 | 55 | 18 | 7.85 |
| 14 | 17* | 11 | 14 | 2 | 420 | 74 | 35.00 |
| | | 1 | 1 | 1 | 9 | 9* | — |
| | | 7 | 9 | 6 | 28 | 11* | 9.33 |
| 6 | 28 | 7 | 12 | — | 480 | 151 | 40.00 |
| | | 3 | 6 | 1 | 111 | 27 | 22.20 |
| | | 4 | 5 | 1 | 57 | 31* | 14.25 |
| | | 2 | 1 | — | 3 | 3 | 3.00 |
| | | 3 | 2 | — | 29 | 27 | 14.50 |
| | | 3 | 2 | 1 | 30 | 27* | 30.00 |
| 0* | — | 3 | 2 | 1 | 8 | 8 | 8.00 |
| 107 | 0 | 2 | 3 | — | 266 | 159 | 88.66 |
| 5 | 5 | | | | | | |
| 6 | 10 | | | | | | |
| 4 | 2 | | | | | | |
| 26 | 9 | | | | | | |
| 363 | 224 | | | | | | |
| 10 | 6 | | | | | | |
| W | | | | | | | |
| — | | | | | | | |

| D.L. Boyd | A.L. Mann | S.J. Milosz | Byes | Leg-byes | Wides | No-balls | Total | Wkts |
|---|---|---|---|---|---|---|---|---|
| | | | | 8 | 2 | 4 | 156 | 10 |
| | | | | 8 | | 5 | 213 | 10 |
| | | | | 5 | 3 | | 290 | 10 |
| | | | | 4 | 3 | 3 | 242 | 10 |
| | | | 4 | 5 | | 10 | 276 | 10 |
| | | | 12 | 6 | 2 | 8 | 288 | 3a |
| | | | 2 | 8 | 5 | 20 | 300 | 10 |
| | | | 1 | 1 | 1 | 2 | 302 | 6b |
| | | | | 3 | 5 | 10 | 303 | 10 |
| | | | 1 | 1 | | 2 | 182 | 10 |
| | | | | 11 | 1 | 5 | 295 | 10 |
| | | | 1 | 4 | 1 | 3 | 321 | 5 |
| 23–7–45–1 | | | 19 | 3 | | 7 | 268 | 10 |
| 11–2–38–0 | | | | 3 | 1 | 6 | 140 | 3 |
| | | | 4 | 10 | 1 | 2 | 161 | 10 |
| | | | 9 | 5 | | 1 | 272 | 10 |
| | 7–2–15–0 | | 1 | 7 | 4 | 6 | 229 | 10 |
| | 5–4–1–0 | | 1 | | | 2 | 38 | 1c |
| 13–2–52–1 | 30–10–71–3 | 30.2–5–72–2 | 5 | 2 | | 7 | 297 | 10 |
| 8–0–30–0 | 10–2–14–2 | 20–7–44–1 | 4 | 6 | 1 | 3 | 161 | 6 |
| 23.2–6–51–2 | 3–0–15–0 | 15–2–39–1 | 3 | 9 | | 8 | 292 | 10 |
| 7–1–27–1 | 4–1–8–0 | 8–4–16–0 | | | | | 74 | 1d |
| | | 26–4–78–1 | 2 | 7 | 4 | 9 | 431 | 7e |
| | | 9–3–24–1 | | 4 | 1 | 5 | 154 | 10 |
| 85.2–18–243–5 *av.* 48.60 | 59–19–124–5 *av.* 24.80 | 108.2–25–273–6 *av.* 45.50 | | | | | | |

Wales were outclassed in its semi-final by Western Australia. Valetta and Shipperd once more displayed their one-day expertise by recording scores of 83 and 67 in the Perth side's winning score of 5/230. In replay Wellham's men could only muster 184: a total to which Wellham himself contributed 64.

In Launceston, South Australia won its way into the final by dismissing Woolley's Taswegians for 163 before replying with 5/167. For South Australia Haysman scored 54 and Brinsley took 4/45; but astonishingly, it was Rodney Hogg who won the Man of the Match Award with his economical fast bowling performance which produced 1 wicket and only 10 runs in his 10 overs. Hogg's winning of the title was significant since it clearly indicates that the criterion for bowling effectiveness in limited-over games is now not the taking of wickets but the restriction of runs.

Western Australia entered the McDonald's Cup Final in a supremely confident mood. It was inconceivable that its young South Australian opponents, denuded of all of their Test players, could mount a serious challenge to the experienced Perth team. Lillee's men approached the contest in a relaxed frame of mind – so relaxed in fact that before their bowlers buckled down to their task, openers Bishop and Hilditch had posted 63 on the scoreboard for the first wicket. Hayman's stay at the crease was not long. It was rather the left-handed O'Connor who proved to be the thorn in the side of Western Australia. He combined first with Sleep to add 67 for the fourth wicket – and subsequently with Brinsley to advance the South Australian score to 240. At the fiftieth over, O'Connor was 94 not out, South Australia was 6/256 and Western Australia was in a state of shock and unexpected apprehension.

The favourites began their reply badly when Clements played the gentle medium-pacer, Brinsley on to his wicket. Wood, Shipperd, and Geoff Marsh thereupon laid the foundations of 3 substantial innings but failed to go on with the job. In desperation the tail-end hitter, Boyd, was elevated in the order to quicken the scoring but discovered to his cost that one could not swing indiscriminately at the accurate Carmichael. Marsh alone struck out bravely and successfully and was rewarded with a half-century. When he was caught at deep mid-on, however, the end was in sight for Western Australia. Graf's undefeated 37 took his side to the very brink of victory – but the overs ran out, and South Australia won by 8 runs.

It was fitting that the young South Australian team should carry off the honours in the McDonald's Cup Competition. The 1983/84 season in Australia was The Year of the Youngster. At state level, selectors opened wide the door to youth in almost unprecedented fashion. The retirement of Greg Chappell, Rod Marsh and Dennis Lillee, marked the end of an era and the final demise of the talented Australian cabal of players established by Ian Chappell in the 1970s. It was a turbulent and, at times, a distinctly distasteful epoch. Now it is at an end and the 'situations vacant' sign hangs on the door of the Australian dressing room. There is abundant natural talent in the ranks of the emergent Australian players. They possess innate ability but, on the evidence of the 1984 tour of the West Indies, lack the wisdom which springs from a combination of knowledge and experience. The getting of wisdom takes time and will fully occupy the attention of Australia's elite young cricketers for the next few years.

SECTION C

# Year of Triumph

The season in New Zealand. Shell Cup and Shell Trophy.
England's tour of New Zealand.
Don Cameron's review of the season.

*Hero's welcome. Man-of-all-seasons Richard Hadlee leaves the field after New Zealand's historic victory at Christchurch in the second Test match. (Adrian Murrell)*

## Shell Trophy

***15, 16 and 17 December 1983***

***at Whangerei***

**Northern Districts** 363 (C.M. Presland 97 not out, C.W. Dickeson 59, G.P. Howarth 57, B.L. Cairns 53, D.A. Stirling 5 for 101) and 178 for 6 dec (L.M. Crocker 96)
**Central Districts** 284 (M.D. Crowe 119, I.D.S. Smith 79, B.L. Cairns 4 for 64) and 197 for 8 (I.R. Snook 52, C.W. Dickeson 4 for 54)

*Match drawn*
*Northern Districts 4 pts, Central Districts 0 pts*

The New Zealand season began a little earlier than usual, and the first day was a generally dour affair. John Wiltshire asked Northern to bat first on a wicket of variable bounce, but the home side, missing the injured John Wright, lunched well at 100 for 1. The pace trio of Gill, Stirling and Robertson brought about a collapse in the afternoon which saw Northern slump to 199 for 7 at tea in spite of Cairns' innings of 53 off 61 balls. Presland and Dickeson batted throughout the last session and next morning took their stand to a record 143. Presland was desperately unlucky to be left short of a maiden century, but the home side could still rejoice as Central slipped to 22 for 4.

Martin Crowe played splendidly for 256 minutes and reached the ninth century of his career. He was given good support by Wiltshire and particularly by Ian Smith who reached his fifty off 41 deliveries and played some sparkling cricket.

Under a dark sky and with a stoppage for rain, Northern scored briskly and Howarth set Central to make 255 in 188 minutes in much brighter weather. They began slowly, but when they increased the tempo wickets began to fall to the spin of Howarth and Dickeson, and in the end Briasco and Toynbee held out for 40 minutes to save the game.

*Martin Crowe began the season in fine style. (Adrian Murrell)*

## Shell Cup

***18 December 1983***

***at Whangerei***

**Central Districts** 163 (M.D. Crowe 101 not out)
**Northern Districts** 167 for 3 (G.P. Howarth 68)

*Northern Districts won by 7 wickets*

A second fine hundred in three days from Martin Crowe was insufficient to pose too many problems for Northern who, led by Geoff Howarth's brisk knock, won with 15 overs to spare.

***26 December 1983***

***at Tauranga***

**Northern Districts** 146 for 9
**Wellington** 148 for 7 (J.V. Coney 59, E.J. Gray 52)

*Wellington won by 3 wickets*

***at Christchurch***

**Auckland** 182 for 9 (M.J. Greatbatch 75)
**Canterbury** 182 for 7

*Canterbury won on losing fewer wickets with scores level*

***at Napier***

**Central Districts** 245 for 7 (J.R. Wiltshire 83, I.R. Snook 65)
**Otago** 162 (R.N. Hoskin 61, D.R. O'Sullivan 4 for 22, D.A. Stirling 4 for 30)

*Central Districts won by 83 runs*

In the first complete round of Shell Cup matches Canterbury owed their narrow victory to David Stead who followed his 3 for 30 with an innings of 33 not out which clinched the game by the narrowest of margins.

In spite of some impressive bowling by Lance Cairns, who took 3 for 12, Wellington won comfortably enough against Northern Districts for whom Lindsay Crocker was top scorer with 44. Evan Gray's 3 for 22 and 52 at a crucial time made him undisputed Man of the Match.

Ian Snook and John Wiltshire led Central Districts to an impressive total, but a stand of 101 between Richard Hoskin and Bruce Blair, who made 47, suggested a surprise victory for Otago. The advent of O'Sullivan and Stirling brought about a collapse, however, and the home side won with ease.

## Shell Trophy

***27, 28 and 29 December 1983***

***at Tauranga***

**Northern Districts** 242 (L.M. Crocker 79, E.J. Gray 5 for 36) and 192 (E.J. Gray 4 for 61)

**Wellington** 263 (C.W. Dickeson 5 for 45) and 91 for 5

*Match drawn*
*Wellington 4 pts, Northern Districts 0 pts*

***at Napier***

**Otago** 322 (D.J. Walker 113, S.J. McCullum 53, D.R. O'Sullivan 4 for 100) and 230 (W.K. Lees 60, D.R. O'Sullivan 4 for 89)
**Central Districts** 289 (J.R. Wiltshire 72, R.E. Hayward 51, S.L. Boock 4 for 65)

*Match drawn*
*Otago 4 pts, Central Districts 0 pts*

***at Christchurch***

**Canterbury** 324 (R.J. Hadlee 93, P.E. McEwan 80, D.R. Hadlee 69, G.B. Troup 4 for 88)
**Auckland** 98 (C.H. Thiele 4 for 36) and 211 (T.J. Franklin 57, P.N. Webb 56, D.R. Hadlee 4 for 44, D.W. Stead 4 for 61)

*Canterbury won by an innings and 12 runs*
*Canterbury 16 pts, Auckland 0 pts*

Wellington had by far the better of the encounter at Tauranga, emphasising the superiority that they had shown in the Shell Cup. The game was destined to be a first innings contest after Northern had taken over six hours to make 242. Crocker played by far the best innings, he alone showing the necessary footwork to deal with the dangerous Gray. Wellington closed the second day at 227 for 8, but Pigott and Grant Cederwall snatched the points next morning. Eventually the visitors were asked to make 172 in just over two hours, but the sides settled for a draw with two overs of the last 20 remaining.

*Neill Mallender performed impressively for Otago throughout the season. (George Herringshaw)*

At McLean Park, Napier, Otago were 143 for 6 when Derek Walker, not selected for the side in 1982–83, joined Dawson. They added 83 and then Walker and Mallender put on 60. Boock helped in a ninth wicket stand of 33 which ended when Walker was bowled by O'Sullivan. He had hit 113, a maiden first-class hundred, a just reward for a busy cricketer who has worked hard at his game and has played for Worcestershire second eleven. It seemed, however, that Central Districts would still snatch a lead through the positive batting of Wiltshire and Hayward, but Stephen Boock bowled quite magnificently taking 4 for 65 in 46.2 overs as well as bringing off memorable catches to dismiss Hayward and Robertson, and Otago led by 33. Warren Less chose to let Otago bat throughout the last day and the game fizzled to a draw.

Canterbury were 149 for 7, the last wickets having gone for 45 runs, when Richard and Dayle Hadlee came together in a stand of 166 which beat a sixty-three-year old Canterbury record. Paul McEwan had played with great confidence earlier, but it was the Hadlees, each of whom batted for three hours, who took the honours. Richard hit a six and fifteen fours; Dayle hit nine fours. Richard Hadlee continued his magnificent form on to the second day, taking 3 for 14 and making three splendid catches as Auckland were routed. Rain prevented play after mid-afternoon, but Canterbury, with Dayle Hadlee's medium pace and David Stead's leg-spin decisive, completed a fine win on the last day.

## Shell Trophy

***31 December 1983, 1 and 2 January 1984***

***at Alexandra***

**Auckland** 302 (T.J. Franklin 106, M.C. Sneddon 64 not out) and 194 (J.J. Crowe 85, S.L. Boock 4 for 59, N.A. Mallender 4 for 66)
**Otago** 278 (R.N. Hoskin 105, S.J. McCullum 57, G.J. Dawson 55) and 219 for 4 (K.R. Rutherford 77, B.R. Blair 50)

*Otago won by 6 wickets*
*Otago 12 pts, Auckland 4 pts*

***at Christchurch***

**Northern Districts** 170 (J.M. Parker 58) and 104 (R.J. Hadlee 4 for 14, D.R. Hadlee 4 for 39)
**Canterbury** 175 (P.E. McEwan 51, C.M. Presland 5 for 49) and 103 for 5 (B.P. Bracewell 4 for 23)

*Canterbury won by 5 wickets*
*Canterbury 16 pts, Northern Districts 0 pts*

***at Wellington***

**Central Districts** 151 (A.C.S. Pigott 4 for 39) and 237 (R.E. Hayward 55, E.J. Gray 4 for 54)
**Wellington** 360 (R.W. Ormiston 104 not out, B.A. Edgar 71, G.N. Cederwall 68) and 29 for 1

*Wellington won by 9 wickets*
*Wellington 16 pts, Central Districts 0 pts*

Otago made a remarkable recovery to beat Auckland at Alexandra. Franklin batted 358 minutes for his century on the first day, and with Martin Snedden taking 151 balls for his 64 not out, Auckland seemed in a strong position. Hoskin and McCullum, in a second wicket stand of 109, gave Otago some hope of first innings points, but only Dawson of the later batsmen played with any authority and they trailed by 83. The slow left-arm of Boock and the medium pace of Mallender disconcerted Auckland's second innings and with Lees in good form behind the stumps, Otago found themselves with a chance of victory in spite of Jeff Crowe's well struck 85 off 121 deliveries. Otago began their task of scoring 219 to win shortly before lunch on the last day and were well served by McCullum and Rutherford who put on 64 in 78 minutes. Hoskin was run out for 1, but Bruce Blair batted well and victory came just after 6.00 when Andrew Jones, in his first Shell Trophy match, swept John Bracewell for 2.

On a pitch which offered bowlers considerable assistance Canterbury gained their second victory when they beat Northern Districts inside two days at Christchurch. The Hadlee brothers were again in devastating form after John Parker played by far the best innings of the first day. McEwan also played well, but Canterbury, needing 100 to win, were 40 for 5 in their second innings when Richard Hadlee joined Leggat. He hit 35 not out and, understandably, was named Man of the Match.

The excellent bowling of Tony Pigott (4 for 39 in 17 overs) was almost frittered away when Wellington were 9 for 3, recovering to 47 for 3 by the close of the first day. Gray left at 87 on the second morning, but Edgar batted with great determination and, using his innings as a firm foundation, Ormiston and Grant Cederwall carried the champions to a commanding position. 209 behind on the first innings, Central closed at 33 for 1 and were 100 for 5 at lunch on the last day. They batted stubbornly in the afternoon, but Gray dismissed Hart, Martin Crowe and Wiltshire as 7 runs were scored and Wellington's victory was assured.

*2 January 1984*

*at Lautoka, Fiji*

**England XI** 274 for 6 (M.W. Gatting 142)
**Fiji President's XI** 76 (N.G.B. Cook 4 for 9)

*England XI won by 198 runs*

*3 January 1984*

*at Suva, Fiji*

**England XI** 146 for 9
**Fiji President's XI** 128 (N.G.B. Cook 4 for 20)

*England XI won by 18 runs*

England played two matches in Fiji on their way to New Zealand. Nick Cook performed well in both. Foster had to bowl off a full run to save England from embarrassment in the second match when the home side's excitement and nerves got the better of them as victory beckoned.

## Shell Cup

*3 January 1984*

*at Alexandra*

**Otago** 186
**Auckland** 191 for 2 (J.F. Reid 69 not out, M.C. Sneddon 55)

*Auckland won by 8 wickets*

*at Christchurch*

**Northern Districts** 180 (C.H. Thiele 4 for 37)
**Canterbury** 181 for 5 (R.T. Latham 71, P.E. McEwan 57)

*Canterbury won by 5 wickets*

*at Wellington*

**Wellington** 134 (D.A. Stirling 4 for 19)
**Central Districts** 135 for 2 (M.D. Crowe 65 not out)

*Central Districts won by 8 wickets*

After the second complete round of matches the Shell Cup remained very open with only Otago pointless. Martin Snedden confirmed his all-round quality with 55 as an opener at Alexandra where Auckland won with just under six overs to spare. Canterbury won with as much time to spare at Christchurch. Lindsay Crocker was again top scorer for Northern with 42, but few others could cope with medium-paced Craig Thiele. A second wicket stand of 112 between Latham and McEwan set the home side on the way to an easy win.

At Basin Reserve, Martin Crowe turned in a splendid all-round performance. He took 3 for 24 as he and Stirling destroyed the home side who offered little resistance after Edgar had gone for 46, and then he led them to a comfortable success with an unbeaten 65.

## Shell Trophy

*5, 6 and 7 January 1984*

*at Dunedin*

**Northern Districts** 229 (G.P. Howarth 80, D.J. Walker 4 for 50) and 339 for 7 dec (A.D.G. Roberts 73 not out, G.P. Howarth 62, S.L. Boock 4 for 144)
**Otago** 318 for 5 dec (S.J. McCullum 121, G.J. Dawson 77) and 151 for 6

*Match drawn*
*Otago 4 pts, Northern Districts 0 pts*

*at Wellington*

**Wellington** 300 (B.A. Edgar 105, R.W. Ormiston 55, C.H. Thiele 5 for 80) and 224 for 4 dec (E.J. Gray 103 not out)
**Canterbury** 297 (P.E. McEwan 114, V.R. Brown 64, E.J. Chatfield 5 for 81) and 15 for 0

*Match drawn*
*Wellington 4 pts, Canterbury 0 pts*

A rain-shortened first day at Dunedin ended with Northern on 161 for 4. Howarth, twice missed, opened the visitors' innings and hit 80 off 107 deliveries. The innings closed at 229 the next day and Otago were in deep trouble at 17 for 3. There then came a thrilling counter-offensive by the two diminutive left-handers, Dawson and McCullum. They added 206, an Otago fourth wicket record, in 132 minutes of brilliant batting. McCullum's 121, with three sixes and sixteen fours, came off 142 balls, and Dawson faced 98 balls. The rest was anti-climax as Northern set Otago to make 251 in well under 3 hours. The game ended in a draw and Northern ended their South Island tour pointless.

The meeting of the giants at Basin Reserve saw Canterbury handicapped by the absence of the injured Richard Hadlee. Bruce Edgar hit a stabilising $5\frac{1}{2}$ hour century on the opening day which took Wellington to a strong position. On a second day curtailed by bad light, Paul McEwan, who hit a career best, and Vaughan Brown added 134 for Canterbury's third wicket in 116 minutes and gave their side every chance

*John Bracewell, Auckland and New Zealand off-break bowler, who shattered England by scoring a maiden century against them in the first match of the tour. (Adrian Murrell)*

of taking first innings points. Dayle Hadlee and Craig Thiele almost secured them on the last morning, but Thiele was caught at slip by Coney off Chatfield, so giving the bowler 5 wickets in an innings for the twenty-first time and Wellington 4 points. Evan Gray hit his third first-class hundred in just over three hours, but the game was destined to be drawn, leaving Canterbury 8 points ahead of Wellington at the top of the table with Otago 4 points behind the champions in third place.

***7, 8 and 9 January 1984***

***at Auckland***

**England XI** 220 (D.I. Gower 84, M.W. Gatting 56, M.C. Snedden 6 for 70) and 321 (R.W. Taylor 86, M.W. Gatting 64)
**Auckland** 282 for 8 dec (J.G. Bracewell 104 not out) and 58 for 1

*Match drawn*

After two pleasant social games in Fiji England started the serious part of their tour with a narrow escape against Auckland. A graceful Gower innings had been the highlight of a moderate first day in which Martin Snedden had revealed his best form. With the home side 109 for 5 at the close, England seemed well placed, but a remarkable maiden century by John Bracewell on the second day transformed the match. He survived a couple of chances but played with great panache and reached his hundred with a six. He also hit thirteen fours in his innings which lasted for 153 deliveries. Auckland led by 63 and with England 105 for 4 at the end of the day, a shock result seemed highly probable. Taylor and Gatting, the overnight batsmen, played with great good sense, however, and the game was saved. Taylor was at his dignified professional best. Gatting was all tenacity and a few lusty blows from Botham enlightened the day.

## Shell Cup

***8 January 1984***

***at Oamuru***

**Otago** 229 (B.R. Blair 89)
**Northern Districts** 122 (D.J. Walker 4 for 22)

*Otago won by 107 runs*

***at Wellington***

**Wellington** 205 for 7 (B.A. Edgar 93 not out)
**Canterbury** 174 (R.T. Latham 67, E.J. Gray 4 for 33)

*Wellington won by 31 runs*

The results of these two matches confused the Shell Cup table even further. Otago, with Lees giving the hard-hitting Bruce Blair good support, gained victory over Northern for whom nothing was going right. Walker and Steve Boock (3 for 25) took a strangle-hold on the visitors' innings and Otago moved to a massive win.

At Basin Reserve Bruce Edgar batted throughout the fifty overs and just finished short of his century. Rod Latham led a spirited reply for Canterbury, but Evan Gray was again in good form.

Wellington, Canterbury and Central Districts shared top spot with two wins from three matches.

## Shell Trophy

***10, 11 and 12 January 1984***

***at Rotorua***

**Northern Districts** 146 (J.G. Bracewell 4 for 22) and 281 (G.P. Howarth 60, J.M. Parker 55 not out, S.R. Tracy 4 for 65, J.G. Bracewell 4 for 77)
**Auckland** 270 (J.J. Crowe 151, T.J. Franklin 59, B.L. Cairns 4 for 70)

*Match drawn*
*Auckland 4 pts, Northern Districts 0 pts*

Northern were in total disarray on the first day and were saved only by a 69-run stand from John Parker and David White. Jeff Crowe stamped Auckland's authority on the game with two sixes and twenty-two fours in what was his first century in New Zealand. It was a powerful innings and one gratifying to the Test selectors. After his dismissal the last 7 wickets fell for 15 runs. Rain claimed $3\frac{1}{2}$ hours of the last day and stubborn innings by Parker and Cairns thwarted Auckland in spite of a marathon spell from John Bracewell.

*Jeff Crowe – a first century in New Zealand, for Auckland against Northern Districts, 10–12 January. (Adrian Murrell)*

***12, 13 and 14 January 1984***

***at Lower Hutt***

**Wellington** 316 (B.A. Edgar 106, J.G. Boyle 63, J.V. Coney 51, B.R. Blair 4 for 44) and 70 for 4
**Otago** 153 (R. Hoskin 66, E.J. Chatfield 4 for 41) and 232 (B.R. Blair 65, S.J. Maguiness 4 for 67, E.J. Chatfield 4 for 80)

*Wellington won by 6 wickets*
*Wellington 16 pts, Otago 0 pts*

The holders moved to the top of the table with a decisive win over Otago. 226 for 2 at tea, Edgar, in a resolute five-hour century having shared century stands with Boyle and Coney, they lost their grip on the game as wickets tumbled in the last session, but splendid bowling on the second day seized the initiative. In buffeting winds they captured the last 9 Otago wickets for 67 runs enabling McSweeney to enforce the follow-on. The collapse was heralded when McSweeney stumped Hoskin after he had 66 out of 86 in 92 minutes. It was the first of McSweeney's nine victims in the match. Otago closed at 119 for 3, but they were all out 5 minutes before lunch on the last day. Even without the injured Pigott, Wellington looked a powerful force capable of taking the title for the third year in succession.

***11, 12 and 13 January 1984***

***at Palmerston North***

**England XI** 294 for 6 dec (C.J. Tavare 89, G. Fowler 83, A.J. Lamb 51) and 300 for 6 dec (G. Fowler 104, I.T. Botham 80, D.W. Randall 66)
**Central Districts** 168 (V.J. Marks 5 for 66) and 163 for 2 (R.T. Hart 67, P.S. Briasco 65 not out)

*Match drawn*

England gained some useful practice at Palmerston North although their failure to win was disappointing. Fowler endorsed his claim for a Test place with two good innings and there were sound knocks from Tavare, Randall, looking very much in form, and Lamb. Botham hit mightily on the last day to make 80 off 38 deliveries. He took three sixes and a four in an over from Briasco and took 32 off an over from Snook, but by no stretch of imagination could these be considered front line bowlers. It was good fun for the crowd. England bowled well on the second day as the home side batted rather dourly. Marks' performance challenged Cook for the spinner's place in the Test side.

***14, 15 and 16 January 1984***

***at Hamilton***

**England XI** 287 for 3 dec (C.L. Smith 138 not out, D.I. Gower 69) and 194 for 2 dec (D.W. Randall 101 not out, C.L. Smith 50)
**Northern Districts** 111 (N.A. Foster 6 for 30) and 293 (C.M. Presland 58, A.D.G. Roberts 58, G.P. Howarth 55, I.T. Botham 4 for 72, N.G.B. Cook 4 for 91)

*England XI won by 78 runs*

On the eve of the first Test match England gained a morale boosting win, but Smith's two fine innings wrecked their selection plans. Smith had had two failures in Fiji and another against Central Districts, but he returned to form as he shared a second wicket stand of 126 with Gower who was all charm and authority. Smith showed a pleasing array of strokes later and batted well in the second innings when Derek Randall was again bubbling with shots and joy. In the home side's first innings Neil Foster bowled with great pace and accuracy to record a career best of 6 for 30. There are many who feel that he was too lacking in experience for this tour, but he was certainly impressive with his early form. Northern showed stiffer resistance at the second attempt, but Botham and Cook wore them down and England won on the first ball of the eleventh over of the last twenty.

## Shell Cup

***15 January 1984***

***at Wellington***

**Otago** 178 (S.J. Richards 61)
**Wellington** 182 for 4 (B.A. Edgar 81 not out)

*Wellington won by 6 wickets*

***at Auckland***

**Central Districts** 123 (G.K. Robertson 57, M.C. Snedden 4 for 17)
**Auckland** 124 for 2

*Auckland won by 8 wickets*

Accurate bowling by Gray restricted Otago who were 83 for 5 before Richards hit 61 out of 94. His brave effort could not thwart Wellington who won with 18 balls to spare. Edgar again batted well, but Gray took the individual award.

With 4 wickets falling for 1 run and Snedden in devastating form, Central Districts owed any respectability to Robertson who came in at 50 for 7 and hit 57 of the last 74 runs. It was an heroic gesture which only delayed the inevitable.

### Shell Trophy

***16, 17 and 18 January 1984***

***at Auckland***

**Central Districts** 205 and 263 (M.D. Crowe 151, A.J. Hunt 4 for 26, G.B. Troup 4 for 45)
**Auckland** 145 (G.K. Robertson 4 for 30) and 81 (M.D. Crowe 5 for 18)

*Central Districts won by 242 runs*
*Central Districts 16 pts, Auckland 0 pts*

***19, 20 and 21 January 1984***

***at Dunedin***

**Otago** 210 (K.R. Rutherford 93) and 43 for 3
**Canterbury** 82 (R.J. Webb 6 for 20)

*Match drawn*
*Otago 4 pts, Canterbury 0 pts*

Central Districts took their first points of the season in dramatic style in Auckland. They batted indifferently on the first day, but, inspired by the brisk medium pace of Peter Visser, making his debut as deputy for the injured Stirling, they had Auckland at 44 for 4 by the close, Visser having 3 for 16 in 12 overs. Auckland, weakened by the absence of Reid and Webb, struggled to within 60 of the visitors' score, but then Martin Crowe hit a magnificent career best, a chanceless 151 in 215 minutes off 181 deliveries; nor was his part in the match ended with his dismissal. Auckland needed 324 to win and all but four balls of the last day in which to get them. They surrendered with one of the worst batting displays in their history, being all out in little over two hours. There was some uneven bounce, but the batting was inexcusably inept and Martin Crowe's medium pace brought him a career best of 5 for 18 in 8 overs.

The match at Dunedin was ruined by rain and Otago's innings was not completed until the last morning. Ken Rutherford, eighteen years old, batted with great freedom to hit eight fours in a career best score made off 171 balls. Canterbury, losing the services of Dayle Hadlee, who was unwell, had a torrid time on a lively pitch against the pace of Richard Webb and Neil Mallender and were all out in 38 overs. Their failure to gain any points was a blow to their chances of catching Wellington.

### Shell Cup

***22 January 1984***

***at Dunedin***

**Otago** 208 for 7 (K.R. Rutherford 62)
**Canterbury** 99

*Otago won by 109 runs*

After Ken Rutherford and Warren Lees, who hit 46, had taken Otago to a good score, Canterbury were never in the match.

*Wright, caught Cook, bowled Botham for 17 at Basin Reserve, Wellington – the scene of the first Test match. (Patrick Eagar)*

### First Test Match
### NEW ZEALAND *v.* ENGLAND

New Zealand won the toss and batted first. They decided to omit Evan Gray from the twelve selected and, rather surprisingly, England preferred Smith to Fowler. For the first hour and a half, with the wicket placid, it seemed that New Zealand would move tranquilly to a sound position, but in the twenty-fifth over Botham, who had bowled with sustained aggression, underpitched slightly and Wright seized upon the offer too hastily and hit the ball straight to mid-on. In Botham's next over Edgar touched a leg-side ball to Taylor, and from this point the innings eroded.

Howarth drove without getting to the pitch of the ball and was taken in the gully, and Martin Crowe, having been comprehensively beaten by Willis once was then bowled by the England captain.

Jeff Crowe and Jeremy Coney had begun to look settled when Cook had Coney taken at silly point. Foster had bowled well without luck, but Jeff Crowe drove at him loosely and was taken behind after a good knock. Hadlee made some flourishes before becoming Botham's fourth victim and Willis accounted for Snedden and Cairns. Snedden was his three hundred and seventh Test wicket and Cairns, brilliantly caught at slip by the diving Gatting, was his record three hundred and eighth. In 84 Test matches he had overtaken Fred Trueman's England record and now

*Jeremy Coney, New Zealand's saviour. A maiden Test century at a crucial moment. (Ken Kelly)*

only Gibbs, 309, and Lillee, 355, stood in front of him.

Seven more runs were added on the second morning before Botham had Smith lbw. It was the twenty-first time that Botham had taken 5 wickets in a Test innings.

At lunch England were 62 for 2, an out of form Tavare was bowled when he nudged a ball onto his off-stump and Chris Smith, first to go, was taken left-handed in the gully when he drove at a wide ball. Both wickets fell to Lance Cairns who had Lamb taken at short-leg and Gower taken at gully off an indecisive jab in quick succession. Then Gatting swung across the line unwisely and was lbw, and England were 115 for 5. It could have been worse. Before he had scored Botham edged straight to Cairns at third slip where, as he had done at Lord's in 1983, the New Zealand medium-pace bowler dropped a simple and vital catch. Botham was also missed by Snedden on 19 and by John Wright on 75, but he deserved his luck. When you hit as hard and as often as he does you are likely to get dropped. In 235 minutes he hit two sixes and twenty-two fours as he scored 138 off only 167 balls. It was his thirteenth Test hundred and if at times it was sedate by his standards, it contained some bludgeoning shots, essays in might, which none in living memory have ever approached.

He and Randall added 232 for the sixth wicket and Randall, so often rejected by the selectors, once more produced that blend of happy spontaneity and technical application which make him so loved by those who watch the game. He batted for six hours, seven minutes and was last out after hitting two sixes and twenty fours.

**FIRST TEST MATCH – NEW ZEALAND *v.* ENGLAND**
20, 21, 22, 23 and 24 January 1984 at Basin Reserve, Wellington

**NEW ZEALAND**

| | FIRST INNINGS | | SECOND INNINGS | |
|---|---|---|---|---|
| J.G. Wright | c Cook, b Botham | 17 | c Foster, b Cook | 35 |
| B.A. Edgar | c Taylor, b Botham | 9 | c Taylor, b Willis | 30 |
| G.P. Howarth† | c Gower, b Botham | 15 | run out | 34 |
| M.D. Crowe | b Willis | 13 | c Botham, b Gatting | 100 |
| J.J. Crowe | c Taylor, b Foster | 52 | lbw, b Botham | 3 |
| J.V. Coney | c Gower, b Cook | 27 | not out | 174 |
| R.J. Hadlee | c Gatting, b Botham | 24 | c Lamb, b Foster | 18 |
| M.C. Snedden | c Taylor, b Willis | 11 | c Taylor, b Foster | 16 |
| I.D.S. Smith* | lbw, b Botham | 24 | b Cook | 29 |
| B.L. Cairns | c Gatting, b Willis | 3 | c sub (Fowler), b Willis | 64 |
| E.J. Chatfield | not out | 4 | b Cook | 0 |
| Extras | b 4, lb 9, nb 7 | 20 | b 4, lb 14, w 2, nb 14 | 34 |
| | | 219 | | 537 |

| | O | M | R | W | O | M | R | W |
|---|---|---|---|---|---|---|---|---|
| Willis | 19 | 7 | 37 | 3 | 37 | 8 | 102 | 2 |
| Foster | 24 | 9 | 60 | 1 | 37 | 12 | 91 | 2 |
| Botham | 27.4 | 8 | 59 | 5 | 36 | 6 | 137 | 1 |
| Cook | 23 | 11 | 43 | 1 | 66.3 | 26 | 153 | 3 |
| Smith | | | | | 3 | 1 | 6 | — |
| Gatting | | | | | 8 | 4 | 14 | 1 |

FALL OF WICKETS
1- 34, 2- 39, 3- 56, 4- 71, 5- 114, 6- 160, 7- 174, 8- 200, 9- 208
1- 62, 2- 79, 3- 153, 4- 165, 5- 279, 6- 302, 7- 334, 8- 402, 9- 520

**ENGLAND**

| | FIRST INNINGS | | SECOND INNINGS | |
|---|---|---|---|---|
| C.J. Tavare | b Cairns | 9 | not out | 36 |
| C.L. Smith | c Hadlee, b Cairns | 27 | not out | 30 |
| D.I. Gower | c Hadlee, b Cairns | 33 | | |
| A.J. Lamb | c M.D. Crowe, b Cairns | 13 | | |
| M.W. Gatting | lbw, b Cairns | 19 | | |
| I.T. Botham | c J.J. Crowe, b Cairns | 138 | | |
| D.W. Randall | c M.D. Crowe, b Hadlee | 164 | | |
| R.W. Taylor* | run out | 14 | | |
| N.G.B. Cook | c Smith, b Cairns | 7 | | |
| N.A. Foster | c Howarth, b Hadlee | 10 | | |
| R.G.D. Willis† | not out | 5 | | |
| Extras | lb 8, nb 16 | 24 | nb 3 | 3 |
| | | 463 | (for no wkt) | 69 |

| | O | M | R | W | O | M | R | W |
|---|---|---|---|---|---|---|---|---|
| Hadlee | 31.5 | 6 | 97 | 2 | | | | |
| Snedden | 21 | 3 | 101 | — | 7 | 2 | 28 | — |
| Cairns | 45 | 11 | 143 | 7 | | | | |
| Chatfield | 28 | 5 | 68 | — | 5 | — | 24 | — |
| M.D. Crowe | 3 | — | 20 | — | 6 | 1 | 11 | — |
| Coney | 4 | 1 | 10 | — | | | | |
| Edgar | | | | | 3 | 1 | 3 | — |
| J.J. Crowe | | | | | 1 | 1 | 0 | — |

FALL OF WICKETS
1- 41, 2- 51, 3- 84, 4- 92, 5- 115, 6- 347, 7- 372, 8- 386, 9- 426

*Umpires:* F.R. Goodall and S.J. Woodward

**Match drawn**

New Zealand, 244 behind on the first innings, lost both openers for 79 and were 191 for 4 at lunch on the fourth day, Howarth having been needlessly run out and Jeff Crowe having become another Botham victim.

Coney, after an uncertain start, settled to help Martin Crowe in a stand of 114. The stand was dominated by Crowe who, at the age of twenty-one, reached a lovely maiden Test hundred. It took him 278 minutes and 275 balls and it included nineteen fours, but the statistics tell little of the authority and the composed elegance of his batting. He showed no sign of weakening until, in the excitement of his achievement, he touched a gentle outswinger to Botham at slip and gave Gatting his first Test wicket.

Hadlee and Snedden fell to the lively Foster before the close which came at 335 for 7 with Coney on 76 not out.

It still seemed that England would grasp victory, but Coney, with unswerving concentration, became New Zealand's hero. In an innings lasting 490 minutes, he reached his maiden Test century, his first century for seven years and the highest score of his career. It was a mighty effort by a jovial and likeable cricketer. He hit a six and twenty-six fours off the 373 balls he faced, and he and Cairns added a record 118 for the ninth wicket, Cairns reaching his highest Test score before becoming Willis' three hundred and tenth Test victim.

## Shell Trophy

***26, 27 and 28 January 1984***

***at Auckland***

**Wellington** 194 (R.H. Vance 59) and 209 (R.H. Vance 56, J.G. Bracewell 5 for 78)
**Auckland** 275 (J.F. Reid 106, J.G. Bracewell 52, S.J. Maguiness 4 for 35) and 130 for 1 (T.J. Franklin 70 not out)

*Auckland won by 9 wickets*
*Auckland 16 pts, Wellington 0 pts*

***at New Plymouth***

**Central Districts** 356 for 2 dec (R.D. Hart 167 not out, P.S. Briasco 157) and 276 for 7 dec (J.R. Wiltshire 105, M.D. Crowe 63)
**Canterbury** 297 (P.E. McEwan 77, V.R. Brown 69, D.R. O'Sullivan 5 for 99) and 150 (D.A. Stirling 4 for 40)

*Central Districts won by 185 runs*
*Central Districts 16 pts, Canterbury 0 pts*

With the surprise victory of the season, Auckland took maximum points from Wellington and threw the Shell Trophy wide open. Some keen bowling had Wellington out for a disappointing 194 in ten minutes under five hours. Auckland lost both openers for 18, but Reid and Jeff Crowe added 72, and John Reid, who batted 339 minutes and faced 283 balls, grafted for the fifth century of his career to put the home side in a good position. He was seventh out after hitting fourteen fours. Vance and Edgar began Wellington's second innings confidently, but their last eight wickets fell for 85, John Bracewell, eager to regain his Test place, bowling with excellent control and turn, and supported by good fielding, being the arch destroyer. Needing 129 in under 3 hours, Auckland scored with gusto as Franklin, Reid and Webb paced them to victory.

Canterbury's hopes of the Shell Trophy diminished and Central's leapt in the match at New Plymouth. On the opening day, Ron Hart and Scott Briasco both hit maiden centuries as they shared a second wicket partnership of 317, a New Zealand record for that wicket, eclipsing the 301 set by Dempster and Allcot at Edgbaston in 1927. They batted with great verve and such a feat by two young batsmen excited the whole country. Canterbury fought back well on the second day to come within 59 of the home side's score with some solid batting, and it seemed as if Central might lose their advantage when they were 35 for 3 in their second knock. Then Martin Crowe played with great authority, and on the last morning skipper John Wiltshire hit a chanceless century which virtually put the game out of Canterbury's reach. Some characterless batting and some keen bowling and fielding by Central brought Canterbury's downfall in under 3 hours. The visitors were handicapped in that Richard Hadlee was unable to bowl in Central's first innings because of a rib injury.

***27, 28 and 29 January 1984***

***at Dunedin***

**England XI** 194 for 8 dec (V.J. Marks 50, N.A. Mallender 4 for 53) and 118 for 4
**Otago** 152 for 9 dec (V.J. Marks 5 for 52)

*Match drawn*

With no play possible on the first day and an hour lost on the second, England's game in Dunedin was doomed to a draw. There was a fine all-round performance from Vic Marks and the bowler to give England most trouble was Northamptonshire's Neil Mallender.

England's main concern was over the fitness of Dilley, Taylor and Foster. Foster broke a toe batting against Willis in the nets and was very doubtful for the second Test match.

## Shell Cup

***29 January 1984***

***at Auckland***

**Auckland** 137
**Wellington** 140 for 5 (R.H. Vance 53)

*Wellington won by 5 wickets*

***at Wanganui***

**Canterbury** 175 (D.A. Stirling 4 for 32)
***Central Districts*** 179 for 8 (R.E. Hayward 63, M.D. Crowe 59)

*Central Districts won by 2 wickets*

***30 January 1984***

***at Auckland***

**Northern Districts** 136
**Auckland** 76 for 2

*Auckland won on faster scoring rate*

Wellington finished top of the Shell Cup qualifying table when they beat Auckland in a somewhat chaotic finish as Coney hit Snedden for 10 off three balls and the number of overs left was in doubt in the rain affected match. Pigott bowled well with 3 for 24, but a first wicket stand of 91 between Edgar and Vance made certain of victory for Wellington.

Auckland came back the following day to beat Northern Districts in a rain-ruined game and this win gave them a somewhat fortuitous second place and the right to meet

*Cricket at Molyneux Park, Alexandra. A festive gathering for England XI v. Otago. (Patrick Eagar)*

Wellington in the final ahead of Central Districts on faster scoring rate. Central had laboured a little in beating Canterbury the previous day.

**Shell Cup – Final Table**

| | *P* | *W* | *L* | *Pts* |
|---|---|---|---|---|
| Wellington | 5 | 4 | 1 | 8 |
| Auckland | 5 | 3 | 2 | 6 |
| Central Districts | 5 | 3 | 2 | 6 |
| Canterbury | 5 | 2 | 3 | 4 |
| Otago | 5 | 2 | 3 | 4 |
| Northern Districts | 5 | 1 | 4 | 2 |

***30 January 1984***

***at Alexandra***

**England XI** 297 for 4 (C.J. Tavare 126, A.J. Lamb 106 not out)
**Otago** 185 for 8 (S.J. McCullum 97 not out, B.R. Blair 53)

*England XI won by 112 runs*

Although not playing in this match, in which Fowler kept wicket, Bob Taylor reported fit and Paul Downton, on standby in South Africa, was able to relax again. Tavare hit 126 off 122 balls. He was dropped on the square-leg boundary when 99 and then dropped three times more, at long-on, by the same fielder. Lamb hit three sixes and ten fours in his unbeaten innings which lasted just over 2 hours. McCullum and Bruce Blair had a third wicket stand of 100 for the home side. It was a festive occasion and many journeyed from central Otago to raise the attendance to 5000 although Alexandra's population is only 4000.

## Shell Trophy

***31 January, 1 and 2 February 1984***

***at Palmerston North***

**Central Districts** 356 (P.S. Briasco 78, P. Blackbourn 58, R.E. Hayward 54) and 239 for 5 dec (R.E. Hayward 102, P. Blackbourn 52 not out)
**Wellington** 246 (E.B. McSweeney 92, G.K. Robertson 5 for 80) and 210 for 8 (P.J. Holland 67)

*Match drawn*
*Central Districts 4 pts, Wellington 0 pts*

***1, 2 and 3 February 1984***

**Auckland** 311 for 8 dec (J.F. Reid 69, J.G. Bracewell 59, T.J. Franklin 58) and 28 for 0
**Northern Districts** 153 (J.G. Bracewell 6 for 32) and 180 (J.M. Parker 69)

*Auckland won by 10 wickets*
*Auckland 16 pts, Northern Districts 0 pts*

Wellington's hold on the Shell Trophy was weakened further when Central Districts reached 355 for 9 on the opening day in Palmerston North. It was powerful batting in the later part of the innings which took Central to their big score. Scott Briasco again batted well, but the last four wickets produced 163 runs after Gray had retired injured from the attack. Wellington, weakened by Test calls and injury, persuaded John Morrison out of retirement, but it was skipper Ervin McSweeney who saved them from humiliation with a bustling 92 in 157 minutes. He came to the wicket at 79 for 5 and hit twelve fours in his innings of 92 off 143 balls. Gary Robertson bowled splendidly, quick and accurate, to return impressive figures on a fast pitch and quick outfield.

Richard Hayward, the former Hampshire left-hander, scored a solid century in the second innings and shared a sixth wicket stand of 103 with Peter Blackbourn who hit two fifties on his first-class debut. Sadly for Central, however, skipper Wiltshire had a bone in his arm broken by a ball from Grant Cederwall.

Needing 350 to win in 230 minutes, Wellington owed much to makeshift opener Holland who held the earlier part of the innings together, but it was finally Ormiston who staved off defeat with a resolute 35 not out.

With their emphatic win over Northern Districts, still struggling to find the form that had been expected of them, Auckland joined Wellington at the top of the table. They batted enterprisingly on the first day so that Snedden was able to declare 90 minutes before the close. The innings was founded on a second wicket stand of 129 between Franklin and Reid, but there was substance all through the middle order. 62 for 0 at the close, Northern Districts collapsed to John Bracewell's off-spin on the second day when 18 wickets fell for 261 runs. Bracewell bowled 53 overs in the day and took 8 for 83. It followed his excellent 59 and he completed a good all-round match with 3 catches. Rain threatened on the last day, but the match took less than an hour to complete.

**Second Test Match**
**NEW ZEALAND *v.* ENGLAND**

New Zealand included Stirling and Boock in their party to the exclusion of Snedden, who had failed to find his form, and Gray, who was rather unlucky to be omitted as he had been twelfth man in the first Test. Stirling was made twelfth man on this occasion and Stephen Boock, the slow left-arm bowler, returned to international cricket. Well as he had been bowling for three years, his return came as something of a surprise. Boock had last played for New Zealand in a one-day international in Australia in December, 1980, and shortly after this match he had asked to return home to New Zealand as he was playing no cricket. His request had been granted, but it was thought by many that he was unlikely to play for New Zealand again. It was good to see the talents of this likeable young man rewarded once more.

With Foster injured, Dilley not fully fit and spin not part of England's plans, Tony Pigott was called from Wellington to join the England side and make his Test debut instead of getting married as he had planned.

There were ominous signs at the start that England were not to have a happy time. Botham produced a massive wide and dropped Edgar at slip off Willis. Pigott was in to the attack sooner than expected and took a wicket with his seventh ball in Test cricket when Edgar played firmly off his legs and was taken by Randall at backward short-leg. By the standards the marvellous Randall had set himself on the tour, it was a straightforward catch.

Wright had looked positive, but Cowans angled the ball across him and had him taken behind. Cowans followed this by clipping Howarth's off stump and on the stroke of lunch Botham had Martin Crowe taken at slip. 87 for 4. It was the nadir of New Zealand's innings, and, in truth, their position was far better than might have been expected in the conditions. The afternoon belonged to them entirely. They scored 116 runs and lost only 1 wicket. Jeff Crowe and Coney added 50 in less than an hour before Crowe shuffled across to Cowans, the most dangerous of the England bowlers, and was lbw.

Coney was taken low at slip in Pigott's first over after tea, but this was simply the signal for Hadlee's all out assault on some erratic England bowling. He made 99 off 81 deliveries. Pigott was the main sufferer, but Botham had one of his worst days, and it was hard to understand why Cowans was not brought back to attack Hadlee while he was hitting his eighteen fours in his 111 minutes. 78 runs in 38 minutes were added with the bubbling Ian Smith.

Hadlee essayed a cut at a ball that was too wide for the shot and was taken by Taylor, who had missed Smith off Cowans. It had been an innings of heroic stature and England had been routed. Willis quickly finished off the tail, but 307 on a doubtful wicket in under 73 overs was mighty scoring.

It became mightier before the close when Boock bowled just one ball after Hadlee and Cairns had sent down 7 overs.

*Richard Hadlee during his devastating innings of 99. (Adrian Murrell)*

*Tavare is taken at first slip by Jeff Crowe off Hadlee. (Adrian Murrell)*

Boock tossed the ball up. It beat Fowler's forward prod and England were 7 for 1. Worse was to come.

Overnight rain and steady drizzle meant that no play was possible until 4.30. Tavare, bat and body in argument, steered the ball to first slip. Incredibly Gower padded up to Hadlee and offered no shot. Randall edged low to second slip and England were 10 for 4, the last 3 wickets having gone to Hadlee without him conceding a run.

*Gower is lbw and Hadlee lifts his arms in triumph. (Adrian Murrell)*

The pitch was not to blame. The New Zealand bowlers kept a good length, did not waste a delivery, offered variety and were backed by imaginative captaincy and fielding of quality and enthusiasm. Even Chatfield, not noted for his fielding, took Botham well at long-leg after he and Lamb had added 31. By the close Lamb, to a faint edge, and Taylor, at slip, had gone and England were 53 for 7.

On the Sunday, Pigott went to Cairns' slower ball, but Willis held out for 40 minutes so indicating what application might have achieved. Nevertheless England were bowled out for 82 and followed-on 225 runs in arrears.

The England second innings began grimly. After 15 runs and 15 overs Tavare was taken behind off Hadlee. Gower pushed at a ball from the same bowler and Cairns clutched the chance at fourth slip. Fowler pushed Boock, making such an impressive return to Test cricket, to silly point and Gatting, driving a little recklessly, was caught at slip. When Botham was taken at silly mid-on first ball it was apparent that the last lingering doubts as to whether New Zealand would achieve an historic victory vanished.

Randall and Taylor showed some spirit and Taylor went down the wicket to hit Boock back over his head, but then he set off on a non-existent run and Edgar's stop and throw gave him no chance. Then Randall was caught at the second attempt and Cowans fell to Man of the Match Hadlee and

*Fowler is caught by Howarth off Boock and England face an innings defeat. (Patrick Eagar)*

New Zealand had won in what was a fraction over 12 hours playing time.

The pitch was condemned by England and there were to have been complaints, but the record books will show that New Zealand gained her greatest Test victory and that England were bowled out for under 100 twice in a Test match for only the third time in a long history of Test cricket.

Whatever the debate, New Zealand's victory was thoroughly deserved, a triumph for fine spirit, dedicated cricket and intelligent leadership.

BELOW: *Gatting, caught Hadlee, bowled Boock 0 and the noose tightens around England's neck. (Adrian Murrell)* RIGHT (above): *The end. Cowans is caught behind for 7 and New Zealand leap in ecstasy at an historic victory. (Patrick Eagar)*

BELOW: *An historic moment in cricket history. The scoreboard at the end of the second Test match. (Adrian Murrell)*

**SECOND TEST MATCH – NEW ZEALAND *v.* ENGLAND**
3, 4 and 5 February 1984 at Lancaster Park, Christchurch

**NEW ZEALAND**

| | FIRST INNINGS | |
|---|---|---|
| J.G. Wright | c Taylor, b Cowans | 25 |
| B.A. Edgar | c Randall, b Pigott | 1 |
| G.P. Howarth† | b Cowans | 9 |
| M.D. Crowe | c Tavare, b Botham | 19 |
| J.J. Crowe | lbw, b Cowans | 47 |
| J.V. Coney | c Botham, b Pigott | 41 |
| R.J. Hadlee | c Taylor, b Willis | 99 |
| I.D.S. Smith* | not out | 32 |
| B.L. Cairns | c Taylor, b Willis | 2 |
| S.L. Boock | c Taylor, b Willis | 5 |
| E.J. Chatfield | lbw, b Willis | 0 |
| Extras | b 8, lb 11, w 2, nb 6 | 27 |
| | | 307 |

| | O | M | R | W |
|---|---|---|---|---|
| Willis | 22.1 | 5 | 51 | 4 |
| Botham | 17 | 1 | 88 | 1 |
| Pigott | 17 | 7 | 75 | 1 |
| Cowans | 14 | 2 | 52 | 3 |
| Gatting | 2 | — | 14 | — |

FALL OF WICKETS
1- 30, 2- 42, 3- 53, 4- 87, 5- 137, 6- 203, 7- 281, 8- 291, 9- 301

**ENGLAND**

| | FIRST INNINGS | | SECOND INNINGS | |
|---|---|---|---|---|
| G. Fowler | b Boock | 4 | c Howarth, b Boock | 10 |
| C.J. Tavare | c J. Crowe, b Hadlee | 3 | c Smith, b Hadlee | 6 |
| D.I. Gower | lbw, b Hadlee | 2 | c Cairns, b Hadlee | 8 |
| A.J. Lamb | c Smith, b Chatfield | 11 | c Coney, b Chatfield | 9 |
| D.W. Randall | c Coney, b Hadlee | 0 | (7) c Cairns, b Hadlee | 25 |
| I.T. Botham | c Chatfield, b Cairns | 18 | c M. Crowe, b Boock | 0 |
| M.W. Gatting | not out | 19 | (5) c Hadlee, b Boock | 0 |
| R.W. Taylor* | c J. Crowe, b Cairns | 2 | run out | 15 |
| A.C.S. Pigott | lbw, b Cairns | 4 | not out | 8 |
| R.G.D. Willis† | b Chatfield | 6 | c Howarth, b Hadlee | 0 |
| N.G. Cowans | c Coney, b Chatfield | 4 | c Smith, b Hadlee | 7 |
| Extras | lb 5, nb 4 | 9 | lb 2, nb 3 | 5 |
| | | 82 | | 93 |

| | O | M | R | W | O | M | R | W |
|---|---|---|---|---|---|---|---|---|
| Hadlee | 17 | 9 | 16 | 3 | 17.5 | 6 | 28 | 5 |
| Cairns | 19 | 5 | 35 | 3 | 9 | 3 | 21 | — |
| Boock | 6 | 3 | 12 | 1 | 13 | 3 | 25 | 3 |
| Chatfield | 8.2 | 3 | 10 | 3 | 11 | 1 | 14 | 1 |

FALL OF WICKETS
1- 7, 2- 9, 3- 10, 4- 10, 5- 41, 6- 41, 7- 47, 8- 58, 9- 72
1- 15, 2- 23, 3- 25, 4- 31, 5- 31, 6- 33, 7- 72, 8- 76, 9- 80

*Umpires:* F.R. Goodall and S.J. Woodward

**New Zealand won by an innings and 132 runs**

*Early success for England. Edgar is lbw to Willis. (Patrick Eagar)*

*Ian Smith in action during his magnificent maiden Test century. (Adrian Murrell)*

**Third Test Match**
**NEW ZEALAND *v.* ENGLAND**

New Zealand, not unnaturally, relied on the team that brought them victory at Christchurch while England dropped Chris Tavare, who had been completely out of form, and brought back Chris Smith so that they had their different opening partnership of the three-match series. Foster returned for Pigott and Marks came in to the exclusion of Gatting.

England had just the early success that they looked for when Edgar was lbw to Willis in the third over. Edgar had had a poor series. Howarth batted with great confidence until he drove at Cowans and was caught at third slip by Randall with his usual aplomb. Martin Crowe was not at his best and was superbly taken at slip, but rain and bad light brought an early close with New Zealand 140 for 3 and John Wright very much in control.

The second day was delayed by overnight rain, and when it began there was to be the end of England's hopes of drawing the series. Wright and Jeff Crowe took their stand to a record 154 before Wright was bowled by Willis. He had faced 297 balls and hit twenty-four fours in a masterly display. If he was overshadowed, it was only because Jeff Crowe, after an apprenticeship that had been hard and at times painful, reached a thoroughly well earned maiden Test hundred.

His triumph was not to be the last. New Zealand began the third day on 354 for 6 and although Crowe added only 13 to his overnight score, New Zealand prospered. A superb catch by Cowans removed Cairns and left Smith unbeaten on 77 with only Boock and Chatfield to come. Boock stayed for four overs and then Chatfield played a determined straight bat while Smith savaged the bowling. One of the day's many stoppages came when he was 97 and there was another as he turned Foster to fine-leg to reach his maiden Test century. He celebrated by hitting Marks for two sixes and then Howarth declared. The chirpy Smith was not finished yet. He caught Fowler off the first ball of the England innings and Gower was bowled by Boock before the close so that England had only honour left to play for.

The honour was restored as Randall, Smith, rather laboriously, and Botham matched New Zealand's offerings. Randall was undoubtedly England's man of the series.

So New Zealand beat England in a Test series for the first time, and it was a triumph well deserved. There is a joy in their approach to the game which is warming and while it is easy to fault England on selection and approach, one should not detract from the fine side that New Zealand have fused together. Boock brought breadth and Smith, even if he is not yet in the top flight of wicket-keepers, has brought a cheerful zest. There is growing stability in the middle order and Hadlee is probably the finest bowler in the world as well as being a very useful hard-hitting batsman. Above all is the quiet charm, intelligence and authority of a captain who has become a national hero.

*Gower is bowled by Boock and New Zealand celebrate. (Adrian Murrell)*

*Randall hits out during his innings of 104. He was unquestionably England's man-of-the-series. (Adrian Murrell)*

**THIRD TEST MATCH – NEW ZEALAND *v.* ENGLAND**
10, 11, 12, 14 and 15 February 1984 at Eden Park, Auckland

**NEW ZEALAND**

| | FIRST INNINGS | | SECOND INNINGS | |
|---|---|---|---|---|
| J.G. Wright | b Willis | 130 | not out | 11 |
| B.A. Edgar | lbw, b Willis | 0 | not out | 0 |
| G.P. Howarth† | c Randall, b Cowans | 35 | | |
| M.D. Crowe | c Botham, b Willis | 16 | | |
| J.J. Crowe | b Marks | 128 | | |
| J.V. Coney | b Cowans | 9 | | |
| R.J. Hadlee | b Marks | 3 | | |
| I.D.S. Smith* | not out | 113 | | |
| B.L. Cairns | c Cowans, b Foster | 28 | | |
| S.L. Boock | lbw, b Marks | 2 | | |
| E.J. Chatfield | not out | 6 | | |
| Extras | lb 19, nb 7 | 26 | lb 1, nb 4 | 5 |
| | (for 9 wkts dec) | 496 | (for no wkt) | 16 |

| | O | M | R | W | O | M | R | W |
|---|---|---|---|---|---|---|---|---|
| Willis | 34 | 7 | 109 | 3 | 3 | 1 | 7 | — |
| Botham | 29 | 10 | 70 | — | | | | |
| Cowans | 36 | 11 | 98 | 2 | 2 | 1 | 4 | — |
| Foster | 30 | 8 | 78 | 1 | | | | |
| Marks | 40.2 | 9 | 115 | 3 | | | | |

FALL OF WICKETS
1- 3, 2- 74, 3- 111, 4- 265, 5- 293, 6- 302, 7- 385, 8- 451, 9- 461

**ENGLAND**

| | FIRST INNINGS | |
|---|---|---|
| G. Fowler | c Smith, b Hadlee | 0 |
| C.L. Smith | c Smith, b Cairns | 91 |
| D.I. Gower | b Boock | 26 |
| A.J. Lamb | lbw, b Cairns | 49 |
| D.W. Randall | c Wright, b Chatfield | 104 |
| R.W. Taylor* | st Smith, b Boock | 23 |
| I.T. Botham | run out | 70 |
| V.J. Marks | c Smith, b Chatfield | 6 |
| N.A. Foster | not out | 18 |
| R.G.D. Willis† | c Smith, b Hadlee | 3 |
| N.G. Cowans | c Cairns, b Boock | 21 |
| Extras | b 7, lb 13, nb 8 | 28 |
| | | 439 |

| | O | M | R | W |
|---|---|---|---|---|
| Hadlee | 43 | 12 | 91 | 2 |
| Cairns | 40 | 20 | 52 | 2 |
| Boock | 61.3 | 28 | 103 | 3 |
| Chatfield | 46 | 21 | 72 | 2 |
| M.D. Crowe | 17 | 5 | 62 | — |
| Coney | 13 | 8 | 13 | — |
| Howarth | 7 | 1 | 18 | — |

FALL OF WICKETS
1- 0, 2- 48, 3- 143, 4- 234, 5- 284, 6- 371, 7- 387, 8- 391, 9- 396

*Umpires:* F.R. Goodall and S.J. Woodward

**Match drawn**

## England *v.* New Zealand – Test Match Averages

### NEW ZEALAND BATTING

| | M | Inns | NOs | Runs | HS | Av | 100s | 50s |
|---|---|---|---|---|---|---|---|---|
| I.D.S. Smith | 3 | 4 | 2 | 198 | 113* | 99.00 | 1 | |
| J.V. Coney | 3 | 4 | 1 | 251 | 174* | 83.66 | 1 | |
| J.J. Crowe | 3 | 4 | | 230 | 128 | 57.50 | 1 | 1 |
| J.G. Wright | 3 | 5 | 1 | 218 | 130 | 54.50 | 1 | |
| M.D. Crowe | 3 | 4 | | 148 | 100 | 37.00 | 1 | |
| R.J. Hadlee | 3 | 4 | | 144 | 99 | 36.00 | | 1 |
| B.L. Cairns | 3 | 4 | | 97 | 64 | 24.25 | | 1 |
| G.P. Howarth | 3 | 4 | | 93 | 35 | 23.25 | | |
| B.A. Edgar | 3 | 5 | 1 | 40 | 30 | 10.00 | | |
| E.J. Chatfield | 3 | 4 | 2 | 10 | 6* | 5.00 | | |
| S.L. Boock | 2 | 2 | | 7 | 5 | 3.50 | | |

Played in one Test: M.C. Snedden 11 and 16

### NEW ZEALAND BOWLING

| | Overs | Mds | Runs | Wkts | Av | Best | 5/inn |
|---|---|---|---|---|---|---|---|
| R.J. Hadlee | 109.4 | 33 | 232 | 12 | 19.33 | 5/28 | 1 |
| S.L. Boock | 80.3 | 34 | 140 | 7 | 20.00 | 3/25 | |
| B.L. Cairns | 113 | 39 | 251 | 12 | 20.91 | 7/143 | 1 |
| E.J. Chatfield | 98.2 | 30 | 188 | 6 | 31.33 | 3/10 | |
| J.V. Coney | 17 | 9 | 23 | 0 | — | 0/10 | |
| M.D. Crowe | 26 | 6 | 93 | 0 | — | 0/11 | |

Bowled in one Test: M.C. Snedden 28–5–129–0; B.A. Edgar 3–1–3–0; G.P. Howarth 7–1–18–0; J.J. Crowe 1–1–0–0

### NEW ZEALAND CATCHES

9–I.D.S. Smith (ct 8/st 1); 3–R.J. Hadlee, M.D. Crowe, J.J. Crowe, G.P. Howarth, J.V. Coney and B.L. Cairns; 1–E.J. Chatfield and J.G. Wright

### ENGLAND BATTING

| | M | Inns | NOs | Runs | HS | Av | 100s | 50s |
|---|---|---|---|---|---|---|---|---|
| C.L. Smith | 2 | 3 | 1 | 148 | 91 | 74.00 | | 1 |
| D.W. Randall | 3 | 4 | | 293 | 164 | 73.25 | 2 | |
| I.T. Botham | 3 | 4 | | 226 | 138 | 56.50 | 1 | |
| N.A. Foster | 2 | 2 | 1 | 28 | 18* | 28.00 | | |
| A.J. Lamb | 3 | 4 | | 82 | 49 | 20.50 | | |
| M.W. Gatting | 2 | 3 | 1 | 38 | 19* | 19.00 | | |
| C.J. Tavare | 2 | 4 | 1 | 54 | 36* | 18.00 | | |
| D.I. Gower | 3 | 4 | | 69 | 33 | 17.25 | | |
| R.W. Taylor | 3 | 4 | | 54 | 23 | 13.50 | | |
| N.G. Cowans | 2 | 3 | | 32 | 21 | 10.66 | | |
| G. Fowler | 2 | 3 | | 14 | 10 | 4.66 | | |
| R.G.D. Willis | 3 | 4 | 1 | 14 | 6 | 4.66 | | |

Played in one Test: N.G.B. Cook 7; V.J. Marks 6; A.C.S. Pigott 4 and 8*

### ENGLAND BOWLING

| | Overs | Mds | Runs | Wkts | Av | Best | 5/inn |
|---|---|---|---|---|---|---|---|
| R.G.D. Willis | 115.1 | 28 | 306 | 12 | 25.50 | 4/51 | |
| M.W. Gatting | 10 | 4 | 28 | 1 | 28.00 | 1/14 | |
| N.G. Cowans | 52 | 24 | 154 | 5 | 30.80 | 3/52 | |
| I.T. Botham | 109.4 | 25 | 354 | 7 | 50.57 | 5/59 | 1 |
| N.A. Foster | 91 | 29 | 229 | 4 | 57.25 | 2/91 | |

Bowled in one Test: V.J. Marks 40.2–9–115–3; C.L. Smith 3–1–6–0; A.C.S. Pigott 17–7–75–2; N.G.B. Cook 89.3–37–196–4

### ENGLAND CATCHES

9–R.W. Taylor; 3–I.T. Botham; 2–D.W. Randall, D.I. Gower and M.W. Gatting;1–C.J. Tavare, N.G.B. Cook, A.J. Lamb, N.A. Foster, N.G. Cowans and sub (G. Fowler)

## First One-Day International
## NEW ZEALAND *v.* ENGLAND

A crowd of 27,000 packed into the ground where England had suffered defeat a few weeks earlier. Once again Howarth won the toss, but, to the surprise of many, he elected to field. On a wicket which threatened to deteriorate rapidly, this seemed an unwise decision.

England omitted Tavare and Gower was asked to open the innings. It was not a successful move for he edged to Jeff Crowe at slip after facing 11 balls. Lamb and Smith were very subdued and it was 22 overs before England reached 50. Smith was 88 minutes, 68 deliveries for his 17 and that included a six off Robertson, a surprise selection in the New Zealand side.

### FIRST ONE-DAY INTERNATIONAL – NEW ZEALAND *v.* ENGLAND
18 February 1984 at Lancaster Park, Christchurch

**ENGLAND**

| | | |
|---|---|---|
| D.I. Gower | c J.J. Crowe, b Hadlee | 3 |
| C.L. Smith | run out | 17 |
| A.J. Lamb | c Robertson, b Hadlee | 43 |
| D.W. Randall | c Cairns, b Hadlee | 70 |
| I.T. Botham | c Smith, b Hadlee | 1 |
| M.W. Gatting | b Hadlee | 0 |
| V.J. Marks | lbw, b Cairns | 28 |
| R.W. Taylor* | run out | 2 |
| N.A. Foster | c Wright, b Cairns | 0 |
| N.G. Cowans | not out | 4 |
| R.G.D. Willis† | | |
| Extras | b 8, lb 4, nb 8 | 20 |
| (50 overs) | (for 9 wickets) | 188 |

| | O | M | R | W |
|---|---|---|---|---|
| Hadlee | 10 | 2 | 32 | 5 |
| Chatfield | 10 | 4 | 20 | — |
| Cairns | 10 | 2 | 41 | 2 |
| Coney | 10 | 1 | 30 | — |
| Robertson | 10 | — | 45 | — |

FALL OF WICKETS
1- 9, 2- 59, 3- 107, 4- 109, 5- 109, 6- 177, 7- 184, 8- 184, 9- 188

**NEW ZEALAND**

| | | |
|---|---|---|
| J.G. Wright | c Taylor, b Willis | 4 |
| B.A. Edgar | c Taylor, b Botham | 10 |
| G.P. Howarth† | run out | 18 |
| M.D. Crowe | run out | 0 |
| J.J. Crowe | b Botham | 0 |
| J.V. Coney | c Botham, b Foster | 19 |
| B.L. Cairns | lbw, b Marks | 23 |
| R.J. Hadlee | c Gower, b Marks | 23 |
| I.D.S. Smith* | c Gower, b Foster | 7 |
| G.K. Robertson | lbw, b Willis | 10 |
| E.J. Chatfield | not out | 0 |
| Extras | lb 9, w 6, nb 5 | 20 |
| (42.1 overs) | | 134 |

| | O | M | R | W |
|---|---|---|---|---|
| Willis | 6.1 | 1 | 18 | 2 |
| Cowans | 10 | 2 | 37 | — |
| Foster | 10 | 4 | 19 | 2 |
| Botham | 6 | 3 | 7 | 2 |
| Marks | 10 | 1 | 33 | 2 |

FALL OF WICKETS
1- 7, 2- 38, 3- 38, 4- 38, 5- 44, 6- 76, 7- 112, 8- 120, 9- 124

**England won by 54 runs**

**SECOND ONE-DAY INTERNATIONAL – NEW ZEALAND *v.* ENGLAND**
22 February 1984 at Basin Reserve, Wellington

**NEW ZEALAND**

| | | |
|---|---|---|
| B.A. Edgar | b Marks | 12 |
| T.J. Franklin | c and b Marks | 6 |
| G.P. Howarth† | lbw, b Marks | 21 |
| M.D. Crowe | c Foster, b Marks | 8 |
| J.J. Crowe | c Foster, b Marks | 1 |
| J.V. Coney | b Botham | 44 |
| R.J. Hadlee | c Randall, b Foster | 21 |
| B.L. Cairns | c Gower, b Foster | 0 |
| I.D.S. Smith* | lbw, b Botham | 0 |
| G.K. Robertson | run out | 11 |
| E.J. Chatfield | not out | 0 |
| Extras | lb 9, w 2 | 11 |
| (47.1 overs) | | 135 |

| | O | M | R | W |
|---|---|---|---|---|
| Willis | 9 | 4 | 17 | — |
| Cowans | 10 | 1 | 33 | — |
| Marks | 10 | 3 | 20 | 5 |
| Botham | 8.1 | 1 | 25 | 2 |
| Foster | 10 | 3 | 29 | 2 |

FALL OF WICKETS
1- 23, 2- 34, 3- 50, 4- 52, 5- 63, 6- 104, 7- 104, 8- 104, 9- 135

**ENGLAND**

| | | |
|---|---|---|
| D.I. Gower | c J.J. Crowe b Chatfield | 21 |
| C.L. Smith | b Hadlee | 70 |
| A.J. Lamb | c and b Chatfield | 6 |
| D.W. Randall | not out | 25 |
| I.T. Botham | b Hadlee | 15 |
| M.W. Gatting | not out | 0 |
| V.J. Marks | | |
| R.W. Taylor* | | |
| N.A. Foster | | |
| N.G. Cowans | | |
| R.G.D. Willis† | | |
| Extras | lb 2 | 2 |
| (45.1 overs) | (for 4 wickets) | 139 |

| | O | M | R | W |
|---|---|---|---|---|
| Hadlee | 10 | 2 | 31 | 2 |
| Robertson | 6 | — | 28 | — |
| Coney | 10 | 1 | 29 | — |
| Chatfield | 10 | 5 | 16 | 2 |
| Cairns | 9.1 | 1 | 33 | — |

FALL OF WICKETS
1- 36, 2- 54, 3- 117, 4- 135

**England won by 6 wickets**

The sensible batting of the England innings came from Randall and Marks who added 68 in 14 overs, but, in spite of the inevitable fine contribution by Randall, England's score did not look to be a winning one.

Within an hour, however, it was quite apparent that England had made a winning score. Wright was beaten twice by Willis before being caught behind in the fifth over. Edgar departed in the thirteenth. Martin Crowe responded to Howarth's call and was left stranded; his brother played on without scoring. Botham bowled meanly and quite quickly and this must have frustrated the New Zealanders for Howarth was run out after Smith had made a brilliant stop at square-leg. 44 for 5 and the match decided. Coney, Cairns and Hadlee did bring some respectability, but England bowled out New Zealand with 7.5 overs of their quota unused. Randall, rightly, took Man of the Match.

### Second One-Day International
### NEW ZEALAND *v.* ENGLAND

England took the one-day series with a most convincing win on a sluggish wicket at Wellington, the issue being virtually decided before lunch by which time the New Zealand innings was in tatters.

Wright was unfit and was replaced by Franklin who, driving half-heartedly, was caught and bowled in the eighteenth over, 23 for 1. By the twenty-eighth over Vic Marks had added 4 more wickets and New Zealand were 63 for 5. Marks scarcely bowled a bad ball, nagged away at middle and leg, and he and the pitch inhibited any forceful shots. It was a most accomplished piece of bowling, demonstrating once more that slow bowling can be at least as effective as medium pace in limited-over cricket.

Hadlee and Coney added 41 in 12 overs, but Foster, who bowled an admirable line and length, dismissed Hadlee and Cairns with successive balls. There were some good blows

*Vic Marks bowling during the international at Wellington. His 5 for 20 was the best bowling performance ever recorded for England in a limited-over international. (Adrian Murrell)*

from Coney and Robertson at the end, but 136 hardly suggested fear for the England batsmen.

Gower began very wildly and perished at point. Smith again batted purposefully and played his best innings for England. He punished the loose ball and reached his fifty in 88 minutes. Randall was dropped at the wicket off Chatfield and Botham was bowled, attempting a back-handed sweep when the scores were level.

### Third One-Day International
### NEW ZEALAND *v.* ENGLAND

Although England had won the series, a record crowd of 45,000 rejoiced in their heroes' victory in the final match. Willis won the toss and batted; it was the first time that he had called correctly in any of the representative games.

Smith had his off-stump knocked back by the last ball of the second over, but Gower and Lamb prospered, adding 67 in 18 overs. Randall was bowled in the twenty-fifth over, Boock showing that his accuracy could have benefitted New Zealand in the earlier games. Lamb now dominated proceedings. He had some support from Botham, but the close of the innings was notable for some bizarre run-outs so that England's 209 was less than had been expected.

Webb, who had replaced the out-of-form Edgar, hit two thunderous fours and was then bowled by Willis. Wright mis-hit Marks to be splendidly caught and bowled in the twelfth over, but there was to be no triumph for the off-spinner this time. Howarth and Martin Crowe added 160 in 32 overs and put the match out of England's reach. Crowe reached a maiden century in limited-over international cricket and took the individual honours.

RIGHT (above): *Chris Smith is bowled by Richard Hadlee.* (below): *Allan Lamb turns the ball to leg in his fine innings of 97 not out. (Adrian Murrell)*

## THIRD ONE-DAY INTERNATIONAL – NEW ZEALAND *v.* ENGLAND
25 February 1984 at Eden Park, Auckland

**ENGLAND**

|  |  |  |
|---|---|---|
| D.I. Gower | lbw, b Chatfield | 35 |
| C.L. Smith | b Hadlee | 5 |
| A.J. Lamb | not out | 97 |
| D.W. Randall | b Boock | 11 |
| I.T. Botham | c Wright, b Coney | 18 |
| M.W. Gatting | c Smith, b Chatfield | 4 |
| V.J. Marks | b Chatfield | 3 |
| R.W. Taylor* | run out | 8 |
| N.A. Foster | run out | 1 |
| N.G. Cowans | run out | 0 |
| R.G.D. Willis† | not out | 7 |
| Extras | b 4, lb 11, w 1, nb 4 | 20 |
| (50 overs) | (for 9 wickets) | 209 |

| | O | M | R | W |
|---|---|---|---|---|
| Hadlee | 10 | 2 | 51 | 1 |
| Cairns | 10 | 2 | 31 | — |
| Chatfield | 10 | 2 | 29 | 3 |
| Boock | 10 | — | 40 | 1 |
| Coney | 10 | — | 38 | 1 |

FALL OF WICKETS
1- 6, 2- 73, 3- 86, 4- 130, 5- 140, 6- 148, 7- 185, 8- 192, 9- 192

**NEW ZEALAND**

|  |  |  |
|---|---|---|
| J.G. Wright | c and b Marks | 14 |
| P.N. Webb | b Willis | 8 |
| G.P. Howarth† | lbw, b Botham | 72 |
| M.D. Crowe | not out | 107 |
| J.V. Coney | not out | 2 |
| J.J. Crowe | | |
| R.J. Hadlee | | |
| B.L. Cairns | | |
| I.D.S. Smith* | | |
| S.L. Boock | | |
| E.J. Chatfield | | |
| Extras | lb 7, w 2 | 9 |
| (45.3 overs) | (for 3 wickets) | 212 |

| | O | M | R | W |
|---|---|---|---|---|
| Willis | 10 | 1 | 36 | 1 |
| Cowans | 9.3 | — | 61 | — |
| Marks | 10 | 1 | 27 | 1 |
| Botham | 7 | 1 | 22 | 1 |
| Foster | 6 | — | 37 | — |
| Smith | 3 | — | 20 | — |

FALL OF WICKETS
1- 22, 2- 34, 3- 194

**New Zealand won by 7 wickets**

Hadlee was named Man of the Series for the six international matches, but Randall ran him very close.

## Shell Trophy

### *24, 25 and 26 February 1984*

**at Christchurch**

**Otago** 195 (W.K. Lees 55, V.R. Brown 7 for 50) and 178 (S.R. McNally 4 for 33)
**Canterbury** 165 (V.R. Brown 53 not out, R.J. Webb 5 for 30) and 210 for 5 (P.E. McEwan 74, A.P. Nathu 70 not out)

*Canterbury won by 5 wickets*
*Canterbury 12 pts, Otago 4 pts*

A match-winning all-round performance by Vaughan Brown was the highlight of Canterbury's win over Otago, a win which took them to the top of the Shell Trophy ahead of Wellington. Rutherford and McCullum put on 63 for Otago's first wicket, but Brown's off-breaks began to bite and the visitors slipped to 110 for 5 and only a good innings from Warren Lees averted total collapse. Canterbury fared little better and were 155 for 6 at the close with the left-handed Brown 44 not out. He was left undefeated next day, but Webb and Bruce Blair finished off the Canterbury innings and gained the points. Brown took three more wickets when Otago batted again, but, in search of 209 for victory, Canterbury closed the day at 35 for 2.

On the last day Paul McEwan reached 50 off 35 deliveries, the fastest fifty of the season and Canterbury gained a surprise victory on a turning wicket. They owed much, too, to debutant Anup Nathu who opened and batted for 250 minutes. Otago were handicapped in that Mallender was unable to bowl and Lees took off the keeper's gloves to bowl 18 accurate overs.

### *2, 3 and 4 March 1984*

**at Christchurch**

**Wellington** 158 (E.J. Gray 55 not out, V.R. Brown 4 for 49) and 149 (E.B. McSweeney 72, C.H. Thiele 5 for 52)
**Canterbury** 323 (R.W. Fulton 59 not out, R.P. Jones 56)

*Canterbury won by an innings and 16 runs*
*Canterbury 16 pts, Wellington 0 pts*

**at Nelson**

**Central Districts** 224 for 8 dec (M.H. Toynbee 52 not out) and 0 for 0 dec
**Auckland** 37 for 3 dec and 178 (P.N. Webb 88, P. Visser 7 for 40)

*Central Districts won by 9 runs*
*Central Districts 16 pts, Auckland 0 pts*

**at Hamilton**

**Otago** 428 (W.K. Lees 99, G.J. Dawson 74, S.J. McCullum 65, I.A. Rutherford 62, C.W. Dickeson 4 for 135)
**Northern Districts** 365 (L.M. Crocker 126, C.M. Kuggeleijn 97, B.G. Cooper 52 not out, P.W. Hills 5 for 67)

*Match drawn*
*Otago 4 pts, Northern Districts 0 pts*

Wellington's two-year reign as champions of New Zealand ended at Lancaster Park when a handful of spectators saw them beaten by an innings by Canterbury who consolidated their lead at the top of the table. All of their 60 points had been gained at Lancaster Park.

Batting first on a warm opening day, Wellington gave a poor performance and it was Vaughan Brown who once more led Canterbury's assault with his off-breaks after McNally and Thiele had made early inroads into the Wellington batting. Evan Gray, with 55 in 128 minutes off 116 balls, was the visitors only success. He hit five fours and a six. Ray Jones and Anup Nathu started briskly for the home side against some wayward bowling by Pigott and the day ended with Canterbury 147 for 4. Consistent batting by the lower order on the second day took them to a commanding position and it seemed they would gain victory in two days, but bad light and rain stopped play early with Wellington at 119 for 7. Only a brisk, brave innings from skipper McSweeney saved them from humiliation and he had the added satisfaction of reaching 100 dismissals quicker than any other New Zealand wicket-keeper, but Canterbury needed only 55 minutes on the last morning to get one hand on the Shell Trophy.

Controversy surrounded Central's win at Nelson which put them in second place within 8 points of Canterbury with one match remaining. The match was ruined by rain and Central forfeited their second innings in an effort to obtain a result after Auckland had declared at 37 for 3. There had been no play on the second day and only 3 hours on the first. Auckland were left to make 188 in 180 minutes and a fierce 88 from Peter Webb, nine fours and a six off 103 balls, nearly took them there.

Central's hero was medium-pacer Peter Visser who did the hat-trick in his third over when he had Fisher caught at slip, bowled Hunt and trapped Knowles lbw. He finished with a career best 7 for 40 to win an exciting match. Much credit was due also to Webb and Hellaby who rescued Auckland from 13 for 5. The match ended in semi-darkness. Central's win was upheld after an enquiry as to whether or not declarations had been arranged between the captains.

Some consistent batting saw Otago to a big score at Hamilton where Warren Lees was run out in going for the quick single that would have brought his century. Northern responded with a maiden first-class hundred from Lindsay Crocker who shared a second wicket stand of 222 in 190 minutes with Chris Kuggeleijn who hit sixteen fours in his 97 before being caught behind off Lindsay. Crocket hit twenty-three fours in his 198-minute innings. It was a thrilling stand, but Northern faded after these two were parted.

### *6, 7 and 8 March 1984*

**at Invercargill**

**Otago** 178 for 9 dec (M.H. Toynbee 4 for 47) and 52 for 1
**Central Districts** 179 for 6 dec

*Match drawn*
*Central Districts 4 pts, Otago 0 pts*

**at Wellington**

**Wellington** 83 for 1 dec (J.G. Boyle 51 not out) and 274 for 7 dec (R.H. Vance 114, E.B. McSweeney 60 not out, J.G. Boyle 55, C.W. Dickeson 4 for 96)
**Northern Districts** 85 for 2 dec and 259 (J.M. Parker 110, A.D.G. Roberts 75, S.J. Maguiness 5 for 72)

*Wellington won by 13 runs*
*Wellington 12 pts, Northern Districts 4 pts*

## England in New Zealand 1984
First Class Matches

| BATTING | v. Auckland (Auckland) 7–9 January 1984 | | v. Central Districts (Palmerston N.) 11–13 January 1984 | | v. Northern Districts (Hamilton) 14–16 January 1984 | | First Test Match (Wellington) 20–24 January 1984 | | v. Otago (Dunedin) 27–29 January 1984 | | Second Test Match (Christchurch) 3–5 February 1984 | | Third Test Match (Auckland) 10–15 February 1984 | | *M* | *Inns* | *NOs* | *Runs* | *HS* | *Av* |
|---|---|---|---|---|---|---|---|---|---|---|---|---|---|---|---|---|---|---|---|---|
| C.J. Tavare | 1 | 2 | 89 | 7 | 7 | 7 | 9 | 36* | 4 | 33* | 3 | 6 | | | 6 | 12 | 2 | 204 | 89 | 20.40 |
| G. Fowler | 18 | 6 | 83 | 104 | | | | | 31 | 7 | 4 | 10 | 0 | — | 5 | 9 | — | 263 | 104 | 29.22 |
| D.I. Gower | 84 | 33 | | | 69 | — | 33 | — | 4 | 38 | 2 | 8 | 26 | — | 6 | 9 | — | 297 | 84 | 33.00 |
| A.J. Lamb | 21 | 15 | 51 | 0 | | | 13 | — | 31 | 29 | 11 | 9 | 49 | — | 6 | 10 | — | 229 | 51 | 22.90 |
| M.W. Gatting | 56 | 64 | | | 17 | 24* | 19 | — | 0 | — | 19* | 0 | | | 5 | 8 | 2 | 199 | 64 | 33.16 |
| I.T. Botham | 0 | 44 | 27 | 80 | — | — | 138 | — | | | 18 | 0 | 70 | — | 6 | 8 | — | 377 | 138 | 47.12 |
| R.W. Taylor | 1 | 86 | — | 18* | — | — | 14 | — | 28 | — | 2 | 15 | 23 | — | 7 | 8 | 1 | 187 | 86 | 26.71 |
| G.R. Dilley | 0 | 28 | — | — | | | | | 17* | — | | | | | 3 | 3 | 1 | 45 | 28 | 22.50 |
| N.G.B. Cook | 6 | 8 | | | — | — | 7 | — | 5* | — | | | | | 4 | 4 | 1 | 26 | 8 | 8.66 |
| N.A. Foster | 21 | 8 | | | — | — | 10 | — | | | | | 18* | — | 4 | 4 | 1 | 57 | 21 | 19.00 |
| R.G.D. Willis | 2* | 4* | — | — | — | — | 5* | — | | | 6 | 0 | 3 | — | 6 | 6 | 3 | 20 | 6 | 6.66 |
| C.L. Smith | | | 6 | 3 | 138* | 50 | 27 | 30* | 16 | 9 | | | 91 | — | 5 | 9 | 2 | 370 | 138* | 52.85 |
| D.W. Randall | | | 26 | 66 | 35* | 101* | 164 | — | | | 0 | 25 | 104 | — | 5 | 8 | 2 | 521 | 164 | 86.83 |
| V.J. Marks | | | 3* | 16* | | | | | 50 | — | | | 6 | — | 3 | 4 | 2 | 75 | 50 | 37.50 |
| N.G. Cowans | | | — | — | — | — | | | — | — | 4 | 7 | 21 | — | 5 | 3 | — | 32 | 21 | 10.66 |
| A.C.S. Pigott | | | | | | | | | | | 4 | 8* | | | 1 | 2 | 1 | 12 | 8* | 12.00 |
| Byes | 4 | 6 | | | | | | | 1 | | | | 7 | | | | | | | |
| Leg-byes | 3 | 12 | 4 | 2 | 8 | 5 | 8 | | 2 | 2 | 5 | 2 | 13 | | | | | | | |
| Wides | | | | | 2 | 2 | | | 2 | | | | | | | | | | | |
| No-balls | 3 | 5 | 5 | 4 | 11 | 5 | 16 | 3 | 3 | | 4 | 3 | 8 | | | | | | | |
| Total | 220 | 321 | 294 | 300 | 287 | 194 | 463 | 69 | 194 | 118 | 82 | 93 | 439 | | | | | | | |
| Wickets | 10 | 10 | 6 | 6 | 3 | 2 | 10 | 0 | 8 | 4 | 10 | 10 | 10 | | | | | | | |
| Result | D | | D | | W | | D | | D | | L | | D | | | | | | | |

*Catches* 17 – R.W. Taylor
6 – C.J. Tavare
5 – D.W. Randall
4 – I.T. Botham, D.I. Gower and R.G.D. Willis
3 – C.L. Smith, N.G. Cowans and N.G.B. Cook
2 – N.A. Foster, M.W. Gatting and G. Fowler (inc. one as sub)
1 – A.J. Lamb and G.R. Dilley

| BOWLING | R.G.D. Willis | N.A. Foster | G.R. Dilley | N.G.B. Cook | M.W. Gatting | N.G. Cowans | I.T. Botham | V.J. Marks | C.L. Smith |
|---|---|---|---|---|---|---|---|---|---|
| *v.* Auckland (Auckland) | 18.4–3–68–2 | 23–5–64–3 | 16–2–70–1 | 32–11–67–2 | | | | | |
| 7–9 January 1984 | 3–2–5–0 | 5–0–25–0 | 4–2–4–1 | 5–2–17–0 | 2–2–0–0 | | | | |
| *v.* Central Districts (Palmerston | 12–5–13–2 | | 13–5–16–1 | | | 18–5–45–2 | 13–4–21–0 | 21.3–11–66–5 | |
| North) 11–13 January 1984 | 5–1–25–1 | | 11–4–31–0 | | | 8–3–25–1 | 8–2–31–0 | 24–6–45–0 | |
| *v.* Northern Districts (Hamilton) | 5–3–6–0 | 11–4–30–6 | | 5–2–19–0 | | 12–4–28–1 | 12–4–21–3 | | |
| 14–16 January 1984 | 11–3–26–0 | 12–2–36–0 | | 32–8–91–4 | | 12–3–52–2 | 21.1–9–72–4 | | |
| First Test Match (Wellington) | 19–7–37–3 | 24–9–60–1 | | 23–11–43–1 | | | 27.4–8–59–5 | | |
| 20–24 January 1984 | 37–8–102–2 | 37–12–91–2 | | 66.3–26–153–3 | 8–4–14–1 | | 36–6–137–1 | | 3–1–6–0 |
| *v.* Otago (Dunedin) | | | 18–8–28–3 | 6–2–15–0 | 8–3–19–1 | 11–5–24–0 | | 19.3–4–52–5 | |
| 27–29 January 1984 | | | | | | | | | |
| Second Test Match (Christchurch) | 22.1–5–51–4 | | | | 2–0–14–0 | 14–2–52–3 | 17–1–88–1 | | |
| 3–5 February 1984 | | | | | | | | | |
| Third Test Match (Auckland) | 34–7–109–3 | 30–8–78–1 | | | | 36–11–98–2 | 29–10–70–0 | 40.2–9–115–3 | |
| 10–15 February 1984 | 3–1–7–0 | | | | | 2–1–4–0 | | | |
| | 169.5–45–<br>449–17<br>*av.* 26.41 | 142–40–<br>384–13<br>*av.* 29.53 | 62–21–<br>149–6<br>*av.* 24.83 | 169.3–62–<br>405–10<br>*av.* 40.50 | 20–9–<br>47–2<br>*av.* 23.50 | 113–34–<br>328–11<br>*av.* 29.81 | 163.5–44–<br>499–14<br>*av.* 35.64 | 105.2–30–<br>278–13<br>*av.* 21.38 | 3–1–<br>6–0<br>— |

Central's attempt to rob Canterbury of the Shell Trophy ended in farce at Invercargill. There was no play on the first day and play did not begin until 2.00 pm on the second when Otago reached 178 for 9. Otago declared overnight and Central took first innings points and then raced through 37 overs in an attempt to avoid penalties for slow over rate earlier in the season, an undignified end to their challenge for the Trophy.

Rain affected the game at Basin Reserve which was virtually resolved on one innings. Boyle and Vance added 100 for Wellington's second wicket and McSweeney hit well, scoring all but 7 of a 66-run stand with Morrison.

Northern were left 150 minutes plus 20 overs to score 273 and reached 174 for 2 before the final hour thanks to Parker and Roberts who added 169 for the third wicket in 131 minutes. Parker, having reached the twenty-first hundred of his career, was out at 209 and Cooper left 7 runs later. The decisive change in fortunes came in the seventeenth of the last twenty overs when Maguiness dismissed Wright, Young and Brendon Bracewell with successive deliveries for the first hat-trick of his career. Northern were now 241 for 8 and the end came when Morrison took a diving catch at slip to dismiss Carrington off Gray with only 4 balls remaining.

### *9, 10 and 11 March 1984*

**at Auckland**

**Canterbury** 293 (P.E. McEwan 155, A.E. Blain 53 not out) and 135 for 3 dec (P.E. McEwan 52)
**Auckland** 178 for 8 dec (A.T.R. Hellaby 50 not out, V.R. Brown 4 for 38) and 87 for 1

*Match drawn*
*Canterbury 4 pts, Auckland 0 pts*

Rain was the eventual winner in the last Shell Trophy match of the season in which new champions Canterbury had the best of the encounter. A sparkling 155 in 242 minutes off 192 balls with twenty-six fours from Paul McEwan was the highlight of the first day. Auckland's reply was tediously slow and rain interruptions hindered progress and finally ended play early after Bull's encouraging declaration.

| A.C.S. Pigott | Byes | Leg-byes | Wides | No-balls | Total | Wkts |
|---|---|---|---|---|---|---|
| | 1 | 12 | | 1 | 283 | 8 |
| | 1 | 3 | | 3 | 58 | 1 |
| | | 6 | 1 | | 168 | 10 |
| | | 3 | | 3 | 163 | 2 |
| | | 3 | 1 | 3 | 111 | 10 |
| | | 4 | | 12 | 293 | 10 |
| | 4 | 9 | | 7 | 219 | 10 |
| | 4 | 14 | 2 | 14 | 537 | 10 |
| | 4 | 3 | 1 | 6 | 152 | 9 |
| 17–7–75–2 | 8 | 11 | 2 | 6 | 307 | 10 |
| | | 19 | | 7 | 496 | 9 |
| | | 1 | | 4 | 16 | 0 |
| 17–7–75–2 *av.* 37.50 | | | | | | |

**Shell Trophy Final Table** (1983 positions in brackets)

| | *P* | *W* | *L* | *D* | *1st Inns Lead* | *Pts* |
|---|---|---|---|---|---|---|
| Canterbury (5) | 8 | 4 | 1 | 3 | 4 | 64 |
| Central Districts (2) | 8 | 3 | 1 | 4 | 5 | 56 |
| Wellington (1) | 8 | 3 | 2 | 3 | 4 | 52 |
| Auckland (6) | 8 | 2 | 4 | 2 | 4 | 40 |
| Otago (3) | 8 | 1 | 2 | 5 | 5 | 32 |
| Northern Districts (4) | 8 | — | 3 | 5 | 2 | 8 |

## Shell Cup Final
## WELLINGTON *v.* AUCKLAND

Early reports suggested that the final had been abandoned because of bad weather and the Cup awarded to Wellington because of their better qualifying record. In the event a soggy 35-over match was played which Auckland won with 9 balls to spare.

Ormiston and Gray had lifted Wellington's innings from drabness and Pigott had played some lusty blows at the close, but Auckland had never really been troubled. Gray bowled well and Franklin dithered for a while and there was anxiety when 4 wickets fell for 8 runs, but Hunt and Snedden stopped further progress by Wellington and saw their side to victory.

Hunt's fielding brought him the individual fielding award and Greatbatch, who had had a poor season in the first-class game, won some consolation as he was named Man of the Match for his fine innings of 47.

*Martin Snedden, dropped from the national side, had some consolation in leading Auckland to victory in the Shell Cup. (George Herringshaw)*

## Auckland 1983–84
First Class Matches

| BATTING | v. Canterbury (Christchurch) 27–29 Dec. 1983 | | v. Otago (Alexandra) 31 December 1983–2 January 1984 | | v. England XI (Auckland) 7–9 January 1984 | | v. Northern Districts (Rotorua) 10–12 January 1984 | | v. Central Districts (Auckland) 16–18 January 1984 | | v. Wellington (Auckland) 26–28 January 1984 | | v. Northern Districts (Auckland) 1–3 February 1984 | | v. Central Districts (Nelson) 2–4 March 1984 | | v. Canterbury (Auckland) 9–11 March 1984 | | M | Inns | NOs | Runs | HS | Av |
|---|---|---|---|---|---|---|---|---|---|---|---|---|---|---|---|---|---|---|---|---|---|---|---|---|---|---|
| P.N. Webb | 4 | 56 | 32 | 14 | 38 | 41* | | | | | 3 | 30 | 16 | 11* | 1 | 88 | 6 | — | 7 | 13 | 2 | 340 | 88 | 30.90 |
| T.J. Franklin | 0 | 57 | 106 | 29 | 0 | 0 | 59 | — | 1 | 18 | 8 | 70* | 58 | 9* | | | 21 | 47* | 8 | 15 | 3 | 483 | 106 | 40.25 |
| J.F. Reid | 7 | 10 | 4 | 21 | 43 | — | 8 | — | | | 106 | 25* | 69 | — | | | | | 6 | 9 | 1 | 293 | 106 | 36.62 |
| J.J. Crowe | 3 | 38 | 34 | 85 | 23 | — | 151 | — | 5 | 18 | 43 | — | | | | | | | 6 | 9 | — | 400 | 151 | 44.44 |
| M.J. Greatbatch | 39 | 0 | 5 | 1 | 2 | 10* | 0 | — | 10 | 10 | | | 1 | — | 28* | 7 | 10 | 6 | 8 | 14 | 2 | 129 | 39 | 10.75 |
| M.C. Snedden | 2 | 0 | 64* | 18 | 27 | — | 5 | — | 1 | 3 | 38* | — | 41 | — | — | 18* | 15 | — | 9 | 12 | 3 | 232 | 64* | 25.77 |
| A.T.R. Hellaby | 10 | 0 | | | 4 | — | | | 34 | 0 | 1 | — | | | — | 46 | 50* | — | 6 | 8 | 1 | 145 | 50* | 20.71 |
| J.G. Bracewell | 17 | 11 | 28 | 4 | 104* | — | 2* | — | 26 | 0 | 52 | — | 59 | — | | | | | 7 | 10 | 2 | 303 | 104* | 37.87 |
| P.J. Kelly | 2 | 22 | 3 | 0 | 0 | — | 2 | — | 2 | 10 | 8 | — | 4 | — | — | 5 | 14 | — | 9 | 12 | — | 72 | 22 | 6.00 |
| G.B. Troup | 0 | 3 | 2* | 6 | 28* | — | 0 | — | 5 | 0 | 0 | — | — | — | — | 0 | 13* | — | 9 | 11 | 3 | 57 | 28* | 7.12 |
| S.R. Tracy | 0* | 9* | | | — | — | 0 | — | 0* | 8 | | | — | — | | | — | — | 6 | 5 | 3 | 17 | 9* | 8.50 |
| A.J. Hunt | | | 10 | 10 | | | 14 | — | 6 | 0 | | | | | 5* | 0 | 12 | 34* | 5 | 9 | 2 | 91 | 34* | 13.00 |
| R.J. Ackland | | | — | 0* | | | 5 | — | | | | | | | | | | | 2 | 2 | 1 | 5 | 5 | 5.00 |
| I.D. Fisher | | | | | | | | | 41 | 13* | 4 | — | 41 | — | 0 | 2 | | | 4 | 6 | 1 | 101 | 41 | 20.20 |
| L.W. Stott | | | | | | | | | | | 5 | — | 0* | — | — | 2 | 11 | — | 4 | 4 | 1 | 18 | 11 | 6.00 |
| R. Brazendale | | | | | | | | | | | | | | | 1 | 0 | | | 1 | 2 | — | 1 | 1 | 0.50 |
| D. Knowles | | | | | | | | | | | | | | | — | 0 | 13 | — | 2 | 2 | — | 13 | 13 | 6.50 |
| Byes | 4 | 5 | 4 | 2 | 1 | 1 | | | 5 | | | 3 | 1 | | 1 | | 4 | | | | | | | |
| Leg-byes | 7 | 3 | 6 | 3 | 12 | 3 | (24) | | 7 | 1 | 2 | 1 | 11 | (8) | 1 | 1 | 6 | | | | | | | |
| Wides | | | | | | | | | | | | | 3 | | | | 1 | | | | | | | |
| No-balls | 3 | | 4 | 1 | 1 | 3 | | | 2 | | 5 | 1 | 7 | | | 9 | 2 | | | | | | | |
| Total | 98 | 214 | 302 | 194 | 283 | 58 | 270 | | 145 | 81 | 275 | 130 | 311 | 28 | 37 | 178 | 178 | 87 | | | | | | |
| Wickets | 10 | 10 | 8 | 10 | 8 | 1 | 10 | | 10 | 10 | 10 | 1 | 8 | 0 | 3 | 10 | 8 | 0 | | | | | | |
| Result | L | | L | | D | | D | | L | | W | | W | | L | | D | | | | | | | |
| Points | 0 | | 4 | | — | | 4 | | 0 | | 16 | | 16 | | 0 | | 0 | | | | | | | |

*Catches* 31 – P.J. Kelly (ct 30/st 1)
9 – A.J. Hunt and J.G. Bracewell
7 – J.F. Reid
6 – T.J. Franklin
5 – M.J. Greatbatch, J.J. Crowe and M.C. Snedden
4 – A.T.R. Hellaby (plus 1 as sub)
3 – L.W. Stott and P.N. Webb
2 – G.B. Troup and I.D. Fisher
1 – S.R. Tracy and D. Knowles

| BOWLING | S.R. Tracy | G.B. Troup | M.C. Snedden | A.T.R. Hellaby | J.G. Bracewell | J.F. Reid | R.J. Ackland | A.J. Hunt | I.D. Fisher |
|---|---|---|---|---|---|---|---|---|---|
| *v.* Canterbury (Christchurch) | 14–1–50–1 | 24–5–88–4 | 26.1–10–74–1 | 11–5–25–2 | 30–10–72–2 | | | | |
| 27–29 December 1983 | | | | | | | | | |
| *v.* Otago (Auckland) | | 18–5–61–1 | 18–1–77–3 | | 33–9–68–3 | | 23–4–63–3 | | |
| 31 Dec. 1983–2 Jan. 1984 | | 9–0–41–0 | 14–5–26–0 | | 32.1–10–82–2 | 5–0–19–0 | 11–2–35–0 | 8–4–10–1 | |
| *v.* England XI (Auckland) | 8.4–1–46–3 | 14–3–59–1 | 18–4–70–6 | 6–0–22–0 | 4–1–13–0 | | | | |
| 7–9 January 1984 | 16–2–49–2 | 22–4–61–2 | 25–9–50–2 | 19.4–9–41–3 | 27–4–90–1 | 4–0–7–0 | | | |
| *v.* Northern Districts (Rotorua) | 17–6–52–2 | 21–6–35–1 | 19–7–28–2 | | 17–8–22–4 | | | | |
| 10–12 January 1984 | 17–2–65–4 | 18–4–59–0 | 17–6–42–1 | | 46.4–18–77–4 | | 21–6–29–1 | 1–1–0–0 | |
| *v.* Central Districts (Auckland) | 10–1–31–2 | 14.5–4–49–3 | 25–9–62–3 | 16–1–48–2 | | | | | |
| 16–18 January 1984 | 9–2–41–0 | 20–8–45–4 | 16–2–57–2 | 2–0–19–0 | 14–5–52–0 | | | 8–2–26–4 | 3–0–11–0 |
| *v.* Wellington (Auckland) | | 17–7–39–2 | 24–5–55–3 | 3–1–7–0 | 31.2–13–56–3 | | | | |
| 26–28 January 1984 | | 20–3–58–3 | 12–5–11–1 | 5–2–6–0 | 46–21–78–5 | 8–4–23–0 | | | |
| *v.* Northern Districts (Auckland) | 7–0–25–0 | 13–2–47–2 | 12–5–24–1 | | 28–13–32–6 | 1–0–7–0 | | | |
| 1–3 February 1984 | 9–2–23–2 | 16–4–54–3 | 8–1–23–0 | | 33–11–63–2 | | | | |
| *v.* Central Districts (Nelson) | | 12–4–24–1 | 14–5–30–2 | 4–0–9–0 | | | | 25–10–60–1 | |
| 2–4 March 1984 | | | | | | | | | |
| *v.* Canterbury (Auckland) | 11–4–42–2 | 20–5–45–3 | 15.4–4–48–2 | 12–3–36–2 | | | | 17–5–42–0 | |
| 9–11 March 1984 | 3–0–13–0 | 5–0–18–0 | 10–4–19–1 | 1–0–6–0 | | | | 3–1–21–0 | |
| | 121.4–21–437–18 *av.* 24.27 | 263.5–64–783–30 *av.* 26.10 | 273.5–82–696–30 *av.* 23.20 | 79.4–21–219–9 *av.* 24.33 | 342.1–123–705–32 *av.* 22.03 | 18–4–56–0 — | 55–12–127–4 *av.* 31.75 | 62–23–159–6 *av.* 26.50 | 3–0–11–0 — |

†C.W. Dickeson retired hurt a D. Knowles 3–2–5–1

## SHELL CUP FINAL – WELLINGTON *v.* AUCKLAND
17 March 1984 at Basin Reserve, Wellington

| WELLINGTON | | |
|---|---|---|
| C. Pickett | b Tracy | 0 |
| J.G. Boyle | b Troup | 7 |
| R.H. Vance | c and b Hellaby | 12 |
| R.W. Ormiston | run out | 37 |
| E.J. Gray | c Webb, b Troup | 20 |
| E.B. McSweeney†* | not out | 20 |
| J.F.M. Morrison | b Troup | 0 |
| A.C.S. Pigott | not out | 17 |
| S.J. Maguiness | | |
| K.B. Marshall | | |
| P. Schofer | | |
| Extras | lb 8, nb 8 | 16 |
| (35 overs) | (for 6 wickets) | 129 |

| | O | M | R | W |
|---|---|---|---|---|
| Tracy | 7 | 4 | 11 | 1 |
| Troup | 7 | — | 26 | 3 |
| Stott | 7 | — | 35 | — |
| Hellaby | 7 | — | 16 | 1 |
| Snedden | 7 | — | 25 | — |

FALL OF WICKETS
1- 1, 2- 9, 3- 48, 4- 87, 5- 90, 6- 90

| AUCKLAND | | |
|---|---|---|
| T.J. Franklin | st McSweeney, b Gray | 4 |
| M.J. Greatbatch | b Gray | 47 |
| P.N. Webb | run out | 19 |
| A.T.R. Hellaby | c Pickett, b Gray | 5 |
| A.J. Hunt | not out | 15 |
| D. Knowles | lbw, b Maguiness | 0 |
| M.C. Snedden† | not out | 28 |
| P.J. Kelly* | | |
| L.W. Stott | | |
| S.R. Tracy | | |
| G.B. Troup | | |
| Extras | b 1, lb 6, w 5 | 12 |
| (33.3 overs) | (for 5 wickets) | 130 |

| | O | M | R | W |
|---|---|---|---|---|
| Pigott | 6 | 2 | 11 | — |
| Marshall | 7 | 1 | 25 | — |
| Gray | 7 | — | 22 | 3 |
| Schofer | 6.3 | — | 34 | — |
| Maguiness | 7 | — | 26 | 1 |

FALL OF WICKETS
1- 20, 2- 78, 3- 80, 4- 85, 5- 86

**Auckland won by 5 wickets**

## First Class Averages

| BATTING | M | Inns | NOs | Runs | HS | Av | 100s | 50s |
|---|---|---|---|---|---|---|---|---|
| P. Blackbourn | 3 | 4 | 2 | 154 | 58 | 77.00 | | 2 |
| A.E. Blain | 3 | 5 | 3 | 122 | 53* | 61.00 | | 1 |
| P.E. McEwan | 8 | 12 | | 713 | 155 | 59.41 | 2 | 5 |
| M.D. Crowe | 9 | 14 | 1 | 649 | 151 | 49.92 | 3 | 1 |
| J.J. Crowe | 9 | 13 | | 630 | 151 | 48.46 | 2 | 2 |
| I.D.S. Smith | 9 | 13 | 4 | 390 | 113* | 43.33 | 1 | 1 |
| P.S. Briasco | 8 | 13 | 2 | 472 | 157 | 42.90 | 1 | 2 |
| J.V. Coney | 8 | 13 | 1 | 513 | 174* | 42.75 | 1 | 1 |
| T.J. Franklin | 8 | 15 | 3 | 483 | 106 | 40.25 | 1 | 4 |
| R.J. Hadlee | 6 | 9 | 1 | 305 | 99 | 38.12 | | 2 |
| J.G. Bracewell | 7 | 10 | 2 | 303 | 104* | 37.87 | 1 | 2 |
| R.W. Fulton | 3 | 5 | 2 | 113 | 59* | 37.66 | | 1 |
| J.F. Reid | 6 | 9 | 1 | 293 | 106 | 36.62 | 1 | 1 |
| E.J. Gray | 8 | 14 | 4 | 362 | 103* | 36.20 | 1 | 1 |
| J.R. Wiltshire | 7 | 11 | 1 | 347 | 105 | 34.70 | 1 | 1 |
| L.M. Crocker | 9 | 17 | | 588 | 126 | 34.58 | 1 | 2 |
| J.G. Wright | 5 | 9 | 1 | 273 | 130 | 34.12 | 1 | |
| A.D.G. Roberts | 9 | 16 | 2 | 475 | 75 | 33.92 | | 3 |
| J.M. Parker | 9 | 17 | 2 | 506 | 110 | 33.73 | 1 | 3 |
| G.J. Dawson | 9 | 15 | 2 | 434 | 77 | 33.38 | | 3 |
| A.J. Jones | 5 | 8 | 3 | 163 | 41* | 32.60 | | |
| B.A. Edgar | 8 | 15 | 1 | 452 | 106 | 32.28 | 2 | 1 |
| S.J. McCullum | 9 | 16 | | 514 | 121 | 32.12 | 1 | 3 |
| R.W. Ormiston | 8 | 13 | 4 | 287 | 104* | 31.88 | 1 | 1 |
| W.K. Lees | 9 | 12 | 1 | 350 | 99 | 31.81 | | 3 |
| G.P. Howarth | 9 | 16 | | 508 | 80 | 31.75 | | 5 |
| I.A. Rutherford | 3 | 5 | 1 | 127 | 62 | 31.75 | | 1 |
| K.R. Rutherford | 8 | 14 | 1 | 408 | 93 | 31.38 | | 2 |
| E.B. McSweeney | 8 | 12 | 1 | 342 | 92 | 31.09 | | 3 |
| P.N. Webb | 7 | 13 | 2 | 340 | 88 | 30.90 | | 2 |
| A.P. Nathu | 3 | 5 | 1 | 121 | 70* | 30.25 | | 1 |
| R.T. Hart | 9 | 15 | 1 | 395 | 167* | 28.21 | 1 | 1 |
| D.R. Hadlee | 6 | 5 | | 140 | 69 | 28.00 | | 1 |
| R.E. Hayward | 9 | 14 | 2 | 331 | 102 | 27.58 | 1 | 3 |
| C.M. Presland | 8 | 15 | 4 | 292 | 97* | 26.54 | | 2 |
| R.H. Vance | 8 | 16 | 2 | 363 | 114 | 25.92 | 1 | 2 |
| V.R. Brown | 8 | 11 | 1 | 259 | 69 | 25.90 | | 3 |
| S.J. Gill | 6 | 9 | 3 | 155 | 37 | 25.83 | | |
| J.G. Boyle | 7 | 13 | 1 | 303 | 63 | 25.25 | | 3 |
| D.J. Walker | 6 | 10 | 1 | 223 | 113 | 24.77 | 1 | |
| M.C. Snedden | 10 | 14 | 3 | 259 | 64* | 23.54 | | 1 |
| B.R. Blair | 8 | 14 | 1 | 299 | 65 | 23.00 | | 2 |
| P.J. Holland | 7 | 12 | 3 | 206 | 67 | 22.88 | | 1 |
| R.N. Hoskin | 8 | 14 | | 313 | 105 | 22.35 | 1 | 1 |
| G.N. Cederwall | 5 | 7 | | 153 | 68 | 21.85 | | 1 |
| A.T.R. Hellaby | 6 | 8 | 1 | 145 | 50* | 20.71 | | 1 |
| M.H. Toynbee | 9 | 13 | 3 | 207 | 52* | 20.70 | | 1 |
| I.R. Snook | 9 | 15 | | 309 | 52 | 20.60 | | 1 |
| R.P. Jones | 3 | 5 | | 103 | 56 | 20.60 | | 1 |
| I.D. Fisher | 4 | 6 | 1 | 101 | 41 | 20.20 | | |
| D.R. O'Sullivan | 7 | 7 | 2 | 101 | 33 | 20.20 | | |
| B.L. Cairns | 9 | 16 | | 288 | 64 | 18.00 | | 2 |
| C.L. Bull | 8 | 11 | 1 | 167 | 40 | 16.70 | | |
| M.J.E. Wright | 7 | 13 | | 205 | 41 | 15.76 | | |
| G.K. Robertson | 9 | 10 | | 155 | 46 | 15.50 | | |
| D.J. White | 7 | 14 | 1 | 177 | 40 | 13.61 | | |
| C.W. Dickeson | 8 | 13 | 2 | 125 | 59 | 11.36 | | 1 |
| M.J. Greatbatch | 8 | 14 | 2 | 129 | 39 | 10.75 | | |

(Qualification – 100 runs, average 10.00)
(C.M. Kuggeleijn played in two matches, scoring 97 and 47 not out)

| L.W. Stott | R. Brazendale | P.N. Webb | *Byes* | *Leg-byes* | *Wides* | *No-balls* | *Total* | *Wkts* |
|---|---|---|---|---|---|---|---|---|
| | | | 5 | 4 | 1 | 5 | 324 | 10 |
| | | | | | | | | |
| | | | | 3 | | 6 | 278 | 10 |
| | | | | | | 6 | 219 | 4 |
| | | | 4 | 3 | | 3 | 220 | 10 |
| | | | 6 | 12 | | 5 | 321 | 10 |
| | | | | (9) | | | 146 | 9† |
| | | | | (9) | | | 281 | 10 |
| | | | 5 | 4 | 1 | 5 | 205 | 10 |
| | | | 10 | 1 | | 1 | 263 | 10 |
| 11–4–24–2 | | | 2 | 2 | 1 | 8 | 194 | 10 |
| 12–4–24–1 | | | 3 | 5 | 1 | | 209 | 10 |
| 8–2–13–1 | | | 2 | 2 | 1 | | 153 | 10 |
| 11–5–15–3 | | | | 2 | | | 180 | 10 |
| 18–8–19–1 | 21–9–59–3 | | | 7 | 1 | 15 | 224 | 8 |
| | | | | | | | | |
| 18–5–65–1 | | | | 6 | 1 | 8 | 293 | 10 |
| 0.3–0–4–0 | | 8–1–40–1 | | 4 | | 5 | 135 | 3a |
| 78.3–28–164–9 *av.* 18.22 | 21–9–59–3 *av.* 19.66 | 8–1–40–1 *av.* 40.00 | | | | | | |

**Canterbury 1983–84**
First Class Matches

## BATTING

| | *v.* Auckland (Christchurch) 27–29 Dec. 1983 | | *v.* Northern Districts (Christchurch) 31 December 1983–2 January 1984 | | *v.* Wellington (Wellington) 5–7 January 1984 | | *v.* Otago (Dunedin) 19–21 January 1984 | | *v.* Central Districts (New Plymouth) 26–28 January 1984 | | *v.* Otago (Christchurch) 24–26 February 1984 | | *v.* Wellington (Christchurch) 2–4 March 1984 | | *v.* Auckland (Auckland) 9–11 March 1984 | | *M* | *Inns* | *NOs* | *Runs* | *HS* | *Av* |
|---|---|---|---|---|---|---|---|---|---|---|---|---|---|---|---|---|---|---|---|---|---|---|
| A.J. Devlin | 20 | — | 0 | — | | | | | 0 | 5 | | | | | | | 3 | 4 | — | 25 | 20 | 6.25 |
| R.T. Latham | 2 | — | 36 | 0 | 5 | 5* | 1 | — | | | | | | | | | 4 | 6 | 1 | 49 | 36 | 9.80 |
| P.E. McEwan | 80 | — | 51 | 10 | 114 | — | 1 | — | 77 | 12 | 46 | 74 | 41 | — | 155 | 52 | 8 | 12 | — | 713 | 155 | 59.41 |
| V.R. Brown | 13 | — | 12 | 0 | 64 | — | 1 | — | 69 | 2 | 53* | 17 | 4 | — | 24 | — | 8 | 11 | 1 | 259 | 69 | 25.90 |
| C.L. Bull | 0 | — | 24 | 11 | 1 | — | 8 | — | 21 | 23 | 6 | 19* | 40 | — | 14 | — | 8 | 11 | 1 | 167 | 40 | 16.70 |
| D.W. Stead | 24 | — | 0 | 6 | | | 18* | — | 23 | 6 | | | | | | | 4 | 6 | 1 | 77 | 24 | 15.40 |
| R.I. Leggat | 4 | — | 1 | 19* | 0 | — | | | | | | | | | | | 3 | 4 | 1 | 24 | 19* | 8.00 |
| R.J. Hadlee | 93 | — | 0 | 35* | | | | | 33 | 0 | | | | | | | 3 | 5 | 1 | 161 | 93 | 40.25 |
| D.R. Hadlee | 69 | — | 7 | — | 48 | — | — | — | | | 6 | — | 10 | — | | | 6 | 5 | — | 140 | 69 | 28.00 |
| A.W. Hart | 4* | — | 10* | — | 12* | — | 19 | — | | | 0 | — | 18 | — | 2 | — | 7 | 7 | 3 | 65 | 19 | 16.25 |
| C.H. Thiele | 0 | — | 5 | — | 2 | — | 4 | — | 0 | 23 | | | 6 | — | 4 | — | 7 | 8 | — | 44 | 23 | 5.50 |
| P.J. Rattray | | | | | 21 | 8* | 14 | — | 14 | 31 | | | | | | | 3 | 5 | 1 | 88 | 31 | 22.00 |
| D.C. Aberhart | | | | | 6 | — | | | | | | | | | | | 1 | 1 | — | 6 | 6 | 6.00 |
| S.N. Bateman | | | | | 1 | — | 0 | — | | | | | | | | | 1 | 2 | — | 1 | 1 | 0.50 |
| A.E. Blain | | | | | | | 1 | — | 16 | 39* | | | | | 53* | 13* | 3 | 5 | 3 | 122 | 53* | 61.00 |
| G.C. Bateman | | | | | | | | | 15 | 5 | | | | | | | 1 | 2 | — | 20 | 15 | 10.00 |
| S.R. McNally | | | | | | | | | 14* | 0 | 0 | — | 47 | — | 5 | — | 4 | 5 | 1 | 66 | 47 | 16.50 |
| R.P. Jones | | | | | | | | | | | 6 | 15 | 56 | — | 3 | 23 | 3 | 5 | — | 103 | 56 | 20.60 |
| A.P. Nathu | | | | | | | | | | | 4 | 70* | 29 | — | 0 | 18 | 3 | 5 | 1 | 121 | 70* | 30.25 |
| R.W. Fulton | | | | | | | | | | | 17 | 2 | 59* | — | 15 | 20* | 3 | 5 | 2 | 113 | 59* | 37.66 |
| A.J. Nuttall | | | | | | | | | | | 12 | 1 | 0 | — | 3 | — | 3 | 4 | — | 16 | 12 | 4.00 |
| K.G. Taylor | | | | | | | | | | | 1 | — | | | | | 1 | 1 | — | 1 | 1 | 1.00 |
| Byes | 5 | | 12 | 3 | 5 | | | | 2 | 2 | 3 | 4 | 5 | | | | | | | | | |
| Leg-byes | 4 | | 3 | 10 | 12 | 1 | (15) | | 6 | | 2 | 6 | 6 | | 6 | 4 | | | | | | |
| Wides | 1 | | 3 | 1 | 1 | | | | 1 | | 4 | 1 | | | 1 | | | | | | | |
| No-balls | 5 | | 11 | 8 | 5 | 1 | | | 6 | 2 | 5 | 1 | 2 | | 8 | 5 | | | | | | |
| Total | 324 | | 175 | 103 | 297 | 15 | 82 | | 297 | 150 | 165 | 210 | 323 | | 293 | 135 | | | | | | |
| Wickets | 10 | | 10 | 5 | 10 | 0 | 9† | | 10 | 10 | 10 | 5 | 10 | | 10 | 3 | | | | | | |
| Result | W | | W | | D | | D | | L | | W | | W | | D | | | | | | | |
| Points | 16 | | 16 | | 0 | | 0 | | 0 | | 12 | | 16 | | 4 | | | | | | | |

*Catches*
18 – A.W. Hart
7 – P.E. McEwan
5 – C.L. Bull and A.E. Blain
4 – R.J. Hadlee
3 – C.H. Thiele, D.W. Stead, R.T. Latham, R.I. Leggat, A.P. Nathu and R.W. Fulton
2 – V.R. Brown, S.R. McNally and A.J. Nuttall
1 – A.J. Devlin, D.C. Aberhart, D.R. Hadlee and R.P. Jones

† D.R. Hadlee absent ill

## BOWLING

| | R.J. Hadlee | C.H. Thiele | D.R. Hadlee | V.R. Brown | A.J. Devlin | D.W. Stead | R.I. Leggat | D.C. Aberhart | S.N. Bateman |
|---|---|---|---|---|---|---|---|---|---|
| *v.* Auckland (Christchurch) | 15–8–14–3 | 12–3–36–4 | 12–8–6–1 | 6–3–7–1 | 3–1–8–0 | 9.3–6–13–1 | | | |
| 27–29 December 1983 | 12–1–31–1 | 14–3–43–1 | 15.4–6–44–4 | 6–3–8–0 | | 18–3–61–4 | 9–2–19–0 | | |
| *v.* Northern Districts (Christchurch) | 17–7–22–3 | 14–3–30–2 | 17–4–45–2 | 11–3–21–1 | | 16.3–3–32–2 | 1–0–4–0 | | |
| 31 Dec. 1983–2 Jan. 1984 | 18–11–14–4 | 10–2–21–0 | 14.1–0–39–4 | 7–3–12–2 | | | | | |
| *v.* Wellington (Wellington) | | 21–3–80–5 | 20–4–43–3 | 22–9–31–0 | | | 5–1–22–0 | 19–5–53–1 | 17–3–51–1 |
| 5–7 January 1984 | | 14–2–36–0 | 6–1–21–0 | 21–8–47–1 | | | 8.4–1–37–0 | 9–1–19–0 | 14–4–36–3 |
| *v.* Otago (Dunedin) | | 27–6–82–1 | | 17–6–18–3 | | 20.2–5–51–3 | | | 15–3–37–2 |
| 19–21 January 1984 | | 5–0–16–1 | | 1–1–0–0 | | 3–0–8–0 | | | 5–1–14–2 |
| *v.* Central Districts (New | | 20–4–73–0 | | 26–10–33–0 | 3–1–8–0 | 24–4–90–1 | | | |
| Plymouth) 26–28 January 1984 | 10–2–16–1 | 19–3–76–1 | | 8–2–39–0 | | 19–6–57–0 | | | |
| *v.* Otago (Christchurch) | | | 15–4–38–1 | 26.4–9–50–7 | | | | | |
| 24–26 February 1984 | | | 9–2–20–1 | 33–9–62–3 | | | | | |
| *v.* Wellington (Christchurch) | | 13.5–4–23–2 | 8–1–31–1 | 16–3–49–4 | | | | | |
| 2–4 March 1984 | | 16.3–6–52–5 | | 10–4–20–1 | | | | | |
| *v.* Auckland (Auckland) | | 19–5–50–1 | | 33–17–38–4 | | | | | |
| 9–11 March 1984 | | 4–0–11–1 | | 6–1–21–0 | | | | | |
| | 72–29–97–12 *av.* 8.08 | 209.2–44–629–24 *av.* 26.20 | 116.5–30–287–17 *av.* 16.88 | 249.4–91–456–27 *av.* 16.88 | 6–2–16–0 — | 110.2–27–312–11 *av.* 28.36 | 23.4–4–82–0 — | 28–6–72–1 *av.* 72.00 | 51–11–138–8 *av.* 17.25 |

a G.C. Bateman 16–0–68–0; 9–2–37–1
b K.G. Taylor 7–1–20–0; 9–4–17–1
c R.P. Jones 2–0–4–0; A.E. Blain 2–0–8–0; A.P. Nathu 2–1–4–0; C.L. Bull 2–0–6–0

| BOWLING | Overs | Mds | Runs | Wkts | Av | Best | 10/m | 5/inn |
|---|---|---|---|---|---|---|---|---|
| R.J. Hadlee | 181.4 | 62 | 329 | 24 | 13.70 | 5/28 | | 1 |
| P. Visser | 88.3 | 21 | 241 | 16 | 15.06 | 7/40 | | 1 |
| D.R. Hadlee | 116.5 | 30 | 287 | 17 | 16.88 | 4/39 | | |
| V.R. Brown | 249.4 | 91 | 456 | 27 | 16.88 | 7/50 | 1 | 1 |
| S.R. McNally | 101 | 28 | 274 | 14 | 19.57 | 4/33 | | |
| S.J. Maguiness | 255.1 | 82 | 546 | 26 | 21.00 | 5/72 | | 1 |
| B.P. Bracewell | 170.2 | 44 | 444 | 21 | 21.14 | 4/23 | | |
| G.K. Robertson | 251.1 | 60 | 728 | 34 | 21.41 | 5/80 | | 1 |
| N.A. Mallender | 177.4 | 35 | 517 | 24 | 21.54 | 4/53 | | |
| J.G. Bracewell | 342.1 | 123 | 705 | 32 | 22.03 | 6/32 | | 2 |
| E.J. Chatfield | 338 | 112 | 676 | 30 | 22.53 | 5/81 | | 1 |
| R.J. Webb | 231 | 50 | 677 | 29 | 23.34 | 6/20 | | 2 |
| D.R. O'Sullivan | 282 | 81 | 739 | 31 | 23.83 | 5/99 | | 1 |
| E.J. Gray | 292.5 | 114 | 651 | 27 | 24.11 | 5/35 | | 1 |
| S.R. Tracy | 121.4 | 21 | 437 | 18 | 24.27 | 4/65 | | |
| B.L. Cairns | 295.1 | 95 | 713 | 29 | 24.58 | 7/143 | | 1 |
| B.R. Blair | 122 | 40 | 278 | 11 | 25.27 | 4/44 | | |
| S.L. Boock | 344 | 141 | 708 | 28 | 25.28 | 4/59 | | |
| G.B. Troup | 263.5 | 64 | 783 | 30 | 26.10 | 4/45 | | |
| D.A. Stirling | 156.3 | 33 | 524 | 20 | 26.20 | 5/101 | | 1 |
| C.H. Thiele | 209.2 | 44 | 629 | 24 | 26.20 | 5/52 | | 2 |
| C.W. Dickeson | 250.2 | 79 | 616 | 23 | 26.78 | 5/45 | | 1 |
| M.C. Snedden | 301.5 | 87 | 825 | 30 | 27.50 | 6/70 | | 1 |
| D.W. Stead | 110.2 | 27 | 312 | 11 | 28.36 | 4/61 | | |
| M.H. Toynbee | 123.2 | 39 | 330 | 11 | 30.00 | 4/47 | | |
| C.M. Presland | 105 | 16 | 379 | 12 | 31.58 | 5/49 | | 1 |
| A.C.S. Pigott | 135 | 33 | 403 | 12 | 33.58 | 4/39 | | |
| S.J. Gill | 140 | 34 | 396 | 11 | 36.00 | 3/57 | | |
| S.M. Carrington | 112 | 20 | 403 | 11 | 36.63 | 3/34 | | |

(Qualification – 10 wickets)

**LEADING FIELDERS**

33–I.D.S. Smith (ct 28/st 5); 32–E.B. McSweeney (ct 28/st 4); 31–P.J. Kelly (ct 30/st 1); 19–W.K. Lees (ct 15/st 4); 18–A.W. Hart; 16–M.D. Crowe; 13–M.J.E. Wright (ct 11/st 2); 12–J.V. Coney; 10–P. Blackbourn (ct 6/st 4) and M.H. Toynbee; 9–B.R. Blair, R.T. Hart, A.J. Hunt and J.G. Bracewell; 8–R.J. Webb, P.S. Briasco, R.E. Hayward and J.J. Crowe

| P.E. McEwan | A.J. Nuttall | S.R. McNally | *Byes* | *Leg-byes* | *Wides* | *No-balls* | *Total* | *Wkts* |
|---|---|---|---|---|---|---|---|---|
| | | | 4 | 7 | | 3 | 98 | 10 |
| | | | 5 | 3 | | | 214 | 10 |
| | | | 8 | 2 | 1 | 5 | 104 | 10 |
| | | | 2 | 11 | | 5 | 104 | 10 |
| | | | 9 | 1 | | 10 | 300 | 10 |
| 5–0–16–0 | | | 5 | 5 | | 2 | 224 | 4 |
| 4–0–10–0 | | | 1 | 8 | | 3 | 210 | 10 |
| | | | | (5) | | | 43 | 3 |
| 3–0–10–0 | | 20–7–55–1 | 4 | 7 | 1 | 7 | 356 | 2a |
| | | 20–7–44–3 | | 4 | | 3 | 276 | 7 |
| 4–1–15–1 | 22–7–50–1 | 5–1–13–0 | 3 | 6 | | | 195 | 10b |
| 5–3–4–1 | 18–9–26–0 | 13–4–33–4 | | (16) | | | 178 | 10 |
| 1–0–2–0 | 4–2–7–0 | 14–3–41–3 | 3 | 2 | | | 158 | 10 |
| | 7–3–11–0 | 17–3–50–3 | 4 | 4 | | 8 | 149 | 10 |
| 1–0–4–0 | 16.3–2–49–2 | 9–3–24–0 | 4 | 6 | 1 | 2 | 178 | 8 |
| | 8–3–19–0 | 3–0–14–0 | | | | | 87 | 1c |
| 23–4–61–2 *av.* 30.50 | 75.3–26–162–3 *av.* 54.00 | 101–28–274–14 *av.* 19.57 | | | | | | |

## CRICKET IN NEW ZEALAND
### by
### DON CAMERON

There is still, Common Market agricultural problems notwithstanding, a general and warm regard in New Zealand for things English and especially for an England cricket team fit and fresh and promising to decorate a New Zealand summer.

We had this pleasant experience some years ago when Geoff Boycott (vice for the injured Mike Brearley) led his men smiling from Auckland airport and genuinely pleased to be among New Zealanders. It might be remarked that Boycott cherished the thought of tour captaincy which had eluded him for so long, and that his men reacted most happily to being among something like home comforts after a short tour of India. Still, they were fresh and keen compared with the England teams which used to regard a New Zealand tour as a tiring and tedious postscript after their four-year expeditions to Australia.

So Alan Smith and Bob Willis and Norman Gifford and Bernard Thomas came genially among us early last January, the players of both sides on the most amiable terms after mixing together in Australia the previous southern summer, and again during the New Zealanders tour of England in mid-1983.

Willis, especially, had the highest hopes for his 'lads', even if he was then and later to mask his true feelings by press-conference remarks which travelled from the droll to the inscrutable, and back again.

Seven weeks later England departed, still of apparent good humour but with Willis' high hopes for his team rather in tatters. He had become the first England captain to lose a Test series in New Zealand, with the incredible New Zealand win at Christchurch sandwiched between two high-scoring no-contests at Wellington and Auckland. He had salvaged a little by winning the first two of the three one-day internationals, but he and his men headed for the plane and the rigours of Pakistan with the hub-bub of the one-day defeat at Eden Park still grumbling in their ears.

Where did England go wrong? The short and not unreasonable answer was that they were undone on a sub-standard pitch at Lancaster Park in the second Test, and that in other matches the results showed that their performances were at least adequate. Willis, to his credit, did not always hide behind that convenient excuse, even if he did tend to go on and on about the state of New Zealand wickets. All history suggested that England, who had only lost once to New Zealand abroad, and once at home, should have performed much better in New Zealand. Willis was aware of this and by the end of the Christchurch Test he did stop his comments about the inadequacies of his batting in one match or his bowling in another to spare the thought that at least at Christchurch New Zealand had batted and bowled much better than England.

But those of us on the sideline who have an old-fashioned regard for the skills of the game, especially those displayed by the past heroes of England, could not help but be amazed at the modest progress, and the steady decline of the England playing standards during the tour. Nor could we escape the plain fact that from halfway through the first Test and onward the New Zealanders played with the growing confidence and polish which Geoff Howarth had been nurturing

## Central Districts 1983–84
First Class Matches

| BATTING | v. Northern Districts (Whangerei) 15–17 Dec. 1983 | | v. Otago (Napier) 27–29 Dec. 1983 | | v. Wellington (Wellington) 31 December 1983–2 January 1984 | | v. England XI (Palmerston North) 11–13 January 1984 | | v. Auckland (Auckland) 16–18 January 1984 | | v. Canterbury (New Plymouth) 26–28 January 1984 | | v. Wellington (Palmerston North) 31 Jan.–2 Feb. 1984 | | v. Auckland (Nelson) 2–4 March 1984 | | v. Otago (Invercargill) 6–8 March 1984 | | *M* | *Inns* | *NOs* | *Runs* | *HS* | *Av* |
|---|---|---|---|---|---|---|---|---|---|---|---|---|---|---|---|---|---|---|---|---|---|---|---|---|
| I.R. Snook | 5 | 52 | 38 | — | 44 | 19 | 17 | 19 | 41 | 19 | 10 | 15 | 1 | 11 | 11 | — | 10 | — | 9 | 15 | — | 309 | 52 | 20.60 |
| R.T. Hart | 0 | 30 | 4 | — | 8 | 27 | 14 | 67 | 1 | 35 | 167* | 6 | 21 | 1 | 11 | — | 3 | — | 9 | 15 | 1 | 395 | 167* | 28.21 |
| P.S. Briasco | 1 | 5* | 16 | — | | | 15 | 65* | 30 | 0 | 157 | 9 | 78 | 26 | 29 | — | 41 | — | 8 | 13 | 2 | 472 | 157 | 42.90 |
| M.D. Crowe | 119 | 0 | 30 | — | 38 | 39 | 41 | — | 17 | 151 | 3* | 63 | | | | | | | 6 | 10 | 1 | 501 | 151 | 55.66 |
| J.R. Wiltshire | 36 | 10 | 72 | — | 4 | 0 | 18 | — | 25 | 25 | — | 105 | 32 | 20* | | | | | 7 | 11 | 1 | 347 | 105 | 34.70 |
| R.E. Hayward | 8 | 23 | 51 | — | 8 | 55 | 8 | 6* | 2 | 0 | — | 12* | 54 | 102 | 0 | — | 2 | — | 9 | 14 | 2 | 331 | 102 | 27.58 |
| M.H. Toynbee | 14 | 1* | 45 | — | 3 | 13 | 5 | — | 19* | 8 | — | 3 | 4 | 5 | 52* | — | 35 | — | 9 | 13 | 3 | 207 | 52* | 20.70 |
| I.D.S. Smith | 79 | 16 | 15 | — | 0 | 22 | 22 | — | 19 | 10* | — | 9* | | | | | | | 6 | 9 | 2 | 192 | 79 | 27.42 |
| S.J. Gill | 7 | 11 | | | 20 | 30* | 0 | — | | | | | 11 | 9* | 37 | — | 30* | — | 6 | 9 | 3 | 155 | 37 | 25.83 |
| D.A. Stirling | 0* | — | 1* | — | 0* | 5 | 0* | — | | | — | 47 | | | | | | | 5 | 6 | 4 | 53 | 47 | 26.50 |
| G.K. Robertson | 0 | 35 | 0 | — | 11 | 5 | 21 | — | 3 | 2 | — | — | 46 | — | 32 | — | — | — | 9 | 10 | — | 155 | 46 | 15.50 |
| D.R. O'Sullivan | | | 4 | — | 10 | 4 | | | 33 | 1 | — | — | 32* | — | 17* | — | — | — | 7 | 7 | 2 | 101 | 33 | 20.20 |
| P. Visser | | | | | | | | | 0 | 0 | | | 8 | — | — | — | — | — | 4 | 3 | — | 8 | 8 | 2.66 |
| P. Blackbourn | | | | | | | | | | | | | 58 | 52* | 0 | — | 44* | — | 3 | 4 | 2 | 154 | 58 | 77.00 |
| C. Smith | | | | | | | | | | | | | | | 12 | — | 0 | — | 2 | 2 | — | 12 | 12 | 6.00 |
| Byes | 1 | 5 | 1 | | 1 | 8 | | | 5 | 10 | 4 | | | | | | 5 | | | | | | | |
| Leg-byes | 5 | 5 | 6 | | 2 | 3 | 6 | 3 | 4 | 1 | 7 | (7) | 3 | 5 | 7 | | 4 | | | | | | | |
| Wides | | | | | | 1 | 1 | | 1 | | 1 | | | 2 | 1 | | | | | | | | | |
| No-balls | 9 | 4 | 6 | | 2 | 6 | | 3 | 5 | 1 | 7 | | 8 | 6 | 15 | | 5 | | | | | | | |
| Total | 284 | 197 | 289 | | 151 | 237 | 168 | 163 | 205 | 263 | 356 | 276 | 356 | 239 | 224 | 0 | 179 | | | | | | | |
| Wickets | 10 | 8 | 10 | | 10 | 10 | 10 | 2 | 10 | 10 | 2 | 7 | 10 | 5 | 8 | 0 | 6 | | | | | | | |
| Result | D | | D | | L | | D | | W | | W | | D | | W | | D | | | | | | | |
| Points | 0 | | 0 | | 0 | | — | | 16 | | 16 | | 4 | | 16 | | 4 | | | | | | | |

*Catches* 24 – I.D.S. Smith (ct 20/st 4)
13 – M.D. Crowe
10 – P. Blackbourn (ct 6/st 4) and M.H. Toynbee
9 – R.T. Hart
8 – P.S. Briasco and R.E. Hayward
4 – S.J. Gill
2 – D.R. O'Sullivan and I.R. Snook
1 – J.R. Wiltshire, P. Visser, C. Smith and sub (Duff)

| BOWLING | G.K. Robertson | S.J. Gill | D.A. Stirling | M.D. Crowe | M.H. Toynbee | P.S. Briasco | R.E. Hayward | I.R. Snook | D.R. O'Sullivan |
|---|---|---|---|---|---|---|---|---|---|
| *v.* Northern Districts (Whangarei) | 23–10–70–2 | 41–8–89–3 | 33.3–9–101–5 | 19–5–53–0 | 3–1–5–0 | 10–4–12–0 | | | |
| 15–17 December 1983 | 11–1–39–2 | 11–1–22–0 | 4–0–25–0 | 8–1–20–0 | 13–3–38–1 | 9–2–28–3 | | | |
| *v.* Otago (Napier) | 19–4–61–0 | | 17–0–71–3 | 23–5–49–2 | 12–7–14–0 | | 1–0–10–0 | | 35.2–8–100–4 |
| 27–29 December 1983 | 21–7–49–3 | | 18–6–33–1 | 2–2–0–0 | 14–4–31–1 | | | 3–1–8–1 | 40.1–19–89–4 |
| *v.* Wellington (Wellington) | 27.4–10–65–3 | 29–9–70–1 | 23–6–70–2 | 14–3–39–1 | 11–2–25–0 | | | | 27–9–71–2 |
| 31 Dec. 1983–2 Jan. 1984 | 4.3–0–10–1 | | 2–0–13–0 | 2–1–4–0 | | | | | |
| *v.* England XI (Palmerston | 14–7–42–1 | 21–5–95–2 | 18–4–67–2 | 11–3–40–0 | 8.2–3–36–1 | 2–0–5–0 | | | |
| North) 11–13 January 1984 | 11–1–41–0 | 16–3–57–3 | 13–1–54–1 | 8–2–32–0 | 3–0–25–2 | 3–1–30–0 | 5–1–23–0 | 1–0–32–0 | |
| *v.* Auckland (Auckland) | 23–9–30–4 | | | 10–4–20–0 | | | | | 9.5–2–32–2 |
| 16–18 January 1984 | 8–0–26–2 | | | 8–0–18–5 | | | | | 13–2–29–3 |
| *v.* Canterbury (New Plymouth) | 21–4–61–3 | | 16–3–50–2 | 14–2–62–0 | 1–0–10–0 | | | | 33.5–9–99–5 |
| 26–28 January 1984 | 12–1–41–3 | | 12–4–40–4 | 7–1–17–1 | | | | | 11–3–48–2 |
| *v.* Wellington (Palmerston North) | 22–1–80–5 | 17–7–41–2 | | | | 3–1–5–0 | | | 17.5–3–60–1 |
| 31 January–2 February 1984 | 14–2–39–2 | 3–0–21–0 | | | 5–2–16–0 | | | | 24–6–65–3 |
| *v.* Auckland (Nelson) | | | | | 10–3–20–1 | 1–1–0–0 | | | 11–6–15–2 |
| 2–4 March 1984 | 16–3–56–3 | 2–1–1–0 | | | 6–0–32–0 | | | | 9–1–39–0 |
| *v.* Otago (Invercargill) | 4–0–18–0 | | | | 19–6–47–4 | | | | 31–6–74–3 |
| 6–8 March 1984 | | | | | 18–8–31–1 | | | | 19–7–18–0 |
| | 251.1–60–728–34 *av.* 21.41 | 140–34–396–11 *av.* 36.00 | 156.3–33–524–20 *av.* 26.20 | 126–29–354–9 *av.* 39.33 | 123.2–39–330–11 *av.* 30.00 | 28–9–80–3 *av.* 26.66 | 6–2–33–0 — | 4–1–40–1 *av.* 40.00 | 282–81–739–31 *av.* 23.83 |

in his team for several years. Steadily, and pleasantly, we came to realise that Howarth's men, once past the cliff-edge of the first Test, developed into a better all-round side than England possessed. That on good pitches or bad the New Zealand batsmen were likely to prosper more than England's, that on good pitches or bad the New Zealand bowlers were likely to cause the false or fatal stroke more often than England's.

For those New Zealanders lately involved with the game and who had rejoiced at New Zealand's recent successes at Test and one-day level the New Zealand success caused joy and only a little surprise. For those of us who had watched and suffered a good deal for New Zealand cricket over long years of poverty the sight of New Zealanders looking more confident, more technically accurate, more likely to seize the main chance, produced a state of bemusement which, as I write, still remains.

A look at the Test figures only adds to the bewilderment. Derek Randall, 293 runs at 73.75, confirms a cricketer of breeding. Ian Botham, 226 at 56, figures somewhat in keeping with this astonishing cricketer and Chris Smith, 154 at 77 after a somnolent 91 in the third Test. But what do we make of Lamb with 82 runs, Mike Gatting with 38, Chris Tavare with 54, David Gower with 69, Graeme Fowler with 14, Bob Taylor with 54?

Or bowling, in which only the indomitable Willis, 12 wickets at 25, looked a bowler of Test-match class or attitude. Botham seven wickets at 50, Norman Cowans five at 30, Neil Foster four at 57 – none of these suggesting Test-match application, all of them hinting the wide gap between reputation and performance.

How different the New Zealand figures. Only four New Zealand bowlers took wickets, Richard Hadlee 12 at 19, Lance Cairns 12 at 20, Stephen Boock seven at 20, Ewen Chatfield six at 31. The batting is equally lop-sided, six men over 140 runs each, Jeff Crowe, Jeremy Coney and John Wright in the 200s, Jeff Crowe, Martin Crowe, Coney and Ian Smith scoring their maiden Test hundreds, Wright, Jeff Crowe and Smith all scoring hundreds in the first innings at Auckland.

A harsh and independent judge would, on this evidence, pass a heavy sentence against England, and very likely without the right of appeal. England may challenge that, protesting that the conditions for the second Test at Lancaster Park were unfair, inferior, and so forth. But a higher court would still uphold the sentence for that second Test showed harshly but completely the wide gap in attitudes between the two teams. Mental attitudes, tactical attitudes, technical attitudes.

It was common knowledge that Lancaster Park had produced inferior pitches before the Test, which had accelerated Canterbury's start in their eventual Shell Trophy victory, and that only a week before the first Test the New Zealand Cricket Council was convinced, on Christchurch-prepared evidence, that the Test should remain at Lancaster Park and not be shifted to the more docile strip at McLean Park in Napier.

But the Test remained at Lancaster Park and England had the unsettling problem of having both Foster and Graham Dilley unfit and had to call in Tony Pigott, then involved with Wellington and bowling indifferently after a run of leg injuries.

New Zealand, in contrast, had, through marvellous centuries by Martin Crowe and Coney, batted itself clear of defeat with a second innings of 537 in the first Test at Wellington. There was an air of positive confidence among the New Zealanders, especially among the batsmen who had done well at Wellington. This confidence echoed from Howarth who won the toss and decided to bat first. Even before a ball was bowled the pitch was described as a minefield, but Howarth had faith in his batsmen, and wanted to press home the batting advantage won at Wellington.

If Willis had similar faith in his bowlers it was seldom repaid. He worked himself as industriously as ever, even if he probably sowed the first seeds of despair among his batsmen when early on he made a ball snarl up past John Wright's nose.

But Botham, on a pitch that suited anyone of some pace and accuracy, bowled like a tipsy tramp. Pigott could not last long even after removing Bruce Edgar. Worse still, the whole bowling tactical plan was awry. The early bowling was short, and Wright, Jeff Crowe and Coney off the back foot peppered away at the mid-wicket fence. Hadlee arrived at 137 for five, and a prime target for short-pitched bowling. Instead, through new tactics or old carelessness, the bowlers gave Hadlee a generous length, he slashed away happily both sides of point on through mid-on. It was heart-in-the-mouth batting, but it worked, 99 from 81 balls, 18 daring slashes to the fence, and with Smith maintaining his confidence gained at Wellington, New Zealand reached the heady heights of 307.

Just to confirm that everything belonged to New Zealand Howarth gave Boock an over at the fag-end of the day and a genial little tweak removed a mesmerised Fowler.

The pitch was not good, but it was usable and, against bowling of such indiscipline that field-placing was difficult, if offered runs at a rapid pace.

Surely England could not bat as badly as they had bowled. They did, in spades. The second day was delayed until 4.30, and then came the complete contrast. Hadlee and Chatfield

| *P. Visser* | *Byes* | *Leg-byes* | *Wides* | *No-balls* | *Total* | *Wkts* |
|---|---|---|---|---|---|---|
| | 15 | 7 | 5 | 6 | 363 | 10 |
| | | 6 | | | 178 | 6 |
| | 2 | 7 | 3 | 5 | 322 | 10 |
| | 6 | 9 | | 5 | 230 | 10 |
| | 8 | 6 | | 6 | 360 | 9 |
| | | 1 | | 1 | 29 | 1 |
| | | 4 | | 5 | 294 | 6 |
| | | 3 | | 3 | 300 | 6 |
| 23–6–49–3 | 5 | 7 | | 2 | 145 | 10 |
| 4–2–7–0 | | 1 | | | 81 | 10 |
| | 2 | 6 | 1 | 6 | 297 | 10 |
| | 2 | | | 2 | 150 | 10 |
| 13–2–48–2 | 3 | 3 | | 6 | 246 | 10 |
| 21–5–64–2 | | 3 | 1 | 1 | 210 | 8 |
| | 1 | 1 | | | 37 | 3 |
| 15.3–4–40–7 | | 1 | | 9 | 178 | 10 |
| 12–2–33–2 | 2 | | 1 | 3 | 178 | 9 |
| | 1 | 1 | 1 | | 52 | 1 |
| 88.3–21–241–16 *av.* 15.06 | | | | | | |

## Northern Districts 1983–84

First Class Matches

| BATTING | v. Central Districts (Whangarei) 15–17 Dec. 1983 | | v. Wellington (Tauranga) 27–29 Dec. 1983 | | v. Canterbury (Christchurch) 31 December 1983–2 January 1984 | | v. Otago (Dunedin) 5–7 January 1984 | | v. Auckland (Rotorua) 10–12 January 1984 | | v. England XI (Hamilton) 14–16 January 1984 | | v. Auckland (Auckland) 1–3 February 1984 | | v. Otago (Hamilton) 2–4 March 1984 | | v. Wellington (Wellington) 6–8 March 1984 | | M | Inns | NOs | Runs | HS | Av |
|---|---|---|---|---|---|---|---|---|---|---|---|---|---|---|---|---|---|---|---|---|---|---|---|---|
| L.M. Crocker | 15 | 96 | 79 | 40 | 19 | 1 | 9 | 22 | 18 | 46 | 15 | 6 | 39 | 6 | 126 | — | 30 | 21 | 9 | 17 | — | 588 | 126 | 34.58 |
| J.G. Wright | | | | | | | | | 2 | 22 | 16 | 15 | | | | | | | 2 | 4 | — | 55 | 22 | 13.75 |
| G.P. Howarth | 57 | 20 | 46 | 11 | 16 | 4 | 80 | 62 | 4 | 60 | 0 | 55 | | | | | | | 6 | 12 | — | 415 | 80 | 34.58 |
| J.M. Parker | 5 | 40 | 13 | 18 | 58 | 6 | 6 | 21 | 34 | 55* | 2 | 31 | 5 | 69 | 32 | — | 1* | 110 | 9 | 17 | 2 | 506 | 110 | 33.73 |
| A.D.G. Roberts | 12 | 1 | 42 | 36 | 7 | 19 | 29 | 73* | 12 | 13 | 22 | 58 | 26 | 28* | 22 | — | — | 75 | 9 | 16 | 2 | 475 | 75 | 33.92 |
| B.L. Cairns | 53 | 0 | 3 | 36 | 5 | 14 | 11 | 22 | 11 | 35 | 0 | 1 | | | | | | | 6 | 12 | — | 191 | 53 | 15.91 |
| M.J.E. Wright | 29 | 2 | 6 | 0 | 7 | 0 | | | | | 24 | 39 | 41 | 37 | 2 | — | 3 | 15 | 7 | 13 | — | 205 | 41 | 15.76 |
| D.J. White | 0 | 4* | 7 | 0 | 12 | 23 | 11 | 40 | 38 | 5 | 6 | 2 | 24 | 5 | | | | | 7 | 14 | 1 | 177 | 40 | 13.61 |
| C.M. Presland | 97* | 9* | 17 | 14 | 13 | 12* | 4 | 43 | 3 | 0 | 6 | 58 | 1 | 1 | | | — | 14* | 8 | 15 | 4 | 292 | 97* | 26.54 |
| B.P. Bracewell | 0 | — | 0 | 30 | 9 | 4 | 5 | — | 10* | 8 | 13* | 0* | 8 | 9 | 3 | — | — | 0 | 9 | 14 | 3 | 99 | 30 | 9.00 |
| C.W. Dickeson | 59 | — | 22 | 0 | 3 | 0 | | | 5* | 14 | 0 | 12 | 0* | 4 | 2 | — | — | 4 | 8 | 13 | 2 | 125 | 59 | 11.36 |
| S.M. Carrington | 3 | — | 0* | 2* | 5* | 3 | 0 | — | | | | | 0 | 4 | 0 | — | — | 4 | 7 | 10 | 3 | 21 | 5* | 3.00 |
| R.D. Broughton | | | | | | | 39 | 11 | | | | | 4 | 2 | | | | | 2 | 4 | — | 56 | 39 | 14.00 |
| G. McKenzie | | | | | | | 12* | 21* | | | | | | | | | | | 1 | 2 | 2 | 33 | 21* | — |
| B. Young | | | | | | | | | 0 | 14 | | | 0 | 13 | 2 | — | — | 0 | 4 | 6 | — | 29 | 14 | 4.83 |
| C.M. Kuggeleijn | | | | | | | | | | | | | | | 97 | — | 47* | 0 | 2 | 2 | 1 | 144 | 97 | 144.00 |
| B.G. Cooper | | | | | | | | | | | | | | | 52* | — | — | 4 | 2 | 2 | 1 | 56 | 52* | 56.00 |
| M.R. McKinnon | | | | | | | | | | | | | | | 14 | — | | | 1 | 1 | — | 14 | 14 | 14.00 |
| Byes | 15 | | 1 | 2 | 8 | 2 | 10 | 5 | | | | | 2 | | 2 | | | 3 | | | | | | |
| Leg-byes | 7 | 6 | 5 | 3 | 2 | 11 | 5 | 7 | (9) | (9) | 3 | 4 | 2 | 2 | 5 | | 3 | 6 | | | | | | |
| Wides | 5 | | | | 1 | | 1 | 4 | | | 1 | | 1 | | 2 | | | | | | | | | |
| No-balls | 6 | | 1 | | 5 | 5 | 7 | 8 | | | 3 | 12 | | | 4 | | 1 | 3 | | | | | | |
| Total | 363 | 178 | 242 | 192 | 170 | 104 | 229 | 339 | 146 | 281 | 111 | 293 | 153 | 180 | 365 | | 85 | 259 | | | | | | |
| Wickets | 10 | 6 | 10 | 10 | 10 | 10 | 10 | 7 | 9† | 10 | 10 | 10 | 10 | 10 | 10 | | 2 | 10 | | | | | | |
| Result | D | | D | | L | | D | | D | | L | | L | | D | | L | | | | | | | |
| Points | 4 | | 0 | | 0 | | 0 | | 0 | | — | | 0 | | 0 | | 4 | | | | | | | |

*Catches* 13 – M.J.E. Wright (ct 11/st 2)
5 – B.P. Bracewell, J.M. Parker and B. Young
4 – C.M. Presland, L.M. Crocker, C.W. Dickeson and A.D.G. Roberts
3 – S.M. Carrington
2 – G.P. Howarth, D.J. White and B.L. Cairns
1 – J.G. Wright, R.D. Broughton and C.M. Kuggeleijn

†C.W. Dickeson retired hurt

| BOWLING | B.P. Bracewell | C.M. Presland | C.W. Dickeson | B.L. Cairns | A.D.G. Roberts | G.P. Howarth | S.M. Carrington | J.M. Parker | D.J. White |
|---|---|---|---|---|---|---|---|---|---|
| *v.* Central Districts (Whangarei) | 15.5–3–52–2 | 7–1–30–1 | 14–4–48–0 | 23–6–64–4 | 6–1–10–0 | | 14–2–50–2 | 1–0–5–0 | 3–0–10–0 |
| 15–17 December 1983 | 8–4–11–0 | | 14–4–54–4 | 13–8–17–0 | | 6–0–45–3 | 7–3–13–1 | | 11–2–43–0 |
| *v.* Wellington (Tauranga) | 21–3–63–1 | 3–0–13–0 | 31.2–13–45–5 | 37–14–68–4 | | 3–1–2–0 | 4–1–11–0 | | 11–2–30–0 |
| 27–29 December 1983 | 2–1–7–0 | | 13–3–36–3 | 11–2–22–2 | | 2–1–1–0 | 4–0–17–0 | 1–1–0–0 | 2–1–2–0 |
| *v.* Canterbury (Christchurch) | 6–3–12–0 | 17–3–49–5 | 2–1–1–0 | 15.1–5–37–2 | 3–0–9–0 | 1–0–4–0 | 14–5–34–3 | | |
| 31 Dec. 1983–2 Jan. 1984 | 9–2–23–4 | 2–0–19–0 | | 8–2–22–0 | | | 6–0–17–0 | | |
| *v.* Otago (Dunedin) | 17–3–64–2 | 9–1–28–1 | | 14–4–46–0 | | 6–0–30–0 | 16–1–65–2 | | |
| 5–7 January 1984 | 9–2–30–3 | 6–1–20–1 | | 7–2–11–0 | 5–1–15–1 | | 6–2–20–0 | | 7–2–14–0 |
| *v.* Auckland (Rotorua) | 21.3–9–34–3 | 14–4–38–2 | | 28–10–70–4 | 10–2–43–1 | 14–2–44–0 | | | 6–2–17–0 |
| 10–12 January 1984 | | | | | | | | | |
| *v.* England XI (Hamilton) | 13–2–43–1 | 15–2–50–1 | 28–9–57–0 | 10–1–41–1 | 15–3–56–0 | 4–0–19–0 | | | |
| 14–16 January 1984 | 7–2–19–0 | 10–1–41–1 | 19–5–35–1 | 16–2–64–0 | 6–1–23–0 | | | | |
| *v.* Auckland (Auckland) | 9–4–9–3 | 8–1–46–0 | 32–6–95–2 | | 15–6–33–1 | | 15–0–60–1 | | 8–1–31–1 |
| 1–3 February 1984 | | | 4–1–13–0 | | | | | | |
| *v.* Otago (Hamilton) | 21–3–52–1 | | 59–20–135–4 | | 12–3–34–0 | | 16–2–86–1 | | |
| 2–4 March 1984 | | | | | | | | | |
| *v.* Wellington (Wellington) | 6–2–15–0 | 8–1–26–0 | 7–6–1–0 | | 8–5–11–0 | | 6–2–19–1 | | |
| 6–8 March 1984 | 5–1–10–1 | 6–1–19–0 | 27–7–96–4 | | 3–1–12–0 | | 4–2–11–0 | 4–0–31–0 | |
| | 170.2–44–444–21 *av.* 21.14 | 105–16–379–12 *av.* 31.58 | 250.2–79–616–23 *av.* 26.78 | 182.1–56–462–17 *av.* 27.17 | 83–23–246–3 *av.* 82.00 | 36–4–145–3 *av.* 48.33 | 112–20–403–11 *av.* 36.63 | 6–1–36–0 — | 48–10–147–1 *av.* 147.00 |

a M.R. McKinnon 31.2–5–113–2 b C.M. Kuggeleijn 17–5–66–1

bowled the full attacking length the new ball demanded. They offered very few loose deliveries while at the other end Cairns ambled in, if anything making the ball swing too much, but still reducing the batsmen to prodding uncertainty. By stumps England were in tatters, 53 for seven. The next day they were gone for 82 and Howarth gleefully sent England back in again.

If the England batting on the first innings had represented bewildered uncertainty, that of the second represented, Randall and Taylor excepted, docile resignation. Rather than try and make the best of a bad pitch, which Randall and Taylor did manfully but with small return, too many of the England batsmen gave up the ghost. It seemed as if they should not be expected to play on such a pitch, that everything was rather beneath their dignity. How else could you explain Botham smiling genially after prodding a catch from the first ball he received, at something below lethal intent, from Boock.

So the sad and benumbing funeral went on until England, in a fraction over two days' playing time, were out for 93, defeated by an innings and 132 runs.

It should be added that Howarth handled his bowlers cleverly and they all, especially Hadlee and Chatfield, bowled the ideal line and length for such a pitch. The catching behind the stumps was also outstanding.

But afterwards some of us sat in the deserted grandstand trying to describe this incredible slaughter, to get it into some kind of perspective. It was plain that England had bowled indifferently and batted with, for the most part, no sense or discipline. Threading through the mind came visions of past Englishmen, especially of men of Kenny Barrington's steel or Ted Dexter's audacity. One could not imagine Barrington capitulating so completely. He would have got the tip of that craggy nose even closer to that defiant chin and he would have fought for survival. Dexter would have batted with bitter reprisal, or Colin Cowdrey with quick-witted technique. It might be unfair to compare the men of the present with the heroes of the past, but these are the men who linger in New Zealanders' minds. The heritage of England cricket is still within New Zealand's soul, and yet here we were watching England players resign, losing their wickets with a smile, regarding a humbling, crushing defeat as simply a matter of 22 yards of ill-mannered turf. For many of us there was the touch of gall amid the sweet taste of success that evening.

There were some macabre touches the next day. Rather than continue a Test on the main Lancaster Park field the Englishmen the next day walked over the field on their way to the practice nets. Some of them, and Alan Smith, dallied by the pitch.

With a mixture of glee and surprise they noted, round about Hadlee's attacking length and line, a largish square of the pitch which was loose. They eased the large piece out and Smith bore it with some haste to some England cricket writers who were also wandering toward the training nets. Smith exhibited the piece of turf with suitable expressions of surprise, perhaps of justification for yesterday's debacle.

What Smith did not realise was that earlier that morning the groundsman and a Canterbury official had ventured out to the pitch with a spade and, in the cause of finding out what problems lurked below, had levered out a chunk of the pitch, examined the subsoil, and then replaced the large divot which Smith later seized upon.

There was never the prospect that anyone would dig large pieces out of the Eden Park used for the third Test, nor that the batsmen would be presented with unmannerly behaviour by the ball. Eden Park has a recent history of producing a docile batting strip which requires very good bowling, or very bad batting, to produce a result. The last time Willis played there New Zealand scored heavily in both innings, led by Howarth with a century in each.

Even before the third Test Willis seemed resigned that the match would be drawn, and New Zealand would take the series. He had really only one option – to bat first, and to take in two spinners, Nick Cook and Vic Marks, who might pin the New Zealand batsmen down on a slow pitch. But Willis reasoned that spinners had not been effective the last time he played on Eden Park, so he left out Cook, lengthened what was politely called his batting, and on the face of it rather hoped that things would turn out right. Howarth overtrumped by winning the toss and batting. Willis might have made the right decision by his own reasoning, but he should have realised that medium-fast bowlers tend to become modest pluggers on Eden Park and anyone on the front foot has no right to get out once the shine has left the ball. Howarth had no reason to take any risk, so Boock was his only spinner, and Howarth simply asked his men for a first innings of 400, preferably going into the third day.

This, amid some breaks for rain, they achieved, with Wright soldiering on with a painful back for a century, Jeff Crowe coming along with his first century in Tests, and Smith impishly clipping another as the England bowling was reduced to a walk. The rest, which included Smith's painstaking, and often painful, 91 and a flowing century from Randall, passed peacefully enough and New Zealand had their series win.

Even considering the erratic England batting, and the variable quality of the bowling, this was a singular achievement for Howarth and his men. Before the series Howarth

| G. McKenzie | M.J.E. Wright | B.G. Cooper | *Byes* | *Leg-byes* | *Wides* | *No-balls* | *Total* | *Wkts* |
|---|---|---|---|---|---|---|---|---|
| | | | 1 | 5 | | 9 | 284 | 10 |
| | | | 5 | 5 | | 4 | 197 | 8 |
| | | | 6 | 6 | | 19 | 263 | 10 |
| | | | 1 | 5 | | | 91 | 5 |
| | | | 12 | 3 | 3 | 11 | 175 | 10 |
| | | | 3 | 10 | 1 | 8 | 103 | 5 |
| 5–1–47–0 | | | 11 | 8 | 2 | 17 | 318 | 5 |
| 6–0–25–1 | | | 6 | 1 | 2 | 7 | 151 | 6 |
| | | | | (24) | | | 270 | 10 |
| | | | | | | | | |
| | | | | 8 | 2 | 11 | 287 | 3 |
| | | | | 5 | 2 | 5 | 194 | 2 |
| | 6–1–15–0 | | 1 | 11 | 3 | 7 | 311 | 8 |
| | 4–1–7–0 | | | (8) | | | 28 | 0 |
| | | | 2 | 3 | 1 | 2 | 428 | 10a |
| | | | | | | | | |
| | | 1–0–5–0 | 2 | 1 | | 3 | 83 | 1 |
| | | 3–1–19–1 | 5 | 5 | | | 274 | 7b |
| 11–1–72–1 *av.* 72.00 | 10–2–22–0 — | 4–1–24–1 *av.* 24.00 | | | | | | |

## Otago 1983–84
First Class Matches

| BATTING | v. Central Districts (Napier) 27–29 Dec. 1983 | | v. Auckland (Alexandra) 31 December 1983–2 January 1984 | | v. Northern Districts (Dunedin) 5–7 January 1984 | | v. Wellington (Hutt) 12–14 January 1984 | | v. Canterbury (Dunedin) 19–21 January 1984 | | v. England XI (Dunedin) 27–29 January 1984 | | v. Canterbury (Christchurch) 24–26 February 1984 | | v. Northern Districts (Hamilton) 2–4 March 1984 | | v. Central Districts (Invercargill) 6–8 March 1984 | | *M* | *Inns* | *NOs* | *Runs* | *HS* |
|---|---|---|---|---|---|---|---|---|---|---|---|---|---|---|---|---|---|---|---|---|---|---|---|
| K.R. Rutherford | 24 | 27 | 2 | 77 | 0 | 2 | | | 93 | 10 | 47 | — | 33 | 20 | 13 | — | 37 | 23* | 8 | 14 | 1 | 408 | 93 |
| S.J. McCullum | 53 | 0 | 57 | 34 | 121 | 20 | 7 | 11 | 11 | 4 | 17 | — | 33 | 39 | 65 | — | 42 | 0 | 9 | 16 | — | 514 | 121 |
| R.N. Hoskin | 20 | 13 | 105 | 1 | 2 | 0 | 66 | 41 | 9 | 0 | 2 | — | 1 | 16 | | | 37 | — | 8 | 14 | — | 313 | 105 |
| B.R. Blair | 22 | 43 | 4 | 50 | 1 | 21 | 2 | 65 | 10 | 4* | 1 | — | 27 | 5 | 44 | — | | | 8 | 14 | 1 | 299 | 65 |
| G.J. Dawson | 31 | 26 | 55 | 29* | 77 | 26 | 36 | 21 | 2 | 20* | 20 | — | 11 | 6 | 74 | — | 0 | — | 9 | 15 | 2 | 434 | 77 |
| A.J. Jones | | | 14 | 22* | 33* | 41* | 17 | 4 | 32 | — | 0 | — | | | | | | | 5 | 8 | 3 | 163 | 41* |
| S.J. Richards | 1 | 15 | | | | | | | | | 25 | — | | | 16 | — | | | 3 | 4 | — | 57 | 25 |
| W.K. Lees | 13 | 60 | 3 | — | — | 3* | 0 | 33 | 27 | — | 11 | — | 55 | 28 | 99 | — | 18 | — | 9 | 12 | 1 | 350 | 99 |
| N.A. Mallender | 12 | 12 | 0 | — | — | — | 0 | 17* | 9* | — | 2 | — | 2* | 4 | | | | | 7 | 9 | 3 | 58 | 17* |
| S.L. Boock | 16* | 9 | 4 | — | — | — | 1 | 14 | 0 | — | 13* | — | | | | | | | 6 | 7 | 2 | 57 | 16* |
| R.J. Webb | 0 | 0* | 4* | — | — | — | 0* | 0 | 4 | — | — | — | 0 | 0* | 4* | — | 1* | — | 9 | 10 | 6 | 13 | 4* |
| D.J. Walker | 113 | 5 | 21 | — | 46* | 22 | 0 | 10 | 1 | — | | | 0 | 5 | | | | | 6 | 10 | 1 | 223 | 113 |
| J.K. Lindsay | | | | | | | 8 | 5 | | | | | 18 | 7 | 1 | — | 5 | — | 4 | 6 | — | 44 | 18 |
| I.A. Rutherford | | | | | | | | | | | | | 6 | 32 | 62 | — | 1 | 26* | 3 | 5 | 1 | 127 | 62 |
| R. Mawhinney | | | | | | | | | | | | | | | 41 | — | 14 | — | 2 | 2 | — | 55 | 41 |
| P.W. Hills | | | | | | | | | | | | | | | 1 | — | 8 | — | 2 | 2 | — | 9 | 8 |
| K. Ibadulla | | | | | | | | | | | | | | | | | 9* | — | 1 | 1 | 1 | 9 | 9* |
| Byes | 2 | 6 | | | 11 | 6 | 2 | 7 | 1 | | 4 | | 3 | | 2 | | 2 | 1 | | | | | |
| Leg-byes | 7 | 9 | 3 | | 8 | 1 | 8 | 4 | 8 | (5) | 3 | | 6 | (16) | 3 | | | 1 | | | | | |
| Wides | 3 | | | | 2 | 2 | 1 | | | | 1 | | | | 1 | | 1 | 1 | | | | | |
| No-balls | 5 | 5 | 6 | 6 | 17 | 7 | 5 | | 3 | | 6 | | | | 2 | | 3 | | | | | | |
| Total | 322 | 230 | 278 | 219 | 318 | 151 | 153 | 232 | 210 | 43 | 152 | | 195 | 178 | 428 | | 178 | 52 | | | | | |
| Wickets | 10 | 10 | 10 | 4 | 5 | 6 | 10 | 10 | 10 | 3 | 9 | | 10 | 10 | 10 | | 9 | 1 | | | | | |
| Result | D | | W | | D | | L | | D | | D | | L | | D | | D | | | | | | |
| Points | 4 | | 12 | | 4 | | 0 | | 4 | | — | | 4 | | 4 | | 0 | | | | | | |

*Catches* 19 – W.K. Lees (ct 15/st 4)
9 – B.R. Blair
8 – R.J. Webb
7 – S.J. McCullum
5 – S.L. Boock
4 – R.N. Hoskin and I.A. Rutherford
3 – A.J. Jones and N.A. Mallender
2 – G.J. Dawson, D.J. Walker, K.R. Rutherford and J.K. Lindsay
1 – R. Mawhinney, P.W. Hills

| BOWLING | N.A. Mallender | R.J. Webb | B.R. Blair | S.L. Boock | A.J. Jones | K.R. Rutherford | G.J. Dawson | R. Mawhinney | D.J. Walker |
|---|---|---|---|---|---|---|---|---|---|
| *v.* Central Districts (Napier) | 25–4–82–3 | 26–1–106–3 | | 46.2–27–65–4 | | | | | 10–2–23–0 |
| 27–29 December 1983 | | | | | | | | | |
| *v.* Auckland (Alexandra) | 26–5–72–2 | 18–3–56–0 | 8–0–35–1 | 32–11–78–2 | | | | | 23–6–43–2 |
| 31 Dec. 1983–2 Jan. 1984 | 21–3–66–4 | 14–2–39–1 | 9–2–24–1 | 25.1–13–59–4 | | | | | |
| *v.* Northern Districts (Dunedin) | 20–3–71–3 | 17–5–38–2 | 11–3–28–0 | 17.4–8–19–1 | | | | | 21–5–50–4 |
| 5–7 January 1984 | 18–2–57–2 | 25–8–74–1 | | 52–19–144–4 | 9–3–26–0 | | 3–2–4–0 | | 8–3–10–0 |
| *v.* Wellington (Hutt) | 19–3–56–1 | 17–5–44–1 | 27–11–44–4 | 40.2–11–81–3 | | | | | 25–11–44–0 |
| 12–14 January 1984 | 6.4–1–24–1 | 4–0–20–1 | | 10–6–20–2 | | | | | |
| *v.* Canterbury (Dunedin) | 13–8–16–2 | 11–5–20–6 | | 14–4–31–0 | | | | | |
| 19–21 January 1984 | | | | | | | | | |
| *v.* England XI (Dunedin) | 20–4–53–4 | 20–2–76–3 | 5–1–4–0 | 18–4–53–1 | | | | | |
| 27–29 January 1984 | 8–2–10–2 | 7–1–17–0 | 8–2–26–1 | 8–4–18–0 | 6–0–31–0 | 1–0–1–0 | 1–0–13–0 | | |
| *v.* Canterbury (Christchurch) | 1–0–6–0 | 14–3–30–5 | 10–3–33–3 | | | | 2–1–12–0 | | 10–6–21–0 |
| 24–26 February 1984 | | 14–4–29–1 | 30–13–54–1 | | | | | | |
| *v.* Northern Districts (Hamilton) | | 25–6–72–2 | 14–5–30–0 | | | 3–0–18–1 | | 15–5–50–0 | |
| 2–4 March 1984 | | | | | | | | | |
| *v.* Central Districts (Invercargill) | | 19–5–56–3 | | | | | | 13–5–22–2 | |
| 6–8 March 1984 | | | | | | | | | |
| | 177.4–35–517–24 *av.* 21.54 | 231–50–677–29 *av.* 23.34 | 122–40–278–11 *av.* 25.27 | 263.3–107–568–21 *av.* 27.04 | 15–3–57–0 — | 4–0–19–1 *av.* 19.00 | 6–3–29–0 — | 28–10–72–2 *av.* 36.00 | 97–33–191–6 *av.* 31.83 |

†D.R. Hadlee absent ill    a S.J. McCullum 0.2–0–0–1    b K. Ibadulla 13–3–43–1

spoke often of New Zealand's failures in England after their historic win at Headingley, and of the need for the players to restore their own confidence, and the home public's pride in the team.

Yet Howarth and his men were somewhere short of Test-match mood when they started the first Test at Wellington. Botham was quickly among them, five wickets in an innings of 219. The score had some respectability when Cairns reduced England to 115 for five, but Cairns dropped Botham at nought, there were two other chances discarded, and Botham (138) and Randall (184) were together in a sixth wicket stand of 232, out of a total of 463 which looked good enough to win the match.

But for two days all New Zealanders seemed to hold their breath as Martin Crowe reached his maiden century, the irrepressible Coney went on to 174 and with substantial help from Cairns and Smith carried New Zealand to 537 and safety.

Cairns with his seven for 143, Crowe and Coney with their hundreds had done the trick for Howarth. They had shown that the England bowling did not have sharp teeth, and that consistent bowling could thwart most of the England batsmen. It was the lift, the precious boost, which the New Zealanders needed, and it was this confidence, a thinly disguised superiority complex, which Howarth and his men took into the historic win in Christchurch.

The public pride in Howarth's men lapped over into the three one-day internationals, so much so that before the first match was played at Lancaster Park the 41,000 seats for the third at Eden Park a week later had already been sold. But while the crowds were big and boisterous the one-day hysteria of past summers was, blessedly, muted. The Test series had been won, and the one-day matches were put in their proper perspective – little cameos of entertainment.

It said much for Willis' steadfast captaincy that he re-assembled his ragged army and won the first and second one-dayers, the first after a magical innings by Randall, the second through an artful display of spin-bowling by Marks. The third at Eden Park brought the flourish New Zealanders wanted – runs at last for Howarth, and a bristling century by Martin Crowe to over-balance a muscular 97 by Lamb.

| J.K. Lindsay | W.K. Lees | P.W. Hills | *Byes* | *Leg-byes* | *Wides* | *No-balls* | *Total* | *Wkts* |
|---|---|---|---|---|---|---|---|---|
| | | | 1 | 6 | | 6 | 289 | 10 |
| | | | 4 | 6 | | 4 | 302 | 8 |
| | | | 2 | 3 | | 1 | 194 | 10 |
| | | | 10 | 5 | 1 | 7 | 229 | 10 |
| | | | 5 | 7 | 4 | 8 | 339 | 7 |
| 10–3–34–0 | | | 2 | 7 | 3 | 1 | 316 | 10 |
| | | | 1 | | | 5 | 70 | 4 |
| | | | | | (15) | | 82 | 9† |
| | | | 1 | 2 | 2 | 3 | 194 | 8 |
| | | | | 2 | | | 118 | 4a |
| 15–3–49–2 | | | 3 | 2 | 4 | 5 | 165 | 10 |
| 24–8–75–1 | 18.2–4–40–1 | | 4 | 6 | 1 | 1 | 210 | 5 |
| 34–9–115–2 | | 30–6–67–5 | 2 | 5 | 2 | 4 | 365 | 10 |
| 1–1–0–0 | | 9–2–44–0 | 5 | 4 | | 5 | 179 | 6b |
| 84–24<br>273–5<br>*av.* 54.60 | 18.2–4–<br>40–1<br>*av.* 40.00 | 39–8–<br>111–0<br>— | | | | | | |

There was, at the tail-end of this Eden Park one-dayer a pleasant touch by Botham which went largely unnoticed. Botham had not had the happiest of tours on the field. His batting seemed brittle, his bowling lacking either verve or concentration. Martin Crowe had recently been signed to play for Botham's county, Somerset. Botham was fielding close in, rather like a half-point, when Crowe cracked the ball for the four which he needed for his century. Botham might have stopped the ball. Instead he made a rather exaggerated leap out of the line of shot. Then as the game ended and the crowd poured on to the field Botham salvaged one of the stumps and presented it to Crowe as they raced off the field.

It was a gracious act. There were many such from Willis and his men, and also from Howarth and his New Zealanders. History will judge Willis' men harshly, perhaps the least-equipped England side to tour New Zealand. But the comradeship between the players, and everyone's willingness to play cricket and forget the nonsense and the aggro did give the tour and the Test series a special mark of distinction.

In a rather more tangible aspect the tour, with its drama and crowd-pulling appeal, also struck a substantial blow for the finances of the New Zealand Cricket Council. The facts and figures are not yet available, but the prospect is that the NZCC will make a profit of close to $200,000 from the summer, and this will give the NZCC more room in which to make its financial manoeuvres.

The cash-register had scarcely stopped ringing before the New Zealanders were away to Sri Lanka for a tour which brought two Test wins and a draw, and a 2–1 lead in the one-day series. Hadlee held almost all the Sri Lankans in thrall, and the temporary eclipse of Bruce Edgar gave away to the restoration of John Reid, the Auckland left-hander, as a batsman of genuine international quality against spin-bowling. The New Zealanders had their problems in Sri Lanka, perhaps in the anti-climax after beating England. The Test series set all kinds of records for slow over-rates, but by the time of the last test Reid with 180 and Hadlee with two bags of five wickets gave New Zealand victory by an innings. Hadlee had 23 wickets in the three Test series and Boock moved back into the Test establishment with 11 wickets.

To the New Zealanders at home it was a strange, rather unreal tour. Only one newspaper correspondent went with the New Zealanders, and Radio New Zealand was not interested enough to send a tour commentator – instead they paid Coney $5000 to provide his off-beat reports. So the tour seemed to exist in some weird kind of vacuum, and did not have the impact it deserved.

However, it completed a summer in which New Zealand won three Tests and drew three, rich fare after the thin pickings of previous years. There were, as well as the NZCC profit, other riches to consider. The Crowe brothers moved up the ladder into international players of genuine ability. Reid moved back into the Test batting ranks. Coney and Wright flourished, in about the same proportion as Howarth and Edgar lapsed into temporary decline. Smith, whose early selections as a wicket-keeper came from his latent ability as a batsman, suddenly blossomed into a decidedly useful accumulator of runs at number 7 or 8.

## Wellington 1983–84
First Class Matches

| BATTING | v. Northern Districts (Tauranga) 27–29 Dec. 1983 | | v. Central Districts (Wellington) 31 December 1983–2 January 1984 | | v. Canterbury (Wellington) 5–7 January 1984 | | v. Otago (Hutt) 12–14 January 1984 | | v. Auckland (Auckland) 26–28 January 1984 | | v. Central Districts (Palmerston North) 31 Jan–2 Feb 1984 | | v. Canterbury (Christchurch) 2–4 March 1984 | | v. Northern Districts (Wellington) 6–8 March 1984 | | M | Inns | NOs | Runs | HS | Av |
|---|---|---|---|---|---|---|---|---|---|---|---|---|---|---|---|---|---|---|---|---|---|---|---|
| R.H. Vance | 18 | 23 | 0 | 10* | 12 | 29 | 3 | 9 | 59 | 56 | 1 | 10 | 14 | 2 | 3* | 114 | 8 | 16 | 2 | 363 | 114 | 25.92 |
| B.A. Edgar | 23 | 33 | 71 | 15 | 105 | 11 | 106 | 15 | 8 | 25 | | | | | | | 5 | 10 | — | 412 | 106 | 41.20 |
| J.G. Boyle | 38 | — | | | 12 | 0 | 63 | 12 | 9 | 4 | 32 | 27 | 0 | 0 | 51* | 55 | 7 | 13 | 1 | 303 | 63 | 25.25 |
| J.V. Coney | 38 | 5 | 5 | — | 38 | 39 | 51 | 11 | 37 | 38 | | | | | | | 5 | 9 | — | 262 | 51 | 29.11 |
| R.W. Ormiston | 4 | 2* | 104* | — | 55 | — | 15 | 0* | 11 | 5 | 2 | 35* | 25 | 21 | — | 8 | 8 | 13 | 4 | 287 | 104* | 31.88 |
| E.J. Gray | 27 | 9* | 41 | — | 27 | 103* | 1 | 17* | 24 | 0 | 39 | 6 | 55* | 0 | — | 13 | 8 | 14 | 4 | 362 | 103* | 36.20 |
| E.B. McSweeney | 5 | 0 | 9 | — | 4 | — | 24 | — | 27 | 24 | 92 | 18 | 7 | 72 | — | 60* | 8 | 12 | 1 | 342 | 92 | 31.09 |
| P.J. Holland | 33 | — | 1 | 2* | 0 | 30* | 28* | — | 2 | 14 | 15 | 67 | 24 | 0 | | | 7 | 12 | 3 | 206 | 67 | 22.88 |
| A.C.S. Pigott | 18 | — | 21 | — | | | | | | | 7 | 26 | 7 | 6 | — | 0 | 5 | 7 | — | 85 | 26 | 12.14 |
| G.N. Cederwall | 27 | 13 | 68 | — | 11 | — | 8 | — | | | 26 | 0 | | | | | 5 | 7 | — | 153 | 68 | 21.85 |
| E.J. Chatfield | 1* | — | — | — | 4* | — | 4 | — | 0* | 1* | | | | | | | 5 | 5 | 4 | 10 | 4* | 10.00 |
| S.J. Maguiness | | | 20 | — | 12 | — | 0 | — | 4 | 25 | 8* | 4* | 14 | 9 | — | 1* | 7 | 10 | 3 | 97 | 25 | 13.85 |
| K.B. Marshall | | | | | | | | | 0 | 8 | | | | | | | 1 | 2 | — | 8 | 8 | 4.00 |
| J.F.M. Morrison | | | | | | | | | | | 11 | 12 | 4 | 12 | — | 7 | 3 | 5 | — | 46 | 12 | 9.20 |
| B.W. Cederwall | | | | | | | | | | | 1 | 0* | 0 | 7 | | | 2 | 4 | 1 | 8 | 7 | 2.66 |
| P. Schofer | | | | | | | | | | | | | 3 | 4* | — | — | 2 | 2 | 1 | 7 | 4* | 7.00 |
| C. Pickett | | | | | | | | | | | | | | | 23 | 6 | 1 | 2 | — | 29 | 23 | 14.50 |
| T. Vogel | | | | | | | | | | | | | | | — | — | 1 | — | | | | — |
| Byes | 6 | 1 | 8 | | 9 | 5 | 2 | 1 | 2 | 3 | 3 | | 3 | 4 | 2 | 5 | | | | | | |
| Leg-byes | 6 | 5 | 6 | 1 | 1 | 5 | 7 | | 2 | 5 | 3 | 3 | 2 | 4 | 1 | 5 | | | | | | |
| Wides | | | | | | | 3 | | 1 | 1 | | 1 | | | | | | | | | | |
| No-balls | 19 | | 6 | 1 | 10 | 2 | 1 | 5 | 8 | | 6 | 1 | | 8 | 3 | | | | | | | |
| Total | 263 | 91 | 360 | 29 | 300 | 224 | 316 | 70 | 194 | 209 | 246 | 210 | 158 | 149 | 83 | 274 | | | | | | |
| Wickets | 10 | 5 | 9 | 1 | 10 | 4 | 10 | 4 | 10 | 10 | 10 | 8 | 10 | 10 | 1 | 7 | | | | | | |
| Result | D | | W | | D | | W | | L | | D | | L | | W | | | | | | | |
| Points | 4 | | 16 | | 4 | | 16 | | 0 | | 0 | | 0 | | 12 | | | | | | | |

*Catches*

32 – E.B. McSweeney (ct 28/st 4)
9 – J.V. Coney
6 – R.H. Vance
5 – P.J. Holland
4 – R.W. Ormiston, E.J. Chatfield and S.J. Maguiness
3 – G.N. Cederwall and E.J. Gray
2 – J.F.M. Morrison and J.G. Boyle
1 – B.A. Edgar, B.W. Cederwall and P. Schofer

| BOWLING | A.C.S. Pigott | E.J. Chatfield | G.N. Cederwall | E.J. Gray | J.V. Coney | P.J. Holland | S.J. Maguiness | K.B. Marshall | P. Schofer |
|---|---|---|---|---|---|---|---|---|---|
| v. Northern Districts (Tauranga) | 19–3–61–0 | 26.1–4–52–3 | 6–2–22–0 | 44–27–35–5 | 10–3–31–1 | 19–7–34–1 | | | |
| 27–29 December 1983 | | 15–6–24–2 | 7–2–31–0 | 24.4–7–61–4 | 12–4–21–3 | 10–1–50–1 | | | |
| v. Central Districts (Wellington) | 17–5–39–4 | 27–14–35–1 | 9.4–4–26–3 | | | | 24–9–46–2 | | |
| 31 Dec. 1983–2 Jan. 1984 | 17–9–24–2 | 29.5–14–50–3 | 13–2–45–1 | 24–13–54–4 | 5–2–6–0 | 7–5–9–0 | 17–6–31–0 | | |
| v. Canterbury (Wellington) | | 30.2–8–81–5 | 5–0–13–0 | 27–8–73–3 | 6–1–31–0 | 4–0–26–0 | 30–10–50–2 | | |
| 5–7 January 1984 | | 6–5–2–0 | 4–3–1–0 | | | 10–6–10–0 | | | |
| v. Otago (Hutt) | | 15.2–5–41–4 | 6–0–27–0 | 25–9–45–3 | | | 22–11–24–3 | | |
| 12–14 January 1984 | | 35–11–80–4 | | 19–7–47–1 | 9–3–26–0 | 3–2–1–0 | 23.3–8–67–4 | | |
| v. Auckland (Auckland) | | 41–10–96–2 | | 35.5–13–89–3 | | 7–2–18–0 | 24–12–35–4 | 8–1–30–1 | |
| 26–28 January 1984 | | 14–5–27–0 | | 11–2–53–1 | | 3–0–20–0 | 4–1–8–0 | 1–0–9–0 | |
| v. Central Districts (Palmerston | 23–3–53–0 | | 20–1–93–3 | 16–7–35–0 | | | 34–10–81–3 | | |
| North) 31 Jan.–2 Feb. 1984 | 9–3–21–1 | | 18–7–44–2 | | | 16–4–48–1 | 22–7–44–0 | | |
| v. Canterbury (Christchurch) | 15–1–63–1 | | | 46–18–76–1 | | 7–1–24–2 | 31–6–74–2 | | 14–4–45–2 |
| 2–4 March 1984 | | | | | | | | | |
| v. Northern Districts (Wellington) | 3–1–11–0 | | | 9–0–42–0 | | | 4.4–0–14–1 | | 1–0–6–0 |
| 6–8 March 1984 | 15–1–56–2 | | | 11.2–3–41–2 | | | 19–2–72–5 | | |
| | 118–26–328–10 av. 32.80 | 239.4–82–488–24 av. 20.33 | 88.4–21–302–9 av. 33.55 | 292.5–114–651–27 av. 24.11 | 42–13–115–4 av. 28.75 | 86–28–240–5 av. 48.00 | 255.1–82–546–26 av. 21.00 | 9–1–39–1 av. 39.00 | 15–4–51–2 av. 25.50 |

a R.H. Vance 1–0–4–0 b T. Vogel 7–3–8–1, 8–0–33–0

On the other hand there must be some concern about the bowling. Hadlee had a splendid season with 35 wickets from six Tests. He sustained his form brilliantly, but one wonders how long his spare frame can sustain the effort. Chatfield was consistently good, Cairns had some dazzling patches and, as mentioned before Boock regained and held his Test position. But where are the new men, especially those to replace Hadlee, coming from? Sean Tracy, a burly young man, had the early distinction of twice quickly defeating Tavare in the Auckland match but his subsequent form was rather disappointing. At various times the selectors included two burly Central Districts' medium-fast bowlers, Derek Stirling and Gary Robertson, in their squads, but Robertson had only a brief appearance in the one-day match at Christchurch. Stirling spent most of his time at twelth man in the Tests, was taken to Sri Lanka and there qualified for unemployment pay. John Bracewell, the off-spinner, and one of the few genuine finger-spinners in the New Zealand game, took wickets and scored runs for Auckland, but rather moved out of the international orbit.

In terms of displaying international-quality players the season was a success in a batting sense, but rather deepened the concern that will be felt when Hadlee finds Test cricket physically too demanding.

The NZCC set a new pattern by having the England tour start in early January, and proceeding in the midst of the Shell Trophy competition – a pattern that will be followed by Pakistan next summer. The new system was not a complete success. The England tour overshadowed the Shell matches, and the quick departure of the New Zealanders to Sri Lanka meant the leading players were not available at the critical time of the domestic season. For some reason or another, too, the Shell Cup one-day finalists, Auckland and Wellington, were found in the first third of the season, but did not play the final until mid-March, when it was very much a non-event.

The same problems will occur next summer, for the New Zealanders will be away to the one-day matches in Australia and then to West Indies as the Shell Trophy matches reach their most interesting stage.

| R.W. Ormiston | B.W. Cederwall | J.F.M. Morrison | *Byes* | *Leg-byes* | *Wides* | *No-balls* | *Total* | *Wkts* |
|---|---|---|---|---|---|---|---|---|
| | | | 1 | 5 | | 1 | 242 | 10 |
| | | | 2 | 3 | | | 192 | 10 |
| | | | 1 | 2 | | 2 | 151 | 10 |
| | | | 8 | 3 | 1 | 6 | 237 | 10 |
| | | | 5 | 12 | 1 | 5 | 297 | 10 |
| | | | | 1 | | 1 | 15 | 0 |
| | | | 2 | 8 | 1 | 5 | 153 | 10 |
| | | | 7 | 4 | | | 232 | 10 |
| | | | | 2 | | 5 | 275 | 10 |
| 0.1–0–4–0 | | | 3 | 1 | | 1 | 130 | 1a |
| | 16.3–5–66–2 | 5–0–17–1 | | 3 | | 8 | 356 | 10 |
| | 13–1–47–1 | 8–3–22–0 | | 5 | 2 | 6 | 239 | 5 |
| | 2–0–8–0 | 7.2–2–20–1 | 5 | 6 | | 2 | 323 | 10 |
| | | | | | | | | |
| | | | | 3 | | 1 | 85 | 2b |
| 6–1–19–0 | | 6–1–26–0 | 3 | 6 | | 3 | 259 | 10 |
| 6.1–1–<br>23–0<br>— | 31.3–6–<br>121–3<br>*av.* 40.33 | 26.2–6–<br>85–2<br>*av.* 42.50 | | | | | | |

Canterbury started well in the trophy competition with two quick outright wins on Lancaster Park but faded in the middle of the race and then moved ahead toward the close of the competition. Central Districts and Auckland managed a late rally, and there were cries of collusion when Central conceded their second innings in a rain-affected match at Nelson, and then bowled out Auckland in conditions so dark the fieldsmen sometimes could not see the ball. The matter was not completely resolved, and in any case Central's last bid to win the trophy was foiled by rain at Invercargill, and Canterbury held first place.

Auckland gained some slight compensation by winning the Shell Cup final before a smattering of spectators at the Basin Reserve. Next summer the one-day final will be played at a more sensible time, but the NZCC will have to decide on a better balance to the season. Rather than be the centrepiece of the home season the Shell series is pushed into the background when it coincides with a tour, and it further loses value when the leading players are seldom available. The selectors are more content for it keeps the Test candidates in action at the time of the internationals. The public are less content, for the trophy crowds were increasingly modest.

The problems were obscured last summer by the drama of the victory over England, but they will remain unless the NZCC produces a balanced programme which maintains public interest, and has the leading players involved as much as possible.

*Hadlee had a splendid season with 35 wickets from six Tests. (Adrian Murrell)*

SECTION D

# Still Learning

The season in Sri Lanka. Zimbabwe on tour.
The Test and limited-over international series against New Zealand.

*Roy Dias – a world-class batsman.*
*(Adrian Murrell)*

The season in Sri Lanka had two main peaks; the first was the visit of the Zimbabwe side in December, 1983, and the second was the series against New Zealand three months later.

Zimbabwe sent a party of fourteen under the captaincy of John Traicos and managed by David Ellman-Brown, whose energy, enthusiasm and administrative ability have done so much to further the cause of his country's cricket in the past few years. Duncan Fletcher and Greg Peckover were unable to accompany the side for business reasons and Jack Heron had announced at the start of the season in Zimbabwe that he would not be available for representative cricket. Other members of the World Cup side missing from the party were Craig Hodgson, who had not found form and Vince Hogg who was somewhat unfortunate to be omitted. Newcomers were fast-medium bowler Jonathan Brent, left-arm medium pacer Malcolm Jarvis and batsmen Colin Robertson and Tommy Dunk.

***3 and 4 December 1983***

***at Maitland Place, Colombo***

**Zimbabwe** 217 (R. Jayawardena 4 for 83)
**Sri Lanka Colts** 162 for 6
*Match drawn*

The visitors struggled against the off-spin of Rochana Jayawardena on a slow pitch in humid conditions. The wicket-keeping of skipper Brendon Kuruppu, a catch and three stumpings, was splendid but his team-mates, although fielding well, failed to hold their chances. Rain brought play to an early close and there were more interruptions on the second day when the bowling of Traicos, 3 for 22 in 25 overs, gave Zimbabwe the initiative.

*Amerasinghe – a remarkable debut in first-class cricket, 16 for 109 in his first two matches. (Adrian Murrell)*

*Brendon Kuruppu plays forward. Robin Brown is the wicket-keeper and Omarshah is at short-leg. (R.G. Nixon)*

***6, 7 and 8 December 1983***

***at Moratuwa***

**Zimbabwe** 210 (K.M. Curran 63, J. Amersinghe 7 for 82) and 133 for 5
**Sri Lanka Board President's XI** 146
*Match drawn*

An injury to Malcolm Jarvis weakened the touring party who were opposed to a strong Sri Lankan side led by Test keeper Guy de Alwis who was injured during the match. The most interesting selection in the President's XI was that of left-arm spinner Jayantha Amerasinghe who was making his first-class debut at the age of 29 and returned match figures of 10 for 110.

Zimbabwe made a disastrous start when Omarshah and Dunk were out for 6. Pycroft and Brown were dropped off successive balls before they added 40. Pycroft was caught off Amerasinghe's third ball in first-class cricket and Houghton was lbw in the spinner's next over. Only Curran played with confidence against flighted deliveries and he and Traicos added 52 for the last wicket.

Fernando and Kaluperuma began with a stand of 75, but off-spinners Hick and Traicos then caused havoc and the side collapsed. Rain ruined the last day when spin was again dominant.

*Robin Brown cuts. de Alwis is the wicket-keeper. (R.G. Nixon)*

*Ian Butchart plays with caution as Amerasinghe's close field clusters in anticipation. (R.G. Nixon)*

ABOVE: *de Mel bowling to Paterson, Pycroft is the non-striker.* BELOW: *Robertson turns de Mel to leg, Paterson is the non-striker.*

## SRI LANKA XI *v.* ZIMBABWE

This match had been billed as an unofficial Test match, and both Zimbabwe and the local press were deeply upset when Sri Lanka declared that they would field an under-25 team. They then decided to include the spinner Amerasinghe and gave no explanation as to why they had reduced the status of the match. There were protests, but to no avail, and Zimbabwe felt robbed of an opportunity to assess their strength against a Test team in Test match conditions.

Zimbabwe were asked to bat first on a slow pitch and struggled against spin and medium pace until rain ended play

*Sri Lanka XI v. Zimbabwe, teams grouped on a historic occasion. Back row (l to r)—Umpire Francis, Mr Rajingham (Zimbabwe Liaison Officer), J.P. Brent, M.P. Jarvis, A.H. Shah, K.M. Curran, I.P. Butchart, C.M. Robertson, G.M. Paterson, P.W.E. Rawson, G.A. Hicks, B. de Silva, V. John, S. Warnakulasurija, J. Amerasinghe, R. Buultjens, R. Jayawardene, M. von Hagt, Umpire. Front row (l to r)—T.W. Dunk, R.D. Brown, A.J. Pycroft, D.L. Houghton, Mr D. Ellman-Brown, A.J. Traicos, Hon. Gamani Dissanayake (President Board of Control), R.S. Madugalle, Nuski Mohamed (Hon. Sec.), team manager, D.S.B. Kuruppu, A.L.F. de Mel, A. Ranatunge, R.J. Ratnayake. (John & Co)*

## SRI LANKAN XI *v.* ZIMBABWE

10, 11, 12 and 13 December 1983 at Colombo

**ZIMBABWE**

| | FIRST INNINGS | | SECOND INNINGS | |
|---|---|---|---|---|
| G.A. Paterson | lbw, b de Mel | 16 | c Ranatunge, b Ratnayake | 1 |
| C.M. Robertson | c Madugalle, b de Mel | 1 | c Madugalle, b de Mel | 17 |
| R.D. Brown | lbw, b Amerasinghe | 21 | b de Mel | 0 |
| A.J. Pycroft | c Kuruppu, b de Mel | 19 | b Jayawardene | 31 |
| K.M. Curran | c Kuruppu, b Ratnayake | 7 | c Buultjens, b Amerasinghe | 32 |
| D.L. Houghton* | b Amerasinghe | 52 | c Jayawardene, b Amerasinghe | 77 |
| T.W. Dunk | c Kuruppu, b Ratnayake | 3 | c Madugalle, b Jayawardene | 0 |
| G.A. Hick | run out | 9 | st Kuruppu, b Ranatunge | 57 |
| P.W.E. Rawson | c Ranatunge, b Ratnayake | 28 | b Amerasinghe | 0 |
| A.J. Traicos† | not out | 8 | b Amerasinghe | 5 |
| M.P. Jarvis | b Ratnayake | 7 | not out | 0 |
| Extras | | 30 | | 8 |
| | | 201 | | 228 |

| | O | M | R | W | O | M | R | W |
|---|---|---|---|---|---|---|---|---|
| de Mel | 24 | 3 | 72 | 3 | 16 | 3 | 49 | 2 |
| Ratnayake | 24 | 5 | 49 | 4 | 11 | 1 | 50 | 1 |
| Amerasinghe | 30 | 10 | 40 | 2 | 32 | 12 | 59 | 4 |
| Jayawardene | 6 | 2 | 10 | — | 15 | 2 | 47 | 2 |
| Ranatunge | | | | | 7.5 | 3 | 15 | 1 |

FALL OF WICKETS

1- 9, 2- 27, 3- 64, 4- 75, 5- 75, 6- 87, 7- 108, 8- 180, 9- 191

1- 3, 2- 7, 3- 18, 4- 82, 5- 98, 6- 117, 7- 210, 8- 210, 9- 222

**SRI LANKAN XI**

| | FIRST INNINGS | | SECOND INNINGS | |
|---|---|---|---|---|
| D.S.B. Kuruppu* | c Curran, b Rawson | 28 | lbw, b Rawson | 2 |
| M. von Hagt | c Houghton, b Rawson | 12 | not out | 6 |
| S. Warnakula-suriya | st Brown, b Traicos | 65 | not out | 4 |
| R.S. Madugalle† | c Houghton, b Rawson | 17 | | |
| A. Ranatunge | c Houghton, b Traicos | 43 | | |
| B. de Silva | c sub (Butchart), b Traicos | 0 | | |
| R. Buultjens | c Jarvis, b Traicos | 19 | | |
| A.L.F. de Mel | c sub (Butchart), b Curran | 17 | | |
| R. Jayawardene | b Curran | 0 | | |
| R.J. Ratnayake | not out | 6 | | |
| J. Amerasinghe | b Traicos | 0 | | |
| Extras | | 24 | | 4 |
| | | 231 | (for 1 wicket) | 16 |

| | O | M | R | W | O | M | R | W |
|---|---|---|---|---|---|---|---|---|
| Curran | 17 | 1 | 51 | 2 | | | | |
| Rawson | 25 | 4 | 81 | 3 | 3 | — | 7 | 1 |
| Jarvis | 11 | 1 | 26 | — | 5 | 2 | 5 | — |
| Traicos | 29.4 | 15 | 30 | 5 | | | | |
| Hick | 10 | 3 | 19 | — | | | | |
| Houghton | | | | | 1 | 1 | 0 | — |
| Dunk | | | | | 1 | 1 | 0 | — |

FALL OF WICKETS

1- 47, 2- 48, 3- 73, 4- 149, 5- 149, 6- 197, 7- 224, 8- 224, 9- 225

1- 4

**Match drawn**

*Rawson slashes Amerasinghe through the off-side. (R.G. Nixon)*

shortly after tea with the visitors at 126 for 7. Play started late the following day, but Rawson gave Houghton excellent support and the last three wickets added 93. Sri Lanka closed at 67 for 2 and would have suffered more the next day had not chances been missed. As it was, Warnakulasuriya batted with good sense and held the innings together. He mixed disciplined defence with some sparkling shots before being stumped by Brown who had taken over temporarily behind the wicket when Houghton was hit in the mouth.

Sri Lanka's lead was only 30, but before the close Zimbabwe were in deep trouble, losing 3 for 18 before Pycroft and Curran hung on grimly.

They battled on the next morning, but 6 were down for 117 when seventeen-year-old Graeme Hick joined Houghton. Houghton batted with his usual panache and Hick without blemish in scoring his maiden first-class fifty. They added 93 and were not parted until after tea. Hick was last out, but by that time the game had been saved.

### First One-Day International

***15 December 1983***

**Zimbabwe** 90 for 6
***v.* Sri Lanka**

*Match abandoned and declared unofficial before start of play*

This was the first international match to be played at Radella since the visit of Dexter's side in 1961–62. Overnight rain delayed the start and made conditions so bad that play was called off officially. An exhibition match was arranged, but this, too, ended in rain. Robin Brown returned to Zimbabwe after this match for business reasons.

### Second One-Day International
### SRI LANKA *v.* ZIMBABWE

Zimbabwe were put in to bat and made a solid start before a middle-order collapse. Houghton and Rawson revived the visitors' innings and 170 from the reduced 45 overs was better than had seemed possible in face of some steady bowling and superb fielding. Then came another downpour and the ground was left unfit for play, fielding in such conditions being an impossibility.

## SECOND ONE-DAY INTERNATIONAL: SRI LANKA *v.* ZIMBABWE
17 December 1983 at Maitland Place, Colombo

**ZIMBABWE**

|  |  |  |
|---|---|---|
| A.H. Omarshah | c de Alwis, b Ranatunga | 8 |
| G.A. Paterson | c Madugalle, b Amerasinghe | 38 |
| G.A. Hick | st de Alwis, b Amerasinghe | 16 |
| A.J. Pycroft | c Amerasinghe, b Ranatunga | 0 |
| D.L. Houghton* | not out | 43 |
| K.M. Curran | c de Mel, b Ratnayake | 10 |
| C.M. Robertson | c de Alwis, b de Mel | 6 |
| I.P. Butchart | c de Alwis, b de Mel | 3 |
| P.W.E. Rawson | not out | 31 |
| A.J. Traicos† | | |
| J.P. Brent | | |
| Extras | | 15 |
| (45 overs) | (for 7 wickets) | 170 |

| | O | M | R | W |
|---|---|---|---|---|
| de Mel | 9 | 1 | 26 | 2 |
| John | 9 | 3 | 41 | — |
| Ratnayake | 9 | 1 | 34 | 1 |
| Ranatunga | 9 | 2 | 26 | 2 |
| Amerasinghe | 9 | — | 28 | 2 |

FALL OF WICKETS
1- 31, 2- 61, 3- 63, 4- 77, 5- 101, 6- 109, 7- 115

**SRI LANKA**

S. Wettimuny
B.S.B. Kuruppu
R.L. Dias
L.R.D. Mendis†
R.S. Madugalle
A. Ranatunga
A.L.F. de Mel
R.G. de Alwis*
R.J. Ratnayake
V. John
J. Amerasinghe

**Match abandoned**

### Third One-Day International
### SRI LANKA *v.* ZIMBABWE

Once again rain delayed the start and reduced the number of overs to 30. Zimbabwe put Sri Lanka in to bat and the home side were given a good start by Wettimuny and Kuruppu. Wettimuny was first to go and Kuruppu and Dias were involved in a serious mix-up which led to Kuruppu sacrificing his wicket. Dias then batted with great power and brilliance and his 68 came off 56 balls. Had Roy Dias played for one of the senior Test nations, he would, in the opinion of many, be ranked among the great batsmen of the world. He has an eloquence of stroke, an ease of timing and a relentless power that make him a most exciting player. His innings confirmed the very high opinion that Zimbabwe held of him. He gained little support. Mendis was not fully fit and only de Mel offered real resistance.

In the conditions, the target of 144 was a formidable one, however. Six wickets fell for 59 and only a brave effort from Curran and Butchart raised hope. So Sri Lanka, through the

## THIRD ONE-DAY INTERNATIONAL: SRI LANKA *v.* ZIMBABWE
18 December 1983 at Colombo

**SRI LANKA**

|  |  |  |
|---|---|---|
| S. Wettimuny | c Houghton, b Butchart | 21 |
| D.S.B. Kuruppu | run out | 16 |
| R.L. Dias | not out | 68 |
| L.R.D. Bendis† | c Hick, b Brent | 11 |
| R.S. Madugalle | c Pycroft, b Hick | 1 |
| A. Ranatunga | run out | 2 |
| A.L.F. de Mel | c Pycroft, b Curran | 10 |
| R.G. de Alwis* | b Curran | 1 |
| R.J. Ratnayake | c Hick, b Curran | 2 |
| V. John | not out | 1 |
| J. Amerasinghe | | |
| Extras | | 10 |
| (30 overs) | (for 8 wickets) | 143 |

| | O | M | R | W |
|---|---|---|---|---|
| Rawson | 6 | 1 | 24 | — |
| Curran | 6 | — | 30 | 3 |
| Butchart | 6 | — | 26 | 1 |
| Traicos | 6 | — | 23 | — |
| Brent | 3 | — | 18 | 1 |
| Hick | 3 | — | 12 | 1 |

FALL OF WICKETS
1- 39, 2- 54, 3- 93, 4- 95, 5- 99, 6- 108, 7- 123, 8- 141

**ZIMBABWE**

|  |  |  |
|---|---|---|
| A.H. Omarshah | run out | 4 |
| G.A. Paterson | lbw, b de Mel | 0 |
| G.A. Hick | c Madugalle, b John | 16 |
| A.J. Pycroft | b Amerasinghe | 24 |
| D.L. Houghton* | b John | 4 |
| K.M. Curran | b de Mel | 21 |
| C.M. Robertson | c de Alwis, b Ranatunga | 2 |
| I.P. Butchart | run out | 19 |
| P.W.E. Rawson | c Madugalle, b Ranatunga | 1 |
| J.P. Brent | run out | 7 |
| A.J. Traicos† | not out | 2 |
| Extras | | 12 |
| (27.5 overs) | | 112 |

| | O | M | R | W |
|---|---|---|---|---|
| de Mel | 5 | — | 21 | 2 |
| John | 6 | — | 19 | 2 |
| Ratnayake | 4.5 | — | 16 | — |
| Amerasinghe | 6 | — | 11 | 1 |
| Ranatunga | 6 | — | 33 | 2 |

FALL OF WICKETS
1- 1, 2- 10, 3- 47, 4- 56, 5- 56, 6- 59, 7- 99, 8- 102, 9- 102

**Sri Lanka won by 31 runs**

brilliance of Dias, achieved the only result of Zimbabwe's tour.

David Ellman-Brown said that the tour had been tough under trying conditions, but very worthwhile. His team had learned much, made new friends and enjoyed wonderful hospitality. The press coverage, he thought, had been magnificent. It was disappointing that Zimbabwe had not met the full Sri Lanka team in a first-class match, and the weather had been dreadful.

For Zimbabwe, many of whose players did not do themselves justice in the heat and humidity, the problem of finding a good opening partnership remained. For Sri Lanka, there was the profit of left-arm spinner Jayantha Amerasinghe who, in two first-class matches, the extent of his career, had taken 16 wickets for 209 runs.

Following their triumph over England, New Zealand arrived in Sri Lanka for a one-month tour. Their party consisted of 14 players, the 11 who beat England in Christchurch plus Reid, Stirling and John Bracewell. From the start they were plagued by rain.

LEFT: *Kevin Curran – a good all-round tour. (Ken Kelly)*
RIGHT: *Brendon Kuruppu – Sri Lanka's solitary batting success in the first one-day international against New Zealand. (Adrian Murrell)*

***29 February, 1 and 2 March 1984***

***at Galle***

**New Zealanders** 245 for 8 dec (J.F. Reid 61, J.J. Crowe 56, J.V. Coney 53 not out, V.B. John 4 for 60) and 57 for 2
**Sri Lanka Colts** 105 (J.G. Bracewell 4 for 20)

*Match drawn*

There was no play possible on the first day, but the home side had some early success on the second when John dismissed Wright and Edgar with only 23 scored. John Reid, returning to a New Zealand side after an absence of three years, led a revival with a fine half-century, and Jeff Crowe, Coney and Cairns bolstered the score. On the last day Sri Lanka Colts collapsed against the spin of Bracewell and Boock, who had 3 for 15, but Wright, leading the side in Howarth's absence, decided not to enforce the follow-on.

**First One-Day International**
**SRI LANKA v. NEW ZEALAND**

Sent in to bat, New Zealand profited from some wayward bowling and slack fielding so that they were able to move to a commanding total. The dominant batsman was John Reid

**FIRST ONE-DAY INTERNATIONAL: SRI LANKA *v.* NEW ZEALAND**
4 March 1984 at Colombo

| NEW ZEALAND | | | |
|---|---|---|---|
| G.P. Howarth† | c Kuruppu, b Ranatunga | 33 |
| J.G. Wright | c and b de Mel | 20 |
| J.F. Reid | c John, b Ratnayeke | 80 |
| M.D. Crowe | c de Mel, b de Silva | 29 |
| J.J. Crowe | not out | 39 |
| R.J. Hadlee | c Ranatunga, b Ratnayeke | 6 |
| B.L. Cairns | b John | 1 |
| J.V. Coney | not out | 4 |
| I.D.S. Smith* | | |
| S.L. Boock | | |
| E.J. Chatfield | | |
| Extras | b 3, lb 6, w 2, nb 11 | 22 |
| (42 overs) | (for 6 wickets) | 234 |

| | O | M | R | W |
|---|---|---|---|---|
| de Mel | 7 | 1 | 40 | 1 |
| John | 9 | 1 | 39 | 1 |
| Ratnayeke | 8 | — | 37 | 2 |
| de Silva | 9 | — | 42 | 1 |
| Ranatunga | 9 | — | 54 | 1 |

FALL OF WICKETS
1- 58, 2- 76, 3- 123, 4- 220, 5- 227, 6- 229

| SRI LANKA | | |
|---|---|---|
| S. Wettimuny | c Coney, b Chatfield | 16 |
| D.S.B. Kuruppu | c Hadlee, b Coney | 38 |
| R.L. Dias | c and b Boock | 9 |
| L.R.D. Mendis† | b Boock | 15 |
| A. Ranatunga | c Coney, b Boock | 16 |
| J.R. Ratnayeke | run out | 1 |
| D.S. de Silva | c J.J. Crowe, b Hadlee | 8 |
| R.S. Madugalle | b Cairns | 5 |
| R.G. de Alwis* | c Smith, b Hadlee | 8 |
| A.L.F. de Mel | b Hadlee | 2 |
| V. John | not out | 6 |
| Extras | b 1, lb 4, w 1 | 6 |
| (37.3 overs) | | 130 |

| | O | M | R | W |
|---|---|---|---|---|
| Cairns | 9 | — | 35 | 1 |
| Hadlee | 8.3 | — | 22 | 3 |
| Chatfield | 4 | — | 24 | 1 |
| Boock | 9 | — | 28 | 3 |
| Coney | 7 | 2 | 15 | 1 |

FALL OF WICKETS
1- 54, 2- 60, 3- 73, 4- 98, 5- 100, 6- 102, 7- 111, 8- 122, 9- 123

**New Zealand won by 104 runs**

who, on his return to international cricket, hit two sixes and two fours in his 80 made off 79 deliveries. He made a hesitant start, but prospered as he and Martin Crowe added 47 in 8.2 overs.

Wettimuny and Kuruppu began quite confidently for Sri Lanka, but Chatfield broke the stand and Boock's nagging accuracy frustrated the middle order and led them to disaster as they sought a run-rate which his control would not allow.

***5, 6 and 7 March 1984***

***at Radella***

**President's XI** 62 for 4
***v.* New Zealanders**

*Match abandoned*

Only 90 minutes play was possible on the first day, 43 on the second and none on the third. Chatfield had 2 for 1. His victims were Wettimuny and skipper Roy Dias for 0. As this was the last first-class game outside Test matches, its abandonment was a great blow to New Zealand's plans for preparation.

**First Test Match**
**SRI LANKA v. NEW ZEALAND**

Already hampered by rain on the tour, New Zealand suffered further frustration when no play was possible on the first day of the first Test match, and no play possible until after lunch on the second day which New Zealand closed at 120 for the loss of Howarth.

Sri Lanka had caused a surprise by omitting de Mel from their side, stating that he was not fully fit, and as Dias also did not play, they could be said to have been without their best bowler and their best batsman. New Zealand relied on both spinners to the exclusion of pace men Chatfield and Stirling and Edgar, completely out of form, also stood down.

*John – his fine bowling failed to bring Sri Lanka victory in the first Test match. (Adrian Murrell)*

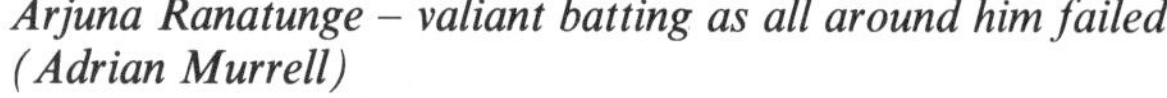

*Arjuna Ranatunge – valiant batting as all around him failed. (Adrian Murrell)*

*Stephen Boock, the destroyer of Sri Lanka. Five wickets in a Test innings for the first time. (Adrian Murrell)*

Howarth moved up to open the innings and batted fluently until falling to John late on the second day. John bowled remarkably well to return his best figures in Test cricket and with Ranatunge giving good support in the field as well as with the ball, Sri Lanka came back well to dismiss New Zealand for 276, less than had been expected at the end of the second day.

Wettimuny fell to Hadlee's fourth ball of the innings and debutant Kaluperuma was taken at silly point, but night-watchman Ratnayake gave Fernando solid support and they ended the day at 50 for 2.

There now seemed no possibility of a result unless New Zealand could bowl Sri Lanka out cheaply, and when Fernando, Ratnayeke, Mendis and Ranatunge went quickly on the fourth morning, it seemed that this would be the case. There was a moderate recovery, but at 155 for 9, the home side were in desperate trouble. Jayantha Amerasinghe, in his first Test match, and Vinothen John then added 60, a Sri Lankan record for the last wicket, John making his highest score in Test cricket and Amerasinghe being top scorer for the innings. It was a most courageous stand and gave Sri Lanka new hope. Wright and Reid fell before the close and a draw now looked inevitable.

Howarth reached his second half century of the match as New Zealand sought quick runs on the final morning. There was some violent hitting from Hadlee and Smith and Howarth declared after lunch, leaving Sri Lanka 130 minutes and 20 overs in which to make 263. Any hopes that they could make this total were quickly dispelled by Hadlee who routed the top of the order batsmen, sending back the first four with only 14 scored. When Boock joined the attack, he immediately sent back Kaluperuma and de Silva and at 18 for 6, Sri Lanka faced the blackest day in their brief Test history.

Some pride was restored by left-hander Arjuna Ranatunge, who hit 51 off 45 balls in swashbuckling style, and Rumesh Ratnayake when they added 42 in 53 minutes after an early stand by Ranatunge and de Alwis had produced 37.

Ranatunge was particularly severe on Bracewell who ultimately had his revenge. The last 3 wickets fell without a run being scored and New Zealand had gained a victory which even Howarth had thought unlikely.

Hadlee had match figures of 8 for 43 and was obviously too much for the Sri Lankans. Stephen Boock had his best Test figures of 5 for 28 in the second innings and it was good to see his rehabilitation in international cricket had been completed.

For Sri Lanka there was dismay and the anger of the crowd emphasised the feeling of bitter disappointment that all must have felt.

## FIRST TEST MATCH: SRI LANKA *v.* NEW ZEALAND
9, 10, 11, 13 and 14 March 1984 at Asgiriya Stadium, Kandy

**NEW ZEALAND**

| | FIRST INNINGS | | SECOND INNINGS | |
|---|---|---|---|---|
| G.P. Howarth† | c de Alwis, b John | 62 | lbw, b John | 60 |
| J.G. Wright | lbw, b John | 45 | c de Alwis, b John | 4 |
| J.F. Reid | c Kaluperuma, b Amerasinghe | 26 | c Ranatunge, b de Silva | 30 |
| M.D. Crowe | c Ratnayake, b de Silva | 26 | (5) st de Alwis, b de Silva | 8 |
| J.J. Crowe | c sub, b John | 20 | (8) c Amerasinghe, b Kaluperuma | 9 |
| J.V. Coney | lbw, b Ratnayake | 25 | (10) not out | 3 |
| R.J. Hadlee | c Ranatunge, b John | 29 | (6) c sub, b Kaluperuma | 27 |
| I.D.S. Smith* | b Ranatunge | 30 | (9) not out | 31 |
| B.L. Cairns | c de Alwis, b Ranatunge | 0 | (7) c Wettimuny, b de Silva | 2 |
| J.G. Bracewell | c de Silva, b John | 2 | (4) c Amerasinghe, b John | 21 |
| S.L. Boock | not out | 4 | | |
| Extras | b 1, lb 1, w 5 | 7 | b 2, lb 1, w 3 | 6 |
| | | 276 | (for 8 wkts dec) | 201 |

| | O | M | R | W | O | M | R | W |
|---|---|---|---|---|---|---|---|---|
| John | 29.1 | 7 | 86 | 5 | 17.5 | 1 | 73 | 3 |
| Ratnayake | 15 | 4 | 45 | 1 | | | | |
| Ranatunge | 9 | 3 | 17 | 2 | 4 | — | 14 | — |
| de Silva | 29 | 6 | 69 | 1 | 21 | 2 | 59 | 3 |
| Amerasinghe | 12 | 3 | 45 | 1 | 8 | 2 | 32 | — |
| Kaluperuma | 6 | 3 | 7 | — | 4 | — | 17 | 2 |

FALL OF WICKETS
1- 97, 2- 124, 3- 163, 4- 169, 5- 210, 6- 236, 7- 266, 8- 266, 9- 272
1- 14, 2- 75, 3- 111, 4- 126, 5- 133, 6- 137, 7- 167, 8- 167

**SRI LANKA**

| | FIRST INNINGS | | SECOND INNINGS | |
|---|---|---|---|---|
| S. Wettimuny | c Coney, b Hadlee | 0 | c Smith, b Hadlee | 5 |
| E.R.N.S. Fernando | c Hadlee, b Boock | 29 | lbw, b Hadlee | 2 |
| S.M.S. Kaluperuma | c Howarth, b Bracewell | 18 | c J. Crowe, b Boock | 5 |
| R.J. Ratnayake | c Smith, b Hadlee | 6 | (9) lbw, b Boock | 12 |
| L.R.D. Mendis† | c Bracewell, b Hadlee | 5 | (4) b Hadlee | 0 |
| R.S. Madugalle | c M. Crowe, b Hadlee | 33 | (5) c Bracewell, b Hadlee | 2 |
| A. Ranatunge | c Bracewell, b Cairns | 20 | (6) c and b Bracewell | 51 |
| D.S. de Silva | b Bracewell | 11 | (7) c Coney, b Boock | 0 |
| R.G. de Alwis* | lbw, b Boock | 26 | (8) c Howarth, b Boock | 19 |
| V.B. John | not out | 27 | c Wright, b Boock | 0 |
| A.M.J.G. Amerasinghe | run out | 34 | not out | 0 |
| Extras | lb 2, nb 4 | 6 | lb 1 | 1 |
| | | 215 | | 97 |

| | O | M | R | W | O | M | R | W |
|---|---|---|---|---|---|---|---|---|
| Hadlee | 20.5 | 7 | 35 | 4 | 7 | 4 | 8 | 4 |
| Cairns | 18 | 3 | 71 | 1 | 4 | 1 | 6 | — |
| M.D. Crowe | 3 | 1 | 4 | — | | | | |
| Boock | 23 | 7 | 63 | 2 | 9 | 3 | 28 | 5 |
| Bracewell | 15 | 4 | 36 | 2 | 7 | 1 | 54 | 1 |

FALL OF WICKETS
1- 0, 2- 38, 3- 55, 4- 55, 5- 61, 6- 89, 7- 120, 8- 132, 9- 155
1- 3, 2- 12, 3- 12, 4- 14, 5- 18, 6- 18, 7- 55, 8- 97, 9- 97

**New Zealand won by 165 runs**

### Second Test Match
### SRI LANKA v. NEW ZEALAND

New Zealand included Chatfield for Bracewell and Sri Lanka thankfully welcomed back Roy Dias, but he was sadly run out for 16 as Sri Lanka, having been put in to bat, dragged through the first day to 145 for 6 at less than two runs an over.

They subsided for 174 on the second morning as Cairns quickly disposed of the tail after Madugalle and Ravi Ratnayeke had offered the best resistance of the innings. New Zealand struggled in their turn. Howarth and Wright began comfortably enough, but John had Wright brilliantly caught at square-leg when the score was 38 and then had Reid caught behind, having first bowled Howarth. Jeff Crowe and Coney led the side out of trouble until Coney skied a de Silva leg-break to mid-off. By the close the visitors had lost five wickets and were still 10 runs in arrears.

In a six-over burst on the third morning Ravi Ratnayeke took 4 for 10 with his medium-fast bowling. He was aided by some excellent close catching and his fine bowling brought him final figures of 5 for 42, the best recorded for Sri Lanka in their short Test career.

Sri Lanka's joy at having swept away the last five New Zealand wickets for 32 runs was short-lived. The New Zealand score had only been boosted by a last wicket stand of 20 between Cairns and Chatfield, but their 198 was still the lowest score made against Sri Lanka in a Test match, but

*Ravi Ratnayeke, 5 for 42, the best bowling recorded for Sri Lanka in a Test match. (second Test) (Adrian Murrell)*

*Martin Crowe – 19 in 221 minutes in the second Test and the anger of the crowd. (George Herringshaw)*

*Sidath Wettimuny – an innings of courage and determination in the second Test. (Adrian Murrell)*

Hadlee dismissed Fernando shortly before lunch and Kaluperuma immediately afterwards. At 13 for 2 Sri Lanka were in desperate trouble, but Wettimuny and Dias batted with courage and some flair to take them to 133 by the end of the day. They were assisted by some uncharacteristic poor catching by the New Zealanders who dropped Dias twice and Wettimuny once.

After the rest day Wettimuny and Dias continued in splendid form and Roy Dias, who hit eighteen fours, reached his second century in seven Test matches and it was the first scored by a Sri Lankan in a home Test. He and Wettimuny added a record 163 for the third wicket. Wettimuny retired hurt shortly before lunch after being hit in the groin by a ball from Hadlee and he was caught without adding to his score when he returned at the fall of the sixth wicket. Wettimuny batted with great determination for his 65 made in 235 minutes.

Mendis declared and left New Zealand to make 266. They

**SECOND TEST MATCH: SRI LANKA *v.* NEW ZEALAND**
16, 17, 18, 20 and 21 March 1984 at Colombo

**SRI LANKA**

| | FIRST INNINGS | | SECOND INNINGS | |
|---|---|---|---|---|
| S. Wettimuny | c Coney, b Chatfield | 26 | c Hadlee, b Chatfield | 65 |
| E.R.N.S. Fernando | b M.D. Crowe | 8 | c J. Crowe, b Hadlee | 0 |
| S.M.S. Kaluperuma | b Boock | 23 | c Wright, b Hadlee | 2 |
| R.L. Dias | run out | 16 | b Cairns | 108 |
| L.R.D. Mendis† | b Hadlee | 1 | (6) b Chatfield | 36 |
| R.S. Madugalle | not out | 44 | (7) c J. Crowe, b Chatfield | 36 |
| A. Ranatunge | c Smith, b Cairns | 6 | (8) run out | 7 |
| J.R. Ratnayeke | lbw, b Hadlee | 22 | (5) c and b Hadlee | 12 |
| D.S. de Silva | c Coney, b Cairns | 0 | not out | 13 |
| R.G. de Alwis* | c Smith, b Cairns | 2 | b Chatfield | 2 |
| V. John | c Smith, b Cairns | 0 | not out | 3 |
| Extras | b 5, lb 7, w 8, nb 6 | 26 | lb 4, nb 1 | 5 |
| | | 174 | (for 9 wkts dec) | 289 |

| | O | M | R | W | O | M | R | W |
|---|---|---|---|---|---|---|---|---|
| Hadlee | 22 | 12 | 27 | 2 | 30 | 13 | 58 | 3 |
| Cairns | 24.5 | 6 | 47 | 4 | 22 | 3 | 79 | 1 |
| Chatfield | 20 | 7 | 35 | 1 | 29 | 9 | 78 | 4 |
| M.D. Crowe | 13 | 5 | 21 | 1 | | | | |
| Boock | 7 | 2 | 18 | 1 | 42 | 16 | 65 | — |
| Coney | | | | | 4 | 3 | 4 | — |

FALL OF WICKETS
1- 25, 2- 66, 3- 68, 4- 69, 5- 99, 6- 111, 7- 152, 8- 153, 9- 165
1- 3, 2- 13, 3- 176, 4- 209, 5- 234, 6- 244, 7- 245, 8- 278, 9- 282

**NEW ZEALAND**

| | FIRST INNINGS | | SECOND INNINGS | |
|---|---|---|---|---|
| G.P. Howarth† | b John | 24 | c Kaluperuma, b John | 10 |
| J.G. Wright | c Dias, b John | 20 | c de Silva, b Ranatunge | 48 |
| J.F. Reid | c de Alwis, b John | 7 | lbw, b John | 0 |
| J.J. Crowe | b Ratnayeke | 50 | c de Alwis, b Ranatunge | 16 |
| J.V. Coney | c John, b de Silva | 30 | (6) not out | 20 |
| R.J. Hadlee | b Ratnayeke | 19 | | |
| S.L. Boock | c Madugalle, b Ratnayeke | 4 | | |
| M.D. Crowe | c Kaluperuma, b Ratnayeke | 0 | (5) not out | 19 |
| I.D.S. Smith* | c Kaluperuma, b Ratnayeke | 7 | | |
| B.L. Cairns | lbw, b de Silva | 14 | | |
| E.J. Chatfield | not out | 9 | | |
| Extras | b 4, lb 6, w 1, nb 3 | 14 | b 4, lb 4, nb 2 | 10 |
| | | 198 | (for 4 wkts) | 123 |

| | O | M | R | W | O | M | R | W |
|---|---|---|---|---|---|---|---|---|
| John | 24 | 1 | 89 | 3 | 21 | 11 | 26 | 2 |
| J.R. Ratnayeke | 21 | 8 | 42 | 5 | 21 | 11 | 17 | — |
| Kaluperuma | 1 | — | 3 | — | 6 | 3 | 10 | — |
| Ranatunge | 4 | 1 | 11 | — | 18 | 7 | 29 | 2 |
| de Silva | 14.3 | 6 | 39 | 2 | 19 | 10 | 31 | — |
| Madugalle | | | | | 1 | 1 | 0 | — |

FALL OF WICKETS
1- 38, 2- 53, 3- 66, 4- 127, 5- 151, 6- 166, 7- 166, 8- 171, 9- 178
1- 10, 2- 10, 3- 48, 4- 89

**Match drawn**

closed at 6 for 0 with an exciting last day in prospect. It was not to be. In the thirteenth over of the innings Howarth drove lazily at Vinothen John and was caught at slip. Reid was lbw first ball and from that point New Zealand batted only for survival. In an innings which lasted 86 overs, 347 minutes, they scored only 123 and earned the wrath of the crowd who were disappointed not only by the batting of Martin Crowe, 19 in 221 minutes, but by the failure of Sri Lanka to register their first Test victory when the efforts of Dias, Ravi Ratnayeke, John and Wettimuny had made it seem possible.

## Third Test Match
## SRI LANKA *v.* NEW ZEALAND

Following their fine showing in the second Test, Sri Lanka entered the last match of the series with hopes of recording their first Test victory, but they were quickly dashed on the opening day when Hadlee and Chatfield had them struggling at 63 for 5. Once again the Sri Lankan top order batsmen had found difficulty in coping with Hadlee's pace.

A most courageous stand between Madugalle and Ranatunge gave the home side new hope and they ended the day at 230 for 8, a remarkable recovery. Chatfield finished off the tail on the second morning to give him his best figures in a

RIGHT: *Ewen Chatfield, his best figures in Test cricket. The destroyers of Sri Lanka in the third test. (George Herringshaw)* BELOW: *(left): Madugalle – brave batting for Sri Lanka in the third Test match.* BELOW: *(right): Richard Hadlee. (Adrian Murrell)*

## THIRD TEST MATCH: SRI LANKA *v.* NEW ZEALAND
24, 25, 26, 28 and 29 March 1984 at Colombo

### SRI LANKA

| | FIRST INNINGS | | SECOND INNINGS | |
|---|---|---|---|---|
| S. Wettimuny | b Hadlee | 4 | c Coney, b Hadlee | 2 |
| S.M.S. Kaluperuma | b Hadlee | 16 | c Coney, b Hadlee | 18 |
| J.R. Ratnayeke | lbw, b Hadlee | 0 | (7) b Boock | 2 |
| R.L. Dias | c Smith, b Chatfield | 10 | absent injured | 0 |
| L.R.D. Mendis† | c J. Crowe, b Chatfield | 19 | (6) b Boock | 10 |
| R.S. Madugalle | not out | 89 | (3) c Wright, b Bracewell | 38 |
| A. Ranatunge | c sub, b Chatfield | 37 | (4) c Wright, b Boock | 50 |
| D.S. de Silva | c Smith, b Hadlee | 17 | (5) c Smith, b Hadlee | 1 |
| R.G. de Alwis* | c Boock, b Hadlee | 28 | (8) c Bracewell, b Hadlee | 10 |
| A.M.J.G Amerasinghe | c Wright, b Chatfield | 15 | (9) b Hadlee | 5 |
| V. John | c and b Chatfield | 12 | (10) not out | 0 |
| Extras | lb 4, nb 5 | 9 | lb 1, nb 5 | 6 |
| | | 256 | | 142 |

| | O | M | R | W | O | M | R | W |
|---|---|---|---|---|---|---|---|---|
| Hadlee | 22 | 4 | 73 | 5 | 16 | 7 | 29 | 5 |
| Chatfield | 22 | 5 | 63 | 5 | 9 | 2 | 27 | — |
| M.D. Crowe | 6 | 2 | 22 | — | 5 | 2 | 13 | — |
| Bracewell | 9 | 2 | 31 | — | 11 | 4 | 35 | 1 |
| Boock | 20 | 9 | 51 | — | 16 | 2 | 32 | 3 |
| Coney | 3 | — | 7 | — | | | | |

FALL OF WICKETS
1- 4, 2- 4, 3- 22, 4- 32, 5- 63, 6- 182, 7- 222, 8- 227, 9- 249
1- 16, 2- 63, 3- 63, 4- 79, 5- 101, 6- 105, 7- 136, 8- 138, 9- 142

### NEW ZEALAND

| | FIRST INNINGS | |
|---|---|---|
| G.P. Howarth† | lbw, b Ratnayeke | 7 |
| J.G. Wright | c de Alwis, b Ratnayeke | 18 |
| J.F. Reid | c and b Amerasinghe | 180 |
| M.D. Crowe | c de Alwis, b Ratnayeke | 45 |
| S.L. Boock | b John | 35 |
| J.J. Crowe | lbw, b John | 18 |
| J.V. Coney | c de Alwis, b Amerasinghe | 92 |
| R.J. Hadlee | c Kaluperuma, b de Silva | 0 |
| I.D.S. Smith* | b John | 42 |
| J.G. Bracewell | c Kaluperuma, b de Silva | 0 |
| E.J. Chatfield | not out | 1 |
| Extras | b 4, lb 10, w 2, nb 5 | 21 |
| | | 459 |

| | O | M | R | W |
|---|---|---|---|---|
| John | 37 | 8 | 99 | 3 |
| Ratnayeke | 40 | 9 | 128 | 3 |
| Ranatunge | 16 | 5 | 18 | — |
| de Silva | 42 | 4 | 95 | 2 |
| Amerasinghe | 30 | 4 | 73 | 2 |
| Kaluperuma | 10 | 2 | 25 | — |

FALL OF WICKETS
1- 13, 2- 32, 3- 132, 4- 214, 5- 253, 6- 386, 7- 391, 8- 429, 9- 436

**New Zealand won by an innings and 61 runs**

## Sri Lanka *v.* New Zealand – Test Match Averages

### SRI LANKA BATTING

| | M | Inns | NOs | Runs | HS | Av | 100s | 50s |
|---|---|---|---|---|---|---|---|---|
| R.S. Madugalle | 3 | 6 | 2 | 242 | 89* | 60.50 | | 1 |
| R.L. Dias | 2 | 3 | | 134 | 108 | 44.66 | 1 | |
| A. Ranatunge | 3 | 6 | | 171 | 51 | 28.50 | | 2 |
| A.M.J.G. Amerasinghe | 2 | 4 | 1 | 54 | 34 | 18.00 | | |
| S. Wettimuny | 3 | 6 | | 102 | 65 | 17.00 | | 1 |
| R.G. de Alwis | 3 | 6 | | 87 | 28 | 14.50 | | |
| V. John | 3 | 6 | 3 | 42 | 27* | 14.00 | | |
| S.M.S. Kaluperuma | 3 | 6 | | 82 | 23 | 13.66 | | |
| L.R.D. Mendis | 3 | 6 | | 71 | 36 | 11.83 | | |
| E.R.N.S. Fernando | 2 | 4 | | 39 | 29 | 9.75 | | |
| J.R. Ratnayeke | 2 | 4 | | 36 | 22 | 9.00 | | |
| D.S. de Silva | 3 | 6 | 1 | 42 | 17 | 8.40 | | |

Played in one Test: R.J. Ratnayake 6 and 12

### SRI LANKA BOWLING

| | Overs | Mds | Runs | Wkts | Av | Best | 10/m | 5/in |
|---|---|---|---|---|---|---|---|---|
| A. Ranatunge | 51 | 16 | 89 | 4 | 22.25 | 2/17 | | |
| V. John | 129 | 28 | 373 | 16 | 23.31 | 5/86 | | 1 |
| J.R. Ratnayeke | 82 | 28 | 187 | 8 | 23.37 | 5/42 | | 1 |
| S.M.S. Kaluperuma | 27 | 8 | 62 | 2 | 31.00 | 2/17 | | |
| D.S. de Silva | 125.3 | 28 | 293 | 8 | 36.62 | 3/59 | | |
| A.M.J.G. Amerasinghe | 50 | 9 | 150 | 3 | 50.00 | 2/73 | | |

Also bowled: R.J. Ratnayake 15–4–45–1; R.S. Madugalle 1–1–0–0

### SRI LANKA FIELDING

9–R.G. de Alwis (ct 8/st 1); 6–S.M.S. Kaluperuma; 3–A.M.J.G. Amerasinghe; 2–A. Ranatunge, D.S. de Silva, and subs; 1–R.J. Ratnayake, S. Wettimuny, R.L. Dias, V. John and R.S. Madugalle

### NEW ZEALAND BATTING

| | M | Inns | NOs | Runs | HS | Av | 100s | 50s |
|---|---|---|---|---|---|---|---|---|
| J. Coney | 3 | 5 | 2 | 170 | 92 | 56.66 | | 1 |
| J.F. Reid | 3 | 5 | | 243 | 180 | 48.60 | 1 | |
| I.D.S. Smith | 3 | 4 | 1 | 110 | 42 | 36.66 | | |
| G.P. Howarth | 3 | 5 | | 163 | 62 | 32.60 | | 2 |
| J.G. Wright | 3 | 5 | | 135 | 48 | 27.00 | | |
| M.D. Crowe | 3 | 5 | 1 | 98 | 45 | 24.50 | | |
| J.J. Crowe | 3 | 5 | | 113 | 50 | 22.60 | | 1 |
| S.L. Boock | 3 | 3 | 1 | 43 | 35 | 21.50 | | |
| R.J. Hadlee | 3 | 4 | | 75 | 29 | 18.75 | | |
| J.G. Bracewell | 2 | 3 | | 23 | 21 | 7.66 | | |
| B.L. Cairns | 2 | 3 | | 16 | 14 | 5.33 | | |

Played in two Tests: E.J. Chatfield 9* and 1*

### NEW ZEALAND BOWLING

| | Overs | Mds | Runs | Wkts | Av | Best | 10/m | 5/inn |
|---|---|---|---|---|---|---|---|---|
| R.J. Hadlee | 117.5 | 47 | 230 | 23 | 10.00 | 5/29 | 1 | 2 |
| E.J. Chatfield | 80 | 23 | 203 | 10 | 20.30 | 5/63 | | 1 |
| S.L. Boock | 117 | 39 | 257 | 11 | 23.36 | 5/28 | | 1 |
| B.L. Cairns | 68.5 | 13 | 203 | 6 | 38.33 | 4/47 | | |
| J.G. Bracewell | 42 | 11 | 156 | 4 | 39.00 | 2/36 | | |
| M.D. Crowe | 27 | 10 | 60 | 1 | 60.00 | 1/21 | | |
| J.V. Coney | 7 | 3 | 11 | 0 | — | 0/4 | | |

### NEW ZEALAND FIELDING

8–I.D.S. Smith; 6–J.V. Coney;
5–J.G. Bracewell and J.G. Wright; 4–J.J. Crowe; 3–R.J. Hadlee; 2–G.P. Howarth; 1– M.D. Crowe, S.L. Boock, E.J. Chatfield and sub

Test match, but Ravi Ratnayeke again raised Sri Lankan morale when he sent back Howarth and Wright to leave New Zealand 32 for 2 at lunch. A determined, sometimes grim, partnership between Reid and Martin Crowe restored New Zealand's advantage. Crowe fell to Ratnayeke before the close which came at 135 for 3. The runs had been scored in 61 overs and provided a most dour day's cricket.

Off the third ball of the third day Reid was missed at slip by Madugalle from the bowling of the impressive Ravi Ratnayeke. It was a costly mistake for by the end of the day Reid had celebrated his recall to international cricket with his highest Test score and was 156 not out. New Zealand were 322 for 5, made at little more than two an over, and they were immune from defeat.

Reid took his score to a career best 180 after the rest day and Coney hit lavishly as their stand realised 133. Leading by 203 on the first innings, New Zealand captured 3 Sri Lankan wickets for 69 before the close and with Dias unable to bat, Sri Lanka faced another defeat.

There was no recovery on the last day in spite of a brave 50 from Ranatunge. Boock combined with Hadlee to bring the Sri Lankan innings to an end shortly after lunch. Hadlee had match figures of 10 for 102, the fourth time he had taken 10 wickets in a Test match. His 23 wickets in the series was a remarkable achievement and won him the individual award.

Sri Lanka were left with much to ponder, particularly on how they were to maintain the necessary top class competition in order to survive at Test level.

*Duleep Mendis – victory in the second one-day international was no comfort for the Test defeats. (Adrian Murrell)*

### Second One-Day International
### SRI LANKA *v.* NEW ZEALAND

Geoff Howarth was still celebrating his thirty-third birthday and his team's triumph in an away series for the first time in 15 years when he was abruptly halted by Sri Lanka's victory in the second of the one-day internationals.

**SECOND ONE-DAY INTERNATIONAL: SRI LANKA *v.* NEW ZEALAND**
31 March 1984 at Moratuwa

| SRI LANKA | | |
|---|---|---|
| S. Wettimuny | b Chatfield | 6 |
| D.S.B.P. Kuruppu | c Wright, b Stirling | 4 |
| R.S. Madugalle | c Coney, b Chatfield | 10 |
| A. Ranatunge | not out | 50 |
| L.R.D. Mendis† | b Cairns | 4 |
| A. de Silva | b Hadlee | 8 |
| J.R. Ratnayeke | run out | 12 |
| U.S.H. Karnain | c Cairns, b M.D. Crowe | 28 |
| R.G. de Alwis* | run out | 1 |
| D.S. de Silva | not out | 18 |
| V. John | | |
| Extras | b 1, lb 10, w 1, nb 4 | 16 |
| (40 overs) | (for 8 wickets) | 157 |

| | O | M | R | W |
|---|---|---|---|---|
| Cairns | 8 | 1 | 11 | 1 |
| Hadlee | 8 | 2 | 27 | 1 |
| Stirling | 5 | 1 | 34 | 1 |
| Chatfield | 8 | — | 29 | 2 |
| Coney | 6 | — | 21 | — |
| M.D. Crowe | 5 | — | 19 | 1 |

FALL OF WICKETS
1- 11, 2- 22, 3- 37, 4- 48, 5- 69, 6- 110, 7- 110, 8- 112

| NEW ZEALAND | | |
|---|---|---|
| J.G. Wright | c Wettimuny, b John | 3 |
| B.A. Edgar | c de Alwis, b Karnain | 12 |
| G.P. Howarth† | b Karnain | 12 |
| B.L. Cairns | b Karnain | 5 |
| M.D. Crowe | c de Alwis, b Karnain | 9 |
| J.J. Crowe | lbw, b Karnain | 9 |
| J.V. Coney | b Ranatunge | 11 |
| R.J. Hadlee | c A. de Silva, b Ranatunge | 13 |
| I.D.S. Smith* | c A. de Silva, b D.S. de Silva | 11 |
| D.A. Stirling | not out | 14 |
| E.J. Chatfield | lbw, b Ranatunge | 5 |
| Extras | b 1, lb 10, nb 1 | 12 |
| (34 overs) | | 116 |

| | O | M | R | W |
|---|---|---|---|---|
| John | 7 | — | 13 | 1 |
| J.R. Ratnayeke | 6 | — | 14 | — |
| Karnain | 8 | 1 | 26 | 5 |
| D.S. de Silva | 5 | — | 28 | 1 |
| Ranatunge | 8 | 1 | 23 | 3 |

FALL OF WICKETS
1- 4, 2- 31, 3- 39, 4- 39, 5- 49, 6- 66, 7- 76, 8- 88, 9- 96

**Sri Lanka won by 41 runs**

## THIRD ONE-DAY INTERNATIONAL: SRI LANKA *v.* NEW ZEALAND
1 April 1984 at Colombo

| NEW ZEALAND | | |
|---|---|---|
| J.G. Wright† | c de Alwis, b J.R. Ratnayeke | 10 |
| B.A. Edgar | b D.S. de Silva | 24 |
| M.D. Crowe | run out | 68 |
| J.F. Reid | c D.S. de Silva, b John | 9 |
| J.J. Crowe | b Ranatunge | 5 |
| J.V. Coney | c and b Ranatunge | 13 |
| R.J. Hadlee | c Madugalle, b Ranatunge | 9 |
| I.D.S. Smith* | run out | 13 |
| B.L. Cairns | not out | 40 |
| S.L. Boock | not out | 8 |
| E.J. Chatfield | | |
| Extras | lb 1, w 1 | 2 |
| (44 overs) | (for 8 wickets) | 201 |

| | O | M | R | W |
|---|---|---|---|---|
| John | 9 | 1 | 43 | 1 |
| J.R. Ratnayeke | 8 | — | 32 | 1 |
| Karnain | 9 | — | 41 | — |
| D.S. de Silva | 9 | — | 34 | 1 |
| Ranatunge | 9 | — | 49 | 3 |

FALL OF WICKETS
1- 16, 2- 45, 3- 63, 4- 77, 5- 114, 6- 124, 7- 153, 8- 154

| SRI LANKA | | |
|---|---|---|
| S. Wettimuny | c Smith, b Hadlee | 33 |
| D.S.B.P. Kuruppu | c Smith, b Hadlee | 3 |
| R.S. Madugalle | c sub, b Boock | 10 |
| A. de Silva | run out | 7 |
| A. Ranatunge | c J.J. Crowe, b Cairns | 13 |
| L.R.D. Mendis† | c Hadlee, b Chatfield | 7 |
| U.S.H. Karnain | c Boock, b Cairns | 1 |
| J.R. Ratnayeke | c Reid, b Chatfield | 7 |
| R.G. de Alwis* | lbw, b Hadlee | 9 |
| D.S. de Silva | not out | 14 |
| V. John | c sub, b Coney | 1 |
| Extras | b 6, lb 4 | 10 |
| (38.1 overs) | | 115 |

| | O | M | R | W |
|---|---|---|---|---|
| Cairns | 7 | 2 | 14 | 2 |
| Hadlee | 6 | — | 19 | 3 |
| Chatfield | 9 | 2 | 13 | 2 |
| Boock | 9 | 1 | 22 | 1 |
| Coney | 6.1 | 1 | 24 | 1 |
| M.D. Crowe | 1 | — | 13 | — |

FALL OF WICKETS
1- 6, 2- 29, 3- 39, 4- 73, 5- 76, 6- 79, 7- 85, 8- 94, 9- 114

**New Zealand won by 86 runs**

With Cairns economic and Chatfield and Hadlee bowling useful spells, it seemed that New Zealand would have little difficulty in winning after they had contained Sri Lanka to 157 in 40 overs. That they reached such a total was due entirely to Ranatunge's unbeaten fifty and some purposeful late batting by Karnain, on his international debut, and Somachandra de Silva.

Wright fell quickly to John, but Edgar and Howarth seemed to be easing New Zealand towards victory when medium paced bowler Uvaisul Karnain was introduced into the attack. In his eight-over spell he dismissed five batsmen to reduce New Zealand to 66 for 6 and win his side the match.

There was consternation from New Zealand when umpires Francis and Vidanagamage led the players off the field at the end of the eighteenth over with the score at 61 for 5 because of bad light. Coney and Martin Crowe, the batsmen, stayed at the wicket and Howarth came on to the field to protest, but the stoppage lasted for 12 minutes. Martin Crowe was out shortly after the resumption and the tail, though giving a livelier performance than their colleagues higher up the order, fell to the spin of Ranatunge and de Silva.

In his first international match, Karnain, a hockey international, was named Man of the Match for a fine all-round performance.

### Third One-Day International
### SRI LANKA v. NEW ZEALAND

New Zealand duly took the limited-over series with a comfortable win in the third match. They were without Howarth, who had an infected tooth, and Wright led the side. A flawless innings from Martin Crowe had moved New Zealand towards a substantial total, but Ranatunge took three quick wickets and when the eighth wicket fell the score was a disappointing 154. Lance Cairns then found his hitting range for the first time on the tour and 47 were added for the ninth wicket. In the last over of the innings he hit John for 26, including three massive sixes over mid-wicket.

Sri Lanka were quickly in trouble to Hadlee and with Chatfield and Boock able to provide a mid-innings brake, New Zealand won easily.

*Geoff Howarth – victory abroad to add to victory at home. Adrian Murrell)*

**First Class Averages**

**BATTING**

| | M | Inns | NOs | Runs | HS | Av | 100s | 50s |
|---|---|---|---|---|---|---|---|---|
| R.S. Madugalle | 5 | 8 | 2 | 259 | 89* | 43.16 | | 1 |
| R.L. Dias | 3 | 4 | | 134 | 108 | 33.50 | 1 | |
| A. Ranatunge | 6 | 9 | 1 | 245 | 51 | 30.62 | | 2 |
| S. Warnakulasuriya | 4 | 4 | 1 | 77 | 65 | 25.66 | | 1 |
| E.R.N.S. Fernando | 4 | 6 | | 117 | 48 | 19.50 | | |
| S. Wettimuny | 4 | 7 | | 125 | 65 | 17.85 | | 1 |
| S.M.S. Kaluperuma | 6 | 8 | | 134 | 30 | 16.75 | | |
| R.G. de Alwis | 5 | 7 | | 95 | 28 | 13.57 | | |
| A.M.J.G. Amerasinghe | 5 | 6 | 1 | 60 | 34 | 12.00 | | |

(Qualification – 50 runs)

**BOWLING**

| | Overs | Mds | Runs | Wkts | Av | Best | 10/m | 5/in |
|---|---|---|---|---|---|---|---|---|
| A.M.J.G. Amerasinghe | 168 | 46 | 379 | 19 | 19.94 | 7/82 | 1 | 1 |
| V. John | 151 | 34 | 439 | 20 | 21.95 | 5/86 | | 1 |
| A. Ranatunge | 80.5 | 27 | 154 | 7 | 22.00 | 2/17 | | |
| A.L.F. de Mel | 40 | 6 | 119 | 5 | 23.80 | 3/72 | | |
| R.J. Ratnayake | 50 | 10 | 144 | 6 | 24.00 | 4/49 | | |
| J.R. Ratnayeke | 102.2 | 31 | 259 | 9 | 28.77 | 5/42 | | 1 |
| D.S. de Silva | 125.3 | 28 | 293 | 8 | 36.62 | 3/59 | | |

(Qualification – 5 wickets)

**FIELDING**

10–R.G. de Alwis (ct 9/st 1); 8–S.M.S. Kaluperuma; 5–A. Ranatunge; 4–R.S. Madugalle, A.M.J.G. Amerasinghe and R. Buultjens; 3–D.S.B. Kuruppu

**SECTION E**

# Fading Glory

The season in South Africa.
Castle Currie Cup and Castle Bowl. Nissan Shield. The tour of the 'rebel' West Indians.
South Africa *v.* West Indian XI International Series.

The editor is indebted to Peter Sichel of the *Protea Cricket Annual of South Africa* for supplying statistics for much of this section.

*Alan Kourie – bowled more overs and took more wickets than any other South African bowler. (Adrian Murrell)*

## Fading Glory

The Season in South Africa. Castle Currie Cup and Castle Bowl. Nissan Shield. The tour of the 'rebel' West Indians. South Africa *v.* West Indian XI International Series.

The editor is indebted to Peter Sichel of the Protea Cricket Annual of South Africa for supplying statistics for much of this section.

### Castle Currie Cup

***8, 9 and 10 October, 1983***

---

***at Durban***

**Natal** 130 (A.M. Ferreira 6 for 26) and 211 (R.M. Bentley 63, M.B. Logan 60, P.A. Robinson 6 for 46)
**Northern Transvaal** 93 (P.B. Clift 4 for 6, G. Miller 4 for 24) and 252 for 9 (D. J. Richardson 108)

*Northern Transvaal won by 1 wicket*
*Northern Transvaal 15 pts, Natal 5 pts*

A shortened Currie Cup programme meant that each side would play four matches and the top four teams would play off. In the opening match, dominated by players who spend the summer in England, Northern Transvaal won an exciting game after being behind for most of the match, Ackermann and Robinson adding 18 for the last wicket.

### Nissan Shield

***15 October, 1983***

---

***at Cape Town***

**Western Province 'B'** 93 (S.T. Clarke 5 for 10)
**Transvaal** 95 for 1

*Transvaal won by 9 wickets*

*Steve Jefferies of Western Province. He worked hard to force his way into the South African side. (Ken Kelly)*

***at Oude Libertas***

**Northern Transvaal** 195 (G. McMillan 51, S. Jones 5 for 20)
**Boland** 122 (A.M. Ferreira 4 for 14)

*Northern Transvaal won by 73 runs*

The limited-over competition, formerly known as the Datsun shield, 55 overs, began with two matches in which Sylvester Clarke dominated and Gordon McMillan saved Northern Transvaal from embarrassment.

***22 October 1983***

---

***at Bloemfontein***

**Natal** 207 for 9
**Orange** Free State 124

*Natal won by 83 runs*

***at Kimberley***

**Transvaal** 354 for 9 (H.R. Fotheringham 101, K.A. McKenzie 89, R.G. Pollock 71, P. McLaren 4 for 60)
**Griqualand West** 173 for 7 (M.J.D. Doherty 70, K. Sharp 50, S.T. Clarke 4 for 9)

*Transvaal won by 181 runs*

***at Pretoria***

**Western Province** 216 for 9 (G.A. Gooch 55, P.H. Rayner 52, P.A. Robinson 4 for 56)
**Northern Transvaal** 149 (M. Yachad 62)

*Western Province won by 67 runs*

### Castle Currie Cup

***29, 30 and 31 October 1983***

---

***at Durban***

**Natal** 367 for 4 dec (B.J. Whitfield 116, R.A. Smith 75, M.B. Logan 63, R.M. Bentley 53)
**Western Province** 205 (A.P. Kuiper 61, M.J. Procter 5 for 63, G. Miller 4 for 71) and 420 for 5 (R.F. Pienaar 151 not out, A.P. Kuiper 104, P.N. Kirsten 62)

*Match drawn*
*Natal 8 pts, Western Province 3 pts*

***at Johannesburg***

**Transvaal** 262 (S.J. Cook 82) and 153 (A.J. Kourie 50 not out, W.K. Watson 5 for 44)
**Eastern Province** 148 (I.K. Daniell 66, R.W. Hanley 7 for 31) and 123 (R.W. Hanley 5 for 22)

*Transvaal won by 144 runs*
*Transvaal 19 pts, Eastern Province 5 pts*

### Castle Bowl

***at Constantia***

**Natal 'B'** 209 (P.H. Williams 58, D. Norman 4 for 41, M.D. Mellor 4 for 75) and 189 (G.N. Lister-James 61, D. Norman 4 for 47)
**Western Province 'B'** 235 (E.J. Hodkinson 6 for 70) and 169 for 4

*Western Province 'B' won by 6 wickets*
*Western Province 'B' 18 pts, Natal 'B' 7 pts*

***29, 31 October and 1 November 1983***

---

***at Bloemfontein***

**Orange Free State** 341 for 5 dec (R.A. le Roux 188, J.J. Strydom 60)

*Omar Henry (Western Province). A competent all-rounder and one of the first coloured players to hold his own in a Currie Cup side. (Ken Kelly)*

**Eastern Province 'B'** 150 (A. Sidebottom 4 for 21) and 117 (C.J.P.G. van Zyl 4 for 37)

*Orange Free State won by an innings and 74 runs*
*Orange Free State 17 pts, Eastern Province 'B' 1 pt*

A career best from Roy Pienaar in a fifth wicket stand with Kuiper who hit the second century of his career saved Western Province after they had been forced to follow-on in Durban, and career best bowling by 'Spook' Hanley won the match for Transvaal at Johannesburg. The most notable achievement in the opening Bowl matches was a career best 188 by Ray le Roux which set up Orange Free State's big win.

## Castle Bowl

### *3, 4 and 5 November 1983*

***at Pietersburg***

**Northern Transvaal 'B'** 381 for 8 dec (S. Vercueil 87, A. Geringer 61, C.P.L. de Lange 51) and 214 for 3 dec (V.F. du Preez 117 not out, L. van Rensburg 51)
**Eastern Province 'B'** 266 (D.G. Emslie 99) and 212 for 6 (D.G. Emslie 90 not out)

*Match drawn*
*Eastern Province 'B' 8 pts, Northern Transvaal 'B' 7 pts*

### *4, 5 and 6 November 1983*

***at Johannesburg***

**Transvaal 'B'** 317 for 9 dec (B. Roberts 73, W. Kirsh 65, C.R. Norris 51 not out) and 91 for 2
**Griqualand West** 120 (C.R. Norris 7 for 31) and 285 (N.E. Wright 91)

*Transvaal 'B' won by 8 wickets*
*Transvaal 'B' 19 pts, Griqualand West 3 pts*

## Castle Currie Cup

### *4, 5 and 7 November 1983*

***at Pretoria***

**Transvaal** 288 for 6 dec (S.J. Cook 50, H.R. Fotheringham 54) and 222 for 7 dec (S.J. Cook 74 not out, I.F.N. Weideman 5 for 82)
**Northern Transvaal** 233 (N.T. Day 65, M. Yachad 61) and 199 for 6

*Match drawn*
*Transvaal 6 pts, Northern Transvaal 4 pts*

### *5, 6 and 7 November 1983*

***at Cape Town***

**Eastern Province** 373 (P. Willey 11, D.H. Howell 74 not out) and 209 (W. Larkins 110, D.L. Hobson 5 for 75, G.S. le Roux 4 for 53)
**Western Province** 587 for 7 dec (G.A. Gooch 163, L. Seeff 128, O. Henry 79 not out, P.N. Kirsten 58, J.E. Emburey 52 not out, P. Willey 4 for 145)

*Western Province won by an innings and 5 runs*
*Western Province 22 pts, Eastern Province 6 pts*

Career bests with bat and ball by left-hander Craig Norris at Johannesburg were totally overshadowed by events at Cape Town where Gooch, a six and twenty fours, and Lawrie Seeff put on a record 293 for Western Province's first wicket. Then John Emburey, 52 off 22 balls, hit six sixes in 7 balls in a game dominated by Englishmen, both Willey and Larkins hitting their first centuries in the Currie Cup.

## Castle Bowl

### *10, 11 and 12 November 1983*

***at Oude Libertas, Stellenbosch***

**Boland** 280 (A. du Toit 117) and 241 for 9 dec
**Western Province 'B'** 225 (I.M. Wingreen 72, S.A. Jones 4 for 28) and 147 for 5 (S.T. Jefferies 55 not out)

*Match drawn*
*Boland 6 pts, Western Province 5 pts*

### *12, 13 and 14 November 1983*

***at Kimberley***

**Griqualand West** 195 (M.D. Moxon 51, M.R. Ballantyne 5 for 35, I. Foulkes 4 for 56) and 307 (A.P. Beukes 91, M.D. Moxon 60)
**Border** 401 for 9 dec (R.C. Ontong 145, I. Foulkes 74, J.G. Thomas 68, A.P. Beukes 4 for 86) and 112 for 8

*Border won by 2 wickets*
*Border 18 pts, Griqualand West 3 pts*

## Castle Currie Cup

*12, 13 and 14 November 1983*

***at Port Elizabeth***

**Eastern Province** 415 (W. Larkins 116, I.K. Daniell 81, G.S. Cowley 73, D.J. Thomas 6 for 105)
**Natal** 242 (R.A. Smith 109, R.M. Bentley 50, J.A. Carse 4 for 43) and 239 for 4 (M.B. Logan 84, R.A. Smith 54)

*Match drawn*
*Eastern Province 7 pts, Natal 4 pts*

In spite of the efforts of Yorkshire's Martyn Moxon, Glamorgan's Ontong and Thomas took Border to victory in the Bowl match at Kimberley while two good innings from the exciting Robin Smith helped Natal to draw at St George's Park in the Currie Cup match.

## Castle Bowl

*18, 19 and 20 November 1983*

***at Johannesburg***

**Transvaal 'B'** (M.J. Rindel 81, B.W. Proctor 5 for 50) and 119 (G.P. Hurlbatt 4 for 36, E.J. Hodkinson 4 for 45)
**Natal 'B'** 157 (C.D. Mitchley 5 for 65, T.H. Parrymore 4 for 49) and 233 for 7 (G.V. Tramontino 66, S.M. Hedley 55, G.N. Lister-James 54 not out)

*Natal 'B' won by 3 wickets*
*Natal 'B' 15 pts, Transvaal 'B' 9 pts*

## Currie Cup

*19, 20 and 21 November 1983*

***at Cape Town***

**Western Province** 244 (P.N. Kirsten 100) and 316 for 6 dec. (P.N. Kirsten 80)
**Transvaal** 279 (R.G. Pollock 154, D.L. Hobson 5 for 43) and 176 for 2 (C.E.B. Rice 85 not out, S.J. Cook 58)

*Match drawn*
*Transvaal 10 pts, Western Province 8 pts*

Two dropped catches by Graham Gooch allowed Graeme Pollock to recapture his form and hit a six and twenty-five fours in his innings of 154. Predictably, the meeting between the two top sides ended in stalemate. Grant Lister-James again played well to steer Natal 'B' to victory.

*19, 21 and 22 November 1983*

***at Pretoria***

**Northern Transvaal** 288 for 9 dec (W.F. Morris 73 not out, L.J. Barnard 60, C.E.H. Croft 4 for 41) and 136 for 5 dec
**West Indians** 153 (I.F.N. Weideman 4 for 35) and 183 for 5 (A.I. Kallicharran 92)

*Match drawn*

Norther Transvaal recovered from 98 for 5 thanks to a fierce innings from number nine, Morris, and Weideman and Barnard (3 for 6) bowled them to a lead, but Kallicharran restored sanity in the opening match of the 'rebel' West Indians tour.

*24 November 1983*

***at Stellenbosch***

**Boland** 132 for 8
**West Indians** 133 for 6

*West Indians won by 4 wickets*

*25, 26 and 28 November 1983*

***at Cape Town***

**West Indians** 291 (M.A. Lynch 105, S.F.A. Bacchus 61, D.L. Hobson 5 for 92, J.E. Emburey 4 for 63) and 300 (C.L. King 75, F.D. Stephenson 73, D.L. Hobson 7 for 129)
**Western Province** 322 for 8 dec (P.N. Kirsten 71, P.H. Rayner 54, K.S. McEwan 54) and 57 for 1

*Match drawn*

The leg-breaks of Denys Hobson suggested a weakness in the West Indian side, but King and Stephenson made typically violent responses.

## *Castle Currie Cup*

*26, 27 and 28 November 1983*

***at Johannesburg***

**Transvaal** 532 for 6 dec (R.G. Pollock 147, S.J. Cook 122, H.R. Fotheringham 64, K.A. McKenzie 59)
**Natal** 300 (P.B. Clift 64, T.R. Madsen 63, A.J.S. Smith 72, C.D. Mitchley 4 for 46) and 201 for 4 (R.M. Bentley 110 not out)

*Match drawn*
*Transvaal 9 pts, Natal 6 pts*

## Castle Bowl

*26, 27 and 28 November 1983*

***at Pietermaritzburg***

**Boland** 179 (G.J. Parsons 56, M.D. Clare 5 for 65)
**Natal 'B'** 66 for 5

*Match drawn*
*Natal 'B' 5 pts, Boland 3 pts*

Rain ruined the Bowl match, but at Johannesburg a ninth wicket stand of 85 revived Natal who eventually saved the match thanks to Bentley's century.

*30 November 1983*

***at East London***

**West Indians** 247 for 6 (S.F.A. Bacchus 65, E.N. Trotman 62 not out)
**Border** 119 (B.D. Julien 4 for 25)

*West Indians won by 128 runs*

## Castle Bowl

*30 November, 1 and 2 December 1983*

***at Bloemfontein***

**Griqualand West** 108 (G.R. Grobler 4 for 23) and 177 (C.J.P.G. van Zyl 4 for 42)
**Orange Free State** 500 for 6 dec (J.J. Strydom 119 not out, R.J. East 108, R.A. le Roux 64, C.J. Richards 60)

*Orange Free State won by an innings and 215 runs*
*Orange Free State 20 pts, Griqualand West 2 pts*

A fifth wicket stand of 142 between East and Strydom was the basis of Free State's big score.

*2, 3 and 4 December 1983*

***at Durban***

**West Indians** 397 (S.F.A. Bacchus 88, C.L. King 67, A.I. Kallicharran 55, M.D. Clare 4 for 68) and 168 for 9 dec (A.I. Kallicharran 79)
**Natal** 239 (M.J. Procter 102, E.A. Moseley 4 for 36) and 160 for 3 (R.M. Bentley 65, D. Bestall 58 not out)

*Match drawn*

## Castle Currie Cup

*2 and 3 December 1983*

***at Pretoria***

**Northern Transvaal** 230 (P.J.A. Visagie 56, N.T. Day 50, A.P. Kuiper 6 for 55) and 128 (E.O. Simons 4 for 30)
**Western Province** 282 (K.S. McEwan 67, A.P. Kuiper 67, A.M. Ferreira 5 for 76) and 79 for 2

*Western Province won by 8 wickets*
*Western Province 20 pts, Northern Transvaal 8 pts*

A career best bowling performance by Adrian Kuiper who also batted well helped Western Province to victory in two days.

### First One-Day International
### SOUTH AFRICA *v.* WEST INDIAN XI

*7 December 1983*

***at Johannesburg***

**South Africa** 233 for 7 (P.N. Kirsten 55)
**West Indian XI** 235 for 8 (A.I. Kallicharran 80, C.L. King 63 not out)

*West Indian XI won by 2 wickets*

In the first limited-over international, a day–night match, the West Indian XI recovered from a poor start to win an exciting victory with 4 balls to spare.

In a consistent batting display, South Africa reached a satisfactory 233 from their 50 overs, the highlights of the innings being a stand of 78 between Kirsten and Pollock and some good hitting from Rice and le Roux towards the close.

West Indies started disastrously, losing both openers for 12, but at the supper break, they were 36 for 2 off 12 overs. Kallicharran, 20 not out at the interval, continued in eloquent form and found a good partner in King who, although troubled by cramp, bludgeoned runs in his usual manner. The pair added 97 and Rowe also played sensibly. A minor collapse gave hints of a South African victory, but Collis King found the help he needed in David Murray and they added 39 for the ninth wicket to take their side to a narrow victory.

*10 December 1983*

***at Bloemfontein***

**West Indians** 290 for 6 (S.F.A. Bacchus 103, A.T. Greenidge 70 not out)
**Orange Free State** 232 for 6 (W.M. van der Merwe 67 not out, R.A. le Roux 58)

*West Indians won by 58 runs*

This match turned out to be something of a celebration when, following the first one-day international, there was dispute over the financial arrangements for the tour which were ultimately resolved.

## Nissan Shield

*10 December 1983*

***at Port Elizabeth***

**Eastern Province** 185 (W. Larkins 69, H.A. Page 4 for 32)
**Transvaal** 191 for 4 (R.G. Pollock 59 not out, H.R. Fotheringham 52)

*Transvaal won by 6 wickets*

***at Cape Town***

**Natal** 190 for 9
**Western Province** 195 for 4

*Western Province won by 6 wickets*

*12, 13 and 14 December 1983*

***at East London***

**South African Universities** 264 and 190 (B. McBride 63, R.C. Ontong 5 for 44)
**Border** 243 for 9 dec and 159 for 8 (R.C. Ontong 54, D. Cullinan 53)

*Match drawn*

***at Port Elizabeth***

**Eastern Province** 314 for 9 dec (D.G. Emslie 60, I.K. Daniell 50)

*Ezra Moseley – the scourge of South Africa in the one-day internationals. (Adrian Murrell)*

and 161 for 9 dec (D.G. Emslie 50 not out, H.L. Alleyne 4 for 26, A.I. Kallicharran 4 for 26)
**West Indians** 242 for 7 dec (E.N. Trotman 96, W.K. Watson 4 for 70) and 181 for 7

*Match drawn*

***17, 18 and 19 December 1983***

***at Johannesburg***

**West Indians** 230 (E.H. Mattis 51, C.D. Mitchley 6 for 53) and 172 (A.J. Kourie 4 for 58)
**Transvaal** 310 for 9 dec (K.A. McKenzie 84) and 94 for 6

*Transvaal won by 4 wickets*

A career best bowling performance by Cyril Mitchley, the medium-pacer, and some hard hitting by Kevin McKenzie made possible Transvaal's win over the tourists, their first defeat of the tour, although in the end the bowling of Alleyne and Clarke nearly frustrated the South African champions who won with 11 balls to spare.

## Castle Bowl

***17, 18 and 19 December 1983***

***at Pietermaritzburg***

**Natal 'B'** 160 (P.L. Symcox 4 for 52) and 249 for 9 dec (J.W. Stephenson 50, G.E. McMillan 4 for 64)
**Northern Transvaal 'B'** 224 (P.L. Symcox 89, K.R. Cooper 6 for 84) and 186 for 6 (C.P.L. de Lange 53)

*Northern Transvaal 'B' won by 4 wickets*
*Northern Transvaal 'B' 17 pts, Natal 'B' 5 pts*

## Castle Currie Cup

***17, 18 and 19 December 1983***

***at Port Elizabeth***

**Northern Transvaal** 363 for 9 dec (M. Yachad 108, L.J. Barnard 68) and 147 for 4 (V.F. du Preez 52 not out)
**Eastern Province** 325 for 9 dec (W. Larkins 94, D.J. Brickett 61)

*Match drawn*
*Northern Transvaal 7 pts, Eastern Province 6 pts*

Eastern Province took sufficient points to oust Natal from fourth place and qualify for the semi-finals. They were 162 for 7, but Brickett, Watson and van Vuuren, the last three batsmen, doubled the score.

**Currie Cup Log**

| | *P* | *W* | *L* | *D* | *Points* *Batting* | *Bowling* | *Pts* |
|---|---|---|---|---|---|---|---|
| Western Province | 4 | 2 | – | 2 | 19 | 14 | 53 |
| Transvaal | 4 | 1 | – | 3 | 16 | 18 | 44 |
| Northern Transvaal | 4 | 1 | 1 | 2 | 7 | 17 | 34 |
| Eastern Province | 4 | – | 2 | 2 | 12 | 12 | 24 |
| Natal | 4 | – | 1 | 3 | 10 | 13 | 23 |

## Castle Bowl

***21, 22 and 23 December 1983***

***at Port Elizabeth***

**Eastern Province 'B'** 379 for 9 dec (I.L. Howell 109, R.G. Fensham 97, A.P. Nel 82) and 228 for 9 dec (R.G. Fensham 64, M.B. Minaar 4 for 74)
**Western Province 'B'** 342 (J.D. du Toit 128, P.D. Swart 81, B. deK Robey 7 for 88) and 270 for 4 (I.M. Wingreen 97, T.A. Clarke 79 not out)

*Western Province 'B' won by 6 wickets*
*Western Province 'B' 19 pts, Eastern Province 'B' 8 pts*

***26, 27 and 28 December***

***at East London***

**Northern Transvaal 'B'** 178 (A. Geringer 50) and 229 (C.P.L. de Lange 63, J.G. Thomas 4 for 27, R.C. Ontong 4 for 86)
**Border** 249 (M.B. Minaar 60) and 161 for 3 (M.D. Tramontino 59)

*Border won by 7 wickets*
*Border 17 pts, Northern Transvaal 'B' 6 pts*

Border and Western Province 'B' continued their climb to the top of the Castle Bowl with comfortable wins. There were career bests for medium pacer Robey and batsman du Toit and the Glamorgan pair, Ontong, the skipper, and Thomas, were again in fine form for Border.

### First International
### SOUTH AFRICA *v.* WEST INDIAN XI

The West Indians recovered from early setbacks to move to a commanding position in the first of the four unofficial 'Tests' against South Africa. Rowe decided to bat when he won the toss, but his batsmen made an uncertain start. Trotman lashed 21 from 27 deliveries before he was out and with Bacchus retiring hurt after dislocating a finger when hit on the hand by le Roux and Lynch and King falling within the space of six balls, the visitors slumped to 87 for 3.

Rowe and Kallicharran then added 154 in 201 minutes before Kallicharran fell to le Roux for a most elegant 103. Rowe continued into the second day and reached 157 in just over seven hours. It was a faultless innings, emphasising once again the glories of this batsman which have never been seen as often as was initially promised. Stephenson and Parry helped Rowe in brisk stands as the innings moved towards the point of declaration. Moseley and Parry finished in violent form and South Africa faced a daunting 529.

The match was doomed to a draw on the third day when rain restricted play to two hours. Kirsten and Cook had added 130 in 167 minutes but not without some fortune. Kirsten was dropped by Rowe at slip off Stephenson shortly after Cook's dismissal and he and Pollock began the last day together.

Pollock was not his fluent self but still scored valuable runs before falling to Parry. At 239 for 3, South Africa appeared to be batting out the match with ease, but Sylvester Clarke took 4 for 24 in 5 overs with the second new ball and the home side collapsed to 333 all out. Only Kourie of the later batsmen offered any resistance to Clarke and Moseley and South Africa followed-on 296 runs behind.

Cook and Fotheringham batted out time, but a chastened South African side contemplated the lack of penetration in their pace attack and the absence of any young pace bowlers who seriously threatened le Roux and Jefferies.

OPPOSITE: *Lawrence Rowe – captain of the West Indian XI and still one of the world's finest batsmen. (Adrian Murrell)*

## FIRST INTERNATIONAL – SOUTH AFRICA *v.* WEST INDIAN XI
23, 24, 26 and 27 December 1983 at Durban

**WEST INDIAN XI**

| | FIRST INNINGS | |
|---|---|---|
| S.F.A. Bacchus | retired hurt | 19 |
| E.N. Trotman | c Pollock, b le Roux | 21 |
| M.A. Lynch | c Hobson, b Kourie | 26 |
| A.I. Kallicharran | c Hobson, b le Roux | 103 |
| C.L. King | c Jefferies, b Rice | 0 |
| L.G. Rowe† | lbw, b Jefferies | 157 |
| D.A. Murray* | c Kourie, b le Roux | 32 |
| F.D. Stephenson | b Hobson | 53 |
| D.R. Parry | not out | 63 |
| E.A. Moseley | not out | 33 |
| S.T. Clarke | | |
| Extras | b 5, lb 9, w 2, nb 6 | 22 |
| | (for 7 wkts dec) | 529 |

| | O | M | R | W |
|---|---|---|---|---|
| le Roux | 27 | 2 | 88 | 3 |
| Jefferies | 31 | 3 | 132 | 1 |
| Rice | 21 | 4 | 65 | 1 |
| Kourie | 36 | 5 | 123 | 1 |
| Hobson | 19 | 1 | 95 | 1 |
| Kirsten | 1 | — | 4 | — |

FALL OF WICKETS
1- 34, 2- 86, 3- 87, 4- 241, 5- 311, 6- 392, 7- 481

**SOUTH AFRICA**

| | FIRST INNINGS | | SECOND INNINGS | |
|---|---|---|---|---|
| S.J. Cook | c Murray, b Clarke | 69 | not out | 30 |
| H.R. Fotheringham | lbw, b Moseley | 0 | not out | 22 |
| P.N. Kirsten† | c Murray, b Moseley | 84 | | |
| R.G. Pollock | b Parry | 62 | | |
| K.S. McEwan | c sub, b Moseley | 11 | | |
| C.E.B. Rice | c and b Parry | 7 | | |
| A.J. Kourie | b Clarke | 32 | | |
| R.V. Jennings* | b Clarke | 18 | | |
| G.S. le Roux | c Stephenson, b Clarke | 11 | | |
| S.T. Jefferies | b Clarke | 0 | | |
| D.L. Hobson | not out | 12 | | |
| Extras | b 4, lb 9, w 1, nb 13 | 27 | lb 2, nb 5 | 7 |
| | | 333 | (for no wkt) | 59 |

| | O | M | R | W | O | M | R | W |
|---|---|---|---|---|---|---|---|---|
| Clarke | 32.1 | 11 | 105 | 5 | 3 | — | 9 | — |
| Moseley | 26 | 5 | 76 | 3 | 4 | 2 | 8 | — |
| Stephenson | 21 | 5 | 61 | — | 6 | 1 | 16 | — |
| Parry | 25 | 7 | 62 | 2 | | | | |
| King | 2 | 1 | 2 | — | 6 | 2 | 13 | — |
| Kallicharran | | | | | 5 | 2 | 6 | — |

FALL OF WICKETS
1- 2, 2- 132, 3- 219, 4- 239, 5- 249, 6- 257, 7- 302, 8- 313, 9- 313

**Match drawn**

### Second International
### SOUTH AFRICA *v.* WEST INDIAN XI

The South Africans fielded an unchanged side for the second international. The West Indians brought in Mattis for the injured Bacchus and Julien for Moseley. Mattis was the first out after he and Trotman had put on 31 for the first wicket and his dismissal heralded a West Indian collapse, five wickets falling for 18 runs, four of them to the slow left-arm Kourie who had tantalised the West Indian touring side in 1982–83.

Collis King, who was missed off Jefferies when 2, curbed his naturally aggressive style to play a responsible innings and save his side from total humiliation. He and David Murray added 107 for the sixth wicket and King batted for over 3 hours for his 83. Parry and Julien added an invaluable 64 in 90 minutes for the 9th wicket, but the visitors were all out for 252 shortly before the end of the first day.

The South Africans began very slowly on the second day, but after a solid start from Cook and Fotheringham, Kirsten and Pollock joined in a stand of 183. Kirsten batted dourly and Pollock, at first subdued, reached his full range of glory in the after tea session when runs came at more than a run a minute. Pollock fell shortly before the close of play and Kirtsen added only 1 before he was out to Julien on the third morning. McEwan and Rice kept the score moving, however, although it took Rice 56 minutes to open his score. Then he hit four sixes and six fours and South Africa took a lead of 152 on the first innings.

This lead became formidable when West Indies lost 4 for

## SECOND INTERNATIONAL – SOUTH AFRICA *v.* WEST INDIAN XI

30 and 31 December 1983, 1 and 2 January 1984 at Cape Town

**WEST INDIAN XI**

| | FIRST INNINGS | | SECOND INNINGS | |
|---|---|---|---|---|
| E.N. Trotman | c Jennings, b Kourie | 28 | c Jennings, b Jefferies | 1 |
| E.H. Mattis | lbw, b Jefferies | 6 | c Rice, b Kourie | 26 |
| M.A. Lynch | c Jennings, b Kourie | 2 | run out | 23 |
| A.I. Kallicharran | c Fotheringham, b Kourie | 8 | lbw, b Kourie | 17 |
| C.L. King | c Kourie, b Jefferies | 83 | c Pollock, b Jefferies | 26 |
| L.G. Rowe† | c and b Kourie | 0 | (7) c Cook, b Hobson | 31 |
| D.A. Murray* | lbw, b Rice | 39 | (8) c Fotheringham, b Kourie | 40 |
| F.D. Stephenson | c Pollock, b Kourie | 7 | (9) lbw, b le Roux | 7 |
| B.D. Julien | not out | 33 | (10) c Kirsten, b le Roux | 18 |
| D.R. Parry | c and b le Roux | 30 | (6) c Pollock, b Rice | 58 |
| S.T. Clarke | lbw, b Jefferies | 0 | not out | 3 |
| Extras | b 7, lb 6, w 1, nb 2 | 16 | b 4, lb 7, w 6, nb 1 | 18 |
| | | 252 | | 268 |

**SOUTH AFRICA**

| | FIRST INNINGS | | SECOND INNINGS | |
|---|---|---|---|---|
| S.J. Cook | c Murray, b Clarke | 45 | not out | 40 |
| H.R. Fotheringham | c Julien, b Stephenson | 20 | not out | 71 |
| P.N. Kirsten† | c Parry, b Julien | 88 | | |
| R.G. Pollock | c Murray, b Parry | 102 | | |
| K.S. McEwan | c Murray, b Clarke | 32 | | |
| C.E.B. Rice | not out | 71 | | |
| A.J. Kourie | lbw, b Clarke | 1 | | |
| R.V. Jennings* | lbw, b Parry | 8 | | |
| G.S. le Roux | c Mattis, b Clarke | 11 | | |
| S.T. Jefferies | c Julien, b Parry | 1 | | |
| D.L. Hobson | c and b Clarke | 1 | | |
| Extras | lb 17, w 7 | 24 | lb 5, w 1 | 6 |
| | | 404 | (for no wkt) | 117 |

| | O | M | R | W | O | M | R | W |
|---|---|---|---|---|---|---|---|---|
| le Roux | 17 | 6 | 34 | 1 | 17.3 | 5 | 50 | 2 |
| Jefferies | 20 | 5 | 63 | 3 | 16 | 6 | 62 | 2 |
| Kourie | 22 | 6 | 66 | 5 | 27 | 11 | 61 | 3 |
| Hobson | 20 | 5 | 49 | — | 15 | 2 | 36 | 1 |
| Rice | 8 | 1 | 24 | 1 | 15 | 7 | 21 | 1 |
| Kirsten | | | | | 6 | 1 | 20 | — |

| | O | M | R | W | O | M | R | W |
|---|---|---|---|---|---|---|---|---|
| Clarke | 37.5 | 19 | 92 | 5 | 6 | — | 23 | — |
| Julien | 24 | 6 | 71 | 1 | 2 | — | 11 | — |
| Stephenson | 27 | 5 | 95 | 1 | 2 | — | 11 | — |
| Parry | 36 | 8 | 79 | 3 | 8 | — | 36 | — |
| King | 5 | 1 | 21 | — | 3 | — | 22 | — |
| Kallicharran | 3 | — | 22 | — | 0.2 | — | 8 | — |

FALL OF WICKETS (West Indian XI)
1- 31, 2- 38, 3- 46, 4- 49, 5- 49, 6- 156, 7- 183, 8- 183, 9- 247
1- 5, 2- 53, 3- 63, 4- 86, 5- 100, 6- 178, 7- 206, 8- 232, 9- 260

FALL OF WICKETS (South Africa)
1- 61, 2- 84, 3- 267, 4- 273, 5- 315, 6- 318, 7- 364, 8- 393, 9- 398

**South Africa won by 10 wickets**

89 before the close. Had not Jefferies dropped an easy chance offered by Kallicharran off Kourie when 1, the West Indian position would have been even worse.

The West Indians had another escape on the last morning when Parry was missed at slip by Pollock off le Roux, but King fell and it was left to Rowe and Murray to try to save the match. They looked as if they would do so until Rowe hit a leg-side full toss from leg-spinner Hobson straight to Cook at mid-on. Julien failed to bat with the necessary caution and South Africa were left to make 177 in 65 minutes. They needed only 21.2 overs as Cook and, in particular, Fotheringham savaged some short-pitched bowling and raced to victory.

## Castle Bowl

### *31 December 1983, 1 and 2 January 1984*

#### *at East London*

**Natal 'B'** 374 (S.M. Hedley 86, B.W. Proctor 58 not out, G.N. Lister-James 53) and 252 for 5 dec (M.D. Mellor 87 not out, N.P. Daniels 75)
**Border** 281 for 4 dec (N. Minnaar 82, I. Foulkes 55 not out, E.T. Laughlin 50 not out) and 227 for 5 (D. Cullinan 106 not out)

*Match drawn*
*Border 6 pts, Natal 'B' 6 pts*

#### *at Johannesburg*

**Transvaal 'B'** 157 (C.J.P.G. van Zyl 4 for 27) and 204 (B. Roberts 89)
**Orange Free State** 164 (H.A. Page 5 for 44) and 186 for 9 (A. Sidebottom 59, H.A. Page 4 for 47)

*Match drawn*
*Transvaal 'B' 5 pts, Orange Free State 5 pts*

The two drawn matches produced a maiden hundred for Cullinan and a best bowling performance by Hugh Page.

### *5, 6 and 7 January 1984*

#### *at Bloemfontein*

**Western Province 'B'** 312 (T.N. Lazard 117, C.J.P.G. van Zyl 5 for 57) and 149 for 6 dec (P.D. Swart 52, W.M. van der Merwe 4 for 31)
**Orange Free State** 220 (R.A. le Roux 78, C.J. Richards 73) and 100 for 6 (M.B. Minnaar 4 for 29)

*Match drawn*
*Orange Free State 6 pts, Western Province 'B' 6 pts*

### *6, 7 and 9 January 1984*

#### *at Pretoria*

**Transvaal 'B'** 195 (M.S. Venter 75, G.L. Ackermann 5 for 50) and 143 (E. Klopper 5 for 42)
**Northern Transvaal 'B'** 212 (G.L. Ackermann 67, P.J.A. Visagie 51, H.A. Page 4 for 54, C.D. Mitchley 4 for 90) and 132 for 5

*Northern Transvaal 'B' won by 5 wickets*
*Northern Transvaal 'B' 17 pts, Transvaal 'B' 5 pts*

There was a maiden hundred for Lazard at Bloemfontein and another good knock by Jack Richards who was not keeping wicket for Orange Free State. Northern Transvaal 'B' moved up to challenge the leaders.

### Second One-Day International
### SOUTH AFRICA *v.* WEST INDIAN XI

***6 January 1984***

***at Port Elizabeth***

**West Indian XI** 260 for 8 (E.A. Moseley 63 not out, S.T. Jefferies 4 for 79)
**South Africa** 262 for 6 (H.R. Fotheringham 78)

*South Africa won by 4 wickets*

West Indies recovered well from a dreadful start which saw half the side out for 77. Rowe and the ever-dependable Murray nearly doubled the score and Ezra Moseley hit a violent 63, sharing an eighth wicket partnership of 68 with Sylvester Clarke which helped their side to an impressive 260 off 50 overs.

South Africa started indifferently and after 14 overs they were 55 for the loss of Cook and Kirsten who was still on probation as captain. Fotheringham and Pollock then added 69 in 46 minutes and although both were out, Ken McEwan, Rice, Kuiper and le Roux steered South Africa to a comfortable win with 5.2 overs remaining and so levelled the series.

Fotheringham batted with great panache and hit two sixes and nine fours.

### Third One-Day International
### SOUTH AFRICA *v.* WEST INDIAN XI

***8 January 1984***

***at Durban***

**South Africa** 220 (K.S. McEwan 50, E.A. Moseley 4 for 53)
**West Indian XI** 194 for 4

*West Indian XI won on faster scoring rate*

Reverting to an all pace attack, the West Indians never allowed the South African batsmen to settle and only when McEwan and Rice added 74 for the fifth wicket did the batting look confident. Kirsten had looked sound after coming in at a difficult time and Kuiper also batted well to help the South African score to 220. Moseley followed his ferocious innings of the previous match with 4 for 53, but Clarke looked the most hostile and menacing of the West Indian bowlers.

Trotman and Greenidge gave the West Indians their best start of the tour, but Clive Rice dismissed them with consecutive deliveries. Kallicharran and Lynch added 53 in 68 minutes, but when Rowe came to the wicket at 111 for 3, the West Indians were behind the required run rate. Bad light had reduced the West Indian target after 23 minutes had been lost and Rowe quickly increased the tempo of the innings. Kallicharran left at 147 and from the last 8 overs of the innings, Rowe and Murray plundered 67 runs with some violent hitting and the West Indians had won with ease.

### Fourth One-Day International
### SOUTH AFRICA *v.* WEST INDIAN XI

***10 January 1984***

***at Cape Town***

**South Africa** 149 (E.A. Moseley 4 for 38)
**West Indian XI** 150 for 2 (E.N. Trotman 94 not out)

*West Indian XI won by 8 wickets*

The West Indians lost Rowe through illness on the day before the match and Kallicharran took over the captaincy. Any misgivings that the tourists may have had in Rowe's absence were quickly dispersed when Ezra Moseley tore into the South African batting and reduced them to 49 for 4, a plight from which they never totally recovered. Moseley, well supported by the other pace bowlers, bowled quickly and accurately and apart from some elegant shots by Pollock and some brave batting by Kuiper, the South Africans had no answer to the speed and attacking line of the West Indian bowlers.

Trotman and Greenidge gave the West Indians a brisk start and soon made it obvious that the visitors would win with ease. Trotman was belligerent from the opening over and he finished on 94 not out as the West Indians won with 10.1 overs to spare so taking a 3-1 lead in the six-match series.

### Third International
### SOUTH AFRICA *v.* WEST INDIAN XI

Deposed as captain, Peter Kirsten nevertheless did much to save his side from complete humiliation on the opening day at Johannesburg. Kallicharran, who had taken over leadership of the West Indian side from Rowe who had influenza, won the toss and asked South Africa to bat. Both openers went for 34 before Kirsten and Pollock came together and attacked the bowling. Pollock hit 41 from 31 deliveries, but their good work was undone when the last five South African wickets went for 9 runs. Alleyne destroyed the middle order and Moseley brought the innings to an abrupt close with 3 wickets in 4 balls.

The West Indians started badly, but a riotous 54 from Collis King rescued them. He hit 28 from the first 11 balls he received, and his fifty, with two sixes and seven fours, came off 34 deliveries. The visitors closed the day at 106 for 4, but King was out without addition the next morning and in spite of a patient knock from David Murray, 43 in just under two hours, and a spirited innings by Stephenson, they gained a lead of only 33. Kuiper finished off the tail quickly.

The South African second innings followed the same pattern as the first, and once more it was Kirsten and Pollock, with 83 in an hour, who rescued them. Pollock hit 46 off 33 balls, but the game tilted back in favour of West Indies at the end of the day when Hartley Alleyne took wickets with the last two balls so leaving himself on a hat-trick overnight.

Ken McEwan, who was off the field for most of the match through illness and had dropped down to number eight, was out second ball on the third morning to give Alleyne 3 wickets in 4 balls, but Rice and Kourie lifted South Africa to 236.

There then began a tense period when, chasing 204 for victory, West Indies slipped to 99 for 6 shortly after tea. King and Stephenson, uncharacteristically subdued, added 44 in 75 minutes before Kuiper had Stephenson caught behind. Moseley hit three fours but left at 172 and West Indies closed at 180 for 8.

Collis King, suffering from chicken pox, had stood firm, curbing his natural tendency to attack in an effort to coax victory, and on the last morning, he and Clarke pushed and

## THIRD INTERNATIONAL – SOUTH AFRICA *v.* WEST INDIAN XI

13, 14, 16 and 17 January 1984 at Johannesburg

**SOUTH AFRICA**

| | FIRST INNINGS | | SECOND INNINGS | |
|---|---|---|---|---|
| S.J. Cook | lbw, b Clarke | 7 | c Greenidge, b Alleyne | 17 |
| H.R. Fotheringham | b Moseley | 8 | lbw, b Moseley | 4 |
| P.N. Kirsten | c Murray, b Alleyne | 67 | c King, b Moseley | 61 |
| R.G. Pollock | c Murray, b Alleyne | 41 | b Stephenson | 46 |
| K.S. McEwan | c Murray, b Alleyne | 0 | (8) c Stephenson, b Alleyne | 0 |
| C.E.B. Rice† | c Trotman, b Stephenson | 4 | (5) c Murray, b Clarke | 47 |
| A.P. Kuiper | lbw, b Alleyne | 16 | (6) c Mattis, b Alleyne | 10 |
| A.J. Kourie | not out | 7 | (9) b Alleyne | 31 |
| R.V. Jennings* | c sub, b Moseley | 1 | (7) lbw, b Alleyne | 0 |
| W.K. Watson | lbw, b Moseley | 0 | not out | 6 |
| R.W. Hanley | c Murray, b Moseley | 0 | c Stephenson, b Clarke | 0 |
| Extras | lb 4, nb 5 | 9 | b 3, lb 5, w 4, nb 2 | 14 |
| | | 160 | | 236 |

| | O | M | R | W | O | M | R | W |
|---|---|---|---|---|---|---|---|---|
| Clarke | 13 | 6 | 17 | 1 | 24.3 | 5 | 74 | 2 |
| Moseley | 10.4 | 2 | 45 | 4 | 14 | 1 | 55 | 2 |
| Alleyne | 12 | 1 | 54 | 4 | 14 | 1 | 62 | 5 |
| Stephenson | 9 | 2 | 34 | 1 | 4 | — | 31 | 1 |
| King | 1 | — | 1 | — | | | | |

FALL OF WICKETS
1- 16, 2- 34, 3- 91, 4- 92, 5- 102, 6- 151, 7- 154, 8- 160, 9- 160
1- 6, 2- 44, 3- 127, 4- 149, 5- 169, 6- 169, 7- 169, 8- 216, 9- 236

**WEST INDIAN XI**

| | FIRST INNINGS | | SECOND INNINGS | |
|---|---|---|---|---|
| E.N. Trotman | c Fotheringham, b Hanley | 3 | c Pollock, b Watson | 4 |
| A.T. Greenidge | c Jennings, b Kuiper | 20 | c Kourie, b Kuiper | 43 |
| E.H. Mattis | lbw, b Watson | 0 | b Watson | 32 |
| M.A. Lynch | lbw, b Rice | 9 | c Jennings, b Rice | 7 |
| C.L. King | c Jennings, b Watson | 54 | (8) c sub, b Rice | 42 |
| D.A. Murray* | c Pollock, b Kuiper | 43 | c Pollock, b Rice | 3 |
| A.I. Kallicharran† | lbw, b Hanley | 18 | (5) c Pollock, b Watson | 7 |
| F.D. Stephenson | not out | 30 | (7) c Jennings, b Kuiper | 20 |
| E.A. Moseley | c Pollock, b Kuiper | 0 | c Hanley, b Watson | 14 |
| S.T. Clarke | lbw, b Kuiper | 9 | not out | 23 |
| H.L. Alleyne | c sub, b Kuiper | 0 | not out | 0 |
| Extras | lb 3, w 1, nb 3 | 7 | lb 3, w 2, nb 5 | 10 |
| | | 193 | (for 9 wkts) | 205 |

| | O | M | R | W | O | M | R | W |
|---|---|---|---|---|---|---|---|---|
| Watson | 16 | 5 | 42 | 2 | 16.2 | 3 | 63 | 4 |
| Hanley | 13 | 4 | 26 | 2 | 9 | 1 | 27 | — |
| Rice | 6 | 1 | 46 | 1 | 12 | — | 50 | 3 |
| Kuiper | 11.5 | — | 50 | 5 | 11 | — | 32 | 2 |
| Kourie | 6 | 1 | 22 | — | 5 | 1 | 23 | — |

FALL OF WICKETS
1- 6, 2- 11, 3- 23, 4- 69, 5- 106, 6- 142, 7- 154, 8- 154, 9- 189
1- 4, 2- 72, 3- 86, 4- 94, 5- 97, 6- 99, 7- 143, 8- 172, 9- 200

**West Indian XI won by 1 wicket**

nudged the score along until, 4 short of the target, King lashed at Rice and was caught at long-off by Jefferies, substituting for McEwan. It was a splendid catch. Next over Clarke turned Watson off his toes for 4 and the series was level 1–1 after an enthralling match.

## Castle Bowl

***19, 20 and 21 January 1984***

***at Kimberley***

**Eastern Province 'B'** 358 (J.W. Furstenburg 71, N. Mandy 62, A. Nel 53) and 33 for 0
**Griqualand West** 189 (B. deK Robey 5 for 48) and 199 (F.W. Swarbrook 54, A.L. Hobson 4 for 72)

*Eastern Province 'B' won by 10 wickets*
*Eastern Province 'B' 21 pts, Griqualand West 4 pts*

***21, 22 and 23 January 1984***

***at Constantia***

**West Province 'B'** 374 for 5 dec (T.N. Lazard 121, T.A. Clarke 81, L. Seeff 70) and 1 for 0
**Transvaal 'B'** (M.B Minnaar 5 for 59) and 213 (L. Selsick 60, J. During 4 for 43)

*Western Province 'B' won by 10 wickets*
*Western Province 'B' 22 pts, Transvaal 'B' 2 pts*

## Fifth One-Day International
## SOUTH AFRICA *v.* WEST INDIAN XI

***21 January 1984***

***at Johannesburg***

**South Africa** 279 for 3 (M. Yachad 123 not out, S.J. Cook 87)
**West Indian XI** 208 for 7 (L.G. Rowe 87, A.T. Greenidge 68)

*West Indian XI won on faster scoring rate*

A controversial win by the tourists gave them a 4–1 winning lead in the series and drew severe criticism of the umpires from Clive Rice, the South African skipper.

A crowd of 28,000 saw Cook and Yachad, who was replacing Fotheringham, put on a dashing 156 for the first wicket, and Yachad, in his international debut, carried his bat for a sparkling 123 in which he did not give a chance.

Faced with a daunting target of 280, the West Indians were 36 for 3, but rain halted play for an hour when the tourists were well behind the run rate. The umpires decreed, however, that play could resume, although obviously the fielding conditions were dreadful, and that the West Indian target would be reduced to 208 in 37 overs.

Led by Rowe and Greenidge, the West Indians scored at more than seven runs an over in the final session. Both batsmen and King fell in the space of 11 runs so that the visitors were 180 for 6 with less than 6 overs remaining.

Stephenson was run out on 196, but Moseley hit the winning runs with 2.3 overs to spare.

### Sixth One-Day International
### SOUTH AFRICA *v.* WEST INDIAN XI

***23 January 1984***

***at Pretoria***

**South Africa** 227 for 7 (C.E.B. Rice 54)
**West Indian XI** 54 (R.W. Hanley 6 for 22)

*South Africa won by 173 runs*

Put in to bat after losing the toss for the fifth time in the series, South Africa adopted the policy of attack and inspired by skipper Clive Rice who shared two half-century stands, they scored freely in the afternoon after an uncertain start.

Their 227 was commendable, but few could have foreseen that it would bring them so decisive a victory. Rupert 'Spook' Hanley worked up a fierce pace on a wicket which gave him some assistance. He dismissed Trotman with his third ball and added the wickets of Kallicharran, Lynch and Mattis before tea. After the break he accounted for Murray and Moseley, and with the dangerous King run out, West Indies were shot out for a miserable 54. Not surprisingly, Hanley took the Man of the Match award, but the individual award for the series went to Lance Rowe.

The overwhelming victory was some consolation for South Africa who had lost the series 4–2.

***25 January 1984***

***at Kimberley***

**West Indians** 316 for 9 (E.H. Mattis 84, M.A. Lynch 73, P. McLaren 4 for 39)
**Griqualand West** 193 (A.P. Beukes 66)

*West Indians won by 123 runs*

## Castle Bowl

***26, 27 and 28 January 1984***

***at Oude Libertas, Stellenbosch***

**Transvaal 'B'** 290 (B. Roberts 89, M.S. Venter 74, G.J. Parsons 4 for 54) and 129 (P. Anker 6 for 50)
**Boland** 265 for 7 dec (S.A. Jones 63 not out, S. Nackerdien 63) and 155 for 5

*Boland won by 5 wickets*
*Boland 14 pts, Transvaal 'B' 6 pts*

### Fourth International
### SOUTH AFRICA *v.* WEST INDIAN XI

A glorious innings by Ken McEwan, thought by many to be the best of the season, lightened the first day for South Africa. Going to the wicket at 16 for 3, he hit 120 out of 151 with twenty-one fours. Clarke had dismissed Kirsten and Pollock in four deliveries and with David Murray excelling behind the stumps, South Africa were 267 for 8 when bad light ended play.

*William Watson took his opportunity well as South Africa's opening bowler. (Adrian Murrell)*

*The destroyer of South Africa – Sylvester Clarke, West Indian fast bowler. (Adrian Murrell)*

## FOURTH INTERNATIONAL – SOUTH AFRICA *v.* WEST INDIAN XI

27, 28, 30 and 31 January 1984 at Port Elizabeth

### SOUTH AFRICA

| | FIRST INNINGS | | SECOND INNINGS | |
|---|---|---|---|---|
| S.J. Cook | c Murray, b Stephenson | 26 | c Murray, b Clarke | 2 |
| M. Yachad | c Murray, b Moseley | 6 | lbw, b Alleyne | 31 |
| P.N. Kirsten | c Murray, b Clarke | 0 | b Clarke | 4 |
| R.G. Pollock | c Mattis, b Clarke | 0 | c Murray, b Clarke | 42 |
| K.S. McEwan | c Kallicharran, b Moseley | 120 | c Murray, b Alleyne | 0 |
| C.E.B. Rice† | c Murray, b Clarke | 23 | c Clarke, b Stephenson | 12 |
| A.P. Kuiper | c Murray, b Stephenson | 5 | c Alleyne, b Clarke | 14 |
| A.J. Kourie | not out | 63 | c Murray, b Stephenson | 4 |
| D.J. Richardson* | lbw, b Alleyne | 13 | b Stephenson | 3 |
| W.K. Watson | c Murray, b Clarke | 8 | not out | 4 |
| R.W. Hanley | b Clarke | 0 | b Clarke | 0 |
| Extras | b 2, lb 8, w 3 | 13 | b 6, lb 3, w 2 | 11 |
| | | 277 | | 127 |

| | O | M | R | W | O | M | R | W |
|---|---|---|---|---|---|---|---|---|
| Clarke | 23 | 7 | 36 | 5 | 13.4 | 3 | 32 | 5 |
| Moseley | 20 | 2 | 93 | 2 | 8 | 1 | 22 | — |
| Stephenson | 18 | 2 | 61 | 2 | 15 | 2 | 47 | 3 |
| Alleyne | 16 | 2 | 55 | 1 | 10 | 3 | 15 | 2 |
| King | 5 | 1 | 19 | — | | | | |

FALL OF WICKETS

1- 11, 2- 16, 3- 16, 4- 54, 5- 100, 6- 117, 7- 206, 8- 264, 9- 277

1- 4, 2- 9, 3- 66, 4- 87, 5- 103, 6- 109, 7- 117, 8- 122, 9- 124

### WEST INDIAN XI

| | FIRST INNINGS | | SECOND INNINGS | |
|---|---|---|---|---|
| E.N. Trotman | c Pollock, b Hanley | 43 | c Kuiper, b Kirsten | 77 |
| S.F.A. Bacchus | c Kirsten, b Rice | 66 | c sub, b Watson | 76 |
| E.H. Mattis | c Kourie, b Kuiper | 15 | lbw, b Hanley | 1 |
| A.I. Kallicharran† | c Cook, b Watson | 16 | not out | 32 |
| C.L. King | c Kuiper, b Watson | 0 | (6) not out | 10 |
| L.G. Rowe | lbw, b Kuiper | 16 | | |
| D.A. Murray* | run out | 8 | | |
| F.D. Stephenson | not out | 19 | (5) c sub, b Kourie | 1 |
| E.A. Moseley | c Kourie, b Kuiper | 4 | | |
| S.T. Clarke | c Kuiper, b Watson | 0 | | |
| H.L. Alleyne | lbw, b Kourie | 4 | | |
| Extras | lb 6, w 1, nb 1 | 8 | b 4, lb 5 | 9 |
| | | 199 | (for 4 wkts) | 206 |

| | O | M | R | W | O | M | R | W |
|---|---|---|---|---|---|---|---|---|
| Watson | 24 | 10 | 46 | 3 | 9 | — | 46 | 1 |
| Hanley | 15 | 4 | 30 | 1 | 8 | — | 38 | 1 |
| Kourie | 11 | 1 | 23 | 1 | 19 | 5 | 65 | 1 |
| Kuiper | 18 | 3 | 57 | 3 | 4 | — | 25 | — |
| Rice | 13 | 2 | 35 | 1 | 3 | — | 9 | — |
| Kirsten | | | | | 6 | 1 | 14 | 1 |

FALL OF WICKETS

1- 83, 2- 113, 3- 136, 4- 136, 5- 160, 6- 170, 7- 176, 8- 180, 9- 185

1- 130, 2- 133, 3- 182, 4- 186

**West Indian XI won by 6 wickets**

## South Africa *v.* West Indian XI – International Match Averages

### SOUTH AFRICA BATTING

| | M | Inns | NOs | Runs | HS | Av | 100s | 50s |
|---|---|---|---|---|---|---|---|---|
| P.N. Kirsten | 4 | 6 | | 304 | 88 | 50.66 | | 4 |
| R.G. Pollock | 4 | 6 | | 293 | 102 | 48.83 | 1 | 1 |
| S.J. Cook | 4 | 8 | 2 | 236 | 69 | 39.33 | | 1 |
| A.J. Kourie | 4 | 6 | 2 | 138 | 63* | 34.50 | | 1 |
| C.E.B. Rice | 4 | 6 | 1 | 164 | 71* | 32.80 | | 1 |
| H.R. Fotheringham | 3 | 6 | 2 | 125 | 71* | 31.25 | | 1 |
| K.S. McEwan | 4 | 6 | | 163 | 120 | 27.16 | 1 | |
| A.P. Kuiper | 2 | 4 | | 45 | 16 | 11.25 | | |
| W.K. Watson | 2 | 4 | 2 | 18 | 8 | 9.00 | | |
| R.V. Jennings | 3 | 4 | | 27 | 18 | 6.75 | | |
| R.W. Hanley | 2 | 4 | | 0 | 0 | 0.00 | | |

Played in two matches: G.S. le Roux 11 and 11; S.T. Jefferies 0 and 1; D.L. Hobson 12* and 1

Played in one match: M. Yachad 6 and 31; D.J. Richardson 13 and 3

### SOUTH AFRICA BOWLING

| | Overs | Mds | Runs | Wkts | Av | Best | 5/inn |
|---|---|---|---|---|---|---|---|
| A.P. Kuiper | 44.5 | 3 | 164 | 10 | 16.40 | 5/50 | 1 |
| W.K. Watson | 65.2 | 18 | 197 | 10 | 19.70 | 4/63 | |
| G.S. le Roux | 61.3 | 13 | 172 | 6 | 28.66 | 3/88 | |
| R.W. Hanley | 45 | 9 | 121 | 4 | 30.25 | 2/26 | |
| C.E.B. Rice | 78 | 15 | 250 | 8 | 31.25 | 3/50 | |
| A.J. Kourie | 126 | 30 | 383 | 11 | 34.81 | 5/66 | 1 |
| P.N. Kirsten | 13 | 2 | 38 | 1 | 38.00 | 1/14 | |
| S.T. Jefferies | 67 | 14 | 257 | 6 | 42.83 | 3/63 | |
| D.L. Hobson | 54 | 8 | 180 | 2 | 90.00 | 1/36 | |

### SOUTH AFRICA CATCHES

10–R.G. Pollock; 7–R.V. Jennings; 6–A.J. Kourie; 4–subs; 3–A.P. Kuiper and H.R. Fotheringham; 2–S.J. Cook, P.N. Kirsten and D.L. Hobson; 1–S.T. Jefferies, G.S. le Roux, C.E.B. Rice and R.W. Hanley

### WEST INDIANS BATTING

| | M | Inns | NOs | Runs | HS | Av | 100s | 50s |
|---|---|---|---|---|---|---|---|---|
| S.F.A. Bacchus | 2 | 3 | 1 | 161 | 76 | 80.50 | | 2 |
| D.R. Parry | 2 | 3 | 1 | 151 | 63* | 75.50 | | 2 |
| L.G. Rowe | 3 | 4 | | 204 | 157 | 51.00 | 1 | |
| C.L. King | 4 | 7 | 1 | 215 | 83 | 35.83 | | 2 |
| A.I. Kallicharran | 4 | 7 | 1 | 201 | 103 | 33.50 | 1 | |
| D.A. Murray | 4 | 6 | | 165 | 43 | 27.50 | | |
| F.D. Stephenson | 4 | 7 | 2 | 137 | 53 | 27.40 | | 1 |
| E.N. Trotman | 4 | 7 | | 177 | 77 | 25.28 | | 1 |
| E.A. Moseley | 3 | 4 | 1 | 51 | 33* | 17.00 | | |
| M.A. Lynch | 3 | 5 | | 67 | 26 | 13.40 | | |
| E.H. Mattis | 3 | 6 | | 80 | 32 | 13.33 | | |
| S.T. Clarke | 4 | 5 | 2 | 35 | 23* | 11.66 | | |
| H.L. Alleyne | 2 | 3 | 1 | 4 | 4 | 2.00 | | |

Played in one match: B.D. Julien 33* and 18; A.T. Greenidge 20 and 43

### WEST INDIANS BOWLING

| | Overs | Mds | Runs | Wkts | Av | Best | 5/inn |
|---|---|---|---|---|---|---|---|
| H.L. Alleyne | 52 | 7 | 186 | 12 | 15.50 | 5/62 | 1 |
| S.T. Clarke | 153.1 | 51 | 388 | 23 | 16.86 | 5/32 | 4 |
| E.A. Moseley | 82.4 | 13 | 299 | 11 | 27.18 | 4/45 | |
| D.R. Parry | 69 | 15 | 177 | 5 | 35.40 | 3/79 | |
| F.D. Stephenson | 102 | 17 | 356 | 8 | 44.50 | 4/45 | |
| A.I. Kallicharran | 8.2 | 2 | 36 | 0 | — | 0/6 | |
| C.L. King | 22 | 5 | 78 | 0 | — | 0/1 | |

Bowled in one match: B.D. Julien 26–6–82–1

### WEST INDIANS CATCHES

20–D.A. Murray; 3–E.H. Mattis and F.D. Stephenson; 2–D.R. Parry, B.D. Julien, S.T. Clarke and subs; 1–E.N. Trotman, A.T. Greenidge, C.L. King, A.I. Kallicharran and H.L. Alleyne

South Africa added only 10 next morning but seized the initiative when they captured 6 wickets for 54 runs in the final session. Bacchus and Trotman had batted studiously, but what followed was wasteful. The West Indians added 19 on the third morning and then decided the match through the fast bowling of Clarke who was in devastating form and routed South Africa. Pollock was hit on the ear and had to have four stitches and the whole side looked shattered.

In 18 overs before the close of the third day, the tourists scored 103 for 0, Bacchus 65, Trotman 36. Bacchus began with 11 off Watson's first over and 15 off the next from Hanley, including a six out of the ground. He was more subdued on the last day and was out to a lazy shot. Kallicharran played sensibly and Stephenson was promoted to end the match, but he was caught on the long-on boundary and it was left to King. The difference between the two sides was Sylvester Clarke who had match figures of 10 for 68.

## Castle Bowl

***2, 3 and 4 February 1984***

***at Kimberley***

**Griqualand West** 176 (G.L. Ackermann 4 for 72) and 384 for 8 dec (K. Sharp 98, N.E. Wright 65, K. Dugmore 51, G.E. McMillan 5 for 69)
**Northern Transvaal 'B'** 273 (S. Vercueil 78) and 58 for 1

*Match drawn*
*Northern Transvaal 'B' 9 pts, Griqualand West 4 pts*

## Nissan Shield

***4 February 1984***

***at Johannesburg***

**Transvaal** 293 for 5 (K.A. McKenzie 109, M.S. Venter 100 not out)
**Eastern Province** 141 (S.T. Clarke 4 for 15)

*Transvaal won by 152 runs*

***at Durban***

**Western Province** 246 (G.A. Gooch 60)
**Natal** 219 (B.J. Whitfield 50)

*Western Province won by 27 runs*

## Castle Currie Cup – Semi-Finals

***10, 11, 12 and 13 February 1984***

***at Johannesburg***

**Transvaal** 252 (H.R. Fotheringham 99) and 488 (S.J. Cook 166, H.R. Fotheringham 115, R.G. Pollock 53, A.M. Ferreira 6 for 115)
**Northern Transvaal** 199 (N.T. Day 70, S.T. Clarke 6 for 62) and 307

*Transvaal won by 234 runs*

***at Port Elizabeth***

**Western Province** 293 (G.A. Gooch 67, P.H. Rayner 54, T.G. Shaw 5 for 127) and 353 for 6 dec (G.A. Gooch 171, A.P. Kuiper 64 not out)
**Eastern Province** 334 (G.S. Cowley 98, T.G. Shaw 66, S.T. Jefferies 4 for 86) and 245 (P. Willey 88, S.T. Jefferies 6 for 45)

*Western Province won by 67 runs*

As expected the two giants reached the final, but there was some brave resistance. The highlight of the game at Wanderers was an opening stand of 226 by Cook and Fotheringham in Transvaal's second innings. At St George's Park, Cowley and Shaw added 150 for Eastern Province's eighth wicket to give their side an unexpected lead, but Graham Gooch hit a masterly 171 and with Steve Jefferies again bowling well, Western snatched victory in spite of some stubborn middle order batting.

## Castle Bowl

***11, 13 and 14 February 1984***

***at East London***

**Boland** 156 (S.A. Jones 82, J.G. Thomas 4 for 36) and 351 (P. Anker 54, S.A. Jones 53, A. du Toit 51, J.G. Thomas 4 for 77)
**Border** 386 (J. Hosking 98 not out, R.C. Ontong 76, I. Foulkes 60) and 122 for 3 (R.C. Ontong 79 not out)

*Border won by 7 wickets*
*Border 20 pts, Boland 3 pts*

***16, 17 and 18 February 1984***

***at Durban***

**Natal 'B'** 322 for 7 dec (D.A. Scott 110 not out) and 142 for 2 (P.H. Williams 53 not out)
**Griqualand West** 296 (F.W. Swarbrook 63, M.D. Clare 4 for 66)

*Match drawn*
*Natal 'B' 9 pts, Griqualand West 8 pts*

***at Port Elizabeth***

**Boland** 278 (S.A. Jones 76, P. Anker 50 not out) and 194 (A. du Toit 52, A.L. Hobson 6 for 73)
**Eastern Province 'B'** 286 for 9 dec (I.L. Howell 55) and 187 for 5 (M.B. Billson 62 not out)

*Eastern Province 'B' won by 5 wickets*
*Eastern Province 'B' 20 pts, Boland 6 pts*

***17, 18 and 20 February 1984***

***at Pretoria***

**Orange Free State** 132 (G. Grobler 5 for 48) and 264 (C.M. Casalis 60, C.J. Richards 55, G. Grobler 4 for 74)
**Northern Transvaal 'B'** 243 (P.L. Symcox 57, C.P.L. de Lange 57. W.M. van der Merwe 4 for 42, A. Sidebottom 4 for 42) and 156 for 9 (W.M. van der Merwe 4 for 26, C.J.P.G. van Zyl 4 for 52)

*Northern Transvaal 'B' won by 1 wicket*
*Northern Transvaal 'B' 18 pts, Orange Free State 3 pts*

A remarkable last wicket stand of 51 between Simons and Geringer brought a fine and unexpected victory.

## Castle Currie Cup Final

***24, 25, 26 and 27 February 1984***

***at Newlands, Cape Town***

**Transvaal** 425 for 7 dec (R.G. Pollock 94, S.J. Cook 93, A.I. Kallicharran 73) and 179 (K.A. McKenzie 61 not out, S.T. Jefferies 7 for 105)
**Western Province** 327 (P.N. Kirsten 57, R.F. Pienaar 51, R.W. Hanley 4 for 85) and 136 (A.J. Kourie 6 for 57)

*Transvaal won by 141 runs*

Transvaal retained the Currie Cup in convincing fashion. Jimmy Cook and Alvin Kallicharran added 162 for the second wicket after Fotheringham had gone for 14. A fifth wicket stand of 110 between Pollock and McKenzie took the holders to a formidable total and they grasped the game firmly when Hanley had Gooch lbw for 11. Solid batting in the middle order gave Western Province some hope and Jefferies, with a career best bowling performance, gave his side a real chance on the third day, but Alan Kourie's slow left-arm decided the issue and when he dismissed both Gooch (15) and Kirsten (22) victory was assured.

**West Indian Team in South Africa 1983–4**
First Class Matches

| BATTING | v. Northern Transvaal (Pretoria) 19–22 Nov. 1983 | | v. Western Province (Capetown) 25–28 Nov. 1983 | | v. Natal (Durban) 2–4 December 1983 | | v. Eastern Province (Port Elizabeth) 12–14 Dec. 1983 | | v. Transvaal (Johannesburg) 17–19 Dec. 1983 | | v. South Africa (Durban) 23–27 Dec. 1983 | | v. South Africa (Cape Town) 30 December 1983–3 January 1984 | | v. South Africa (Johannesburg) 13–17 Jan. 1984 | | v. South Africa (Port Elizabeth) 27–31 Jan. 1984 | | M | Inns | NOs | Runs | H/S | Av |
|---|---|---|---|---|---|---|---|---|---|---|---|---|---|---|---|---|---|---|---|---|---|---|---|---|
| S.F.A. Bacchus | 0 | 9 | 61 | 40 | 88 | 7 | 3 | 29 | 24 | 10 | 19* | — | | | | | 66 | 76 | 7 | 13 | 1 | 432 | 88 | 36.00 |
| A.T. Greenidge | 9 | 11 | 19 | 14 | 36 | 1 | 11 | 22 | 2 | 20 | | | | | 20 | 43 | | | 6 | 12 | | 208 | 43 | 17.33 |
| E.H. Mattis | 35 | 7 | | | | | | | 51 | 8 | | | 6 | 26 | 0 | 32 | 15 | 1 | 5 | 10 | | 181 | 51 | 18.10 |
| A.I. Kallicharran | 4 | 92 | 0 | 11 | 55 | 79 | 4 | 19 | | | 103 | — | 8 | 17 | 18 | 7 | 16 | 32* | 8 | 15 | 1 | 465 | 103 | 33.21 |
| L.G. Rowe | 23 | 36 | 23 | 2 | 47 | 0 | | | 47 | 1 | 157 | — | 0 | 31 | | | 16 | — | 7 | 12 | | 383 | 157 | 31.91 |
| E.N. Trotman | 20 | 11* | | | | | 96 | 20 | 10 | 30 | 21 | — | 28 | 1 | 3 | 4 | 43 | 77 | 7 | 13 | 1 | 364 | 96 | 30.33 |
| D.A. Murray | 2 | 10* | 14 | 6 | 13* | — | 40* | 6 | 35 | 12 | 32 | — | 39 | 40 | 43 | 3 | 8 | — | 9 | 15 | 3 | 303 | 43 | 25.25 |
| E.A. Moseley | 35 | — | | | 8 | 18 | | | 30 | 22 | 33* | — | | | 0 | 14 | 4 | — | 6 | 9 | 1 | 164 | 35 | 20.50 |
| A.L. Padmore | 7 | — | 9* | 2* | | | — | — | | | | | | | | | | | 3 | 3 | 2 | 18 | 9* | 18.00 |
| H.L. Alleyne | 1 | — | 4 | 2 | | | — | — | | | | | | | 0 | 0* | 4 | — | 5 | 6 | 1 | 11 | 4 | 2.20 |
| C.E.H. Croft | 3* | — | | | 0 | 4* | | | 5* | 0* | | | | | | | | | 3 | 5 | 4 | 12 | 5* | 12.00 |
| M.A. Lynch | | | 105 | 39 | 40 | 20 | | | 0 | 37 | 26 | — | 2 | 23 | 9 | 7 | | | 6 | 11 | | 308 | 105 | 28.00 |
| C.L. King | | | 19 | 75 | 67 | 32 | 7 | 35* | | | 0 | — | 83 | 26 | 54 | 42 | 0 | 10* | 7 | 13 | 2 | 450 | 83 | 40.90 |
| F.D. Stephenson | | | 11 | 73 | | | 46 | 10 | | | 53 | — | 7 | 7 | 30* | 20 | 19* | 1 | 6 | 11 | 2 | 277 | 73 | 30.77 |
| S.T. Clarke | | | 8 | 18 | | | | | 12 | 1 | — | — | 0 | 3* | 9 | 23* | 0 | — | 6 | 9 | 2 | 74 | 23* | 10.57 |
| B.D. Julien | | | | | 22 | 1 | 27 | 18 | | | | | 33* | 18 | | | | | 3 | 6 | 1 | 119 | 33* | 23.80 |
| D.R. Parry | | | | | 11 | 5 | 5* | 3* | 6 | 26 | 63* | — | 30 | 58 | | | | | 5 | 9 | 3 | 207 | 63* | 34.50 |
| Byes | | | | 4 | 4 | | | 4 | 2 | | 5 | | 4 | 4 | | | | 4 | | | | | | |
| Leg-byes | 7 | 2 | 14 | 13 | 5 | 1 | 3 | 9 | 1 | 2 | 9 | | 7 | 7 | 3 | 3 | 6 | 5 | | | | | | |
| Wides | 2 | 3 | 1 | 1 | 1 | | | | 3 | 1 | 2 | | 1 | 6 | 1 | 2 | 1 | | | | | | | |
| No-balls | 5 | 2 | 3 | | | | | 4 | 2 | 2 | 6 | | 4 | 1 | 3 | 5 | 1 | | | | | | | |
| Total | 153 | 183 | 291 | 300 | 397 | 168 | 242 | 179 | 230 | 172 | 529 | | 252 | 268 | 193 | 205 | 199 | 206 | | | | | | |
| Wickets | 10 | 5 | 10 | 10 | 10 | 9 | 7 | 7 | 10 | 10 | 7 | | 10 | 10 | 10 | 9 | 10 | 4 | | | | | | |
| Result | D | | D | | D | | D | | L | | D | | L | | W | | W | | | | | | | |

*Catches* 39 – D.A. Murray
5 – A.I. Kallicharran
4 – E.N. Trotman, F.D. Stephenson and A.T. Greenidge
3 – S.F.A. Bacchus, E.H. Mattis, L.G. Rowe, S.T. Clarke, D.R. Parry and subs
2 – H.L. Alleyne and B.D. Julien
1 – E.A. Moseley, A.L. Padmore, C.E.H. Croft, M.A. Lynch and C.L. King

| BOWLING | E.A. Moseley | H.L. Alleyne | C.E.H. Croft | A.L. Padmore | S.T. Clarke | F.D. Stephenson | C.L. King | A.T. Greenidge | B.D. Julien |
|---|---|---|---|---|---|---|---|---|---|
| v. Northern Transvaal (Pretoria) | 18–3–66–1 | 21–6–64–1 | 13–4–41–4 | 25–5–103–3 | | | | | |
| 19–22 November 1983 | 13–4–32–1 | 12–1–37–1 | 13–2–20–2 | 11–1–37–0 | | | | | |
| v. Western Province (Cape Town) | | 20–7–76–2 | | 23–4–52–0 | 27–6–87–3 | 15–1–64–2 | 6–2–33–1 | | |
| 25–28 November 1983 | | 2–0–7–0 | | 3–1–4–0 | 7–1–15–0 | 7–1–24–1 | | 1–0–1–0 | |
| v. Natal (Durban) | 19–6–36–4 | | 14–1–55–2 | | | | | | 17–1–76–2 |
| 2–4 December 1983 | 9–3–23–2 | | 8–1–39–0 | | | | 10–1–35–0 | | 2–0–20–0 |
| v. Eastern Province (Port | | 15–3–51–0 | | 36–7–53–2 | | 28–6–73–1 | 7–1–30–3 | | 14–4–37–1 |
| Elizabeth) 12–14 Dec. 1983 | | 12–5–26–4 | | 10–2–28–0 | | 14–5–42–1 | 7–0–15–0 | | |
| v. Transvaal (Johannesburg) | 22–5–92–2 | | 18–2–95–1 | | 21–7–45–2 | | | | |
| 17–19 December 1983 | 11.1–0–49–3 | | | | 12–2–38–3 | | | | |
| v. South Africa (Durban) | 26–5–76–3 | | | | 32.1–11–105–5 | 21–5–61–0 | 2–1–2–0 | | |
| 23–27 December 1983 | 4–2–8–0 | | | | 3–0–9–0 | 6–1–16–0 | 6–2–13–0 | | |
| v. South Africa (Cape Town) | | | | | 37.5–13–92–5 | 27–5–95–1 | 5–1–21–0 | | 24–5–71–1 |
| 30 Dec. 1983–3 Jan. 1984 | | | | | 6–0–23–0 | 2–0–11–0 | 3–0–22–0 | | 2–0–11–0 |
| v. South Africa (Johannesburg) | 10.4–2–45–4 | 12–1–54–4 | | | 13–6–17–1 | 9–2–34–1 | 1–0–1–0 | | |
| 13–17 January 1984 | 14–1–55–2 | 14–1–62–5 | | | 24.3–5–74–2 | 4–0–31–1 | | | |
| v. South Africa (Port Elizabeth) | 20–2–93–2 | 16–2–55–1 | | | 23–7–36–5 | 18–2–61–2 | 5–1–19–0 | | |
| 27–31 January 1984 | 8–1–22–0 | 10–3–15–2 | | | 13.4–3–32–5 | 15–2–47–3 | | | |
| | 174.5–34–<br>597–24<br>*av.* 24.87 | 134–29–<br>447–20<br>*av.* 22.35 | 66–10–<br>250–9<br>*av.* 27.77 | 108–20–<br>277–5<br>*av.* 55.40 | 220.1–61–<br>573–31<br>*av.* 18.48 | 166–30–<br>559–13<br>*av.* 43.00 | 52–9–<br>191–4<br>*av.* 47.75 | 1–0–<br>1–0<br>— | 59–10–<br>215–4<br>*av.* 53.75 |

## Nissan Shield Final

*3 March 1984*

***at Johannesburg***

**Transvaal** 305 for 5 (A.I. Kallicharran 107, S.J. Cook 51)
**Western Province** 216 (R.F. Pienaar 84)

*Transvaal won by 89 runs*

Clive Rice's side completed the double and were indebted to two West Indians. Alvin Kallicharran hit a six and ten fours in his 177-minute innings and Western Province were reduced to 28 for 4, mainly by Sylvester Clarke who took 23 wickets at 6.30 apiece in the competition.

## Castle Bowl

*10, 11 and 12 March 1984*

***at Constantia***

**Western Province 'B'** 191 and 313 for 9 dec (T.A. Clarke 138 not out, R.C. Ontong 4 for 109)
**Border** 113 (R.R. Lawrenson 4 for 35, M.B. Minnaar 4 for 42) and 139 (N. Minnaar 55, A.G. Elgar 6 for 24)

*Western Province 'B' won by 252 runs*
*Western Province 'B' 16 pts, Border 5 pts*

*15, 16 and 17 March 1984*

***at Uitenhage***

**Border** 263 (B. deK Robey 4 for 74) and 252 for 9 dec (D. Cullinan 84, H. Austin 4 for 89)
**Eastern Province 'B'** 203 (R.C. Ontong 4 for 13) and 230 (I.L. Howell 56, D. Callaghan 50, R.C. Ontong 4 for 74)

*Border won by 82 runs*
*Border 19 pts, Eastern Province 'B' 7 pts*

***at Oude Libertas, Stellenbosch***

**Boland** 307 (A. du Toit 74, P. Anker 59, C.J.P.G. van Zyl 6 for 50) and 209 for 7 dec (L.J. Kets 87, S.A. Jones 68, W.M. van der Merwe 5 for 40)
**Orange Free State** 171 and 217 (R.J. East 88, C.M. Casalis 58, P. Anker 6 for 88)

*Boland won by 128 runs*
*Boland 20 pts, Orange Free State 4 pts*

In their final match Border fell 37 runs short of gaining the point that they needed to join Western Province 'B' at the top of the Castle Bowl table.

**Castle Bowl Log**

| | *P* | *W* | *L* | *D* | *Points* *Batting* | *Bowling* | *Pts* |
|---|---|---|---|---|---|---|---|
| Western Province 'B' | 6 | 4 | – | 2 | 23 | 23 | 86 |
| Border | 6 | 4 | 1 | 1 | 17 | 28 | 85 |
| Northern Transvaal 'B' | 6 | 3 | 1 | 2 | 17 | 27 | 74 |
| Eastern Province 'B' | 6 | 2 | 3 | 1 | 21 | 24 | 65 |
| Orange Free State | 6 | 2 | 2 | 2 | 8 | 27 | 55 |
| Boland | 6 | 2 | 2 | 2 | 12 | 20 | 52 |
| Natal 'B' | 6 | 1 | 2 | 3 | 10 | 27 | 47 |
| Transvaal 'B' | 6 | 1 | 4 | 1 | 13 | 24 | 47 |
| Griqualand West | 6 | – | 4 | 2 | 8 | 16 | 24 |

## Benson & Hedges Floodlit Cup Final

*30 March 1984*

***at Johannesburg***

**Eastern Province** 124 (I.K. Daniell 85)
**Natal** 125 for 3

*Natal won by 7 wickets*

| D.R. Parry | A.I. Kallicharran | E.H. Mattis | *Byes* | *Leg-byes* | *Wides* | *No-balls* | *Total* | *Wkts* |
|---|---|---|---|---|---|---|---|---|
| | | | 1 | 5 | 6 | 2 | 288 | 9 |
| | | | | 6 | 3 | 1 | 136 | 5 |
| | | | | 4 | 1 | 5 | 322 | 8 |
| | | | 1 | 2 | 1 | 2 | 57 | 1 |
| 19–5–57–2 | | | 1 | 5 | 3 | 6 | 239 | 10 |
| 12–4–33–0 | | | | 4 | 1 | 5 | 160 | 3 |
| 18–1–53–2 | | | 5 | 3 | 3 | 6 | 314 | 9 |
| 7–3–9–0 | 6.1–1–26–4 | | 5 | 6 | | 4 | 161 | 9 |
| 21–3–61–2 | | 0.4–0–0–1 | 4 | 9 | | 4 | 310 | 9 |
| | | | | 6 | 1 | | 94 | 6 |
| 25–7–62–2 | | | 4 | 9 | 1 | 13 | 333 | 10 |
| | 5–2–6–0 | | 2 | | | 5 | 59 | 0 |
| 36–8–79–3 | 3–0–22–0 | | | 17 | 6 | 1 | 404 | 10 |
| 8–0–36–0 | 0.2–0–8–0 | | | 5 | 1 | | 117 | 0 |
| | | | | 4 | | 5 | 160 | 10 |
| | | | 3 | 5 | 4 | 2 | 236 | 10 |
| | | | 2 | 8 | 3 | | 277 | 10 |
| | | | 6 | 3 | 2 | | 127 | 10 |
| 146–31–390–11 *av.* 35.45 | 14.3–3–62–4 *av.* 15.50 | 0.4–0–0–1 *av.* 0.00 | | | | | | |

### First Class Averages

| **BATTING** | **M** | **Inns** | **NOs** | **Runs** | **HS** | **Av** | **100s** | **50s** |
|---|---|---|---|---|---|---|---|---|
| T.N. Lazard | 3 | 6 | 1 | 290 | 121 | 58.00 | 2 | |
| T.A. Clarke | 6 | 11 | 3 | 459 | 138* | 57.37 | 1 | 2 |
| S.J. Cook | 11 | 21 | 3 | 1016 | 166 | 56.44 | 2 | 6 |
| S.A. Jones | 6 | 11 | 3 | 428 | 82 | 53.50 | | 5 |
| R.A. Smith | 4 | 7 | 1 | 309 | 109 | 51.50 | 1 | 2 |
| G.A. Gooch | 7 | 13 | 1 | 615 | 171 | 51.25 | 2 | 1 |
| D.G Emslie | 6 | 10 | 2 | 398 | 99 | 49.75 | | 4 |
| R.G. Pollock | 11 | 19 | 1 | 894 | 154 | 49.66 | 3 | 3 |
| D. Cullinan | 5 | 10 | 2 | 376 | 106* | 47.00 | 1 | 2 |
| R.C. Ontong | 7 | 14 | 1 | 610 | 145 | 46.92 | 1 | 3 |
| W. Larkins | 5 | 8 | | 369 | 116 | 46.12 | 2 | 1 |
| R.M. Bentley | 5 | 9 | 1 | 362 | 110* | 45.25 | 1 | 4 |
| P.N. Kirsten | 11 | 19 | 1 | 805 | 100 | 44.72 | 1 | 9 |
| J.P. Hosking | 3 | 5 | 1 | 177 | 98* | 44.25 | | 1 |
| T.R. Madsen | 4 | 7 | 3 | 171 | 63 | 42.75 | | 1 |
| I.L. Howell | 5 | 10 | 1 | 376 | 109 | 41.77 | 1 | 2 |
| C.M. Casalis | 3 | 4 | | 166 | 60 | 41.50 | | 2 |
| M.B. Logan | 4 | 7 | | 289 | 84 | 41.28 | | 3 |
| P. Hawtrey | 4 | 6 | 2 | 164 | 48 | 41.00 | | |
| R.F. Pienaar | 8 | 13 | 2 | 448 | 151* | 40.72 | 1 | 1 |
| P.J.A. Visagie | 6 | 11 | 3 | 321 | 56 | 40.12 | | 2 |
| A.P. Kuiper | 9 | 15 | 2 | 510 | 104 | 39.23 | 1 | 3 |
| R.A. le Roux | 6 | 10 | | 387 | 188 | 38.70 | 1 | 2 |
| A. du Toit | 6 | 11 | | 415 | 117 | 37.72 | 1 | 3 |

| | | | | | | | | |
|---|---|---|---|---|---|---|---|---|
| P.D. Swart | 6 | 11 | 2 | 337 | 81 | 37.44 | | 2 |
| K.S. McEwan | 7 | 11 | 1 | 371 | 120 | 37.10 | 1 | 2 |
| I. Foulkes | 7 | 14 | 4 | 370 | 74 | 37.00 | | 3 |
| A.J.S. Smith | 5 | 7 | 2 | 183 | 72 | 36.60 | | 1 |
| K.A. McKenzie | 7 | 12 | 1 | 400 | 84 | 36.36 | | 3 |
| G.E. McMillan | 7 | 12 | 6 | 218 | 49* | 36.33 | | |
| O. Henry | 5 | 8 | 3 | 180 | 79* | 36.00 | | 1 |
| J.D. du Toit | 4 | 6 | 1 | 180 | 128 | 36.00 | 1 | |
| P. Anker | 6 | 8 | 2 | 215 | 59 | 35.83 | | 3 |
| M.D. Moxon | 3 | 6 | | 213 | 60 | 35.50 | | 2 |
| P. Willey | 6 | 10 | | 354 | 111 | 35.40 | 1 | 1 |
| C.J. Richards | 4 | 7 | | 242 | 73 | 34.57 | | 3 |
| J.J. Strydom | 6 | 10 | 1 | 307 | 119* | 34.11 | 1 | 1 |
| A. Sidebottom | 5 | 7 | 2 | 170 | 59 | 34.00 | | 1 |
| S. Vercueil | 6 | 11 | 2 | 306 | 87 | 34.00 | | 2 |
| N.P. Daniels | 4 | 7 | 1 | 202 | 75 | 33.66 | | 1 |
| B.W. Proctor | 6 | 6 | 3 | 101 | 58* | 33.66 | | 1 |
| I.M. Wingreen | 6 | 11 | | 369 | 97 | 33.54 | | 2 |
| A. Geringer | 6 | 10 | 1 | 299 | 61 | 33.20 | | 2 |
| H.R. Fotheringham | 10 | 19 | 2 | 555 | 115 | 32.64 | 1 | 4 |
| R.J. East | 6 | 10 | | 321 | 108 | 32.10 | 1 | 1 |
| M.B. Billson | 4 | 6 | 1 | 160 | 62* | 32.00 | | 1 |
| N.T. Day | 6 | 12 | | 384 | 70 | 32.00 | | 3 |
| P.A. Robinson | 5 | 8 | 3 | 159 | 49 | 31.80 | | |
| R.G. Fensham | 4 | 8 | | 254 | 97 | 31.75 | | 2 |
| G.S. Cowley | 5 | 8 | 1 | 222 | 98 | 31.71 | | 2 |
| H.W.H. Bergins | 6 | 10 | 3 | 217 | 43* | 31.00 | | |
| D.K. Pearse | 6 | 9 | 2 | 217 | 48* | 31.00 | | |
| P.H. Williams | 6 | 11 | 1 | 310 | 58 | 31.00 | | 2 |
| A.I. Kallicharran | 10 | 19 | 1 | 555 | 103 | 30.83 | 1 | 4 |
| G.N. Lister-James | 5 | 8 | 1 | 215 | 61 | 30.71 | | 3 |
| C.E.B. Rice | 11 | 19 | 3 | 490 | 85* | 30.62 | | 2 |
| B. Roberts | 6 | 11 | | 336 | 89 | 30.54 | | 3 |
| M.D. Mellor | 4 | 8 | 1 | 213 | 87* | 30.42 | | 1 |
| K.C. Dugmore | 3 | 5 | | 150 | 51 | 30.00 | | 1 |
| A.J. Kourie | 11 | 18 | 4 | 415 | 63* | 29.64 | | 2 |
| J.W. Furstenburg | 4 | 8 | 1 | 205 | 71 | 29.28 | | 1 |
| P.L. Symcox | 6 | 11 | | 319 | 89 | 29.00 | | 2 |
| C.R. Norris | 6 | 11 | 2 | 257 | 51* | 28.55 | | 1 |
| M.J.R. Rindel | 3 | 6 | 1 | 141 | 81 | 28.20 | | 1 |
| I.K. Daniell | 6 | 10 | | 280 | 81 | 28.00 | | 3 |
| J.E. Emburey | 7 | 8 | 3 | 138 | 52* | 27.60 | | 1 |
| C.P.L. de Lange | 6 | 11 | | 303 | 63 | 27.54 | | 4 |
| N. Mandy | 3 | 6 | 1 | 137 | 62 | 27.40 | | 1 |
| T.G. Shaw | 5 | 9 | 1 | 219 | 66 | 27.37 | | 1 |
| M.S. Venter | 7 | 14 | | 382 | 75 | 27.28 | | 1 |
| L. Seeff | 8 | 15 | 1 | 381 | 128 | 27.21 | 1 | 1 |
| S.M. Hedley | 5 | 10 | | 271 | 86 | 27.10 | | 2 |
| G.S. le Roux | 5 | 5 | | 135 | 46 | 27.00 | | |
| D.J. Brickett | 6 | 8 | 1 | 188 | 61 | 26.85 | | 1 |
| V.F. du Preez | 7 | 14 | 3 | 295 | 117* | 26.81 | 1 | 1 |
| H.A. Page | 9 | 15 | 4 | 290 | 35 | 26.36 | | |
| P.H. Rayner | 8 | 14 | 1 | 342 | 54 | 26.30 | | 2 |
| W.F. Morris | 5 | 7 | 1 | 157 | 73* | 26.16 | | 1 |
| D.H. Howell | 6 | 10 | 1 | 235 | 74* | 26.11 | | 1 |
| M.J. Procter | 5 | 7 | 1 | 156 | 102 | 26.00 | 1 | |
| M. Yachad | 7 | 14 | | 350 | 108 | 25.00 | | |
| A.P. Beukes | 6 | 11 | | 274 | 91 | 24.90 | | 1 |
| N.E. Wright | 6 | 11 | | 274 | 91 | 24.90 | | 2 |
| N. Minnaar | 6 | 12 | | 298 | 82 | 24.83 | | 3 |
| B. McBride | 7 | 14 | 3 | 273 | 63 | 24.81 | | 1 |
| B.J. Whitfield | 5 | 9 | | 223 | 116 | 24.77 | 1 | |
| L.J. Barnard | 6 | 12 | | 297 | 68 | 24.75 | | 2 |
| F.W. Swarbrook | 4 | 6 | | 144 | 63 | 24.00 | | 2 |
| M.D. Tramontino | 7 | 14 | | 335 | 59 | 23.92 | | 1 |
| S.T. Jefferies | 6 | 10 | 2 | 186 | 55* | 23.25 | | 1 |
| A.P. Nel | 5 | 9 | | 209 | 82 | 23.22 | | 2 |
| K. Sharp | 6 | 11 | | 254 | 98 | 23.09 | | 1 |
| A.D. Methven | 3 | 5 | | 115 | 39 | 23.00 | | |
| P.L. Selsick | 3 | 6 | 1 | 114 | 60 | 22.80 | | 1 |
| G.J. Parsons | 6 | 10 | 1 | 205 | 56 | 22.77 | | 1 |
| W.E. Schonegevel | 3 | 5 | | 111 | 38 | 22.20 | | |
| G.D. Tullis | 5 | 6 | | 130 | 46 | 21.66 | | |
| D.J. Richardson | 7 | 14 | | 297 | 108 | 21.21 | 1 | |
| J.W. van Heerden | 6 | 10 | 1 | 190 | 42 | 21.11 | | |
| V.G. Cresswell | 5 | 9 | | 185 | 45 | 20.55 | | |
| R.V. Jennings | 9 | 14 | 4 | 205 | 46* | 20.50 | | |
| K.D. Verdoorn | 6 | 12 | 2 | 203 | 49 | 20.30 | | |
| N.M. Lambrechts | 6 | 11 | | 223 | 34 | 20.27 | | |
| M.R. Ballantyne | 7 | 10 | 2 | 161 | 41* | 20.12 | | |

(Qualification–100 runs, average 20.00)
(D.A. Scott (Natal 'B') 110 not out)

| BOWLING | Overs | Mds | Runs | Wkts | Av | Best | 10/m | 5/inn |
|---|---|---|---|---|---|---|---|---|
| K.G. Bauermeister | 49.5 | 10 | 131 | 11 | 11.90 | 3/10 | | |
| A. Grobler | 58.1 | 13 | 159 | 12 | 13.25 | 4/23 | | |
| C.J.P.G. van Zyl | 171.3 | 42 | 546 | 39 | 14.00 | 6/50 | | 2 |
| A. Sidebottom | 114.1 | 31 | 243 | 16 | 15.18 | 4/21 | | |
| C.R. Norris | 132 | 43 | 330 | 20 | 16.50 | 7/31 | | 1 |
| S.A. Jones | 111.3 | 30 | 255 | 14 | 18.21 | 4/28 | | |
| S.T. Clarke | 391 | 122 | 895 | 49 | 18.26 | 6/62 | 1 | 5 |
| G. Grobler | 129.1 | 26 | 420 | 23 | 18.26 | 5/48 | | 1 |
| J. During | 139.4 | 31 | 313 | 17 | 18.41 | 4/43 | | |
| E. Klopper | 104.3 | 16 | 297 | 16 | 18.56 | 5/42 | | 1 |
| R.C. Ontong | 279.5 | 78 | 717 | 38 | 18.86 | 5/44 | | 1 |
| W.M. van der Merwe | 146.3 | 38 | 404 | 21 | 19.23 | 5/40 | | 1 |
| G.J. Parsons | 144.1 | 31 | 409 | 21 | 19.47 | 4/54 | | |
| G.M. Gower | 130 | 38 | 278 | 14 | 19.85 | 3/43 | | |
| G.L. Ackermann | 189 | 44 | 676 | 34 | 19.88 | 5/50 | | 1 |
| R.W. Hanley | 280 | 86 | 708 | 35 | 20.22 | 7/31 | 1 | 2 |
| D. Norman | 147 | 29 | 472 | 23 | 20.52 | 4/41 | | |
| G. Hurlbatt | 76.1 | 12 | 251 | 12 | 20.91 | 4/36 | | |
| G.E. McMillan | 204 | 48 | 481 | 23 | 20.91 | 5/69 | | 1 |
| W.F. Morris | 89.2 | 26 | 210 | 10 | 21.00 | 3/6 | | |
| P. Anker | 227.2 | 70 | 610 | 29 | 21.03 | 6/50 | | 2 |
| A.L. Hobson | 96.1 | 15 | 294 | 13 | 22.61 | 6/73 | | 1 |
| A.P. Kuiper | 180.5 | 25 | 617 | 27 | 22.85 | 5/55 | | 2 |
| J.G. Thomas | 216.3 | 48 | 576 | 25 | 23.04 | 4/27 | | |
| M.B. Minnaar | 265 | 83 | 607 | 26 | 23.34 | 5/59 | | 1 |
| E.J. Hodkinson | 119 | 22 | 374 | 16 | 23.37 | 6/70 | | 1 |
| A.M. Ferreira | 219.5 | 54 | 635 | 27 | 23.51 | 6/26 | | 2 |
| C.D. Mitchley | 290 | 63 | 752 | 31 | 24.25 | 6/53 | | 2 |
| H.A. Page | 209.5 | 51 | 610 | 25 | 24.40 | 5/44 | | 1 |
| W.K. Watson | 235 | 57 | 693 | 27 | 25.66 | 5/44 | | 1 |
| S.J. Jefferies | 276.2 | 49 | 823 | 32 | 25.71 | 7/105 | | 2 |
| B. Roberts | 86.4 | 12 | 264 | 10 | 26.40 | 2/27 | | |
| D.L. Hobson | 270.2 | 50 | 1009 | 38 | 26.55 | 7/129 | 1 | 4 |
| B.W. Protctor | 99 | 25 | 293 | 11 | 26.63 | 5/50 | | 1 |
| B. deK Robey | 172.2 | 47 | 519 | 19 | 27.31 | 7/88 | | 1 |
| P. Willey | 225.2 | 50 | 576 | 20 | 28.80 | 4/145 | | |
| C.J. Coetzee | 77.4 | 12 | 284 | 10 | 28.40 | 3/58 | | |
| I. Foulkes | 196.5 | 40 | 628 | 22 | 28.54 | 4/56 | | |
| K.R. Cooper | 96.5 | 20 | 291 | 10 | 29.10 | 6/84 | | 1 |
| M.D. Clare | 174.4 | 30 | 497 | 17 | 29.23 | 5/65 | | 1 |
| T.G. Shaw | 211.2 | 50 | 614 | 21 | 29.23 | 5/127 | | 1 |
| G. Miller | 206.5 | 48 | 528 | 18 | 29.33 | 5/43 | | 2 |
| P. McLaren | 131.4 | 19 | 444 | 15 | 29.60 | 3/37 | | |
| H.W. Raath | 118.3 | 22 | 333 | 11 | 30.27 | 4/52 | | |
| P.A. Robinson | 131.1 | 23 | 487 | 16 | 30.43 | 6/46 | | 1 |
| A.J. Kourie | 431.1 | 117 | 1167 | 38 | 30.71 | 6/57 | | 2 |
| M.K. van Vuuren | 117 | 21 | 372 | 12 | 31.00 | 3/74 | | |
| N.V. Radford | 118 | 31 | 344 | 11 | 31.27 | 3/37 | | |
| J.A. Carse | 152.4 | 26 | 517 | 16 | 32.31 | 4/43 | | |
| G.S. le Roux | 130.3 | 22 | 438 | 13 | 33.69 | 4/53 | | |
| M.J. Procter | 173.1 | 49 | 474 | 12 | 33.85 | 5/63 | | 1 |
| C.E.B. Rice | 146 | 25 | 475 | 14 | 33.92 | 3/50 | | |
| A.P. Beukes | 203.1 | 55 | 515 | 15 | 34.33 | 4/86 | | |
| I.F.N. Weideman | 155.5 | 37 | 450 | 13 | 34.61 | 5/82 | | 1 |
| M.R. Ballantyne | 104 | 17 | 362 | 10 | 36.20 | 5/35 | | 1 |
| G.P. van Rensburg | 101 | 15 | 371 | 10 | 37.10 | 3/53 | | |
| J.E. Emburey | 274 | 70 | 670 | 17 | 39.41 | 4/63 | | |

(Qualification–10 wickets)

## LEADING FIELDERS

32–R.V. Jennings; 24–S. Vercueil (ct 23/st 1); 22–R.J. East; 21–B. McBride (ct 19/st 2) and R.J. Ryall (ct 20/st 1); 20–J.W. Stephenson; 19–G.D. Tullis (ct 17/st 2); 18–N.T. Day (ct 17/st 1), D.H. Howell (ct 16/st 2) and A.J. Kourie; 15–V.G. Cresswell (ct 11/st 4), L.H. Fick (ct 13/st 2) and I. Foulkes; 14–R.G. Pollock: 12–C.J. Richards, K.J. Rule (ct 11/st 1) and J.J. Strydom; 11–H.R. Fotheringham and N. Minnaar

SECTION F

# Towards Maturity

The season in Zimbabwe.
Zimbabwe *v.* Young West Indies and Young India.

Facts and Figures by John R. Ward.

*Peter Rawson – fast bowler and hard hitting batsman.*
*(Ken Kelly)*

Zimbabwean cricket followers really did not know what to expect from their team before their participation in the 1983 Prudential World Cup. As a new venture, and Zimbabwe's baptism into competitive international cricket, it created a great interest and excitement throughout the country, and a wide range of predictions. When it was over, the balance could be seen to be in favour of the optimists. The victory over Australia in the first match of the competition was the great triumph, particularly as Zimbabwe had not been able to beat Young Australia in Zimbabwe a few months before. Then came the memorable match against India at Tunbridge Wells when Kapil Dev's famous innings brought his side back from the depths of 17 for 5. There are many Zimbabwe followers who believe that had Rawson and Curran continued to bowl, Zimbabwe would have won and Kapil Dev's innings would never have been allowed. Such conjecture is an integral part of cricket talk.

Zimbabwe's fielding won high praise and the team returned proud and happy, already looking forward to the next World Cup, but the immediate problem was to deal with the Young West Indies touring team.

***5 October 1983***

***at Harare South***

**Young West Indies** 241 for 3 (T.R.O. Payne 95, O.W. Peters 65, P.V. Simmonds 57)
**Zimbabwe Country Districts** 222 for 9 (R.D. Brown 76, A. Waller 51)
*Young West Indies won by 19 runs*

The second Young West Indies side to visit Zimbabwe was not as strong as its predecessor. It consisted of some very promising young players, some in their mid-twenties, but none who had played Test cricket. Faoud Bacchus, originally selected as captain, elected to go to South Africa instead and Timur Mohammed took over as captain. The replacement for Bacchus was Shane Julien, a superb athlete, who turned out to be one of the most exciting players in the side.

In the opening match the home side put up a good fight and were 163 for 3, but the later batsmen fell to Estwick as they tried to force the pace.

**First International**
**ZIMBABWE *v.* YOUNG WEST INDIES**

Zimbabwe included Graeme Hick, the seventeen-year-old schoolboy who had been taken to England with the World Cup squad simply to gain experience. He became the youngest player to represent Zimbabwe.

Although losing Omarshah early on, Zimbabwe made a sound start and passed 250 with only 4 wickets down. The highlight of the home side's innings was a sparkling 82 in just over an hour from Dave Houghton. Traicos declared at the overnight score. He had succeeded Fletcher as captain. Fletcher had resigned as captain, but had made himself available for home international matches. In November, Fletcher was named Zimbabwe's sportsman of the year and was awarded the John Hopley Trophy.

Zimbabwe took a firm grip on the game on the second day when they bowled out Young West Indies for 140 in under three hours. Hogg and Rawson did the early damage as 5 wickets fell for 34. Hogg had been injured during the World

ABOVE: *Graeme Hick who made his international debut against Young West Indies. (Ken Kelly)* BELOW: *Robin Brown plays and misses. Grant Paterson is the non-striker.*

## FIRST INTERNATIONAL – ZIMBABWE *v.* YOUNG WEST INDIES
7, 8 and 10 October 1983 at Harare Sports Club

**ZIMBABWE**

| | FIRST INNINGS | | SECOND INNINGS | |
|---|---|---|---|---|
| G.A. Paterson | c Payne, b Ferris | 39 | | |
| A. Omarshah | c and b Ferris | 0 | (7) c Peters, b Butts | 10 |
| R.D. Brown | c Butts, b Ferris | 42 | (1) c Eddy, b Walsh | 29 |
| A.J. Pycroft | c Worrell, b Butts | 38 | not out | 49 |
| D.L. Houghton* | c Worrell, b Walsh | 82 | (2) c Worrell, b Ferris | 9 |
| K.M. Curran | c Mohammad, b Butts | 48 | (3) run out | 5 |
| D.A.G. Fletcher | c Worrell, b Butts | 4 | (5) b Butts | 6 |
| G.A. Hick | not out | 28 | (6) b Butts | 12 |
| P.W.E. Rawson | lbw, b Ferris | 23 | (8) c Worrell, b Walsh | 1 |
| A.J. Traicos† | | | (9) not out | 5 |
| V.R. Hogg | | | | |
| Extras | | 18 | | 17 |
| | (for 8 wkts dec) | 322 | (for 7 wkts) | 143 |

| | O | M | R | W | O | M | R | W |
|---|---|---|---|---|---|---|---|---|
| Ferris | 19.4 | 5 | 75 | 4 | 9 | 2 | 32 | 1 |
| Walsh | 22 | 6 | 64 | 1 | 16 | 7 | 36 | 2 |
| Butts | 35 | 8 | 107 | 3 | 14.5 | 2 | 58 | 3 |
| Kallicharran | 16 | 1 | 54 | — | | | | |
| Timur Mohammed | 2 | — | 4 | — | | | | |

FALL OF WICKETS
1- 8, 2- 72, 3- 97, 4- 179, 5- 251, 6- 260, 7- 275, 8- 322
1- 17, 2- 22, 3- 75, 4- 84, 5- 104, 6- 124, 7- 129

**YOUNG WEST INDIES**

| | FIRST INNINGS | | SECOND INNINGS | |
|---|---|---|---|---|
| A.A. Lyght | c Pycroft, b Rawson | 9 | c Houghton, b Fletcher | 77 |
| O.W. Peters | c Houghton, b Hogg | 4 | lbw, b Traicos | 40 |
| T.R.O. Payne | c Hick, b Hogg | 16 | c Fletcher, b Rawson | 28 |
| Timur Mohammed† | st Houghton, b Traicos | 45 | c Rawson, b Traicos | 7 |
| S.W. Julien | lbw, b Hogg | 0 | c Pycroft, b Rawson | 27 |
| V.A. Eddy | c Omarshah, b Traicos | 0 | c Pycroft, b Traicos | 56 |
| D.I. Kallicharran | c Rawson, b Traicos | 22 | c Houghton, b Rawson | 30 |
| M.C. Worrell* | c Hick, b Rawson | 27 | c and b Rawson | 3 |
| C. Butts | c Hick, b Rawson | 0 | c Brown, b Hogg | 37 |
| G.J.F. Ferris | not out | 6 | (11) not out | 0 |
| C.A. Walsh | c Curran, b Rawson | 8 | (10) b Rawson | 0 |
| Extras | | 3 | | 19 |
| | | 140 | | 324 |

| | O | M | R | W | O | M | R | W |
|---|---|---|---|---|---|---|---|---|
| Hogg | 8 | 6 | 6 | 3 | 14 | 2 | 60 | 1 |
| Rawson | 16 | 5 | 45 | 4 | 24 | 2 | 97 | 5 |
| Traicos | 13 | 2 | 35 | 3 | 29 | 7 | 72 | 3 |
| Curran | 3 | — | 28 | — | 5 | — | 33 | — |
| Hick | 2 | — | 23 | — | 6 | — | 13 | — |
| Fletcher | | | | | 10 | 1 | 28 | 1 |
| Omarshah | | | | | 3 | 2 | 2 | — |

FALL OF WICKETS
1- 9, 2- 25, 3- 30, 4- 30, 5- 34, 6- 74, 7- 126, 8- 126, 9- 128
1- 110, 2- 143, 3- 159, 4- 159, 5- 194, 6- 245, 7- 253, 8- 305, 9- 305

**Zimbabwe won by 3 wickets**

Cup and out of form in league matches so that his selection had been opposed, but he bowled well in tandem with Rawson although he was less effective when the tourists were asked to follow-on.

Andrew Lyght made nonsense of the first innings collapse with 77 in just over an hour before being first out at 110. There was more consistency in the batting and eventually Zimbabwe were left to score 143 to win.

*Ali Omarshah drives George Ferris through the covers.*

Incredibly, the first one-day international was played on the Sunday in the middle of this match, rather in the way that a John Player League game punctuates a county championship match in England, and both Paterson and Omarshah had been injured and were unable to open Zimbabwe's second innings. The home side were forced to struggle very hard for what had looked to be an easy victory and it was only a dogged fighting innings by Andy Pycroft that saw them home.

*Duncan Fletcher bowling against the Young West Indies at Harare Sports Club. Timur Mohammed is the non-striker.*

### First One-Day International
### ZIMBABWE *v.* YOUNG WEST INDIES

This match, as has been stated, was sandwiched in the middle of the first-class game. The visitors were soon in trouble against some accurate bowling. They displayed their inexperience at this form of cricket and lost wickets to injudicious shots. Timur Mohammed, Derek Kallicharran and Roddy Estwick effected a recovery with some determined batting, but, after a solid start, Zimbabwe never seemed in danger of losing.

Grant Paterson batted impressively in spite of being injured and Andy Pycroft and Duncan Fletcher finally settled matters with a partnership of 85 after Houghton and Curran had failed to score.

***12 October 1983***

***at Hwange***

**Young West Indies** 202 (A.A. Lyght 91, J.P. Brent 4 for 41)
**Young Zimbabwe** 206 for 6 (C.M. Robertson 72)

*Young Zimbabwe won by 4 wickets*

This was an encouraging win for Zimbabwe cricket. Andrew Lyght batted brilliantly, but he had little support. Medium-fast bowler Jonathan Brent was the man who most troubled the tourists. Robertson, on the verge of the national side, batted splendidly and Butchart, too, batted well as the home side won the 50-over match with 4 balls to spare.

### Second One-Day International
### ZIMBABWE *v.* YOUNG WEST INDIES

Once more it was Andy Pycroft who was the backbone of the Zimbabwe innings, scoring briskly and playing some delightful shots after his team had begun badly.

The disasters of the beginning of the Zimbabwe innings were as nothing compared to the visitors who lost Lyght and Payne to successive balls in Rawson's opening over. There was some brave batting by the middle order, but the West Indians were always struggling in deteriorating light. Eventually, the umpires ended the match with six overs still remaining and the West Indians needing 39 off 36 balls which, with Fletcher having dismissed Eddy and Kallicharran, they were unlikely to achieve.

Zimbabwe won the match on a far superior scoring rate.

### Third One-Day International
### ZIMBABWE *v.* YOUNG WEST INDIES

This was the most one-sided match of the tour. The visitors were savaged by a fourth wicket stand of 126 between Pycroft and Houghton and they never recovered. Rawson dismissed the first three West Indian batsmen with only 24 scored and although Timur Mohammed played a gallant captain's innings, there was never any hope of Young West Indies winning the match.

This victory gave Zimbabwe a 3–0 lead in the 4-match series.

***18 and 19 October 1983***

***at Mutare***

**Young Zimbabwe** 200 (G.C. Wallace 74, C.A. Walsh 5 for 52) and 172 (C. Butts 5 for 46)
**Young West Indies** 215 (S.W. Julien 67) and 163 for 5 (S.W. Julien 72)

*Young West Indies won by 5 wickets*

Young Zimbabwe were 55 for 6 before Gary Wallace and Derek Hawtrey put on 82. The tourists struggled in their turn

**FIRST ONE-DAY INTERNATIONAL – ZIMBABWE *v.* YOUNG WEST INDIES**
9 October 1983 at Harare Sports Club

**YOUNG WEST INDIES**

|  |  |  |
|---|---|---|
| O.W. Peters | c Fletcher, b Curran | 12 |
| A.A. Lyght | c Houghton, b Curran | 6 |
| T.R.O. Payne* | c Paterson, b Butchart | 28 |
| Timur Mohammed† | c Brown, b Butchart | 48 |
| S.W. Julien | b Butchart | 14 |
| V.A. Eddy | b Butchart | 7 |
| D.I. Kallicharran | c Peckover, b Curran | 60 |
| R.O. Estwick | run out | 30 |
| C. Butts | c Fletcher, b Rawson | 19 |
| C.A. Walsh | not out | 1 |
| G.J.F. Ferri | not out | 1 |
| Extras | | 13 |
| (50 overs) | (for 9 wickets) | 239 |

| | O | M | R | W |
|---|---|---|---|---|
| Rawson | 10 | 3 | 37 | 1 |
| Curran | 10 | 1 | 49 | 3 |
| Fletcher | 10 | 1 | 37 | — |
| Butchart | 10 | — | 58 | 4 |
| Traicos | 10 | — | 45 | — |

FALL OF WICKETS
1- 14, 2- 25, 3- 74, 4- 104, 5- 123, 6- 123, 7- 178, 8- 219, 9- 237

**ZIMBABWE**

|  |  |  |
|---|---|---|
| A.H. Omarshah | run out | 14 |
| G.A. Paterson | c Julien, b Butts | 66 |
| R.D. Brown | c Ferris, b Butts | 23 |
| A.J. Pycroft | not out | 68 |
| D.L. Houghton* | lbw, b Ferris | 0 |
| K.M. Curran | run out | 0 |
| D.A.G. Fletcher | run out | 41 |
| G.E. Peckover | c Payne, b Ferris | 3 |
| I.P. Butchart | not out | 3 |
| P.W.E. Rawson | | |
| A.J. Traicos† | | |
| Extras | | 23 |
| (49.2 overs) | (for 7 wickets) | 241 |

| | O | M | R | W |
|---|---|---|---|---|
| Ferris | 9.2 | 2 | 28 | 2 |
| Estwick | 9 | 1 | 41 | — |
| Walsh | 10 | 1 | 48 | — |
| Eddy | 5 | — | 22 | — |
| Julien | 6 | — | 27 | — |
| Butts | 10 | — | 52 | 2 |

FALL OF WICKETS
1- 27, 2- 114, 3- 124, 4- 128, 5- 129, 6- 214, 7- 229

**Zimbabwe won by 3 wickets**

## SECOND ONE-DAY INTERNATIONAL – ZIMBABWE *v.* YOUNG WEST INDIES
15 October 1983 at Queens Ground, Bulawayo

**ZIMBABWE**

|  |  |  |
|---|---|---|
| A.H. Omarshah | c and b Walsh | 7 |
| G.E. Peckover | c Mohammed, b Ferris | 3 |
| R.D. Brown | c Julien, b Butts | 32 |
| A.J. Pycroft | b Ferris | 66 |
| D.L. Houghton* | b Walsh | 32 |
| D.A.G. Fletcher | run out | 4 |
| K.M. Curran | b Walsh | 2 |
| I.P. Butchart | not out | 21 |
| G.A. Hick | not out | 16 |
| P.W.E. Rawson | | |
| A.J. Traicos† | | |
| Extras | | 42 |
| (50 overs) | (for 7 wickets) | 225 |

| | O | M | R | W |
|---|---|---|---|---|
| Estwick | 10 | 5 | 13 | — |
| Ferris | 10 | 3 | 49 | 2 |
| Walsh | 10 | 2 | 45 | 3 |
| Butts | 10 | — | 37 | 1 |
| Simmonds | 10 | 1 | 39 | — |

FALL OF WICKETS
1- 15, 2- 16, 3- 89, 4- 171, 5- 177, 6- 180, 7- 184

**YOUNG WEST INDIES**

|  |  |  |
|---|---|---|
| A.A. Lyght | b Rawson | 0 |
| P.V. Simmonds | c Houghton, b Butchart | 34 |
| T.R.O. Payne* | c Houghton, b Rawson | 0 |
| Timur Mohammed† | c Houghton, b Rawson | 15 |
| V.A. Eddy | c Houghton, b Fletcher | 46 |
| S.W. Julien | c Pycroft, b Traicos | 42 |
| D.I. Kallicharran | b Fletcher | 25 |
| R.O. Estwick | not out | 3 |
| C. Butts | not out | 2 |
| C.A. Walsh | | |
| G.J.F. Ferris | | |
| Extras | | 20 |
| (44 overs) | (for 7 wickets) | 187 |

| | O | M | R | W |
|---|---|---|---|---|
| Rawson | 10 | 3 | 29 | 3 |
| Curran | 7 | — | 40 | — |
| Butchart | 10 | 1 | 40 | 1 |
| Traicos | 10 | 1 | 31 | 1 |
| Fletcher | 7 | 1 | 27 | 2 |

FALL OF WICKETS
1- 0, 2- 0, 3- 35, 4- 62, 5- 129, 6- 171, 7- 177

**Zimbabwe won on faster scoring rate**

with Peters, Payne, Simmonds, Worrell and Kallicharran all failing to reach double figures, but Shane Julien and Timur Mohammed batted well and there were useful contributions from Butts, Estwick and Walsh at the end which secured a first innings lead.

The off-spin of Butts caused the home side problems in the second innings and the last 8 wickets fell for 90 runs. Aggressive batting from Lyght and Julien put Young West Indies on the way to victory.

### Second International
### ZIMBABWE *v.* YOUNG WEST INDIES

A splendid game of cricket, ending in near darkness, brought the Young West Indies tour to a close. Rawson removed four of the first five West Indian batsmen cheaply, but Lyght stood firm and at last found a worthy partner in Kallicharran. Lyght reached a cultured century before being run out at the bowler's end by wicket-keeper Dave Houghton

## THIRD ONE-DAY INTERNATIONAL – ZIMBABWE *v.* YOUNG WEST INDIES
16 October 1983 at Queens Ground, Bulawayo

**ZIMBABWE**

|  |  |  |
|---|---|---|
| R.D. Brown | b Estwick | 2 |
| A.M. Omarshah | c Julien, b Walsh | 23 |
| D.A.G. Fletcher | c Payne, b Walsh | 24 |
| D.L. Houghton* | c Simmonds, b Walsh | 66 |
| A.J. Pycroft | c Eddy, b Butts | 83 |
| I.P. Butchart | b Ferris | 1 |
| G.A. Hick | c Simmonds, b Ferris | 20 |
| G.E. Peckover | not out | 10 |
| P.W.E. Rawson | not out | 15 |
| A.J. Traicos† | | |
| V.R. Hogg | | |
| Extras | | 30 |
| (50 overs) | (for 7 wickets) | 274 |

| | O | M | R | W |
|---|---|---|---|---|
| Estwick | 10 | — | 41 | 1 |
| Ferris | 10 | 1 | 39 | 2 |
| Walsh | 9 | — | 44 | 3 |
| Simmonds | 6 | — | 37 | — |
| Butts | 10 | 1 | 38 | 1 |
| Eddy | 2 | — | 20 | — |
| Lyght | 1 | — | 13 | — |
| Kallicharran | 2 | — | 12 | — |

FALL OF WICKETS
1- 3, 2- 45, 3- 70, 4- 196, 5- 198, 6- 237, 7- 240

**YOUNG WEST INDIES**

|  |  |  |
|---|---|---|
| A.A. Lyght | b Rawson | 4 |
| P.V. Simmonds | c Pycroft, b Rawson | 2 |
| S.W. Julien | c Fletcher, b Rawson | 11 |
| Timur Mohammed† | c Peckover, b Butchart | 74 |
| T.R.O. Payne* | c Houghton, b Hogg | 7 |
| V.A. Eddy | b Butchart | 15 |
| D.I. Kallicharran | run out | 0 |
| R.O. Estwick | lbw, b Traicos | 3 |
| C. Butts | b Butchart | 0 |
| C.A. Walsh | not out | 15 |
| G.J.F. Ferris | b Butchart | 0 |
| Extras | | 12 |
| (40 overs) | | 143 |

| | O | M | R | W |
|---|---|---|---|---|
| Rawson | 6 | 2 | 13 | 3 |
| Hogg | 10 | 3 | 19 | 1 |
| Fletcher | 6 | — | 16 | — |
| Butchart | 10 | 2 | 45 | 4 |
| Traicos | 8 | 1 | 38 | 1 |

FALL OF WICKETS
1- 6, 2- 7, 3- 24, 4- 46, 5- 109, 6- 109, 7- 126, 8- 126, 9- 138

**Zimbabwe won by 131 runs**

who thought and reacted very quickly. Lyght had played a couple of delightful innings on the tour but he was very inconsistent. Indeed, Kallicharran was perhaps the only West Indian batsman to show consistency and responded well to a crisis. He helped Lyght in a stand of 122 and both he and Butts passed fifty.

Ferris troubled the early Zimbabwe batsmen all of whom got out just as they had seemed to have negotiated initial problems. Once again it was Andy Pycroft who gave the Zimbabwe innings substance and he received good support from Houghton and Curran.

Traicos declared 25 runs behind so that his bowlers could attack the opposition before the close of the second day. His initiative was rewarded when Lyght snicked to slip in the first over. Simmonds drove uppishly to mid-on at the end of the day and Curran dived to take a fine catch, but unfortunately touched the ground with the ball as he fell. Simmonds was rightly given not out, a decision which some of the Zimbabwean players wrongly questioned.

At the beginning of the last day a draw looked certain, but, in a sensational first over, Curran had Simmonds lbw with his second ball and Timur Mohammed brilliantly caught by Robertson at cover off the next. The left-hander had tried to pull over mid-wicket, but he had got a top edge and the ball swirled high over cover. Robertson lost sight of it, but picked it up at the last moment and spun round to take the catch.

Julien played some elegant shots before being bowled by Rawson and Kallicharran played another tigerish, fighting innings. Rawson's three wickets brought him to 50 in only 8 first-class matches, a remarkable achievement. He has taken five wickets or more in an innings on 6 occasions.

Zimbabwe needed 212 for victory in approximately 4 hours. Ferris and Walsh bowled well and the West Indian fielding was excellent. Once more Pycroft and Houghton made amends for the lapses of the early batsmen. Pycroft stayed almost to the end, caught on the fine-leg boundary in attempting the winning hit. In extremely poor light, with West Indies bowling at a very slow rate, Butchart came and went. Fletcher was steady and with three balls remaining and the scores level, Graeme Hick came out into the gloom and square-cut Estwick magnificently for 4, so giving Zimbabwe victory in the series.

## Fourth One-Day International
## ZIMBABWE *v.* YOUNG WEST INDIES

Once again a limited-over international was played in the middle of the three-day game, but, although Zimbabwe had already won the series, this match produced some of the finest batting seen in the country for a long time.

The tourists lost their openers quickly, Lyght falling to a marvellous running catch by debutant Jonathan Brent. He raced from third man to square leg, covering more than 30 yards. After this there was little joy for the Zimbabwean bowlers. Timur Mohammed and Shane Julien tore the bowling to shreds in a third wicket stand of 213 runs in $2\frac{1}{2}$ hours, both reaching attractive and accomplished centuries.

Zimbabwe's target of 299 looked next to impossible, but Gerald Peckover, the former hockey international, thought otherwise. He batted with stylish aggression and ran some outrageous singles in an effort to maintain the required scoring rate. He reached his first century for Zimbabwe in

**SECOND INTERNATIONAL – ZIMBABWE *v.* YOUNG WEST INDIES**
21, 22 and 24 October 1983 at Harare Sports Club

**YOUNG WEST INDIES**

| | FIRST INNINGS | | SECOND INNINGS | |
|---|---|---|---|---|
| A.A. Lyght | run out | 114 | c Pycroft, b Rawson | 0 |
| P.V. Simmonds | b Rawson | 1 | lbw, b Curran | 9 |
| S.W. Julien | c Houghton, b Rawson | 4 | b Rawson | 43 |
| Timur Mohammed† | b Rawson | 1 | c Robertson, b Curran | 0 |
| V.A. Eddy | c Brown, b Rawson | 8 | c Robertson, b Curran | 5 |
| D.I. Kallicharran | c Hick, b Butchart | 64 | b Traicos | 72 |
| M.C. Worrell* | b Butchart | 5 | lbw, b Traicos | 13 |
| C. Butts | c Rawson, b Curran | 51 | c Hick, b Butchart | 21 |
| R.O. Estwick | c Butchart, b Rawson | 27 | c Traicos, b Butchart | 4 |
| C.A. Walsh | lbw, b Rawson | 6 | c Pycroft, b Rawson | 12 |
| G.J.F. Ferris | not out | 0 | not out | 0 |
| Extras | | 8 | | 7 |
| | | 289 | | 186 |

| | O | M | R | W | O | M | R | W |
|---|---|---|---|---|---|---|---|---|
| Rawson | 19.5 | 3 | 77 | 6 | 11 | 2 | 73 | 3 |
| Curran | 10 | 3 | 20 | 1 | 8 | 1 | 46 | 3 |
| Traicos | 28 | 6 | 75 | — | 13.5 | 4 | 38 | 2 |
| Hick | 18 | 3 | 57 | — | | | | |
| Fletcher | 5 | 1 | 19 | — | | | | |
| Butchart | 10 | 4 | 33 | 2 | 6 | — | 22 | 2 |

FALL OF WICKETS
1- 15, 2- 19, 3- 13, 4- 64, 5- 186, 6- 196, 7- 208, 8- 259, 9- 289
1- 0, 2- 34, 3- 34, 4- 57, 5- 57, 6- 124, 7- 157, 8- 161, 9- 179

**ZIMBABWE**

| | FIRST INNINGS | | SECOND INNINGS | |
|---|---|---|---|---|
| A.H. Omarshah | c Lyght, b Ferris | 19 | c Julien, b Ferris | 8 |
| C.M. Robertson | st Worrell, b Kallicharran | 22 | c Lyght, b Ferris | 1 |
| R.D. Brown | c Worrell, b Walsh | 11 | c Worrell, b Walsh | 16 |
| A.J. Pycroft | c Worrell, b Walsh | 90 | c Simmonds, b Walsh | 75 |
| D.L. Houghton* | c Julien, b Ferris | 35 | b Ferris | 48 |
| K.M. Curran | c Worrell, b Walsh | 33 | c Estwick, b Walsh | 21 |
| D.A.G. Fletcher | b Walsh | 17 | not out | 16 |
| G.A. Hick | c Worrell, b Walsh | 12 | (9) not out | 4 |
| I.P. Butchart | not out | 5 | (8) c Worrell, b Estwick | 2 |
| P.W.E. Rawson | not out | 4 | | |
| A.J. Traicos† | | | | |
| Extras | | 16 | | 24 |
| | (for 8 wkts dec) | 264 | (for 7 wkts) | 215 |

| | O | M | R | W | O | M | R | W |
|---|---|---|---|---|---|---|---|---|
| Ferris | 15 | 5 | 44 | 2 | 17 | 3 | 46 | 3 |
| Estwick | 9 | 3 | 19 | — | 10.4 | 2 | 24 | 1 |
| Walsh | 19 | 6 | 40 | 5 | 23 | 3 | 82 | 3 |
| Kallicharran | 20 | 2 | 96 | 1 | 5 | — | 26 | — |
| Butts | 15 | 3 | 48 | — | 2 | — | 13 | — |
| Simmonds | 1 | — | 1 | — | | | | |

FALL OF WICKETS
1- 27, 2- 54, 3- 60, 4- 160, 5- 225, 6- 230, 7- 255, 8- 256
1- 14, 2- 26, 3- 51, 4- 123, 5- 181, 6- 209, 7- 211

**Zimbabwe won by 3 wickets**

## FOURTH ONE-DAY INTERNATIONAL – ZIMBABWE *v.* YOUNG WEST INDIES

23 October 1983 at Harare Sports Club

**YOUNG WEST INDIES**

|  |  |  |
|---|---|---|
| A.A. Lyght | c Brent, b Curran | 8 |
| P.V. Simmonds | c Pycroft, b Rawson | 9 |
| Timur Mohammed† | c Pycroft, b Butchart | 102 |
| S.W. Julien | c Robertson, b Butchart | 142 |
| R.O. Estwick | b Butchart | 1 |
| T.R.O. Payne* | not out | 23 |
| D.I. Kallicharran | not out | 1 |
| V.A. Eddy | | |
| C. Butts | | |
| C.A. Walsh | | |
| G.J.F. Ferris | | |
| Extras | | 12 |
| (50 overs) | (for 5 wickets) | 298 |

| | O | M | R | W |
|---|---|---|---|---|
| Rawson | 9 | 1 | 66 | 1 |
| Curran | 9 | 1 | 60 | 1 |
| Brent | 6 | 1 | 30 | — |
| Traicos | 10 | — | 50 | — |
| Fletcher | 7 | — | 40 | — |
| Butchart | 9 | 1 | 40 | 3 |

FALL OF WICKETS
1- 17, 2- 18, 3- 231, 4- 271, 5- 294

**ZIMBABWE**

|  |  |  |
|---|---|---|
| C.M. Robertson | c Payne, b Estwick | 0 |
| G.E. Peckover | c Payne, b Ferris | 102 |
| R.D. Brown | c Butts, b Walsh | 25 |
| D.A.G. Fletcher | st Payne, b Butts | 25 |
| A.J. Pycroft | b Simmonds | 0 |
| D.L. Houghton* | c Estwick, b Butts | 35 |
| K.M. Curran | c Mohammed, b Estwick | 28 |
| I.P. Butchart | b Ferris | 9 |
| P.W.E. Rawson | c Payne, b Ferris | 0 |
| J.P. Brent | not out | 6 |
| A.J. Traicos† | not out | 1 |
| Extras | | 51 |
| (50 overs) | (for 9 wickets) | 282 |

| | O | M | R | W |
|---|---|---|---|---|
| Estwick | 10 | 1 | 46 | 2 |
| Ferris | 10 | 2 | 28 | 3 |
| Walsh | 10 | — | 47 | 1 |
| Eddy | 5 | — | 30 | — |
| Butts | 10 | 1 | 48 | 2 |
| Simmonds | 5 | — | 32 | 1 |

FALL OF WICKETS
1- 9, 2- 92, 3- 139, 4- 140, 5- 206, 6- 228, 7- 244, 8- 244, 9- 279

**Young West Indies won by 16 runs**

magnificent fashion and while he was at the wicket, Zimbabwe had a chance of victory. It could not last, however, and although Curran made a brave bid for victory in dying light of the day, Zimbabwe were beaten after a valiant struggle.

Sadly, this was Peckover's last game for his country as he decided to emigrate to South Africa. His fielding will be greatly missed as will his opening batting.

The Young West Indies returned home with a rather poor record. Few of their batsmen had performed as well as their records suggested that they would, but Ferris and Walsh, supported by Estwick, showed that West Indies have strength in depth in pace bowling and were a hostile combination. Clyde Butts was an accurate off-spinner and Michael Worrell a most accomplished and impressive young wicket-keeper.

Zimbabwe toured Sri Lanka and gave a creditable account of themselves in difficult conditions so that they looked forward with optimism to the visit of the Young Indian side. On paper, the Indian side looked a strong one. Led by Shastri, the side included four others, Navot Singh, Maninder, Sivaramakrishnan and vice-captain Srikkanth, who had played Test cricket. As it transpired the team was disappointing with only Shastri showing any form with the bat. The bowling of Maninder Singh and Prabhakar was impressive, but they were confronted by some very poor batting from Zimbabwe whose cricket, in the second half of the season, seemed to take a step backwards.

*Charlie Locke of Zimbabwe Country Districts bowls to Rajput in the opening match of the Young India tour.*

***29 February 1984***

***at Harare South Country Club***

**Young India** 241 for 3 (R.J. Shastri 103 not out, M. Azaruddin 71 not out)
**Zimbabwe Country Districts** 205 (G.A. Paterson 62)
*Young India won by 36 runs*

The tourists made an impressive start with Shastri and Azaruddin sharing an unbeaten 4th wicket stand of 175. Paterson and Brown put on 97 for the first wicket, but the Indian spinners teased the later batsmen to destruction and Kulkarni finished the innings when he bowled 3 batsmen in 4 balls with his fast-medium.

### First International
### ZIMBABWE *v.* YOUNG INDIA

Showing signs of a surfeit of limited-over cricket, Zimbabwe wasted the opportunity given them of batting first on a good

LEFT: *Graeme Hick plays defensively to the bowling of Maninder Singh. Maninder Singh was the main threat to Zimbabwe's batsmen. (R.G.Nixon)*

CENTRE: *Duncan Fletcher pulls Prabhakar.* RIGHT: *Malcolm Jarvis looks aggrieved as Rajput plays and misses. (R.G. Nixon)*

wicket. No-one seemed prepared to build an innings and both Houghton and Butchart fell to rash shots after starting well. Inevitably, it was Pycroft who produced the most accomplished knock of the day. More aggressive than usual, he hit 54 off 57 deliveries. Maninder Singh took the honours for India with his controlled left-arm spin, devastating against undisciplined batting.

The Zimbabwe opening attack looked innocuous, but Rawson, perhaps stung by being pulled through mid-wicket for 4, produced a fierce delivery to trap Srikkanth and this heralded an Indian collapse as 3 more wickets fell in the quarter of an hour before the close, each to a poor stroke, and with the visitors on 47 for 4, Zimbabwe were right back in the game.

Ravi Shastri has rarely batted better than he did on the following day. Coming to the wicket at 57 for 5, he hit 101 out of 154 in 166 minutes. Traicos had bowled with great economy, but Shastri hit him for four fours in as many overs. He then hit Curran for three successive fours immediately after lunch. It was glorious batting, but when he was out

**FIRST INTERNATIONAL – ZIMBABWE *v.* YOUNG INDIA**
2, 3 and 5 March 1984 at Harare Sports Club

**ZIMBABWE**

| | FIRST INNINGS | | SECOND INNINGS | |
|---|---|---|---|---|
| R.D. Brown | c Srikkanth, b Maninder | 9 | c Viswanath, b Prabhakar | 18 |
| G.A. Paterson | c Rajput, b Prabhakar | 28 | c Maninder, b Kulkarni | 5 |
| G.A. Hick | b Kulkarni | 23 | c Viswanath, b Prabhakar | 15 |
| A.J. Pycroft* | lbw, b Shastri | 54 | st Viswanath, b Maninder | 0 |
| D.L. Houghton | b Maninder | 30 | c Viswanath, b Prabhakar | 5 |
| K.M. Curran | c Viswanath, b Maninder | 11 | c and b Maninder | 16 |
| D.A.G. Fletcher | c Azauruddin, b Maninder | 4 | not out | 35 |
| I.P. Butchart | st Viswanath b Maninder | 32 | (9) c Rajput, b Maninder | 4 |
| P.W.E. Rawson | b Sivaramakrisham | 8 | (10) c sub, b Maninder | 3 |
| A.J. Traicos† | not out | 2 | (8) c Shastri, b Maninder | 0 |
| M.P. Jarvis | c Viswanath, b Sivaramakrisham | 2 | c Viswanath, b Maninder | 5 |
| Extras | | 19 | | 12 |
| | | 222 | | 118 |

| | O | M | R | W | O | M | R | W |
|---|---|---|---|---|---|---|---|---|
| Kulkarni | 11 | 1 | 33 | 1 | 3 | 1 | 7 | 1 |
| Prabhakar | 10 | 3 | 19 | 1 | 14 | 6 | 22 | 3 |
| Maninder Singh | 32 | 6 | 95 | 5 | 17 | 5 | 43 | 6 |
| Sivaramakrishnan | 9 | 2 | 30 | 2 | 3 | — | 11 | — |
| Shastri | 12 | 1 | 26 | 1 | 8 | 1 | 23 | — |

FALL OF WICKETS
1- 44, 2- 45, 3- 115, 4- 136, 5- 161, 6- 176, 7- 183, 8- 216, 9- 218
1- 7, 2- 38, 3- 39, 4- 44, 5- 51, 6- 80, 7- 86, 8- 90, 9- 96

**YOUNG INDIA**

| | FIRST INNINGS | | SECOND INNINGS | |
|---|---|---|---|---|
| K. Srikkanth | lbw, b Rawson | 18 | c Houghton, b Rawson | 16 |
| Navjot Singh | st Houghton b Traicos | 14 | c Butchart, b Curran | 0 |
| L.S. Rajput | lbw, b Rawson | 14 | not out | 23 |
| M. Azaruddin | c Paterson, b Traicos | 0 | not out | 10 |
| M.D. Gunjal | c Fletcher, b Curran | 2 | | |
| Maninder Singh | c Fletcher, b Rawson | 6 | | |
| R.J. Shastri† | c Brown, b Jarvis | 101 | | |
| S. Viswanath* | c Hick, b Traicos | 16 | | |
| L. Sivaramakrishnan | c Pycroft, b Curran | 27 | | |
| M. Prabhakar | not out | 51 | | |
| R.R. Kulkarni | c Brown, b Fletcher | 32 | | |
| Extras | | 11 | | 0 |
| | | 292 | (for 2 wkts) | 49 |

| | O | M | R | W | O | M | R | W |
|---|---|---|---|---|---|---|---|---|
| Rawson | 24 | 9 | 73 | 3 | 5 | — | 19 | 1 |
| Jarvis | 9 | 1 | 38 | 1 | | | | |
| Curran | 18 | 4 | 61 | 2 | 3 | 1 | 16 | 1 |
| Traicos | 19 | 6 | 80 | 3 | | | | |
| Butchart | 4 | — | 20 | — | | | | |
| Fletcher | 3 | 1 | 5 | 1 | | | | |
| Hick | 2 | 1 | 4 | — | 2 | — | 14 | — |

FALL OF WICKETS
1- 24, 2- 43, 3- 43, 4- 46, 5- 161, 6- 176, 7- 183, 8- 216, 9- 218
1- 7, 2- 38, 3- 39, 4- 44, 5- 51, 6- 80, 7- 86, 8- 90, 9- 96

*Umpires:* B. McLoughlin and A. Wilmot

**Young India won by 8 wickets**

**FIRST ONE-DAY INTERNATIONAL – ZIMBABWE *v.* YOUNG INDIA**
4 March 1984 at Harare Sports Club

| YOUNG INDIA | | |
|---|---|---|
| S. Khandkar | c Houghton, b Curran | 24 |
| K. Srikkanth | run out | 18 |
| L.S. Rajput | c and b Traicos | 1 |
| M. Azaruddin | c Traicos, b Butchart | 50 |
| R.J. Shastri† | st Houghton, b Traicos | 10 |
| M.R. Srinivasaprasad | c Houghton, b Fletcher | 0 |
| S. Viswanath* | st Houghton, b Hick | 13 |
| M. Prabhakar | not out | 27 |
| R.R. Kulkarni | b Butchart | 6 |
| Maninder Singh | not out | 21 |
| G. D'Monte | | |
| Extras | | 6 |
| (50 overs) | (for 8 wickets) | 176 |

| | O | M | R | W |
|---|---|---|---|---|
| Rawson | 7 | 1 | 13 | — |
| Curran | 9 | 1 | 32 | 1 |
| Fletcher | 7 | — | 24 | 1 |
| Traicos | 10 | 1 | 26 | 2 |
| Brent | 4 | — | 22 | — |
| Hick | 6 | — | 22 | 1 |
| Butchart | 7 | — | 31 | 2 |

FALL OF WICKETS
1- 33, 2- 37, 3- 49, 4- 68, 5- 73, 6- 119, 7- 119, 8- 132

| ZIMBABWE | | |
|---|---|---|
| R.D. Brown | c Srinivasaprasad, b Rajput | 38 |
| G.A. Paterson | st Viswanath, b Maninder | 27 |
| D.A.G. Fletcher | b Rajput | 27 |
| A.J. Pycroft | not out | 38 |
| D.L. Houghton* | c Azaruddin, b Rajput | 20 |
| K.M. Curran | not out | 9 |
| G.A. Hick | | |
| I.P. Butchart | | |
| P.W.E. Rawson | | |
| A.J. Traicos† | | |
| J.P. Brent | | |
| Extras | | 20 |
| (47.1 overs) | (for 4 wickets) | 179 |

| | O | M | R | W |
|---|---|---|---|---|
| Kulkarni | 9 | 4 | 26 | — |
| Prabhakar | 8 | 1 | 35 | — |
| Shastri | 10 | — | 27 | — |
| Maninder Singh | 10 | 1 | 21 | 1 |
| Rajput | 10 | 1 | 46 | 3 |
| Srikkanth | 0.1 | — | 4 | — |

FALL OF WICKETS
1- 45, 2- 89, 3- 108, 4- 154

*Umpires:* I. Robinson and P. Latham

**Zimbabwe won by 6 wickets**

Young India were still 11 short of Zimbabwe's score. The last wicket stand was, in retrospect, the decisive phase of the match. Prabhakar, the young student who had batted high in the order for Delhi in the Ranji Trophy and was to return to score a century for them in the final of the competition, looked every bit as sound a batsman as Shastri and he and Kulkarni added 81 for the last wicket.

Prabhakar then brought devastation with his bowling and when Maninder Singh took over he was once again aided by some totally irresponsible batting. Only Duncan Fletcher seemed prepared to bat with application and sense. He was not out at the close of the second day with the score at 86 for 7, and although he cajolled a few more runs on the Monday, there was no effective recovery and Zimbabwe were out for 118 after one of the most abject displays of batting that they had given since their days in the Currie Cup.

### First One-Day International
### ZIMBABWE *v.* YOUNG INDIA

Playing with greater sense than they had done on the previous day in the three-day international, Zimbabwe beat Young India with ease.

The tourists had begun well, but the opening stand ended in disaster when Srikkanth was run out after a mix-up. Azaruddin played very well, but Shastri, who had savaged Traicos the previous day, fell victim to that bowler when he was beaten in the flight and stumped by Houghton who had an excellent day behind the stumps with four dismissals.

The Young India score was moderate and presented no difficulties to a side who were prepared to apply themselves. Each batsman played with responsibility and the target was reached with ease.

Fletcher was named Man of the Match for his good all-round cricket.

### Second One-Day International
### ZIMBABWE *v.* YOUNG INDIA

A good crowd attended the first international match to be staged at Mutare, but the Young Indians gave a very disappointing display. On a hot, humid day only Azaruddin and Rajput, in a third wicket stand of 76, played with any authority. Paterson and Fletcher gave Zimbabwe a splendid start and Graeme Hick gave further indication of his rich promise with four sixes and six fours in an innings of 62 not out which won him the Man of the Match award.

***10 March 1984***

***at Bulawayo Athletic Club***

**Young Zimbabwe** 204 for 6 (G.A. Paterson 64, I.P. Butchart 51 not out)
**Young India** 208 for 6
*Young India won by 4 wickets*

Young Zimbabwe began badly, losing 4 for 22 against the pace of D'Monte and Prabhakar. Paterson and Waller added 111 in less than 90 minutes and skipper Ian Butchart hit 51 off 40 deliveries. In reply, Srikkanth hit 42 off 28 balls and consistent batting saw the visitors to victory with just under 5 overs to spare.

## SECOND ONE-DAY INTERNATIONAL – ZIMBABWE *v.* YOUNG INDIA
7 March 1984 at Mutare Sports Club

| YOUNG INDIA | | |
|---|---|---|
| L.S. Rajput | run out | 65 |
| K. Srikkanth | b Rawson | 6 |
| S. Khandkar | b Rawson | 0 |
| M. Azaruddin | c and b Traicos | 47 |
| R.J. Shastri† | b Butchart | 11 |
| Navjot Singh | b Hick | 8 |
| S. Viswanath* | c Houghton, b Fletcher | 17 |
| M. Prabhakar | b Curran | 8 |
| L. Sivarama-krishnan | c Brent, b Fletcher | 1 |
| Maninder Singh | not out | 3 |
| R.R. Kulkarni | c Traicos, b Rawson | 2 |
| Extras | | 16 |
| (45.2 overs) | | 184 |

| | O | M | R | W |
|---|---|---|---|---|
| Rawson | 7.2 | 1 | 27 | 3 |
| Curran | 7 | 1 | 25 | 1 |
| Fletcher | 10 | — | 34 | 2 |
| Traicos | 10 | — | 40 | 1 |
| Butchart | 7 | — | 22 | 1 |
| Hick | 4 | — | 20 | 1 |

FALL OF WICKETS
1- 36, 2- 36, 3- 112, 4- 137, 5- 141, 6- 161, 7- 177, 8- 179, 9- 181

| ZIMBABWE | | |
|---|---|---|
| G.A. Paterson | st Viswanath, b Sivaramakrishnan | 44 |
| D.A.G. Fletcher | lbw, b Sivaramakrishnan | 36 |
| G.A. Hick | not out | 62 |
| A.J. Pycroft | retired hurt | 11 |
| D.L. Houghton* | c and b Sivaramakrishnan | 13 |
| K.M. Curran | not out | 8 |
| C.M. Robertson | | |
| K.G. Walton | | |
| I.P. Butchart | | |
| P.W.E. Rawson | | |
| A.J. Traicos† | | |
| Extras | | 13 |
| (40.2 overs) | (for 3 wickets) | 187 |

| | O | M | R | W |
|---|---|---|---|---|
| Kulkarni | 5 | — | 12 | — |
| Prabhakar | 3 | — | 21 | — |
| Shastri | 6 | — | 39 | — |
| Maninder Singh | 10 | 2 | 50 | — |
| Sivaramakrishnan | 10 | 1 | 34 | 3 |
| Rajput | 6.2 | 2 | 18 | — |

FALL OF WICKETS
1- 82, 2- 103, 3- 163

**Zimbabwe won by 7 wickets**

### Third One-Day International
### ZIMBABWE *v.* YOUNG INDIA

Zimbabwe took a winning 3–0 lead in the series with an exciting victory in front of the largest crowd at a match in Bulawayo for several years.

Azaruddin again showed his preference for the limited-over game with an aggressive innings and Shastri hit a sound fifty. Fletcher bowled well for Zimbabwe who faced a moderate target.

Grant Paterson batted with confidence and victory seemed assured, but there was a middle-order collapse and the

## THIRD ONE-DAY INTERNATIONAL – ZIMBABWE *v.* YOUNG INDIA
11 March 1984 at Bulawayo Athletic Club

| YOUNG INDIA | | |
|---|---|---|
| L.S. Rajput | lbw, b Rawson | 6 |
| K. Srikkanth | b Fletcher | 14 |
| S. Khandkar | run out | 25 |
| M. Azaruddin | c Rawson, b Traicos | 43 |
| R.J. Shastri† | c Hick, b Fletcher | 53 |
| M.D. Gunjal | c Brown, b Butchart | 24 |
| M. Prabhakar | run out | 2 |
| S. Viswanath* | c Butchart, b Fletcher | 1 |
| R.R. Kulkarni | c and b Fletcher | 0 |
| Maninder Singh | b Butchart | 4 |
| G. D'Monte | not out | 0 |
| Extras | | 9 |
| (49.4 overs) | | 181 |

| | O | M | R | W |
|---|---|---|---|---|
| Rawson | 10 | 2 | 41 | 1 |
| Butchart | 9.4 | 1 | 36 | 2 |
| Hick | 10 | 2 | 24 | — |
| Fletcher | 10 | 1 | 41 | 4 |
| Traicos | 8.3 | 1 | 20 | 1 |
| Houghton | 1.3 | — | 10 | — |

FALL OF WICKETS
1- 8, 2- 40, 3- 60, 4- 103, 5- 155, 6- 167, 7- 175, 8- 177, 9- 177

| ZIMBABWE | | |
|---|---|---|
| G.A. Paterson | c Viswanath, b Shastri | 62 |
| D.A.G. Fletcher | c Viswanath, b D'Monte | 5 |
| G.A. Hick | c Azaruddin, b Kulkarni | 10 |
| D.L. Houghton | st Viswanath, b Maninder | 16 |
| A.J. Pycroft | b Maninder | 15 |
| K.M. Curran | c and b Maninder | 10 |
| R.D. Brown | not out | 43 |
| I.P. Butchart | c D'Monte, b Shastri | 3 |
| K.G. Walton | st Viswanath, b Shastri | 2 |
| P.W.E. Rawson | c Khandkar, b Kulkarni | 5 |
| A.J. Traicos† | not out | 0 |
| Extras | | 14 |
| (49.4 overs) | (for 9 wickets) | 185 |

| | O | M | R | W |
|---|---|---|---|---|
| Prabhakar | 7.4 | 1 | 31 | — |
| D'Monte | 4 | — | 27 | 1 |
| Kulkarni | 10 | 2 | 21 | 2 |
| Rajput | 8 | 1 | 32 | — |
| Maninder Singh | 10 | 1 | 20 | 3 |
| Shastri | 10 | — | 40 | 3 |

FALL OF WICKETS
1- 15, 2- 47, 3- 91, 4- 99, 5- 127, 6- 136, 7- 159, 8- 170, 9- 179

**Zimbabwe won by 1 wicket**

Indian bowling was tight. Robin Brown stood firm, but there was little support from the tail.

Traicos had injured a hand while bowling and Houghton had finished his over while Brown kept wicket. Now Traicos had to bat at a crucial time with his hand injured. At the start of the last over, three runs were needed for victory. Brown levelled the scores with a two and then drove a boundary through mid-wicket with two balls remaining.

***14 March 1984***

***at Hwange***

**Young India** 208
**Young Zimbabwe** 176 (K.G. Walton 67 not out, L. Sivaramakrishnan 4 for 17)
*Young India won by 50 runs*

In spite of an uneven batting display, Young India reached 208 and the home side rarely looked like making a challenge. Kevin Walton carried his bat and won a place in the national side. The rest showed little idea of how to cope with leg-spin.

### Second International
### ZIMBABWE *v.* YOUNG INDIA

This match was scheduled for four days, but so pitiful was the batting of both sides that, but for rain and bad light, it would have been finished in two.

Rawson and Curran soon had the tourists in deep trouble and, in spite of Shastri's determination and class, they never effectively recovered. The Indian captain found support only from Kulkarni who stayed long enough to see the score past the 100. Maninder Singh ran lethargically and was thrown out by Pycroft so that Shastri was left undefeated on 42. Traicos, having placed himself at mid-on because of his injured hand instead of his usual position in the gully, found himself taking the first two catches of the innings from simple lofted drives. Rawson and Curran had 4 wickets each although Rawson was very expensive in the context of the match.

Zimbabwe showed batting incompetence to equal the Indians'. Paterson was out to the first ball he faced, Brown lasted a little longer and Hick attempted too much too soon. Pycroft and Fletcher brought some sanity to the batting, but Fletcher was caught behind just before the close of the first day and Pycroft went next morning without adding to his overnight score.

The innings continued its decline and it was only a last wicket stand between Rawson and Traicos that gave Zimbabwe the lead. It was a shabby performance. Some more limp batting was to come, but credit should also be given to some fine bowling by Rawson. Bowling unchanged, he took 7 for 49 to bring his total of wickets in the four first-class games to 33, a remarkable achievement. He was well supported by Curran, and their bowling seemed to have made possible an easy victory for Zimbabwe. The easy victory looked destined to become a humiliating defeat as batsmen scurried back to the pavilion after inept displays. At the end of a bewildering second day Zimbabwe were 50 for 6 with Walton on 0 and Curran on 9. 22 wickets had fallen in a bewildering day for 185 runs.

Walton and Curran nudged the score to 60 before Walton fell to Maninder Singh. Butchart then joined Curran and showed a welcome positivity. Curran was lbw to Prabhakar at 86 and the task seemed daunting, but Rawson proved the ideal partner for Butchart and he alone could take total credit from the match in which he scored 17 without being dismissed and took 11 for 119.

### Fourth One-Day International
### ZIMBABWE *v.* YOUNG INDIA

A somewhat soggy match resulted in Zimbabwe winning comfortably. Fletcher's tight bowling was decisive and brought him the individual award. Brown gave the Zimbabwe innings solidity and Pycroft batted in his usual vein.

### Fifth One-Day International
### ZIMBABWE *v.* YOUNG INDIA

This match was not on the original programme, but was arranged when the scheduled four-day match finished more than a day early. The Zimbabwe Cricket Union declared that the game should be counted as a full international on a par with the other one-day matches against Young India.

Walton played by far his best innings in representative cricket and made possible a good score by Zimbabwe. Young India seemed to be slipping to a big defeat until Viswanath played a fine innings which nearly brought them victory. As it was, Rawson and Curran gnawed away at the tail and Zimbabwe took the series 5–0.

Viswanath was named Man of the Match, a deserved honour, not only for his valiant fifty, but for his impressive wicket-keeping throughout the tour.

*Peter Rawson – 11 for 119 against Young India in the Second International and 33 wickets in 4 first-class matches in the season. (Ken Kelly)*

## SECOND INTERNATIONAL – ZIMBABWE *v.* YOUNG INDIA
16, 17 and 20 March 1984 at Harare Sports Club

### YOUNG INDIA

| | FIRST INNINGS | | SECOND INNINGS | |
|---|---|---|---|---|
| K. Srikkanth | c Traicos, b Rawson | 0 | (5) c Houghton, b Curran | 14 |
| Navjot Singh | c Hick, b Butchart | 21 | c Walton, b Rawson | 11 |
| L.S. Rajput | c Traicos, b Curran | 6 | (1) c Traicos, b Rawson | 1 |
| M. Azaruddin | c Houghton, b Curran | 0 | c Houghton, b Rawson | 2 |
| M.D. Gunjal | c Walton, b Rawson | 29 | (3) c Butchart, b Curran | 43 |
| R.J. Shastri† | not out | 42 | c Hick, b Rawson | 4 |
| S. Viswanath* | c Houghton, b Rawson | 0 | lbw, b Rawson | 1 |
| M. Prabhakar | c Houghton, b Rawson | 0 | c Pycroft, b Rawson | 2 |
| L. Sivarama-krishnan | c Fletcher, b Curran | 0 | c Walton, b Rawson | 0 |
| R.R. Kulkarni | c Walton, b Curran | 12 | c Houghton, b Curran | 22 |
| Maninder Singh | run out | 0 | not out | 2 |
| Extras | | 2 | | 4 |
| | | 112 | | 106 |

| | O | M | R | W | O | M | R | W |
|---|---|---|---|---|---|---|---|---|
| Rawson | 16.1 | 2 | 70 | 4 | 15 | 2 | 49 | 7 |
| Curran | 14 | 2 | 29 | 4 | 12.4 | 3 | 36 | 3 |
| Butchart | 2 | — | 11 | 1 | 2 | — | 17 | — |

FALL OF WICKETS
1- 0, 2- 11, 3- 13, 4- 40, 5- 67, 6- 69, 7- 69, 8- 70, 9- 108
1- 7, 2- 18, 3- 20, 4- 37, 5- 46, 6- 52, 7- 82, 8- 82, 9- 82

*Umpires:* A. Wilmot and D. Arnott

**Zimbabwe won by 2 wickets**

### ZIMBABWE

| | FIRST INNINGS | | SECOND INNINGS | |
|---|---|---|---|---|
| R.D. Brown | c Navjot, b Prabhakar | 7 | c Viswanath, b Kulkarni | 3 |
| G.A. Paterson | c Viswanath, b Prabhakar | 0 | c Navjot, b Kulkarni | 8 |
| G.A. Hick | c Azaruddin, b Maninder | 18 | b Maninder | 8 |
| A.J. Pycroft | c Viswanath, b Prabhakar | 34 | c Viswanath, b Prabhakar | 1 |
| D.A.G. Fletcher | c Viswanath, b Maninder | 24 | b Prabhakar | 16 |
| D.L. Houghton* | c Rajput, b Maninder | 2 | b Maninder | 4 |
| K.G. Walton | c Rajput, b Prabhakar | 4 | c Srikkanth, b Maninder | 17 |
| K.M. Curran | c Navjot, b Prabhakar | 6 | lbw, b Prabhakar | 12 |
| I.P. Butchart | st Viswanath, b Maninder | 0 | not out | 29 |
| P.W.E. Rawson | not out | 11 | not out | 6 |
| A.J. Traicos† | c Viswanath, b Maninder | 3 | | |
| Extras | | 5 | | 1 |
| | | 114 | (for 8 wkts) | 105 |

| | O | M | R | W | O | M | R | W |
|---|---|---|---|---|---|---|---|---|
| Kulkarni | 4 | — | 12 | — | 6 | 2 | 7 | 2 |
| Prabhakar | 18 | 7 | 40 | 5 | 25 | 5 | 48 | 3 |
| Maninder Singh | 16.2 | 3 | 41 | 5 | 19.3 | 4 | 49 | 3 |
| Sivaramakrishnan | 2 | — | 16 | — | | | | |

FALL OF WICKETS
1- 4, 2- 25, 3- 25, 4- 85, 5- 85, 6- 91, 7- 99, 8- 99, 9- 99
1- 8, 2- 12, 3- 13, 4- 34, 5- 40, 6- 41, 7- 60, 8- 86

Young Indian captain Ravi Shastri did not play in this match. He announced later that he had stood down as a protest against what he called poor umpiring, claiming that several decisions had gone against his team at vital moments during the tour, and that the umpires had allowed themselves to be unduly influenced by heavy appeals from the Zimbabwe players.

Unfortunately, whatever acceptance his comments might have received from his own country, he could not be taken seriously in Zimbabwe. The Young Indians quickly became well-known for the great number of ludicrous appeals they made on the field, and on a number of occasions, for a particularly confident appeal, the entire team, even the deep fielders, would converge on the umpire, repeating their appeal and shouting, 'That's out! That's out!' If the appeal was rejected, they would continue to argue or throw tantrums on the field. Zimbabwe were very mild compared with this. Good ambassadors for their country off the field, these young men need to appreciate that the majority of Zimbabwe cricket followers are only able to judge Indian cricketers by what they saw of them *on* the field of play.

In spite of the considerable success in the limited-over matches and the victories over both the touring sides in first-class matches, there was some disappointment at the end of the season in Zimbabwe. After the euphoria of the showing in the World Cup, there were some who had thought that the country was on the verge of Test status, but the displays against the Young Indians disproved this notion. The fielding remained of the highest standard, and the bowling was generally good, but the batting was another story. None of the batsmen, except Pycroft at times, looked ready to make the transition to five-day Test matches; the 'limited-over mentality' was often far too evident.

Zimbabwe's cricket administrators are well aware of the need for the players to gain more first-class experience and are pursuing an ambitious programme which would bring full-strength English and Australian Test sides to Zimbabwe en route to play each other in the next Ashes series. Overseas

### First Class Averages

| BATTING | M | Inns | NOs | Runs | HS | Av | 100s | 50s |
|---|---|---|---|---|---|---|---|---|
| A.J. Pycroft | 4 | 8 | 1 | 341 | 90 | 48.71 | | 3 |
| D.L. Houghton | 4 | 8 | | 215 | 82 | 26.87 | | 1 |
| D.A.G. Fletcher | 4 | 8 | 2 | 122 | 35* | 20.33 | | |
| G.A.Hick | 4 | 8 | 2 | 120 | 28* | 20.00 | | |
| K.M. Curran | 4 | 8 | | 152 | 48 | 19.00 | | |
| I.P. Butchart | 3 | 6 | 2 | 72 | 32 | 18.00 | | |
| R.D. Brown | 4 | 8 | | 135 | 42 | 16.87 | | |
| G.A. Paterson | 3 | 5 | | 80 | 39 | 16.00 | | |
| P.W.E. Rawson | 4 | 7 | 3 | 56 | 23 | 14.00 | | |

(Qualification – 50 runs, average 10.00)

| BOWLING | Overs | Mds | Runs | Wkts | Av | Best | 5/in | 10/m |
|---|---|---|---|---|---|---|---|---|
| P.W.E. Rawson | 131 | 25 | 503 | 33 | 14.24 | 7/49 | 3 | 1 |
| K.M. Curran | 73.4 | 14 | 269 | 14 | 19.21 | 4/29 | | |
| I.P. Butchart | 24 | 4 | 103 | 5 | 20.60 | 2/22 | | |
| A.J. Traicos | 102.5 | 25 | 300 | 11 | 27.27 | 3/35 | | |

(Qualification – 5 wickets)

**LEADING FIELDERS**

13–D.L. Houghton (ct 11/st 2); 8–G.A. Hick; 7–A.J. Pycroft; 4–P.W.E. Rawson, D.A.G. Fletcher, A.J. Traicos, R.D. Brown and K.G. Walton

tours are also planned.

As yet, there are not the resources to run a first-class domestic competition, but for the first time some of the inter-provincial matches were played over three days. As usual, Mashonaland had little difficulty in vanquishing all opposition, but it was encouraging to see signs of a cricketing renaissance in Matabeleland, the Bulawayo area. The return to the area of Tommy Dunk, the veteran national player, was one of the causes of the resurgence, but much credit must go to the new coach, the former New Zealand Test bowler Bob Blair. He has done wonders in generating enthusiasm and improving techniques in all levels of cricket in the province. Large crowds attending the representative matches were a testament to this upsurge in enthusiasm.

### FOURTH ONE-DAY INTERNATIONAL – ZIMBABWE *v.* YOUNG INDIA
18 March 1984 at Harare Sports Club

**YOUNG INDIA**

|  |  |  |
|---|---|---|
| S. Khandkar | c Houghton, b Rawson | 3 |
| L.S. Rajput | c Curran, b Fletcher | 38 |
| M.D. Gunjal | c Fletcher, b Curran | 5 |
| K. Srikkanth | c Rawson, b Fletcher | 1 |
| R.J. Shastri† | c Houghton, b Butchart | 4 |
| M. Azaruddin | b Butchart | 0 |
| S. Viswanath* | c Houghton, b Fletcher | 4 |
| L. Sivarama-krishnan | b Butchart | 3 |
| M. Prabhakar | c Houghton, b Curran | 14 |
| R.R. Kulkarni | not out | 0 |
| Maninder Singh | c Houghton, b Curran | 0 |
| Extras | | 6 |
| (29 overs) | | 78 |

| | O | M | R | W |
|---|---|---|---|---|
| Rawson | 7 | 1 | 18 | 1 |
| Curran | 8 | 2 | 20 | 3 |
| Fletcher | 6 | 2 | 10 | 3 |
| Butchart | 7 | 1 | 22 | 3 |
| Traicos | 1 | — | 2 | — |

FALL OF WICKETS
1- 20, 2- 36, 3- 39, 4- 50, 5- 52, 6- 60, 7- 60, 8- 74, 9- 78

**ZIMBABWE**

|  |  |  |
|---|---|---|
| R.D. Brown | not out | 38 |
| G.A. Paterson | c Viswanath, b Kulkarni | 5 |
| G.A. Hick | c and b Maninder | 1 |
| A.J. Pycroft | b Sivaramakrishnan | 23 |
| D.L. Houghton* | not out | 6 |
| A.C. Waller | | |
| D.A.G. Fletcher | | |
| K.M. Curran | | |
| I.P. Butchart | | |
| P.W.E. Rawson | | |
| A.J. Traicos† | | |
| Extras | | 8 |
| (27 overs) | (for 3 wickets) | 81 |

| | O | M | R | W |
|---|---|---|---|---|
| Prabhakar | 4 | 2 | 7 | — |
| Kulkarni | 8 | 1 | 18 | 1 |
| Sivaramakrishnan | 6 | — | 24 | 1 |
| Maninder Singh | 9 | 2 | 24 | 1 |

FALL OF WICKETS
1- 13, 2- 28, 3- 62

**Zimbabwe won by 7 wickets**

### FIFTH ONE-DAY INTERNATIONAL – ZIMBABWE *v.* YOUNG INDIA
21 March 1984 at Harare Sports Club

**ZIMBABWE**

|  |  |  |
|---|---|---|
| R.D. Brown | c Khandkar, b Prabhakar | 11 |
| K.G. Walton | c Srikkanth, b Sivaramakrishnan | 81 |
| G.A. Hick | c Gunjal, b Sivaramakrishnan | 13 |
| A.J. Pycroft | c Gunjal, b Sivaramakrishnan | 28 |
| G.A. Paterson | b Prabhakar | 40 |
| D.A.G. Fletcher | run out | 5 |
| D.L. Houghton* | b D'Monte | 0 |
| K.M. Curran | run out | 0 |
| I.P. Butchart | not out | 6 |
| P.W.E. Rawson | b D'Monte | 16 |
| A.J. Traicos† | c Rajput, b D'Monte | 0 |
| Extras | | 10 |
| (49.3 overs) | | 210 |

| | O | M | R | W |
|---|---|---|---|---|
| Prabhakar | 10 | 1 | 34 | 2 |
| D'Monte | 9.3 | 1 | 45 | 3 |
| Rajput | 10 | 2 | 31 | — |
| Sivaramakrishnan | 10 | 1 | 41 | 3 |
| Maninder Singh | 10 | — | 49 | — |

FALL OF WICKETS
1- 24, 2- 53, 3- 126, 4- 154, 5- 175, 6- 175, 7- 175, 8- 184, 9- 210

**YOUNG INDIA**

|  |  |  |
|---|---|---|
| M.R. Sriniva-saprasad | c Houghton, b Curran | 19 |
| K. Srikkanth† | c Curran, b Traicos | 38 |
| S. Khandkar | run out | 16 |
| L.S. Rajput | c Butchart, b Hick | 5 |
| M.D. Gunjal | c Curran, b Fletcher | 26 |
| Navjot Singh | c Butchart, b Hick | 1 |
| S. Viswanath* | b Rawson | 53 |
| M. Prabhakar | c Hick, b Fletcher | 6 |
| L. Sivarama-krishnan | c Rawson, b Curran | 6 |
| Maninder Singh | c Houghton, b Rawson | 11 |
| G. D'Monte | not out | 0 |
| Extras | | 10 |
| (47.4 overs) | | 191 |

| | O | M | R | W |
|---|---|---|---|---|
| Rawson | 6.4 | 1 | 35 | 2 |
| Curran | 10 | 1 | 39 | 2 |
| Traicos | 10 | 2 | 17 | 1 |
| Hick | 8 | — | 35 | 2 |
| Butchart | 6 | — | 31 | — |
| Fletcher | 7 | 1 | 24 | 2 |

FALL OF WICKETS
1- 43, 2- 68, 3- 84, 4- 85, 5- 99, 6- 136, 7- 150, 8- 168, 9- 191

**Zimbabwe won by 19 runs**

SECTION G

# Triumph Long Awaited

The season in Pakistan. The Patron's Trophy.
The Quaid-e-Azam Trophy. The Wills Cup. Pakistan *v.* England.
Pakistan Under-23 *v.* Sri Lanka Under-23.
Tony Lewis on England in Pakistan.
The First Asia Cup, in Sharjah.

*Pakistan rules. The crowd at Lahore.*
*(Adrian Murrell)*

The season in Pakistan was a turbulent one. The failure in the Prudential World Cup was a bitter disappointment and when Imran Khan failed to regain fitness in time to bowl in Australia a controversy began which reverberated throughout the year. The selection committee decided, with some justification, that Imran should not lead the side to Australia as he was not fit, but the then President of the B.C.C.P., Air Marshall Nur Khan, vetoed their decision and named Imran as captain. At this the selectors resigned en masse.

Following the debacle in Australia when three players were flown out to re-enforce the side, Air Marshall Nur Khan himself resigned and Lt Gen Ghulam Safdar Butt became the head of the Pakistan Board of Control.

Against this background and an overlong and arduous international programme which meant that the leading players were once again not available for domestic competitions an attempt was made to play two first-class tournaments, the upgraded Patron's Trophy and the Quaid-e-Azam. This meant a record 88 matches and, eventually, no time for the P.A.C.O. Pentagular tournament, one of the country's premier competitions.

*Tauseef Ahmed, 54 wickets in the season gave him a place in the Pakistan Test side. (Adrian Murrell)*

Let us consider for one moment the season that confronted a leading Pakistani cricketer. If he were a contracted player in England, he would have had only a few days between returning from England in late September, 1983, and joining the Pakistan side on their month-long tour of India. On the completion of that tour he had to fly to Australia and when he returned from there it was just in time to play in the Test series and one-day internationals against England. As soon as the England tour was over he was off to Sharjah for the first Asia Cup competition. By then it was time to begin the season in England again. Pakistan domestic cricket had seen nothing of him and an insane international programme was taking a further step towards killing the goose that lays the golden eggs. Certainly there was indication of this by the lack of public support for the Test series against England.

## B.C.C.P. PATRON'S TROPHY

Since 1979–80 the Patron's Trophy had served as a second-class competition which was a qualifying tournament for the Quaid-e-Azam Trophy. In 1983 the Board decided to upgrade the tournament and to reserve it for zonal and associated teams rather than allow commercial sides to compete. This was a wise move and one forwarded by Imran Khan in his autobiography.

Nineteen teams competed and were divided into four groups. Sadly, many of the facilities provided for the players during the competition were primitive for the associations have not the resources of the commercial organisations who look after their players well.

### Group A

***2, 3 and 4 October 1983***

***at Race Course Ground, Quetta***

**Quetta** 257 (Younus Ata 90, Samiullah Khan 4 for 43) and 180 (Younus Ata 70)
**Sukkur** 130 (Asif Baloch 7 for 46) and 219 for 3 (Rizwan Yousuf 116 not out)

*Match drawn*
*Quetta 10 pts, Sukkur 4 pts*

Two good innings by opening batsman Younus Ata and some fine spin bowling from Asif Baloch put the home side in a commanding position, but Rizwan Yousuf who lost opening partner Arshad Ali through obstructing the field hit a splendid century and saved the match.

***4, 5 and 6 October 1983***

***at National Stadium, Karachi***

**Hyderabad** 146 and 130 (Nadeem Jamal 62, Abdur Raqeeb 6 for 31)
**Karachi Blues** 226 (Mazharullah 4 for 39) and 51 for 0

*Karachi Blues won by 10 wickets*
*Karachi Blues 17 pts, Hyderabad 4 pts*

The strong Karachi Blues side, which included six Test players, overwhelmed Hyderabad in the first match at the National Stadium. The wicket was never easy and the visitors struggled against Sikhander Bakht, Tauseef Ahmed and Abdur Raqeeb who had match figures of 9 for 53. Rizwan-uz-Zaman batted well for his 41 for the home side and there were sensible innings from Ejaz Faqih and Anil Dalpat so that Karachi Blues took a first innings lead of 80. Wickets fell steadily when Hyderabad batted again and the home side won with ease.

***6, 7 and 8 October 1983***

***at Race Course Ground, Quetta***

**Lahore City Blues** 157 (Tariq Baloch 7 for 53) and 218 (Raj Hans 4 for 54)
**Quetta** 144 (Sohail Khan 5 for 42) and 206 for 8 (Naved Nawaz 57, Sohail Khan 4 for 44)

*Match drawn*
*Lahore City Blues 6 pts, Quetta 4 pts*

***7, 8 and 9 October 1983***

***at National Stadium, Karachi***

**Sukkur** 64 (Tauseef Ahmed 4 for 12) and 81
**Karachi Blues** 299 for 3 (Siddiq Patni 123 not out, Haroon Rashid 92, Mahmood Rasheed 51 not out)

*Karachi Blues won by an innings and 154 runs*
*Karachi Blues 18 pts, Sukkur 1 pt*

Bowlers dominated the match at Quetta where the home side finished 26 runs short of victory with two wickets standing. At Karachi, Karachi Blues routed Sukkur. The visitors failed to reach a hundred in either innings and Siddiq Patni and Haroon Rashid put on 155 for the Blues second wicket before Haroon was run out. Mahmood Rasheed then hit furiously scoring 51 out of an unfinished stand of 96.

***11, 12 and 13 October 1983***

***at National Stadium, Karachi***

**Karachi Blues** 261 for 8 (Nasir Valika 63) and 112 for 3
**Lahore City Blues** 82 (Rashid Khan 8 for 39) and 290 (Aamer Sohail 68, Sikhander Bakht 5 for 100)

*Karachi Blues won by 7 wickets*
*Karachi Blues 18 pts, Lahore City Blues 4 pts*

***at Niaz Stadium, Hyderabad***

**Hyderabad** 274 for 6 (Zulfiqar Ali 147) and 196 for 7 dec (Meer Hyder 57, Arif Amin 4 for 54)
**Sukkur** 180 (Abdul Nabi 57, Haaris A. Khan 5 for 51) and 122 (Nasir Khan 56)

*Hyderabad won by 168 runs*
*Hyderabad 18 pts, Sukkur 4 pts*

Having reached 261 for 8 in their 75 overs, Karachi Blues, inspired by Rashid Khan, who included the hat-trick in his 8 for 39, routed the Lahore side and enforced the follow-on. Some dogged batting in the second innings, particularly by the late order, nearly saved the game for Lahore City Blues, but the home side scored at almost six an over to achieve a fine win.

In Hyderabad, Zulfiqar Ali dominated the home side's innings with a fine hundred after both openers had been lost for 43. Sukkur's poor form continued and, although avoiding the follow-on, they were well beaten with Haaris A. Khan having match figures of 8 for 78.

***14, 15 and 16 October 1983***

***at National Stadium, Karachi***

**Lahore City Blues** 299 for 8 (Tariq Mansoor 57, Abdul Nabi 6 for 86)
**Sukkur** 108 and 312 for 5 (Arshad Ali 105 not out, Aqeel Ahmed 83)

*Match drawn*
*Lahore City Blues 10 pts, Sukkur 4 pts*

***at Niaz Stadium, Hyderabad***

**Quetta** 245 (Navad Nawaz 59, Salman Tahir 57, Asif Baloch 53, Haaris A. Khan 5 for 81) and 309 for 7 (Salman Tahir 82, Raj Hans 66, Murtaza Khan 61, Zakir Khan 51)
**Hyderabad** 297 for 9 (Meer Hyder 88, Ghulam Ali 78, Nadeem Jamal 63, Asif Baloch 4 for 125)

*Match drawn*
*Hyderabad 10 pts, Quetta 7 pts*

Batsmen dominated the game in Karachi where, having been 17 for 4 at one time in their first innings and following-on 191 runs behind, Sukkur were saved by Arshad Ali's patient century. He and Aqeel Ahmed added 154 for the fifth wicket. The game in Hyderabad was similarly dominated by the bat and Quetta's second innings degenerated into farce as nine bowlers were used.

*Sikhander Bakht played a vital part in bowling Karachi Blues to a place in the BCCP Patron's Trophy Final. (Adrian Murrell)*

*Shoaib Mohammad, 151 not out v. Quetta, 18 October and eventually a place in the Test side (Adrian Murrell)*

***18, 19 and 20 October 1983***

***at National Stadium, Karachi***

**Karachi Blues** 320 for 2 (Shoaib Mohammad 151 not out, Nasir Valika 104 not out)
**Quetta** 70 (Sikhander Bakht 5 for 29, Jalal-ud-Din 4 for 30) and 75 (Iqbal Sikander 5 for 20)

*Karachi Blues won by an innings and 175 runs*
*Karachi Blues 18 pts, Quetta 1 pt*

An unbroken stand of 229 by Shoaib Mohammad and Nasir Valika for the third wicket emphasised Karachi Blues dominance of Group A. Their bowlers having been hit for 4.26 an over, the Quetta batsmen suffered in their turn as they were shot out for 70 in 21.1 overs and, following-on, managed only 5 runs and 10.2 overs more. Sikhander Bakht had match figures of 7 for 43.

The match between Lahore City Blues and Hyderabad scheduled for 21, 22 and 23 October at Lahore was never played.

**Group A Final Table**

| | *P* | *W* | *L* | *D* | *Pts* |
|---|---|---|---|---|---|
| Karachi Blues | 4 | 4 | — | — | 71 |
| Hyderabad | 3 | 1 | 1 | 1 | 32 |
| Quetta | 4 | — | 1 | 3 | 22 |
| Lahore City Blues | 3 | — | 1 | 2 | 20 |
| Sukkur | 4 | — | 2 | 2 | 13 |

**Group B**

***5, 6 and 7 October 1983***

***at Bahawal Stadium, Bahawalpur***

**Bahawalpur** 202 for 6 (Moghees-ud-Din 57 not out) and 362 for 6 dec (Azhar Abbas 108, Farooq Shera 84, Tanvir Shah 63)
**Multan** 191 (Javed Ilyas 70, Mohammad Altaf 7 for 52) and 86 for 0

*Match drawn*
*Bahawalpur 8 pts, Multan 4 pts*

The match was destined to be drawn when Bahawalpur for whom Azhar Abbas and Tanvir Shah shared a second wicket stand of 101 batted on in their second innings.

***9, 10 and 11 October 1983***

***at Qaddafi Stadium, Lahore***

**Multan** 122 (Tahir Baig 6 for 47) and 133 for 3 (Saleemullah 59)
**Lahore City Greens** 220 (Ameer Akbar 80, Saleem Taj 68, Masood Anwar 8 for 44)

*Match drawn*
*Lahore City Greens 8 pts, Multan 4 pts*

In spite of splendid bowling by spinner Masood Anwar, Lahore City Greens took a first innings lead of 98 thanks largely to a stand of 139 for the second wicket between Saleem Taj and Ameer Akbar. Multan fought back well, but rain prevented any play on the last day.

***13, 14 and 15 October 1983***

***at Bahawal Stadium, Bahawalpur***

**Karachi Greens** 277 for 3 (Kamal Najamuddin 86, Feroze Najamuddin 82 not out, Moin Mumtaz 54 not out) and 284 for 5 dec (Kamal Najamuddin 111 not out, Zafar Ali 77)
**Bahawalpur** 229 and 234 for 7 (Qasim Shera 64 not out)

*Match drawn*
*Karachi Greens 10 pts, Bahawalpur 5 pts*

Karachi Greens always held the advantage in this match from the time that Feroze Najamuddin and Moin Mumtaz joined in an unbeaten fourth wicket stand of 116. Kamal Majamuddin played two fine innings, but, eventually, Karachi left themselves insufficient time to dismiss the home side.

***18, 19 and 20 October 1983***

***at Bahawal Stadium, Bahawalpur***

**Lahore City Greens** 224 (Shahid Anwar 62, Mohammad Altaf 4 for 85) and 300 (Ameer Akbar 62, Babar Altaf 59 not out, Akram Raza 59, Mohammad Altaf 5 for 82)
**Bahawalpur** 203 for 9 (Moghees-ud-Din 55, Zahid Khan 4 for 58) and 191 for 3 (Naseer Ahmed 63)

*Match drawn*
*Lahore City Greens 8 pts, Bahawalpur 6 pts*

An evenly contested match in which the batsmen held sway for most of the time was doomed for a draw when Lahore City Greens failed to make a challenging declaration.

### *18, 19 and 20 October 1983*

#### *at Sahiwal Stadium, Sahiwal*

**Karachi Greens** 320 for 9 dec (Kamal Najammudin 108, Zafar Mehdi 61, Zafar Ali 54, Javed Ilyas 4 for 95) and 267 for 3 dec (Khalid Alvi 104 not out, Bharat Kumar 70, Sajid Ali 56)
**Multan** 274 (Javed Ilyas 92) and 314 for 6 (Ijaz Ahmed 117, Saleemullah 107)

*Multan won by 4 wickets*
*Multan 18 pts, Karachi Greens 8 pts*

A magnificent match saw Multan achieve a memorable victory when they scored the 314 that they needed to win at nearly seven runs an over. Karachi Greens had seemed to be in control of the match for most of the time and when Khalid Alvi hit a fine second innings century the game seemed to be out of Multan's reach. Two sparkling centuries by Ijaz Ahmed and opening batsman Saleemullah, however, brought Multan their sensational victory. The pair added 208 for the second wicket.

### *22, 23 and 24 October 1983*

#### *at Qaddafi Stadium, Lahore*

**Karachi Greens** 234 (Mohinder Kumar 67, Tahir Baig 4 for 54) and 216 (Feroze Najamuddin 58 not out)
**Lahore City Greens** 267 for 6 dec (Akram Raza 71, Saleem Taj 54 not out) and 44 (Saleem Jaffer 5 for 11, Mohinder Kumar 4 for 31)

*Karachi Greens won by 139 runs*
*Karachi Greens 16 pts, Lahore City Greens 8 pts*

33 runs in arrears on the first innings and able to set Lahore City Greens a target of only 184, Karachi Greens snatched a remarkable victory and so won a place in the semi-finals ahead of Multan. In 19.1 overs on the last day, opening bowlers Saleem Jaffer and Mohinder Kumar bowled out Lahore Greens for 44, only Akram Raza reaching double figures. That the wicket gave them assistance was undeniable, but they were aided also by some limp batting.

**Group B Final Table**

| | *P* | *W* | *L* | *D* | *Pts* |
|---|---|---|---|---|---|
| Karachi Greens | 3 | 1 | 1 | 1 | 34 |
| Multan | 3 | 1 | — | 2 | 26 |
| Lahore City Greens | 3 | — | 1 | 2 | 24 |
| Bahawalpur | 3 | — | — | 3 | 19 |

## Group C

### *5, 6 and 7 October 1983*

#### *at D.P. Stadium, Faisalabad*

**Sargodha** 185 (Mohammad Aslam 73, Tanvir Afzal 4 for 39, Wasim Haider 4 for 46) and 260 for 4 dec (Tasnim Abidi 150 not out)
**Faisalabad** 222 (Tahir Rasheed 61) and 61 for 1 (Bilal Ahmed 51)

*Match drawn*
*Faisalabad 8 pts, Sargodha 5 pts*

#### *at the Municipal Stadium, Gujranwala*

**Lahore City Whites** 231 (Ali Zia 73, Aamer Malik 60, Aamer Wasim 6 for 56, Sajjad Bashir 4 for 42) and 218 for 3 dec (Rameez Raja 101 not out, Aamer Malik 74)
**Gujranwala** 116 (Ali Zia 4 for 15) and 100 (Mohsin Kamal 4 for 36)

*Lahore City Whites won by 233 runs*
*Lahore City Whites 17 pts, Gujranwala 4 pts*

A second innings century from Tasnim Abidi who had been one of the few batsmen to show confidence in the first innings saved Sargodha at Faisalabad after the home side had looked to have the edge. Predictably, in Gujranwala, the home side, who bowled well, were overwhelmed by Lahore City Whites whose all-round strength was impressive.

### *9, 10 and 11 October 1983*

#### *at Iqbal Stadium, Faisalabad*

**Faisalabad** 114 (Sajjad Bashir 6 for 32) and 365 for 9 (Mohammad Ashraf 121, Anwar Awais 102, Azam Khan 54 not out)
**Gujranwala** 319 (Zakir Mirza 120, Abid Sarwar 58, Tanvir Afzal 6 for 113)

*Match drawn*
*Gujranwala 10 pts, Faisalabad 4 pts*

#### *at LCCA Ground, Lahore*

**Karachi Whites** 240 (Zafar Ahmed 52) and 128 for 4 (Anwar Miandad 50 not out)
**Sargodha** 213 (Arshad Pervez 54, Tasnim Abidi 50)

*Match drawn*
*Karachi Whites 9 pts, Sargodha 6 pts*

Faisalabad seemed to be heading for defeat at the Iqbal Stadium when a brave third wicket stand lifted them from 9 for 2 to 255 before Anwar Awais fell to Tahir Mahmood. The other hero and centurion was Mohammad Ashraf, but earlier it had appeared that the home side had no hope. Opening bowler Sajjad Bashir, with match figures of 9 for 83, had bowled Gujranwala into a good position which had been emphasised by Zakir Mirza's fine hundred. Then came the great recovery.

At Lahore, rain prevented any play on the last day when the match was interestingly balanced.

### *13, 14 and 15 October 1983*

#### *at the Municipal Stadium, Gujranwala*

**Sargodha** 214 (Arshad Pervez 86, Azhar Sultan 58 not out, Tahir Mahmood 4 for 22) and 245 for 9 dec (Zahid Mahmood 83)
**Gujranwala** 213 (Mohammad Aslam 6 for 52) and 118 for 6

*Match drawn*
*Sargodha 8 pts, Gujranwala 6 pts*

#### *at LCCA Ground, Lahore*

**Lahore City Whites** 194 (Mohiuddin Khan 5 for 37) and 167 for 5 (Mohiuddin Khan 4 for 60)
**Karachi Whites** 287 (Zafar Ahmed 60 not out, Umar Rasheed 56)

*Match drawn*
*Karachi Whites 10 pts, Lahore City Whites 5 pts*

Sargodha recovered from 13 for 2 to reach 214 thanks to some middle-order substance. They seemed heading for a good first innings lead until Sajjad Bashir and Abid Nazir added 51 for Gujranwala's last wicket. Eventually the home side were left to make 247 at six an over, a task that was beyond them. Time lost to rain hampered chances of a result in Lahore.

### *18, 19 and 20 October 1983*

#### *at LCCA Ground, Lahore*

**Faisalabad** 57 (Afzaal Butt 4 for 13, Mohsin Kamal 4 for 21) and 146 (Mian Fayyaz 4 for 48)
**Lahore City Whites** 373 for 2 (Saadat Ali 183, Abdus Sami 122, Shafiq Ahmed 58 not out)

*Lahore City Whites won by an innings and 170 runs*
*Lahore City Whites 18 pts, Faisalabad 1 pt*

#### *at the Municipal Stadium, Gujranwala*

**Gujranwala** 293 for 9 (Ijaz Ahmed 82, Tahir Mahmood 77, Zakir Mirza 58, Aftab Baloch 5 for 44) and 140 (Amin Lakhani 5 for 22)
**Karachi Whites** 295 for 8 (Zahid Ahmed 59, Umar Rasheed 52, Javed Chaudhri 4 for 96) and 141 for 3

*Karachi Whites won by 7 wickets*
*Karachi Whites 18 pts, Gujranwala 8 pts*

Faisalabad were routed in Lahore where Afzaal Butt, Mohsin Kamal and Shafeeq Ahmed, two wickets with the two balls he bowled, shot them out in 16.2 overs. Saadat Ali and Abdus Sami put on 293 for Lahore City's first wicket and runs came at five an over. At their second attempt, Faisalabad again batted poorly and this time it was the spin of Mian Fayyaz and Shahid Aziz which accounted for them.

At Gujranwala, a stalemate first innings was turned to a comfortable victory for the visitors by the bowling of Amin Lakhani who took 5 for 22 in 8.5 overs as the last five Gujranwala second innings wickets went down for 5 runs.

### *22, 23 and 24 October 1983*

#### *at Iqbal Stadium, Faisalabad*

**Karachi Whites** 241 (Anwar Miandad 60, Tanvir Afzal 4 for 68) and 205 for 8 dec (Anwar Miandad 67, Zahid Ahmed 50, Tanvir Shaukat 4 for 67)
**Faisalabad** 124 (Mohiuddin Khan 6 for 48) and 158 (Amin Lakhani 4 for 39, Zahid Ahmed 4 for 44)

*Karachi Whites won by 164 runs*
*Karachi Whites 17 pts, Faisalabad 4 pts*

#### *at LCCA Ground, Lahore*

**Lahore City Whites** 282 for 7 (Abdus Sami 78, Rameez Raja 76) and 231 for 4 dec (Rameez Raja 74 not out, Saadat Ali 57)
**Sargodha** 205 for 9 (Arshad Pervez 53, Shahid Aziz 5 for 69) and 211 (Arshad Pervez 84 not out, Shahid Aziz 4 for 65)

*Lahore City Whites won by 97 runs*
*Lahore City Whites 18 pts, Sargodha 6 pts*

By beating Sargodha in Lahore, Lahore City Whites won the Group C competition and moved into the semi-finals. The spin of Shahid Aziz was the decisive factor, but the home side's batting, too, played a significant part. With quick runs needed in the second innings to allow time to bowl out the visitors, Lahore City Whites scored at six runs an over. Stubborn resistance at the end of the Sargodha second innings threatened to thwart Lahore, but Mohsin Kamal returned to take the last two wickets. Arshad Pervez batted splendidly to lift his side from the depths of 63 for 5.

In Faisalabad, the home side offered little to threaten the supremacy of the Karachi side who gave a solid team performance.

**Group C Final Table**

| | *P* | *W* | *L* | *D* | *Pts* |
|---|---|---|---|---|---|
| Lahore City Whites | 4 | 3 | — | 1 | 58 |
| Karachi Whites | 4 | 2 | — | 2 | 54 |
| Gujranwala | 4 | — | 2 | 2 | 28 |
| Sargodha | 4 | — | 1 | 3 | 25 |
| Faisalabad | 4 | — | 2 | 2 | 17 |

## Group D

### *5, 6 and 7 October 1983*

#### *at Pindi Club, Rawalpindi*

**Hazara** 200 (Kifayat Hussain 57, M. Rafiq Malik 4 for 62)
**Dera Ismail Khan** 39 (Shafiq Iqbal 4 for 6) and 103 (Rafat Nawaz 6 for 32)

*Hazara won by an innings and 78 runs*
*Hazara 16 pts, Dera Ismail Khan 4 pts*

### *6, 7 and 8 October 1983*

#### *at Services Ground, Peshawar*

**Peshawar** 161 (Abdul Wahab 5 for 58) and 218 for 7 dec (Aftab Ahmed 62 not out)
**Rawalpindi** 199 (Imtinan Zamir 58) and 66 for 6 (Zakir Khan 4 for 46)

*Match drawn*
*Rawalpindi 7 pts, Peshawar 4 pts*

Dera Ismail Khan, predictably the weakest side in the group, gave a dreadful performance in Rawalpindi. They had done well to bowl out Hazara in 68.1 overs, but then succumbed themselves in 24.5 overs for 39. Javed Chughtai, who batted for 76 minutes, was the only man to reach double figures. Following-on, they fared a little better at the second attempt with Shafiq Ahmed and Mohammad Irfan offering some resistance, but Rafat Nawaz finished with match figures of 9 for 45 and Hazara, having been dismissed for 220, found themselves innings victors.

Rawalpindi found conditions difficult in Peshawar and were happy to settle for a draw in the end.

### *9, 10 and 11 October 1983*

#### *at Jinnah Park, Sialkot*

**Lahore Division** 194 (Shahid Tanvir 59) and 129 (Zakir Khan 4 for 30)
**Peshawar** 133 and 191 for 9 (Abdur Rahim 87 not out, Shahid Tanvir 4 for 98)

*Peshawar won by 1 wicket*
*Peshawar 14 pts, Lahore Division 5 pts*

#### *at Pindi Club, Rawalpindi*

**Rawalpindi** 319 for 8 (Imtinan Zamir 57, Sabih Azhar 50 not out)
**Hazara** 79 (Abdul Wahab 5 for 41) and 75 (Mohammad Riaz 4 for 16)

*Rawalpindi won by an innings and 165 runs*
*Rawalpindi 18 pts, Hazara 4 pts*

A magnificent stand for the last wicket, with number eleven Waheed Khan scoring 31 not out, the second highest score, gave Peshawar a memorable victory in Sialkot. Lahore Division had led comfortably on the first innings and seemed set for victory, but Abdur Rahim batted heroically and at last found the necessary support in the unlikely form of Waheed who hit fiercely and helped to bring off the highly improbable.

There was a more predictable win for Rawalpindi who totally outclassed Hazara to take maximum points.

### *13, 14 and 15 October 1983*

***at Pindi Club, Rawalpindi***

**Lahore Division** 59 (Mohammad Riaz 7 for 20) and 118 (Mohammad Riaz 6 for 39)
**Rawalpindi** 203 for 5 dec (Masood Anwar 82, Mohammad Riaz 52, Raja Afaq 50 not out)

*Rawalpindi won by an innings and 26 runs*
*Rawalpindi 16 pts, Lahore Division 3 pts*

***at Services Ground, Peshawar***

**Dera Ismail Khan** 150 (Arif Khattak 59) and 79 (Aamer Mirza 4 for 18)
**Peshawar** 257 for 3 (Aamer Mirza 105 not out, Aftab Ahmed 51 not out)

*Peshawar won by an innings and 28 runs*
*Peshawar 18 pts, Dera Ismail Khan 2 pts*

On a doubtful wicket in Rawalpindi Lahore Division were bowled out in 31.4 overs after being put in to bat. The spin of Mohammad Riaz was quickly employed and he finished with the remarkable match figures of 13 for 59. In order to make up for time lost to rain, Rawalpindi batted briskly and declared before routing the Lahore side a second time.

In Peshawar, Dera Ismail Khan chose to bat on winning the toss and reached 150 for the only time in the season. Peshawar responded positively and declared as soon as Aamer Mirza reached his century. Needing 107 to avoid an innings defeat, Dera Ismail Khan lost 6 for 56 and slipped to another disaster.

### *18, 19 and 20 October 1983*

***at Services Ground, Peshawar***

**Rawalpindi** 406 for 8 dec (Masood Anwar 184, Imtinan Zamir 100, Arif Khattak 5 for 46)
**Dera Ismail Khan** 76 (Asif Afridi 4 for 18) and 120 (Mohammad Riaz 4 for 25, Raja Afaq 4 for 37)

*Rawalpindi won by an innings and 210 runs*
*Rawalpindi 18 pts, Dera Ismail Khan 4 pts*

***at Jinnah Park, Sialkot***

**Lahore Division** walk over
*v.* **Hazara**

*Lahore Division 14 pts, Hazara 0 pts*

Hazara failed to turn up in Sialkot and Lahore Division were awarded the match. In Peshawar, Rawalpindi, with Masood Anwar and Imtinan Zamir adding 209 for the third wicket, totally outplayed Dera Ismail Khan.

### *22, 23 and 24 October 1983*

***at Jinnah Park, Sialkot***

**Dera Ismail Khan** 74 (Shahid Tanvir 5 for 39, Aziz Malik 4 for 22) and 134 (Shahid Tanvir 4 for 47)
**Lahore Division** 252 for 5 dec (Sarfraz Azeem 109, Nadeem A. Lodhi 76)

*Lahore Division won by an innings and 44 runs*
*Lahore Division 18 pts, Dera Ismail Khan 3 pts*

***at Services Ground, Peshawar***

**Peshawar** 265 for 9 dec (Zakir Khan 100 not out) and 65 for 0
**Hazara** 111 (Iqbal Butt 7 for 30) and 217 (Nasim Fazal 97 not out, Iqbal Butt 5 for 61)

*Peshawar won by 10 wickets*
*Peshawar 18 pts, Hazara 4 pts*

Dera Ismail Khan suffered their fourth innings defeat in four matches when they fell to the fine bowling of Shahid Tanvir and an accomplished century by Sarfraz Azeem. He and Nadeem Ahmed Lodhi added 132 for the fourth wicket.

Some splendid seam bowling by Iqbal Butt, match figures of 12 for 91, sent Hazara tumbling to defeat in Peshawar. Peshawar's earlier hero was Zakir Khan. He came in at 93 for 7 and scored a blistering hundred. Faridoon Khan joined him in an unbeaten last wicket stand of 113, but Peshawar were helped by some indifferent fielding and 46 extras.

**Group D Final Table**

| | *P* | *W* | *L* | *D* | *Pts* |
|---|---|---|---|---|---|
| Rawalpindi | 4 | 3 | — | 1 | 59 |
| Peshawar | 4 | 3 | — | 1 | 54 |
| Lahore Division | 4 | 2 | 2 | — | 40 |
| Hazara | 4 | 1 | 3 | — | 24 |
| Dera Ismail Khan | 4 | — | 4 | — | 13 |

**Semi-Finals**

### 27, 28, 29 and 30 October 1983

**at National Stadium, Karachi**

**Karachi Blues** 312 for 9 (Haroon Rashid 83, Iqbal Sikander 78, Sikhander Bakht 52, Mohinder Kumar 4 for 80, Saleem Jaffer 4 for 99) and 395 for 3 dec (Iqtidar Ali 200 not out, Shoaib Mohammad 94, Ejaz Faqih 78)
**Karachi Greens** 197 (Kamal Najamuddin 69) and 231 for 6 (Zafar Ali 101 not out)

*Match drawn*
*Karachi Blues won on first innings*

***at Qaddafi Stadium, Lahore***

**Lahore City Whites** 292 for 8 (Masood Iqbal 68 not out) and 295 (Shafiq Ahmed 91, Mohammad Riaz 4 for 93)
**Rawalpindi** 186 (Afzaal Butt 6 for 55, Mohsin Kamal 4 for 39) and 80 for 4

*Match drawn*
*Lahore City Whites won on first innings*

Karachi Blues were 27 for 4 and 84 for 5 before Haroon Rashid and Iqbal Sikander effected a recovery with a stand of 127. Sikhander Bakht then hit lustily and Blues reached a commendable 312 in their 85 overs. The Greens passed 100 with only two wickets down, but they lost their last 8 wickets

*Sarfraz Nawaz, captain of Lahore City Whites, bowled splendidly in the Patron's Final but could not save his side from defeat. (Adrian Murrell)*

for 92 runs and, with such a first innings supremacy, it was unlikely that Karachi Blues would be denied a place in the final. The second innings was highlighted by an opening stand of 209 between Iqtidar Ali and Shoaib Mohammad, and Iqtidar Ali went on to complete 200 which included a six and nineteen fours. It was a remarkable innings in that in three other visits to the crease in the tournament, Iqtidar could muster only 11 runs.

There was a match of similar pattern in Lahore where an even batting display took the City Whites to 292 in 85 overs after they had been put in. Although Sarfraz Nawaz was wicketless from his 20 overs, the seam bowling of Afzaal Butt and Mohsin Kamal proved too much for Rawalpindi and gave Lahore City Whites a considerable first innings advantage which again proved decisive.

## The Final

As was written in *The Pakistan Cricketer* by the distinguished commentator on the game, Gul Hameed Bhatti, 'It is useless to mention that facilities for the players during the Patron's competition were primitive. At places there wasn't even running water, or soap and towels. So much so that many prominent players of the Karachi team refused to travel to Lahore for the final because they would have had to travel third-class by train and stay in some seedy hotel.' The other blight on the final was that, as it was televised live, the attendance was poor.

In the event, a low-scoring match provided a thrilling contest with Karachi Blues snatching a narrow victory. Karachi won the toss and asked Lahore to bat. The decision was rewarded when the City Whites were bowled out for 153

### B.C.C.P. PATRON'S TROPHY FINAL – LAHORE CITY WHITES *v.* KARACHI BLUES
2, 3, 4 and 5 November 1983 at Qaddafi Stadium, Lahore

**LAHORE CITY WHITES**

| | FIRST INNINGS | | SECOND INNINGS | |
|---|---|---|---|---|
| Abdul Sami | c Anil, b Jalal | 16 | c Iqbal, b Jalal | 0 |
| Saadat Ali | c Siddiq, b Kamal | 42 | lbw, b Jalal | 10 |
| Shafiq Ahmed | b Nadeem | 4 | c Iqbal, b Jalal | 44 |
| Rameez Raja | c Anil, b Kamal | 6 | b Jalal | 5 |
| Ali Zia | c Nadeem, b Kamal | 12 | b Nadeem | 41 |
| Naved Anjum | c Iqtidar, b Iqbal | 7 | c Ejaz, b Nadeem | 19 |
| Mansoor Rana | c Anil, b Kamal | 5 | lbw, b Jalal | 0 |
| Masood Iqbal* | c Shoaib, b Iqbal | 7 | b Nadeem | 7 |
| Sarfraz Nawaz† | c Nadeem, b Kamal | 9 | run out | 3 |
| Afzaal Butt | c Iqbal, b Jalal | 18 | c Anil, b Nadeem | 0 |
| Mohsin Kamal | not out | 16 | not out | 2 |
| Extras | b 1, lb 4, nb 6 | 11 | b 1, lb 1, w 1, nb 2 | 5 |
| | | 153 | | 146 |

| | O | M | R | W | O | M | R | W |
|---|---|---|---|---|---|---|---|---|
| Jalal-ud-Din | 16.4 | 4 | 40 | 2 | 22 | 2 | 79 | 5 |
| Nadeem Yousuf | 12 | 1 | 29 | 1 | 15.1 | 5 | 33 | 4 |
| Iqbal Sikander | 20 | 7 | 39 | 2 | 6 | 1 | 13 | — |
| Kamal Merchant | 18 | 8 | 34 | 5 | 5 | 2 | 14 | — |
| Tauseef Ahmed | | | | | 1 | — | 2 | — |

FALL OF WICKETS
1- 42, 2- 47, 3- 73, 4- 74, 5- 91, 6- 95, 7- 100, 8- 113, 9- 117
1- 0, 2- 29, 3- 31, 4- 54, 5- 101, 6- 117, 7- 135, 8- 144, 9- 144

**KARACHI BLUES**

| | FIRST INNINGS | | SECOND INNINGS | |
|---|---|---|---|---|
| Shoaib Mohammad | lbw, b Sarfraz | 11 | b Naved | 49 |
| Siddiq Patni | c Masood, b Sarfraz | 18 | b Afzaal | 0 |
| Iqtidar Ali | lbw, b Afzaal | 5 | c Masood, b Sarfraz | 4 |
| Mahmood Rashid | b Sarfraz | 23 | c Ali, b Mohsin | 9 |
| Ejaz Faqih† | lbw, b Mohsin | 3 | c Masood, b Mohsin | 13 |
| Anil Dalpat* | lbw, b Sarfraz | 12 | lbw, b Mohsin | 2 |
| Iqbal Sikander | c Masood, b Afzaal | 1 | not out | 40 |
| Nadeem Yousuf | c and b Afzaal | 16 | c Shafiq, b Naved | 27 |
| Kamal Merchant | lbw, b Afzaal | 0 | not out | 11 |
| Jalal-ud-Din | lbw, b Afzaal | 0 | | |
| Tauseef Ahmed | not out | 9 | | |
| Extras | b 7, lb 4, w 3, nb 13 | 27 | b 7, lb 3, w 4, nb 8 | 22 |
| | | 125 | (for 7 wkts) | 177 |

| | O | M | R | W | O | M | R | W |
|---|---|---|---|---|---|---|---|---|
| Afzaal Butt | 18.4 | 9 | 31 | 5 | 20 | 6 | 37 | 1 |
| Sarfraz Nawaz | 23 | 11 | 42 | 4 | 28 | 10 | 37 | 1 |
| Mohsin Kamal | 10 | 3 | 25 | 1 | 20 | 3 | 51 | 3 |
| Naved Anjum | | | | | 8.5 | 2 | 30 | 2 |

FALL OF WICKETS
1- 31, 2- 36, 3- 71, 4- 75, 5- 92, 6- 93, 7- 103, 8- 103, 9- 105
1- 2, 2- 19, 3- 42, 4- 47, 5- 71, 6- 103, 7- 144

**Karachi Blues won by 3 wickets**

in 66.4 overs, only Saadat Ali, with a typically pugnacious 42, offering serious resistance.

Karachi Blues began steadily, but the relentless seam attack of Afzaal, Sarfraz and Mohsin Kamal proved too much for them and they lost their last 9 wickets for 94.

It was again the seam bowlers who triumphed as Jalal-ud-Din and Nadeem Yousuf gnawed away at the Lahore batting to give Karachi Blues a hope of victory. It seemed a very slim hope when, needing the highest score of the match, they lost 6 wickets for 71 runs, but Iqbal Sikander, who had batted consistently well throughout the competition after his barren trip to India, found a stable partner in Nadeem Yousuf and then in Kamal Merchant and an exciting victory was achieved.

## Quaid-e-Azam Trophy

The Quaid-e-Azam Trophy, Pakistan's leading national competition, was open only to commercial and departmental teams. H.B.F.C. and P.A.C.O. qualified for the competition as they were finalists in the B.C.C.P. Patron's Trophy in 1982–83 and State Bank were added after winning a qualifying non-first-class tournament.

***19, 20, 21 and 22 November 1983***

***at L.C.C.A. Ground, Lahore***

**Habib Bank** 215 (Aslam Qureshi 54, Shahid Mahboob 4 for 74) and 378 for 4 dec (Azhar Khan 103 not out, Saleem Malik 83, Agha Zahid 81, Tehsin Javed 62 not out)
**P.A.C.O.** 267 (Shaukat Mirza 137 not out) and 199 for 2 (Shaukat Mirza 70 not out, Tanvir Ahmed 68 not out)
*Match drawn*

***at Iqbal Stadium, Faisalabad***

**Allied Bank** 294 (Salman Qizilbash 73, Feroze Najamuddin 71, Naved Anjum 6 for 67, Pervez Shah 4 for 63) and 255 (Rameez Raja 73, Pervez Shah 5 for 67, Hafeez-ur-Rehman 4 for 44)
**Railways** 342 for 8 (Naved Anjum 116, Musleh-ud-Din 97, Manzoor Elahi 50, Raees-ur-Rehman 6 for 82) and 175 for 9 (Musleh-ud-Din 52, Jalal-ud-Din 4 for 58)
*Match drawn*

***at Niaz Stadium, Hyderabad***

**H.B.F.C.** 267 for 9 (Tariq Alam 60) and 203 (Tahir Rasheed 64, Afzaal Butt 6 for 70)
**National Bank** 255 (Ali Zia 81, Saleem Pervez 60, Tariq Wahab 4 for 87) and 218 for 5 (Sajid Ali 60)
*National Bank won by 5 wickets*

The match in Lahore saw some remarkable recoveries. Habib Bank, having been put in to bat, were 98 for 7 before Aslam Qureshi and the tail wagged to very good effect. In reply, P.A.C.O. were 10 for 2 and 51 for 3, but Shaukat Mirza and Shahid Mahboob added 111, a stand completely dominated by Shaukat. Habib scored heavily in their second innings and a draw become inevitable.

Splendid all-round cricket by Naved Anjum could not bring victory to Railways. Following his century, there was an eighth wicket stand of 100 between Manzoor Elahi and Musleh-ud-Din who, unfortunately, was run out three short of his hundred. Needing 208 in as many minutes to win the match, Railways made a bold bid, but wickets tumbled to Jalal-ud-Din and they were pleased to hang on for a draw when the ninth wicket fell at the end of the fifty-fourth over.

National Bank, runners-up in 1982–83, made a positive start in their attempt to reclaim the title when they came back from a small first innings deficit to beat H.B.F.C. with ease. They owed much to some fine bowling from Afzaal Butt who brought his season's tally to 32 wickets. Needing 216 for victory, National Bank were given a fine start by Mohammad Jamil, promoted to opener, and Sajid Ali who put on 61 and consistent batting saw the win easily accomplished.

***25, 27, 28 and 29 November 1983***

***at National Stadium, Karachi***

**State Bank** 114 (Ehtesham-ud-Din 4 for 19) and 243 (Tariq Javed 124, Ehtesham-ud-Din 8 for 61)
**United Bank** 241 for 6 (Shafiq Ahmed 124) and 117 for 1 (Siddiq Patni 52 not out)
*United Bank won by 9 wickets*

***at Niaz Stadium, Hyderabad***

**Muslim Commercial Bank** 189 (Babar Basharat 75, Kazim Mehdi 4 for 57) and 348 for 9 dec (Ejaz Faqih 81, Azmut Rana 55, Asif Ali 50 not out, Tariq Wahab 5 for 90)
**H.B.F.C.** 264 for 9 (Tahir Rasheed 69 not out, Munir-ul-Haq 53) and 205 for 6 (Noor-ul-Qamar 62)
*Match drawn*

***at Qaddafi Stadium, Lahore***

**Pakistan International Airlines** 259 for 6 (Rashid Israr 77 not

*Mohsin Kamal, Lahore City and Allied Bank. His splendid bowling in the Patron's and Quaid-e-Azam Trophies earned him a Test debut against England. (Adrian Murrell)*

out, Naeem Ahmed 64) and 382 for 8 dec (Shoaib Mohammad 111, Asif Mohammad 73, Rizwan-uz-Zaman 58, Anil Dalpat 52 not out, Liaqat Ali 5 for 122)
**Habib Bank** 303 for 4 (Arshad Pervez 144 not out, Sultan Rana 88) and 52 for 2

*Match drawn*

***at Iqbal Stadium, Faisalabad***

**National Bank** 333 for 7 (Alia Zia 93, Asad Rauf 53) and 147 for 6 (Shoain Habib 4 for 29)
**Allied Bank** 176 (Zafar Ahmed 53 not out) and 302 (Rameez Raja 149)

*National Bank won by 4 wickets*

***at L.C.C.A. Ground, Lahore***

**Railways** 144 (Ghaffar Kazmi 4 for 54) and 200 (Abdus Sami 55, Shahid Mahboob 6 for 54)
**P.A.C.O.** 143 and 202 for 9 (Naved Anjum 4 for 51)

*P.A.C.O. won by 1 wicket*

State Bank's debut in the competition proved an unhappy one as Shafiq Ahmed, with ten fours in his 124, and the veteran medium-pace bowler Ehtesham-ud-Din put United Bank in a commanding position. Once achieved, the command was never relinquished and Siddiq Patni and Haroon Rashid had no difficulty in stroking them to victory.

In Hyderabad, Muslim Commercial Bank struggled against H.B.F.C. in the opening stages of the game. A solid batting performance in the second innings put the match beyond H.B.F.C.'s reach, but they could certainly claim a moral victory.

A fourth wicket stand of 106 between Arshad Pervez and Sultan Rana took Habib Bank into the lead against P.I.A., but an opening stand of 114 by Shoaib Mohammad, enhancing his claim for a Test place with an assured century, and Rizwan-uz-Zaman nullified the advantage that the Bank side had achieved and, inevitably, the game was drawn.

In Lahore, National Bank won their second match of the season and so took the lead in the embryo competition. Consistent batting was followed by a highly professional bowling performance and Allied Bank were forced to follow-on. A superb century from Rameez Raja brought them back into the game, but the leaders were nudged to a four-wicket win.

P.A.C.O. won a thrilling game in Lahore. One run behind on the first innings, they owed much to Shahid Mahboob. He had match figures of 9 for 90 and then, after P.A.C.O. had lost 9 for 171, he engaged in a last wicket stand of 31 with Arshad Nawaz which brought a fine victory.

### *1, 2, 3 and 4 December 1983*

***at Bagh-e-Jinnah Ground, Lahore***

**Habib Bank** 371 for 4 (Saleem Malik 132, Arshad Pervez 131) and 299 for 7 dec (Azhar Khan 109, Anwar Miandad 65, Ali Ahmed 4 for 120)
**H.B.F.C.** 281 (Saadat Ali 73, Tahir Rasheed 67, Saleem Malik 5 for 36) and 246 for 6 (Raees Ahmed 119 not out)

*Match drawn*

***at Punjab University, Lahore***

**Allied Bank** 249 for 6 (Salman Qizilbash 73, Rameez Raja 71) and 293 for 5 dec (Iqtidar Ali 76, Talat Masood 75, Salim Yousuf 69, Salman Qizilbash 53)
**State Bank** 255 (Saleem Mohiuddin, Jalal-ud-Din 4 for 100) and 143 (Jalal-ud-Din 6 for 49, Shoaib Habib 4 for 36)

*Allied Bank won by 144 runs*

***at Bahawal Stadium, Bahawalpur***

**Muslim Commercial Bank** 288 (Anwar-ul-Haq 64, Shahid Butt 4 for 93) and 273 (Mohiuddin Khan 57, Tauseef Ahmed 5 for 90)
**United Bank** 237 for 9 dec (Shafiq Ahmed 67, Mahmood Rasheed 54, Ejaz Faqih 4 for 75) and 135 for 4

*Match drawn*

***at Qaddafi Stadium, Lahore***

**Pakistan International Airlines** 297 for 6 (Naeem Ahmed 63, Rizwan-uz-Zaman 52, Iqbal Sikander 51) and 254 for 7 dec (Iqbal Sikander 111 not out, Asif Mohammad 54)
**P.A.C.O.** 228 (Shaukat Mirza 70) and 260 for 8 (Shaukat Mirza 77, Hasan Jamil 5 for 97)

*Match drawn*

***at Jinnah Park, Sialkot***

**National Bank** 100 (Shahid Pervez 4 for 26) and 358 for 9 dec (Sajid Ali 146, Saleem Pervez 105)
**Railways** 234 for 9 (Abdus Sami 54, Iqbal Qasim 4 for 63) and 132 (Naved Anjum 51, Iqbal Qasim 5 for 42)

*National Bank won by 92 runs*

Arshad Pervez and Saleem Malik joined in a second wicket stand of 259 to take Habib Bank to an unassailable position against H.B.F.C. The newcomers fought well, but Saleem Malik continued with his Man of the Match performance with 5 of the last 7 wickets which fell for 53 runs. There was more heavy scoring from the Bank side, but the placid wicket had ensured a draw.

It was the bowling of Jalal-ud-Din which was the dominant factor in bringing about the downfall of State Bank. The first innings had ended with honours even, but, set 288 to win, State Bank collapsed before the pace man and the spin of Shoaib Habib and the last 9 wickets fell for 63. Jalal-ud-Din returned match figures of 10 for 149.

A rather dour game at Bahawalpur resulted in stalemate and, at the Qaddafi Stadium, P.A.C.O. hung on for a draw, Ghaffar Kazmi and Arshad Nawaz holding out for some time when P.I.A. looked set for victory.

National Bank were shot out by a good all-round bowling performance at Sialkot and Railways took a formidable first innings lead with solid contributions from the tail. 134 in arrears and 30 for 1 in their second innings, National Bank were saved by a stand of 248 between Sajid Ali and Saleem Pervez. Asked to make 225 to win, Railways, dispirited, lost 3 for 28 and Iqbal Qasim took over to give National their third win. They already looked destined to be champions.

### *7, 8, 9 and 10 December 1983*

***at Punjab University, Lahore***

**United Bank** 282 (Sadiq Mohammad 124, Raees Ahmed 4 for 50, Ali Ahmed 4 for 97) and 236 (Haroon Rashid 50, Raees Ahmed 5 for 51)
**H.B.F.C.** 288 for 8 (Ijaz Ahmed 82, Tariq Alam 67 not out, Rafat Alam 50, Ehtesham-ud-Din 4 for 79) and 232 for 5 (Saadat Ali 99, Sagheer Abbas 63 not out)

*H.B.F.C. won by 5 wickets*

***at Qaddafi Stadium, Lahore***

**Allied Bank** 311 for 4 (Rameez Raja 149, Iqtidar Ali 72, Saleem Yousuf 59 not out) and 298 (Iqtidar Ali 80, Rameez Raja 68, Jamshed Hussain 4 for 85)
**Habib Bank** 359 for 6 dec (Azhar Khan 155, Sultan Rana 132, Jalal-ud-Din 4 for 92) and 156 for 6 (Jalal-ud-Din 5 for 76)

*Match drawn*

***at Bahawal Stadium, Bahawalpur***

**Pakistan International Airlines** 215 for 8 (Asif Mohammad 57, Ejaz Faqih 6 for 76) and 223 (Iqbal Sikander 69, Hasan Jamil 50, Ilyas Khan 5 for 58, Mohiuddin Khan 4 for 49.
**Muslim Commercial Bank** 201 (Anwar-ul-Haq 80, Asif Ali 65, Iqbal Sikander 5 for 74) and 213 (Zahid Ahmed 5 for 39)

*Pakistan International Airlines won by 24 runs*

***at L.C.C.A. Ground, Lahore***

**National Bank** 307 for 8 (Sajid Ali 97, Afzaal Ahmed 63, Saleem Pervez 51, Arshad Nawaz 4 for 78, Ghaffar Kazmi 4 for 96) and 360 for 9 dec (Sajid Ali 141, Ali Zia 111, Asad Rauf 56, Yahya Toor 5 for 48)
**P.A.C.O.** 166 (Iqbal Qasim 5 for 48, Ali Zia 4 for 52) and 422 (Tanvir Ahmed 151, Moin Mumtaz 126, Qaiser Hussain 60 not out, Iqbal Qasim 4 for 109)

*National Bank won by 79 runs*

***at Jinnah Park, Sialkot***

**Railways** 227 (Mohammad Arif snr 4 for 84) and 151 (Mansoor Rana 65, Aziz Ahmed 5 for 49)
**State Bank** 134 (Naved Anjum 5 for 42) and 201 (Naved Anjum 4 for 59)

*Railways won by 43 runs*

H.B.F.C. won their first match in the tournament when, in spite of a century by the evergreen Sadiq Mohammad, they beat United Bank by 5 wickets. They owed much to the bowling of Raees and to the virulent batting of Saadat Ali who played a brilliant innings of 99 to make a victory possible.

In a high-scoring game in the Qaddafi Stadium, Rameez Raja played two exciting innings, Azhar Khan and Sultan Rana shared a 4th wicket stand of 274 and Jalal-ud-Din once more made one wonder why the Test selectors had turned their backs on him.

P.I.A. squeezed an exciting victory over Muslim Commercial Bank, Iqbal Sikander having a fine all-round match with 8 wickets for 167.

The dominance of National Bank continued and they moved further ahead at the top of the table with their fourth win in as many matches. Determined batting throughout the order and excellent spin bowling by Iqbal Qasim and Ali Zia gave them a first innings lead of 141 and when Ali Zia followed his bowling feat with a fine century, P.A.C.O. were left to make 502 to win, a seemingly impossible task. They were 96 for 3 before Tanvir Ahmed and Moin Mumtaz joined in a stand of 172. There followed another brave innings by Qaiser Hussain and, remarkably, P.A.C.O. came within 80 runs of their target, the most honourable defeat of the season.

A low-scoring game at Sialkot saw Naved Anjum again bowl well and Railways won a good victory over the luckless State Bank side.

*Saleem Malik. He was in magnificent form for Habib Bank. (Adrian Murrell)*

***13, 14, 15 and 16 December 1983***

***at Iqbal Stadium, Faisalabad***

**P.A.C.O.** 184 (Ghaffar Kazmi 56 not out, Jalal-ud-Din 5 for 97, Raees-ur-Rehman 4 for 37) and 315 (Ghaffar Kazmi 131, Moin Mumtaz 92, Raees-ur-Rehman 5 for 90, Jalal-ud-Din 5 for 108)
**Allied Bank** 303 for 6 dec (Iqtidar Ali 104, Rameez Raja 63, Salman Qizilbash 58, Shahid Mahboob 4 for 122) and 199 for 4 (Iqtidar Ali 57 not out)

*Allied Bank won by 6 wickets*

***at Bahawal Stadium, Bahawalpur***

**Habib Bank** 262 (Sultan Rana 112, Jamshed Hussain 68, Ejaz Faqih 6 for 72) and 242 (Azhar Khan 79, Ilyas Khan 4 for 55)
**Muslim Commercial Bank** 212 (Mohiuddin Khan 51, Ejaz Faqih 50, Abdur Raqeeb 4 for 62) and 145 for 3

*Match drawn*

***at Punjab University, Lahore***

**P.I.A.** 242 (Naeem Ahmed 56, Shahid Mohammad 50, Shahid Butt 4 for 68) and 132 (Ehtesham-ud-Din 4 for 73)
**United Bank** 286 for 8 (Sadiq Mohammad 117, Shafiq Ahmed 62, Iqbal Sikander 4 for 101) and 89 for 8 (Hasan Jamil 5 for 43)

*United Bank won by 2 wickets*

***at Qaddafi Stadium, Lahore***

**Railways** 107 (Tariq Wahab 7 for 49) and 437 (Mansoor Rana 121, Talat Mirza 89, Naved Anjum 64, Munawwar Javed 57, Raees Ahmed 4 for 94)
**H.B.F.C.** 186 (Saadat Ali 90, Navad Anjum 4 for 54) and 250 (Saadat Ali 125)

*Railways won by 108 runs*

*at L.C.C.A. Ground, Lahore*

**National Bank** 313 for 6 (Sajid Ali 111, Asad Rauf 73, Ali Zia 62)
**State Bank** 151 and 161 (Afzaal Butt 7 for 104)

*National Bank won by an innings and 1 run*

With their fifth successive win, National Bank moved into an almost impregnable position at the top of the table. Their innings was founded on a third wicket stand of 138 between opener Sajid Ali and Asad Rauf. State Bank lost Tariq Javed without a run scored and later had Imtiaz Ahmed forced to retire hurt without scoring and unable to bat in the second innings. They lost their last five wickets for 35 and had to follow-on. Afzaal Butt took the first six second innings wickets to fall and bowled unchanged to take 7 for 104 in 18 overs, runs coming cheaply as men clustered round the bat.

United Bank were indebted to a second wicket stand of 125 between Sadiq Mohammad and Shafiq Ahmed for the first innings lead. A balanced attack accounted for P.I.A. cheaply when they batted again, but United Bank, needing only 89 to win at three an over, found themselves in dreadful trouble at 37 for 5 and 67 for 8. The collapse was caused by Hassan Jamil, who had not bowled in the first innings, and Raja Akbar. At last Shafiq Ahmed, who only batted with sense, found a dependable partner in Saud Khan and the pair took United Bank to victory, Shafiq finishing on 34 not out.

Habib Bank recovered from 82 for 7 to 262 thanks mainly to an eighth wicket stand of 138 between Jamshed Hussain and Sultan Rana. Muslim Commercial Bank, too, had their troubles and lost half their wickets for 59, but solid batting at the close of the innings took them to within 50 of their opponents. Habib Bank batted dreadfully slowly in their second innings, Ejaz Faqih taking 3 for 84 in 53 overs, and the game meandered to a draw.

P.A.C.O. seemed to be facing an innings defeat when, 119 behind on the first innings, they slipped to 91 for 7 in their second. Coming in at number 9, Ghaffar Kazmi hit 131 and shared an eighth wicket stand of 197 with Moin Mumtaz. It was a glorious bid to save the game, but Allied Bank were eventual winners.

Railways made a remarkable recovery to beat H.B.F.C. Bowled out in 42.4 overs, Tariq Wahab bowling unchanged, they trailed by 79 on the first innings, but, inspired by Mansoor Rana's century, they reached 437 in their second innings with some even batting. Accurate and determined bowling and fielding then took them to a fine victory in spite of Saadat Ali's second accomplished knock of the match.

### *19, 20, 21 and 22 December 1983*

*at L.C.C.A. Ground, Lahore*

**H.B.F.C.** 147 (Naeem Ahmed 5 for 54, Aziz Ahmed 4 for 34) and 358 (Saadat Ali 119, Noor-ul-Qamar 77)
**State Bank** 224 (Saleem Mohiuddin 64, Mohammad Arif snr 58, Ali Ahmed 6 for 62) and 161 (Ali Ahmed 4 for 54)

*H.B.F.C. won by 120 runs*

*at Qaddafi Stadium, Lahore*

**Habib Bank** 160 (Afzaal Butt 5 for 65) and 283 (Tehsin Javed 76, Sultan Rana 56, Arshad Pervez 54, Anwar Khan 5 for 65, Jahanzeb Khan 4 for 91)
**National Bank** 258 (Saleem Pervez 117, Aslam Qureshi 4 for 55) and 70 for 6 (Jamshed Hussain 4 for 39)

*Match drawn*

*at Jinnah Park, Sialkot*

**Muslim Commercial Bank** 229 (Asif Ali 74, Azmat Rana 56) and 238 (Azmat Rana 71)
**Railways** 149 (Talat Mirza 64, Ejaz Faqih 6 for 42) and 318 (Manzoor Elahi 53, Naved Anjum 51, Ilyas Khan 4 for 58)

*Match tied*

*at Bahawal Stadium, Bahawalpur*

**Pakistan International Airlines** 263 for 8 (Asif Mohammad 56, Iqbal Sikander 56, Amin Lakhani 5 for 111) and 222 for 8 dec (Shoaib Mohammad 65)
**Allied Bank** 126 (Saleem Yousuf 51) and 212 (Amin Lakhani 54 not out, Salman Qizilbash 54, Iqbal Sikander 6 for 75, Zahid Ahmed 4 for 71)

*Pakistan International Airlines won by 147 runs*

*at Sahiwal Stadium, Sahiwal*

**United Bank** 282 (Shafiq Mohammad 90, Sadiq Mohammad 80, Shahid Mahboob 5 for 76) and 355 (Shafiq Ahmed 125, Sadiq Mohammad 99, Arshad Nawaz 6 for 85)
**P.A.C.O.** 150 (Tauseef Ahmed 5 for 38) and 113 (Shahid Aziz 6 for 29)

*United Bank won by 374 runs*

United Bank reasserted their challenge to retain the Quaid-e-Azam Trophy when they overwhelmed P.A.C.O. in Sahiwal. Second wicket stands of 82 and 147 by Sadiq Mohammad and Shafiq Ahmed provided the substance of each United Bank innings and the bowling of Shahid Aziz (9 for 60) and Tauseef Ahmed (8 for 90) was too much for P.A.C.O.

P.I.A. gave a solid team performance to beat Allied Bank, Iqbal Sikander having a good all-round match, and H.B.F.C., with Saadat Ali again in inspiring form, came from behind to beat State Bank who themselves had recovered from 6 for 3 in their first innings, Saleem Ahmed and Mohammad Arif snr adding 112 for the ninth wicket.

Needing ten runs an over to win, National Bank ran into their first trouble of the season as, in the rush, wickets tumbled and they had to settle for a draw against Habib Bank.

The great excitement, however, was at Sialkot. Railways staged another of their sensational recoveries. They trailed by 80 runs on the first innings and when Muslim Commercial Bank reached 238 in their second innings and had a day in which to bowl out Railways it seemed that the Bank must win. Railways batted with determination and consistency in their effort to make 319 to win, but the ninth wicket fell at 298 and wicket-keeper Zulqarnian joined Haroon Rashid. They edged the score closer and closer, but, with the scores level, Ejaz Faqih bowled Zulqarnian with the fifth ball of his forty-first over and the match was tied.

### *25, 26, 27 and 28 December 1983*

*at Sahiwal Stadium, Sahiwal*

**P.A.C.O.** 312 for 7 (Qaiser Hussain 103 not out, Ghaffar Kazmi 74) and 415 for 5 (Qaiser Hussain 129 not out, Yahya Toor 101 not out, Tanvir Ahmed 56)
**Muslim Commercial Bank** 321 for 6 dec (Asif Ali 93, Ejaz Faqih 84 not out, Babar Basharat 73, Shahid Mahboob 4 for 93)

*Match drawn*

*at Bahawal Stadium, Bahawalpur*

**Pakistan International Airlines** 257 for 5 (Shoaib Mohammad

103 not out, Shahid Mohammad 58) and 275 for 5 dec (Rizwan-uz-Zaman 56, Asif Mohammad 54, Naeem Ahmed 52 not out)
**State Bank** 150 (Iqbal Sikander 6 for 40) and 201 (Mohammad Arif snr 50)

*Pakistan International Airlines won by 181 runs*

***at Jinnah Park, Sialkot***

**Allied Bank** 206 (Saleem Yousuf 103) and 220 (Rameez Raja 61)
**H.B.F.C.** 266 for 6 dec (Munir-ul-Haq 100 not out, Rafat Alam 69) and 161 for 2 (Saadat Ali 87 not out)

*H.B.F.C. won by 8 wickets*

***at Qaddafi Stadium, Lahore***

**Railways** 71 (Atiq-ur-Rehman 5 for 49) and 143 (Liaqat Ali 4 for 51, Atiq-ur-Rehman 4 for 64)
**Habib Bank** 276 (Azhar Khan 55, Pervez Shah 5 for 63, Naved Anjum 5 for 94)

*Habib Bank won by an innings and 62 runs*

***26, 27, 28 and 29 December 1983***

***at Punjab University, Lahore***

**National Bank** 285 for 9 (Ali Zia 128) and 241 (Shahid Butt 6 for 104)
**United Bank** 266 (Mahmood Rasheed 116 not out, Alia 5 for 81) and 262 for 6 (Siddiq Patni 89, Mahmood Rasheed 53)

*United Bank won by 4 wickets*

United Bank closed the gap on National Bank when they inflicted the first defeat of the season on the leaders. National batted solidly and bowled well enough to take a narrow first innings lead in spite of Mahmood Rasheed's fine century which included two sixes and ten fours. Again National batted consistently, but United Bank, in their quest for victory, were inspired by a third wicket stand of 103 between Sadiq Patni, the sheet anchor, and Mahmood Rasheed who hit seven fours in his sparkling 53. Then Haroon Rashid completed the work with a mature 49 not out after three wickets had fallen for 10 runs.

Shoaib Mohammad brought himself a step closer to the Test side with another elegant hundred as P.I.A. outplayed State Bank who nestled at the bottom of the table. H.B.F.C., the opening partnership of Munir-ul-Haq and Saadat Ali again prospering, always had the better of the match in Sialkot in spite of Saleem Yousuf's excellent century.

For once Railways could not manage a recovery. On a doubtful wicket they were routed by Atiq-ur-Rehman, who had match figures of 9 for 113 and Liaqat Ali, 6 for 60. Habib Bank batted with a discipline and sense which Railways could not match.

In Sahiwal a high-scoring game ended inevitably in a draw; Ejaz Faqih bowled 107 overs in the match and took 5 for 261.

***31 December 1983, 1, 2 and 3 January 1984***

***at Qaddafi Stadium, Lahore***

**National Bank** 338 for 7 (Ijaz Ahmed 74, Taslim Arif 60 not out, Saleem Pervez 59, Sajid Ali 56, Ejaz Faqih 4 for 109) and 266 for 8 dec (Mohammad Jamil 77, Sajid Ali 60, Ilyas Khan 4 for 62)
**Muslim Commercial Bank** 196 (Afzaal Butt 5 for 70, Anwar Khan 4 for 29) and 322 (Ejaz Faqih 68, Azmat Rana 59, Mohiuddin Khan 51, Anwar-ul-Haq 50, Afzaal Butt 7 for 134)

*National Bank won by 86 runs*

***at Jinnah Park, Sialkot***

**Habib Bank** 261 (Arshad Pervez 111, Tauseef Ahmed 4 for 76) and 184 (Agha Zahid 65, Tehsin Javed 50, Shahid Aziz 7 for 44)
**United Bank** 286 for 5 (Shafiq Ahmed 94 not out, Sadiq Mohammad 53, Haroon Rashid 53, Azhar Khan 5 for 101) and 149 (Liaqat Ali 7 for 62)

*Habib Bank won by 10 runs*

***at Bahawal Stadium, Bahawalpur***

**State Bank** 222 for 9 (Ahsan Jawwad 77 not out) and 177 (Tariq Javed 72, Shahid Mahboob 7 for 66)
**P.A.C.O.** 330 for 8 (Shaukat Mirza 112 not out, Shahid Mahboob 56) and 70 for 2

*P.A.C.O. won by 8 wickets*

***at National Stadium, Karachi***

**Pakistan International Airlines** 264 for 7 (Iqbal Sikander 86, Shahid Mohammad 63) and 271 for 5 dec (Rizwan-uz-Zaman 139 not out, Shoaib Mohammad 78, Manzoor Elahi 4 for 56)
**Railways** 252 for 9 (Naved Anjum 52, Zakir Butt 50, Zahid Ahmed 4 for 57) and 156 for 4 (Abdus Sami 61 not out, Naved Anjum 54 not out)

*Match drawn*

National Bank's leadership of the Quaid-e-Azam Trophy became firmer than ever when, beating Muslim Commercial Bank in a tense game in Lahore, they increased their lead as United Bank slipped to defeat by a narrow margin in Sialkot. United Bank had seemed to have taken a grip on the game with good first innings batting and even better bowling by Shahid Aziz. Habib Bank found their own hero, however, in former Test opening bowler Liaqat Ali who bowled Shahid Butt when United Bank were still 11 short of their target.

State Bank crashed to defeat yet again as Shahid Mahboob had match figures of 10 for 129. In Karachi there was some good batting and bowling, but the match ended in stalemate.

***5, 6, 7 and 8 January 1984***

***at Bagh-e-Jinnah Ground, Lahore***

**National Bank** 323 (Ali Zia 130, Sajid Ali 97, Zahid Ahmed 4 for 93) and 385 (Taslim Arif 125, Saleem Pervez 80, Ijaz Ahmed 67 not out, Zahid Ahmed 4 for 81)
**Pakistan International Airlines** 255 for 6 (Rizwan-uz-Zaman 62, Naeem Ahmed 62, Iqbal Qasim 4 for 83) and 216 for 4 (Rizwan-uz-Zaman 94, Asif Mohammad 52 not out)

*Match drawn*

***6, 7, 8 and 9 January 1984***

***at Qaddafi Stadium, Lahore***

**State Bank** 161 (Nasir Javed 81 not out, Atiq-ur-Rehman 6 for 60) and 124 (Ahsan Jawwad 59 not out, Atiq-ur-Rehman 4 for 39)
**Habib Bank** 350 for 2 (Arshad Pervez 181, Tehsin Javed 110 not out)

*Habib Bank won by an innings and 65 runs*

***at Bahawal Stadium, Bahawalpur***

**H.B.F.C.** 379 for 8 (Saadat Ali 208, Munir-ul-Haq 61, Raees Ahmed 52) and 280 (Munir-ul-Haq 132 not out, Ghaffar Kazmi 4 for 84)
**P.A.C.O.** 321 (Shaukat Mirza 68, Moin Mumtaz 67, Ghaffar Kazmi

54 not out, Kazim Mehdi 5 for 41) and 287 (Shaukat Mirza 116, Tanvir Ahmed 52, Izhar Ahmed 6 for 86)

*H.B.F.C. won by 51 runs*

***7, 8, 9 and 10 January 1984***

***at Punjab University, Lahore***

**Muslim Commercial Bank** 225 (Ejaz Faqih 100 not out, Shoaib Habib 5 for 59) and 222 (Babar Basharat 72, Salahuddin 52, Ejaz Faqih 50 not out, Amin Lakhani 8 for 82)
**Allied Bank** 184 (Ejaz Faqih 5 for 66) and 137 (Ejaz Faqih 5 for 51)

*Muslim Commercial Bank won by 126 runs*

***at Hyderabad***

**United Bank** *v.* **Railways Postponed**

*Railways walk over*

The match in Hyderabad was postponed and rescheduled for late February, but United Bank would not accept the venue and Railways were awarded a walk-over.

National Bank dominated the high-scoring game with P.I.A., but the pitch was the only winner.

A second wicket stand of 259 between Arshad Pervez and Tehsin Javed was the highlight of Habib Bank's humiliation of State Bank. Saadat Ali continued his magnificent scoring for H.B.F.C. and Munir-ul-Haq again gave him splendid support. Shaukat Mirza batted well for P.A.C.O. as H.B.F.C. won a fine game. A wonderful all-round performance by skipper Ejaz Faqih took Muslim Commercial Bank to an easy win over Allied.

ABOVE: *Saadat Ali – 1649 runs, a new record for a season in Pakistan.* BELOW: *Anil Dalpat, 69 dismissals, a record for a season in Pakistan. His exciting displays behind the stumps won him the place as Wasim Bari's successor. (Adrian Murrell)*

***12, 13, 14 and 15 January 1984***

***at Qaddafi Stadium, Lahore***

**Muslim Commercial Bank** 378 for 6 dec (Azmat Rana 172, Mohiuddin Khan 104 not out, Matloob Elahi 4 for 101)
**State Bank** 73 and 57

*Muslim Commercial Bank won by an innings and 248 runs*

***at L.C.C.A. Ground, Lahore***

**H.B.F.C.** 322 for 9 (Saadat Ali 97, Irshad Ahmed 54, Zahid Ahmed 6 for 120) and 432 for 5 dec (Raees Ahmed 110, Ijaz Ahmed 104, Saadat Ali 84, Noor-ul-Qamar 54 not out)
**Pakistan International Airlines** 313 for 7 (Zahid Ahmed 121, Aftab Baloch 76) and 225 for 4 (Aqeel Memon 105 not out, Kamran Rasheed 63)

*Match drawn*

State Bank's ultimate misery came in their ninth defeat in as many matches when, because of injury and illness, they batted six men short in each innings against Muslim Commercial Bank and batted for a total of 26.2 overs. The winners had been 98 for 5 at one time, but Azmat Rana and Mohiuddin added 173 and then Mohiuddin and Zagham Burki added 107.

Runs flowed in H.B.F.C.'s match with P.I.A., but, in scoring 97 and 84, Saadat Ali brought his total of runs for the season to 1649, so beating Zaheer's ten-year old record. His aggregate for the Quaid-e-Azam Trophy was 1217, a record for the competition. Anil Dalpat behind the stumps and Ali Zia in the field also set new records for a Pakistan domestic season.

*30 and 31 January, 1 and 2 February 1984*

*at National Stadium, Karachi*

**Allied Bank** 131 (Sikhander Bakht 6 for 44) and 162 (Zafar Ahmed 53 not out, Sikhander 6 for 81)
**United Bank** 244 (Nasir Shah 86, Amin Lakhani 5 for 52) and 50 for 1

*United Bank won by 9 wickets*

Having conceded the match against Railways, United Bank needed to win this match to confirm second place to National Bank who had regained the title. Sikhander Bakht and Ehtesham-ud-Din were twice too much for the Allied batsmen and, after a consistent, if not inspiring batting display, United won with ease.

**Quaid-e-Azam Trophy Final Table**
(1982–83 positions in brackets)

| | *P* | *W* | *L* | *D* | *Tied* | *Pts* |
|---|---|---|---|---|---|---|
| National Bank (2) | 9 | 6 | 1 | 2 | — | 128 |
| United Bank (1) | 9 | 5 | 3 | 1 | — | 103 |
| H.B.F.C. (—) | 9 | 4 | 2 | 3 | — | 102 |
| Habib Bank (4) | 9 | 3 | — | 6 | — | 98 |
| Pakistan International A. (5) | 9 | 3 | 1 | 5 | — | 94 |
| Railways (3) | 9 | 3 | 3 | 2 | 1 | 84 |
| Muslim Commercial Bank (6) | 9 | 2 | 2 | 4 | 1 | 83 |
| P.A.C.O. (—) | 9 | 2 | 4 | 3 | — | 75 |
| Allied Bank (7) | 9 | 2 | 5 | 2 | — | 71 |
| State Bank (—) | 9 | — | 9 | — | — | 38 |

A Sri Lankan Under-23 side toured Pakistan during January and February. They played five two-day matches, all of which were drawn, and three four-day international matches which were accorded first-class status.

*15, 16, 17 and 18 January 1984*

*at National Stadium, Karachi*

**Pakistan Under-23** 393 for 6 dec (Rameez Raja 145, Shoaib Mohammad 112, Sajid Ali 77)
**Sri Lanka Under-23** 143 (Shahid Mahboob 5 for 29) and 224 (S.M.S. Kaluperuma 62 not out, Shahid Mahboob 4 for 43)

*Pakistan Under-23 won by an innings and 26 runs*

The three-match series against the Sri Lankan tourists gave the Pakistan selectors the opportunity to reward young players who had done well in the domestic competitions and the players seized their chances splendidly. Shoaib and Sajid added 122 for Pakistan's second wicket and Shoaib and Rameez put on 159 for the third. The mature innings played by these last two batsmen did much to win them places in the side to face England two months later.

The Sri Lankans fared badly against the opening attack of Shahid Mahboob and Atiq-ur-Rehman while Naved Anjum continued his season of success with 3 for 58 in the second innings. The Sri Lankans were disappointing, but Kaluperuma, who batted number seven in the second innings instead of opening, batted with great spirit.

*26, 27, 28 and 29 January 1984*

*at Qaddafi Stadium, Lahore*

**Sri Lanka Under-23** 314 for 9 dec (S. Warbakulasuriya 62, Akram Raza 4 for 63) and 196 for 6 (D.S.B. Kuruppu 55, A. Ranatunga 51)
**Pakistan Under-23** 257 for 8 dec (Shoaib Mohammad 101 not out, R.J. Ratnayake 5 for 93)

*Match drawn*

The Sri Lankans gave a much better account of themselves in the second match with an even batting display. In contrast, Pakistan were 91 for 5, but Shoaib, with his second hundred stood firm after Ratnayake had troubled the other batsmen. Pakistan declared 57 in arrears and the game degenerated into farce as ten players bowled in Sri Lanka's second innings.

*7, 8, 9 and 10 February 1984*

*at Pindi Club, Rawalpindi*

**Sri Lanka Under-23** 383 (S.M.S. Kaluperuma 132 not out, A. Ranatunga 88, Shahid Mahboob 5 for 104) and 163 for 2 (S. Warnakulasuriya 81 not out, C.P. Amerasinghe 72 not out)
**Pakistan Under-23** 397 for 7 dec (Rizwan-uz-Zaman 189, K.G. Perera 4 for 76)

*Match drawn*

The match was dominated by two fine innings. At 83 for 5, Kaluperuma joined Ranatunga and the pair added 113. Kaluperuma then added 116 with Karnain and ended with his highest score in first-class cricket. The Pakistan innings was shaped by one player, Rizwan-uz-Zaman, who reached a career best. When Sri Lanka batted again they lost Kuruppu and Deepal without a run scored, but Warbakulasuriya and Amerasinghe batted out against ten different bowlers.

## The Wills Cup

Following the Quaid-e-Azam Trophy and preceding the arrival of the England party was the national limited-over competition, the Wills Cup. Ten teams competed in two leagues and the top two teams in each league qualified for the semi-finals.

**Group A**

| | *P* | *W* | *L* | *Pts* | *Run Rate* |
|---|---|---|---|---|---|
| United Bank | 5 | 5 | — | 20 | 4.66 |
| Pakistan Int. Airlines | 5 | 4 | 1 | 16 | 4.48 |
| Karachi | 5 | 3 | 2 | 12 | 4.36 |
| Allied Bank | 5 | 2 | 3 | 8 | 4.28 |
| State Bank | 5 | 1 | 4 | 4 | 3.45 |
| Railways | 5 | — | 5 | 0 | 3.49 |

**Group B**

| | *P* | *W* | *L* | *Pts* | *Run Rate* |
|---|---|---|---|---|---|
| H.B.F.C. | 5 | 4 | 1 | 16 | 5.59 |
| Habib Bank | 5 | 4 | 1 | 16 | 5.23 |
| Muslim Commercial Bank | 5 | 3 | 2 | 12 | 5.67 |
| P.A.C.O. | 5 | 2 | 3 | 8 | 4.83 |
| National Bank | 5 | 2 | 3 | 8 | 4.66 |
| Lahore City | 5 | — | 5 | 0 | 4.30 |

**Semi-Finals**

*22 February 1984*

***at National Stadium, Karachi***

**Pakistan International Airlines** 218 (Zaheer Abbas 75)
**H.B.F.C.** 213 for 5 (Saadat Ali 73, Raees Ahmed 65)

*Pakistan International Airlines won by 5 runs*

***at Niaz Stadium, Hyderabad***

**United Bank** 124
**Habib Bank** 125 for 2 (Saleem Malik 52 not out)

*Habib Bank won by 8 wickets*

Zaheer Abbas won the toss in Karachi and elected to bat. Shoaib Mohammad gave the innings a sound start with his 32, but it was Zaheer, with 75 off 77 deliveries, who gave H.B.F.C. the problem of scoring at 4.92 an over. H.B.F.C. had made an excellent impression in their first season and the Quaid-e-Azam Trophy and Saadat Ali, the most successful batsman of the season, moved to the attack immediately with a dashing 73. In the absence of Irshad Ahmed, H.B.F.C. were being led by Noor-ul-Qamar and, rather unwisely, he chose to juggle his batting order when a cool head would have brought victory. Raees Ahmed was out just before the final bid for the target was made and H.B.F.C. finished five runs short although they still had 5 wickets in hand. P.I.A., on the other hand, had been bowled out with three balls of their 45 overs remaining.

In Hyderabad, United Bank gave a limp display. Mohsin Khan asked them to bat first on a wicket still damp from preparation and a crowd of 5000 saw them bowled out in 42.5 overs with only Nasir Valika, 34, and Shafiq Ahmed, 29, batting with any real purpose. Saleem Malik, who had opened the bowling with Liaqat Ali and accounted for Mansoor Akhtar and Mahmood Rasheed, now turned his attention to batting and in 58 minutes hit a six, off Sikhan-dher Bakht, and seven fours. Arshad Pervez also batted well, with two sixes off the slow left-arm spinner Shahid Butt. Habib Bank won with ease and Saleem was named Man of the Match, an honour which Saadat Ali had received in Karachi.

**Final**

*24 February 1984*

***at Qaddafi Stadium, Lahore***

**Pakistan International Airlines** 181 (Shoaib Mohammad 51)
**Habib Bank** 182 for 3 (Mohsin Khan 86, Arshad Pervez 63 not out)

*Habib Bank won by 7 wickets*

Having won the three previous Wills One-Day Finals, P.I.A.'s reign came to an end when they were well beaten by Habib Bank. Zaheer again decided to bat when he won the toss, but his side were bowled out in 39.4 overs for a meagre 181. Rizwan and Asif Mohammad went cheaply, but Shoaib and Zaheer added 100 in 96 minutes, Zaheer hitting two fours and a six in his 48. When they were separated, however, there was a middle-order collapse, 4 wickets falling for 8 runs. The collapse was brought about by Abdul Qadir who took 3 for 49 in his 9 overs.

Zahid Ahmed hit 26 in 35 minutes and Anil Dalpat hit a brisk 19, but the final score of 181 was bitterly disappointing after the third wicket century stand.

Habib Bank lost Saleem Malik and Agha Zahid with only 6 runs scored, but Mohsin Khan, named Man of the Match, and Arshad Pervez added 152, a record stand for the competition. Habib reached their target with 4 overs remaining.

The individual prizes for the best performances in the competition went to Qasim Umar (batting), Naeem Ahmed (bowling), Sultan Rana (fielding) and Anil Dalpat (wicket-keeping).

## First Test Match
## PAKISTAN *v. ENGLAND*

It was something of a surprise, and perhaps a comment on selection, that England, with three opening batsmen in their party to choose from, decided to omit two of them and to ask Gatting to open. It was decided to play both spinners, which was welcome, but the absence of any warm up matches and the intensity of the Pakistan part of the tour with one international following upon another made form-finding and team-selection a hazardous business.

Pakistan's problems were great. Imran had wisely decided that he would miss the series and give his injured shin a proper chance to heal. Javed Miandad had been hit in the mouth by a ball from Lillee when playing in a benefit match and was unfit. Wasim Bari, one of the truly great cricketers and fine men of the world, had announced his retirement from Test cricket at the end of the tour of Australia, and Mudassar Nazar reported unfit on the first morning of the Test. It was hardly the ideal preparation for a side whose morale was said to be low and whose selectors had become the victims of politicians from without and within the Pakistan Board of Control.

Zaheer and Sarfraz, both of whom had been in dispute with authority in recent weeks, now found themselves as captain and chief adviser, and they could not have been encouraged when Willis won the toss and England took first knock in hot, dry, dusty and windless conditions. Pakistan included two players new to Test cricket, Rameez Raja, younger brother of Wasim, and wicket-keeper Anil Dalpat, the first Hindu to play for Pakistan.

England's opening stand lasted nearly two hours but produced only 41 grim runs. Sarfraz bowled admirably on a wicket which gave no assistance, but it was Tauseef who took the first wicket when Gatting misjudged the amount his off-spin would turn, anticipating rather too much. Smith spent $3\frac{1}{2}$ hours scoring 28 before he gave Sarfraz a deserved wicket, and the veteran pace bowler then made one leap at Lamb so that he was caught bat-pad. Randall was totally bemused by Abdul Qadir's mixture, and but for some positive shots from Botham and Gower before the close, the day would have been even more miserable than 147 for 4 off 76 overs.

England's innings ended after only 80 minutes on the second morning. In 9 overs Abdul Qadir took 4 wickets for 9 runs and England were out for the lowest score that they had ever made in Pakistan. Botham was taken bat-pad in Qadir's first over. The inability to read whether Qadir was bowling leg-break, top spinner or googly, and which one, accounted for Taylor and Gower, who had batted with great discipline. Cook went at silly point and Willis in the gully after enduring some fierce bouncers from Sarfraz.

LEFT: *(top): The scene for the first Test match at Karachi. Barbed wire fences the crowd as a precaution against student demonstrations.* LEFT: *(centre): Gower, l.b.w., b Abdul Qadir 58.* LEFT: *(bottom): Abdul Qadir, Man of the Match, strikes again. Bob Taylor falls l.b.w.* RIGHT: *(top): Gatting is l.b.w. to Safraz without offering a shot and the England decline begins.* RIGHT: *(bottom): A fifth wicket for Qadir. Cook is brilliantly caught by Saleem Malik. (Adrian Murrell)*

*Gower, caught Mohsin, bowled Tauseef for 57, and Pakistan scent a famous victory. (Adrian Murrell)*

*Botham takes a magnificent acrobatic catch to dismiss Qasim Umar and Pakistan have an attack of the jitters. (Adrian Murrell)*

As if to show their contempt for the paucity of England's batting, Mohsin and Qasim started with some brisk shots. Mohsin hit freely off front or back foot; Qasim, more watchful at first, punched the ball hard. After 19 overs Willis introduced spin and in his third over Cook trapped Qasim. To his chagrin, Rameez was adjudged caught bat-pad at silly point. Just before tea Zaheer played a slashing cut at Botham and was splendidly caught in the gully.

Cook bowled an immaculate length on the line off the off-stump, varying flight and turn, and it was hard to remember that he had yet to play a handful of Tests. He beat Mohsin through the air and had him magnificently taken at slip by Botham off an intended drive. Wasim Raja drove limply to mid-on and although Saleem Malik and Anil Dalpat, who had had a splendid match behind the stumps, held out to the close at 131 for 5, Cook had bowled England back into the game.

Considering how well Cook bowled after being idle for five weeks, it seems unfair to lay any blame on him, but, on the second morning, after Willis had had Anil caught low down

**FIRST TEST MATCH – PAKISTAN *v.* ENGLAND**
2, 3, 4 and 6 March 1984 at National Stadium, Karachi

**ENGLAND**

| | FIRST INNINGS | | SECOND INNINGS | |
|---|---|---|---|---|
| C.L. Smith | c Wasim, b Sarfraz | 28 | lbw, b Sarfraz | 5 |
| M.W. Gatting | b Tauseef | 26 | lbw, b Sarfraz | 4 |
| D.I. Gower | lbw, b Qadir | 58 | c Mohsin, b Tauseef | 57 |
| A.J. Lamb | c Rameez, b Sarfraz | 4 | c Anil, b Qadir | 20 |
| D.W. Randall | b Qadir | 8 | b Qadir | 16 |
| I.T. Botham | c Rameez, b Qadir | 22 | b Tauseef | 10 |
| V.J. Marks | c Rameez, b Sarfraz | 5 | b Qadir | 1 |
| R.W. Taylor* | lbw, b Qadir | 4 | c Mohsin, b Tauseef | 19 |
| N.G.B. Cook | c Saleem, b Qadir | 9 | c Mohsin, b Wasim | 5 |
| R.G.D. Willis† | c Wasim, b Sarfraz | 6 | c Tauseef, b Wasim | 2 |
| N.G. Cowans | not out | 1 | not out | 0 |
| Extras | lb 6, nb 5 | 11 | b 6, lb 6, nb 8 | 20 |
| | | 182 | | 159 |

| | O | M | R | W | O | M | R | W |
|---|---|---|---|---|---|---|---|---|
| Azeem Hafeez | 11 | 3 | 21 | — | 8 | 3 | 14 | — |
| Sarfraz Nawaz | 22.5 | 8 | 42 | 4 | 15 | 1 | 27 | 2 |
| Tauseef Ahmed | 24 | 11 | 33 | 1 | 21 | 6 | 37 | 3 |
| Wasim Raja | 3 | 2 | 1 | — | 3.3 | 1 | 2 | 2 |
| Abdul Qadir | 31 | 12 | 74 | 5 | 31 | 4 | 59 | 3 |

FALL OF WICKETS
1- 41, 2- 90, 3- 94, 4- 108, 5- 154, 6- 159, 7- 164, 8- 165, 9- 180
1- 6, 2- 21, 3- 63, 4- 94, 5- 121, 6- 128, 7- 128, 8- 157, 9- 159

**PAKISTAN**

| | FIRST INNINGS | | SECOND INNINGS | |
|---|---|---|---|---|
| Mohsin Khan | c Botham, b Cook | 54 | b Cook | 10 |
| Qasim Umar | lbw, b Cook | 29 | c Botham, b Cook | 7 |
| Rameez Raja | c Smith, b Cook | 1 | c Botham, b Marks | 1 |
| Zaheer Abbas† | c Lamb, b Botham | 0 | b Cook | 8 |
| Saleem Malik | lbw, b Willis | 74 | run out | 11 |
| Wasim Raja | c Cowans, b Cook | 3 | c Cowans, b Cook | 0 |
| Anil Dalpat* | c Taylor, b Willis | 12 | not out | 16 |
| Abdul Qadir | c Lamb, b Botham | 40 | b Cook | 7 |
| Sarfraz Nawaz | c Botham, b Cook | 8 | not out | 4 |
| Tauseef Ahmed | not out | 17 | | |
| Azeem Hafeez | c Willis, b Cook | 24 | | |
| Extras | lb 5, nb 10 | 15 | b 1, nb 1 | 2 |
| | | 277 | (for 7 wkts) | 66 |

| | O | M | R | W | O | M | R | W |
|---|---|---|---|---|---|---|---|---|
| Willis | 17 | 6 | 33 | 2 | 2 | — | 13 | — |
| Cowans | 12 | 3 | 34 | — | 2.3 | 1 | 10 | — |
| Botham | 30 | 5 | 90 | 2 | | | | |
| Cook | 30 | 12 | 65 | 6 | 14 | 8 | 18 | 5 |
| Marks | 13 | 4 | 40 | — | 12 | 5 | 23 | 1 |

FALL OF WICKETS
1- 67, 2- 79, 3- 80, 4- 96, 5- 105, 6- 138, 7- 213, 8- 229, 9- 240
1- 17, 2- 18, 3- 26, 4- 38, 5- 38, 6- 40, 7- 59

*Umpires:* Khizar Hayat and Shakoor Rana

**Pakistan won by 3 wickets**

*Rameez Raja, on his Test debut, falls to a Botham catch off Marks, but Pakistan win an historic victory. (Adrian Murrell)*

by Taylor, he missed a straight-forward caught and bowled chance offered by Abdul Qadir before he had scored and the miss proved to be crucial. From that point the England game seemed to decline. Saleem, who batted with great good sense and temperament, took Pakistan into the lead. Abdul Qadir made an invaluable 40, and Tauseef and Azeem joined in an unlikely last wicket stand of 37 which took the home side's lead to 95. In the context of the match this was a mighty lead.

Sarfraz dismissed both Smith and Gatting before the close, but Gower and Lamb took the score to 54 and much depended on them.

They added only 9 runs after the rest day before Qadir had Lamb caught behind. Randall struggled painfully against the leg-spinner, bursts of wild aggression being punctuated by nervous gropings. He was bowled by the googly which none in the England side seemed able to read. Frustrated by Qadir, Botham was bowled sweeping off-spinner Tauseef. Gower was taken at slip after an innings lasting 212 minutes. He batted with great resolution when all around him floundered. Taylor played nobly, but the end was swift and inevitable. Abdul Qadir was credited with only 3 wickets, but his command of the game was immeasurable. He dominated the England innings, holding such psychological sway with his fingers spinning avidly and his aggression comparable to that of a demon fast bowler, that his opponents were bemused and frustrated into submission. Pakistan were left to make 65 to beat England in Pakistan for the first time.

Cook was introduced after only three overs of the Pakistan innings and Qasim slashed his second ball and was caught well at slip. In his next over Mohsin swung wildly and was bowled. Zaheer hit two fours and then essayed a cut at a ball pitched on middle and drifting to leg. Saleem looked positive and twice hit Marks grandly, but then charged up the pitch while Rameez stood his ground and was run out. Rameez had been solid, but strokeless, and edged Marks to slip. Wasim Raja tried the bold approach. He hit Cook high towards the boundary where Cowans took the ball inches inside the fence. Had he missed the ball, it would have been 6. Pakistan were 40 for 6. They had been conquered by Cook on their nerves when in sight of success. England dared to believe the impossible probable.

But Abdul Qadir had not brought his country to the point of victory to see it wasted. He gave the calm, impressive Anil Dalpat the support and solidity that was needed. At 59 he survived an appeal for lbw, but he was bowled next ball. Cowans had replaced Marks, but bowled wastefully. In any case, it was too late. Sarfraz, bristling with determination, slashed Cowans for four and Pakistan had won an historic victory.

## First One-Day International
## PAKISTAN *v.* ENGLAND

England introduced those of their party who had had no cricket for nearly a month which, whilst necessary for practice for the individuals concerned, tended to devalue international cricket if a first choice team was not being selected.

A crowd of 40,000 packed into the ground before the start and saw Tavare, still completely out of touch, go early when he sparred outside the off-stump in the fifth over. Gower was also in poor form and the England start was slow. Fowler, who ran well and batted with enthusiasm, and Lamb added 70 in 12 overs, but this was the only flair in the England

*Rashid Khan, second in the first-class averages, and good bowling in the first one-day international. (George Herringshaw)*

## FIRST ONE-DAY INTERNATIONAL – PAKISTAN *v.* ENGLAND
9 March 1984 at Gaddafi Stadium, Lahore

| ENGLAND | | | |
|---|---|---|---|
| | G. Fowler* | b Sarfraz Nawaz | 43 |
| | C.J. Tavare | c Ashraf Ali, b Rashid Khan | 4 |
| | D.I. Gower | c Qasim Umar, b Shahid Mahboob | 7 |
| | A.J. Lamb | run out | 57 |
| | D.W. Randall | run out | 16 |
| | I.T. Botham | not out | 18 |
| | M.W. Gatting | b Sarfraz Nawaz | 9 |
| | G.R. Dilley | lbw, b Sarfraz Nawaz | 1 |
| | V.J. Marks | b Rashid Khan | 2 |
| | N.A. Foster | not out | 6 |
| | R.G.D. Willis† | | |
| | Extras | lb 13, w 6, nb 2 | 21 |
| | (40 overs) | (for 8 wickets) | 184 |

| | O | M | R | W |
|---|---|---|---|---|
| Rashid Khan | 8 | 1 | 28 | 2 |
| Shahid Mahboob | 8 | 2 | 28 | 1 |
| Mudassar Nazar | 8 | 1 | 34 | — |
| Sarfraz Nawaz | 8 | — | 33 | 3 |
| Wasim Raja | 8 | — | 40 | — |

FALL OF WICKETS
1- 11, 2- 24, 3- 94, 4- 134, 5- 147, 6- 160, 7- 164, 8- 173

| PAKISTAN | | | |
|---|---|---|---|
| | Mohsin Khan | b Dilley | 39 |
| | Saadat Ali | run out | 44 |
| | Qasim Umar | c Fowler, b Marks | 11 |
| | Zaheer Abbas† | not out | 59 |
| | Saleem Malik | c Tavare, b Willis | 11 |
| | Mudassar Nazar | not out | 8 |
| | Wasim Raja | | |
| | Shahid Mahboob | | |
| | Ashraf Ali* | | |
| | Sarfraz Nawaz | | |
| | Rashid Khan | | |
| | Extras | b 1, lb 5, w 1, nb 8 | 15 |
| | (38.4 overs) | (for 4 wickets) | 187 |

| | O | M | R | W |
|---|---|---|---|---|
| Willis | 7.4 | 1 | 25 | 1 |
| Dilley | 8 | — | 38 | 1 |
| Botham | 7 | — | 43 | — |
| Marks | 8 | 1 | 32 | 1 |
| Foster | 8 | — | 34 | — |

FALL OF WICKETS
1- 79, 2- 96, 3- 120, 4- 156

**Pakistan won by 6 wickets**

innings. Botham came in with only 6 overs left and was denied much of the strike and the England total was very disappointing. Eight overs of leg-spin from Wasim Raja again posed problems for a side whose feet seemed set in concrete.

Pakistan, who were not at full strength, were well served by Mohsin and Saadat who made 72 off the first 20 overs. Mohsij played on to Dilley and Saadat was run out when Fowler, fumbling, regathered and threw down the wicket to make his one positive contribution as wicket-keeper. Foster held a good catch to dismiss Qasim, but Zaheer batted with great fluency and although 60 were needed from the last 10 overs, the result never seemed in doubt and Zaheer took the individual award.

*The groundsman prepares. (Adrian Murrell)*

### Second Test Match
### PAKISTAN *v.* ENGLAND

Rarely can a side have begun a Test match in such distressing circumstances as England at Faisalabad. Shortly before the match, with rumours and allegations as to unsavoury behaviour by certain members of the team when in New Zealand permeating the press, Ian Botham was forced to return to England for an operation on his knee. Then Willis was found to be unwell and, as it transpired, unable to take any further part in the tour. With Cowans also not fully fit, the party was reduced to twelve players and Tavare was the one to stand down. By the end of the first day he, too, had become unwell. By the end of the first day on the field, Pakistan, having won the toss, were 257 for 4 and were almost immune from defeat.

No praise can be too high for England, however. Gower led the side admirably, composed and intelligent, and his bowlers responded with fine efforts. Dilley came from the shadows to bowl with fire and enthusiasm and Foster was accurate and hostile. Cook, if not as positive in his approach as he had been in the first Test when he had taken 11 splendid wickets and ended on the losing side, bowled steadily and learned much. Marks had also bowled accurately and wisely on a placid wicket.

England had been encouraged by dismissing Mohsin, Mudassar and Qasim for 70 and it was left to Saleem and Zaheer to restore order with a stand of 130, a stand that was ended when Gatting had the Pakistan captain lbw. Saleem and Wasim Raja continued their stand into the second day and both reached accomplished centuries. Wasim Raja hits in the air much and it has surprised many that his Test career has lasted so long and that his place has survived the

ABOVE: *Qasim Umar turns a ball to leg. Gower and Taylor look on.* RIGHT: *Wasim Raja – an exciting hundred. Gatting at short leg.* BELOW: *Saleem Malik in full flow during his innings of 116. Taylor, Lamb and Cook are apprehensive. (Adrian Murrell)*

challenge of younger Pakistani batsmen, but he is exciting to watch when things go well for him and this was one of the occasions when they did.

Saleem is a greater threat to future Test bowlers. Twenty-one-years old, he has been playing Test cricket for three years. He combines an eloquent array of shots with a mature sense of discipline that marks him as a batsman of exceptional ability. He is pleasing to the eye and bubbles with enthusiasm. He was bowled by a Dilley no-ball at 98 and caught behind off a Dilley no-ball at 114. They were two of the 20 no-balls that Dilley bowled and it seems unbelievable that an international cricketer of four years standing has not yet been able to rectify his run-up problem.

Abdul Qadir reached a maiden Test fifty and Zaheer declared to give England an hour at the end of the day. Fowler was now unwell and could not open, but Gatting and Smith did well and blossomed on the third morning with some fiercely struck shots. It seemed that we would see Gatting's first Test hundred but after an aggressive 75 he was first out when Tauseef made one pop and turn. Gower was unfit to bat at number three and Randall, after an uncertain beginning, batted with his usual competence. Of the batsmen

## SECOND TEST MATCH – PAKISTAN *v.* ENGLAND

12, 13, 14, 16 and 17 March, 1984 at Iqbal Stadium, Faisalabad

**PAKISTAN**

| | FIRST INNINGS | | SECOND INNINGS | |
|---|---|---|---|---|
| Mohsin Khan | c Lamb, b Dilley | 20 | b Dilley | 2 |
| Mudassar Nazar | c Gatting, b Cook | 12 | lbw, b Foster | 4 |
| Qasim Umar | c Gatting, b Foster | 16 | c Taylor, b Dilley | 17 |
| Saleem Malik | c Lamb, b Cook | 116 | c sub (Cowans), b Marks | 76 |
| Zaheer Abbas† | lbw, b Gatting | 68 | not out | 32 |
| Wasim Raja | b Marks | 112 | not out | 5 |
| Abdul Qadir | c Foster, b Dilley | 50 | | |
| Anil Dalpat | lbw, b Dilley | 8 | | |
| Sarfraz Nawaz | not out | 16 | | |
| Tauseef Ahmed | not out | 1 | | |
| Azeem Hafeez | | | | |
| Extras | lb 11, w 2, nb 17 | 30 | lb 1 | 1 |
| | (for 8 wkts dec) | 449 | (for 4 wkts) | 137 |

| | O | M | R | W | O | M | R | W |
|---|---|---|---|---|---|---|---|---|
| Foster | 30 | 7 | 109 | 1 | 5 | 1 | 10 | 1 |
| Dilley | 28 | 6 | 101 | 3 | 9 | — | 41 | 2 |
| Cook | 54 | 14 | 133 | 2 | 16 | 6 | 38 | — |
| Marks | 27 | 9 | 59 | 1 | 8 | 2 | 26 | 1 |
| Gatting | 3 | — | 17 | 1 | 2 | — | 18 | — |
| Fowler | | | | | 1 | — | 3 | — |

FALL OF WICKETS
1- 35, 2- 53, 3- 70, 4- 200, 5- 323, 6- 416, 7- 430, 8- 433
1- 6, 2- 6, 3- 56, 4- 123

**ENGLAND**

| | FIRST INNINGS | |
|---|---|---|
| M.W. Gatting | c Saleem, b Tauseef | 75 |
| C.L. Smith | b Sarfraz | 66 |
| D.W. Randall | b Sarfraz | 65 |
| A.J. Lamb | c Anil Dalpat, b Azeem | 19 |
| D.I. Gower† | st Anil Dalpat, b Mudassar | 152 |
| G. Fowler | c Qasim, b Wasim Raja | 57 |
| R.W. Taylor* | c Saleem, b Abdul Qadir | 0 |
| V.J. Marks | b Sarfraz | 83 |
| G.R. Dilley | not out | 2 |
| N.G.B. Cook | not out | 1 |
| N.A. Foster | | |
| Extras | b 10, lb 4, nb 12 | 26 |
| | (for 8 wkts dec) | 546 |

| | O | M | R | W |
|---|---|---|---|---|
| Azeem Hafeez | 19 | 3 | 71 | 1 |
| Sarfraz Nawaz | 49 | 11 | 129 | 3 |
| Wasim Raja | 26 | 6 | 61 | 1 |
| Abdul Qadir | 51 | 13 | 124 | 1 |
| Tauseef Ahmed | 30 | 10 | 96 | 1 |
| Mudassar Nazar | 14 | 1 | 39 | 1 |

FALL OF WICKETS
1- 127, 2- 163, 3- 214, 4- 245, 5- 361, 6- 361, 7- 528, 8- 545

*Umpires:* Mahboob Shah and Javed Akhtar

**Match drawn**

Lamb alone could find no form. He bats solely on technique and is in need of some inner music to dictate to him.

England finished at 233 for 3 and, after the rest day, David Gower reached a century that was proof of the justice of poetry. He had done so much to revive England at a time of despair and their courageous battle in this match owed much to his quiet, but positive leadership. His innings was one of great determination and, inevitably, of charm, and he was rightly named Man of the Match. Marks gave him fine support as they added 167 for the 7th wicket and Marks reached a score higher than the aggregate of his previous Test innings.

There was more success for Dilley when Pakistan batted again, and further evidence of Saleem's class. The match had long since been drawn.

### Third Test Match
### PAKISTAN *v.* ENGLAND

With Dilley returning to England injured, followed almost immediately by Willis, the party was reduced to twelve players and it was the luckless Tavare, who had had no chance to play himself back into form on the ill-conceived tour, who was again left out. Pakistan chose to pack their side with batting, although surprisingly much of it was young and inexperienced, and to take the field with only three front line bowlers, one of whom, Mohsin Kamal, was making his Test debut. Zaheer won the toss and on the assumption that whatever help the wicket would give to the bowler, it would give early in the match, he asked England to bat. He was to be quickly rewarded for his decision.

Fowler, still not fully fit, dropped to number six and Gatting, who opened in his place, was unquestionably lbw in the second over when he moved across his wicket. Gower became Kamal's first Test victim when he drove unwisely at a wide delivery. Smith was taken at second slip and Randall was caught at silly point off bat and pad although he obviously thought it was only pad. As batsmen so rarely agree with umpires these days, his demonstration of disagreement had little validity. Lamb showed some remembrance of things until he became Abdul Qadir's second victim, caught at short leg, and England were in desperate straits, 83 for 5 on a good wicket.

They were rescued by a splendid stand from Fowler and Marks who batted nearly 4 hours for an impressive and hard-earned 74. Fowler batted for $2\frac{1}{2}$ hours and played some pleasing shots until he tried to hit Qadir over the top. Both batsmen offered chances, but their application and sheer determination earned them some luck. The disappointment to England was that Fowler once more got himself out when he looked to be playing well. Taylor and Foster followed quickly and Marks finally became Qadir's fifth victim, demonstrating that trust in cricket still remained when he walked for a bat-pad catch. He deserved all praise for that and for a fine innings.

England closed at 241 for 9 and did not add to that score the next morning. It seemed a meagre score in spite of the grand efforts of Marks and Fowler, but England bowled with purpose and were well organised by Gower. Foster had

Mohsin Khan lbw after he had an appeal for lbw against Shoaib turned down. Sadly Foster had reacted with a lack of discipline and whatever else comes to England's cricket in the next few years, one hopes a rediscovery of discipline and behaviour is among them.

Qasim and Saleem were tied down by some accurate bowling and keen fielding, but it came as something of a surprise when Marks bowled Saleem. Qasim now found his touch and played some elegant shots as did Rameez, but Foster accounted for both and with Wasim Raja also falling and Zaheer incapacitated and batting with a runner, Pakistan finished the day at 173 for 6 and England in high spirits.

In his first two overs on the third morning Neil Foster dismissed Qadir, a marvellous one-handed catch by Bob Taylor, and Anil Dalpat and so became the first English fast bowler to take five wickets in a Test in Pakistan. Pakistan were 181 for 8 and England had a chance of levelling the series. Their hopes were dashed by a record ninth wicket stand of 161 between Sarfraz, who made his highest Test score, and Zaheer who, although in some pain, still managed to produce some fluent shots. England were upset that Sarfraz was not given out caught behind off Foster before he had reached 20, but as they showed their consternation, it is to be hoped that they resolved to walk without arguing the next time that they touched a ball and the umpire was uncertain or unsighted.

Pakistan had a first innings lead of 102 thanks to Sarfraz's mighty effort and the determination and elegance of their captain. Before the close Fowler had played wildly and been caught behind and Smith had run himself out in a moment of uncertainty. 65 for 2 and much depended on Gower.

LEFT: *(top): Mohsin Khan drops David Gower during his masterly innings of 173.* LEFT: *(bottom): Mohsin Kamal captures Fowler's wicket on his Test debut.* BELOW: *Randall turns away dejectedly after being given out caught controversially for the second time in the match. (Adrian Murrell)*

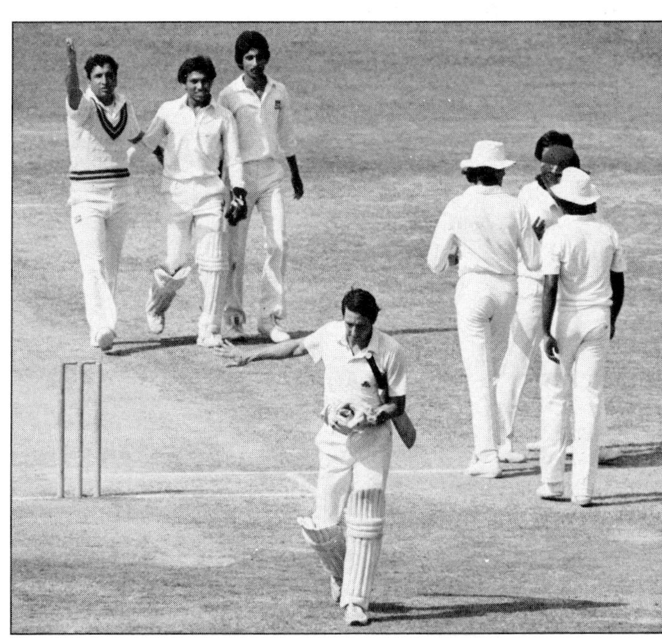

LEFT: *(top): Vic Marks has a close escape during his fighting innings of 74 at Lahore.* LEFT: *(centre): Foster, l.b.w., bowled Qadir 0. Abdul Qadir was Pakistan's man-of-the-series.* LEFT: *(bottom): Bob Taylor just fails to stump Saleem Malik.* RIGHT: *(top): Zaheer Abbas in all his glory despite a groin injury.* RIGHT: *(bottom): Sarfraz Nawaz – a mighty innings. (Adrian Murrell)*

On the rest day Gower stated thankfully that England aimed to play the game with discipline and dignity both in England and Pakistan and everywhere in the world. He gave substance to his words with an innings of character and charm that one could only admire for its maturity, elegance, resolution and example. He and Gatting added 137 for the third wicket. Lamb and Randall went quickly, but Marks again batted well and was only out when going for quick runs on the last morning. Gower declared when Taylor was out; his own innings had lasted for 7 hours, 8 minutes and he had faced 273 balls and hit fifteen fours. He left Pakistan to make 243 in a minimum of 59 overs.

Mohsin Khan began with that independence of spirit that makes him such a glorious player when he is in touch. He breathes elegance and charm and he hits with a crispness. Shoaib, less gifted and less experienced, soon followed his example and a record stand was made that brought Pakistan to the edge of victory. At tea they were 104 for 0; 139 needed from 27 overs. At 173 Shoaib hit a full toss from Cowans straight to Gatting. It seemed to matter little; all that was

## THIRD TEST MATCH – PAKISTAN *v.* ENGLAND

19, 20, 21, 23 and 24 March 1984 at Gaddafi Stadium, Lahore

### ENGLAND

| | FIRST INNINGS | | SECOND INNINGS | |
|---|---|---|---|---|
| C.L. Smith | c Saleem, b Sarfraz | 18 | run out | 15 |
| M.W. Gatting | lbw, b Sarfraz | 0 | (3) run out | 53 |
| D.I. Gower† | c Anil, b Mohsin Kamal | 9 | (4) not out | 173 |
| A.J. Lamb | c Rameez, b Abdul Qadir | 29 | (5) c and b Qadir | 6 |
| D.W. Randall | c Saleem, b Abdul Qadir | 14 | (6) c Saleem, b Qadir | 0 |
| G. Fowler | c Qasim, b Abdul Qadir | 58 | (2) c Anil, b Kamil | 19 |
| V.J. Marks | c Mohsin Khan, b Qadir | 74 | c sub (Akram), b Qadir | 55 |
| R.W. Taylor* | lbw, b Sarfraz | 1 | (10) b Sarfraz | 5 |
| N.A. Foster | lbw, b Abdul Qadir | 6 | (8) lbw, b Qadir | 0 |
| N.G.B. Cook | c Anil, b Sarfraz | 3 | | |
| N.G. Cowans | not out | 3 | (9) st Anil, b Qadir | 3 |
| Extras | b 4, lb 5, w 9, nb 8 | 26 | b 6, lb 3, w 1, nb 5 | 15 |
| | | 241 | (for 9 wkts dec) | 344 |

| | O | M | R | W | O | M | R | W |
|---|---|---|---|---|---|---|---|---|
| Mohsin Kamal | 15 | — | 66 | 1 | 17 | 3 | 59 | 1 |
| Sarfraz Nawaz | 22.5 | 5 | 49 | 4 | 27.4 | 1 | 112 | 1 |
| Abdul Qadir | 30 | 7 | 84 | 5 | 42 | 5 | 110 | 5 |
| Wasim Raja | 11 | 4 | 16 | — | 21 | 5 | 48 | — |

FALL OF WICKETS

1- 5, 2- 20, 3- 47, 4- 77, 5- 83, 6- 203, 7- 205, 8- 222, 9- 237

1- 35, 2- 38, 3- 175, 4- 189, 5- 189, 6- 308, 7- 309, 8- 327, 9- 344

### PAKISTAN

| | FIRST INNINGS | | SECOND INNINGS | |
|---|---|---|---|---|
| Mohsin Khan | lbw, b Foster | 1 | c Smith, b Cowans | 104 |
| Shoaib Mohammad | lbw, b Cowans | 7 | c Gatting, b Cowans | 80 |
| Qasim Umar | c Fowler, b Foster | 73 | run out | 0 |
| Saleem Malik | b Marks | 38 | c Gatting, b Cowans | 7 |
| Rameez Raja | c Smith, b Foster | 26 | (8) not out | 6 |
| Wasim Raja | c Gower, b Cowans | 12 | lbw, b Cowans | 0 |
| Zaheer Abbas† | not out | 82 | (5) c Gatting, b Cowans | 5 |
| Abdul Qadir | c Taylor, b Foster | 3 | | |
| Anil Dalpat* | c Gower, b Foster | 2 | | |
| Sarfraz Nawaz | c Gatting, b Smith | 90 | (7) not out | 10 |
| Mohsin Kamal | c Gower, b Cook | 0 | | |
| Extras | lb 9 | 9 | lb 5 | 5 |
| | | 343 | (for 6 wkts) | 217 |

| | O | M | R | W | O | M | R | W |
|---|---|---|---|---|---|---|---|---|
| Cowans | 29 | 5 | 89 | 2 | 14 | 2 | 42 | 5 |
| Foster | 37 | 8 | 67 | 5 | 15 | 4 | 44 | — |
| Cook | 44 | 12 | 117 | 1 | 18.2 | 2 | 73 | — |
| Marks | 20 | 4 | 59 | 1 | 10 | — | 53 | — |
| Smith | 1 | — | 2 | 1 | 1 | 1 | 0 | — |

FALL OF WICKETS

1- 9, 2- 13, 3-, 99, 4- 138, 5- 151, 6- 168, 7- 175, 8- 181, 9- 342

1- 173, 2- 175, 3- 187, 4- 197, 5- 199, 6- 199

*Umpires:* Khizar Hayat and Amanuliah Khan

**Match drawn**

## Pakistan *v.* England – Test Match Averages

### PAKISTAN BATTING

| | M | Inns | NOs | Runs | HS | Av | 100s | 50s |
|---|---|---|---|---|---|---|---|---|
| Sarfraz Nawaz | 3 | 5 | 3 | 128 | 90 | 64.00 | | 1 |
| Saleem Malik | 3 | 6 | | 322 | 116 | 53.66 | 1 | 2 |
| Zaheer Abbas | 3 | 6 | 2 | 195 | 82* | 48.75 | | 2 |
| Mohsin Khan | 3 | 6 | | 191 | 104 | 31.83 | 1 | 1 |
| Wasim Raja | 3 | 6 | 1 | 132 | 112 | 26.40 | 1 | |
| Abdul Qadir | 3 | 4 | | 100 | 50 | 25.00 | | 1 |
| Qasim Umar | 3 | 6 | | 142 | 73 | 23.66 | | 1 |
| Anil Dalpat | 3 | 4 | 1 | 38 | 16* | 12.66 | | |
| Rameez Raja | 2 | 4 | 1 | 34 | 26 | 11.33 | | |

Played in two Tests: Tauseef Ahmed 1* and 17*, Azeem Hafeez 24
Played in one Test: Shoaib Mohammad 7 and 80, Mohsin Kamal 0, Mudassar Nazar 12 and 4

### PAKISTAN BOWLING

| | Overs | Mds | Runs | Wkts | Av | Best | 5/inn | 10/m |
|---|---|---|---|---|---|---|---|---|
| Abdul Qadir | 185 | 41 | 451 | 19 | 23.73 | 5/74 | 3 | 1 |
| Sarfraz Nawaz | 137.2 | 26 | 359 | 14 | 25.64 | 4/42 | | |
| Tauseef Ahmed | 75 | 27 | 166 | 5 | 33.20 | 3/37 | | |
| Wasim Raja | 64.3 | 18 | 128 | 3 | 42.66 | 2/2 | | |
| Azeem Hafeez | 38 | 9 | 106 | 1 | 106.00 | 1/71 | | |

Bowled in one Test: Mudassar Nazar 14–1–39–1; Mohsin Kamal 32–3–125–2

### PAKISTAN FIELDING

7–Anil Dalpat (ct 5/st 2); 6–Saleem Malik; 4–Mohsin Khan and Rameez Raja; 2–Qasim Umar and Wasim Raja; 1–Abdul Qadir, Tauseef Ahmed and sub

### ENGLAND BATTING

| | M | Inns | NOs | Runs | HS | Av | 100s | 50s |
|---|---|---|---|---|---|---|---|---|
| D.I. Gower | 3 | 5 | 1 | 449 | 173* | 112.25 | 2 | 2 |
| G. Fowler | 2 | 3 | | 134 | 58 | 44.66 | | 2 |
| V.J. Marks | 3 | 5 | | 218 | 83 | 43.60 | | 3 |
| M.W. Gatting | 3 | 5 | | 158 | 75 | 31.60 | | 2 |
| C.L. Smith | 3 | 5 | | 132 | 66 | 26.40 | | 1 |
| D.W. Randall | 3 | 5 | | 103 | 65 | 20.60 | | 1 |
| A.J. Lamb | 3 | 5 | | 78 | 29 | 15.60 | | |
| N.G. Cowans | 2 | 4 | 3 | 7 | 3* | 7.00 | | |
| N.G.B. Cook | 3 | 4 | 1 | 18 | 9 | 6.00 | | |
| R.W. Taylor | 3 | 5 | | 29 | 19 | 5.80 | | |

Played in two Tests: N.A. Foster 6 and 0
Played in one Test: I.T. Botham 22 and 10, R.G.D. Willis 6 and 2, G.R. Dilley 2*

### ENGLAND BOWLING

| | Overs | Mds | Runs | Wkts | Av | Best | 5/inn | 10/m |
|---|---|---|---|---|---|---|---|---|
| N.G. Cowans | 57.3 | 11 | 175 | 7 | 25.00 | 5/42 | 1 | |
| N.G.B. Cook | 176.2 | 54 | 444 | 14 | 31.71 | 5/65 | 2 | 1 |
| N.A. Foster | 87 | 20 | 230 | 7 | 32.85 | 5/67 | 1 | |
| V.J. Marks | 90 | 24 | 260 | 4 | 65.00 | 1/23 | | |

Bowled in one Test: G.R. Dilley 37–6–142–5; C.L. Smith 2–1–2–1; M.W. Gatting 5–0–35–1; G. Fowler 1–0–3–0; I.T. Botham 30–5–90–2; R.G.D. Willis 19–6–46–2

### ENGLAND FIELDING

6–M.W. Gatting; 4–A.J. Lamb and I.T. Botham; 3–C.L. Smith, D.I. Gower, R.W. Taylor and N.G. Cowans (one as sub); 1–G. Fowler, N.A. Foster and R.G.D. Willis

needed now was a constant flow of singles. There was no need for heroics. Qasim was immediately run out. He went for a run. Both batsmen hesitated and then he surrendered although with effort he may have made his ground. Saleem slogged when he need not have done. Zaheer came with his runner and flicked a catch to square leg where Gatting appeared to take his third in a row. Mohsin was caught at long-on after a glorious hundred and Wasim Raja was adjudged lbw so that Cowans had taken 3 wickets in an over and Pakistan could now only play for safety and the series.

England had lost a series to Pakistan for the first time, but they had ended with dignity and some pride restored, and they had to thank David Gower for much of that.

*Gower pulls off a brilliant catch to end Pakistan's first innings. (Adrian Murrell)*

## Second One-Day International
## PAKISTAN *v.* ENGLAND

England ended the saddest tour in their history with a win over Pakistan with 8 balls to spare, yet even at the last there was bewilderment. In order to give Tavare a game, Taylor stood down and Fowler kept wicket. Fowler missed two stumpings and once more emphasised the need for a specialist wicket-keeper in limited-over cricket. Incomprehensibly, Tavare was placed at number 7 and did not bat, and it was hard to see why he could not have come into the side as a straightforward replacement for Lamb whose form had been no better than Tavare's himself.

Mohsin and Saadat gave Pakistan a splendid start with 76 in 21 overs, but the middle order fell away against Gatting and with the spinners proving economical, Chris Smith was brought on when Cowans might have been recalled and was rewarded with two cheap wickets.

When Qadir came on he quickly accounted for Smith, but he was then faced by two left-handers and looked far less menacing. Wickets fell to indiscretions, but Gatting stroked England to a victory which always looked likely and won himself the individual award.

So England ended on a happier note and they now went home to face enquiries and post-mortems about performances on and off the field.

**SECOND ONE-DAY INTERNATIONAL – PAKISTAN *v.* ENGLAND**
26 March 1984 at Karachi

| PAKISTAN | | |
|---|---|---|
| Mohsin Khan | st Fowler, b Cook | 37 |
| Saadat Ali | not out | 78 |
| Wasim Raja | c Fowler, b Gatting | 14 |
| Saleem Malik | c Foster, b Gatting | 2 |
| Qasim Umar | c and b Gatting | 7 |
| Naved Anjum | st Fowler, b Smith | 2 |
| Mudassar Nazar | run out | 6 |
| Abdul Qadir | c Cook, b Smith | 3 |
| Sarfraz Nawaz† | c Gower, b Cowans | 3 |
| Anil Dalpat* | not out | 0 |
| Rashid Khan | | |
| Extras | b 4, lb 4, nb 3 | 11 |
| (40 overs) | (for 8 wickets) | 163 |

| | O | M | R | W |
|---|---|---|---|---|
| Foster | 8 | — | 36 | — |
| Cowans | 5 | — | 20 | 1 |
| Gatting | 8 | 1 | 32 | 3 |
| Marks | 8 | 1 | 22 | — |
| Cook | 8 | — | 34 | 1 |
| Smith | 3 | — | 8 | 2 |

FALL OF WICKETS
1-76, 2-102, 3-107, 4-123, 5-135, 6-145, 7-155, 8-160

| ENGLAND | | |
|---|---|---|
| G. Fowler* | c Anil Dalpat, b Mudassar | 25 |
| C.L. Smith | lbw, b Abdul Qadir | 17 |
| D.I. Gower† | b Mudassar Nazar | 31 |
| A.J. Lamb | c Saleem Malik, b Naved Anjum | 19 |
| M.W. Gatting | not out | 38 |
| D.W. Randall | not out | 19 |
| C.J. Tavare | | |
| V.J. Marks | | |
| N.A. Foster | | |
| N.G.B. Cook | | |
| N.G. Cowans | | |
| Extras | b 1, lb 8, w 3, nb 3 | 15 |
| (38.4 overs) | (for 4 wickets) | 164 |

| | O | M | R | W |
|---|---|---|---|---|
| Rashid Khan | 8 | — | 31 | — |
| Sarfraz Nawaz | 7.4 | 1 | 24 | — |
| Mudassar Nazar | 8 | 1 | 22 | 2 |
| Abdul Qadir | 8 | — | 33 | 1 |
| Wasim Raja | 5 | — | 30 | — |
| Naved Anjum | 2 | — | 9 | 1 |

FALL OF WICKETS
1-37, 2-79, 3-88, 4-119

*Umpires:* Mehboob Shah and Shakil Khan

**England won by 6 wickets**

## England in Pakistan
by TONY LEWIS

It would be kindest to let this brief tour wither; not to nourish it by recalling the unhappiness; to let it die without decent burial. England flew from their losing series in New Zealand and promptly lost the first of three Test matches in Pakistan. That was in Karachi. When they moved off to Lahore there were two Fleet Street reporters waiting in the Lahore Hilton International Hotel to put extraordinary information before the players. They were not cricket reporters. They were foot-in-the-door news hounds from the *Mail on Sunday* who had come to confront some of the team with accusations of drug taking and sexual promiscuity while they were playing in New Zealand.

The word affidavit was thrown about. A girl named Mary Burgess had written her name in cricket history. She had given the *Mail on Sunday* a sworn statement that she had witnessed Ian Botham in a drug-taking sequence in a private room. 'I looked into his eyes and thought "Wow!" He looked straight through me. He was spaced out – his eyes were down in his cheeks.'

There were others who attacked the England team, and Botham was not the only player accused.

There followed inferences that drug-taking, late night drinking sessions and a high rate of sexual activity had impaired their performances on the field. England lost the series to New Zealand, the first in history, and Christchurch, venue of the second Test was their undoing, on and off the field.

Thus it can be realised how the morale of the England side was hit on Sunday 11 March in Lahore when trunk telephone calls to Britain produced the full venom of the *Mail on Sunday*'s story. England by this time had lost the first one-day international against Pakistan to add to the Karachi defeat. Ian Botham returned to England. At the press conference, the tour manager Alan Smith insisted that Botham had gone back for an operation to his knee. Of course, everyone close to the game knew that he had been struggling on a collapsing knee for some time. Indeed it was said to be a congenital condition which had been with him since the age of twelve. The whole world cruelly winked and saw his departure as proof of his New Zealand guilt. To complete the background to this tour, I must publish the statement of the England manager Alan Smith. 'I have been asked to comment on stories which are currently appearing in English newspapers. Gossip reached me about one month ago in New Zealand. I made inquiries at the time and found absolutely nothing substantiated.

'No member of the team was then carrying any named substances and I have categoric assurances that no-one is now. As far as I know, our team has been well received and liked wherever we have been – on the field and off the field. I have had quite a number of comments to that effect. I deplore current attempts to unsettle members of the team. The results may not have been all that we wished for, but this has been due to lack of form and not to any fault in team spirit, which has been excellent throughout.'

With such troubled minds, England arrived in Pakistan. Every time the muezzin wailed his plea to Allah from the mosque it sounded like a lament for England cricket. It would not go away. Conversations with the players were false because there were topics which were taboo. We heard that Botham was suing the offending newspaper. Life in Pakistan became *sub judice*. The players behaved as if they were on a Sunday School outing ... in a minefield.

The show had to go on and it brought a moment of historic joy to Pakistan. Like New Zealand, they too were to win a series against England for the first time in their history.

The cricketing tale begins in Karachi. Zaheer Abbas was made captain for the series. Imran Khan was still unable to play because of injury. It was feared that he would never bowl fast again. Javed Miandad had been struck on the head by a ball from Dennis Lillee in a benefit match in India. He was about to fly to New York for serious medical investigations. These two missed this series.

The Karachi pitch turned from the start and fizzed a bit. England looked hopelessly stodgy in conditions which called for delicacy and 'touch' play against the leg-spin and googlies of Abdul Qadir and the off-spinners of Tauseef Ahmed. Sarfraz Nawaz, too, as he has done so often, wobbled the ball around in the air and off the seam all through the innings. Only David Gower, 58, appeared to have the confidence to wait for the ball to come onto the bat: the rest launched into firm drives and pushes even though they had no idea which way Qadir was spinning the ball.

However, Nick Cook, the young left arm spinner produced a performance which decimated the relatively inexperienced Pakistanis. Pakistan were reduced to 138–6. Then, Willis, the captain, by strangely over bowling Botham, by feeding Qadir, now a batsman of threat, with slow spin, instead of the faster variety which he did not relish, helped Pakistan to a total of 277 and a lead of 95 on the first innings.

It was crucial. Only Gower in England's second innings resisted. 159 all out left Pakistan 65 to win.

As so often happens when small scores are required for historic wins – this would be the first Test ever won by Pakistan in Pakistan – batting proved to be agony. England's fielders preyed around the pads and it was with some relief to Pakistan that the winning run came when 7 wickets were down. Cook took 11 wickets in the match. This beat Tony Lock's best bowling record for England in Pakistan, 8–225 at Dacca in 1961–62. However, the ominous warning came from Abdul Qadir. He took 8 wickets in this Test, but more importantly, he threatened to be the major difference between the sides.

Thus it turned out. The next two Tests were played on slow pitches, unhelpful to bowlers, at Faisalabad and Lahore. Qadir sent England batsmen to bed dreaming bad dreams.

Qadir is a small, stocky bundle of mischief, a delight to watch if not to play. He is said to have two googlies, the one he shows freely, and the one he does not. Like all outstanding spin bowlers he has a fast loop in the air which gives him extra bounce. This allows him to station a cage of close fielders around hesitant, prodding batsmen scooping up the ricochetes off bat and pad.

In fact England played him much better in the second Test at Faisalabad. Gatting led the way, Randall and Smith followed, but the huge total of 546–8 was based on a magnificent 152 from Gower. Gower, like Qadir and eventually like Salim Malik and Sarfraz, was to become an outstanding figure of the series.

Gower had replaced the sick Willis as England captain and indeed, when Willis was found to be suffering from a mild variety of hepititis Gower took over the tour as Willis returned home early.

England were far more astute in the field under Gower. He chided those who tended to play act, such as Dilley, Foster and Cook who wasted energy while showing their disapproval of umpires. He also stayed firm with an umpire who tried to make him hurry up his over rate in spite of the fact that there was a minimum requirement to bowl 77 on each Test match day. Gower's tactical awareness was obvious. His batting thrived on the responsibility. He confirmed it by playing a mammoth 7 hour and 8 minute 173 not out at Lahore. The good things of the tour emerged when he led – the arrival of Neil Foster as a top class fast bowler, the restatement of Norman Cowan's potential, Mike Gatting's move to batting authority in Tests, Chris Smith's dedication to improvement. Also, if it was needed, an impeccable contribution behind the stumps by Bob Taylor.

Gower almost produced a miracle in the final Test at Lahore. He declared, leaving Pakistan to score 243 in 59 overs. Moshin Khan sent them racing towards it with a stylish century. The son of Hanif Mohammad, Chaoib scampered after him. Panic struck, wickets tumbled and Pakistan had to block it out at the end with 6 wickets down.

In Salim Malik Pakistan have found probably the most promising young player in the world. He is not yet 21. His batting at Karachi on the turner indicated his class: his century at Faisalabad confirmed it. His defence is relaxed and well organised, he shows no fear of fast bowling, he has the delicate touches as well as cannonball power off the back or front foot, to off or to leg.

Sarfraz Nawaz who has reached the age of obscuring his age, bowled beautifully throughout and in one glorious innings at Lahore scored a virtuoso 90, putting on 161 with a limping Zaheer and removing his side from all danger of defeat.

There was one serious question to be asked about this series. Why did so few spectators turn up to watch it? A personal view is that we were watching Test match overkill. Not a pretty sight. Empty concrete terraces. It was possible to conclude that only the players' bank balances benefit from whistle-stop cricket. Short tours drop no roots, do not spread the game. No youngsters of 'Pindi or Peshawar could dream of a Gower cover drive, or a sweep by Salim, because the cricket was never taken there. No child in Sialkot saw the mighty Botham or the giant Saffraz. The instant circus moved swiftly and was not seen. There was no time to build heroes. England left Pakistan almost as they came in, anonymously under their white sun hats, a losing team. It is one winter many of them will wish had never been. Not the Pakistanis of course. Triumphs long awaited are rightly to be savoured.

## First Class Averages

| BATTING | M | Inns | NOs | Runs | HS | Av | 100s | 50s |
|---|---|---|---|---|---|---|---|---|
| Kamal Najamuddin | 3 | 5 | 1 | 374 | 111* | 93.50 | 2 | 2 |
| Qasim Shera | 3 | 5 | 2 | 201 | 64* | 67.00 | | 1 |
| Saadat Ali | 14 | 27 | 1 | 1649 | 208 | 63.42 | 4 | 7 |
| Javed Ilyas | 3 | 5 | 1 | 236 | 92 | 59.00 | | 2 |
| Arshad Pervez | 12 | 20 | 2 | 1051 | 181 | 58.38 | 4 | 5 |
| Rizwan-uz-Zaman | 11 | 18 | 3 | 864 | 189 | 57.60 | 2 | 5 |
| Saleem Malik | 6 | 11 | 0 | 607 | 132 | 55.18 | 2 | 3 |
| Aamer Mirza | 4 | 7 | 3 | 220 | 105* | 55.00 | 1 | |
| Tasnim Abidi | 4 | 7 | 1 | 328 | 150* | 54.66 | 1 | 1 |
| Saleem Taj | 3 | 5 | 1 | 217 | 68 | 54.25 | | 2 |
| Shafiq Ahmed | 12 | 22 | 3 | 1007 | 125 | 53.00 | 2 | 6 |
| Zafar Ali | 4 | 7 | 1 | 317 | 101* | 52.83 | 1 | 2 |
| Masood Anwar | 5 | 7 | 0 | 365 | 184 | 52.14 | 1 | 1 |
| Azhar Khan | 10 | 17 | 4 | 676 | 155 | 52.00 | 3 | 2 |
| Munir-ul-Haq | 6 | 12 | 3 | 461 | 132* | 51.22 | 2 | 2 |
| Sajid Ali | 14 | 24 | 0 | 1180 | 146 | 49.16 | 3 | 7 |
| Shaukat Mirza | 11 | 22 | 4 | 882 | 137* | 49.00 | 3 | 4 |
| Sadiq Mohammad | 7 | 14 | 1 | 635 | 124 | 48.84 | 2 | 3 |
| Shoaib Mohammad | 15 | 26 | 3 | 1118 | 151* | 48.60 | 5 | 4 |
| Azmat Rana | 7 | 12 | 1 | 531 | 172 | 48.27 | 1 | 4 |
| Tehsin Javed | 9 | 14 | 4 | 476 | 110* | 47.60 | 1 | 2 |
| Imtinan Zamir | 4 | 6 | 1 | 238 | 100 | 47.60 | 1 | 2 |
| Saleemullah | 3 | 6 | 1 | 234 | 107 | 46.80 | 1 | 1 |
| Ameer Akbar | 3 | 5 | 0 | 231 | 80 | 46.20 | | 2 |
| Zafar Ahmed | 13 | 23 | 9 | 632 | 60* | 45.14 | | 4 |
| Ijaz Faqih | 12 | 20 | 3 | 751 | 100* | 44.17 | 1 | 6 |
| Iqtidar Ali | 12 | 22 | 3 | 834 | 200* | 43.89 | 2 | 4 |
| Ali Zia | 13 | 25 | 1 | 1021 | 130 | 42.54 | 3 | 4 |
| Qaiser Hussein | 9 | 16 | 3 | 552 | 129* | 42.46 | 2 | 1 |
| Iqbal Sikander | 12 | 19 | 3 | 677 | 111* | 42.31 | 1 | 5 |
| Sarfraz Azeem | 3 | 5 | 0 | 205 | 109 | 41.00 | 1 | |
| Rameez Raja | 20 | 36 | 4 | 1294 | 149 | 40.43 | 4 | 7 |
| Meer Haider | 3 | 5 | 0 | 202 | 88 | 40.40 | | 2 |
| Moin Mumtaz | 11 | 20 | 2 | 704 | 126 | 39.11 | 1 | 3 |
| Haroon Rasheed | 13 | 20 | 3 | 647 | 92 | 38.05 | | 4 |
| Tanvir Ahmed | 8 | 16 | 2 | 530 | 151 | 37.85 | 1 | 3 |
| Siddiq Patni | 7 | 13 | 2 | 414 | 123* | 37.63 | 1 | 2 |
| Saleem Pervez | 9 | 17 | 0 | 637 | 117 | 37.47 | 2 | 4 |
| Asif Mohammad | 10 | 17 | 1 | 596 | 73 | 37.25 | | 6 |
| Ghaffar Kazmi | 10 | 15 | 3 | 447 | 131 | 37.25 | 1 | 3 |
| Tahir Mahmood | 4 | 7 | 1 | 221 | 77 | 36.83 | | 1 |
| Sultan Rana | 9 | 14 | 0 | 513 | 132 | 36.64 | 2 | 2 |
| Zakir Mirza | 4 | 7 | 0 | 253 | 120 | 36.14 | 1 | 1 |
| Azhar Abbas | 3 | 6 | 0 | 216 | 108 | 36.00 | 1 | |
| Zahid Ahmed | 12 | 20 | 5 | 536 | 121 | 35.73 | 1 | 2 |
| Naseer Ahmed | 3 | 6 | 0 | 210 | 63 | 35.00 | | 1 |
| Mahmood Rasheed | 12 | 20 | 3 | 583 | 116* | 34.29 | 1 | 3 |
| Aamer Sohail | 4 | 6 | 0 | 204 | 68 | 34.00 | | 1 |
| Naeem Ahmed | 9 | 17 | 2 | 507 | 64 | 33.80 | | 5 |
| Naved Anjum | 16 | 28 | 3 | 828 | 116 | 33.12 | 1 | 5 |
| Raees Ahmed | 9 | 18 | 1 | 560 | 119* | 32.94 | 2 | 1 |
| Aftab Baloch | 13 | 18 | 5 | 428 | 76 | 32.92 | | 1 |
| Ijaz Ahmed | 8 | 13 | 0 | 418 | 117 | 32.15 | 2 | 1 |
| Tariq Alam | 8 | 14 | 4 | 321 | 67* | 32.10 | | 2 |
| Manzoor Elahi | 11 | 20 | 4 | 503 | 53 | 31.43 | | 2 |
| Salman Qizilbash | 9 | 18 | 0 | 553 | 73 | 30.72 | | 5 |
| Salman Tahir | 4 | 8 | 0 | 245 | 82 | 30.62 | | 2 |
| Younis Ata | 4 | 8 | 0 | 244 | 90 | 30.50 | | 2 |
| Ijaz Ahmed | 5 | 10 | 1 | 271 | 74 | 30.11 | | 2 |
| Asif Ali | 9 | 16 | 1 | 450 | 93 | 30.00 | | 4 |
| Tahir Rasheed | 9 | 17 | 4 | 385 | 67 | 29.61 | | 3 |
| Rafat Alam | 7 | 12 | 0 | 352 | 69 | 29.33 | | 2 |
| Arshad Ali | 4 | 8 | 1 | 205 | 105* | 29.28 | 1 | |
| Ahsan Jawwad | 8 | 14 | 2 | 350 | 77* | 29.16 | | 2 |
| Anwar Miandad | 13 | 20 | 4 | 466 | 67 | 29.12 | | 4 |
| Abdus Sami | 13 | 25 | 1 | 695 | 122 | 28.95 | 1 | 4 |
| Rizwan Yousuf | 4 | 8 | 1 | 200 | 116* | 28.57 | 1 | |
| Jamshed Hussain | 7 | 8 | 0 | 219 | 68 | 27.37 | | 1 |
| Anwar-ul-Haq | 9 | 15 | 0 | 406 | 80 | 27.06 | | 3 |
| Agha Zahid | 9 | 16 | 0 | 430 | 81 | 26.87 | | 2 |
| Mohammad Jamil | 8 | 14 | 4 | 266 | 7 | 26.60 | | 1 |
| Shahid Mohammad | 6 | 11 | 0 | 289 | 63 | 26.27 | | 3 |
| Asad Rauf | 10 | 18 | 1 | 444 | 73 | 26.11 | | 3 |
| Farooq Shera | 6 | 10 | 1 | 235 | 84 | 26.11 | | 1 |

| | | | | | | | | |
|---|---|---|---|---|---|---|---|---|
| Saleem Yousuf | 13 | 25 | 3 | 564 | 103 | 25.63 | 1 | 3 |
| Mohiuddin Khan | 13 | 20 | 2 | 459 | 104* | 25.50 | 1 | 3 |
| Tariq Javed | 12 | 19 | 1 | 453 | 124 | 25.16 | 1 | 1 |
| Yahya Toor | 9 | 16 | 2 | 342 | 101* | 24.42 | 1 | |
| Taslim Arif | 9 | 17 | 2 | 364 | 125 | 24.26 | 1 | 1 |
| Babar Basharat | 9 | 16 | 0 | 384 | 75 | 24.00 | | 3 |
| Noor-ul-Qamar | 7 | 13 | 1 | 278 | 77 | 23.16 | | 3 |
| Talat Mirza | 6 | 12 | 0 | 270 | 89 | 22.50 | | 2 |
| Salahuddin | 8 | 15 | 1 | 307 | 52 | 21.92 | | 1 |
| Feroze Najamuddin | 12 | 21 | 3 | 394 | 82* | 21.88 | | 3 |
| Nasir Javed | 10 | 17 | 1 | 347 | 81* | 21.68 | | 1 |
| Musleh-ud-Din | 7 | 14 | 0 | 301 | 97 | 21.50 | | 2 |
| Nasir Valika | 10 | 15 | 2 | 268 | 104* | 20.61 | 1 | 1 |
| Zafar Mehdi | 8 | 13 | 1 | 245 | 61 | 20.41 | | 1 |
| Saleem Mohiuddin | 5 | 10 | 0 | 203 | 64 | 20.30 | | 2 |
| Masood Iqbal | 12 | 17 | 2 | 288 | 68* | 19.20 | | 1 |
| Mansoor Rana | 12 | 20 | 0 | 382 | 121 | 19.10 | 1 | 1 |
| Umar Rasheed | 11 | 21 | 0 | 396 | 56 | 18.85 | | 2 |
| Umar Rasheed | 11 | 21 | 0 | 396 | 56 | 18.85 | | 2 |
| Anil Dalpat | 19 | 23 | 6 | 315 | 52* | 18.52 | | 1 |
| Pervez Shah | 6 | 12 | 0 | 210 | 42 | 17.50 | | |
| Mohammad Arif Sr | 9 | 16 | 0 | 269 | 58 | 16.81 | | 2 |
| Shoaib Habib | 12 | 20 | 2 | 300 | 49 | 16.66 | | |
| Farrukh Zaman | 12 | 16 | 2 | 221 | 36 | 15.78 | | |
| Shahzad Bashir | 8 | 16 | 0 | 244 | 45 | 15.25 | | |
| Shahid Mahboob | 16 | 23 | 1 | 267 | 56 | 12.18 | | 1 |

(Qualification – 200 runs, average 10.00)

| BOWLING | Overs | Mdns | Runs | Wkts | Av | Best | 10/m | 5/inn |
|---|---|---|---|---|---|---|---|---|
| Mohammad Riaz | 104.2 | 26 | 223 | 28 | 7.96 | 7/20 | 1 | 2 |
| Rashid Khan | 39 | 9 | 92 | 11 | 8.36 | 8/39 | | 1 |
| Shahid Aziz | 152 | 47 | 348 | 29 | 12.00 | 7/44 | | 3 |
| Abdul Wahab | 60.3 | 14 | 139 | 11 | 12.63 | 5/41 | | 2 |
| Iqbal Butt | 149 | 33 | 335 | 24 | 13.95 | 7/30 | 1 | 2 |
| Zakir Khan | 80 | 14 | 226 | 16 | 14.12 | 4/30 | | |
| Shahid Tanvir | 109 | 12 | 275 | 19 | 14.47 | 5/39 | | 1 |
| Ehtesham-ud-Din | 175 | 42 | 494 | 33 | 14.96 | 8/61 | 1 | 1 |
| Khatib Rizwan | 115 | 30 | 260 | 17 | 15.29 | 3/10 | | |
| Haaris A. Khan | 116.2 | 37 | 246 | 15 | 16.40 | 5/51 | | 2 |
| Saleem Jaffer | 73 | 15 | 199 | 12 | 16.58 | 5/11 | | 1 |
| Tahir Mahmood | 65 | 14 | 172 | 10 | 17.20 | 4/22 | | |
| Iqbal Qasim | 324.1 | 109 | 617 | 35 | 17.62 | 5/42 | | 2 |
| Tahir Baig | 81 | 17 | 214 | 12 | 17.83 | 6/47 | | 1 |
| Hafeez-ur-Rehman | 83.1 | 15 | 202 | 11 | 18.36 | 4/44 | | |
| Naved Anjum | 365 | 80 | 1022 | 55 | 18.58 | 6/67 | | 3 |
| Zahid Khan | 69.1 | 10 | 190 | 10 | 19.00 | 4/58 | | |
| Masood Anwar | 84 | 20 | 231 | 12 | 19.25 | 8/44 | | 1 |
| Nadeem Yousuf | 62 | 10 | 194 | 10 | 19.40 | 4/33 | | |
| Atiq-ur-Rehman | 147.5 | 30 | 506 | 26 | 19.46 | 6/60 | 1 | 2 |
| Shahid Pervez | 98.4 | 24 | 234 | 12 | 19.50 | 4/26 | | |
| Sajjad Bashir | 88 | 20 | 275 | 14 | 19.64 | 6/32 | | 1 |
| Sohail Khan | 97 | 17 | 238 | 12 | 19.83 | 5/42 | | 1 |
| Raja Afaq | 96.5 | 20 | 259 | 13 | 19.92 | 4/37 | | |
| Mohsin Kamal | 172.1 | 28 | 568 | 28 | 20.28 | 4/21 | | |
| Afzaal Butt | 417.1 | 75 | 1362 | 66 | 20.63 | 7/104 | 1 | 7 |
| Sikander Bakht | 273.1 | 35 | 952 | 46 | 20.69 | 6/44 | 1 | 4 |
| Mohammad Altaf | 152.3 | 19 | 455 | 21 | 21.66 | 7/52 | | 2 |
| Pervez Shah | 164 | 35 | 459 | 21 | 21.85 | 5/63 | | 2 |
| Liaqat Ali | 304.2 | 50 | 897 | 41 | 21.87 | 7/62 | | 2 |
| Tauseef Ahmed | 526.1 | 149 | 1224 | 54 | 22.66 | 5/38 | | 2 |
| Zahid Ahmed | 302.2 | 64 | 827 | 36 | 22.97 | 6/120 | | 2 |
| Jalal-ud-Din | 388 | 56 | 1339 | 58 | 23.08 | 6/49 | 2 | 5 |
| Wasim Haider | 67 | 8 | 231 | 10 | 23.10 | 4/46 | | |
| Aslam Qureshi | 154.5 | 32 | 440 | 19 | 23.15 | 4/55 | | |
| Musleh-ud-Din | 73.3 | 13 | 278 | 12 | 23.16 | 3/24 | | |
| Iqbal Sikander | 399.4 | 91 | 1144 | 49 | 23.34 | 6/40 | | 4 |
| Ijaz Faqih | 539.5 | 107 | 1258 | 53 | 23.73 | 6/42 | 1 | 5 |
| Abdul Qadir | 185 | 41 | 451 | 19 | 23.73 | 5/74 | 1 | 3 |
| Raees-ur-Rehman | 176.4 | 17 | 714 | 30 | 23.80 | 6/82 | | 2 |
| Tariq Wahab | 157.2 | 39 | 478 | 20 | 23.90 | 7/49 | | 2 |
| Ali Zia | 278.3 | 50 | 768 | 32 | 24.00 | 5/81 | | 1 |
| Anwar Khan | 159.2 | 33 | 456 | 19 | 24.00 | 5/65 | | 1 |
| Mohammad Aslam | 84.2 | 14 | 244 | 10 | 24.40 | 6/52 | | 1 |
| Tanvir Afzal | 113.3 | 13 | 397 | 16 | 24.81 | 6/113 | | 1 |
| Amin Lakhani | 418.5 | 84 | 1167 | 47 | 24.82 | 8/82 | 1 | 4 |
| Sarfraz Nawaz | 247.2 | 57 | 597 | 24 | 24.87 | 4/42 | | |
| Farrukh Zaman | 242.4 | 33 | 700 | 28 | 25.00 | 3/40 | | |
| Hasan Jamil | 113 | 20 | 405 | 16 | 25.31 | 5/43 | | 2 |
| Jamshed Hussain | 104 | 14 | 405 | 16 | 25.31 | 4/39 | | |
| Aamer Wasim | 99.2 | 13 | 280 | 11 | 25.45 | 6/56 | | 1 |
| Mohinder Kumar | 95.2 | 19 | 358 | 14 | 25.57 | 4/31 | | |
| Abdur Raqeeb | 342.5 | 96 | 768 | 30 | 25.60 | 6/31 | | 1 |
| Asif Afridi | 275.2 | 49 | 846 | 33 | 25.63 | 4/18 | | |
| Haroon Rasheed | 113.4 | 8 | 390 | 15 | 26.00 | 3/14 | | |
| Shahid Mahboob | 596.2 | 110 | 1939 | 74 | 26.20 | 7/66 | 1 | 5 |
| Mohiuddin Khan | 282.3 | 35 | 975 | 37 | 26.35 | 6/48 | | 2 |
| Waheed Niazi | 88.1 | 18 | 265 | 10 | 26.50 | 3/43 | | |
| Aftab Baloch | 291.1 | 76 | 663 | 25 | 26.52 | 5/44 | | 1 |
| Ilyas Khan | 264 | 50 | 640 | 24 | 26.66 | 5/58 | | 1 |
| Saleem Malik | 84 | 6 | 294 | 11 | 26.72 | 5/36 | | 1 |
| Asif Baloch | 153.2 | 20 | 455 | 17 | 26.76 | 7/46 | | 1 |
| Jahanzeb Khan | 115.3 | 13 | 405 | 15 | 27.00 | 4/91 | | |
| Tahir Mahmood | 78 | 8 | 299 | 11 | 27.18 | 3/12 | | |
| Raees Ahmed | 271.5 | 34 | 826 | 30 | 27.53 | 5/51 | | 1 |
| Kazim Mehdi | 308.4 | 66 | 800 | 29 | 27.57 | 5/41 | | 1 |
| Ali Ahmed | 304 | 51 | 949 | 34 | 27.91 | 6/62 | 1 | 1 |
| Shahid Butt | 387.5 | 80 | 979 | 35 | 27.97 | 6/104 | | 1 |
| Shoaib Habib | 295.2 | 66 | 718 | 25 | 28.72 | 5/59 | | 1 |
| Abdul Nabi | 102.5 | 15 | 319 | 11 | 29.00 | 6/86 | | 1 |
| Yahya Toor | 89.2 | 6 | 363 | 12 | 30.25 | 5/48 | | 1 |
| Arshad Nawaz | 349 | 96 | 829 | 26 | 31.88 | 6/85 | | 1 |
| Aziz Ahmed | 304 | 71 | 832 | 26 | 32.00 | 5/49 | | 1 |
| Mian Fayyaz | 123.4 | 24 | 321 | 10 | 32.10 | 4/48 | | |
| Nadeem Ghauri | 215.3 | 57 | 464 | 14 | 33.14 | 3/37 | | |
| Rafat Alam | 113 | 18 | 427 | 12 | 35.58 | 2/19 | | |
| Mohammad Arif Sr | 256.4 | 54 | 743 | 21 | 35.83 | 4/84 | | |
| Matloob Elahi | 105 | 15 | 359 | 10 | 35.90 | 4/101 | | |
| Tanvir Shaukat | 70.5 | 6 | 362 | 10 | 36.20 | 4/67 | | |
| Izhar Ahmed | 186.2 | 49 | 439 | 12 | 36.58 | 6/86 | | 1 |
| Naeem Ahmed | 102.5 | 7 | 454 | 12 | 37.83 | 5/54 | | 1 |
| Raja Akbar | 242 | 51 | 800 | 21 | 38.09 | 3/31 | | |
| Ghaffar Kazmi | 361 | 52 | 1258 | 32 | 39.31 | 4/54 | | |
| Akram Raza | 154.4 | 39 | 435 | 11 | 39.54 | 4/63 | | |
| Moin Mumtaz | 135 | 20 | 557 | 13 | 42.84 | 3/52 | | |
| Zaigham Burki | 221.3 | 53 | 662 | 15 | 44.13 | 3/75 | | |
| Azhaf Khan | 184.3 | 27 | 510 | 11 | 46.36 | 5/101 | | 1 |
| Manzoor Elahi | 169.3 | 21 | 677 | 13 | 52.07 | 4/56 | | |

(Qualification – 10 wickets)

**LEADING FIELDERS**

Anil Dalpat–69 (ct 52/st 17); Masood Iqbal–36 (ct 35/st 1); Zulquarnain–35 (ct 33/st 2); Saleem Yousuf–32 (ct 26/st 6); Tahir Rasheed–31 (ct 23/st 8); Shahid Munir–29 (ct 15/st 14); Arif-ud-Din–21 (ct 11/st 10); Taslim Arif–21 (ct 19/st 2); Mansoor Khan–16 (ct 8/st 8); Azhar Abbas–15 (ct 11/st 4); Shahzad Bashir–13 (ct 11/st 2); Wasim Arif–12 (ct 12/st 0); Nasir Atiq–11 (ct 6/st 5); Pervez Alam–10 (ct 7/st 3); Nisar Ahmed–10 (ct 10/st 0); Waheed Mirza–10 (ct 9/st 1); Iqtidar Khwaja–10 (ct 6/st 4).

Note: Masood Iqbal's dismissals include 2 catches held while not keeping wicket. Waheed Mirza's tally includes one such catch.

Following the end of the series with England, Pakistan joined India and Sri Lanka in Sharjah for the inaugural Asia Cup. The players who received benefits from the Cup were Imran Khan, Maqsood Ahmed, Bedi and Durani. The next Asia Cup is planned for 1986 when more countries are likely to compete.

## Asia Cup – Match One
## PAKISTAN *v.* SRI LANKA

The inaugural Asia Cup, sponsored by Rothmans, began with a surprise when pre-tournament favourites Pakistan were comfortably beaten by Sri Lanka. Pakistan had a

ABOVE: *The first Asia Cup. The flags fly over Sharjah. (Adrian Murrell)* RIGHT: *Roy Dias (Sri Lanka) – a match-winning 57 not out against Pakistan. (Patrick Eagar)*

stronger side than the one which had played England with Javed, Zaheer and Mudassar fit again. Sarfraz, originally dropped for indiscreet comments, was forgiven and reinstated, a familiar pattern.

Put in to bat on a humid day, Pakistan began well with a brisk stand between Saadat Ali and Mohsin Khan, but thereafter their innings lost momentum. Zaheer hit both spinners, de Silva and Ranatunge, over long-off for sixes, but he was caught in the same area shortly before lunch after an 82-minute innings and Pakistan floundered.

Sri Lanka began soundly and then increased their rate of scoring. Roy Dias was the backbone of the innings and when Mendis was deceived by Qadir's googly and bowled, Ranatunge hit boldly to prevent the leg-spinner from getting on top. He hit a six and four to square-leg in one over before

**ASIA CUP – MATCH ONE: PAKISTAN *v.* SRI LANKA**
6 April 1984 at Sharjah

| PAKISTAN | | |
|---|---|---|
| Mohsin Khan | c Dias, b D.S. de Silva | 27 |
| Saadat Ali | c Kuruppu, b Ranatunge | 30 |
| Mudassar Nazar | c Kuruppu, b Karnain | 1 |
| Zaheer Abbas† | c Ratnayake, b Ratanunge | 47 |
| Javed Miandad | b John | 9 |
| Saleem Malik | run out | 17 |
| Abdul Qadir | b D.S. de Silva | 7 |
| Shahid Mahboob | not out | 18 |
| Sarfraz Nawaz | c John, b Ranatunge | 5 |
| Anil Dalpat* | c Ranatunge, b Ratnayake | 5 |
| Rashid Khan | not out | 0 |
| Extras | b 8, lb 9, w 3, nb 1 | 21 |
| (46 overs) | (for 9 wickets) | 187 |

| | O | M | R | W |
|---|---|---|---|---|
| John | 10 | 3 | 27 | 1 |
| Ratnayake | 9 | — | 33 | 1 |
| Karnain | 7 | 1 | 19 | 1 |
| Ranatunge | 10 | — | 38 | 3 |
| D.S. de Silva | 10 | — | 49 | 2 |

FALL OF WICKETS
1- 59, 2- 60, 3- 84, 4- 110, 5- 142, 6- 154, 7- 157, 8- 165, 9- 185

| SRI LANKA | | |
|---|---|---|
| S. Wettimuny | run out | 18 |
| D.S.B. Kuruppu* | c Anil Dalpat, b Mudassar Nazar | 25 |
| R.L. Dias | not out | 57 |
| L.R.D. Mendis† | b Abdul Qadir | 20 |
| A. Ranatunge | st Anil Dalpat, b Abdul Qadir | 26 |
| R.S. Madugalle | c Zaheer Abbas, b Sarfraz Nawaz | 4 |
| A. de Silva | not out | 14 |
| U.S.H. Karnain | | |
| D.S. de Silva | | |
| J.R. Ratnayake | | |
| V. John | | |
| Extras | b 4, lb 14, w 6, nb 2 | 26 |
| (43.3 overs) | (for 5 wickets) | 190 |

| | O | M | R | W |
|---|---|---|---|---|
| Shahid Mahboob | 9 | 1 | 30 | — |
| Rashid Khan | 8 | 2 | 26 | — |
| Mudassar Nazar | 7 | — | 25 | 1 |
| Sarfraz Nawaz | 10 | 1 | 36 | 1 |
| Abdul Qadir | 9 | — | 42 | 2 |
| Saadat Ali | 0.3 | — | 5 | — |

FALL OF WICKETS
1- 52, 2- 67, 3- 105, 4- 163, 5- 170

*Umpires:* H.D. Bird and Swaroop Kishan

**Sri Lanka won by 5 wickets**

being well stumped by Anil Dalpat. Madugalle went quickly, but Dias saw his side to victory with 15 balls to spare.

### Asia Cup – Match Two
### INDIA v. SRI LANKA

After Manoj Prabhakar and Chetan Sharma had reduced Sri Lanka to 26 for 4 with Dias and Mendis among the fallen, there was never any doubt as to the outcome of the second match in the first Asia Cup. Veteran Madan Lal produced an accurate spell which complemented the work of the young pace men and frustrated any hopes of a revival by Sri Lanka.

Khanna and Parkar, both firm strikers of the ball, scored at $4\frac{1}{2}$ an over to bring an easy victory and the wicket-keeper, who had scored heavily for Delhi in the Ranji Trophy, reached an accomplished fifty.

### Asia Cup – Match Three
### INDIA v. PAKISTAN

India took the first Asia Cup in a somewhat unremarkable fashion when they beat Pakistan with ease in the third and last match of the competition. Khanna and Parkar gave India a good start and there were consistent contributions from all batsmen. In contrast Pakistan were laboured. Without breaking through as they had done against Sri

*Khanna and Parkar leave the field in triumph after India had beaten Sri Lanka by 10 wickets. (Patrick Eagar)*

**ASIA CUP – MATCH TWO: INDIA v. SRI LANKA**
8 April 1984 at Sharjah

| SRI LANKA | | | |
|---|---|---|---|
| | S. Wettimuny | c Madan Lal, b Prabhakar | 12 |
| | D.S.B. Kuruppu* | c Khanna, b Chetan Sharma | 0 |
| | R.L. Dias | c Vengsarkar, b Prabhakar | 5 |
| | L.R.D. Mendis† | c Patil, b Chetan Sharma | 1 |
| | R.S. Madugalle | b Madan Lal | 38 |
| | A. Ranatunge | run out | 9 |
| | A. de Silva | lbw, b Madan Lal | 11 |
| | U.S.H. Karnain | lbw, b Madan Lal | 0 |
| | J.R. Ratnayake | b Shastri | 2 |
| | D.S. de Silva | not out | 8 |
| | V. John | c Gavaskar, b Chetan Sharma | 2 |
| | Extras | lb 4, w 3, nb 1 | 8 |
| | (41 overs) | | 96 |

| | O | M | R | W |
|---|---|---|---|---|
| Chetan Sharma | 8 | 1 | 22 | 3 |
| Prabhakar | 10 | 3 | 16 | 2 |
| Binny | 7 | — | 25 | — |
| Madan Lal | 8 | 2 | 11 | 3 |
| Shastri | 7 | 1 | 13 | 1 |
| Kirti Azad | 1 | — | 1 | — |

FALL OF WICKETS
1- 1, 2- 17, 3- 20, 4- 26, 5- 53, 6- 79, 7- 81, 8- 82, 9- 86

| INDIA | | | |
|---|---|---|---|
| | S.C. Khanna* | not out | 51 |
| | G.A.M.H. Parkar | not out | 32 |
| | D.B. Vengsarkar | | |
| | S.M. Gavaskar† | | |
| | S.M. Patil | | |
| | R.J. Shastri | | |
| | Kirti Azad | | |
| | R.M.H. Binny | | |
| | S. Madan Lal | | |
| | M. Prabhakar | | |
| | Chetan Sharma | | |
| | Extras | b 1, w 12, nb 1 | 14 |
| | (21.4 overs) | (for no wicket) | 97 |

| | O | M | R | W |
|---|---|---|---|---|
| John | 6 | 1 | 30 | — |
| Ratnayake | 4 | — | 27 | — |
| Karnain | 2 | — | 4 | — |
| D.S. de Silva | 6 | — | 21 | — |
| Madugalle | 0.4 | — | 1 | — |

FALL OF WICKETS
None

*Umpires:* H.D. Bird and Shakoor Rana

**India won by 10 wickets**

## ASIA CUP – MATCH THREE: INDIA *v.* PAKISTAN
13 April 1984 at Sharjah

| INDIA | | | |
|---|---|---|---|
| | S.C. Khanna* | c and b Mudassar | 56 |
| | G.A.M.H. Parkar | run out | 22 |
| | D.B. Vengsarkar | b Shahid Mahboob | 14 |
| | S.M. Patil | c Saleem Malik, b Sarfraz Nawaz | 43 |
| | S.M. Gavaskar† | not out | 36 |
| | R.J. Shastri | | |
| | Kirti Azad | | |
| | R.M.H. Binny | | |
| | S. Madan Lal | | |
| | M. Prabharkar | | |
| | C. Sharma | | |
| | Extras | | 17 |
| | (46 overs) | (for 4 wickets) | 188 |

| | O | M | R | W |
|---|---|---|---|---|
| Azeem Hafeez | 7 | — | 41 | — |
| Sarfraz Nawaz | 10 | 1 | 37 | 1 |
| Shahid Mahboob | 10 | 1 | 23 | 1 |
| Abdul Qadir | 10 | — | 36 | — |
| Mudassar Nazar | 9 | — | 34 | 1 |

FALL OF WICKETS
1- 54, 2- 88, 3- 110, 4- 188

| PAKISTAN | | | |
|---|---|---|---|
| | Mohsin Khan | c Parkar, b Shastri | 35 |
| | Saadat Ali | run out | 13 |
| | Mudassar Nazar | st Khanna, b Shastri | 18 |
| | Zaheer Abbas† | c Madan Lal, b Binny | 27 |
| | Saleem Malik | run out | 15 |
| | Qasim Umar | c Prabhakar, b Binny | 16 |
| | Shahid Mahboob | run out | 0 |
| | Abdul Qadir | run out | 0 |
| | Sarfraz Nawaz | c Patil, b Binny | 4 |
| | Anil Dalpat* | st Khanna, b Shastri | 1 |
| | Azeem Hafeez | not out | 0 |
| | Extras | | 5 |
| | (39.4 overs) | | 134 |

| | O | M | R | W |
|---|---|---|---|---|
| Chetan Sharma | 7 | — | 18 | — |
| Prabhakar | 7 | — | 17 | — |
| Binny | 9.4 | — | 33 | 3 |
| Madan Lal | 7 | 1 | 21 | — |
| Shastri | 10 | — | 40 | 3 |

FALL OF WICKETS
1- 22, 2- 69, 3- 70, 4- 91, 5- 125, 6- 125, 7- 125, 8- 128, 9- 133

*Umpires:* H.D. Bird and H.C. Felsinger

**India won by 54 runs**

Lanka Chetan Sharma and Prabharkar bowled frugally and Pakistan fell well behind the required rate. So great was their frustration that four men were run out in a desperate bid to achieve quick runs. India were not to be denied and won with ease.

**Asia Cup**

| | *P* | *W* | *L* | *Pts* |
|---|---|---|---|---|
| India | 2 | 2 | — | 4 |
| Sri Lanka | 2 | 1 | 1 | 2 |
| Pakistan | 2 | — | 2 | 0 |

*Sharjah and the first Asia Cup. (Adrian Murrell)*

ABOVE: *The victorious Indian side. (Adrian Murrell)*

BELOW: *Gavaskar holds aloft the Asia Cup. (Adrian Murrell)*

SECTION H

# Kings of Cricket

The season in the West Indies.
The Test and one-day international series against Australia.

*Clive Lloyd – 100 Test matches for the West Indies.*
*(George Herringshaw)*

Once again the West Indian domestic season began bereft of its top players. There were, of course, further defections to the side playing in South Africa, and the West Indian team was engaged in its long and arduous tour of India and Australia when the home season started. It seems that throughout the world domestic competitions are suffering as international cricket threatens us with death by indigestion.

## Jones Cup, 1983–84

### *8, 9, 10 and 11 October 1983*

***at Bourda, Georgetown, Guyana***

**Demerara** 319 (S. Bamfield 100, A.F.D. Jackman 60, S. Ganouri 7 for 91) and 286 (S. Ganouri 5 for 65)
**Berbice** 496 for 9 dec (T.R. Etwaroo 198, K. Singh 88, M. Chin 57, C. Armstrong 4 for 119) and 45 for 4

*Match drawn*

A high-scoring game representing something of a prelude to the season proper ended in a draw when Berbice failed in their dash to score 110 at more than ten an over. Etwaroo and Singh added 184 for Berbice's 5th wicket and Ganouri had match figures of 12 for 157.

## Beaumont Cup, 1984

### *5, 6, 7 and 8 January*

***at Guaracara Park, Pointe-a-Pierre***

**South-Central Trinidad** 267 (R. Nanan 75 not out, R. Sampath 55) and 189 (K.C. Williams 5 for 29)
**North-East Trinidad and Tobago** 212 (C. Rampersad 50) and 245 for 8 (P.V. Simmonds 68)

*North-East Trinidad and Tobago won by 2 wickets*

A well fought match in which the balance changed throughout the four days saw Joseph and Mahabir finally give North-East victory with an unbeaten ninth wicket stand of 19. A sixth wicket stand of 98 between Sampath and skipper Nanan revived South-Central when they looked in danger of collapse, and their 267 was enough to give them a useful first innings lead. A fine spell by Williams had them in trouble at the end of the third day when they were 77 for 5. A last wicket stand of 64 between Ramnath and Antoine lifted them to 189 and left North-East a target of 245. They began solidly, but slipped from 216 for 4 to 226 for 8 before Joseph and Mahabir brought victory.

### *20, 21, 22 and 23 January*

***at Kennington Oval, Bridgetown***

**Trinidad and Tobago** 174 (M.A. Small 5 for 57) and 214 (P. Moosai 78)
**Barbados** 237 (H. Joseph 5 for 83) and 152 for 4 (A. Gilkes 85 not out)

*Barbados won by 6 wickets*
*Barbados 16 pts, Trinidad and Tobago 0 pts*

***at Sabina Park, Kingston***

**Guyana** 411 (A.A. Lyght 122, W.H.F. White 105, A.D.F. Jackman 78) and 134 (C.A. Walsh 6 for 35)
**Jamaica** 347 (M.C. Neita 133, O.W. Peters 72, R.F. Joseph 6 for 114) and 200 for 4 (T. Corke 62, M.C. Neita 61)

*Jamaica won by 6 wickets*
*Jamaica 16 pts, Guyana 5 pts*

*Milton Small who had figures of 8 for 110 on his first-class debut for Barbados against Trinidad on 20 January and eventually forced his way into the Test side. (Adrian Murrell)*

### *21, 22, 23 and 24 January*

***at Castries***

**Leeward Islands** 228 for 9 dec (A.L. Kelly 69)
**Windward Islands** 92 for 4

*Match abandoned*
*Leeward Islands 4 pts, Windward Islands 4 pts*

The opening round of matches in the Shell Shield provided a major upset when reigning champions Guyana were beaten by Jamaica, bottom in 1983. A century opening stand between Lyght and Seeram established Guyana's innings. Lyght went on to a career best 122 and William White hit a maiden first-class century to take the visitors to a commanding position. Jamaica fought back well through Ordeimo Peters and Mark Neita who reached a maiden first-class hundred. Ray Joseph cut off the tail when he returned with the new ball and his 6 for 114 was also a career best.

Not to be outdone, Courtney Walsh bowled briskly for the home side to record his career best and with good support from Clement Thompson, he routed Guyana. With ample time in which to get the 199 needed to win, Jamaica were brought to the brink of success by a 94-run third wicket partnership from Corke and Man of the Match Neita.

In a low scoring game in Bridgetown, the Man of the Match was Milton Small with a career best 5 for 57 and match figures of 8 for 110. Trinidad lost 6 wickets in reaching a hundred and only some hard hitting by skipper Ranjie Nanan and pace man Gray gave the innings a boost. Barbados batted solidly throughout the order and only Harold Joseph's off-breaks and Ganesh Mahabir's leg-spin posed real problems as they took a lead of 63. They were held up for a time by Prakash Moosai who hit his highest first-class score, but Gilkes did the same for the home side as they moved to a comfortable win.

There was no play possible on the first two days and none until after lunch on the third day at Mindoo Phillip Park, Castries so that an indecisive draw was inevitable.

***28, 29, 30 and 31 January***

***at Kennington Oval, Bridgetown***

**Barbados** 231 (T.R.O. Payne 75) and 304 for 9 dec (C.A. Best 108, G.L. Linton 80 not out)

**Windward Islands** 212 (L.C. Sebastien 96 not out, G.L. Linton 5 for 75, N.A. Phillips 4 for 35) and 45 for 2

*Match drawn*
*Barbados 8 pts, Windward Islands 4 pts*

***at Sabina Park, Kingston***

**Leeward Islands** 337 (R.M. Otto 131, A. Merrick 62 not out, C.A. Walsh 4 for 90) and 71 for 3
**Jamaica** 165 (A. Merrick 5 for 45) and 241 (M.C. Neita 51, N.C. Guishard 4 for 53)

*Leeward Islands won by 7 wickets*
*Leeward Islands 16 pts, Jamaica 0 pts*

***at Queen's Park Oval, Port-of-Spain***

**Guyana** 250 (A.D.F. Jackman 61, R. Nanan 5 for 56) and 197 (Timur Mohammed 66 not out, R. Nanan 4 for 45)
**Trinidad and Tobago** 344 (P. Moosai 97, A. Rajah 72, D.I. Kallicharran 4 for 135) and 20 for 3

*Match drawn*
*Trinidad and Tobago 8 pts, Guyana 4 pts*

*Andy Roberts. A Test career may have closed but he still performed splendidly for Leeward Islands. Match figures of 10 for 144 v Barbados, 3–6 February. (Adrian Murrell)*

The dethronement of Guyana continued as only rain at lunch on the last day in Trinidad saved them from another defeat. Ranjie Nanan was the home side's hero with his telling off-breaks. Trinidad were struggling at 87 for 4 when Prakash Moosai, improving on his career best of the previous match, and Anmeal Rajah added 164 to take the home side solidly into the lead.

Guyana were without the injured Etwaroo in their second knock and in spite of a brave, defiant innings from skipper Timur Mohammed, they fell to Nanan and Joseph. There was a shock for Trinidad, needing 104 to win, when Simmonds, Dharson and Suraj were shot out before lunch.

Rain prevented any play on the final day in Bridgetown where Barbados, 90 for 5 at lunch on the first day, recovered to 231. It seemed that Windward Islands would take a big lead when they closed at 81 for 1, but the leg-breaks of George Linton who had a splendid all-round match with a career best 80 not out in the second innings and the medium pace of Neil Phillips with his best bowling figures gave Barbados a surprise lead. Carlisle Best's maiden century put Barbados in a commanding position before the rain.

Leeward Islands took only three days to beat Jamaica in Kingston and so bring the home side down to earth after their heady victory over Guyana. Ralston Otto's maiden first-class hundred and a marvellous all-round performance by Anthony Merrick who had career bests with bat and ball took Leeward to the ascendancy. The last 6 Jamaican wickets fell for 32 and they were forced to follow-on. They fared a little better in their second innings, but Noel Guishard's off-breaks ended stubborn middle order resistance and Leeward scored the runs needed for victory at nearly 5 an over to end the match on the third day.

***3, 4, 5 and 6 February***

***at Basseterre, St Kitts***

**Barbados** 303 (G.L. Linton 83, C.A. Best 82, A.M.E. Roberts 6 for 80) and 287 (H. Braithwaite 86, T.R.O. Payne 75, A.M.E. Roberts 4 for 64, E.T. Willett 4 for 93)
**Leeward Islands** 273 (R.M. Otto 134, N.C. Guishard 85, R.O. Estwick 6 for 68) and 174 for 7

*Match drawn*
*Barbados 8 pts, Leeward Islands 4 pts*

***at Guaracara Park, Pointe-a-Pierre***
**Jamaica** 151 and 302 (C.A. Davidson 77, M.C. Neita 70, G. Mahabir 4 for 57)

**Trinidad and Tobago** 227 (C.A. Walsh 5 for 80) and 153 (E.L. Wilson 4 for 48)

*Jamaica won by 73 runs*
*Jamaica 16 pts, Trinidad and Tobago 5 pts*

***at Bourda Oval, Georgetown***
**Guyana** 261 (R. Seeram 57, C. Lambert 52, S.J. Hinds 6 for 97) and 136 for 3 (A.A. Lyght 63)
**Windward Islands** 223 (N. Phillip 63, L.C. Sebastien 53, C. Butts 6 for 79)

*Match drawn*
*Guyana 8 pts, Windward Islands 4 pts*

Rain hampered Guyana's chances of forcing their first win of the season when they had the better of exchanges with Windward Islands, and Barbados were thwarted by Leeward resistance after Milton Small had taken three quick wickets to make victory look possible.

Andy Roberts bowled splendidly on the opening day, but Best and George Linton, who bettered his score of the

**Barbados 1984**
First Class Matches

| BATTING | *v.* Trinidad & Tobago (Bridgetown) 20–23 January 1984 | | *v.* Windward Islands (Bridgetown) 28–31 January 1984 | | *v.* Leeward Islands (Basseterre) 3–6 February 1984 | | *v.* Jamaica (Bridgetown) 11–14 February 1984 | | *v.* Guyana (Georgetown) 17–19 February 1984 | | *v.* Australia (Bridgetown) 24–27 March 1984 | | *M* | *Inns* | *NOs* | *Runs* | *HS* | *Av* |
|---|---|---|---|---|---|---|---|---|---|---|---|---|---|---|---|---|---|---|
| C.A. Best | 46 | 22 | 16 | 108 | 82 | 20 | 33 | 65 | 5 | 14 | 20 | 43 | 6 | 12 | — | 474 | 108 | 39.50 |
| A. Gilkes | 22 | 85* | 19 | 40 | 36 | 3 | | | | | 104 | 75 | 4 | 8 | 1 | 384 | 104 | 54.85 |
| T.R.O. Payne | 25 | 11 | 75 | 2 | 22 | 75 | 27 | 76 | 59 | 0 | 16 | 51* | 6 | 12 | 1 | 439 | 76 | 39.90 |
| H. Braithwaite | 40 | 32* | 22 | 12 | 0 | 86 | 18 | 4 | 4 | 11 | | | 5 | 10 | 1 | 229 | 86 | 25.44 |
| L.N. Reifer | 14 | — | 0 | 1 | 5 | 1 | | | | | | | 3 | 5 | — | 21 | 14 | 4.20 |
| G.L. Linton | 19 | — | 3 | 80* | 83 | 29* | 5 | 25 | 7 | 9* | | | 5 | 9 | 3 | 260 | 83 | 43.33 |
| M.C. Worrell | 20 | 1 | 36 | 16 | 0 | 3 | 47* | 3 | | | 26* | — | 5 | 9 | 2 | 152 | 47* | 21.71 |
| N.A. Phillips | 34 | — | 25 | 9 | 28 | 5 | 45 | 10 | 2 | 18 | 35 | 5* | 6 | 11 | 1 | 216 | 45 | 21.60 |
| R.M. Ellcock | 2 | — | 18 | 10 | | | | | 5 | 1 | | | 3 | 5 | — | 36 | 18 | 7.20 |
| R.O. Estwick | 7 | 0 | 0 | 5 | 5* | 9 | 0 | 0* | 2* | 0 | 0 | — | 6 | 11 | 3 | 28 | 9 | 3.50 |
| M.A. Small | 0* | — | 2* | 0* | 2 | 1 | 0 | — | | | 8 | — | 5 | 7 | 3 | 13 | 8 | 3.33 |
| D. Cumberbatch | | | | | 11 | 42 | 14 | 2 | 1 | 1 | 0 | — | 4 | 7 | — | 71 | 42 | 10.14 |
| T. Hunte | | | | | | | 70 | 47 | 72 | 15 | 1 | 29 | 3 | 6 | — | 234 | 72 | 39.00 |
| G.N. Reifer | | | | | | | 24 | 45 | 11 | 51 | | | 2 | 4 | — | 131 | 51 | 32.75 |
| C.G. Greenidge | | | | | | | | | 45 | 15 | | | 1 | 2 | — | 60 | 45 | 30.00 |
| D.L. Haynes | | | | | | | | | | | 70 | 15 | 1 | 2 | — | 85 | 70 | 42.50 |
| S.R. Greaves | | | | | | | | | | | 5 | 2 | 1 | 2 | — | 7 | 5 | 3.50 |
| Byes | 1 | | | 12 | 3 | 5 | 8 | 1 | 8 | 5 | 2 | | | | | | | |
| Leg-byes | 6 | 1 | 2 | 3 | 18 | 5 | 8 | 3 | 1 | 4 | 3 | 3 | | | | | | |
| Wides | | | 1 | | | | 2 | | | | | 2 | | | | | | |
| No-balls | 1 | | 12 | 6 | 8 | 3 | 20 | 9 | 10 | 4 | 12 | 8 | | | | | | |
| Total | 237 | 152 | 231 | 304 | 303 | 287 | 321 | 290 | 232 | 148 | 302 | 233 | | | | | | |
| Wickets | 10 | 4 | 10 | 9 | 10 | 10 | 10 | 10 | 10 | 10 | 10 | 5 | | | | | | |
| Result | W | | D | | D | | W | | L | | D | | | | | | | |
| Points | 16 | | 8 | | 8 | | 16 | | 0 | | — | | | | | | | |

*Catches* 17 – M.C. Worrell, 10 – T.R.O. Payne, 9 – C.A. Best, 4 – N.A. Phillips, 3 – G. Linton, R.O. Estwick, T.A. Hunte and H. Braithwaite, 2 – L.N. Reifer, A. Gilkes, D. Cumberbatch and subs, 1 – M.A. Small and D.L. Haynes

| BOWLING | R.O. Estwick | R.M. Ellcock | M.A. Small | G.L. Linton | N.A. Phillips | D. Cumberbatch | C.A. Best | S.R. Greaves | T.A. Hunte |
|---|---|---|---|---|---|---|---|---|---|
| *v.* Trinidad and Tobago | 15–2–60–2 | 10–2–35–1 | 17–2–57–5 | 7–3–17–1 | 1.1–0–1–1 | | | | |
| (Bridgetown) 20–23 January | 10–2–31–3 | 12–2–49–2 | 19–2–53–3 | 15.3–3–45–2 | 9–0–29–0 | | | | |
| *v.* Windward Islands | 8–0–29–1 | 7–1–27–0 | 15–4–34–0 | 27.4–3–75–5 | 14–1–35–4 | | | | |
| (Bridgetown) 28–31 January | | 5–1–17–1 | 7–2–16–1 | 2–0–8–0 | | | | | |
| *v.* Leeward Islands | 19–3–68–6 | | 17.2–1–64–3 | 11–1–53–0 | 13–2–39–1 | 18–3–47–0 | | | |
| (Basseterre) 3–6 February | 11–1–27–0 | | 18–1–51–3 | 17–7–32–2 | 15–2–30–1 | 11–2–29–1 | | | |
| *v.* Jamaica (Bridgetown) | 11–0–64–0 | | 16–3–57–3 | 11–0–46–3 | 12–1–34–3 | 7–1–30–1 | | | |
| 11–14 February | 13–2–38–3 | | | 23–3–91–3 | 20–3–52–3 | 3.4–1–16–1 | | | |
| *v.* Guyana (Georgetown) | 17–1–76–3 | 5.1–1–31–2 | | 14–0–65–1 | 16–5–34–0 | 28–2–67–3 | | | |
| 17–19 February | 6.3–0–19–1 | 3–0–26–0 | | | 7–0–31–0 | 10–1–24–0 | | | |
| *v.* Australians (Bridgetown) | 23–3–86–3 | | 19–5–60–0 | | 19–3–73–0 | 15–3–74–3 | | 6–1–23–0 | 2–0–10–0 |
| 24–27 March | 25–5–106–1 | | 20–2–78–1 | | 11–1–40–0 | 26–4–98–2 | 5–2–19–0 | | |
| | 158.3–19–604–23 *av.* 26.26 | 42.1–7–185–6 *av.* 30.83 | 148.2–20–470–19 *av.* 24.73 | 128.1–20–432–17 *av.* 25.41 | 137.1–18–398–13 *av.* 30.61 | 118.4–17–385–11 *av.* 35.00 | 5–2–19–0 — | 6–1–23–0 — | 2–0–10–0 — |

previous match, gave the visitors' innings substance. Leeward Islands were 77 for 6, 4 wickets having gone to Roddy Estwick who finished with a career best 6 for 68, when Ralston Otto was joined by Noel Guishard. They added 183 and both batsmen hit career best scores. Their lead having been restricted to 30, Barbados needed runs at a good rate and Braithwaite and Payne batted well, but the home side's bowling was never easy to score from, Eddy bowling 7 overs for 3 runs with his off-breaks. Small gave Leeward some fright when he dismissed the out-of-form Julien, Buffonge and Man of the Match Otto in quick succession, but a draw always seemed likely.

Jamaica, trailing on the first innings, recovered well to beat Trinidad and challenge Barbados at the top of the Shell Shield table. Jamaica had struggled on the first day and Cleveland Davidson's 43 was the only innings of substance in a rain-marred opening to the match.

150 for 7 at lunch on the third day, Trinidad were given a boost when K.C. Williams and Harold Joseph added 51 for the ninth wicket. Jamaica fought back well and owed much to Davidson and Neita who put on 84 for the fourth wicket. The later batsmen went for quick runs and the last 5 wickets went for 19 runs.

Trinidad needed 227 to win and went for brisk runs, but Courtenay Walsh's pace and Errol Wilson's off-breaks were a disconcerting combination and with Robert Haynes' leg-breaks also causing problems, they were soon in trouble. They scored at the rate of nearly six an over at the start, but wickets fell just as quickly and at tea they were 71 for 4. There was no recovery and in one spell after tea 5 wickets fell for 21 runs.

***11, 12, 13 and 14 February***

***at Albion, Berbice***

**Guyana** 427 for 9 dec (C.B. Lambert 123, A.A. Lyght 95, Timur Mohammed 62, W.H.F. White 53, D. Thompson 4 for 94)
**Leeward Islands** 208 (S.I. Williams 63, L. Lawrence 56, D.I. Kallicharran 5 for 59, C. Butts 5 for 78) and 586 (V.A. Eddy 120, R.M. Otto 91, L. Lawrence 68, N.C. Guishard 62, A.M.E. Roberts 54)

*Match drawn*
*Guyana 8 pts, Leeward Islands 4 pts*

| | Byes | Leg-byes | Wides | No-balls | Total | Wkts |
|---|---|---|---|---|---|---|
| | 1 | 3 | | 9 | 174 | 10 |
| | 3 | 4 | 1 | 5 | 214 | 10 |
| | 4 | 8 | 1 | 4 | 212 | 10 |
| | 4 | | | 3 | 45 | 2 |
| | 2 | | 1 | | 273 | 10 |
| | 1 | 4 | | | 174 | 7 |
| | 8 | 6 | 4 | 7 | 245 | 10 |
| | 4 | 1 | 1 | 2 | 202 | 10 |
| | 1 | 6 | | 7 | 280 | 10 |
| | 4 | | | 5 | 104 | 1 |
| | 1 | 5 | 5 | 2 | 332 | 6 |
| | 6 | 9 | | 5 | 356 | 4 |

***at Arnos Vale, Kingstown***

**Windward Islands** 374 (L.A. Lewis 128, L.C. Sebastien 107, G. Mahabir 4 for 84)
**Trinidad and Tobago** 130 (A. Rajah 61, N. Phillip 5 for 47, S.J. Hinds 4 for 17) and 215 (P.V. Simmonds 66, T. Kentish 4 for 73, S.J. Hinds 4 for 76)

*Windward Islands won by an innings and 29 runs*
*Windward Islands 16 pts, Trinidad and Tobago 0 pts*

***at Kensington Oval, Bridgetown***

**Barbados** 321 (T. Hunte 70, E.L. Wilson 5 for 63) and 290 (T.R.O. Payne 76, C.A. Best 65, R.C. Haynes 4 for 78)
**Jamaica** 245 (M.C. Neita 108) and 202 (A. Morgan 57)

*Barbados won by 164 runs*
*Barbados 16 pts, Jamaica 0 pts*

When Walsh was caught by substitute Broomes off the bowling of Cumberbatch just before tea on the last day at Bridgetown Barbados had beaten Jamaica by 164 runs and were assured of first place in the Shell Shield although it was still possible for Jamaica to share the title if they won their final match.

Barbados had held control since Best and Hunte began the match with an opening stand of 101. Solid batting throughout the order took the home side to 246 for 7 by the close and they were all out just under an hour before lunch on the second day. Jamaica struggled in the afternoon and were 126 for 5 before Mark Neita played a quite magnificent innings. He completely dominated the day and no other batsman

*Norbert Phillip, a valiant captain of Windward Islands, fast bowler and powerful hitter. He bowled his side to success against Trinidad and Tobago, 11–14 February. (George Herringshaw)*

reached 40, indeed Jamaica's next highest scorers were opener Williams (36) and Haynes (20). Jamaica were all out early on the third morning and by lunch Best and Hunte had completed their second century stand of the match.

Declaring at their overnight score, Barbados left themselves the last day in which to bowl out Jamaica. Only 2 wickets fell before lunch, but the last 8 wickets fell for 91 runs.

Windward Islands beat Trinidad inside three days. A century opening partnership between Sebastien and John was followed by a career best from Linton Lewis. Trinidad were routed by Norbert Phillip's pace and Stanley Hinds' off-

**Guyana 1984**
First Class Matches

| BATTING | v. Jamaica (Kingston) 20–23 January 1984 | | v. Trinidad (Port of Spain) 28–31 January 1984 | | v. Windward Islands (Georgetown) 3–6 February 1984 | | V. Leeward Islands (Berbice) 11–14 February 1984 | | v. Barbados (Georgetown) 17–19 February 1984 | | v. Australians (Georgetown) 24–27 February 1984 | | M | Inns | NOs | Runs | HS | Av |
|---|---|---|---|---|---|---|---|---|---|---|---|---|---|---|---|---|---|---|
| A.A. Lyght | 122 | 42 | 2 | 6 | 17 | 63 | 95 | — | 31 | 25 | 38 | 0 | 6 | 11 | — | 441 | 122 | 40.09 |
| C.B. Lambert | | | | | 52 | 49 | 123 | — | 23 | 68* | 52 | 4 | 4 | 7 | 1 | 371 | 123 | 61.83 |
| A.F.D. Jackman | 78 | 31 | 61 | 38 | 19 | — | 5 | — | 100 | 2* | 125 | 22 | 6 | 10 | 1 | 481 | 125 | 53.44 |
| Timur Mohammed | 1 | 3 | 38 | 66* | 32 | 1* | 62 | — | 18 | — | 68 | 22 | 6 | 10 | 2 | 311 | 68 | 38.87 |
| R. Seeram | 37 | 0 | 20 | 35 | 57 | 10* | 22 | — | | | 37 | 52 | 5 | 9 | 1 | 270 | 57 | 33.75 |
| D.I. Kallicharran | | | 15 | 22 | 8 | — | 7 | — | 48 | — | 22 | 4 | 5 | 7 | — | 126 | 48 | 18.00 |
| R.A. Harper | | | | | | | | | 7 | — | 5 | 86 | 2 | 3 | — | 98 | 86 | 32.66 |
| M.R. Pydanna | 7 | 11 | 8 | 20 | 5 | 4 | 14* | — | 18 | — | 23* | 56 | 6 | 10 | 2 | 166 | 56 | 20.75 |
| C. Butts | 25 | 5 | 31 | 1 | 16 | — | 28 | — | 0 | — | 8 | 3* | 6 | 9 | 1 | 117 | 31 | 14.62 |
| R.F. Joseph | 4* | 0 | 0* | 0 | 0* | — | — | — | 0* | — | 1* | 0* | 6 | 8 | 6 | 5 | 4* | 2.50 |
| G.E. Charles | | | | | | | | | 11 | — | — | — | 2 | 1 | — | 11 | 11 | 11.00 |
| W.H.F. Whyte | 105 | 18 | 1 | 4 | 4 | — | 53 | — | 10 | — | | | 5 | 7 | — | 195 | 105 | 27.85 |
| K. Singh | 25 | 1 | 39 | 0 | 34 | — | 9 | — | | | | | 4 | 6 | — | 108 | 39 | 18.00 |
| S. Ganouri | 0 | 11 | | | | | | | | | | | 1 | 2 | — | 11 | 11 | 5.50 |
| L. Fraser | 0 | 0* | | | | | | | | | | | 1 | 2 | 1 | 0 | 0* | 0.00 |
| T.R. Etwaroo | | | 22 | — | | | | | | | | | 1 | 6 | — | 22 | 22 | 22.00 |
| Byes | 2 | 4 | 3 | | 7 | 4 | 1 | | 1 | 4 | 8 | 10 | | | | | | |
| Leg-byes | | | 8 | 2 | 6 | 4 | 6 | | 6 | | 14 | | | | | | | |
| Wides | | 1 | | 1 | | | 1 | | | | 1 | | | | | | | |
| No-balls | 5 | 7 | 2 | 2 | 4 | 1 | 1 | | 7 | 5 | 15 | 1 | | | | | | |
| Total | 411 | 134 | 250 | 197 | 261 | 136 | 427 | | 280 | 104 | 417 | 260 | | | | | | |
| Wickets | 10 | 10 | 10 | 9† | 10 | 3 | 9 | | 10 | 1 | 8 | 8 | | | | | | |
| Result | L | | D | | D | | D | | W | | D | | | | | | | |
| Points | 5 | | 4 | | 8 | | 8 | | 16 | | — | | | | | | | |

*Catches*
17–M.R. Pydanna (ct 12/st 5)
10–W.H.F. Whyte (ct 9/st 1)
8–C.B. Lambert
7–A.F.D. Jackman
6–R. Seeram
4–A.A. Lyght
3–K. Singh and D.I. Kallicharran
1–Timur Mohammed, C. Butts, R.F. Joseph and G.E. Charles (plus one as sub)

†T.R. Etwaroo absent injured

| BOWLING | R.F. Joseph | G.E. Charles | C. Butts | R.A. Harper | D.I. Kallicharran | W.H.A. Whyte | R. Seeram | K. Singh | A.A. Lyght |
|---|---|---|---|---|---|---|---|---|---|
| v. Jamaica (Kingston) | 33–4–114–6 | | 46–6–104–2 | | | | | 5–1–15–0 | |
| 20–23 January | 17–4–39–1 | | 25–4–70–0 | | | 10–7–16–2 | | 4–1–8–0 | |
| v. Trinidad and Tobago | 26–6–57–1 | | 32–16–33–1 | | 47–7–135–4 | 17–5–47–2 | | 19–5–49–1 | |
| (Port of Spain) 28–31 January | 4–0–13–2 | | | | | | | 4–2–7–1 | |
| v. Windward Islands | 11–1–31–0 | | 41.5–15–79–6 | | 41–10–89–3 | 3–1–5–0 | | 6–1–12–1 | |
| (Georgetown) 3–6 February | | | | | | | | | |
| v. Leeward Islands | 5–0–33–0 | | 33–6–78–5 | | 32.5–6–59–5 | 4–0–14–0 | | 3–0–22–0 | |
| (Berbice) 11–14 February | 12–0–55–0 | | 65–12–203–4 | | 50–11–161–3 | 2–0–12–0 | 12–1–37–0 | 4–0–33–0 | |
| v. Barbados (Georgetown) | 11–2–49–1 | 8–1–27–0 | 31–17–40–3 | 24.3–7–72–6 | 7–1–35–0 | | | | |
| 17–19 February | 8–1–39–2 | 2–0–5–0 | 28.5–12–45–3 | 23–13–30–5 | 8–0–20–0 | | | | |
| v. Australians (Georgetown) | 23–5–96–1 | 9–2–45–0 | 38–4–132–3 | 34–2–124–2 | 11–1–51–0 | | 1–0–3–0 | | |
| 24–27 February | 14–4–47–2 | | 20–4–64–2 | 24–6–45–0 | 27–3–95–1 | | | | 3–1–9–0 |
| | 164–27–573–16 av. 35.81 | 19–3–77–0 — | 360.4–96–848–29 av. 29.24 | 105.3–28–271–13 av. 20.84 | 223.5–39–645–16 av. 40.31 | 36–13–94–4 av. 23.50 | 13–1–40–0 — | 45–10–146–3 av. 48.66 | 3–1–9–0 — |

a A.D.F. Jackman 4.3–0–25–2
M.R. Pydanna 1–0–17–0
b C.B. Lambert 2–0–11–0
c A.D.F. Jackman 1–0–2–0

breaks and fared little better when they followed-on as the combined off-breaks of Hinds and Kentish took Windward to victory.

Clayton Lambert's maiden century and a first wicket stand of 202 with Andrew Lyght put Guyana in an unassailable position. Runs flowed into the second day and in spite of a century opening partnership between Lawrence and Shirlon Williams, Leeward was forced to follow-on, 10 wickets falling for 88 runs to the off-breaks of Butts and the leg-breaks of Kallicharran. There was another century opening stand, but 3 wickets were down before the arrears were cleared. It was a fourth wicket partnership of 198 between Ralston Otto and Victor Eddy which saved the game and with runs being plundered thereafter, Leeward moved to a massive 586 and Guyana were thwarted in spite of using 9 bowlers.

### *17, 18, 19 and 20 February*

#### *at Bourda Oval, Georgetown*

**Barbados** 232 (T. Hunte 72, T.R.O. Payne 59, R.A. Harper 6 for 72) and 148 (G.N. Reifer 51, R.A. Harper 5 for 30)
**Guyana** 280 (A.D.F. Jackman 100) and 104 for 1 (C.B. Lambert 68 not out)

*Guyana won by 9 wickets*
*Guyana 16 pts, Barbados 0 pts*

#### *at Queen's Park, St George's*

**Jamaica** 120 (J. Etienne 4 for 17)
**Windward Islands** 78 for 8 (C.A. Walsh 5 for 34)

*Match abandoned*
*Jamaica 4 pts, Windward Islands 4 pts*

### *18, 19, 20 and 21 February*

#### *at Basseterre, St Kitt's*

**Australians** 429 for 7 dec (K.C. Wessels 126 retired hurt, A.R. Border 74, K.J. Hughes 61, E.A.E. Baptiste 4 for 95) and 250 for 7 dec (K.C. Wessels 86)
**Leeward Islands** 305 (S.W. Julien 123, E.A.E. Baptiste 57 not out, C.G. Rackemann 6 for 105) and 170 (N.C. Guishard 50)

*Australians won by 204 runs*

| S. Ganouri | L. Fraser | Timur Mohammed | *Byes* | *Leg-byes* | *Wides* | *No-balls* | *Total* | *Wkts* |
|---|---|---|---|---|---|---|---|---|
| 23–2–67–2 | 7–0–23–0 | 4–0–12–0 | 9 | 3 | | 5 | 347 | 10 |
| 6–1–23–0 | 5–1–13–0 | 6.1–0–17–1 | 9 | 5 | | 1 | 200 | 4 |
| | | 2–0–8–0 | 9 | 6 | | 8 | 344 | 10 |
| | | | | | | 2 | 20 | 3 |
| | | | 5 | 2 | 2 | 3 | 223 | 10 |
| | | | 1 | 1 | 3 | 1 | 208 | 10 |
| | | 4–2–22–1 | 16 | 5 | 12 | 3 | 586 | 10a |
| | | | 8 | 1 | | 10 | 232 | 10 |
| | | | 5 | 4 | | 4 | 148 | 10 |
| | | | 2 | 3 | 2 | 8 | 467 | 6b |
| | | | 12 | 2 | 1 | 5 | 276 | 5c |
| 29–3–90–2 *av.* 45.00 | 12–1–36–0 — | 16.1–2–59–2 *av.* 29.50 | | | | | | |

Barbados were confirmed as champions when rain ruined the match at St George's. There was no play on the first and third days and no play before tea on the second. John, with 44, was the only batsman to show ability to cope with the conditions.

Teams welcomed back their Test players and Roger Harper had a devastating effect upon the match in Georgetown where Guyana beat Barbados for the first time in eighteen years. Greenidge, Hunte and Payne took Barbados to 165 for 2, but Harper's off-breaks totally bemused the later batsmen. Guyana owed their narrow lead to a splendid hundred by Andrew Jackman and a spirited 48 from Kallicharran, but by the close of the second day, when Barbados were 79 for 4, the deposed champions had taken a firm grip on the game. There was no recovery and Guyana scored at 4 an over to win by tea on the third day.

The Australians began their tour in encouraging style. Wessels with fifteen fours and a six shook off all signs of jet lag until retiring with an injured ankle. He and Hughes put on 125 for the third wicket. The home side had three off-spinners in their side to counter the Australian left-handers, but Border and Hookes cut loose and Hookes hit Thompson for three successive sixes. Australia declared at their overnight score and fielded substitutes with Phillips and Ritchie arriving late having over-slept. Alderman took a wicket with his first ball in the West Indies when he had Lawrence taken low at second slip, but Shane Julien who had had a dreadful time since moving from Windward Islands played a somewhat unorthodox innings and hit thirteen fours and a six in his 174-minute stay which lifted the home side. Baptiste hit a six and five fours in a spirited 57, but Rackemann finished off the tail to give the tourists a comfortable lead. Wessels was again in fine form and Australia moved into an impregnable position. At lunch on the last day Leeward Islands were 96 for 6, and lost another wicket shortly after. Nearly all the wickets had fallen as batsmen played attacking shots against the pace men. Guishard halted the slump, but Lawrence and Eddy were the only others to reach double figures.

### *23, 24, 25 and 26 February*

#### *at St John's, Antigua*

**Trinidad and Tobago** 337 (R. Nanan 98 not out, P.V. Simmonds 72, A. Rajah 50) and 289 for 3 (A. Rajah 141 not out, P. Moosai 66 not out)
**Leeward Islands** 613 for 5 dec (R.B. Richardson 162, R.M. Otto 136, L. Lawrence 118, S.W. Julien 90)

*Match drawn*
*Leeward Islands 8 pts, Trinidad and Tobago 4 pts*

#### *at Georgetown*

**Australians** 467 for 6 dec (A.R. Border 113, S.B. Smith 105, G.M. Ritchie 64, D.W. Hookes 61, D.M.J. Jones 58) and 276 for 5 dec (S.B. Smith 116, R.B. Phillips 62, D.M.J. Jones 60)
**Guyana** 417 for 8 dec (A.F.D. Jackman 125, Timur Mohammed 68, C.B. Lambert 52, R.M. Hogg 5 for 114) and 260 for 8 (R.A. Harper 86, M.R. Pydanna 56, R. Seeram 52, T.G. Hogan 5 for 95)

*Match drawn*

Leading the Australian side, Allan Border emulated Kim Hughes by winning the toss. On a perfect batting wicket the Australians enjoyed themselves and Border hit three sixes and twelve fours in his innings. Ritchie scored 64 off 69 balls

## Trinidad and Tobago 1984
First Class Matches

| BATTING | v. Barbados (Bridgetown) 20–23 January 1984 | | v. Guyana (Port of Spain) 28–31 January 1984 | | v. Jamaica (Pointe-à-Pierre) 3–6 February 1984 | | v. Windward Islands (Kingston) 11–13 February 1984 | | v. Leeward Islands (St John's) 23–26 February 1984 | | v. Australians (Pointe-à-Pierre) 9–12 March 1984 | | M | Inns | NOs | Runs | HS | Av |
|---|---|---|---|---|---|---|---|---|---|---|---|---|---|---|---|---|---|---|
| R.S. Gabriel | | | | | | | | | | | 8 | 10 | 1 | 2 | — | 18 | 10 | 9.00 |
| P.V. Simmonds | 42 | 6 | 5 | 15 | 33 | 0 | 28 | 66 | 72 | 22 | 4 | 42 | 6 | 12 | — | 335 | 72 | 27.91 |
| H.A. Gomes | | | | | | | | | 1 | 3 | 23 | 8 | 2 | 4 | — | 35 | 23 | 8.75 |
| A.L. Logie | | | | | | | | | | | 12 | 13 | 1 | 2 | — | 25 | 13 | 12.50 |
| A. Rajah | 2 | 3 | 72 | 1* | 23 | 34 | 61 | 8 | 40 | 141* | 100 | 39 | 6 | 12 | 2 | 534 | 141* | 53.40 |
| P. Moosai | 7 | 78 | 97 | — | | | | | 25 | 66* | 33 | 20 | 4 | 7 | 1 | 326 | 97 | 54.33 |
| R. Nanan | 30 | 46 | 17 | — | 32 | 10 | 0 | 1 | 98* | — | 38 | 40* | 6 | 10 | 2 | 312 | 98* | 39.00 |
| C. Rampersad | 10 | 45 | 29 | 0* | 4 | 27 | 26 | 1 | 10 | — | 61 | 10 | 6 | 11 | 1 | 223 | 61 | 22.30 |
| A. Gray | 31* | 3* | 29 | — | | | | | 14 | — | 41* | 3 | 4 | 6 | 3 | 121 | 41* | 40.33 |
| H. Joseph | 0 | 0 | 6 | — | 24 | 24 | 0 | 26 | 0 | — | 0 | 26 | 6 | 10 | — | 106 | 26 | 10.60 |
| D. St Hilaire | | | | | | | | | 2 | — | 0 | 0 | 2 | 3 | — | 2 | 2 | 0.66 |
| W. Debisette | 9 | 10 | | | | | | | | | | | 1 | 2 | — | 19 | 10 | 9.50 |
| A. Dharson | 9 | 4 | 7 | 1 | 17 | 9 | | | | | | | 3 | 6 | — | 47 | 17 | 7.83 |
| G. Sahadeo | 18 | 1 | 9 | — | 6 | 1 | 5 | 37* | | | | | 4 | 7 | 1 | 77 | 37* | 12.83 |
| G. Mahabir | 3 | 5 | 11* | — | 0* | 5* | 0 | 20 | 0 | — | | | 5 | 8 | 3 | 44 | 20 | 8.80 |
| J. Suraj | | | 39 | 1 | 0 | 6 | | | | | | | 2 | 4 | — | 46 | 39 | 11.50 |
| R. Sampath | | | | | 30 | 24 | 0 | 16 | | | | | 2 | 4 | — | 70 | 30 | 17.50 |
| K.C. Williams | | | | | 48 | 3 | 0* | 4 | | | | | 2 | 4 | 1 | 55 | 48 | 18.33 |
| K.R. Bainey | | | | | | | 0 | 22 | 44 | 49 | | | 2 | 4 | — | 115 | 49 | 28.75 |
| K. Williams | | | | | | | 0 | 8 | | | | | 1 | 2 | — | 8 | 8 | 8.00 |
| Byes | 1 | 3 | 9 | | 4 | | | 1 | 2 | | | 4 | | | | | | |
| Leg-byes | 3 | 4 | 6 | | 3 | 4 | 3 | 4 | 4 | 1 | 12 | 6 | | | | | | |
| Wides | | 1 | | | | | | | 3 | | | 1 | | | | | | |
| No-balls | 9 | 5 | 8 | 2 | 3 | 6 | 7 | 1 | 12 | 7 | 4 | | | | | | | |
| Total | 174 | 214 | 344 | 20 | 227 | 153 | 130 | 215 | 337 | 289 | 336 | 222 | | | | | | |
| Wickets | 10 | 10 | 10 | 3 | 10 | 10 | 10 | 10 | 10 | 3 | 10 | 10 | | | | | | |
| Results | L | | D | | L | | L | | D | | D | | | | | | | |
| Points | 0 | | 8 | | 5 | | 0 | | 4 | | — | | | | | | | |

*Catches* 8–C. Rampersad (ct 7/st 1)
P.V. Simmonds and
G. Sahadeo (ct 4/st 4)
7–A. Rajah
4–R. Sampath (inc. 2 as sub)

2–A. Dharson,
R. Nanan,
H.A. Gomes
P. Moosai,
J. Suraj and H. Joseph

1–A. Gray,
G. Mahabir,
K.R. Bainey
and sub (Singh)

| BOWLING | A. Gray | D. St Hilaire | H. Joseph | R. Nanan | H.A. Gomes | P.V. Simmonds | G. Mahabir | K.C. Williams | R. Sampath |
|---|---|---|---|---|---|---|---|---|---|
| v. Barbados (Bridgetown) 20–23 January | 13–3–37–2 | | 37.1–7–83–5 | 33–12–48–0 | | 5–0–11–0 | 29–9–51–3 | | |
| | 2–0–11–0 | | 26.4–5–56–1 | 24–7–40–1 | | | 19–7–44–1 | | |
| v. Guyana (Port of Spain) 28–31 January | 12–2–48–3 | | 24–3–76–0 | 37.3–13–56–5 | | 3–1–12–0 | 15–1–47–2 | | |
| | 5–0–23–1 | | 27–5–64–3 | 20.4–9–45–4 | | 10–2–20–0 | 17–5–43–0 | | |
| v. Jamaica (Pointe-à-Pierre) 3–6 February | | | 18.4–4–42–3 | 22–7–21–3 | | | 13–3–30–3 | 6–1–24–0 | 5–0–22–0 |
| | | | 36–7–97–3 | 19–3–75–0 | | | 25.1–7–57–4 | 12–0–37–1 | 8–1–13–1 |
| v. Windward Islands (Kingston) 11–13 February | | | 44–5–100–0 | 54–10–108–2 | | 1–0–10–0 | 26.2–3–84–4 | 12–2–34–3 | 13–4–23–0 |
| v. Leeward Islands (St John's) 23–26 February | 19–0–102–1 | 12–0–93–1 | 38–5–105–0 | 51–8–114–0 | 14–2–56–2 | | 37–2–120–1 | | |
| v. Australians (Pointe-à-Pierre) 9–12 March | 23–4–89–2 | 18–1–90–3 | 28–5–80–2 | 21.2–2–62–3 | 7–1–28–0 | 2–0–7–0 | | | |
| | 2–0–2–0 | 2–0–7–0 | 2–0–9–0 | 2–1–13–0 | | | | | |
| | 76–9–312–9 *av.* 34.66 | 32–1–190–4 *av.* 47.50 | 281.3–46–712–17 *av.* 41.88 | 284.3–72–582–18 *av.* 32.33 | 21–3–84–2 *av.* 42.00 | 21–3–60–0 — | 181.3–37–476–18 *av.* 26.44 | 30–3–95–4 *av.* 23.75 | 26–5–58–1 *av.* 58.00 |

a T.R. Etwaroo absent injured
b C. Rampersad 5–4–5–0

*Mylton Pydanna (Barbados). Given few opportunities with the West Indian side in India, he returned to perform as capably as ever behind the stumps in the Shell Shield. (Adrian Murrell)*

*Ricardo Ellcock who returned to Barbados to bowl well in the Shell Shield triumph. (Ken Kelly)*

and confirmed the opinion that here was a neat, poised and powerful player. Smith and Border put on 180 for the third wicket and after tea Hookes and Jones put on 113 for the fifth in exciting style. Guyana responded with a third wicket stand of 196 between Andy Jackman and Timur Mohammed and they declared at lunch on the third day which was shortened by the weather. Hogg, although experiencing run-up problems, bowled remarkably well and extracted pace from a placid pitch. Smith hit his second hundred of the match and played himself into the Test side and when Lawson struck two quick blows the home side were in trouble. Timur and Jackman hung on until lunch, but Hogan caused a collapse in mid-afternoon. Harper and Pydanna batted well to save the game for with Charles out with a fractured hand, Guyana were in trouble. Hogan exploited the rough well, but the tourists missed several chances and this cost them the match.

The Shell Shield ended with a record 613 for 5 by Leeward Islands. Trinidad closed the first day at 305 for 6, but were out quickly the next morning. Richardson and Lawrence began the home side's reply with a stand of 290, and Julien and Otto added 120 for the third wicket. Runs came at $3\frac{1}{2}$ an over and the only failure in the Leeward side was Viv Richards with 37. Declaring an hour before the close of the third day, Leeward were unable to bowl out Trinidad a second time and Rajah batted impressively.

| P. Moosai | R.S. Gabriel | A. Rajah | *Byes* | *Leg-byes* | *Wides* | *No-balls* | *Total* | *Wkts* |
|---|---|---|---|---|---|---|---|---|
| | | | 1 | 6 | | 1 | 237 | 10 |
| | | | | 1 | | | 152 | 3 |
| | | | 3 | 8 | | 2 | 250 | 10 |
| | | | | 2 | 1 | 2 | 197 | 9a |
| | | | 7 | 5 | 1 | | 151 | 10 |
| | | | 15 | 8 | | | 302 | 10 |
| | | | 6 | 9 | 1 | | 374 | 10 |
| | | | 10 | 13 | 2 | 2 | 613 | 5 |
| | | | 5 | 9 | 2 | 10 | 370 | 10 |
| 3-2-4-0 | 3-2-6-0 | 4-3-10-1 | | | 3 | 5 | 56 | 1b |
| 3-2-<br>4-0 | 3-2-<br>6-0 | 4-3-<br>10-1 | | | | | | |
| — | — | *av.* 10.00 | | | | | | |

**Shell Shield – Final Table**

| | *P* | *W* | *L* | *D* | *NR* | *Pts* |
|---|---|---|---|---|---|---|
| Barbados (3) | 5 | 2 | 1 | 2 | — | 48 |
| Guyana (1) | 5 | 1 | 1 | 3 | — | 41 |
| Jamaica (6) | 5 | 2 | 2 | — | 1 | 36 |
| Leeward Islands (4) | 5 | 1 | — | 3 | 1 | 36 |
| Windward Islands (2) | 5 | 1 | — | 2 | 2 | 32 |
| Trinidad & Tobago (5) | 5 | — | 3 | 2 | — | 17 |

(1983 positions in brackets)

## First One-Day International
## WEST INDIES *v.* AUSTRALIA

Woolley chipped a bone in his hand in the match against Guyana and was not available for the first one-day international, but as Australia decided to omit both spinners, the absence of a specialist wicket-keeper mattered less. West Indies were badly hit by injuries. Marshall, Holding and Baptiste were not able to play and Clive Lloyd declared himself not fully fit so that Milton Small, after a brief but successful career, made his international debut.

The West Indian pace bowling, Garner apart, was unimpressive, but the Australians failed to take full advantage of some wayward bowling and it was 17 overs before a boundary was scored. On a perfect pitch Wessels and Smith occupied 25 overs for their opening stand of 106, and Ritchie failed to lift the scoring rate while Hughes and Border fell quickly to Gomes' off-spin. It was left to Dean Jones to score some brisk, unorthodox runs and the last 10 overs produced 66 runs.

The success of the spin in the West Indies attack could not have encouraged the Australian pace men and they were poorly supported in the field where three chances were missed as Haynes and Richardson added 167 for the second wicket. Haynes stroked West Indies to a comfortable victory.

**Jamaica 1984**
First Class Matches

| BATTING | *v.* Guyana (Kingston) 20–23 January 1984 | | *v.* Leeward Islands (Kingston) 28–30 January 1984 | | *v.* Trinidad and Tobago (Point-à-Pierre) 3–6 February 1984 | | *v.* Barbados (Bridgetown) 11–14 February 1984 | | *v.* Windward Islands (St George's) 17–20 February 1984 | | *M* | *Inns* | *NOs* | *Runs* | *HS* | *Av* |
|---|---|---|---|---|---|---|---|---|---|---|---|---|---|---|---|---|
| O.W. Peters | 72 | 19 | 40 | 31 | 20 | 47 | 15 | 11 | 15 | — | 5 | 9 | — | 270 | 72 | 30.00 |
| A.B. Williams | 34 | 18 | 30 | 41 | 36 | 5 | 36 | 2 | 18 | — | 5 | 9 | — | 220 | 41 | 24.44 |
| T. Corke | 12 | 62 | 9 | 6 | 15 | 37 | 1 | 26 | | | 4 | 8 | — | 168 | 62 | 21.00 |
| M.C. Neita | 133 | 61 | 22 | 51 | 1 | 70 | 108 | 36 | 0 | — | 5 | 9 | — | 482 | 133 | 53.55 |
| C.A. Davidson | 32 | 17* | 16 | 41 | 43 | 77 | 10 | 8 | 4 | — | 5 | 9 | 1 | 248 | 77 | 31.00 |
| M.A. Tucker | 1 | 8* | 4 | 21 | | | | | | | 2 | 4 | 1 | 34 | 21 | 11.33 |
| R.C. Haynes | 26 | — | 3 | 2 | 3 | 8 | 20 | 23 | 8 | — | 5 | 8 | — | 93 | 26 | 11.62 |
| P.A.O. Francis | 18 | — | 6 | 29 | 6 | 1 | 7 | 0 | 2 | — | 5 | 8 | — | 69 | 29 | 8.62 |
| K. McLeod | 1 | — | 5 | 3 | | | 0 | 6 | | | 3 | 5 | — | 15 | 6 | 3.00 |
| C.U. Thompson | 0 | — | 4* | 2* | 7 | 2 | | | 23 | — | 4 | 6 | 2 | 38 | 23 | 9.50 |
| C.A. Walsh | 1* | — | 0 | 1 | 0* | 6 | 19 | 14 | 8* | — | 5 | 8 | 3 | 49 | 19 | 9.80 |
| J.A. Gordon | | | | | 7 | 22 | | | 18 | — | 2 | 3 | — | 47 | 22 | 15.66 |
| E.L. Wilson | | | | | 0 | 4* | 0* | 11* | 4 | — | 3 | 5 | 3 | 19 | 11* | 9.50 |
| A. Morgan | | | | | | | 4 | 57 | 10 | — | 2 | 3 | — | 71 | 57 | 23.66 |
| Byes | 9 | 9 | 11 | 2 | 7 | 15 | 8 | 4 | 1 | | | | | | | |
| Leg-byes | 3 | 5 | 6 | 6 | 5 | 8 | 6 | 1 | 2 | | | | | | | |
| Wides | | | | | 1 | | 4 | 1 | | | | | | | | |
| No-balls | 5 | 1 | 9 | 5 | | | 7 | 2 | 7 | | | | | | | |
| Total | 347 | 200 | 165 | 241 | 151 | 302 | 245 | 202 | 120 | | | | | | | |
| Wickets | 10 | 4 | 10 | 10 | 10 | 10 | 10 | 10 | 10 | | | | | | | |
| Result | W | | L | | W | | L | | Ab. | | | | | | | |
| Points | 16 | | 0 | | 16 | | 0 | | 4 | | | | | | | |

*Catches* 12 – P.A.O. Francis, 11 – O.W. Peters, 5 – C.A. Davidson, 3 – C.A. Walsh, 2 – K. McLeod, T. Corke and A.B. Williams, 1 – R.C. Haynes and sub (J.A. Gordon)

| BOWLING | C.A. Walsh | K. McLeod | C.U. Thompson | R.C. Haynes | M.A. Tucker | M.C. Neita | T. Corke | E.L. Wilson | J.A. Gordon |
|---|---|---|---|---|---|---|---|---|---|
| *v.* Guyana (Kingston) | 19–0–108–1 | 17.3–3–49–3 | 26–7–64–2 | 18–1–80–0 | 39–14–80–3 | 2–0–7–0 | 5–0–21–0 | | |
| 20–23 January | 9–1–35–6 | 5–0–27–0 | 11.3–2–40–3 | 1–0–7–0 | 6–0–21–1 | | | | |
| *v.* Leeward Islands | 25–5–90–4 | 18–4–54–0 | 20–2–68–2 | 20–0–79–1 | 20.3–9–33–2 | 1–0–8–0 | | | |
| (Kingston) 28–30 January | 8–0–33–2 | 2–0–7–0 | 5–0–29–1 | | | | | | |
| *v.* Trinidad and Tobago | 26–4–80–5 | | 7–1–34–0 | 11.5–1–49–2 | | | | 26–3–50–2 | 4–2–7–0 |
| (Pointe-à-Pierre) 3–6 February | 9–0–51–3 | | 5–1–16–0 | 10.4–1–34–2 | | | | 14–1–48–4 | |
| *v.* Barbados (Bridgetown) | 23–2–79–2 | 15–3–48–1 | | 39–9–89–1 | | | 8–0–26–0 | 39–19–63–5 | |
| 11–14 February | 20–3–93–2 | 11–1–46–2 | | 28–7–78–4 | | | 2–0–11–0 | 23–7–52–0 | |
| *v.* Windward Islands | 15–2–34–5 | | 10–2–32–1 | 2–1–4–0 | | | | 2–0–6–0 | |
| (St George's) 17–20 February | | | | | | | | | |
| | 154–17–603–30 | 68.3–11–231–6 | 84.3–15–283–9 | 130.3–20–420–10 | 65.3–20–134–6 | 3–0–15–0 | 15–0–58–0 | 104–30–219–11 | 4–2–7–0 |
| | *av.* 20.06 | *av.* 38.50 | *av.* 31.44 | *av.* 42.00 | *av.* 22.33 | — | — | *av.* 19.90 | — |

## First Test Match
## WEST INDIES *v.* AUSTRALIA

Only 71 minutes play were possible on the first day during which Australia reached 55 for 3. Garner took 3 wickets in 33 balls at a cost of 19 runs. Smith, on his Test debut, was taken high above his head by Dujon after the ball had leapt off the batsman's glove and Wessels fell to a tumbling catch at slip. Hughes, rather unluckily, was out to the last ball before the final stoppage.

Australia fared badly on the second day when only an innings of great character from Ritchie, who batted for 225 minutes and hit a six and eleven fours, saved them from total humiliation as Garner and Harper routed the middle order. Harper exploited roughness outside the off-stump to trouble the left-handers and three wickets fell for 9 runs, including the wicket of Ritchie, as Australia slumped to 182 for 9. There followed a remarkable record stand of 92 between Hogg and Hogan, both of whom hit their best scores in Test cricket, which raised Australian hopes.

West Indies had closed the second day at 20 for 0, but Lawson, bowling very quickly and very accurately, had Greenidge out with his fourth ball of the third day and later had Richardson dismissed. Lawson had been fined earlier for rudeness to the umpire. Haynes batted carefully, but Hogan, revelling in success in the match, destroyed the middle order and Australia took an unexpected lead of 49.

23 for 0 overnight, Australia were struggling at 78 for 5 at lunch, Garner and Daniel having done the damage. Wessels was first to fall, taken at first slip. Ritchie and Hughes went in successive overs, the first lbw, the second taken at short-leg. Smith batted 93 minutes before edging a leg-cutter to Dujon. Hookes was bowled by a ball that kept low.

Border and Phillips added 125 in the afternoon to revive Australia's hopes. Uncertain at first, Border batted doggedly until run out. Phillips, the more fluent, finished the day on 71, but added only 5 more on the last morning. There were some brisk runs from Lawson and Hogan, however, and Hughes left West Indies 260 minutes in which to make 323 to win.

Greenidge, in glorious form, and Haynes put the 100 up in the twenty-seventh over, but although they continued to bat with great panache, the task was too great and the chase was ended with 4 of the last 20 overs still remaining, but with a new record first wicket partnership for West Indies against Australia having been established.

| C.A. Davidson | Byes | Leg-byes | Wides | No-balls | Total | Wkts |
|---|---|---|---|---|---|---|
| | 2 | | | 5 | 411 | 10 |
| | 4 | | 1 | 7 | 134 | 10 |
| | 1 | 4 | | 9 | 337 | 10 |
| | | 2 | | 6 | 71 | 3 |
| | 4 | 3 | | 3 | 227 | 10 |
| | | 4 | | 6 | 153 | 10 |
| | 8 | 8 | 2 | 20 | 321 | 10 |
| 1–0–6–0 | 1 | 3 | | 9 | 290 | 9 |
| | 2 | | | | 78 | 8 |
| 1–0–6–0 — | | | | | | |

ABOVE: *Courtenay Walsh. A splendid season for Jamaica. His 30 first-class wickets won him a place in the party to tour England. (Adrian Murrell).* BELOW: *Gordon Greenidge who shared a record first wicket partnership of 250 with Desmond Haynes in the first Test. (Allsport)*

## FIRST ONE-DAY INTERNATIONAL – WEST INDIES *v.* AUSTRALIA
29 February 1984 at Berbice, Guyana

**AUSTRALIA**

|  |  |  |
|---|---|---|
| K.C. Wessels | c Small, b Richards | 44 |
| S.B. Smith | b Gomes | 60 |
| G.M. Ritchie | run out | 46 |
| K.J. Hughes† | b Gomes | 2 |
| A.R. Border | b Gomes | 2 |
| D.M.J. Jones | not out | 43 |
| W.B. Phillips* | not out | 0 |
| G.F. Lawson | | |
| R.M. Hogg | | |
| C.G. Rackemann | | |
| T.M. Alderman | | |
| Extras | b 7, lb 18, nb 9 | 34 |
| (50 overs) | (for 5 wickets) | 231 |

| | O | M | R | W |
|---|---|---|---|---|
| Garner | 10 | 1 | 35 | — |
| Daniel | 5 | — | 19 | — |
| Davis | 10 | 1 | 66 | — |
| Small | 5 | — | 14 | — |
| Richards | 10 | — | 38 | 1 |
| Gomes | 10 | — | 34 | 3 |

FALL OF WICKETS
1- 106, 2- 137, 3- 143, 4- 159, 5- 222

**WEST INDIES**

|  |  |  |
|---|---|---|
| C.G. Greenidge | c Phillips, b Rackemann | 23 |
| D.L. Haynes | not out | 133 |
| R.B. Richardson | c Jones, b Alderman | 61 |
| I.V.A. Richards† | not out | 4 |
| A.L. Logie | | |
| P.J. Dujon* | | |
| H.A. Gomes | | |
| J. Garner | | |
| W.W. Daniel | | |
| M.A. Small | | |
| W.W. Davis | | |
| Extras | lb 5, nb 7 | 12 |
| (48 overs) | (for 2 wickets) | 233 |

| | O | M | R | W |
|---|---|---|---|---|
| Lawson | 10 | 3 | 26 | — |
| Alderman | 10 | — | 62 | 1 |
| Hogg | 8 | — | 40 | — |
| Rackemann | 10 | 1 | 54 | 1 |
| Border | 6 | 1 | 22 | — |
| Wessels | 4 | — | 24 | — |

FALL OF WICKETS
1- 62, 2- 229

**West Indies won by 8 wickets**

## FIRST TEST MATCH – WEST INDIES *v.* AUSTRALIA
2, 3, 4, 6 and 7 March 1984 at Bourda, Georgetown

**AUSTRALIA**

| | FIRST INNINGS | | SECOND INNINGS | |
|---|---|---|---|---|
| S.B. Smith | c Dujon, b Garner | 3 | (2) c Dujon, b Garner | 12 |
| K.C. Wessels | c Lloyd, b Garner | 4 | (1) c Lloyd, b Daniel | 20 |
| G.M. Ritchie | c Davis, b Harper | 78 | lbw, b Garner | 3 |
| K.J. Hughes† | b Garner | 18 | c Haynes, b Daniel | 0 |
| A.R. Border | b Garner | 5 | run out | 54 |
| D.W. Hookes | c Dujon, b Harper | 32 | b Garner | 10 |
| W.B. Phillips* | c Greenidge, b Harper | 16 | b Daniel | 76 |
| G.F. Lawson | c Richards, b Harper | 11 | not out | 35 |
| T.G. Hogan | not out | 42 | lbw, b Davis | 18 |
| T.M. Alderman | lbw, b Garner | 1 | (11) not out | 3 |
| R.M. Hogg | lbw, b Garner | 52 | (10) b Davis | 6 |
| Extras | b 2, lb 3, w 1, nb 11 | 17 | b 10, lb 15, nb 11 | 36 |
| | | 279 | (for 9 wkts dec) | 273 |

| | O | M | R | W | O | M | R | W |
|---|---|---|---|---|---|---|---|---|
| Garner | 27.2 | 10 | 75 | 6 | 24 | 5 | 67 | 3 |
| Daniel | 12 | 3 | 60 | — | 27 | 4 | 86 | 3 |
| Davis | 19 | 2 | 45 | — | 14 | 3 | 35 | 2 |
| Harper | 24 | 7 | 56 | 4 | 15 | 4 | 27 | — |
| Gomes | 15 | 1 | 35 | — | 11 | 2 | 25 | — |
| Richards | 5 | 2 | 3 | — | 6 | 2 | 8 | — |

FALL OF WICKETS
1- 6, 2- 23, 3- 55, 4- 63, 5- 139, 6- 166, 7- 180, 8- 180, 9- 182
1- 37, 2- 41, 3- 42, 4- 50, 5- 60, 6- 185, 7- 209, 8- 248, 9- 263

**WEST INDIES**

| | FIRST INNINGS | | SECOND INNINGS | |
|---|---|---|---|---|
| C.G. Greenidge | c Wessels, b Lawson | 16 | not out | 120 |
| D.L. Haynes | lbw, b Hogg | 60 | not out | 103 |
| R.B. Richardson | lbw, b Lawson | 19 | | |
| I.V.A. Richards | c Phillips, b Hogg | 8 | | |
| H.A. Gomes | c Border, b Hogan | 10 | | |
| C.H. Lloyd† | c Phillips, b Alderman | 36 | | |
| P.J. Dujon* | b Hogan | 21 | | |
| R.A. Harper | b Hogan | 10 | | |
| J. Garner | not out | 16 | | |
| W.W. Davis | c Ritchie, b Hogan | 11 | | |
| W.W. Daniel | lbw, b Lawson | 4 | | |
| Extras | lb 7, nb 12 | 19 | b 10, lb 13, nb 4 | 27 |
| | | 230 | (for no wkt) | 250 |

| | O | M | R | W | O | M | R | W |
|---|---|---|---|---|---|---|---|---|
| Lawson | 20.4 | 4 | 59 | 3 | 18 | — | 54 | — |
| Alderman | 21 | 3 | 64 | 1 | 11 | — | 43 | — |
| Hogg | 12 | — | 44 | 2 | 13 | — | 56 | — |
| Hogan | 25 | 9 | 56 | 4 | 19 | 2 | 74 | — |

FALL OF WICKETS
1- 29, 2- 72, 3- 93, 4- 110, 5- 154, 6- 181, 7- 191, 8- 203, 9- 225

*Umpires:* D.M. Archer and D.J. Narine

**Match drawn**

***9, 10, 11 and 12 March***

***at Pointe-a-Pierre***

**Trinidad and Tobago** 336 (A. Rajah 100, C. Rampersad 61) and 222 (T.G. Hogan 4 for 74)
**Australians** 370 (K.C. Wessels 89, K.J. Hughes 73) and 56 for 1
*Match drawn*

The Australians won the toss for the fifth time in as many matches and reduced Trinidad to 82 for 4 at lunch. It was Alderman who started the home side's problems when Gabriel mistimed a hook. Gomes scored 23 in under an hour, but it was Aneil Rajah, Trinidad's outstanding batsman of the season, who rescued the home side. They were all out on the second morning and the visitors were 293 for 5 by the close, Hughes having batted well below form and Trinidad having missed many chances. Hogan and Maguire provided aggression late in the innings as the last five wickets fell for 77 and Australia were out just before lunch on the third day. Rain ended play half-an-hour after lunch and Trinidad batted until shortly before tea on the final day, leaving Australia 75 minutes in which to make 189. Hughes was angered by the home side's tactics and batted rather ungraciously.

### Second One-Day International
### WEST INDIES *v.* AUSTRALIA

Australia drew level in the one-day series with a somewhat fortuitous win in Port of Spain. The pitch was damp and the start was delayed by half-an-hour so that the quota of overs was reduced from 50 to 45, but, as it transpired, Australia could only manage to bowl 37 overs in the three hours allotted, a scandalously slow rate.

Hughes won the toss and asked West Indies to bat. The home side welcomed back Malcolm Marshall, but he still seemed far from fit. Ritchie was unfit for Australia who again relied on the make-shift wicket-keeping of Phillips rather than the specialist Woolley. Rackemann could not be considered, but Jones, at first doubtful, was able to play.

Lawson dismissed Haynes and Richardson in the same over, but there followed some dreadful fielding errors. Greenidge and Richards twice each and Lloyd once were all missed off not too difficult chances. Wessels, at square-leg, for whom catching in one-day games had become something of a nightmare, and Hookes at slip were among the offenders, but Maguire dropped the simplest of return catches from Richards when the batsman was on 34. Richards played finely on a difficult wicket and hit 67 from 71 deliveries with some flashing shots. Lloyd celebrated being dropped by hitting four fours in the final over.

Hookes was bowled by Garner at 30, but Wessels, Hughes and Smith gave the Australian innings the substance needed to force a win although it must be said that the wicket had now become easier. There was a spate of run outs as the target and the end of the overs neared. Wessels made his 67 from 32 overs and when he left only 34 were needed, but the end came when Small, who still looked too excited for international cricket, made a wild overthrow which yielded 5 runs. There were just two balls remaining.

*Roger Harper, 4 for 56 with his off-breaks in the first Test. (Adrian Murrell)*

### Second Test Match
### WEST INDIES *v.* AUSTRALIA

For the first time on the tour Kim Hughes lost the toss and Richards, leading the West Indies in the absence of the injured Lloyd, asked Australia to bat first on a wicket that was green and damp. The pitch persuaded West Indies to give Small his first Test cap and to omit Harper, a decision they must have regretted later. Beset by illness, Australia brought in Jones for his Test debut in place of Smith. Phillips, who kept the wicket-keeping spot to the exclusion of the specialist Woolley, was asked to combine that duty with opening.

Garner dismissed Wessels with the fifth ball of the match, caught at fourth slip, and with the fifth ball of his next over he bowled Ritchie who moved too far across his stumps. Phillips fell to a ball that reared fiercely and, after Hughes and Border had halted the West Indian advance for about half an hour, Hughes became Garner's fourth victim when he touched the ball to the wicket-keeper. The Australians were glad of the rain that ended play for the day shortly after with the score at 55 for 4. Garner had bowled quickly and obtained a prodigious amount of lift. In 8 overs he had taken 4 for 22. Marshall, in contrast, could find neither control nor pace and still looked far from match fit after his absence through injury.

Hookes flitted briefly on the second day, but Jones gave Border admirable support in a stand of 103, and then Lawson, growing in stature as an all-rounder, helped in a stand of 49. Daniel finished off the Australian tail on the third morning, the second day having also suffered from curtailment, and Allan Border was left unbeaten on 98, an innings of great resource in that he had batted through an uncertain start and played with relentless determination to lift his side from a dismal position.

By the end of the third day West Indies had moved to within 37 of the Australian total with only 4 wickets lost. They began their innings midway through the afternoon and

**Leeward Islands 1984**
First Class Matches

| BATTING | v. Windward Islands (Castries) 21–24 January 1984 | | v. Jamaica (Kingston) 28–30 January 1984 | | v. Barbados (Basseterre) 3–6 February 1984 | | v. Guyana (Berbice) 11–14 February 1984 | | v. Australians (Basseterre) 18–21 February 1984 | | v. Trinidad and Tobago (St John's) 23–26 February 1984 | | *M* | *Inns* | *NOs* | *Runs* | *HS* | *Av* |
|---|---|---|---|---|---|---|---|---|---|---|---|---|---|---|---|---|---|---|
| R.B. Richardson | | | | | | | | | 7 | 0 | 162 | — | 2 | 3 | — | 169 | 162 | 56.33 |
| L. Lawrence | 14 | — | 0 | 25 | 5 | 42 | 56 | 68 | 0 | 33 | 118 | — | 6 | 10 | — | 361 | 118 | 36.10 |
| S.W. Julien | 0 | — | 5 | 5 | 0 | 8 | 9 | 29 | 123 | 2 | 90 | — | 6 | 10 | — | 271 | 123 | 27.10 |
| R.M. Otto | 42 | — | 131 | 12* | 134 | 12 | 14 | 91 | 20 | 4 | 136 | — | 6 | 10 | 1 | 596 | 136 | 66.22 |
| V.A. Eddy | 45 | — | 42 | 2* | 13 | 31* | 19 | 120 | 11 | 38 | 33* | — | 6 | 10 | 3 | 354 | 120 | 50.57 |
| S.I. Williams | 23 | — | 0 | — | 0 | 31 | 63 | 42 | 31 | 2 | 10* | — | 6 | 9 | 1 | 202 | 63 | 25.25 |
| E.A.E. Baptiste | | | | | | | | | 57* | 3 | — | — | 2 | 2 | 1 | 60 | 57* | 60.00 |
| N.C. Guishard | 0 | — | 29 | — | 85 | 9 | 1 | 62 | 3 | 50 | — | — | 6 | 8 | — | 239 | 85 | 29.87 |
| A. Merrick | 15 | — | 62* | — | 4 | — | 11 | 34 | 16 | 5 | — | — | 6 | 7 | 1 | 147 | 62* | 24.50 |
| J.B. Harris | | | | | | | | | 5 | 12 | | | 1 | 2 | — | 17 | 12 | 8.50 |
| D. Thompson | | | | | | | 0 | 2* | 2 | 0* | | | 2 | 4 | 2 | 4 | 2* | 2.00 |
| A.L. Kelly | 69 | — | | | | | | | | | | | 1 | 1 | — | 69 | 69 | 69.00 |
| A.M.E. Roberts | 9 | — | 30 | — | 3 | 5* | 22 | 54 | | | — | — | 5 | 6 | 1 | 123 | 54 | 24.60 |
| E.T. Willett | 2* | — | 13 | — | 2* | — | 1* | — | | | | | 4 | 5 | 3 | 19 | 13 | 9.50 |
| G.J.F. Ferris | — | — | 11 | — | | | | | | | | | 2 | 1 | — | 11 | 11 | 11.00 |
| F. Buffonge | | | 0 | 19 | 24 | 17 | | | | | | | 2 | 4 | — | 60 | 24 | 15.00 |
| U.V.C. Lawrence | | | | | 0 | 14 | 6 | 47 | | | | | 2 | 4 | — | 67 | 47 | 16.75 |
| I.V.A. Richards | | | | | | | | | | | 37 | — | 1 | 1 | — | 37 | 37 | 37.00 |
| Byes | | | 1 | | 2 | 1 | 1 | 16 | 4 | 8 | 10 | | | | | | | |
| Leg-byes | 5 | | 4 | 2 | | 4 | 1 | 5 | 12 | 10 | 13 | | | | | | | |
| Wides | 1 | | | | 1 | | 3 | 12 | 4 | | 2 | | | | | | | |
| No-balls | 3 | | 9 | 6 | | | 1 | 3 | 10 | 3 | 2 | | | | | | | |
| Total | 228 | | 337 | 71 | 273 | 174 | 208 | 586 | 305 | 170 | 613 | | | | | | | |
| Wickets | 9 | | 10 | 3 | 10 | 7 | 10 | 10 | 10 | 10 | 5 | | | | | | | |
| Result | Ab. | | W | | D | | D | | L | | D | | | | | | | |
| Points | 4 | | 16 | | 4 | | 4 | | — | | 8 | | | | | | | |

*Catches* 14 – S.I. Williams (ct 10/st 4)
7 – R.M. Otto
4 – L. Lawrence, E.T. Willett and S. Julien
3 – A. Merrick
2 – F. Buffonge and I.V.A. Richards
1 – A.M.E. Roberts, E.A.E. Baptist, N.C. Guishard and sub

| BOWLING | A. Merrick | J.B. Harris | E.A.E. Baptiste | D. Thompson | N.C. Guishard | V.A. Eddy | R.M. Otto | A.M.E. Roberts | G.J.F. Ferris |
|---|---|---|---|---|---|---|---|---|---|
| *v.* Windward Islands | 7–1–30–1 | | | | 3–0–8–0 | | | 8–2–15–3 | 5–0–27–0 |
| (Castries) 21–24 January | | | | | | | | | |
| *v.* Jamaica (Kingston) | 11.4–3–45–5 | | | | 6–1–14–1 | | | 10–1–25–2 | 11–1–35–1 |
| 28–30 January | 15–2–78–3 | | | | 25–9–53–4 | 4–1–7–0 | | 12.5–6–26–2 | |
| *v.* Barbados (Basseterre) | 16.2–1–64–1 | | | | 13–3–30–0 | 5–0–15–0 | | 23–4–80–6 | |
| 3–6 February | 23–3–54–1 | | | | 16–4–36–0 | 7–5–3–1 | | 30–8–64–4 | |
| *v.* Guyana (Berbice) | 17–2–63–2 | | | 34–9–94–4 | 41–6–105–1 | 8–1–17–0 | | 9–0–48–0 | |
| 11–14 February | | | | | | | | | |
| *v.* Australians (Basseterre) | 12–4–41–0 | 12–2–71–0 | 25–4–95–4 | 19–3–66–0 | 18–1–91–2 | 10–0–42–0 | 1–0–12–0 | | |
| 18–21 February | | 15–3–41–0 | 19–5–51–2 | | 34–9–102–2 | 14–1–42–3 | | | |
| *v.* Trinidad and Tobago | 23.2–5–73–3 | | 20–2–90–2 | | 19–2–62–1 | 3–2–2–0 | | 25–5–73–3 | |
| (St John's) 23–26 February | 25–3–121–1 | | 7–4–15–1 | | 19–6–46–0 | 11–3–36–0 | | 25–8–43–1 | |
| | 150.2–24–<br>569–17<br>*av.* 33.47 | 27–5–<br>112–0<br>— | 71–15–<br>251–9<br>*av.* 27.88 | 53–12–<br>160–4<br>*av.* 40.00 | 194–41–<br>547–11<br>*av.* 49.72 | 62–13–<br>164–4<br>*av.* 41.00 | 1–0–<br>12–0<br>— | 142.5–34–<br>374–21<br>*av.* 17.80 | 16–1–<br>62–1<br>*av.* 62.00 |

## SECOND ONE-DAY INTERNATIONAL – WEST INDIES *v.* AUSTRALIA
14 March 1984 at Port of Spain

| **WEST INDIES** | | | |
|---|---|---|---|
| | C.G. Greenidge | c Lawson, b Wessels | 63 |
| | D.L. Haynes | b Lawson | 1 |
| | R.B. Richardson | c Phillips, b Lawson | 0 |
| | I.V.A. Richards | c Alderman, b Maguire | 67 |
| | C.H. Lloyd† | not out | 31 |
| | P.J. Dujon* | c Maguire, b Alderman | 16 |
| | M.D. Marshall | run out | 0 |
| | J. Garner | not out | 0 |
| | H.A. Gomes | | |
| | W.W. Daniel | | |
| | M.A. Small | | |
| | Extras | b 1, lb 8, w 3 | 12 |
| | (37 overs) | (for 6 wickets) | 190 |

| | O | M | R | W |
|---|---|---|---|---|
| Lawson | 9 | 1 | 40 | 2 |
| Alderman | 9 | 2 | 39 | 1 |
| Hogg | 6 | — | 49 | — |
| Maguire | 9 | 1 | 28 | 1 |
| Wessels | 4 | — | 25 | 1 |

FALL OF WICKETS
1- 25, 2- 25, 3- 135, 4- 145, 5- 173, 6- 178

| **AUSTRALIA** | | | |
|---|---|---|---|
| | K.C. Wessels | c Richards, b Daniel | 67 |
| | D.W. Hookes | b Garner | 14 |
| | S.B. Smith | c Richards, b Small | 27 |
| | K.J. Hughes† | run out | 18 |
| | D.M.J. Jones | run out | 3 |
| | A.R. Border | not out | 26 |
| | W.B. Phillips* | run out | 10 |
| | G.F. Lawson | not out | 0 |
| | J.N. Maguire | | |
| | T.M. Alderman | | |
| | R.M. Hogg | | |
| | Extras | b 7, lb 15, w 2, nb 5 | 29 |
| | (36.4 overs) | (for 6 wickets) | 194 |

| | O | M | R | W |
|---|---|---|---|---|
| Garner | 9.4 | 2 | 24 | 1 |
| Daniel | 9 | — | 56 | — |
| Small | 9 | — | 40 | 1 |
| Marshall | 9 | — | 52 | — |

FALL OF WICKETS
1- 30, 2- 98, 3- 143, 4- 157, 5- 162, 6- 188

**Australia won by 4 wickets**

Greenidge made 24 in 35 minutes before falling to a spiteful ball from Hogg which brushed his gloves. Hogg also ran out Haynes and Richardson and Gomes fell each side of tea to leave the home side uncertainly placed on 129 for 4. Richards and Logie took command for the rest of the day and when play was resumed on the fourth day they took their stand to exactly 100 before Richards fell to the twelfth ball of the morning. This was the break-through that Australia had needed, but they were now to be thwarted by a brilliant innings from Jeff Dujon. He quickly caught up Logie who had a 43-run start on him and the pair added 158 before Logie, nervous in the 90s, fell to Hogan, having been dropped at slip 4 runs earlier.

Dujon was quite magnificent, emphasising once again that his advance in the past six months had been greater than any other West Indian player. He reached his second Test century

| E.T. Willett | U.Y.C. Lawrence | I.V.A. Richards | Byes | Leg-byes | Wides | No-balls | Total | Wkts |
|---|---|---|---|---|---|---|---|---|
| 2–0–6–0 | | | 4 | 2 | | 9 | 92 | 4 |
| | | | | | | | | |
| 11–0–29–1 | | | 11 | 6 | | 9 | 165 | 10 |
| 25–5–69–1 | | | 2 | 6 | | 5 | 241 | 10 |
| 19–7–52–2 | 9–1–41–1 | | 3 | 18 | | 8 | 303 | 10 |
| 44.4–13–93–4 | 11–1–27–0 | | 5 | 5 | | 3 | 287 | 10 |
| 36.5–8–93–2 | | | 1 | 6 | 1 | 1 | 427 | 9 |
| | | | | | | | | |
| | | | 5 | 6 | 1 | 10 | 429 | 7 |
| | | | 4 | 10 | | 11 | 250 | 7 |
| | | 10–2–31–1 | 2 | 4 | 3 | 12 | 337 | 10 |
| | | 14–5–27–0 | | 1 | | 7 | 289 | 3 |
| 138.3–33–342–10 *av.* 34.20 | 20–2–68–1 *av.* 68.00 | 24–7–58–1 *av.* 58.00 | | | | | | |

*Jeff Dujon, an elegant batsman and stylish wicket-keeper, hit 130 in the second Test match. (George Herringshaw)*

in 212 minutes off 153 balls with twelve fours and two sixes, hooks off two successive balls by Hogg. He finished on 130 and West Indies had a lead of 213.

Australia suffered further when Phillips was run out by Logie's direct hit from cover in the first over of their second innings. Ritchie plundered the wayward Marshall, but Small claimed him as his first Test victim when he bowled him between bat and pad. Garner found a way through Wessels' defence and Australia closed miserably at 55 for 3.

On the last day Border stood firm, but every time a partnership had developed two wickets went quickly and at 196 for 8 Australia faced defeat. Hogg battled gamely with Border to avoid that indignity, but when he fell to Richards there were still two hours remaining and Australia had a lead of 25. When the last hour began Australia were still only 57 runs ahead and a West Indian victory still seemed certain, but Alderman faced 83 balls without giving a chance and West Indies conceded the draw when Border reached his hundred, one of the great fighting Test innings and the climax for him of what had been a memorable match. He had batted for 4¾

**Windward Islands 1984**
First Class Matches

| BATTING | *v.* Leeward Islands (Castries) 21–24 January 1984 | | *v.* Barbados (Bridgetown) 28–31 January 1984 | | *v.* Guyana (Georgetown) 3–6 February 1984 | | *v.* Trinidad & Tobago (Kingston) 11–14 February 1984 | | *v.* Jamaica (St George's) 17–20 February 1984 | | *v.* Australians (Castries) 14–17 April 1984 | | *M* | *Inns* | *NOs* | *Runs* | *HS* | *Av* |
|---|---|---|---|---|---|---|---|---|---|---|---|---|---|---|---|---|---|---|
| L.C. Sebastien | 7 | — | 96* | 12 | 53 | — | 107 | — | 0 | — | 2 | 77 | 6 | 8 | 1 | 354 | 107 | 50.57 |
| L.D. John | 31 | — | 22 | 0 | 2 | — | 59 | — | 44 | — | 114 | 88 | 6 | 8 | — | 360 | 114 | 45.00 |
| L.A. Lewis | 13* | — | 32 | 15* | 23 | — | 128 | — | 14 | — | 61 | 12* | 6 | 8 | 2 | 298 | 128 | 49.66 |
| C.A. Elwin | 7 | — | 0 | — | 7 | — | | | | | | | 3 | 3 | — | 14 | 7 | 4.66 |
| A.D. Texeira | 15 | — | 5 | 11* | 33 | — | 1 | — | | | | | 4 | 5 | 1 | 65 | 33 | 16.25 |
| I. Cadette | 4* | — | 2 | — | 13 | — | 11 | — | 7* | — | 14 | — | 6 | 6 | 2 | 51 | 14 | 12.75 |
| D.J. Collymore | — | — | 9 | — | 5 | — | | | | | 16 | — | 4 | 3 | — | 30 | 16 | 10.00 |
| N. Phillip | — | — | 4 | — | 63 | — | 35 | — | 8 | — | 13 | — | 6 | 5 | — | 123 | 63 | 24.60 |
| T. Kentish | — | — | 0 | — | 5* | — | 0 | — | 1* | — | 26* | — | 6 | 5 | 3 | 32 | 26* | 16.00 |
| S.J. Hinds | — | — | 14 | — | 0 | — | 5 | — | 0 | — | 37 | — | 6 | 5 | — | 56 | 37 | 11.20 |
| J. Etienne | — | — | 11 | — | | | | | — | — | | | 3 | 1 | — | 11 | 11 | 11.00 |
| C. Walters | | | | | | | 2 | — | 1 | — | 0 | 1* | 3 | 4 | 1 | 4 | 2 | 1.33 |
| J.D. Charles | | | | | 7 | — | 10 | — | 1 | — | 14 | 4 | 4 | 5 | — | 36 | 14 | 7.20 |
| S. Murphy | | | | | | | 0* | — | | | | | 1 | 1 | 1 | 0 | 0* | — |
| K. Hobson | | | | | | | | | 0 | — | | | 1 | 1 | — | 0 | 0 | 0.00 |
| W.W. Davis | | | | | | | | | | | 12 | — | 1 | 1 | — | 12 | 12 | 12.00 |
| Byes | 4 | | 4 | 4 | 5 | | 6 | | 2 | | 5 | 5 | | | | | | |
| Leg-byes | 2 | | 8 | | 2 | | 9 | | | | 8 | 1 | | | | | | |
| Wides | | | 1 | | 2 | | 1 | | | | 8 | | | | | | | |
| No-balls | 9 | | 4 | 3 | 3 | | | | | | 7 | 2 | | | | | | |
| Total | 92 | | 212 | 45 | 223 | | 374 | | 78 | | 337 | 190 | | | | | | |
| Wickets | 4 | | 10 | 2 | 10 | | 10 | | 8 | | 10 | 3 | | | | | | |
| Result | Ab. | | D | | D | | W | | Ab. | | D | | | | | | | |
| Points | 4 | | 4 | | 4 | | 16 | | 4 | | — | | | | | | | |

*Catches* 13 – I. Cadette (ct 12/st 1); 6 – A.D. Texeira and J.D. Charles; 5 – S.J. Hinds, T. Kentish and L.C. Sebastian; 3 – L.D. John and J. Etienne; 2 – D.J. Collymore, L.A. Lewis, L.A. Lewis; 1 – K. Hobson

| BOWLING | N. Phillip | D.J. Collymore | T. Kentish | S.J. Hinds | J. Etienne | S. Murphy | J.D. Charles | L.A. Lewis | L.C. Sebastien |
|---|---|---|---|---|---|---|---|---|---|
| *v.* Leeward Islands | 10–1–45–1 | 23.3–1–70–3 | 12–2–37–2 | 15–3–28–0 | 21–7–43–3 | | | | |
| (Castries) 21–24 January | | | | | | | | | |
| *v.* Barbados (Bridgetown) | 11–1–57–2 | 18–1–74–3 | 8–1–18–2 | 16.3–1–58–3 | 8–1–22–0 | | | | |
| 28–31 January | 19–3–51–3 | 9–2–18–0 | 35–8–88–3 | 50–9–115–2 | 7–0–17–0 | | | | |
| *v.* Guyana (Georgetown) | 16–1–62–2 | 10.3–3–23–1 | 32–3–62–1 | 35–4–97–6 | | | 1–0–2–0 | 2–0–2–0 | |
| 3–6 February | 3–0–12–0 | | 17–6–38–1 | 8–2–32–0 | | | 4–0–17–0 | 2–0–11–0 | 5–1–18–2 |
| *v.* Trinidad and Tobago | 17–1–47–5 | | 7–1–15–0 | 12.4–5–17–4 | | 11–1–48–1 | | | |
| (Kingston) 11–14 February | 4–0–16–0 | | 32–8–73–4 | 23–1–76–4 | | 11–2–34–1 | 2.3–1–11–1 | | |
| *v.* Jamaica (St George's) | 13–2–24–1 | | 14–4–19–2 | 19–8–33–2 | 14.5–8–17–4 | | | | |
| 17–20 February | | | | | | | | | |
| *v.* Australians (Castries, | 10–0–54–1 | 22–1–73–2 | 26.2–6–70–1 | 17–1–83–3 | | | | | |
| St Lucia) 14–17 April | 11–0–58–0 | 19–3–70–1 | 26–1–72–2 | 8–2–34–0 | | | 2–0–16–0 | | 3–0–22–0 |
| | 114–9–426–15 *av.* 28.40 | 102–11–328–10 *av.* 32.80 | 209.2–40–492–18 *av.* 27.33 | 204.1–36–573–24 *av.* 23.87 | 50.5–16–99–7 *av.* 14.14 | 22–3–82–2 *av.* 41.00 | 9.3–1–46–1 *av.* 46.00 | 4–0–13–0 — | 8–1–40–2 *av.* 20.00 |

*David Hookes, 103 not out v Barbados, 24–27 March. (George Herringshaw)*

*Gus Logie who hit 97 in his only Test innings of the series. (Allsport)*

hours and hit twelve fours. He was undoubtedly Man of the Match, a match which had been ordained by the brilliance of Dujon and the courageous best Test score of Terry Alderman.

***24, 25, 26 and 27 March***

***at Bridgetown***

**Australians** 322 for 6 dec (G.M. Ritchie 99, G.M. Wood 76, R.D. Woolley 56 not out) and 356 for 4 dec (D.W. Hookes 103 not out, S.B. Smith 66, K.J. Hughes 65)
**Barbados** 302 (A.S. Gilkes 104, D.L. Haynes 70) and 233 for 5 (A.S. Gilkes 75, T.R.O. Payne 51 not out)
*Match drawn*

| K. Hobson | W.W. Davis | *Byes* | *Leg-byes* | *Wides* | *No-balls* | *Total* | *Wkts* |
|---|---|---|---|---|---|---|---|
| | | | 5 | 1 | 3 | 228 | 9 |
| | | | 2 | 1 | 12 | 231 | 10 |
| | | 12 | 3 | | 6 | 304 | 9 |
| | | 7 | 6 | | 4 | 261 | 10 |
| | | 4 | 4 | | 1 | 136 | 3 |
| | | | 3 | | 7 | 130 | 10 |
| | | 1 | 4 | | 1 | 215 | 10 |
| 13–3–24–1 | | 1 | 2 | | 7 | 120 | 10 |
| | 15–1–76–2 | 1 | 5 | | 13 | 362 | 10 |
| | 20–3–59–3 | 5 | 8 | 1 | 14 | 344 | 6 |
| 13–3–24–1 *av.* 24.00 | 35–4–135–5 *av.* 27.00 | | | | | | |

Graeme Wood arrived as a replacement for the injured Wessels and immediately made his mark as he and Ritchie added 140 for the second wicket on the opening day. There was some late hitting by Woolley and Hughes declared at the overnight score. Rackemann, playing his first game after injury, was naturally below his best and Haynes and Gilkes put on 150 for the Shell Shield champion's first wicket. Gilkes, profitting from a dropped slip catch when 3, reached a maiden first-class hundred and, although Barbados lost their last 9 wickets for 103 runs, they came to within 30 of the Australian score. Australia batted solidly at the second attempt, obviously with an eye to the forthcoming Test, and Hookes, in danger of losing his place, hit sixteen fours in an innings which lasted 163 minutes. Gilkes was again top scorer for the home side as the game was drawn.

## Third Test Match
## WEST INDIES *v.* AUSTRALIA

The West Indies selected a more balanced side and welcomed the return of Holding after injury as well as recalling Harper. They were handicapped when Logie withdrew on the eve of the match and this probably helped Richardson retain his place in the side. Lloyd won the toss and asked Australia to bat, the belief being that the first morning was the only period when the Bridgetown wicket would be of any advantage to the bowlers.

## SECOND TEST MATCH – WEST INDIES *v.* AUSTRALIA
16, 17, 18, 20 and 21 March 1984 at Port-of-Spain, Trinidad

### AUSTRALIA

| | FIRST INNINGS | | SECOND INNINGS | |
|---|---|---|---|---|
| K.C. Wessels | c Gomes, b Garner | 4 | lbw, b Garner | 4 |
| W.B. Phillips* | c Dujon, b Garner | 4 | run out | 0 |
| G.M. Ritchie | b Garner | 1 | b Small | 26 |
| K.J. Hughes† | c Dujon, b Garner | 24 | lbw, b Marshall | 33 |
| A.R. Border | not out | 98 | (6) not out | 100 |
| D.W. Hookes | b Garner | 23 | (7) c Richardson, b Gomes | 21 |
| D.M.J. Jones | c and b Richards | 48 | (8) b Richards | 5 |
| G.F. Lawson | c and b Daniel | 14 | (9) b Marshall | 20 |
| T.G. Hogan | c Greenidge, b Daniel | 0 | (5) c Logie, b Daniel | 38 |
| R.M. Hogg | c Marshall, b Daniel | 11 | c Garner, b Richards | 9 |
| T.M. Alderman | c Richardson, b Garner | 1 | not out | 21 |
| Extras | b 6, lb 4, nb 17 | 27 | b 6, lb 1, w 1, nb 14 | 22 |
| | | 255 | (for 9 wkts) | 299 |

| | O | M | R | W | O | M | R | W |
|---|---|---|---|---|---|---|---|---|
| Garner | 28.1 | 9 | 60 | 6 | 15 | 4 | 35 | 1 |
| Marshall | 19 | 2 | 73 | — | 22 | 3 | 73 | 2 |
| Daniel | 15 | 3 | 40 | 3 | 9 | 3 | 11 | 1 |
| Small | 10 | 3 | 24 | — | 14 | 2 | 51 | 1 |
| Gomes | 10 | — | 33 | — | 27 | 5 | 53 | 1 |
| Richards | 10 | 4 | 15 | 1 | 25 | 5 | 65 | 2 |
| Logie | | | | | 0.1 | — | 4 | — |

FALL OF WICKETS
1- 4, 2- 7, 3- 16, 4- 50, 5- 85, 6- 185, 7- 234, 8- 234, 9- 253
1- 1, 2- 35, 3- 41, 4- 114, 5- 115, 6- 153, 7- 162, 8- 196, 9- 238

### WEST INDIES

| | FIRST INNINGS | |
|---|---|---|
| C.G. Greenidge | c Phillips, b Hogg | 24 |
| D.L. Haynes | run out | 53 |
| R.B. Richardson | c Wessels, b Alderman | 23 |
| I.V.A. Richards† | c Phillips, b Alderman | 76 |
| H.A. Gomes | b Lawson | 3 |
| A.L. Logie | lbw, b Hogan | 97 |
| P.J. Dujon* | b Hogan | 130 |
| M.D. Marshall | lbw, b Lawson | 10 |
| J. Garner | not out | 24 |
| W.W. Daniel | not out | 6 |
| M.A. Small | | |
| Extras | b 7, lb 12, w 2, nb 1 | 22 |
| | (for 8 wkts dec) | 468 |

| | O | M | R | W |
|---|---|---|---|---|
| Lawson | 32 | 3 | 132 | 2 |
| Hogg | 31 | 2 | 103 | 1 |
| Alderman | 35 | 9 | 91 | 2 |
| Hogan | 28 | 3 | 123 | 2 |

FALL OF WICKETS
1- 35, 2- 93, 3- 124, 4- 129, 5- 229, 6- 387, 7- 430, 8- 462

**Match drawn**

## THIRD TEST MATCH – WEST INDIES *v.* AUSTRALIA
30 and 31 March, 1, 3 and 4 April 1984 at Kennington Oval, Bridgetown

### AUSTRALIA

| | FIRST INNINGS | | SECOND INNINGS | |
|---|---|---|---|---|
| S.B. Smith | c Dujon, b Marshall | 10 | (2) b Marshall | 7 |
| G.M. Wood | c Dujon, b Holding | 68 | (1) lbw, b Garner | 20 |
| G.M. Ritchie | c and b Harper | 57 | c Haynes, b Marshall | 0 |
| K.J. Hughes† | c Dujon, b Holding | 20 | c Lloyd, b Holding | 25 |
| A.R. Border | c Richardson b Marshall | 38 | (6) c Dujon, b Holding | 8 |
| D.W. Hookes | c Dujon, b Garner | 30 | (7) b Holding | 9 |
| T.G. Hogan | b Garner | 40 | (5) c Richardson, b Holding | 2 |
| W.B. Phillips* | c Dujon, b Garner | 120 | b Marshall | 1 |
| G.F. Lawson | b Baptiste | 10 | c Harper, b Marshall | 2 |
| R.M. Hogg | c Garner, b Harper | 3 | not out | 5 |
| T.M. Alderman | not out | 2 | b Marshall | 0 |
| Extras | b 14, lb 8, nb 9 | 31 | b 1, lb 6, nb 11 | 18 |
| | | 429 | | 97 |

| | O | M | R | W | O | M | R | W |
|---|---|---|---|---|---|---|---|---|
| Garner | 33.5 | 6 | 110 | 3 | 8 | 4 | 9 | 1 |
| Marshall | 26 | 2 | 83 | 2 | 15.5 | 1 | 42 | 5 |
| Holding | 30 | 5 | 94 | 2 | 15 | 4 | 24 | 4 |
| Baptiste | 17 | 5 | 34 | 1 | 3 | — | 14 | — |
| Harper | 43 | 9 | 86 | 2 | 2 | 1 | 1 | — |

FALL OF WICKETS
1- 11, 2- 114, 3- 158, 4- 171, 5- 223, 6- 263, 7- 307, 8- 330, 9- 336
1- 13, 2- 13, 3- 63, 4- 65, 5- 68, 6- 80, 7- 85, 8- 85, 9- 92

### WEST INDIES

| | FIRST INNINGS | | SECOND INNINGS | |
|---|---|---|---|---|
| C.G. Greenidge | run out | 64 | not out | 10 |
| D.L. Haynes | b Hogg | 145 | not out | 11 |
| R.B. Richardson | not out | 131 | | |
| I.V.A. Richards | b Lawson | 6 | | |
| E.A.E. Baptiste | b Lawson | 11 | | |
| P.J. Dujon* | b Alderman | 2 | | |
| C.H. Lloyd† | b Hogg | 76 | | |
| M.D. Marshall | b Hogg | 10 | | |
| R.A. Harper | b Hogg | 19 | | |
| J. Garner | c Phillips, b Hogg | 9 | | |
| M.A. Holding | c Smith, b Hogg | 0 | | |
| Extras | lb 25, nb 11 | 36 | | 0 |
| | | 509 | (for no wkt) | 21 |

| | O | M | R | W | O | M | R | W |
|---|---|---|---|---|---|---|---|---|
| Lawson | 33.2 | 4 | 150 | 2 | 2 | 1 | 3 | — |
| Alderman | 42.4 | 6 | 152 | 1 | 1.5 | — | 18 | — |
| Hogg | 33 | 4 | 77 | 6 | | | | |
| Hogan | 34 | 8 | 97 | — | | | | |
| Border | 3 | 1 | 8 | — | | | | |

FALL OR WICKETS
1- 132, 2- 277, 3- 289, 4- 313, 5- 316, 6- 447, 7- 465, 8- 493, 9- 509

*Umpires:* D.M. Archer and L. Barker

**West Indies won by 10 wickets**

*Richie Richardson, heir apparent to Viv Richards as 'king' of Antigua. He hit centuries in the third and fourth Test matches.*
*(Adrian Murrell)*

## FOURTH TEST MATCH – WEST INDIES *v.* AUSTRALIA

7, 8, 9 and 10 April 1984 at St John's, Antigua

### AUSTRALIA

| | FIRST INNINGS | | SECOND INNINGS | |
|---|---|---|---|---|
| W.B. Phillips | c Dujon, b Garner | 5 | c Dujon, b Garner | 23 |
| G.M. Ritchie | c Holding, b Marshall | 6 | b Garner | 22 |
| A.R. Border | c Dujon, b Baptiste | 98 | c Greenidge, b Baptiste | 19 |
| K.J. Hughes† | c Marshall, b Harper | 24 | c Richards, b Marshall | 29 |
| D.M.J. Jones | b Harper | 1 | c Dujon, b Garner | 11 |
| D.W. Hookes | c Richardson b Baptiste | 51 | c Greenidge, b Holding | 29 |
| R.D. Woolley* | c Dujon, b Baptiste | 13 | lbw, b Marshall | 8 |
| T.G. Hogan | c Harper, b Holding | 14 | c Baptiste, b Garner | 6 |
| G.F. Lawson | b Holding | 4 | not out | 17 |
| J.N. Maguire | not out | 15 | b Marshall | 0 |
| C.G. Rackemann | b Holding | 12 | b Garner | 0 |
| Extras | b 5, lb 4, nb 10 | 19 | b 19, lb 7, nb 10 | 36 |
| | | 262 | | 200 |

| | O | M | R | W | O | M | R | W |
|---|---|---|---|---|---|---|---|---|
| Marshall | 19 | 2 | 70 | 1 | 17 | 5 | 51 | 3 |
| Garner | 18 | 5 | 34 | 1 | 20.5 | 2 | 63 | 5 |
| Holding | 19.5 | 3 | 42 | 3 | 14 | 2 | 22 | 1 |
| Harper | 19 | 4 | 58 | 2 | 6 | — | 24 | — |
| Baptiste | 17 | 2 | 42 | 3 | 8 | 2 | 14 | 1 |
| Richards | 5 | — | 7 | — | | | | |

FALL OF WICKETS
1- 14, 2- 14, 3- 67, 4- 78, 5- 201, 6- 208, 7- 217, 8- 224, 9- 246
1- 50, 2- 57, 3- 97, 4- 116, 5- 150, 6- 167, 7- 176, 8- 185, 9- 185

### WEST INDIES

| | FIRST INNINGS | |
|---|---|---|
| C.G. Greenidge | c Ritchie, b Lawson | 0 |
| D.L. Haynes | b Lawson | 21 |
| R.B. Richardson | c Woolley, b Rackemann | 154 |
| I.V.A. Richards | c Woolley, b Rackemann | 178 |
| P.J. Dujon* | c Hughes, b Rackemann | 28 |
| C.H. Lloyd† | c Jones, b Rackemann | 38 |
| M.D. Marshall | c Hookes, b Maguire | 6 |
| E.A.E. Baptiste | b Maguire | 6 |
| R.A. Harper | c Ritchie, b Maguire | 27 |
| J. Garner | c Hogan, b Rackemann | 10 |
| M.A. Holding | not out | 3 |
| Extras | b 12, lb 14, nb 1 | 27 |
| | | 498 |

| | O | M | R | W |
|---|---|---|---|---|
| Lawson | 49 | 4 | 125 | 2 |
| Rackemann | 42.4 | 6 | 160 | 5 |
| Maguire | 44 | 9 | 122 | 3 |
| Hogan | 30 | 9 | 65 | — |

FALL OF WICKETS
1- 0, 2- 43, 3- 351, 4- 390, 5- 405, 6- 426, 7- 442, 8- 468, 9- 491

**West Indies won by an innings and 36 runs**

This seemed to be the case when Smith fell in the fourth over and Ritchie was missed at gully by Holding before he scored, but thereafter there was little movement and Wood and Ritchie added 103 comfortable runs. Holding took the wickets of Hughes and Wood in the space of 3 overs in the final session, but Australia could not have been disappointed by their close of play score of 227 for 5.

They faltered on the second day until a magnificently aggressive century by Wayne Phillips put them in a seemingly commanding position. His innings lasted only 227 minutes and in the second session of the day he scored 92 out of 120. The last two Australian wickets added 99 to which Hogg contributed 3 and Alderman 2. Phillips was last out when he top-edged a bouncer from Garner. It was a splendid innings and Hogg and Alderman had also shown the batting determination that they had shown previously in the series.

West Indies closed the day at 57 for 0 and on the third day Greenidge and Haynes took their stand to 132 in just over three hours. Haynes then shared a stand of 145 with Richardson who was quite unable to find his touch. He took 75 minutes to reach double figures and batted for $4\frac{1}{4}$ hours to finish the day on 61 not out. West Indies went in to the rest day on 301 for 3 and with Hogg and Lawson nursing injuries, a draw looked certain.

Baptiste and Dujon fell quickly on the fourth morning, but Clive Lloyd whose batting has ripened to a vintage richness as his career draws to a close, hit 76 off 77 deliveries. He hit three sixes and eight fours and prompted Richardson to a freedom of stroke play that he had not shown on the third day. They added 131 in 111 minutes and Richardson reached his second Test century. Hogg took the last 5 wickets for 28 runs to return remarkable figures of 6 for 77, a splendid bowling performance in such conditions against such opponents, and West Indies were all out 25 minutes before tea.

By the close Australia were 61 for 4. The innings was completely undermined by Malcolm Marshall and on the last day he and Michael Holding bowled unchanged to send Australia to an ignominious defeat in 73 minutes. Nightwatchman Hogan skied the second ball of the day to mid-wicket and a procession followed. Border hung out his bat. Hookes and Phillips played on. There was a magnificent low slip catch by Harper and Australia were left totally demoralised.

Holding had returned to Test cricket with his vigour undiminished. Marshall had regained his pace and control, and Clive Lloyd was close to fulfilling an ambition and leading West Indies to victory in the home series against Australia.

For Australia the darkness continued with the news that Graeme Wood's short tour was over. He was returning home with a broken finger.

### Fourth Test Match
### WEST INDIES *v.* AUSTRALIA

Australia were badly hit by injuries which deprived them of Hogg and Alderman as well as Wood who had been forced to return home. Hughes won the toss, but his batsmen failed to take advantage of a good wicket. They were 78 for 4 and it was a fifth wicket stand of 123 between Border and Hookes that improved the situation. They were separated by Baptiste who, in a spell after tea, took 3 wickets in 6 overs to put West Indies in complete control. Australia closed at 238 for 8 and were thankful for the additional runs that the last two wickets produced on the second morning.

In lowering cloudy conditions West Indies began badly when Greenidge was taken at third slip off the second ball of the innings which swung viciously. Both Lawson and Rackemann bowled a full length in an effort to exploit the conditions and suffered a little in consequence, but Lawson beat Haynes with a splendid in-swinger and West Indies were 43 for 2.

By the end of the day they were 11 runs ahead of Australia with only two men out. In the last session of the day Richardson and Richards savaged the tired Australian attack. Richardson ran to his second century in successive Tests, a feat that was especially pleasing to him as it was achieved on his home ground. Richards, too, delighted his home crowd and the pair added 308, a record for West Indies third wicket against Australia. Well as young Richardson batted he was overshadowed by the master who gave a brilliant exhibition of batting even by his high standards. In an innings lasting 375 minutes he hit thirty fours and reached his highest score against Australia. He was caught behind, the first of Rackemann's five victims, shortly before lunch, but Richardson batted on until the afternoon when his innings of 7 hours 4 minutes came to a close as he edged to Woolley. He had hit a six and twenty-two fours.

West Indies closed the third day at 493 for 9 and the innings lasted only 4 balls on the fourth morning. Ritchie and Phillips began quite well as Australia strove to score 236 needed to make West Indies bat again, but Garner dismissed them in quick succession after they had put on 50. By lunch Australia were 90 for 2 and shortly after the break Border, the most dependable of the Australian batsmen, sliced Baptiste to gully. Hughes and Jones followed and at tea Australia were 166 for 5.

On the resumption Marshall increased his pace and the irrepressible Garner returned to frustrate and destroy. Five wickets fell for 34 runs and Australia hurried to another defeat.

An enormous difference in class between the two teams had become most apparent.

***14, 15, 16 and 17 April***

***at Castries, St Lucia***

**Australians** 362 (S.B. Smith 127, G.R.J. Matthews 54) and 344 for 6 dec (D.M.J. Jones 95, D.W. Hookes 74, A.R. Border 54 not out, R.D. Woolley 52 not out)
**Windward Islands** 337 (L.D. John 114, L.A. Lewis 61) and 190 for 3 (L.D. John 88, L.C. Sebastien 77)
*Match drawn*

A fine century by Steve Smith re-asserted his claim for a Test place. He shared an opening stand of 122 with Matthews, another player in need of encouragement. A chanceless century by opener Lance John was the basis of the home side's reply. John shared a third wicket stand of 136 with Linton Lewis, but the later batting fell away until Kentish and Hinds hit fiercely in a ninth wicket stand of 50. Dean Jones, opening in place of Matthews who was ill, hit twelve fours and two sixes in his innings of 95 which lasted 193

ABOVE AND BELOW: *The King in two moods. Viv Richards, 178 in the fourth Test. (Adrian Murrell)*

## THIRD ONE-DAY INTERNATIONAL – WEST INDIES *v.* AUSTRALIA

19 April 1984 at Castries, St Lucia

| AUSTRALIA | | | |
|---|---|---|---|
| | S.B. Smith | b Garner | 6 |
| | W.B. Phillips* | b Marshall | 0 |
| | G.M. Ritchie | c Dujon, b Garner | 0 |
| | A.R. Border | c Dujon, b Garner | 90 |
| | K.J. Hughes† | b Holding | 78 |
| | D.W. Hookes | c Dujon, b Marshall | 22 |
| | D.M.J. Jones | c and b Marshall | 0 |
| | T.G. Hogan | c and b Marshall | 0 |
| | G.F. Lawson | run out | 2 |
| | J.N. Maguire | not out | 1 |
| | C.G. Rackemann | not out | 0 |
| | Extras | b 1, lb 2, w 2, nb 2 | 7 |
| | (45 overs) | (for 9 wickets) | 206 |

| | O | M | R | W |
|---|---|---|---|---|
| Garner | 10 | — | 33 | 3 |
| Marshall | 10 | 2 | 34 | 4 |
| Holding | 10 | — | 57 | 1 |
| Baptiste | 8 | — | 42 | — |
| Harper | 7 | — | 37 | — |

FALL OF WICKETS
1- 2, 2- 6, 3- 8, 4- 158, 5- 198, 6- 199, 7- 202, 8- 205, 9- 205

| WEST INDIES | | | |
|---|---|---|---|
| | C.G. Greenidge | c Lawson, b Hogan | 42 |
| | D.L. Haynes | not out | 102 |
| | R.B. Richardson | c Hogan, b Maguire | 6 |
| | A.L. Logie | c Phillips, b Maguire | 28 |
| | P.J. Dujon* | not out | 13 |
| | T.R.O. Payne | | |
| | E.A.E. Baptiste | | |
| | M.D. Marshall | | |
| | R.A. Harper | | |
| | J. Garner | | |
| | M.A. Holding† | | |
| | Extras | b 4, lb 10, w 2, nb 1 | 17 |
| | (41.4 overs) | (for 3 wickets) | 208 |

| | O | M | R | W |
|---|---|---|---|---|
| Lawson | 10 | 1 | 43 | — |
| Rackemann | 10 | — | 56 | — |
| Maguire | 10 | — | 57 | 2 |
| Hogan | 10 | — | 31 | 1 |
| Border | 1 | — | 3 | — |
| Jones | 0.4 | — | 4 | — |

FALL OF WICKETS
1- 96, 2- 119, 3- 180

*Umpires:* Sadiq Mohammed and P. White

**West Indies won by 7 wickets**

minutes. His sixes came in one over from Collymore which produced 25 runs. Well as Jones batted, the rest of the Australian batting was erratic until Hookes stabilised affairs. Border and Woolley hit well at the end and Hughes was able to declare. Davis, omitted from the West Indian side to tour England, was the best of the Windward bowlers.

Sebastien and John reached 50 in 9 overs, but they then lost momentum and their stand of 151 took 172 minutes. Play ended a quarter of an hour after tea on the last day because of rain.

### Third One-Day International
### WEST INDIES *v.* AUSTRALIA

Michael Holding led the West Indian side in the absence of both Lloyd, who was injured, and Richards, who withdrew because of the death of a friend. The absence of two leading batsmen gave an opportunity to Thelston Payne who, in the event, was asked only to field, his batting prowess not being needed.

Holding won the toss and asked Australia to bat on a wicket that was hard in true. Marshall bowled Phillips in his first over and Smith and Ritchie fell to rash shots so that Australia were 8 for 3. It was in this context that Border and Hughes came together and produced a magnificent and brave stand of 150 in 30 overs. There was a flourish from Hookes and Australia finished on a thankful 206.

In 19 overs Greenidge and Haynes, with a regular ration of boundaries, put on 96. Greenidge hit two sixes and three fours in his 42. Haynes continued to flourish and West Indies moved to an easy win with 20 balls to spare. Haynes hit two sixes and eleven fours in what was his fourth century against the Australian bowlers in the season.

### *22 April*

***at Montego Bay, Jamaica***

**Australians** 171 for 1 (S.B. Smith 84 not out, W.P. Phillips 64) (33 overs)
***v.* Jamaica**
*Match abandoned*

As there was no play possible on the first day of the scheduled first-class match, two one-day matches were arranged. Play was abandoned in the first of these because of rain and the second was unable to start. Smith and Phillips shared a first wicket stand of 121.

### Fourth One-Day International
### WEST INDIES *v.* AUSTRALIA

Desmond Haynes hooked Rodney Hogg for 6 to complete his fifth century of the season against the Australians and to give West Indies another overwhelming victory. This win gave them the one-day series by 3–1 to complement the winning lead that they had already taken in the Test series.

The Australian innings had been founded on a second wicket stand of 89 between Smith and Ritchie, but the later batsmen had found it as difficult as ever to plunder quick runs against the tight West Indian attack in which spin was used more liberally than usual.

**FOURTH ONE-DAY INTERNATIONAL – WEST INDIES *v.* AUSTRALIA**
26 April 1984 at Kingston, Jamaica

| AUSTRALIA | | | |
|---|---|---|---|
| S.B. Smith | b Harper | 50 | |
| W.B. Phillips* | c Logie, b Garner | 13 | |
| G.M. Ritchie | c Haynes, b Garner | 84 | |
| A.R. Border | b Harper | 28 | |
| K.J. Hughes† | c Greenidge, b Garner | 8 | |
| D.W. Hookes | b Marshall | 0 | |
| G.R.J. Matthews | b Marshall | 10 | |
| T.G. Hogan | not out | 1 | |
| G.F. Lawson | | | |
| R.M. Hogg | | | |
| J.N. Maguire | | | |
| Extras | b 5, lb 2, w 4, nb 4 | 15 | |
| (50 overs) | (for 7 wickets) | 209 | |

| | O | M | R | W |
|---|---|---|---|---|
| Garner | 10 | — | 47 | 3 |
| Marshall | 10 | 1 | 26 | 2 |
| Baptiste | 5 | — | 19 | — |
| Holding | 8 | — | 44 | — |
| Harper | 10 | 1 | 41 | 2 |
| Richards | 7 | — | 25 | — |

FALL OF WICKETS
1- 22, 2- 111, 3- 161, 4- 185, 5- 187, 6- 205, 7- 209

| WEST INDIES | | |
|---|---|---|
| C.G. Greenidge | b Maguire | 34 |
| D.L. Haynes | not out | 104 |
| R.B. Richardson | not out | 51 |
| I.V.A. Richards† | | |
| A.L. Logie | | |
| P.J. Dujon* | | |
| M.D. Marshall | | |
| E.A.E. Baptiste | | |
| R.A. Harper | | |
| J. Garner | | |
| M.A. Holding | | |
| Extras | b 5, lb 8, w 4, nb 5 | 22 |
| (47.4 overs) | (for 1 wicket) | 211 |

| | O | M | R | W |
|---|---|---|---|---|
| Lawson | 8 | — | 39 | — |
| Hogg | 8.4 | — | 51 | — |
| Maguire | 6 | 1 | 16 | 1 |
| Hogan | 10 | 1 | 31 | — |
| Matthews | 10 | 1 | 42 | — |
| Border | 5 | — | 19 | — |

FALL OF WICKET
1- 80

*Umpires:* L. Barker and J. Gayle

**West Indies won by 9 wickets**

### Fifth Test Match
### WEST INDIES *v.* AUSTRALIA

Hogg, fit again, returned to the Australia side in place of Rackemann who had taken five wickets in the fourth Test. Matthews replaced Jones and Smith came back at the expense of Woolley, the specialist wicket-keeper again being sacrificed because of the inadequacies of the batsmen. The West Indies were unchanged so that Lloyd played his one hundredth Test match.

The West Indies were in total control from the start. Australia lost both openers for 23 and Smith was put out of the match with a hand injury. Border and Hughes hinted recovery, but the West Indian attack was too good for most of the visiting batsmen.

In reply, West Indies were solid rather than spectacular. Greenidge took over two hours to reach fifty, but he and Haynes once again showed total dominance of the Australian attack and put on 162 before Haynes was bowled by Hogan. There had been an excess of short-pitched deliveries, particularly from Hogg who was retaliating for the tactics used by Garner and Marshall. Following Haynes' dismissal, Richards and Richardson went quickly, but West Indies reached 205 for 3 at tea on the second day.

Greenidge followed shortly after the break and had the tenacious Australian bowling been supported by adequate fielding, the West Indian position would have been worse. Lloyd was missed at long-leg and Dujon was dropped by Phillips. As it was, the lead was restricted at 106, a good effort by the bowlers although it was hard to understand why Matthews bowled only two overs as, presumably, he had been included for his off-spin bowling, always more likely to trouble the West Indians than pace.

The Australians began their second innings after lunch on the third day and by tea they were 81 for 3. This represented a recovery by Border and Hughes after three wickets had gone for 27. Hughes was out shortly after tea and by the close they

*Desmond Haynes. He totally dominated the one-day series with three centuries. (George Herringshaw)*

## FIFTH TEST MATCH – WEST INDIES *v.* AUSTRALIA

28, 29 and 30 April and 2 May 1984 at Kingston, Jamaica

### AUSTRALIA

| | FIRST INNINGS | | SECOND INNINGS | |
|---|---|---|---|---|
| W.B. Phillips* | c Dujon, b Garner | 12 | b Garner | 2 |
| S.B. Smith | c Greenidge, b Marshall | 9 | absent injured | 0 |
| A.R. Border | c Dujon, b Marshall | 41 | not out | 60 |
| G.M. Ritchie | c Dujon, b Marshall | 5 | b Holding | 8 |
| K.J. Hughes† | c Harper, b Holding | 19 | c Greenidge, b Marshall | 23 |
| D.W. Hookes | b Harper | 36 | c Dujon, b Marshall | 7 |
| G.R.J. Matthews | st Dujon, b Harper | 7 | (2) b Holding | 7 |
| T.G. Hogan | c and b Garner | 25 | (7) b Marshall | 10 |
| G.F. Lawson | c Harper, b Garner | 15 | (8) b Marshall | 4 |
| R.M. Hogg | not out | 1 | (9) b Marshall | 14 |
| J.N. Maguire | b Baptiste | 9 | (10) b Garner | 0 |
| Extras | b 8, lb 4, w 1, nb 7 | 20 | b 17, lb 4, nb 4 | 25 |
| | | 199 | | 160 |

| | O | M | R | W | O | M | R | W |
|---|---|---|---|---|---|---|---|---|
| Marshall | 18 | 4 | 37 | 3 | 23 | 3 | 51 | 5 |
| Garner | 17 | 4 | 42 | 3 | 16.4 | 6 | 28 | 2 |
| Holding | 12 | 2 | 43 | 1 | 11 | 4 | 20 | 2 |
| Baptiste | 11 | 3 | 39 | 1 | 6 | 3 | 11 | — |
| Harper | 20 | 7 | 26 | 2 | 9 | 2 | 25 | — |
| Richards | | | | | 2 | — | 4 | — |

FALL OF WICKETS
1- 22, 2- 23, 3- 34, 4- 73, 5- 113, 6- 124, 7- 142, 8- 181, 9- 190
1- 7, 2- 15, 3- 27, 4- 89, 5- 109, 6- 125, 7- 131, 8- 159, 9- 160

### WEST INDIES

| | FIRST INNINGS | | SECOND INNINGS | |
|---|---|---|---|---|
| C.G. Greenidge | c Ritchie, b Hogan | 127 | not out | 32 |
| D.L. Haynes | b Hogan | 60 | not out | 15 |
| R.B. Richardson | c Phillips, b Lawson | 0 | | |
| I.V.A. Richards | run out | 2 | | |
| C.H. Lloyd† | c Phillips, b Lawson | 20 | | |
| P.J. Dujon* | c Phillips, b Maguire | 23 | | |
| M.D. Marshall | c Hookes, b Maguire | 19 | | |
| E.A.E. Baptiste | c Lawson, b Maguire | 27 | | |
| R.A. Harper | c Phillips, b Maguire | 0 | | |
| J. Garner | c Phillips, b Lawson | 7 | | |
| M.A. Holding | not out | 0 | | |
| Extras | b 1, lb 11, nb 8 | 20 | b 2, lb 3, nb 3 | 8 |
| | | 305 | (for no wkt) | 55 |

| | O | M | R | W | O | M | R | W |
|---|---|---|---|---|---|---|---|---|
| Lawson | 30 | 8 | 91 | 3 | 5 | — | 24 | — |
| Hogg | 16 | 2 | 67 | — | 5.4 | — | 18 | — |
| Hogan | 30 | 8 | 68 | 2 | | | | |
| Maguire | 16.4 | 2 | 57 | 4 | 1 | — | 8 | — |
| Matthews | 2 | — | 10 | — | | | | |

FALL OF WICKETS
1- 162, 2- 169, 3- 174, 4- 213, 5- 228, 6- 260, 7- 274, 8- 274, 9- 297

*Umpires:* D.M. Archer and L. Barker

**West Indies won by 10 wickets**

*Allan Border – a lone figure of defiance in Australia's disasters. (Adrian Murrell)*

were 135 for 7, with Smith unable to bat, and the game lost.

It ended before lunch on the fourth day when West Indies won by 10 wickets to take the series 3–0. Australia were totally outclassed, Border alone showing the tenacity and technique to cope with the West Indian pace attack. The averages for the series make chastening reading for the Australians. Garner's 31 wickets was a West Indian record against Australia.

## First Class Averages

| BATTING | M | Inns | NOs | Runs | HS | Av | 100s | 50s |
|---|---|---|---|---|---|---|---|---|
| T.R. Etwaroo | 2 | 3 | 1 | 230 | 198 | 115.00 | 1 | |
| D.L. Haynes | 6 | 10 | 3 | 553 | 145 | 79.00 | 2 | 4 |
| R.B. Richardson | 7 | 8 | 1 | 496 | 162 | 70.85 | 3 | |
| R.M. Otto | 6 | 10 | 1 | 596 | 136 | 66.22 | 3 | 1 |
| C.G. Greenidge | 6 | 10 | 3 | 453 | 127 | 64.71 | 2 | 1 |
| A. Gilkes | 4 | 8 | 1 | 383 | 104 | 54.85 | 1 | 2 |
| M.C. Neita | 5 | 9 | | 482 | 133 | 53.55 | 2 | 3 |
| A.F.D. Jackman | 7 | 12 | 1 | 583 | 125 | 53.00 | 2 | 3 |
| C.B. Lambert | 5 | 9 | 1 | 418 | 123 | 52.25 | 1 | 4 |
| A. Rajah | 7 | 14 | 2 | 619 | 141* | 51.83 | 2 | 3 |
| I.V.A. Richards | 6 | 6 | | 307 | 178 | 51.16 | 1 | 1 |
| L.C. SEbastien | 6 | 8 | 1 | 354 | 107 | 50.57 | 1 | 3 |
| V.A. Eddy | 6 | 10 | 3 | 354 | 120 | 50.57 | 1 | |
| L.A. Lewis | 6 | 8 | 2 | 298 | 128 | 49.66 | 1 | 1 |

## West Indies v. Australia – Test Match Averages

### WEST INDIES BATTING

| | M | Inns | NOs | Runs | HS | Av | 100s | 50s |
|---|---|---|---|---|---|---|---|---|
| D.L. Haynes | 5 | 8 | 3 | 468 | 145 | 93.60 | 2 | 3 |
| R.B. Richardson | 5 | 5 | 1 | 327 | 154 | 81.75 | 2 | |
| C.G. Greenidge | 5 | 8 | 3 | 393 | 127 | 78.60 | 2 | 1 |
| I.V.A. Richards | 5 | 5 | | 270 | 178 | 54.00 | 1 | 1 |
| C.H. Lloyd | 4 | 4 | | 170 | 76 | 42.50 | | 1 |
| P.J. Dujon | 5 | 5 | | 204 | 130 | 40.80 | 1 | |
| J. Garner | 5 | 5 | 2 | 66 | 24* | 22.00 | | |
| E.A.E. Baptiste | 3 | 3 | | 44 | 27 | 14.66 | | |
| R.A. Harper | 4 | 4 | | 56 | 27 | 14.00 | | |
| M.D. Marshall | 4 | 4 | | 45 | 19 | 11.25 | | |
| M.A. Holding | 3 | 3 | 2 | 3 | 3* | 3.00 | | |

Played in two Tests: W.W. Daniel 4 and 6*; H.A. Gomes 10 and 3
Played in one Test: A.L. Logie 97; W.W. Davis 11; M.A. Small did not bat

### WEST INDIES BOWLING

| | Overs | Mdns | Runs | Wkts | Av | Best | 5/inn |
|---|---|---|---|---|---|---|---|
| J. Garner | 208.5 | 55 | 523 | 31 | 16.87 | 6/60 | 3 |
| M.A. Holding | 101.5 | 20 | 245 | 13 | 18.84 | 4/24 | |
| M.D. Marshall | 159.5 | 25 | 480 | 21 | 22.85 | 5/42 | 1 |
| E.A. E. Baptiste | 62 | 15 | 154 | 6 | 25.66 | 3/42 | |
| W.W. Daniel | 63 | 13 | 197 | 7 | 28.14 | 3/40 | |
| R.A. Harper | 138 | 34 | 303 | 10 | 30.30 | 4/56 | |
| I.V.A. Richards | 53 | 13 | 102 | 3 | 34.00 | 2/65 | |
| H.A. Gomes | 63 | 8 | 146 | 1 | 146.00 | 1/53 | |

Bowled in one Test: W.W. Davis 33–5–80–2; A.L. Logie 0.1–0–4–0; M.A. Small 24–5–75–1

### WEST INDIES CATCHES

22–P.J. Dujon (ct 21/st 1); 7–C.G. Greenidge; 5–R.B. Richardson; 4–R.A. Harper; 3–J. Garner and C.H. Lloyd; 2–I.V.A. Richards, M.D. Marshall and D.L. Haynes; 1–E.A.E. Baptiste, W.W. Davis, H.A. Gomes, W.W. Daniel, A.L. Logie and M.A. Holding

### AUSTRALIA BATTING

| | M | Inns | NOs | Runs | HS | Av | 100s | 50s |
|---|---|---|---|---|---|---|---|---|
| A.R. Border | 5 | 10 | 3 | 521 | 100* | 74.41 | 1 | 4 |
| W.B. Phillips | 5 | 10 | | 259 | 120 | 25.90 | 1 | 1 |
| D.W. Hookes | 5 | 10 | | 248 | 51 | 24.80 | | 1 |
| T.W. Hogan | 5 | 10 | 1 | 195 | 42* | 21.66 | | |
| K.J. Hughes | 5 | 10 | | 215 | 33 | 21.50 | | |
| G.M. Ritchie | 5 | 10 | | 206 | 78 | 20.60 | | 2 |
| R.M. Hogg | 4 | 8 | 2 | 101 | 52 | 16.83 | | 1 |
| G.F. Lawson | 5 | 10 | 2 | 132 | 35* | 16.50 | | |
| D.M.J. Jones | 2 | 4 | | 65 | 48 | 16.25 | | |
| T.M. Alderman | 3 | 6 | 3 | 28 | 21* | 9.33 | | |
| S.B. Smith | 3 | 5 | | 41 | 12 | 8.20 | | |
| K.C. Wessels | 2 | 4 | | 32 | 20 | 8.00 | | |
| J.N. Maguire | 2 | 4 | 1 | 24 | 15* | 8.00 | | |

Played in one Test: G.M. Wood 68 and 20; R.D. Woolley 13 and 8; C.G. Rackemann 12 and 0; G.R.J. Matthews 7 and 7

### AUSTRALIA BOWLING

| | Overs | Mdns | Runs | Wkts | Av | Best | 5/inn |
|---|---|---|---|---|---|---|---|
| J.N. Maguire | 61.4 | 11 | 187 | 7 | 26.71 | 4/57 | |
| R.M. Hogg | 110.4 | 8 | 365 | 9 | 40.55 | 6/77 | 1 |
| G.F. Lawson | 190.1 | 24 | 638 | 12 | 53.16 | 3/59 | |
| T.M. Hogan | 166 | 37 | 483 | 8 | 60.37 | 4/56 | |
| T.M. Alderman | 111.3 | 18 | 368 | 4 | 87.50 | 2/91 | |

Also bowled: A.R. Border 3–1–8–0; G.R.J. Matthews 2–0–10–0; C.G. Rackemann 42.4–6–160–5

### AUSTRALIA CATCHES

10–W.B. Phillips; 4–G.M. Ritchie; 2–R.D. Woolley, D.W. Hookes and K.C. Wessels; 1–A.R. Border, S.B. Smith, K.J. Hughes, D.M.J. Jones, T.G. Hogan and G.F. Lawson

*Joel Garner, the scourge of Australia, 31 wickets in the series. (Ken Kelly)*

| | | | | | | | | |
|---|---|---|---|---|---|---|---|---|
| R. Moosai | 5 | 9 | 1 | 362 | 97 | 45.25 | | 3 |
| L.D. John | 6 | 8 | | 360 | 114 | 45.00 | 1 | 2 |
| R. Nanan | 7 | 12 | 3 | 403 | 98* | 44.77 | | 2 |
| G.L. Linton | 5 | 9 | 3 | 260 | 83 | 43.33 | | 2 |
| C.H. Lloyd | 4 | 4 | | 170 | 76 | 42.50 | | 1 |
| P.J. Dujon | 5 | 5 | | 204 | 130 | 40.80 | 1 | |
| A.A. Lyght | 6 | 11 | | 441 | 122 | 40.09 | 1 | 2 |
| T.R.O. Payne | 6 | 12 | 1 | 439 | 76 | 39.90 | | 5 |
| C.A. Best | 6 | 12 | | 474 | 108 | 39.50 | 1 | 2 |
| T. Hunte | 3 | 6 | | 234 | 72 | 39.00 | | 2 |
| Timur Mohammed | 6 | 10 | 2 | 311 | 68 | 38.87 | | 3 |
| L. Lawrence | 6 | 10 | | 361 | 118 | 36.10 | 1 | 2 |
| R. Seeram | 6 | 11 | 1 | 344 | 57 | 34.40 | | 2 |
| G.N. Reifer | 2 | 4 | | 131 | 51 | 32.75 | | 1 |
| C.A. Davidson | 5 | 9 | 1 | 248 | 77 | 31.00 | | 1 |
| O.W. Peters | 5 | 9 | | 270 | 72 | 30.00 | | 1 |
| N.C. Guishard | 6 | 8 | | 239 | 85 | 29.87 | | 3 |
| A. Gray | 5 | 8 | 3 | 145 | 41* | 29.00 | | |
| P.V. Simmonds | 7 | 14 | | 404 | 72 | 28.85 | | 3 |
| W.H.F. Whyte | 6 | 9 | | 245 | 105 | 27.22 | 1 | 1 |
| S.W. Julien | 6 | 10 | | 271 | 123 | 27.10 | 1 | |
| K.R. Bainey | 3 | 6 | | 161 | 49 | 26.83 | | |
| E.A.E. Baptiste | 5 | 5 | 1 | 104 | 57* | 26.00 | | 1 |
| H. Braithwaite | 5 | 10 | 1 | 229 | 86 | 25.44 | | 1 |
| V.I. Williams | 6 | 9 | 1 | 202 | 63 | 25.25 | | 1 |
| K. Singh | 5 | 8 | | 199 | 88 | 24.87 | | 1 |
| N. Phillip | 6 | 5 | | 123 | 63 | 24.60 | | 1 |
| A.M.E. Roberts | 5 | 6 | 1 | 123 | 54 | 24.60 | | 1 |

## Australians in West Indies 1984
First Class Matches

| BATTING | *v.* Leeward Islands (Basseterre) 18–21 February 1984 | | *v.* Guyana (Georgetown) 24–27 February 1984 | | First Test Match (Georgetown) 2–7 March 1984 | | *v.* Trinidad & Tobago (Point-à-Pierre) 9–12 March 1984 | | Second Test Match (Port-of-Spain) 16–21 March 1984 | | *v.* Barbados (Bridgetown) 24–24 March 1984 | | Third Test Match (Bridgetown) 31 March–4 April 1984 | | Fourth Test Match (St John's, Antigua) 7–10 April 1984 | | *v.* Windward Islands (Castries, St Lucia) 14–17 April 1984 | | Fifth Test Match (Kingston) 28 April–2 May 1984 | |
|---|---|---|---|---|---|---|---|---|---|---|---|---|---|---|---|---|---|---|---|---|
| W.B. Phillips | 27 | 23 | 1 | 62 | 16 | 76 | 19 | 12* | 4 | 0 | 21* | 52* | 120 | 1 | 5 | 23 | | | 12 | 2 |
| K.C. Wessels | 126* | 86 | | | 4 | 20 | 89 | — | 4 | 4 | | | | | | | | | | |
| G.M. Ritchie | 14 | 40 | 64 | 0 | 78 | 3 | 46 | — | 1 | 26 | 99 | — | 57 | 0 | 6 | 22 | 12 | 12 | 5 | 8 |
| K.J. Hughes | 61 | 3 | | | 18 | 0 | 73 | 10* | 24 | 33 | 27 | 65 | 20 | 25 | 24 | 29 | 22 | 10 | 19 | 23 |
| A.R. Border | 74 | 17 | 113 | — | 5 | 54 | | | 98* | 100* | | | 38 | 8 | 98 | 19 | 46 | 54* | 41 | 60* |
| D.W. Hookes | 66 | 24 | 61 | 3* | 32 | 10 | | | 23 | 21 | 22 | 103* | 30 | 9 | 51 | 29 | 22 | 74 | 36 | 7 |
| R.D. Woolley | 27* | 5 | 27* | — | | | 18 | — | | | 56* | — | | | 13 | 8 | 30 | 52* | | |
| T.G. Hogan | 2 | 23* | — | 3 | 42* | 18 | 25 | — | 0 | 38 | | | 40 | 2 | 14 | 6 | | | 25 | 10 |
| J.N. Maguire | 3 | 4* | | | | | 19 | — | | | — | — | | | 15* | 0 | 9 | — | 9 | 0 |
| C.G. Rackemann | 7* | — | | | | | | | | | — | — | | | 12 | 0 | 6 | — | | |
| T.M. Alderman | — | — | | | 1 | 3* | 0* | — | 1 | 21* | | | 2* | 0 | | | 13* | — | | |
| S.B. Smith | | | 105 | 116 | 3 | 12 | 10 | — | | | 9 | 66 | 10 | 7 | | | 127 | 5 | 9 | — |
| D.M.J. Jones | | | 58 | 60 | | | | | 48 | 5 | 9 | 47 | | | 1 | 11 | 2 | 95 | | |
| G.R.J. Matthews | | | 23* | 12* | | | 45 | 26 | | | — | — | | | | | 54 | 14 | 7 | 7 |
| G.F. Lawson | | | — | — | 11 | 35* | | | 14 | 20 | | | 10 | 2 | 4 | 17* | | | 15 | 4 |
| R.M. Hogg | | | — | — | 52 | 6 | 0 | — | 11 | 9 | | | 3 | 5* | | | | | 1* | 14 |
| G.M. Wood | | | | | | | | | | | 76 | 3 | 68 | 20 | | | | | | |
| Byes | 5 | 4 | 2 | 12 | 2 | 10 | 5 | | 6 | 6 | 1 | 6 | 14 | 1 | 5 | 19 | 1 | 5 | 8 | 17 |
| Leg-byes | 6 | 10 | 3 | 2 | 3 | 15 | 9 | | 4 | 1 | 5 | 9 | 8 | 6 | 4 | 7 | 5 | 8 | 4 | 4 |
| Wides | 1 | | 2 | 1 | 1 | | 2 | 3 | | 1 | 5 | | | | | | | 1 | 1 | |
| No-balls | 10 | 11 | 8 | 5 | 11 | 11 | 10 | 5 | 17 | 14 | 2 | 5 | 9 | 11 | 10 | 10 | 13 | 14 | 7 | 4 |
| Total | 429 | 250 | 467 | 276 | 279 | 273 | 370 | 56 | 255 | 299 | 332 | 356 | 429 | 97 | 262 | 200 | 362 | 344 | 199 | 160 |
| Wickets | 7 | 7 | 6 | 5 | 10 | 9 | 10 | 1 | 10 | 9 | 6 | 4 | 10 | 10 | 10 | 10 | 10 | 6 | 10 | 10 |
| Result | W | | D | | D | | D | | D | | D | | L | | L | | D | | L | |

*Catches* 16–W.B. Phillips
12–R.D. Woolley (ct 11/st 1)
9–K.J. Hughes
6–G.M. Ritchie
5–S.B. Smith
4–D.W. Hookes, T.M. Alderman and G.R.J. Matthews
3–A.R. Border, K.C. Wessels, J.N. Maguire and subs
2–C.G. Rackemann, R.M. Hogg and D.M. Jones
1–T.G. Hogan and G.F. Lawson

| BOWLING | C.G. Rackemann | T.M. Alderman | J.N. Maguire | T.G. Hogan | A.R. Border | K.C. Wessells | G.F. Lawson | R.M. Hogg | D.M.J. Jones |
|---|---|---|---|---|---|---|---|---|---|
| *v.* Leeward Islands | 33–5–105–6 | 16–2–52–3 | 21–4–59–1 | 17–1–73–0 | 1–1–0–0 | | | | |
| (Basseterre) 18–21 February | 9.4–1–42–3 | 16–5–47–3 | 15–3–37–3 | 7–2–13–1 | | 3–0–13–0 | | | |
| *v.* Guyana (Georgetown) | | | | 25–3–66–2 | | | 18–1–99–0 | 27–4–114–5 | 4–0–13–0 |
| 24–27 February | | | | 33–8–95–5 | | | 11–4–31–2 | 4–0–15–0 | |
| First Test Match | | 21–3–64–1 | | 25–9–56–4 | | | 20.4–4–59–3 | 12–0–44–2 | |
| (Georgetown) 2–7 March | | 11–0–43–0 | | 19–2–74–0 | | | 18–0–54–0 | 13–0–56–0 | |
| *v.* Trinidad and Tobago | | 15–5–62–2 | 25.2–6–67–4 | 14–2–65–2 | | 1–0–1–0 | | 23–3–75–1 | |
| (Pointe-à-Pierre) 9–12 March | | 16–4–29–1 | 16–5–46–2 | 19.1–3–74–4 | | | | | |
| Second Test Match | | 35–9–91–2 | | 28–3–123–2 | | | 32–3–132–2 | 31–2–103–1 | |
| (Port of Spain) 16–21 March | | | | | | | | | |
| *v.* Barbados (Bridgetown) | 28–1–121–3 | | 30–4–83–3 | | | | | | 1.3–0–10–1 |
| 24–27 March | 11–1–45–0 | | 8–0–47–1 | | | | | | 10–1–39–1 |
| Third Test Match (Bridgetown) | | 42.4–6–152–1 | | 34–8–97–0 | 3–1–8–0 | | 33.2–4–150–2 | 33–4–77–6 | |
| 30 March–4 April | | 1.5–0–18–0 | | | | | 2–1–3–0 | | |
| Fourth Test Match (St John's, | 42.4–6–160–5 | | 44–9–122–3 | 30–9–65–0 | | | 49–4–125–2 | | |
| Antigua) 7–10 April | | | | | | | | | |
| *v.* Windward Islands (Castries, | 13–2–47–2 | 19–1–75–2 | 16–1–48–2 | | 6.1–0–27–1 | | | | 4–0–12–0 |
| St Lucia) 14–17 April | 9.4–1–26–0 | 10–2–21–0 | 17–4–70–3 | | | | | | |
| Fifth Test Match (Kingston) | | | 16.4–2–57–4 | 30–8–68–2 | | | 30–8–91–3 | 16–2–67–0 | |
| 28 April–2 May | | | 1–0–8–0 | | | | 5–0–24–0 | 5.4–0–18–0 | |
| | 148–17–546–19 *av.* 28.73 | 203.3–37–654–15 *av.* 43.60 | 210–38–644–26 *av.* 24.76 | 281.1–58–869–22 *av.* 39.50 | 10.1–2–35–1 *av.* 35.00 | 4–0–14–0 — | 219–29–768–14 *av.* 54.85 | 164.4–15–569–15 *av.* 37.93 | 19.3–1–74–2 *av.* 37.00 |

a S.B. Smith 1–0–5–0

| M | Inns | NOs | Runs | HS | Av |
|---|---|---|---|---|---|
| 9 | 18 | 3 | 476 | 120 | 31.73 |
| 4 | 7 | 1 | 333 | 126* | 55.50 |
| 10 | 18 | — | 493 | 99 | 27.38 |
| 9 | 18 | 1 | 486 | 73 | 28.58 |
| 8 | 15 | 4 | 825 | 113 | 75.00 |
| 9 | 18 | 2 | 623 | 103* | 38.93 |
| 6 | 9 | 4 | 236 | 56* | 47.20 |
| 8 | 14 | 2 | 248 | 42* | 20.66 |
| 6 | 8 | 2 | 59 | 19 | 9.83 |
| 4 | 4 | — | 25 | 12 | 6.25 |
| 6 | 8 | 5 | 41 | 21* | 13.66 |
| 7 | 12 | — | 479 | 127 | 39.91 |
| 5 | 10 | — | 336 | 95 | 33.60 |
| 5 | 8 | 2 | 188 | 54 | 31.33 |
| 6 | 10 | 2 | 132 | 35* | 16.50 |
| 6 | 9 | 2 | 101 | 52 | 14.42 |
| 2 | 4 | — | 167 | 76 | 41.75 |

| G.R.J. Matthews | D.W. Hookes | G.M. Ritchie | Byes | Leg-byes | Wides | No-balls | Total | Wkts |
|---|---|---|---|---|---|---|---|---|
| | | | 4 | 12 | 4 | 10 | 305 | 10 |
| | | | 8 | 10 | | 3 | 170 | 10 |
| 26–8–80–1 | 4–0–23–0 | | 8 | 14 | 1 | 15 | 417 | 8 |
| 17–3–53–0 | 9–0–47–0 | 1–0–4–1 | 10 | | | 1 | 260 | 8a |
| | | | | 7 | | 12 | 230 | 10 |
| | | | 10 | 13 | | 4 | 250 | 0 |
| 13–0–54–1 | | | | 12 | | 4 | 336 | 10 |
| 19–3–63–2 | | | 4 | 6 | 1 | | 222 | 10 |
| | | | 7 | 12 | 2 | 1 | 468 | 8 |
| 31–6–83–3 | | | 2 | 3 | | 12 | 302 | 10 |
| 27–5–76–2 | 5–0–17–1 | 1–0–6–0 | | 3 | 2 | 8 | 233 | 5 |
| | | | | 25 | | 11 | 509 | 10 |
| | | | | | | | 21 | 0 |
| | | | 12 | 14 | | 1 | 498 | 10 |
| | 20–0–115–3 | | 5 | 8 | 8 | 7 | 337 | 10 |
| 15–2–53–0 | 3–0–14–0 | | 5 | 1 | | 2 | 190 | 3 |
| 2–0–10–0 | | | 1 | 11 | | 8 | 305 | 10 |
| | | | 2 | 3 | | 3 | 55 | 0 |
| 150–27–472–9 *av.* 52.44 | 41–0–216–4 *av.* 54.00 | 2–0–10–1 *av.* 10.00 | | | | | | |

| | | | | | | | |
|---|---|---|---|---|---|---|---|
| A. Merrick | 6 | 7 | 1 | 147 | 62* | 24.50 | 1 |
| A.B. Williams | 5 | 9 | | 220 | 41 | 24.44 | |
| C. Rampersad | 7 | 13 | 1 | 274 | 61 | 22.83 | 2 |
| R.A. Harper | 6 | 7 | | 154 | 86 | 22.00 | 1 |
| M.C. Worrell | 5 | 9 | 2 | 152 | 47* | 21.71 | |
| N.A. Phillips | 6 | 11 | 1 | 216 | 45 | 21.60 | |
| R. Sampath | 3 | 6 | | 129 | 55 | 21.50 | |
| T. Corke | 4 | 8 | | 168 | 62 | 21.00 | 1 |
| M.R. Pydanna | 6 | 10 | 2 | 166 | 56 | 20.75 | 1 |
| D.I. Kallicharran | 5 | 7 | | 126 | 48 | 18.00 | |
| C. Butts | 6 | 9 | 1 | 117 | 31 | 14.62 | |
| A. Dharson | 4 | 8 | | 103 | 34 | 12.87 | |
| H. Joseph | 7 | 12 | 1 | 134 | 26 | 12.18 | |

(Qualification – 100 runs, average 10.00)

| BOWLING | Overs | Mdns | Runs | Wkts | Av | Best | 5/in | 10/m |
|---|---|---|---|---|---|---|---|---|
| K.C. Williams | 54.1 | 10 | 133 | 10 | 13.30 | 5/63 | 1 | |
| J. Garner | 208.5 | 55 | 223 | 31 | 16.87 | 6/60 | 3 | |
| S. Ganouri | 99.3 | 25 | 246 | 14 | 17.57 | 7/91 | 2 | 1 |
| A.M.E. Roberts | 142.5 | 34 | 374 | 21 | 17.80 | 6/80 | 1 | 1 |
| M.A. Holding | 101.5 | 20 | 245 | 13 | 18.84 | 4/24 | | |
| E.L. Wilson | 104 | 30 | 219 | 11 | 19.90 | 5/63 | 1 | |
| C.A. Walsh | 154 | 17 | 603 | 30 | 20.06 | 6/35 | 3 | |
| M.D. Marshall | 159.5 | 25 | 480 | 21 | 22.85 | 5/42 | 1 | |
| S.J. Hinds | 204.1 | 36 | 573 | 24 | 23.87 | 6/97 | 1 | |
| R.A. Harper | 243.3 | 62 | 574 | 23 | 24.95 | 6/72 | 2 | 1 |
| G. Mahabir | 208.5 | 40 | 575 | 23 | 25.00 | 4/57 | | |
| G.L. Linton | 128.1 | 20 | 432 | 17 | 25.41 | 5/75 | 1 | |
| R.O. Estwick | 158.3 | 19 | 604 | 23 | 26.26 | 6/68 | 1 | |
| E.A.E. Baptiste | 133 | 30 | 405 | 15 | 27.00 | 4/95 | | |
| M.A. Small | 172.2 | 25 | 545 | 20 | 27.25 | 5/57 | 1 | |
| T. Kentish | 209.2 | 40 | 492 | 18 | 27.33 | 4/73 | | |
| N. Phillip | 114 | 9 | 426 | 15 | 28.40 | 5/47 | 1 | |
| C. Butts | 360.4 | 96 | 848 | 29 | 29.24 | 6/79 | 2 | |
| N.A. Phillips | 137.1 | 18 | 398 | 13 | 30.61 | 4/35 | | |
| R. Nanan | 284.3 | 72 | 582 | 18 | 32.33 | 5/56 | 1 | |
| D.J. Collymore | 102 | 11 | 328 | 10 | 32.80 | 3/70 | | |
| A. Merrick | 150.2 | 24 | 569 | 17 | 33.47 | 5/45 | 1 | |
| E.T. Willett | 138.3 | 33 | 342 | 10 | 34.20 | 4/93 | | |
| D. Cumberbatch | 118.4 | 17 | 385 | 11 | 35.00 | 3/67 | | |
| H. Joseph | 312.3 | 51 | 819 | 22 | 37.22 | 5/82 | 1 | |
| R.F. Joseph | 195 | 32 | 679 | 16 | 38.68 | 6/114 | 1 | |
| D.I. Kallicharran | 223.5 | 39 | 645 | 16 | 40.31 | 5/59 | 1 | |
| A. Gray | 96 | 9 | 406 | 10 | 40.60 | 3/48 | | |
| R.C. Haynes | 130.3 | 20 | 420 | 10 | 42.00 | 4/78 | | |
| N.C. Guishard | 194 | 41 | 547 | 11 | 49.72 | 4/53 | | |

(Qualification – 10 wickets)

## LEADING FIELDERS

22–P.J. Dujon (ct 21/st 1); 17–M.R. Pydanna (ct 12/st 5) and M.C. Worrell; 14–S.I. Williams (ct 10/st 4); 13–G. Sahadeo (ct 8/st 5) and I. Cadette (ct 12/st 1); 12–P.A.O. Francis and C. Rampersad (ct 10/st 2); 11–C.B. Lambert, O.W. Peters and P.V. Simmonds; 10–W.H.F. Whyte (ct 9/st 1)

SECTION I

# The English Season

Brittanic Assurance County Championship.
John Player League. NatWest Trophy. Benson and Hedges Cup.
England *v.* West Indies. England *v.* Sri Lanka.
Review of the season by David Lemmon.
Book reviews.

*England* v. *West Indies at Headingley.*
*(Ken Kelly)*

*Jonathan Agnew began an excellent season with a career best 8 for 47 for Leicestershire against Cambridge University, 18 April. (David Munden)*

### *18, 19 and 20 April*

**at Cambridge**

**Leicestershire** 353 for 6 dec (P. Willey 141 not out, J.C. Balderstone 105) and 361 for 3 dec (I.P. Butcher 109, M.D. Haysman 102 not out, N.E. Briers 73, M.A. Garnham 65 not out)
**Cambridge University** 127 (J.P. Agnew 8 for 47) and 65

*Leicestershire won by 522 runs*

The sun shone. A fine crowd gathered and we renewed old friendships. It was a glorious beginning to an English season and Fenner's a beautiful setting, a place where all dreams seem possible. Sadly, the two oldest Universities can no longer boast teams of first-class standard. The better cricketers are now at other universities and Cambridge had even lost their captain, Pollock, to studies. Incomprehensibly, Peck, a cricketer of moderate accomplishment, had been asked to lead the side in Pollock's absence although he was now a schoolmaster and ineligible for the Varsity match. His presence therefore denied a place to one of the promising young cricketers in residence.

Willey reached a hundred in his first game for Leicestershire. Balderstone hit the first century of the season, a just triumph for such a noble cricketer in his benefit year. Butcher and Haysman, the South Australian, also hit hundreds, but, most interestingly, Agnew, once described by Ray Illingworth as England's fastest young bowler, took a career best 8 for 47. The opposition was very weak. The margin of victory was the biggest in England for 50 years and to add to Cambridge's woes, Price broke a finger.

### *21, 23 and 24 April*

**at Cambridge**

**Essex** 463 for 4 dec (C. Gladwin 162, G.A. Gooch 89, K.S. McEwan 69, K.W.R. Fletcher 59) and 259 for 3 dec (D.R. Pringle 96, B.R. Hardie 68, S. Turner 50)
**Cambridge University** 222 (A.E. Lea 119, J.K. Lever 4 for 44) and 116 for 4

*Match drawn*

**at Oxford**

**Nottinghamshire** 355 for 6 dec (B.C. Broad 88, R.T. Robinson 79, J.D. Birch 52) and 222 for 0 dec (B.C. Broad 108 not out, R.T. Robinson 100 not out)
**Oxford University** 154 (J.D. Carr 64, R.A. Pick 5 for 33, P.M. Such 5 for 34) and 163 (R.A. Pick 5 for 25)

*Nottinghamshire won by 258 runs*

The slaughter of the innocents moved into its second phase. Gooch and Gladwin, who hit a maiden first-class century, put on 145 for Essex's first wicket in the first innings and Pringle, 96 off 76 balls, and Hardie, 156 in the second. No Essex batsman was dismissed for under 50. Cambridge had a hero in Lea who, with the advantage of two chances, batted $6\frac{1}{4}$ hours for his hundred in his second first-class game. Breddy and Cotterell batted for 170 minutes to save the game for the home side.

At Oxford, Pick and Such, pace and spin, twice mutilated the university. Broad had a remarkable debut for his new county and Bruce French had nine dismissals in an excellent display of wicket-keeping.

### *25, 26 and 27 April*

**at Lord's**

**M.C.C.** 235 for 6 dec (M.C.J. Nicholas 76 not out, T.A. Lloyd 60) and 215 dec (T.A. Lloyd 102 not out, M.W. Gatting 75 not out)
**Essex** 210 (G.A. Gooch 78, K.S. McEwan 70, N.F. Williams 4 for 55) and 173

*M.C.C. won by 67 runs*

**at Cambridge**

**Hampshire** 448 for 3 dec (T.E. Jesty 248, V.P. Terry 137) and 226 for 3 dec (R.J. Parks 89, D.R. Turner 76)
**Cambridge University** 106 (E. Reifer 4 for 43) and 207 (E. Reifer 4 for 65)

*Hampshire won by 361 runs*

**at Oxford**

**Glamorgan** 301 for 9 dec (Younis Ahmed 158 not out, A.L. Jones 56, D.A. Thorne 4 for 81) and 193 for 2 dec (R.C. Ontong 59 not out, J.A. Hopkings 56)
**Oxford University** 163 (M.W.W. Selvey 6 for 31) and 126 (M.R. Cullinan 51, S.R. Barwick 7 for 38)

*Glamorgan won by 205 runs*

The season's first showpiece, Champion County *v.* M.C.C., destroyed by rain in 1983, saw the Club victorious and several thousand spectators at Lord's to watch them. Lloyd and Smith began with a stand of 103 for M.C.C., but Smith, laboured and strokeless, was outshone by his partner. Andy

Lloyd did even better in the second innings with a fine century as he and Gatting shared an unbeaten stand of 170. Lloyd is an intelligent and determined player and his performance in this match must have enhanced his prospects of a place in an England side desperately in needed of character and application. Gooch gave a taste of the forbidden fruit with an exotic display and McEwan was languid and regal. Neil Williams prompted the Essex decline in the second innings when he dismissed Gooch, East and McEwan in one over, two to fine catches by Downton, but the Champions were handicapped by an injury to Fletcher which threatened to keep him out for some weeks.

Both universities suffered further mutilation. Younis made an impressive debut for Glamorgan with 158 out of 222 in under 4 hours and Selvey and Barwick enjoyed bowling. At Cambridge, Jesty and Terry shared a second wicket stand of 302 and both hit career bests as did Bobby Parks in the second innings. Reifer gave a good indication of his value without ever suggesting that he was another Marshall. Another Hampshire player, Nicholas, made a good impression at Lord's where Gower was praised for his captaincy.

***28, 29 and 30 April***

***at Bristol***

**Kent** 412 for 7 dec (R.A. Woolmer 153, D.G. Aslett 140)

**Gloucestershire** 204 and 354 for 4 (Zaheer Abbas 157 not out, A.W. Stovold 57, P.W. Romaines 52)

*Match drawn*
*Kent 7 pts, Gloucestershire 4 pts*

***at Southampton***

**Essex** 449 for 5 dec (G.A. Gooch 220, K.S. McEwan 89) and 18 for 0
**Hampshire** 276 (M.C.J. Nicholas 147) and 189 (N.E.J. Pocock 55, N.A. Foster 4 for 49)

*Essex won by 10 wickets*
*Essex 23 pts, Hampshire 5 pts*

***at Trent Bridge***

**Nottinghamshire** 175 (G. Monkhouse 4 for 41) and 327 for 5 dec (C.E.B. Rice 86, J.D. Birch 75, B.C. Broad 63)
**Surrey** 129 (A. Needham 50, P.M. Such 5 for 52, R.J. Hadlee 4 for 8) and 148 (R.D.V. Knight 58 not out, R.J. Hadlee 4 for 14)

*Nottinghamshire won by 225 runs*
*Nottinghamshire 21 pts, Surrey 4 pts*

***at Taunton***

**Somerset** 298 for 5 dec (P.M. Roebuck 145, J.G. Wyatt 87) and 249 for 5 dec. (P.M. Roebuck 69, P.W. Denning 53 not out)
**Yorkshire** 242 (M.D. Moxon 61, A. Sidebottom 54 not out, D.L. Bairstow 53, J.D. Love 53)

*Yorkshire won by 3 wickets*
*Yorkshire 18 pts, Somerset 7 pts*

*Chris Gladwin (Essex) – a maiden century in the first match of his second season, 162* v. *Cambridge University, 21 April. (Adrian Murrell)*

*An England contender. Bruce French of Notts. Nine dismissals in the match against Oxford University, 21–24 April. (George Herringshaw)*

*On his way to a hundred and an England place, Andy Lloyd turns a ball past Brian Hardie as Stuart Turner looks on. M.C.C. v. Essex, 25–27 April. (Adrian Murrell)*

***at Edgbaston***

**Warwickshire** 438 for 5 dec (A.I. Kallicharran 200 not out, T.A. Lloyd 110, G.W. Humpage 53) and 301 for 4 dec (A.I. Kallicharran 117 not out, G.W. Humpage 86 not out)
**Northamptonshire** 391 for 5 dec (G. Cook 102, R.J. Bailey 100 not out, A.J. Lamb 57) and 157 for 3 (A.J. Lamb 67 not out)

*Match drawn*
*Warwickshire 5 pts, Northamptonshire 5 pts*

***at Worcester***

**Sussex** 207 (A.P. Pridgeon 4 for 78) and 222 (G.D. Mendis 116, J.D. Inchmore 4 for 71)
**Worcestershire** 281 (D.J. Humphries 88 not out, T.S. Curtis 69, I.A. Greig 4 for 91) and 151 for 4 (D.M. Smith 53 not out)

*Worcestershire won by 6 wickets*
*Worcestershire 23 pts, Sussex 6 pts*

***28, 30 April and 1 May***

***at Chesterfield***

**Leicestershire** 297 (P. Willey 102, D.I. Gower 70, G. Miller 4 for 32) and 249 for 4 dec (I.P. Butcher 130)
**Derbyshire** 214 (K.J. Barnett 114) and 321 (B. Roberts 80, I.S. Anderson 79, A. Hill 53, J.P. Agnew 5 for 100)

*Leicestershire won by 11 runs*
*Leicestershire 23 pts, Derbyshire 6 pts*

***at Lord's***

**Middlesex** 373 for 7 dec (C.T. Radley 128 not out, M.W. Gatting 55, P.R. Downton 52) and 20 for 0
**Glamorgan** 174 and 218 (N.G. Cowans 4 for 48)

*Middlesex won by 10 wickets*
*Middlesex 24 pts, Glamorgan 3 pts*

***at Oxford***

**Oxford University** 90 (P.J.W. Allott 4 for 21) and 290 (J.D. Carr 123, R.M. Edbrooke 58)
**Lancashire** 495 for 7 dec (J. Abrahams 123, D.P. Hughes 105, S.T. Jefferies 65, J.A. Ormrod 50, P.J.W. Allott 50 not out, J.D. Carr 5 for 155)

*Lancashire won by an innings and 115 runs*

The Britannic Assurance County Championship began in glorious weather and six of the eight matches produced a result. On Sunday evening Worcestershire stood top of the table having beaten Sussex in two days. On a fiery wicket Sussex lost Standing injured and Mendis, bowled in Pridgeon's first over, the first wicket of the season. They never recovered and, by the end of the first day, Worcestershire were 43 runs ahead thanks to a thumping innings from Humphries. Inchmore, Ellcock and Pridgeon bowled well on a wicket that gave them assistance on the Sunday and the only Sussex resistance came from an heroic display by Mendis who dominated the innings. Smith guided the home side to a creditable win late in the day after they had been 27 for 2.

Woolmer and Aslett shared a third wicket stand of 207 at Bristol and then Gloucestershire succumbed to Jarvis and Ellison, but, following on, they were given a sound start by Stovold and Romaines and Zaheer halted the threat of Underwood with a typically fluent century.

Leading Essex in the absence of Fletcher, Graham Gooch hit a career best at Southampton. In an exciting display of stroke-making, he hit five sixes and twenty-five fours in his five-hour innings. He and McEwan, a batsman of classical beauty, added 182 at 5 an over. It was glorious stuff. Mark Nicholas followed his innings at Lord's with an accomplished and impressive century, but Foster, Lever and Pringle, growing in strength as an all-rounder, saw Essex to a fine win.

Middlesex, runners-up in 1983, gained maximum points in the game against Glamorgan. Radley, batting at number 5, gave the middle order substance with a professionally acquired hundred. The all-round strength of the Middlesex attack was too much for Glamorgan and Cowans showed good early season form.

The wicket at Trent Bridge again caused raised eye-brows, but Notts, with Clive Rice scoring well in both innings, achieved a massive victory which argued that strokes could be made and runs scored by the batsmen who had both technique and character. Surrey displayed neither of these qualities in two dreadfully limp innings and Richard Hadlee had match figures of 8 for 22 in 27.4 overs.

The surprise performance was Yorkshire's win at Taunton. Somerset dominated the match for the first two days, but, commendable as was the opening stand of 246 by Roebuck and Wyatt after Somerset had been put in by Bairstow, it bordered on the tedious and the home side took

ABOVE: *The M.C.C. team* v. *Essex at Lord's (Back Row) N. Williams, Nicholas, Cowans, Cowdrey, Lloyd, R.G. Williams (Front Row) Smith, Gatting, Gower (capt), Downton, Cook. (Adrian Murrell)* RIGHT: *J.D. Carr, a fine all-round cricketer. 123 and 5 for 155 for Oxford University* v. *Lancashire, 28–30 April. (Adrian Murrell)*

only 3 bonus points. Boycott fell before the end of the day and Yorkshire trailed by 56 runs on the first innings, and for the smallness of the margin, they had to thank a late hard-hit fifty from Sidebottom. Eventually, Botham asked Yorkshire to make 306 to win at nearly 4 runs an over, and they reached the target mainly due to an energetic and inspiring innings from Bairstow who, at least, suggested that he would make them believe that all is possible.

In a run feast at Edgbaston, Alvin Kallicharran scored 317 runs without being dismissed, joining the score of batsmen who have scored two hundred and one hundred in a match. Perhaps more significant was that Andy Lloyd scored another impressive century and Robert Bailey hit a maiden hundred in a match which was always destined for a draw.

There were problems at Chesterfield where David Gower was taken into hospital with a poisoned hand after scoring a brisk 70 to complement Peter Willey's workman-like century. Kim Barnett, the most mature young batsman in the country, hit a fine hundred in reply, but the Derbyshire middle order disintegrated and Leicestershire gained a sub-

LEFT: *Alvin Kallicharran, 200 not out and 117 not out for Warwickshire against Northants at Edgbaston, 28–30 April. He was only the third batsman to score a not out double century and a not out century in the same match. George Sharp is behind the stumps. (Ken Kelly)*

BELOW: *Robert Bailey, an exciting young batsman, on his way to a maiden century in the same match. (Ken Kelly)*

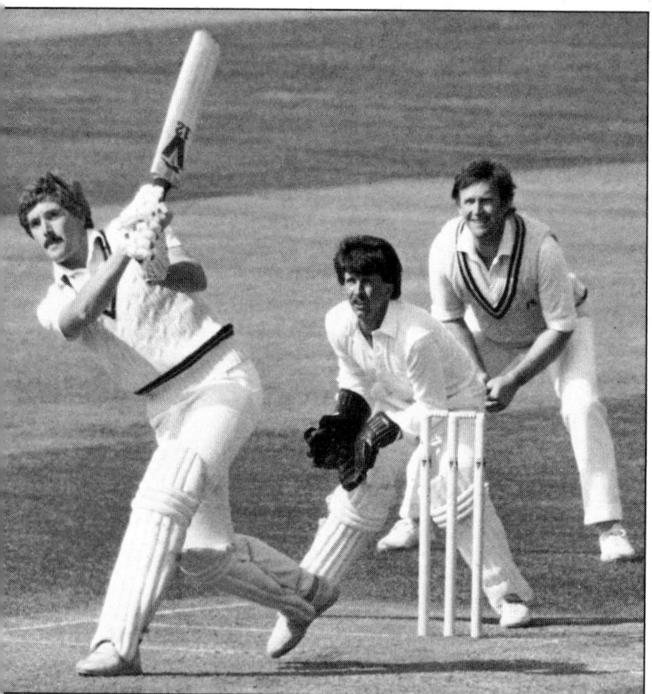

stantial lead which was built upon by Ian Butcher's second century of the season. Set to make 333, Derbyshire lost Barnett at 28 when he dragged a ball from Agnew on to his stumps, but Anderson and Hill added 106. A middle order collapse saw 5 men fall for 56 runs, but Bruce Roberts, the 21-year old Zimbabwe all-rounder, played a wonderful innings which, sadly, ended with the home side just short of their target. It was a magnificent game of cricket and Jonathan Agnew produced another fine spell of bowling to give further indication of his advance.

At Oxford, Carr had career bests in batting and bowling, a morale booster for Oxford and Lancashire won by an innings.

## John Player League

### *29 April*

**_at Leicester_**

**Leicestershire** 177 for 8 (P. Willey 60, P.G. Newman 4 for 44)
**Derbyshire** 181 for 3 (K.J. Barnett 65, J.E. Morris 60 not out)

*Derbyshire (4 pts) won by 7 wickets*

The opening match in the Sunday League saw Wright and Barnett put on 87 for Derbyshire's first wicket, Morris bat with authority, Garnham sustain an eye injury and Derbyshire win with 3.4 overs to spare.

### *2, 3 and 4 May*

**_at Canterbury_**

**Essex** 202 (K.S. McEwan 63, R.M. Ellison 4 for 35) and 113 (G.A. Gooch 84, R.M. Ellison 5 for 27)
**Kent** 183 (D.R. Pringle 7 for 53) and 136 for 7

*Kent won by 3 wickets*
*Kent 21 pts, Essex 6 pts*

**_at Old Trafford_**

**Lancashire** 269 (D.P. Hughes 72) and 190 for 2 (G. Fowler 70)
**Derbyshire** 394 (G. MIller 130, R.J. Finney 52, D.G. Moir 51, L.L. McFarlane 4 for 65)

*Match drawn*
*Lancashire 4 pts, Derbyshire 5 pts*

**_at Trent Bridge_**

**Nottinghamshire** 291 for 9 dec and 188 for 5 (D.W. Randall 75 not out)
**Leicestershire** 196 and 219 for 6 (I.P. Butcher 62, G.J. Parsons 54 not out)

*Match drawn*
*Nottinghamshire 7 pts, Leicestershire 4 pts*

**_at The Oval_**

**Surrey** 318 for 7 dec (R.D.V. Knight 87, M.A. Lynch 60, C.J. Richards 56 not out) and 225 for 9 dec (M.A. Lynch 66, D.B. Pauline 65, D.J. Capel 5 for 28)
**Northamptonshire** 300 (A.J. Lamb 74, R.J. Bailey 65) and 244 for 4 (R.J. Boyd-Moss 79)

*Northamptonshire won by 6 wickets*
*Northamptonshire 23 pts, Surrey 8 pts*

*Geoff Miller (Derbyshire) – a maiden hundred after a decade of endeavour. 2–4 May. (Ken Kelly)*

***at Worcester***

**Glamorgan** 309 for 8 dec (S.P. Henderson 90) and 134 (S.P. Henderson 56, R.M. Ellcock 4 for 34, A.E. Warner 5 for 27)
**Worcestershire** 209 (P.A. Neale 73, W.W. Davis 4 for 73) and 168 (D.N. Patel 59, S.R. Barwick 7 for 55)

*Glamorgan won by 66 runs*
*Glamorgan 24 pts, Worcestershire 5 pts*

***at Cambridge***

**Sussex** 359 for 5 dec (I.A. Greig 106 not out, P.W.G. Parker 100 not out, G.D. Mendis 69) and 141 for 2 dec (C.M. Wells 61 not out, A.P. Wells 53 not out)
**Cambridge University** 156 (C.R. Andrew 51, D.A. Reeve 5 for 22) and 132 for 4 (S.N. Siddiqi 52)

*Match drawn*

***at Oxford***

**Somerset** 365 for 1 dec (P.M. Roebuck 152 not out, J.G. Wyatt 103, M.D. Crowe 100 not out) and 186 for 4 dec (N.F.M. Popplewell 50)
**Oxford University** 171 (M.R. Davis 6 for 82) and 241 (J.D. Carr 100)

*Somerset won by 139 runs*

In three days mutilated by bad weather, the highlight was Geoff Miller's maiden century after 12 years of first-class cricket. It was made possible in an eighth wicket stand of 108 with Newman.

In a seam bowler's paradise at Canterbury, Derek Pringle bowled Essex to a narrow first innings lead, but, in spite of Gooch's commanding 84, Essex were beaten in a tense finish by Tavare's patience and a career best 5 for 27 from Richard Ellison upon whom England should call in the near future.

Seamers thrived at Worcester, too. Steve Barwick emulated his career best performance (8 for 42) on the same ground a year earlier and bowled Glamorgan to a fine victory.

With Gower in Hospital, Leicestershire owed much to Garnham and Parsons who held out for the last 25 overs at Trent Bridge to thwart the home side.

Set to make 247 in 47 overs, Northants, in spite of losing Geoff Cook with a broken jaw, beat Surrey with an over to spare. Capel had 5 for 28, a career best, and Boyd-Moss, with stands of 78 with Larkins and 72 in 10 overs with Lamb, were the stars of a fine win.

At Fenner's and in The Parks, county professionals sharpened averages and recorded career bests against moderate opposition, but Carr gave hope for the future with his second century of the season.

## Benson and Hedges Cup

***5 May***

***at Chelmsford***

**Essex** 222 for 8 (B.R. Hardie 62 not out, G.A. Gooch 57)
**Gloucestershire** 217 for 9 (Zaheer Abbas 67)

*Essex (2 pts) won by 5 runs*
*(Gold Award –* B.R. Hardie)

***at Swansea***

**Glamorgan** 178 for 9 (R.C. Ontong 81, I.T. Botham 4 for 51)
**Somerset** 182 for 7 (P.W. Denning 63)

*Somerset (2 pts) won by 3 wickets*
*(Gold Award –* R.C. Ontong)

***at Southampton***

**Combined Universities** 154 (K.A. Haynes 67)
**Hampshire** 155 for 1 (C.L. Smith 82 not out)

*Hampshire (2 pts) won by 9 wickets*
*(Gold Award –* C.L. Smith)

***at Lord's***

**Kent** 220 for 9 (R.M. Ellison 72, W.W. Daniel 5 for 31)
**Middlesex** 143 (J.E. Emburey 50)

*Kent (2 pts) won by 77 runs*
*(Gold Award –* R.M. Ellison)

***at Northampton***

**Northamptonshire** 256 for 3 (W. Larkins 83, R.J. Bailey 77, A.J. Lamb 56 not out)
**Scotland** 230 (R.G. Swan 55)

*Northamptonshire (2 pts) won by 26 runs*
*(Gold Award –* A.J. Lamb)

***at Trent Bridge***

**Nottinghamshire** 210 for 7 (D.W. Randall 57)
**Worcestershire** 181 (C.E.B. Rice 4 for 60)

*Nottinghamshire (2 pts) won by 29 runs*
*(Gold Award –* B. French)

***at Leeds***

**Leicestershire** 172 for 9 (P. Willey 54)
**Yorkshire** 178 for 3

*Yorkshire (2 pts) won by 7 wickets*
*(Gold Award* – P. Willey)

***at Bowdon***

**Minor Counties** 219 for 4 (R.E. Hayward 78 not out, N.A. Riddell 59 not out)
**Lancashire** 223 for 4 (J. Abrahams 66 not out, S.J. O'Shaughnessy 50)

*Lancashire (2 pts) won by 6 wickets*
*(Gold Award* – R.E. Hayward)

There were no surprises in the first round of matches in the Benson and Hedges Cup, but, at Bowdon, Minor Counties, with Hayward and Riddell adding an undefeated 130 for the fifth wicket, then dismissed Fowler and Ormrod with only 4 scored. O'Shaughnessy and Hughes effected a recovery and Abrahams and Fairbrother took Lancashire to victory by scoring the last 106 runs.

Doughty and Graveney hit splendidly for Gloucestershire at Chelmsford when all seemed lost, but their brave effort ended in defeat at 8.15.

Bruce French took the individual honours at Trent Bridge

LEFT: *Richard Ellison, Gold Award winner, brought Kent victory after they looked doomed to defeat by Middlesex in the Benson and Hedges match at Lord's, 5 May. (Adrian Murrell)*
BELOW: *Derek Aslett batting for Kent against Middlesex, Benson and Hedges Cup. (Adrian Murrell)*

with a vital 48 not out which helped lift Notts from 125 for 6 to 210 off their 55 overs. Bailey and Larkins began the Northants innings with a stand of 149 against Scotland, but the visitors died very bravely. Hampshire, Yorkshire and Somerset won with ease although the latter had some alarms until steadied by the veterans Rose and Denning.

The outstanding performance of the day belonged to Kent who recovered from 24 for 4 through the efforts of Aslett, Ellison and Johnson and then, with Alderman in their attack, bowled out Middlesex, the holders, for 143, Ellison taking 2 for 3 to complement his earlier aggressive batting.

***5, 7, and 8 May***

***at Edgbaston***

**Warwickshire** 275 (G.J. Lord 55) and 189 (T.A. Lloyd 50, M.A. Feltham 5 for 62)
**Surrey** 247 (D.B. Pauline 57, N. Gifford 4 for 62) and 132 for 7 (R.D.V. Knight 50 not out, G.C. Small 4 for 50)

*Match drawn*
*Warwickshire 7 pts, Surrey 6 pts*

Roger Knight's dour defence saw him through the last 33 overs of the match and saved Surrey from defeat in a match which was notable for a career best from medium-pacer Feltham in his second county game and for the Warwickshire debut of Scots grave-digger Willie Morton who was not asked to bowl his left-arm spin and was then carried from the field with an injured back in the second innings, an unhappy debut.

*Emburey, Williams, Gatting and Downton in pursuit. (Adrian Murrell)*

**John Player League**

***6 May***

***at Chelmsford***

**Essex** 173 for 9 (D.R. Pringle 81)
**Nottinghamshire** 174 for 4 (B.C. Broad 56, C.E.B. Rice 55)

*Nottinghamshire (4 pts) won by 6 wickets*

***at Swansea***

**Glamorgan** 223 for 5 (J.A. Hopkins 73)
**Gloucestershire** 153 for 8

*Glamorgan (4 pts) won by 70 runs*

***at Southampton***

**Hampshire** 226 for 4 (M.C.J. Nicholas 77 not out, T.E. Jesty 62)
**Sussex** 227 for 7 (A.P. Wells 71 not out)

*Sussex (4 pts) won by 3 wickets*

***at Lord's***

**Kent** 83
**Middlesex** 84 for 3

*Middlesex (4 pts) won by 7 wickets*

***at Edgbaston***

**Surrey** 223 for 9 (M.A. Lynch 60, A.R. Butcher 53, A.M. Ferreira 4 for 49)
**Warwickshire** 226 for 6 (A.I. Kallicharran 65, D.L. Amiss 52)

*Warwickshire (4 pts) won by 4 wickets*

*Warwickshire players crowd the bat as they try to force a win over Surrey, 5–8 May. (Ken Kelly)*

***at Bradford***

**Worcestershire** 173 for 7
**Yorkshire** 142

*Worcestershire (4 pts) won by 31 runs*

Yorkshire's run of success was ended by the spin of Illingworth and Patel who brought a Worcestershire victory when all seemed lost. Yorkshire's last 7 wickets fell for 41 runs. Kent could not stage their Saturday recovery and were trounced at Lord's while Gloucestershire found the late journey from Chelmsford to Swansea too demanding. Essex had no such journey, but, in spite of Pringle's fine knock, they were beaten by consistent Notts batting.

There was exciting hitting at Southampton. Hampshire scored 99 from their last 10 overs, Nicholas hitting four sixes in his last 14 balls, but Alan Wells hit 6 and 4 from the first two balls of the last over to win the match. An equally exciting climax at Edgbaston saw Paul Smith and Ferreira hit 81 off 51 balls to win with 4 deliveries to spare.

***9, 10 and 11 May***

***at Derby***

**Glamorgan** 144 (G. Miller 6 for 30) and 145 for 5
**Derbyshire** 364 (W.P. Fowler 116, J.G. Wright 67, J.F. Steele 5 for 101, W.W. Davis 4 for 63)

*Match drawn*
*Derbyshire 8 pts, Glamorgan 4 pts*

***at Southampton***

**Gloucestershire** 290 (A.J. Wright 74, R.C. Russell 63, T.M. Tremlett 5 for 48) and 288 for 3 dec (P.W. Romaines 90, C.W.J. Athey 69, Zaheer Abbas 67 not out)
**Hampshire** 252 for 1 dec (C.L. Smith 125, V.P. Terry 105 not out) and 187 for 7 (C.L. Smith 67)

*Match drawn*
*Hampshire 7 pts, Gloucestershire 3 pts*

***at Old Trafford***

**Kent** 296 (C. Penn 115, G.W. Johnson 50, S.N.V. Waterton 50, P.J.W. Allott 5 for 56) and 75 for 0 dec
**Lancashire** 96 for 2 dec and 166 for 9

*Match drawn*
*Lancashire 3 pts, Kent 3 pts*

***at Leicester***

**Leicestershire** 256 for 9 dec (M.A. Garnham 57 not out) and 110 for 3 dec (J.C. Balderstone 50)
**Worcestershire** 214 for 7 dec (D.J. Humphries 52) and 150 for 5 (N.G.B. Cook 4 for 45)

*Match drawn*
*Leicestershire 5 pts, Worcestershire 5 pts*

***at Northampton***

**Northamptonshire** 210 (D.J. Capel 51, N.A. Foster 6 for 79) and 145 (A.J. Lamb 64 not out, J.K. Lever 4 for 43)
**Essex** 348 for 7 dec (B.R. Hardie 99, C. Gladwin 94, K.S. McEwan 68, N.A. Mallender 4 for 69) and 8 for 0

*Essex won by 10 wickets*
*Essex 24 pts, Northamptonshire 5 pts*

***at Hove***

**Surrey** 179 (G.S. le Roux 4 for 41) and 205 for 2 (G.P. Howarth 108 not out)
**Sussex** 340 (D.A. Reeve 61, J.R.T. Barclay 51, G.S. Le Roux 50, S.T. Clarke 4 for 105)

*Match drawn*
*Sussex 8 pts, Surrey 5 pts*

***at Leeds***

**Yorkshire** 301 for 5 dec (G. Boycott 73, K. Sharp 64, D.L. Bairstow 62 not out) and 35 for 1 dec
**Nottinghamshire** 36 for 3 dec and 294 (B.C. Broad 62, B.N. French 55, A. Sidebottom 4 for 51, S.J. Dennis 4 for 77)

*Yorkshire won by 6 runs*
*Yorkshire 21 pts, Nottinghamshire 2 pts*

***at Cambridge***

**Cambridge University** 181 (N. Gifford 4 for 52) and 151 (C. Lethbridge 4 for 41)
**Warwickshire** 370 for 9 dec (A.I. Kallicharran 180, D.L. Amiss 54, S.N. Siddiqi 5 for 90)

*Warwickshire won by an innings and 38 runs*

***at Oxford***

**Middlesex** 359 for 6 dec (W.N. Slack 145, M.W. Gatting 102 not out, M.D. Petchey 4 for 65) and 150 for 2 dec (K.P. Tomlins 103 not out)
**Oxford University** 257 for 7 dec (G.J. Toogood 68, R.M. Edbrooke 66) and 55 for 6 (N.F. Williams 4 for 19)

*Match drawn*

With rain interfering everywhere there were some challenging declarations and exciting finishes. Kent, 84 for 5 in their first innings, were rescued by Chris Penn's maiden first-class century. Eventually, Lancashire, set to make 276 in 89 overs, were thankful to Zaidi and McFarlane for salvation after being 25 for 4.

At Leicester, Worcestershire needed 11 off the last over but fell 3 runs short of their target in spite of a fine effort by Curtis.

A batsman's match at Southampton ended in a draw as Hampshire failed in their bid to make 327 in 61 overs. At the end, the home side were thankful to draw although they had the first innings heroes when Smith and Terry put on 223 for the first wicket.

Surrey staged another rearguard action after three defeats in four matches. Howarth and Knight batted with resolution to save the game with an unbeaten stand of 123. Earlier, Reeve, a career best 61, and le Roux had added 109 in 32 overs for the ninth wicket to put Sussex in command.

An innings of 45 not out in 69 overs by John Steele saved Glamorgan from defeat at Derby. Miller had bowled the home side into a good position and this had been enhanced by Fowler's maiden first-class hundred, a fierce effort, and a last wicket stand of 64 between Taylor and Mortensen who, unfortunately, injured his back while making his career best 40 not out and could not bowl.

The Essex seam attack thrived at Northampton where the home side lost Boyd-Moss with a broken thumb, a victim of Foster's fast spell. Gladwin batted well for his championship best. McEwan hit lavishly and Hardie supplied the necessary substance on the second day to put Essex top of the embryo table.

They were followed by Yorkshire who, after declarations to repair lost time, beat Notts by 6 runs with two balls to spare. Bairstow set Notts to make 301 in 77 overs and they began well with Robinson and Randall adding 102 for the second wicket, but after tea they slipped to 194 for 6 as Rice and Hadlee went in successive overs. French rallied the cause and 10 were needed from the last over, but Dennis bowled Cooper with his fourth delivery and the White Rose rejoiced.

*Two maiden centurions, 9–11 May.* ABOVE: *Fowler (Derbyshire) 116* v. *Glamorgan. (Trevor Jones)* BELOW: *Chris Penn (Kent) 115* v. *Lancashire. (Adrian Murrell)*

Middlesex enjoyed batting practice at The Parks and Alvin Kallicharran, with his third century of the summer, brought his aggregate to 522 at an average of 174 as a strong Warwickshire side savaged Cambridge University.

## Benson and Hedges Cup

### *12 May*

#### *at Bristol*

**Hampshire** 239 for 9 (T.E. Jesty 51, D.R. Turner 50, D.V. Lawrence 5 for 48)
**Gloucestershire** 240 for 2 (P.W. Romaines 98 not out, A.W.Stovold 78)

*Gloucestershire (2pts) won by 8 wickets*
*(Gold Award* – P.W. Romaines)

#### *at Canterbury*

**Kent** 201 for 7
**Glamorgan** 144 (R.M. Ellison 4 for 28)

*Kent (2 pts) won by 57 runs*
*(Gold Award* – S.T. Jefferies)

#### *at Old Trafford*

**Nottinghamshire** 100 (S.T. Jefferies 4 for 15)
**Lancashire** 104 for 3

*Lancashire (2 pts) won by 7 wickets*
*(Gold Award* – S.T. Jefferies)

#### *at Leicester*

**Warwickshire** 229 for 7 (D.L. Amiss 115, G.W. Humpage 55, J.P. Agnew 5 for 43)
**Leicestershire** 202 (P. Willey 57)

*Warwickshire (2 pts) won by 7 wickets*
*(Gold Award* – D.L. Amiss)

#### *at Taunton*

**Sussex** 279 for 5 (J.R.T. Barclay 81, P.W.G. Parker 70)
**Somerset** 205 (V.J. Marks 75 not out)

*Sussex (2 pts) won by 74 runs*
*(Gold Award* – J.R.T. Barclay)

#### *at Worcester*

**Derbyshire** 257 for 7 (A. Hill 74, J.E. Morris 51)
**Worcestershire** 257 for 9 (D.B. D'Oliveira 57)

*Derbyshire (2 pts) won by losing fewer wickets*
*(Gold Award* – D.B. D'Oliveira)

#### *at Perth*

**Yorkshire** 231 for 7 (J.D. Love 88)
**Scotland** 186 for 7 (S.N. Hartley 4 for 39)

*Yorkshire (2 pts) won by 45 runs*
*(Gold Award* – J.D. Love)

#### *Oxford*

**Combined Universities** 193 for 6 (A.J.T. Miller 91, J.D. Carr 50)
**Surrey** 194 for 9 (M.A. Lynch 85)

*Surrey (2 pts) won by 1 wicket*
*(Gold Award* – A.J.T. Miller)

The second round of Benson and Hedges Cup matches produced no surprises but much excitement and tense finishes.

Lancashire, that most hospitable of clubs, overwhelmed Notts at Old Trafford. Jefferies took the individual honours in a strong bowling performance, but there was a fine contribution from Watkinson, the wickets of Robinson and Rice, and from O'Shaughnessy.

*Steve Jefferies, Gold Award for Lancashire, 12 May. (David Munden)*

Barclay and Parker added 115 for Sussex's second wicket to set up the victory over Somerset and Love's innings was too much for brave Scotland.

Warwickshire were 28 for 3, including Kallicharran for 0, two of them to the impressive Agnew, but Amiss and Humpage added 118. Any young player who wants to understand what is meant by technique should watch an innings by Dennis Amiss. Leicestershire could never muster the required rate after Small had destroyed their middle order.

Ellison again provided heroics for Kent with top score of 38 not out and four wickets, all of them leading batsmen, and Paul Romaines, that hard working player, and Andy Stovold put on 169 for Gloucestershire's first wicket in the high-scoring contest with Hampshire.

There was drama at Oxford where Surrey, needing 194 to beat the much criticised Combined Universities side, were 38 for 3, and, in spite of the efforts of Lynch and Knight, still 7 runs short when the ninth wicket fell. Clarke and Pocock brought victory on the first ball of the last over.

A third wicket stand of 109 in 20 overs between Alan Hill and John Morris, an elegant and promising young batsman, took Derbyshire to a good position. Worcestershire, 105 for 4, were revived by D'Oliveira and Neale, and there were important contributions from Humphries and Inchmore, but when the last ball arrived the home side were 4 short of victory. Ellcock swung hard on the off, but, as they went for a fourth run, Illingworth was run out and Derbyshire had won the match.

## John Player League

### *13 May*

***at Old Trafford***

**Northamptonshire** 187 for 5 (D.J. Wild 51)
**Lancashire** 191 for 2 (S.J. O'Shaughnessy 76 not out, G. Fowler 54)

*Lancashire (4 pts) won by 8 wickets*

***at Lord's***

**Essex** 214 for 5 (C. Gladwin 75)
**Middlesex** 214 for 5 (W.N. Slack 71)

*Match tied. Middlesex 2 pts, Essex 2 pts*

**at Taunton**

**Hampshire** 219 for 4 (C.L. Smith 88, V.P. Terry 65)
**Somerset** 184 for 8

*Hampshire (4 pts) won by 35 runs*

***at The Oval***

**Glamorgan** 152 for 6
**Surrey** 153 for 6

*Surrey (4 pts) won by 4 wickets*

***at Worcester***

**Nottinghamshire** 241 for 1 (C.E.B. Rice 98 not out, R.T. Robinson 97 not out)
**Worcestershire** 242 for 5 (C.L. King 101 not out)

*Worcestershire (4 pts) won by 5 wickets*

Fowler and O'Shaughnessy put on 92 for Lancashire's first wicket to make light of Northants score and Smith and Terry began Hampshire's innings with a stand of 136 at Taunton. Good catching helped to bring Hampshire a comfortable win. Surrey won a rather dour struggle at The Oval, but, at Worcester, after Robinson and Rice had shared an unbeaten second wicket stand of 200 for Notts, Collis King hit 101 not out off 81 balls, the last of his 10 fours bringing victory with 9 balls to spare.

Gladwin again batted with panache at Lord's and Middlesex, after reaching 148 for the loss of Barlow, reached the last over needing 10 to win. Tomlins and Downton hit 7 of them and 2 came from Downton's pull off the last ball to level the scores.

*Paul Romaines, a match-winning innings and a Gold Award, Gloucestershire v. Hampshire, 12 May. (George Herringshaw)*

***at Leicester***

**Northamptonshire** 239 for 6 (A.J. Lamb 80, R.J. Bailey 61)
**Leicestershire** 243 for 4 (P. Willey 88 not out)

*Leicestershire (2 pts) won by 6 wickets*
*(Gold Award –* P. Willey)

***At Edgbaston***

**Warwickshire** 254 (A.M. Ferreira 71, T.A. Lloyd 70)
**Yorkshire** 247 for 8 (S.N. Hartley 65 not out, M.D. Moxon 58, K. Sharp 57)

*Warwickshire (2 pts) won by 7 runs*
*(Gold Award –* S.N. Hartley)

*Edgbaston 1984. (Ken Kelly)*

## Benson and Hedges Cup

### *15 May*

***at Derby***

**Nottinghamshire** 282 for 4 (B.C. Broad 122, R.T. Robinson 71)
**Derbyshire** 223 (A. Hill 87)

*Nottinghamshire (2 pts) won by 59 runs*
*(Gold Award –* B.C. Broad)

***at Bristol***

**Combined Universities** 243 (A.J.T. Miller 101, J.D. Carr 66)
**Gloucestershire** 216 (P.W. Romaines 60)

*Combined Universities (2 pts) won by 27 runs*
*(Gold Award –* A.J.T. Miller)

*Chris Old breaks the wicket and Sharp is run out after a misunderstanding with Gold Award winner Hartley. (Ken Kelly)*

***at Worcester***

**Minor Counties** 205 for 8 (R.E. Hayward 61)
**Worcestershire** 209 for 3 (D.N. Patel 69 not out, C.L. King 61)

*Worcestershire (2 pts) won by 7 wickets*
*(Gold Award* – D.N. Patel)

***15 and 16 May***

***at Chelmsford***

**Surrey** 150
**Essex** 152 for 4

*Essex (2 pts) won by 6 wickets*

***At Lord's***

**Sussex** 214 (W.M. Gatting 4 for 49)
**Middlesex** 215 for 8 (C.T. Radley 65 not out)

*Middlesex (2 pts) won by 2 wickets*
*(Gold Award* – J.E. Emburey)

***16 May***

**Kent** 160 (M.D. Crowe 4 for 24)
**Somerset** 161 for 8 (B.C. Rose 61, K.B.S. Jarvis 4 for 38)

*Somerset (2 pts) won by 2 wickets*
*(Gold Award* – M.D. Crowe)

A third wicket stand of 133 between Lamb and Bailey of 133 was nullified by Peter Willey's inspiring 88 not out, his partnership of 87 in 11 overs for the fifth wicket with Boon bringing victory with 2 overs to spare.

An opening stand of 148 in 37 overs by Broad, who took his first Gold Award, and Robinson helped Notts to their highest score in the competition and to a comfortable win at Derby.

Essex, with Turner bowling niggardly, and Worcestershire, with Patel and King adding 109 for the third wicket, had easy victories, but Warwickshire, recovering from 14 for 2, beat Yorkshire narrowly in a fine contest. They were rescued by Andy Lloyd's determination and some good hitting from Old and Ferreira. Yorkshire fought bravely as Moxon and Sharp added 100 and Hartley hit with glorious certainty, but Willis, returning to cricket for the first time since his illness in Pakistan, bowled well and thwarted them.

Middlesex recovered from 61 for 4 to beat Sussex. They owed their victory to Emburey's clean hitting and Radley's solidity. Gatting had produced a good spell of bowling to blunt Sussex earlier in the day. A fine all-round performance by Martin Crowe, who put on 88 for the third wicket with Rose, helped Somerset to stumble to victory in difficult conditions at Canterbury.

The performance of the round, however, was at Bristol where Miller and Carr added 135 in 30 overs for the third wicket as Combined Universities reached their highest score in the competition and Miller became their first centurion. Gloucestershire began their innings well enough, but Carr and Hayes caused a middle order collapse to bring the Universities side a memorable victory.

## Benson and Hedges Cup

***17 May***

***at Old Trafford***

**Worcestershire** 237 for 9 (D.N. Patel 90 not out, M.J. Weston 52, M. Watkinson 4 for 58)
**Lancashire** 240 for 7 (S.J. O'Shaughnessy 51, J.D. Inchmore 6 for 29)

*Lancashire (2 pts) won by 3 wickets*
*(Gold Award* – J.D.Inchmore)

***at Taunton***

**Middlesex** 189 for 9
**Somerset** 193 for 3 (N.F.M. Popplewell 67)

*Somerset (2 pts) won by 7 wickets*
*(Gold Award* – N.F.M. Popplewell)

ABOVE LEFT: *Chris Broad. (David Munden)* ABOVE RIGHT: *Tim Robinson (George Herringshaw) 148 in 37 overs for Notts* v. *Derbyshire, 15 May. Chris Broad took his first Gold Award.* BELOW LEFT: *Anton Ferreira during his furious assault on the Yorkshire bowling, 15 May. (Ken Kelly)* BELOW RIGHT: *Norman Gifford is run out off the last ball of the Warwickshire innings. (Ken Kelly)*

*at Hove*

**Glamorgan** 165
**Sussex** 169 for 3 (G.D. Mendis 56)

*Sussex (2 pts) won by 7 wickets*
*(Gold Award* – G.D. Mendis)

*at Glasgow*

**Scotland** 204 for 5 (C.J. Warner 59, O. Henry 59)
**Leicestershire** 207 for 4

*Leicestershire (2 pts) won by 6 wickets*
*(Gold Award* – O. Henry)

*17 and 18 May*

*at Northampton*

**Northamptonshire** 248 for 8 (W. Larkins 62)
**Warwickshire** 252 for 8 (A.I. Kallicharran 122, D.L. Amiss 79, D.S. Steele 4 for 35)

*Warwickshire (2 pts) won by 2 wickets*
*(Gold Award* – A.I. Kallicharran)

*A Gold Award on his first team debut, 17 May, Stephen Andrew (Hampshire). (Sporting Pictures)*

*at The Oval*

**Hampshire** 223 for 7
**Surrey** 117

*Hampshire (2 pts) won by 106 runs*
*(Gold Award* – S.J.W. Andrew)

*at Shrewsbury*

**Minor Counties** 197 for 8
**Derbyshire** 201 for 6 (G. Miller 65 not out, W.P. Fowler 53)

*Derbyshire (2 pts) won by 4 wickets*
*(Gold Award* – W.P. Fowler)

**Combined Universities 1984**
Benson and Hedges Cup

| BATTING | v. Hampshire (Southampton) 5 May | v. Surrey (Oxford) 12 May | v. Gloucestershire (Bristol) 15 May | v. Essex 17 & 18 May | *Runs* |
|---|---|---|---|---|---|
| A.J.T. Miller | 3 | 91 | 101 | 41 | 236 |
| R.M. Edbrooke | 7 | 1 | 6 | 11 | 25 |
| G.J. Toogood | 8 | 18 | 0 | 2 | 28 |
| C.R. Andrew | 4 | | | | 4 |
| J.D. Carr | 8 | 50 | 66 | 10 | 134 |
| K.A. Hayes | 67 | 10 | 21 | 24 | 122 |
| D.A. Thorne | 4 | 7 | 28* | 1 | 40 |
| P.G. Roebuck | 13 | | | | 13 |
| A.G. Davies | 13 | 0* | 12 | 20 | 45 |
| T.A. Cotterell | 6 | — | 0 | 3 | 9 |
| P. Garlick | 0* | — | 0 | — | 0 |
| J.G. Franks | | 3* | 0 | 22* | 25 |
| A.D.H. Grimes | | — | 0 | 1* | 1 |
| Byes | 1 | 2 | | | |
| Leg-byes | 5 | 8 | 6 | 5 | |
| Wides | 12 | 1 | 1 | 6 | |
| No-balls | 3 | 2 | 2 | 6 | |
| Total | 154 | 193 | 243 | 152 | |
| Wickets | 10 | 6 | 10 | 8 | |
| Result | L | L | W | L | |
| Points | 0 | 0 | 2 | 0 | |

*Catches* 8 – A.G. Davies (ct 7/st 1)
2 – K.A. Hayes and T.A. Cotterell
1 – D.A. Thorne

| BOWLING | P Garlick | P.G. Roebuck | K.A. Hayes | C.R. Andrew | T.A. Cotterell | J.D. Carr | A.D.H. Grimes |
|---|---|---|---|---|---|---|---|
| v. Hampshire (Southampton) 5 May | 9–3–15–0 | 2–0–9–0 | 9–2–23–0 | 11–0–41–0 | 11–3–35–1 | 5–0–22–0 | |
| v. Surrey (Oxford) 12 May | 11–2–31–3 | | 11–2–33–1 | | 11–1–34–0 | 10.1–1–38–1 | 11–0–40–3 |
| v. Gloucestershire (Bristol) 15 May | 9–1–36–1 | | 11–2–40–3 | | 11–1–42–2 | 8.4–0–22–3 | 10–0–45–1 |
| v. Essex (Cambridge) 17 and 18 May | 9–1–26–1 | | 8–3–23–0 | | 5–0–29–0 | 5.3–0–29–1 | 11–0–44–2 |
| Wickets | 5 | 0 | 4 | 0 | 3 | 5 | 6 |

*Kim Barnett, Derbyshire's fine young captain. A consistent scorer and challenging for an England place. (George Herringshaw)*

ABOVE: *Graham Clinton returned to the Surrey side to win a Benson and Hedges Gold Award and give them a surprise place in the quarter-finals. (George Herringshaw)* BELOW: *John Inchmore (Worcestershire), 6 for 29 and on the losing side, 17 May. (Ken Kelly)*

***at Cambridge***

**Combined Universities** 152 for 8
**Essex** 156 for 4 (K.S. McEwan 72, D.R. Pringle 51 not out)

*Essex (2 pts) won by 6 wickets*
*(Gold Award –* K.S. McEwan)

Although rain hindered, it did not ruin any of the matches. Essex lost Gooch and Fletcher for 7, but on the Friday, McEwan, Gladwin and Pringle all hit well to bring victory over the Universities with 16.3 overs to spare. Hampshire, relying on consistent batting, overwhelmed Surrey who were dismissed for their lowest score in the competition thanks to

| | *Byes* | *Leg-byes* | *Wides* | *No-balls* | *Total* | *Wkts* |
|---|---|---|---|---|---|---|
| | 1 | 1 | 8 | | 155 | 1 |
| | 4 | 4 | 10 | | 194 | 9 |
| | 4 | 10 | 16 | 1 | 216 | 10 |
| | 1 | 3 | 1 | | 156 | 4 |

a remarkable debut by Stephen Andrew who took the wickets of Pauline, Butcher and Lynch for 12 runs in 7 overs and took the Gold Award at the first attempt.

Inchmore took the first 6 Lancashire wickets at a personal cost of 29 runs, but the home side were taken to victory by Fairbrother and Jefferies adding 34 in 5 overs. Patel played beautifully for Worcestershire and made one ponder as to why he is ignored when lesser off-spin all-rounders gain international honours.

Leicestershire won with four balls to spare at Hamilton Crescent, a lovely ground, and Sussex won a docile match at Hove with 7.3 overs to spare. Derbyshire were troubled by David Surridge's fine bowling, a sad loss to the first-class game, and needed a good all-round performance from Fowler to see them home. Warwickshire, dependant on a second wicket stand of 134 between Kallicharran and Amiss, won with an over to spare at Northampton and qualified for the quarter-finals along with Essex and Somerset who put out the holders, Middlesex, who were quite dreadful. They batted poorly on a miserable day and their out-cricket was terrible. Popplewell and Roebuck began Somerset's innings with a stand of 114.

**Minor Counties 1984**
Benson and Hedges Cup

| BATTING | v. Lancashire (Bowdon) 5 May | v. Worcestershire (Worcester) 15 May | v. Derbyshire (Shrewsbury) 17 May | v. Nottinghamshire (Trent Bridge) 19 May | Runs |
|---|---|---|---|---|---|
| S.G. Plumb | 9 | 7 | 34 | 21 | 71 |
| W.M. Osman | 25 | 10 | 8 | 5 | 48 |
| S. Greensword | 26 | 20 | 0 | | 46 |
| D. Bailey | 0 | 0 | 1 | 16 | 17 |
| R.E. Hayward | 78* | 61 | 21 | 39 | 199 |
| N.A. Riddell | 59* | 18 | 49 | 9 | 135 |
| N.T. O'Brien | — | 0 | 3 | 23 | 26 |
| F.E. Collyer | — | 49 | 42 | 6 | 97 |
| T.S. Smith | — | 1* | 4* | 2 | 7 |
| D. Surridge | — | — | — | 1* | 1 |
| W.G. Merry | — | | | — | — |
| A. Ramage | | 14* | 23* | | 37 |
| S. Ogrizivic | | | | 4* | 4 |
| Byes | | 2 | 4 | | |
| Leg-byes | 11 | 8 | 6 | 8 | |
| Wides | 9 | 10 | 1 | 2 | |
| No-balls | 2 | 5 | 1 | 3 | |
| Total | 219 | 205 | 197 | 139 | |
| Wickets | 4 | 8 | 8 | 8 | |
| Results | L | L | L | L | |
| Points | 0 | 0 | 0 | 0 | |

*Catches* 4 – F.E. Collyer
3 – N.A. Riddell
2 – N.T. O'Brien
1 – W.M. Osman, D. Surridge, T.S. Smith and R.E. Hayward

| BOWLING | W.G. Merry | D. Surridge | T.S. Smith | S. Greensword | N.T. O'Brien | S.G. Plumb | D. Bailey | A. Ramage | S. Ogrizovic |
|---|---|---|---|---|---|---|---|---|---|
| v. Lancashire (Bowdon) 5 May | 8–4–16–1 | 8–2–20–1 | 10–0–51–0 | 11–5–31–1 | 7–0–26–1 | 8.2–1–46–0 | 1–0–10–0 | | |
| v. Worcestershire (Worcester) 15 May | | 10–3–34–1 | 9–1–49–0 | 6–0–25–0 | 3–0–27–0 | 2.5–1–18–1 | 5–0–30–0 | 7–2–11–0 | |
| v. Derbyshire (Shrewsbury) 17 May | | 10–1–31–3 | 6–1–27–0 | 10–2–38–0 | 7–2–18–0 | 8.3–1–44–1 | | 11–4–34–1 | |
| v. Nottinghamshire (Trent Bridge) 19 May | 10–0–52–0 | 9.5–1–26–4 | | | | 2–0–10–0 | 6–0–15–0 | | 11–5–21–2 |
| Wickets | 1 | 9 | 0 | 1 | 1 | 2 | 0 | 1 | 2 |

## Benson and Hedges Cup

### *19 May*

#### *at Derby*

**Derbyshire** 210 for 8
**Lancashire** 165 for 9 (G. Fowler 92)

*Derbyshire (2 pts) won by 45 runs*
*(Gold Award* – R.J. Finney)

#### *at Cardiff*

**Middlesex** 163 (W.W. Davis 5 for 29)
**Glamorgan** 165 for 3 (J.A. Hopkins 62 not out)

*Glamorgan (2 pts) won by 7 wickets*
*(Gold Award* – W.W. Davis)

#### *at Southampton*

**Essex** 254 for 4 (K.W.R. Fletcher 76, G.A. Gooch 51, D.R. Pringle 51 not out)
**Hampshire** 227 for 8 (V.P. Terry 72, D.R. Pringle 4 for 46)

*Essex (2 pts) won by 27 runs*
*(Gold Award* – D.R. Pringle)

#### *at Trent Bridge*

**Minor Counties** 139 for 8 (C.E.B. Rice 5 for 28)
**Nottinghamshire** 140 for 6 (R.J. Hadlee 67 not out, D. Surridge 4 for 26)

*Nottinghamshire (2 pts) won by 4 wickets*
*(Gold Award* – R.J. Hadlee)

#### *at The Oval*

**Surrey** 202 (G.S. Clinton 94)
**Gloucestershire** 164

*Surrey (2 pts) won by 38 runs*
*(Gold Award* – G.S. Clinton)

#### *at Hove*

**Kent** 227 for 7 (G.W. Johnson 60)
**Sussex** 230 for 9 (C.M. Wells 60, P.W.G. Parker 57 not out)

*Sussex (2 pts) won by 1 wicket*
*(Gold Award* – C.M. Wells)

***at Edgbaston***

**Warwickshire** 262 for 7 (G.W. Humpage 100 not out, C.M. Old 57, W.A. McPate 4 for 54)
**Scotland** 133 (S.M. Old 5 for 19)

*Warwickshire (2 pts) won by 129 runs*
*(Gold Award –* C.M. Old)

***at Bradford***

**Northamptonshire** 251 for 7 (A.J. Lamb 92, R.J. Bailey 75)
**Yorkshire** 252 for 3 (G. Boycott 106, K. Sharp 87)

*Yorkshire (2 pts) won by 7 wickets*
*(Gold Award –* G. Boycott)

The final round of matches in the zonal groups saw Middlesex's discomfort continue and Warwickshire, with Humpage collecting the third century in the season's competition by a Warwickshire player, complete a hundred per cent record in Group A.

Yorkshire joined Warwickshire in the quarter-finals when Boycott, winning his ninth Gold Award, and Sharp outbatted the efforts of Bailey and Lamb to put on 146 for the third wicket and help their side to win with 1.3 overs to spare.

Hampshire needed to beat Essex in Group D to qualify, but, in spite of another impressive spell from young Andrew, they failed against the all-round power of the Essex attack and the forceful batting of Gooch, Pringle and Fletcher. To everyone's bewilderment, not least of all their own, Surrey joined Essex as qualifiers. Clinton returned to give their batting substance and Gloucestershire floundered against a good attack in which Feltham and Knight were prominent.

Derbyshire beat Lancashire to finish level on points at the top of Group B only to be ousted by mathematics. Notts, the group winners, struggled against the splendid Surridge and were 59 for 5 before Hadlee restored sanity and self-respect.

The most crucial match of the day was at Hove where the winners would join Somerset as Group C qualifiers. Kent owed much to Aslett and Johnson who added 88 and they reached 227 which looked as if it would be a winning score. Mendis and Barclay were out for 43 and Parker retired after being hit over the eye by Alderman, but the Wells brothers took the score to 177. Then 7 wickets fell for 37 runs so that the bloodstained Parker and number eleven Waller needed 9 from the last over. Parker took 7 off the first three balls, but the fourth was scoreless. Waller swung the fifth over mid-on for 4 and victory.

| | *Byes* | *Leg-byes* | *Wides* | *No-balls* | *Total* | *Wkts* |
|---|---|---|---|---|---|---|
| | 4 | 6 | 10 | 3 | 223 | 4 |
| | | 9 | 5 | 1 | 209 | 3 |
| | 1 | 2 | 4 | 2 | 201 | 6 |
| | 1 | 5 | 10 | | 140 | 6 |

**Benson and Hedges Cup – Group Tables**

| GROUP A | *P* | *W* | *L* | *Pts* |
|---|---|---|---|---|
| Warwickshire | 4 | 4 | — | 8 |
| Yorkshire | 4 | 3 | 1 | 6 |
| Leicestershire | 4 | 2 | 2 | 4 |
| Northamptonshire | 4 | 1 | 3 | 2 |
| Scotland | 4 | — | 4 | 0 |
| GROUP B | | | | |
| Nottinghamshire | 4 | 3 | 1 | 6 |
| Lancashire | 4 | 3 | 1 | 6 |
| Derbyshire | 4 | 3 | 1 | 6 |
| Worcestershire | 4 | 1 | 3 | 2 |
| Minor Counties | 4 | — | 4 | 0 |
| GROUP C | | | | |
| Sussex | 4 | 3 | 1 | 6 |
| Somerset | 4 | 3 | 1 | 6 |
| Kent | 4 | 2 | 2 | 4 |
| Glamorgan | 4 | 1 | 3 | 2 |
| Middlesex | 4 | 1 | 3 | 2 |
| GROUP D | | | | |
| Essex | 4 | 4 | — | 8 |
| Surrey | 4 | 2 | 2 | 4 |
| Hampshire | 4 | 2 | 2 | 4 |
| Gloucestershire | 4 | 1 | 3 | 2 |
| Combined Universities | 4 | 1 | 3 | 2 |

### *19, 20 and 21 May*

***at Worcester***

**West Indians** 412 for 9 dec (C.G. Greenidge 138, D.L. Haynes 89, P.J. Dujon 52 not out)
**Worcestershire** 124 for 1 (T.S. Curtis 82 not out)

*Match drawn*

### *19, 21 and 22 May*

***at Leicester***

**Leicestershire** 318 (J.J. Whitaker 160, G.J. Parsons 55, M.D. Crowe 5 for 66) and 57 for 3
**Somerset** 338 (M.D. Crowe 77, B.C. Rose 70, P.M. Roebuck 64, P. Willey 6 for 78)

*Match drawn*
*Somerset 8 pts, Leicestershire 6 pts*

The West Indies' tour began with damp weather on the second and third days after Greenidge and Haynes had begun with a stand of 206 on the Saturday. Curtis batted with great spirit on the last afternoon.

Rain washed out the last day at Leicester, but the first day was memorable for a maiden century from Whitaker who came in at 30 for 4 and added 126 for the seventh wicket with Parsons.

ABOVE: *The West Indies arrive. The team picture at Worcester. (Ken Kelly)* BELOW: *Desmond Haynes during his innings of 89. (Ken Kelly)*

*Tim Curtis during his spirited reply for Worcestershire* v. *West Indians. (Ken Kelly)*

ABOVE: *A nasty moment for the West Indies. Viv Richards slips. (All Sport)* BELOW: *James Whitaker, a glorious maiden first-class century for Leicestershire* v. *Somerset, 19 May, saved his side. (David Munden)*

### John Player League

***20 May***

***at Derby***

**Lancashire** 133 (B. Roberts 4 for 29)
**Derbyshire** 136 for 4

*Derbyshire (4 pts) won by 6 wickets*

***at Cardiff***

**Glamorgan** 64 for 3
*v* Middlesex

*Match abandoned. Glamorgan 2 pts, Middlesex 2 pts*

**at Canterbury**

*Match abandoned. Kent 2 pts, Surrey 2 pts*

***at Leicester***

**Somerset** 189 for 8
**Leicestershire** 22 for 1

*Match abandoned. Leicestershire 2 pts, Somerset 2 pts*

***at Northampton***

**Northamptonshire** 118 for 4 (W. Larkins 69)
*v* **Warwickshire**

*Match abandoned. Northamptonshire 2 pts, Warwickshire 2 pts*

***at Hove***

*Match abandoned.*
*Sussex 2 pts, Gloucestershire 2 pts*

***at Hull***

**Nottinghamshire** 169 for 7 (B.C. Broad 54, G.B. Stevenson 4 for 29)
**Yorkshire** 150 (E.E. Hemmings 4 for 32)

*Nottinghamshire (4 pts) won by 19 runs*

Cold, wet weather frustrated many including David Gower who, on returning from his illness, was 14 not out when the rain arrived. Derbyshire won convincingly with 5 overs to spare and had to thank a good spell from Roberts. Yorkshire looked on the right path at Hull, but Hemmings and Rice bowled tightly on a suspect wicket in miserable conditions and snatched victory for the visitors.

***23, 24 and 25 May***

***at Chesterfield***

**Surrey** 306 (C.J. Richards 109, G. Miller 5 for 117) and 246 for 5 (D.B. Pauline 88, R.D.V. Knight 59)
**Derbyshire** 302 for 8 (A. Hill 89, J.H. Hampshire 66)

*Match drawn*
*Derbyshire 8 pts, Surrey 7 pts*

***at Chelmsford***

**Nottinghamshire** 264 (R.J. Hadlee 71 not out, D.W. Randall 56, N.A. Foster 4 for 86) and 87 for 0
**Essex** 93 (K. Saxelby 4 for 15) and 257 (G.A. Gooch 108, K.W.R. Fletcher 83, R.J. Hadlee 6 for 52)

*Nottinghamshire won by 10 wickets*
*Nottinghamshire 23 pts, Essex 4 pts*

***at Cardiff***

**Gloucestershire** 286 for 4 dec (P.W. Romaines 141 not out, P. Bainbridge 67 not out) and 229 for 5 dec (A.W. Stovold 90, A.J. Wright 51 not out)
**Glamorgan** 251 for 1 dec (A.L. Jones 129, J.A. Hopkins 116 not out) and 61 for 1

*Match drawn*
*Glamorgan 4 pts, Gloucestershire 3 pts*

***at Lord's***

**Middlesex** 139 (B.J. Griffiths 5 for 32, A. Walker 4 for 50) and 199 (M.W. Gatting 71, R.W. Hanley 5 for 58, B.J. Griffiths 4 for 71)
**Northamptonshire** 202 (D.J. Wild 59) and 54 for 4

*Match drawn*
*Northamptonshire 6 pts, Middlesex 4 pts*

***at Hove***

**Sussex** 109 (T.M. Tremlett 4 for 26, S.J.W. Andrew 4 for 30) and 450 for 9 (C.M. Wells 203)
**Hampshire** 298 (T.E. Jesty 96, V.P. Terry 75)

*Match drawn*
*Hampshire 7 pts, Sussex 4 pts*

***at Nuneaton***

**Lancashire** 369 for 5 dec (J. Abrahams 201 not out, J. Simmons 72 not out) and 186 for 8 dec (C. Maynard 50 not out)
**Warwickshire** 253 for 3 dec (A.I. Kallicharran 101, T.A. Lloyd 76) and 245 for 6 (D.L. Amiss 80, G.W. Humpage 67, P.J.W. Allott 5 for 54)

*Match drawn*
*Warwickshire 5 pts, Lancashire 5 pts*

***at Worcester***

**Leicestershire** 222 (D.I. Gower 103) and 196 (M.A. Garnham 74, J.J. Whitaker 61)
**Worcestershire** 174 (M.J. Weston 54, G.J. Parsons 5 for 42) and 221 (P.A. Neale 80)

*Leicestershire won by 23 runs*
*Leicestershire 22 pts, Worcestershire 4 pts*

***at Taunton***

**Somerset** 116 (R.A. Harper 5 for 32) and 125 (J.G. Wyatt 69, M.D. Marshall 5 for 31)
**West Indians** 342 (R.A. Harper 73, H.A. Gomes 72, C.H. Lloyd 72, R.B. Richardson 50)

*West Indians won by an innings and 101 runs*

Leicestershire moved ahead of Essex in the Britannic Assurance County Championship when they took 22 points from Worcestershire at New Road. David Gower, named as England's captain, returned from blood poisoning with a stylish century and his seam attack bowled Leicestershire to a 48-run lead. 39 for 5 in their second innings, the visitors were rescued by Whitaker and Garnham who added 122. Left 99 overs in which to make 245, Worcestershire lost 3 for 20, but a brave, dogged innings from skipper Neale effected a fighting recovery which was ultimately denied by Cook, Parsons and Agnew.

Nottinghamshire moved into a challenging position by beating the champions at Chelmsford. Fletcher asked Notts to bat and both openers were dismissed for 5, but solid middle order batting brought a commendable score. Essex lost their last 9 wickets for 33 and followed-on. Gooch hit a sparkling century, but this time the last 8 wickets went down for 52 and Notts cruised to victory. A burst of 5 for 11 in 5

*Kevin Saxelby's bowling was decisive in the vital championship victory that Notts had over Essex at Chelmsford, 23–25 May. (David Munden)*

overs plus his 71 made Hadlee the Man of the Match, a position not new to him.

Jack Richards lifted Surrey at Chesterfield with an accomplished hundred after they had been in danger at 148 for 6. Thereafter the match followed a pedestrian path. In the drawn game at Cardiff, Paul Romaines engaged in two century stands as he proved once more his value to Gloucestershire with an innings of skill and application, but he had to give pride of place to Hopkins and Alan Lewis Jones who put on 240 for Glamorgan's first wicket, Jones hitting a maiden century after 11 years in first-class cricket.

The gloom of Middlesex continued as they fell to the Northants' seamers at Lord's. Cowans struck back, but weather determined a draw. Hampshire took the initiative on the first day at Hove where Andrew, 18 years old and in his first championship match, impressed as he had done in the Benson and Hedges Cup. Terry and Jesty saw the visitors past 220 with only 2 wickets down, but the fourth batting point was lost. Facing an innings defeat, Sussex were saved by Colin Wells who hit two sixes and twenty-five fours in a six-hour career best 203.

There was a maiden double century for Lancashire skipper John Abrahams at Nuneaton, and a fourth century of the season for Alvin Kallicharran, his ninth in 20 innings. Rain ended what was a well contested match after Amiss and Humpage had added 151 in 29 overs in the bid to reach 303 off 64 overs, the last 8 being lost.

West Indies beat Somerset with ominous ease as Roger Harper displayed a rich vein of all-round talent.

ABOVE: *The reward for years of waiting. Alan Lewis Jones, a maiden century, 23–25 May. (Trevor Jones)* BELOW: *John Abrahams, a career best for Lancashire* v. *Warwickshire, 23–25 May. (George Herringshaw)*

### *26, 27 and 28 May*

**at Leeds**

**Yorkshire** 188 (D.L. Bairstow 62, P.J.W. Allott 6 for 31) and 16 for 2

**Lancashire** 288 for 7 dec (G. Fowler 107, J.A. Ormrod 60, A. Sidebottom 4 for 50)

*Match drawn*
*Lancashire 6 pts, Yorkshire 4 pts*

**at Swansea**

**Glamorgan** 175 (A.L. Jones 50, J. Garner 5 for 19) and 88 (E.A.E. Baptiste 4 for 17
**West Indians** 489 for 6 dec (I.V.A. Richards 170, R.B. Richardson 111, H.A. Gomes 73, A.L. Logie 71, S.R. Barwick 4 for 135)

*West Indians won by an innings and 226 runs*

### *26, 28 and 29 May*

**at Derby**

**Derbyshire** 294 for 9 dec (J.G. Wright 86, K.J. Barnett 63, C.E.B. Rice 4 for 61) and 177 for 4 dec (K.J. Barnett 50)
**Nottinghamshire** 218 for 2 dec (C.E.B. Rice 77 not out, D.W. Randall 55 not out) and 166 for 7 (R.T. Robinson 54)

*Match drawn*
*Nottinghamshire 4 pts, Derbyshire 2 pts*

**at Chelmsford**

**Surrey** 235 (A.R. Butcher 79, M.A. Lynch 68) *v* **Essex**

*Match drawn*
*No points*

***at Canterbury***

**Kent** 179 for 4 dec (D.J. Tavare 69, D.G. Aslett 68) and 0 for 0 dec
**Hampshire** 0 for 0 dec and 56 (D.L. Underwood 7 for 21)

*Kent won by 123 runs*
*Kent 17 pts, Hampshire 1 pt*

***at Leicester***

**Northamptonshire** 264 for 9 dec (A.J. Lamb 65, J.P. Agnew 4 for 84) and 67 for 2 dec
**Leicestershire** 0 for 0 dec and 335 for 6 (P. Willey 104, D.I. Gower 74, J.J. Whitaker 68 not out)

*Leicestershire won by 4 wickets*
*Leicestershire 20 pts, Northamptonshire 3 pts*

***at Lord's***

**Middlesex** 177 for 9 dec
**Sussex** 178 for 5 (J.R.T. Barclay 73 not out)

*Sussex won by 5 wickets*
*Sussex 12 pts, Middlesex 0 pts*

ABOVE: *Paul Smith had career bests for Warwickshire, 26–28 May. Here he scores off Illingworth. Humphries is the wicket-keeper and McEvoy is at slip.* BELOW: *Pridgeon bowls to Humpage. (Ken Kelly)*

***at Taunton***

**Somerset** 150 for 7 dec and 155 for 6 dec
**Gloucestershire** 103 for 6 dec and 72 (I.T. Botham 4 for 14, M.R. Davis 4 for 25)

*Somerset won by 130 runs*
*Somerset 19 pts, Gloucestershire 3 pts*

***at Edgbaston***

**Warwickshire** 200 for 8 dec (G.W. Humpage 100 not out) and 264 for 4 dec (D.L. Amiss 84 not out, P.A. Smith 81)
**Worcestershire** 172 for 7 dec (M.J. Weston 51, C.M. Old 5 for 52) and 127 for 5 (P.A. Smith 4 for 41)

*Match drawn*
*Warwickshire 5 pts, Worcestershire 4 pts*

Rain ruined the Bank Holiday week-end and the cricket. At Lord's and Chelmsford play was possible only on the final day. Surrey chose to ignore those who support the game and the spirit of the game itself by batting throughout the day at Chelmsford. Sussex beat Middlesex with 11 balls to spare in a match played in the right spirit.

In the Roses match, Yorkshire were 12 for 4 but Bairstow hit some lusty blows to give some respectability. There was no play on the second day and Fowler and Ormrod took their stand to 159 before the first wicket fell and the inevitable draw.

There was no play on the first day at Taunton, but, on an exciting last day, 22 wickets fell and 312 runs were scored. Botham set Gloucestershire to make 203 in 45 overs. The pitch was dry and venomous, but Gloucestershire's second innings batting took eccentric avenues as they crashed to 41 for 6 and were finally beaten with 37 balls to spare.

The forfeiture of innings after a blank second day and a start delayed until 1.40 on the last day brought a sensational finish at Canterbury where Hampshire, needing 180 in 59 overs, were bowled out by Derek Underwood, revelling in the conditions, for 56 in 26.2 overs.

Warwickshire and Worcestershire could come to no such agreements at Edgbaston where Humpage's brisk hundred illuminated the first day and Paul Smith, that energetic, enthusiastic and most promising all-rounder, recorded career best bowling and championship best batting performances to infuse life into a dying match.

Notts were thankful to draw at Derby after being set to make 254 on a turning pitch. There was a first innings century stand between Rice and Randall, but much of the batting was too measured in conditions that were never easy.

The most enterprising cricket was at Leicester where, after forfeiture and declaration, Leicestershire were set to make 332 off 76 overs. Gower hit 74 out of 125, helping the recovery from 32 for 2, and Willey, who played a match-winning innings against his old county, and Garnham added 84 in 15 overs. Five runs were needed off the last over with Whitaker, who again batted with great determination and flair, and Parsons at the wicket. Parsons faced the last ball with the scores level and off-drove Hanley for 4 to win the match and keep Leicestershire at the top of the table.

Mutilated by Garner on the first day and by Garner, Holding and Baptiste on the last and savaged by Richardson, Richards and the rest of the West Indian batsmen on the second day, Glamorgan suffered their heaviest defeat at the hands of a touring side. The West Indian power looked frightening.

## John Player League

### 27 May

**at Chelmsford**

**Essex** 186 for 2 (G.A. Gooch 75 not out, C. Gladwin 68)
**Surrey** 156 for 6

*Essex (4 pts) won by 30 runs*

**at Bristol**

*Match abandoned.*
*Gloucestershire 2 pts, Somerset 2 pts*

**at Leicester**

*Match abandoned.*
*Leicestershire 2 pts, Sussex 2 pts*

**at Lord's**

**Northamptonshire** 135 for 4 (A.J. Lamb 61 not out)
**Middlesex** 137 for 5 (G.D Barlow 53)

*Middlesex (4 pts) won by 5 wickets*

**at Trent Bridge**

*Match abandoned.*
*Nottinghamshire 2 pts, Derbyshire 2 pts*

**at Edgbaston**

*Match abandoned.*
*Warwickshire 2 pts, Worcestershire 2 pts*

Rain prevented play in all but two matches. At Lord's, 22 overs were played and Middlesex won with 4 balls to spare to go top of the table. At Chelmsford, in a 21-over match, Gooch and Gladwin gave a spectacular display of hitting with an opening partnership of 125 in 15 overs which set up victory over Surrey.

### 29 May

**at Liverpool**

**West Indians** 297 for 6 (C.G. Greenidge 186 not out, H.A. Gomes 87)
**Lancashire** 241 for 7 (G. Fowler 94)

*West Indians won by 56 runs*

Greenidge and Gomes added 229 in 41 overs after the tourists had been 3 for 2. Lancashire responded well with Fowler hitting fiercely. A crowd of 8000 watched a superb day's cricket and the match was a total triumph for the organisation by the Lancashire club.

### 30, 31 May and 1 June

**at Southampton**

**Somerset** 134 (C.A. Connor 4 for 31) and 201 (P.W. Denning 66, M.D. Crowe 53, T.M. Tremlett 4 for 43, E.L. Reifer 4 for 52)
**Hampshire** 333 for 9 dec (V.P. Terry 68, M.C.J. Nicholas 65, N.G. Cowley 51, C.H. Dredge 4 for 59) and 5 for 0

*Hampshire won by 10 wickets*
*Hampshire 24 pts, Somerset 4 pts*

**at Dartford**

**Middlesex** 310 (R.O. Butcher 104, C.T. Radley 61, K.B.S. Jarvis 4 for 66) and 129 for 6 dec
**Kent** 188 (N.R. Taylor 66, N.F. Williams 4 for 55) and 253 for 3 (D.G. Aslett 129 not out, R.A. Woolmer 86)

*Kent won by 7 wickets*
*Kent 19 pts, Middlesex 7 pts*

*Roland Butcher in action during his exciting back-to-form century for Middlesex against Kent at Dartford, 30 May. (Adrian Murrell)*

*Kent* v. *Middlesex at Dartford, 30 May–1 June. (Adrian Murrell)*

*at Northampton*

**Northamptonshire** 378 for 5 dec (W. Larkins 151, D.J. Wild 91, G. Cook 56) and 14 for 0
**Lancashire** 289 (N.H. Fairbrother 72, J. Simmons 54, R.W. Hanley 5 for 77)
*Match drawn*
*Northamptonshire 6 pts, Lancashire 4 pts*

***at The Oval***

**Surrey** 300 for 5 dec (A.R. Butcher 117 not out, G.S. Clinton 65) and 222 for 3 dec (A.R. Butcher 114, G.S. Clinton 78 not out)
**Glamorgan** 260 for 4 dec (J.A. Hopkins 128 not out, S.P. Henderson 53) and 261 for 9 (J.A. Hopkins 65, P.I. Pocock 4 for 37)
*Match drawn*
*Surrey 5 pts, Glamorgan 5 pts*

***at Edgbaston***

**Warwickshire** 338 for 4 dec (A.I. Kallicharran 116, D.L. Amiss 100 not out) and 49 for 1
**Nottinghamshire** 296 for 4 dec (C.E.B. Rice 129, B.C. Broad 64)
*Match drawn*
*Warwickshire 5 pts, Nottinghamshire 4 pts*

***at Worcester***

**Essex** 266 (P.J. Prichard 86, D.E. East 63, R.M. Ellcock 4 for 62) and 55 for 2
**Worcestershire** 222 (D.L. Acfield 6 for 58)
*Match drawn*
*Sussex 6 pts, Yorkshire 5 pts*

***at Sheffield***

**Yorkshire** 342 for 8 dec (J.D. Love 61, K. Sharp 54) and 80 for 1
**Sussex** 267 for 4 dec (P.W.G. Parker 67 not out, A.P. Wells 56 not out)
*Match drawn*
*Sussex 6 pts, Yorkshire 5 pts*

***at Oxford***

**Gloucestershire** 162 (P.W. Romaines 56, J.D. Carr 5 for 57) and 255 for 3 dec (P. Bainbridge 117 not out, A.J. Wright 80)
**Oxford University** 72 (D.A. Graveney 5 for 28) and 51 for 0
*Match drawn*

Only at Dartford, The Oval and Southampton was play possible on the last day. At Dartford, Middlesex, having been rescued by a thrilling century from Roland Butcher, who had been badly out of form, lost to a remarkable innings by Derek Aslett. Butcher and Radley added 159 for the fourth wicket in the first innings and, ultimately, Kent were set to make 252 in 57 overs on a wicket giving a little encouragement to spin. They were 28 for 2, but Woolmer and Aslett put on 171 in 38 overs. Aslett, magnificent on the off-side, hit a six and sixteen fours, and Kent won with 6.4 overs to spare.

Cardigan Connor took four wickets on his debut for Hampshire who, with Tremlett taking 3 wickets in 12 balls on the last afternoon, won with ease against Somerset threatened only by the weather.

Butcher, leading Surrey in the absence of Howarth, hit a century in each innings against Glamorgan who were set to make 263 in 58 overs. John Hopkins hit his second century in eight days, a solid effort rather than an exciting one, and was the backbone of the bid for victory which, having looked possible, ended with Glamorgan 2 runs and Surrey 1 wicket short in a splendid finish.

In the first edition of *Pelham Cricket Year* we prophesied a great future for Paul Prichard who was 13 at the time of writing and not then on the Essex staff. He made his first-class debut at Worcester and went in when Ellcock had reduced the visitors to 22 for 4. He hit 86 in a mature innings and saved his side. Acfield bowled Essex to dominance, but Ellcock and Pridgeon added 71 for the last wicket.

Larkins hit a six and seventeen fours in a glorious 151

against Lancashire and he and Duncan Wild, who scored a career best 91, added 136 for the second wicket. Amiss and Kallicharran, his fifth of the season, hit centuries in a run feast at Edgbaston where Rice struck the ball hard and elegantly on the second day.

Sussex bowled rather poorly at Sheffield but redeemed themselves a little with the bat. At Oxford, the wicket was appreciated by the spinners in the first innings, but it eased for Phil Bainbridge to hit his first century of the season and share a third wicket stand of 139 with Anthony Wright before the rain.

### First Texaco One-Day International
### ENGLAND *v.* WEST INDIES

England introduced Andy Lloyd to international cricket, a justifiable selection, surprisingly chose Fowler and recalled Miller in the absence of the injured Marks and once again elected for a lesser wicket-keeper in the hope of some crumbs of runs. Cowans and Randall were the players omitted from England's party of 13.

All began well for England. Botham ran out Haynes in his first over and then had Greenidge caught behind off a ball which moved late. Richardson was caught and bowled off a ball that held back and Miller, in a good spell when the wicket was giving him a little help, completely bemused Gomes, had Lloyd taken on the square-leg boundary according to a prearranged plan and captured Dujon first ball when the batsman swept irresponsibly. Miller also drew Richards forward and beat him down the leg-side when the batsman was on 44. It would have been a marvellous stumping, but that is why you pick the best wicket-keeper. Bairstow, to his credit, performed capably and ran out Marshall with a splendid throw. At lunch, West Indies were 107 for 7. England were winning easily, but Richards was still there. He had hit Botham for 16 in one over and was suggesting awesome power.

*Aslett just fails to catch Barlow, Kent* v. *Middlesex at Dartford, 30 May–1 June. (Tom Morris)*

Baptiste stayed until the score was 161 and he was caught behind off the returning Botham. Garner fell in the forty-first over, Richards 96 not out. He had been glorious until this

RIGHT: *Alan Butcher – a century in each innings for Surrey against Glamorgan at The Oval, 30 May–1 June. (George Herringshaw)* LEFT: *Paul Prichard (Essex). Six years ago we prophesised an exciting future for this young batsman. At the age of 19, he made his championship debut at Worcester and scored 86 to rescue his side. (Sporting Pictures)*

## FIRST TEXACO ONE-DAY INTERNATIONAL – ENGLAND *v.* WEST INDIES
31 May 1984 at Old Trafford, Manchester

**WEST INDIES**

| | | |
|---|---|---|
| D.L. Haynes | run out | 1 |
| C.G. Greenidge | c Bairstow, b Botham | 9 |
| R.B. Richardson | c and b Willis | 6 |
| I.V.A. Richards | not out | 189 |
| H.A. Gomes | b Miller | 4 |
| C.H. Lloyd† | c Pringle, b Miller | 8 |
| P.J. Dujon* | c Gatting, b Miller | 0 |
| M.D. Marshall | run out | 4 |
| E.A.E. Baptiste | c Bairstow, b Botham | 26 |
| J. Garner | c and b Foster | 3 |
| M.A. Holding | not out | 12 |
| Extras | b 4, lb 2, w 1, nb 3 | 10 |
| (55 overs) | (for 9 wickets) | 272 |

| | O | M | R | W |
|---|---|---|---|---|
| Willis | 11 | 2 | 38 | 1 |
| Botham | 11 | — | 67 | 2 |
| Foster | 11 | — | 61 | 1 |
| Miller | 11 | 1 | 32 | 3 |
| Pringle | 11 | — | 64 | — |

FALL OF WICKETS
1-5, 2-11, 3-46, 4-63, 5-89, 6-98, 7-106, 8-161, 9-166

**ENGLAND**

| | | |
|---|---|---|
| G. Fowler | c Lloyd, b Garner | 1 |
| T.A. Lloyd | c Dujon, b Holding | 15 |
| M.W. Gatting | lbw, b Garner | 0 |
| D.I. Gower† | c Greenidge, b Marshall | 15 |
| A.J. Lamb | c Richardson, b Gomes | 75 |
| I.T. Botham | c Richardson, b Baptiste | 2 |
| D.L. Bairstow* | c Garner, b Richards | 13 |
| G. Miller | b Richards | 7 |
| D.R. Pringle | c Garner, b Holding | 6 |
| N.A. Foster | b Garner | 24 |
| R.G.D. Willis | not out | 1 |
| Extras | b 6, nb 3 | 9 |
| (50 overs) | | 168 |

| | O | M | R | W |
|---|---|---|---|---|
| Garner | 8 | — | 18 | 3 |
| Holding | 11 | 2 | 23 | 2 |
| Baptiste | 11 | — | 38 | 1 |
| Marshall | 6 | 1 | 20 | 1 |
| Richards | 11 | 1 | 45 | 2 |
| Gomes | 3 | — | 15 | 1 |

FALL OF WICKETS
1-7, 2-8, 3-33, 4-48, 5-51, 6-80, 7-100, 8-115, 9-162

*Umpires:* D.J. Constant and D.R. Shepherd

**West Indies won by 104 runs**

*Before the match Cedric Rhoades, the hospitable Lancashire chairman, presents Clive Lloyd with a silver salver to commemorate his 100 Test appearances. (Ken Kelly)*

point, now he transcended adjectives. In 14 overs, he and Holding added a record 106 for the last wicket, Richards made 93 of them. His century came from 112 balls, his next 50 came off 35. Holding was allowed to face only 27 of the 81 deliveries of the partnership.

Viv Richards played the greatest innings seen in a limited-over international, surpassing Kapil Dev's 175 against Zimbabwe in 1983 which was also made in dramatic circumstances. Richards, with swaggering confidence, hit five sixes and twenty-one fours as he faced 170 balls. All of his shots

*Friends and adversaries. Botham and Richards in contemplation. (George Herringshaw)*

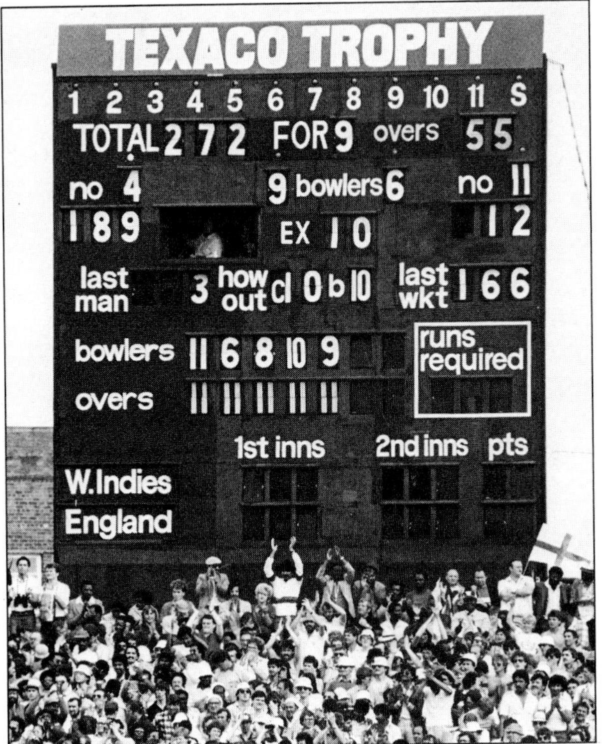


ABOVE: *Richards, number 4, 189 not out – the highest score in a limited-over international. (George Herringshaw)* BELOW: *Viv Richards hits Foster for an audacious off-side four. (Ken Kelly)*

were splendid, some of them, Botham into the pavilion, Pringle out of the ground, Foster over mid-off, were breathtaking. It is unlikely that those who watched it will ever see its like again.

What followed, inevitably, was an anti-climax. Fowler was taken at slip off Dujon's gloves. Gatting briefly suggested uncertainty and pain. Gower and Botham perished to fine catches. Lloyd played encouragingly for 11 overs before being brilliantly caught behind. Lamb looked less secure than others but stayed to the end. It mattered little now for the outcome had long since been decided and we were still relishing the memory of Richards in all his glory as we will for the rest of our lives.

### Second Texaco One-Day International
### ENGLAND *v.* WEST INDIES

Overnight rain delayed the start and the match was reduced to 50 overs. Gower decided to ask the West Indies to bat first and his decision was totally justified when, in frugal opening spells, Willis, Botham and Pringle exploited a little moisture in the pitch and reduced West Indies to 43 for 4. Haynes and Richardson contributed to their own destructions by playing across the line. The decisive wicket fell when Richards swept at Miller and top-edged the ball to Pringle at short fine-leg. Pringle was the hero again when he bowled Gomes, but Lloyd and Dujon hinted salvation.

Lloyd hit Miller for 6 after lunch, but when Miller returned to the attack the West Indian captain was caught at long-on. England bowled well and fielded magnificently, securing two run-outs as their reward. For their part, the West Indies were surprisingly lack-lustre.

## SECOND TEXACO ONE-DAY INTERNATIONAL – ENGLAND *v.* WEST INDIES
2 June 1984 at Trent Bridge, Nottingham

| WEST INDIES | | | |
|---|---|---|---|
| C.G. Greenidge | c Botham, b Pringle | | 20 |
| D.L. Haynes | lbw, b Willis | | 4 |
| R.B. Richardson | c Gower, b Pringle | | 10 |
| I.V.A. Richards | c Pringle, b Miller | | 3 |
| H.A. Gomes | b Pringle | | 15 |
| C.H. Lloyd† | c Pringle, b Miller | | 52 |
| P.J. Dujon* | run out | | 21 |
| M.D. Marshall | run out | | 20 |
| E.A.E. Baptiste | lbw, b Willis | | 19 |
| M.A. Holding | b Botham | | 0 |
| J. Garner | not out | | 6 |
| Extras | lb 7, nb 2 | | 9 |
| (48.3 overs) | | | 179 |

| ENGLAND | | | |
|---|---|---|---|
| G. Fowler | b Baptiste | | 25 |
| T.A. Lloyd | c Dujon, b Baptiste | | 49 |
| D.I. Gower† | lbw, b Marshall | | 36 |
| A.J. Lamb | b Gomes | | 11 |
| I.T. Botham | c Gomes, b Holding | | 15 |
| M.W. Gatting | b Garner | | 6 |
| D.L. Bairstow* | b Holding | | 9 |
| G. Miller | not out | | 3 |
| D.R. Pringle | not out | | 2 |
| N.A. Foster | | | |
| R.G.D. Willis | | | |
| Extras | b 4, lb 14, nb 6 | | 24 |
| (47.5 overs) | (for 7 wickets) | | 180 |

| | O | M | R | W |
|---|---|---|---|---|
| Willis | 9.3 | — | 26 | 2 |
| Botham | 9 | 1 | 33 | 1 |
| Pringle | 10 | 3 | 21 | 3 |
| Miller | 10 | 2 | 44 | 2 |
| Foster | 10 | — | 46 | — |

| | O | M | R | W |
|---|---|---|---|---|
| Garner | 9 | 1 | 22 | 1 |
| Holding | 8.5 | 1 | 29 | 2 |
| Marshall | 10 | 1 | 30 | 1 |
| Baptiste | 10 | 2 | 31 | 2 |
| Richards | 5 | — | 23 | — |
| Gomes | 5 | — | 21 | 1 |

FALL OF WICKETS
1- 24, 2- 38, 3- 39, 4- 43, 5- 75, 6- 128, 7- 148, 8- 160, 9- 161

FALL OF WICKETS
1- 75, 2- 103, 3- 131, 4- 145, 5- 157, 6- 173, 7- 177

*Umpires:* H.D. Bird and D.G. Oslear

**England won by 3 wickets**

In search of 180, England were given a fine start by Lloyd and Fowler who added 75 before Fowler was bowled between bat and pad. They survived a torrid time from Garner and Lloyd in particular played with great determination and good sense. Gower applied himself well, but Botham, Lamb and Bairstow perished wildly. Poor Gatting, unkindly received by the Notts crowd, was in total disarray, but Miller and Man of the Match Pringle took England to what was only their fourth win over West Indies in one-day internationals.

LEFT: *England off to a fine start. Willis exults and Haynes is lbw. (Adrian Murrell)* BELOW: *Gomes is bowled by Pringle. (Adrian Murrell)*

TOP: *Clive Lloyd plays a lone hand for West Indies. Botham, Gomes and Bairstow look on. (Adrian Murrell)* ABOVE: *Fowler is bowled by Baptiste to end England's opening stand. (Ken Kelly)* RIGHT: *Man of the Match Derek Pringle. (Adrian Murrell)*

### Third Texaco One-Day International
### ENGLAND *v.* WEST INDIES

England's hopes of surprising all and taking the Texaco Trophy were ended by a competent all-round performance by the West Indies and another display of arrogant mastery by Viv Richards. Once more England were given a sound start by Lloyd and Fowler. They scored at three an over until Holding bowled Fowler. Lloyd succumbed to Harper on the last ball before lunch and Lamb was run out immediately after the interval when he underestimated Harper's brilliant fielding. Botham hit Harper onto the roof of the Grandstand and then was caught quite brilliantly by him at mid-wicket, the tall off-spinner taking the ball shin high on the run when Botham pulled Baptiste. Harper's fielding and tidy bowling earned him the individual award.

Gower, who had been named England's captain for the summer earlier in the day, struggled for 21 overs and where acceleration had been hoped for, there was a tumbling of wickets as Marshall, returning faster and fiercer than in the previous matches, strangled attempts at quick scoring. England closed on a disappointing 196 with only two fours to their credit.

LEFT: *Andy Lloyd pulls Harper to the boundary. (Ken Kelly)*
BELOW: *Joel Garner – eleven overs of unrelenting accuracy. (Adrian Murrell)*

## THIRD TEXACO ONE-DAY INTERNATIONAL – ENGLAND *v.* WEST INDIES
*4 June, 1984 at Lord's*

| ENGLAND | | |
|---|---|---|
| G. Fowler | b Holding | 34 |
| T.A. Lloyd | b Harper | 37 |
| D.I. Gower† | b Marshall | 29 |
| A.J. Lamb | run out | 0 |
| I.T. Botham | c Harper, b Baptiste | 22 |
| D.W. Randall | c Dujon, b Marshall | 8 |
| D.L. Bairstow* | b Marshall | 8 |
| G. Miller | b Holding | 10 |
| D.R. Pringle | lbw, b Garner | 8 |
| N.A. Foster | not out | 4 |
| R.G.D. Willis | not out | 6 |
| Extras | b 1, lb 17, w 4, nb 8 | 30 |
| (55 overs) | (for 9 wickets) | 196 |

| | O | M | R | W |
|---|---|---|---|---|
| Garner | 11 | 4 | 17 | 1 |
| Holding | 11 | — | 33 | 2 |
| Marshall | 11 | — | 38 | 3 |
| Baptiste | 11 | 1 | 40 | 1 |
| Harper | 11 | — | 38 | 1 |

FALL OF WICKETS
1- 60, 2- 91, 3- 91, 4- 128, 5- 144, 6- 151, 7- 167, 8- 177, 9- 182

| WEST INDIES | | |
|---|---|---|
| C.G. Greenidge | c Bairstow, b Pringle | 32 |
| D.L. Haynes | c Randall, b Miller | 18 |
| H.A. Gomes | not out | 56 |
| I.V.A. Richards | not out | 84 |
| C.H. Lloyd† | | |
| P.J. Dujon* | | |
| M.D. Marshall | | |
| R.A. Harper | | |
| E.A.E. Baptiste | | |
| M.A. Holding | | |
| J. Garner | | |
| Extras | b 1, w 2, nb 4 | 7 |
| (46.5 overs) | (for 2 wickets) | 197 |

| | O | M | R | W |
|---|---|---|---|---|
| Willis | 10.5 | 2 | 52 | — |
| Botham | 8 | — | 25 | — |
| Miller | 9 | 1 | 35 | 1 |
| Pringle | 8 | — | 38 | 1 |
| Foster | 11 | 1 | 40 | — |

FALL OF WICKETS
1- 50, 2- 63

*Umpires:* D.G.L. Evans and B.J. Meyer

**West Indies won by 8 wickets**

Neither Haynes nor Greenidge showed any signs of mastering the wicket or the bowling and when Haynes was magnificently caught on the square-leg boundary by the diving Randall and Greenidge was caught behind off Pringle England looked to have a chance of victory.

Pringle had bowled well as had Willis and Foster and the other England bowlers, but Richards hit him for four fours in the first two overs he received from him. Suddenly the batting was on a different level and the game was over. Richards hit 84 off 65 balls with ten fours and four sixes, three of the sixes were off Willis' last seven deliveries. Gomes gained in confidence and looked a very good player and England contemplated what was in store for the rest of the summer.

### *2, 4, and 5 June*

#### *at Derby*

**Middlesex** 274 (W.N. Slack 93, P.R. Downton 88, P.G. Newman 4 for 76) and 60 for 1
**Derbyshire** 314 (K.J. Barnett 144)

*Match drawn*
*Derbyshire 8 pts, Middlesex 7 pts*

#### *at Swansea*

**Worcestershire** 466 for 6 dec (D.N. Patel 153, D.J. Humphries 100 not out, M.J. Weston 60, D.B. D'Oliveira 51)
**Glamorgan** 230 (J.A. Hopkins 59, D.N. Patel 4 for 58, R.K. Illingworth 4 for 60) and 93 for 8 (R.K. Illingworth 5 for 32)

*Match drawn*
*Worcestershire 8 pts, Glamorgan 4 pts*

#### *at Bournemouth*

**Hampshire** 303 (T.M. Tremlett 74, V.P. Terry 54) and 127 (M. Hendrick 5 for 17, R.J. Hadlee 5 for 35)
**Nottinghamshire** 308 for 5 dec (R.J. Hadlee 100 not out, B.N. French 70 not out, B.C. Broad 54) and 124 for 8 (C.A. Connor 4 for 39)

*Nottinghamshire won by 2 wickets*
*Nottinghamshire 23 pts, Hampshire 5 pts*

#### *at Canterbury*

**Kent** 175 (J.N. Shepherd 4 for 39) and 70 (G. Sainsbury 5 for 19, J.N. Shepherd 5 for 30)
**Gloucestershire** 130 (P.W. Romaines 73, T.M. Alderman 4 for 30) and 116 for 6

*Gloucestershire won by 4 wickets*
*Gloucestershire 20 pts, Kent 5 pts*

LEFT: *Gower bowled Marshall 29. (Ken Kelly)*

### at Old Trafford

**Surrey** 221 (R.D.V. Knight 60, A.R. Butcher 52, J. Simmons 5 for 71) and 251 (G.S. Clinton 66, J. Simmons 5 for 85)
**Lancashire** 219 (J.A. Ormrod 67, P.I. Pocock 7 for 74) and 251 for 8 (N.H. Fairbrother 62)

*Match drawn*
*Lancashire 6 pts, Surrey 6 pts*

### at Hinckley

**Essex** 189 (N. Phillip 71, A.M.E. Roberts 4 for 23) and 183 for 2 (G.A. Gooch 113 not out)
**Leicestershire** 226 (N. Phillip 5 for 48)

*Match drawn*
*Leicestershire 6 pts, Essex 5 pts*

### at Horsham

**Sussex** 338 for 4 dec (C.M. Wells 127 not out, G.D. Mendis 107, P.W.G. Parker 76) and 21 for 0
**Northamptonshire** 200 and 178 (J.R.T. Barclay 4 for 32)

*Sussex won by 10 wickets*
*Sussex 24 pts, Northamptonshire 3 pts*

### at Middlesbrough

**Yorkshire** 309 (J.D. Love 112)
**Somerset** 141 for 6 (S.D. Fletcher 4 for 24)

*Match drawn*
*Yorkshire 6 pts, Somerset 4 pts*

Rain on the last day prevented play at Derby, Hinckley and Middlesbrough where Yorkshire were in a good position after Love's century had restored them from 15 for 3 on the Saturday. Fletcher decided to bat first on a green pitch at Hinckley and Essex suffered as Andy Roberts, returning to first-class cricket at Leicestershire's request, reduced them to 105 for 7. Norbert Phillip hit a lusty 71 and then bowled Essex back into contention. Gooch hit a fine, brisk hundred, but the rain spoiled a good finish. The same could be said of the game at Derby where Slack and Downton took Middlesex from 87 for 6 to 200 and Barnett and Bob Taylor added 172 in 54 overs for the home side's fifth wicket.

Play was delayed until 4.15 on the last day at Swansea where Glamorgan hung on grimly against the spin of Illingworth and Patel. A cultured century on the first day and 100 in 101 minutes by Humphries had put Worcestershire in an unassailable position.

Notts moved to within two points of Leicestershire when a magnificent all-round performance by Hadlee helped them to victory at Bournemouth. Notts were 134 for 5 before he and French added 174 in 49 overs. He and Hendrick then destroyed Hampshire's second innings and when Notts faltered in their quest for 123 he hit a brisk 37.

Gloucestershire gained their first victory of the season in a grim struggle at Canterbury. Shepherd and Sainsbury had 17 wickets between them and Bainbridge and Athey brought steadiness when it looked as if Gloucestershire might fail in their task.

*Hinckley Cricket Club. (David Munden)*

*Richard Hadlee – match-winner for Notts against Hampshire at Bournemouth, 2–5 June, with both bat and ball. (George Herringshaw)*

In an exciting finish at Old Trafford, Lancashire fell three runs short of their target of 254 in 59 overs. Jack Simmons gave Lancashire hope of victory with 10 for 156 in the match, but 13 runs off the last over proved a little too much after Fairbrother and Simmons had added 51 quick runs for the sixth wicket.

The only thing that nearly prevented Sussex overwhelming Northants was bad light on the last day. Colin Wells and Parker consolidated the advantage given by Mendis' fine hundred by adding 200 for the fourth wicket on the opening day. Wells hit four sixes and ten fours, and good all round bowling maintained the Sussex dominance.

### John Player League

***3 June***

***at Derby***

**Derbyshire** 180 for 7 (J.E. Morris 57)
**Middlesex** 181 for 5 (R.O. Butcher 82)

*Middlesex (4 pts) won by 5 wickets*

***at Southampton***

**Nottinghamshire** 235 for 5 (C.E.B. Rice 87, J.D. Birch 54)
**Hampshire** 230 for 6 (V.P. Terry 110)

*Nottinghamshire (4 pts) won by 5 runs*

***at Canterbury***

**Kent** 235 for 6 (R.M. Ellison 84)
**Gloucestershire** 222 for 8 (C.W.J. Athey 79, R.M. Ellison 4 for 52)

*Kent (4 pts) won by 13 runs*

***at Old Trafford***

**Lancashire** 153
**Surrey** 154 for 6 (A.R. Butcher 73)

*Surrey (4 pts) won by 4 wickets*

***at Hinckley***

**Essex** 148 for 7 (G.A. Gooch 51)
**Leicestershire** 118 (P. Willey 51)

*Essex (4 pts) won by 30 runs*

***at Horsham***

**Sussex** 236 (P.W.G. Parker 77, D.J. Capel 4 for 61)
**Northamptonshire** 165 (D.J. Capel 53 not out)

*Sussex (4 pts) won by 71 runs*

***at Worcester***

**Worcestershire** 89 for 7 (J.F. Steele 4 for 19)
*v.* **Glamorgan**

*Match abandoned*
*Worcestershire 2 pts, Glamorgan 2 pts*

***at Middlesbrough***

**Somerset** 233 for 5 (P.M. Roebuck 84)
**Yorkshire** 234 for 3 (G.B. Stevenson 81 not out, G. Boycott 67)

*Yorkshire (4 pts) won by 7 wickets*

Middlesex won the top-of-the-table clash at Derby in thrilling style, Butcher hitting seven sixes in his 82 off 57 balls. Like the game at Derby, the one at Hinckley was reduced in overs, but Essex won comfortably after Gooch and Gladwin had put on 47 in 12 overs. Having put Notts in, Hampshire, chasing 236, scored only 12 off 7 overs, but Terry and Jesty added 89 in 12 overs. Terry hit four sixes and four fours in his 110, but Hampshire failed in their task after he was run out at 211.

Pocock's 3 for 18 in 8 overs did much to help Surrey to victory at Old Trafford and Sussex won with ease in spite of Capel's all-round performance at Horsham. In a glorious game at Canterbury, Ellison and Athey played spectacular innings, but Ellison's bowling stole the day for Kent.

Yorkshire, the reigning champions, won their first match of the season when Stevenson, coming in with 100 needed off 11 overs, hit 81 off 29 balls with ten sixes and saw them to victory with 21 balls to spare. Breathtaking stuff!

***6 June***

***at Arundel***

**West Indians** 140 (C.H. Lloyd 53)
**Lavinia, Duchess of Norfolk's XI** 76

*West Indians won by 64 runs*

*Martyn Moxon in action during his Gold Award innings in the Benson and Hedges quarter-final at Hove. (Adrian Murrell)*

Winning the toss, Lancashire asked Essex to bat first on a pitch of unpredictable bounce under lowering cloud which encouraged movement. Gooch managed only 4 in 12 overs which rather emphasised the conditions and Essex were always struggling. Fletcher batted capably and there were some encouraging, hearty blows from David East, but the middle order was strangled by a fine spell from O'Shaughnessy. With Pringle bowling well and Fowler run out by Fletcher, Lancashire were 35 for 3 before Abrahams, who hit the ball more positively than anyone, and Hughes added 107 in 29 overs. There was some hesitancy when Pringle struck again, but a violent 13 from Maynard ended speculation.

In spite of le Roux's and Alan Wells' fifties, Sussex were never really in the hunt against Yorkshire for whom Moxon gave further indication of maturity and elegance.

Warwickshire's innings was founded on an opening partnership of 102 in 27 overs from Andy Lloyd and Paul Smith. Kallicharran, Humpage and Amiss then pillaged mercilessly and Somerset were set a daunting task. At 23 for 3, they were reeling drunkenly, but Martin Crowe played with great authority. He and Popplewell added 79, but Crowe, who hit thirteen fours, was run out by Botham who then ran himself out when he did not realise that the ball was already in the wicket-keeper's gloves as he set off for a single.

Rain delayed play at Trent Bridge for a day and Notts were put in in difficult conditions which Surrey failed to exploit sufficiently. Randall and Rice added 164 in 23 overs and 100 came off the last 10 overs as Surrey wilted. They wilted even more when they batted, being dismissed for a dispirited 89 in 35.3 overs. The gap between the sides was enormous.

## Benson and Hedges Cup

### Quarter-Finals

***6 June***

**at Chelmsford**

**Essex** 157
**Lancashire** 158 for 6 (J. Abrahams 53, D.R. Pringle 5 for 35)

*Lancashire won by 4 wickets*
(*Gold Award* – J. Abrahams)

**at Hove**

**Yorkshire** 260 for 5 (M.D. Moxon 79, S.N. Hartley 55 not out)
**Sussex** 223 (A.P. Wells 51, G.S. le Roux 50)

*Yorkshire won by 37 runs*
(*Gold Award* – M.D. Moxon)

**at Edgbaston**

**Warwickshire** 282 for 5 (T.A. Lloyd 77, A.I. Kallicharran 63)
**Somerset** 216 (M.D Crowe 89)

*Warwickshire won by 66 runs*
(*Gold Award* – T.A. Lloyd)

***7 June***

**at Trent Bridge**

**Nottinghamshire** 256 for 3 (D.W. Randall 103 not out, C.E.B. Rice 94)
**Surrey** 89

*Nottinghamshire won by 167 runs*
(*Gold Award* – C.E.B. Rice)

***7 and 8 June***

**at Oxford**

**West Indians** 341 for 7 dec. (D.L. Haynes 100, A.L. Logie 96, R.B. Richardson 88)
**Combined Universities** 78 and 120 for 2 (A.J.T. Miller 56)

*Match drawn*

***9, 10 and 11 June***

**at Milton Keynes**

**Northamptonshire** 220 (R.J. Bailey 95, D.J. Capel 63, M.D. Marshall 4 for 36, M.A. Small 4 for 52) and 220 for 5 dec (E.A.E. Baptiste 4 for 49)
**West Indians** 268 (H.A. Gomes 109 not out) and 50 for 0

*Match drawn*

***9, 11 and 12 June***

**at Ilford**

**Warwickshire** 334 (A.I. Kallicharran 100, T.A. Lloyd 72, J.K. Lever 5 for 89) and 119 (D.R. Pringle 4 for 13, J.K. Lever 4 for 46)
**Essex** 114 (A.M. Ferreira 4 for 44) and 374 (K.S. McEwan 97, C. Gladwin 92, G.A. Gooch 54, N. Gifford 4 for 144)

*Essex won by 35 runs*
*Essex 19 pts, Warwickshire 8 pts*

**at Gloucester**

**Gloucestershire** 313 (P.W. Romaines 103, C.W.J. Athey 70, A.J. Wright 70, R.J. Finney 5 for 58) and 287 for 4 dec (A.W. Stovold 97, P.W. Romaines 66, P. Bainbridge 64 not out)

**Derbyshire** 331 for 9 dec (D.G. Moir 98, K.J. Barnett 74, B. Roberts 66) and 195 for 7 (D.A. Graveney 4 for 57)

*Match drawn*
*Derbyshire 6 pts, Gloucestershire 5 pts*

### at Tunbridge Wells

**Yorkshire** 297 (M.D. Moxon 110, G. Boycott 59, D.L. Underwood 4 for 27) and 234 for 5 dec (G. Boycott 104 not out, K. Sharp 99)
**Kent** 277 (R.A. Woolmer 58, I.G. Swallow 4 for 52) and 121 for 7 (A. Sidebottom 6 for 41)

*Match drawn*
*Kent 7 pts, Yorkshire 6 pts*

### at Old Trafford

**Lancashire** 296 (S.J. O'Shaughnessy 86, N.H. Fairbrother 55) and 159 (G.S. le Roux 4 for 44)
**Sussex** 303 for 7 dec (P.W.G. Parker 92, G.D. Mendis 80, A.P. Wells 57, S.T. Jefferies 4 for 74)

*Sussex won by 6 wickets*
*Sussex 23 pts, Lancashire 6 pts*

### at Trent Bridge

**Glamorgan** 170 (E.E. Hemmings 6 for 50) and 191 (W.W. Davis 50, E.E. Hemmings 6 for 73)
**Nottinghamshire** 349 for 8 dec (D.W. Randall 79, R.J. Hadlee 71, B.C. Broad 57, J.F. Steele 4 for 100) and 16 for 0

*Nottinghamshire won by 10 wickets*
*Nottinghamshire 22 pts, Glamorgan 4 pts*

### at Bath

**Middlesex** 473 for 7 dec (M.W. Gatting 258, P.H. Edmonds 55, W.N. Slack 53) and 88 for 2
**Somerset** 516 (N.F.M. Popplewell 133, M.D. Crowe 125, B.C. Rose 97, P.H. Edmonds 6 for 111)

*Match drawn*
*Somerset 5 pts, Middlesex 4 pts*

### at The Oval

**Surrey** 115 (J.P. Agnew 5 for 44) and 266 (M.A. Lynch 144, J.P. Agnew 5 for 76)
**Leicestershire** 259 (M.A. Garnham 84, P.B. Clift 58, T.J. Boon 51, S.T. Clarke 6 for 62) and 123 for 7

*Leicestershire won by 3 wickets*
*Leicestershire 23 pts, Surrey 4 pts*

### at Worcester

**Hampshire** 316 for 3 dec (T.E. Jesty 143 not out, D.R. Turner 70 not out, V.P. Terry 63) and 304 for 4 dec (T.E. Jesty 141, M.C.J. Nicholas 100)
**Worcestershire** 328 for 5 dec (R.N. Kapil Dev 95, D.M. Smith 83 not out, D.N. Patel 52) and 296 for 6 (P.A. Neale 66, M.J. Weston 54)

*Worcestershire won by 4 wickets*
*Worcestershire 21 pts, Hampshire 5 pts*

Dropped from the England side, Mike Gatting responded in typical fashion with 258 in 276 minutes including eight sixes and thirty-two fours. Somerset replied with a third wicket stand of 249 in 76 overs by Crowe and Popplewell, but thereafter boredom set in as, even with Botham unfit to bat, they reached 516 and a draw.

There were runs of a more positive nature at Worcester. Trevor Jesty hit a century in each innings, but Kapil Dev, in his first championship game for the home side, hit a violent 95 in the first innings and played a part in their reaching 293 in 63 overs to win the match. Victory came with two balls to spare, which was hard on Jesty and Nicholas who had added 238 earlier in the day.

Robert Bailey gave further indication of his talent with 95 against the tourists for whom Gomes clinched a Test place. Paul Romaines was another to give fresh evidence of undoubted application and talent with a hundred on the slow

*Northants* v. *West Indies at Milton Keynes. (Adrian Murrell)*

*Mike Gatting leaves the field after his mighty innings of 258 for Middlesex against Somerset at Bath, 9 June. (David Munden)*

wicket at Gloucester which, in spite of the brave efforts of both sides, determined a draw. Moir hit a career best 98 as he and Roberts saved Derbyshire's first innings and Bob Taylor took his first wicket in first-class cricket.

A fluent century from Moxon, a practical one from Boycott and a hard-hit 99 from Sharp set up the possibility of a Yorkshire win at Tunbridge Wells which was nearly fulfilled by Sidebottom's opening burst which reduced Kent to 18 for 4, but they survived.

Sussex showed some excellent form against bottom-of-the-table Lancashire who suffered a grievous blow when they lost wicket-keeper Maynard with a broken finger while batting.

The three leading counties all won. Leicestershire, with Boon, Garnham and Clift lifting them from 45 for 4, almost won in two days at The Oval in spite of Lynch's century. Agnew, with 10 for 120, was again most impressive. Notts led all the way against Glamorgan who succumbed twice to Hemmings, 12 for 123, and were victims of consistent batting by the home side.

The most remarkable win of the season took place at Ilford where Warwickshire reached 334 on the Saturday with Kallicharran hitting his sixth hundred of the season. On the Monday, Essex lost their last 6 wickets for 14 runs and had to follow-on. Gooch and Gladwin began the second innings with a stand of 99 and there were fine innings from McEwan, Prichard and Pringle while Foster also made a valuable contribution, but Warwickshire needed only 155 to win in 56 overs. Lever dismissed Lloyd and Kallicharran at 6 and although Warwickshire went to 58 before Acfield struck, the last 8 wickets fell for 61 and Essex had won. They bowled well and fielded zestfully to suggest that they would not surrender their title lightly. Lever and Pringle were heroes.

*Trevor Jesty, a century in each innings for Hampshire against Worcestershire 9–11 June, but still he finished on the losing side. (George Herringshaw)*

## John Player League

### *10 June*

***at Ilford***

**Essex** 239 for 8 (G.A. Gooch 74)
**Warwickshire** 191 for 9 (C.M. Old 58, N. Phillip 4 for 37)

*Essex (4 pts) won by 42 runs*

***at Gloucester***

**Derbyshire** 272 for 4 (J.E. Morris 104, G. Miller 78 not out)
**Gloucestershire** 203 for 5 (Zaheer Abbas 64, P. Bainbridge 50 not out)

*Gloucestershire (4 pts) won by 5 wickets*

***at Canterbury***

**Kent** 164 for 8 (R.M. Ellison 55 not out)
**Yorkshire** 167 for 4 (M.D. Moxon 77)

*Yorkshire (4 pts) won by 6 wickets*

***at Old Trafford***

**Sussex** 157 for 8
**Lancashire** 159 for 2 (G. Fowler 75, J.A. Ormrod 57)

*Lancashire (4 pts) won by 8 wickets*

***at Trent Bridge***

**Nottinghamshire** 177 for 7 (J.D. Birch 72 not out)
**Glamorgan** 178 for 5 (A.L. Jones 71)

*Glamorgan (4 pts) won by 5 wickets*

***at Bath***

**Somerset** 201 for 8 (P.M. Roebuck, 70, B.C. Rose 51)
**Middlesex** 202 for 9 (K.P. Tomlins 59, M.W. Gatting 58)

*Middlesex (4 pts) won by 1 wicket*

***at The Oval***

**Leicestershire** 212 for 3 (J.J. Whitaker 107 not out)
**Surrey** 215 for 7 (A.R. Butcher 59)

*Surrey (4 pts) won by 3 wickets*

***at Worcester***

**Hampshire** 185 for 7
**Worcestershire** 186 for 3 (D.M. Smith 66 not out, M.J. Weston 60)

*Worcestershire (4 pts) won by 7 wickets*

Two fine young batsmen, Morris and Whitaker, hit excellent centuries and found themselves on the losing sides. Morris' Derbyshire were unlucky in that Gloucestershire's target was reduced to 203 in 29 overs by rain. Surrey batted consistently to win with a ball to spare. Middlesex maintained their lead with victory off the last ball by 1 wicket when Wayne Daniel struck a two. Essex and Worcestershire won easily to hold second and third places, but Notts lost at home to Glamorgan and lost ground.

Fowler and Ormrod gave Lancashire a comfortable win with an opening stand of 142 and Moxon and Boycott put on 108 for Yorkshire's first wicket at Canterbury, Moxon hitting his best Sunday League score.

LEFT: *Alan Hill (Derbyshire) has never enjoyed a better season. (George Herringshaw)* RIGHT: *Tim Boon (103 not out) – a maiden century in first-class cricket and Peter Willey (159 not out) stand before the Leicester score-board which shows their fourth wicket record partnership of 290* v. *Warwickshire. (David Munden)*

***13, 14 and 15 June***

***at Ilford***

**Essex** 333 for 9 dec (K.S. McEwan 101, C. Gladwin 80, K.W.R. Fletcher 75, R.J. Finney 4 for 36, B. Roberts 4 for 77) and 258 for 7 dec (G.A. Gooch 76, P.J. Prichard 69, P.G. Newman 4 for 62)
**Derbyshire** 256 (A. Hill 83, W.P. Fowler 61 not out, N. Phillip 4 for 60) and 276 (A. Hill 84, J.G. Wright 53, G.A. Gooch 4 for 54)

*Essex won by 59 runs*
*Essex 24 pts, Derbyshire 5 pts*

***at Gloucester***

**Gloucestershire** 328 for 3 dec (A.W. Stovold 126, Zaheer Abbas 76 not out, C.W.J. Athey 62) and 162 for 3 dec (P.W. Romaines 71, Zaheer Abbas 64 not out)
**Worcestershire** 225 for 9 dec (D.A. Graveney 6 for 73) and 91 for 9

*Match drawn*
*Gloucestershire 6 pts, Worcestershire 2 pts*

***at Basingstoke***

**Hampshire** 203 (V.P. Terry 50, G.B. Stevenson 4 for 35) and 255 (M.C.J. Nicholas 128)
**Yorkshire** 401 (M.D. Moxon 68, K. Sharp 64, R.G. Lumb 55, G. Boycott 53, T.M. Tremlett 5 for 63) and 83 for 5 (T.M. Tremlett 4 for 33)

*Match drawn*
*Yorkshire 7 pts, Hampshire 3 pts*

***at Tunbridge Wells***

**Kent** 114 (I.A. Greig 4 for 39) and 142 (C.S. Cowdrey 63, G.S. le Roux 5 for 19)
**Sussex** 257 (A.P. Wells 93, G.D. Mendis 65)

*Sussex won by an innings and 1 run*
*Sussex 23 pts, Kent 3 pts*

***at Leicester***

**Leicestershire** 382 for 3 dec (P. Willey 159 not out, T.J. Boon 103 not out) and 241 (J.J. Whitaker 73)
**Warwickshire** 330 for 3 dec (A.I. Kallicharran 155, K.D. Smith 93) and 161 (P.B. Clift 4 for 17, J.P. Agnew 4 for 61)

*Leicestershire won by 132 runs*
*Leicestershire 21 pts, Warwickshire 5 pts*

***at Lord's***

**Surrey** 395 for 8 dec (M.A. Lynch 112, A. Needham 70, A.J. Stewart 69 not out, R.D.V. Knight 57, J.E. Emburey 4 for 68) and 226 for 6 dec (A.R. Butcher 67)
**Middlesex** 320 (C.T. Radley 118 not out, W.N. Slack 94, M.W. Gatting 58, A. Needham 4 for 48) and 237 (N.G. Cowans 66, G.D. Barlow 59, A. Needham 5 for 82)

*Surrey won by 64 runs*
*Surrey 23 pts, Middlesex 6 pts*

***at Bath***

**Lancashire** 369 for 5 dec (S.J. O'Shaughnessy 159 not out, D.P. Hughes 113) and 201 for 8 dec (J.A. Ormrod 95 not out, V.J. Marks 6 for 63)

**Somerset** 303 for 9 dec (M.D Crowe 113, J.W. Lloyds 73 not out, P.J.W. Allott 7 for 72) and 179 for 8 (J.G. Wyatt 61, M.D. Crowe 54, J. Simmons 5 for 31)

*Match drawn*
*Lancashire 8 pts, Somerset 6 pts*

***at Cambridge***

**Glamorgan** 318 for 4 dec (S.P. Henderson 108, Younis Ahmed 62) and 164 for 1 dec (A.L. Jones 82, C.J.C. Rowe 60 not out)
**Cambridge University** 119 (J.G. Thomas 4 for 23) and 155 (A.G. Davies 59 not out)

*Glamorgan won by 208 runs*

For the second time in a week Essex won a thrilling victory at Ilford. Gladwin and McEwan led a spirited assault on a Derbyshire attack which looked very weak without Mortensen and Miller and three Derbyshire wickets, all lbw as at Gloucester, were captured before the close. Hill and Fowler revived the visitors, but Gooch and Prichard lashed the Derbyshire bowling again and Fletcher declared at lunchtime leaving Derbyshire to make 336 in 82 overs. They went for the runs with Hill again batting finely and Morris looking an exciting player, but Gooch brought about a middle order collapse and with Lever returning to provide the kill, Taylor being lbw without playing a shot first ball for the second time in the match, Essex won with 3.3 overs to spare.

Leicestershire stayed ahead of them with a good win over Warwickshire who collapsed in their second innings as they had done at Ilford. Kallicharran became the first man to a thousand runs with his seventh century of the season, but the honours went to Peter Willey and Tim Boon who shared a fourth wicket record stand of 290, Boon hitting the first century of his career.

ABOVE: *Steve O'Shaughnessy, 159 not out for Lancashire against Somerset. A rapidly maturing cricketer. (George Herringshaw)* BELOW LEFT: *Essex jubilation. Gladwin, Turner, Fletcher and Phillip celebrate two marvellous victories in Ilford week which put them on the way to retaining the championship. (Adrian Murrell)* BELOW: *Downton, caught Richards bowled Knight 7, and Surrey take a firm grip on the match with Middlesex at The Oval, 23–26 June. (Tom Morris)*

ABOVE: *Lethbridge, caught Garnham, bowled Clift and Warwickshire, 82 for 7, face defeat by Leicestershire, 13–15 June. (David Munden)* BELOW: *Andy Needham – match-winning bowling for Surrey against Middlesex at Lords. (Adrian Murrell)*

There was a third wicket stand of 216 between the evergreen Hughes and O'Shaughnessy at Bath. O'Shaughnessy hit two sixes and twenty-one fours in a career best, but in a high-scoring match it was the off-spinners who nearly brought a decision.

There was high-scoring on the slow Gloucester wicket too, but David Graveney, with 9 wickets in the match, nearly brought the home side victory. Martyn Moxon again displayed his class and Mark Nicholas gave another clarion call to the selectors, but it was Tim Tremlett's accuracy which thwarted Yorkshire who failed by 2 runs to make 85 off 12 overs to win the match at Basingstoke.

A weakened and seemingly dispirited Kent were beaten in two days by Sussex for whom Alan Wells hit a career best 93. There was more spirit at Lord's where Surrey beat Middlesex, their first win there for 13 years. Put in to bat, Surrey owed much to a third wicket stand of 167 between Monte Lynch and Roger Knight while Alec Stewart emphasised his potential. Middlesex looked in danger of having to follow-on, but Radley and Slack batted with customary sense and eventually they were left to make 302 in 55 overs. Barlow and Slack bustled to 113, but 8 wickets then fell for 27 runs, Needham's off-spin proving devastating until he was savaged by Cowans who lashed a career best. Surrey achieved their first win of the season when Daniel was caught off Clarke with 17 balls remaining.

Glamorgan won at Fenner's for the first time, welcoming not only an accomplished hundred by Henderson, but the return of Javed Miandad.

## First Cornhill Test Match
## ENGLAND *v.* WEST INDIES

Rarely can England have had such a depressing start to a Test match. There was the pre-match announcement that Bob Willis was to retire from first-class cricket at the end of the season and then, after Gower had won the toss, Fowler was caught off his glove on the leg-side, Randall chopped on to Garner and Gower taken at slip off a poor shot. Lamb played an equally poor shot to be acrobatically caught at slip and worst of all, poor Andy Lloyd, beginning his Test career with some confident strokes, was hit on the side of the head by a ball from Marshall in the seventh over and was taken to hospital to take no further part in the match. Marshall was later warned for consistently bowling short and the length became fuller, but the damage had long since become irreparable.

*In his first Test innings Andy Lloyd is felled by a Marshall bouncer and takes no further part in the series. (Ken Kelly)*

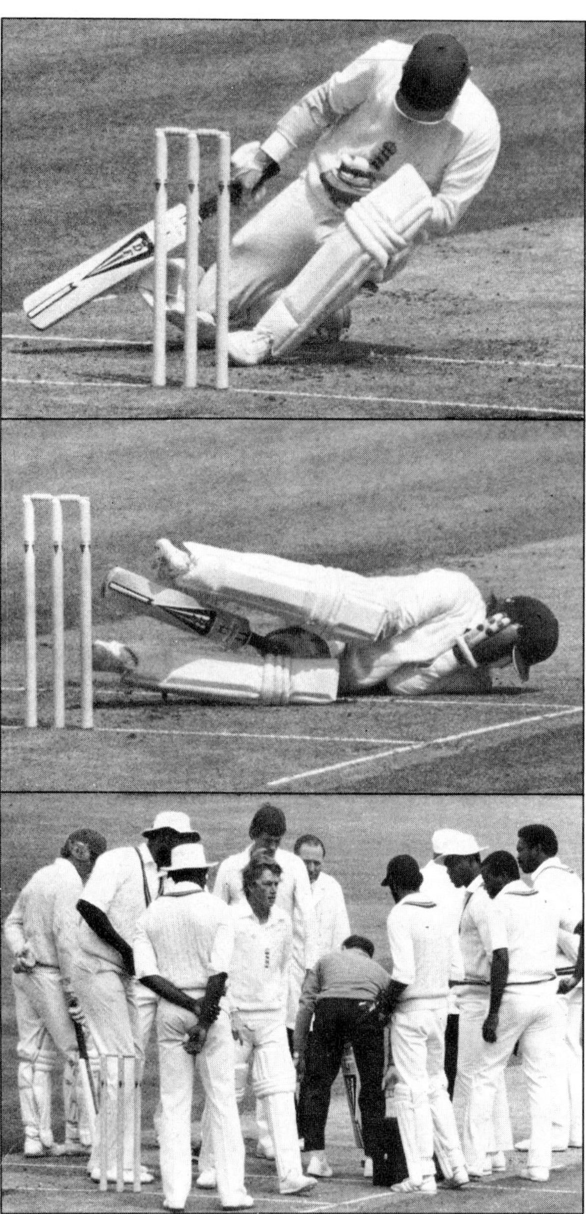

England's position would have been even worse had Botham been caught at slip by Harper before he scored as he should have been, particularly by so fine a fielder. Downton also had a lucky escape in not being adjudged lbw to a Holding yorker, but thereafter, Botham, in his swashbuckling style, and Downton, with determination and phlegmatic application, gave England some ray of hope.

Downton certainly earned his place with his batting performances in this match although it is hard to see why he was picked if, as the chairman of selectors stated, he was not the best available wicket-keeper. Does one state that A is the best batsman in England and then select B? I think not. Therefore why not accord the same policy in the selection of the wicket-keeper?

Garner's aggression, Dujon's fine keeping and the all-round quality of the West Indian out-cricket was too much for England who now gained some encouragement when Willis had Greenidge and Haynes lbw in the same over, but, by the end of the second day, West Indies were 230 runs ahead with 3 wickets standing. It was a bad day for England. Their tactics seemed lacking and West Indies took full

*A dejected skipper. Gower is caught at slip. (Adrian Murrell)*

advantage. Richards and Gomes hit 106 off 28 overs before lunch and as half chances went begging, they added 206 for the third wicket before Richards drove straight to mid-off. Gomes and Lloyd were both caught at slip, but not before the first had reached a pleasing, effortless hundred and the second had punished some tired bowling. Worse was to follow for England.

On the Saturday, in an exhilarating stand, Holding, with four sixes and eight fours, and Baptiste, with eleven fours added 150 in 29 overs in under two hours for the ninth wicket, a record. It was a crescendo to the innings, a wonderful battery of blistering strokes.

ABOVE: *Geoff Miller is caught behind. West Indies celebrate. (Ken Kelly)* BELOW: *Dujon brilliantly taken at silly mid-off by Gower. (Adrian Murrell)*

*Clive Lloyd catches Allan Lamb after a juggling act. (Ken Kelly)*

ABOVE: *Eldine Baptiste lashes his way to 87 not out.* BELOW: *Umpire Bird warns Marshall about intimidatory bowling. (Ken Kelly)*

ABOVE: *Michael Holding in violent assault on the England bowling. (Adrian Murrell)* BELOW: *Garner is caught by Lamb to give Pringle his fifth wicket. (Ken Kelly)*

*Downton's brave innings is ended, caught Greenidge, bowled Harper. (Ken Kelly)*

England batted again 415 in arrears. Fowler, Randall, Gower and Lamb were out to dreadful strokes and, on the Monday, in spite of Downton's tenacious innings and some spirit from Pringle and Willis at the close it was over soon after lunch. England were beaten by an innings and 180 runs, the fourth heaviest defeat in their history. Garner returned his best figures in Test cricket and there were many wounds to lick and much to ponder.

## FIRST CORNHILL TEST MATCH – ENGLAND *v.* WEST INDIES

*14, 15, 16 and 18 June 1984 at Edgbaston, Birmingham*

### ENGLAND

| | FIRST INNINGS | | SECOND INNINGS | |
|---|---|---|---|---|
| G. Fowler | c Dujon, b Garner | 0 | lbw, b Garner | 7 |
| T.A. Lloyd | retired hurt | 10 | absent hurt | 0 |
| D.W. Randall | b Garner | 0 | c Lloyd, b Garner | 1 |
| D.I. Gower† | c Harper, b Holding | 10 | c Dujon, b Garner | 12 |
| A.J. Lamb | c Lloyd, b Baptiste | 15 | c Richards, b Marshall | 13 |
| I.T. Botham | c Garner, b Harper | 64 | lbw, b Garner | 38 |
| G. Miller | c. Dujon, b Holding | 22 | c Harper, b Marshall | 11 |
| D.R. Pringle | c Dujon, b Holding | 4 | not out | 46 |
| P.R. Downton* | lbw, b Garner | 33 | (2) c Greenidge, b Harper | 56 |
| N.G.B. Cook | c Lloyd, b Marshall | 2 | (9) run out | 9 |
| R.G.D. Willis | not out | 10 | (10) c Dujon, b Garner | 22 |
| Extras | b 8, lb 5, nb 8 | 21 | b 1, lb 5, w 4, nb 10 | 20 |
| | | 191 | | 235 |

| | O | M | R | W | O | M | R | W |
|---|---|---|---|---|---|---|---|---|
| Marshall | 14 | 4 | 37 | 1 | 23 | 7 | 65 | 2 |
| Garner | 14.3 | 2 | 53 | 4 | 23.5 | 7 | 55 | 5 |
| Holding | 16 | 4 | 44 | 2 | 12 | 3 | 29 | — |
| Baptiste | 11 | 3 | 28 | 1 | 5 | 1 | 18 | — |
| Harper | 4 | 1 | 8 | 1 | 13 | 3 | 48 | 1 |

FALL OF WICKETS
1- 1, 2- 5, 3- 45, 4- 49, 5- 89, 6- 103, 7- 168, 8- 173, 9- 191
1- 17, 2- 21, 3- 37, 4- 65, 5- 127, 6- 138, 7- 181, 8- 193, 9- 235

### WEST INDIES

| | FIRST INNINGS | |
|---|---|---|
| C.G. Greenidge | lbw, b Willis | 19 |
| D.L. Haynes | lbw, b Willis | 8 |
| H.A. Gomes | c Miller, b Pringle | 143 |
| I.V.A. Richards | c Randall, b Cook | 117 |
| P.J. Dujon* | c Gower, b Miller | 23 |
| C.H. Lloyd† | c Pringle, b Botham | 71 |
| M.D. Marshall | lbw, b Pringle | 2 |
| R.A. Harper | b Pringle | 14 |
| E.A.E. Baptiste | not out | 87 |
| M.A. Holding | c Willis, b Pringle | 69 |
| J. Garner | c Lamb, b Pringle | 0 |
| Extras | b 6, lb 17, w 2, nb 28 | 53 |
| | | 606 |

| | O | M | R | W |
|---|---|---|---|---|
| Willis | 25 | 3 | 108 | 2 |
| Botham | 34 | 7 | 127 | 1 |
| Pringle | 31 | 5 | 108 | 5 |
| Cook | 38 | 6 | 127 | 1 |
| Miller | 15 | 1 | 83 | 1 |

FALL OF WICKETS
1- 34, 2- 35, 3- 241, 4- 294, 5- 418, 6- 418, 7- 421, 8- 455, 9- 605

*Umpires:* H.D. Bird and B.J. Meyer

**West Indies won by an innings and 180 runs**

*16, 18 and 19 June*

*at Chelmsford*

**Northamptonshire** 204 (R.J. Bailey 75, J.K. Lever 5 for 72) and 315 for 6 (G. Cook 84, R.G. Williams 65, W. Larkins 55)
**Essex** 417 (K.W.R. Fletcher 131, C. Gladwin 72, K.S. McEwan 51, A. Walker 4 for 85)

*Match drawn*
*Essex 8 pts, Northamptonshire 4 pts*

*at Cardiff*

**Lancashire** 337 for 8 dec (J. Abrahams 83, N.H. Fairbrother 66, J.A. Ormrod 62, M.R. Chadwick 52) and 251 for 6 dec (N.H. Fairbrother 68, S.T. Jefferies 55 not out, R.C. Ontong 5 for 80)
**Glamorgan** 306 (Younis Ahmed 83, Javed Miandad 63, I. Folley 5 for 65) and 169 for 8 (I. Folley 4 for 58)

*Match drawn*
*Lancashire 8 pts, Glamorgan 5 pts*

*at Southampton*

**Leicestershire** 325 for 8 dec (P. Willey 156, T.J. Boon 75) and 172 (R.J. Maru 6 for 75)
**Hampshire** 244 (A.M.E. Roberts 5 for 53) and 190 (C.L. Smith 75, M.C.J. Nicholas 55)

*Leicestershire won by 63 runs*
*Leicestershire 24 pts, Hampshire 3 pts*

*at Lord's*

**Warwickshire** 231 (P.A. Smith 80, N.G. Cowans 6 for 64) and 122
**Middlesex** 139 (C. Lethbridge 4 for 35) and 94 (G.C. Small 5 for 41, A.M. Ferreira 4 for 26)

*Warwickshire won by 120 runs*
*Warwickshire 22 pts, Middlesex 4 pts*

*at Trent Bridge*

**Gloucestershire** 113 (R.J. Hadlee 7 for 35) and 160 (R.J. Hadlee 4 for 41)
**Nottinghamshire** 398 for 7 dec (J.D. Birch 110 not out, R.T. Robinson 78, C.B. Broad 71)

*Nottinghamshire won by an innings and 125 runs*
*Nottinghamshire 24 pts, Gloucestershire 2 pts*

*at Guildford*

**Surrey** 208 (A.J. Stewart 73) and 262 for 6 (A.R. Butcher 135 not out)
**Sussex** 355 for 9 dec (D.A. Reeve 119, J.R.T. Barclay 76)

*Match drawn*
*Sussex 7 pts, Surrey 2 pts*

*at Harrogate*

**Derbyshire** 439 (J.G. Wright 141, J.E. Morris 116, K.J. Barnett 50, P. Carrick 6 for 165) and 175 for 7 dec (J. E. Morris 76, P. Carrick 5 for 60)
**Yorkshire** 352 for 4 dec (G. Boycott 153 not out, K. Sharp 104, P. Robinson 74 not out) and 204 for 6 (M.D. Moxon 74)

*Match drawn*
*Yorkshire 6 pts, Derbyshire 5 pts*

*at Worcester*

**Cambridge University** 217 (A.E. Lea 61, D.N. Patel 4 for 56) and 196 (D.N. Patel 5 for 28)
**Worcestershire** 395 for 5 dec (D.N. Patel 197, T.S. Curtis 129) and 21 for 0

*Worcestershire won by 10 wickets*

*at Oxford*

**Oxford University** 184 (K.B.S. Jarvis 4 for 43, G.W. Johnson 4 for 65) and 178 (D.A. Thorne 69 not out, K.B.S. Jarvis 5 for 30, G.W. Johnson 5 for 52)
**Kent** 419 (R.M. Ellison 106, C.J. Tavare 102, K.A. Hayes 4 for 58)

*Kent won by an innings and 57 runs*

Essex failed to make headway at the top of the Britannic Assurance County Championship after good bowling by Lever on the opening day, a fine century from Fletcher and more positive batting from Gladwin had put them in a commanding position. Northants held out on the last day with Cook, Williams and Capel doing well, but it was Bailey who again impressed with elegant aggression.

Meanwhile Leicestershire and Notts maintained their bid for the title with easy wins. Notts won through Hadlee's masterly bowling and John Birch's century on his twenty-ninth birthday. Leicester, again indebted to Boon and Willey who added 171 for the fourth wicket, withstood Maru's career best left-arm spin and 120 stand between Smith and Nicholas to capture the last 8 wickets for 54 runs and win the match at Southampton.

Folley's new form of bowling, left-arm spin, earned him career best figures at Cardiff but could not force a Lancashire victory, and Dermot Reeve's maiden century, a splendid

BELOW: *(left): Dermot Reeve, an exciting all-rounder. Sent in as night-watchman for Sussex against Surrey at Guildford, he hit a maiden century. (Adrian Murrell)* BELOW: *(right): John Morris, one of the brightest prospects in England. A maiden century for Derbyshire v. Yorkshire at Harrogate. (George Herringshaw)*

achievement when, going in as night-watchman, he shared a third wicket stand of 190 with Barclay, failed to bring victory for Sussex. Butcher hit his third hundred of the season on the last afternoon.

There was a maiden hundred, too, at Harrogate where John Morris, a twenty-year old of charm and positive composure, fulfilled the elegant promise of recent weeks with an exquisite innings which emulated team-mate John Wright. Philip Robinson, who sweltered on his debut while Wright and Morris added 190, played superbly in both his innings but could not bring Yorkshire victory.

Patel and Curtis hit career bests against poor Cambridge and Richard Ellison, that exciting cricketer, hit a maiden hundred at Oxford where Chris Tavare suggested a return to form. At Lord's, Middlesex's unhappiness continued as they were beaten in two days by Warwickshire who owed much to the effervescent Paul Smith, 65 for 5 when he came in, and the growing maturity of another young man, Robin Dyer. Gladstone Small and Anton Ferreira bowled them to victory on the second day against a side who seemed to have lost all confidence in the three-day game.

## John Player League

***17 June***

***at Chesterfield***

**Yorkshire** 225 for 6
**Derbyshire** 181

*Yorkshire (4 pts) won by 44 runs*

***at Chelmsford***

**Essex** 158 for 6 (C. Gladwin 61)
**Northamptonshire** 155 for 4

*Essex (4 pts) won by 3 runs*

***at Cardiff***

**Glamorgan** 127 for 8
**Lancashire** 130 for 5

*Lancashire (4 pts) won by 5 wickets*

***at Basingstoke***

**Hampshire** 188 for 3 (C.L. Smith 95)
**Leicestershire** 192 for 3 (P. Willey 67, J.J. Whitaker 57 not out)

*Leicestershire (4 pts) won by 7 wickets*

***at Lord's***

**Middlesex** 157 for 5 (M.W. Gatting 74)
**Warwickshire** 86

*Middlesex (4 pts) won by 71 runs*

***at Trent Bridge***

**Gloucestershire** 191 for 6 (C.W.J. Athey 59, J.N. Shepherd 52 not out)
**Nottinghamshire** 138 (J.N. Shepherd 4 for 33)

*Gloucestershire (4 pts) won by 53 runs*

***at Bath***

**Kent** 173 for 6 (C.S. Cowdrey 55 not out)
**Somerset** 176 for 2 (M.D. Crowe 78, P.M. Roebuck 68 not out)

*Somerset (4 pts) won by 8 wickets*

***at Guildford***

**Sussex** 38 for 1 *v* **Surrey**

*Match abandoned*
*Surrey 2 pts, Sussex 2 pts*

Middlesex routed Warwickshire in a game reduced to 24 overs and Essex, with Gladwin again sparkling, fielded and bowled well to beat Northants in a 27-over game and maintain second place. Notts fell away again after some lusty blows by John Shepherd and Kent's indifferent form continued as Crowe and Roebuck stroked Somerset to victory with a 114-run second wicket stand. Lancashire won comfortably at Cardiff in spite of a good spell from Mike Selvey and Yorkshire batted consistently at Chesterfield. Hampshire languished at the bottom even though Chris Smith showed a welcome return to form. Willey and Whitaker added 106 for the visitors and stole the match.

## Benson and Hedges Cup

**Semi-Finals**

***20 June***

***at Leeds***

**Warwickshire** 276 for 4 (A.I. Kallicharran 85, G.W. Humpage 58 not out, R.I.H.B. Dyer 54)
**Yorkshire** 273 for 8 (K. Sharp 83, M.D. Moxon 50)

*Warwickshire won by 3 runs*
(*Gold Award* – D.L. Bairstow)

***20 and 21 June***

***at Trent Bridge***

**Nottinghamshire** 223 for 6
**Lancashire** 224 for 4 (M.R. Chadwick 87, G. Fowler 53)

*Lancashire won by 6 wickets*
(*Gold Award* – M.R. Chadwick)

In one of the great one-day cricket matches, Warwickshire beat Yorkshire at Headingley although the issue was in doubt until the last ball. Bairstow won the toss and asked Warwickshire to bat and although Sidebottom had David

*Early success for Yorkshire at Leeds. David Smith is caught by Bairstow, Man of the Match, off Sidebottom. (Ken Kelly)*

ABOVE: *Mark Chadwick – Gold Award winner at Trent Bridge (George Herringshaw)*

BELOW: *Kallicharran's fine innings is at an end as he is run out. (George Herringshaw)*

Smith caught behind at 11, Yorkshire had little else to enthuse about. Kallicharran was in the form he had shown all season and was clipping the ball to all parts of the field almost as soon as he had come to the wicket. He was given splendid support by Robin Dyer who did admirably as substitute for the injured Lloyd. Dyer fell when Oldham joined the attack and Kallicharran was run out when he attempted a second run to a Carrick mis-field, but Humpage and Paul Smith hit fiercely after a valuable contribution from Amiss, 86 coming from the last ten overs of the innings.

Old, who bowled a good spell, had Boycott caught behind in the twelth over, but Moxon played well reaching 50 off 81 balls before being lbw sweeping. Ferreira had suffered in his first spell, but he returned to take three wickets in successive overs, one of them being Sharp who had batted with great panache. Ferreira's earlier waywardness had given Yorkshire a sniff of victory however and Bairstow and Stevenson added 71 in 10 overs to bring glory in sight. They both fell to Small in the fifty-fourth over and Willis' accuracy and accumulated wisdom denied Yorkshire the ten that they needed off the last over.

At Trent Bridge, Notts were put in to bat and struggled against a good seam attack which was well supported in the field. When a storm ended play at 4.30 on the Wednesday

*Two successes for Ferreira: (left): Sharp is bowled. (right): Robinson is caught behind. (Ken Kelly)*

Lancashire were 41 for 0 off 12.2 overs, the game was in the balance, but next morning, with Rice unable to bowl and aided by some poor catching and indifferent bowling, Fowler and Chadwick took their opening stand to 103. Lancashire, with young Chadwick taking the honours, batted consistently and sailed into their first Benson and Hedges Final after five years of falling at the last hurdle.

## Tilcon Trophy

### Semi-Finals

***20 June***

***at Harrogate***

**Northamptonshire** 294 for 7 (D.J. Capel 87 not out)
**Derbyshire** 182 (N.A. Mallender 4 for 44)

*Northamptonshire won by 112 runs*

***21 June***

**Leicestershire** 228 for 7 (M.D. Haysman 91 not out)
**Sussex** 147 (P.B. Clift 4 for 49)

*Leicestershire won by 81 runs*

### Final

**Leicestershire** 280 for 8 (P. Willey 95, J.J. Whitaker 50)
**Northamptonshire** 231 (R.G. Williams 78)

*Leicestershire won by 49 runs*

***21 and 22 June***

***at Dublin***

**West Indians** 584 for 6 dec (H.A. Gomes 153, A.L. Logie 129, R.B. Richardson 78, T.R.O. Payne 73 not out, R.A. Harper 64, C.G. Greenidge 54)
**Ireland** 187 for 9 (J.F. Short 54, R.A. Harper 4 for 58)

*Match drawn*

***23, 24 and 25 June***

***at Chelmsford***

**West Indians** 322 for 8 dec (P.J. Dujon 107, A.L. Logie 85, C.G. Greenidge 77, N.A. Foster 4 for 46) and 277 for 9 dec (C.G. Greenidge 62, I.V.A. Richards 60)
**Essex** 267 for 9 dec (G.A. Gooch 101, R.A. Harper 6 for 85) and 164 for 6 (D.R. Pringle 53 not out)

*Match drawn*

***23, 25 and 26 June***

***at Derby***

**Derbyshire** 199 (R.M. Ellison 4 for 34) and 161 (J.G. Wright 62, K.B.S. Jarvis 4 for 41)
**Kent** 305 (C.S. Cowdrey 95) and 58 for 2

*Kent won by 8 wickets*
*Kent 23 pts, Derbyshire 4 pts*

***at Bristol***

**Hampshire** 351 for 4 dec (V.P. Terry 175 not out, C.L. Smith 78) and 214 for 7 dec (V.P. Terry 73, D.A. Graveney 5 for 83)
**Gloucestershire** 300 for 5 dec (P.W. Romaines 63, P. Bainbridge 58 not out) and 215 for 8 (A.W. Stovold 67, C.W.J. Athey 51, R.J. Maru 4 for 64)

*Match drawn*
*Gloucestershire 5 pts, Hampshire 5 pts*

*Paul Terry (Hampshire) 175 not out* v. *Gloucestershire, 23–25 June. His magnificent batting brought him to the notice of the England selectors. (Sporting Pictures)*

ABOVE: *Tim Robinson edges through slip on his way to his 171. Agnew is the suffering bowler.* RIGHT: *Chris Broad superbly caught at slip by Ian Butcher off Nick Cook. (David Munden)* BELOW: *Roger Knight – instrumental in Surrey's rout of Middlesex at The Oval, 23–25 June. (George Herringshaw)*

***at Old Trafford***

**Lancashire** 183 and 196 (R.K. Illingworth 5 for 58)
**Worcestershire** 303 (D.M. Smith 77, M.J. Weston 61, J. Simmons 5 for 104) and 74 for 5

*Match drawn*
*Worcestershire 8 pts, Lancashire 5 pts*

***at Leicester***

**Nottinghamshire** 404 (R.T. Robinson 171, A.M.E. Roberts 5 for 104) and 128 for 0 (R.T. Robinson 85 not out)
**Leicestershire** 257 (I.P. Butcher 54, E.E. Hemmings 4 for 69)

*Match drawn*
*Nottinghamshire 7 pts, Leicestershire 5 pts*

***at Northampton***

**Yorkshire** 329 (M.D. Moxon 90, A.A. Metcalfe 58, D.S. Steele 4 for 97)
**Northamptonshire** 135 (S.D. Fletcher 4 for 42) and 160 (M.J. Bamber 51, P. Carrick 6 for 32)

*Yorkshire won by an innings and 34 runs*
*Yorkshire 23 pts, Northamptonshire 2 pts*

***at The Oval***

**Middlesex** 155 (R.D.V. Knight 4 for 7) and 90 (S.T. Clarke 4 for 28)
**Surrey** 399 (M.A. Lynch 118, C.J. Richards 64, G. Monkhouse 51)

*Surrey won by an innings and 154 runs*
*Surrey 24 pts, Middlesex 4 pts*

***at Hove***

**Glamorgan** 300 for 7 dec (Younis Ahmed 122, J.A. Hopkins 74) and 243 for 8 dec (R.C. Ontong 70, I.A. Greig 4 for 68)
**Sussex** 300 for 7 dec (C.M. Wells 138 not out, D.A. Reeve 52, W.W. Davis 5 for 68) and 227 for 9 (A.M. Green 81, R.C. Ontong 4 for 60)

*Match drawn*
*Sussex 6 pts, Glamorgan 5 pts*

***at Edgbaston***

**Somerset** 354 for 8 dec (P.M. Roebuck 102, N.F.M. Popplewell 90) and 315 for 5 dec (M.D. Crowe 152 not out, B.C. Rose 60)
**Warwickshire** 301 for 5 dec (D.L. Amiss 80, K.D. Smith 77) and 252 (A.M. Ferreira 61, I.T. Botham 4 for 64)

*Somerset won by 116 runs*
*Somerset 22 pts, Warwickshire 6 pts*

In a grim top of the table struggle Leicestershire batted into the third day in an attempt to match Notts' mammoth score which was founded on Tim Robinson's fine innings. Hampered by rain and respect for each other, the two leading sides drew. Kent moved quietly into fifth place when they overwhelmed the luckless Derbyshire whose bowling remained thin and who were beaten early on the last day.

Worcestershire were thwarted by stoppages at Old Trafford. They needed 77 in 9 overs at the end, but failed by 3 runs after some brave hitting.

With twenty-four fours to his credit, Paul Terry hit a career best at Bristol. It was a fine innings in a mainly dull match which breathed a little life on the last day when Hampshire nearly snatched victory.

Glamorgan also nearly snatched victory at Hove where Sussex, chasing 244 in 46 overs, finished 17 short with one wicket standing. Younis and Colin Wells had first innings centuries and Davis and Ontong, with his off-spin, almost won the game for the visitors.

Yorkshire won a resounding victory at Northampton where Carrick's spin and Bairstow's acrobatic catching and stumpings grasped victory in 80 minutes on the last day. The sadness was that Martyn Moxon, selected to play for England on the Sunday, cracked a rib and had to postpone his Test debut.

Put in to bat at Edgbaston, Somerset, enjoying a second wicket stand of 172 between Roebuck and Popplewell, and a masterly century by Martin Crowe in the second innings, romped to victory as Warwickshire subsided to some lively bowling by Botham who forced Old to retire hurt when he struck him on the helmet.

For Surrey there was total triumph at The Oval where Lynch was again in splendid form and Middlesex performed so badly that team changes were announced after an emergency meeting. Nothing seemed to be going well for Middlesex, but Surrey had seized a new start to the season to coincide with the opening of their splendid new facilities.

Meanwhile, Graham Gooch, the first Englishman to a thousand runs, became the first man to take a century off the West Indian tourists. Supporters wept for England.

## John Player League

### *24 June*

#### *at Derby*

**Kent** 255 for 6 (C.S. Cowdrey 59, D.G. Aslett 58)
**Derbyshire** 256 for 9 (D.G. Moir 79)

*Derbyshire (4 pts) won by 1 wicket*

#### *at Bristol*

**Hampshire** 262 for 7 (M.C.J. Nicholas 108, C.L. Smith 58)
**Gloucestershire** 140

*Hampshire (4 pts) won by 122 runs*

#### *at Old Trafford*

**Lancashire** 199 for 6 (G. Fowler 64)
**Worcestershire** 102 (S.T. Jefferies 4 for 20)

*Lancashire (4 pts) won by 97 runs*

#### *at Leicester*

**Leicestershire** 186 for 8 (R.A. Pick 4 for 36)
**Nottinghamshire** 188 for 4 (B.C. Broad 62)

*Nottinghamshire (4 pts) won by 6 wickets*

#### *at Luton*

**Northamptonshire** 209 for 4 (G. Cook 64)
**Yorkshire** 210 for 6 (M.D. Moxon 61)

*Yorkshire (4 pts) won by 4 wickets*

#### *at The Oval*

**Middlesex** 248 for 5 (M.W. Gatting 103 not out, W.N. Slack 66)
**Surrey** 174 (M.A. Lynch 65 not out)

*Middlesex (4 pts) won by 74 runs*

#### *at Hove*

**Sussex** 211 for 6
**Glamorgan** 173 for 8

*Sussex (4 pts) won by 38 runs*

#### *at Edgbaston*

**Somerset** 192 for 9
**Warwickshire** 188 for 6 (D.L. Amiss 54)

*Somerset (4 pts) won by 4 runs*

Middlesex moved 10 points clear at the top of the table when they won with ease at The Oval. Slack and Gatting added 131 for the third wicket. Gatting faced only 61 deliveries and hit six sixes in his first century in limited-over cricket.

Chris Broad celebrated his selection for England by pacing Notts to victory while Mark Nicholas hit his first John Player League century and shared a Hampshire fourth wicket league record stand of 122 with Chris Smith.

There were four stumpings at Luton where Yorkshire, with Moxon and Sharp batting well, kept Northants without a win. The outstanding performance of the day, however, was at Derby where the home side, chasing a target of 256, were 142 for 8 when Bob Taylor joined Dallas Moir. They added a league record 105 in 11 overs and brought Derbyshire to the brink of victory. Moir hit six fours and four sixes in his 79 made off 50 balls and when he was run out going for a quick single 9 were needed off 6 balls. The end came with two balls remaining when Taylor swung Ellison over square-leg for 6.

### *27, 28 and 29 June*

#### *at Chesterfield*

**Essex** 468 for 7 dec (G.A. Gooch 227, B.R. Hardie 58)
**Derbyshire** 187 (B.J.M. Maher 66) and 364 for 9 (J.H. Hampshire 101 not out, J.E. Morris 79)

*Match drawn*
*Essex 8 pts, Derbyshire 3 pts*

#### *at Swansea*

**Glamorgan** 327 (A.L. Jones 122) and 359 for 4 dec (R.C. Ontong 204 not out, Younis Ahmed 53)
**Middlesex** 438 for 9 dec (P.H. Edmonds 142, S.R. Barwick 4 for 78)

*Match drawn*
*Middlesex 8 pts, Glamorgan 7 pts*

#### *at Bournemouth*

**Hampshire** 356 (V.P. Terry 136, N.G. Cowley 80) and 11 (C.M. Wells 4 for 42)
**Sussex** 232 (D.A. Reeve 65) and 127 (R.J. Maru 4 for 23)

*Hampshire won by 108 runs*
*Hampshire 23 pts, Sussex 4 pts*

### at Old Trafford

**Lancashire** 197 (D.V. Lawrence 5 for 64) and 281 for 8 dec (J. Abrahams 81, J. Simmons 63)
**Gloucestershire** 190 (A.W. Stovold 73, S.T. Jefferies 5 for 56) and 150 for 5 (C.W.J. Athey 80)

*Match drawn*
*Lancashire 5 pts, Gloucestershire 5 pts*

### at Northampton

**Warwickshire** 400 for 9 dec (D.L. Amiss 121, A.M. Ferreira 76 not out, G.W. Humpage 55) and 208 for 4 dec (A.I. Kallicharran 65, R.I.H.B. Dyer 55)
**Northamptonshire** 333 for 8 dec (G. Cook 82, W. Larkins 78, A.M. Ferreira 4 for 87) and 236 for 8 (W. Larkins 63, G. Cook 56, N. Gifford 5 for 79)

*Match drawn*
*Warwickshire 7 pts, Northamptonshire 5 pts*

### at Trent Bridge

**Nottinghamshire** 390 for 5 dec (R.T. Robinson 169, D.W. Randall 136) and 259 for 5 dec (D.W. Randall 73, S.B. Hassan 70)
**Yorkshire** 341 (D.L. Bairstow 91, S.J. Dennis 53 not out, R.J. Hadlee 4 for 75, K.E. Cooper 4 for 93) and 122 for 3 (K. Sharp 52 not out)

*Match drawn*
*Nottinghamshire 8 pts, Yorkshire 6 pts*

### at Taunton

**Leicestershire** 254 (C.H. Dredge 4 for 48) and 276 for 9 dec (J.J. Whitaker 67, M.A. Garnham 53, M.R. Davis 5 for 82)
**Somerset** 192 (M.D. Crowe 70 not out, A.M.E. Roberts 7 for 74) and 341 for 4 (M.D. Crowe 190, P.M. Roebuck 128)

*Somerset won by 6 wickets*
*Somerset 21 pts, Leicestershire 7 pts*

### at Worcester

**Worcestershire** 436 for 6 dec (D.M. Smith 189 not out, T.S. Curtis 65, D.B. D'Oliveira 60)
**Kent** 180 (R.K. Illingworth 4 for 21) and 303 for 4 (D.G. Aslett 109, C.J. Tavare 96)

*Match drawn*
*Worcestershire 8 pts, Kent 2 pts*

### at Banstead

**Surrey** 361 for 7 dec (K. Medlycott 117 not out, N.J. Falkner 101 not out, A.J. Pollock 4 for 104)
**Cambridge University** 201 (A.G. Davis 69, M.A. Feltham 4 for 57) and 162 for 4 (P.G. Roebuck 54 not out)

*Match drawn*

The glory of Gooch continued as England gathered at Lord's to face West Indies without him. He hit a career best 227 off 224 balls at Chesterfield. His innings included five sixes and

ABOVE: *Martin Crowe. A marvellous innings of 190 in Somerset's glorious victory over Leicestershire at Taunton, 27–29 June. (George Herringshaw)* RIGHT: *David Lawrence – fine bowling for Gloucestershire against Lancashire at Old Trafford. (Adrian Murrell)*

*Graham Gooch. As England wallowed he savaged attacks all over the country as Essex fought to retain the Championship. (Adrian Murrell)* INSET: *Keith Medlycott (Surrey) joined the elite group of players who have scored a century on their first-class debut, 27 June* v. *Cambridge University. (Sporting Pictures)*

thirty-two fours and he dominated the weakened Derbyshire attack in stands of 142 with Gladwin and 155 with Fletcher. 121 for 4 in their second innings at the end of the second day, Derbyshire looked doomed to defeat, but John Hampshire hit his first hundred of the season and batted throughout the last day to thwart Essex.

Nottinghamshire and Leicestershire were also thwarted. A glorious second wicket partnership of 265 between Robinson and Randall put Notts in the ascendancy at Trent Bridge and Yorkshire, 115 for 6, were wilting before Bairstow, in typically aggressive mood, and Dennis, with a violent maiden fifty, rallied them and saved the match. Leicestershire suffered a worse fate than Notts. Thanks to Andy Roberts' bowling, they seemed totally in charge at Taunton and set Somerset to make an improbable 341 in 87 overs. In a brilliant display of batting, Peter Roebuck and Martin Crowe added a record 319 in 80 overs for the third wicket and Somerset gained an historic victory with 7 balls to spare.

Leicestershire (166 points), Notts (145) and Essex (127) led the table at the end of June, but Sussex's chances of moving into third place were dashed by Hampshire who, with Terry hitting a century and becoming the first batsman eligible to play for England to reach a thousand runs and Maru exploiting a turning wicket, won a comfortable victory at Bournemouth.

David Smith hit a career best at Worcester, but Kent, with Aslett again prominent and Tavare furthering his recovery, drew the match after a first innings collapse.

A second century of the season for Alan Lewis Jones and career bests by Phil Edmonds and Rodney Ontong were the highlights of the game at Swansea where the restructured Middlesex side could not force victory. Batsmen enjoyed themselves on the placid pitch at Northampton where both sides strove for a win on the last day. Dennis Amiss hit an accomplished century and George Sharp broke a finger shortly after hearing that he had become a father. Honours were even in a tense struggle at Old Trafford where David Lawrence had a career best on the first day and the weather was not kind.

At Banstead, Surrey were 172 for 7 against Cambridge and then Neil Falkner and Keith Medlycott, making their first-class debuts, both hit hundreds and added an unbeaten 189.

## Second Cornhill Test Match
## ENGLAND *v.* WEST INDIES

There was an air of foreboding when Lloyd won the toss and asked England to bat, but, on a first day, punctuated by showers, there were signs of encouragement for England as Fowler and Broad put on 101 for the first wicket. Fowler enjoyed some luck but played with a greater sense of maturity than one had seen before and Broad, big and purposeful, allied a sound defence to an eagerness to play forceful shots and he hit eight resounding fours. His innings ended when Marshall, having gone round the wicket, had him caught behind on the leg-side one-handed as he fended a ball off his hip. It was a most encouraging innings and it was ended by a fine catch. In a fine spell of bowling Marshall accounted for Gower immediately and troubled Lamb and Fowler, but they survived until the second day.

It was on the Friday, however, that the England innings lost its way. Marshall compensated for the absence of Holding with some fierce bowling and Lamb and Gatting, lbw without playing a shot, fell to him. There was a flourish from Botham, some sense from Downton and Fowler completed a tenacious hundred. He batted for just over six hours and while his innings had technical blemishes none could doubt its courage.

Marshall finished with 6 wickets and there was a remarkable run out when Baptiste hit the stumps at the bowler's end from fine-leg as Miller dawdled.

England's hopes soared as Greenidge, at slip, Gomes, splendidly at short-leg, and Haynes, lbw, fell to Botham with

*Chris Broad. A most determined debut. (Adrian Murrell)*

*Gomes is caught at short-leg by Gatting. One of Botham's eight wickets. (Ken Kelly)*

only 35 scored. Ominously, Richards and Lloyd batted out the day, but Richards was adjudged lbw early on the Saturday, a decision which caused doubt, and Lloyd could never get going again.

Dujon mishooked impetuously, but Baptiste, with an array of exquisite boundaries, and Marshall raised West Indies to within reach of England. The hero of the day, however, was Ian Botham. He ran in to bowl with all his old fire and recaptured the late swing which had made him the scourge of Australia in 1981. His figures of 8 for 103 were the best returned by an English bowler against West Indies in England.

Leading by 41, England allowed their advantage to lapse as Broad was taken at second slip off Garner and Small grabbed the wickets of Fowler and Gower. Gatting batted as well as anyone we had seen in the match and it seemed that at last we would see his confirmation as a Test batsman, but once more he offered no shot to Marshall and trudged back angrily and sadly with England on 88 for 4. He had gained his inclusion when Moxon withdrew and we wondered if he would ever been seen on the Test field again.

The England innings on the Monday was notable for the revival brought about by Lamb and Botham who added 128. Botham batted with good sense and completed a fine match which did much to silence growing criticism and Lamb, whose place had been very much in doubt, reached a praiseworthy hundred. There was hesitancy at the end of the day when England unwisely elected to come off for bad light, so throwing away an initiative they had gained.

It all seemed academic the next morning when 13 runs were added in 20 minutes for the loss of Lamb and Pringle who was the recipient of a harsh lbw decision for the second time in the match. Gower asked West Indies to make 342 to win and none felt that England was in danger of defeat.

LEFT: *Lamb reaches his century. The pleasure is obvious.* BELOW: *A pensive skipper. David Gower on the point of declaration. (Adrian Murrell)*

At 57, Haynes was run out by Lamb when Greenidge turned down his call and he slipped. It was the first time for seven Tests that West Indies had lost a wicket in their second innings. It was England's solitary success. In a marvellous display of batting Greenidge and Gomes added a record 287. Gomes again played with a composure that makes him such an essential balance to this fine West Indian side. He was missed at slip by Pringle off Foster, who afterwards went wayward, but his was a splendid innings. If it did not receive the ultimate accolades, it was because Gomes was partnering

ABOVE: *A solitary success for England. Haynes is run out by Lamb. (Ken Kelly)* RIGHT: *Greenidge in glory.* BELOW: *Gomes lashes a four off Miller past Gatting. (Adrian Murrell)*

Greenidge who played one of the most glorious innings ever seen in a Test match. Off 242 balls he made 214 with twenty-nine fours and two sixes. It was the highest score ever made by a West Indian at Lord's and it was one of the great match-winning innings of history. He was given a life by Botham and one by Lamb, but these were minor imperfections in a day of glory.

England were shattered and, inevitably, there were cries for mass executions, but it is the splendour of Greenidge and Gomes that will be remembered when all else is forgotten.

ABOVE: *An historic scoreboard. West Indies win by 9 wickets. (Ken Kelly)* LEFT: *The victors run from the field in triumph. Gomes and Greenidge. (Adrian Murrell)*

## SECOND CORNHILL TEST MATCH – ENGLAND *v.* WEST INDIES

*28, 29, 30 June, 2 and 3 July 1984 at Lord's*

**ENGLAND**

| | FIRST INNINGS | | SECOND INNINGS | |
|---|---|---|---|---|
| G. Fowler | c Harper, b Baptiste | 106 | lbw, b Small | 11 |
| B.C. Broad | c Dujon, b Marshall | 55 | c Harper, b Garner | 0 |
| D.I. Gower† | lbw, b Marshall | 3 | c Lloyd, b Small | 21 |
| A.J. Lamb | lbw, b Marshall | 23 | c Dujon, b Marshall | 110 |
| M.W. Gatting | lbw, b Marshall | 1 | lbw, b Marshall | 29 |
| I.T. Botham | c Richards, b Baptiste | 30 | lbw, b Garner | 81 |
| P.R. Downton* | not out | 23 | lbw, b Small | 4 |
| G. Miller | run out | 0 | b Harper | 9 |
| D.R. Pringle | lbw, b Garner | 2 | lbw, b Garner | 8 |
| N.A. Foster | c Harper, b Marshall | 6 | not out | 9 |
| R.G.D. Willis | b Marshall | 2 | | |
| Extras | b 4, lb 14, w 2, nb 15 | 35 | b 4, lb 7, w 1, nb 6 | 18 |
| | | 286 | (for 9 wkts dec) | 300 |

**WEST INDIES**

| | FIRST INNINGS | | SECOND INNINGS | |
|---|---|---|---|---|
| C.G. Greenidge | c Miller, b Botham | 1 | not out | 214 |
| D.L. Haynes | lbw, b Botham | 12 | run out | 17 |
| H.A. Gomes | c Gatting, b Botham | 10 | not out | 92 |
| I.V.A. Richards | lbw, b Botham | 72 | | |
| C.H. Lloyd† | lbw, b Botham | 39 | | |
| P.J. Dujon* | c Fowler, b Botham | 8 | | |
| M.D. Marshall | c Pringle, b Willis | 29 | | |
| E.A.E. Baptiste | c Downton, b Willis | 44 | | |
| R.A. Harper | c Gatting, b Botham | 8 | | |
| J. Garner | c Downton, b Botham | 6 | | |
| M.A. Small | not out | 3 | | |
| Extras | lb 5, w 1, nb 7 | 13 | b 4, lb 4, nb 13 | 21 |
| | | 245 | (for 1 wkt) | 344 |

| | O | M | R | W | O | M | R | W |
|---|---|---|---|---|---|---|---|---|
| Garner | 32 | 10 | 67 | 1 | 30.3 | 3 | 91 | 3 |
| Small | 9 | — | 38 | — | 12 | 2 | 40 | 3 |
| Marshall | 36.5 | 10 | 85 | 6 | 22 | 6 | 85 | 2 |
| Baptiste | 20 | 6 | 36 | 2 | 26 | 8 | 48 | — |
| Harper | 8 | — | 25 | — | 8 | 1 | 18 | 1 |

| | O | M | R | W | O | M | R | W |
|---|---|---|---|---|---|---|---|---|
| Willis | 19 | 5 | 48 | 2 | 15 | 5 | 48 | — |
| Botham | 27.4 | 6 | 103 | 8 | 20.1 | 2 | 117 | — |
| Pringle | 11 | — | 54 | — | 8 | — | 44 | — |
| Foster | 6 | 2 | 13 | — | 12 | — | 69 | — |
| Miller | 2 | — | 14 | — | 11 | — | 45 | — |

FALL OF WICKETS (England)
1- 101, 2- 106, 3- 183, 4- 185, 5- 243, 6- 248, 7- 251, 8- 255, 9- 264
1- 5, 2- 33, 3- 36, 4- 88, 5- 216, 6- 230, 7- 273, 8- 290, 9- 300

FALL OF WICKETS (West Indies)
1- 1, 2- 18, 3- 35, 4- 138, 5- 147, 6- 173, 7- 213, 8- 231, 9- 241
1- 57

*Umpires:* D.G.L. Evans and B.J. Meyer

**West Indies won by 9 wickets**

***30 June, 2 and 3 July***

***at Swansea***

**Glamorgan** 427 for 4 dec (Javed Miandad 212 not out, A.L. Jones 92, G.C. Holmes 84 not out) and 178
**Leicestershire** 389 (T.J. Boon 113, A.M.E. Roberts 89, G.J. Parsons 52) and 175 for 8 (J.F. Steele 5 for 68)

*Match drawn*
*Glamorgan 8 pts, Leicestershire 5 pts*

***at Liverpool***

**Middlesex** 313 (C.T. Radley 88, I. Folley 5 for 101) and 169 (J.E. Emburey 57, P.J.W. Allott 6 for 46)
**Lancashire** 208 (M. Watkinson 77) and 141 for 9 (J. Abrahams 58 not out, S.J. O'Shaughnessy 51)

*Match drawn*
*Middlesex 7 pts, Lancashire 5 pts*

***at Northampton***

**Northamptonshire** 255 (W. Larkins 108, R.G. Williams 50, M.R. Davis 7 for 55) and 270 (R.J. Bailey 114, R.G. Williams 65, M.R. Davis 4 for 64, G.V. Palmer 4 for 78)
**Somerset** 501 for 5 dec (P.M. Roebuck 159, P.W. Denning 90, V.J. Marks 53 not out) and 25 for 0

*Somerset won by 10 wickets*
*Somerset 24 pts, Northamptonshire 4 pts*

***at The Oval***

**Hampshire** 154 (S.T. Clarke 4 for 28) and 238 (V.P. Terry 102, S.T. Clarke 5 for 41)
**Surrey** 296 (M.A. Lynch 104, C.J. Richards 53, N.G. Cowley 4 for 33) and 100 for 7

*Surrey won by 3 wickets*
*Surrey 23 pts, Hampshire 5 pts*

***at Hastings***

**Kent** 92 (N.R. Taylor 52, C.M. Wells 5 for 25) and 243 (D.L. Underwood 111, T.M. Alderman 52 not out)
**Sussex** 143 (C.M. Wells 51, K.B.S. Jarvis 4 for 34, T.M. Alderman 4 for 46) and 192 (C.M. Wells 81, T.M. Alderman 5 for 60)

*Match tied*
*Kent 12 pts, Sussex 12 pts*

***at Edgbaston***

**Gloucestershire** 257 (Zaheer Abbas 68, C.M. Old 4 for 58) and 163 (C.W.J. Athey 77 not out, C.M. Old 4 for 45)
**Warwickshire** 252 (D.L. Amiss 87, J.N. Shepherd 5 for 116) and 169 for 3 (A.I. Kallicharran 62)

*Warwickshire won by 7 wickets*
*Warwickshire 23 pts, Gloucestershire 7 pts*

***at Worcester***

**Worcestershire** 400 for 6 dec (D.J. Humphries 133 not out, M.J. Weston 67, P.A. Neale 60, D.M. Smith 52) and 270 for 7 dec (P.A. Neale 69, D.G. Moir 4 for 77)
**Derbyshire** 347 for 8 dec (J.E. Morris 103, B. Roberts 72 not out, W.P. Fowler 58) and 254 for 7 (K.J. Barnett 104)

*Match drawn*
*Worcestershire 7 pts, Derbyshire 6 pts*

*David Humphries (Worcestershire) enjoying his best season with the bat, 133 not out against Derbyshire, 30 June. (George Herringshaw)*

*Bruce Roberts, Derbyshire's fine acquisition, an all-rounder from Zimbabwe. (Mike Powell)*

*at Leeds*

**Yorkshire** 183 (J.K. Lever 5 for 69) and 188 (P.E. Robinson 50, N. Phillip 4 for 47)
**Essex** 524 for 7 dec (G.A. Gooch 131, K.W.R. Fletcher 106, B.R. Hardie 94, K.S. McEwan 68)

*Essex won by an innings and 153 runs*
*Essex 24 pts, Yorkshire 3 pts*

*at Trent Bridge*

**Cambridge University** 237 (A.G. Davies 68, T.A. Cotterell 52) and 245 for 6 dec (C.R. Andrew 101 not out, P.G.P. Roebuck 62)
**Nottinghamshire** 256 for 6 dec (M. Newell 76, J.D. Birch 69) and 227 for 3 (S.B. Hassan 103 not out, P. Johnson 63, J.D. Birch 54 not out)

*Nottinghamshire won by 7 wickets*

With Leicestershire failing to win at Swansea, Essex moved closer to the top when they inflicted the heaviest defeat on Yorkshire that the White Rose had ever suffered in their 93 years at Headingley. 100 for 1 at lunch on the Saturday, Yorkshire were bowled out in the afternoon by the Essex seamers and by the close Gooch was out for 131 and Essex were in the lead. The carnage became horrendous on Monday as Hardie and Fletcher added 163 in 45 overs for the sixth wicket to take Essex to their highest score ever against Yorkshire. Lever than broke the back of the batting for the second time and Phillip and Acfield finished the job early on the last day.

Javed Miandad hit his highest score in the United Kingdom on the first day at Swansea, but Tim Boon's highest championship score and Andy Roberts' volatile career best brought parity for the visitors who were eventually left to make 217 in 50 overs. They were almost lured to defeat by the slow left-arm of their former all-rounder John Steele.

Nottinghamshire, giving career debuts to several youngsters, beat Cambridge University for whom Andrew hit a maiden century. Humphries continued his best ever season with the bat with a thumping career best at New Road, but Morris, such an exciting young player, reached his second century of the season and gave Derbyshire hope. They were asked to make 324 in 60 overs and Kim Barnett hit a powerful hundred to take them to 152 for 1, but they then lost 6 wickets for 65 runs before Fowler and Finney earned a draw.

Chris Old bowled well to help Warwickshire to a comfortable win over luckless Gloucestershire who had Zaheer and Brassington injured, the latter breaking a bone in his hand in his come-back match. In spite of Paul Terry's fifth century of the season, Hampshire succumbed to Lynch's powerful batting and the speed of Clarke and Thomas. Surrey, troubled by Tim Tremlett's late movement and a rare spell from Trevor Jesty, made hard work of victory.

The success of Somerset continued. Davis' seven wickets nullified Larkins' uncharacteristically dour hundred and Roebuck's career best gave the visitors total supremacy. At 23 for 5, Northants were in dreadful trouble, but Bailey batted magnificently to give another indication of his exciting potential, and to save Northants from the indignity of an innings defeat. Here is a young batsman of high quality.

Allott gave the England selectors another reminder at Liverpool and Watkinson hit a career best to revive Lancashire's first innings, but it was Jefferies who survived 12 overs and Abrahams who eventually saved the home side from defeat.

Wickets tumbled on the first day at Hastings where fine catches were held and bowlers performed well in an encouraging atmosphere, but on the second day, Underwood, who had come in as night-watchman after the fall of 21 wickets in the day, hit the first century of his noble career while all around him floundered. He was given late support by Knott and there were lusty blows from Alderman who reached a maiden fifty. Needing 193 to win, Sussex reached 186 for 6 with Colin Wells hitting forcefully until he pulled Alderman to mid-wicket. Four runs later Greig was caught in the deep off Ellison who had le Roux taken at slip next ball, 190 for 9. Waller and Smith hit singles, but Alderman had Smith taken at slip, again by Tavare, and a marvellous match was tied.

## John Player League

*1 July*

*at Swansea*

**Leicestershire** 291 for 5 (J.J. Whitaker 132, P. Willey 106)
**Glamorgan** 262 (Javed Miandad 53)

*Leicestershire (4 pts) won by 29 runs*

*at Old Trafford*

**Lancashire** 186 for 9
**Middlesex** 132 (R.O. Butcher 63)

*Lancashire (4 pts) won by 54 runs*

*at Northampton*

**Somerset** 174 for 8 (M.D. Crowe 57, R.W. Hanley 4 for 50)
**Northamptonshire** 175 for 3 (R.G. Williams 81 not out)

*Northamptonshire (4 pts) won by 7 wickets*

*at The Oval*

**Hampshire** 199 for 6 (C.L. Smith 55)
**Surrey** 203 for 5 (A.R. Butcher 52)

*Surrey (4 pts) won by 5 wickets*

*at Hastings*

**Kent** 222 for 5 (N.R. Taylor 72, C.S. Cowdrey 60)
**Sussex** 140 (D.L. Underwood 6 for 12)

*Kent (4 pts) won by 82 runs*

*at Edgbaston*

**Warwickshire** 215 for 5 (G.W. Humpage 109 not out)
**Gloucestershire** 166 for 7

*Warwickshire (4 pts) won by 49 runs*

*at Worcester*

**Worcestershire** 222 for 8 (D.N. Patel 98)
**Derbyshire** 200 (R.J. Finney 50 not out)

*Worcestershire (4 pts) won by 22 runs*

*at Leeds*

**Essex** 206 for 8 (A. Sidebottom 4 for 32)
**Yorkshire** 189 for 9 (A.A. Metcalfe 71, J.K. Lever 4 for 21)

*Essex (4 pts) won by 17 runs*

When, in his second over, John Lever had Boycott and Sharp caught behind by David East he became the first bowler to reach 300 wickets in the John Player League. He was also

ABOVE: *Mark Davis (Somerset), 11 for 119 against Northamptonshire. A rapidly maturing bowler of class. (George Herringshaw)* RIGHT: *John Lever of Essex, the first bowler to reach 300 wickets in the John Player League. The most consistent wicket-taker in English cricket over the past five seasons. None gives more to the game. (David Munden)* BELOW: *Years of endeavour and success. Derek Underwood, 300 wickets in the John Player League, 1 July, and the next day a maiden century in first-class cricket. England may still have need of him. (Adrian Murrell)*

instrumental in bringing Essex victory at Headingley and taking them to within 6 points of Middlesex who, in a listless display, were outbatted, outfielded and outbowled by an enthusiastic and energetic Lancashire side.

Thirty minutes after Lever's three hundreth wicket at Leeds, Derek Underwood reached the 300 mark at Hastings and celebrated by taking five more wickets, three of them stumped by Knott, in the rout of Sussex.

Leicestershire made their highest score in the competition when Whitaker, 132 off 117 balls, and Willey, 106 off 80 balls, reached a 4th wicket record stand of 178 in 23 overs. Glamorgan responded bravely, but lost by 29 runs.

Geoff Humpage carried his bat through the innings at Edgbaston and put Warwickshire in an unassailable position while Dipak Patel, in spite of injuring an ankle, had a fine all-round match at New Road to keep Worcestershire level on points with Lancashire and Surrey in third place. At the other end of the table, Northants had their first win of the season.

## NatWest Bank Trophy – Round One

***4 July***

***at Kendal***

**Cumberland** 121 (K.J. Barnett 6 for 24)
**Derbyshire** 124 for 1 (J.G. Wright 73 not out)

*Derbyshire won by 9 wickets*
(*Man of the Match* – J.G. Wright)

***at Darlington***

**Northamptonshire** 209 for 8 (W. Larkins 77, S. Greensword 4 for 28)
**Durham** 198

*Northamptonshire won by 11 runs*
(*Man of the Match* – S. Greensword)

***at Chelmsford***

**Essex** 327 for 6 (G.A. Gooch 133, K.S. McEwan 75, A.A. Lilley 59 not out)
**Scotland** 137

*Essex won by 190 runs*
(*Man of the Match* – G.A. Gooch)

***at Swansea***

**Glamorgan** 147 for 9
**Nottinghamshire** 148 for 4 (D.W. Randall 71)

*Nottinghamshire won by 6 wickets*
(*Man of the Match* – D.W. Randall)

***at St Albans***

**Somerset** 153 for 9
**Hertfordshire** 137

*Somerset won by 16 runs*
(*Man of the Match* – B.G. Evans)

***at Canterbury***

**Kent** 232 for 7 (C.S. Cowdrey 64)
**Berkshire** 143

*Kent won by 89 runs*
(*Man of the Match* – C.S. Cowdrey)

***at Old Trafford***

**Lancashire** 272 for 7 (G. Fowler 101)
**Buckinghamshire** 199 for 8 (D.E. Smith 54, P.J.W. Allott 4 for 34)

*Lancashire won by 73 runs*
(*Man of the Match* – G. Fowler)

***at Norwich***

**Hampshire** 239 for 8 (M.C.J. Nicholas 63, V.P. Terry 50)
**Norfolk** 121 (N.G. Cowley 5 for 24)

*Hampshire won by 118 runs*
(*Man of the Match* – N.G. Cowley)

***at Jesmond***

**Middlesex** 233 for 9 (C.T. Radley 64 not out)
**Northumberland** 143 (M.E. Younger 57)

*Middlesex won by 90 runs*
(*Man of the Match* – M.E. Younger)

***at Telford***

**Shropshire** 229 for 5 (Mushtaq Mohammad 80, S. Gale 68)
**Yorkshire** 192

*Shropshire won by 37 runs*
(*Man of the Match* – Mushtaq Mohammad)

ABOVE: *The crowd watch the first round NatWest Trophy match at Kendal in leisurely fashion. (David Munden)* BELOW: *The architect of the sensational victory by Shropshire over Yorkshire, Mushtaq Mohammad, Man of the Match at Telford, 4 July. (Ken Kelly)*

***at Stone***

**Staffordshire** 151 for 8 (J.N. Shepherd 4 for 20)
**Gloucestershire** 152 for 2 (C.W.J. Athey 70 not out, P.W. Romaines 52)

*Gloucestershire won by 8 wickets*
(*Man of the Match* – J.N. Shepherd)

***at The Oval***

**Ireland** 157 for 7 (S.S.J. Warke 77, J.A. Prior 50)
**Surrey** 161 for 3 (G.S. Clinton 79 not out)

*Surrey won by 7 wickets*
(*Man of the Match* – J.A. Prior)

***at Hove***

**Sussex** 231 for 8 (A.M. Green 74)
**Devon** 169 for 9 (J.R.T. Barclay 5 for 53)

*Sussex won by 62 runs*
(*Man of the Match* – A.M. Green)

***at Edgbaston***

**Warwickshire** 392 for 5 (A.I. Kallicharran 206, K.D. Smith 101)
**Oxfordshire** 165 for 8 (G. Ford 62, A.I. Kallicharran 6 for 32)

*Warwickshire won by 227 runs*
(*Man of the Match* – A.I. Kallicharran)

***at Swindon***

**Leicestershire** 354 for 7 (J.J. Whitaker 155, D.I. Gower 77, N.E. Briers 59, J. Spencer 4 for 82)
**Wiltshire** 209 for 6 (J.M. Rice 75 not out)

*Leicestershire won by 145 runs*
(*Man of the Match* – J.J. Whitaker)

***at Worcester***

**Suffolk** 149 (D.N. Patel 4 for 22, M.J. Weston 4 for 30)
**Worcestershire** 152 for 4 (T.S. Curtis 54 not out)

*Worcestershire won by 6 wickets*
(*Man of the Match* – T.S. Curtis)

There were some brave performances by Minor Counties in the first round of the NatWest Trophy, Durham and Hertfordshire almost pulling off surprises and Shropshire causing the only sensation by beating Yorkshire convincingly.

Shropshire were 62 for 3, but Mushtaq and Gale added 102 and Yorkshire, chasing 230, were reduced to 80 for 5, three of them victims of Mushtaq's leg-spinners. There was a rally by Carrick and Stevenson, but the task was too great and Yorkshire were knocked out by a minor county for the

**Scotland 1984**
Limited-over Matches

| BATTING | v. Northamptonshire (Northampton) 5 May B&H | v. Yorkshire (Perth) 12 May B&H | v. Leicestershire (Glasgow) 17 May B&H | v. Warwickshire (Edgbaston) 19 May B&H | v. Essex (Chelmsford) 4 July NW | *Runs* |
|---|---|---|---|---|---|---|
| W.A. Donald | 32 | 36 | 22 | 9 | 5 | 104 |
| C.J. Warner | 25 | 24 | 59 | 9 | 6 | 123 |
| R.G. Swan | 55 | 27 | 10 | 16 | 41 | 149 |
| T.B. Racionzer | 40 | 17 | 18 | 5 | 0 | 80 |
| O. Henry | 15 | 24 | 59 | 5 | 8 | 111 |
| R.S. Weir | 26 | 5 | 10* | 9 | | 50 |
| A.B.M. Ker | 23 | 25 | 0* | 4 | 12 | 64 |
| D. De Neef | 0 | 9 | — | | 15 | 24 |
| H.G.F. Johnston | 1 | | | 20 | | 21 |
| W.A. McPate | 0 | 1* | — | 15 | 13* | 29 |
| J.D. Knight | 2* | — | — | 8* | | 10 |
| J.E. Ker | | 2* | — | 12 | 13 | 27 |
| A. Brown | | | | | 6 | 6 |
| P.G. Duthie | | | | | 0 | 0 |
| Byes | 1 | 4 | 2 | 1 | 2 | |
| Leg-byes | 9 | 11 | 22 | 11 | 9 | |
| Wides | | 1 | 1 | 4 | 6 | |
| No-balls | 1 | | 1 | 5 | 1 | |
| Total | 230 | 186 | 204 | 133 | 137 | |
| Wickets | 10 | 8 | 5 | 10 | 10 | |
| Result | L | L | L | L | L | |
| Points | 0 | 0 | 0 | 0 | — | |

*Catches* 3 – O. Henry
2 – T. B. Racionzer, A.B.M. Ker and A. Brown
1 – C.J. Warner, J.D. Knight, R.G. Swan and W.A. McPate

| BOWLING | D. de Neff | W.A. McPate | O. Henry | W.A. Donald | H.G.F. Johnston | T.B. Racionzer | J.E. Ker | P.G. Duthie |
|---|---|---|---|---|---|---|---|---|
| v. Northamptonshire (Northampton) 5 May B&H | 11–0–61–0 | 11–4–59–0 | 11–1–37–1 | 11–0–35–2 | 7–0–35–0 | 4–0–23–0 | | |
| v. Yorkshire (Perth) 12 May B&H | 11–2–65–1 | 9–1–34–0 | 11–1–53–1 | 11–3–30–2 | | 2–0–9–0 | 11–3–25–1 | |
| v. Leicestershire (Glasgow) 17 May B&H | 3.2–0–26–0 | 9–1–36–0 | 11–3–31–0 | 11–2–32–0 | | 9–0–36–1 | 11–0–37–2 | |
| v. Warwickshire (Edgbaston) 19 May B&H | | 11–2–54–4 | 11–1–44–0 | 7–0–27–0 | 4–0–27–0 | 11–1–60–0 | 11–1–35–3 | |
| v. Essex (Chelmsford) 4 July NW | 12–1–37–3 | 10–2–58–1 | 12–0–65–0 | 8–0–25–0 | | 4–0–29–1 | 8–1–59–0 | 6–0–35–1 |
| Wickets | 4 | 5 | 2 | 4 | 0 | 2 | 6 | 1 |

LEFT: *Kallicharran is congratulated by Paul Smith for his innings of 206 out of 371.* RIGHT: *The scoreboard – 206 out of 371 in only 58 overs. (Ken Kelly)*

second time. The accuracy of Malcolm Nash and the penetration of Barnard were decisive factors.

Cowdrey continued with his run of fifties in limited-over cricket and there were glories for Gooch, inevitably, and Fowler, but the outstanding individual performance of the day was by Alvin Kallicharran. In 45 overs, he hit the first double century in limited-over cricket in England and he and David Smith added a record 197 for the 2nd wicket. Kallicharran hit four sixes and twenty-five fours and, after Oxfordshire had passed 100 for the loss of one wicket, he bowled his off-spin to take 6 for 32 in 12 overs. Warwickshire's score was the highest in a limited-over competition.

| | Byes | Leg-byes | Wides | No-balls | Total | Wkts |
|---|---|---|---|---|---|---|
| | | 3 | 2 | 1 | 256 | 3 |
| | | 9 | 5 | 1 | 231 | 7 |
| | 1 | | 5 | 3 | 207 | 4 |
| | | 6 | 7 | 2 | 262 | 7 |
| | 1 | 10 | 1 | 7 | 327 | 6 |

**4, 5 and 6 July**

***at Lord's***

**Cambridge University** 271 for 7 dec (I.D. Burnley 86, M.N. Breddy 61, J.D. Carr 4 for 93) and 195 (I.D. Burnley 70, D.A. Thorne 5 for 39)
**Oxford University** 206 for 1 dec (A.J.T. Miller 128 not out, G.J. Toogood 52 not out) and 261 for 5 (G.J. Toogood 109, J.D. Carr 68)

*Oxford University won by 5 wickets*

After a dour first day, Oxford University breathed life into the match with some challenging batting, Miller, a left-hander of real class, and Toogood adding 148. Cambridge collapsed to Thorne on the last morning and Oxford had to make 261 in 220 minutes. The decisive batting came after tea when Carr and Toogood, who reached a maiden first-class hundred, added 102 in 43 minutes. Toogood's fine innings

## Cambridge University 1984
First Class Matches

| BATTING | v. Leicestershire (Cambridge) 18–20 April | | v. Essex (Cambridge) 21–24 April | | v. Hampshire (Cambridge) 25–27 April | | v. Sussex (Cambridge) 2–4 May | | v. Warwickshire (Cambridge) 9–11 May | | v. Glamorgan (Cambridge) 13–15 June | | v. Worcestershire (Worcester) 16–19 June | | v. Surrey (Banstead) 27–29 June | | v. Nottinghamshire (Trent Bridge) 30 June–3 July | | v. Oxford University (Lord's) 4–6 July | |
|---|---|---|---|---|---|---|---|---|---|---|---|---|---|---|---|---|---|---|---|---|---|---|
| C.R. Andrew | 14 | 7 | 6 | 9 | 13 | 26 | 51 | 38 | | | 10 | 20 | 1 | 19 | 6 | 6 | 48 | 101* | 0 | 30 |
| A.E. Lea | 4 | 0 | 119 | 11 | 20 | 38 | 11 | 5 | 12 | 10 | 3 | 2 | 61 | 7 | | | 11 | 32 | 39 | 10 |
| S.N. Siddiqi | 48 | 0 | | | 12 | 32 | 29 | 52 | 9 | 16 | 0 | 20 | | | | | 1 | 0 | | |
| M. Breddy | 35 | 19 | 36 | 46* | 15 | 2 | 9 | 8 | 5 | 35 | 5 | 1 | 3 | 6 | 5 | 28 | 0 | 3 | 61 | 17 |
| I.G. Peck | 2 | 2 | | | 0 | 49* | 9 | — | 23 | 12 | | | | | | | | | | |
| T.A. Cotterell | 0 | 9 | 10 | 41* | 16 | 25 | 0 | — | 29 | 3 | 0 | 14 | 19 | 11 | 4 | — | 52 | — | — | 14 |
| A.K. Golding | 4 | 6 | 0 | — | 4 | 16 | 29 | — | 14 | 18 | 0 | 5 | 44 | 39 | 10 | — | | | | |
| I.E.W. Sanders | 0 | 9 | | | | | | | | | | | | | | | | | | |
| S.G.P. Hewitt | 1* | 3* | 2* | — | 14* | 0 | | | | | | | | | | | | | | |
| P. Garlick | 2 | 0 | 0 | — | 0 | 0 | 0 | — | 0* | 0 | 0 | 0 | 1* | 0* | 0* | — | 6* | — | — | 4* |
| D.G. Price | — | — | | | | | | | 49 | 9 | 24 | 1 | 35 | 42 | 34 | 0 | 0 | — | 25 | 20 |
| G.F.H. McDonnell | | | 1 | 5 | 1 | 0 | | | | | | | | | | | | | | |
| N.P. Thomas | | | 0 | 0 | | | | | | | | | | | | | | | | |
| P.C. Richardson | | | 7 | — | | | | | | | | | | | | | | | | |
| A.J. Pollock | | | 32 | — | | | | | | | 30 | 6 | 3 | 1 | 11 | — | 1 | — | 4 | 9 |
| A.D.H. Grimes | | | | | 0 | 9 | 5* | — | 11 | 9* | 0 | 0 | 0 | 11 | 13 | — | | | — | 0 |
| P.G.P. Roebuck | | | | | | | 4 | 24* | | | | | 20 | 28 | 9 | 54* | 23 | 62 | 31 | 6 |
| A.G. Davies | | | | | | | 1 | 2* | 20 | 10 | 27* | 59* | 0 | 5 | 69 | 20* | 68 | 2 | 17* | 8 |
| T. Travers | | | | | | | | | 5 | 15 | | | | | | | | | | |
| I.D. Burnley | | | | | | | | | | | | | | | 17 | 21 | 12 | 26 | 86 | 70 |
| Byes | 1 | 3 | 2 | 3 | 3 | 4 | 5 | | | 8 | 4 | 7 | 7 | 17 | 3 | 10 | 1 | 5 | 3 | 1 |
| Leg-byes | 11 | 3 | 6 | 2 | 3 | 3 | 3 | 1 | 4 | 6 | 3 | 11 | 14 | 5 | 9 | 3 | 8 | 9 | 5 | 6 |
| Wides | 1 | | | | | 1 | | 1 | | | 5 | | 1 | 1 | 10 | 3 | 2 | 1 | | |
| No-balls | 4 | 4 | 1 | 1 | 5 | 2 | | 1 | | | 8 | 9 | 8 | 4 | 1 | 17 | 4 | 4 | | |
| Total | 127 | 65 | 222 | 118 | 106 | 207 | 156 | 132 | 181 | 151 | 119 | 155 | 217 | 196 | 201 | 162 | 237 | 245 | 271 | 195 |
| Wickets | 9† | 9 | 10 | 4 | 10 | 10 | 10 | 4 | 10 | 10 | 10 | 10 | 10 | 10 | 10 | 4 | 10 | 6 | 7 | 10 |
| Result | L | | D | | L | | D | | L | | L | | L | | D | | L | | L | |

*Catches* 11 – A.G. Davies (ct 9/st 2)
4 – S.G.P. Hewitt (ct 3/st 1)
3 – A.J. Pollock, D.G. Price and T.A. Cotterell
2 – A.E. Lea, I.G. Peck, A.K. Golding, M. Breddy, C.R. Andrew, A.D.H. Grimes and P.G.P. Roebuck
1 – N.P. Thomas, I.D. Burnley, S.N. Siddiqi and P. Garlick

†D.G. Price absent hurt

| BOWLING | I.E.W. Sanders | P. Garlick | A.K. Golding | T.A. Cotterell | C.R. Andrew | A.E. Lea | A.J. Pollock | P.C. Richardson | A.D.H. Grimes |
|---|---|---|---|---|---|---|---|---|---|
| v. Leicestershire (Cambridge) | 22–5–78–2 | 12–2–55–0 | 16–1–82–1 | 15–2–47–0 | 27–6–77–3 | | | | |
| 18–20 April | 3–0–15–1 | 16–0–70–0 | 24–2–105–0 | 37–5–106–2 | 5–0–30–0 | 4–0–25–0 | | | |
| v. Essex (Cambridge) | | 13–2–65–0 | 14–0–96–0 | 14–1–95–1 | | 2–1–10–0 | 30–8–95–2 | 18–0–92–1 | |
| 21–24 April | | 10–1–65–0 | 8–0–48–1 | 14–0–63–2 | | | 8–0–47–0 | 3–0–30–0 | |
| v. Hampshire (Cambridge) | | 16.3–3–77–2 | 25–5–120–0 | 26–2–98–0 | 9–1–56–0 | | | | 12–1–77–0 |
| 25–27 April | | 9–3–26–0 | 25–4–77–1 | 18–3–43–2 | 7–0–42–0 | | | | 8–0–28–0 |
| v. Sussex (Cambridge) | | 20–0–110–1 | 19–1–75–1 | 33–7–95–3 | 8–0–32–0 | | | | 5–0–34–0 |
| 2–4 May | | 14–2–69–2 | | | 2–0–16–0 | | | | 15–3–55–0 |
| v. Warwickshire (Cambridge) | | 23–3–104–1 | 26.1–3–100–2 | 9–0–45–0 | | | | | 17–5–24–1 |
| 9–11 May | | | | | | | | | |
| v. Glamorgan | | 16–3–47–1 | 10–1–44–0 | 15–4–41–0 | 13–1–56–1 | | 12.4–1–62–0 | | 18–5–48–1 |
| 13–15 June | | 8–0–26–0 | 6–0–16–0 | 7–0–27–1 | 12–5–30–0 | 3–1–15–0 | 11–3–36–0 | | 5–1–8–0 |
| v. Worcestershire (Worcester) | | 25–4–87–1 | 12–0–59–0 | 26–2–83–1 | 8–0–33–0 | | 14.1–2–54–3 | | 15–2–58–0 |
| 16–19 June | | 1.3–0–11–0 | | | | | | | 2–0–10–0 |
| v. Surrey (Banstead) | | 28–6–97–2 | | 17–4–56–0 | 9–0–31–0 | | 29–6–104–4 | | 14–2–51–1 |
| 27–29 June | | | | | | | | | |
| v. Nottinghamshire (Trent Bridge) | | 14–0–76–0 | | 23.4–6–60–1 | 10–4–21–0 | 8–3–27–2 | 20–5–66–2 | | |
| 30 June–3 July | | 6–0–44–0 | | 13–1–82–0 | 8–0–31–0 | | 15.3–3–64–2 | | |
| v. Oxford University (Lord's) | | 12–0–46–1 | | 14–5–48–0 | 20.1–6–38–0 | 2–0–15–0 | 10–2–32–0 | | 6–1–21–0 |
| 4–6 July | | 9–2–17–1 | | 12–0–85–0 | 20.2–2–75–2 | | 11–2–60–1 | | 6–2–13–0 |
| | 25–5–93–3 *av.* 31.00 | 253–31–1092–12 *av.* 91.00 | 185.1–17–822–6 *av.* 137.00 | 293.4–42–1074–13 *av.* 82.61 | 158.3–25–568–6 *av.* 94.66 | 19–5–92–2 *av.* 46.00 | 161.2–32–620–14 *av.* 44.28 | 21–0–122–1 *av.* 122.00 | 123–22–427–3 *av.* 142.33 |

| | M | Inns | NOs | Runs | H/S | Av |
|---|---|---|---|---|---|---|
| | 9 | 18 | 1 | 405 | 101* | 23.82 |
| | 9 | 18 | | 395 | 119 | 21.94 |
| | 6 | 12 | | 219 | 52 | 18.25 |
| | 10 | 20 | 1 | 339 | 61 | 17.84 |
| | 4 | 7 | 1 | 97 | 49* | 16.16 |
| | 10 | 16 | 1 | 247 | 52 | 16.46 |
| | 8 | 13 | | 189 | 44 | 14.53 |
| | 1 | 2 | | 9 | 9 | 4.50 |
| | 3 | 5 | 4 | 20 | 14* | 20.00 |
| | 10 | 15 | 6 | 13 | 6* | 1.44 |
| | 7 | 11 | | 239 | 49 | 21.72 |
| | 2 | 4 | | 7 | 5 | 1.75 |
| | 1 | 2 | | 0 | 0 | 0.00 |
| | 1 | 1 | | 7 | 7 | 7.00 |
| | 6 | 9 | | 97 | 32 | 10.77 |
| | 7 | 11 | 2 | 58 | 13 | 6.44 |
| | 5 | 10 | 2 | 261 | 62 | 32.62 |
| | 7 | 14 | 5 | 308 | 69 | 34.22 |
| | 1 | 2 | | 20 | 15 | 10.00 |
| | 3 | 6 | | 232 | 86 | 38.66 |

| S.N. Siddigi | Byes | Leg-byes | Wides | No-balls | Total | Wkts |
|---|---|---|---|---|---|---|
| | 7 | 1 | | 6 | 353 | 6 |
| | 2 | 3 | | 5 | 361 | 3 |
| | 7 | | 1 | 2 | 463 | 4 |
| | 1 | | | 5 | 259 | 3 |
| | 6 | 7 | | 7 | 448 | 3 |
| | 1 | 5 | | 4 | 226 | 3 |
| | 1 | 3 | | 9 | 359 | 5 |
| | | 1 | | | 141 | 2 |
| 23–6–90–5 | 4 | 2 | 1 | | 370 | 9 |
| | 8 | 3 | 8 | 1 | 318 | 4 |
| | 1 | 3 | 2 | | 164 | 1 |
| | 4 | 8 | 4 | 5 | 395 | 5 |
| | | | | | 21 | 0 |
| | 4 | 14 | 4 | | 361 | 7 |
| | | 3 | 3 | | 256 | 5 |
| | 1 | 3 | 2 | | 227 | 3 |
| | | 5 | | 1 | 206 | 1 |
| | 1 | 8 | 2 | | 261 | 5 |
| 23–6–<br>90–5<br>*av.* 18.00 | | | | | | |

*Bowler turned batsman, Dallas Moir, a ferocious maiden century for Derbyshire* v. *Warwickshire at Chesterfield, 9 July. (George Herringshaw)*

was ended by Pollock, but Hayes, with two sixes, and the stylish Bristowe took Oxford to victory with 5 overs to spare, their first win at Lord's for 8 years.

### *5 and 6 July*

#### *at Colwyn Bay*

**West Indians** 401 (C.G. Greenidge 93, P.J. Dujon 71, E.A.E. Baptiste 65, C.H. Lloyd 59) and 275 for 2 dec (R.B. Richardson 149, T.R.O. Payne 71 not out)
**League Cricket Conference** 136 (R.A. Harper 4 for 23) and 76 for 8 (C.A. Walsh 6 for 26)

*Match drawn*

### *7, 8 and 9 July*

#### *at Leicester*

**Leicestershire** 283 (I.P. Butcher 118, P.B. Clift 54) and 136 for 5
**West Indians** 506 for 5 dec (H.A. Gomes 143, A.L. Logie 141, C.G. Greenidge 56 not out, D.L. Haynes 50, P.B. Clift 4 for 120)

*Match drawn*

### *7, 9 and 10 July*

#### *at Chesterfield*

**Warwickshire** 444 for 8 dec (G.W. Humpage 205, D.L. Amiss 86) and 279 for 6 dec (A.I. Kallicharran 87, D.L. Amiss 55 not out, R.I.H.B. Dyer 53)
**Derbyshire** 432 for 8 dec (A. Hill 125, D.G. Moir 107, G. Miller 79) and 142 for 5

*Match drawn*
*Derbyshire 6 pts, Warwickshire 6 pts*

#### *at Southend*

**Essex** 141 (C. Gladwin 60, W.W. Davis 5 for 57, M.W.W. Selvey 4 for 40) and 241 for 5 (D.E. East 81, C. Gladwin 59)
**Glamorgan** 333 for 7 dec (A.L. Jones 114)

*Match drawn*
*Glamorgan 8 pts, Essex 3 pts*

**Oxford University 1984**
First Class Matches

| BATTING | v. Nottinghamshire (Oxford) 21–24 April | | v. Glamorgan (Oxford) 25–27 April | | v. Lancashire (Oxford) 28 April–1 May | | v. Somerset (Oxford) 2–4 May | | v. Middlesex (Oxford) 9–11 May | | v. Gloucestershire (Oxford) 30 May–1 June | | v. Kent (Oxford) 16–19 June | | v. Cambridge Univ. (Lord's) 4–6 July | | *M* | *Inns* | *NOs* | *Runs* | *H/S* | *Av* |
|---|---|---|---|---|---|---|---|---|---|---|---|---|---|---|---|---|---|---|---|---|---|---|
| A.J.T. Miller | 21 | 17 | 2 | 15 | 1 | 7 | 0 | 0 | | | | | | | 128* | 5 | 5 | 10 | 1 | 196 | 128* | 21.77 |
| R.M. Edbrooke | 9 | 37 | 33 | 17 | 31 | 58 | 7 | 22 | 66 | 2 | 1 | 19* | 42 | 41 | 20 | 15 | 8 | 16 | 1 | 420 | 66 | 28.00 |
| K.A. Hayes | 0 | 0 | 20 | 4 | 1 | 37 | 0 | 36 | 5 | 0 | 36 | — | 9 | 11 | — | 35* | 8 | 14 | 1 | 194 | 37 | 14.92 |
| G.J. Toogood | 17 | 37 | 39 | 2 | 14 | 0 | 28 | 30 | 68 | 4 | 3 | — | 22 | 0 | 52* | 109 | 8 | 15 | 1 | 425 | 109 | 30.35 |
| D.A. Thorne | 0 | 5 | 33 | 5 | 0 | 10 | 2 | 37 | 43 | 13* | 0 | — | 17 | 69* | — | 3 | 8 | 14 | 2 | 237 | 69* | 19.75 |
| J.D. Carr | 64 | 35 | | | 10 | 123 | 15 | 100 | 12 | 4 | 1 | — | 35 | 1 | — | 68 | 7 | 12 | | 468 | 123 | 39.00 |
| J.G. Franks | 36 | 7* | 10 | 0 | 11 | 4 | 28 | 0 | 42* | 5 | 0 | — | 0 | 27 | — | — | 8 | 13 | 2 | 170 | 42* | 15.45 |
| M.R. Cullinan | 6 | 2 | 0 | 51 | 1 | 13 | 59 | 8 | 0 | 4 | | | 0 | 11 | — | — | 7 | 12 | | 155 | 59 | 12.91 |
| H.T. Rawlinson | 0 | 0 | 8 | 1 | | | | | | | | | 19* | 7 | — | — | 4 | 6 | 1 | 35 | 19* | 7.00 |
| J.R. Turnbull | 0 | 3 | 0 | 1 | | | 2* | 0* | | | 0* | — | 6 | 0 | | | 5 | 9 | 3 | 12 | 6 | 2.00 |
| M.P. Lawrence | 0* | 14 | 0* | 17* | 0 | 3 | 1 | 2 | — | — | 10 | — | 0 | 2 | — | — | 8 | 11 | 3 | 49 | 17* | 6.12 |
| W. Bristowe | | | 7 | 5 | | | | | — | 8* | 13 | 30* | 26 | 0 | — | 15* | 5 | 8 | 3 | 104 | 30* | 20.80 |
| S. Hewitt | | | | | 12 | 16* | 22 | 4 | 2 | — | 4 | — | | | | | 4 | 6 | 1 | 60 | 22 | 12.00 |
| J. Brettel | | | | | 0* | 0 | | | | | | | | | | | 1 | 2 | 1 | 0 | 0* | 0.00 |
| M.D. Petchey | | | | | | | | | — | — | | | | | | | 1 | — | | | | — |
| A.A.G. Mee | | | | | | | | | | | 2 | — | | | | | 1 | 1 | | 2 | 2 | 2.00 |
| Byes | | 4 | | 4 | 2 | 7 | 2 | | 1 | 4 | 1 | | | 4 | | 1 | | | | | | |
| Leg-byes | | 2 | 8 | 1 | 5 | 2 | 3 | 1 | 6 | 3 | | | 4 | 3 | 5 | 8 | | | | | | |
| Wides | | | 3 | | 1 | 5 | | | 1 | 1 | | | | 1 | | 2 | | | | | | |
| No-balls | 1 | | | 3 | 1 | 5 | 2 | 1 | 11 | 7 | 1 | 2 | 4 | 1 | 1 | | | | | | | |
| Total | 154 | 163 | 163 | 126 | 90 | 290 | 171 | 241 | 257 | 55 | 72 | 51 | 184 | 178 | 206 | 261 | | | | | | |
| Wickets | 10 | 10 | 10 | 10 | 10 | 10 | 10 | 10 | 7 | 6 | 10 | 0 | 10 | 10 | 1 | 5 | | | | | | |
| Result | L | | L | | L | | L | | D | | D | | L | | W | | | | | | | |
| Points | — | | — | | — | | — | | — | | — | | — | | — | | | | | | | |

*Catches*

9 – J.G. Franks (ct 8/st 1) and J.D. Carr
6 – D.A. Thorne
4 – K.A. Hayes, M.P. Lawrence and R.M. Edbrooke
3 – M.R. Cullinan (ct 2/st 1) and G.J. Toogood
2 – W. Bristowe, J.R. Turnbull and H.T. Rawlinson
1 – J. Brettel, A.J.T. Miller and A.A.G. Mee

| BOWLING | D.A. Thorne | J.R. Turnbull | H.T. Rawlinson | J.D. Carr | M.P. Lawrence | K.A. Hayes | G.J. Toogood | S.G.P. Hewitt | M. Brettel |
|---|---|---|---|---|---|---|---|---|---|
| v. Nottinghamshire (Oxford) | 22–2–79–2 | 10–1–41–0 | 8–2–33–0 | 16–5–47–0 | 31–2–94–2 | 15–3–51–2 | | | |
| 21–24 April | 10–1–41–0 | 3–0–28–0 | 14–1–64–0 | 2–0–5–0 | 13–2–47–0 | 6–1–23–0 | | | |
| v. Glamorgan (Oxford) | 37–2–81–4 | 11–3–35–1 | 33.5–4–114–3 | | 17–5–55–1 | 6–2–9–0 | 1–1–0–0 | | |
| 25–27 April | 18–4–56–1 | 5–0–18–0 | 14–4–47–0 | | 13–0–43–1 | | 6–2–15–0 | | |
| v. Lancashire (Oxford) | 13–3–32–1 | | | 55–15–155–5 | 40–10–137–0 | | 10–1–52–0 | 13–1–27–0 | 15–3–74–1 |
| 28 April–1 May | | | | | | | | | |
| v. Somerset (Oxford) | | 23–6–78–1 | | 34–5–115–0 | 18–0–77–0 | | 8–1–32–0 | 11–2–53–0 | |
| 2–4 May | | 9–0–53–1 | | 9–0–28–1 | 18–4–57–1 | | 7–0–27–0 | 3–0–6–0 | |
| v. Middlesex (Oxford) | 6–2–12–0 | | | 28–9–79–1 | 25–1–100–0 | | 3–0–23–0 | 12.5–1–64–1 | |
| 9–11 May | | | | 11.4–3–35–0 | 8–1–26–0 | 7–2–16–0 | | 18–4–52–2 | |
| v. Gloucestershire (Oxford) | 13–2–25–0 | 7–1–23–0 | | 28.2–12–57–5 | 13–6–29–2 | 10–4–19–2 | | | |
| 30 May–1 June | 11–1–45–0 | 10–3–34–0 | | 24–4–74–0 | 12–2–38–1 | | 9.5–0–30–1 | 7–0–30–1 | |
| v. Kent (Oxford) | 21–4–86–1 | 13–4–44–0 | 15–3–53–0 | 36–14–75–0 | 31.5–11–79–3 | 24–8–58–4 | 5–1–15–1 | | |
| 16–19 June | | | | | | | | | |
| v. Cambridge University | 23–8–60–1 | | 6–3–14–0 | 34–6–93–4 | 31.2–10–62–1 | 12–5–33–0 | 1–0–1–1 | | |
| (Lord's) 4–6 July | 26.1–12–39–5 | | 5–1–21–1 | 35–16–49–2 | 17–7–25–1 | 15–3–50–1 | 4–3–4–0 | | |
| | 200.1–41–556–15 *av.* 37.06 | 91–18–354–3 *av.* 118.00 | 95.5–18–346–4 *av.* 86.50 | 313–89–812–18 *av.* 45.11 | 291.1–61–869–13 *av.* 66.84 | 95–28–259–9 *av.* 28.77 | 54.5–9–199–3 *av.* 66.33 | 64.5–8–232–4 *av.* 58.00 | 15–3–74–1 *av.* 74.00 |

### at Maidstone

**Lancashire** 404 for 4 dec (G. Fowler 226, J.A. Ormrod 73) and 0 for 0 dec
**Kent** 74 for 1 dec and 279 for 8 (N.R. Taylor 108, C.J. Tavare 79, J. Simmons 5 for 59)

*Match drawn*
*Lancashire 4 pts, Kent 1 pt*

### at Uxbridge

**Worcestershire** 321 (P.A. Neale 77, P.H. Edmonds 4 for 101) and 211 (D.N. Patel 82, D.B. D'Oliveira 50)
**Middlesex** 377 (M.W. Gatting 104, W.N. Slack 100, R.O. Butcher 64, C.T. Radley 59, A.P. Pridgeon 5 for 50, R.M. Ellcock 4 for 69) and 156 for 3 (C.T. Radley 57 not out)

*Middlesex won by 7 wickets*
*Middlesex 24 pts, Worcestershire 5 pts*

### at Northampton

**Northamptonshire** 322 (R.J. Bailey 82, D.S. Steele 66 not out, D. Ripley 61, D.J. Thomas 5 for 63) and 230 for 6 dec (W. Larkins 89, R.J. Boyd-Moss 86)
**Surrey** 304 for 5 dec (G.P. Howarth 113, R.D.V. Knight 50) and 261 (A.R. Butcher 63, M.A. Lynch 53

*Northamptonshire won by 7 runs*
*Northamptonshire 22 pts, Surrey 8 pts*

### at Trent Bridge

**Nottinghamshire** 233 (R.T. Robinson 59, D.W. Randall 53) and 242 for 5 dec (D.W. Randall 110 not out, R.J. Hadlee 67)
**Sussex** 161 (P.M. Such 4 for 34, R.J. Hadlee 4 for 41) and 172 (P.W.G. Parker 56 not out, A.P. Wells 54, R.J. Hadlee 4 for 6)

*Nottinghamshire won by 142 runs*
*Nottinghamshire 22 pts, Sussex 5 pts*

### at Taunton

**Somerset** 397 for 4 dec (P.M. Roebuck 101, I.T. Botham 87, J.W. Lloyds 61 not out, N.A. Felton 58, M.D. Crowe 51 not out)
**Hampshire** 244 (J.J.E. Hardy 94 not out, M.C.J. Nicholas 53, M.R. Davis 6 for 83) and 166 for 8 (R.J. Parks 53 not out)

*Match drawn*
*Somerset 8 pts, Hampshire 3 pts*

### at Bradford

**Gloucestershire** 381 for 5 dec (P.W. Romaines 120, J.N. Shepherd 76 not out, A.W. Stovold 54, C.W.J. Athey 52) and 226 for 5 dec (C.W.J. Athey 114 not out)
**Yorkshire** 328 for 3 dec (R.G. Lumb 165 not out, S.N. Hartley 104 not out) and 281 for 2 (G. Boycott 126 not out, K. Sharp 95)

*Yorkshire won by 8 wickets*
*Yorkshire 21 pts, Gloucestershire 5 pts*

After a week of terrible traumas Yorkshire showed signs of rehabilitation with a fine win at Bradford. They toiled on the Saturday as Paul Romaines, who should be on the England selectors' list, led the Gloucestershire charge, but Lumb, with a career best 165, and Hartley added 247 in 65 overs for the fourth wicket to keep Yorkshire in the match. Athey then chose to make his first century for Gloucestershire, against his old county, and Graveney asked Yorkshire to make 280 in 53 overs. Boycott and Sharp had a magnificent stand of 195 in 32 overs for the second wicket and sealed the match, victory coming with 17 balls to spare.

Ian Butcher hit a welcome century against the West Indians who then plundered runs themselves before settling for a draw in face of mounting injuries. There was a draw too at Taunton where Hardy made a career best for Hampshire but could not help save the follow-on. Eventual salvation came from a dogged eighth wicket stand by Parks and Tremlett.

Graeme Fowler, enjoying a golden spell, hit the first double century of his career, but rain marred the match at Maidstone and although Taylor and Tavare made a spirited effort to take Kent to 331 in 97 overs, Jack Simmons broke through and the home side were happy to save the game. The same applied to Essex who, grumbling about the perfect wicket at Southend, managed to get out for 141 after being 84 for 0. They batted disgracefully against some good seam bowling by Selvey and Davis and after Jones' century, a habit he had quickly acquired since tasting success, Essex were happy to lose the second day's play and draw.

Middlesex won their first match since May Day. Gatting hit his usual century on being dropped from the England

| A.J.T. Miller | M.D. Petchey | M.R. Cullinan | *Byes* | *Leg-byes* | *Wides* | *No-balls* | *Total* | *Wkts* |
|---|---|---|---|---|---|---|---|---|
| | | | 5 | 2 | 3 | | 355 | 6 |
| | | | | 11 | | 1 | 220 | 0 |
| | | | 2 | 3 | 2 | | 301 | 9 |
| | | | 4 | 10 | | | 193 | 2 |
| | | | 14 | 4 | | | 495 | 7 |
| | | | | | | | | |
| | | | 4 | 6 | | | 365 | 1 |
| 1–0–4–1 | | | 6 | 5 | | | 186 | 4 |
| | 25–6–65–4 | | 1 | 9 | 3 | 3 | 359 | 6 |
| | 9–1–17–0 | | 1 | 1 | | 2 | 150 | 2 |
| | | | 8 | 1 | | | 162 | 10 |
| | | | 1 | 3 | | | 255 | 3 |
| | | 2–1–4–1 | | 3 | 1 | 1 | 419 | 10 |
| | | | | | | | | |
| | | | 3 | 5 | | | 271 | 7 |
| | | | 1 | 6 | | | 195 | 10 |
| 1–0–4–1 *av.* 4.00 | 34–7–82–4 *av.* 20.50 | 2–1–4–1 *av.* 4.00 | | | | | | |

Cricket at Grace Road, Leicester. (David Munden)

team, the last 7 Worcestershire second innings wickets fell for 31 and Middlesex, needing 156 in 46 overs, won with 6 overs to spare. In a spirited and sporting game at Northampton, Surrey, pursuing 269 in 48 overs, were beaten with 3 balls to spare after Howarth and Butcher had begun the chase with 92 in 18 overs. Ripley had a career best and three stumpings in a fine match.

Geoff Humpage appeared to have hammered Warwickshire to a commanding position at Chesterfield, but on the Monday, Alan Hill, enjoying a season of great consistency, and Dallas Moir added 150 in 24 overs for the seventh wicket to bring Derbyshire to equality. Moir's maiden hundred came in 95 minutes and, in a violent assault on the bowling, he hit six sixes and twelve fours. With such heavy scoring, there was little chance of a result, particularly as Barnett was injured and Derbyshire slipped to 17 for 4 at the second attempt.

Notts moved closer to the top with a relentless win over Sussex. It was the panache of Randall and Hadlee which set up the victory and, ultimately, the devastating bowling of the incomparable New Zealander.

### John Player League

*8 July*

---

*at Derby*

**Derbyshire** 240 for 9 (G. Miller 71 not out, K.J. Barnett 55, G.C. Small 5 for 57)
**Warwickshire** 206 (G. Miller 4 for 32, B. Roberts 4 for 49)

*Derbyshire (4 pts) won by 34 runs*

*at Southend*

**Essex** 262 for 4 (K.W.R. Fletcher 84 not out, K.S. McEwan 59)
**Glamorgan** 171 for 8 (H. Morris 55 not out, N. Phillip 4 for 20)

*Essex (4 pts) won by 91 runs*

*at Maidstone*

**Kent** 200 (C.S. Cowdrey 75)
**Lancashire** 194 (D.P. Hughes 92, T.M. Alderman 5 for 36)

*Kent (4 pts) won by 6 wickets*

*at Lord's*

**Worcestershire** 188 for 8
**Middlesex** 118

*Worcestershire (4 pts) won by 70 runs*

*at Northampton*

**Surrey** 262 for 7 (M.A. Lynch 103, A.R. Butcher 64)
**Northamptonshire** 288 for 8 (W. Larkins 64)

*Surrey (4 pts) won by 34 runs*

*at Trent Bridge*

**Sussex** 156 for 9
**Nottinghamshire** 157 for 4

*Nottinghamshire (4 pts) won by 6 wickets*

*at Scarborough*

**Gloucestershire** 228 for 6 (A.W. Stovold 62, P.W. Jarvis 4 for 45)
**Yorkshire** 229 for 3 (A.A. Metcalfe 115 not out, K. Sharp 61)

*Yorkshire (4 pts) won by 7 wickets*

With Gooch back in the side Essex overwhelmed Glamorgan and with Middlesex crumbling to Worcestershire they moved

*Richard Lumb (Yorkshire) – centuries in successive matches including a career best 165 not out v. Gloucestershire, 9 July and then he announced his retirement. (Sporting Pictures (UK) Ltd)*

to two points behind the leaders with two games in hand. Lynch hit 103 off 66 balls and added 105 with Allan Butcher to maintain Surrey's challenge and Nottinghamshire also kept in touch with an easy win over Sussex.

Lancashire slipped when Alderman thwarted them and David Hughes, in particular, with two balls remaining. Miller had a fine all-round game in Derbyshire's success and Metcalfe, who hit a glorious maiden Sunday league hundred, and Sharp put on 141 in 26 overs for Yorkshire's second wicket in the victory over Gloucestershire in a game that was marred by racialist taunts.

*11, 12 and 13 July*

---

*at Southend*

**Essex** 322 (P.J. Prichard 68, G.A. Gooch 64, J. Simmons 6 for 51)
**Lancashire** 76 (J.K. Lever 6 for 26, N.A. Foster 4 for 30) and 200 (N.H. Fairbrother 61, J.K. Lever 4 for 55)

*Essex won by an innings and 46 runs*
*Essex 24 pts, Lancashire 4 pts*

*at Cardiff*

**Yorkshire** 415 for 9 dec (R.G. Lumb 144, K. Sharp 132, R.C. Ontong 4 for 101) and 262 for 4 dec (G. Boycott 101 not out, K. Sharp 62)

*Hugh Morris (Glamorgan), a young player of rich talent. A maiden century v. Yorkshire at Cardiff, 12 July. (Sporting Pictures (UK) Ltd)*

**Glamorgan** 357 for 9 dec (H. Morris 114 not out, R.C. Ontong 70, S.J. Dennis 5 for 124) and 92 for 0

*Match drawn*
*Glamorgan 7 pts, Yorkshire 6 pts*

***at Southampton***

**Hampshire** 194 (J.J.E. Hardy 55, B.J. Griffiths 5 for 63) and 201 for 3 dec (T.E. Jesty 86 not out, J.J.E. Hardy 64 not out)
**Northamptonshire** 135 for 4 dec (G. Cook 50) and 264 for 8 (W. Larkins 82)

*Northamptonshire won by 2 wickets*
*Northamptonshire 20 pts, Hampshire 2 pts*

***at Maidstone***

**Kent** 279 (D.G. Aslett 55, C.S. Cowdrey 54, G. Miller 4 for 61) and 152 (G. Miller 4 for 22)
**Derbyshire** 251 for 5 dec (K.J. Barnett 84, W.P. Fowler 60 not out) and 127 (D.L. Underwood 4 for 25)

*Kent won by 53 runs*
*Kent 21 pts, Derbyshire 7 pts*

***at Leicester***

**Sussex** 240 (G.J. Parsons 5 for 46) and 250 for 7 dec (A.P. Wells 105 not out, G.J. Parsons 4 for 59)
**Leicestershire** 115 (D.A. Reeve 4 for 39) and 258 for 8 (I.P. Butcher 102, C.E. Waller 6 for 75)

*Match drawn*
*Sussex 6 pts, Leicestershire 4 pts*

***at Uxbridge***

**Middlesex** 307 (C.P. Metson 96, M.W. Gatting 55, P. Bainbridge 4 for 76) and 176 for 4 dec (R.O. Butcher 56 not out)
**Gloucestershire** 251 for 9 dec (J.N. Shepherd 87, N.F. Williams 4 for 72) and 222 for 7 (J.N. Shepherd 56 not out, J.E. Emburey 4 for 55)

*Match drawn*
*Middlesex 8 pts, Gloucestershire 7 pts*

***at Trent Bridge***

**Somerset** 249 (J.W. Lloyds 63, V.J. Marks 55, R.J. Hadlee 4 for 45) and 282 for 3 dec (M.D. Crowe 74, N.F.M. Popplewell 62 retired hurt, N.A. Felton 61)
**Nottinghamshire** 203 (C.E.B. Rice 61, V.J. Marks 4 for 41) and 202 for 5 (C.E.B. Rice 80)

*Match drawn*
*Somerset 6 pts, Nottinghamshire 5 pts*

***at Worcester***

**Warwickshire** 252 (C.M. Old 70, P.J. Newport 5 for 51) and 223 for 4 (D.L. Amiss 101 not out, R.I.H.B. Dyer 64)
**Worcestershire** 445 for 7 dec (R.N. Kapil Dev 94, D.B. d'Oliveira 74, P.A. Neale 86 not out, A.P. Pridgeon 67)

*Match drawn*
*Worcestershire 8 pts, Warwickshire 5 pts*

In spite of interruptions by rain, Essex routed Lancashire at Southchurch Park and moved to the top of the Brittanic Assurance County Championship. Put in to bat, they were given a good start by Gooch and Gladwin, and Paul Prichard later played with mature authority on a difficult wicket in difficult conditions. Lancashire, Simmons apart, bowled poorly although there was much to admire in the wicket-keeping of John Stanworth. The visitors batted even worse than they had bowled and Lever, in spite of a niggling injury, twice tore them apart so that Essex snatched victory on the last afternoon.

Both Notts and Leicestershire, the other main contenders, failed to win, indeed Leicestershire were indebted to a century from Ian Butcher for their salvation. The highlights of the match at Grace Road were some fine bowling from Gordon Parsons and hard-hit maiden century by the talented and eager Alan Wells. Notts batted poorly in a dour struggle with Somerset for whom Simon Turner kept wicket impressively in his second championship match.

Philip Newport had a career best bowling performance at New Road and Paul Pridgeon, batting as night-watchman, hit the first fifty of his career. There was a flurry of runs from Neale, Kapil Dev and d'Oliveira, but, on the last day, the honours went to Dennis Amiss who hit the eighty-eighth century of his career, passed 1000 runs for the season, the twentieth time he had accomplished the feat, and moved into the top twenty of the most prolific scorers in first-class cricket.

Another century by Richard Lumb and a fine hundred by that forceful and classy player, Kevin Sharp, dominated the first day at Cardiff, but Hugh Morris hit a maiden century on the second day after which the game dragged to a meaningless draw. Morris is a stylish young player and his century emphasised the assessment that here is a batsman who could serve England well in the near future.

*Chris Broad is caught by Lloyd off Harper for 32. (Ken Kelly)*

In conditions of more help to bowlers than batsmen, Derbyshire had a glimpse of victory at Maidstone, but 181 turned out to be too great a target. Alan Hill carried his bat for 48 while Underwood and Alderman reaped a harvest of wickets and grabbed victory for Kent.

Gloucestershire, another side in search of comfort, had Middlesex reeling at 119 for 7, but reserve wicket-keeper Colin Metson played the best innings of his first-class career and in stands of 94 with Williams and 74 with Hughes, he lifted Middlesex to 4 batting points. In reply, Gloucestershire struggled to 84 for 6, but they were rescued by Shepherd's onslaught and Trembath's perseverance. Eventually, Gatting asked the visitors to make 233 in 45 overs and Shepherd's fierce hitting nearly brought a brave and unexpected victory after Zaheer's earlier sluggishness.

The most exciting events were at Southampton where Northants won on the last ball of the match. On the first day Griffiths and Wild bowled out Hampshire and Northants moved to 123 for 1 at which point Cowley took 3 wickets without conceding a run. There was no play on the second day and Northants declared at the beginning of the last day. Hampshire went for quick runs and Jesty hit Boyd-Moss for five sixes and a two in one over while he and Hardy, an impressive, determined left-hander, added 151 in 56 minutes of scintillating batting. Northants were left to make 261 in 48 overs. Larkins gave them an excellent foundation with an imperious 82. Boyd-Moss, having conceded 94 runs in 9 overs, was out first ball to stamp Friday the thirteenth indelibly on his memory, but firm batting from Wild, Williams, Steele and Ripley took Northants to the last over needing 6 to win. Alan Walker steered the last ball to the third man boundary to give Northants a gleeful victory.

**Third Cornhill Test Match**
**ENGLAND *v.* WEST INDIES**

For the first time since 1921 England lost the first three Tests of a five match series when West Indies gained victory at Headingley with depressing ease.

England omitted Cowans again and won the toss. Batting first, they suffered a tense and torrid opening which saw Fowler and Gower both lbw offering no shot. Terry, obviously nervous, flashed outside the off-stump once too often and was well taken at third slip by Harper. Broad batted doggedly and had seemed to have overcome the worst when he cut at Harper while unbalanced and was caught at slip by Lloyd. It appeared that England had gained an unlikely bonus when Marshall was forced to leave the field with a broken thumb. It was stated that he would take no further part in the match, but later events were to prove that a false presumption.

Lamb and Botham restored the England innings with some sensible batting and added 85 before Botham was caught down the leg-side. Downton showed courage until falling at slip shortly after Lamb had reached a fine hundred in $3\frac{1}{2}$ hours. It was by far his best innings for England, combining disciplined defence with the determination never to let the bowler take command.

He was out straight away on the second morning when the last four England wickets added only 33. England were heartened when Greenidge was caught at slip just before lunch and Haynes was bowled by Allott shortly after. The Lancashire bowler marked his return to Test cricket with a

*Michael Holding reaches 200 Test wickets* LEFT: *Alott is bowled – 198.* CENTRE: *Cook is bowled – 199.* RIGHT: *Pringle is caught at mid-wicket – Haynes, the catcher, offers his congratulations. (Ken Kelly)*

fine spell, accurate and hostile, and he captured Richards when the batsman hit lazily to mid-on.

Lloyd and Gomes added 70 before Lloyd was caught at silly point. Dujon looked elegant and ominous for an hour before he became the first of three Allott victims, and, in spite of some lusty blows by Holding, England ended the day happily. West Indies were 31 runs behind and had only 3 wickets standing, one of them the injured Marshall.

BELOW: *Larry Gomes, 104 not out, an innings of majestic calm.* RIGHT: *Michael Holding in violent mood – again. (Adrian Murrell)*

*Premature elation – Richards is caught by Pringle off Allott. (Ken Kelly)*

Their hopes were dashed the next morning when Holding continued his violent assault, particularly on Willis, and, with three sixes and five fours, hit 59 off 55 balls. At the other end was the ever watchful Gomes who accumulates runs almost unnoticed. He played with quiet charm and mature authority and while he lacks the flamboyant personality of those around him, he is the calm balance in the side and, arguably, the most vital member of the batting line up.

Garner was run out trying to give him the strike, but as the players prepared to leave the field Marshall emerged, his left wrist in plaster. Gomes responded to this brave support by driving Willis back over his head to reach a magnificent century. Marshall hit a one-handed four and then edged to slip to give Allott his sixth deserved wicket.

Marshall's part in the match was not finished. He opened the bowling and made a ball lift viciously so that Broad could only parry it to square-leg. Garner had Terry lbw, but Gower and Fowler, revealing the same strength of character he had shown at Lord's, batted defiantly to add 91. Gower fell to a perfectly pitched ball from Harper which turned and took the edge and Fowler was caught and bowled one-handed by Marshall who then had Lamb lbw so that 3 wickets had fallen for 3 runs. Botham batted with a sense of responsibility but just before the close he received a fierce away cutter from Garner and was caught behind.

On the Monday the last four England wickets fell in half an hour and by lunch West Indies were 74 for 0. After the break, Haynes, having been dropped at slip, was caught at extra cover and Greenidge was held at short-leg. This was the first time in ten Tests that West Indies had lost 2 wickets in their second innings. Gomes was dropped off Pringle by Gower at slip and Richards was missed second ball. For England it was a miserable, demoralizing end. For West Indies it was total triumph, with Gomes' memorable hundred and Marshall's heroic 7 for 53, his best figures in Test cricket while his left hand was in plaster.

ABOVE: *Malcolm Marshall one-handed. (Adrian Murrell)*
BELOW: *Gower is caught by Dujon off Harper and with him go England's hopes (Ken Kelly)*

*Allott is lbw to Marshall, one of Marshall's seven wickets, his best return in Test cricket. (Ken Kelly)*

## THIRD CORNHILL TEST MATCH – ENGLAND *v.* WEST INDIES
12, 13, 14 and 16 July 1984 at Headingley, Leeds

### ENGLAND

| | FIRST INNINGS | | SECOND INNINGS | |
|---|---|---|---|---|
| G. Fowler | lbw, b Garner | 10 | c and b Marshall | 50 |
| B.C. Broad | c Lloyd, b Harper | 32 | c Baptiste, b Marshall | 2 |
| V.P. Terry | c Harper, b Holding | 8 | lbw, b Garner | 1 |
| D.I. Gower† | lbw, b Garner | 2 | c Dujon, b Harper | 43 |
| A.J. Lamb | b Harper | 100 | lbw, b Marshall | 3 |
| I.T. Botham | c Dujon, b Baptiste | 45 | c Dujon, b Garner | 14 |
| P.R. Downton* | c Lloyd, b Harper | 17 | c Dujon, b Marshall | 27 |
| D.R. Pringle | c Haynes, b Holding | 19 | (9) lbw, b Marshall | 2 |
| P.J.W. Allott | b Holding | 3 | (10 lbw, b Marshall | 4 |
| N.G.B. Cook | b Holding | 1 | (8) c Lloyd, b Marshall | 0 |
| R.G.D. Willis | not out | 4 | not out | 5 |
| Extras | b 4, lb 7, nb 18 | 29 | lb 6, nb 2 | 8 |
| | | 270 | | 159 |

| | O | M | R | W | O | M | R | W |
|---|---|---|---|---|---|---|---|---|
| Garner | 30 | 11 | 73 | 2 | 16 | 7 | 37 | 2 |
| Marshall | 6 | 4 | 6 | — | 26 | 9 | 53 | 7 |
| Holding | 29.2 | 8 | 70 | 4 | 7 | 1 | 31 | — |
| Baptiste | 13 | 1 | 45 | 1 | | | | |
| Harper | 19 | 6 | 47 | 3 | 16 | 8 | 30 | 1 |

FALL OF WICKETS
1- 13, 2- 43, 3- 53, 4- 87, 5- 172, 6- 236, 7- 237, 8- 244, 9- 254
1- 10, 2- 13, 3- 104, 4- 106, 5- 107, 6- 135, 7- 138, 8- 140, 9- 146

### WEST INDIES

| | FIRST INNINGS | | SECOND INNINGS | |
|---|---|---|---|---|
| C.G. Greenidge | c Botham, b Willis | 10 | c Terry, b Cook | 49 |
| D.L. Haynes | b Allott | 18 | c Fowler, b Cook | 43 |
| H.A. Gomes | not out | 104 | not out | 2 |
| I.V.A. Richards | c Pringle, b Allott | 15 | not out | 22 |
| C.H. Lloyd† | c Gower, b Cook | 48 | | |
| P.J. Dujon* | lbw, b Allott | 26 | | |
| E.A.E. Baptiste | c Broad, b Allott | 0 | | |
| R.A. Harper | c Downton, b Allott | 0 | | |
| M.A. Holding | c Allott, b Willis | 59 | | |
| J. Garner | run out | 0 | | |
| M.D. Marshall | c Botham, b Allott | 4 | | |
| Extras | lb 3, nb 15 | 18 | lb 2, nb 13 | 15 |
| | | 302 | (for 2 wkts) | 131 |

| | O | M | R | W | O | M | R | W |
|---|---|---|---|---|---|---|---|---|
| Willis | 18 | — | 123 | 2 | 8 | 1 | 40 | — |
| Allott | 26.5 | 7 | 61 | 6 | 7 | 2 | 24 | — |
| Botham | 7 | — | 45 | — | | | | |
| Pringle | 13 | 3 | 26 | — | 8.3 | 2 | 25 | — |
| Cook | 9 | 1 | 29 | 1 | 9 | 2 | 27 | 2 |

FALL OF WICKETS
1- 16, 2- 43, 3- 78, 4- 148, 5- 201, 6- 206, 7- 206, 8- 288, 9- 290
1- 106, 2- 108

*Umpires:* D.J. Constant and D.G.L. Evans

**West Indies won by 8 wickets**

***14, 16 and 17 July***

***at Cardiff***

**Somerset** 187 (J.G. Thomas 5 for 56) and 295 (B.C. Rose 123, M.D. Crowe 74, J.G. Thomas 5 for 67)
**Glamorgan** 211 (R.C. Ontong 97, M.D. Crowe 4 for 37) and 272 for 8 (A.L. Jones 85, R.C. Ontong 72 not out, V.J. Marks 4 for 91)

*Glamorgan won by 2 wickets*
*Glamorgan 22 pts, Somerset 5 pts*

***at Bristol***

**Gloucestershire** 327 for 6 dec (P. Bainbridge 134 not out, A.W. Stovold 53) and 90 (J.K. Lever 8 for 37)
**Essex** 300 for 2 dec (C. Gladwin 94, K.S. McEwan 88 not out, K.W.R. Fletcher 69 not out) and 121 for 2

*Essex won by 8 wickets*
*Essex 22 pts, Gloucestershire 4 pts*

***at Portsmouth***

**Lancashire** 298 for 7 dec (J. Abrahams 67, D.W. Varey 61, J.A. Ormrod 51) and 277 for 1 dec (J.A. Ormrod 139 not out, S.J. O'Shaughnessy 103 not out)
**Hampshire** 300 for 8 dec (T.E. Jesty 131) and 279 for 2 (M.C.J. Nicholas 158, D.R. Turner 76 not out)

*Hampshire won by 8 wickets*
*Hampshire 22 pts, Lancashire 6 pts*

***at Lord's***

**Yorkshire** 121 (N.G. Cowans 4 for 25, N.F. Williams 4 for 58) and 203 (S.N. Hartley 54)
**Middlesex** 303 for 8 dec (M.W. Gatting 131 not out, R.O. Butcher 62, C. Shaw 4 for 68) and 22 for 1

*Middlesex won by 9 wickets*
*Middlesex 24 pts, Yorkshire 3 pts*

***at Northampton***

**Kent** 250 for 6 dec and 204 for 5 dec (N.R. Taylor 86 not out)
**Northamptonshire** 124 (T.M. Alderman 5 for 34, R.M. Ellison 4 for 22) and 330 (D.J. Wild 128, G. Cook 59, D.J. Capel 54)

*Match tied*
*Kent 15 pts, Northamptonshire 10 pts*

***at Trent Bridge***

**Worcestershire** 138 (R.A. Pick 4 for 52) and 178 (P.A. Neale 83, R.J. Hadlee 5 for 61)
**Nottinghamshire** 153 (R.N. Kapil Dev 5 for 57, A. P. Pridgeon 4 for 58) and 164 for 5 (D.W. Randall 70)

*Nottinghamshire won by 5 wickets*
*Nottinghamshire 21 pts, Worcestershire 4 pts*

***at the Oval***

**Surrey** 260 (G.S. Clinton 113 not out, P.G. Newman 7 for 104) and 266 for 4 dec (G.S. Clinton 67, A.J. Stewart 60 not out, M.A. Lynch 55)
**Derbyshire** 250 for 5 dec (W.P. Fowler 76 not out, A. Hill 71) and 201 (A. Hill 50, P.I. Pocock 5 for 43)

*Surrey won by 75 runs*
*Surrey 21 pts, Derbyshire 7 pts*

***at Edgbaston***

**Warwickshire** 227 for 8 dec (D.L. Amiss 94, P.A. Smith 57, C.E. Waller 4 for 72) and 173 for 5 dec (A.I. Kallicharran 83 not out)
**Sussex** 122 for 4 dec and 123 for 4

*Match drawn*
*Warwickshire 3 pts, Sussex 3 pts*

ABOVE: *J.G. Thomas – 10 for 123 in Glamorgan's win over Somerset, 14–17 July. (George Herringshaw)*

The Trent Bridge wicket came in for much criticism when 23 wickets fell on the Monday and Notts won in two days to go top of the Britannic Assurance County Championship for 24 hours. Pick bowled well on the Saturday when Banks alone offered serious resistance and Kapil Dev had three wickets in 4 balls on the Monday, but Neale, Randall and Rice were the only batsmen to surmount the uneven bounce.

Essex struggled on the first day after putting Gloucestershire in. Romaines dourly and then Bainbridge more aggressively took the home side to a good score, but ferocious Essex batting on the second day claimed full batting points. Gladwin passed his thousand runs for the season, his first full one, and looked set for a maiden championship hundred when he pulled Graveney's first delivery into the hands of mid-wicket. Fletcher declared in arrears, but five Gloucestershire wickets had gone down before the close for 59 runs and John Lever, with career best bowling figures, completed the rout next day as Essex moved to a most impressive victory.

Middlesex overcame the loss of the first day's play to beat Yorkshire late on the last day. Hartley and Carrick offered stubborn resistance, but the innings fell apart after tea. Bairstow, hit in the face in the first innings, was unable to bat. Gatting again batted splendidly for his county and made one sigh for him to repeat this form at Test level.

Warwickshire and Sussex could conjure no magic for a rain-marred game at Edgbaston, but Surrey, inspired by the reliable Clinton, recovered from 103 for 7 to beat Derbyshire for whom Newman awakened memories of what was once prophesied for him. Pat Pocock's spin was the ultimate factor in giving Surrey victory.

Glamorgan beat Somerset for the first time in fourteen years in a thrilling finish at Cardiff. Ontong's determined innings had given Glamorgan first innings advantage, but Rose and Crowe took Somerset from 31 for 3 to 176 before both fell to Ontong. Greg Thomas had innings and match career best figures and the home side were left to make 272 in 67 overs. They collapsed from 135 for 1, but Ontong's determination took them to victory with 7 balls to spare.

In a match notable for the weaknesses of the attacks, Hampshire hit 276 in 51.3 overs to beat Lancashire. Nicholas and Turner batted flamboyantly to take their side to victory and Jesty had scored a lively century in the first innings. Ormrod, who hit his first hundred for Lancashire, and O'Shaughnessy, maturing into a fine all-rounder, added 214 in 114 minutes for Lancashire's second wicket in the second innings.

Kent seemed to be well on top when they asked Northants to make 331 in 80 overs, but Duncan Wild chose this moment to make a brave and quite magnificent maiden century. He hit a six and nineteen fours and he and David Capel added 117 for the fourth wicket. It was hard to maintain the momentum and when Griffiths, the number eleven of number elevens, joined Walker, 17 were needed in $2\frac{1}{2}$ overs. They scrambled and scurried and Griffiths was run out on the last ball of the match going for what would have been the winning bye. It was the first tie in 745 championship matches at Northampton, but Kent's second of the season. It was a credit to the attitude of both sides.

OPPOSITE: *Duncan Wild – a magnificent maiden hundred for Northants in the tied match with Kent, 17 July. (George Herringshaw)*

## John Player League

***15 July***

***at Cardiff***

**Glamorgan** 189 for 7 (Javed Miandad 56, J.A. Hopkins 51)
**Somerset** 192 for 3 (N.A. Felton 84 not out)

*Somerset (4 pts) won by 7 wickets*

***at Bristol***

**Essex** 238 for 8 (K.S. McEwan 89, B.R. Hardie 52, C.W.J. Athey 4 for 50)
**Gloucestershire** 94

*Essex (4 pts) won by 144 runs*

***at Portsmouth***

**Hampshire** 206 for 7 (D.R. Turner 63)
**Lancashire** 210 for 6 (N.H. Fairbrother 54 not out)

*Lancashire (4 pts) won by 4 wickets*

***at Lord's***

**Yorkshire** 131 for 7
**Middlesex** 134 for 3

*Middlesex (4 pts) won by 7 wickets*

***at Tring***

**Kent** 175 (M.R. Benson 88)
**Northamptonshire** 172 for 6 (W. Larkins 79)

*Northamptonshire (4 pts) won by 4 wickets*

***at The Oval***

**Surrey** 185 for 7 (D.J. Thomas 60, R.D.V. Knight 57 not out)
**Derbyshire** 99

*Surrey (4 pts) won by 86 runs*

***at Edgbaston***

**Warwickshire** 227 for 5 (D.L. Amiss 54, G.W. Humpage 54, A.I. Kallicharran 51)
**Sussex** 209 for 9

*Warwickshire (4 pts) won by 18 runs*

***at Worcester***

**Leicestershire** 204 for 6
**Worcestershire** 198 for 9

*Leicestershire (4 pts) won by 6 runs*

Middlesex maintained their two-point lead at the top of the table by beating Yorkshire easily in a match reduced to 25 overs. Essex breathed down their necks by overwhelming Gloucestershire, McEwan and Hardie sharing a century stand. Worcestershire's challenge faltered when they lost momentum and wickets against Leicestershire for whom Ian Carmichael of South Australia appeared. Born in Yorkshire, he was in England on an Esso Scholarship and had been playing for Essex II. Surrey and Lancashire moved into third and fourth places. Jack Simmons hit 45 off 22 balls to bring his side 4 points at Portsmouth.

## NatWest Trophy – Round Two

***18 July***

***at Northampton***

**Northamptonshire** 247 for 5 (R.G. Williams 94, A.J. Lamb 65)
**Worcestershire** 117 (N.A. Mallender 7 for 37)

*Northamptonshire won by 130 runs*
(*Man of the Match* – N.A. Mallender)

***at Chelmsford***

**Essex** 121 (G.A. Gooch 64)
**Surrey** 122 for 5

*Surrey won by 5 wickets*
(*Man of the Match* – G.A. Gooch)

***at Trent Bridge***

**Middlesex** 228 (M.W. Gatting 67, P.R. Downton 62, K. Saxelby 4 for 28)
**Nottinghamshire** 223 for 8 (B.C. Broad 65, C.E.B. Rice 57)

*Middlesex won by 5 runs*
(*Man of the Match* – J.E. Emburey)

***at Southampton***

**Kent** 250 for 8 (C.S. Cowdrey 71, D.G. Aslett 67, E.L. Reifer 4 for 46)
**Hampshire** 99 (T.M. Alderman 4 for 21)

*Kent won by 151 runs*
(*Man of the Match* – C.S. Cowdrey)

***at Bristol***

**Lancashire** 349 for 6 (G. Fowler 122, J. Abrahams 51)
**Gloucestershire** 281 (P.W. Romaines 56, A.W. Stovold 53, P. Bainbridge 51, J. Simmons 5 for 37)

*Lancashire won by 68 runs*
(*Man of the Match* – G. Fowler)

***at Hove***

**Somerset** 288 for 3 (M.D. Crowe 114, P.M. Roebuck 98)
**Sussex** 220 for 9 (G.D. Mendis 55)

*Somerset won by 68 runs*
(*Man of the Match* – M.D. Crowe)

***at Edgbaston***

**Warwickshire** 305 for 8 (R.I.H.B. Dyer 119, G.W. Humpage 77)
**Shropshire** 202 (J. Foster 56)

*Warwickshire won by 103 runs*
(*Man of the Match* – R.I.H.B. Dyer)

***18 and 19 July***

***at Leicester***

**Leicestershire** 301 for 7 (D.I. Gower 156)
**Derbyshire** 181

*Leicestershire won by 120 runs*
(*Man of the Match* – D.I. Gower)

With his first century for Warwickshire Robin Dyer, who had had a fine month since winning a first team place, ensured that giant-killers Shropshire would advance no further in the competition. He and Humpage added 149 after Amiss and Kallicharran had gone for 33. Gower hit 156 off 128 balls, his last fifty coming in 4 overs, and Derbyshire could never respond to this onslaught.

Lamb and Williams took Northants from 49 for 3 to 199. The final score of 247 did not look too formidable, but Neil Mallender bowled like a man inspired, fast and straight to take his best haul in any competition.

Essex seem to have the black spot on them in this tournament. At Chelmsford they did nothing right. Their team selection was questionable as was the decision to bat first in overcast conditions although, in fairness, Surrey

*A disastrous day for Hampshire, David Turner is run out when a drive from Jesty is deflected onto the wicket by Ellison, 17 July. (Tom Morris)*

*Man of the Match Robin Dyer during his innings of 119 for Warwickshire against Shropshire. David Ashley is the wicket-keeper. (Ken Kelly)*

COURAGE
BITTER
ORIGINAL GRAVITY 1034-1038
STORE AND SERVE COOL

would have done the same had they won the toss. Gladwin fell first ball to Thomas who bowled well and Essex struggled from then on. Gooch batted 52 overs for his 64, an uncharacteristic innings which told something of the wicket and something of the lack of application of his colleagues. Essex bowled almost as well as Surrey had done, but catches were dropped and Butcher steered the visitors to the quarter finals.

A stand of 110 between Aslett and Cowdrey and some lusty blows from Ellison set Kent on the road to victory against Hampshire who batted poorly and were outplayed in every department of the game.

Lancashire reached a massive 349 for 6 against the weak Gloucestershire attack. They were indebted to a fine innings from Fowler, enjoying a purple patch, and to some hard hitting by the middle order. Gloucestershire, for whom little had gone right for some weeks, replied in a spirited vein and Stovold and Romaines began with 116, but Jack Simmons blunted the late order with his accurate off-breaks.

Roebuck and Crowe added 188 for Somerset's second wicket and virtually decided the outcome of the game at Hove. They benefitted from missed chances, but Crowe, in particular, with a six and fourteen fours, showed a wide range of fine shots.

The match of the round was at Trent Bridge, the graveyard of the hopes of so many visitors. Downton, showing his England resolution, and Gatting put on 92 in 21 overs for Middlesex's third wicket and at 170 for 2 in 43 overs, Middlesex were prospecting. Hadlee cut short the elation and the later batsmen floundered against Saxelby. Broad and Robinson gave Notts a solid start, but Gatting's captaincy and the magnificent spin bowling of Edmonds and Emburey, who, crucially, conceded only 52 runs in their 24 overs and accounted for both openers, frustrated the home side. Rice played splendidly and Notts reached the last 3 overs needing 24 to win with 5 wickets standing. Hadlee was well taken at short-leg and Hemmings was run out. Thirteen were needed off the last over. Rice hooked Cowans to fine-leg where Williams took the catch and Notts fell short of their target.

***19 and 20 July***

***at West Bromwich***

**West Indians** 556 for 7 dec (D.L. Haynes 169, T.R.O. Payne 120, I.V.A. Richards 109, P.J. Dujon 77) and 9 for 0
**Minor Counties** 240 (S.R. Atkinson 76)

*Match drawn*

***21, 22 and 23 July***

***at Derby***

**West Indians** 459 (C.G. Greenidge 113, D.L. Haynes 83, A. L. Logie 65, P.J. Dujon 57)
**Derbyshire** 89 (W.W. Davis 5 for 39) and 201 (G. Miller 74 not out, W.W. Davis 5 for 32, R.A. Harper 4 for 41)

*West Indians won by an innings and 169 runs*

After the run feast of the first day and a half, Greenidge and Haynes put on 172 for the first wicket, the tourists twice shattered Derbyshire. Winston Davis, who had been called into the side as replacement for the injured Small, made an emphatic bid for a Test place with match figures of 10 for 71. He bowled very quickly.

**Benson and Hedges Cup Final**
**LANCASHIRE *v.* WARWICKSHIRE**

Lancashire arrived at Lord's bottom of the Britannic Assurance County Championship and one of the most unlikely finalists of the competition's history. Warwickshire were firm

*Dyer caught Maynard bowled Watkinson 11. (Patrick Eagar)*

*Humpage caught Maynard bowled Allott 8. (Patrick Eagar)*

favourites and, with Willis' impending retirement, they had sentiment on their side. They troubled many by a strange team selection. Two young players, Dyer and Paul Smith, were asked to open the innings. David Smith was omitted and, most strangely, Asif Din won a place at the expense of Lethbridge, David Smith or Thorne. Sadly, Lancashire decided to omit their young wicket-keeper John Stanworth, a player of immense talent, and to recall Maynard, recovered from injury and the stronger batsman.

Abrahams won the toss and asked Warwickshire to take first knock on a wicket that gave some help to the bowler in steamy conditions. He was quickly rewarded for his enterprise when Smith mishooked to mid-wicket where Fairbrother took an easy catch. Dyer batted solidly for 16 overs. It was his job to give base to the innings and he is a young man of charm, talent and determination. Kallicharran batted with a panache which never quite suggested domination and Warwickshire reached 100 in the thirtieth over. Almost on the stroke of lunch Amiss steered the ball to Maynard, but, 109 for 3, Kallicharran and Humpage at the crease, there was no need why Warwickshire should not eat happily.

Thirteen overs and five balls later they were 134 for 9. Willis was cheered to the wicket and 5 runs were added before the final curtain. It was the most miserable batting performance in a final since Warwickshire's display in the NatWest final of 1982. Allott and Simmons, in particular, bowled well for Lancashire and Jefferies, Watkinson and O'Shaughnessy had come up with vital wickets. The fielding was magnificent and Abrahams' organization of his forces splendidly authoritative and intelligent. How he has grown in stature since becoming captain.

No side has ever won a Benson and Hedges Final by scoring 139 when batting first and there was never any likelihood that Warwickshire would do so now. Fowler was caught behind at 23, but Ormrod and O'Shaughnessy batted sensibly. There was a flutter of excitement when Lancashire were 71 for 4 and, momentarily, it seemed that the game might be in the balance. It wasn't. Fairbrother, who needs luck at the beginning of an innings, survived and played with confident aggression. Hughes revived memories of earlier days and Lancashire, most deservedly, took the Benson and Hedges Cup for the first time.

*Fowler caught Humpage bowled Willis. (Patrick Eagar)*

ABOVE: *Kallicharran drives Simmons.* BELOW: *Willis bowls to Fairbrother. (Patrick Eagar)*

Sadly, the end was marred by the situation of farce as spectators hovered on the edge of the pitch and the players sought only the refuge of the pavilion. A final of such importance should not be degraded by such indignity.

Peter May named John Abrahams for the Gold Award for his leadership and there can't be too many Gold Award winners who have scored 0 and not bowled and still come out with the accolade.

*John Abrahams with the Benson and Hedges Cup. (Patrick Eagar)*

ABOVE: *David Hughes who made 35.* BELOW: *John Abrahams with the Lancashire players. (Patrick Eagar)*

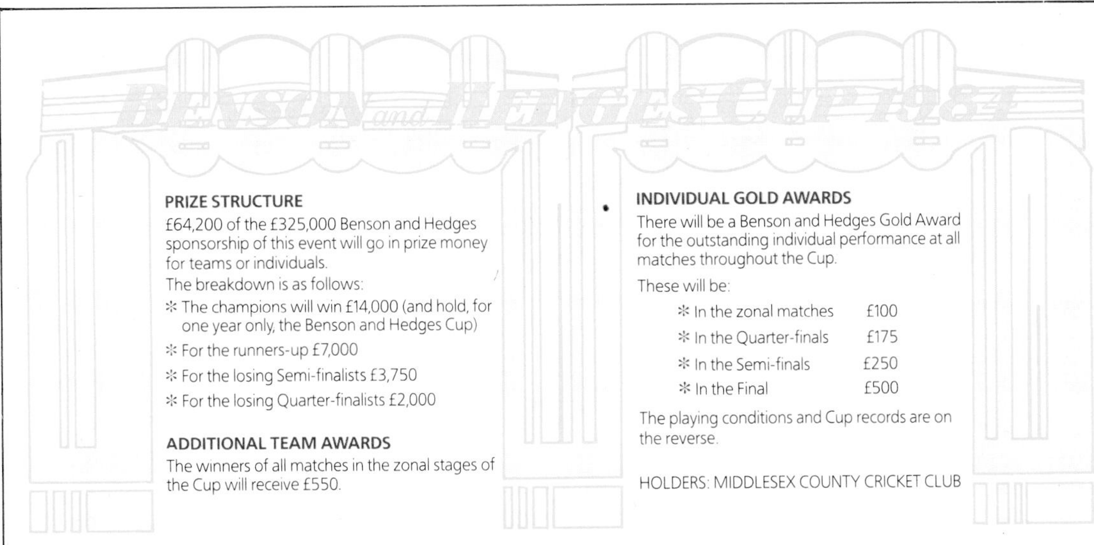


**PRIZE STRUCTURE**

£64,200 of the £325,000 Benson and Hedges sponsorship of this event will go in prize money for teams or individuals.

The breakdown is as follows:

- The champions will win £14,000 (and hold, for one year only, the Benson and Hedges Cup)
- For the runners-up £7,000
- For the losing Semi-finalists £3,750
- For the losing Quarter-finalists £2,000

**ADDITIONAL TEAM AWARDS**

The winners of all matches in the zonal stages of the Cup will receive £550.

**INDIVIDUAL GOLD AWARDS**

There will be a Benson and Hedges Gold Award for the outstanding individual performance at all matches throughout the Cup.

These will be:

- In the zonal matches £100
- In the Quarter-finals £175
- In the Semi-finals £250
- In the Final £500

The playing conditions and Cup records are on the reverse.

HOLDERS: MIDDLESEX COUNTY CRICKET CLUB

## MARYLEBONE CRICKET CLUB

### FINAL

15p **LANCASHIRE v. WARWICKSHIRE** 15p

at Lord's Ground, Saturday, July 21st, 1984

Any alterations to teams will be announced over the public address system

**LANCASHIRE**

| |  |  |  |
|---|---|---|---|
| 1 | G. Fowler | c Humpage b Willis | 7 |
| 2 | J. A. Ormrod | c Humpage b Ferreira | 24 |
| 3 | S. J. O'Shaughnessy | c Humpage b Ferreira | 22 |
| 4 | D. P. Hughes | not out | 35 |
| ‡5 | J. Abrahams | c Humpage b Smith | 0 |
| 6 | N. H. Fairbrother | not out | 36 |
| 7 | S. T. Jefferies | | |
| 8 | J. Simmons | | |
| *9 | C. Maynard | | |
| 10 | M. Watkinson | | |
| 11 | P. J. W. Allott | | |
| | B , l-b 6, w 1, n-b 9, | | 16 |
| | | Total | 140 |

FALL OF THE WICKETS

1...23 2...43 3...70 4...71 5... 6... 7... 8... 9... 10...

| Bowling Analysis | O. | M. | R. | W. | Wd. | N-b |
|---|---|---|---|---|---|---|
| Willis | 9 | 0 | 19 | 1 | ... | ... |
| Small | 4 | 0 | 30 | 0 | ... | 7 |
| Ferreira | 11 | 2 | 26 | 2 | ... | ... |
| Old | 10.4 | 3 | 23 | 0 | ... | ... |
| Smith | 6 | 0 | 20 | 1 | 1 | 2 |
| Gifford | 2 | 1 | 6 | 0 | ... | ... |
| | ... | ... | ... | ... | ... | ... |

**WARWICKSHIRE**

| |  |  |  |
|---|---|---|---|
| 1 | P. A. Smith | c Fairbrother b Allott | 0 |
| 2 | R. I. H. B. Dyer | c Maynard b Watkinson | 11 |
| 3 | A. I. Kallicharran | c Abrahams b Jefferies | 70 |
| 4 | D. L. Amiss | c Maynard b Watkinson | 20 |
| *5 | G. W. Humpage | c Maynard b Allott | 8 |
| 6 | A. M. Ferreira | c and b O'Shaughnessy | 4 |
| 7 | C. M. Old | b O'Shaughnessy | 5 |
| 8 | M. A. Asif Din | c Ormrod b Jefferies | 3 |
| 9 | G. C. Small | l b w b Jefferies | 2 |
| 10 | N. Gifford | not out | 2 |
| ‡11 | R. G. D. Willis | c Jefferies b Allott | 2 |
| | B , l-b 4, w , n-b 8, | | 12 |
| | | Total | 139 |

FALL OF THE WICKETS

1...1 2...48 3...102 4...115 5...121 6...127 7...132 8...133 9...134 10...139

| Bowling Analysis | O. | M. | R. | W. | Wd. | N-b |
|---|---|---|---|---|---|---|
| Allott | 8.4 | 0 | 15 | 3 | ... | ... |
| Jefferies | 11 | 2 | 28 | 3 | ... | 3 |
| Watkinson | 9 | 0 | 23 | 2 | ... | 3 |
| O'Shaughnessy | 11 | 1 | 43 | 2 | ... | 2 |
| Simmons | 11 | 3 | 18 | 0 | ... | ... |
| | ... | ... | ... | ... | ... | ... |
| | ... | ... | ... | ... | ... | ... |

‡ Captain * Wicket-keeper

Umpires—D. J. Constant & D. G. L. Evans

Scorers—A. Lowe, S. P. Austin & E. Solomon

Toss won by—Lancashire who elected to field

RESULT—Lancashire won by 6 wickets

The playing conditions for the Benson & Hedges Cup Competition are printed on the back of this score card.

**Total runs scored at end of each over:—**

Lancashire 1 2 3 4 5 6 7 8 9 10 11 12 13 14 15 16 17 18 19 20
21 22 23 24 25 26 27 28 29 30 31 32 33 34 35 36 37 38 39 40
41 42 43 44 45 46 47 48 49 50 51 52 53 54 55

Warwickshire 1 2 3 4 5 6 7 8 9 10 11 12 13 14 15 16 17 18 19 20
21 22 23 24 25 26 27 28 29 30 31 32 33 34 35 36 37 38 39 40
41 42 43 44 45 46 47 48 49 50 51 52 53 54 55

Reproduced by kind permission of M.C.C.

# How Travel Key can shrink the cost of business rail travel.

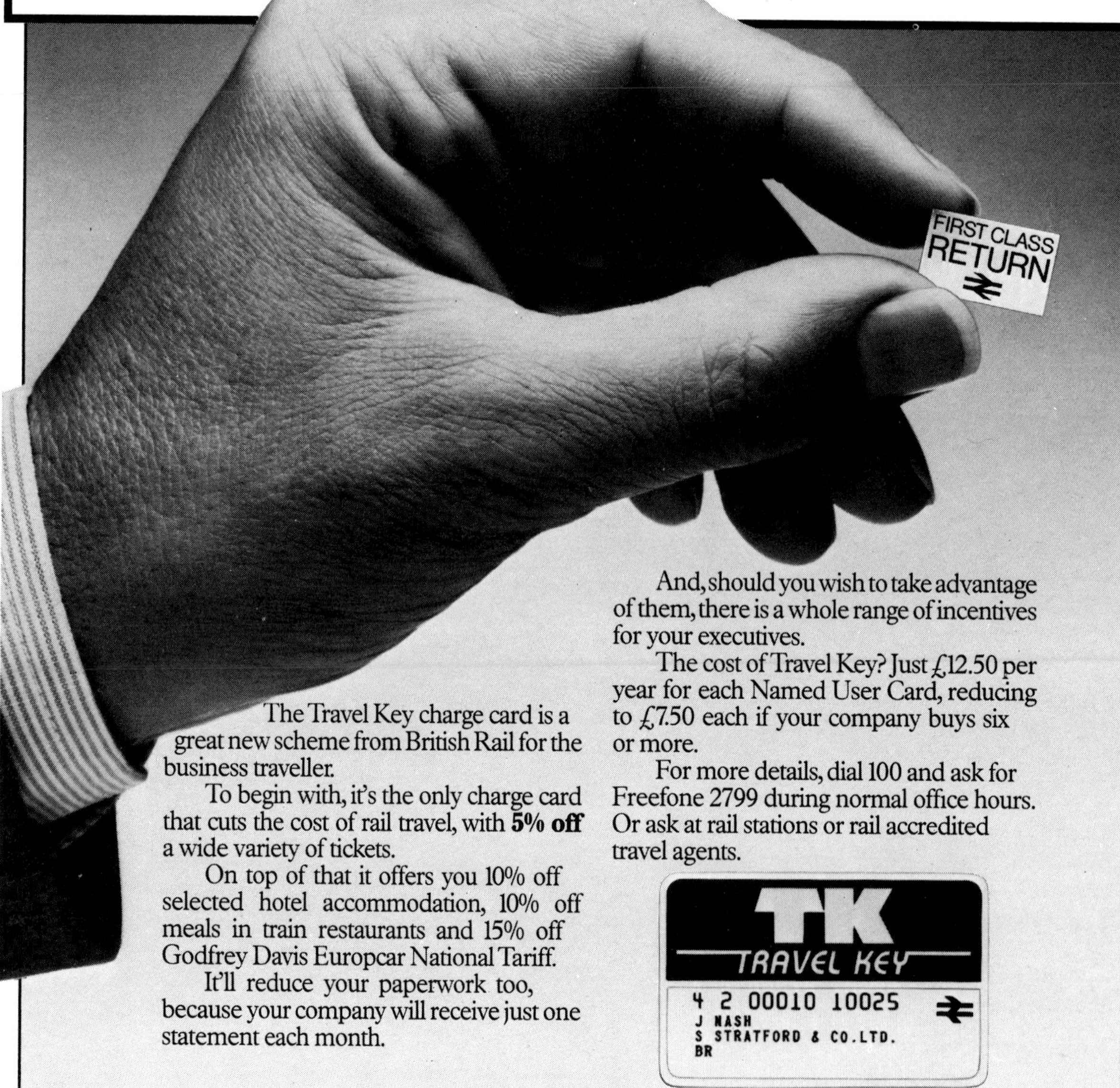


The Travel Key charge card is a great new scheme from British Rail for the business traveller.

To begin with, it's the only charge card that cuts the cost of rail travel, with **5% off** a wide variety of tickets.

On top of that it offers you 10% off selected hotel accommodation, 10% off meals in train restaurants and 15% off Godfrey Davis Europcar National Tariff.

It'll reduce your paperwork too, because your company will receive just one statement each month.

And, should you wish to take advantage of them, there is a whole range of incentives for your executives.

The cost of Travel Key? Just £12.50 per year for each Named User Card, reducing to £7.50 each if your company buys six or more.

For more details, dial 100 and ask for Freefone 2799 during normal office hours. Or ask at rail stations or rail accredited travel agents.

## John Player League

***22 July***

***at Bournemouth***

**Hampshire** 233 for 9 (M.C.J. Nicholas 94, C. Shaw 5 for 41)
**Yorkshire** 202 (K. Sharp 74, C.A. Connor 4 for 16)

*Hampshire (4 pts) won by 31 runs*

***at Canterbury***

**Kent** 213 for 5 (R.M. Ellison 83)
**Essex** 216 for 3 (G.A. Gooch 99, K.S. McEwan 52 not out)

*Essex (4 pts) won by 7 wickets*

***at Leicester***

**Gloucestershire** 210 for 6 (C.W.J. Athey 77, E.J. Cunningham 56)
**Leicestershire** 212 for 2 (N.E. Briers 86 not out, D.I. Gower 75)

*Leicestershire (4 pts) won by 8 wickets*

***at Trent Bridge***

**Nottinghamshire** 215 for 7
**Northamptonshire** 216 for 6 (A.J. Lamb 99)

*Northamptonshire (4 pts) won by 4 wickets*

***at Taunton***

**Somerset** 208 for 8 (M.D. Crowe 53)
**Lancashire** 209 for 3 (S.J. O'Shaughnessy 91, G. Fowler 54)

*Lancashire (4 pts) won by 7 wickets*

***at Worcester***

**Sussex** 168 for 7
**Worcestershire** 167 (T.S. Curtis 59)

*Sussex (4 pts) won by 1 run*

Essex moved to the top of the John Player League when Gooch's power upset Ellison's earlier celebration at being named in the England party for the fourth Test. Ellison had hit 83 in 21 overs and Kent had scored 56 from their last 5 overs, but Gooch's dominant 99 in 33 overs led Essex to the top with 5 balls to spare.

Lancashire celebrated their Benson and Hedges victory by crushing Somerset, Fowler and O'Shaughnessy beginning with a stand of 101. Worcestershire's challenge faded as they failed to scramble 8 runs from the last over after bad pacing earlier in the innings. Lamb, who came to the wicket after one ball of the Northants innings, inspired his side to a fine win at Trent Bridge, but Gloucestershire's bravery could not bring them a first victory over Leicestershire for whom Briers and Gower shared a second wicket stand of 122.

***25, 26 and 27 July***

***at Buxton***

**Lancashire** 211 (J. Simmons 58, G. Miller 6 for 84, R.J. Finney 4 for 57) and 231 (N.H. Fairbrother 102, R.J. Finney 5 for 55)
**Derbyshire** 313 (R.J. Finney 78, K.J. Barnett 59, J.G. Wright 56, J.H. Hampshire 55, N.V. Radford 5 for 95) and 131 for 3 (K.J. Barnett 62, A. Hill 56 not out)

*Derbyshire won by 7 wickets*
*Derbyshire 24 pts, Lancashire 6 pts*

***at Bristol***

**Leicestershire** 301 for 7 dec (J.C. Balderstone 83, P. Willey 57, J.N. Shepherd 4 for 75) and 220 for 6 dec (T.J. Boon 82 not out, J.C. Balderstone 76)
**Gloucestershire** 200 and 246 for 6 (A.W. Stovold 139 not out, P. Willey 4 for 76)

*Match drawn*
*Leicestershire 8 pts, Gloucestershire 5 pts*

***at Northampton***

**Northamptonshire** 338 (R.J. Bailey 95, G. Cook 71) and 190 (D.J. Capel 70, P.H. Edmonds 4 for 42)
**Middlesex** 324 (M.W. Gatting 146, C.T. Radley 58, J.E. Emburey 54, R.G. Williams 4 for 83) and 208 for 3 (M.W. Gatting 91 not out, W.N. Slack 91)

*Middlesex won by 7 wickets*
*Middlesex 23 pts, Northamptonshire 7 pts*

***at Taunton***

**Glamorgan** 353 for 7 dec (A.L. Jones 100, Javed Miandad 83) and 231 for 1 dec (G.C. Holmes 90, J.A. Hopkins 86 not out)
**Somerset** 308 for 8 dec (P.M. Roebuck 63, M.R. Davis 60 not out, V.J. Marks 53) and 112 for 4

*Match drawn*
*Somerset 7 pts, Glamorgan 7 pts*

***at The Oval***

**Surrey** 255 for 3 dec (G. Monkhouse 100 not out, G.S. Clinton 78) and 162 for 8 dec (C.J. Richards 57 not out, K.B.S. Jarvis 5 for 49)
**Kent** 171 for 9 dec (C.S. Cowdrey 59) and 143 for 7

*Match drawn*
*Surrey 7 pts, Kent 2 pts*

***at Edgbaston***

**Warwickshire** 472 (G.W. Humpage 101, A.I. Kallicharran 84, P.A. Smith 69, A.M. Ferreira 54) and 227 for 4 dec (D.L. Amiss 98 not out, R.I.H.B. Dyer 76)
**Hampshire** 398 for 7 dec (D.R. Turner 153, J.J.E. Hardy 95, N.G. Cowley 58) and 176 (G.C. Small 4 for 35)

*Warwickshire won by 125 runs*
*Warwickshire 23 pts, Hampshire 7 pts*

***at Scarborough***

**Yorkshire** 188 (D.L. Bairstow 94, J.D. Inchmore 4 for 37) and 221 for 3 (M.D. Moxon 126 not out, P.E. Robinson 55 not out)
**Worcestershire** 402 (P.A. Neale 143, D.N. Patel 90, P.W. Jarvis 6 for 115)

*Match drawn*
*Worcestershire 7 pts, Yorkshire 2 pts*

***at Cleethorpes***

**Nottinghamshire** 311 for 8 dec (P. Johnson 80, J.D. Birch 60, D.W. Randall 52) and 210 for 6 dec (R.T. Robinson 115 not out)
**Sri Lankans** 199 (R.G. de Alwis 74, E.E. Hemmings 7 for 47) and 123 for 2

*Match drawn*

Leicestershire failed to close the gap at the top of the table when Andy Stovold denied them victory with 139 not out in 280 minutes. He and Paul Romaines began with a stand of 123 which raised hopes of a Gloucestershire victory. Willey took four quick wickets to blunt the challenge and the home side drew with honour. The great achievement was by Derbyshire, however, who gained their first championship victory of the season. Neil Fairbrother hit a maiden century for Lancashire, but Roger Finney's good all-round cricket and dependable batting brought the home side a deserved and much needed win.

With Mike Gatting again in devastating form, Middlesex moved into fifth place in the table, the early season troubles forgotten. Set to make 205 in 60 overs, Middlesex won with 12.5 overs to spare, Slack and Gatting sharing a second wicket stand of 142. Two very promising young batsmen, Bailey and Capel, had performed very well for Northants, but one of the delights of the match was Phil Edmonds' teasing, intelligent spin which made possible his side's victory burst.

Alan Lewis Jones continued to show his appetite for centuries and there was a fine forceful innings from Holmes as well as a maiden first-class fifty from Davis which, with Simon Turner's 27 not out, helped to save the follow-on for Somerset against Glamorgan. Graham Monkhouse, sent in as night-watchman, hit his maiden century in first-class cricket in the rain-blighted game at The Oval.

The Sri Lankans began their short tour in damp conditions at Cleethorpes. They performed capably, but the main honours went to Tim Robinson and Eddie Hemmings whose off-spin always demanded respect.

Yorkshire, 30 for 6 on the first morning, were rallied by Bairstow and Booth, but Phil Neale, with his first century of the season, and Patel led Worcestershire to a big lead. Moxon, restored to fitness, reminded the Test selectors of his presence with an accomplished, match-saving century in the second innings.

After massive first innings scores, which included delightful hundreds from two likeable men, Geoff Humpage and David Turner and another indication of Hardy's potential, Norman Gifford made an astute declaration and brought Warwickshire to victory with one ball to spare. He had been tempted by sentiment to allow Amiss to complete his century after the veteran and the so promising Robin Dyer had added 117 for the third wicket, but the closure proved just right. Tremlett and Connor were left to survive 28 balls to save the match for Hampshire, but Small had Tremlett lbw with the fifth ball of the last over.

ABOVE: *Gordon Greenidge – a second double century in the series. Allott is hit for four.* BELOW: *Jeff Dujon drives Cowans on his way to a majestic century. (Adrian Murrell)*

## Fourth Cornhill Test Match
## ENGLAND *v.* WEST INDIES

With Bob Willis unwell, England brought in Cowans and, sadly and surprisingly, omitted Ellison from the chosen twelve. Pat Pocock returned to Test cricket, having watched lesser men occupy the off-spinner's place for a number of years. There was still no mention of Edmonds, the best slow left-arm bowler in the country. West Indies included Winston Davis, recruited from Glamorgan, in place of the injured Marshall, and Walsh must have wondered why he had been selected for the tour in the first place.

West Indies won the toss and were soon in trouble. Haynes mis-hooked Botham to long-leg where Cowans judged a good catch. Cowans had been given the new ball and he really bowled dreadfully. When Allott appeared the game looked different. He recaptured the form of Headingley and in his first five overs had Gomes taken at slip, Richards caught at mid-wicket and Lloyd taken by Downton. At 70 for 4, West Indies were reeling and England rejoiced. The joy was short-lived. In an afternoon and early evening of glorious batting, Greenidge and Dujon added 197 in 69 overs.

We have repeatedly stated that Dujon is the most improved player in the West Indian side and now he revealed his full potential with fluent stroke-making. He is an aesthetically pleasing batsman and time becomes suspended when watching him in full flow. He was out shortly before the close when he gloved a bouncer to the wicket-keeper.

At the other end, Greenidge, curbing his natural inclination to attack, was playing an innings of discipline and power. He was now joined by night-watchman Winston Davis who stayed well into the second day to end all England's hopes of victory. They were together for some three hours and added 170 before Davis, after playing straight and positively, was bowled by Pocock who bowled quite beautifully on the second morning. Davis had given one chance when Lamb missed a simple catch off Cook.

For Greenidge no praise can be too high. With his side stumbling, he curtailed his aggressive tendencies and played the longest and highest innings of his career, nine and three quarter hours for 223. He was frequently having to restart after stoppages for drizzle and bad light, but his unwavering concentration brought West Indies from the brink of disaster to the position of dominance. This was a mighty innings, his second double century of the series, yet totally different in character from the match-winning innings at Lord's. He hit thirty fours and faced 425 balls.

Pocock bowled Baptiste and also captured the wickets of Greenidge and Garner. He and Allott stood far above the rest of the attack which was often very bad.

England began well as Fowler and Broad, again showing courage and determination put on 90 after a late start on the Saturday. Then the innings fell apart. Shortly before tea Fowler played on to Baptiste and shortly after Terry was hit by Davis and retired with a broken arm. Broad was caught at slip. Gower played wildly and was caught behind. Botham fell to a high catch in the gully and Downton went at slip. Lamb and Allott batted out the day.

They continued to give hope that England would avoid the follow-on on the Monday morning, but Allott was tempted to try to hook the second new ball and was caught at square-leg. Cook helped Lamb to add 29 and Pocock showed sound defence until his off-stump was knocked back by Garner. Cowans fell immediately and, with Lamb on 98 not out, England were still 23 short of salvation.

At this point Terry, his broken arm hidden under his sweater, appeared from the pavilion. Lamb had strike and played five deliveries without scoring. He hit the sixth for two to reach his third century in successive Tests, a marvellous achievement. The achievement was blighted, however, in that he had mistaken the appearance of the injured Terry as a chance for him to reach personal glory rather for him to try to save England from following-on. It was unsavoury cricket and the total lack of communication in the England dressing room was bewildering.

A shocked Terry faced two balls, swinging one-handed at both, the second knocking his stumps over.

England followed-on and Holding bowled Fowler with the second ball of the innings. Downton, at number three, showed his customary tenacity and Broad looked solid until offering no stroke to Harper. The off-break bowler accounted for both Downton and Lamb and had Botham taken at short-leg so that Allott was back again at the end of the day to try to save the match.

The game was all over in 42 minutes on the last day. Allott, missed in the first over by Haynes off Harper, was bowled by a ball of full length in the second. Cook pushed at the first

*Winston Davis – night-watchman supreme. (Adrian Murrell)*

*Paul Terry. (Adrian Murrell)*

*Allan Lamb – his third century in successive Test matches. (Adrian Murrell)*

ball he faced and was caught behind. Pocock drove Harper to mid-off for an easy catch. Cowans swung lavishly at Harper, hitting him for 4 and 6. Then he missed and the ball struck him and trickled back onto the stumps while he held his posture. It was a symbolically ludicrous and dismal end for England.

Harper, a really magnificent cricketer and probably a future West Indies captain, finished with his best figures in Test cricket. Greenidge was unchallenged as Man of the Match and Gower reached his first fifty of the series, small comfort for a side who were totally outclassed.

*England's second innings destroyer – Roger Harper. (Adrian Murrell)*

**FOURTH CORNHILL TEST MATCH – ENGLAND *v.* WEST INDIES**
26, 27, 28, 30 and 31 July 1984 at Old Trafford, Manchester

**WEST INDIES**

| | FIRST INNINGS | |
|---|---|---|
| C.G. Greenidge | c Downton, b Pocock | 223 |
| D.L. Haynes | c Cowans, b Botham | 2 |
| H.A. Gomes | c Botham, b Allott | 30 |
| I.V.A. Richards | c Cook, b Allott | 1 |
| C.H. Lloyd† | c Downton, b Allott | 1 |
| P.J. Dujon* | c Downton, b Botham | 101 |
| W.W. Davis | b Pocock | 77 |
| E.A.E. Baptiste | b Pocock | 6 |
| R.A. Harper | not out | 39 |
| M.A. Holding | b Cook | 0 |
| J. Garner | c Terry, b Pocock | 7 |
| Extras | b 4, lb 6, w 2, nb 1 | 13 |
| | | 500 |

| | O | M | R | W |
|---|---|---|---|---|
| Botham | 29 | 5 | 100 | 2 |
| Cowans | 19 | 2 | 76 | — |
| Allott | 28 | 9 | 76 | 3 |
| Cook | 39 | 6 | 114 | 1 |
| Pocock | 45.3 | 14 | 121 | 4 |

FALL OF WICKETS
1- 11, 2- 60, 3- 62, 4- 70, 5- 267, 6- 437, 7- 443, 8- 470, 9- 471

*Umpires:* H.D. Bird and D.O. Oslear

**West Indies won by an innings and 64 runs**

**ENGLAND**

| | FIRST INNINGS | | SECOND INNINGS | |
|---|---|---|---|---|
| G. Fowler | b Baptiste | 38 | b Holding | 0 |
| B.C. Broad | c Harper, b Davis | 42 | lbw, b Harper | 21 |
| V.P. Terry | b Garner | 7 | absent hurt | 0 |
| D.I. Gower† | c Dujon, b Baptiste | 4 | not out | 57 |
| A.J. Lamb | not out | 100 | b Harper | 9 |
| I.T. Botham | c Garner, b Baptiste | 6 | c Haynes, b Harper | 1 |
| P.R. Downton* | c Harper, b Garner | 0 | (3) b Harper | 24 |
| P.J.W. Allott | c Gomes, b Davis | 26 | (7) b Garner | 14 |
| N.G.B. Cook | b Holding | 13 | (8) c Dujon, b Garner | 0 |
| P.I. Pocock | b Garner | 0 | (9) c Garner, b Harper | 0 |
| N.G. Cowans | b Garner | 0 | (10) b Harper | 14 |
| Extras | b 5, lb 21, nb 18 | 44 | b 9, lb 3, w 1, nb 3 | 16 |
| | | 280 | | 156 |

| | O | M | R | W | O | M | R | W |
|---|---|---|---|---|---|---|---|---|
| Garner | 22.2 | 7 | 51 | 4 | 12 | 4 | 25 | 2 |
| Davis | 20 | 2 | 71 | 2 | 3 | 1 | 6 | — |
| Harper | 23 | 10 | 33 | — | 28.4 | 12 | 57 | 6 |
| Holding | 21 | 2 | 50 | 1 | 11 | 2 | 21 | 1 |
| Baptiste | 19 | 8 | 31 | 3 | 11 | 5 | 29 | — |
| Richards | | | | | 1 | — | 2 | — |

FALL OF WICKETS
1- 90, 2- 112, 3- 117, 4- 138, 5- 147, 6- 228, 7- 257, 8- 278, 9- 278
1- 0, 2- 39, 3- 77, 4- 99, 5- 101, 6- 125, 7- 127, 8- 128, 9- 156

***28, 29 and 30 July***

**at The Oval**

**Surrey** 250 for 9 dec (G.P. Howarth 77, A. Needham 54) and 208 for 8 dec (V.B. John 5 for 89)
**Sri Lankans** 194 (L.R.D. Mendis 67 not out) and 105

*Surrey won by 159 runs*

***28, 30 and 31 July***

***at Chelmsford***

**Essex** 329 (K.W.R. Fletcher 122, B.R. Hardie 78, R.K. Illingworth 4 for 51) and 243 (G.A. Gooch 75, D.N. Patel 5 for 117)
**Worcestershire** 217 (T.S. Curtis 52) and 172 (R.N. Kapil Dev 71, N.A. Foster 5 for 57)

*Essex won by 183 runs*
*Essex 24 pts, Worcestershire 6 pts*

*Ian Butcher. Consistency as Leicestershire's opener brought him his county cap. (David Munden)*

***at Swansea***

**Derbyshire** 332 (A. Hill 65, J.H. Hampshire 62) and 188 for 9 dec
**Glamorgan** 224 (Javed Miandad 64, D.G. Moir 5 for 62) and 271 for 8 (J. Derrick 57 not out, D.G. Moir 4 for 97)

*Match drawn*
*Derbyshire 7 pts, Glamorgan 5 pts*

***at Bristol***

**Northamptonshire** 239 (D.S. Steele 70, R.G. Williams 61, J.N. Shepherd 4 for 64) and 258 for 6 dec (D.S. Steele 78 not out, D.A. Graveney 4 for 64)
**Gloucestershire** 277 (P.W. Romaines 91, C.W.J. Athey 52) and 86 for 4

*Match drawn*
*Gloucestershire 7 pts, Northamptonshire 4 pts*

***at Lord's***

**Hampshire** 350 for 6 dec (D.R. Turner 117, M.C.J. Nicholas 96, P.H. Edmonds 4 for 104) and 153 (N.G. Cowley 57 not out, S.P. Hughes 4 for 27)
**Middlesex** 291 (R.O. Butcher 116, J.E. Emburey 53, C.A. Connor 4 for 67) and 215 for 1 (M.W. Gatting 128 not out, W.N. Slack 52 not out)

*Middlesex won by 9 wickets*
*Middlesex 21 pts, Hampshire 8 pts*

***at Trent Bridge***

**Lancashire** 154 (R.J. Hadlee 4 for 49) and 213 (E.E. Hemmings 4 for 81)
**Nottinghamshire** 364 (R.T. Robinson 117, B.N. French 98, S.T. Jefferies 4 for 109) and 4 for 0

*Nottinghamshire won by 10 wickets*
*Nottinghamshire 23 pts, Lancashire 4 pts*

***at Hove***

**Somerset** 235 (V.J. Marks 59 not out, C.M. Wells 4 for 52) and 185 (G.S. le Roux 6 for 57)
**Sussex** 417 for 3 dec (G.D. Mendis 209 not out, A.M. Green 79, P.W.G. Parker 69) and 4 for 1

*Sussex won by 9 wickets*
*Sussex 24 pts, Somerset 2 pts*

***at Edgbaston***

**Kent** 366 for 7 dec (R.M. Ellison 79 not out, N.R. Taylor 73, C.J. Tavare 62) and 125 (A.M. Ferreira 4 for 27, G.C. Small 4 for 56)
**Warwickshire** 301 for 6 dec (D.L. Amiss 68, A.M. Ferreira 62 not out, G.W. Humpage 56) and 193 for 2 (R.I.H.B. Dyer 75 not out, P.A. Smith 52)

*Warwickshire won by 8 wickets*
*Warwickshire 22 pts, Kent 5 pts*

***at Sheffield***

**Leicestershire** 327 for 4 dec (I.P. Butcher 130, J.C. Balderstone 59, G.J. Parsons 53 not out) and 265 for 7 dec (G.J. Parsons 58)
**Yorkshire** 303 for 8 dec (J.D. Love 84, D.L. Bairstow 65, K. Sharp 53) and 204 for 6 (G. Boycott 74)

*Match drawn*
*Leicestershire 7 pts, Yorkshire 5 pts*

Essex and Notts forged ahead of the field at the top of the Britannic Assurance County Championship as Leicestershire, after Butcher's century on the opening day, were well held by Yorkshire for whom Love hit an impressive 84 before breaking a finger. Essex, put in to bat by Neale, recovered from an uneasy start through a stand of 166 for the fourth wicket between Hardie and Fletcher. The Essex captain reached an effortless hundred and Worcestershire failed against the all-round strength of the home attack. Gooch then had a quick run spree and, with Foster and Acfield to the fore, Essex bowled out Worcestershire by early afternoon on the last day in spite of some fierce blows from Kapil Dev. Notts' win was equally impressive and equally quick. Lancashire succumbed rapidly on the first day and Robinson reached his fifth century of the season on the Monday when Bruce French was out for a career best, two short of a hundred. The match ended early on the last day.

Middlesex had their fourth win in five matches as Mike Gatting hit the fastest hundred of the summer. He reached his century in 85 minutes as Middlesex raced to victory with 61 overs to spare. Hampshire had begun well when David Turner, neat and attractive, had hit his second century in successive matches, but Middlesex, thanks to Roland Butcher, fought back to parity after being 143 for 7. Hampshire were handicapped by the withdrawal from the match of Tim Tremlett. Sadly, the news reached Lord's that his father had died. Maurice Tremlett was a good man who gave many people great pleasure. He will be much missed, but his son, a young man of ability and charm, is continuing a fine tradition.

Derbyshire and Glamorgan fought a fine match in spite of interruptions for rain. Derbyshire batted positively to set Glamorgan a target of 297 at approximately 5 runs an over. Glamorgan slipped to 227 for 8, but Derrick and Davies, two of the younger members of the side, added 54 and saved the match. It was during this game that Bob Taylor announced that he was to retire from first-class cricket. It came as little surprise after his unjustifiable omission from the England side. He is one of the greatest wicket-keepers in the history of the game and also one of cricket's kindest and most courteous of men.

Rain also marred events at Bristol where Gloucestershire glimpsed victory after taking a first innings lead of 38, but, ultimately, were grateful for a draw when they slipped to 34 for 4 in their second innings.

Sussex overwhelmed Somerset. Garth le Roux had his best bowling figures of the season and Gehan Mendis hit the highest score of his career, sharing stands of 197 with Green, 146 with Parker and 74 with Alan Wells. Mendis hit twenty-six fours in an innings which was particularly attractive for its powerful driving and delicate cutting. Somerset were handicapped by injuries to Davis and Dredge, who had sunstroke.

After an opening day of fine stroke-making Kent fell apart at Edgbaston where Ferreira, Small and Lethbridge bowled well on a good wicket. Needing 191 to win, Warwickshire were given a good start by Paul Smith, 52 in 48 minutes, and Robin Dyer who continued to impress with neat and sound batsmanship.

The Sri Lankans lost the second match of their tour and suffered injuries to de Alwis and de Mel. There were some encouraging signs in the batting of Mendis and the bowling of John and de Silva, but The Oval wicket came in for some criticism.

## John Player League

*29 July*

**at Chelmsford**

**Worcestershire** 178 for 9 (G.A. Gooch 4 for 33)
**Essex** 180 for 4 (D.R. Pringle 77 not out, K.S. McEwan 68)

*Essex (4 pts) won by 6 wickets*

**at Ebbw Vale**

**Glamorgan** 277 for 6 (Younis Ahmed 103 not out, Javed Miandad 69)
**Derbyshire** 153 (G.C. Holmes 5 for 2)

*Glamorgan (4 pts) won by 124 runs*

**at Bristol**

**Gloucestershire** 214 for 6 (Zaheer Abbas 102)
**Northamptonshire** 218 for 3 (R.J. Boyd-Moss 99, R.J. Bailey 77 not out)

*Northamptonshire (4 pts) won by 7 wickets*

**at Lord's**

**Hampshire** 164 for 8
**Middlesex** 165 for 5 (C.T. Radley 62)

*Middlesex (4 pts) won by 5 wickets*

**at Trent Bridge**

**Nottinghamshire** 233 for 4 (D.W. Randall 54 not out)
**Lancashire** 210 for 7 (D.P. Hughes 67)

*Nottinghamshire (4 pts) won by 23 runs*

**at Hove**

**Sussex** 211 for 5 (A.M. Green 78)
**Somerset** 191 for 9 (M.D. Crowe 75, D.A. Reeve 4 for 31)

*Sussex (4 pts) won by 20 runs*

**at Edgbaston**

**Kent** 234 for 7 (M.R. Benson 78, D.G. Aslett 72)
**Warwickshire** 153 (A.I. Kallicharran 73)

*Kent (4 pts) won by 81 runs*

**at Bradford**

**Yorkshire** 230 for 7 (J.D. Love 69 not out, M.D. Moxon 52)
**Leicestershire** 229 for 5 (N.E. Briers 108)

*Yorkshire (4 pts) won by 1 run*

Essex and Middlesex moved clear of the pack with comfortable wins. Essex, having lost Gooch, who bowled very well, and Gladwin for 21, were revived by McEwan and Pringle adding 127. Middlesex were 23 for 3, but Radley and Butcher righted matters. Lancashire lost ground at Trent Bridge.

Northants were indebted to a third wicket stand of 146 by Bailey and Boyd-Moss, two fine young players. Boyd-Moss' 99 was his Sunday best. Kent swamped Warwickshire, Amiss falling to Penn's second ball of the innings, and Sussex had no trouble with the injury hit Somerset. Briers, like Zaheer Abbas, hit a century and finished on the losing side. Leicestershire needed two off the last ball, but Garnham's straight drive was fielded by bowler Hartley who threw down the wicket to give his side victory by 1 run.

Younis, returning to the Glamorgan side, relished a stand of 147 for the third wicket with Javed Miandad. Derbyshire were handicapped by the withdrawal of Miller, injured in pre-match practice, but they hit fiercely for 25 overs. Then Holmes joined the attack and took 5 for 2 in 14 deliveries.

## NatWest Trophy – Round Three

*1 August*

***at Lord's***

**Middlesex** 276 for 8 (G.D. Barlow 158)
**Lancashire** 105 (W.W. Daniel 5 for 14)

*Middlesex won by 171 runs*
(*Man of the Match* – G.D. Barlow)

***at Northampton***

**Leicestershire** 238 for 9 (I.P. Butcher 81)
**Northamptonshire** 242 for 7 (R.J. Boyd-Moss 88 not out)

*Northamptonshire won by 3 wickets*
(*Man of the Match* – R.J. Boyd-Moss)

***at Taunton***

**Kent** 275 for 5 (C.J. Tavare 103, M.R. Benson 96)
**Somerset** 265 for 5 (N.A. Felton 87, P.M. Roebuck 81, B.C. Rose 54 not out)

*Kent won by 10 runs*
(*Man of the Match* – C.J. Tavare)

***at Edgbaston***

**Warwickshire** 305 for 5 (A.I. Kallicharran 101, K.D. Smith 74, D.L. Amiss 73 not out)
**Surrey** 195 (D.J. Thomas 53, C.M. Old 4 for 45)

*Warwickshire won by 110 runs*
(*Man of the Match* – A.I. Kallicharran)

*Graham Barlow, 158 in the NatWest Quarter Final at Lord's. The highest score by an Englishman in the competition. A splendid return to form in his benefit year. (George Herringshaw)*

Middlesex, the favourites, had the easiest of victories over Lancashire. Graham Barlow, who had been in poor form in his benefit year, returned to the side as Tomlins was injured and hit the highest score that an Englishman has made in the competition. He and Slack put on 73 in 23 overs for the first wicket and Barlow's mighty innings did not end until he was run out off the first ball of the last over. Daniel bowled at a furious pace to demoralise the Lancashire batting. He was ably supported by Hughes and by some magnificent catching, particularly by Edmonds, the enigma of English cricket.

Warwickshire, after a cautious start, bludgeoned Surrey to submission at Edgbaston. Kallicharran, with his tenth hundred of the summer, and David Smith, showing a welcome return to form, added 137 for the third wicket and Amiss scored briskly. Howarth, Clinton and Knight were out for 17 and the game was virtually decided.

A third batsman to return to form was Chris Tavare, the nightmares of the winter becoming fainter, who hit 103 and shared a second wicket stand of 167 with Benson. Poor Simon Turner, the most promising wicket-keeper, dropped both batsmen. He was not alone in a day of dropped catches. Knott and Johnson dropped Roebuck and Johnson dropped Felton, the easiest of caught and bowled chances. Underwood later missed a similar chance. Felton, who batted with splendid aggression, and Roebuck put on 134 for the first wicket before Felton was caught in the deep by Johnson off Underwood. Crowe was magnificently caught by Knott and Botham went first ball, lbw to Underwood. Roebuck's strokes seem to have evaporated since he was made an opener and in spite of Rose's brave attack, the holders failed by ten runs.

The loss of five wickets for 21 runs in 7 overs in mid-innings ended Leicestershire's chances of making a big total after Balderstone and Butcher had begun with a stand of 88. The vital dismissal was when Larkins yorked Gower for 24. Northants had to work hard for victory even though they reached 124 for 2 at tea. They owed much to the sensible aggression of Boyd-Moss and victory came when Mallender hit Roberts to the long-leg boundary on the first ball of the final over.

*1, 2 and 3 August*

***at Trent Bridge***

**West Indians** 361 for 4 (A.L. Logie 122 not out, I.V.A. Richards 81, D.L. Haynes 69)
*v.* **Nottinghamshire**

*Match drawn*

Haynes and Gomes put on 105 in 32 overs and Logie hit a sparkling century off 132 balls with sixteen fours. Then came the rain.

*4, 5 and 6 August*

***at Lord's***

**West Indians** 211 (R.A. Harper 58, N.G. Cowans 4 for 52) and 224

for 6 dec (A.L. Logie 84 not out, D.L. Haynes 62)
**Middlesex** 177 for 4 dec (M.W. Gatting 50 not out) and 87 for 2

*Match drawn*

### *4, 6 and 7 August*

#### *at Southampton*

**Warwickshire** 295 for 9 dec (D.L. Amiss 69, R.I.H.B. Dyer 61, P.A. Smith 54, T.M. Tremlett 4 for 61) and 194 for 5 dec (A.I. Kallicharran 59 not out)
**Hampshire** 212 for 3 dec (C.L. Smith 110 not out, D.R. Turner 68) and 125 for 4

*Match drawn*
*Hampshire 6 pts, Warwickshire 4 pts*

#### *at Canterbury*

**Kent** 355 (C.J. Tavare 117, J.P. Agnew 5 for 71) and 126 for 3 (C.S. Cowdrey 51 not out)
**Leicestershire** 197 (T.M. Alderman 5 for 25, D.L. Underwood 4 for 22)

*Match drawn*
*Kent 8 pts, Leicestershire 3 pts*

#### *at Old Trafford*

**Lancashire** 151 (P.W. Jarvis 6 for 61)
**Yorkshire** 124 for 5

*Match drawn*
*Yorkshire 4 pts, Lancashire 3 pts*

#### *at Northampton*

**Northamptonshire** 158 (G. Cook 80, G. Miller 5 for 40, D.G. Moir 4 for 39) and 272 for 5 dec (G. Cook 102, R.J. Boyd-Moss 87)
**Derbyshire** 150 for 4 dec (J.G. Wright 84, N.A. Mallender 4 for 45)

*Match drawn*
*Derbyshire 5 pts, Northamptonshire 2 pts*

#### *at Weston-super-Mare*

**Somerset** 293 for 9 dec (N.A. Felton 101) and 104 for 4 dec
**Surrey** 217 (A.R. Butcher 85, G.P. Howarth 50, S.C. Booth 4 for 76, V.J. Marks 4 for 80) and 157 for 9 (V.J. Marks 5 for 55, S.C. Booth 4 for 57)

*Match drawn*
*Somerset 7 pts, Surrey 6 pts*

#### *at Eastbourne*

**Sussex** 259 (P.W.G. Parker 114, A.M. Green 52, D.L. Acfield 6 for 44) and 133 for 8 dec (D.R. Pringle 4 for 16)
**Essex** 197 (N.A. Foster 54 not out, D.A. Reeve 4 for 35) and 115 for 2 (C. Gladwin 66 not out)

*Match drawn*
*Sussex 7 pts, Essex 4 pts*

#### *at Worcester*

**Nottinghamshire** 202 (R.J. Hadlee 70, A.P. Pridgeon 4 for 39) and 167 for 5 (B.C. Broad 53)
**Worcestershire** 261 for 5 dec (T.S. Curtis 70, R.N. Kapil Dev 69 not out)

*Match drawn*
*Worcestershire 7 pts, Nottinghamshire 4 pts*

#### *at Cheltenham*

**Gloucestershire** 278 for 4 dec (S.H. Wootton 97, P.W. Romaines 83, E.J. Cunningham 61 not out) and 116 for 6 (V.B. John 6 for 58)
**Sri Lankans** 286 for 1 dec (S. Wettimuny 123 not out, S.A.R. Silva 91, R.S. Madugalle 57 not out)

*Match drawn*

Rain blighted the holiday matches to such an extent that none produced a result. Middlesex gave the West Indians their biggest fright of the tour when they had them at 83 for 5 on the Saturday, and Gatting's captaincy nearly produced a result in spite of the weather.

There was no play possible on the last day at Canterbury where Tavare had hit a back-to-form century and at Old Trafford where the bowlers were very much on top. Kim Barnett made a challenging declaration at Northampton but got no response from the home side and efforts by Nicholas and Gifford to produce a result. Nick Pocock had announced his retirement and it was expected that Jesty would lead

LEFT: *Robin Boyd-Moss (Northants) recovered his best form after injury and was awarded his county cap. (George Herringshaw)* BELOW: *Cricket at Canterbury (Adrian Murrell)*

Hampshire until the end of the season, but twenty minutes before the start of the game at Southampton, Jesty, who had been leading the side for most of the season in Pocock's absence, was told that Nicholas had been appointed captain.

Somerset, with spinners Marks and the excitingly promising left-arm Booth to the fore, set Surrey the task of scoring 181 in 35 overs, but an exciting finish saw the visitors 24 runs short and Somerset needing only one more wicket. Felton's stylish hundred in the first innings had made Somerset's bid possible.

Nottinghamshire's chances of catching Essex were blunted by Worcestershire who dominated the rain-ruined match. The leaders trailed badly to Sussex on the first innings, Parker scoring a hundred and Foster's 54 rescued Essex from 97 for 6, but the Essex target was eventually 196 in 51 overs. They were totally in command with Gladwin 66 not out in under 33 overs before a storm ended matters.

The Sri Lankans were denied victory by rain at Cheltenham. Their exciting, elegant batting had put them in command, Wettimuny, a fine centurion, and Silva put on 190 for the first wicket. Vinothen John took all six Gloucestershire second innings wickets before the rain.

### John Player League

***5 August***

***at Portsmouth***

**Hampshire** 219 for 5 (C.L. Smith 88 not out, D.R. Turner 74)
**Warwickshire** 218 for 7 (A.I. Kallicharran 62)
*Hampshire (4 pts) won by 1 run*

***at Canterbury***

**Leicestershire** 120 for 8 (C.S. Cowdrey 5 for 28)
**Kent** 56 for 1
*Match abandoned*
*Kent 2 pts, Leicestershire 2 pts*

***at Old Trafford***

**Yorkshire** 124 for 9
**Lancashire** 127 for 5 (G. Fowler 57)
*Lancashire (4 pts) won by 5 wickets*

***at Northampton***

**Northamptonshire** 216 for 8 (A.J. Lamb 83, R.J. Finney 4 for 38)
**Derbyshire** 185 (W.P. Fowler 51)
*Northamptonshire (4 pts) won by 31 runs*

***at Weston-Super-Mare***

**Surrey** 99 (V.J. Marks 4 for 11)
**Somerset** 103 for 7
*Somerset (4 pts) won by 3 wickets*

***at Eastbourne***

**Essex** 104 (A.N. Jones 5 for 28)
**Sussex** 105 for 4 (G.D. Mendis 58 not out)
*Sussex (4 pts) won by 6 wickets*

LEFT: *Vic Marks – a month of miracles in August.* BELOW: *Cheltenham (Adrian Murrell)*

With Middlesex idle, Essex lost a glorious chance of consolidating their position at the top of the table when the bowling of Adrian Jones reduced them to 87 for 9 at Eastbourne. Only brisk hitting by David East took them to a hundred, but Sussex were never in danger and ended Essex's run of nine consecutive wins. In protest at the shabby treatment he had received, Trevor Jesty resigned as Hampshire's vice-captain, but was in the side that beat Warwickshire off the last ball. Lancashire held on to third place with a comfortable win in the Roses Match.

***8, 9 and 10 August***

**at Cheltenham**

**Glamorgan** 258 (H. Morris 81) and 243 for 6 dec (G.C. Holmes 64, J.A. Hopkins 52)
**Gloucestershire** 252 for 8 dec (A.J. Wright 56, A.W. Stovold 56, J.F. Steele 4 for 47) and 207 for 8 (C.W.J. Athey 72, R.C. Ontong 4 for 56)

*Match drawn*
*Gloucestershire 6 pts, Glamorgan 5 pts*

**at Canterbury**

**Kent** 236 (C.S. Cowdrey 102, G.W. Johnson 84) and 246 for 8 dec (M.R. Benson 120, L. Potter 57) Surrey 183 (M.A. Lynch 80, T.M. Alderman 5 for 52) and 124

*Kent won by 175 runs*
*Kent 22 pts, Surrey 4 pts*

**at Southport**

**Northamptonshire** 380 for 9 dec (D.J. Wild 144, R.J. Boyd-Moss 105)
**Lancashire** 70 (R.W. Hanley 6 for 21) and 280 (S.J. O'Shaughnessy 75, N.H. Fairbrother 65, D.S. Steele 5 for 86)

*Northamptonshire won by an innings and 30 runs*
*Northamptonshire 23 pts, Lancashire 1 pt*

**at Leicester**

**Leicestershire** 206 (P. Willey 85, G.J. Parsons 63, A. Sidebottom 5 for 39) and 363 for 5 dec (P. Willey 167, J.J. Whitaker 54 not out)
**Yorkshire** 306 (M.D. Moxon 67, P.B. Clift 4 for 70)

*Match drawn*
*Leicestershire 6 pts, Yorkshire 6 pts*

**at Lord's**

**Middlesex** 329 for 9 dec (M.W. Gatting 116, C.P. Metson 64, P.H. Edmonds 58 not out, D.R. Pringle 6 for 66) and 245 (R.O. Butcher 78)
**Essex** 364 for 7 dec (B.R. Hardie 80 not out, D.R. Pringle 63, S. Turner 59 not out) and 214 for 6 (G.A. Gooch 105 not out)

*Essex won by 4 wickets*
*Essex 22 pts, Middlesex 7 pts*

**at Trent Bridge**

**Nottinghamshire** 361 (C.E.B. Rice 64, D.W. Randall 57, R.J. Hadlee 56, R.T. Robinson 54, G. Miller 4 for 65, D.G. Moir 4 for 80) and 131 (D.G. Moir 6 for 60)
**Derbyshire** 139 (J.H. Hampshire 53 not out, R.J. Hadlee 4 for 30, E.E. Hemmings 4 for 45) and 381 (K.J. Barnett 90, G. Miller 86, R.J. Finney 73)

*Derbyshire won by 28 runs*
*Derbyshire 19 pts, Nottinghamshire 8 pts*

**at Weston-super-Mare**

**Somerset** 472 for 7 dec (V.J. Marks 134, J.W. Lloyds 113 not out, N.F.M. Popplewell 88, M.D. Crowe 53)
**Worcestershire** 160 and 298 for 7 (P.A. Neale 105, T.S. Curtis 76)

*Match drawn*
*Somerset 6 pts, Worcestershire 3 pts*

**at Eastbourne**

**Sussex** 389 for 6 dec (C.M. Wells 132 not out, P.W.G. Parker 122, N. Gifford 4 for 102)
**Warwickshire** 150 (D.A. Reeve 4 for 28) and 137 (C.M. Wells 5 for 59)

*Sussex won by an innings and 102 runs*
*Sussex 22 pts, Warwickshire 2 pts*

**at Southampton**

**Hampshire** 312 for 6 dec (R.A. Smith 132) and 291 for 4 dec (C.L. Smith 102 not out, R.A. Smith 97)
**Sri Lankans** 336 for 9 dec (P.A. de Silva 75, L.R.D. Mendis 64, A. Ranatunga 50) and 102 for 3

*Match drawn*

Lancashire's miserable time in the Britannic Assurance County Championship continued when they were beaten in two days by Northamptonshire. A superb second championship century by Duncan Wild was the backbone of the Northants innings and 'Spook' Hanley had his best figures for the county as Lancashire were bowled out twice in a day. O'Shaughnessy, 27 not out and 75, was the only batsman to offer real determination although Fairbrother played with his customary gusto in the second innings.

Marks reached his first hundred for Somerset and Lloyds and Popplewell helped in the recovery after an uncertain start, but Worcestershire, thanks to Neale, hung on for a draw. Willey batted dourly to save Leicestershire in an uninspiring match at Grace Road and Glamorgan were thwarted in a close finish at Cheltenham.

Chris Cowdrey, somewhat surprisingly being spoken of as a Test prospect, saved Kent from 42 for 5 in a stand of 149 with Johnson, and Benson was in glorious form in the second innings to show that he is a real England batsman of the near future. Alderman had bowled Kent to a lead and Surrey crumbled at the second attempt.

Parker, with his second century of Eastbourne week, and Colin Wells batted Sussex to a formidable position and then Wells joined Reeve in bringing about Warwickshire's downfall and Sussex victory by an innings.

Robin Smith, qualified for England in 1985, gave two magnificent displays against the Sri Lankans at Southampton. He is unquestionably one of the most exciting stroke players in the world. Brother Chris, recovering from a lean season, reached his thousand runs with a second innings century. The Sri Lankans again demonstrated exciting batting and bowling that lacked penetration.

All else was dwarfed, however, by the two matches concerning the top of the table sides. At Trent Bridge, Clive Rice decided to bat first on a wicket that looked of doubtful quality. Notts scored consistently after the early loss of Hassan and with the wicket showing signs of deterioration and taking spin, Derbyshire were bowled out for 139 and followed-on. They showed pluck and determination. Kim Barnett, as ever, led by example, and Miller and Finney, a very useful all-rounder, shared a sixth wicket stand of 135 in 28 overs. They exploited some dreadfully loose bowling and slack fielding. Notts still needed only 160 to win in 35 overs and had reached half their target with three men out, but totally irresponsible batting, swinging wildly when only steady singles were needed threw the match away and Derbyshire, with Dallas Moir ten wickets in the match, won a remarkable victory after being outplayed for two days.

Essex went 22 points clear with a wonderful victory at Lord's. Gatting's fine hundred and some powerful hitting by Metson and Edmonds put Middlesex in control on the first day, but Essex batted like a side eager to win on the second day when Hardie and Pringle, who had an excellent all-round match, added 112 for the fifth wicket and benefitted from dropped catches. David East and the old warrior Stuart Turner then hit lustily and Essex reached 364 in 97 overs. Both Middlesex openers were out before the end of the second day, but Butcher stood firm after Gatting's earlier defiance and Essex were left the improbable task of scoring 211 in 33 overs. Gladwin, appreciating that 6.5 an over was much to ask, began furiously, but all was overshadowed by Gooch who hit one of the most magnificent hundreds ever seen at Lord's and saw Essex to a memorable victory with 7 balls to spare.

## Fifth Cornhill Test Match
## ENGLAND *v.* WEST INDIES

West Indies were at full strength again and won the toss. England gave new caps to Richard Ellison and to Jonathan Agnew who, after a couple of years of promise and no fulfilment, was enjoying a good season but could scarcely have expected to find himself opening the England bowling. Chris Tavare, showing the power of playing a good innings on television, returned to the England side although his record in first-class cricket during the year hardly warranted a recall.

Lloyd elected to bat and must have regretted his decision as, with the ball moving appreciably, West Indies slumped to 70 for 6. Three wickets went down before lunch, the last one being Gomes who was stunningly caught by Botham at close slip to give Ellison his first Test wicket.

The second ball of the afternoon was hooked by Richards into the hands of Allott on the leg boundary. Dujon and Marshall fell to good slip catches, but Lloyd and Baptiste, who had some good fortune against the enthusiastic Ellison, added 54. Lloyd played with a blend of serenity and aggression in what was most certainly his last Test in England.

Botham reached 300 Test wickets and now no record seems safe from him and England's good day was only marred when Garner beat and bowled Broad before the close. Pocock came in as night-watchman and the next morning he withstood a battery of short-pitched bowling with courage for 46 minutes before being caught off Marshall from a ball which could just as easily have injured him. Fowler had retired hurt after being struck on the arm, a blow which left him numbed although he was able to resume later.

Marshall bowled very quickly and very fiercely and he, Holding and Garner savaged the England batting to give West Indies a first innings lead of 28. Tavare was caught down the leg side, Gower off a ball that rose and followed him like an exocet missile. Botham waged brief retaliation before being left helpless by a ferocious ball from Marshall. Lamb was lbw and although Ellison played encouragingly, one could only feel some sympathy for England's batsmen who faced a battering of intimidatory bowling without either umpire finding it necessary or politic to invoke Law 42.

England's hopes of victory, which had soared on the first

*Botham reaches 300 Test wickets.* LEFT: *Greenidge is lbw – 298.* CENTRE: *Richards is caught on the boundary – 299.* RIGHT: *Dujon is caught at slip by Tavare taking the ball above his head – 300. (Ken Kelly)*

*Fowler, caught Richards, bowled Baptiste.* INSET: *Agnew on his Test debut. (Ken Kelly)*

## FIFTH CORNHILL TEST MATCH – ENGLAND *v.* WEST INDIES

9, 10, 11, 13 and 14 August 1984 at Kennington Oval

### WEST INDIES

| | FIRST INNINGS | | SECOND INNINGS | |
|---|---|---|---|---|
| C.G. Greenidge | lbw, b Botham | 22 | c Botham, b Agnew | 34 |
| D.L. Haynes | b Allott | 10 | b Botham | 125 |
| H.A. Gomes | c Botham, b Ellison | 18 | c Tàvare, b Ellison | 1 |
| I.V.A. Richards | c Allott, b Botham | 8 | lbw, b Agnew | 15 |
| P.J. Dujon* | c Tavare, b Botham | 3 | (6) c Lamb, b Ellison | 49 |
| C.H. Lloyd† | not out | 60 | (5) c Downton, b Ellison | 36 |
| M.D. Marshall | c Gower, b Ellison | 0 | (8) c Lamb, b Botham | 12 |
| E.A.E. Baptiste | c Fowler, b Allott | 32 | (7) c Downton, b Allott | 5 |
| R.A. Harper | b Botham | 18 | c Downton, b Allott | 17 |
| M.A. Holding | lbw, b Botham | 0 | lbw, b Botham | 30 |
| J. Garner | c Downton, b Allott | 6 | not out | 10 |
| Extras | b 1, lb 4, w 7, nb 1 | 13 | lb 12 | 12 |
| | | 190 | | 346 |

| | O | M | R | W | O | M | R | W |
|---|---|---|---|---|---|---|---|---|
| Agnew | 12 | 3 | 46 | — | 14 | 1 | 51 | 2 |
| Allott | 17 | 7 | 25 | 3 | 26 | 1 | 96 | 2 |
| Botham | 23 | 8 | 72 | 5 | 22.3 | 2 | 103 | 3 |
| Ellison | 18 | 3 | 34 | 2 | 26 | 7 | 60 | 3 |
| Pocock | | | | | 8 | 3 | 24 | — |

FALL OF WICKETS
1- 19, 2- 45, 3- 64, 4- 64, 5- 67, 6- 70, 7- 124, 8- 154, 9- 154
1- 51, 2- 52, 3- 69, 4- 132, 5- 214, 6- 247, 7- 264, 8- 293, 9- 329

### ENGLAND

| | FIRST INNINGS | | SECOND INNINGS | |
|---|---|---|---|---|
| G. Fowler | c Richards, b Baptiste | 31 | c Richards, b Marshall | 7 |
| B.C. Broad | b Garner | 4 | c Greenidge, b Holding | 39 |
| P.I. Pocock | c Greenidge, b Marshall | 0 | (10) c and b Holding | 0 |
| C.J. Tavare | c Dujon, b Holding | 16 | (3) c Richards, b Garner | 49 |
| D.I. Gower† | c Dujon, b Holding | 12 | (4) lbw, b Holding | 7 |
| A.J. Lamb | lbw, b Marshall | 12 | (5) c Haynes, b Holding | 1 |
| I.T. Botham | c Dujon, b Marshall | 14 | (6) c Marshall, b Garner | 54 |
| P.R. Downton* | c Lloyd, b Garner | 16 | (7) lbw, b Garner | 10 |
| R.M. Ellison | not out | 20 | (8) c Holding, b Garner | 13 |
| P.J.W. Allott | b Marshall | 16 | (9) c Lloyd, b Holding | 4 |
| J.P. Agnew | b Marshall | 5 | not out | 2 |
| Extras | b 2, lb 4, nb 10 | 16 | lb 2, w 1, nb 13 | 16 |
| | | 162 | | 202 |

| | O | M | R | W | O | M | R | W |
|---|---|---|---|---|---|---|---|---|
| Garner | 18 | 6 | 37 | 2 | 18.4 | 3 | 51 | 4 |
| Marshall | 17.5 | 5 | 35 | 5 | 22 | 5 | 71 | 1 |
| Holding | 13 | 2 | 55 | 2 | 13 | 2 | 43 | 5 |
| Baptiste | 12 | 4 | 19 | 1 | 8 | 3 | 11 | — |
| Harper | 1 | 1 | 0 | — | 8 | 5 | 10 | — |

FALL OF WICKETS
1- 10, 2- 22, 3- 45, 4- 64, 5- 83, 6- 84, 7- 116, 8- 133, 9- 156
1- 15, 2- 75, 3- 88, 4- 90, 5- 135, 6- 181, 7- 186, 8- 200, 9- 200

*Umpires:* B.J. Meyer and D.J. Constant

**West Indies won by 172 runs**

## Cornhill Test Match Averages – England *v.* West Indies

### ENGLAND BATTING

| | M | Inns | NOs | Runs | HS | Av | 100s | 50s |
|---|---|---|---|---|---|---|---|---|
| A.J. Lamb | 5 | 10 | 1 | 386 | 110 | 42.88 | 3 | |
| I.T. Botham | 5 | 10 | | 347 | 81 | 34.70 | | 3 |
| G. Fowler | 5 | 10 | | 260 | 106 | 26.00 | 1 | 1 |
| B.C. Broad | 4 | 8 | | 195 | 55 | 24.37 | | 1 |
| P.R. Downton | 5 | 10 | 1 | 210 | 56 | 23.33 | | 1 |
| R.G.D. Willis | 3 | 5 | 3 | 43 | 22 | 21.50 | | |
| D.I. Gower | 5 | 10 | 1 | 171 | 57* | 19.00 | | 1 |
| D.R. Pringle | 3 | 6 | 1 | 81 | 46* | 16.20 | | |
| P.J.W. Allott | 3 | 6 | | 67 | 26 | 11.16 | | |
| G. Miller | 2 | 4 | | 42 | 22 | 10.50 | | |
| V.P. Terry | 2 | 3 | | 16 | 8 | 5.33 | | |
| N.G.B. Cook | 3 | 6 | | 25 | 13 | 4.16 | | |
| P.I. Pocock | 2 | 4 | | 0 | 0 | 0.00 | | |

Played in one Test: T.A. Lloyd 10*; D.W. Randall 1 and 0; M.W. Gatting 1 and 29; N.A. Foster 6 and 9*; N.G. Cowans 0 and 14; C.J. Tavare 16 and 49; R.M. Ellison 20* and 13; J.P. Agnew 5 and 2*

### WEST INDIES BATTING

| | M | Inns | NOs | Runs | HS | Av | 100s | 50s |
|---|---|---|---|---|---|---|---|---|
| C.G. Greenidge | 5 | 8 | 1 | 572 | 223 | 81.71 | 2 | |
| H.A. Gomes | 5 | 8 | 3 | 400 | 143 | 80.00 | 2 | 1 |
| C.H. Lloyd | 5 | 6 | 1 | 255 | 71 | 51.00 | | 2 |
| I.V.A. Richards | 5 | 7 | 1 | 250 | 117 | 41.66 | 1 | 1 |
| P.J. Dujon | 5 | 6 | | 210 | 101 | 35.00 | 1 | |
| E.A.E. Baptiste | 5 | 6 | 1 | 174 | 87* | 34.80 | | 1 |
| M.A. Holding | 5 | 5 | | 158 | 69 | 31.66 | | 2 |
| D.L. Haynes | 5 | 8 | | 235 | 125 | 29.37 | 1 | |
| R.A. Harper | 5 | 6 | 1 | 96 | 39* | 19.20 | | |
| M.D. Marshall | 4 | 5 | | 47 | 29 | 9.40 | | |
| J. Garner | 5 | 6 | 1 | 29 | 10* | 5.80 | | |

Played in one Test: M.A. Small 3*; W.W. Davis 77

### ENGLAND BOWLING

| | Overs | Mds | Runs | Wkts | Av | Best | 5/inn |
|---|---|---|---|---|---|---|---|
| R.M. Ellison | 44 | 10 | 94 | 5 | 18.80 | 3/60 | |
| P.J.W. Allott | 104.5 | 26 | 282 | 14 | 20.14 | 6/61 | 1 |
| I.T. Botham | 163.2 | 30 | 667 | 19 | 35.10 | 8/103 | 2 |
| P.I. Pocock | 53.3 | 17 | 145 | 4 | 36.25 | 4/121 | |
| J.P. Agnew | 26 | 4 | 97 | 2 | 48.50 | 2/51 | |
| D.R. Pringle | 71.3 | 10 | 257 | 5 | 51.40 | 5/108 | 1 |
| N.G.B. Cook | 95 | 15 | 297 | 5 | 59.40 | 2/27 | |
| R.G.D. Willis | 85 | 14 | 367 | 6 | 61.16 | 2/48 | |
| G. Miller | 28 | 1 | 142 | 1 | 142.00 | 1/83 | |
| N.G. Cowans | 19 | 2 | 76 | 0 | — | | |
| N.A. Foster | 18 | 2 | 82 | 0 | — | | |

### WEST INDIES BOWLING

| | Overs | Mds | Runs | Wkts | Av | Best | 5/inn |
|---|---|---|---|---|---|---|---|
| M.D. Marshall | 167.4 | 50 | 437 | 24 | 18.20 | 7/53 | 3 |
| J. Garner | 217.5 | 60 | 540 | 29 | 18.62 | 5/55 | 1 |
| R.A. Harper | 128.4 | 47 | 276 | 13 | 21.23 | 6/57 | 1 |
| M.A. Holding | 122.2 | 24 | 343 | 15 | 22.86 | 5/43 | 1 |
| M.A. Small | 21 | 2 | 78 | 3 | 26.00 | 3/40 | |
| E.A.E. Baptiste | 125 | 39 | 265 | 8 | 33.12 | 3/31 | |
| W.W. Davis | 23 | 3 | 77 | 2 | 38.50 | 2/71 | |
| I.V.A. Richards | 1 | — | 2 | 0 | — | | |

### ENGLAND CATCHES

10–P.R. Downton; 5—I.T. Botham; 3—G. Fowler, D.I. Gower, A.J. Lamb and D.R. Pringle; 2–V.P. Terry, G. Miller, M.W. Gatting, C.J. Tavare and P.J.W. Allott; 1–N.G.B. Cook, N.G. Cowans, D.W. Randall, R.G.D. Willis and B.C. Broad

### WEST INDIES CATCHES

16–P.J. Dujon; 9–C.H. Lloyd; 8–R.A. Harper; 5–I.V.A. Richards; 3–D.L. Haynes, C.G. Greenidge and J. Garner; 2–M.A. Holding and M.D. Marshall; 1–H.A. Gomes and E.A.E. Baptiste

day, evaporated on the third when Desmond Haynes, so long out of form, stroked his side to a position with a century of effortless grace and unerring concentration. There was good support from Lloyd and the dashing Dujon, but Botham was at his most wayward and Gower at his least energetic or inventive. Ellison bowled encouragingly and Agnew took his first Test wickets, yet the outcricket remained depressingly unimaginative and unable to cope with the West Indian batsmen. Harper, Holding and Garner hit strongly at the close, and the visitors, having been 69 for 3, with Richards and Gomes out, ended on 346 so that England needed 375 to win.

They were 71 for the loss of Fowler at tea on the fourth day, but soon after they were 90 for 4 as Holding, bowling off his long run and with all his old grace and speed, tore the heart out ot the innings. Broad was caught in the gully off his glove as the ball rose steeply. Gower was lbw as the ball cut back and kept low and Lamb was sensationally caught at short-leg by Haynes, one-handed to his right.

Tavare played well until caught at slip and Botham, with some heartening and exciting shots, carried England's hopes into the last day. They were soon dashed. Botham hooked a Garner bouncer into the hands of Marshall at long leg. Botham's fifty had come off 49 balls. It was at least a gesture of spirited defiance, but it was a last flicker. Downton was lbw to Garner; in his first over, Holding had Allott caught at

*Gower falls to Holding and a miserable summer for the England captain draws to a close. (Ken Kelly)*

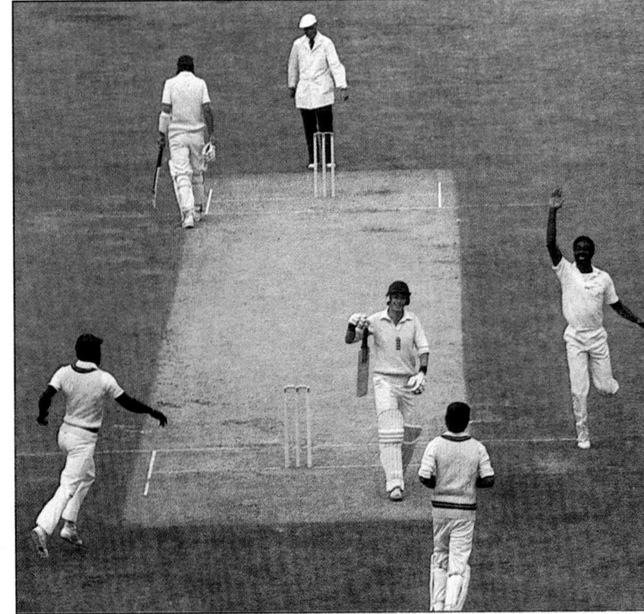

## West Indians in England 1984
First Class Matches

| BATTING | v. Worcestershire (Worcester) 19–21 May | | v. Somerset (Taunton) 23–25 May | | v. Glamorgan (Swansea) 26–28 May | | v. Northamptonshire (Milton Keynes) 9–11 June | | First Test Match (Edgbaston) 14–18 June | | v. Essex (Chelmsford) 23–25 June | | Second Test Match (Lord's) 28 June–3 July | | v. Leicestershire (Leicester) 7–9 July | | Third Test Match (Leeds) 12–16 July | | v. Derbyshire (Derby) 21–23 July | | Fourth Test Match (Old Trafford) 26–31 July | |
|---|---|---|---|---|---|---|---|---|---|---|---|---|---|---|---|---|---|---|---|---|---|---|
| C.G. Greenidge | 138 | — | | | 4 | — | 11 | 36* | 19 | — | 77 | 62 | 1 | 214* | 56* | — | 10 | 49 | 113 | — | 223 | — |
| D.L. Haynes | 89 | — | 20 | — | | | 12 | 12* | 8 | — | | | 12 | 17 | 50 | — | 18 | 43 | 83 | — | 2 | — |
| R.B. Richardson | 19 | — | 50 | — | 111 | — | | | | | 5 | 41 | | | 45 | — | | | 30 | — | | |
| I.V.A. Richards | 12 | — | | | 170 | — | 41 | — | 117 | — | 9 | 60 | 72 | — | 2 | — | 15 | 22* | 0 | — | 1 | — |
| A.L. Logie | 2 | — | 0 | — | 71 | — | | | | | 85 | 2 | | | 141 | — | | | 65 | — | | |
| P.J. Dujon | 52* | — | 12 | — | 18 | — | 27 | — | 23 | — | 107 | 24 | 8 | — | | | 26 | — | 57 | — | 101 | — |
| E.A.E. Baptiste | 6 | — | | | — | — | 16 | — | 87* | — | | | 44 | — | | | 0 | — | 0 | — | 6 | — |
| R.A. Harper | 42 | — | 73 | — | 16* | — | | | 14 | — | — | 12 | 8 | — | — | — | 0 | — | 31 | — | 39* | — |
| J. Garner | 29 | — | | | — | — | | | 0 | — | — | 3 | 6 | — | | | 0 | — | | | 7 | — |
| M.A. Holding | 0 | — | | | — | — | | | 69 | — | | | | | | | 59 | — | | | 0 | — |
| C.A. Walsh | 2* | — | 0 | — | | | 0 | — | | | — | — | | | — | — | | | 0* | — | | |
| C.H. Lloyd | | | 72 | — | — | — | 8 | — | 71 | — | | | 39 | — | | | 48 | — | | | 1 | — |
| T.R.O. Payne | | | 1 | — | | | 15 | — | | | 19* | 34* | | | 41* | — | | | 44 | — | | |
| M.A. Small | | | 2* | — | | | 1 | — | | | — | — | 3* | — | — | — | | | | | | |
| M.D. Marshall | | | 34 | — | | | 15 | — | 2 | — | | | 29 | — | — | — | 4 | — | | | | |
| H.A. Gomes | | | 72 | — | 73 | — | 109* | — | 143 | — | 4* | 6 | 10 | 92* | 143 | — | 104* | 2* | | | 30 | — |
| W.W. Davis | | | | | | | | | | | | | | | | | | | 11 | — | 77 | — |
| Byes | | | | | | | | 2 | 6 | | | | | 4 | 1 | | | | | | 4 | |
| Leg-byes | 19 | | 3 | | 12 | | 9 | | 17 | | 1 | 17 | 5 | 4 | 6 | | 3 | 2 | 4 | | 6 | |
| Wides | | | 2 | | 4 | | | | 2 | | 2 | 4 | 1 | | 5 | | | | | | 2 | |
| No-balls | 2 | | 1 | | 10 | | 4 | | 28 | | 13 | 12 | 7 | 13 | 16 | | 15 | 13 | 21 | | 1 | |
| Total | 412 | | 342 | | 489 | | 268 | 50 | 606 | | 322 | 277 | 245 | 344 | 506 | | 302 | 131 | 459 | | 500 | |
| Wickets | 9 | | 10 | | 6 | | 10 | 0 | 10 | | 5 | 8 | 10 | 1 | 5 | | 10 | 2 | 10 | | 10 | |
| Result | D | | W | | W | | D | | W | | D | | W | | D | | W | | W | | W | |

*Catches*
27 – P.J. Dujon
14 – R.A. Harper
12 – C.H. Lloyd and I.V.A. Richards
9 – D.L. Haynes
5 – T.R.O. Payne (ct 4/st 1) and C.G. Greenidge
4 – J. Garner
3 – M.D. Marshall, M.A. Holding, A.L. Logie and R.B. Richardson
2 – H.A. Gomes
1 – M.A. Small, W.W. Davis, E.A.E. Baptiste and sub

| BOWLING | J. Garner | M.A. Holding | E.A.E. Baptiste | C.A. Walsh | R.A. Harper | I.V.A. Richards | M.D. Marshall | M.A. Small | H.A. Gomes |
|---|---|---|---|---|---|---|---|---|---|
| v. Worcestershire (Worcester) | 8–5–12–0 | 10–5–15–0 | 8–0–33–1 | 9–3–36–0 | 7–3–9–0 | 3–1–10–0 | | | |
| 19–21 May | | | | | | | | | |
| v. Somerset (Taunton) | | | | 15–3–37–1 | 19.3–9–32–5 | | 11–4–13–2 | 13–7–9–0 | 3–2–2–1 |
| 23–25 May | | | | 10–2–30–1 | 5–0–17–0 | | 19.2–7–31–5 | 14–1–36–3 | |
| v. Glamorgan (Swansea) | 16–10–19–5 | 25.3–9–61–3 | 19–7–32–0 | | 17–7–30–2 | | | | 1–1–0–0 |
| 26–28 May | 14–5–21–3 | 14–3–27–3 | 11.2–5–17–4 | | | | | | |
| v. Northamptonshire (Milton | | | 22–6–48–2 | 14–4–34–0 | | 5–0–10–0 | 17.4–4–36–4 | 21–5–52–4 | 11–2–21–0 |
| Keynes) 9–11 June | | | 19–4–49–4 | 15–2–60–1 | | 4–2–17–0 | 15–4–36–0 | 5–0–27–0 | 9–1–17–0 |
| First Test Match | 14.3–2–53–4 | 16–4–44–2 | 11–3–28–1 | | 4–1–8–1 | | 14–4–37–1 | | |
| (Edgbaston) 14–18 June | 23.5–7–55–5 | 12–3–29–0 | 5–1–18–0 | | 13–3–48–1 | | 23–7–65–2 | | |
| v. Essex (Chelmsford) | 12-1–25–0 | | | 17–3–76–1 | 30.1–3–85–6 | 12–1–27–0 | | 9–1–41–2 | |
| 23–25 June | 3–0–7–2 | | | 9–1–40–1 | 18–10–26–2 | 8–2–22–0 | | 10–1–53–1 | 3–0–13–0 |
| Second Test Match | 32–10–67–1 | | 20–6–36–2 | | 8–0–25–0 | | 36.5–10–85–6 | 9–0–38–0 | |
| (Lord's) 28 June–3 July | 30.3–3–91–3 | | 26–8–48–0 | | 8–1–18–1 | | 22–6–85–2 | 12–2–40–3 | |
| v. Leicestershire (Leicester) | | | | 16.1–4–71–3 | 30–9–73–3 | 16–3–60–2 | 10–3–28–2 | 7–0–25–0 | 1–0–1–0 |
| 7–9 July | | | | 13–2–50–2 | 11–3–16–0 | 17–8–27–1 | | | 14–8–25–1 |
| Third Test Match | 30–11–73–2 | 29.2–8–70–4 | 13–1–45–1 | | 19–6–47–3 | | 6–4–6–0 | | |
| (Leeds) 12–26 July | 16–7–37–2 | 7–1–31–0 | | | 16–8–30–1 | | 26–9–53–7 | | |
| v. Derbyshire (Derby) | | | | 13–4–33–3 | 5–4–4–2 | | | | |
| 21–23 July | | | 17–3–73–0 | 10–2–37–0 | 23.5–9–41–4 | 8–3–10–0 | | | |
| Fourth Test Match | 22.2–7–51–4 | 21–2–50–1 | 19–8–31–3 | | 23–10–33–0 | | | | |
| (Old Trafford) 26–31 July | 12–4–25–2 | 11–2–21–1 | 11–5–29–0 | | 28.4–12–57–6 | 1–0–2–0 | | | |
| v. Nottinghamshire (Trent | | | | | | | | | |
| Bridge) 1–3 August | | | | | | | | | |
| v. Middlesex (Lord's) | | 7–1–40–0 | | 7–1–28–1 | 3–1–14–0 | | 9–2–34–1 | | |
| 4–6 August | | | | 8–1–25–0 | 4–1–9–0 | | 11–1–31–2 | | 2–1–2–0 |
| Fifth Test Match | 18–6–37–2 | 13–2–55–2 | 12–4–19–1 | | 1–1–0–0 | | 17.5–5–35–5 | | |
| (The Oval) 9–14 August | 18.4–3–51–4 | 13–2–43–5 | 8–3–11–0 | | 8–5–10–0 | | 22–5–71–1 | | |
| | 270.5–81–624–39 *av.* 16.00 | 178.5–42–486–21 *av.* 23.14 | 221.2–64–517–19 *av.* 27.21 | 156.1–32–557–14 *av.* 39.78 | 302.1–106–632–37 *av.* 17.08 | 74–20–185–3 *av.* 61.66 | 260.4–75–646–40 *av.* 16.15 | 100–17–321–13 *av.* 24.69 | 44–15–81–2 *av.* 40.50 |

a M.R. Davis, retired hurt, absent injured
b T.A. Lloyd, retired hurt, absent injured
c J.H. Hampshire, absent hurt
d V.P. Terry, absent hurt

| v. Nottingham (Trent Bridge) 1–3 August | | v. Middlesex (Lord's) 4–6 August | | Fifth Test Match (The Oval) 9–14 August | | M | Inns | NOs | Runs | H/S | Av |
|---|---|---|---|---|---|---|---|---|---|---|---|
| | | | | 22 | 34 | 11 | 16 | 3 | 1069 | 223 | 82.23 |
| 69 | — | 0 | 62 | 10 | 125 | 12 | 17 | 1 | 632 | 125 | 39.50 |
| 6 | — | 0 | 28 | | | 8 | 10 | — | 335 | 111 | 33.50 |
| 81 | — | | | 8 | 15 | 12 | 15 | 1 | 625 | 170 | 44.64 |
| 122* | — | 13 | 84* | | | 8 | 10 | 2 | 585 | 141 | 73.12 |
| | | 29 | 22* | 3 | 49 | 12 | 15 | 2 | 558 | 107 | 42.92 |
| — | — | | | 32 | 5 | 10 | 9 | 1 | 196 | 87* | 24.50 |
| — | — | 58 | — | 18 | 17 | 13 | 12 | 2 | 328 | 73 | 32.80 |
| | | | | 6 | 10* | 8 | 8 | 1 | 61 | 29 | 8.71 |
| | | 31 | — | 0 | 30 | 7 | 7 | — | 189 | 69 | 27.00 |
| — | — | 0 | — | | | 8 | 5 | 2 | 2 | 2* | 0.66 |
| 29* | — | | | 60* | 36 | 9 | 9 | 2 | 364 | 72 | 52.00 |
| — | — | 35 | 2 | | | 7 | 8 | 3 | 191 | 44 | 38.20 |
| | | | | | | 5 | 3 | 2 | 6 | 3* | 6.00 |
| | | 7 | 0 | 0 | 12 | 8 | 9 | | 103 | 34 | 11.44 |
| 27 | — | 4 | 3 | 18 | 1 | 12 | 17 | 5 | 841 | 143 | 70.08 |
| — | — | 6* | 18 | | | 4 | 4 | 1 | 112 | 77 | 37.33 |
| | | 4 | | 1 | | | | | | | |
| 20 | | 5 | 1 | 4 | 12 | | | | | | |
| 2 | | 3 | | 7 | | | | | | | |
| 5 | | 16 | 4 | 1 | | | | | | | |
| 361 | | 211 | 224 | 190 | 346 | | | | | | |
| 4 | | 10 | 6 | 10 | 10 | | | | | | |
| D | | D | | W | | | | | | | |

| C.G. Greenidge | W.W. Davis | Byes | Leg-byes | Wides | No-balls | Total | Wkts |
|---|---|---|---|---|---|---|---|
| | | 1 | 1 | | 7 | 124 | 1 |
| | | | | | | | |
| | | 6 | 5 | 1 | 11 | 116 | 9 a |
| | | 2 | 4 | 1 | 4 | 125 | 9 |
| | | | 12 | 8 | 13 | 175 | 10 |
| | | 9 | 7 | | 7 | 88 | 10 |
| | | 2 | 8 | | 9 | 220 | 10 |
| | | 1 | 7 | | 6 | 220 | 5 |
| | | 8 | 5 | 8 | | 191 | 9 b |
| | | 1 | 5 | 4 | 10 | 235 | 9 |
| | | 4 | 5 | 1 | 3 | 267 | 9 |
| | | | | 1 | 2 | 164 | 6 |
| | | 4 | 14 | 2 | 15 | 286 | 10 |
| | | 4 | 7 | 1 | 6 | 300 | 9 |
| | | 5 | 2 | 3 | 15 | 283 | 10 |
| 9–6–11–1 | | 1 | 4 | | 2 | 136 | 5 |
| | | 4 | 7 | | 18 | 270 | 10 |
| | | | 6 | | 2 | | |
| | 18–5–39–5 | 2 | 4 | | 7 | 89 | 10 |
| | 9–1–32–5 | | 5 | 1 | 2 | 201 | 9 c |
| | 20–2–71–2 | 5 | 21 | | 18 | 280 | 10 |
| | 3–1–6–0 | 9 | 3 | 1 | 3 | 156 | 9 d |
| | | | | | Abandoned | | |
| | | | | | | | |
| | 12–3–42–2 | 2 | 4 | | 13 | 177 | 4 |
| | 4–1–9–0 | 2 | 6 | | 3 | 87 | 2 |
| | | 2 | 4 | | 10 | 162 | 10 |
| | | | 2 | 1 | 13 | 202 | 10 |
| 9–6–11–1 *av.* 11.00 | 66–13–199–14 *av.* 14.21 | | | | | | |

slip and held a return catch from Pocock who had failed to score in four innings; and finally Ellison was taken in the gully.

West Indies had won the series 5–0, the first time England had suffered such indignity in England, and it represented just about the difference in the two sides.

The match was followed by a presentation 'ceremony' which I hope is the last I will witness for it was totally without dignity and it brought discredit to the game.

### *11, 12 and 13 August*

#### *at Canterbury*

**Sri Lankans** 340 for 7 dec (A. Ranatunga 118, P.A. de Silva 59)
**Kent** 182 (D.S. de Silva 5 for 39, V.B. John 5 for 50) and 420 for 5 dec (D.G. Aslett 221 not out, M.R. Benson 65, A.D.E. Samarayake 4 for 142)

*Match drawn*

### *11, 13 and 14 August*

#### *at Derby*

**Derbyshire** 475 (J.G. Wright 177, G. Miller 76 not out, W.P. Fowler 57, D.A. Reeve 4 for 130)
**Sussex** 135 (I.J. Gould 58, R.J. Finnet 4 for 19) and 151 (C.M. Wells 60, G. Miller 5 for 41, D.G. Moir 5 for 62)

*Derbyshire won by an innings and 189 runs*
*Derbyshire 24 pts, Sussex 2 pts*

#### *at Chelmsford*

**Essex** 200 (P.J. Prichard 54) and 264 (G.A. Gooch 87, S.C. Booth 4 for 50)
**Somerset** 180 (J.K. Lever 5 for 54) and 199 (V.J. Marks 60, B.C. Rose 59, J.K. Lever 5 for 62)

*Essex won by 85 runs*
*Essex 22 pts, Somerset 5 pts*

#### *at Cardiff*

**Glamorgan** 142 and 425 for 7 dec (Javed Miandad 171, A.L. Jones 132, R.C. Ontong 54)
**Hampshire** 328 (D.R. Turner 89, N.G. Cowley 76, T.M. Tremlett 68 not out, J.G. Thomas 4 for 49)

*Match drawn*
*Hampshire 6 pts, Glamorgan 2 pts*

#### *at Cheltenham*

**Gloucestershire** 280 (A.J. Wright 139, C.W.J. Athey 65, S.T. Clarke 4 for 38) and 225 for 6 (J.N. Shepherd 62 not out, A.W. Stovold 54)
**Surrey** 367 (R.D.V. Knight 142, G.P. Howarth 55, D.V. Lawrence 5 for 103)

*Match drawn*
*Gloucestershire 5 pts, Surrey 5 pts*

#### *at Leicester*

**Lancashire** 218 (P.B. Clift 5 for 67) and 285 for 4 dec (J. Abrahams 100 not out, M. Watkinson 59)
**Leicestershire** 139 (S.T. Jefferies 6 for 67) and 124 (M. Watkinson 6 for 39)

*Lancashire won by 240 runs*
*Lancashire 22 pts, Leicestershire 4 pts*

#### *at Lord's*

**Middlesex** 152 (C.T. Radley 52, K. Saxelby 5 for 43, R.J. Hadlee 4 for 55) and 149 (K.E. Cooper 8 for 44)

*After eight years of uninterrupted Test cricket which have brought him more than three thousand runs and two hundred wickets Ian Botham decided that he needed a rest. He stated that he was not available for the England party to tour India. (A.S.P.)*

**Nottinghamshire** 344 (R.J. Hadlee 210 not out, W.W. Daniel 4 for 85)

*Nottinghamshire won by an innings and 43 runs*
*Nottinghamshire 25 pts, Middlesex 5 pts*

***at Wellingborough***

**Worcestershire** 351 for 9 dec (T.S. Curtis 124, M.J. Weston 66) and 193 for 5 dec (D.N. Patel 55 not out)
**Northamptonshire** 263 (R.J. Bailey 64, M.J. Weston 4 for 44, P.J. Newport 4 for 47) and 215 for 5 (G. Cook 91, R.J. Bailey 53)

*Match drawn*
*Worcestershire 8 pts, Northamptonshire 5 pts*

***at Leeds***

**Warwickshire** 285 (G.W. Humpage 112, C.M. Old 52, A. Sidebottom 6 for 64) and 242 for 7 dec (G.W. Humpage 77, D.L. Amiss 54)
**Yorkshire** 153 (C.M. Old 5 for 53, A.M. Ferreira 4 for 61) and 183 (G. Boycott 55 not out, C.M. Old 6 for 46)

*Warwickshire won by 191 runs*
*Warwickshire 23 pts, Yorkshire 5 pts*

A century which began on Saturday evening and ended on Tuesday morning and spanned more than six hours brought the Cheltenham Festival to a dull conclusion. The centurion was Roger Knight who could not match the sparkle that Tony Wright showed in hitting a maiden hundred on the first day. There was another fine maiden century at Canterbury where Ranatunga hit cleanly and often. Somachandra de Silva's leg-breaks and John's swing troubled Kent who followed-on. Aslett then hit the first double century of his career and the match was saved.

Centuries by Javed Miandad and Alan Lewis Jones saved Glamorgan who once more settled for a tedious draw and in spite of a fine innings from Curtis and good all-round cricket from Weston, the promising Worcestershire side could not force a win at Wellingborough.

It took only two days for Derbyshire, having acquired a taste for victory, to beat Sussex. John Wright, on one of his infrequent appearances, gave a magnificent display for the home side and first Finney and then spinners Miller and Moir bowled out Sussex twice in less than a day. There was victory in two days for Nottinghamshire at Lord's too in one of the most remarkable matches of the season which produced one of the finest individual performances of the season. Hadlee and Saxelby exploited conditions and wicket to bowl out Middlesex cheaply, but the visitors fared even worse when Daniel staggered them to 17 for 4. Hadlee then joined Johnson and dominated a stand of 124. By the end of the day he had scored 127 out of 178 and on the Monday reached the first double century of his career and led his side to maximum points. He and Such, a career best 16, added 57 for the last wicket. Middlesex then succumbed to the career best bowling of Kevin Cooper and Notts moved strongly to challenge Essex for the title.

Paul Prichard squeezed Essex to a second batting point on the opening day at Chelmsford and then John Lever took ten wickets in the match and, with Gooch in violent mood in the second innings, the champions beat a depleted Somerset side.

Leicestershire's challenge, like Middlesex's faded as they provided Lancashire with their first championship win of the season. The bowling of Jefferies and Watkinson, a career best, and the calm influence of John Abrahams brought Lancashire their much needed win. It ended a run of 26

ABOVE: *Mike Watkinson's career best at Leicester helped to bring Lancashire's first championship victory of the season (David Munden).* BELOW: *Kevin Cooper, 8 for 44 against Middlesex at Lord's, 11–13 August, and Notts maintain pressure on Essex at the top of the championship. (George Herringshaw)*

## Derbyshire C.C.C.
Limited-Over Matches – 1984

| BATTING | v. Leicestershire (Leicester) 29 April (J.P.) | v. Worcestershire (Worcester) 12 May (B.&H.) | v. Nottinghamshire (Derby) 15 May (B.&H.) | v. Minor Counties (Shrewsbury) 17/18 May (B.&H.) | v. Lancashire (Derby) 19 May (B.&H.) | v. Lancashire (Derby) 20 May (J.P.) | v. Nottinghamshire (Trent Bridge) 27 May (J.P.) | v. Middlesex (Derby) 3 June (J.P.) | v. Gloucestershire (Gloucester) 10 June (J.P.) | v. Yorkshire (Chesterfield) 17 June (J.P.) | v. Northamptonshire (Harrogate) 20 June (T.T.) | v. Kent (Derby) 24 June (J.P.) | v. Worcestershire (Worcester) 1 July (J.P.) | v. Cumberland (Kendal) 4 July (N.W.) | v. Warwickshire (Derby) 8 July (J.P.) | v. Surrey (The Oval) 15 July (J.P.) | v. Leicestershire (Leicester) 18/19 July (N.W.) | v. Glamorgan (Ebbw Vale) 29 July (J.P.) |
|---|---|---|---|---|---|---|---|---|---|---|---|---|---|---|---|---|---|---|
| K.J. Barnett | 65 | 34 | 11 | 14 | 29 | 44 | | 5 | 41 | 21 | | 1 | 16 | 37 | 55 | | 16 | 39 |
| J.G. Wright | 35 | 20 | 39 | 24 | 12 | 0 | | 6 | 14 | 46 | | 34 | 7 | 73* | 5 | 37 | 46 | 6 |
| J.E. Morris | 60* | 51 | | 5 | 24 | 4 | | 57 | 104 | 16 | 26 | 16 | 18 | — | 45 | 1 | 8 | |
| J.H. Hampshire | 8 | 21* | 5 | 1 | | | | | | | | | | | | | | 22 |
| G. Miller | 5* | 7 | 25 | 65* | 26 | 29* | | | 78* | | | 18 | | — | 71* | 11 | 1 | |
| W.P. Fowler | — | 6 | 1 | 53 | 16 | 26* | | 9 | 19* | 30 | 9 | 41 | 7 | — | 26 | 7 | 1 | 2 |
| R.J. Finney | — | 6 | 9 | 28 | 46 | — | | 40* | — | 19 | 18 | | 50* | — | 2 | 1 | | 0 |
| B. Roberts | — | | 0 | 2* | 11 | — | | 3 | — | 0 | 72 | 7 | 33 | — | 3 | | 3 | 24* |
| R.W. Taylor | — | — | 6 | — | 6* | — | | — | — | | | 29* | | — | | | 1 | 1 |
| P.G. Newman | — | 18* | 21 | — | 2* | — | | 4 | — | 24 | 15 | 6 | 7 | — | | 0* | 35 | |
| O.H. Mortensen | — | | | | — | | | — | — | 2 | | | | | | | | |
| A. Hill | | 74 | 87 | | 25 | 26 | | 43 | 6 | 8 | 2* | 8 | 33 | 13* | 8 | 4 | 25 | 29 |
| C.J. Tunnicliffe | | — | | — | | | | 3* | | | 2 | | | | | 4 | | |
| D.G. Moir | | | 1* | | | — | | | | 2 | 0 | 79 | 8 | — | 4 | 25 | 23 | 8 |
| B.J.M. Maher | | | | | | | | | | 8* | | | 3 | | 0 | 3 | | |
| I.S. Anderson | | | | | | | | | | | 6 | | | | | | | 2 |
| C. Marples | | | | | | | | | | | 19 | | | | | | | |
| J.P. Taylor | | | | | | | | | | | 0 | | | | | | | |
| I. Broome | | | | | | | | | | | | 2* | 7 | | 9* | 0 | 2* | 0 |
| Byes | 1 | 1 | 1 | 1 | | 1 | | | 4 | | 6 | 1 | | | | 4 | | 4 |
| Leg-byes | 3 | 11 | 7 | 2 | 9 | 3 | | 4 | 1 | 3 | | 13 | 6 | 1 | 8 | 2 | 11 | 12 |
| Wides | | 6 | 7 | 4 | 4 | 2 | | 2 | 4 | 1 | 2 | | 4 | | 1 | | 4 | 4 |
| No-balls | 4 | 2 | 3 | 2 | | 1 | | 4 | 1 | 1 | 5 | 1 | 1 | | 3 | | 5 | |
| Total | 181 | 257 | 223 | 201 | 210 | 136 | | 180 | 272 | 181 | 182 | 256 | 200 | 124 | 240 | 99 | 181 | 153 |
| Wickets | 3 | 7 | 10 | 6 | 8 | 4 | | 7 | 4 | 10 | 10 | 9 | 10 | 1 | 9 | 10 | 10 | 10 |
| Result | W | W | L | W | W | W | Ab. | L | L | L | L | W | L | W | W | L | L | L |
| Points | 4 | 2 | 0 | 2 | 2 | 4 | 2 | 0 | 0 | 0 | — | 4 | 0 | — | 4 | 0 | — | 0 |

*Catches*

23 – R.W. Taylor (ct 21/st 2)
14 – W.P. Fowler
11 – K.J. Barnett
7 – D.G. Moir and G. Miller
6 – J.G. Wright
5 – B. Roberts and A. Hill
4 – P.G. Newman and J.E. Morris
3 – R.J. Finney and C.J. Tunnicliffe
2 – J.H. Hampshire, C. Marples
B.J.M. Maher (ct 1/st 1) and
O.H. Mortensen
1 – I.S. Anderson and sub

| BOWLING | O.H. Mortensen | R.J. Finney | G. Miller | W.P. Fowler | P.G. Newman | C.J. Tunnicliffe | K.J. Barnett | D.G. Moir | B. Roberts |
|---|---|---|---|---|---|---|---|---|---|
| (J.P.) *v.* Leicestershire (Leicester) 29 April | 8–1–46–1 | 8–1–38–0 | 8–3–11–1 | 8–1–29–1 | 8–0–44–4 | | | | |
| (B.&H.) *v.* Worcestershire (Worcester) 12 May | | 9–0–62–0 | 11–2–38–1 | 11–1–54–2 | 11–0–50–1 | 11–5–28–2 | 2–0–10–1 | | |
| (B.&H.) *v.* Nottinghamshire (Derby) 15 May | | 9–0–32–0 | 11–0–39–0 | 3–0–23–1 | 11–2–44–1 | | | 11–1–43–0 | 10–0–79–2 |
| (B.&H.) *v.* Minor C. (Shrewsbury) 17/18 May | | 6–0–29–0 | 11–2–20–1 | | 11–1–39–3 | 11–3–29–1 | 6–2–21–1 | | 10–1–47–2 |
| (B.&H.) *v.* Lancashire (Derby) 19 May | 11–2–30–3 | 11–5–20–2 | 11–2–31–3 | | 11–1–47–1 | | 1–0–2–0 | | 10–1–25–0 |
| (J.P.) *v.* Lancashire (Derby) 20 May | | 8–3–17–2 | 8–2–18–1 | | 7–1–19–2 | | | 8–1–25–1 | 7.2–0–29–4 |
| (J.P.) *v.* Nottinghamshire (Trent Br.) 27 May | | | | | | | | | |
| (J.P.) *v.* Middlesex (Derby) 3 June | 6–0–24–1 | 6–0–21–1 | | | 5–0–46–1 | 4.4–0–49–0 | | | 6–0–26–2 |
| (J.P.) *v.* Gloucestershire (Gloucester) 10 June | 7–0–26–1 | 6–0–41–0 | 7.5–0–89–3 | | 8–0–34–1 | | | | |
| (J.P.) *v.* Yorkshire (Chesterfield) 17 June | 8–2–27–0 | 3–0–24–0 | | | 8–1–37–1 | | 5–0–40–1 | 8–1–36–2 | 8–0–48–2 |
| (T.T.) *v.* Northants. (Harrogate) 20 June | | 2–0–18–0 | | 8–0–48–1 | 7–0–32–2 | 11–0–35–0 | | 11–3–33–1 | 6–0–48–1 |
| (J.P.) *v.* Kent (Derby) 24 June | | | 8–0–50–0 | | 8–0–36–0 | | | 8–0–54–3 | 8–0–76–2 |
| (J.P.) *v.* Worcestershire (Worcester) 1 July | | 8–1–24–1 | | 4–0–31–3 | 6–0–37–2 | | | 8–0–27–0 | 6–1–46–1 |
| (N.W.) *v.* Cumberland (Kendal) 4 July | | 8–3–8–2 | 12–4–14–0 | 2–0–6–0 | 12–2–25–1 | | 9.2–0–24–6 | 12–5–19–1 | 4–0–11–0 |
| (J.P.) *v.* Warwickshire (Derby) 8 July | | 8–0–32–0 | 8–0–32–4 | | | | | 8–0–29–1 | 7.2–0–49–4 |
| (J.P.) *v.* Surrey (The Oval) 15 July | | 5–0–44–1 | | | 8–1–37–2 | 4–0–43–0 | | | |
| (N.W.) *v.* Leicestershire (Leicester) 18 July | | | 12–3–25–0 | | 12–1–73–0 | | | 12–1–39–2 | 12–1–73–2 |
| (J.P.) *v.* Glamorgan (Ebbw Vale) 29 July | | 6–0–45–1 | | 4–0–30–0 | | | 8–0–61–1 | 8–1–36–1 | 8–0–51–1 |
| (J.P.) *v.* Northants. (Northampton) 5 Aug. | | 8–0–38–4 | 8–0–38–0 | 4–0–26–1 | | | 4–0–30–0 | 8–0–29–0 | |
| (J.P.) *v.* Sussex (Heanor) 12 August | | 8–0–56–1 | 8–0–38–1 | | | | | 8–0–48–0 | 8–0–35–2 |
| (J.P.) *v.* Somerset (Taunton) 19 August | 8–1–26–2 | 7–0–41–2 | 4–0–19–1 | | | | | 8–0–56–0 | 4–0–29–0 |
| (Asda) *v.* Yorkshire (Scarborough) 29 Aug. | 10–2–21–0 | 10–3–37–1 | | 5–0–33–1 | | | | 10–0–38–2 | 8–0–48–2 |
| (J.P.) *v.* Essex (Derby) 2 September | 8–0–28–2 | 8–0–54–1 | | 3–0–16–0 | | | | 8–1–32–1 | 5–0–46–2 |
| (J.P.) *v.* Hampshire (Derby) 9 September | 8–1–25–3 | | 0.4–0–8–0 | | | | | | |
| Wickets | 13 | 19 | 16 | 10 | 22 | 3 | 10 | 15 | 29 |

| v. Northamptonshire (Northampton) 5 August (J.P.) | v. Sussex (Heanor) 12 August (J.P.) | v. Somerset (Derby) 19 August (J.P.) | v. Yorkshire (Scarborough) 29 August (Asda) | v. Essex (Derby) 2 September (J.P.) | v. Hampshire (Derby) 9 September (J.P.) | Runs |
|---|---|---|---|---|---|---|
| 29 | 12 | 1 | 22 | 131* | 0 | 623 |
| 13 | 24 | 33 | | 1 | 33 | 508 |
| 24 | | | 0 | 10 | 25 | 494 |
| 0 | | 8 | 2 | | 16* | 83 |
| 36 | 6 | 22 | | | 8* | 408 |
| 51 | 21 | 10 | 0 | 3 | 24 | 362 |
| 2 | 12 | 14 | 16 | — | | 263 |
| | 47 | 8 | 6 | 44* | — | 263 |
| 4* | 4* | 8* | 0 | — | — | 59 |
| | | | | | | 132 |
| | | 5 | 1* | — | | 8 |
| 13 | 28 | | 18 | — | — | 450 |
| | | | | | | 9 |
| 5 | 5 | 5 | 0 | — | — | 165 |
| | | | | | | 14 |
| | 23 | | 22 | 8 | | 61 |
| | | | | | | 19 |
| 0 | 4 | 1 | | | — | 5 |
| | | | | | | 20 |
| 1 | | | 1 | 5 | | |
| 7 | 12 | 3 | 1 | 8 | 6 | |
| | 3 | 10 | 3 | | 2 | |
| | | | 6 | 5 | 2 | |
| 185 | 201 | 128 | 98 | 215 | 116 | |
| 10 | 10 | 10 | 10 | 4 | 4 | |
| L | L | L | L | L | L | |
| 0 | 0 | 0 | — | 0 | 0 | |

| J.P. Taylor | I. Broome | A. Hill | Byes | Leg-byes | Wides | No-balls | Total | Wkts |
|---|---|---|---|---|---|---|---|---|
| | | | 1 | 6 | 2 | | 177 | 8 |
| | | | 1 | 5 | 5 | 4 | 257 | 9 |
| | | | 1 | 9 | 10 | 2 | 282 | 4 |
| | | | 4 | 6 | 1 | 1 | 197 | 8 |
| | | | 3 | 4 | 3 | | 165 | 9 |
| | | | 5 | 13 | 5 | 2 | 135 | 10 |
| | | | Match Abandoned | | | | | |
| | | | 4 | 7 | 4 | | 181 | 5 |
| | | | | 10 | 3 | | 203 | 5 |
| | | | 6 | 5 | 2 | | 225 | 6 |
| 10–0–60–2 | | | 1 | 8 | 5 | 6 | 294 | 7 |
| | 8–0–21–1 | | 3 | 8 | 7 | | 255 | 6 |
| | 8–0–39–1 | | 2 | 13 | 3 | | 222 | 8 |
| | | | 1 | 7 | 6 | | 121 | 10 |
| | 8–0–45–1 | | | 15 | 3 | 1 | 206 | 10 |
| | 8–0–53–3 | | | 6 | 2 | | 185 | 7 |
| | 12–0–74–2 | | 6 | 7 | | 4 | 301 | 7 |
| | 6–1–35–2 | | 6 | 8 | 3 | 2 | 277 | 6 |
| 8–1–41–2 | | | 1 | 7 | 6 | | 216 | 8 |
| 8–0–38–2 | | | 2 | 8 | 6 | | 231 | 6 |
| 7–0–47–0 | | | 1 | 10 | 13 | | 242 | 5 |
| | | 7–1–26–1 | | 11 | | 6 | 220 | 7 |
| | | 8–0–32–3 | | 9 | 2 | 1 | 220 | 9 |
| 8–0–46–1 | | | 1 | 5 | 2 | 2 | 89 | 4 |
| 7 | 10 | 4 | | | | | | |

## English Counties Form Charts

The statistics of all limited-over cricket matches follow in pages 348 to 385. The games covered are:

John Player League (J.P.) — Tilcon Trophy (T.T.)
Benson and Hedges (B.&H.) — Asda Trophy (Asda)
National Westminster Bank Trophy (N.W.)

Once again averages are not produced as it is felt that they have little relevance in limited-over cricket where batsmen often sacrifice their wickets for quick runs and bowlers are ordered to contain rather than capture wickets.
In the batting tables a blank indicates that a batsman did not *play* in a game, a dash (—) that he did not *bat*.

championship matches without a win, stretching back to July, 1983.

The bludgeoning bat of Geoff Humpage and the accuracy and movement of Chris Old brought Warwickshire victory at Headingley. Old had ten wickets in the match, the first Yorkshireman to take 10 wickets for and against Yorkshire in the championship.

### John Player League

***12 August***

***at Heanor***

**Sussex** 231 for 6 (A.M. Green 83, C.M. Wells 62)
**Derbyshire** 201 (G.S. le Roux 4 for 30, A.N. Jones 4 for 43)
*Sussex (4 pts) won by 30 runs*

***at Chelmsford***

**Essex** 199 for 7
**Somerset** 180 for 6 (N.F.M. Popplewell 72)
*Essex (4 pts) won by 19 runs*

***at Cardiff***

**Hampshire** 229 for 6 (R.A. Smith 104, M.C.J. Nicholas 58)
**Glamorgan** 228 for 8 (A.L. Jones 55, G.C. Holmes 54, T.M. Tremlett 4 for 43)
*Hampshire (4 pts) won by 1 run*

***at Cheltenham***

**Surrey** 193 for 9 (R.D.V. Knight 59, M.A. Lynch 50, D.V. Lawrence 4 for 33)
**Gloucestershire** 197 for 4 (P.W. Romaines 82, C.W.J. Athey 51)
*Gloucestershire (4 pts) won by 6 wickets*

***at Leicester***

**Leicestershire** 171 for 6 (N.E. Briers 50)
**Lancashire** 177 for 2 (S.J. O'Shaughnessy 101 not out, J. Abrahams 59)
*Lancashire (4 pts) won by 8 wickets*

***at Lord's***

**Nottinghamshire** 223 for 4 (R.J. Hadlee 75 not out, R.T. Robinson 51)
**Middlesex** 211 for 8 (C.T. Radley 51)
*Nottinghamshire (4 pts) won by 12 runs*

**Essex C.C.C.**
Limited-Over Matches – 1984

| BATTING | v. Gloucestershire (Chelmsford) 5 May (B.&H.) | v. Nottinghamshire (Chelmsford) 6 May (J.P.) | v. Middlesex (Lord's) 13 May (J.P.) | v. Surrey (Chelmsford) 15/16 May (B.&H.) | v. Combined Univ. (Cambridge) 17/18 May (B.&H.) | v. Hampshire (Southampton) 19 May (B.&H.) | v. Surrey (Chelmsford) 27 May (J.P.) | v. Leicestershire (Hinkley) 3 June (J.P.) | v. Lancashire (Chelmsford) 6 June (B.&H.) | v. Warwickshire (Ilford) 10 June (J.P.) | v. Northamptonshire (Chelmsford) 17 June (J.P.) | v. Yorkshire (Leeds) 1 July (J.P.) | v. Scotland (Chelmsford) 4 July (N.W.) | v. Glamorgan (Southend) 8 July (J.P.) | v. Gloucestershire (Bristol) 15 July (J.P.) | v. *Surrey* (Chelmsford) 18 July (N.W.) | v. Kent (Canterbury) 22 July (J.P.) | v. Worcestershire (Chelmsford) 29 July (J.P.) |
|---|---|---|---|---|---|---|---|---|---|---|---|---|---|---|---|---|---|---|
| G.A. Gooch | 57 | 1 | 12 | 29 | 2 | 51 | 75* | 51 | 4 | 74 | 4 | 17 | 133 | 27 | 15 | 64 | 99 | 3 |
| C. Gladwin | 23 | 4 | 75 | 41 | 26 | 20 | 68 | 20 | 25 | 30 | 61 | 10 | 1 | 22 | 29 | 0 | 24 | 10 |
| B.R. Hardie | 62* | 18 | 2 | 14* | — | 8* | — | 7 | 9 | 6* | 11* | 40 | 0 | — | 52 | 22 | — | — |
| K.S. McEwan | 16 | 5 | 30 | 49* | 72 | 37 | 3 | 8 | 4 | 18 | 14 | 35 | 75 | 59 | 89 | 1 | 52* | 68 |
| D.R. Pringle | 7 | 81 | 38 | 11 | 51* | 51* | 17* | | 0 | 48 | | | | 12 | | 0 | 14 | 77* |
| N. Phillip | 0 | 15 | | | | | — | 13 | | 0 | 21 | 6 | 7 | 44* | 8 | 0 | — | 7* |
| S. Turner | 0 | 34 | 8* | — | 0* | — | — | 1 | 4 | 0 | — | 7 | | — | 1 | | — | — |
| D.E. East | 33 | 2 | — | — | — | — | — | 6* | 22 | 0 | — | 19* | 25* | — | 25* | 0 | — | — |
| N.A. Foster | 0 | 4 | — | — | — | — | | | 9 | | | | — | | | 3 | | |
| J.K. Lever | 1* | 2* | — | — | — | — | — | — | 13 | 14* | — | — | — | — | 3* | 15* | — | — |
| D.L. Acfield | — | 0* | — | — | — | — | | — | 5* | — | | | — | | — | 1 | — | — |
| K.W.R. Fletcher | | | 36* | 1 | 0 | 76 | — | 30* | 48 | 33 | 13 | 39 | 8 | 84* | 5 | 7 | 14* | 3 |
| A.W. Lilley | | | | | | | — | 1 | | | 21 | 16 | 59* | | 1 | | | |
| R.E. East | | | | | | | | | | | — | 2* | | — | | | | |
| Byes | 1 | | 1 | | 1 | 1 | 3 | | | 2 | | 6 | 1 | | | 1 | 1 | 1 |
| Leg-byes | 12 | 6 | 7 | 2 | 3 | 5 | 12 | 10 | 7 | 10 | 9 | 8 | 10 | 9 | 4 | 3 | 9 | 7 |
| Wides | 7 | 1 | 3 | 1 | 1 | 4 | 8 | 1 | 5 | 1 | 2 | | 1 | 2 | 3 | 1 | 2 | 4 |
| No-balls | 3 | | 2 | 4 | | 1 | | | 2 | 3 | 2 | 1 | 7 | 3 | 3 | 3 | 1 | |
| Total | 222 | 173 | 214 | 152 | 156 | 254 | 186 | 148 | 157 | 239 | 158 | 206 | 327 | 262 | 238 | 121 | 216 | 180 |
| Wickets | 8 | 9 | 5 | 4 | 4 | 4 | 2 | 7 | 10 | 8 | 6 | 8 | 6 | 4 | 8 | 10 | 3 | 4 |
| Result | W | L | Tie | W | W | W | W | W | L | W | W | W | W | W | W | L | W | W |
| Points | 2 | 0 | 2 | 2 | 2 | 2 | 4 | 4 | — | 4 | 4 | 4 | — | 4 | 4 | — | 4 | 4 |

*Catches*
21 – D.E. East (ct 19/st 2)
10 – K.S. McEwan
8 – N. Philip
7 – B.R. Hardie
6 – C. Gladwin and G.A. Gooch
5 – J.K. Lever
4 – S. Turner and K. W. R. Fletcher
3 – D.R. Pringle
2 – D. L. Acfield, N.A. Foster and sub
1 – A. W. Lilley and R.E. East

| BOWLING | J.K. Lever | N.A. Foster | D.R. Pringle | S. Turner | N. Phillip | D.L. Acfield | G.A. Gooch | R.E. East | A.W. Lilley |
|---|---|---|---|---|---|---|---|---|---|
| (B.&H.) v. Gloucestershire (Chelmsford) 5 May | 11–1–33–2 | 11–1–46–3 | 11–0–51–2 | 11–0–38–1 | 11–2–30–1 | | | | |
| (J.P.) v. Nottinghamshire (Chelmsford) 6 May | 7.4–1–28–2 | 6–0–31–0 | 8–1–30–0 | 2–1–8–0 | 7–0–36–0 | 8–0–29–0 | | | |
| (J.P.) v. Middlesex (Lord's) 13 May | 8–0–42–2 | 6–0–23–0 | 8–0–27–0 | 7–1–34–1 | | 7–1–33–0 | 4–0–34–1 | | |
| (B.&H.) v. Surrey (Chelmsford) 15/16 May | 11–4–18–1 | 9–1–33–1 | 10–4–25–3 | 11–3–17–3 | | 5–1–23–1 | 4–0–11–1 | | |
| (B.&H.) v. Combined Universities (Cambridge) 17/18 May | 11–2–30–1 | 11–1–38–2 | 11–6–20–2 | 11–2–24–1 | | | 11–2–23–2 | | |
| (B.&H.) v. Hampshire (Southampton) 19 May | 11–1–52–2 | 11–0–67–0 | 11–0–46–4 | 11–2–27–0 | | 11–3–21–1 | | | |
| (J.P.) v. Surrey (Chelmsford) 27 May | 5–0–33–3 | | 4–0–22–0 | 4–0–33–2 | 4–0–37–0 | | 4–0–22–1 | | |
| (J.P.) v. Leicestershire (Hinckley) 3 June | 6–4–5–2 | | | 5–0–24–2 | 5.3–0–22–2 | 6–0–29–0 | 6–1–30–2 | | |
| (B.&H.) v. Lancashire (Chelmsford) 6 June | 9.5–3–20–0 | 11–1–30–0 | 10–3–35–5 | 11–3–14–0 | | 7–1–21–0 | 4–0–24–0 | | |
| (J.P.) v. Warwickshire (Ilford) 10 June | 8–1–38–1 | | 8–0–51–0 | 8–2–32–3 | 8–0–37–4 | 7–0–25–1 | | | |
| (J.P.) v. Northants. (Chelmsford) 17 June | 7–0–42–1 | | | 6–0–33–1 | 7–0–33–0 | | 4–0–18–2 | 3–0–18–0 | |
| (J.P.) v. Yorkshire (Leeds) 1 July | 8–0–21–4 | | | 8–0–40–2 | 8–0–23–2 | | 8–1–53–0 | 8–0–35–2 | |
| (N.W.) v. Scotland (Chelmsford) 4 July | 8–2–16–1 | 7–1–19–0 | | | 6–2–13–2 | 12–7–9–3 | | | 7–3–19–2 |
| (J.P.) v. Glamorgan (Southend) 8 July | 4–0–13–1 | | 6–0–24–1 | 8–0–42–2 | 8–2–20–4 | | 4–0–23–0 | 8–0–26–0 | |
| (J.P.) v. Gloucestershire (Bristol) 15 July | 4–1–9–0 | | | 6–2–8–3 | 6–0–15–3 | 8–1–25–0 | 8–0–22–1 | | 0.3–0–0–2 |
| (N.W.) v. Surrey (Chelmsford) 18 July | 8.1–0–34–1 | 12–4–24–2 | 10–2–32–1 | | 4–1–11–0 | 12–5–16–1 | | | |
| (J.P.) v. Kent (Canterbury) 22 July | 8–0–34–2 | | 8–0–59–0 | 8–0–43–0 | 8–1–26–1 | 2–0–9–0 | 6–0–32–1 | | |
| (J.P.) v. Worcestershire (Chelmsford) 29 July | 8–0–35–2 | | 6–0–19–1 | 4–1–13–1 | 6–1–25–0 | 8–1–27–1 | 8–1–33–4 | | |
| (J.P.) v. Sussex (Eastbourne) 5 August | | | 8–2–15–1 | 6.2–0–25–0 | 8–1–26–3 | | 6–0–31–0 | | |
| (J.P.) v. Somerset (Chelmsford) 12 August | 8–0–38–3 | | 8–0–24–2 | 8–1–27–0 | 4–0–18–0 | 4–0–24–0 | 8–0–33–0 | | |
| (J.P.) v. Hampshire (Colchester) 19 August | 8–0–47–0 | | 8–0–31–2 | 7–0–52–0 | 3–0–20–0 | 6–0–35–0 | 8–0–53–1 | | |
| (J.P.) v. Derbyshire (Derby) 2 September | | 7–1–25–1 | 6–0–38–0 | 8–0–56–0 | 6–0–14–1 | 8–0–35–2 | 5–0–29–0 | | |
| (J.P.) v. Lancashire (Old Trafford) 9 Sept. | | | 3–0–23–0 | 3.3–1–12–0 | 3–0–18–0 | 4–0–19–1 | | | |
| Wickets | 31 | 9 | 24 | 22 | 23 | 11 | 16 | 2 | 4 |

| v. Sussex (Eastbourne) 5 August (J.P.) | v. Somerset (Chelmsford) 12 August (J.P.) | v. Hampshire (Colchester) 19 August (J.P.) | v. Derbyshire (Derby) 2 September (J.P.) | v. Lancashire (Old Trafford) 9 September (J.P.) | Runs |
|---|---|---|---|---|---|
| 8 | 38 | 125* | 64 | 0 | 953 |
| 8 | 8 | 9 | 0 | 4 | 518 |
| 0 | | — | 9 | 26* | 286 |
| 22 | 42 | 61 | 18 | 11 | 789 |
| 9 | 33 | 28 | 18 | 12 | 507 |
| 14 | 0 | 19* | 0 | 7 | 161 |
| 0 | 8* | — | 36* | 1 | 100 |
| 17* | 5* | — | 13 | 2 | 169 |
| | | | 10 | 3 | 29 |
| | — | — | | | 48 |
| 1 | — | — | 0* | 4 | 11 |
| 15 | 41 | 3 | 40 | 1 | 497 |
| 4 | 11 | | | | 113 |
| | | | | | 2 |
| 5 | 11 | 7 | 9 | 1 | |
| · | 2 | 2 | 2 | 1 | |
| 1 | | | 1 | 2 | |
| 104 | 199 | 254 | 220 | 75 | |
| 10 | 7 | 4 | 9 | 10 | |
| L | W | W | W | L | |
| 0 | 4 | 4 | 4 | 0 | |

| B.R. Hardie | K.W.R. Fletcher | Byes | Leg-byes | Wides | No-balls | Total | Wkts |
|---|---|---|---|---|---|---|---|
| | | 2 | 8 | 5 | 4 | 217 | 9 |
| | | 7 | | 3 | 2 | 174 | 4 |
| | | 1 | 15 | 3 | 2 | 214 | 5 |
| | | 4 | | 12 | 7 | 150 | 10 |
| | | | | | | | |
| | | | 5 | 6 | 6 | 152 | 8 |
| | | 1 | 10 | 1 | 2 | 227 | 8 |
| | | 1 | 7 | | 1 | 156 | 6 |
| | | 2 | 4 | | 2 | 118 | 10 |
| | | | 10 | 1 | 3 | 158 | 6 |
| | | | 7 | | 1 | 191 | 9 |
| | | 2 | 5 | 3 | 1 | 155 | 4 |
| | | | 11 | 2 | 3 | 188 | 10 |
| 8–1–16–1 | 4.3–0–27–1 | 2 | 9 | 6 | 1 | 137 | 10 |
| 2–0–11–0 | | 1 | 6 | 3 | 2 | 171 | 8 |
| | | | 10 | 2 | 3 | 94 | 10 |
| | | | 1 | 4 | | 122 | 5 |
| | | | 8 | 1 | 1 | 213 | 5 |
| | | 4 | 12 | 5 | 5 | 178 | 9 |
| | | | 4 | 2 | 2 | 105 | 4 |
| | | | 11 | 2 | 3 | 180 | 6 |
| | | | 9 | | 5 | 252 | 6 |
| | | 5 | 8 | | 5 | 215 | 4 |
| | | | 6 | | 1 | 79 | 1 |
| 1 | 1 | | | | | | |

*Robin Smith – an exciting batsman who will be qualified for Hampshire and England in 1985. (Sporting Pictures (UK) Ltd.)*

***at Wellingborough***

**Worcestershire** 157 for 9
**Northamptonshire** 158 for 5
*Northamptonshire (4 pts) won by 5 wickets*

***at Scarborough***

**Warwickshire** 251 for 5 (G.W. Humpage 81, K.D. Smith 53)
**Yorkshire** 238 for 9 (S.N. Hartley 73, G.C. Small 4 for 32)
*Warwickshire (4 pts) won by 13 runs*

For the second week running Hampshire won by 1 run as Tremlett denied Glamorgan on the last ball of the match. Earlier Robin Smith, who is likely to be the most talked of batsman in England in 1985, hit his first Sunday League hundred. Lancashire, with a fine century from the ever-improving Steve O'Shaughnessy and Notts kept up their challenge, but Notts' victory at Lord's meant that Essex went six points clear. Pringle and Fletcher had given the Essex innings a needed boost against Somerset, but the visitors were cruising to victory when they reached 109 in 22 overs before Popplewell, having hit 72 off 71 balls, was lbw to Pringle. A run later Crowe was run out by a marvellous throw from Gladwin who hit the stumps from the boundary with a flat throw. From thereon the tight bowling of Lever, Turner and Pringle denied the game to Somerset.

**Glamorgan C.C.C.**
Limited-Overs Matches – 1984

| BATTING | v. Somerset (Swansea) 5 May (B.&H.) | v. Gloucestershire (Swansea) 6 May (J.P.) | v. Kent (Canterbury) 12 May (B.&H.) | v. Surrey (The Oval) 13 May (J.P.) | v. Sussex (Hove) 17 May (B.&H.) | v. Middlesex (Cardiff) 19 May (B.&H.) | v. Middlesex (Cardiff) 20 May (J.P.) | v. Worcestershire (Worcester) 3 June (J.P.) | v. Nottinghamshire (Trent Bridge) 10 June (J.P.) | v. Lancashire (Cardiff) 17 June (J.P.) | v. Sussex (Hove) 24 June (J.P.) | v. Leicestershire (Swansea) 1 July (J.P.) | v. Nottinghamshire (Swansea) 4 July (N.W.) | v. Essex (Southend) 8 July (J.P.) | v. Somerset (Cardiff) 15 July (J.P.) | v. Derbyshire (Ebbw Vale) 29 July (J.P.) | v. Hampshire (Cardiff) 12 August (J.P.) | v. Northamptonshire (Swansea) 19 August (J.P.) |
|---|---|---|---|---|---|---|---|---|---|---|---|---|---|---|---|---|---|---|
| J.A. Hopkins | 0 | 73 | 34 | 43 | 28 | 62* | 10 | — | 23 | 31 | 8 | 15 | 29 | 5 | 51 | 12 | 20 | |
| A.L. Jones | 4 | 29 | | | 18 | 20 | 15 | — | 71 | 0 | 1 | 23 | 7 | 7 | 2 | 47 | 55 | 15 |
| R.C. Ontong | 81 | 38 | | | 5 | 38 | 17* | | 9 | 0 | 45 | 9 | 2 | 30 | 20 | 13 | 14 | 23 |
| Younis Ahmed | 12 | 34* | | | 48 | 16 | 13 | — | 7 | 24 | 15 | 34 | 18 | 1 | 18 | 103* | 17 | 5 |
| S.P. Henderson | 4 | 20* | 0 | 0 | 0 | 7* | — | — | 31 | | | | | | | | | 65* |
| J.F. Steele | 28 | 0 | 18 | 38* | 7 | — | — | — | — | 23 | 16 | 0 | 31 | 9 | 8* | — | 5* | — |
| T. Davies | 18 | — | 3 | 8* | 23 | — | — | — | — | 19* | 9* | 38* | 1 | 15 | 1* | — | 3* | 1* |
| J.G. Thomas | 3 | 7 | 17 | 5 | 3 | — | — | — | 21* | 19 | 12 | 4 | | | 14 | 11 | 2 | 33 |
| W.W. Davis | 8 | — | 2 | — | 4 | — | — | — | — | | | | 5 | 5 | | | | — |
| M.W.W. Selvey | 0* | — | 4* | — | 13 | | — | | — | 4* | 5* | 9 | 6* | 7* | — | | | |
| S.R. Barwick | 0* | | 18 | — | 8* | | | | | — | — | | 2* | — | — | — | — | |
| C.J.C. Rowe | | — | 5 | 25 | | | | — | | | | | 30 | | | | | |
| D.A. Francis | | | 23 | 2 | | | | | | | | | | | | | | |
| H. Morris | | | 10 | 16 | | | | | | | | | | 55* | | | | 26 |
| G.C. Holmes | | | | | | — | — | — | 8* | 2 | 36 | 44 | 13 | 25 | 7 | 1 | 54 | 26 |
| R.C. Green | | | | | | — | | — | | | | | | | | | | |
| Javed Miandad | | | | | | | | | | 0 | 22 | 53 | | | 56 | 69 | 44 | |
| B.J. Lloyd | | | | | | | | | | | | 27 | | | | | | |
| J. Derrick | | | | | | | | | | | | | | | | 2* | 1 | 7 |
| Byes | | 6 | 2 | 1 | 1 | | | | | | | 1 | 1 | 1 | 1 | 6 | | 4 |
| Leg-byes | 12 | 13 | 5 | 10 | 4 | 11 | 8 | | 7 | 3 | 4 | 5 | | 6 | 8 | 8 | 11 | 8 |
| Wides | 4 | 3 | | 3 | 3 | 5 | 1 | | | 1 | | | 1 | 3 | 2 | 3 | 1 | 1 |
| No-balls | 4 | | 3 | 1 | | 6 | | | 1 | 1 | | | 1 | 2 | 1 | 2 | 1 | |
| Total | 178 | 223 | 144 | 152 | 165 | 165 | 64 | | 178 | 127 | 173 | 262 | 147 | 171 | 189 | 277 | 228 | 214 |
| Wickets | 9 | 5 | 10 | 6 | 10 | 3 | 3 | | 5 | 8 | 8 | 10 | 9 | 8 | 7 | 6 | 8 | 7 |
| Result | L | W | L | L | L | W | Ab. | Ab. | W | L | L | L | L | L | L | W | L | W |
| Points | 0 | 4 | 0 | 0 | 0 | 2 | 2 | 2 | 4 | 0 | 0 | 0 | — | 0 | 0 | 4 | 0 | 4 |

*Catches*
24 – T. Davies (ct 17/st 7)
14 – J.F. Steele
11 – A.L. Jones
8 – R.C. Ontong and J.A. Hopkins
5 – J.G. Thomas
3 – M.W.W. Selvey and G.C. Holmes
2 – W.W. Davis
1 – H. Morris, Younis Ahmed, Javed Miandad, J. Derrick and S.P. Henderson

| BOWLING | S.R. Barwick | W.W. Davis | J.F. Steele | M.W.W. Selvey | R.C. Ontong | J.G. Thomas | C.J.C. Rowe | R.C. Green | G.C. Holmes |
|---|---|---|---|---|---|---|---|---|---|
| (B.&H.) *v.* Somerset (Swansea) 5 May | 4–0–23–0 | 11–0–47–2 | 11–2–28–2 | 7–1–22–1 | 11–4–22–2 | 5–0–25–0 | | | |
| (J.P.) *v.* Gloucestershire (Swansea) 6 May | | 8–0–32–1 | 8–1–16–0 | 8–0–40–2 | 6–2–21–1 | 8–0–29–3 | 1–0–10–0 | | |
| (B.&H.) *v.* Kent (Canterbury) 12 May | 11–2–31–0 | 11–1–55–2 | 11–1–21–2 | 11–2–25–2 | | 11–1–57–1 | | | |
| (J.P.) *v.* Surrey (The Oval) 13 May | 7–0–24–0 | 7.5–0–30–0 | 8–2–18–3 | 7–0–36–0 | | 8–3–28–3 | | | |
| (B.&H.) *v.* Sussex (Hove) 17 May | 1–0–10–0 | 7–2–18–0 | 11–1–43–0 | 10–0–31–2 | 11–1–29–0 | 7.3–1–27–1 | | | |
| (B.&H.) *v.* Middlesex (Cardiff) 19 May | | 9.2–2–29–5 | 11–2–32–3 | | 11–3–22–1 | 10–1–28–0 | | 11–2–36–1 | |
| (J.P.) *v.* Middlesex (Cardiff) 20 May | | | | | | | | | |
| (J.P.) *v.* Worcestershire (Worcester) 3 June | | 7–1–19–1 | 8–0–19–4 | | | 4–0–12–1 | | 3–0–13–0 | 3–0–10–1 |
| (J.P.) *v.* Nottinghamshire (Trent Br.) 10 June | | 8–0–34–1 | 8–2–20–1 | 8–1–29–1 | 7–0–40–1 | 7–0–34–1 | | | 2–0–9–1 |
| (J.P.) *v.* Lancashire (Cardiff) 17 June | 7–1–13–0 | | 8–0–15–1 | 8–0–25–3 | 8–0–34–0 | 7–1–28–1 | | | |
| (J.P.) *v.* Sussex (Hove) 24 June | 8–0–59–0 | | 8–0–32–2 | 8–0–22–1 | | 8–0–46–3 | | | 8–2–30–0 |
| (J.P.) *v.* Leicestershire (Swansea) 1 July | | | 8–0–39–1 | 6–0–67–0 | 3–0–30–1 | 8–0–58–1 | | | 8–0–38–1 |
| (N.W.) *v.* Nottinghamshire (Swansea) 4 July | 4.2–0–15–0 | 8–1–29–0 | 8–3–20–1 | | 12–3–34–1 | | 10–3–37–2 | | |
| (J.P.) *v.* Essex (Southend) 8 July | 8–1–50–0 | 8–1–63–0 | 8–0–27–3 | 8–0–49–0 | 8–0–59–1 | | | | |
| (J.P.) *v.* Somerset (Cardiff) 15 July | 8–0–31–0 | | 8–0–25–0 | 7.1–0–42–0 | 8–0–37–2 | 8–0–50–1 | | | |
| (J.P.) *v.* Derbyshire (Ebbw Vale) 29 July | 4–1–11–1 | | 8–0–46–1 | | 3–0–31–1 | 4–1–7–0 | | | 2.2–1–2–5 |
| (J.P.) *v.* Hampshire (Cardiff) 12 August | 4–0–25–0 | | 8–1–26–1 | | 8–0–41–1 | 8–2–41–2 | | | 4–0–28–0 |
| (J.P.) *v.* Northants. (Swansea) 19 August | | 8–1–33–1 | 8–0–38–1 | | 8–0–43–1 | 4–0–22–0 | | | 4–0–24–1 |
| (J.P.) *v.* Yorkshire (Leeds) 26 August | | 8–0–41–1 | 8–1–22–2 | | 8–1–24–0 | 4–1–12–1 | | | 8–0–38–3 |
| (J.P.) *v.* Warwickshire (Edgbaston) 2 Sept. | | 7–1–27–0 | 8–1–37–2 | | 8–0–45–3 | 6.3–0–34–0 | | | 3–0–21–0 |
| (J.P.) *v.* Kent (Canterbury) 9 September | | 6.2–0–16–3 | 8–1–31–1 | | 8–3–17–2 | 7–1–35–2 | | | 3–0–26–1 |
| Wickets | 1 | 17 | 31 | 12 | 18 | 21 | 2 | 1 | 13 |

| v. Yorkshire (Leeds) 26 August (J.P.) | v. Warwickshire (Edgbaston) 2 September (J.P.) | v. Kent (Canterbury) 9 September (J.P.) | Runs |
|---|---|---|---|
| | 18 | 6 | 468 |
| 32 | 22 | 0 | 368 |
| 48* | 32 | 6 | 430 |
| 14 | 36 | | 415 |
| 2 | 5 | 63 | 197 |
| — | — | 3* | 186 |
| 4* | — | 4 | 147 |
| 33 | 14* | 1 | 199 |
| — | — | 3 | 27 |
| | | | 48 |
| | | | 28 |
| | | | 60 |
| | | | 25 |
| 1 | | 3 | 111 |
| 21 | 73 | 53 | 363 |
| | | | — |
| | | | 244 |
| | | | 27 |
| 4 | 6* | 17* | 37 |
| 1 | | | |
| 10 | 14 | 9 | |
| 9 | 6 | 4 | |
| | | 1 | |
| 179 | 226 | 173 | |
| 7 | 6 | 9 | |
| W | L | W | |
| 4 | 0 | 4 | |

| B.J. Lloyd | J. Derrick | Byes | Leg-byes | Wides | No-balls | Total | Wkts |
|---|---|---|---|---|---|---|---|
| | | 8 | 2 | | 5 | 182 | 7 |
| | | | 2 | 1 | 2 | 153 | 8 |
| | | 2 | 7 | 1 | 2 | 201 | 7 |
| | | | 11 | 4 | 2 | 153 | 6 |
| | | 2 | 6 | | 3 | 169 | 3 |
| | | 2 | 8 | 3 | 3 | 163 | 10 |
| | | Match Abandoned | | | | | |
| | | 4 | 6 | 6 | | 89 | 7 |
| | | | 6 | 4 | 1 | 177 | 7 |
| | | 4 | 5 | 2 | 4 | 130 | 5 |
| | | | 15 | 6 | 1 | 211 | 6 |
| 7–0–47–0 | | 1 | 6 | 5 | | 291 | 5 |
| | | 2 | 9 | | 2 | 148 | 4 |
| | | | 9 | 2 | 3 | 262 | 4 |
| | | | 4 | 2 | 1 | 192 | 3 |
| | 8–0–36–2 | 4 | 12 | 4 | | 153 | 10 |
| | 8–0–61–1 | 4 | 3 | | | 229 | 6 |
| | 8–0–32–1 | 1 | 14 | 5 | 1 | 213 | 5 |
| | 4–0–12–1 | 4 | 19 | 5 | 1 | 178 | 9 |
| | 6–0–47–2 | | 12 | 6 | | 229 | 7 |
| | 4–0–23–1 | | 6 | 2 | | 156 | 10 |
| 0 | 8 | | | | | | |

## NatWest Trophy – Semi Finals

### *15 August*

### *at Edgbaston*

**Warwickshire** 224 (A.I. Kallicharran 86)
**Kent** 226 for 4 (M.R. Benson 113 not out)

*Kent won by 6 wickets*
*(Man of the Match – M.R. Benson)*

### *15 and 16 August*

### *at Lord's*

**Northamptonshire** 226 for 6 (R.J. Bailey 56 not out, W. Larkins 52)
**Middlesex** 228 for 2 (M.W. Gatting 88 not out, W.N. Slack 79)

*Middlesex won by 8 wickets*
*(Man of the Match – W. N. Slack)*

*Mark Benson – match-winning innings for Kent in the NatWest Semi-Final at Edgbaston. (Adrian Murrell)*

## Gloucestershire C.C.C.
Limited-Over Matches – 1984

| BATTING | v. Essex (Chelmsford) 5 May (B.&H.) | v. Glamorgan (Swansea) 6 May (J.P.) | v. Hampshire (Bristol) 12 May (B.&H.) | v. Combined Univ. Bristol 15 May (B.&H.) | v. Surrey (The Oval) 19 May (B.&H.) | v. Sussex (Hove) 20 May (J.P.) | v. Somerset (Bristol) 27 May (J.P.) | v. Kent (Canterbury) 3 June (J.P.) | v. Derbyshire (Gloucester) 10 June (J.P.) | v. Nottinghamshire (Trent Bridge) 17 June (J.P.) | v. Hampshire (Bristol) 24 June (J.P.) | v. Warwickshire (Edgbaston) 1 July (J.P.) | v. Staffordshire (Stone) 4 July (N.W.) | v. Yorkshire (Scarborough) 8 July (J.P.) | v. Essex (Bristol) 15 July (J.P.) | v. Lancashire (Bristol) 18 July (N.W.) | v. Leicestershire (Leicester) 22 July (J.P.) | v. Northamptonshire (Bristol) 29 July (J.P.) |
|---|---|---|---|---|---|---|---|---|---|---|---|---|---|---|---|---|---|---|
| A.W. Stovold | 44 | 1 | 78 | 31 | 16 | | | 29 | 29 | 25 | 12 | 12 | 11 | 62 | 9 | 53 | 14* | 18 |
| P.W. Romaines | 7 | 32 | 98* | 60 | 5 | | | 18 | 20 | 1 | 3 | 22 | 52 | 39 | 8 | 56 | 2 | 30 |
| C.W.J. Athey | 2 | 15 | 35* | 4 | 10 | | | 79 | 22 | 59 | 6 | 38 | 70* | 27 | 3 | 7 | 77 | 9 |
| Zaheer Abbas | 67 | 7 | 2 | 24 | 22 | | | 12 | 64 | | 46 | | | | 5 | 21 | 28 | 102 |
| A.J. Wright | 7 | | — | 0 | 7 | | | | 3 | 9 | | 0 | — | 0* | | | | |
| R.J. Doughty | 31 | 1 | — | 13 | 25 | | | 21* | 2* | 8 | | | | | | | | |
| D.A. Graveney | 26 | 9 | — | 31 | 5 | | | 1 | — | — | 22 | 14 | — | — | | 20* | | — |
| J.N. Shepherd | 2 | 24 | — | 7 | 10 | | | 10 | | 52* | 4 | 2 | — | 12 | | 2 | 1 | 36* |
| R.C. Russell | 10 | 43 | — | 8 | 4 | | | 9 | — | — | 6 | | — | 2* | 14 | 16 | 1* | 5* |
| D.V. Lawrence | 1* | — | — | | | | | 1* | — | — | 17 | — | — | — | | 0 | — | |
| G.E. Sainsbury | 1* | 6* | — | 1 | 0* | | | — | — | — | 4* | — | — | | 0 | 3 | — | — |
| J.H. Childs | | 10* | | 6* | | | | | | | | | | | | | | |
| P. Bainbridge | | | | | 48 | | | 33 | 50* | 28 | 4 | 17 | 5* | 19 | 18 | 51 | 19 | 4 |
| C.R. Trembath | | | | | | | | | | | 1 | | | — | 5 | | | |
| E.J. Cunningham | | | | | | | | | | | | 40* | — | 44 | 17 | 18 | 56 | 2 |
| A.J. Brassington | | | | | | | | | | | | 1* | | | | | | |
| C. Dale | | | | | | | | | | | | | | | 0 | | — | — |
| D.A. Burrows | | | | | | | | | | | | | | | 0* | | | |
| C.A. Walsh | | | | | | | | | | | | | | | | | | |
| Byes | 2 | | 4 | 4 | 1 | | | | | | | | 4 | 4 | | | | |
| Leg-byes | 8 | 2 | 9 | 10 | 3 | | | 5 | 10 | 6 | 2 | 18 | 2 | 7 | 10 | 25 | 10 | 3 |
| Wides | 5 | 1 | 8 | 16 | 5 | | | 1 | 3 | 1 | 11 | 1 | 2 | 11 | 2 | 3 | | 1 |
| No-balls | 4 | 2 | 6 | 1 | 3 | | | 3 | | 2 | 2 | 1 | 6 | 1 | 3 | 6 | 2 | 4 |
| Total | 217 | 153 | 240 | 216 | 164 | | | 222 | 203 | 191 | 140 | 166 | 152 | 228 | 94 | 281 | 210 | 214 |
| Wickets | 9 | 8 | 2 | 10 | 10 | | | 8 | 5 | 6 | 10 | 7 | 2 | 6 | 10 | 10 | 6 | 6 |
| Result | L | L | W | L | L | Ab. | Ab. | L | W | W | L | L | W | L | L | L | L | L |
| Points | 0 | 0 | 2 | 0 | 0 | 2 | 2 | 0 | 4 | 4 | 0 | 0 | — | 0 | 0 | — | 0 | 0 |

*Catches*

18 – R.C. Russell (ct 15/st 3)
11 – C.W.J. Athey and D.A. Graveney
10 – A.W. Stovold
8 – P.W. Romaines
6 – G.E. Sainsbury
5 – P. Bainbridge
4 – A.J. Wright and D.V. Lawrence
3 – J.N. Shepherd
2 – E.J. Cunningham
1 – A.J. Brassington, Zaheer Abbas and sub

| BOWLING | D.V. Lawrence | J.N. Shepherd | G.E. Sainsbury | R.J. Doughty | C.W.J. Athey | J.H. Childs | D.A. Graveney | P. Bainbridge | C.R. Trembath |
|---|---|---|---|---|---|---|---|---|---|
| (B.&H.) *v.* Essex (Chelmsford) 5 May | 11–1–52–1 | 11–3–42–2 | 11–0–40–0 | 11–2–32–2 | 11–1–33–3 | | | | |
| (J.P.) *v.* Glamorgan (Swansea) 6 May | 8–0–45–1 | 8–0–31–1 | 7–2–26–0 | 2–0–15–1 | 4–0–25–0 | 4–0–30–0 | 6–0–29–0 | | |
| (B.&H.) *v.* Hampshire (Bristol) 12 May | 11–1–48–5 | 11–0–39–2 | 11–0–43–1 | 11–2–37–0 | 5–0–30–0 | | 6–1–30–0 | | |
| (B.&H.) *v.* Combined Universities (Bristol) 15 May | | 10.3–2–40–2 | 11–1–39–1 | 2–0–18–0 | 9–0–48–4 | 11–1–53–0 | 11–1–36–1 | | |
| (B.&H.) *v.* Surrey (The Oval) 19 May | | 11–2–35–3 | 9–3–21–2 | 6–0–24–0 | 9–1–32–1 | | 9–0–26–1 | 11–1–38–1 | |
| (J.P.) *v.* Sussex (Hove) 20 May | | | | | | | | | |
| (J.P.) *v.* Somerset (Bristol) 27 May | | | | | | | | | |
| (J.P.) *v.* Kent (Canterbury) 3 June | 7–0–65–0 | 8–0–45–0 | 7–0–31–0 | 1–0–15–1 | | | 8–1–35–2 | 8–0–31–2 | |
| (J.P.) *v.* Derbyshire (Gloucester) 10 June | 7–0–58–0 | | 8–1–57–0 | 4–0–30–0 | 4–0–31–0 | | 8–0–29–1 | 8–0–57–2 | |
| (J.P.) *v.* Nottinghamshire (Trent Br.) 17 June | 5.1–0–14–1 | 8–0–33–4 | 5–2–19–3 | 0.5–0–6–0 | 3.1–0–12–0 | | 4–0–7–0 | 8–0–29–1 | |
| (J.P.) *v.* Hampshire (Bristol) 24 June | 8–0–52–2 | 8–0–44–0 | 7–0–56–2 | | | | 6–0–32–0 | 8–0–47–3 | 1–0–15–0 |
| (J.P.) *v.* Warwickshire (Edgbaston) 1 July | 8–0–35–3 | 8–0–48–1 | 8–2–36–0 | | 1–0–7–0 | | 7–0–30–0 | 8–0–44–1 | |
| (N.W.) *v.* Staffordshire (Stone) 4 July | 10–2–34–1 | 12–3–20–4 | 12–4–22–1 | | 2–0–15–0 | | 12–5–20–2 | 12–2–27–0 | |
| (J.P.) *v.* Yorkshire (Scarborough) 8 July | 8–1–42–2 | 8–0–31–0 | | | 3–0–34–0 | | 5–0–34–0 | 8–0–34–0 | 7.1–0–37–0 |
| (J.P.) *v.* Essex (Bristol) 15 July | | | 8–0–44–2 | | 7–0–50–4 | | | 8–0–28–0 | 4–0–28–0 |
| (N.W.) *v.* Lancashire (Bristol) 18 July | 12–1–82–1 | 12–1–68–1 | 12–1–58–3 | | 6–0–36–0 | | 6–0–32–0 | 12–2–32–1 | |
| (J.P.) *v.* Leicestershire (Leicester) 22 July | 6–0–30–0 | 6.1–0–48–0 | 7–0–31–1 | | | | | 8–0–59–0 | |
| (J.P.) *v.* Northamptonshire (Bristol) 29 July | | 8–0–31–1 | 7.3–0–38–0 | | 1–0–15–0 | | 8–0–24–1 | 8–0–42–0 | |
| (J.P.) *v.* Surrey (Cheltenham) 12 August | 8–0–33–4 | 8–0–29–1 | 8–0–37–2 | 8–0–42–0 | | | | 8–0–44–2 | |
| (J.P.) *v.* Worcestershire (Worcester) 19 Aug. | 6–0–26–1 | 8–1–30–1 | 8–3–25–1 | | | | 8–1–17–1 | | |
| (J.P.) *v.* Lancashire (Moreton-in-Marsh) 26 August | 7.3–0–32–4 | 8–0–26–1 | | | | 7–0–36–1 | 2–0–15–0 | 7–0–51–2 | |
| (J.P.) *v.* Middlesex (Bristol) 9 September | 7–0–34–3 | 8–0–19–1 | 7–0–24–1 | | | | | 8–0–39–1 | |
| Wickets | 29 | 25 | 20 | 4 | 12 | 1 | 9 | 16 | 0 |

| v. Surrey (Cheltenham) 12 August (J.P.) | v. Worcestershire (Worcester) 19 August (J.P.) | v. Lancashire (M'ton-in-Marsh) 26 August (J.P.) | v. Middlesex (Bristol) 9 September (J.P.) | Runs |
|---|---|---|---|---|
| 27* | 22 | 12 | 43* | 548 |
| 82 | 2 | 14 | 10 | 561 |
| 51 | 5 | 24 | 20 | 563 |
| | | | | 400 |
| 14 | | | | 40 |
| — | 2 | | | 103 |
| — | 2 | — | 5* | 135 |
| 4 | 6 | 26* | 1 | 199 |
| | | 11* | 10 | 139 |
| — | 10* | — | — | 29 |
| — | 5 | | — | 20 |
| | | — | | 16 |
| 7* | 5 | 30 | 6 | 344 |
| | | | | 6 |
| — | 30 | 50 | 47 | 304 |
| | | | | 1 |
| | | | | 0 |
| | | | | 0 |
| | 14 | 9 | — | 23 |
| 1 | 8 | 8 | 2 | |
| 10 | 15 | 5 | 5 | |
| 1 | | 6 | | |
| | 1 | 2 | 3 | |
| 197 | 127 | 197 | 152 | |
| 4 | 10 | 6 | 6 | |
| W | L | W | W | |
| 4 | 0 | 4 | 4 | |

| D.A. Burrows | C. Dale | C.A. Walsh | Byes | Leg-byes | Wides | No-balls | Total | Wkts |
|---|---|---|---|---|---|---|---|---|
| | | | 1 | 12 | 7 | 3 | 222 | 8 |
| | | | 6 | 13 | 3 | | 223 | 5 |
| | | | 2 | 8 | 2 | | 239 | 9 |
| | | | | | | | | |
| | | | | 6 | 1 | 2 | 243 | 10 |
| | | | | 10 | 13 | 3 | 202 | 10 |
| | | | | Match Abandoned | | | | |
| | | | | Match Abandoned | | | | |
| | | | | 10 | 3 | | 235 | 6 |
| | | | 4 | 1 | 4 | 1 | 272 | 4 |
| | | | | 7 | 7 | 4 | 138 | 10 |
| | | | 1 | 13 | 2 | | 262 | 7 |
| | | | 1 | 11 | 2 | 1 | 215 | 5 |
| | | | | 12 | 1 | | 151 | 8 |
| | | | | 9 | 7 | 1 | 229 | 3 |
| 5-0-32-1 | 8-0-46-1 | | | 4 | 3 | 3 | 238 | 8 |
| | | | 3 | 25 | 12 | 1 | 349 | 6 |
| | 8-0-35-1 | | | 5 | 4 | | 212 | 2 |
| | 7-0-58-0 | | | 5 | 5 | | 218 | 3 |
| | | | | 4 | 3 | 1 | 193 | 9 |
| | | 6·4-2-20-0 | | 7 | 3 | | 128 | 6 |
| | | | | | | | | |
| | | 7-2-15-1 | | 8 | 8 | 1 | 192 | 10 |
| | | 8-1-37-1 | | 10 | 1 | 1 | 165 | 7 |
| 1 | 2 | 2 | | | | | | |

*Wilf Slack – Man of the Match at Lord's in the NatWest Semi-Final. (Adrian Murrell)*

On a steamy morning Warwickshire struggled. The Smith brothers were both out with 14 scored and it was left to the determination of Robin Dyer and the stroke-making of Alvin Kallicharran, who enjoyed some luck, to establish a base to the innings. It was Old who gave Kallicharran the middle order support he needed and they added 62 for the sixth wicket, but 224 never looked to be a winning score. Kent lost Taylor at 26, but Tavare helped Benson in a stand of 59 and although Aslett and Cowdrey went cheaply, Benson and the hard-hitting Ellison scored the last 90 runs, troubled only by the accuracy of Gifford.

Overcast weather took the match at Lord's into a second day, but Middlesex always looked to be the winners. Northants, hampered by injury and silly selection which weakened their attack, batted fitfully after Edmonds had dropped Cook off Cowans' third ball of the match. Edmonds made amends with a brilliant catch in the gully to dismiss Boyd-Moss and Larkins, never at his best, was lbw to Daniel. Lamb perished at mid-off and it was left to the exciting stroke-play of Bailey to give the Northants innings any quality. Barlow and Slack began the Middlesex reply with a stand of 55 and Gatting and Slack added 130 for the second wicket against some very moderate bowling. Middlesex strolled to victory with 5.5 overs to spare.

### *16 August*

### *at Arundel*

**Duchess of Norfolk's XI** 212 for 6 (C. Gladwin 57, D.S. de Silva 4 for 31)
**Sri Lankans** 216 for 9 (D.S.B. Kuruppu 58)
*Sri Lankans won by 4 wickets*

*Bobby Parks – six catches for Hampshire against Essex at Colchester to equal the county record. A wicket-keeper of quiet charm. (George Herringshaw)*

**18, 19 and 20 August**

***at Hove***

**Sri Lankans** 193 (S. Wettimuny 73, P.A. de Silva 62, C.M. Wells 4 for 50) and 235 (J.R. Ratnayeke 66)
**Sussex** 345 for 6 dec (P.W.G. Parker 181, I.A. Greig 50, A.L.F. de Mel 4 for 111)

*Match drawn*

**18, 20 and 21 August**

***at Colchester***

**Hampshire** 189 (T.E. Jesty 74, J.K. Lever 5 for 84, N.A. Foster 4 for 40) and 312 (T.E. Jesty 120, N.A. Foster 5 for 61)
**Essex** 329 (K.S. McEwan 142 not out, T.M. Tremlett 4 for 75) and 173 for 2 (G.A. Gooch 79, C. Gladwin 64)

*Essex won by 8 wickets*
*Essex 24 pts, Hampshire 4 pts*

***at Swansea***

**Glamorgan** 314 for 6 dec (R.C. Ontong 69, H. Morris 60, Younis Ahmed 59, R.G. Williams 4 for 115) and 90 for 4
**Northamptonshire** 161 (R.J. Boyd-Moss 73, J.F. Steele 4 for 27) and 242 (W. Larkins 86, R.C. Ontong 5 for 73, J.F. Steele 4 for 92)

*Glamorgan won by 6 wickets*
*Glamorgan 23 pts, Northamptonshire 2 pts*

***at Folkestone***

**Nottinghamshire** 212 (B.C. Broad 58, R.T. Robinson 56, R.J. Hadlee 51, T.M. Alderman 5 for 44) and 367 for 4 dec (C.E.B. Rice 152 not out, P. Johnson 133)
**Kent** 231 (M.R. Benson 54) and 285 for 9 (M.R. Benson 115, N.R. Taylor 67)

*tch drawn*
*6 pts, Nottinghamshire 6 pts*

***at Old Trafford***

**Warwickshire** 244 (D.L. Amiss 118, P.A. Smith 89, P.J.W. Allott 5 for 44) and 327 for 4 dec (A.I. Kallicharran 117, R.I.H.B. Dyer 84, G.W. Humpage 61 not out)
**Lancashire** 300 for 9 dec (S.J. O'Shaughnessy 129) and 221 (N.H. Fairbrother 66, J. Simmons 59, G.C. Small 5 for 42)

*Warwickshire won by 50 runs*
*Warwickshire 22 pts, Lancashire 8 pts*

***at Leicester***

**Middlesex** 391 for 6 dec (W.N. Slack 106, G.D. Barlow 96, M.W. Gatting 64, R.O. Butcher 62) and 215 for 6 dec (R.O. Butcher 81)
**Leicestershire** 313 (J.C. Balderstone 72, T.J. Boon 70, D.I. Gower 64) and 134 for 5 (M.A. Garnham 54)

*Match drawn*
*Middlesex 8 pts, Leicestershire 5 pts*

***at Taunton***

**Derbyshire** 373 (K.J. Barnett 120, A. Hill 99, C.H. Dredge 4 for 70) and 226 for 7 (J.G. Wright 77, K.J. Barnett 56, V.J. Marks 7 for 83)
**Somerset** 508 (V.J. Marks 116 not out, I.T. Botham 90, N.A. Felton 52, G. Miller 5 for 187)

*Match drawn*
*Derbyshire 7 pts, Somerset 6 pts*

***at The Oval***

**Yorkshire** 175 (P.I. Pocock 6 for 30) and 148 (D.J. Thomas 4 for 57)
**Surrey** 518 for 5 dec (G.S. Clinton 192, A.R. Butcher 118, M.A. Lynch 85, R.D.V. Knight 77)

*Surrey won by an innings and 195 runs*
*Surrey 24 pts, Yorkshire 1 pt*

***at Worcester***

**Gloucestershire** 356 for 4 dec (P.W. Romaines 114, C.W.J. Athey 108 not out) and 232 for 6 dec (A.J. Wright 82)
**Worcestershire** 303 for 7 dec (P.A. Neale 73, R.N. Kapil Dev 58 not out) and 289 for 5 (R.N. Kapil Dev 62 not out, D.B. d'Oliveira 57 not out)

*Worcestershire won by 5 wickets*
*Worcestershire 21 pts, Gloucestershire 7 pts*

A maximum-point win at Colchester and Notts' failure to force victory at Folkestone took Essex 38 points clear at the top of the Britannic Assurance County Championship. The win at Colchester was a notable one. There were two fine innings from Trevor Jesty and six catches in an innings for the immaculate and courteous Bobby Parks who thereby equalled his Hampshire record. These Hampshire feats tended to be overshadowed by the brilliance of the Essex cricket. John Lever became the first bowler to reach 100 wickets for the season and Graham Gooch became the first batsman to reach two thousand runs. Ken McEwan hit a lovely century to ensure four batting points and he and Foster, an ever-improving batsman, put on 90 for the eighth wicket. Gooch and Gladwin began Essex's second innings with a stand of 125 and the runs came at nearly seven an over.

Meanwhile Notts, thanks to a fourth wicket stand of 260 in 62 overs between Rice and Johnson, who hit a career best, set Kent to make 349 in 87 overs. Benson, who again played magnificently, and Taylor put on 178 in 44 overs, but 4 wickets fell for 12 runs and eventually Notts needed to take two wickets in the last 8 overs. Graham Johnson was out with one over left, but Alderman defended doggedly to deny Notts.

Sussex considered 84 in 12 overs too much to ask and declined to attempt it so that Sri Lanka achieved a draw after Parker's earlier fluent and commanding innings. Glamorgan eked out a good win over Northants and owed their spinners much.

The consistent Alan Hill and the engaging Kim Barnett seemed to have batted Derbyshire to a position of strength at Taunton, but Botham was in fierce mood and Marks, enjoying a mouth of wonder, hit another hundred and followed it with seven wickets so that Derbyshire struggled to survive.

Barlow and Slack began the Middlesex innings with a stand of 192, but lapses in the field by both sides thwarted a result. Leicestershire were forced to ban Garnham following this match for verbal abuse in a second team game. It was his second suspension within a few weeks and one despaired for cricket if not for a young player who had seemed to have promise.

Moxon and Boycott withdrew from the Yorkshire side shortly before the start of the match at The Oval and one had visions of more northern politics. Yorkshire were twice bowled out for under two hundred and took only one point from a match in which Clinton, hitting a career best, and Butcher put on 277 for Surrey's first wicket. After 100 overs Surrey were 335 for 1 and runs continued to be plundered from a weak, dispirited attack.

Poor Gloucestershire began so well with stands of 113 and 93 and centuries for Athey and the under-praised Romaines, one of the most reliable opening batsmen in the country. Worcestershire trailed on the first innings and, in search of 286 in 64 overs, were 180 for 5 when Kapil Dev joined d'Oliveira. They hit 109 off 79 balls and won the match with 19 balls to spare.

It was poor Lancashire, too, for, having taken maximum bonus points thanks to another fine hundred from Steve O'Shaughnessy, they were bowled out 51 short of their target of 272 in 64 overs. Small did the damage with a new ball burst and it was only a late flourish by Fairbrother and Simmons that brought any hope. The first Warwickshire innings had been a remarkable affair with Amiss and Paul Smith adding 191 for the fifth wicket and nobody else reaching double figures. In Paul Smith and Robin Dyer, Warwickshire have two of the very best young players to have established themselves in the past few seasons.

ABOVE: *Kapil Dev – fierce hitting for Worcestershire against Gloucestershire. (David Munden)* BELOW: *Kevin Sharp of Yorkshire, a batsman of maturity and polish. A career best of 173 against Derbyshire at Chesterfield, 22 August. (Adrian Murrell)*

## John Player League

***19 August***

***at Colchester***

**Essex** 254 for 4 (G.A. Gooch 125 not out, K.S. McEwan 61)
**Hampshire** 252 for 6 (D.R. Turner 114, M.C.J. Nicholas 59, R.A. Smith 51)

*Essex (4 pts) won by 2 runs*

***at Swansea***

**Northamptonshire** 213 for 5 (A.J. Lamb 65, W. Larkins 63)
**Glamorgan** 214 for 7 (S.P. Henderson 65 not out)

*Glamorgan (4 pts) won by 3 wickets*

**Hampshire C.C.C.**
Limited-Over Matches – 1984

| **BATTING** | *v.* Combined Univ. (Southampton) 5 May (B.&H.) | *v.* Sussex (Southampton) 6 May (J.P.) | *v.* Gloucestershire (Bristol) 12 May (B.&H.) | *v.* Somerset (Taunton) 13 May (J.P.) | *v.* Surrey (The Oval) 17/18 May (B.&H.) | *v.* Essex (Southampton) 19 May (B.&H.) | *v.* Nottinghamshire (Bournemouth) 3 June (J.P.) | *v.* Worcestershire (Worcester) 10 June (J.P.) | *v.* Leicestershire (Basingstoke) 17 June (J.P.) | *v.* Gloucestershire (Bristol) 24 June (J.P.) | *v.* Surrey (The Oval) 1 July (J.P.) | *v.* Norfolk (Norwich) 8 July (N.W.) | *v.* Lancashire (Portsmouth) 15 July (J.P.) | *v.* Kent (Southampton) 18 July (N.W.) | *v.* Yorkshire (Bournemouth) 22 July (J.P.) | *v.* Middlesex (Lord's) 29 July (J.P.) | *v.* Warwickshire (Portsmouth) 5 August (J.P.) | *v.* Glamorgan (Cardiff) 12 August (J.P.) |
|---|---|---|---|---|---|---|---|---|---|---|---|---|---|---|---|---|---|---|
| V.P. Terry | 38 | 30 | 23 | 65 | 33 | 72 | 110 | 6 | 45 | 25 | 40 | 50 | | 0 | 14 | | | |
| C.L. Smith | 82* | 7 | 5 | 88 | 3 | 24 | 30 | 11 | 95 | 58 | 55 | 4 | 43 | 2 | 46 | 41 | 88* | 29 |
| M.C.J. Nicholas | 25* | 77* | 30 | 12 | 49 | 13 | 11 | 34 | 19* | 108 | 0 | 63 | | 8 | 94 | 17 | 3 | 58 |
| T.E. Jesty | — | 62 | 51 | 21 | 25 | 39 | 42 | 8 | 18 | 0 | 41 | 2 | 32 | 35 | 7 | 1 | 16 | 7 |
| D.R. Turner | — | 15 | 50 | 22* | 40 | 40 | | 24 | — | 45 | 11 | 20 | 63 | 1 | 45 | 8 | 74 | 7 |
| N.E.J. Pocock | — | 21* | 22 | — | 25 | 4 | | 48* | — | 3* | 23* | 33* | 20 | 2 | | | | |
| N.G. Cowley | — | — | 11 | — | 23* | 1 | 1 | 5 | — | 0 | 4 | 30 | 15 | 0 | 3 | 33 | 5* | 14* |
| T.M. Tremlett | — | — | 17 | — | — | — | 6* | 35 | — | 1* | — | 3 | 5* | 17 | 1 | 6 | — | 2* |
| R.J. Parks | — | — | 4 | — | 3* | 11* | — | — | — | — | — | 5* | 1 | 25 | 6* | 4* | — | — |
| E.L. Reifer | — | — | 14* | 3* | 12 | 8 | 5 | 2* | — | 6 | 10* | 6 | 2* | 1 | 0 | 0 | | |
| S.J. Malone | — | — | | — | | | | | | | | | | | | | | |
| K.St J.D. Emery | | | — | | | | | | | | | | | | | | | |
| S.J.W. Andrew | | | | | — | 1* | | | | | — | | — | | | — | — | — |
| J.J.E. Hardy | | | | | | | 10* | | | | | | 10 | | 1 | 42 | 17 | 1 |
| R.J. Maru | | | | | | | — | | | | | | | | | | | |
| C.A. Connor | | | | | | | — | — | — | — | | — | — | 3* | 0* | 0* | — | — |
| R.A. Smith | | | | | | | | | | | | | | | | | 1 | 104 |
| Byes | 1 | 4 | 2 | | | 1 | | 5 | | 1 | 1 | | | | 1 | 1 | 1 | 4 |
| Leg-byes | 1 | 6 | 8 | 4 | 7 | 10 | 14 | 4 | 6 | 13 | 12 | 5 | 8 | 2 | 6 | 11 | 9 | 3 |
| Wides | 8 | 2 | 2 | 4 | 2 | 1 | 1 | 2 | 3 | 2 | 2 | 5 | 6 | 1 | 8 | | 5 | |
| No-balls | | 2 | | | 1 | 2 | | 1 | 2 | | | 13 | 1 | 2 | 1 | | | |
| Total | 155 | 226 | 239 | 219 | 223 | 227 | 230 | 185 | 188 | 262 | 199 | 239 | 206 | 99 | 233 | 164 | 219 | 229 |
| Wickets | 1 | 4 | 9 | 4 | 7 | 8 | 6 | 7 | 3 | 7 | 6 | 8 | 7 | 10 | 9 | 8 | 5 | 6 |
| Result | W | L | L | W | W | L | L | L | L | W | L | W | L | L | W | L | W | W |
| Points | 2 | 0 | 0 | 4 | 2 | 0 | 0 | 0 | 0 | 4 | 0 | — | 0 | — | 4 | 0 | 4 | 4 |

*Catches*

24 – R.J. Parks (ct 20/st 4)
13 – N.E.J. Pocock
10 – V.P. Terry
7 – R.A. Smith
6 – D.R. Turner, M.C.J. Nicholas, N.G. Cowley and T.E. Jesty
5 – C.L. Smith and T.M. Tremlett
3 – E.L. Reifer
2 – J.J.E. Hardy and S.J.W. Andrew
1 – G.A. Connor and sub

| **BOWLING** | S.J. Malone | T.M. Tremlett | T.E. Jesty | E.L. Reifer | N.G. Cowley | M.C.J. Nicholas | K.St J.D. Emery | S.J.W. Andrew | C.A. Connor |
|---|---|---|---|---|---|---|---|---|---|
| (B.&H,) *v.* Combined Universities (Southampton) 5 May | 9–3–28–2 | 11–4–19–2 | 11–2–47–1 | 8.2–3–20–3 | 10–2–19–0 | | | | |
| (J.P.) *v.* Sussex (Southampton) 6 May | 8–0–45–2 | 8–0–42–2 | | 8–0–43–1 | 8–2–29–1 | 7.2–0–55–1 | | | |
| (B.&H.) *v.* Gloucestershire (Bristol) 12 May | | 11–2–57–1 | 8–0–41–0 | 9.5–4–26–0 | 10–3–35–0 | 11–0–38–0 | 3–0–16–0 | | |
| (J.P.) *v.* Somerset (Taunton) 13 May | 8–0–37–2 | 8–0–31–1 | | 8–0–28–2 | 8–2–36–1 | 8–0–39–2 | | | |
| (B.&H.) *v.* Surrey (The Oval) 17/18 May | | 10–1–27–2 | | 7.1–0–19–3 | 9–4–17–1 | 6–0–31–1 | | 7–0–12–3 | |
| (B.&H.) *v.* Essex (Southampton) 19 May | | 11–1–35–0 | | 11–1–57–0 | 11–3–32–0 | 11–1–71–1 | | 11–1–48–3 | |
| (J.P.) *v.* Nottinghamshire (Brnmth) 3 June | | 8–0–46–2 | | 8–0–47–1 | 8–0–46–0 | 8–0–44–1 | | | 8–0–46–1 |
| (J.P.) *v.* Worcestershire (Worcester) 10 June | | 7–2–27–0 | | 8–1–34–1 | 8–0–35–1 | 8–0–42–1 | | | 6–0–28–0 |
| (J.P.) *v.* Leicestershire (Basingstoke) 17 June | | 8–0–33–0 | | 6.3–0–48–0 | 8–2–36–2 | 6–0–24–0 | | | 8–0–43–1 |
| (J.P.) *v.* Gloucestershire (Bristol) 24 June | | 8–0–43–2 | | 4–0–15–1 | 8–2–20–2 | 4–0–25–0 | | | 7–1–14–3 |
| (J.P.) *v.* Surrey (The Oval) 1 July | | 8–0–24–1 | 2–0–17–1 | 7–1–30–0 | 6–0–35–1 | 8–0–35–1 | | 7.5–0–45–1 | |
| (N.W.) *v.* Norfolk (Norwich) 4 July | | 10–3–24–3 | | 9–3–31–1 | 11.2–2–24–5 | 7–3–13–0 | | | 6–3–9–1 |
| (J.P.) *v.* Lancashire (Portsmouth) 15 July | | 7.5–0–60–1 | | 7–0–33–1 | 8–1–48–1 | | | 6–0–16–1 | 8–0–41–2 |
| (N.W.) *v.* Kent (Southampton) 18 July | | 12–1–44–1 | | 12–1–46–4 | 12–0–43–0 | 12–2–53–1 | | | 12–1–54–0 |
| (J.P.) *v.* Yorkshire (Bournemouth) 22 July | | 8–0–32–1 | | 7–0–38–1 | 8–0–57–0 | 7–0–41–1 | | | 6.5–1–15–4 |
| (J.P.) *v.* Middlesex (Lord's) 29 July | | 8–0–17–1 | 6–0–39–0 | 7–0–31–0 | | | | 7.4–0–38–1 | 8–3–22–3 |
| (J.P.) *v.* Warwickshire (Portsmouth) 5 Aug. | | 8–0–53–0 | 8–0–40–1 | | 8–0–45–2 | | | 8–0–37–0 | 8–0–31–2 |
| (J.P.) *v.* Glamorgan (Cardiff) 12 August | | 8–0–43–4 | 8–0–39–0 | | 8–0–34–1 | | | 8–0–42–0 | 8–0–57–1 |
| (J.P.) *v.* Essex (Colchester) 19 August | | 8–0–38–2 | 8–0–59–0 | | 8–1–44–1 | | | 8–0–50–0 | 8–0–54–1 |
| (J.P.) *v.* Kent (Bournemouth) 26 August | | 8–0–36–0 | 8–0–39–1 | | 8–0–56–2 | | | 5–0–22–0 | 7.3–0–32–0 |
| (Asda) *v.* Lancashire (Scarborough) 30 Aug. | | 8–0–40–1 | 6–0–9–0 | 8.3–1–32–1 | 10–1–34–1 | 6–0–25–3 | | | 9–0–38–2 |
| (Asda) *v.* Yorkshire (Scarborough) 31 August | | 10–3–33–2 | 10–2–29–2 | 5–0–27–1 | 10–0–41–0 | 5–0–17–0 | | | 10–1–51–2 |
| (J.P.) *v.* Northamptonshire (Southampton) 2 September | | | 8–1–36–1 | | 8–1–35–1 | 8–0–31–2 | | 8–0–38–3 | 8–0–33–1 |
| (J.P.) *v.* Derbyshire (Derby) 9 September | | | 6–0–21–1 | | 5–0–15–1 | 5.1–0–32–0 | | 4–0–16–0 | 6–1–22–1 |
| Wickets | 6 | 29 | 8 | 21 | 24 | 15 | 0 | 12 | 25 |

| v. Essex (Colchester) 19 August (J.P.) | v. Kent (Bournemouth) 26 August (J.P.) | v. Lancashire (Scarborough) 30 August (Asda) | v. Yorkshire (Scarborough) 31 August (Asda) | v. Northamptonshire (Southampton) 2 September (J.P.) | v. Derbyshire (Derby) 9 September (J.P.) | Runs |
|---|---|---|---|---|---|---|
| | | | | | | 551 |
| 6 | 37* | 37 | 14* | 64* | 22* | 891 |
| 59 | 16 | 14 | 37 | 24 | 26 | 797 |
| 3 | 18 | 84* | 20* | 18 | 6 | 556 |
| 114 | 75 | 43 | 81 | 4 | 4 | 786 |
| | | 1 | — | | | 202 |
| 3 | 23 | 0 | — | 4 | 14* | 189 |
| 1* | 10 | — | — | — | | 104 |
| — | 1* | — | — | 4* | — | 64 |
| | | 1* | — | | | 70 |
| | | | | | | — |
| | | | | | | — |
| — | — | | | — | — | 1 |
| 1* | 0 | | | 58 | — | 140 |
| | | | | | — | — |
| — | — | — | — | — | — | 3 |
| 51 | 12 | 60 | 46 | 6 | 7 | 287 |
| | | 3 | | 4 | 1 | |
| 9 | 7 | 4 | 13 | 2 | 5 | |
| | 1 | 1 | 6 | 1 | 2 | |
| 5 | | | 3 | | 2 | |
| 252 | 200 | 248 | 220 | 189 | 89 | |
| 6 | 7 | 6 | 3 | 6 | 4 | |
| L | L | W | W | W | W | |
| 0 | 0 | — | — | 4 | 4 | |

| C.L. Smith | D.R. Turner | *Byes* | *Leg-byes* | *Wides* | *No-balls* | *Total* | *Wkts* |
|---|---|---|---|---|---|---|---|
| | | 1 | 5 | 12 | 3 | 154 | 10 |
| | | | 9 | 4 | | 227 | 7 |
| | | 4 | 9 | 8 | 6 | 240 | 2 |
| | | | 8 | 5 | | 184 | 8 |
| | | | 4 | 5 | 2 | 117 | 10 |
| | | 1 | 5 | 4 | 1 | 254 | 4 |
| | | 1 | 5 | | | 235 | 5 |
| 1.2–0–7–0 | | | 9 | 1 | 3 | 186 | 3 |
| | | | | | | | |
| | | | 8 | | | 192 | 3 |
| 2.1–1–3–2 | 1–0–5–0 | | 2 | 11 | 2 | 140 | 10 |
| | | | 11 | 6 | | 203 | 5 |
| | | | 6 | 6 | 8 | 121 | 10 |
| | | | 7 | 2 | 3 | 210 | 6 |
| | | | 6 | 3 | 1 | 250 | 8 |
| | | 1 | 8 | 9 | | 202 | 10 |
| | | 4 | 8 | 3 | 3 | 165 | 5 |
| | | | 6 | 5 | 1 | 218 | 7 |
| | | | 11 | 1 | 1 | 228 | 8 |
| | | | 7 | 2 | | 254 | 4 |
| | | 4 | 12 | 2 | | 203 | 3 |
| | | | 16 | 11 | | 205 | 10 |
| | | | 9 | 8 | 4 | 219 | 7 |
| | | | | | | | |
| | | | 6 | 4 | 3 | 186 | 8 |
| | | | 6 | 2 | 2 | 116 | 4 |
| 2 | 0 | | | | | | |

**Kent C.C.C.**
Limited-Over Matches – 1984

| BATTING | v. Middlesex (Lord's) 5 May (B.&H.) | v. Middlesex (Lord's) 6 May (J.P.) | v. Glamorgan (Canterbury) 12 May (B.&H.) | v. Somerset (Canterbury) 16 May (B.&H.) | v. Sussex (Hove) 19 May (B.&H.) | v. Surrey (Canterbury) 20 May (J.P.) | v. Gloucestershire (Canterbury) 3 June (J.P.) | v. Yorkshire (Canterbury) 10 June (J.P.) | v. Somerset (Bath) 17 June (J.P.) | v. Derbyshire (Derby) 24 June (J.P.) | v. Sussex (Hastings) 1 July (J.P.) | v. Berkshire (Canterbury) 4 July (N.W.) | v. Lancashire (Maidstone) 8 July (J.P.) | v. Northamptonshire (Tring) 15 July (J.P.) | v. Hampshire (Southampton) 18 July (N.W.) | v. Essex (Canterbury) 22 July (J.P.) | v. Warwickshire (Edgbaston) 29 July (J.P.) | v. Somerset (Taunton) 1 August (N.W.) |
|---|---|---|---|---|---|---|---|---|---|---|---|---|---|---|---|---|---|---|
| R.A. Woolmer | 0 | | 26 | 34 | 17 | | | | | | | | | | | | | |
| N.R. Taylor | 2 | 12 | 26 | 0 | 24 | | | | | 46 | 72 | 31 | 22 | 0 | 8 | 13 | 27 | 24 |
| C.J. Tavare | 15 | 12 | 31 | 3 | 0 | | 6 | 10 | 1 | 12* | 13* | 20 | 3 | 18 | 4 | 34* | 0 | 103 |
| D.G. Aslett | 45 | 6 | 13 | 46 | 42 | | 32 | 0 | 32 | 58 | 1 | 19 | 13 | 3 | 67 | 29 | 72 | 17 |
| C.S. Cowdrey | 5 | | | | | | 15 | 43 | 55* | 59 | 60 | 64 | 75 | 21 | 71 | 33 | 14 | 0 |
| R.M. Ellison | 72 | | 38* | 19 | 15 | | 84 | 55* | 19 | 43 | 5 | 10 | 14 | 28 | 41* | 83 | 14 | 15* |
| A.P.E. Knott | 41 | 2 | 21 | 7 | 20* | | 29* | 8 | 16 | | — | 7 | 6 | 5 | 1 | — | | — |
| G.W. Johnson | 13 | 13 | 31 | 3 | 60 | | 18 | 20 | 23 | 12* | 23* | 21* | 2 | 2 | 2 | 11* | 7* | 4* |
| D.L. Underwood | 0 | 0 | 0* | 10 | 7* | | — | 0 | — | | — | 0* | 1 | 0 | 11 | — | — | — |
| T.M. Alderman | 4* | 4* | — | 0 | — | | — | 1* | — | — | — | — | 11 | 5* | — | — | — | — |
| K.B.S. Jarvis | 1* | 0 | — | 1* | — | | — | — | — | — | — | — | 2* | 0 | — | — | | — |
| K.D. Masters | | | | | | | | | | | | | | | | | | |
| S.G. Hinks | | 1 | | | | | | | | | | | | | | | | |
| C. Penn | | 13 | 3 | 17 | 14 | | 0* | 9 | 5* | 3 | | | | | | | 0 | |
| L. Potter | | 7 | | | | | 38 | 9 | 5 | 4 | 37 | 41 | | | | | | |
| S. Marsh | | | | | | | | | | — | | | | | | | | |
| M.R. Benson | | | | | | | | | | | | | 43 | 88 | 35 | 0 | 78 | 96 |
| S.N.V. Waterton | | | | | | | | | | | | | | | | | 6* | |
| Byes | 4 | | 2 | 1 | | | | | | 3 | 2 | | | | | | 1 | 1 |
| Leg-byes | 8 | 4 | 7 | 13 | 23 | | 10 | 4 | 9 | 8 | 4 | 7 | 6 | 4 | 6 | 8 | 10 | 9 |
| Wides | 8 | 7 | 1 | 6 | 2 | | 3 | 5 | 5 | 7 | 4 | | 1 | | 3 | 1 | 4 | 6 |
| No-balls | 2 | 2 | 2 | | 3 | | | | 3 | | 1 | 12 | 1 | 1 | 1 | 1 | 1 | |
| Total | 220 | 83 | 201 | 160 | 227 | | 235 | 164 | 173 | 255 | 222 | 232 | 200 | 175 | 250 | 213 | 234 | 275 |
| Wickets | 9 | 10 | 7 | 10 | 7 | | 6 | 8 | 6 | 6 | 5 | 7 | 10 | 10 | 8 | 5 | 7 | 5 |
| Result | W | L | W | L | L | Ab. | W | L | L | L | W | W | W | W | W | L | W | W |
| Points | 2 | 0 | 2 | 0 | 0 | 2 | 4 | 0 | 0 | 0 | 4 | — | 4 | 4 | — | 0 | 4 | — |

*Catches*

21 – A.P.E. Knott (ct 15/st 6)
13 – T.M. Alderman
9 – D.G. Aslett
7 – C.J. Tavare
6 – N.R. Taylor
5 – C.S. Cowdrey and G.W. Johnson
4 – D.L. Underwood, L. Potter, M.R. Benson and S.N.V. Waterton (ct 2/st 2)
3 – C. Penn
2 – R.A. Woolmer and R.M. Ellison
1 – K.B.S. Jarvis and S. Marsh

| BOWLING | K.B.S. Jarvis | T.M. Alderman | C.S. Cowdrey | R.M. Ellison | D.L. Underwood | R.A. Woolmer | C. Penn | G.W. Johnson | K.D. Masters |
|---|---|---|---|---|---|---|---|---|---|
| (B.&H.) *v.* Middlesex (Lord's) 5 May | 8–1–20–1 | 7–3–9–2 | 7–1–20–1 | 5–2–3–2 | 11–2–35–2 | 9–1–37–2 | | | |
| (J.P.) *v.* Middlesex (Lord's) 6 May | 7–3–16–1 | 8–5–12–1 | | | 8–2–26–0 | | 6.3–0–19–1 | | |
| (B.&H.) *v.* Glamorgan (Canterbury) 12 May | 9–0–17–1 | 11–1–33–1 | | 10–3–28–4 | 11–1–28–2 | 9–1–18–1 | 3–0–10–0 | | |
| (B.&H.) *v.* Somerset (Canterbury) 16 May | 10.4–2–38–4 | 11–1–39–2 | | 11–2–25–0 | 11–4–21–2 | 4–0–9–0 | 7–0–19–0 | | |
| (B.&H.) *v.* Sussex (Hove) 19 May | 10.5–0–64–2 | 11–2–32–2 | | 11–2–32–2 | 8–0–38–0 | 11–1–38–0 | 3–1–13–0 | | |
| (J.P.) *v.* Surrey (Canterbury) 20 May | | | | | | | | | |
| (J.P.) *v.* Gloucestershire (Canterbury) 3 June | 8–0–42–1 | 8–0–36–0 | | 8–0–52–4 | 7–0–50–0 | | 8–1–33–0 | | |
| (J.P.) *v.* Yorkshire (Canterbury) 10 June | 8–1–25–1 | 7–0–25–2 | | 8–0–33–1 | 7–0–44–0 | | 6–1–29–0 | | |
| (J.P.) *v.* Somerset (Bath) 17 June | 4–0–19–0 | 7–0–35–0 | 5–0–28–0 | 5.1–1–26–1 | 7–0–39–0 | | 4–0–24–0 | | |
| (J.P.) *v.* Derbyshire (Derby) 24 June | 8–0–47–2 | 8–0–49–1 | 8–0–45–2 | 7.4–0–43–1 | | | 8–0–57–2 | | |
| (J.P.) *v.* Sussex (Hastings) 1 July | 5.5–0–31–2 | 8–0–34–0 | 8–0–37–1 | 5–0–13–1 | 8–3–12–6 | | | | |
| (N.W.) *v.* Berkshire (Canterbury) 4 July | 12–4–23–3 | 12–3–35–1 | 12–0–33–1 | 12–4–14–1 | 12–4–19–3 | | | | |
| (J.P.) *v.* Lancashire (Maidstone) 8 July | 6–0–35–0 | 7.4–0–36–5 | 8–0–41–1 | 8–0–39–3 | 8–1–22–0 | | | 2–0–9–0 | |
| (J.P.) *v.* Northamptonshire (Tring) 15 July | 7–1–37–1 | 8–0–39–0 | 3–0–17–0 | 8–0–40–3 | 8–2–13–1 | | | 4–0–18–0 | |
| (J.P.) *v.* Hampshire (Southampton) 18 July | 12–4–28–1 | 9.3–3–21–4 | 6–0–19–1 | 6–0–10–1 | 10–4–16–1 | | | | |
| (J.P.) *v.* Essex (Canterbury) 22 July | 6–0–34–0 | 8–0–47–2 | 8–0–41–0 | 7.1–0–37–0 | 8–0–26–1 | | | 2–0–18–0 | |
| (J.P.) *v.* Warwickshire (Edgbaston) 29 July | | 5.5–0–23–2 | 7–0–28–2 | 5–0–19–1 | 8–1–22–2 | | 7–0–45–3 | | |
| (N.W.) *v.* Somerset (Taunton) 1 August | 12–1–30–1 | 12–2–58–2 | 2–0–12–0 | 12–0–64–0 | 12–0–61–2 | | | 10–0–32–0 | |
| (J.P.) *v.* Leicestershire (Canterbury) 5 Aug. | 7–1–29–0 | 7–1–23–1 | 7–0–28–5 | 6–0–22–1 | 6–2–7–1 | | | | |
| (N.W.) *v.* Warwickshire (Edgbaston) 15 Aug. | 12–2–23–0 | 11.3–2–55–3 | 12–1–50–2 | 12–5–30–2 | 12–2–38–2 | | | | |
| (J.P.) *v.* Notts. (Folkestone) 19 August | | 7.3–0–44–2 | 8–0–32–1 | | 8–0–26–1 | | 8–0–45–0 | 8–0–31–0 | |
| (J.P.) *v.* Hampshire (Brnmth) 26 August | | 8–1–48–2 | 8–0–40–1 | | 8–0–26–2 | | 8–0–51–1 | 8–1–27–1 | |
| (N.W.) *v.* Middlesex (Lord's) 1 September | 12–1–47–3 | 12–0–53–0 | 12–1–48–0 | 12–2–53–2 | 12–2–25–1 | | | | |
| (J.P.) *v.* Worcestershire (Worcester) 2 Sept. | | | | 8–0–33–0 | | | 8–1–41–1 | 8–0–39–2 | 5.3–0–27–0 |
| (J.P.) *v.* Glamorgan (Canterbury) 9 Sept. | 8–0–38–3 | 7–2–26–3 | 8–0–27–0 | 8–1–23–1 | 8–0–45–2 | | | | |
| Wickets | 27 | 38 | 18 | 41 | 31 | 3 | 8 | 3 | 0 |

| v. Leicestershire (Canterbury) 5 August (J.P.) | v. Warwickshire (Edgbaston) 15 August (N.W.) | v. Nottinghamshire (Folkestone) 19 August (J.P.) | v. Hampshire (Bournemouth) 26 August (J.P.) | v. Middlesex (Lord's) 1 September (N.W.) | v. Worcestershire (Worcester) 2 September (J.P.) | v. Glamorgan (Canterbury) 9 September (J.P.) | | Runs |
|---|---|---|---|---|---|---|---|---|
| | | | | | | | | 77 |
| 25 | 3 | 5 | 51 | 49 | 31 | 5 | | 476 |
| 5* | 30 | 1 | | 28 | 3 | 7 | | 359 |
| — | 9 | 60 | 15 | 11 | 2 | 10 | | 602 |
| — | 1 | 21 | — | 58 | | 24 | | 619 |
| — | 49* | | | 23* | 27 | 39 | | 693 |
| | — | — | — | | | | | 163 |
| — | — | 32* | — | 0 | 2 | | | 299 |
| — | — | — | — | — | | 7 | | 36 |
| — | — | — | — | — | | 0* | | 25 |
| — | — | | | — | | 0 | | 4 |
| | | | | | 0 | | | 0 |
| 21* | | | 52* | | 5 | 30 | | 109 |
| | | 2* | — | | 9 | | | 75 |
| | | 31 | 35* | | 18 | 11 | | 236 |
| — | | | | | 1* | | | 1 |
| | 113* | 17 | 32 | 37 | 62 | | | 601 |
| | | | | 4* | | 15 | | 25 |
| 1 | 2 | | 4 | 10 | 1 | | | |
| 3 | 11 | 12 | 12 | 8 | 9 | 6 | | |
| 1 | 6 | | 2 | 3 | | 2 | | |
| | 2 | 2 | | 1 | 11 | | | |
| 56 | 226 | 183 | 203 | 232 | 181 | 156 | | |
| 1 | 4 | 6 | 3 | 6 | 10 | 10 | | |
| Ab. | W | L | W | L | L | L | | |
| 2 | — | 0 | 4 | — | 0 | 0 | | |

| S.G. Hinks | Byes | Leg-byes | Wides | No-balls | Total | Wkts |
|---|---|---|---|---|---|---|
| | | 8 | 8 | 3 | 143 | 10 |
| | | 1 | 5 | 5 | 84 | 3 |
| | 2 | 5 | | 3 | 144 | 10 |
| | | 5 | 1 | 4 | 161 | 8 |
| | | 5 | 5 | 3 | 230 | 9 |
| | | Match Abandoned | | | | |
| | | 5 | 1 | 3 | 222 | 8 |
| | | 8 | 3 | | 167 | 4 |
| | | 3 | 1 | 1 | 176 | 2 |
| | 1 | 13 | | 1 | 256 | 9 |
| | | 5 | 6 | 2 | 140 | 10 |
| | | 15 | 4 | | 143 | 9 |
| | | 4 | 6 | 2 | 194 | 10 |
| | | 4 | 4 | | 172 | 6 |
| | | 2 | 1 | 2 | 99 | 10 |
| | 1 | 9 | 2 | 1 | 216 | 3 |
| | | 3 | 11 | 2 | 153 | 10 |
| | | 5 | 3 | | 265 | 5 |
| | | 10 | | 1 | 120 | 8 |
| | | 16 | 8 | 4 | 224 | 10 |
| | | 5 | 1 | 2 | 186 | 4 |
| | | 7 | 1 | | 200 | 7 |
| | | 7 | 1 | 2 | 236 | 6 |
| 8-1-36-1 | 2 | 4 | 1 | 1 | 184 | 4 |
| | | 9 | 4 | 1 | 173 | 9 |
| 1 | | | | | | |

### *at Folkestone*

**Kent** 183 for 6 (D.G. Aslett 60, R.J. Hadlee 4 for 20)
**Nottinghamshire** 186 for 4 (R.T. Robinson 86)
*Nottinghamshire (4 pts) won by 6 wickets*

### *at Old Trafford*

**Lancashire** 157 for 7
**Warwickshire** 160 for 7 (K.D. Smith 53)
*Warwickshire (4 pts) won by 3 wickets*

### *at Leicester*

**Middlesex** 243 for 8 (M.W. Gatting 109, C.T. Radley 51)
**Leicestershire** 136 (J.E. Emburey 4 for 14)
*Middlesex (4 pts) won by 107 runs*

### *at Taunton*

**Somerset** 242 for 5 (I.T. Botham 73)
**Derbyshire** 128
*Somerset (4 pts) won by 114 runs*

### *at The Oval*

**Surrey** 205 for 7
**Yorkshire** 193 for 9
*Surrey (4 pts) won by 12 runs*

### *at Worcester*

**Gloucestershire** 127 (R.K. Illingworth 4 for 11)
**Worcestershire** 128 for 6
*Worcestershire (4 pts) won by 4 wickets*

Essex maintained their six-point lead at the top of the John Player League with an astounding win over Hampshire who, for the third week running, came to the last ball with the result in the balance. Gooch hit a mighty century for Essex and shared a second wicket stand of 116 with McEwan. Essex's 254 looked formidable, but Nicholas and David Turner began with 124 and although Jesty went 19 runs later, Turner and Robin Smith took their side to the point of victory with a stand of 95 in 11 blazing overs. Turner was run out in attempting a second run and Robin Smith was run out next ball, a no-ball, as he charged insanely down the wicket. His elder brother was also run out and Hampshire needed 8 off Pringle's last over. There were four singles and then Cowley missed a full toss on leg stump and was bowled. Tremlett could manage only a single to mid-off.

Middlesex, inspired by a Gatting century, trounced Leicestershire and Notts maintained their challenge with victory at Folkestone. The Lancashire challenge slipped as they lost with 5 balls to spare.

## *22, 23 and 24 August*

### *at Chesterfield*

**Yorkshire** 439 (K. Sharp 173, A.A. Metcalfe 60, P.E. Robinson 54, D.L. Bairstow 50)
**Derbyshire** 253 (R.J. Finney 60, W.P. Fowler 50, S. Oldham 4 for 59) and 156
*Yorkshire won by an innings and 30 runs*
*Yorkshire 24 pts, Derbyshire 5 pts*

## Lancashire C.C.C.

Limited-Over Matches – 1984

| BATTING | v. Minor Counties (Bowden) 5 May (B.&H.) | v. Nottinghamshire (Old Trafford) 12 May (B.&H.) | v. Northamptonshire (Old Trafford) 13 May (J.P.) | v. Worcestershire (Old Trafford) 17 May (B.&H.) | v. Derbyshire (Derby) 19 May (B.&H.) | v. Derbyshire (Derby) 20 May (J.P.) | v. Surrey (Old Trafford) 3 June (J.P.) | v. Essex (Chelmsford) 6 June (B.&H.) | v. Sussex (Old Trafford) 10 June (J.P.) | v. Glamorgan (Cardiff) 17 June (J.P.) | v. Nottinghamshire (Trent Bridge) 20/21 June (B.&H.) | v. Worcestershire (Old Trafford) 24 June (J.P.) | v. Middlesex (Old Trafford) 1 July (J.P.) | v. Buckinghamshire (Old Trafford) 4 July (N.W.) | v. Kent (Maidstone) 8 July (J.P.) | v. Hampshire (Portsmouth) 15 July | v. Gloucestershire (Bristol) 18 July (N.W.) | v. Warwickshire (Lord's) 21 July (B.&H.) |
|---|---|---|---|---|---|---|---|---|---|---|---|---|---|---|---|---|---|---|
| G. Fowler | 1 | 16 | 54 | 31 | 92 | 1 | | 10 | 75 | | 53 | 64 | | 101 | 8 | | 122 | 7 |
| J.A. Ormrod | 0 | 0 | | | | | 37 | 14 | 57 | 29 | | | 15 | 40 | | 3 | 4 | 24 |
| S.J.O'Shaughnessy | 50 | 41 | 76* | 51 | 3 | 3 | 25 | 3 | 2* | 9 | 16 | 6 | 6 | 12 | 3 | 4 | 21 | 22 |
| D.P. Hughes | 38 | 38* | 25* | 14 | 16 | 6 | 3 | 48* | | 4 | 17* | 9 | 47 | 36 | 92 | 36 | 38 | 35* |
| J. Abrahams | 66* | 1* | 23 | 10 | 7 | 38 | 17 | 53 | — | 16 | 22 | 12 | 37 | 13 | 34 | 30 | 51 | 0 |
| N.H. Fairbrother | 45* | — | — | 38* | 1 | 3 | 17 | 0 | 13* | 15 | 21* | 15 | 34 | 35 | 3 | 54* | 36 | 36* |
| M. Watkinson | — | — | — | — | 2* | 5 | 9* | — | — | — | — | 22* | 2 | 2* | 6 | 0 | — | — |
| S.T. Jefferies | — | — | — | 39 | 2 | 1 | 10 | — | — | 35* | — | 28 | 22 | 0 | 31 | 26 | 23* | — |
| C. Maynard | — | — | — | 8* | 14 | 26 | 22 | 13 | | | | | | | | — | | — |
| P.J.W. Allott | — | — | — | — | 15* | 3* | 0 | — | — | — | — | — | 6 | — | 4* | | — | — |
| L.L. McFarlane | — | | | | | | | | | | | | | | | | | |
| J. Simmons | | — | — | 0 | 1 | 18 | 6 | 3* | — | 7* | — | 24* | 8 | 10* | 1 | 45* | 13* | — |
| N.V. Radford | | | — | | | 4 | | | | | | | | | | — | | |
| D.W. Varey | | | | 27 | 2 | | | | | | | | | | | | | |
| D.J. Makinson | | | | | | | 2 | | — | — | | — | 2* | | 0 | — | | |
| J. Stanworth | | | | | | | | | — | — | — | — | — | — | 0 | | — | |
| M.R. Chadwick | | | | | | | | | | | 87 | | | | | | | |
| B.P. Patterson | | | | | | | | | | | | | | | | | | |
| K.A. Hayes | | | | | | | | | | | | | | | | | | |
| C.H. Lloyd | | | | | | | | | | | | | | | | | | |
| Byes | 4 | 4 | | 1 | 3 | 5 | | | 2 | 4 | | 1 | | 1 | | | 3 | |
| Leg-byes | 6 | 1 | 4 | 14 | 4 | 13 | 4 | 10 | 7 | 5 | 3 | 13 | 4 | 12 | 4 | 7 | 25 | 6 |
| Wides | 10 | 3 | 4 | 7 | 3 | 5 | 1 | 1 | 1 | 2 | 2 | 4 | 2 | 9 | 6 | 2 | 12 | 1 |
| No-balls | 3 | | 5 | | | 2 | | 3 | 2 | 4 | 3 | 1 | 1 | 1 | 2 | 3 | 1 | 9 |
| Total | 223 | 104 | 191 | 240 | 165 | 133 | 153 | 158 | 159 | 130 | 224 | 199 | 186 | 272 | 194 | 210 | 349 | 140 |
| Wickets | 4 | 3 | 2 | 7 | 9 | 10 | 10 | 6 | 2 | 5 | 4 | 6 | 9 | 7 | 10 | 6 | 6 | 4 |
| Result | W | W | W | W | L | L | L | W | W | W | W | W | W | W | L | W | W | W |
| Points | 2 | 2 | 4 | 2 | 0 | 0 | 0 | – | 4 | 4 | — | 4 | 4 | — | 0 | 4 | — | — |

*Catches*

26 – C. Maynard
13 – N.H. Fairbrother
12 – J. Abrahams
10 – S. J. O'Shaughnessy, M. Watkinson and J. Stanworth
9 – D.P. Hughes
7 – S.T. Jefferies
5 – P.J.W. Allott and J. Simmons
4 – G. Fowler and J.A. Ormrod
1 – N.V. Radford and D.J. Makison

| BOWLING | P.J.W. Allott | L.L. McFarlane | M. Watkinson | S.T. Jefferies | S.J. O'Shaughnessy | D.P. Hughes | J. Simmons | N.V. Radford | D.J. Makison |
|---|---|---|---|---|---|---|---|---|---|
| (B.&H.) v. Minor Counties (Bowden) 5 May | 11–1–47–0 | 11–0–50–0 | 9–3–15–2 | 11–5–27–1 | 7–1–25–0 | 6–1–33–1 | | | |
| (B.&H.) v. Notts. (Old Trafford) 12 May | 8–2–10–1 | | 8–2–13–2 | 9.4–3–15–4 | 11–4–25–0 | 3–1–7–0 | 11–2–20–2 | | |
| (J.P.) v. Northants. (Old Trafford) 13 May | 8–2–24–0 | | 8–2–46–2 | 8–2–15–0 | 6–0–26–1 | | 7–1–37–1 | 6–1–26–0 | |
| (B.&H.) v. Worcs. (Old Trafford) 17 May | 11–0–57–1 | | 11–0–58–4 | 11–2–34–1 | 11–1–45–2 | | 11–1–31–1 | | |
| (B.&H.) v. Derbyshire (Derby) 19 May | 11–2–33–1 | | 11–0–60–3 | 11–2–35–0 | 11–3–28–1 | | 11–0–41–3 | | |
| (J.P.) v. Derbyshire (Derby) 20 May | 8–1–26–1 | | 5–0–26–0 | 8–1–36–0 | | | 6–0–20–1 | 8–0–21–2 | |
| (J.P.) v. Surrey (Old Trafford) 3 June | 8–0–50–2 | | 4.1–0–32–2 | 8–0–27–1 | 2–0–6–0 | | 8–2–15–1 | | 5–1–16–0 |
| (B.&H.) v. Essex (Chelmsford) 6 June | 11–2–33–3 | | 10–1–36–1 | 11–2–36–0 | 11–5–10–3 | | 11–1–25–1 | | |
| (J.P.) v. Sussex (Old Trafford) 10 June | 8–0–25–1 | | 6–1–18–1 | 7–0–38–1 | 6–0–19–1 | | 5–0–25–1 | | 8–0–20–3 |
| (J.P.) v. Glamorgan (Cardiff) 17 June | 8–1–18–2 | | 8–1–24–0 | 4–0–26–1 | 8–4–15–2 | | 4–0–14–0 | | 8–0–25–1 |
| (B.&H.) v. Notts. (Trent Bridge) 20/21 June | 11–3–39–0 | | 11–1–52–1 | 11–1–45–2 | 9–0–37–1 | | 11–5–23–2 | | |
| (J.P.) v. Worcs. (Old Trafford) 24 June | 5–2–4–2 | | 5–0–22–0 | 6.1–1–20–4 | 3–0–6–1 | | 5–0–19–0 | | 8–0–24–2 |
| (J.P.) v. Middlesex (Old Trafford) 1 July | 6–1–16–2 | | 4–1–14–1 | 5–0–18–1 | 5–0–18–3 | | 7–3–22–1 | | 7–0–29–0 |
| (N.W.) v. Bucks. (Old Trafford) 4 July | 11–2–34–4 | | 9–2–29–0 | 12–1–45–0 | 12–3–27–1 | | 12–4–33–1 | | |
| (J.P.) v. Kent (Maidstone) 8 July | 6.4–0–30–2 | | 5–0–44–2 | 8–1–24–1 | 8–0–32–0 | | 5–0–34–2 | | 6–0–28–3 |
| (J.P.) v. Hampshire (Portsmouth) 15 July | | | 6–0–34–0 | 7–0–31–2 | 8–0–24–2 | | 2–0–23–0 | 7–0–32–2 | 8–0–47–1 |
| (N.W.) v. Gloucestershire (Bristol) 18 July | 9–0–36–1 | | 8–0–48–0 | 9.5–0–43–3 | 12–0–54–1 | | 12–2–37–5 | | |
| (B.&H.) v. Warwickshire (Lord's) 21 July | 8.4–0–15–3 | | 9–0–23–2 | 11–2–28–3 | 11–1–43–2 | | 11–3–18–0 | | |
| (J.P.) v. Somerset (Taunton) 22 July | 8–1–29–1 | | 6–0–26–1 | 6–0–27–2 | 4–0–26–0 | | 7–0–28–0 | | 8–0–51–3 |
| (J.P.) v. Notts. (Trent Bridge) 29 July | | | 5–0–33–1 | 8–0–54–0 | 7–1–32–0 | | 8–0–31–2 | 7–1–31–1 | 5–0–32–0 |
| (N.W.) v. Middlesex (Lord's) 1 August | 12–2–41–2 | | 12–1–63–3 | | 12–2–36–1 | | 12–0–46–0 | | |
| (J.P.) v. Yorkshire (Old Trafford) 5 August | 8–1–13–0 | | 5–0–17–1 | 8–1–19–2 | 4–0–21–0 | | 8–0–20–1 | 7–1–22–1 | |
| (J.P.) v. Leicestershire (Leicester) 12 Aug. | | | 5–0–12–0 | 5–0–31–0 | 7–1–37–1 | | 8–0–17–1 | 7–0–28–2 | 2–0–11–0 |
| (J.P.) v. Warwickshire (Old Trafford) 19 Aug. | 8–2–26–1 | | 7–0–36–1 | 8–1–28–1 | 5–1–23–0 | | 8–1–27–0 | 3.1–0–10–2 | |
| (J.P.) v. Glos. (Moreton-in-Marsh) 26 Aug. | | | 8–1–31–0 | | 8–0–24–3 | | 8–2–31–1 | 8–0–37–1 | 7–0–48–1 |
| (Asda) v. Hampshire (Scarborough) 30 Aug | | 10–1–42–2 | 10–1–54–2 | | 10–2–43–1 | | 8–1–54–0 | | |
| (J.P.) v. Essex (Old Trafford) 9 September | | | 8–0–25–3 | | | | 8–1–19–4 | 5–1–12–0 | 5–0–15–2 |
| Wickets | 30 | 2 | 35 | 30 | 27 | 1 | 31 | 11 | 16 |

| v. Somerset (Taunton) 22 July (J.P.) | v. Nottinghamshire (Trent Bridge) 29 July (J.P.) | v. Middlesex (Lord's) 1 August (N.W.) | v. Yorkshire (Old Trafford) 5 August (J.P.) | v. Leicestershire (Leicester) 12 August (J.P.) | v. Warwickshire (Old Trafford) 19 August (J.P.) | v. Gloucestershire (M'ton-in-Marsh) 26 August (J.P.) | v. Hampshire (Scarborough) 30 August (Asda) | v. Essex (Old Trafford) 9 September (J.P.) | Runs |
|---|---|---|---|---|---|---|---|---|---|
| 54 | | 14 | 57 | | 26 | | 5 | 50 | 841 |
| | 27 | 19 | | 7 | | 1 | 63 | | 340 |
| 91 | 15 | 7 | 3 | 101* | 5 | 12 | 13 | 21* | 621 |
| 24* | 67 | 13 | 23 | 0* | 23 | 63 | 47 | — | 762 |
| 27 | 7 | 0 | 11 | — | 5 | | 4 | — | 484 |
| 0* | 29 | 13 | 7 | 59 | 10 | 29 | 1 | — | 514 |
| — | 19* | 6 | — | — | 32* | 3 | 5 | — | 113 |
| — | 26 | | 15* | — | 21 | | | | 279 |
| — | — | 5* | — | — | 20* | 0 | 15 | — | 123 |
| — | | 7 | — | | — | | | | 335 |
| | | | | | | | 2* | | 2 |
| — | 3 | 1 | 6* | — | 0 | 9 | 6 | — | 161 |
| | 3* | | — | — | — | 0 | | — | 7 |
| | | | | | | | | | 29 |
| — | — | | | — | | 0* | | — | 4 |
| | | | | | | | | | 0 |
| | | | | | | | | | 87 |
| | | 4 | | | | | | | 4 |
| | | | | | | 53 | 17 | 1* | 71 |
| | | | | | | 5 | | | 5 |
| | 1 | 1 | | 4 | 2 | | | | |
| 8 | 7 | 5 | 4 | 4 | 9 | 8 | 16 | 6 | |
| 5 | 3 | 7 | 1 | 2 | 2 | 8 | 11 | | |
| | 3 | 3 | | | 2 | 1 | | 1 | |
| 209 | 210 | 105 | 127 | 177 | 157 | 192 | 205 | 79 | |
| 3 | 7 | 10 | 5 | 2 | 7 | 10 | 10 | 1 | |
| W | L | L | W | W | L | L | L | W | |
| 4 | 0 | — | 4 | 4 | 0 | 0 | — | 4 | |

| J. Abrahams | B.P. Patterson | K.A. Hayes | Byes | Leg-byes | Wides | No-balls | Total | Wkts |
|---|---|---|---|---|---|---|---|---|
| | | | | 11 | 9 | 2 | 219 | 4 |
| | | | | 2 | 7 | 1 | 100 | 10 |
| | | | | 12 | | 1 | 187 | 5 |
| | | | | 9 | 3 | | 237 | 9 |
| | | | | 9 | 4 | | 210 | 8 |
| | | | 1 | 3 | 2 | 1 | 136 | 4 |
| | | | 4 | 2 | 2 | | 154 | 6 |
| 1–0–3–0 | | | | 7 | 5 | 2 | 157 | 10 |
| | | | | 9 | 2 | 1 | 157 | 8 |
| | | | | 3 | 1 | 1 | 127 | 8 |
| 2–0–11–0 | | | | 4 | 5 | 7 | 223 | 6 |
| | | | | 6 | 1 | | 102 | 10 |
| | | | 6 | 9 | | | 132 | 10 |
| 4–1–16–1 | | | | 6 | 2 | 7 | 199 | 8 |
| | | | | 6 | 1 | 1 | 200 | 10 |
| | | | | 8 | 6 | 1 | 206 | 7 |
| 6–0–29–0 | | | | 25 | 3 | 6 | 281 | 10 |
| | | | | 4 | | 8 | 139 | 10 |
| | | | 1 | 16 | 3 | 1 | 208 | 8 |
| | | | 3 | 12 | 3 | 2 | 233 | 4 |
| | 12–0–69–1 | | 3 | 9 | 3 | 6 | 276 | 8 |
| | | | | 9 | 2 | 1 | 124 | 9 |
| 6–0–24–0 | | | | 6 | 2 | 3 | 171 | 6 |
| | | | 3 | 4 | 2 | 1 | 160 | 7 |
| | | 1–0–5–0 | 8 | 5 | 6 | 2 | 197 | 6 |
| 10–0–30–1 | | 2–0–17–0 | 3 | 4 | 1 | | 248 | 6 |
| | | | | 1 | 1 | 2 | 75 | 10 |
| 2 | 1 | 0 | | | | | | |

*Chris Cowdrey, the architect of Kent's victory over Essex at Colchester. An all-rounder on the brink of the England side. (David Munden)*

### at Colchester

**Essex** 90 (T.M. Alderman 4 for 19, K.B.S. Jarvis 4 for 45) and 118 (T.M. Alderman 5 for 27)
**Kent** 201 (C.S. Cowdrey 125 not out) and 10 for 0

*Kent won by 10 wickets*
*Kent 22 pts, Essex 4 pts*

### at Bournemouth

**Hampshire** 188 (T.E. Jesty 86, P.H. Edmonds 4 for 67) and 139 (P.H. Edmonds 8 for 53)
**Middlesex** 240 (G.D. Barlow 93, R.J. Maru 7 for 79) and 91 for 3

*Middlesex won by 7 wickets*
*Middlesex 22 pts, Hampshire 5 pts*

### at Blackpool

**Lancashire** 235 (J. Simmons 72, M.R. Chadwick 61, E.E. Hemmings 5 for 78) and 193 (M. Watkinson 61, R.J. Hadlee 5 for 40)
**Nottinghamshire** 365 for 9 dec (P. Johnson 104, R.T. Robinson 72, D.W. Randall 60) and 64 for 0

*Nottinghamshire won by 10 wickets*
*Nottinghamshire 24 pts, Lancashire 4 pts*

### at Leicester

**Gloucestershire** 250 (J.N. Shepherd 61) and 195 (A.W. Stovold 66, P. Willey 5 for 40)
**Leicestershire** 456 (J.C. Balderstone 181 not out, T.J. Boon 144, J.N. Shepherd 4 for 99)

*Leicestershire won by an innings and 11 runs*
*Leicestershire 24 pts, Gloucestershire 4 pts*

**Leicestershire C.C.C.**
Limited-Over Matches – 1984

| BATTING | v. Derbyshire (Leicester) 29 April (J.P.) | v. Yorkshire (Leeds) 5 May (B.&H.) | v. Warwickshire (Leicester) 12 May (B.&H.) | v. Northamptonshire (Leicester) 15 May (B.&H.) | v. Scotland (Glasgow) 17 May (B.&H.) | v. Somerset (Leicester) 20 May (J.P.) | v. Sussex (Leicester) 27 May (J.P.) | v. Essex (Hinkley) 3 June (J.P.) | v. Surrey (The Oval) 10 June (J.P.) | v. Hampshire (Basingstoke) 17 June (J.P.) | v. Sussex (Harrogate) 21 June (T.T.) | v. Northamptonshire (Harrogate) 22 June (T.T.) | v. Nottinghamshire (Leicester) 24 June (J.P.) | v. Glamorgan (Swansea) 1 July (J.P.) | v. Wiltshire (Swindon) 4 July (N.W.) | v. Worcestershire (Worcester) 15 July (J.P.) | v. Derbyshire (Leicester) 18 July (N.W.) | v. Gloucestershire (Leicester) 22 July (J.P.) |
|---|---|---|---|---|---|---|---|---|---|---|---|---|---|---|---|---|---|---|
| D.I. Gower | 13 | | | | | 14* | | | 11 | | 32 | 45 | 48 | | 77 | | 156 | 75 |
| I.P. Butcher | 29 | 19 | 15 | 43 | 42 | 1 | | 3 | 19 | 22 | 1 | 16 | 13 | 0 | | 35 | 30 | — |
| N.E. Briers | 0 | 42 | 29 | 8 | 38 | 6* | | 5 | — | 38 | 19 | 31 | 10 | 19 | 59 | 47 | 20 | 86* |
| P. Willey | 60 | 54 | 57 | 88* | 40 | — | | 51 | 38 | 67 | 23 | 95 | 1 | 106 | 4 | 45 | 26 | 42* |
| J.J. Whitaker | 41 | 11 | 6 | 46 | 45 | — | | 0 | 107* | 57* | 21 | 50 | 6 | 132 | 155 | 30 | 16 | 0 |
| M.A. Garnham | 2 | 14 | 6 | — | — | — | | 13 | 16* | 0* | 8 | 12 | 26* | 7* | 19 | 0* | 6* | — |
| T.J. Boon | 12* | | | 36* | 5* | | | 14 | — | — | 1 | 2 | 48 | — | 3* | 13 | 22* | — |
| J.P. Agnew | 1 | 3 | 23* | — | — | — | | 0* | — | — | | | — | — | — | — | — | — |
| L.B. Taylor | 0 | 1* | 0 | — | — | — | | | | | | | | | | | | |
| N.G.B. Cook | 10* | 3* | 23 | — | — | — | | 0 | | | — | — | | — | — | | | |
| G.J.F. Ferris | — | | | | | | | | | | | | | | | | | |
| J.C. Balderstone | | 0 | 2 | | | | | | | | | | | | | | | |
| M.D. Haysman | | 1 | 24 | 15 | 28* | — | | | | | 91* | 3 | | | | | | |
| G.J. Parsons | | 3 | 7 | — | — | — | | 6 | — | — | 16* | 14* | 10 | — | 1 | — | — | — |
| P.B. Clift | | | | | | | | 17 | — | — | — | 1* | 13 | 1* | 10* | | 4 | — |
| A.M.E. Roberts | | | | | | | | 1 | — | — | | | — | 14 | 19 | 19 | 4 | — |
| R.A. Cobb | | | | | | | | | | — | | | | | | | | |
| J.P. Addison | | | | | | | | | | | | | | | | — | | |
| I.R. Carmichael | | | | | | | | | | | | | | | | — | | |
| P.J. Whitticase | | | | | | | | | | | | | | | | | | |
| Byes | 1 | 8 | 4 | | 1 | | | 2 | 6 | | | 2 | | 1 | 2 | 2 | 6 | |
| Leg-byes | 6 | 6 | 4 | 3 | | | | 4 | 8 | 8 | 8 | 6 | 7 | 6 | | 12 | 7 | 5 |
| Wides | 2 | 5 | 1 | 2 | 5 | 1 | | | 2 | | 1 | | 1 | 5 | 4 | 1 | | 4 |
| No-balls | | 2 | 1 | 2 | 3 | | | 2 | 5 | | 7 | 3 | 3 | | 1 | | 4 | |
| Total | 177 | 172 | 202 | 243 | 207 | 22 | | 118 | 212 | 192 | 228 | 280 | 186 | 291 | 354 | 204 | 301 | 212 |
| Wickets | 8 | 9 | 10 | 4 | 4 | 1 | | 10 | 3 | 3 | 7 | 8 | 8 | 5 | 7 | 6 | 7 | 2 |
| Result | L | L | L | W | W | Ab. | Ab. | L | L | W | W | W | L | W | W | W | W | W |
| Points | 0 | 0 | 0 | 2 | 2 | 2 | 2 | 0 | 0 | 4 | — | — | 0 | 4 | — | 4 | — | 4 |

*Catches* 18 – M.A. Garnham (ct 14/st 4)
11 – P. Willey
10 – T.J. Boon
8 – G.J. Parsons and M.D. Haysman
7 – I.P. Butcher, N.G.B. Cook and P.B. Clift
6 – N.E. Briers
5 – J.J. Whitaker
4 – J.P. Agnew
3 – D.I. Gower
2 – A.M.E. Roberts
1 – J.C. Balderstone, R. A. Cogg and P.J. Whitticase

| BOWLING | G.J.F. Ferris | J.P. Agnew | P. Willey | N.G.B. Cook | L.B. Taylor | N.E. Briers | G.J. Parsons | P.B. Clift | A.M.E. Roberts |
|---|---|---|---|---|---|---|---|---|---|
| (J.P.) *v.* Derbyshire (Leicester) 29 April | 8–0–46–1 | 6–1–22–1 | 8–1–19–0 | 8–0–31–1 | 5.2–0–40–0 | 1–0–15–0 | | | |
| (B.&H.) *v.* Yorkshire (Leeds) 5 May | | 8–0–29–1 | 7–1–25–0 | 6–0–30–0 | 9–3–31–0 | 9–2–27–1 | 11–2–21–1 | | |
| (B.&H.) *v.* Warwickshire (Leicester) 12 May | | 11–2–43–5 | 8–1–20–0 | 11–3–37–1 | 8–3–31–0 | 8–0–41–0 | 11–1–43–1 | | |
| (B.&H.) *v.* Northants (Leicester) 15 May | | 11–1–36–2 | 11–4–28–0 | 11–1–37–1 | 11–0–60–3 | | 11–0–54–0 | | |
| (B.&H.) *v.* Scotland (Glasgow) 17 May | | 8–3–12–2 | 11–1–29–0 | 11–2–25–1 | 9–4–39–0 | 5–0–25–0 | 11–1–48–0 | | |
| (J.P.) *v.* Somerset (Leicester) 20 May | | 8–0–46–1 | 8–0–32–0 | 8–0–30–2 | 8–0–38–2 | | 8–1–33–1 | | |
| (J.P.) *v.* Sussex (Leicester) 27 May | | | | | | | | | |
| (J.P.) *v.* Essex (Hinckley) 3 June | | 6–0–33–0 | 6–0–25–2 | | | | 6–1–17–1 | 6–0–30–2 | 7–0–32–2 |
| (J.P.) *v.* Surrey (The Oval) 10 June | | 8–1–54–1 | 8–2–18–3 | | | | 8–0–45–0 | 7.5–0–43–2 | 8–0–41–1 |
| (J.P.) *v.* Hampshire (Basingstoke) 17 June | | 7–0–39–1 | 8–0–24–0 | | | | 7–1–33–0 | 8–0–48–1 | 8–0–33–0 |
| (T.T.) *v.* Sussex (Harrogate) 21 June | | | 11–5–22–2 | 11–1–35–2 | | | 7–0–22–1 | 10.3–2–49–4 | |
| (T.T.) *v.* Northants. (Harrogate) 22 June | | | 11–0–20–1 | 8–1–42–2 | | 11–2–51–1 | 10–2–32–3 | 10–1–54–3 | |
| (J.P.) *v.* Nottinghamshire (Leicester) 24 June | | 8–0–35–2 | 8–1–29–1 | | | | 8–0–25–1 | 7.2–0–46–0 | 7–0–30–0 |
| (J.P.) *v.* Glamorgan (Swansea) 1 July | | 8–0–54–1 | 8–0–42–3 | 1–0–10–0 | | | 8–0–61–2 | 6–0–47–2 | 7.4–0–42–2 |
| (J.P.) *v.* Wiltshire (Swindon) 4 July | | 7–2–24–1 | 12–0–45–0 | 12–4–33–2 | | 7–0–32–1 | 6–2–11–2 | 10–2–39–0 | 5–1–8–0 |
| (J.P.) *v.* Worcestershire (Worcester) 15 July | | 8–1–43–3 | 8–1–33–2 | | | | 8–0–45–0 | | 8–0–35–1 |
| (N.W.) *v.* Derbyshire (Leicester) 18/19 July | | 12–0–36–2 | 12–1–33–3 | | | | 7.4–2–32–2 | 9–1–32–1 | 8–0–28–1 |
| (J.P.) *v.* Gloucestershire (Leicester) 22 July | | 8–2–33–0 | 8–2–37–0 | | | | 8–0–50–2 | 8–1–48–2 | 8–1–30–2 |
| (J.P.) *v.* Yorkshire (Bradford) 29 July | | 8–2–44–1 | 8–0–26–2 | | | | 8–0–55–0 | 8–0–57–1 | |
| (N.W.) *v.* Northants. (Northampton) 1 Aug. | | 12–1–48–2 | 12–0–34–1 | | | | 12–0–44–0 | 12–1–43–2 | 11–1–64–1 |
| (J.P.) *v.* Kent (Canterbury) 5 August | | 3–0–13–0 | | | | | 6–0–23–1 | 3–1–15–0 | |
| (J.P.) *v.* Lancashire (Leicester) 12 August | | | 8–0–20–0 | 6–1–32–0 | | 2–0–24–0 | 5.5–0–44–1 | 8–1–29–0 | |
| (J.P.) *v.* Middlesex (Leicester) 19 August | | | 6–0–49–1 | 3–0–37–0 | | 6–1–29–3 | 8–0–43–1 | 8–0–43–1 | |
| (J.P.) *v.* Northants (Northampton) 26 Aug. | | | 8–1–41–1 | 4–0–25–0 | 8–0–21–1 | | 4–0–14–0 | 7.3–0–27–3 | |
| (J.P.) *v.* Warwickshire (Edgbaston) 9 Sept. | | | | | | | | | |
| Wickets | 1 | 26 | 22 | 12 | 6 | 6 | 20 | 24 | 10 |

| v. Yorkshire (Bradford) 29 July (J.P.) | v. Northamptonshire (Northampton) 1 August (N.W.) | v. Kent (Canterbury) 5 August (J.P.) | v. Lancashire (Leicester) 12 August (J.P.) | v. Middlesex (Leicester) 19 August (J.P.) | v. Northamptonshire (Northampton) 26 August (J.P.) | v. Warwickshire (Edgbaston) 9 September (J.P.) | *Runs* |
|---|---|---|---|---|---|---|---|
| | 24 | 4 | | 8 | | 43 | 550 |
| 31 | 81 | 4 | 15 | 10* | 4 | — | 433 |
| 108 | 7 | 14 | 50 | 0 | 41 | 4 | 681 |
| 44 | 25 | 33 | 3 | 14 | 70 | 18* | 1004 |
| | | 17 | 41 | 11 | 16 | 45 | 853 |
| 20 | 4 | | 16* | 13 | | | 182 |
| — | 1 | 0 | 10 | 24 | 6 | 2* | 199 |
| — | 4* | 4 | | | | | 35 |
| | | | | | 0* | — | 1 |
| | | | — | 13 | 0 | | 49 |
| | | | | | | | — |
| — | 33 | | | | | | 35 |
| | | | | | | | 162 |
| 0 | 23 | 15 | 22 | 20 | 5 | — | 142 |
| 10* | 18* | 13* | 3* | 7 | 30* | — | 127 |
| | 5 | | | | | | 62 |
| — | | | — | | | | — |
| | | | | | | | — |
| — | | — | — | 1 | — | — | 1 |
| | | 5* | | | — | — | 5 |
| 2 | 1 | | | 4 | | | |
| 10 | 7 | 10 | 6 | 7 | 4 | 12 | |
| 4 | 1 | | 2 | | 1 | 3 | |
| | 4 | 1 | 3 | 4 | 2 | 1 | |
| 229 | 238 | 120 | 171 | 136 | 179 | 128 | |
| 5 | 9 | 8 | 6 | 10 | 7 | 3 | |
| L | L | Ab. | L | L | L | Ab. | |
| 0 | — | 2 | 0 | 0 | 0 | 2 | |

| M.D. Haysman | I.R. Carmichael | J.J. Whitaker | *Byes* | *Leg-byes* | *Wides* | *No-balls* | *Total* | *Wkts* |
|---|---|---|---|---|---|---|---|---|
| | | | 1 | 3 | | 4 | 181 | 3 |
| | | | 3 | 8 | 4 | | 178 | 3 |
| | | | | 7 | 6 | 1 | 229 | 7 |
| | | | 4 | 10 | 1 | 9 | 239 | 6 |
| | | | 2 | 22 | 1 | 1 | 204 | 5 |
| | | | 1 | 3 | 4 | 2 | 189 | 8 |
| | | | Match Abandoned | | | | | |
| | | | | 10 | 1 | | 148 | 7 |
| | | | | 14 | | | 215 | 7 |
| | | | | 6 | 3 | 2 | 188 | 3 |
| 4–1–18–1 | | | 1 | | | | 147 | 10 |
| 3–0–15–0 | | | | 13 | 3 | 1 | 231 | 10 |
| | | | 1 | 17 | 5 | | 188 | 4 |
| | | | 1 | 5 | | | 262 | 10 |
| | | 1–0–5–0 | 2 | 3 | 7 | | 209 | 6 |
| | 8–1–30–2 | | 2 | 10 | | | 198 | 9 |
| | | | | 11 | 4 | 5 | 181 | 10 |
| | | | | 10 | | 2 | 210 | 6 |
| | 8–0–35–2 | | | 12 | 1 | | 230 | 7 |
| | | | 1 | 5 | 3 | | 242 | 7 |
| | | | 1 | 3 | 1 | | 56 | 1 |
| | 5–0–18–1 | | 4 | 4 | 2 | | 177 | 2 |
| | 8–0–34–2 | | 1 | 4 | 3 | | 243 | 8 |
| | 8–0–32–0 | | | 16 | 7 | | 183 | 7 |
| | | | Match Abandoned | | | | | |
| 1 | 7 | 0 | | | | | | |

### *at Northampton*

**Sussex** 391 for 9 dec (A.P. Wells 127, J.R.T. Barclay 82, I.J. Gould 84, B.J. Griffiths 4 for 89) and 214 for 4 dec (A.P. Wells 64 not out, I.A. Greig 64 not out)
**Northamptonshire** 303 for 5 dec (R.J. Bailey 106 not out) and 306 for 4 (W. Larkins 183 not out)

*Northamptonshire won by 6 wickets*
*Northamptonshire 23 pts, Sussex 6 pts*

### *at The Oval*

**Somerset** 157 (D.J. Thomas 6 for 36) and 226 (V.J. Marks 76, G.V. Palmer 73 not out, D.J. Thomas 4 for 67)
**Surrey** 401 (R.D.V. Knight 114, G.P. Howarth 55)

*Surrey won by an innings and 18 runs*
*Surrey 24 pts, Somerset 4 pts*

### *at Edgbaston*

**Glamorgan** 326 (Younis Ahmed 90, G.C. Holmes 60, J.A. Hopkins 50, N. Gifford 6 for 83) and 218 for 5 dec (Younis Ahmed 68 not out, W.A. Morton 4 for 85)
**Warwickshire** 194 (W.W. Davis 4 for 43) and 182 (G.W. Humpage 89, J.F. Steele 5 for 42)

*Glamorgan won by 168 runs*
*Glamorgan 24 pts, Warwickshire 4 pts*

### *at Glasgow*

**Scotland** 244 (C.J. Warner 70) and 255 for 8 (C.J. Warner 53, T.B. Racionzer 51)
**Ireland** 356 (J.D. Monteith 95, J.A. Prior 87, S.J. Warke 54, J. Thomson 4 for 116)

*Match drawn*

Just as all were expecting Essex to move into an unassailable lead in the championship, they were beaten in two days by Kent and with Notts taking maximum points at Blackpool, the lead was cut to 18 points. Chris Cowdrey put Essex in at Colchester and with Prichard and McEwan the only Essex batsmen to reach double figures in the match, the home side folded twice to a side which bowled better, particularly Alderman, and batted better, Cowdrey himself playing a quite superbly determined and aggressive innings on a difficult pitch. Alderman leant great service in a ninth wicket stand of 96 in 23 overs. Essex sorely missed the injured Lever, but their batting had no excuses and it was an unhappy day for Gladwin who was awarded his county cap in the morning and was out twice before the close of the first day.

A sparkling hundred in two hours by Paul Johnson gave Notts dominance over Lancashire and the visitors swept to victory as Richard Hadlee took his hundredth wicket and neared the 'double'.

A spinners' wicket at Bournemouth saw Maru record a career best and Edmonds do the same in the second innings and win the game for Middlesex as well as to make one wonder further why he was not in the England side. Another career best came at Chesterfield where Kevin Sharp's 173 in Yorkshire's trouncing of Derbyshire was also a reminder to selectors. Never has the rehabilitation of a batsman been so complete and so welcome.

Chris Balderstone gave notice that his career would be continuing with the highest score of his career as he shared a third wicket stand of 242 with Tim Boon who also made an

**Middlesex C.C.C.**
Limited-Over Matches – 1984

| BATTING | v. Kent (Lord's) 5 May (B.&H.) | v. Kent (Lord's) 6 May (J.P.) | v. Essex (Lord's) 13 May (J.P.) | v. Sussex (Lord's) 15/16 May (B.&H.) | v. Somerset (Taunton) 17 May (B.&H.) | v. Glamorgan (Cardiff) 19 May (B.&H.) | v. Glamorgan (Cardiff) 20 May (J.P.) | v. Northamptonshire (Lord's) 27 May (J.P.) | v. Derbyshire (Derby) 3 June (J.P.) | v. Somerset (Bath) 10 June (J.P.) | v. Warwickshire (Lord's) 17 June (J.P.) | v. Surrey (The Oval) 24 June (J.P.) | v. Lancashire (Old Trafford) 1 July (J.P.) | v. Northumberland (Jesmond) 4 July (N.W.) | v. Worcestershire (Lord's) 8 July (J.P.) | v. Yorkshire (Lord's) 15 July (J.P.) | v. Nottinghamshire (Trent Bridge) 18 July (N.W.) | v. Hampshire (Lord's) 29 July (J.P.) |
|---|---|---|---|---|---|---|---|---|---|---|---|---|---|---|---|---|---|---|
| W.N. Slack | 10 | 0 | 71 | 12 | 12 | 14 | — | 2* | 10 | 0 | | 66 | 0 | 43 | 0 | 11* | 31 | 4 |
| K.P. Tomlins | 10 | 1* | 14* | 9 | 40 | 28 | — | 7 | 18* | 59 | 24* | 2 | 0 | | 13 | | | |
| M.W. Gatting | 1 | 25 | 29 | 29 | 47 | 43 | — | 13 | | 58 | 74 | 103* | | 17 | 42 | 35 | 67 | 3 |
| R.O. Butcher | 8 | 6 | 9 | | | 4 | — | 5* | 82 | 1 | 2 | 5 | 63 | 4 | 5 | 16* | 2 | 44 |
| C.T. Radley | 1 | 41* | | 65* | 7 | | | 48 | 40 | 19 | 0 | 42 | 1 | 64* | 6 | 20 | 25 | 62 |
| J.E. Emburey | 50 | — | 11 | 48 | 1 | 10 | — | — | 9* | 18* | 10 | — | 0 | 31 | 3 | — | 11 | — |
| P.H. Edmonds | 11 | — | | | | | | — | — | 12 | 7* | — | 10 | 30 | 6 | — | 7 | 25* |
| P.R. Downton | 7 | — | 13* | 23 | 28 | 22* | — | 0 | 2 | 4 | | 2* | | 1 | 4 | | 62 | |
| N.F. Williams | 18* | | — | 2 | 23 | | | | — | | — | | 2 | 10 | 17* | — | 3* | — |
| W.W. Daniel | 2 | — | — | 5* | 0 | | — | — | — | 2* | — | — | 1* | 0* | 1 | — | 1 | — |
| N.G. Cowans | 6 | — | — | — | 5* | 5 | — | — | | 0 | — | — | 10 | 11 | 9 | | 0 | |
| S.P. Hughes | | — | — | 0 | 8* | 4 | — | | — | | | | | | | | | |
| G.D. Barlow | | | 46 | 5 | 1 | 0 | — | 53 | 5 | 16 | 30 | 5 | 30 | 11 | | 44 | | 0 |
| K.D. James | | | | | | 14 | — | | | | | | | | | | | |
| G.D. Rose | | | | | | 3 | | | | | | | | | | | | |
| C.P. Metson | | | | | | | | | | | — | | 0 | | | — | | — |
| C.R. Cook | | | | | | | | | | | | | | | | — | | 9* |
| A.J.T. Miller | | | | | | | | | | | | | | | | | 0 | |
| Byes | | | 1 | 1 | 1 | 2 | | | 4 | 1 | | 1 | 6 | 1 | | 1 | | 4 |
| Leg-byes | 8 | 1 | 15 | 11 | 12 | 8 | | 8 | 7 | 11 | 7 | 20 | 9 | 9 | 10 | 5 | 10 | 8 |
| Wides | 8 | 5 | 3 | 5 | 3 | 3 | | 1 | 4 | 1 | 3 | 2 | | 1 | 2 | 2 | 6 | 3 |
| No-balls | 3 | 5 | 2 | | 1 | 3 | | | | | | | | | | | 3 | 3 |
| Total | 143 | 84 | 214 | 215 | 189 | 163 | | 137 | 181 | 202 | 157 | 248 | 132 | 233 | 118 | 134 | 228 | 165 |
| Wickets | 10 | 3 | 5 | 8 | 9 | 10 | | 5 | 5 | 9 | 5 | 5 | 10 | 9 | 10 | 3 | 10 | 5 |
| Result | L | W | Tie | W | L | L | Ab. | W | W | W | W | W | L | W | L | W | W | W |
| Points | 0 | 4 | 2 | 2 | 0 | 0 | 2 | 4 | 4 | 4 | 4 | 4 | 0 | — | 0 | 4 | — | 4 |

*Catches*

16 – P.R. Downton (ct 13/st 3)
10 – R.O. Butcher, M.W. Gatting and P.H. Edmonds
6 – G.D. Barlow and C.P. Metson (ct 4/st 2)
5 – J.E. Emburey
4 – W.N. Slack, C.T. Radley and N.F. Williams
3 – W.W. Daniel and K.P. Tomlins
2 – S.P. Hughes
1 – N.G. Cowans, G. Rose and sub

| BOWLING | W.W. Daniel | N.C. Cowans | N.F. Williams | M.W. Gatting | J.E. Emburey | P.H. Edmunds | S.P. Hughes | W.N. Slack | K.D. James |
|---|---|---|---|---|---|---|---|---|---|
| (B.&H.) *v.* Kent (Lord's) 5 May | 11–4–31–5 | 11–0–49–3 | 11–0–49–0 | 8–0–22–1 | 11–2–25–0 | 4–1–22–0 | | | |
| (J.P.) *v.* Kent (Lord's) 6 May | 6.5–2–7–3 | 8–0–26–2 | | | 8–3–10–3 | 7–2–14–1 | 7–0–13–1 | | |
| (J.P.) *v.* Essex (Lord's) 13 May | 8–0–53–1 | 8–0–25–0 | 8–0–46–1 | | 7–0–30–1 | | 8–0–36–2 | 1–0–11–0 | |
| (B.&H.) *v.* Sussex (Lord's) 15/16 May | 9.5–1–35–3 | 8–1–21–1 | 7–0–22–1 | 10–0–49–4 | 11–3–26–0 | | 9–0–43–0 | | |
| (B.&H.) *v.* Somerset (Taunton) 17 May | 6–1–30–0 | 9.1–1–32–0 | 6–1–38–0 | | 11–3–22–1 | | 11–1–43–2 | 2–0–8–0 | |
| (B.&H.) *v.* Glamorgan (Cardiff) 19 May | | 11–3–22–1 | | 3.4–0–23–1 | 11–3–22–0 | | 11–3–23–0 | 3–0–10–0 | 8–0–28–0 |
| (J.P.) *v.* Glamorgan (Cardiff) 20 May | 5.2–1–12–1 | 8–0–24–1 | | | | | 1–0–8–0 | | 4–1–11–0 |
| (J.P.) *v.* Northamptonshire (Lord's) 27 May | 4–0–16–1 | 4–0–30–0 | | 3–0–22–0 | 5–0–22–1 | 5–0–27–1 | | 1–0–8–0 | |
| (J.P.) *v.* Derbyshire (Derby) 3 June | 6–1–20–1 | | 6–0–25–1 | | 6–0–32–3 | 4–0–35–0 | 4–0–43–1 | 4–0–15–1 | |
| (J.P.) *v.* Somerset (Bath) 10 June | 8–0–32–2 | 8–0–42–2 | | 5–0–29–1 | 8–1–35–1 | 8–1–26–0 | | 3–0–22–1 | |
| (J.P.) *v.* Warwickshire (Lord's) 17 June | 4–0–16–3 | 2–0–11–1 | 5–0–16–1 | 0.3–0–1–1 | 5–0–18–2 | 5–1–14–2 | | | |
| (J.P.) *v.* Surrey (The Oval) 24 June | 8–0–20–2 | 4–0–15–0 | | 3–0–19–0 | 7.5–0–28–2 | 8–0–43–2 | | 8–1–33–1 | |
| (J.P.) *v.* Lancashire (Old Trafford) 1 July | 8–0–32–3 | 8–0–28–1 | 8–0–22–0 | | 4–0–33–1 | 5–0–27–3 | | 6–0–37–1 | |
| (N.W.) *v.* Northumberland (Jesmond) 4 July | 9–2–25–0 | 9–3–19–2 | 10–4–20–1 | 2–0–8–1 | 12–1–20–3 | 12–2–30–1 | | | |
| (J.P.) *v.* Worcestershire (Lord's) 8 July | 8–0–38–3 | 8–0–48–0 | 8–0–30–3 | 1–0–6–0 | 8–2–28–1 | 8–2–22–0 | | | |
| (J.P.) *v.* Yorkshire (Lord's) 15 July | 5–0–26–2 | | 5–0–29–2 | | 5–0–20–0 | 5–1–15–1 | | 5–0–28–1 | |
| (N.W.) *v.* Notts. (Trent Bridge) 18 July | 12–1–43–1 | 9–1–53–2 | 12–1–50–0 | | 12–1–24–1 | 12–1–28–1 | | 3–0–8–1 | |
| (J.P.) *v.* Hampshire (Lord's) 29 July | 7–0–25–0 | | 8–1–38–3 | 8–0–21–2 | 4–0–23–1 | 3–0–20–0 | | 8–0–25–2 | |
| (N.W.) *v.* Lancashire (Lord's) 1 August | 8.4–1–14–5 | 5–1–35–0 | | 9–4–14–2 | | | 7–2–26–3 | | |
| (J.P.) *v.* Nottinghamshire (Lord's) 12 Aug. | 8–0–64–0 | | 4–0–17–0 | 8–0–48–1 | 8–1–36–1 | 8–0–29–2 | | 4–0–14–0 | |
| (N.W.) *v.* Northants. (Lord's) 15/16 Aug. | 12–2–33–3 | 7–0–26–0 | 5–1–19–1 | | 12–2–24–0 | 12–0–47–1 | | 12–0–49–1 | |
| (J.P.) *v.* Leicestershire (Leicester) 19 Aug. | 5–2–7–3 | | 8–1–33–1 | 8–0–30–2 | 4.2–0–14–4 | 8–0–35–0 | | | |
| (J.P.) *v.* Sussex (Hove) 26 August | 8–0–31–2 | | 8–0–28–0 | 5–0–30–1 | 8–2–19–0 | 3–0–28–0 | | 8–0–40–1 | |
| (N.W.) *v.* Kent (Lord's) 1 September | 12–1–41–2 | 9–2–24–0 | | | 12–1–27–1 | 5–0–33–0 | 10–0–52–0 | 12–2–33–1 | |
| (J.P.) *v.* Gloucestershire (Bristol) 9 Sept. | 8–1–27–2 | | 5–0–19–0 | | 7–1–33–2 | 8–0–38–2 | | 5–0–25–0 | |
| Wickets | 48 | 16 | 15 | 17 | 29 | 17 | 9 | 11 | 0 |

| v. Lancashire (Lord's) 1 August (N.W.) | v. Nottinghamshire (Lord's) 12 August (J.P.) | v. Northamptonshire (Lord's) 15/16 Aug. (N.W.) | v. Leicestershire (Leicester) 19 August (J.P.) | v. Sussex (Hove) 26 August (J.P.) | v. Kent (Lord's) 1 September (N.W.) | v. Gloucestershire (Bristol) 9 September (J.P.) | Runs |
|---|---|---|---|---|---|---|---|
| 23 | 8 | 79 | 24* | 18 | 20 | 6 | 464 |
| | | | 10 | 3 | | 12 | 250 |
| 6 | 35 | 88* | 109 | 6 | 37 | 6 | 873 |
| 11 | 13 | — | 2 | 32 | 15 | 34 | 363 |
| 11 | 51 | 17* | 51 | 10 | 67 | 26 | 674 |
| 9 | 23* | — | 4 | 6 | 17* | 12* | 273 |
| 12 | 3 | — | 4 | 0 | 5* | 4* | 136 |
| 12 | | — | 2 | | 40 | 20 | 242 |
| | 2 | — | 2* | 2 | | — | 81 |
| — | | — | — | 1 | — | — | 13 |
| 12* | | — | | | — | | 58 |
| 1* | | | | | — | | 13 |
| 158 | 49 | 24 | 27 | 7 | 25 | 33 | 569 |
| | | | | | | | 14 |
| | | | | | | | 3 |
| | 7* | | | 15* | | | 22 |
| | 1 | | | | | | 10 |
| | | | | | | | 0 |
| 3 | 7 | 7 | 1 | 4 | | | |
| 9 | 11 | 6 | 4 | 8 | 7 | 10 | |
| 3 | 1 | 7 | 3 | 5 | 1 | 1 | |
| 6 | | | | 3 | 2 | 1 | |
| 276 | 211 | 228 | 243 | 120 | 236 | 165 | |
| 8 | 8 | 2 | 8 | 10 | 6 | 7 | |
| W | L | W | W | L | W | L | |
| — | 0 | — | 4 | 0 | — | 0 | |

| G.D. Rose | K.P. Tomlins | Byes | Leg-byes | Wides | No-balls | Total | Wkts |
|---|---|---|---|---|---|---|---|
| | | 4 | 8 | 8 | 2 | 220 | 9 |
| | | | 4 | 7 | 2 | 83 | 10 |
| | | 1 | 7 | 3 | 2 | 214 | 5 |
| | | | 8 | 7 | 3 | 214 | 10 |
| | | | 10 | 2 | 8 | 193 | 3 |
| 4–0–15–0 | | | 11 | 5 | 6 | 165 | 3 |
| | | | 8 | 1 | | 64 | 3 |
| | | 2 | 4 | 4 | | 135 | 4 |
| | | | 4 | 2 | 4 | 180 | 7 |
| | | | 8 | 4 | 3 | 201 | 8 |
| | | 6 | | 4 | | 86 | 10 |
| | | | 10 | 6 | | 174 | 10 |
| | | | 4 | 2 | 1 | 186 | 9 |
| | | 1 | 9 | 1 | | 133 | 10 |
| | | | 9 | 5 | 2 | 188 | 8 |
| | | 6 | 3 | 2 | 2 | 131 | 7 |
| | | 3 | 7 | 4 | 3 | 223 | 8 |
| | | 1 | 11 | | | 164 | 8 |
| | | 1 | 5 | 7 | 3 | 105 | 10 |
| | | | 10 | 5 | | 223 | 4 |
| | | 5 | 15 | 3 | 5 | 226 | 6 |
| | 1–0–2–0 | 4 | 7 | | 4 | 136 | 10 |
| | | | 6 | 9 | 3 | 194 | 4 |
| | | 10 | 8 | 3 | 1 | 232 | 6 |
| | | 2 | 5 | | 3 | 152 | 6 |
| 0 | 0 | | | | | | |

*Chris Balderstone returned to the Leicestershire side in his benefit year and hit a career best 181 not out against Gloucestershire, 22–24 August. (David Munden)*

impressive career best. The limp and luckless Gloucestershire were the victims and they were beaten by an innings when Peter Willey found the wicket assisting him.

Surrey continued their massive scoring and overwhelmed Somerset, David Thomas taking 10 for 103. Glamorgan also continued their run of success under Ontong's leadership and won well at Edgbaston where Younis showed his return to form and fitness was complete.

Sussex seemed well in charge at Northampton where Alan Wells followed his career best of the first innings with a brisk partnership of 107 with Ian Greig in the second. Robin Bailey had responded sparklingly for Northants, but the home side were left to make 303 in 62 overs. That they succeeded was due entirely to a wonderful innings from Wayne Larkins who hit 183 off 186 balls with four sixes and seventeen fours. Victory was achieved with three overs to spare.

## Cornhill Test Match
## ENGLAND *v.* SRI LANKA

England fielded the same eleven that had lost the fifth Test against West Indies at The Oval. Gower won the toss and, with the atmosphere heavy, he asked Sri Lanka to bat. The conditions seemed ideal for the bowlers, but they could summon little swing, although Allott was not given the opportunity to try before lunch.

Silva, after a lusty blow, was lbw to Botham and Madugalle, having looked composed, was bowled by Ellison in the thirteenth over. Thereafter we witnessed, for the best part of two days, the most attractive batting of the summer and, arguably, the most attractive we have seen here for several seasons. Wettimuny was more than a rock. He was all off-side charm. The ball was driven gracefully through the covers or cut with wristy precision. He and Dias added 101 before Dias clipped Pocock into the hands of square leg.

Wettimuny, joined by the chunky, cheerful, pugnacious Ranatunga, reached a century on his first appearance at Lord's and made his country's debut there, as well as his own, a memorable one. Sri Lanka ended a shortened day at 226 for 3, and the entertainment on the second day grew richer still.

ABOVE: *Sidath Wettimuny on his way to his magnificent 190, the highest innings by a Sri Lankan in a Test match and a century on his debut at Lord's.* RIGHT: *Amal Silva, a maiden first-class century in the Lord's Test and a second the following day.* BELOW: *Duleep Mendis, the Sri Lankan captain, hooks Botham into the Mound Stand for six on his way to his exciting century. (Ken Kelly)*

The fourth wicket stand between Wettimuny and Ranatunga had added 148 before Agnew, having had Ranatunga missed at slip by Lamb, a miss symbolic of some sloppy England out-cricket, clipped his off stump. If England thought that they had now broken through, they were mistaken.

Mendis and Wettimuny added 80 in 80 minutes before tea. There was an unnecessary delay through the tardiness of umpires, but there was no tardiness in the Sri Lankan batting. Scorning the opportunity to leave the field because of gloom, Mendis, who had reached 50 off 52 balls, took only another 60 to reach his hundred, a jewel of an innings. Of the many glorious strokes none was more memorable than the three sixes he hit into the Mound Stand off Botham's short deliveries. The England bowler gestured for more fielders on the leg side, presumably he wanted them in the stands.

Pocock was kept out of the attack far too long and, in short, England were dreadful. Their attitude to the game compared to the joy and enthusiasm of the Sri Lankans made a shabby contrast.

Wettimuny's 636-minute innings came to an end on the third morning. He had twenty-one fours and his innings will be cherished by all those lucky enough to see it as will that of Mendis' who hit Pocock to Fowler on the mid-on boundary.

*The teams for the historic Test match – Sri Lanka's first in England. (Adrian Murrell)*

**CORNHILL TEST MATCH – ENGLAND *v.* SRI LANKA**
23, 24, 25, 27 and 28 August 1984 at Lord's

**SRI LANKA**

| | FIRST INNINGS | | SECOND INNINGS | |
|---|---|---|---|---|
| S. Wettimuny | c Downton, b Allott | 190 | c Gower, b Botham | 13 |
| S.A.R. Silva* | lbw, b Botham | 8 | not out | 102 |
| R.S. Madugalle | b Ellison | 5 | b Botham | 3 |
| R.L. Dias | c Lamb, b Pocock | 32 | lbw, b Botham | 38 |
| A. Ranatunga | b Agnew | 84 | lbw, b Botham | 0 |
| L.R.D. Mendis† | c Fowler, b Pocock | 111 | (7) c Fowler, b Botham | 94 |
| P.A. de Silva | c Downton, b Agnew | 16 | (6) c Downton, b Pocock | 3 |
| A.L.F. de Mel | not out | 20 | c Ellison, b Botham | 14 |
| J.R. Ratnayeke | not out | 5 | not out | 7 |
| D.S. de Silva | | | | |
| V.B. John | | | | |
| Extras | b 2, lb 8, w 2, nb 8 | 20 | b 5, lb 4, nb 11 | 20 |
| | (for 7 wkts dec) | 491 | (for 7 wkts dec) | 294 |

| | O | M | R | W | O | M | R | W |
|---|---|---|---|---|---|---|---|---|
| Agnew | 32 | 3 | 123 | 2 | 11 | 3 | 54 | — |
| Botham | 29 | 6 | 114 | 1 | 27 | 6 | 90 | 6 |
| Ellison | 28 | 6 | 70 | 1 | 7 | — | 36 | — |
| Pocock | 41 | 17 | 75 | 2 | 29 | 10 | 78 | 1 |
| Allott | 36 | 7 | 89 | 1 | 1 | — | 2 | — |
| Lamb | | | | | 1 | — | 6 | — |
| Tavare | | | | | 3 | 3 | 0 | — |
| Fowler | | | | | 1 | — | 8 | — |

FALL OF WICKETS
1- 17, 2- 43, 3- 144, 4- 292, 5- 442, 6- 456, 7- 464
1- 19, 2- 27, 3- 111, 4- 115, 5- 118, 6- 256, 7- 276

**ENGLAND**

| | FIRST INNINGS | |
|---|---|---|
| G. Fowler | c Madugalle, b John | 25 |
| B.C. Broad | c Silva, b de Mel | 86 |
| C.J. Tavare | c Ranatunga, b D.S. de Silva | 14 |
| D.I. Gower† | c Silva, b de Mel | 55 |
| A.J. Lamb | c Dias, b John | 107 |
| I.T. Botham | c sub (Vonhagt), b John | 6 |
| R.M. Ellison | c Ratnayeke, b D.S. de Silva | 41 |
| P.R. Downton* | c Dias, b de Mel | 10 |
| P.J.W. Allott | b de Mel | 0 |
| P.I. Pocock | c Silva, b John | 2 |
| J.P. Agnew | not out | 1 |
| Extras | b 5, lb 7, w 5, nb 6 | 23 |
| | | 370 |

| | O | M | R | W |
|---|---|---|---|---|
| de Mel | 37 | 10 | 110 | 4 |
| John | 39.1 | 12 | 98 | 4 |
| Ratnayeke | 22 | 5 | 50 | — |
| D.S. de Silva | 45 | 16 | 85 | 2 |
| Ranatunga | 1 | 1 | 0 | — |
| Madugalle | 3 | — | 4 | — |

FALL OF WICKETS
1- 49, 2- 105, 3- 190, 4- 210, 5- 218, 6- 305, 7- 354, 8- 354, 9- 369

*Umpires:* H.D. Bird and D.G.L. Evans

**Match drawn**

## Northamptonshire C.C.C.
Limited-Over Matches – 1984

| BATTING | v. Scotland (Northampton) 5 May (B.&H.) | v. Lancashire (Old Trafford) 13 May (J.P.) | v. Leicestershire (Leicester) 15 May (B.&H.) | v. Warwickshire (Northampton) 17/18 May (B.&H.) | v. Yorkshire (Bradford) 19 May (B.&H.) | v. Warwickshire (Northampton) 20 May (J.P.) | v. Middlesex (Lord's) 27 May (J.P.) | v. Sussex (Horsham) 3 June (J.P.) | v. Essex (Chelmsford) 17 June (J.P.) | v. Derbyshire (Harrogate) 20 June (T.T.) | v. Leicestershire (Harrogate) 22 June (T.T.) | v. Yorkshire (Luton) 24 June (J.P.) | v. Somerset (Northampton) 1 July (J.P.) | v. Durham (Darlington) 4 July (N.W.) | v. Surrey (Northampton) 8 July (J.P.) | v. Kent (Tring) 15 July (J.P.) | v. Worcestershire (Northampton) 18 July (N.W.) | v. Nottinghamshire (Trent Bridge) 22 July (J.P.) |
|---|---|---|---|---|---|---|---|---|---|---|---|---|---|---|---|---|---|---|
| R.J. Bailey | 77 | 27 | 61 | 22 | 75 | 1 | 38 | 0 | 9 | 21 | 0 | 5 | 27* | 7 | 46 | 24 | 19* | 23 |
| W. Larkins | 83 | 20 | 31 | 62 | 13 | 69 | 7 | 21 | 30 | 24 | 17 | 43 | 16 | 77 | 64 | 79 | 6 | 0 |
| R.J. Boyd-Moss | 17 | | | | | | | | 42* | | | | 39 | 15 | 39 | 9 | | 20 |
| A.J. Lamb | 56* | 38* | 80 | 30 | 92 | 8 | 61* | | | | 38 | 21 | | 17 | 22 | | 65 | 99 |
| D.J. Capel | 17* | 6 | 5 | | | | 5* | 53* | 4* | 87* | | | | | | 15 | 9* | |
| D.J. Wild | — | 51 | 8* | 48 | 7 | 12 | — | 12 | — | 11 | 22 | 21* | — | 1 | 10 | 34 | 5 | 0* |
| D.S. Steele | — | — | 2* | 12 | 6* | — | | | | 37 | 4 | | | | 14 | 1* | | |
| G. Sharp | — | 8* | 11 | 22* | 0 | 1* | | 4 | — | 9 | 8 | — | | | | | | |
| N.A. Mallender | — | — | — | 7 | — | — | | | — | 9* | 0 | — | — | 10 | 4* | — | — | — |
| R.W. Hanley | — | — | — | 1* | — | — | — | 3 | | | | | — | 3* | — | | | |
| B.J. Griffiths | — | — | — | — | — | — | — | 0 | — | — | 0* | — | | | | — | — | — |
| R.G. Williams | | 24 | | 5 | 12 | 20* | 5 | 0 | 27 | 46 | 78 | 44* | 81* | 33 | 12 | | 94 | 43 |
| M.J. Bamber | | | 17 | 29 | 40 | | 9 | 26 | | | | — | — | | | | | |
| A. Walker | | | | | | — | — | 7 | — | — | 2 | — | — | — | — | — | — | — |
| D. Ripley | | | | | | | — | | | | | | — | 27* | 15 | 1* | — | 8* |
| G. Cook | | | | | | | | 33 | 32 | 30 | 45 | 64 | 3 | 2 | | 1 | 23 | 4 |
| Byes | | | 4 | 5 | | 3 | 2 | | 2 | 1 | | | | 4 | 2 | | 4 | 4 |
| Leg-byes | 3 | 12 | 10 | 4 | 4 | | 4 | 5 | 5 | 8 | 13 | 7 | 3 | 7 | | 4 | 9 | 7 |
| Wides | 2 | | 1 | 1 | 2 | 3 | 4 | 1 | 3 | 5 | 3 | 2 | 6 | 6 | | 4 | 12 | 2 |
| No-balls | 1 | 1 | 9 | | | 1 | | | 1 | 6 | 1 | 2 | | | | | 1 | 6 |
| Total | 256 | 187 | 239 | 248 | 251 | 118 | 135 | 165 | 155 | 294 | 231 | 209 | 175 | 209 | 228 | 172 | 247 | 216 |
| Wickets | 3 | 5 | 6 | 8 | 7 | 4 | 4 | 10 | 4 | 7 | 10 | 4 | 3 | 8 | 8 | 6 | 5 | 6 |
| Result | W | L | L | L | L | Ab. | L | L | L | W | L | L | W | W | L | L | W | W |
| Points | 2 | 0 | 0 | 0 | 0 | 2 | 0 | 0 | 0 | — | — | 0 | 4 | — | 0 | 0 | — | 4 |

*Catches*

13 – W. Larkins
12 – D. Ripley (ct 10/st 2)
9 – A.J. Lamb
8 – G. Cook
7 – D.J. Capel and R.J. Bailey
6 – G. Sharp (ct 4/st 2) and D.J. Wild
5 – D.S. Steele and A. Walker
4 – N.A. Mallender
3 – R.G. Williams and R.J. Boyd-Moss
1 – M.J. Bamber, R.W. Hanley and B.J. Griffiths

| BOWLING | R.W. Hanley | N.A. Mallender | B.J. Griffiths | D.J. Capel | W. Larkins | D.S. Steele | R.G. Williams | A. Walker | D.J. Wild |
|---|---|---|---|---|---|---|---|---|---|
| (B.&H.) v. Scotland (Northampton) 5 May | 11–5–37–3 | 10.3–1–38–1 | 11–0–56–0 | 8–1–28–1 | 4–1–22–1 | 10–0–38–3 | | | |
| (J.P.) v. Lancashire (Old Trafford) 13 May | 7.3–1–38–0 | 4–0–30–0 | 5–0–17–0 | 7–1–39–1 | | 7–1–32–1 | 8–0–22–0 | | |
| (B.&H.) v. Leicestershire (Leicester) 15 May | 10–2–36–0 | 10–0–45–2 | 11–1–55–0 | 11–0–61–2 | | 11–1–39–0 | | | |
| (B.&H.) v. Warks. (Northampton) 17/18 May | 10–1–42–2 | 11–1–49–0 | 11–1–53–2 | | 2–0–14–0 | 9–0–35–4 | 11–1–52–0 | | |
| (B.&H.) v. Yorkshire (Bradford) 19 May | 11–2–43–1 | 10.3–1–34–1 | 11–0–51–0 | | 7–0–35–0 | 11–1–59–0 | 2–0–16–0 | | |
| (J.P.) v. Warwickshire (Northampton) 20 May | | | | | | | | | |
| (J.P.) v. Middlesex (Lord's) 27 May | 4–0–18–1 | | 3.2–0–25–0 | 5–0–24–1 | 1–0–8–0 | | 3–0–26–0 | 5–0–27–2 | |
| (J.P.) v. Sussex (Horsham) 3 June | 8–0–49–1 | | 6–0–23–0 | 8–0–61–4 | 5–0–43–0 | | 5–0–46–0 | 8–2–12–3 | |
| (J.P.) v. Essex (Chelmsford) 17 June | | 6–0–48–3 | 6–0–22–0 | 4–0–32–1 | | | | 4–0–23–0 | 7–1–20–1 |
| (T.T.) v. Derbyshire (Harrogate) 20 June | | 8–0–44–4 | 8–3–16–2 | 4–0–17–1 | | 4–0–26–0 | | 6–1–32–0 | 9–1–34–3 |
| (T.T.) v. Leicestershire (Harrogate) 22 June | | 4–0–41–0 | 6–0–24–1 | | | 11–0–60–1 | 11–3–22–3 | 9–1–31–1 | 10–0–60–1 |
| (J.P.) v. Yorkshire (Luton) 24 June | | 8–0–47–0 | 7.1–0–41–1 | | | | 8–0–38–1 | 8–1–24–1 | 8–0–46–2 |
| (J.P.) v. Somerset (Northampton) 1 July | 8–0–50–4 | 8–2–22–1 | | | | | 8–1–33–2 | 8–2–33–1 | 8–0–24–0 |
| (N.W.) v. Durham (Darlington) 4 July | 11–0–46–2 | 12–4–16–2 | | | | | 12–5–32–1 | 11.5–1–43–2 | 12–2–36–1 |
| (J.P.) v. Surrey (Northampton) 8 July | 7–0–37–2 | 7–0–40–2 | | | 1–0–5–0 | | 7–0–60–0 | 8–1–52–1 | 8–0–47–1 |
| (J.P.) v. Kent (Tring) 15 July | | 8–0–33–3 | 8–2–13–0 | 3–0–21–1 | | 3–0–30–0 | | 7.3–0–32–3 | 8–0–41–2 |
| (N.W.) v. Worcs. (Northampton) 18 July | | 12–3–37–7 | 5–1–19–0 | | | | 1–1–0–0 | 6–1–23–1 | 12–4–36–2 |
| (J.P.) v. Notts. (Trent Bridge) 22 July | | 8–0–52–1 | 8–0–37–0 | | | | 8–0–36–2 | 8–0–35–3 | 8–0–38–1 |
| (J.P.) v. Gloucestershire (Bristol) 29 July | 7–2–32–0 | 8–0–47–1 | | 3–0–24–0 | | | 6–0–42–1 | 8–0–31–1 | 8–0–30–2 |
| (N.W.) v. Leics. (Northampton) 1 August | 12–1–34–1 | 12–0–54–1 | | 3–0–16–1 | 12–1–41–1 | | | 9–1–33–2 | 12–0–47–3 |
| (J.P.) v. Derbyshire (Northampton) 5 Aug. | 7.1–0–22–3 | 8–1–31–1 | 8–1–50–1 | 8–0–45–2 | | | | | 8–0–29–3 |
| (J.P.) v. Worcs. (Wellingborough) 12 August | 5–0–11–1 | 7–0–29–1 | 5–0–24–2 | | 6–0–16–1 | 8–0–34–1 | | | 8–0–33–2 |
| (N.W.) v. Middlesex (Lord's) 15/16 August | | 12–2–36–0 | | | 7.5–0–32–0 | | 12–2–30–0 | 11–1–46–0 | 11–0–50–1 |
| (J.P.) v. Glamorgan (Swansea) 19 August | | 8–2–36–2 | | | 4–0–22–1 | 5–0–38–1 | 8–2–33–2 | 6.4–0–33–0 | 8–0–39–1 |
| (J.P.) v. Leicestershire (Northampton) 26 Aug. | | 8–1–40–1 | 8–0–25–1 | 2–0–10–1 | | | 8–0–25–0 | 8–0–34–2 | 6–0–38–1 |
| (J.P.) v. Hampshire (Southampton) 2 Sept. | | 7.2–0–35–2 | | 8–0–45–1 | | | 8–0–32–0 | 8–0–35–0 | 8–0–35–1 |
| Wickets | 21 | 36 | 10 | 17 | 4 | 11 | 12 | 23 | 28 |

| v. Gloucestershire (Bristol) 29 July (J.P.) | v. Leicestershire (Northampton) 1 August (N.W.) | v. Derbyshire (Northampton) 5 August (J.P.) | v. Worcestershire (Wellingborough) 12 August (J.P.) | v. Middlesex (Lord's) 15/16 Aug. (N.W.) | v. Glamorgan (Swansea) 19 August (J.P.) | v. Leicestershire (Northampton) 26 August (J.P.) | v. Hampshire (Southampton) 2 September (J.P.) | Runs |
|---|---|---|---|---|---|---|---|---|
| 77* | 23 | 17 | 19* | 56* | 12 | 36* | 14 | 736 |
| 1 | 17 | 2 | 49 | 52 | 63 | 9 | 2 | 857 |
| 99 | 88* | 39 | 21 | 0 | 10 | 42 | 23 | 503 |
|  | 28 | 83 |  | 35 | 65 |  | 49 | 887 |
| 17* | 15 | 13 | 32 | 23* |  | 2 | 35* | 338 |
| — | 5 | 4 | 3 | 11 | 9* | 4 | 15 | 293 |
|  |  |  | — |  | — |  |  | 76 |
|  |  |  |  |  |  |  | 8 | 71 |
| — | 6* | 3* | — | — | — | 5* | 8* | 52 |
| — | — | 6* | — |  |  |  |  | 13 |
|  |  | — | — |  |  | — |  | 0 |
| — |  |  |  | 3 | 18* | 10 | 11 | 566 |
|  |  |  |  |  |  |  |  | 121 |
| — | — |  |  | — | — | — | — | 9 |
| — | 8 | 24 | 2* | — | — | 1 |  | 86 |
| 14 | 43 | 11 | 17 | 18 | 15 | 51 | 8 | 414 |
|  | 1 | 1 |  | 5 | 1 |  |  |  |
| 5 | 5 | 7 | 8 | 15 | 14 | 16 | 6 |  |
| 5 | 3 | 6 | 4 | 3 | 5 | 7 | 4 |  |
|  |  |  | 3 | 5 | 1 |  | 3 |  |
| 218 | 242 | 216 | 158 | 226 | 213 | 183 | 186 |  |
| 3 | 7 | 8 | 5 | 6 | 5 | 7 | 8 |  |
| W | W | W | W | L | L | W | L |  |
| 4 | — | 4 | 4 | — | 0 | 4 | 0 |  |

| G. Cook | R.J. Bailey | Byes | Leg-byes | Wides | No-balls | Total | Wkts |
|---|---|---|---|---|---|---|---|
|  |  | 1 | 9 |  | 1 | 230 | 10 |
|  |  |  | 4 | 4 | 5 | 191 | 2 |
|  |  |  | 3 | 2 | 2 | 243 | 4 |
|  |  |  | 3 | 3 | 1 | 252 | 8 |
|  |  |  | 4 | 3 | 7 | 252 | 3 |
|  |  | Match Abandoned |  |  |  |  |  |
|  |  |  | 8 | 1 |  | 137 | 5 |
|  |  |  | 2 |  |  | 236 | 8 |
|  |  |  | 9 | 2 | 2 | 158 | 6 |
|  |  | 6 |  | 2 | 5 | 182 | 10 |
| 4-0-31-1 |  | 2 | 6 |  | 3 | 280 | 8 |
|  |  | 13 |  | 1 |  | 210 | 6 |
|  |  | 5 | 5 |  | 2 | 174 | 8 |
|  |  | 6 | 14 | 2 | 3 | 198 | 10 |
|  |  | 8 | 9 | 3 | 1 | 262 | 7 |
|  |  |  | 4 |  | 1 | 175 | 10 |
|  |  |  | 2 |  |  | 117 | 10 |
|  |  |  | 3 | 7 | 7 | 215 | 7 |
|  |  |  | 3 | 1 | 4 | 214 | 6 |
|  |  | 1 | 7 | 1 | 4 | 238 | 9 |
|  |  | 1 | 7 |  |  | 185 | 10 |
|  |  | 1 | 8 | 1 |  | 157 | 9 |
|  | 1-0-14-0 | 7 | 6 |  | 7 | 228 | 2 |
|  |  | 4 | 8 | 1 |  | 214 | 7 |
|  |  |  | 4 | 1 | 2 | 179 | 7 |
|  |  | 4 | 2 | 1 |  | 189 | 6 |
| 1 | 0 |  |  |  |  |  |  |

He had hit eleven fours as well as his three sixes and his 111 had been scored off 143 balls. It was glorious stuff. Aravinda de Silva showed frightening power and ability for one so young and inexperienced and Sri Lanka declared. Drabness followed.

Broad and Fowler started briskly enough until Fowler flashed wildly and was well taken at slip, but we endured some dreadfully dull batting for the rest of the day and had the Sri Lankan catching matched their enthusiasm, they would have had England in deep trouble.

Broad looked set for a maiden Test century, but was caught behind off a good ball. Gower made fifty and Lamb reached his fourth Test hundred of the summer, a remarkable achievement, but he has still to convince the supporters that he is English and that feat may be beyond him. The follow-on, and some face, was saved, and Sri Lanka chose to entertain on the last day.

They had a most uneasy start, and when they were 118 for 5 there was a possibility that they would be bowled out cheaply and England would be set a reachable target, but Silva reached an attacking maiden century and Mendis once again produced some glorious strokes until skying Botham who was now bowling slow. Botham finished with six wickets and moved ahead of Trueman in the list of top wicket-takers in Tests.

England chose to dawdle and be flippant, Botham making low bows to the crowd when taking his first wicket. Sri Lanka played all the best cricket and were a delight to watch. One sighed for an England side with discipline and dignity.

*Somachandra de Silva in teasing form in spite of injury. Ratnayeke is the fielder. (Adrian Murrell)*

## Nottinghamshire C.C.C.
Limited-Over Matches – 1984

| BATTING | v. Worcestershire (Trent Bridge) 5 May (B.&H.) | v. Essex (Chelmsford) 6 May (J.P.) | v. Lancashire (Old Trafford) 12 May (B.&H.) | v. Worcestershire (Worcester) 13 May (J.P.) | v. Derbyshire (Derby) 15 May (B.&H.) | v. Minor Counties (Trent Bridge) 19 May (B.&H.) | v. Yorkshire (Hull) 20 May (J.P.) | v. Derbyshire (Trent Bridge) 27 May (J.P.) | v. Hampshire (Southampton) 3 June (J.P.) | v. Surrey (Trent Bridge) 6 June (B.&H.) | v. Glamorgan (Trent Bridge) 10 June (J.P.) | v. Gloucestershire (Trent Bridge) 17 June (J.P.) | v. Lancashire (Trent Bridge) 20/21 June (B.&H.) | v. Leicestershire (Leicester) 24 June (J.P.) | v. Glamorgan (Swansea) 4 July (N.W.) | v. Sussex (Trent Bridge) 8 July (J.P.) | v. Middlesex (Trent Bridge) 18 July (N.W.) | v. Northamptonshire (Trent Bridge) 22 July (J.P.) |
|---|---|---|---|---|---|---|---|---|---|---|---|---|---|---|---|---|---|---|
| B.C. Broad | 5 | 56 | 2 | 27 | 122 | 3 | 54 | | 14 | 18 | 1 | 1 | 49 | 62 | 8 | 12 | 65 | 19 |
| R.T. Robinson | 35 | — | 16 | 97* | 71 | 15 | 19 | | 32 | 32 | 27 | 15 | 9 | 13 | 21 | 23 | 46 | 32 |
| D.W. Randall | 57 | 5 | 34 | — | 1* | 8 | 11 | | | 103* | 26 | | 9 | 47* | 71 | 38* | 4 | 32 |
| C.E.B. Rice | 7 | 55 | 1 | 98* | 34 | 3 | 4 | | 87 | 94 | 6 | 0 | 43 | 8 | 13* | 21 | 57 | 27 |
| J.D. Birch | 6 | 1* | 8 | — | 30* | 10 | 32 | | 54 | 0* | 72* | 1 | 22 | 3 | 0* | 30 | 3 | 39 |
| R.J. Hadlee | 5 | 32* | 0 | — | 2 | 67* | 19 | | 35 | — | 12 | 13 | 45* | 32* | — | 25* | 6 | 47 |
| S.B. Hassan | 25 | | 18 | — | — | 17 | 14* | | 1* | — | | 22 | | | | | | |
| B.N. French | 48* | — | 8 | — | — | 1* | 3 | | — | — | 4 | 7 | 25* | | — | — | 16 | 1* |
| E.E. Hemmings | 0* | — | 0 | — | — | — | 5* | | — | — | 14* | 17* | — | — | 22 | — | 1 | 0 |
| K. Saxelby | — | — | 3* | — | — | — | — | | — | — | — | 1 | — | | — | — | 7* | — |
| K.E. Cooper | — | — | 0 | — | — | — | — | | — | | — | 31 | — | — | — | — | — | — |
| P. Johnson | | 13 | | | | | | | 6* | | 4 | 12 | 5 | — | | | | |
| M. Hendrick | | | | | | | | | | — | | | | | | | | |
| C.W. Scott | | | | | | | | | | | | | | — | | | | |
| R.A. Pick | | | | | | | | | | | | | | — | — | — | 1* | 1* |
| K.P. Evans | | | | | | | | | | | | | | | | | | |
| M.K. Bore | | | | | | | | | | | | | | | | | | |
| Byes | 4 | 7 | | | 1 | 1 | | | 1 | 2 | | | | 1 | 2 | | 3 | |
| Leg-byes | 8 | 3 | 2 | 6 | 9 | 5 | 7 | | 5 | 3 | 6 | 7 | 4 | 17 | 9 | 3 | 7 | 3 |
| Wides | 4 | | 7 | 12 | 10 | 10 | 1 | | | 4 | 4 | 7 | 5 | 5 | | 5 | 4 | 7 |
| No-balls | 6 | 2 | 1 | 1 | 2 | | | | | | 1 | 4 | 7 | | 2 | | 3 | 7 |
| Total | 210 | 174 | 100 | 241 | 282 | 140 | 169 | | 235 | 256 | 177 | 138 | 223 | 188 | 148 | 157 | 223 | 215 |
| Wickets | 7 | 4 | 10 | 1 | 4 | 6 | 7 | | 5 | 3 | 7 | 10 | 6 | 4 | 4 | 4 | 8 | 7 |
| Result | W | W | L | L | W | W | W | Ab. | W | W | L | L | L | W | W | W | L | L |
| Points | 2 | 4 | 0 | 0 | 2 | 2 | 4 | 2 | 4 | — | 0 | 0 | — | 4 | — | 4 | — | 0 |

*Catches*
37 – B.N. French (ct 29/st 8)
10 – R.J. Hadlee
6 – D.W. Randall, E.E. Hemmings and R.T. Robinson
5 – J.D. Birch, K.E. Cooper and C.E.B. Rice
3 – B.C. Broad and P. Johnson
2 – K. Saxelby, M. Hendrick, C.W. Scott and R.A. Pick
1 – S.B. Hassan, K.P. Evans and sub

| BOWLING | R.J. Hadlee | K.E. Cooper | K. Saxelby | E.E. Hemmings | C.E.B. Rice | B.C. Broad | M. Hendrick | R.A. Pick | K.P. Evans |
|---|---|---|---|---|---|---|---|---|---|
| (B.&H.) v. Worcestershire (Trent Bridge) 5 May | 9.2–3–21–1 | 11–1–31–2 | 10–2–23–0 | 11–1–31–0 | 11–0–60–4 | | | | |
| (J.P.) v. Essex (Chelmsford) 6 May | 8–0–37–2 | 8–2–20–2 | 8–0–47–2 | 8–1–26–0 | 8–0–36–2 | | | | |
| (B.&H.) v. Lancashire (Old Trafford) 12 May | 7–3–17–1 | 11–3–18–1 | 5–1–16–0 | 8–3–21–0 | 5–2–10–0 | 2.4–0–14–0 | | | |
| (J.P.) v. Worcestershire (Worcester) 13 May | 8–0–42–0 | 8–1–31–0 | 8–0–62–2 | 7–0–53–0 | 7.3–0–43–2 | | | | |
| (B.&H.) v. Derbyshire (Derby) 15 May | 9–3–34–2 | 11–0–38–2 | 11–0–45–2 | 8–1–39–0 | 9–0–34–3 | 3–0–15–1 | | | |
| (B.&H.) v. Minor Cos. (Trent Br.) 19 May | 11–5–8–1 | 11–3–30–0 | 11–4–32–1 | 11–2–28–1 | 11–2–28–5 | | | | |
| (J.P.) v. Yorkshire (Hull) 20 May | 7–1–16–1 | 6–0–31–0 | 8–0–26–1 | 8–1–32–4 | 7.1–1–31–3 | | | | |
| (J.P.) v. Derbyshire (Trent Bridge) 27 May | | | | | | | | | |
| (J.P.) v. Hampshire (Southampton) 3 June | 8–2–32–1 | 8–0–57–0 | 8–0–34–0 | 8–0–50–2 | 8–0–42–0 | | | | |
| (B.&H.) v. Surrey (Trent Bridge) 6 June | 5–2–9–2 | | 8–1–12–3 | 9.3–2–12–3 | 7–0–30–2 | | 6–0–20–0 | | |
| (J.P.) v. Glamorgan (Trent Bridge) 10 June | 7–0–27–1 | 8–0–41–0 | 7–0–32–0 | 8–0–32–1 | 8–0–38–1 | | | | |
| (J.P.) v. Gloucestershire (Trent Br.) 17 June | 8–1–24–1 | 8–2–30–1 | 8–1–35–2 | 8–1–39–1 | 8–0–54–0 | | | | |
| (B.&H.) v. Lancashire (Trent Br.) 20/21 June | 10–3–19–1 | 11–1–44–0 | 9.2–1–48–0 | 11–2–32–1 | | 11–0–73–2 | | | |
| (J.P.) v. Leicestershire (Leicester) 24 June | 8–1–28–2 | 8–1–28–0 | | 8–0–42–0 | | 8–0–41–2 | | 8–1–36–4 | |
| (N.W.) v. Glamorgan (Swansea) 4 July | 12–5–23–2 | 12–5–22–2 | 12–4–31–2 | 12–1–29–2 | | | | 12–1–39–1 | |
| (J.P.) v. Sussex (Trent Bridge) 8 July | 8–0–28–2 | 8–2–17–2 | 8–2–23–0 | 8–1–29–2 | | | | 8–0–45–1 | |
| (N.W.) v. Middlesex (Trent Br.) 18 July | 12–4–33–2 | 12–3–26–0 | 11.5–5–28–4 | 12–1–58–2 | | | | 12–0–64–1 | |
| (J.P.) v. Northants. (Trent Bridge) 22 July | 8–0–50–3 | 8–0–43–0 | 8–0–33–2 | 8–0–25–1 | | | | 7–0–46–0 | |
| (J.P.) v. Lancashire (Trent Bridge) 29 July | 8–1–33–0 | 8–0–46–1 | 8–1–44–3 | 8–0–41–2 | | | | 8–0–32–1 | |
| (J.P.) v. Middlesex (Lord's) 12 August | 8–1–31–1 | 8–0–32–3 | 5–0–35–0 | 8–0–37–2 | | | | 7–0–30–1 | 4–0–27–0 |
| (J.P.) v. Kent (Folkestone) 19 August | 8–1–20–4 | 8–1–40–0 | 8–0–38–0 | 8–0–36–2 | | | | 8–0–35–0 | |
| (J.P.) v. Warwickshire (Trent Bridge) 26 Aug. | 8–1–34–2 | 8–0–35–1 | | 8–0–62–0 | | | | 8–0–49–1 | 8–0–47–1 |
| (J.P.) v. Surrey (Trent Bridge) 2 Sept. | 5–0–14–1 | 8–0–32–1 | 8–0–59–0 | 8–0–39–3 | | 2–0–29–0 | | 8–0–45–0 | |
| (J.P.) v. Somerset (Taunton) 9 September | 6–1–10–2 | 8–1–32–1 | | 8–0–43–2 | 5–0–28–1 | | | 7–0–36–0 | |
| Wickets | 35 | 19 | 24 | 31 | 23 | 5 | 0 | 10 | 1 |

| v. Lancashire (Trent Bridge) 29 July (J.P.) | v. Middlesex (Lord's) 12 August (J.P.) | v. Kent (Folkestone) 19 August (J.P.) | v. Warwickshire (Trent Bridge) 26 August (J.P.) | v. Surrey (Trent Bridge) 2 September (J.P.) | v. Somerset (Taunton) 9 September (J.P.) | Runs |
|---|---|---|---|---|---|---|
| | | 30 | | 17 | 26 | 591 |
| 47 | 51 | 86 | 55 | 16 | 37 | 795 |
| 54* | 26 | 23* | 18 | 66* | 11* | 644 |
| 44 | 25 | 28 | 51 | 45 | 5 | 756 |
| 31 | | | 13 | | | 355 |
| 8* | 75* | 8 | 21 | 58 | 14 | 524 |
| | | | | | | 97 |
| — | 17* | | | 11 | — | 141 |
| — | — | | 8 | — | — | 67 |
| — | — | | | 5* | | 16 |
| — | — | | — | — | — | 31 |
| 29 | 14 | 3* | 10 | 2 | — | 98 |
| | | | | | | — |
| | | | 9 | | | 9 |
| — | — | | 0 | — | — | 2 |
| | — | | 27* | | | 27 |
| | | | | | — | — |
| 3 | | | 5 | | 4 | |
| 12 | 10 | 5 | 8 | 9 | 4 | |
| 3 | 5 | 1 | 3 | 4 | 1 | |
| 2 | | 2 | 2 | 1 | | |
| 233 | 223 | 186 | 230 | 234 | 102 | |
| 4 | 4 | 4 | 9 | 6 | 3 | |
| W | W | W | L | W | W | |
| 4 | 4 | 4 | 0 | 4 | 4 | |

| M.K. Bore | Byes | Leg-byes | Wides | No-balls | Total | Wkts |
|---|---|---|---|---|---|---|
| | | 10 | 4 | 1 | 181 | 10 |
| | | 6 | 1 | | 173 | 9 |
| | 4 | 1 | 3 | | 104 | 3 |
| | | 8 | 2 | 1 | 242 | 5 |
| | 1 | 7 | 7 | 3 | 223 | 10 |
| | | 8 | 2 | 3 | 139 | 8 |
| | 7 | 5 | 1 | 1 | 150 | 10 |
| | Match Abandoned | | | | | |
| | | 14 | 1 | | 230 | 6 |
| | 2 | 2 | 2 | | 89 | 10 |
| | | 7 | | 1 | 178 | 3 |
| | | 6 | 1 | 2 | 191 | 6 |
| | | 3 | 2 | 3 | 224 | 4 |
| | | 7 | 1 | 3 | 186 | 8 |
| | 1 | | 1 | 1 | 147 | 9 |
| | | 11 | 2 | 1 | 156 | 9 |
| | | 10 | 6 | 3 | 228 | 10 |
| | 4 | 7 | 2 | 6 | 216 | 6 |
| | 1 | 7 | 3 | 3 | 210 | 7 |
| | 7 | 11 | 1 | | 211 | 8 |
| | | 12 | | 2 | 183 | 6 |
| | | 3 | 1 | | 231 | 5 |
| | | 4 | 5 | 4 | 231 | 5 |
| 2-0-19-0 | 4 | 6 | 2 | 1 | 181 | 6 |
| 0 | | | | | | |

## *25, 27 and 28 August*

### *at Bristol*

**Gloucestershire** 321 (C.W.J. Athey 113, P.W. Romaines 66, P. Bainbridge 50, L.L. McFarlane 4 for 78) and 220 for 9 dec (P. Bainbridge 60, J.N. Shepherd 52, L.L. McFarlane 4 for 72)
**Lancashire** 178 (G.E. Sainsbury 5 for 32) and 195 for 9 (N.H. Fairbrother 81, D.A. Graveney 4 for 31)

*Match drawn*
*Gloucestershire 8 pts, Lancashire 5 pts*

### *at Bournemouth*

**Kent** 147 (C.A. Connor 7 for 37) and 189 (C. Penn 65, M.R. Benson 52, T.M. Tremlett 4 for 29)
**Hampshire** 114 (G.W. Johnson 5 for 38, D.L. Underwood 4 for 34) and 178 (D.L. Underwood 8 for 87)

*Kent won by 44 runs*
*Kent 20 pts, Hampshire 4 pts*

### *at Northampton*

**Northamptonshire** 266 (D.J. Capel 81, W. Larkins 65, I.R. Carmichael 4 for 59, G.J. Parsons 4 for 62) and 255 for 9 dec (D.J. Capel 79, R.J. Bailey 55)
**Leicestershire** 247 (J.J. Whitaker 99, R.G. Williams 4 for 22) and 117 for 5

*Match drawn*
*Northamptonshire 7 pts, Leicestershire 6 pts*

### *at Trent Bridge*

**Warwickshire** 261 (G.W. Humpage 89, D.L. Amiss 70, R.J. Hadlee 6 for 55) and 205 (D.L. Amiss 62, E.E. Hemmings 6 for 49)
**Nottinghamshire** 350 for 6 dec (D.W. Randall 113, R.T. Robinson 97) and 117 for 3

*Nottinghamshire won by 7 wickets*
*Nottinghamshire 24 pts, Warwickshire 5 pts*

### *at The Oval*

**Essex** 314 for 8 dec (K.S. McEwan 104, G.A. Gooch 81) and 274 for 5 dec (G.A. Gooch 160 not out, K.S. McEwan 84)
**Surrey** 327 for 8 dec (R.D.V. Knight 109, M.A. Lynch 58, A.J. Stewart 54) and 179 (A. Needham 57, N.A. Foster 5 for 78)

*Essex won by 82 runs*
*Essex 23 pts, Surrey 7 pts*

*Ken McEwan, two fine innings in Essex's splendid victory at The Oval, 25–28 August. (Adrian Murrell)*

## Somerset C.C.C.
Limited-Over Matches – 1984

| BATTING | v. Glamorgan (Swansea) 5 May (B.&H.) | v. Sussex (Taunton) 12 May (B.&H.) | v. Hampshire (Taunton) 13 May (J.P.) | v. Kent (Canterbury) 16 May (B.&H.) | v. Middlesex (Taunton) 17 May (B.&H.) | v. Leicestershire (Leicester) 20 May (J.P.) | v. Gloucestershire (Bristol) 27 May (J.P.) | v. Yorkshire (Middlesbrough) 3 June (J.P.) | v. Warwickshire (Edgbaston) 6 June (B.&H.) | v. Middlesex (Bath) 10 June (J.P.) | v. Kent (Bath) 17 June (J.P.) | v. Warwickshire (Edgbaston) 24 June (J.P.) | v. Northamptonshire (Northampton) 1 July (J.P.) | v. Hertfordshire (St. Albans) 4 July (N.W.) | v. Glamorgan (Cardiff) 15 July (J.P.) | v. Sussex (Hove) 18 July (N.W.) | v. Lancashire (Taunton) 22 July (J.P.) | v. Sussex (Hove) 29 July (J.P.) |
|---|---|---|---|---|---|---|---|---|---|---|---|---|---|---|---|---|---|---|
| P.W. Denning | 63 | 39 | 7 | 9 | — | | | 45 | 9 | 4 | 25 | 8 | 10 | | | | | |
| P.M. Roebuck | 10 | 4 | 6 | 0 | 34 | 31 | | 84 | 0 | 70 | 68* | 13 | 19 | 21 | 37 | 98 | 45 | |
| M.D. Crowe | 2 | 1 | 7 | 41 | 19* | 27 | | 28 | 89 | 0 | 78 | 21 | 57 | 11 | 3 | 114 | 53 | 75 |
| B.C. Rose | 44* | 6 | 34 | 61 | 5 | 35 | | 39 | 0 | 51 | — | 31 | 29 | 36* | 41 | — | 3 | 10 |
| I.T. Botham | 14 | 33 | 39 | 9 | 48* | 1 | | | 27 | 21 | | 44 | | 15 | | 30* | 49 | |
| N.F.M. Popplewell | 0 | 22 | 36 | 9 | 67 | 16 | | 31 | 26 | 8 | 0* | 29 | 16 | 25 | — | — | 12 | 17 |
| V.J. Marks | 23 | 75* | 18 | 18 | — | 19 | | | 6 | 7 | — | 6 | 23 | 10 | 20* | 5* | 9 | 20 |
| J.W. Lloyds | 8 | 1 | | | | 4 | | 1* | | | — | | 3 | 7 | — | | 1 | 5 |
| T. Gard | 3* | 4 | — | 2* | — | 11 | | — | 19 | 1 | — | 8* | 1* | | | | | |
| C.H. Dredge | — | 1 | 7 | 0* | — | 3* | | — | 17* | 14* | — | 9 | | 9 | — | — | | 16* |
| M.R. Davis | — | 7 | 1* | 2 | — | — | | — | 3 | — | — | — | — | 0* | | | | 2* |
| G.V. Palmer | | | 16 | — | — | 32* | | — | 4 | 10* | — | 6 | 4 | | — | — | 7* | 0 |
| P.H.L. Wilson | | | | | | | | — | | | | | — | | — | — | — | |
| S.J. Turner | | | | | | | | | | | | | | 7 | — | — | 4* | 4 |
| J.G. Wyatt | | | | | | | | | | | | | | 0 | | | | 14 |
| N.A. Felton | | | | | | | | | | | | | | | 84* | 29 | 4 | 14 |
| D. Breakwell | | | | | | | | | | | | | | | | | | |
| R.L. Ollis | | | | | | | | | | | | | | | | | | |
| Byes | 8 | | | | | 1 | | | 1 | | | | 5 | | | | 1 | |
| Leg-byes | 2 | 8 | 8 | 5 | 10 | 3 | | 4 | 10 | 8 | 3 | 8 | 5 | 8 | 4 | 6 | 16 | 9 |
| Wides | | 1 | 5 | 1 | 2 | 4 | | | | 4 | 1 | 4 | | 3 | 2 | 1 | 3 | 5 |
| No-balls | 5 | 3 | | 4 | 8 | 2 | | 1 | 5 | 3 | 1 | 5 | 2 | 1 | 1 | 5 | 1 | |
| Total | 182 | 205 | 184 | 161 | 193 | 189 | | 233 | 216 | 201 | 176 | 192 | 174 | 153 | 192 | 288 | 208 | 191 |
| Wickets | 7 | 10 | 9 | 8 | 3 | 8 | | 5 | 10 | 8 | 2 | 9 | 8 | 9 | 3 | 3 | 8 | 9 |
| Results | W | L | L | W | W | Ab. | Ab. | L | L | L | W | W | L | W | W | W | L | L |
| Points | 2 | 0 | 0 | 2 | 2 | 2 | 2 | 0 | — | 0 | 4 | 4 | 0 | — | 4 | — | 0 | 0 |

*Catches*

10 – T. Gard (ct 7/st 3)
8 – I.T. Botham and C.H. Dredge
7 – N.F.M. Popplewell
5 – M.R. Davis, M.D. Crowe and P.W. Denning
4 – J.W. Lloyds and V.J. Marks
3 – J.G. Wyatt, N.A. Felton and S.J. Turner (ct 1/st 2)
2 – B.C. Rose, G.V. Palmer and subs
1 – P.M. Roebuck, P.H.L. Wilson and R.L. Ollis

| BOWLING | I.T. Botham | M.R. Davis | M.D. Crowe | V.J. Marks | C.H. Dredge | G.V. Palmer | P.H.L. Wilson | N.F.M. Popplewell | J.W. Lloyds |
|---|---|---|---|---|---|---|---|---|---|
| (B.&H.) v. Glamorgan (Swansea) 5 May | 11–0–51–4 | 11–5–17–1 | 11–0–34–2 | 11–3–19–0 | 11–0–37–0 | | | | |
| (B.&H.) v. Sussex (Taunton) 12 May | 11–0–64–2 | 11–2–45–0 | 11–0–65–1 | 11–3–31–0 | 11–0–53–2 | | | | |
| (J.P.) v. Hampshire (Taunton) 13 May | 8–0–37–1 | 8–0–25–0 | 3–0–17–0 | 7–0–47–0 | 7–0–43–2 | 7–0–42–1 | | | |
| (B.&H.) v. Kent (Canterbury) 16 May | 11–3–20–2 | 10–2–17–1 | 10–1–24–4 | 11–1–37–0 | 7–1–21–1 | 6–1–21–0 | | | |
| (B.&H.) v. Middlesex (Taunton) 17 May | 11–2–32–1 | 11–4–22–1 | 11–1–27–3 | 5–0–33–0 | 11–1–32–1 | 7–1–26–1 | | | |
| (J.P.) v. Leicestershire (Leicester) 20 May | 3–0–4–1 | 3.1–1–8–0 | | | 1–0–9–0 | | | | |
| (J.P.) v. Gloucestershire (Bristol) 27 May | | | | | | | | | |
| (J.P.) v. Yorkshire (Middlesbrough) 3 June | | 8–0–29–0 | 6–0–70–0 | | 6.3–1–21–0 | 6–0–39–0 | 8–0–42–3 | 2–0–25–0 | |
| (B.&H.) v. Warwickshire (Edgbaston) 6 June | 11–1–45–1 | 10–0–40–0 | 7–1–32–0 | 11–2–52–1 | 11–0–66–2 | 5–0–32–0 | | | |
| (J.P.) v. Middlesex (Bath) 10 June | 8–1–46–2 | 8–1–27–1 | 8–0–40–0 | 8–0–35–2 | 8–0–41–3 | | | | |
| (J.P.) v. Kent (Bath) 17 June | | 8–2–19–1 | 5–0–18–2 | 8–1–36–0 | 7–2–29–1 | 8–0–37–0 | | 3–0–17–0 | |
| (J.P.) v. Warwickshire (Edgbaston) 24 June | 8–0–33–0 | 8–1–14–0 | 5–0–30–1 | 8–0–31–2 | 7–0–50–2 | 4–0–24–1 | | | |
| (J.P.) v. Northants. (Northampton) 1 July | | 8–0–25–1 | 4–0–28–0 | 8–0–27–0 | | 5–0–31–1 | 5–1–20–1 | | 7–1–35–0 |
| (N.W.) v. Hertfordshire (St Albans) 4 July | 6–1–21–2 | 8–3–20–0 | 6–2–13–1 | 12–5–15–3 | 11.2–1–29–3 | | | 7–3–8–0 | 9–1–18–0 |
| (J.P.) v. Glamorgan (Cardiff) 15 July | | | 8–1–28–0 | 8–1–37–1 | 8–0–32–1 | 8–0–39–0 | 8–0–41–2 | | |
| (N.W.) v. Sussex (Hove) 18 July | 12–4–35–3 | | 12–2–29–2 | 12–1–32–2 | 6–1–14–0 | 8–0–47–1 | 10–1–47–1 | | |
| (J.P.) v. Lancashire (Taunton) 22 July | 7–0–46–1 | | 7–0–30–1 | 8–1–31–1 | | 8–0–35–0 | 2–0–21–0 | | 4–0–33–0 |
| (J.P.) v. Sussex (Hove) 29 July | | 3.4–0–15–0 | 8–0–37–1 | 8–0–45–1 | 7–0–27–0 | 5.2–0–28–0 | | 8–0–40–3 | |
| (N.W.) v. Kent (Taunton) 1 August | 12–1–51–1 | | 12–2–33–3 | 12–1–34–0 | | 12–0–55–0 | | 5–0–41–0 | |
| (J.P.) v. Surrey (Weston-super-Mare) 5 Aug. | 7–1–11–2 | 8–0–21–2 | 8–2–20–2 | 8–4–11–4 | | | | | 7–2–16–0 |
| (J.P.) v. Essex (Chelmsford) 12 August | | 8–3–30–3 | 8–0–46–0 | 8–0–29–1 | 8–0–34–1 | 5–0–32–1 | | 3–0–15–0 | |
| (J.P.) v. Derbyshire (Taunton) 19 August | 4–0–13–1 | | 4–0–14–2 | 8–2–35–2 | 4–0–16–0 | 8–0–30–2 | | 2–0–7–1 | |
| (J.P.) v. Worcestershire (Taunton) 26 August | | | 6–0–24–1 | 5–1–20–0 | 5–0–15–0 | 5.3–1–32–1 | 6–0–26–0 | | |
| (J.P.) v. Notts. (Taunton) 9 September | 4.3–0–26–1 | | | 8–1–35–2 | 5–0–32–0 | | | | |
| Wickets | 25 | 12 | 26 | 22 | 19 | 9 | 7 | 4 | 0 |

| v. Kent (Taunton) 1 August (N.W.) | v. Surrey (Weston-s-Mare) 5 August (J.P.) | v. Essex (Chelmsford) 12 August (J.P.) | v. Derbyshire (Taunton) 19 August (J.P.) | v. Worcestershire (Taunton) 26 August (J.P.) | v. Nottinghamshire (Taunton) 9 September (J.P.) | Runs |
|---|---|---|---|---|---|---|
| | | | | | 10 | 229 |
| 81 | 19 | | 20 | 25 | 17 | 702 |
| 16 | 15 | 0 | 26 | 15 | 52 | 750 |
| 54* | 1 | 20 | 31 | | 45 | 576 |
| 0 | 1 | | 73 | | 7 | 411 |
| 0 | 9 | 72 | 41* | 14 | 30 | 480 |
| 19* | 0 | 28 | 9* | 18 | 3* | 336 |
| — | 28* | | | | | 58 |
| | — | — | — | 0 | — | 49 |
| | | — | — | 1 | — | 77 |
| | — | — | | | | 15 |
| — | 10* | 4* | — | 3 | — | 96 |
| | | | | 1* | | 1 |
| — | | | | | | 15 |
| | | 2* | — | 21 | | 37 |
| 87 | 7 | 32 | 18 | 13 | 4* | 292 |
| — | | | | | | — |
| | | 6 | | 2 | | 8 |
| | 4 | | 1 | | 4 | |
| 5 | 8 | 11 | 10 | 8 | 6 | |
| 3 | | 2 | 13 | | 2 | |
| | 1 | 3 | | | 1 | |
| 265 | 103 | 180 | 242 | 121 | 181 | |
| 5 | 7 | 6 | 5 | 10 | 6 | |
| L | W | L | W | L | L | |
| — | 4 | 0 | 4 | 0 | 0 | |

| D. Breakwell | B.C. Rose | Byes | Leg-byes | Wides | No-balls | Total | Wkts |
|---|---|---|---|---|---|---|---|
| | | | 12 | 4 | 4 | 178 | 9 |
| | | 1 | 15 | 5 | | 279 | 5 |
| | | | 4 | 4 | | 219 | 4 |
| | | 1 | 13 | 6 | | 160 | 10 |
| | | 1 | 12 | 3 | 1 | 189 | 9 |
| | | | | 1 | | 22 | 1 |
| | | Match Abandoned | | | | | |
| | | | 5 | 1 | 2 | 234 | 3 |
| | | 2 | 8 | 3 | 2 | 282 | 5 |
| | | 1 | 11 | 1 | | 202 | 9 |
| | | | 9 | 5 | 3 | 173 | 6 |
| | | 1 | 4 | 1 | | 188 | 6 |
| | | | 3 | 6 | | 175 | 3 |
| | | 1 | 11 | 1 | | 137 | 10 |
| | | 1 | 8 | 2 | 1 | 189 | 7 |
| | | 2 | 7 | 6 | 1 | 220 | 9 |
| | | | 8 | 5 | | 209 | 3 |
| | | | 13 | 5 | 1 | 211 | 5 |
| 7-0-45-0 | | 1 | 9 | 6 | | 275 | 5 |
| | | 1 | 7 | 12 | | 99 | 10 |
| | | | 11 | 2 | | 199 | 7 |
| | 0.2-0-0-1 | | 3 | 10 | | 128 | 10 |
| | | | 2 | 1 | 2 | 122 | 2 |
| | | 4 | 4 | 1 | | 102 | 3 |
| 0 | 1 | | | | | | |

### *at Hove*

**Sussex** 163 (N.G. Cowans 4 for 51) and 263 (A.M. Green 61)
**Middlesex** 243 (M.W. Gatting 76, R.O. Butcher 55, G.S. le Roux 4 for 67) and 186 for 3 (G.D. Barlow 63 not out, R.O. Butcher 51 not out)
*Middlesex won by 7 wickets*
*Middlesex 22 pts, Sussex 5 pts*

### *at Worcester*

**Somerset** 269 (V.J. Marks 108) and 152 (M.D. Crowe 50, R.N. Kapil Dev 5 for 30)
**Worcestershire** 222 (T.S. Curtis 85, G.V. Palmer 4 for 58) and 203 for 3 (T.S. Curtis 87 not out, P.A. Neale 75 not out)
*Worcestershire won by 7 wickets*
*Worcestershire 22 pts, Somerset 6 pts*

### *at Bradford*

**Glamorgan** 305 (J.A. Hopkins 73) and 201 (H. Morris 58, A. Sidebottom 4 for 34)
**Yorkshire** 283 (P.E. Robinson 92, G. Boycott 65, A. Sidebottom 53, R.C. Ontong 7 for 96) and 41 for 0
*Match drawn*
*Glamorgan 7 pts, Yorkshire 6 pts*

The race for the championship continued with both Notts and Essex winning well. Hadlee led the assault on the Warwickshire batting on the first day, Humpage and Amiss with a fourth wicket stand of 91 offering the stiffest resistance. The highlight of the Notts innings was a second wicket partnership of 178 by Robinson and Randall. Both batsmen were aided by missed catches and slack fielding, but they scored briskly and put Notts in a commanding position. Richard Hadlee then came to the wicket and scored 39. His twenty-first run brought him 1000 runs for the season and so he became the first cricketer since Fred Titmus in 1967 to achieve the 'double'. No praise can be too high for this feat, once quite common, and if one man can ever be said to make a side, that man is Hadlee with Notts. It was Hemmings' off-spin, however, which undid Warwickshire's second innings and set up Notts' comfortable win.

Essex's victory at The Oval was a magnificent one. Put in to bat, Essex struggled a little, but Gooch and McEwan, profiting from missed chances, put on 156 for the third wicket and Essex took 4 batting points. Knight seemed to have ended Essex's chances when he took Surrey to a 13-run lead on a placid pitch. Essex went for quick runs from the start of their second innings and scored at nearly six an over. Gooch and McEwan put on 208 in 145 minutes of thrilling batting. Gooch was at his devastating best and in reaching 2348 runs for the season established a new record for his county. At Lord's, a few miles away, England laboured. Surrey were set to make 262 in 59 overs on a wicket that was still perfect, but they were handicapped by injury to Howarth and illness to Butcher. Eager Essex bowling and fielding brought the champions victory with 13 overs to spare.

There was no such excitement at Bradford where Glamorgan again showed a negative approach and in the bottom of the table contest at Bristol, Graveney, fearing defeat where little chance existed, threw away the chance of victory by batting on and setting Lancashire to make 364 in 88 overs. Graveney bowled well, but Gloucestershire failed by one wicket and their own timidity.

The success of Marks continued, but Worcestershire,

## Surrey C.C.C.
Limited-Over Matches – 1984

| BATTING | v. Warwickshire (Edgbaston) 6 May (J.P.) | v. Combined Univ. (Oxford) 12 May (B.&H.) | v. Glamorgan (The Oval) 13 May (J.P.) | v. Essex (Chelmsford) 15/16 May (B.&H.) | v. Hampshire (The Oval) 17/18 May (B.&H.) | v. Gloucestershire (The Oval) 19 May (B.&H.) | v. Kent (Canterbury) 20 May (J.P.) | v. Essex (Chelmsford) 27 May (J.P.) | v. Lancashire (Old Trafford) 3 June (J.P.) | v. Nottinghamshire (Trent Bridge) 8 June (B.&H.) | v. Leicestershire (The Oval) 10 June (J.P.) | v. Sussex (Guildford) 17 June (J.P.) | v. Middlesex (The Oval) 24 June (J.P.) | v. Hampshire (The Oval) 1 July (J.P.) | v. Ireland (The Oval) 4 July (N.W.) | v. Northamptonshire (Northampton) 8 July (J.P.) | v. Derbyshire (The Oval) 15 July (J.P.) | v. Essex (Chelmsford) 18 July (N.W.) |
|---|---|---|---|---|---|---|---|---|---|---|---|---|---|---|---|---|---|---|
| A.R. Butcher | 53 | 16 | 0 | 10 | 6 | | | 40 | 73 | 17 | 59 | — | 18 | 52 | 16 | 64 | 2 | 35* |
| G.P. Howarth | 38 | 9 | | | | | | | 9 | 16 | 32 | — | 17 | 23 | 4 | 18 | 3 | 18 |
| M.A. Lynch | 60 | 85 | 11 | 0 | 0 | 11 | | 16 | 36 | 4 | 23 | — | 65* | 29 | 19* | 103 | 4 | 10 |
| A.J. Stewart | 1 | | 47 | 5 | 10 | 7 | | 21 | 9 | | 4 | — | 4 | 34 | — | 2 | 28 | |
| A. Needham | 18 | 11 | 25 | 20 | 29 | 30 | | 0* | 0 | | | — | | | | | | |
| D.J. Thomas | 9 | | | | | | | 48 | 2* | 19 | 27 | — | 3 | — | — | 23 | 60 | 11* |
| R.D.V. Knight | 9 | 37 | 12 | 23 | 28 | 7 | | — | 4 | 2 | 17 | — | 16 | 8 | 36 | 17 | 57* | 17 |
| C.J. Richards | 3 | 0 | 12* | 25 | 0 | 0 | | 2* | 13* | 11 | 29 | — | 29 | 8* | — | 6 | 1 | 2 |
| M.A. Feltham | 4* | 2 | 5* | 4 | 22* | 17 | | — | | | 1* | | 1 | | | 8* | 1* | — |
| S.T. Clarke | 0 | 4* | — | 17 | 2 | 4 | | 11 | — | 4 | — | — | 0 | — | — | — | 21 | — |
| P.I. Pocock | 2* | 8* | — | 0 | 1 | 2* | | | — | 0* | — | — | 4 | — | — | — | — | — |
| D.B. Pauline | | 0 | | 19 | 6 | | | 9 | | 3 | | | | | | | | |
| G. Monkhouse | | 4 | — | 4* | | | | — | — | 2 | | — | 1 | — | — | — | — | — |
| N.J. Falkner | | | 24 | | | 2 | | | | | | | | | | | | |
| P.A. Waterman | | | | | 2 | | | | | | | | | | | | | |
| G.S. Clinton | | | | | | 94 | | | | 5 | | | | | 79* | | | 24 |
| I.R. Payne | | | | | | 2 | | | | | 9* | | | — | | | | |
| D.M. Ward | | | | | | | | | | | | | | 32* | | | | |
| N.S. Taylor | | | | | | | | | | | | | | | | | | |
| Byes | 4 | 4 | | 4 | | | | 1 | 4 | 2 | | | | | | 8 | | |
| Leg-byes | 17 | 4 | 11 | | 4 | 10 | | 7 | 2 | 2 | 14 | | 10 | 11 | 3 | 9 | 6 | 1 |
| Wides | 5 | 10 | 4 | 12 | 5 | 13 | | | 2 | 2 | | | 6 | 6 | 4 | 3 | 2 | 4 |
| No-balls | | | 2 | 7 | 2 | 3 | | 1 | | | | | | | | 1 | | |
| Total | 223 | 194 | 153 | 150 | 117 | 202 | | 156 | 154 | 89 | 215 | | 174 | 203 | 161 | 262 | 185 | 122 |
| Wickets | 9 | 9 | 6 | 10 | 10 | 10 | | 6 | 6 | 10 | 7 | | 10 | 5 | 3 | 7 | 7 | 5 |
| Results | L | W | W | L | L | W | Ab. | L | W | L | W | Ab. | L | W | W | W | W | W |
| Points | 0 | 2 | 4 | 0 | 0 | 2 | 2 | 0 | 4 | — | 4 | 2 | 0 | 4 | — | 4 | 4 | — |

*Catches*

29 – C.J. Richards (ct 20/st 9)
9 – M.A. Lynch
7 – A.J. Stewart and G.P. Howarth
6 – S.T. Clarke
5 – R.D.V. Knight and A.R. Butcher
4 – G. Monkhouse and P.I. Pocock
3 – D.J. Thomas and M.A. Feltham
1 – A. Needham

| BOWLING | M.A. Feltham | D.J. Thomas | P.I. Pocock | R.D.V. Knight | S.T. Clarke | G. Monkhouse | A. Needham | A.R. Butcher | P.A. Waterman |
|---|---|---|---|---|---|---|---|---|---|
| (J.P.) v. Warwickshire (Edgbaston) 6 May | 8–0–41–3 | 8–0–58–0 | 8–0–36–1 | 8–0–45–1 | 7.2–0–42–0 | | | | |
| (B.&H.) v. Combined Univ. (Oxford) 12 May | 10–2–29–1 | | 11–4–25–1 | 5–1–16–0 | 11–3–35–1 | 11–1–43–3 | 7–0–32–0 | | |
| (J.P.) v. Glamorgan (The Oval) 13 May | 8–1–26–1 | | 8–2–15–1 | 8–0–29–1 | 8–0–29–1 | 8–0–38–0 | | | |
| (B.&H.) v. Essex (Chelmsford) 15/16 May | 8–1–36–0 | | 4–0–12–0 | 8–2–19–1 | 10–4–25–2 | 9–1–49–1 | | 0.3–0–4–0 | |
| (B.&H.) v. Hampshire (The Oval) 17/18 May | 11–1–52–2 | | 11–3–29–1 | 11–1–37–1 | 11–1–27–1 | | 1–0–8–0 | | 10–0–60–0 |
| (B.&H.) v. Gloucestershire (The Oval) 19 May | 9.3–2–25–3 | | 11–2–41–1 | 11–3–18–2 | 9–2–26–2 | | | | |
| (J.P.) v. Kent (Canterbury) 20 May | | | | | | | | | |
| (J.P.) v. Essex (Chelmsford) 27 May | 4–0–19–1 | 4–0–46–0 | | 4–0–33–1 | 5–0–39–0 | 4–0–26–0 | | | |
| (J.P.) v. Lancashire (Old Trafford) 3 June | | 8–0–39–0 | 8–3–18–3 | 7–0–35–0 | 7–0–23–3 | 6–0–33–3 | | | |
| (B.&H.) v. Notts. (Trent Bridge) 6 June | | 11–2–67–1 | 11–2–44–0 | 11–0–49–1 | 11–3–34–1 | 11–0–53–0 | | | |
| (J.P.) v. Leicestershire (The Oval) 10 June | 8–0–29–1 | 8–0–31–0 | 8–0–48–0 | 8–1–45–1 | 8–0–38–1 | | | | |
| (J.P.) v. Sussex (Guildford) 17 June | | 1–0–3–0 | 0.1–0–0–0 | | 4–1–10–0 | 5–0–18–1 | | | |
| (J.P.) v. Middlesex (The Oval) 24 June | 4–0–26–0 | 5–0–40–0 | 8–0–54–2 | 7–0–37–0 | 7–0–41–2 | 8–0–27–1 | | | |
| (J.P.) v. Hampshire (The Oval) 1 July | | 8–3–16–2 | | 8–1–34–1 | 8–0–26–2 | 8–0–53–1 | | | |
| (N.W.) v. Ireland (The Oval) 4 July | | 12–4–33–1 | 12–2–32–0 | 12–6–13–3 | 12–4–24–2 | 12–2–48–0 | | | |
| (J.P.) v. Northants. (Northampton) 8 July | 7–0–44–0 | 5–0–41–2 | 8–0–38–2 | 5–0–25–3 | 5–0–26–0 | 8–0–52–1 | | | |
| (J.P.) v. Derbyshire (The Oval) 15 July | 3–0–18–1 | 8–1–42–3 | 1.3–0–4–3 | 1–0–7–1 | 5–2–22–1 | | | | |
| (N.W.) v. Essex (Chelmsford) 18 July | 4–2–5–1 | 9–1–20–2 | 10–2–21–2 | 12–2–19–2 | 12–3–28–0 | 9.5–0–20–2 | | | |
| (N.W.) v. Warwickshire (Edgbaston) 1 Aug. | 9–2–35–0 | 7–0–42–0 | 11–0–64–1 | 9–1–38–0 | 12–2–42–2 | 12–2–52–2 | | | |
| (J.P.) v. Somerset (Weston-super-Mare) 5 Aug. | | 6–0–24–1 | 8–3–16–2 | | 8–3–18–3 | 3–0–11–0 | 8–4–17–1 | | |
| (J.P.) v. Glos. (Cheltenham) 12 August | 8–1–42–1 | 8–0–34–1 | | 6–0–27–0 | 7.2–0–37–2 | 8–0–31–0 | 2–0–14–0 | | |
| (J.P.) v. Yorkshire (The Oval) 19 August | | 8–0–40–1 | 8–1–23–2 | 8–0–48–3 | 8–2–19–1 | 7–1–49–1 | | | |
| (J.P.) v. Notts. (Trent Bridge) 2 Sept. | 2.2–0–32–0 | 8–0–38–1 | 8–0–52–1 | 8–0–36–1 | 8–0–21–0 | 4–0–41–1 | | | |
| (J.P.) v. Worcestershire (The Oval) 9 Sept. | 4–1–25–0 | | 4–1–9–1 | | 4–1–11–0 | 8–0–34–1 | | | |
| Wickets | 15 | 15 | 24 | 23 | 27 | 18 | 1 | 0 | 0 |

| v. Warwickshire (Edgbaston) 1 August (N.W.) | v. Somerset (Weston-s-Mare) 5 August (J.P.) | v. Gloucestershire (Cheltenham) 12 August (J.P.) | v. Yorkshire (The Oval) 19 August (J.P.) | v. Nottinghamshire (Trent Bridge) 2 September (J.P.) | v. Worcestershire (The Oval) 9 September (J.P.) | Runs |
|---|---|---|---|---|---|---|
| 13 | 8 | 14 | 26 | 70 | 21 | 613 |
| 11 | 9 | 6 | 5 | | | 218 |
| 11 | 2 | 50 | 36 | 32 | 28 | 635 |
| | 4 | 26 | 16 | 53* | 14 | 285 |
| | 1 | 9 | 7 | 14 | 4 | 168 |
| 53 | 12 | 3 | 19 | 24 | | 313 |
| 1 | | 59 | 27 | 22* | | 399 |
| 38 | 28 | 6 | 26* | 3 | 0 | 242 |
| 4 | 2 | 1* | | — | 0 | 72 |
| 29 | 8 | 11 | 25* | — | 1 | 137 |
| 8* | 5* | | — | — | 3 | 33 |
| | | | | | | 37 |
| 8 | 0 | 0* | — | — | 16 | 35 |
| | | | | | | 26 |
| | | | | | | 2 |
| 4 | | | | | | 206 |
| | | | | | | 11 |
| | | | | | 59* | 91 |
| | | | | | 9* | 9 |
| | 1 | | | | 2 | |
| 6 | 7 | 4 | 8 | 4 | 6 | |
| 6 | 12 | 3 | 8 | 5 | 2 | |
| 3 | | 1 | 2 | 4 | 1 | |
| 195 | 99 | 193 | 205 | 231 | 166 | |
| 10 | 10 | 9 | 7 | 5 | 9 | |
| L | L | L | W | L | L | |
| — | 0 | 0 | 4 | 0 | 0 | |

| I.R. Payne | A.J. Stewart | N.S. Taylor | Byes | Leg-byes | Wides | No-balls | Total | Wkts |
|---|---|---|---|---|---|---|---|---|
| | | | 1 | 2 | | 1 | 226 | 6 |
| | | | 2 | 8 | 1 | 2 | 193 | 6 |
| | | | 1 | 10 | 3 | 1 | 152 | 6 |
| | | | | 2 | 1 | 4 | 152 | 4 |
| | | | | 7 | 2 | 1 | 223 | 7 |
| 11–3–42–2 | | | 1 | 3 | 5 | 3 | 164 | 10 |
| | | | Match Abandoned | | | | | |
| | | | 3 | 12 | 8 | | 186 | 2 |
| | | | | 4 | 1 | | 153 | 10 |
| | | | 2 | 3 | 4 | | 256 | 3 |
| | | | 6 | 8 | 2 | 5 | 212 | 3 |
| | | | 2 | 5 | | | 38 | 1 |
| | | | 1 | 20 | 2 | | 248 | 5 |
| 8–0–55–0 | | | 1 | 12 | 2 | | 199 | 6 |
| | | | | 7 | | | 157 | 7 |
| | | | 2 | | | | 228 | 8 |
| | | | 4 | 2 | | | 99 | 10 |
| | | | 1 | 3 | 1 | 3 | 121 | 10 |
| | | | | 24 | 8 | | 305 | 5 |
| | 0.3–0–4–0 | | 4 | 8 | | 1 | 103 | 7 |
| | | | 1 | 10 | 1 | | 197 | 4 |
| | | | 4 | 9 | 1 | | 193 | 9 |
| | | | | 9 | 4 | 1 | 234 | 6 |
| | | 4–0–17–0 | | 5 | | | 101 | 2 |
| 2 | 0 | 0 | | | | | | |

needing 200 in 101 overs, moved to victory easily with a stand of 151 between Curtis and Neale, both of whom were enjoying their best seasons. Leicestershire and Northants could not contrive a result, but Cardigan Connor had a career best with his medium pace at Bournemouth only to see the spinners become dominant and Underwood win the match for Kent after an eighth wicket second innings stand of 82 by Penn and Johnson had made it possible. Sussex were lifted by a last wicket stand of 56 from Waller and Jones, but Middlesex, with Gatting and Butcher again prominent, were always on top.

## John Player League

### *26 August*

***at Moreton-in-Marsh***

**Gloucestershire** 197 for 6 (E.J. Cunningham 50)
**Lancashire** 192 (D.P. Hughes 63, K.A. Hayes 53, D.V. Lawrence 4 for 32)

*Gloucestershire (4 pts) won by 5 runs*

***at Bournemouth***

**Hampshire** 200 for 7 (D.R. Turner 75)
**Kent** 203 for 3 (S.G. Hinks 52 not out, N.R. Taylor 51)

*Kent (4 pts) won by 7 wickets*

***at Northampton***

**Leicestershire** 179 for 7 (P. Willey 70)
**Northamptonshire** 183 for 7 (G. Cook 51)

*Northamptonshire (4 pts) won by 3 wickets*

***at Trent Bridge***

**Warwickshire** 231 for 5 (D.L. Amiss 107 not out)
**Nottinghamshire** 230 for 9 (R.T. Robinson 55, C.E.B. Rice 51, G.C. Small 4 for 38)

*Warwickshire (4 pts) won by 1 run*

***at Taunton***

**Somerset** 121
**Worcestershire** 122 for 2

*Worcestershire (4 pts) won by 8 wickets*

***at Hove***

**Sussex** 194 for 4 (P.W.G. Parker 81 not out)
**Middlesex** 120 (C.M. Wells 4 for 31)

*Sussex (4 pts) won by 74 runs*

***at Leeds***

**Yorkshire** 178 for 9
**Glamorgan** 179 for 7 (P.W. Jarvis 4 for 28)

*Glamorgan (4 pts) won by 3 wickets*

When Middlesex sank quietly at Hove and Pick was bowled by Gladstone Small on the last ball of the match at Trent Bridge so giving Warwickshire victory by one run, Essex became John Player League Champions for 1984. They had no game, but with both their nearest rivals losing the title was theirs. It was something of an anti-climax, but it was a well-deserved triumph for an excellent all-round team who played with an eagerness and unquenchable belief in themselves.

**Sussex C.C.C.**
Limited-Over Matches – 1984

| BATTING | v. Hampshire (Southampton) 6 May (J.P.) | v. Somerset (Taunton) 12 May (B.&H.) | v. Middlesex (Lord's) 15/16 May (B.&H.) | v. Glamorgan (Hove) 17 May (B.&H.) | v. Kent (Hove) 19 May (B.&H.) | v. Gloucestershire (Hove) 20 May (J.P.) | v. Leicestershire (Leicester) 27 May (J.P.) | v. Northamptonshire (Horsham) 3 June (J.P.) | v. Yorkshire (Hove) 6 June (B.&H.) | v. Lancashire (Old Trafford) 10 June (J.P.) | v. Surrey (Guildford) 17 June (J.P.) | v. Leicestershire (Harrogate) 21 June (T.T.) | v. Glamorgan (Hove) 24 June (J.P.) | v. Kent (Hastings) 1 July (J.P.) | v. Devon (Hove) 4 July (N.W.) | v. Nottinghamshire (Trent Bridge) 8 July (J.P.) | v. Warwickshire (Edgbaston) 15 July (J.P.) | v. Somerset (Hove) 18 July (N.W.) |
|---|---|---|---|---|---|---|---|---|---|---|---|---|---|---|---|---|---|---|
| G.D. Mendis | 27 | 47 | 23 | 56 | 27 | | | 2 | 41 | 2 | | | | 3 | 26 | 10 | 21 | 55 |
| I.J. Gould | 1 | — | 7 | — | 2 | | | 4 | 7 | 32 | 6 | | 38 | 17 | — | 6 | 25 | 31 |
| P.W.G. Parker | 22 | 70 | 36 | 42* | 57* | | | 77 | 5 | 14 | 8* | 7 | 27 | 14 | 43 | 4 | 27 | 37 |
| C.M. Wells | 44 | 34 | 45 | 27 | 60 | | | 15 | 0 | 1 | — | 13 | 38 | 4 | 14 | 9 | 0 | 2 |
| A.P. Wells | 71* | 15 | 20 | 5* | 29 | | | 49 | 51 | 18 | — | 7 | 10 | 4 | 0 | 23 | 16 | 24 |
| I.A. Greig | 7 | 11* | 13 | — | 18 | | | 43 | 27 | 40 | — | 11 | 16 | 29 | 34 | 48 | 6 | 21 |
| G.S. Le Roux | 34 | 0* | 8 | — | 5 | | | 9 | 50 | 4 | | | 47* | 3 | 22 | 2 | 48 | |
| C.P. Phillipson | 8 | — | 13 | — | 0 | | | 19 | | 3 | — | 28 | 3* | 39 | 2 | 25 | 36 | |
| J.R.T. Barclay | 0* | 81 | 15 | 28 | 9 | | | 2* | 14 | 20* | — | 25 | — | 10 | 4* | 0* | 0 | 7* |
| D.A. Reeve | — | — | 16 | — | 5 | | | 14* | 14 | 11* | — | 25 | — | 1 | 1* | 15 | 14* | 12 |
| A.C.S. Pigott | — | | | | | | | | 3* | | | | | | | | | |
| C.E. Waller | | — | 0* | — | 5* | | | — | 0 | — | — | 9 | — | 3* | | — | — | 1 |
| A.M. Green | | | | | | | | | | | 17* | 10 | 10 | | 74 | | | 11 |
| A.N. Jones | | | | | | | | | | | — | 1* | | | | | | 3* |
| D.J. Smith | | | | | | | | | | | | 10 | | | | | | |
| Byes | | 1 | | 2 | | | | | | | 2 | 1 | | | | | 15 | 2 |
| Leg-byes | 9 | 15 | 8 | 6 | 5 | | | 2 | 5 | 9 | 5 | | 15 | 5 | 8 | 11 | | 7 |
| Wides | 4 | 5 | 7 | | 5 | | | | 4 | 2 | | | 6 | 6 | 3 | 2 | 1 | 6 |
| No-balls | | | 3 | 3 | 3 | | | | 2 | 1 | | | 1 | 2 | | 1 | | 1 |
| Total | 227 | 279 | 214 | 169 | 230 | | | 236 | 223 | 157 | 38 | 147 | 211 | 140 | 231 | 156 | 209 | 220 |
| Wickets | 7 | 5 | 10 | 3 | 9 | | | 8 | 10 | 8 | 1 | 10 | 6 | 10 | 8 | 9 | 9 | 9 |
| Result | W | W | L | W | W | Ab. | Ab. | W | L | L | Ab. | L | W | L | W | L | L | L |
| Points | 4 | 2 | 0 | 2 | 2 | 2 | 2 | 4 | — | 0 | 2 | — | 4 | 0 | — | 0 | 0 | — |

*Catches*
17 – I.J. Gould (ct 14/st 3)
11 – P.W.G. Parker and G.D. Mendis
9 – C.P. Phillipson
7 – A.P. Wells and D.A. Reeve
6 – J.R.T. Barclay
4 – G.S. Le Roux and A.M. Green
3 – C.E. Waller and A.N. Jones
2 – I.A. Greig
1 – C.M. Wells and D.J. Smith

| BOWLING | C.M. Wells | G.S. Le Roux | I.A. Greig | D.A. Reeve | A.C.S. Pigott | J.R.T. Barclay | C.E. Waller | C.P. Phillipson | A.N. Jones |
|---|---|---|---|---|---|---|---|---|---|
| (J.P.) v. Hampshire (Southampton) 6 May | 8–1–29–0 | 8–1–53–1 | 8–0–52–1 | 8–0–53–0 | 8–1–25–2 | | | | |
| (B.&H.) v. Somerset (Taunton) 12 May | 11–2–39–3 | 5–0–18–1 | 11–0–37–1 | 6–1–25–0 | | 11–2–45–2 | 9–2–29–0 | 2–0–0–1 | |
| (B.&H.) v. Middlesex (Lord's) 15/16 May | 11–0–41–0 | 10–2–40–3 | 11–0–44–1 | 9.4–0–31–2 | | 6–0–21–1 | 5–0–21–0 | | |
| (B.&H.) v. Glamorgan (Hove) 17 May | 8–1–23–2 | 9–1–24–1 | 11–1–30–0 | 10–1–34–3 | | 6–0–23–1 | 11–2–23–3 | | |
| (B.&H.) v. Sussex (Hove) 19 May | 10–0–38–2 | 10–0–37–1 | 11–1–32–2 | 11–1–51–1 | | 1–0–7–0 | 11–1–34–0 | | |
| (J.P.) v. Gloucestershire (Hove) 20 May | | | | | | | | | |
| (J.P.) v. Leicestershire (Leicester) 27 May | | | | | | | | | |
| (J.P.) v. Northamptonshire (Horsham) 3 June | 8–2–22–3 | 5.5–0–33–1 | 5–0–26–1 | 6–1–28–2 | | 3–0–22–1 | 8–0–28–1 | | |
| (B.&H.) v. Yorkshire (Hove) 6 June | 7–0–28–1 | 11–3–46–1 | 3–0–16–0 | 11–0–72–1 | 5–2–15–0 | 7–0–37–0 | 11–1–40–1 | | |
| (J.P.) v. Lancashire (Old Trafford) 10 June | 8–2–21–0 | 8–0–27–0 | 5–0–21–0 | 5.3–0–25–1 | | 6–0–26–1 | 6–0–27–0 | | |
| (J.P.) v. Surrey (Guildford) 17 June | | | | | | | | | |
| (T.T.) v. Leicestershire (Harrogate) 21 June | 6–0–31–0 | | 11–3–14–1 | | | 6–0–48–0 | 11–1–34–2 | 10–1–56–2 | 11–0–29–2 |
| (J.P.) v. Glamorgan (Hove) 24 June | 8–2–20–2 | 8–1–36–2 | 8–1–43–1 | 8–0–32–3 | | | 8–0–38–0 | | |
| (J.P.) v. Kent (Hastings) 1 July | 8–1–32–1 | 7–0–28–1 | 8–0–58–0 | 7–1–32–2 | | 4–0–25–1 | 2–0–15–0 | 3–0–21–0 | |
| (N.W.) v. Devon (Hove) 4 July | 12–4–21–1 | 9–2–13–0 | 12–3–27–2 | 12–2–29–0 | | 12–0–53–5 | | | |
| (J.P.) v. Notts. (Trent Bridge) 8 July | 3–0–13–0 | 5–1–17–0 | 6.4–0–29–0 | 6–0–19–1 | | 8–1–33–1 | 7–0–38–1 | | |
| (J.P.) v. Warwickshire (Edgbaston) | 8–1–22–0 | 8–0–37–1 | 6–0–62–1 | 8–1–43–1 | | 2–0–12–0 | 7–0–42–2 | | |
| (N.W.) v. Somerset (Hove) 18 July | 12–1–38–0 | | 11–1–49–0 | 11–1–54–0 | | 8–0–46–2 | 8–0–40–0 | | 10–1–49–1 |
| (J.P.) v. Worcestershire (Worcester) 22 July | 8–2–16–2 | | 7–0–39–2 | 4–0–27–2 | | 8–0–44–2 | 8–0–24–0 | | 5–0–13–0 |
| (J.P.) v. Somerset (Hove) 29 July | 8–1–21–0 | 8–0–37–2 | 6–0–33–1 | 7–0–31–4 | | 8–0–34–2 | | | 3–0–21–0 |
| (J.P.) v. Essex (Eastbourne) 5 August | 8–0–26–2 | 7.4–0–12–2 | 8–1–21–1 | 3–0–11–0 | | | | | 7–1–28–5 |
| (J.P.) v. Derbyshire (Heanor) 12 August | 8–0–28–1 | 6.4–1–30–4 | 8–0–48–0 | 7–0–37–1 | | | | | 8–0–43–4 |
| (J.P.) v. Middlesex (Hove) 26 August | 7.4–1–31–4 | 4–2–8–0 | 8–1–29–2 | | | 7–1–24–2 | | | 4–1–8–1 |
| (J.P.) v. Yorkshire (Hove) 9 September | 8–1–26–2 | 4–1–7–0 | | 5.4–0–21–3 | | 6–0–23–3 | | | 3–0–14–0 |
| Wickets | 26 | 21 | 17 | 27 | 2 | 24 | 10 | 3 | 13 |

| v. Worcestershire (Worcester) 22 July (J.P.) | v. Somerset (Hove) 29 July (J.P.) | v. Essex (Eastbourne) 5 August (J.P.) | v. Derbyshire (Heanor) 12 August (J.P.) | v. Middlesex (Hove) 26 August (J.P.) | v. Yorkshire (Hove) 9 September (J.P.) | Runs |
|---|---|---|---|---|---|---|
| | 12* | 58* | 31 | 47 | 25 | 513 |
| 4 | | — | 1* | — | | 181 |
| 9 | 21 | 2 | 12 | 81* | 69 | 684 |
| 2 | 4* | 19 | 62 | 2* | 16 | 411 |
| 43 | 70 | 7 | 2 | 2 | 51 | 517 |
| 40 | 4 | 10* | 16 | 13 | 0* | 407 |
| | 3 | — | 8* | — | — | 243 |
| 3 | | | | — | | 179 |
| 19* | — | — | — | — | — | 234 |
| 6* | — | — | — | | — | 134 |
| | | | | | | 3 |
| — | | | | | | 18 |
| 35 | 78 | 1 | 83 | 31 | 30 | 380 |
| — | — | — | — | — | — | 4 |
| | — | | | | — | 10 |
| | | | 2 | | 4 | |
| 5 | 13 | 4 | 8 | 6 | 15 | |
| 2 | 5 | 2 | 6 | 9 | 1 | |
| | 1 | 2 | | 3 | 1 | |
| 168 | 211 | 105 | 231 | 194 | 212 | |
| 7 | 5 | 4 | 6 | 4 | 5 | |
| W | W | W | W | W | W | |
| 4 | 4 | 4 | 4 | 4 | 4 | |

| A.P. Wells | P.W.G. Parker | A.M. Green | Byes | Leg-byes | Wides | No-balls | Total | Wkts |
|---|---|---|---|---|---|---|---|---|
| | | | 4 | 6 | 2 | 2 | 226 | 4 |
| | | | | 8 | 1 | 3 | 205 | 10 |
| | | | 1 | 11 | 5 | | 215 | 8 |
| | | | 1 | 4 | 3 | | 165 | 10 |
| | | | | 23 | 2 | 3 | 227 | 7 |
| | | | Match Abandoned | | | | | |
| | | | Match Abandoned | | | | | |
| | | | | 5 | 1 | | 165 | 10 |
| | | | | 3 | 3 | | 260 | 5 |
| | | | 2 | 7 | 1 | 2 | 159 | 2 |
| | | | Match Abandoned | | | | | |
| | | | | 8 | 1 | 7 | 228 | 7 |
| | | | | 4 | | | 173 | 8 |
| | | | 2 | 4 | 4 | 1 | 222 | 5 |
| 1-0-1-0 | 1-0-7-0 | 1-0-7-0 | | 8 | 1 | 2 | 169 | 9 |
| | | | | 3 | 5 | | 157 | 4 |
| | | | | 2 | 4 | 3 | 227 | 5 |
| | | | | 6 | 1 | 5 | 288 | 3 |
| | | | | 2 | 2 | | 167 | 10 |
| | | | | 9 | 5 | | 191 | 9 |
| | | | | 5 | | 1 | 104 | 10 |
| | | | | 12 | 3 | | 201 | 10 |
| | | | 4 | 8 | 5 | 3 | 120 | 10 |
| | | | | 5 | 1 | 1 | 98 | 8 |
| 0 | 0 | 0 | | | | | | |

## *29, 30 and 31 August*

### *at Chelmsford*

**Essex** 329 (P.J. Prichard 93, G.A. Gooch 62, D.R. Pringle 50 not out, D.E. East 50, J.E. Emburey 5 for 94) and 233 for 4 dec (G.A. Gooch 71, P.J. Prichard 64)
**Middlesex** 223 (G.D. Barlow 58) and 218 for 2 (W.N. Slack 122 not out)

*Match drawn*
*Essex 8 pts, Middlesex 4 pts*

### *at Swansea*

**Glamorgan** 266 for 5 dec (J. Derrick 69 not out, Younis Ahmed 62, A.L. Jones 53)
**Surrey** 17 for 0

*Match drawn*
*Glamorgan 3 pts, Surrey 2 pts*

### *at Trent Bridge*

**Nottinghamshire** 450 for 7 dec (C.E.B. Rice 103, B.C. Broad 94, R.T. Robinson 86, R.J. Hadlee 78, D.S. Steele 5 for 122)
**Northamptonshire** 129 (M.K. Bore 5 for 30) and 224 (R.G. Williams 50 not out, E.E. Hemmings 6 for 93, M.K. Bore 4 for 94)

*Nottinghamshire won by an innings and 97 runs*
*Nottinghamshire 24 pts, Northamptonshire 3 pts*

### *at Taunton*

**Kent** 290 (N.R. Taylor 139, I.T. Botham 5 for 57) and 314 (D.G. Aslett 152, V.J. Marks 8 for 141)
**Somerset** 494 (P.M. Roebuck 125, N.F.M. Popplewell 78, M.D. Crowe 72, I.T. Botham 54) and 63 for 5

*Match drawn*
*Somerset 6 pts, Kent 3 pts*

### *at Hove*

**Sussex** 348 for 6 dec (P.W.G. Parker 140, C.M. Wells 121, J.N. Shepherd 4 for 91)
**Gloucestershire** 137 (I.A. Greig 4 for 50) and 130 (C.W.J. Athey 56, A.N. Jones 5 for 29, G.S. le Roux 4 for 24)

*Sussex won by an innings and 81 runs*
*Sussex 23 pts, Gloucestershire 1 pt*

### *at Edgbaston*

**Sri Lankans** 301 for 7 dec (S.A.R. Silva 161 not out) and 276 for 5 dec (M.D. Vonhagt 75, S.A.R. Silva 70, R.S. Madugalle 51 not out)
**Warwickshire** 242 for 3 dec (R.I.H.B. Dyer 80, A.I. Kallicharran 79 not out) and 246 for 7 (R.I.H.B. Dyer 60, K.D. Smith 54, J.R. Ratnayeke 4 for 93)

*Match drawn*

In 37 overs before lunch on the first day at Trent Bridge, Broad and Robinson put on 177 and set Notts on course for a resounding two-day win over Northants. Even allowing for the mediocrity of the opposing attack, the Notts openers performed splendidly and Rice, Johnson and Hadlee plundered quick runs in the afternoon so that the declaration came when Rice reached his century with four balls of the hundred overs remaining. Larkins fell at 28 and the next morning Northants were bowled out before lunch. Their main destroyer was Mike Bore and he and Hemmings routed Northants again when they followed-on.

This victory brought Notts to within one point of Essex who were denied victory by Middlesex. Put in to bat, Essex reached maximum points thanks to a brisk knock from

**Warwickshire C.C.C.**
Limited-Over Matches – 1984

## BATTING

| BATTING | v. Surrey (Edgbaston) 6 May (J.P.) | v. Leicestershire (Leicester) 12 May (B.&H.) | v. Yorkshire (Edgbaston) 15 May (B.&H.) | v. Northamptonshire (Northampton) 17/18 May (B.&H.) | v. Scotland (Edgbaston) 19 May (B.&H.) | v. Northamptonshire (Northampton) 20 May (J.P.) | v. Worcestershire (Edgbaston) 27 May (J.P.) | v. Somerset (Edgbaston) 6 June (B.&H.) | v. Essex (Ilford) 10 June (J.P.) | v. Middlesex (Lord's) 17 June (J.P.) | v. Yorkshire (Leeds) 20 June (B.&H.) | v. Somerset (Edgbaston) 24 June (J.P.) | v. Gloucestershire (Edgbaston) 1 July (J.P.) | v. Oxfordshire (Edgbaston) 4 July (N.W.) | v. Derbyshire (Derby) 8 July (J.P.) | v. Sussex (Edgbaston) 15 July (J.P.) | v. Shropshire (Edgbaston) 18 July (N.W.) | v. Lancashire (Lord's) 21 July (B.&H.) |
|---|---|---|---|---|---|---|---|---|---|---|---|---|---|---|---|---|---|---|
| T.A. Lloyd | 4 | 6 | 70 | 9 | 33 | — | | 77 | 10 | | | | | | | | | |
| D.L. Amiss | 52 | 115 | 38 | 79 | 34 | — | | 36 | 13 | 11 | 44 | 54 | 11 | 17 | 43 | 54 | 6 | 20 |
| A.I. Kallicharran | 65 | 0 | 6 | 122* | 5 | — | | 63 | 29 | 4 | 85 | 38 | 5 | 206 | 21 | 51 | 3 | 70 |
| G.W. Humpage | 0 | 55 | 10 | 1 | 100* | — | | 34* | 1 | 6 | 58* | 31 | 109* | 2 | 12 | 54 | 77 | 8 |
| Asif Din | 15 | | 1 | | | — | | 9 | 22 | 6 | | | | | 14 | — | | 3 |
| G.J. Lord | 1 | | | | | | | | | | | | 21 | | | | | |
| A.M. Ferreira | 36* | 21 | 71 | 4 | 3 | — | | 11* | 0 | 8 | — | 25 | 9* | 1* | 25 | 0 | 21 | 4 |
| P.A. Smith | 49* | 7* | | 2 | 9 | — | | 37 | 0 | 6 | 9* | 1 | 1 | 41* | 8 | 19* | 6 | 0 |
| C. Lethbridge | — | 0 | | 11 | 6 | | | | | 4 | | 17* | — | | | — | | |
| N. Gifford | — | — | 8 | 3* | — | — | | — | 7 | 6* | — | — | — | — | 10 | — | 6* | 2* |
| G.C. Small | — | — | 1 | 0 | 0* | — | | — | 40* | 1 | — | — | — | — | 22 | | 9* | 2 |
| K.D. Smith | | 11 | 1 | | | | | | | 9 | 7 | | | 101 | | | | |
| C.M. Old | | 0* | 33 | 14 | 57 | — | | — | 58 | | — | 4* | — | — | 22 | 37 | 22 | 5 |
| R.G.D. Willis | | | 0* | — | — | — | | — | 3* | | — | — | | — | 1* | | — | 2 |
| R.I.H.B. Dyer | | | | | | | | | | 15 | 54 | 12 | 44 | 10 | 9 | 3* | 119 | 11 |
| S. Wall | | | | | | | | | | | | | | | | — | | |
| D.A. Thorne | | | | | | | | | | | | | | | | | 8 | |
| W.A. Morton | | | | | | | | | | | | | | | | | | |
| Byes | 1 | | 1 | | | | | 2 | | 6 | | 1 | 1 | 6 | | | 2 | |
| Leg-byes | 2 | 7 | 9 | 3 | 6 | | | 8 | 7 | | 12 | 4 | 11 | 2 | 15 | 2 | 11 | 4 |
| Wides | | 6 | 3 | 3 | 7 | | | 3 | | 4 | 3 | 1 | 2 | 5 | 3 | 4 | 14 | |
| No-balls | 1 | 1 | 2 | 1 | 2 | | | 2 | 1 | | 4 | | 1 | 1 | 1 | 3 | 1 | 8 |
| Total | 226 | 229 | 254 | 252 | 262 | | | 282 | 191 | 86 | 276 | 188 | 215 | 392 | 206 | 227 | 305 | 139 |
| Wickets | 6 | 7 | 10 | 8 | 7 | | | 5 | 9 | 10 | 4 | 6 | 5 | 5 | 10 | 5 | 8 | 10 |
| Result | W | W | W | W | W | Ab. | Ab. | W | L | L | W | L | W | W | L | W | W | L |
| Points | 4 | 2 | 2 | 2 | 2 | 2 | 2 | — | 0 | 0 | — | 0 | 4 | — | 0 | 4 | — | — |

*Catches*

37 – G.W. Humpage (ct 32/st 5)
12 – D.L. Amiss
7 – P.A. Smith
5 – N. Gifford and R.G.D. Willis
4 – A.I. Kallicharran, R.I.H.B. Dyer and C. Lethbridge
3 – A.M. Ferreira
2 – D.A. Thorne, C.M. Old and G.C. Small
1 – Asif Din

## BOWLING

| BOWLING | G.C. Small | P.A. Smith | A.M. Ferreira | C. Lethbridge | A.I. Kallicharran | N. Gifford | C.M. Old | R.G.D. Willis | S. Wall |
|---|---|---|---|---|---|---|---|---|---|
| (J.P.) v. Surrey (Edgbaston) 6 May | 8–0–28–1 | 5–0–23–0 | 8–0–49–4 | 5–0–28–0 | 6–0–41–0 | 8–0–28–1 | | | |
| (B.&H.) v. Leicestershire (Leicester) 12 May | 10–2–41–3 | 3–0–8–0 | 10.5–2–53–1 | 8–1–32–2 | | 11–0–34–1 | 11–1–24–2 | | |
| (B.&H.) v. Yorkshire (Edgbaston) 15 May | 11–1–54–3 | | 11–1–58–0 | | | 11–0–56–1 | 11–1–40–1 | 11–5–24–1 | |
| (B.&H.) v. Northants. (Northampton) 17/18 May | 11–1–62–0 | | 11–1–51–2 | | | 11–1–25–3 | 11–0–50–0 | 11–0–50–1 | |
| (B.&H.) v. Scotland (Edgbaston) 19 May | 6–2–10–0 | 4–0–16–1 | 5–0–15–0 | 5–0–18–1 | 5–0–11–0 | 11–3–19–0 | 11–4–19–5 | 6–4–4–0 | |
| (J.P.) v. Northants. (Northampton) 20 May | 4–0–12–0 | | 8–1–38–2 | | | | 8–0–30–1 | 4.4–0–31–0 | |
| (J.P.) v. Worcestershire (Edgbaston) 27 May | | | | | | | | | |
| (B.&H.) v. Somerset (Edgbaston) 6 June | 8–1–26–2 | | 9–0–49–0 | | | 10.1–1–45–3 | 11–0–50–1 | 9–1–30–2 | |
| (J.P.) v. Essex (Ilford) 10 June | 8–2–50–3 | 1–0–4–1 | 8–1–27–3 | | | 7–0–47–0 | 8–1–31–0 | 8–0–64–1 | |
| (J.P.) v. Middlesex (Lord's) 17 June | 5–0–25–2 | 5–0–37–0 | 5–0–18–0 | 4–0–38–1 | | 5–0–29–1 | | | |
| (B.&H.) v. Yorkshire (Leeds) 20 June | 11–1–46–2 | | 11–1–59–3 | | | 11–1–62–1 | 11–1–41–1 | 11–1–50–1 | |
| (J.P.) v. Somerset (Edgbaston) 24 June | 8–0–41–3 | | 8–0–28–1 | 8–0–45–1 | | | 8–0–34–0 | 8–1–27–2 | |
| (J.P.) v. Gloucestershire (Edgbaston) 1 July | 8–0–31–0 | | 8–0–34–3 | 8–1–39–1 | | 8–0–29–2 | 8–2–13–1 | | |
| (N.W.) v. Oxfordshire (Edgbaston) 4 July | 6–2–5–0 | 12–0–48–1 | 3–2–2–0 | | 12–4–32–6 | 12–3–22–0 | 8–2–18–0 | 7–2–14–1 | |
| (J.P.) v. Derbyshire (Derby) 8 July | 8–0–57–5 | | 4–0–34–0 | | 4–0–35–0 | 8–1–29–1 | 8–1–25–1 | 8–0–48–1 | |
| (J.P.) v. Sussex (Edgbaston) 15 July | | 2–0–14–0 | 8–1–38–2 | 6–0–35–1 | | 7–0–51–3 | 8–1–16–1 | | 8–1–39–2 |
| (N.W.) v. Shropshire (Edgbaston) 18 July | 11–2–36–2 | 3.4–0–10–3 | 12–3–22–1 | | 2–0–14–0 | 12–3–24–2 | 12–1–56–2 | 7–3–13–0 | |
| (J.P.) v. Lancashire (Lord's) 21 July | 4–0–30–0 | 6–0–20–1 | 11–2–26–2 | | | 2–1–6–0 | 10.4–3–23–0 | 9–0–19–1 | |
| (J.P.) v. Kent (Edgbaston) 29 July | 8–0–45–1 | | 7–1–25–2 | 7–0–40–1 | | 7–0–40–1 | | | |
| (N.W.) v. Surrey (Edgbaston) 1 August | 8–4–16–1 | | 8–2–36–2 | 12–0–46–1 | | 12–0–37–2 | 11.1–1–45–4 | | |
| (J.P.) v. Hampshire (Portsmouth) 5 Aug. | 8–0–43–3 | | 8–0–52–1 | | | 8–0–35–0 | 8–1–23–1 | | |
| (J.P.) v. Yorkshire (Scarborough) 12 August | 8–0–32–4 | | 8–0–46–2 | | | 8–0–55–1 | 8–0–47–0 | | |
| (N.W.) v. Kent (Edgbaston) 15 August | 11–1–42–2 | 1–0–14–0 | 12–1–34–2 | 12–0–57–0 | | 10–3–19–0 | 12–2–39–0 | | |
| (J.P.) v. Lancashire (Old Trafford) 19 August | 7–0–37–1 | | 8–1–25–0 | 8–2–18–3 | | 8–0–32–2 | 8–2–23–0 | | |
| (J.P.) v. Notts. (Trent Bridge) 26 August | 8–0–38–4 | 2–0–19–0 | 8–0–42–2 | 8–0–62–2 | | 8–0–25–0 | 6–0–26–0 | | |
| (J.P.) v. Glamorgan (Edgbaston) 2 Sept. | 8–0–47–1 | 3–0–20–0 | 7–0–32–2 | | | 6–0–32–1 | 8–0–30–2 | | 8–0–45–0 |
| (J.P.) v. Leicestershire (Edgbaston) 9 Sept. | 4–0–22–0 | | 4–0–28–0 | | | 7–0–15–2 | 8–1–33–1 | | 2.1–0–14–0 |
| Wickets | 43 | 7 | 37 | 14 | 6 | 28 | 24 | 11 | 2 |

| v. Kent (Edgbaston) 29 July (J.P.) | v. Surrey (Edgbaston) 1 August (N.W.) | v. Hampshire (Portsmouth) 5 August (J.P.) | v. Yorkshire (Scarborough) 12 August (J.P.) | v. Kent (Edgbaston) 15 August (N.W.) | v. Lancashire (Old Trafford) 19 August (J.P.) | v. Nottinghamshire (Trent Bridge) 26 August (J.P.) | v. Glamorgan (Edgbaston) 2 September (J.P.) | v. Leicestershire (Edgbaston) 9 September (J.P.) | *Runs* |
|---|---|---|---|---|---|---|---|---|---|
| | | | | | | | | | 209 |
| 0 | 73* | 24 | 25 | 2 | 12 | 107* | 67 | — | 937 |
| 73 | 101 | 62 | 13 | 86 | 15 | 3 | 5 | — | 1131 |
| 16 | 2 | 27 | 81 | 20 | 8 | 43 | 22 | — | 777 |
| | | | | | | | | | 70 |
| | | | | | | | | | 22 |
| 12 | 7* | 33* | 39* | 9 | 9 | — | 41* | — | 389 |
| 15 | 11 | 15 | 29* | 0 | 39* | 25* | 11 | — | 340 |
| 0 | — | | | 19 | 6* | — | | | 63 |
| 5* | — | — | — | 2* | — | — | — | — | 49 |
| 1 | — | — | — | 4 | — | — | 4* | — | 84 |
| | 74 | 14 | 53 | 5 | 53 | 0 | 24 | — | 352 |
| | — | 14* | — | 26 | 7 | 12 | 17 | — | 328 |
| | | | | | | | | | 6 |
| 5 | 5 | 15 | 0 | 23 | | 37 | 20 | — | 382 |
| | | | | | | | — | — | — |
| 0 | | 2 | — | | 1 | | | | 11 |
| 10 | | | | | | | | | 10 |
| | | | | | 3 | | | | |
| 3 | 24 | 6 | 9 | 16 | 4 | 3 | 12 | | |
| 11 | 8 | 5 | 2 | 8 | 2 | 1 | 6 | | |
| 2 | | 1 | | 4 | 1 | | | | |
| 153 | 305 | 218 | 251 | 224 | 160 | 231 | 229 | | |
| 10 | 5 | 7 | 5 | 10 | 7 | 5 | 7 | | |
| L | W | L | W | L | W | W | W | Ab. | |
| 0 | — | 0 | 4 | — | 4 | 4 | 4 | 2 | |

ABOVE: *David East (Essex) one of England's most exciting prospects. An ebullient wicket-keeper and hard-hitting batsman. (Adrian Murrell)* BELOW: *Mike Bore bowled Notts to victory over Northants in his first championship match of the season, 29–31 August and took them to within one point of Essex at the top of the table. (George Herringshaw)*

| W.A. Morton | D.A. Thorne | *Byes* | *Leg-byes* | *Wides* | *No-balls* | *Total* | *Wkts* |
|---|---|---|---|---|---|---|---|
| | | 4 | 17 | 5 | | 223 | 9 |
| | | 4 | 4 | 1 | 1 | 202 | 10 |
| | | | 12 | 1 | 2 | 247 | 8 |
| | | 5 | 4 | 1 | | 248 | 8 |
| | | 1 | 11 | 4 | 5 | 133 | 10 |
| | | 3 | | 3 | 1 | 118 | 4 |
| | | Match Abandoned | | | | | |
| | | 1 | 10 | | 5 | 216 | 10 |
| | | 2 | 10 | 1 | 3 | 239 | 8 |
| | | | 7 | 3 | | 157 | 5 |
| | | | 7 | 6 | 2 | 273 | 8 |
| | | | 8 | 4 | 5 | 192 | 9 |
| | | | 18 | 1 | 1 | 166 | 7 |
| | | | 12 | 5 | 7 | 165 | 8 |
| | | | 8 | 1 | 3 | 240 | 9 |
| | | 15 | | 1 | | 209 | 9 |
| | | 4 | 12 | 1 | 10 | 202 | 10 |
| | | | 6 | 1 | 9 | 140 | 4 |
| 4–0–25–0 | 7–0–43–1 | 1 | 10 | 4 | 1 | 234 | 7 |
| | | | 6 | 6 | 3 | 195 | 10 |
| | 8–0–51–0 | 1 | 9 | 5 | | 219 | 5 |
| | 8–0–38–1 | 1 | 10 | 7 | 2 | 238 | 9 |
| | | 2 | 11 | 6 | 2 | 226 | 4 |
| | 1–0–7–0 | 2 | 9 | 2 | 2 | 157 | 7 |
| | | 5 | 8 | 3 | 2 | 230 | 9 |
| | | | 14 | 6 | | 226 | 6 |
| | | | 12 | 3 | 1 | 128 | 3 |
| 0 | 2 | | | | | | |

## Worcestershire C.C.C.
Limited-Over Matches – 1984

| BATTING | v. Nottinghamshire (Trent Bridge) 5 May (B.&H.) | v. Yorkshire (Bradford) 6 May (J.P.) | v. Derbyshire (Worcester) 12 May (B.&H.) | v. Nottinghamshire (Worcester) 13 May (J.P.) | v. Minor Counties (Worcester) 15 May (B.&H.) | v. Lancashire (Old Trafford) 17 May (B.&H.) | v. Warwickshire (Edgbaston) 27 May (J.P.) | v. Glamorgan (Worcester) 3 June (J.P.) | v. Hampshire (Worcester) 10 June (J.P.) | v. Lancashire (Old Trafford) 24 June (J.P.) | v. Derbyshire (Worcester) 1 July (J.P.) | v. Suffolk (Worcester) 4 July (N.W.) | v. Middlesex (Lord's) 8 July (J.P.) | v. Leicestershire (Worcester) 15 July (J.P.) | v. Northamptonshire (Northampton) 18 July (N.W.) | v. Sussex (Worcester) 22 July (J.P.) | v. Essex (Chelmsford) 29 July (J.P.) | v. Northamptonshire (Wellingborough) 12 August (J.P.) |
|---|---|---|---|---|---|---|---|---|---|---|---|---|---|---|---|---|---|---|
| M.J. Weston | 11 | 14 | 25 | 16 | 53 | 52 | | 4 | 60 | 6 | 26 | 1 | 17 | 30 | 10 | | 15 | 2 |
| T.S. Curtis | 40 | 1 | 44 | 8 | 3 | 11 | | | | 12 | | 54* | | | 22 | 59 | 32 | 17 |
| D.N. Patel | 32 | 12 | 4 | 47 | 69* | 90* | | 20 | 20 | 2 | 98 | 16 | 33 | 41 | 28 | 4 | 43 | 36 |
| D.M. Smith | 2 | | 27 | 19 | 8* | 2 | | 6 | 66* | 12 | 2 | 31 | 22 | | | | | 22 |
| P.A. Neale | 23 | 28 | 22 | 4* | — | 10 | | 15* | 15* | 30 | 46 | 20 | 33 | 32 | 0 | 5 | 3 | 13 |
| D.B. D'Oliveira | 16 | 28 | 57 | 36 | — | 0 | | 8 | — | 3 | 8 | 18* | 29 | 0 | 1 | 14 | 4 | 10 |
| D.J. Humphries | 1 | 5 | 20 | — | — | 8 | | 3 | — | 13 | 8 | — | 17* | 7 | 0 | 4 | 2 | |
| J.D. Inchmore | 27 | 19 | 29 | — | — | 25 | | 0 | — | 14 | 2* | — | 12 | 33* | 0 | 13 | 3 | 5 |
| R.K. Illingworth | 0 | 9* | 10 | | | | | 0* | — | 1* | 0 | — | 1 | 1 | 22 | 4 | 12* | |
| R.M. Ellcock | 12 | — | 4* | | | | | — | | 0 | | | | | | | | 0 |
| A.P. Pridgeon | 2* | — | — | — | — | 3* | | — | — | 2 | — | — | — | 0* | 5* | 1* | 6* | 4* |
| M.S.A. McEvoy | | 27* | | | | | | 17 | | | | | | | | | | |
| C.L. King | | | | 101* | 61 | 22 | | | | | | | | | | | | |
| A.E. Warner | | | | — | — | 2 | | | — | | | | | | | 2 | | |
| R.N. Kapil Dev | | | | | | | | | 12 | | 14 | — | 8 | 24 | 2 | 40 | 9 | |
| P.J. Newport | | | | | | | | | | | — | | 0* | 15 | 25 | | | 24 |
| D.A. Banks | | | | | | | | | | | | | | 3 | | 17 | 23 | |
| P. Moores | | | | | | | | | | | | | | | | | | 14* |
| Byes | | 1 | 1 | | | | | 4 | | | 2 | | | 2 | | | 4 | 1 |
| Leg-byes | 10 | 18 | 5 | 8 | 9 | 9 | | 6 | 9 | 6 | 13 | 3 | 9 | 10 | 2 | 2 | 12 | 8 |
| Wides | 4 | 10 | 5 | 2 | 5 | 3 | | 6 | 1 | 1 | 3 | 9 | 5 | | | 2 | 5 | 1 |
| No-balls | 1 | 1 | 4 | 1 | 1 | | | | 3 | | | | 2 | | | | 5 | |
| Total | 181 | 173 | 257 | 242 | 209 | 237 | | 89 | 186 | 102 | 222 | 152 | 188 | 198 | 117 | 167 | 178 | 157 |
| Wickets | 10 | 7 | 9 | 5 | 3 | 9 | | 7 | 3 | 10 | 8 | 4 | 8 | 9 | 10 | 10 | 9 | 9 |
| Result | L | W | L | W | W | L | Ab. | Ab. | W | L | W | W | W | L | L | L | L | L |
| Points | 0 | 4 | 0 | 4 | 2 | 0 | 2 | 2 | 4 | 0 | 4 | — | 4 | 0 | — | 0 | 0 | 0 |

*Catches*
22 – D.J. Humphries (ct 16/st 6)
11 – R.N. Kapil Dev
7 – D.M. Smith
6 – J.D. Inchmore, D.N. Patel and M.J. Weston
5 – P.A. Neale
4 – T.S. Curtis and P. Moores (ct 3/st 1)
3 – R.K. Illingworth, P.J. Newport and A.P. Pridgeon
2 – C.L. King and D.B. D'Oliveira
1 – M.S.A. McEvoy, A.E. Warner, D.A. Banks and sub

| BOWLING | R.M. Ellcock | A.P. Pridgeon | J.D. Inchmore | R.K. Illingworth | D.N. Patel | D.B. D'Oliveira | A.E. Warner | C.L. King | R.N. Kapil Dev |
|---|---|---|---|---|---|---|---|---|---|
| (B.&H.) v. Notts. (Trent Bridge) 5 May | 11–2–45–2 | 10–1–29–1 | 10–2–28–3 | 11–2–29–1 | 6–0–27–0 | 7–0–30–0 | | | |
| (J.P.) v. Yorkshire (Bradford) 6 May | 6.4–0–23–2 | 8–1–26–1 | 7–0–22–1 | 8–0–38–3 | 8–2–18–3 | | | | |
| (B.&H.) v. Derbyshire (Worcester) 12 May | 7–1–36–0 | 5–1–14–0 | 11–1–37–3 | 10–0–63–1 | 11–0–40–1 | 11–0–47–0 | | | |
| (J.P.) v. Notts. (Worcester) 13 May | | 8–0–42–0 | 8–1–32–0 | | 8–1–37–1 | 5–0–39–0 | 8–0–39–0 | 3–0–33–0 | |
| (B.&H.) v. Min. Cos (Worcester) 15 May | | 10–3–31–2 | 11–1–46–2 | | 11–2–39–2 | 1–0–4–0 | 11–0–47–1 | 11–5–13–0 | |
| (B.&H.) v. Lancashire (Old Trafford) 17 May | | 11–1–73–1 | 11–0–29–6 | | 11–2–20–0 | 2–0–20–0 | 11–1–46–0 | 7–0–30–0 | |
| (J.P.) v. Warwickshire (Leicester) 27 May | | | | | | | | | |
| (J.P.) v. Glamorgan (Worcester) 3 June | | | | | | | | | |
| (J.P.) v. Hampshire (Worcester) 10 June | | 6–0–19–1 | 7–1–31–1 | 4–0–22–1 | 8–0–40–1 | | 7–0–34–1 | | 8–0–27–2 |
| (J.P.) v. Lancashire (Old Trafford) 24 June | 7–0–37–1 | 6–1–24–0 | 8–0–42–2 | 7–0–29–1 | 8–1–19–1 | 4–0–29–1 | | | |
| (J.P.) v. Derbyshire (Worcester) 1 July | | 5–0–14–1 | 7–1–35–0 | 8–0–43–3 | 8–0–36–3 | 2–0–15–1 | | | 6.5–0–46–1 |
| (N.W.) v. Suffolk (Worcester) 4 July | | 11–3–14–1 | 12–3–30–1 | 5.1–1–12–0 | 7.2–0–22–4 | | | | 10–2–19–0 |
| (J.P.) v. Middlesex (Lord's) 8 July | | 5–1–14–1 | 8–0–24–2 | 3–0–13–2 | 8–0–35–1 | | | | 7.3–0–20–3 |
| (J.P.) v. Leicestershire (Worcester) 15 July | | 8–0–44–1 | 7–1–32–1 | 8–0–57–2 | 8–0–30–2 | | | | 6–4–15–0 |
| (N.W.) v. Northants. (Northampton) 18 July | | 12–0–63–0 | 12–3–29–2 | 6–1–24–0 | 12–0–51–1 | | | | 12–1–27–1 |
| (J.P.) v. Sussex (Worcester) 22 July | | 6–0–36–1 | 8–0–20–1 | 8–1–21–3 | 8–0–32–1 | 5–0–26–1 | | | 5–0–26–0 |
| (J.P.) v. Essex (Chelmsford) 29 July | | 7–0–34–0 | 7.4–0–36–0 | 8–0–35–0 | 6–0–30–1 | 1–0–7–0 | | | 8–0–26–3 |
| (J.P.) v. Northants. (Wellingborough) 12 Aug. | 7.3–0–40–2 | 8–2–23–0 | 8–0–25–2 | | 8–0–29–1 | | | | |
| (J.P.) v. Gloucestershire (Worcester) 19 Aug | | 7.5–1–31–2 | 8–0–17–2 | 8–2–11–4 | 8–0–26–0 | | | | 7–1–18–2 |
| (J.P.) v. Somerset (Taunton) 26 August | | 6–0–22–0 | | 8–0–31–1 | 8–0–26–3 | | | | 4–1–8–0 |
| (J.P.) v. Kent (Worcester) 2 September | | 4–0–12–0 | 7–0–33–2 | | 4–0–29–0 | | | | 6.5–0–43–1 |
| (J.P.) v. Surrey (The Oval) 9 September | 8–0–23–2 | 8–0–41–1 | | | 8–0–30–1 | | | | |
| Wickets | 9 | 14 | 31 | 22 | 27 | 3 | 2 | 0 | 13 |

| v. Gloucestershire (Worcester) 19 August (J.P.) | v. Somerset (Taunton) 26 August (J.P.) | v. Kent (Worcester) 2 September (J.P.) | v. Surrey (The Oval) 9 September (J.P.) | Runs |
|---|---|---|---|---|
| 3 | 11 | 34 | 31 | 421 |
| 26 | 27 | 75* | 48* | 479 |
| 37 | 48* | 0 | 15 | 695 |
| 2 | 31* | 19 | 2* | 273 |
| 19* | — | 27* | — | 345 |
| 31 | — | — | — | 263 |
| | — | — | — | 88 |
| — | | — | | 182 |
| — | — | | | 60 |
| | | | — | 16 |
| — | — | — | — | 23 |
| | | | | 44 |
| | | | | 184 |
| | | | | 4 |
| 0 | — | 21 | | 130 |
| | — | — | — | 64 |
| | | | — | 43 |
| 0* | | | | 14 |
| | | 2 | | |
| 7 | 2 | 4 | 5 | |
| 3 | 1 | 1 | | |
| | 2 | 1 | | |
| 128 | 122 | 184 | 101 | |
| 6 | 2 | 4 | 2 | |
| W | W | W | W | |
| 4 | 4 | 4 | 4 | |

| M.J. Weston | P.J. Newport | Byes | Leg-byes | Wides | No-balls | Total | Wkts |
|---|---|---|---|---|---|---|---|
| | | 4 | 8 | 4 | 6 | 210 | 7 |
| | | 6 | 7 | | 2 | 142 | 10 |
| | | 1 | 11 | 6 | 2 | 257 | 7 |
| | | | 6 | 12 | 1 | 241 | 1 |
| | | 2 | 8 | 10 | 5 | 205 | 8 |
| | | 1 | 14 | 7 | | 240 | 7 |
| | | | Match Abandoned | | | | |
| | | | Match Abandoned | | | | |
| | | 5 | 4 | 2 | 1 | 185 | 7 |
| | | 1 | 13 | 4 | 1 | 199 | 6 |
| | | | 6 | 4 | 1 | 200 | 10 |
| 12–5–30–4 | | 5 | 5 | 7 | 5 | 149 | 10 |
| | | | 10 | 2 | | 118 | 10 |
| | 3–0–11–0 | 2 | 12 | 1 | | 204 | 6 |
| | 6–0–27–0 | 4 | 9 | 12 | 1 | 247 | 5 |
| | | | 5 | 2 | | 168 | 7 |
| | | 1 | 7 | 4 | | 180 | 4 |
| | 7–1–26–0 | | 8 | 4 | 3 | 158 | 5 |
| | | 8 | 15 | | 1 | 127 | 10 |
| 2.5–0–6–3 | 6–0–20–3 | | 8 | | | 121 | 10 |
| 8–1–24–4 | 8–0–19–1 | 1 | 9 | | 11 | 181 | 10 |
| 8–0–39–0 | 8–0–22–2 | 2 | 6 | 2 | 1 | 166 | 9 |
| 11 | 6 | | | | | | |

Gooch, a vital partnership by East and Pringle and an immaculate innings from the technically sound, temperamentally cool Paul Prichard. By the close Middlesex were 10 for 3, Emburey, Hughes and Gatting having gone, but the resolution of Barlow, Williams and Butcher in particular saved the follow-on, and Essex again went for brisk runs on a wicket that never helped the bowlers as had been prophesied. Middlesex were set to make 340 in 95 overs, and they were given a sound start, but Gatting declined to attempt to win and sent in Downton at number three who batted 18 overs for 5. Gatting was quoted as saying that the asking rate, 3.5, was too much, forgetting perhaps that he had asked Essex to make 6.5 an over at Lord's. The Middlesex attitude showed contempt for the paying customers and for the game itself and was unforgiveable in that they had won the toss, chosen to bat last and were never in any real danger of losing. Fletcher was angered, but he might pause to contemplate too that his captaincy is now the slowest in the championship.

The marvels of Marks in August continued lavishly with career best bowling, but Aslett's best championship innings of the summer held up Somerset who could not reach the target of 111 in 13 overs. There was no play on the last day at Swansea and almost none on the second, and Sussex, with Parker and Colin Wells displaying high quality batting, routed Gloucestershire. Adrian Jones confirmed his promise as a quick bowler with a career best in the second innings.

Amal Silva, his maiden first-class hundred achieved at Lord's the day before, reached his second century at Edgbaston and finished on 161 not out. He is a pugnacious, eager batsman, but while he took a couple of exciting catches at Lord's and his wicket-keeping was always enthusiastic, his keeping is not always balanced and it is as a batsman that one expects to see him flourish. He and Vonhagt put on 141 for the first wicket in the second innings, but the match was drawn. There were two good knocks from Robin Dyer who completed his thousand runs for the season, of which he had only played three-quarters, and gave emphasis to his sound technique and temperament.

## Asda Trophy

### *at Scarborough*

**29 August**

**Yorkshire** 220 for 7 (G. Boycott 60)
**Derbyshire** 98 (P. Carrick 5 for 13)

*Yorkshire won by 122 runs*
(*Man of the Match* – P. Carrick)

**30 August**

**Hampshire** 248 for 6 (T.E. Jesty 84 not out, R.A. Smith 60)
**Lancashire** 205 (J.A. Ormrod 63)

*Hampshire won by 43 runs*
(*Man of the Match* – T.E. Jesty)

**Final**

**31 August**

**Yorkshire** 219 for 7 (D.L. Bairstow 57)
**Hampshire** 220 for 3 (D.R. Turner 81)

*Hampshire won by 7 wickets*
(*Man of the Match* – D.R. Turner)

*Batsman of the Series:* D.R. Turner
*Bowler of the Series:* P. Carrick

**Yorkshire C.C.C.**
Limited-Over Matches – 1984

| BATTING | v. Leicestershire (Leeds) 5 May (B.&H.) | v. Worcestershire (Bradford) 6 May (J.P.) | v. Scotland (Perth) 12 May (B.&H.) | v. Warwickshire (Edgbaston) 15 May (B.&H.) | v. Northamptonshire (Bradford) 19 May (B.&H.) | v. Nottinghamshire (Hull) 20 May (J.P.) | v. Somerset (Middlesbrough) 3 June (J.P.) | v. Sussex (Hove) 6 June (B.&H.) | v. Kent (Canterbury) 10 June (J.P.) | v. Derbyshire (Chesterfield) 17 June (J.P.) | v. Warwickshire (Leeds) 20 June (J.P.) | v. Northamptonshire (Luton) 24 June (J.P.) | v. Essex (Leeds) 1 July (J.P.) | v. Shropshire (Telford) 4 July (N.W.) | v. Gloucestershire (Scarborough) 8 July (J.P.) | v. Middlesex (Lord's) 15 July (J.P.) | v. Hampshire (Bournemouth) 22 July (J.P.) | v. Leicestershire (Bradford) 29 July (J.P.) |
|---|---|---|---|---|---|---|---|---|---|---|---|---|---|---|---|---|---|---|
| G. Boycott | 6 | 23 | 22 | 5 | 106 | | 67 | 31 | 35 | 14 | 21 | 41 | 2 | 27 | 2 | 8 | 5 | 13 |
| M.D. Moxon | 32 | 33 | 4 | 58 | 7 | 15 | 36 | 79 | 77 | 34 | 50 | 61 | | 16 | | | 5 | 52 |
| K. Sharp | 49 | 24 | 31 | 57 | 87* | 7 | 7 | 32 | 13* | | 83 | 45* | 0 | 19 | 61 | 0 | 74 | 0 |
| J.D. Love | 37* | 2 | 88 | 1 | 7* | 28 | 35* | 32 | | | 16 | 14 | 22 | | | | | 69* |
| S.N. Hartley | 39* | 10 | 24 | 65* | | | — | 55* | 8 | 24 | | | | 7 | 1* | 23 | 26 | 42 |
| D.L. Bairstow | — | 6 | 27 | 6 | — | 14 | | 4 | 14 | 20 | 39 | 8 | 2 | 2 | — | 14 | | 19 |
| P. Carrick | — | 0 | 8 | 24 | — | 1 | — | — | — | 1* | 5* | — | 28* | 37 | — | 25 | 21 | 13* |
| A. Sidebottom | — | 10 | 9* | | | | — | 21* | — | — | 1 | 9* | 8 | 14 | | | | — |
| S.J. Dennis | — | 3 | — | 10 | — | 7 | | | | | | | | | — | — | 3 | |
| S.D. Fletcher | — | 8 | | — | | | — | — | — | — | — | — | 5 | | — | | | |
| S. Oldham | — | 8* | — | 1* | — | 5* | — | — | — | — | 3* | — | 8 | 19 | — | — | | — |
| I.G. Swallow | | | 3* | 5 | — | 2 | | | | | | | | | | | | |
| R.G. Lumb | | | | | 31 | 39 | | | — | | | | | | | | | |
| G.B. Stevenson | | | | | — | 12 | 81* | — | 9* | 41* | 36 | 0 | 6 | 26 | | | | 6 |
| A.A. Metcalfe | | | | | | 6 | | | | 39 | | 18 | 71 | 0 | 115* | 31 | 3 | |
| S.J. Rhodes | | | | | | | | | | 39 | | | | | | | 6 | |
| P.E. Robinson | | | | | | | | | | | 4 | | 21 | | 33 | 11 | 21 | 3 |
| P.A. Booth | | | | | | | | | | | | | | 6* | | | | |
| P.W. Jarvis | | | | | | | | | | | | | | | — | — | 4 | |
| C. Shaw | | | | | | | | | | | | | | | | 6* | 16* | |
| Byes | 3 | 6 | | | | 7 | | | | 6 | | 13 | | 2 | | 6 | 1 | |
| Leg-byes | 8 | 7 | 9 | 12 | 4 | 5 | 5 | 3 | 8 | 5 | 7 | | 11 | 7 | 9 | 3 | 8 | 12 |
| Wides | 4 | | 5 | 1 | 3 | 1 | 1 | 3 | 3 | 2 | 6 | 1 | 2 | 8 | 7 | 2 | 9 | 1 |
| No-balls | | 2 | 1 | 2 | 7 | 1 | 2 | | | | 2 | | 3 | 2 | 1 | 2 | | |
| Total | 178 | 142 | 231 | 247 | 252 | 150 | 234 | 260 | 167 | 225 | 273 | 210 | 189 | 192 | 229 | 131 | 202 | 230 |
| Wickets | 3 | 10 | 7 | 8 | 3 | 10 | 3 | 5 | 4 | 6 | 8 | 6 | 10 | 10 | 3 | 7 | 10 | 7 |
| Result | W | L | W | L | W | L | W | W | W | W | L | W | L | L | W | L | L | W |
| Points | 2 | 0 | 2 | 0 | 2 | 0 | 4 | — | 4 | 4 | — | 4 | 0 | — | 4 | 0 | 0 | 4 |

*Catches*

31 – D.L. Bairstow (ct 29/st 2)
13 – M.D. Moxon
9 – K. Sharp
7 – S.N. Hartley
6 – S. Oldham
5 – G. Boycott and A.A. Metcalfe
3 – S.D. Fletcher, I.G. Swallow, P. Carrick and S.J. Rhodes
2 – A. Sidebottom, J.D. Love, G.B. Stevenson, P.E. Robinson, P.W. Jarvis and subs
1 – R.G. Lumb

| BOWLING | S.J. Dennis | S. Oldham | A. Sidebottom | S.D. Fletcher | S.N. Hartley | M.D. Moxon | P. Carrick | I.G. Swallow | G.B. Stevenson |
|---|---|---|---|---|---|---|---|---|---|
| (B.&H.) *v.* Leicestershire (Leeds) 5 May | 9–1–23–2 | 11–4–17–2 | 9–3–15–2 | 5–0–30–0 | 7–2–18–0 | 3–0–22–0 | 11–1–26–2 | | |
| (J.P.) *v.* Worcestershire (Bradford) 6 May | 7–0–31–0 | 8–0–16–2 | 7–0–23–1 | 8–0–25–1 | 3–0–23–0 | | 5–0–25–1 | | |
| (B.&H.) *v.* Scotland (Perth) 12 May | 8–3–22–0 | 9–1–29–2 | 5–1–13–0 | | 11–0–39–4 | | 11–2–27–0 | 11–1–40–1 | |
| (B.&H.) *v.* Warwickshire (Edgbaston) 15 May | 11–4–43–1 | 9–3–29–3 | | 10–0–55–1 | 3–0–22–0 | | 11–0–40–3 | 11–2–50–1 | |
| (B.&H.) *v.* Northants. (Bradford) 19 May | 11–0–41–3 | 11–2–48–2 | | | | 11–0–45–1 | 11–4–53–0 | 3–0–19–0 | 8–0–39–0 |
| (J.P.) *v.* Nottinghamshire (Hull) 20 May | 6–0–27–1 | 8–0–38–0 | | | | 4–0–16–1 | 8–0–20–1 | 4–0–31–0 | 8–0–29–4 |
| (J.P.) *v.* Somerset (Middlesbrough) 3 June | | 7–0–41–0 | 8–0–44–2 | 7–0–39–1 | | 4–0–21–0 | 8–0–37–1 | | 6–0–46–1 |
| (B.&H.) *v.* Sussex (Hove) 6 June | | 11–0–24–3 | 11–1–38–0 | 9.3–0–42–2 | 6–0–36–0 | 6–0–23–1 | | | 10–0–49–3 |
| (J.P.) *v.* Kent (Canterbury) 10 June | | 8–2–22–2 | 8–1–20–3 | 7–0–38–1 | 1–0–8–0 | 7–0–47–1 | | | 7–0–20–1 |
| (J.P.) *v.* Derbyshire (Chesterfield) 17 June | | 7.3–0–41–2 | 8–0–28–0 | 7–0–31–2 | | | 8–0–34–3 | | 7–0–42–3 |
| (B.&H.) *v.* Warwickshire (Leeds) 20 June | | 11–0–38–1 | 11–1–51–2 | 11–1–48–0 | | 5–0–21–0 | 6–1–29–0 | | 11–0–70–0 |
| (J.P.) *v.* Northamptonshire (Luton) 24 June | | 8–0–29–1 | 8–0–27–0 | 8–0–51–0 | | 3–0–21–0 | 5–0–29–2 | | 8–0–41–1 |
| (J.P.) *v.* Essex (Leeds) 1 July | | 8–2–27–1 | 8–1–32–4 | 8–0–46–1 | | | 2–0–15–0 | | 8–0–45–2 |
| (N.W.) *v.* Shropshire (Telford) 4 July | 12–1–56–2 | 12–1–44–2 | | | 2–0–6–0 | | 12–3–28–1 | | 11–1–46–0 |
| (J.P.) *v.* Glos. (Scarborough) 8 July | 6–0–36–0 | 8–1–25–2 | | 7–0–57–0 | | | 5–0–26–0 | | |
| (J.P.) *v.* Middlesex (Lord's) 15 July | 4–0–18–0 | 5–0–25–0 | | | 3.3–0–32–2 | | | | |
| (J.P.) *v.* Hampshire (Bournemouth) 22 July | 6–0–47–0 | | | | 4–0–28–1 | | 8–1–37–0 | | |
| (J.P.) *v.* Leicestershire (Bradford) 29 July | | 8–0–46–0 | 8–0–42–1 | | 7–0–51–0 | | 8–0–30–0 | | 8–0–33–2 |
| (J.P.) *v.* Lancashire (Old Trafford) 5 Aug. | | 8–0–27–1 | 8–2–23–0 | | 5–0–17–2 | | | | 7.5–3–30–2 |
| (J.P.) *v.* Warwickshire (Scarborough) 12 Aug. | | 8–0–46–1 | 8–0–32–1 | | 1–0–19–0 | | 7–0–33–0 | | 5–0–54–1 |
| (J.P.) *v.* Surrey (The Oval) 19 August | | 8–1–33–2 | 7–0–38–2 | | 6–0–26–1 | | 2–0–16–0 | | 8–0–37–1 |
| (J.P.) *v.* Glamorgan (Leeds) 26 August | | 8–0–26–2 | | | | 5–0–43–0 | | | 8–2–24–1 |
| (Asda) *v.* Derbyshire (Scarborough) 29 Aug. | | 10–0–21–1 | 7–0–18–2 | | | | 9–5–13–5 | | |
| (Asda) *v.* Hampshire (Scarborough) 31 Aug. | | 10–0–33–0 | 10–3–27–0 | | | 6–0–34–1 | 10–0–41–0 | | |
| (J.P.) *v.* Sussex (Hove) 9 September | | 8–0–24–2 | 8–0–47–0 | | | 4–0–32–0 | 4–0–24–0 | | 8–0–45–3 |
| Wickets | 9 | 34 | 20 | 9 | 10 | 5 | 19 | 2 | 25 |

| v. Lancashire (Old Trafford) 5 August (J.P.) | v. Warwickshire (Scarborough) 12 August (J.P.) | v. Surrey (The Oval) 19 August (J.P.) | v. Glamorgan (Leeds) 26 August (J.P.) | v. Derbyshire (Scarborough) 29 August (Asda) | v. Hampshire (Scarborough) 29 August (Asda) | v. Sussex (Hove) 9 September (J.P.) | Runs |
|---|---|---|---|---|---|---|---|
| | 16 | | 6 | 60 | 6 | 21 | 537 |
| 23 | 10 | | 18 | 25 | 4 | 3 | 642 |
| 7 | 23 | 8 | 30 | 5 | 26 | 3 | 691 |
| | | 13 | | | 32 | | 396 |
| 3 | 73 | 3 | 7 | 30 | 23 | 14* | 477 |
| 8 | 42 | 15 | 17 | 16 | 57 | 16 | 346 |
| 9 | 40* | 43* | | 39* | 34* | 0 | 328 |
| 8 | 1 | 1 | | 2* | 15* | 0* | 99 |
| | | | | | | | 23 |
| | | | | | | | 13 |
| — | 7* | 5* | 0* | — | — | — | 56 |
| | | | | | | | 10 |
| | | | | | | | 70 |
| 14* | 3 | 29 | 19 | | | 9 | 291 |
| 4 | | 40 | 7 | 0 | | 23 | 357 |
| | | | | | | | 45 |
| 35 | 3 | 13 | 10 | 26 | 1 | 2 | 183 |
| | | | | | | | 6 |
| | | | 9* | — | — | | 15 |
| 1 | 0 | 9 | 26 | | | | 58 |
| | 1 | 4 | 4 | | | | |
| 9 | 10 | 9 | 19 | 11 | 9 | 5 | |
| 2 | 7 | 1 | 5 | 6 | 8 | 1 | |
| 1 | 2 | | 1 | | 4 | 1 | |
| 124 | 238 | 193 | 178 | 220 | 219 | 98 | |
| 9 | 9 | 9 | 9 | 7 | 7 | 8 | |
| L | L | L | L | W | L | L | |
| 0 | 0 | 0 | 0 | — | — | 0 | |

| G. Boycott | C. Shaw | P.W. Jarvis | Byes | Leg-byes | Wides | No-balls | Total | Wkts |
|---|---|---|---|---|---|---|---|---|
| | | | 8 | 6 | 5 | 2 | 172 | 9 |
| | | | 1 | 18 | 10 | 1 | 173 | 7 |
| | | | 4 | 11 | 1 | | 186 | 8 |
| | | | 1 | 9 | 3 | 2 | 254 | 10 |
| | | | | 4 | 2 | | 251 | 7 |
| | | | | 7 | 1 | | 169 | 7 |
| | | | | 4 | | 1 | 233 | 5 |
| | | | | 5 | 4 | 2 | 223 | 10 |
| | | | | 4 | 5 | | 164 | 8 |
| | | | | 3 | 1 | 1 | 181 | 10 |
| | | | | 12 | 3 | 4 | 276 | 4 |
| | | | | 7 | 2 | 2 | 209 | 4 |
| 6-1-26-0 | | | 6 | 8 | | 1 | 206 | 8 |
| | | | 1 | 8 | 7 | | 229 | 5a |
| 6-0-16-0 | | 8-0-45-4 | 4 | 7 | 11 | 1 | 228 | 6 |
| | 5-0-26-0 | 5-0-25-1 | 1 | 5 | 2 | | 134 | 3 |
| 6-0-27-0 | 8-0-41-5 | 7-0-37-3 | 1 | 6 | 8 | 1 | 233 | 9 |
| 1-0-11-0 | | | 2 | 10 | 4 | | 229 | 5 |
| | 5-1-25-0 | | | 4 | 1 | | 127 | 5 |
| 5-1-18-0 | 6-0-38-2 | | | 9 | 2 | | 251 | 5 |
| | 8-0-37-1 | | | 8 | 8 | 2 | 205 | 7 |
| 7.2-0-26-0 | 1.5-0-11-0 | 8-1-28-4 | 1 | 10 | 9 | | 179 | 7b |
| 3.3-0-6-2 | | 5-0-29-0 | 1 | 1 | 3 | 6 | 98 | 10 |
| 2-0-13-1 | | 9.1-1-50-1 | | 13 | 6 | 3 | 220 | 3 |
| 8-1-19-0 | | | 4 | 15 | 1 | 1 | 212 | 5 |
| 3 | 8 | 13 | | | | | | |

## NatWest Trophy Final
## MIDDLESEX *v.* KENT

Kent were distressed that Alan Knott was unfit for the final, Waterton deputised. Middlesex chose Hughes ahead of Williams who had started the season as an England probable. Tavare won the toss and Kent batted.

Benson, one off-drive of classical dimension, and Taylor gave them the best possible start. Daniel and Cowans who both bowled to a width that may have been deemed illegal on a Sunday, were negotiated, and 50 came in the seventeenth over when Taylor straight drove Cowans for four. All went serenely for Kent and they seemed to be moving sweetly to lunch when, in the thirtieth over, Benson leant forward to Emburey, held his pose, and was stumped with ease. In the next over, Taylor missed a ball from Slack and Kent were 98 for 2.

*Neil Taylor hits out. (Adrian Murrell)*

ABOVE: *Benson is stumped by Downton off Emburey and Middlesex have gained the breakthrough. (Tom Morris)*
LEFT: *Disaster for Kent. Aslett is run out. (Adrian Murrell)*
BELOW: *Kent hope. Roland Butcher is bowled by the splendid Underwood (Tom Morris)*

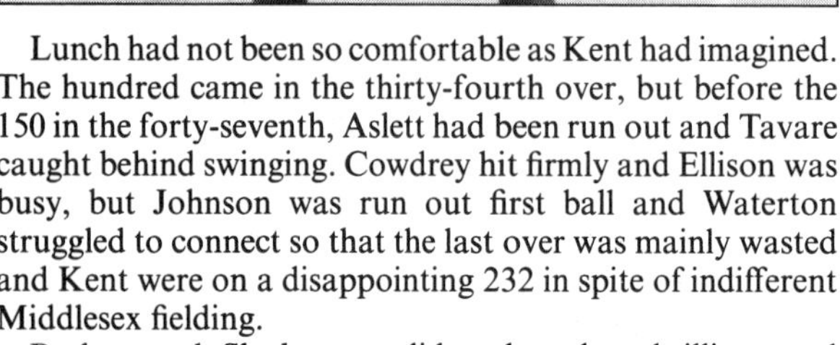

Lunch had not been so comfortable as Kent had imagined. The hundred came in the thirty-fourth over, but before the 150 in the forty-seventh, Aslett had been run out and Tavare caught behind swinging. Cowdrey hit firmly and Ellison was busy, but Johnson was run out first ball and Waterton struggled to connect so that the last over was mainly wasted and Kent were on a disappointing 232 in spite of indifferent Middlesex fielding.

Barlow and Slack are solid rather than brilliant and advanced the score to 39 before Barlow swatted at Jarvis in the twelfth over. The 50 came in the sixteenth over, but in the twentieth, Slack was bowled by Ellison, who, like Alderman, was very disappointing.

Gatting had come to the wicket to the most hostile reception one can remember hearing at Lord's, and it was the more marked as this was a sedate day with little noise. Perhaps the crowd were discrediting him for his attitude at Chelmsford the previous day. They had justification. One hopes that some day our leading cricketers will realise that their position is such because people pay to watch them.

Gatting drove Jarvis to mid-on and Kent appeared to be winning, but their fielding was almost as lethargic as

*Middlesex hope. Man of the Match Clive Radley.* INSET: *(left): Tension. Downton and Tavare: catcher and victim.* INSET: *(right): Moment of truth. Emburey hits Ellison to leg for four and wheels in joy as Middlesex have won off the last ball of the match. Edmonds' face shows the tension. (Adrian Murrell)*

Middlesex's. Now came the crux of the match as Radley and Downton added 97 vital runs in fading light. Radley is a batsman who reaches forty without one realising he has played a shot and he was justifiably named Man of the Match for his hurrying and scurrying which brought Middlesex to the point of victory. Radley was out in the fifty-sixth over and the attacking Downton an over later.

Nine were needed off the last two overs and with 9 balls to go, Underwood, who had bowled splendidly and had been unwisely taken off after sending down 9 overs for 12 runs, dropped Emburey off a simple offering.

Seven were needed off the last over bowled by Ellison and one could not agree with Tavare's field-setting which conceded a run a ball.

Middlesex needed one run off the last ball and Ellison bowled an over-pitched delivery on middle and leg which Emburey turned gleefully for four – had the insurging crowd allowed it to reach the boundary.

# National Westminster Bank Trophy 1984

The County winning the Trophy will receive a prize of £14,000, the losing Finalist £7,000, the losing Semi-finalists £3,750 each and the losing Quarter-finalists £2,000 each.

## MARYLEBONE CRICKET CLUB

# NatWest Bank Trophy Final

15p **KENT v. MIDDLESEX** 15p

at Lord's Ground, †Saturday, September 1st, 1984

**KENT**

| |  |  |  |
|---|---|---|---|
| 1 | N. R. Taylor | b Slack | 49 |
| 2 | M. R. Benson | st Downton b Emburey | 37 |
| ‡3 | C. J. Tavare | c Downton b Daniel | 28 |
| 4 | D. G. Aslett | run out | 11 |
| 5 | C. S. Cowdrey | c Radley b Daniel | 58 |
| 6 | R. M. Ellison | not out | 23 |
| 7 | G. W. Johnson | run out | 0 |
| *8 | S. N. V. Waterton | not out | 4 |
| 9 | D. L. Underwood | | |
| 10 | T. M. Alderman | | |
| 11 | K. B. S. Jarvis | | |
| | B 10, l-b 8, w 3, n-b 1, | | 22 |
| | | Total... | 232 |

FALL OF THE WICKETS

1...96 2...98 3...135 4...163 5...217 6...217 7... 8... 9... 10...

| Bowling Analysis | O. | M. | R. | W. | Wd. | N-b |
|---|---|---|---|---|---|---|
| Cowans | 9 | 2 | 24 | 0 | ... | ... |
| Daniel | 12 | 1 | 41 | 2 | 1 | ... |
| Hughes | 10 | 0 | 52 | 0 | 1 | ... |
| Edmonds | 5 | 0 | 33 | 0 | ... | ... |
| Slack | 12 | 2 | 33 | 1 | 1 | 1 |
| Emburey | 12 | 1 | 27 | 1 | ... | ... |
| | ... | ... | ... | ... | ... | ... |

**MIDDLESEX**

| |  |  |  |
|---|---|---|---|
| 1 | G. D. Barlow | c Waterton b Jarvis | 25 |
| 2 | W. N. Slack | b Ellison | 20 |
| ‡3 | M. W. Gatting | c Tavare b Jarvis | 37 |
| 4 | R. O. Butcher | b Underwood | 15 |
| 5 | C. T. Radley | c Tavare b Ellison | 67 |
| *6 | P. R. Downton | c Cowdrey b Jarvis | 40 |
| 7 | J. E. Emburey | not out | 17 |
| 8 | P. H. Edmonds | not out | 5 |
| 9 | S. P. Hughes | | |
| 10 | N. G. Cowans | | |
| 11 | W. W. Daniel | | |
| | B , l-b 7, w 1, n-b 2, | | 10 |
| | | Total... | 236 |

FALL OF THE WICKETS

1...39 2...60 3...88 4...124 5...211 6...217 7... 8... 9... 10...

| Bowling Analysis | O. | M. | R. | W. | Wd. | N-b |
|---|---|---|---|---|---|---|
| Alderman | 12 | 0 | 53 | 0 | ... | ... |
| Jarvis | 12 | 1 | 47 | 3 | ... | ... |
| Ellison | 12 | 2 | 53 | 2 | ... | ... |
| Cowdrey | 12 | 1 | 48 | 0 | 1 | ... |
| Underwood | 12 | 2 | 25 | 1 | ... | 2 |
| | ... | ... | ... | ... | ... | ... |
| | ... | ... | ... | ... | ... | ... |

**Any alterations to teams will be announced over the public address system**

RULES—1 The Match will consist of one innings per side and each innings is limited to 60 overs.
2 No one bowler may bowl more than 12 overs in an innings.
3 Hours of play: 10.30 a.m. to 7.10 p.m. In certain circumstances the Umpires may order extra time.

Luncheon Interval 12.45 p.m.—1.25 p.m. Tea Interval will be 20 minutes and will normally be taken at 4.30 p.m.

‡Captain *Wicket-keeper

Umpires—H. D. Bird & B. J. Meyer Scorers—J. Foley, H. P. Sharp & E. Solomon

†This match is intended to be completed in one day, but three days have been allocated in case of weather interference

**Kent won the toss**

**Middlesex won by 4 wickets**

Total runs scored at end of each over:

| | | | | | | | | | | | | | | | | | | | | |
|---|---|---|---|---|---|---|---|---|---|---|---|---|---|---|---|---|---|---|---|---|
| **First Innings** | 1 | 2 | 3 | 4 | 5 | 6 | 7 | 8 | 9 | 10 | 11 | 12 | 13 | 14 | 15 | 16 | 17 | 18 | 19 | 20 |
| | 21 | 22 | 23 | 24 | 25 | 26 | 27 | 28 | 29 | 30 | 31 | 32 | 33 | 34 | 35 | 36 | 37 | 38 | 39 | 40 |
| | 41 | 42 | 43 | 44 | 45 | 46 | 47 | 48 | 49 | 50 | 51 | 52 | 53 | 54 | 55 | 56 | 57 | 58 | 59 | 60 |
| **Second Innings** | 1 | 2 | 3 | 4 | 5 | 6 | 7 | 8 | 9 | 10 | 11 | 12 | 13 | 14 | 15 | 16 | 17 | 18 | 19 | 20 |
| | 21 | 22 | 23 | 24 | 25 | 26 | 27 | 28 | 29 | 30 | 31 | 32 | 33 | 34 | 35 | 36 | 37 | 38 | 39 | 40 |
| | 41 | 42 | 43 | 44 | 45 | 46 | 47 | 48 | 49 | 50 | 51 | 52 | 53 | 54 | 55 | 56 | 57 | 58 | 59 | 60 |

Nothing leaves a stronger impression.

## Sri Lankans in England 1984
First Class Matches

| BATTING | *v.* Nottinghamshire (Cleethorpes) 25–27 July | | *v.* Surrey (The Oval) 28–30 July | | *v.* Gloucestershire (Cheltenham) 4–7 August | | *v.* Hampshire (Southampton) 8–10 August | | *v.* Kent (Canterbury) 11–14 August | | *v.* Sussex (Hove) 18–21 August | | Test Match (Lord's) 23–28 August | | *v.* Warwickshire (Edgbaston) 29–31 August | | *v.* D.B. Close's XI (Scarborough) 2–4 September | |
|---|---|---|---|---|---|---|---|---|---|---|---|---|---|---|---|---|---|---|
| S. Wettimuny | 39 | 10 | 7 | 17 | 123* | — | | | 14 | — | 73 | 0 | 190 | 13 | | | 19 | — |
| M.D. Von | 3 | 43 | 27 | 9 | | | 29 | 5 | 12 | — | | | | | 48 | 75 | | |
| A.R. Silva | 4 | 27* | | | 91 | — | 21 | 29 | | | 0 | 25 | 8 | 102* | 161* | 70 | 20 | — |
| R.L. Dias | 31 | — | 9 | 4 | — | — | 25 | 22 | 31 | — | 2 | 11 | 32 | 38 | 10 | 9 | — | — |
| L.R.D. Mendis | 23 | 26* | 67* | 24 | — | — | 64 | — | 20 | — | 12 | 1 | 111 | 94 | | | | |
| A.L.F. de Mel | 0 | — | 11 | — | | | 37 | — | | | 12 | 23 | 20* | 14 | | | — | — |
| R.G. de Alwis | 74 | — | — | — | | | | | | | | | | | | | | |
| D.S. de Silva | 0 | — | 10 | 8 | — | — | | | 37* | — | | | — | — | | | | |
| R.J. Ratnayeke | 1 | — | 1 | 0 | — | — | 0 | 21* | | | 10* | 66 | 5* | 7* | 21 | 31* | — | — |
| M.M. Yusuf | 2* | — | | | — | — | | | — | — | | | | | — | — | | |
| V.B. John | 4 | — | 0 | 0* | — | — | | | — | — | | | — | — | | | | |
| R.S. Madugalle | | | 47 | 8 | 57* | — | 4 | 23* | | | 0 | 27 | 5 | 3 | 24 | 51* | 87* | — |
| A. Ranatunga | | | 0 | 30 | | | 50 | — | 118 | — | 1 | 46 | 84 | 0 | 4 | 13 | 73* | — |
| P.A. de Silva | | | | | — | — | 75 | — | 59 | — | 62 | 15 | 16 | 3 | 6 | — | 0 | — |
| S.D. Arunasiri | | | | | | | 0* | — | | | 0 | 5 | | | — | — | — | — |
| A. Samaranayake | | | | | | | — | — | — | — | 5 | 9* | | | — | — | — | — |
| D.S.B. Kuruppu | | | | | | | | | 25 | — | | | | | 0 | 9 | 4 | — |
| Byes | | 6 | 1 | 1 | 2 | | 5 | | 2 | | | | 2 | 5 | | 2 | | |
| Leg-byes | 7 | 7 | 3 | 1 | 9 | | 4 | | 10 | | 11 | 3 | 8 | 4 | 8 | 4 | 5 | |
| Wides | | | | 1 | 1 | | 1 | 1 | 1 | | | 3 | 2 | | 1 | | | |
| No-balls | 11 | 4 | 11 | 2 | 3 | | 21 | 1 | 11 | | 5 | 1 | 8 | 11 | 18 | 12 | 8 | |
| Total | 199 | 123 | 194 | 105 | 286 | | 336 | 102 | 340 | | 193 | 235 | 491 | 294 | 301 | 276 | 216 | |
| Wickets | 10 | 2 | 9† | 8† | 1 | | 9 | 3 | 7 | | 10 | 10 | 7 | 7 | 7 | 5 | 4 | |
| Result | D | | L | | D | | D | | D | | D | | D | | D | | D | |

*Catches* 12 – A.R. Silva
6 – subs
5 – J.R. Ratnayeke, R.L. Dias, A. Ranatunga and D.S.B. Kuruppu (ct 4/st 1)
3 – R.G. de Alwis, A.L.F. de Mel, P.A. de Silva, R.S. Madugalle and A. Samaranayake
2 – S. Wettimuny, D.S. de Silva, M.D. Vonhagt and S.R. Arunasiri
1 – L.R.D. Mendis and V.B. John

† R.G. de Alwis, absent hurt
A.L.F. de Mel, absent hurt (2nd innings)

| BOWLING | A.L.F. de Mel | V.B. John | J.R. Ratnayeke | D.S. de Silva | M.M. Yusuf | A. Ranatunga | S. Wettimuny | R.S. Madugalle | A. Samarana-yake |
|---|---|---|---|---|---|---|---|---|---|
| *v.* Nottinghamshire | 19–3–51–2 | 16–2–66–3 | 11–1–40–1 | 25–5–71–1 | 11–2–56–0 | | | | |
| (Cleethorpes) 25–27 July | 13–1–58–2 | 13–3–43–0 | 9–1–32–1 | 19–2–46–2 | 5–1–25–1 | | | | |
| *v.* Surrey (The Oval) | 20–5–44–3 | 14.4–3–74–2 | 9–4–29–2 | 23–9–75–1 | | 5–2–6–1 | | | |
| 28–30 July | | 22.4–3–89–5 | 18–3–45–1 | 8–2–29–1 | | 3–2–13–0 | 5–1–7–1 | 2–0–8–0 | |
| *v.* Gloucestershire | | 23–7–71–1 | 14–3–43–1 | 25–8–68–1 | 19–2–62–0 | 7–1–22–0 | | | |
| (Cheltenham) 4–7 August | | 14.2–2–58–6 | 11–2–33–0 | 16–7–19–0 | | | | | |
| *v.* Hampshire (Southampton) | 9–2–20–1 | | 22–1–89–2 | | | 12–1–44–2 | | | 14.2–4–42–0 |
| 8–10 August | | | 17–1–63–1 | | | 11–1–36–1 | | 15–3–34–1 | 10–2–52–1 |
| *v.* Kent (Canterbury) | | 24.4–10–50–5 | | 25–10–39–5 | 6–2–13–0 | 8–1–28–0 | | | 8–3–22–0 |
| 11–14 August | | 23–4–54–0 | | 30–3–100–0 | 23–3–66–0 | 7–0–28–1 | | | 33–3–142–4 |
| *v.* Sussex (Hove) | 29.2–6–111–4 | | 19–4–68–1 | | | 7–2–13–0 | | 8–3–18–1 | 19–4–47–0 |
| 18–21 August | | | | | | | | | |
| Test Match (Lord's) | 37–10–110–4 | 39.1–12–98–4 | 22–5–50–0 | 45–16–85–2 | | 1–1–0–0 | | 3–0–4–0 | |
| 23–28 August | | | | | | | | | |
| *v.* Warwickshire | | | 23–9–44–1 | | 7–0–41–0 | 3–1–11–0 | | | 23–7–62–2 |
| (Edgbaston) 29–31 August | | | 21.2–2–93–4 | | 3–0–19–0 | 5–0–26–1 | | | 29–0–95–2 |
| *v.* D.B. Close's XI | 26–4–76–3 | | 31–7–101–1 | | | | | 3–0–11–0 | 7–1–37–0 |
| (Scarborough) 2–4 September | | | | | | | | | |
| | 153.2–31–470–19 *av.* 24.73 | 190.3–46–603–26 *av.* 23.19 | 227.2–43–730–16 *av.* 45.62 | 216–62–532–13 *av.* 40.92 | 74–10–282–1 *av.* 282.00 | 69–12–227–6 *av.* 37.83 | 5–1–7–1 *av.* 7.00 | 31–6–75–2 *av.* 37.50 | 143.2–24–499–9 *av.* 55.44 |

a L.R.D. Mendis 1–0–2–0

| m | Inns | NOs | Runs | H/S | Av |
|---|---|---|---|---|---|
| 7 | 11 | 1 | 505 | 190 | 50.50 |
| 5 | 9 | — | 251 | 75 | 27.88 |
| 7 | 12 | 3 | 558 | 161* | 62.00 |
| 9 | 12 | — | 224 | 38 | 18.66 |
| 7 | 10 | 2 | 442 | 111 | 55.25 |
| 6 | 7 | 1 | 117 | 37 | 19.50 |
| 2 | 1 | — | 74 | 74 | 74.00 |
| 5 | 4 | 1 | 55 | 37* | 18.33 |
| 8 | 11 | 5 | 163 | 66 | 27.16 |
| 4 | 1 | 1 | 2 | 2* | — |
| 5 | 3 | 1 | 4 | 4 | 2.00 |
| 7 | 12 | 4 | 336 | 87* | 42.00 |
| 7 | 11 | 1 | 419 | 118 | 41.90 |
| 7 | 8 | — | 236 | 75 | 29.50 |
| 4 | 3 | 1 | 5 | 5 | 2.50 |
| 5 | 2 | 1 | 14 | 9* | 14.00 |
| 3 | 4 | — | 38 | 25 | 9.50 |

| S.E. Arunasiri | R.L. Dias | P.A. de Silva | No-balls | Total | Wkts | Byes | Leg-byes | Wides |
|---|---|---|---|---|---|---|---|---|
| | | | 1 | 4 | 4 | 18 | 311 | 7 |
| 1 | | | | 1 | | 5 | 210 | 6 |
| | | | 7 | 4 | 1 | 10 | 250 | 9 |
| | | | 4 | 7 | | 6 | 208 | 8 |
| | | | | 8 | | 4 | 278 | 4 |
| | | | | 2 | 4 | | 116 | 6 |
| 19–3–87–0 | 2–1–9–1 | | | 7 | 3 | 11 | 312 | 6 |
| 10.5–0–74–0 | | 4–0–19–0 | 5 | 2 | 1 | 3 | 291 | 4 a |
| | | | 11 | 7 | 2 | 10 | 182 | 10 |
| | 4–2–9–0 | | 1 | 12 | | 8 | 420 | 5 |
| 24–9–57–0 | | | 1 | 10 | 2 | 18 | 345 | 6 |
| | | | 5 | 7 | 5 | 6 | 370 | 10 |
| 11–1–53–0 | | | | 12 | 5 | 14 | 242 | 3 |
| | | | 2 | 6 | | 5 | 246 | 7 |
| 25–8–65–1 | | | 2 | 9 | 1 | 6 | 308 | 5 |
| 89.5–21–336–1 *av.* 336.00 | 6–3–18–1 *av.* 18.00 | 4–0–19–0 — | | | | | | |

## John Player League

***2 September***

***at Derby***

**Derbyshire** 215 for 4 (K.J. Barnett 131 not out)
**Essex** 220 for 9 (G.A. Gooch 64)

*Essex (4 pts) won by 1 wicket*

***at Southampton***

**Northamptonshire** 186 for 8
**Hampshire** 189 for 6 (C.L. Smith 64 not out, J.J.E. Hardy 58)

*Hampshire (4 pts) won by 4 wickets*

***at Trent Bridge***

**Surrey** 231 for 5 (A.R. Butcher 70, A.J. Stewart 53 not out)
**Nottinghamshire** 234 for 6 (D.W. Randall 66 not out, R.J. Hadlee 58)

*Nottinghamshire (4 pts) won by 4 wickets*

***at Edgbaston***

**Glamorgan** 226 for 6 (G.C. Holmes 73)
**Warwickshire** 229 for 7 (D.L. Amiss 67)

*Warwickshire (4 pts) won by 3 wickets*

***at Worcester***

**Kent** 181 (M.R. Benson 62, M.J. Weston 4 for 24)
**Worcestershire** 184 for 4 (T.S. Curtis 75 not out)

*Worcestershire (4 pts) won by 6 wickets*

*Clive Rice, Nottinghamshire, a bold and valiant skipper. (George Herringshaw)*

| **Derbyshire C.C.C.** First-Class Matches – Batting, 1984 | v. Leicestershire (Chesterfield) 30 April–1 May | | v. Lancashire (Old Trafford) 2–4 May | | v. Glamorgan (Derby) 9–11 May | | v. Surrey (Chesterfield) 23–25 May | | v. Nottinghamshire (Derby) 26–29 May | | v. Middlesex (Derby) 2–5 June | | v. Gloucestershire (Gloucester) 9–12 June | | v. Essex (Ilford) 13–15 June | | v. Yorkshire (Harrogate) 16–19 June | | v. Kent (Derby) 23–26 June | | v. Essex (Chesterfield) 27–29 June | | v. Worcestershire (Worcester) 30 June–3 July | | v. Warwickshire (Chesterfield) 7–10 July | | v. Kent (Maidstone) 11–13 July | |
|---|---|---|---|---|---|---|---|---|---|---|---|---|---|---|---|---|---|---|---|---|---|---|---|---|---|---|---|---|
| K.J. Barnett | 114 | 14 | 2 | — | 17 | — | 34 | — | 63 | 50 | 144 | — | 74 | 47 | 1 | 26 | 50 | 10* | 17 | 36 | 17 | 24 | 16 | 104 | 29 | — | 84 | 0 |
| I.S. Anderson | 4 | 79 | 9 | — | 13 | — | 16 | — | 34 | 14 | 4 | — | 0 | 27 | 13 | 7 | 17 | 20 | | | 34 | 38 | 2 | 29 | | | | |
| A. Hill | 19 | 53 | 47 | — | 3 | — | 89 | — | 12 | 46* | 0 | — | 0 | 39 | 83 | 84 | 6 | 16 | 11 | 0 | 5 | 25 | 4 | 4 | 125 | 1 | 6 | 48* |
| J.H. Hampshire | 0 | 4 | 18 | — | 18 | — | 66 | — | 1 | — | 1 | — | | | | | | | | | 4 | 101* | 27 | 2 | 27 | 7 | 45 | 0 |
| G. Miller | 0 | 0 | 130 | — | 5 | — | 15 | — | 4 | — | | | 3 | 7* | | | | | 13 | 0 | | | | | 79 | 47 | 13 | 13 |
| W.P. Fowler | 20 | 1 | 16 | — | 116 | — | 1 | — | | | 1 | — | | | 61* | 1 | 12 | 6 | 29 | 19 | 1 | 1 | 58 | 28* | | | 60* | 2 |
| R.J. Finney | 24 | 49 | 52 | — | 0 | — | 28 | — | 4 | — | 1 | — | 1 | 0* | 1 | 34 | 4 | 3 | 2 | 5 | 30 | 28 | 4 | 5* | 9 | 6* | 23* | 20 |
| B. Roberts | 0 | 80 | | | | | 8 | — | 40 | — | 36* | — | 66 | 41 | 0 | 6* | 45 | 29* | 5 | 3 | 9 | 27 | 72* | 14 | 0 | 14* | | |
| P.G. Newman | 0 | 10 | 40 | — | 19 | — | 19* | — | 21 | — | 34 | — | | | 9 | 0 | 1 | — | 1 | 6 | 11 | 7 | 38 | — | — | — | — | 0 |
| R.W. Taylor | 6 | 7* | 0 | — | 46 | — | 13* | — | — | 0 | 44 | — | 26* | — | 0 | 0 | | | 20 | 11* | | | | | | | | |
| O.H. Mortensen | 1* | 2 | 2* | — | 40* | — | | | | | 1 | — | — | — | | | | | | | | | | | | | | |
| D.G. Moir | | | 51 | — | | | | | 11* | 31 | | | 98 | 22 | 0 | 5 | 18 | — | | | 3* | 26* | 4* | 21 | 107 | — | — | 6 |
| J.G. Wright | | | | | 67 | — | | | 86 | 33* | | | 48 | 6 | 41 | 53 | 141 | 0 | 40 | 62 | | | | | | | | |
| D.E. Malcolm | | | | | | | — | — | | | | | | | | | | | | | | | | | — | 7 | | |
| J.P. Taylor | | | | | | | | | | | 11 | — | | | | | | | | | | | | | | | | |
| J.E. Morris | | | | | | | | | | | | | 0 | 0 | 34 | 48 | 116 | 76 | 22 | 17 | 0 | 79 | 103 | 26 | 5 | 49 | 15 | 22 |
| B.J.M. Maher | | | | | | | | | | | | | | | | | 9* | 11 | | | 66 | 0 | — | — | 7* | 0 | — | 0 |
| I. Broome | | | | | | | | | | | | | | | | | | | 26* | 0 | | | | | | | | |
| Byes | 4 | 1 | 12 | | 4 | | 1 | | 8 | | 1 | | 5 | | | 1 | | | | | | 6 | 1 | 4 | | 1 | | |
| Leg-byes | 3 | 5 | 11 | | 4 | | 1 | | 8 | 2 | 7 | | 7 | 6 | 6 | 7 | 11 | 3 | 5 | | 4 | 1 | 8 | 6 | 7 | 6 | 2 | 4 |
| Wides | 1 | | | | 3 | | 1 | | 2 | 1 | 2 | | 1 | | 2 | 1 | | | | | | 1 | 2 | 4 | 3 | | 1 | |
| No-balls | 18 | 16 | 4 | | 9 | | 10 | | | | 27 | | 2 | | 5 | 3 | 9 | 1 | 8 | 2 | 3 | | 8 | 7 | 34 | 11 | 2 | 5 |
| Total | 214 | 321 | 394 | | 364 | | 302 | | 294 | 177 | 314 | | 331 | 195 | 256 | 276 | 439 | 175 | 199 | 161 | 187 | 364 | 347 | 254 | 432 | 142 | 251 | 127 |
| Wickets | 10 | 10 | 10 | | 10 | | 8 | | 9 | 4 | 10 | | 9 | 7 | 10 | 10 | 10 | 7 | 10 | 10 | 10 | 9 | 8 | 7 | 8 | 5 | 5 | 10 |
| Result | L | | D | | D | | D | | D | | D | | D | | L | | D | | L | | D | | D | | D | | L | |
| Points | 6 | | 5 | | 8 | | 8 | | 2 | | 8 | | 6 | | 5 | | 5 | | 4 | | 3 | | 6 | | 6 | | 7 | |

*Catches* 31 – R.W. Taylor (ct 26/st 5), 23 – G. Miller, 21 – K.J. Barnett, 20 – J.H. Hampshire, 18 – B.J.M. Maher, 17 – D.G. Moir, 16 – W.P. Fowler, 14 – I.S. Anderson, 13 – A. Hill, 12 – B. Roberts, 9 – J.G. Wright, 7 – subs, 5 – R.J. Finney

## English Counties Form Charts

The statistics of all first-class matches are given on pages 392 to 461. The games covered are:

Britannic Assurance County Championship.
Matches against touring and representative sides.

In the batting tables a blank indicates that a batsman did not *play* in a game, a dash (—) that he did not *bat*. A dash (—) is placed in the batting averages if a player had 2 innings or less, and in the bowling figures if no wicket was taken.

RIGHT: *Paul Downton, Middlesex and England. (David Munden)*

OPPOSITE: *(left): Farewell to one of the greatest wicket-keepers and finest gentlemen ever to grace the game. Bob Taylor retired. (Adrian Murrell) (right): Farewell to Bob Willis. His passing from the game was quiet and without the ceremonies that were his due. None has ever given more for England. (George Herringshaw)*

| v. Surrey (The Oval) 14–17 July | | v. West Indians (Derby) 21–23 July | | v. Lancashire (Buxton) 25–27 July | | v. Glamorgan (Swansea) 28–31 July | | v. Northamptonshire (Northampton) 4–7 August | | v. Nottinghamshire (Trent Bridge) 8–10 August | | v. Sussex (Derby) 11–14 August | | v. Somerset (Taunton) 18–21 August | | v. Yorkshire (Chesterfield) 22–24 August | | v. Leicestershire (Leicester) 5–7 September | | v. Hampshire (Derby) 8–11 September | | M | Inns | NOs | Runs | H/S | Av |
|---|---|---|---|---|---|---|---|---|---|---|---|---|---|---|---|---|---|---|---|---|---|---|---|---|---|---|---|
| | | 5 | 26 | 59 | 62 | 9 | 44 | 5 | — | 18 | 90 | 12 | — | 120 | 56 | 4 | 6 | 19 | 102* | 107* | 17 | 24 | 41 | 3 | 1734 | 144 | 45.63 |
| | | | | | | 39 | 26* | | | 6 | 16 | 7 | — | | | | | | | | | 14 | 23 | 1 | 454 | 79 | 20.63 |
| 71 | 50 | 5 | 2 | 5 | 56* | 65 | 0 | 37 | — | 7 | 1 | 9 | — | 99 | 4 | 25 | 8 | 61 | 8 | 38 | 75 | 25 | 44 | 3 | 1352 | 125 | 32.97 |
| 12 | 48 | 2 | — | 55 | 1* | 62 | 45 | 4 | — | 53* | 33 | 47 | — | 38 | 1 | 37 | 1 | 19 | — | — | 13* | 21 | 32 | 4 | 792 | 101* | 28.28 |
| 32* | 20 | 0 | 74* | 0 | — | 44 | 15 | — | — | 16 | 86 | 76* | — | 45 | 0 | 27 | 49 | 77 | — | — | 1* | 20 | 30 | 5 | 891 | 130 | 35.64 |
| 76* | 27* | 2 | 6 | 15 | 0 | 5 | 0 | 0* | — | 0 | 30 | 57 | — | 3 | 46 | 50 | 29 | 8 | 52* | 101* | 8 | 22 | 38 | 8 | 948 | 116 | 31.60 |
| — | 4 | 9 | 18 | 78 | — | 7 | 8 | — | — | 1 | 73 | 5 | — | 35 | 16* | 60 | 0 | 32 | — | | | 24 | 37 | 5 | 679 | 78 | 21.21 |
| 0 | 1 | | | 4 | — | | | | | | | 20 | — | 13 | 17 | | | 4 | — | — | — | 17 | 26 | 5 | 554 | 80 | 26.38 |
| — | 1 | 8* | 38 | | | | | | | 0 | 6 | | | | | | | | | | | 16 | 21 | 2 | 269 | 40 | 14.15 |
| | | | | 13* | — | 20 | 10 | — | — | 7 | 20* | 5 | — | 1 | — | 2 | 11 | 41* | — | — | — | 18 | 22 | 7 | 303 | 46 | 20.20 |
| | | | | | | | | | | | | | | | | 0* | 8 | 9 | — | — | — | 8 | 8 | 4 | 63 | 40* | 15.75 |
| — | 15 | 0 | 0 | 15 | — | 0 | 12 | — | — | 0 | 0 | 45 | — | 0* | 0* | 16 | 27 | 1 | — | — | — | 20 | 28 | 6 | 534 | 107 | 24.27 |
| | | | | 56 | 6 | 47 | 17 | 84 | — | | | 177 | — | 12 | 77 | | | | | 61 | 87 | 12 | 21 | 1 | 1201 | 177 | 60.05 |
| — | 0 | 3 | 0 | | | | | | | 23 | 3 | | | | | 4 | 0* | | | | | 7 | 8 | 1 | 40 | 23 | 5.71 |
| | | | | | | | | — | — | | | | | 0 | — | | | | | | | 3 | 2 | | 11 | 11 | 5.50 |
| 10 | 14 | 29 | 23 | 1 | — | | | 14* | — | | | | | | | 1 | 2 | 135 | 44 | 2 | 61 | 15 | 28 | 1 | 948 | 135 | 35.11 |
| 33 | 1 | 13 | 6 | | | | | | | | | | | | | | | | | | | 7 | 11 | 2 | 146 | 66 | 16.22 |
| | | | | | | 8* | 1* | | | | | | | | | | | | | | | 2 | 4 | 3 | 35 | 26* | 35.00 |
| | 6 | 2 | | 6 | | 8 | 4 | 1 | | | 14 | 9 | | 1 | 4 | 3 | 2 | 1 | | 2 | | | | | | | |
| 3 | 11 | 4 | 5 | 1 | 1 | 9 | 5 | 3 | | 5 | 5 | 4 | | 4 | 1 | 1 | 2 | 9 | 1 | 7 | 3 | | | | | | |
| | | | 1 | | | 5 | | | | 1 | | | | 1 | 4 | | | | | | 9 | | | | | | |
| 13 | 3 | 7 | 2 | 5 | 5 | 4 | 1 | 1 | | 2 | 4 | 2 | | 1 | | 23 | 11 | 15 | 4 | 4 | 3 | | | | | | |
| 250 | 201 | 89 | 201 | 313 | 131 | 332 | 188 | 150 | | 139 | 381 | 475 | | 373 | 226 | 253 | 156 | 431 | 211 | 322 | 277 | | | | | | |
| 5 | 10 | 10 | 9† | 10 | 3 | 10 | 9 | 4 | | 10 | 10 | 10 | | 10 | 7 | 10 | 10 | 10 | 2 | 3 | 5 | | | | | | |
| L | | L | | W | | D | | D | | W | | W | | D | | L | | D | | W | | | | | | | |
| 7 | | — | | 24 | | 7 | | 5 | | 19 | | 24 | | 7 | | 5 | | 4 | | 21 | | | | | | | |

† J.H. Hampshire absent hurt

4 – J.E. Morris, D.E. Malcolm and O.H. Mortensen
3 – P.G. Newman
2 – J.P. Taylor
1 – I. Broome

| **Derbyshire C.C.C.** First Class Matches – Bowling, 1984 | P.G. Newman | O.H. Mortensen | R.J. Finney | B. Roberts | G. Miller | W.P. Fowler | D.G. Moir | K.J. Barnett | A. Hill |
|---|---|---|---|---|---|---|---|---|---|
| *v.* Leicestershire (Chesterfield)<br>28 April–1 May | 20–2–77–3<br>17–0–76–0 | 22–4–78–1<br>13–2–40–2 | 16–4–52–2<br>6–1–26–0 | 9–0–53–0<br>15–3–42–0 | 21–9–32–4<br>29–14–43–2 | <br>5–1–13–0 | | | |
| *v.* Lancashire (Old Trafford)<br>2–4 May | 7–0–33–1<br>4–1–9–0 | 21.3–6–44–3<br>5–1–24–0 | 15–1–50–3<br>3–0–20–0 | | 35–19–49–2<br>16–3–30–0 | 6–1–20–0<br>16–2–22–0 | 29–5–71–1<br>23–10–30–1 | <br>9–2–21–0 | <br>4–3–5–0 |
| *v.* Glamorgan (Derby)<br>9–11 May | 24–7–40–1<br>21–9–43–3 | 22–8–47–2 | 11–6–11–1<br>12–5–25–1 | | 24–10–30–6<br>27–15–28–1 | <br>8–5–12–0 | | <br>9–1–24–0 | |
| *v.* Surrey (Chesterfield)<br>23–25 May | 14–1–36–0<br>22–6–50–1 | | 10–0–31–3<br>17–6–47–1 | 3–1–3–0<br>12–2–45–3 | 39–10–117–5<br>10–1–21–0 | 20–4–80–1<br>3–1–8–0 | | | |
| *v.* Nottinghamshire (Derby)<br>26–29 May | 17–1–63–0<br>9–0–34–3 | | 11–1–33–0<br>6–0–14–0 | 5–0–19–1 | <br>26–11–41–3 | | 26–7–59–0<br>18–3–53–1 | <br>1–0–14–0 | |
| *v.* Middlesex (Derby)<br>2–5 June | 20.4–4–76–4<br>8–0–28–0 | 20–7–37–3<br>9–3–10–0 | 18–4–46–1<br>5–1–10–1 | 15–1–54–2<br>2–0–4–0 | | | | | |
| *v.* Gloucestershire<br>(Gloucester) 9–12 June | | 20–5–42–0 | 19.3–2–58–5 | 3–0–21–0 | 42–10–86–2<br>17–5–34–0 | | 39–12–99–3<br>18–4–40–0 | <br>8–2–21–0 | <br>12–2–39–1 |
| *v.* Essex (Ilford)<br>13–15 June | 25–9–85–0<br>18–2–62–4 | | 21.1–7–46–4<br>18–4–57–1 | 18–4–77–4<br>5–0–28–0 | | 10–2–28–1 | 32–10–84–0<br>11–2–71–2 | | <br>1–0–1–0 |
| *v.* Yorkshire (Harrogate)<br>16–19 June | 17–5–51–3<br>11–0–58–2 | | 15–3–43–0<br>10–1–36–0 | 6–1–21–0<br>11–1–31–2 | | 9–0–35–0 | 28–7–83–0<br>14–3–51–1 | 9–0–49–0<br>2–0–10–0 | 8–1–22–1<br>2–1–12–0 |
| *v.* Kent (Derby)<br>23–26 June | 26.5–6–63–3<br>8–3–17–1 | | 23–4–43–1<br>7–1–17–1 | 25–5–78–3<br>5–2–14–0 | 14–2–36–1 | | | | |
| *v.* Essex (Chesterfield)<br>27–29 June | 27–4–123–3 | | 23–3–74–0 | 16–0–91–0 | | 4–0–29–1 | 29–3–119–3 | 3–0–15–0 | |
| *v.* Worcestershire (Worcester)<br>30 June–3 July | 16–2–74–0<br>11–3–35–2 | | 16–3–70–2<br>18–2–59–0 | 8–0–44–0<br>16–2–57–1 | | 13.3–4–44–0<br>5–1–21–0 | 33–7–123–3<br>27.1–13–77–4 | <br>1–0–8–0 | |
| *v.* Warwickshire (Chesterfield)<br>7–10 July | 23–0–108–3<br>18–5–52–1 | | 12–1–58–0<br>10–0–52–1 | 5–0–24–0<br>10–2–35–0 | 28–5–94–1<br>6–0–25–0 | | 21–4–62–1<br>9–4–26–1 | | |
| *v.* Kent (Maidstone)<br>11–13 July | 18–6–39–0<br>12–1–31–2 | | 21–6–47–1<br>11–4–29–2 | | 20.3–7–61–4<br>14.2–6–22–4 | | 20–8–47–2<br>17–8–33–1 | | |
| *v.* Surrey (The Oval)<br>14–17 July | 30.5–5–104–7<br>17–3–71–1 | | 24–8–69–2<br>11–2–29–1 | <br>6–2–20–1 | 5–1–13–0<br>6–1–37–0 | <br>1–0–4–0 | 9–3–20–0<br>15–1–67–0 | | <br>2–1–7–0 |
| *v.* West Indians (Derby)<br>21–23 July | 31–4–116–2 | | 18.5–3–66–2 | | 19–6–56–2 | | 19–2–77–1 | | |
| *v.* Lancashire (Buxton)<br>25–27 July | | | 24–7–57–4<br>18–4–55–5 | 5–3–9–0<br>8–2–20–1 | 32.2–8–84–6<br>27.5–10–46–3 | | 14–3–49–0<br>21–5–80–1 | <br>1–1–0–0 | <br>4–0–15–0 |
| *v.* Glamorgan (Swansea)<br>28–31 July | | | 14–4–60–3<br>5–0–26–1 | | 33–11–74–1<br>27.5–3–117–3 | | 30.5–10–62–5<br>26–5–97–4 | | |
| *v.* Northamptonshire<br>(Northampton) 4–7 August | | | 9–1–35–1<br>2–2–0–0 | | 29–10–40–5<br>33–10–59–2 | <br>8–1–29–0 | 19–2–39–4<br>36–17–40–2 | | <br>14–1–72–1 |
| *v.* Nottinghamshire<br>(Trent Bridge) 8–10 August | 12–0–63–0 | | 16–3–57–0 | | 35.2–13–65–4<br>16.2–2–69–3 | | 32–8–80–4<br>17–0–60–6 | | |
| *v.* Sussex (Derby)<br>11–14 August | | | 12–5–19–4<br>5–0–16–0 | 6–0–20–3<br>4–1–20–0 | 15–2–44–2<br>21.5–5–41–5 | | 11.2–3–38–1<br>22–6–62–5 | | |
| *v.* Somerset (Taunton)<br>18–21 August | | | 25–4–98–3 | 9–1–28–0 | 51–10–187–5 | | 31–9–86–0 | | |
| *v.* Yorkshire (Chesterfield)<br>22–24 August | | 25–6–92–3 | 22.3–8–62–3 | | 32–6–110–2 | | 30–6–91–2 | | |
| *v.* Leicestershire (Leicester)<br>5–7 September | | 14–2–46–0<br>11–2–32–2 | 14–2–33–0<br>9–2–34–2 | 17–4–38–1<br>11–2–50–0 | 30–5–87–1<br>29–11–65–3 | | 21–2–87–0<br>19–4–74–2 | | |
| *v.* Hampshire (Derby)<br>8–11 September | | 21–7–52–2<br>9–2–26–0 | | 19–5–80–0<br>3–0–18–0 | 26–7–77–0<br>31–8–74–4 | 9–1–53–2 | 19–3–68–0<br>36.3–7–114–4 | | 3–1–18–0 |
| | 505.2–89–<br>1717–50<br>*av.* 34.34 | 212.3–55–<br>570–18<br>*av.* 31.66 | 584–125–<br>1770–62<br>*av.* 28.54 | 277–44–<br>1044–22<br>*av.* 47.45 | 869.2–256–<br>2094–86<br>*av.* 24.34 | 117.3–23–<br>398–5<br>*av.* 79.60 | 822.5–206–<br>2419–65–<br>*av.* 37.21 | 43–6–<br>162–0<br>— | 47–9–<br>173–3<br>*av.* 57.66 |

a J.H. Hampshire 1–1–0–0
b R.W. Taylor 6.2–1–23–1
J.G. Wright 15–2–81–1

c J.E. Morris 3–0–18–0
d J.E. Morris 6–0–35–1
I. Broome 10–3–45–1

e J.G. Wright 1–0–3–0
I. Broome 0.1–0–4–0
f J.E. Morris 2–0–20–0

g I. Broome 6–2–17–1
3–1–16–0
h J.G. Wright 6–0–30–0

| J.P. Taylor | I.S. Anderson | D.E. Malcolm | *Byes* | *Leg-byes* | *Wides* | *No-balls* | *Total* | *Wkts* |
|---|---|---|---|---|---|---|---|---|
| | | | | 1 | 1 | 3 | 297 | 10 |
| | | | 6 | 2 | | 1 | 249 | 4 |
| | | | | 2 | | | 269 | 10 |
| | 5-3-3-0 | | 15 | 9 | | 2 | 190 | 2a |
| | | | | 6 | | 10 | 144 | 10 |
| | | | 1 | 4 | 2 | 6 | 145 | 5 |
| | | 6.2-0-26-1 | 1 | 8 | 2 | 2 | 306 | 10 |
| | | 15-3-61-0 | | 9 | 1 | 4 | 246 | 5 |
| | 15-1-37-1 | | 1 | 4 | 1 | 1 | 218 | 2 |
| | 1-0-2-0 | | 2 | 3 | 1 | 2 | 166 | 7 |
| 9-2-23-0 | 4-0-20-0 | | 1 | 9 | 4 | 4 | 274 | 10 |
| 1.2-0-6-0 | | | | 1 | | 1 | 60 | 1 |
| | | | | 6 | | 1 | 313 | 10 |
| | 14-3-47-1 | | 1 | | 1 | | 287 | 4b |
| | | | | 8 | | 5 | 333 | 9 |
| | 9-2-30-0 | | 1 | 5 | 2 | 1 | 258 | 7 |
| | 2-0-21-0 | | 5 | 2 | | 2 | 352 | 4c |
| | | | 1 | 5 | | | 204 | 6 |
| | | | | 4 | 1 | | 305 | 10d |
| | | | | 1 | 1 | 1 | 58 | 2e |
| | | | 7 | 6 | 1 | 3 | 468 | 7 |
| | 5-1-16-1 | | 1 | 6 | 1 | 1 | 400 | 6f |
| | | | 1 | 6 | 1 | 5 | 270 | 7 |
| | | 17-3-80-3 | 4 | 9 | 1 | 4 | 444 | 8 |
| | | 14-1-76-2 | | 2 | 1 | 10 | 279 | 6 |
| | | 18-4-78-3 | 2 | 2 | 3 | | 279 | 10 |
| | | 9-1-33-1 | | | 1 | 3 | 152 | 10 |
| | | 12-1-48-0 | | 1 | 1 | 4 | 260 | 10 |
| | | 8-3-18-1 | | 2 | 4 | 7 | 266 | 4 |
| | | 24-3-119-3 | | 4 | | 21 | 459 | 10 |
| | | | | 9 | | 3 | 211 | 10 |
| | | | 4 | 4 | 1 | 6 | 231 | 10 |
| | | | | 3 | | 8 | 224 | 10g |
| | | | 8 | 6 | | 1 | 271 | 8 |
| 7-0-39-0 | | | | 1 | 1 | 3 | 158 | 10 |
| 4-0-28-0 | | | 4 | 10 | | | 272 | 5h |
| | | 17-3-68-2 | | 10 | 5 | 13 | 361 | 10 |
| | | | | 2 | | | 131 | 10 |
| | | | 3 | 9 | 1 | 1 | 135 | 10 |
| | | | | 12 | | | 151 | 10 |
| 28-4-92-2 | | | | 11 | 1 | 5 | 508 | 10 |
| | | 16-2-67-0 | 2 | 6 | 1 | 8 | 439 | 10 |
| | | | 8 | 3 | | 3 | 305 | 2 |
| | | | | 2 | | 2 | 259 | 9 |
| | | | | 5 | | | 353 | 4 |
| | | | 4 | 7 | 1 | 1 | 245 | 8 |
| 49.2-6-188-2 *av.* 94.00 | 55-10-176-3 *av.* 58.66 | 156.2-24-674-16 *av.* 42.12 | | | | | | |

ABOVE: *'Jack' Russell of Gloucestershire – maintained his form in a season troubled by injury and a losing side.* BELOW: *Keith Fletcher – all smiles as Essex take the John Player League. (George Herringshaw)*

| Essex C.C.C. First-Class Matches – Batting, 1984 | v. Cambridge Univ. (Cambridge) 21–24 April | | v. M.C.C. (Lord's) 25–27 April | | v. Hampshire (Southampton) 28–30 April | | v. Kent (Canterbury) 2–4 May | | v. Northamptonshire (Northampton) 9–11 May | | v. Nottinghamshire (Chelmsford) 23–25 May | | v. Surrey (Chelmsford) 26–29 May | | v. Worcestershire (Worcester) 30 May–1 June | | v. Leicestershire (Hinkley) 2–5 June | | v. Warwickshire (Ilford) 9–12 June | | v. Derbyshire (Ilford) 13–15 June | | v. Northamptonshire (Chelmsford) 16–19 June | | v. West Indians (Chelmsford) 23–25 June | | v. Derbyshire (Chesterfield) 27–29 June | |
|---|---|---|---|---|---|---|---|---|---|---|---|---|---|---|---|---|---|---|---|---|---|---|---|---|---|---|---|---|
| G.A. Gooch | 89 | — | 78 | 8 | 220 | 10* | 10 | 84 | 1 | 0* | 33 | 108 | — | — | 7 | 20* | 0 | 113* | 21 | 54 | 16 | 76 | 22 | — | 101 | 2 | 227 | — |
| C. Gladwin | 162 | — | 16 | 43 | 42 | 6* | 10 | 13 | 94 | 8* | 1 | 2 | — | — | 7 | 15 | 0 | 21 | 4 | 92 | 80 | 0 | 72 | — | 8 | 26 | 39 | — |
| K.W.R. Fletcher | 59 | — | 5 | — | | | | | 5 | — | 0 | 83 | — | — | 1 | — | 13 | — | 28 | 12 | 75 | 15 | 131 | — | 32 | 28* | 44 | — |
| K.S. McEwan | 69 | — | 70 | 0 | 89 | — | 63 | 4 | 68 | — | 17 | 13 | — | — | 0 | 7* | 43 | 37* | 4 | 97 | 101 | 20 | 51 | — | 39 | 14 | 48 | — |
| B.R. Hardie | 41* | 68 | 0 | 31 | 6* | — | 49* | 0 | 99 | — | 15 | 11 | — | — | 46 | — | 6 | — | 30 | 0 | 23 | 15 | 17 | — | 15 | 36 | 58 | — |
| D.R. Pringle | 33* | 96 | 2 | 0 | 44* | — | 5 | 0 | 25 | — | 0 | 2 | — | — | | | | | 8 | 25 | | | | | 5 | 53* | | |
| S. Turner | — | 50 | 14 | 5 | | | | | 13* | — | 0 | 4* | — | — | 21 | — | 2 | — | | | 9 | 11* | | | | | 4* | — |
| D.E. East | — | 29* | 0 | 0 | — | — | 0 | 1 | 7 | — | 24 | 16 | — | — | 63 | 9 | 14 | 2 | 5 | 6 | 7 | 1* | 10 | — | 1 | 0 | 0 | — |
| N.A. Foster | — | 10* | 1 | 41* | — | — | 13 | 1 | 5* | — | 0 | 0 | — | — | | | | | 0 | 25 | | | 7 | — | 34 | — | | |
| J.K. Lever | — | — | 11 | 37 | — | — | 0 | 5* | — | — | 0 | 14 | — | — | 4 | — | 9* | — | 0 | 1* | 6* | — | 16* | — | | | | |
| D.L. Acfield | — | — | 1* | 4 | — | — | 0 | 1 | — | — | 0* | 0 | | | 0* | — | 1 | — | 0* | 0 | — | — | | | | | — | — |
| K.R. Pont | | | | | 28 | — | 32 | 1 | | | | | | | | | | | | | | | | | | | | |
| N. Phillip | | | | | 4 | — | 6 | 0 | | | | | | | 10 | — | 71 | — | | | 0 | 42 | 29 | — | 9* | — | 31 | — |
| A.W. Lilley | | | | | | | | | | | | | — | — | | | | | | | | | | | | | | |
| P.J. Prichard | | | | | | | | | | | | | | | 86 | — | 21 | — | 5 | 31 | 3 | 69 | 14 | — | 10 | 2 | — | — |
| R.E. East | | | | | | | | | | | | | | | | | | | | | | | 22 | — | — | — | — | — |
| Byes | 7 | 1 | | | 1 | 1 | | | 9 | | | 1 | | | 7 | | 1 | 4 | | 2 | | 1 | 3 | | 4 | | 7 | |
| Leg-byes | | | 5 | 2 | 7 | | 10 | | 11 | | 3 | 2 | | | 10 | 1 | 4 | 5 | 8 | 4 | 8 | 5 | 1 | | 5 | | 6 | |
| Wides | 1 | | | | 2 | | 1 | 1 | 1 | | | | | | 2 | | 4 | 1 | | | | 2 | 3 | | 1 | 1 | 1 | |
| No-balls | 2 | 5 | 7 | 2 | 6 | 1 | 3 | 2 | 11 | | | 1 | | | 2 | 3 | | | 1 | 25 | 5 | 1 | 19 | | 3 | 2 | 3 | |
| Total | 463 | 259 | 210 | 173 | 449 | 18 | 202 | 113 | 349 | 8 | 93 | 257 | | | 266 | 55 | 189 | 183 | 114 | 374 | 333 | 258 | 417 | | 267 | 164 | 468 | |
| Wickets | 4 | 3 | 10 | 9† | 5 | 0 | 10 | 10 | 7 | 0 | 10 | 10 | | | 10 | 2 | 10 | 2 | 10 | 10 | 9 | 7 | 10 | | 9 | 6 | 7 | |
| Result | D | | L | | W | | L | | W | | L | | D | | D | | D | | W | | W | | D | | D | | D | |
| Points | — | | — | | 23 | | 6 | | 24 | | 4 | | 0 | | 6 | | 5 | | 19 | | 24 | | 8 | | — | | 8 | |

*Catches* 77 – D.E. East (ct 76/st 1); 26 – B.R. Hardie and G.A. Gooch; 22 – K.W.R. Fletcher; 20 – K.S. McEwan; 14 – C. Gladwin; 11 – D.R. Pringle; 10 – J.K. Lever, D.L. Acfield and P.J. Prichard; 9 – N.A. Foster; 4 – S. Turner

Essex celebrated their John Player League title with a win in the grand manner. Derbyshire were inspired by a truly magnificent 131 not out from skipper Kim Barnett. He hit two sixes and twelve fours and shared an unbeaten fifth wicket stand of 158 in 21 overs with Roberts. Barnett's innings was the highest made for Derbyshire in a one-day game. Essex lost Gladwin in the opening over, but Gooch and Fletcher urged them to 190 for 8. Ultimately they needed two off the last ball and Stuart Turner, who batted quite superbly for 36 not out, straight drove Roberts for 6 to win the match.

Worcestershire kept in the hunt for place money with a comfortable win over Kent and Notts, with Hadlee scoring the fastest televised fifty, beat Surrey for whom Thomas got rather agitated and had to be spoken to by captain and umpires.

### *2, 3 and 4 September*

### *at Scarborough*

**D.B. Close's XI** 308 for 5 dec (D.L. Haynes 111, G. Fowler 61)
**Sri Lankans** 216 for 4 (R.S. Madugalle 87 not out, A. Ranatunga 73 not out)
*Match drawn*

The last match of the Sri Lanka tour was ruined when rain made play impossible on the last day. The visitors were 49 for 4, three wickets to Moxon, but Madugalle and Ranatunga put on 157 in 166 minutes before the weather worsened. So the Sri Lankans returned home without a victory to their credit, but they left behind an abiding impression of charm, courtesy and batting of the highest quality in the classical manner.

### *5, 6 and 7 Septermber*

### *at Cardiff*

**Warwickshire** 438 for 7 dec (A.I. Kallicharran 155, G.W. Humpage 127, P.A. Smith 74) and 242 for 2 dec (D.L. Amiss 115 not out, R.I.H.B. Dyer 106 not out)
**Glamorgan** 313 for 6 dec (J.A. Hopkins 98, G.C. Holmes 67, Younis Ahmed 56 not out) and 230 for 6 (Younis Ahmed 80)
*Match drawn*
*Glamorgan 7 pts, Warwickshire 6 pts*

OPPOSITE: *(left): Stuart Turner of Essex. (right): Brian Hardie of Essex. (Trevor Jones)*

| v. Yorkshire (Leeds) 30 June–3 July | | v. Glamorgan (Southend) 7–10 July | | v. Lancashire (Southend) 11–13 July | | v. Gloucestershire (Bristol) 14–17 July | | v. Worcestershire (Chelmsford) 28–31 July | | v. Sussex (Eastbourne) 4–7 August | | v. Middlesex (Lord's) 8–10 August | | v. Somerset (Chelmsford) 11–14 August | | v. Hampshire (Colchester) 18–21 August | | v. Kent (Colchester) 22–24 August | | v. Surrey (The Oval) 25–28 August | | v. Middlesex (Chelmsford) 29–31 August | | v. Lancashire (Old Trafford) 8–11 September | | M | Inns | NOs | Runs | H/S | Av |
|---|---|---|---|---|---|---|---|---|---|---|---|---|---|---|---|---|---|---|---|---|---|---|---|---|---|---|---|---|---|---|---|---|---|
| 131 | — | | | 64 | — | 38 | 26 | 4 | 75 | 39 | 24 | 49 | 105* | 31 | 87 | 42 | 79 | 5 | 8 | 81 | 160* | 62 | 71 | 70 | 8* | 26 | 45 | 7 | 2559 | 227 | 67.34 |
| 30 | — | 60 | 59 | 36 | — | 94 | 21 | 31 | 21 | 9 | 66* | 26 | 15 | 3 | 36 | 16 | 64 | 6 | 1 | 24 | 2 | 0 | 15 | | | 26 | 45 | 3 | 1396 | 162 | 33.23 |
| 106 | — | 0 | 1 | 4 | — | 69* | 36* | 122 | 22 | 2 | 15* | 18 | 8 | 15 | 2 | 16 | — | 0 | 8 | 22 | 0 | 5 | 14* | 40 | — | 25 | 37 | 5 | 1056 | 131 | 33.00 |
| 68 | — | 5 | 21 | 13 | — | 88* | 36* | 7 | 10 | 10 | 0 | 4 | 19 | 1 | 31 | 142* | 12* | 25 | 44 | 104 | 84 | 29 | 16 | 132 | — | 27 | 44 | 6 | 1755 | 142* | 46.18 |
| 94 | — | 29 | 33* | 21 | — | — | — | 78 | 3 | 32 | — | 80* | 10* | 36 | 14 | 0 | — | 8 | 0 | 10 | 2* | 20 | — | 41 | — | 27 | 38 | 7 | 1077 | 99 | 34.74 |
| | | 0 | 13* | | | | | | | 12 | — | 63 | 25 | 0 | 14 | 17 | — | 2 | 1 | 43 | 0 | 50* | 28* | 11 | — | 18 | 29 | 6 | 577 | 96 | 25.08 |
| — | — | | | | | — | — | | | | | 59* | 5 | | | | | | | | | | | | | 12 | 13 | 5 | 197 | 59* | 24.62 |
| 0 | — | 4 | 81 | 35 | — | — | — | 1 | 39 | 11 | — | 24 | 16 | 23 | 12 | 4 | — | 2 | 3 | 8 | — | 50 | — | 2 | — | 27 | 37 | 2 | 510 | 81 | 14.57 |
| | | 0 | — | 8 | — | — | — | 22* | 22 | 54* | — | | | 13 | 11 | 48 | — | 1* | 0 | 3* | — | 3 | — | 19 | — | 21 | 25 | 7 | 341 | 54* | 18.94 |
| — | — | 1* | — | 8 | — | — | — | 0 | 30 | 13 | — | — | — | 3 | 11* | 1 | — | | | — | — | 1 | — | 11 | — | 24 | 22 | 7 | 182 | 37 | 12.13 |
| — | — | 0 | — | 7* | — | — | — | 1 | 3* | 5 | — | — | — | 1* | 4 | 1 | — | 4 | 1* | — | — | 1 | — | 6* | — | 24 | 22 | 9 | 41 | 7* | 3.15 |
| | | | | | | | | | | | | | | | | | | | | | | | | | | 2 | 3 | — | 61 | 32 | 20.33 |
| 33* | — | 1 | — | 31 | — | | | 19 | 0 | | | | | | | | | 4 | 3 | | | | | | | 13 | 17 | 2 | 293 | 71 | 19.53 |
| | | | | | | | | | | | | | | | | | | | | | | | | | | 1 | — | | | | — |
| 37 | — | 26 | 15 | 68 | — | — | — | 26 | 9 | 2 | — | 8 | — | 54 | 21 | 24 | 14* | 22 | 37 | 8 | 13 | 93 | 64 | 100 | 6* | 20 | 29 | 2 | 888 | 100 | 32.88 |
| | | | | | | | | | | | | | | | | | | | | | | | | 8 | — | 4 | 2 | — | 30 | 22 | 15.00 |
| 3 | | | 2 | 2 | | | | | 4 | | 2 | 3 | 4 | 4 | 5 | | | | | 5 | 1 | 1 | 4 | | | † K.W.R. Fletcher absent hurt | | | | | |
| 17 | | 2 | 4 | 11 | | 4 | 1 | 12 | 3 | 7 | 6 | 13 | 7 | 12 | 6 | 10 | 1 | 4 | 4 | 4 | 7 | 10 | 14 | 3 | | | | | | | |
| 3 | | 2 | | | | | | 2 | 2 | | 1 | | | | 5 | 3 | | | 5 | 2 | | | | | | | | | | | |
| 2 | | 11 | 12 | 14 | | 7 | 1 | 4 | | 1 | 1 | 17 | | 4 | 5 | 5 | 3 | 7 | 3 | | 5 | 4 | 7 | 3 | | | | | | | |
| 524 | | 141 | 241 | 322 | | 300 | 121 | 329 | 243 | 197 | 115 | 364 | 214 | 200 | 264 | 329 | 173 | 90 | 118 | 314 | 274 | 329 | 233 | 446 | 14 | | | | | | |
| 7 | | 10 | 5 | 10 | | 2 | 2 | 10 | 10 | 10 | 2 | 7 | 6 | 10 | 10 | 10 | 2 | 10 | 10 | 8 | 5 | 10 | 4 | 10 | 0 | | | | | | |
| W | | D | | W | | W | | W | | D | | W | | W | | W | | L | | W | | D | | W | | | | | | | |
| 24 | | 3 | | 24 | | 22 | | 24 | | 4 | | 22 | | 22 | | 24 | | 4 | | 23 | | 8 | | 24 | | | | | | | |

3 – N. Phillip
2 – R.E. East
1 – K.R. Pont

| **Essex C.C.C.** First-Class Matches – Bowling, 1984 | J.K. Lever | N.A. Foster | D.L. Acfield | D.R. Pringle | S. Turner | G.A. Gooch | C. Gladwin | K.W.R. Fletcher | N. Phillip |
|---|---|---|---|---|---|---|---|---|---|
| *v.* Cambridge University | 22.5–6–44–4 | 23–10–41–1 | 23–11–35–1 | 17–4–42–1 | 17–6–45–2 | 3–1–2–1 | 1–0–4–0 | | |
| (Cambridge) 21–24 April | 14–4–27–1 | 6–1–9–0 | 15–9–16–2 | 9–3–10–0 | 11–3–19–1 | 1–0–5–0 | 4–0–18–0 | 4–2–8–0 | |
| *v.* M.C.C. (Lord's) | 19–3–33–3 | 20–3–68–1 | 8–4–15–0 | 20–6–43–1 | 18–8–40–0 | 7–1–25–1 | | | |
| 25–27 April | 18–5–57–2 | 15–3–34–1 | 11–1–46–0 | 7–1–31–0 | 13–1–32–0 | | | | |
| *v.* Hampshire (Southampton) | 28–7–75–3 | 19.2–4–52–3 | 19–9–35–0 | 20–8–41–2 | | | | | 15–2–55–1 |
| 28–30 April | 15–1–43–1 | 24–6–49–4 | 14–3–47–1 | 10.4–1–35–3 | | | | | 4–0–11–0 |
| *v.* Kent (Canterbury) | 15–3–35–2 | 21–6–60–1 | | 22.1–6–53–7 | | | | | 7–0–24–0 |
| 2–4 May | 11–1–19–3 | 9–2–32–1 | | 16–4–55–2 | | | | | 6–0–17–1 |
| *v.* Northamptonshire | 9–1–39–1 | 21–4–79–6 | | 18.5–5–68–2 | 4–1–14–0 | | | | |
| (Northampton) 9–11 May | 17.5–5–43–4 | 12–2–42–3 | | 3–0–18–0 | 9–1–30–2 | | | | |
| *v.* Nottinghamshire | 21–4–69–1 | 27–5–86–4 | 11–4–16–0 | 17.2–3–56–3 | 20–10–27–2 | | | | |
| (Chelmsford) 23–25 May | 9–0–42–0 | 7–1–26–0 | | 7–2–18–0 | | | | | |
| *v.* Surrey (Chelmsford) | 20–9–48–2 | 15–1–46–2 | | 19–7–45–2 | 14–4–35–2 | 10–3–23–0 | 5–1–13–0 | | |
| 26–29 May | | | | | | | | | |
| *v.* Worcestershire (Worcester) | 23–6–78–1 | | 26–9–58–6 | | 21–13–21–2 | 4–1–7–0 | | | 14–4–47–1 |
| 30 May–1 June | | | | | | | | | |
| *v.* Leicestershire (Hinckley) | 26–5–76–1 | | 17–3–26–0 | | 21–6–44–2 | 10–3–19–2 | | | 23.1–8–48–5 |
| 2–5 June | | | | | | | | | |
| *v.* Warwickshire (Ilford) | 30–6–89–5 | 23–5–66–2 | 26–7–68–0 | 21–6–72–1 | | 9.1–3–23–1 | | | |
| 9–12 June | 17–3–46–4 | 6–1–17–0 | 17–4–30–2 | 6.1–1–13–4 | | | | | |
| *v.* Derbyshire (Ilford) | 24–5–99–3 | | 17–8–36–2 | | 14–4–34–1 | 6–1–14–0 | | | 14.5–2–60–4 |
| 13–15 June | 18–3–62–3 | | 12.3–4–32–1 | | 22–4–51–0 | 9–0–54–4 | | | 17–3–65–2 |
| *v.* Northamptonshire | 23.2–5–72–5 | 14–2–42–1 | | | | 16–6–35–3 | | | 5–0–38–1 |
| (Chelmsford) 16–19 June | 31–5–92–1 | 20–5–73–1 | | | | 30–8–50–3 | | | 10–1–22–1 |
| *v.* West Indians | | 18–5–46–4 | | 17–0–75–0 | | 22–5–62–0 | | | 13–1–43–0 |
| (Chelmsford) 23–25 June | | 16–2–91–2 | | 18–3–73–2 | | | | | 12–2–33–2 |
| *v.* Derbyshire (Chesterfield) | | | 16–3–44–1 | | 15–4–29–3 | 6–1–11–2 | | | 21–6–65–1 |
| 27–29 June | | | 23–4–63–2 | | 23–9–43–1 | 29–5–86–2 | | | 29–2–89–2 |
| *v.* Yorkshire (Leeds) | 24.4–6–69–5 | | 1–0–1–1 | | 11–5–17–1 | 6–1–19–0 | | | 20–5–68–3 |
| 30 June–3 July | 26–6–72–3 | | 19–5–44–3 | | 6–2–17–0 | | | | 14.2–2–47–4 |
| *v.* Glamorgan (Southend) | 29–4–102–3 | 35–9–107–2 | 3–1–12–0 | 23–4–60–1 | | | | | 12–5–30–1 |
| 7–10 July | | | | | | | | | |
| *v.* Lancashire (Southend) | 13–5–26–6 | 16.1–8–30–4 | 2–1–4–0 | | | | | | 2–0–11–0 |
| 11–13 July | 16.2–4–55–4 | 14–2–34–2 | 17–7–36–3 | | | 7–2–21–1 | | | 7–1–42–0 |
| *v.* Gloucestershire (Bristol) | 26–6–72–2 | 23–2–76–1 | 38–11–98–2 | | 14–2–43–0 | 7–2–26–1 | | | |
| 14–17 July | 23.3–7–37–8 | 22–7–47–2 | 4–2–2–0 | | 1–1–0–0 | | | | |
| *v.* Worcestershire | 21–6–81–2 | 14–2–50–3 | 17.5–5–41–1 | | | | | | 11–2–32–3 |
| (Chelmsford) 28–31 July | 11–1–28–1 | 17.1–1–57–5 | 18–5–63–3 | | | | | | 3–0–14–0 |
| *v.* Sussex (Eastbourne) | 23–5–42–0 | 24–5–80–3 | 21.4–6–44–6 | 20–4–40–0 | | 17–3–44–1 | | | |
| 4–7 August | 18–4–45–3 | 6–0–32–0 | 14–3–25–0 | 11.4–6–16–4 | | | | | |
| *v.* Middlesex (Lord's) | 24–4–87–0 | | 25–4–87–0 | 24.4–8–66–6 | 19–7–50–0 | 11–6–16–2 | | | |
| 8–10 August | 21–9–57–2 | | 4–1–9–0 | 24–6–79–3 | 12–4–26–2 | 23–3–57–3 | | | |
| *v.* Somerset (Chelmsford) | 31–14–54–5 | 18.1–4–49–2 | | 16–4–48–1 | | 4–2–5–1 | | | |
| 11–14 August | 20.1–4–62–5 | 19–7–49–1 | 10–3–20–1 | 17–7–31–1 | | 10–1–26–1 | | | |
| *v.* Hampshire (Colchester) | 20.1–2–84–5 | 17–7–40–4 | | 14–3–48–0 | | 4–2–9–1 | | | |
| 18–21 August | 16–4–54–1 | 19.5–4–61–5 | 17–2–57–0 | 24–6–88–3 | | 13–4–33–1 | | | |
| *v.* Kent (Colchester) | | 17–2–51–3 | 2–0–6–1 | 17–2–48–1 | | 12–1–35–2 | | | 15–2–50–2 |
| 22–24 August | | 1.4–0–10–0 | 1–1–0–0 | | | | | | |
| *v.* Surrey (The Oval) | 15–3–59–1 | 22–4–62–2 | 35.2–9–79–2 | 12–1–57–1 | | 20–3–62–2 | | | |
| 25–28 August | 14–3–44–2 | 16–3–78–5 | 8.2–2–29–2 | 4–1–15–0 | | 3–1–9–0 | | | |
| *v.* Middlesex (Chelmsford) | 18–4–47–1 | 19–3–57–3 | 20–11–36–2 | 16.1–1–45–3 | | 9–2–22–1 | | | |
| 29–31 August | 23–5–43–1 | 12–6–24–0 | 27–10–44–1 | 8–2–41–0 | | | 5–0–13–0 | 5–0–20–0 | |
| *v.* Lancashire (Old Trafford) | 15–1–61–2 | 12.5–2–39–2 | 7–2–13–0 | 19–0–75–4 | | 10–3–33–1 | | | |
| 8–11 September | 14–1–81–4 | 7–3–24–1 | 10–0–51–0 | 9–2–22–1 | | 3–0–17–1 | | | |
| | 874.5–195–<br>2550–116<br>*av.* 21.98 | 669.1–149–<br>2016–87<br>*av.* 23.17 | 577.4–174–<br>1368–46<br>*av.* 29.73 | 508.4–117–<br>1527–59<br>*av.* 25.88 | 285–95–<br>617–21<br>*av.* 29.38 | 321.1–74–<br>850–38<br>*av.* 22.36 | 15–1–<br>48–0<br>— | 9–2–<br>28–0<br>— | 275.2–48–<br>911–34<br>*av.* 26.79 |

a R.J. Boyd-Moss, retired hurt, absent hurt
b M.R. Davis absent hurt
c A.R. Butcher absent ill
d D.E. East 3–0–11–0

| A.W. Lilley | R.E. East | P.J. Prichard | Byes | Leg-byes | Wides | No-balls | Total | Wkts |
|---|---|---|---|---|---|---|---|---|
| | | | 2 | 6 | | 1 | 222 | 10 |
| | | | 3 | 2 | | 1 | 118 | 4 |
| | | | 1 | 8 | | 2 | 235 | 6 |
| | | | 6 | 7 | | 2 | 215 | 3 |
| | | | | 4 | | 14 | 276 | 10 |
| | | | 1 | 1 | | 2 | 189 | 10 |
| | | | | 4 | | 7 | 183 | 10 |
| | | | | 3 | | 10 | 136 | 7 |
| | | | | 7 | | 3 | 210 | 9 |
| | | | 4 | 4 | 1 | 3 | 145 | 9a |
| | | | 8 | | | 2 | 264 | 10 |
| | | | | 1 | | | 87 | 0 |
| 5.2–2–11–2 | | | 5 | 5 | | 4 | 235 | 10 |
| | | | | 5 | | 6 | 222 | 10 |
| | | | 2 | 3 | | 8 | 226 | 10 |
| | | | 4 | 9 | 1 | 2 | 334 | 10 |
| | | | 2 | 9 | | 2 | 119 | 10 |
| | | | | 6 | 2 | 5 | 256 | 10 |
| | | | 1 | 7 | 1 | 3 | 276 | 10 |
| | 7–2–11–0 | | 1 | 5 | | | 204 | 10 |
| | 35–14–56–0 | | | 12 | 5 | 5 | 315 | 6 |
| | 26–6–80–1 | | | 1 | 2 | 13 | 322 | 5 |
| | 12–2–47–2 | | | 17 | 4 | 12 | 277 | 8 |
| | 27–12–31–3 | | | 4 | | 3 | 187 | 10 |
| | 37–10–75–2 | | 1 | 1 | 1 | | 364 | 9 |
| | | | | 5 | 1 | 3 | 183 | 10 |
| | | | 5 | 2 | | 1 | 188 | 10 |
| | | | 1 | 12 | 2 | 7 | 333 | 7 |
| | | | 4 | 1 | | | 76 | 10 |
| | | | 5 | 6 | | 1 | 200 | 10 |
| | | | 2 | 7 | 2 | 1 | 327 | 6 |
| | | | | 4 | | | 90 | 10 |
| | | | 4 | 7 | | 2 | 217 | 10 |
| | | | 5 | 2 | 3 | | 172 | 10 |
| | | | 1 | 6 | | 2 | 259 | 10 |
| | | | 2 | 10 | 1 | 2 | 133 | 8 |
| | | | 2 | 6 | | 15 | 329 | 9 |
| | | | | 5 | | 12 | 245 | 10 |
| | | | 4 | 14 | | 6 | 180 | 10 |
| | | | | 3 | 4 | 4 | 199 | 9b |
| | | | 4 | 2 | 1 | 1 | 189 | 10 |
| | | | | 10 | 1 | 8 | 312 | 10 |
| | | | | 3 | 1 | 7 | 201 | 10 |
| | | | | | | | 10 | 0 |
| | | | | 5 | 2 | 1 | 327 | 8 |
| | | | | 2 | 2 | | 179 | 9c |
| | | | 9 | 2 | 2 | 3 | 223 | 10 |
| | | 1–0–5–0 | 8 | 5 | 1 | 3 | 218 | 2d |
| | | | | 4 | | 4 | 229 | 10 |
| | 8.4–2–24–3 | | 8 | 2 | | | 229 | 10 |
| 5.2–2–11–2 *av.* 5.50 | 152.4–48–324–11 *av.* 29.45 | 1–0–5–0 — | | | | | | |

### *at Bristol*

**Somerset** 390 (M.D. Crowe 108, N.F.M. Popplewell 74, I.T. Botham 69, D.V. Lawrence 5 for 58)
**Gloucestershire** 234 (A.W. Stovold 88, P. Bainbridge 68, V.J. Marks 4 for 46) and 73 (I.T. Botham 4 for 43)

*Somerset won by an innings and 83 runs*
*Somerset 24 pts, Gloucestershire 6 pts*

### *at Leicester*

**Derbyshire** 431 (J.E. Morris 135, G. Miller 77, A. Hill 61) and 211 for 2 dec (K.J. Barnett 102 not out, W.P. Fowler 52 not out)
**Leicestershire** 305 for 2 dec (J.C. Balderstone 143 not out, T.J. Boon 123 not out) and 259 for 9 (J.J. Whitaker 117)

*Match drawn*
*Leicestershire 7 pts, Derbyshire 4 pts*

### *at Lord's*

**Middlesex** 272 for 9 dec (C.T. Radley 61, G.W. Johnson 4 for 75) and 190 for 1 dec (M.W. Gatting 100 not out, W.N. Slack 71 not out)
**Kent** *285 for 9 dec (M.R. Benson 127, L. Potter 61, J.E. Emburey 4 for 83)*

*Match drawn*
*Middlesex 5 pts, Kent 6 pts*

### *at Hove*

**Sussex** 436 for 9 dec (P.W.G. Parker 103, G.S. le Roux 68 not out, A.P. Wells 59, E.E. Hemmings 5 for 111) and 141 for 6 dec
**Nottinghamshire** 300 for 9 dec (D.W. Randall 65, P. Johnson 53, C.E. Waller 4 for 55) and 93 for 4

*Match drawn*
*Sussex 6 pts, Nottinghamshire 5 pts*

*Robin Dyer hit his maiden century at Cardiff for Warwickshire against Glamorgan. (Mike Powell)*

**Glamorgan C.C.C.**
First-Class Matches – Batting, 1984

| | v. Oxford University (Oxford) 25–27 April | | v. Middlesex (Lord's) 28 April–1 May | | v. Worcestershire (Worcester) 2–4 May | | v. Derbyshire (Derby) 9–11 May | | v. Gloucestershire (Cardiff) 23–25 May | | v. West Indians (Swansea) 26–28 May | | v. Surrey (The Oval) 30 May–1 June | | v. Worcestershire (Swansea) 2–5 June | |
|---|---|---|---|---|---|---|---|---|---|---|---|---|---|---|---|---|
| J.A. Hopkins | 2 | 56 | 19 | 34 | 16 | 1 | 6 | 2 | 116* | 25* | 0 | 7 | 128* | 65 | 59 | 28 |
| A.L. Jones | 56 | 32 | 4 | 24 | 24 | 20 | 10 | — | 129 | 26 | 50 | 3 | 18 | 40 | 17 | 5 |
| R.C. Ontong | 28 | 59* | 48 | 5 | 34 | 1 | | | 1* | 3* | 10 | 0 | 16 | 19 | | |
| Younis Ahmed | 158* | — | 3 | 6 | 17 | 4 | | | — | — | 33 | 16 | 17 | 47 | 1 | 28 |
| S.P. Henderson | 4 | 32* | 14 | 0 | 90 | 56 | 11 | 28 | — | — | 0 | 3 | 53 | 38 | 22 | 8 |
| D.A. Francis | 0 | — | | | | | 20 | 7 | | | | | | | | |
| J.F. Steele | 18 | — | 33 | 33 | 32 | 7 | 37* | 45* | — | — | 5 | 1 | 11* | 5 | 26 | 0 |
| T. Davies | 3 | — | 0 | 3 | 28 | 0 | 3 | 4* | — | — | 20 | 11 | — | 12 | 0 | 0* |
| J.G. Thomas | 1 | — | 7 | 27 | 23 | 8 | 0 | 27 | | | | | | | 27 | 6 |
| M.W.W. Selvey | 8 | — | 0 | 17 | 0* | 4 | 0 | — | — | — | 14* | 7 | — | 2* | | |
| S.R. Barwick | 16* | — | 0 | 12 | — | 2* | 25 | — | — | — | 2 | 10* | — | 3* | | |
| W.W. Davis | | | 22* | 41* | 10* | 8 | 0 | — | — | — | 7 | 0 | — | 2 | 0 | — |
| C.J.C. Rowe | | | | | | | 16 | 19 | | | | | | | 14 | 2 |
| M.R. Price | | | | | | | | | — | — | 1 | 7 | | | | |
| G.C. Holmes | | | | | | | | | | | | | — | 13 | 44 | 14 |
| R.C. Green | | | | | | | | | | | | | | | 3* | — |
| Javed Miandad | | | | | | | | | | | | | | | | |
| H. Morris | | | | | | | | | | | | | | | | |
| J. Derrick | | | | | | | | | | | | | | | | |
| Byes | 2 | 4 | 1 | 1 | 12 | 9 | | 1 | | 3 | | 9 | 4 | 4 | 9 | |
| Leg-byes | 3 | 10 | 7 | 5 | 8 | 13 | 6 | 4 | 2 | 4 | 12 | 7 | 3 | 9 | 4 | 2 |
| Wides | 2 | | 1 | 2 | | | | 2 | 1 | | 8 | | 8 | | 1 | |
| No-balls | | | 15 | 8 | 15 | 1 | 10 | 6 | 2 | | 13 | 7 | 2 | 2 | 3 | |
| Total | 301 | 193 | 174 | 218 | 309 | 134 | 144 | 145 | 251 | 61 | 175 | 88 | 260 | 261 | 230 | 93 |
| Wickets | 9 | 2 | 10 | 10 | 8 | 10 | 10 | 5 | 1 | 1 | 10 | 10 | 4 | 9 | 10 | 8 |
| Result | W | | L | | W | | D | | D | | L | | D | | D | |
| Points | — | | 3 | | 24 | | 4 | | 4 | | — | | 5 | | 4 | |

| | v. Nottinghamshire (Trent Bridge) 9–12 June | | v. Cambridge Univ. (Cambridge) 13–15 June | | v. Lancashire (Cardiff) 16–19 June | | v. Sussex (Hove) 23–26 June | | v. Middlesex (Swansea) 27–29 June | | v. Leicestershire (Swansea) 30 June–3 July | |
|---|---|---|---|---|---|---|---|---|---|---|---|---|
| J.A. Hopkins | 37 | 29 | | | 36 | 7 | 74 | 32 | 5 | 26 | 9 | 0 |
| A.L. Jones | 17 | 1 | 38 | 82 | 13 | 34 | 44 | 19 | 122 | 8 | 92 | 0 |
| R.C. Ontong | 43 | 0 | 41* | — | 25 | 11 | 2 | 70 | 27 | 204* | 14 | 29 |
| Younis Ahmed | 0 | 32 | 62 | — | 83 | 15 | 122 | 11 | 21 | 53 | 0 | 35 |
| S.P. Henderson | 17 | 3 | 108 | — | | | | | | | | |
| D.A. Francis | | | | | | | | | | | | |
| J.F. Steele | 4 | 8 | | | 2 | 6 | 24* | 47* | 28 | — | — | 4 |
| T. Davies | 4 | 7 | — | — | 1 | 9 | 4 | 31 | 32 | — | — | 24 |
| J.G. Thomas | | | — | — | 7 | 28* | | | | | — | 6 |
| M.W.W. Selvey | 1 | 0* | | | 11* | 0* | — | — | 3* | — | — | 11 |
| S.R. Barwick | 3* | 3 | — | — | 5 | — | — | 3* | 6 | — | — | 5* |
| W.W. Davis | 36 | 50 | | | | | 12* | 1 | 27 | — | | |
| C.J.C. Rowe | | | — | 60* | | | 0 | 16 | 0 | 9* | | |
| M.R. Price | | | | | | | | | | | | |
| G.C. Holmes | 1 | 43 | 33* | — | 49 | 0 | 5 | 0 | 25 | 28 | 84* | 15 |
| R.C. Green | | | — | — | | | | | | | | |
| Javed Miandad | | | 16 | 16* | 63 | 48 | | | | | 212* | 39 |
| H. Morris | | | | | | | | | | | | |
| J. Derrick | | | | | | | | | | | | |
| Byes | | 6 | 8 | 1 | 1 | 3 | | | 8 | | 4 | 6 |
| Leg-byes | 6 | 7 | 3 | 3 | 4 | 6 | 3 | 3 | 5 | 15 | 11 | 3 |
| Wides | | | 8 | 2 | 1 | 1 | 3 | 1 | | | | |
| No-balls | 1 | 2 | 1 | | 5 | 1 | 7 | 9 | 18 | 16 | 1 | 1 |
| Total | 170 | 191 | 318 | 164 | 306 | 169 | 300 | 243 | 327 | 359 | 427 | 178 |
| Wickets | 10 | 10 | 4 | 2 | 10 | 8 | 7 | 8 | 10 | 4 | 4 | 10 |
| Result | L | | W | | D | | D | | D | | D | |
| Points | 4 | | — | | 5 | | 5 | | 7 | | 8 | |

*Catches* 53–T. Davies (ct 43/st 10), 33–J.F. Steele, 30–A.L. Jones, 18–J.A. Hopkins, 15–R.C. Ontong, 13–Younis Ahmed, 10–G.C. Holmes, 9–J.G. Thomas and M.W.W. Selvey, 8–J. Derrick, 7–W.W. Davis, 6–S.R. Barwick, 4–S.P. Henderson and Javed Miandad

LEFT: *Dennis Amiss, Warwickshire. Hit his nineteenth century in first-class cricket at Cardiff. (A.S.P.)*

### *at Worcester*

**Northamptonshire** 342 for 9 dec (R.G. Williams 169, R.J. Boyd-Moss 63) and 240 for 3 dec (A.J. Lamb 133 not out, R.J. Boyd-Moss 51)
**Worcestershire** 282 (D.N. Patel 54, W. Larkins 5 for 59) and 304 for 6 (M.J. Weston 145 not out, D.M. Smith 71)

*Worcestershire won by 4 wickets*
*Worcestershire 22 pts, Northamptonshire 8 pts*

### *at Scarborough*

**Hampshire** 254 for 6 dec (M.C.J. Nicholas 70, R.A. Smith 62) and 155 for 2 dec (D.R. Turner 56 not out)
**Yorkshire** 108 for 1 dec and 252 for 9
*Match drawn*
*Hampshire 3 pts, Yorkshire 2 pts*

When the penultimate round of matches in the Britannic Assurance County Championship began, Essex, who had no game, led Nottinghamshire by one point. In reality, Nottinghamshire had to win only one of their two remaining games to take the title. They travelled to Hove first and Rice,

| v. Essex (Southend) 7–10 July | | v. Yorkshire (Cardiff) 11–13 July | | v. Somerset (Cardiff) 14–17 July | | v. Somerset (Taunton) 25–27 July | | v. Derbyshire (Swansea) 28–31 July | | v. Gloucestershire (Cheltenham) 8–10 August | | v. Hampshire (Cardiff) 11–14 August | | v. Northamptonshire (Swansea) 18–21 August | | v. Warwickshire (Edgbaston) 22–24 August | | v. Yorkshire (Bradford) 25–28 August | | v. Surrey (Swansea) 29–31 August | | v. Warwickshire (Cardiff) 5–7 September | | v. Kent (Canterbury) 8–11 September | | M | Inns | NOs | Runs | H/S | Av |
|---|---|---|---|---|---|---|---|---|---|---|---|---|---|---|---|---|---|---|---|---|---|---|---|---|---|---|---|---|---|---|---|
| 6 | — | 2 | 43* | 3 | 19 | 28 | 86* | 3 | 30 | 18 | 52 | 0 | 0 | 41 | 38 | 50 | 30 | 73 | 8 | 3 | — | 98 | 21 | 13 | 16 | 26 | 50 | 5 | 1500 | 128* | 33.33 |
| 14 | — | 34 | 43* | 11 | 85 | 100 | 41* | 35 | 16 | 5 | 15 | 8 | 132 | 14 | 2 | 9 | 27 | 2 | 11 | 53 | — | 38 | 10 | 11 | 67 | 27 | 51 | 2 | 1811 | 132 | 36.95 |
| 26 | — | 70 | — | 97* | 72* | 18 | — | 9 | 11 | 10 | 25 | 42 | 54 | 69 | 2 | 12 | 6 | 46 | 0 | 23* | — | 9 | 13 | 6 | 10 | 25 | 45 | 8 | 1320 | 204* | 35.67 |
| 44 | — | 6 | — | | | | | | | | | | | 59 | 25* | 90 | 68* | 25 | 37 | 62 | — | 56* | 80 | 44 | 9 | 21 | 35 | 4 | 1369 | 158* | 44.16 |
| | | | | | | | | | | | | | | | | | | | | | | | | | | 10 | 17 | 1 | 487 | 108 | 30.43 |
| | | | | | | | | | | | | | | | | | | | | | | | | | | 2 | 3 | — | 27 | 20 | 9.00 |
| 32* | — | 46 | — | 15 | 16 | 16 | — | 0 | 17 | 38 | 34 | 22 | 29 | 11* | — | 46 | 7* | 25 | 16* | | | 10 | 4* | 60* | 0* | 26 | 41 | 12 | 820 | 60* | 28.27 |
| 14 | — | 25 | — | 0 | 11 | 31* | — | 43 | 21* | 13 | — | 6 | 1* | — | — | 6 | — | 9* | 15 | — | — | — | — | 6 | 1* | 27 | 35 | 7 | 398 | 43 | 14.21 |
| | | 0 | — | 17 | 0 | — | — | 13* | 11 | 2 | — | 4 | — | — | — | 12 | — | 15 | 15* | — | — | 1* | 36* | 11 | 10 | 20 | 26 | 5 | 314 | 36* | 14.95 |
| — | — | 20 | — | 8 | 5* | | | | | | | | | | | | | | | | | | | | | 15 | 18 | 8 | 111 | 20 | 11.10 |
| — | — | 3* | — | 3 | — | — | — | 4 | — | 0 | — | 0* | — | | | | | | | | | | | | | 20 | 19 | 9 | 105 | 25 | 10.50 |
| 29* | — | | | | | | | | | | | | | — | — | 8* | — | 22 | 2 | — | — | — | — | 0 | 1 | 17 | 20 | 6 | 278 | 50 | 19.85 |
| | | | | | | | | 9 | 10 | | | | | | | | | | | | | | | | | 6 | 11 | 2 | 155 | 60* | 17.22 |
| | | | | | | | | | | | | | | | | | | | | — | — | | | | | 3 | 2 | — | 8 | 7 | 4.00 |
| 45 | — | 14 | — | 1 | 34 | 16 | 90 | 1 | 34 | 11 | 64 | 19 | 0 | 33 | 19 | 60 | 49 | 0 | 7 | 19 | — | 67 | 11 | 34 | 57 | 21 | 37 | 2 | 1039 | 90 | 29.68 |
| | | | | | | | | | | | | | | | | | | | | | | | | | | 2 | 1 | 1 | 3 | 3* | — |
| | | | | 24 | 0 | 83 | — | 64 | 49 | 15 | 11 | 21 | 171 | | | | | | | | | | | | | 8 | 15 | 2 | 832 | 212* | 64.00 |
| 1 | — | 114** | — | 6 | 7 | 3 | — | | | 81 | 19* | 0 | 8 | 60 | 1* | 0 | 16 | 48 | 58 | 23 | — | 1* | 29 | 50 | 17 | 12 | 20 | 4 | 542 | 114* | 33.87 |
| | | | | | | 33* | — | 32 | 57* | 40* | 1* | 4 | 20* | 0* | — | 7 | — | 15 | 11 | 69* | — | 0 | — | 53 | 9 | 10 | 15 | 7 | 351 | 69* | 43.87 |
| 1 | | 2 | 1 | 9 | 10 | 3 | 8 | | 8 | 9 | 12 | | | 2 | 1 | 10 | 5 | 5 | 2 | 4 | | 2 | 12 | | 5 | | | | | | |
| 12 | | 7 | 4 | 11 | 11 | 11 | 5 | 3 | 6 | 12 | 7 | 9 | 1 | 9 | 1 | 3 | 8 | 6 | 6 | 9 | | 17 | 7 | 6 | 4 | | | | | | |
| 2 | | 1 | 1 | 2 | | 1 | | | | 2 | 1 | | | 1 | | 1 | 1 | | 1 | | | 5 | | 1 | | | | | | | |
| 7 | | 13 | | 4 | 2 | 10 | 1 | 8 | 1 | 2 | 2 | 7 | 9 | 15 | 1 | 12 | 1 | 15 | 12 | 1 | | 9 | 7 | 1 | 3 | | | | | | |
| 333 | | 357 | 92 | 211 | 272 | 353 | 231 | 224 | 271 | 258 | 243 | 142 | 425 | 314 | 90 | 326 | 218 | 306 | 201 | 266 | | 313 | 230 | 296 | 209 | | | | | | |
| 7 | | 9 | 0 | 10 | 8 | 7 | 1 | 10 | 8 | 10 | 6 | 10 | 7 | 6 | 4 | 10 | 5 | 10 | 9† | 5 | | 6 | 6 | 10 | 9 | | | | | | |
| D | | D | | W | | D | | D | | D | | D | | W | | W | | D | | D | | D | | D | | | | | | | |
| 8 | | 7 | | 22 | | 7 | | 5 | | 5 | | 2 | | 23 | | 24 | | 7 | | 3 | | 7 | | 7 | | | | | | | |

2–C.J.C. Rowe, H. Morris and D.A. Francis

1–R.C. Green and sub

† J.F. Steele retired hurt

on winning the toss, asked Sussex to bat. It was a decision he must have regretted for the home side, with Parker hitting his fifth century in as many weeks, batted into the second day and Notts, having taken only one bowling point, did not reach their 300 until the last morning. There was a flurry of activity then, but the target of 278 in 35 overs in gathering gloom was too much for Notts who settled for a draw and so took a four-point lead over Essex into the final match of the season.

Hampshire and Yorkshire tried to outwit bad weather at Scarborough, but Hampshire were thwarted by Yorkshire's last pair, Sidebottom and Oldham, who survived the last eleven overs, and by their own poor catching. Glamorgan gave up the chase at Cardiff after losing five wickets, but the abiding memory of the match came from Warwickshire. Kallicharran established a new county record with his ninth hundred of the season, three figures being reached before lunch on the first day; Humpage continued his glorious season; Amiss hit his ninetieth century in first-class cricket and shared a third wicket stand of 227 with Robin Dyer, a young man of charm and determination, who hit his maiden century.

Career best bowling by Wayne Larkins and what was, for twenty minutes, the fastest century of the season, by Allan Lamb, gave Northants hope of victory at Worcester, but the home side reached the target of 301 in 63 overs, thanks mainly to a splendid innings from Weston whose second wicket partnership of 149 with Smith was the basis of the victory. Mike Gatting recaptured the fastest century of the season twenty minutes after losing it to Lamb, but the match at Lord's ended on a note of farce after Benson's earlier accomplished hundred. Edmonds did not play in this game, having been suspended by his county for disciplinary reasons.

Poor Gloucestershire seemed doomed for the wooden spoon after being beaten in two days by Somerset. David Lawrence showed his continued improvement as a medium pace bowler, but the home side had little else to cheer them as Crowe reached a good hundred and they subsided from 178 for 3 to 234 all out and, following-on, subsided limply for 73.

Boon and Balderstone were again Leicestershire's heroes. Following their 242 stand against Gloucestershire, they added 259 in 226 minutes for the third wicket against Derbyshire. Centuries from Barnett, who should be an England player, and Morris, who looks likely to be one, enabled Derbyshire to set the home side 338 in 79 overs. They were 51 for 4 and were saved by Whitaker, another young batsman of immense promise.

| Glamorgan C.C.C.<br>First-Class Matches –<br>Bowling, 1984 | J.G. Thomas | S.R. Barwick | M.W.W. Selvey | J.F. Steele | R.C. Ontong | W.W. Davis | C.J.C. Rowe | M.R. Price | G.C. Holmes |
|---|---|---|---|---|---|---|---|---|---|
| *v.* Oxford University (Oxford) 24–26 April | 16–4–49–0<br>15–3–48–0 | 20–8–26–2<br>22–9–38–7 | 16.5–6–31–6 | 11–2–25–1<br>6.3–4–9–2 | 14–6–21–1<br>20–2–23–1 | | | | |
| *v.* Middlesex (Lord's) 28 April–1 May | 8–0–51–0<br>1.3–0–10–0 | 16–2–66–1 | 30–12–67–2 | 13–0–67–0 | 17–0–57–1 | 24–3–56–3<br>2–0–4–0 | | | |
| *v.* Worcestershire (Worcester) 2–4 May | 12–1–55–2<br>6–2–17–0 | 13–6–31–1<br>21.2–5–55–7 | 19–8–41–3<br>4–0–14–0 | 2–2–0–0 | 1–0–8–0<br>3–0–21–0 | 19.2–4–59–4<br>21–6–46–3 | | | |
| *v.* Derbyshire (Derby) 9–11 May | 14–4–62–1 | 12–2–37–0 | 5–1–18–0 | 30–8–101–5 | | 22–4–63–4 | 8–0–63–0 | | |
| *v.* Gloucestershire (Cardiff) 23–25 May | | 21–6–54–0<br>16–6–31–0 | 18–5–39–0<br>5–0–22–0 | 20–6–34–1<br>15–6–23–1 | 16–0–52–0<br>21–9–46–1 | 19–5–36–2<br>15–2–53–2 | | 14–1–53–1<br>15–3–43–1 | |
| *v.* West Indians (Swansea) 26–28 May | | 27.1–5–135–4 | 14–1–53–0 | 23–5–53–0 | 39–6–126–2 | 23–3–83–0 | | 2–0–13–0 | |
| *v.* Surrey (The Oval) 30 May–1 June | | 14–3–49–1<br>10–1–26–2 | 13–3–42–0<br>14–1–62–0 | 20–4–62–0<br>5–1–17–0 | 16.5–1–61–2 | 24–10–55–1<br>18–4–56–0 | | | 11–3–26–1<br>15–1–51–1 |
| *v.* Worcestershire (Swansea) 2–5 June | 27–4–138–2 | | | 29–7–91–1 | | 24–3–73–0 | 23–4–80–1 | | 1–0–4–0 |
| *v.* Nottinghamshire (Trent Bridge) 9–12 June | | 8–2–28–0 | 21–4–47–1 | 45–13–100–4<br>1.5–0–10–0 | 29–7–65–1<br>1–0–6–0 | 26–6–92–2 | | | |
| *v.* Cambridge University (Cambridge) 13–15 June | 11–5–23–4<br>9.5–6–14–2 | 10–6–7–3<br>7–2–18–0 | | | 6–5–3–2<br>30–16–41–3 | | 21–10–30–1<br>31–21–20–3 | | 3–1–3–0 |
| *v.* Lancashire (Cardiff) 16–19 June | 15–4–47–1<br>2–0–12–0 | 16–8–30–1 | 14–0–54–0<br>7–2–24–0 | 30–6–76–3<br>29–10–106–1 | 23–7–65–3<br>33.5–14–80–5 | | | | |
| *v.* Sussex (Hove) 23–26 June | | 19–5–59–2<br>7–0–26–0 | 17–6–53–0<br>9–0–44–1 | 2–0–17–0<br>3–0–17–0 | 10–0–61–0<br>14–1–60–4 | 21.4–5–68–5<br>13–1–63–3 | | | 2–0–11–0 |
| *v.* Middlesex (Swansea) 27–29 June | | 25.2–6–78–4 | 24–3–107–3 | 6–2–13–0 | 18–3–57–0 | 29–8–107–1 | 12–0–43–1 | | |
| *v.* Leicestershire (Swansea) 30 June–3 July | 11–0–58–1 | 11–2–46–1<br>6–0–23–0 | 2–0–17–0 | 30–8–114–2<br>21–4–68–5 | 41–12–113–3<br>26.3–2–77–2 | | | | |
| *v.* Essex (Southend) 7–10 July | | 13–2–29–1<br>20–8–41–2 | 14.4–5–40–4<br>17–4–62–2 | | 14–2–38–0 | 15–2–57–5<br>16–2–82–1 | | | |
| *v.* Yorkshire (Cardiff) 11–13 July | 26–1–120–2<br>7–2–17–1 | 20–5–62–2<br>7–1–18–0 | 20–1–61–0<br>6–1–18–0 | 7.4–0–36–1<br>5–0–9–0 | 29–5–101–4<br>10–2–38–0 | | | | 5–1–21–0<br>6–0–26–1 |
| *v.* Somerset (Cardiff) 14–17 July | 19–6–56–5<br>23–5–67–5 | 14–2–36–1<br>11.5–2–43–2 | 15–4–53–2<br>6–2–28–1 | 3–0–10–1<br>20–8–39–0 | 7.4–2–12–1<br>41–11–104–2 | | | | |
| *v.* Somerset (Taunton) 25–27 July | 20–6–73–3<br>13–2–42–1 | 19–5–45–2<br>9–4–17–1 | | 24–6–58–2<br>11–5–16–2 | 15–4–36–0<br>9–5–17–0 | | | | |
| *v.* Derbyshire (Swansea) 28–31 July | 20–3–60–2<br>8–1–47–2 | 12–0–47–0<br>8–4–11–1 | | 23.1–8–40–2<br>16–0–75–3 | 17–4–42–0 | | 24–2–75–3<br>16–4–45–3 | | |
| *v.* Gloucestershire (Cheltenham) 8–10 August | 17–5–47–0<br>4.5–0–28–0 | 15–6–36–1<br>4–1–11–0 | | 21.5–4–47–4<br>13–0–72–2 | 25–5–52–2<br>20–3–56–4 | | | | |
| *v.* Hampshire (Cardiff) 11–14 August | 26–6–49–4 | 23–4–55–1 | | 16–6–48–0 | 33.3–10–70–2 | | | | |
| *v.* Northamptonshire (Swansea) 18–21 August | 8–4–18–2<br>5–1–14–0 | | | 24–9–27–4<br>38.5–8–92–4 | 30.4–10–64–3<br>38–16–73–5 | 11–1–41–1<br>9–3–29–0 | | | |
| *v.* Warwickshire (Edgbaston) 22–24 August | 10.1–0–45–0 | | | 24–10–32–3<br>21–10–42–5 | 9.2–4–19–2<br>32.2–15–47–2 | 23–8–43–4<br>27–7–72–3 | | | |
| *v.* Yorkshire (Bradford) 25–28 August | 14–5–38–0<br>2–1–4–0 | | | 31.1–6–91–3 | 41–13–96–7 | 11–3–41–0<br>2–2–0–0 | | | 6–1–21–0 |
| *v.* Surrey (Swansea) 29–31 August | 5–2–13–0 | | | | | 5–4–2–0 | | | |
| *v.* Warwickshire (Cardiff) 5–7 September | 12–2–59–1<br>15–3–52–1 | | | 16–3–73–1 | 24–2–84–2<br>2–1–1–0 | 17.5–1–79–1<br>12–2–35–1 | | | 15–2–55–0<br>9–0–38–0 |
| *v.* Kent (Canterbury) 8–11 September | 15–5–50–2<br>17–2–92–3 | | | 4–2–4–0<br>12–2–53–5 | 27–10–52–6<br>32–6–110–1 | 19–4–64–2<br>12–1–67–0 | | | |
| | 435.2–95–<br>1575–47<br>*av.* 33.51 | 477.4–128–<br>1314–50<br>*av.* 26.28 | 311.3–69–<br>997–25<br>*av.* 39.88 | 674–175–<br>1867–68<br>*av.* 27.45 | 837.4–221–<br>2155–74<br>*av.* 29.12 | 480.5–104–<br>1526–48<br>*av.* 31.79 | 135–41–<br>356–12<br>*av.* 29.66 | 31–4–<br>109–2<br>*av.* 54.50 | 73–9–<br>256–3<br>*av.* 85.33 |

a A.L. Jones 7–0–60–1; H. Morris 9–1–45–1; Younis Ahmed 6–3–12–0
b Younis Ahmed 6–0–22–0; J.A. Hopkins 2.2–0–18–0; A.L. Jones 3–0–26–0

| R.C. Green | Javed Miandad | J. Derrick | Byes | Leg-byes | Wides | No-balls | Total | Wkts |
|---|---|---|---|---|---|---|---|---|
| | | | | 8 | 3 | | 163 | 10 |
| | | | 4 | 1 | | 3 | 126 | 10 |
| | | | 1 | 3 | 2 | 3 | 373 | 7 |
| | | | 4 | 2 | | | 20 | 0 |
| | | | 4 | 8 | 1 | 2 | 209 | 10 |
| | | | 3 | 7 | | 5 | 168 | 10 |
| | | | 4 | 4 | 3 | 9 | 364 | 10 |
| | | | | 9 | 1 | 8 | 286 | 4 |
| | | | 1 | 2 | | 8 | 229 | 5 |
| | | | | 12 | 4 | 10 | 489 | 6 |
| | | | | 4 | 1 | | 300 | 5 |
| | | | 1 | 8 | 1 | | 222 | 3 |
| 14.5–3–65–2 | | | 1 | 11 | 1 | 2 | 466 | 6 |
| | | | | 8 | | 9 | 349 | 8 |
| | | | | | | | 16 | 0 |
| 12–3–22–0 | 7–3–14–0 | | 4 | 3 | 5 | 8 | 119 | 10 |
| 5–3–5–0 | 13–4–27–2 | | 7 | 11 | | 9 | 155 | 10 |
| | 8–0–43–0 | | 4 | 8 | 1 | 9 | 337 | 8 |
| | | | 11 | 7 | | 11 | 251 | 6 |
| | | | 4 | 7 | 3 | 17 | 300 | 7 |
| | | | 3 | 9 | | 5 | 227 | 9 |
| | | | 4 | 10 | | 19 | 438 | 9 |
| | 4–1–26–2 | | 7 | 2 | 1 | 5 | 389 | 10 |
| | 0.2–0–0–0 | | | 4 | 1 | 2 | 175 | 8 |
| | | | | 2 | 2 | 1 | 141 | 10 |
| | | | 2 | 4 | | 12 | 241 | 5 |
| | | | 4 | 2 | 2 | 6 | 415 | 9 |
| | | | 12 | 1 | 2 | 4 | 262 | 4a |
| | | | 2 | 10 | 1 | 7 | 187 | 10 |
| | | | 4 | 4 | | 6 | 295 | 10 |
| | | 23–3–81–1 | | 9 | 4 | 2 | 308 | 8 |
| | | 5–3–12–0 | | 5 | 1 | 2 | 112 | 4 |
| | | 19–5–42–3 | 8 | 9 | 5 | 4 | 332 | 10 |
| | | | 4 | 5 | | 1 | 188 | 9 |
| | 9–1–31–0 | 11–3–25–0 | 2 | 6 | 1 | 5 | 252 | 8 |
| | | 6–2–25–1 | 5 | 10 | | | 207 | 8 |
| | 10–0–46–2 | 18–3–51–1 | 2 | 4 | 1 | 2 | 328 | 10 |
| | | | | 2 | | 9 | 161 | 10 |
| | | 4–0–13–0 | 4 | 12 | | 5 | 242 | 10 |
| | | 10.5–4–39–1 | | 6 | | 10 | 194 | 10 |
| | | 4–0–14–0 | | 6 | | 1 | 182 | 10 |
| | | | | 11 | 4 | 2 | 283 | 10 |
| | | 7–3–16–0 | | | | | 41 | 0 |
| | | | | 1 | | 1 | 17 | 0 |
| | | 15–3–69–1 | 3 | 4 | 1 | 11 | 438 | 7 |
| | | 9–2–39–0 | 1 | 2 | | 8 | 242 | 2b |
| | | | 8 | 7 | 2 | 8 | 195 | 10 |
| | | 2–0–15–0 | | 9 | | 4 | 350 | 9 |
| 31.5–9–92–0 — | 51.2–9–187–6 av. 31.16 | 133.5–31–441–8 av. 55.12 | | | | | | |

*Paul Parker hit his fifth hundred in five weeks and thwarted Notts in their title bid, Sussex v. Notts, 5–7 September. (George Herringshaw)*

**Gloucestershire C.C.C.**
First-Class Matches – Batting, 1984

| | v. Kent (Bristol) 28–30 April | | v. Hampshire (Southampton) 9–11 May | | v. Glamorgan (Cardiff) 23–25 May | | v. Somerset (Taunton) 26–29 May | | v. Oxford University (Oxford) 30 May–1 June | | v. Kent (Canterbury) 2–5 June | | v. Derbyshire (Gloucester) 9–12 June | |
|---|---|---|---|---|---|---|---|---|---|---|---|---|---|---|
| A.W. Stovold | 19 | 57 | 18 | 45 | 3 | 90 | 12 | 4 | | | 0 | 0 | 3 | 97 |
| P.W. Romaines | 24 | 52 | 38 | 90 | 141 | 7 | 13 | 5 | 56 | 40 | 73 | 13 | 103 | 66 |
| C.W.J. Athey | 22 | 36 | 4 | 69 | 45 | 12 | 1 | 6 | 26 | 14 | 9 | 38 | 70 | 14 |
| Zaheer Abbas | 10 | 157* | 27 | 67* | 10 | 11 | 0 | 23 | | | 10 | 2 | 20 | 44 |
| P. Bainbridge | 2 | 13 | | | 67* | 31 | 9 | 2 | 4 | 117* | 6 | 47 | 9 | 64* |
| J.N. Shepherd | 47 | — | 0 | — | — | — | 40* | 0 | | | 3 | 8* | 10 | — |
| R.C. Russell | 25 | 13* | 63 | — | — | — | — | 4 | | | 3 | — | 15 | — |
| D.A. Graveney | 4 | — | 4 | — | — | 16* | 14* | 14 | 5 | — | 3 | 4* | 5 | — |
| A.J. Wright | 37 | — | 74 | 6* | 2* | 51* | 10 | 6 | 49 | 80 | 3 | 0 | 70 | — |
| D.V. Lawrence | 4 | — | 3 | — | | | — | 6* | 5 | — | 8 | — | | |
| G.E. Sainsbury | 3* | — | 10* | — | — | — | — | 0 | 0* | — | 0* | — | 0* | — |
| C. Dale | | | 26 | — | — | — | | | 2 | — | | | | |
| R.J. Doughty | | | | | | | | | 4 | — | | | | |
| A.J. Brassington | | | | | | | | | 0 | — | | | | |
| J.H. Childs | | | | | | | | | 2 | — | | | 1 | — |
| E.J. Cunningham | | | | | | | | | | | | | | |
| C.R. Trembath | | | | | | | | | | | | | | |
| D.A. Burrows | | | | | | | | | | | | | | |
| S.H. Wootton | | | | | | | | | | | | | | |
| L.H. Rolls | | | | | | | | | | | | | | |
| C.A. Walsh | | | | | | | | | | | | | | |
| P.G.P. Roebuck | | | | | | | | | | | | | | |
| Byes | 1 | 4 | 6 | | | 1 | | 1 | 8 | 1 | | | | 1 |
| Leg-byes | 3 | 1 | 10 | 9 | 9 | 2 | 4 | 1 | 1 | 3 | 2 | 1 | 6 | |
| Wides | | | 5 | | 1 | | | | | | 1 | | | 1 |
| No-balls | 3 | 1 | 2 | 2 | 8 | 8 | | | | | 9 | 3 | 1 | |
| Total | 204 | 334 | 290 | 288 | 286 | 229 | 103 | 72 | 162 | 255 | 130 | 116 | 313 | 287 |
| Wickets | 10 | 4 | 10 | 3 | 4 | 5 | 6 | 10 | 10 | 3 | 10 | 6 | 10 | 4 |
| Result | D | | D | | D | | L | | D | | W | | D | |
| Points | 4 | | 3 | | 3 | | 3 | | — | | 20 | | 5 | |

| | v. Worcestershire (Gloucester) 13–15 June | | v. Nottinghamshire (Trent Bridge) 16–19 June | | v. Hampshire (Bristol) 23–26 June | | v. Lancashire (Old Trafford) 27–29 June | | v. Warwickshire (Edgbaston) 30 June–3 July | | v. Yorkshire (Bradford) 7–10 July | | v. Middlesex (Uxbridge) 11–13 July | |
|---|---|---|---|---|---|---|---|---|---|---|---|---|---|---|
| A.W. Stovold | 126 | 9 | 0 | 7 | 35 | 67 | 73 | 0 | 30 | 5 | 54 | 4 | 4 | 30 |
| P.W. Romaines | 31 | 71 | 1 | 2 | 63 | 14 | 39 | 32 | 3 | 0 | 120 | 3 | 26 | 7 |
| C.W.J. Athey | 62 | 4 | 15 | 18 | 5 | 51 | 27 | 80 | 1 | 77* | 52 | 114* | 24 | 26 |
| Zaheer Abbas | 76* | 64* | 8 | 4 | 45 | 14 | 4 | 1 | 68 | 9 | | | 0 | 35 |
| P. Bainbridge | 22* | 8* | 34 | 8 | 58* | 1 | 10 | 21 | 8 | 5 | 21 | 16 | 6 | 30 |
| J.N. Shepherd | — | — | 3 | 47 | 32 | 18 | 2 | 6* | 25 | 9 | 76* | — | 87 | 56 |
| R.C. Russell | — | — | 15* | 9 | — | 12 | 1 | — | | | — | — | 28* | — |
| D.A. Graveney | — | — | 10 | 33 | 28* | 24* | 20 | 5* | 25 | 10 | — | — | 28 | 15 |
| A.J. Wright | — | — | 0 | 24 | | | | | 27 | 28 | 15 | 10 | 10 | 7 |
| D.V. Lawrence | | | 17 | 3 | — | 4* | 8 | — | 15 | 0 | — | — | | |
| G.E. Sainsbury | — | — | 2 | 1* | — | — | 0* | — | 9* | 0 | | | | |
| C. Dale | | | | | | | 1 | — | | | — | 49 | 0 | — |
| R.J. Doughty | | | | | | | | | | | | | | |
| A.J. Brassington | | | | | | | | | | 0* | | | | |
| J.H. Childs | — | — | | | — | 1 | | | | | | | | |
| E.J. Cunningham | | | | | | | | | | | 17* | 20* | | |
| C.R. Trembath | | | | | | | | | | | | | 17* | 0* |
| D.A. Burrows | | | | | | | | | | | | | | |
| S.H. Wootton | | | | | | | | | | | | | | |
| L.H. Rolls | | | | | | | | | | | | | | |
| C.A. Walsh | | | | | | | | | | | | | | |
| P.G.P. Roebuck | | | | | | | | | | | | | | |
| Byes | | | | | 13 | 3 | | 4 | 4 | 2 | 5 | 4 | 4 | 5 |
| Leg-byes | 8 | 6 | 7 | 2 | 13 | | 1 | 1 | 10 | 10 | 13 | 4 | 1 | 8 |
| Wides | 2 | | | 1 | 3 | 2 | | | 1 | | 1 | | | |
| No-balls | 1 | | 1 | 1 | 5 | 4 | 4 | | 9 | 8 | 7 | 2 | 16 | 3 |
| Total | 328 | 162 | 113 | 160 | 300 | 215 | 190 | 150 | 257 | 163 | 381 | 226 | 251 | 222 |
| Wickets | 3 | 3 | 10 | 10 | 5 | 8 | 10 | 5 | 10 | 9† | 5 | 5 | 9 | 7 |
| Result | D | | L | | D | | D | | L | | L | | D | |
| Points | 6 | | 2 | | 5 | | 5 | | 7 | | 5 | | 7 | |

*Catches*
36 – R.C. Russell (ct 29/st 7)
26 – C.W.J. Athey
20 – A.W. Stovold (ct 18/st 2)
17 – D.A. Graveney
13 – J.N. Shepherd
12 – P.W. Romaines
11 – A.J. Wright
9 – P. Bainbridge
8 – G.E. Sainsbury
4 – S.H. Wootton
3 – A.J. Brassington (ct 2/st 1)

## John Player League

### *9 September*

***at Derby***

**Derbyshire** 116 for 4
**Hampshire** 89 for 4
*Hampshire (4 pts) won on faster scoring rate*

***at Bristol***

**Middlesex** 165 for 7
**Gloucestershire** 152 for 6
*Gloucestershire (4 pts) won on faster scoring rate*

***at Canterbury***

**Glamorgan** 173 for 9 (S.P. Henderson 63, G.C. Holmes 53)
**Kent** 156
*Glamorgan (4 pts) won by 17 runs*

***at Old Trafford***

**Essex** 75 (J. Simmons 4 for 19)
**Lancashire** 79 for 1 (G. Fowler 50)
*Lancashire (4 pts) won by 9 wickets*

***at Taunton***

**Somerset** 181 for 6 (M.D. Crowe 52)
**Nottinghamshire** 102 for 3
*Nottinghamshire (4 pts) won on faster scoring rate*

***at The Oval***

**Surrey** 166 for 9 (D.M. Ward 59 not out)
**Worcestershire** 101 for 2
*Worcestershire (4 pts) won on faster scoring rate*

***at Hove***

**Sussex** 212 for 5 (P.W.G. Parker 69, A.P. Wells 51)
**Yorkshire** 98 for 8
*Sussex (4 pts) won on faster scoring rate*

***at Edgbaston***

**Leicestershire** 128 for 3 *v* **Warwickshire**
*Match abandoned*
*Warwickshire 2 pts, Leicestershire 2 pts*

With the title already decided and bad weather hampering most matches, the final session of the John Player League was something of an anti-climax. Gloucestershire gained a

| v. Essex (Bristol) 14–17 July | | v. Leicestershire (Bristol) 25–27 July | | v. Northamptonshire (Bristol) 28–31 July | | v. Sri Lankans (Cheltenham) 4–7 August | | v. Glamorgan (Cheltenham) 8–10 August | | v. Surrey (Cheltenham) 11–14 August | | v. Worcestershire (Worcester) 18–21 August | | v. Leicestershire (Leicester) 22–24 August | | v. Lancashire (Bristol) 25–28 August | | v. Sussex (Hove) 29–31 August | | v. Somerset (Bristol) 5–7 September | | v. Middlesex (Bristol) 8–11 September | | M | Inns | NOs | Runs | H/S | Av |
|---|---|---|---|---|---|---|---|---|---|---|---|---|---|---|---|---|---|---|---|---|---|---|---|---|---|---|---|---|---|
| 53 | 0 | 22 | 139* | 13 | 14 | 8 | 26 | 56 | 6 | 8 | 54 | 49* | 1 | 46 | 66 | 0 | 3 | 28 | 0 | 88 | 21 | 3 | 28 | 25 | 50 | 2 | 1524 | 139* | 31.75 |
| 37 | 10 | 0 | 46 | 91 | 6 | 83 | 0 | 43 | 28 | 11 | 23 | 114 | 37 | 0 | 49 | 66 | 4 | 8 | 6 | 7 | 3 | 26 | 13 | 26 | 52 | — | 1844 | 141 | 35.46 |
| 22 | 4 | 42 | 11 | 52 | 28* | 4 | 31 | 23 | 72 | 65 | 20 | 108* | 47 | 20 | 22 | 113 | 18 | 0 | 56 | 8 | 5 | 13 | 106 | 26 | 52 | 4 | 1812 | 114* | 37.75 |
| 20 | 6 | 2 | 1 | | | | | | | | | | | | | | | | | | | | | 14 | 28 | 4 | 738 | 157* | 30.75 |
| 34* | 0 | 35 | 11 | — | — | | | | | | | 9 | 39 | 40 | 27 | 50 | 60 | 7 | 2 | 68 | 7 | 25 | 0 | 22 | 42 | 7 | 1133 | 134* | 32.37 |
| | | 35 | 13 | 14 | 0 | 13* | 26 | 16 | 37 | 2 | 62* | — | 1 | 61 | 6 | 8 | 52 | 28 | 0 | 0 | 9 | 33 | 0 | 24 | 39 | 7 | 885 | 87 | 27.65 |
| 20* | 19 | 20 | — | 19 | 31* | — | 0* | | | | | | | 25 | 0 | 23 | 48 | 1 | 35 | 29 | 13 | 14 | 28 | 21 | 27 | 6 | 513 | 63 | 24.42 |
| 4 | 10 | 11* | 10* | 15 | 0 | — | 0* | 2 | 0 | 20 | 4* | — | — | 19 | 8 | 0 | 6* | 22 | 8 | 4 | 1 | 17* | 2* | 26 | 40 | 13 | 430 | 33 | 15.92 |
| 25 | 29 | 5 | 0 | 15 | — | | | 56 | 37 | 139 | 2 | 41 | 82 | 1 | 2 | 3 | 4 | 8 | 0 | 8 | 5 | | | 22 | 39 | 3 | 971 | 139 | 26.97 |
| | | 0 | — | | | | | 4* | 10* | 4 | — | — | — | 6 | 5 | 4 | 0 | 10 | 0 | 16 | 1 | 2 | 0 | 19 | 25 | 4 | 135 | 17 | 6.42 |
| — | 0* | 5 | — | 0 | — | — | — | — | — | 0* | — | — | — | | | 3* | — | 1* | 5* | 1* | 0* | | | 22 | 20 | 15 | 40 | 10* | 8.00 |
| | | | | 1* | — | | | | | | | | | 21 | 0* | | | | | | | | | 8 | 8 | 2 | 100 | 49 | 16.66 |
| | | | | | | | | | | | | | | | | | | | | | | | | 1 | 1 | | 4 | 4 | 4.00 |
| | | | | | | | | | | | | | | | | | | | | | | | | 2 | 3 | 1 | 22 | 22 | 11.00 |
| | | | | | | — | — | 4* | 0* | 4 | — | | | | | | | | | | | | | 7 | 6 | 2 | 12 | 4* | 3.00 |
| | | | | 24 | — | 61* | 2 | 9 | 2 | 9 | 5 | | | | | | | | | | | 9 | 4 | 6 | 11 | 3 | 162 | 61* | 20.25 |
| — | 8 | | | | | | | | | | | | | | | | | | | | | | | 2 | 3 | 2 | 25 | 17* | 25.00 |
| — | 0 | | | | | | | | | | | | | | | | | | | | | | | 1 | 1 | — | 0 | 0 | — |
| | | | | | | 97 | 25 | 25 | 0 | 5 | 33 | 0 | 9* | | | | | | | | | | | 4 | 8 | 1 | 194 | 97 | 27.71 |
| | | | | | | — | — | | | | | | | | | | | | | | | | | 1 | | | | | — |
| | | | | | | | | | | | | — | — | 4* | 0 | 30 | 8 | 19 | 0 | 1 | 4 | 21 | 9 | 6 | 10 | 1 | 96 | 30 | 10.66 |
| | | | | | | | | | | | | | | | | | | | | | | 5 | 20 | 1 | 2 | — | 25 | 20 | 12.50 |
| 2 | | 4 | 5 | 5 | 3 | | | 2 | 5 | | 13 | 5 | 7 | 5 | 5 | | 1 | | 3 | | 4 | | | | | | | | |
| 7 | 4 | 6 | 5 | 10 | | 8 | 2 | 6 | 10 | 8 | 7 | 12 | 6 | 2 | 2 | 7 | 10 | 1 | 1 | 3 | | 4 | 7 | | | | | | |
| 2 | | 1 | 4 | 2 | | | 4 | 1 | | | | 6 | 1 | | | 2 | 2 | | 6 | 1 | | | | | | | | | |
| 1 | | 12 | 1 | 16 | 4 | 4 | | 5 | | 5 | 2 | 12 | 2 | | 3 | 12 | 4 | 4 | 8 | | | 2 | 10 | | | | | | |
| 27 | 90 | 200 | 246 | 277 | 86 | 278 | 116 | 252 | 207 | 280 | 225 | 356 | 232 | 250 | 195 | 321 | 220 | 137 | 130 | 234 | 73 | 174 | 227 | | | | | | |
| 6 | 10 | 10 | 6 | 9 | 4 | 4 | 6 | 8 | 8 | 10 | 6 | 4 | 6 | 10 | 10 | 10 | 9 | 10 | 10 | 10 | 10 | 10 | 10 | | | | | | |
| L | | D | | D | | D | | D | | D | | L | | L | | D | | L | | L | | L | | | | | | | |
| 4 | | 5 | | 7 | | — | | 6 | | 5 | | 7 | | 4 | | 8 | | 1 | | 6 | | 5 | | | | | | | |

† A.J. Brassington retired hurt
P. Bainbridge absent hurt

–J.H. Childs, Zaheer Abbas and D.V. Lawrence
–C. Dale

surprise win over Middlesex who, having headed the table for much of the season, slumped to fifth place. Notts and Sussex climbed to second and third places by dint of good victories while the champions suffered total indignity at Old Trafford. A young man named David Ward, in his second match of the season, gave notice that he could be a batsman to watch in 1985 with 59 not out at The Oval. He had done very well for Surrey II and is a fine fielder.

**John Player League Final Table**

| | P | W | L | T | NR | Pt |
|---|---|---|---|---|---|---|
| Essex (6) | 16 | 12 | 3 | 1 | 0 | 50 |
| Notts (15) | 16 | 10 | 5 | 0 | 1 | 42 |
| Sussex (4) | 16 | 9 | 4 | 0 | 3 | 42 |
| Lancashire (8) | 16 | 10 | 6 | 0 | 0 | 40 |
| Middlesex (8) | 16 | 9 | 5 | 1 | 1 | 40 |
| Worcs (11) | 16 | 9 | 5 | 0 | 2 | 40 |
| Warwicks (15) | 16 | 7 | 6 | 0 | 3 | 34 |
| Surrey (11) | 16 | 7 | 7 | 0 | 2 | 32 |
| Hampshire (5) | 16 | 7 | 9 | 0 | 0 | 28 |
| Glamorgan (10) | 16 | 6 | 8 | 0 | 2 | 28 |
| Kent (3) | 16 | 6 | 8 | 0 | 2 | 28 |
| Northants (15) | 16 | 6 | 9 | 0 | 1 | 26 |
| Gloucs (14) | 16 | 5 | 9 | 0 | 2 | 24 |
| Leics (11) | 16 | 4 | 8 | 0 | 4 | 24 |
| Somerset (2) | 16 | 5 | 9 | 0 | 2 | 24 |
| Yorkshire (1) | 16 | 6 | 10 | 0 | 0 | 24 |
| Derbyshire (6) | 16 | 4 | 11 | 0 | 1 | 18 |

1983 positions in brackets.

### *8, 10 and 11 September*

#### *at Derby*

**Hampshire** 353 for 4 dec (D.R. Turner 124, C.L. Smith 121, N.G. Cowley 58 not out) and 245 for 8 dec (D.R. Turner 69, G. Miller 4 for 74, D.G. Moir 4 for 114)
**Derbyshire** 323 for 3 dec (K.J. Barnett 107 not out, W.P. Fowler 101 not out, J.G. Wright 61) and 277 for 5 (J.G. Wright 87, A. Hill 75, J.E. Morris 61)

*Derbyshire won by 5 wickets*
*Derbyshire 21 pts, Hampshire 5 pts*

#### *at Bristol*

**Gloucestershire** 174 (N.G. Cowans 5 for 63, W.W. Daniel 4 for 53) and 227 (C.W.J. Athey 106, S.P. Hughes 4 for 49)
**Middlesex** 191 (R.O. Butcher 61, C.A. Walsh 6 for 70) and 213 for 3 (M.W. Gatting 72 not out, R.O. Butcher 65)

*Middlesex won by 7 wickets*
*Middlesex 21 pts, Gloucestershire 5 pts*

| **Gloucestershire C.C.C.** First-Class Matches – Bowling, 1984 | D.V. Lawrence | J.N. Shepherd | G.E. Sainsbury | P. Bainbridge | D.A. Graveney | C. Dale | C.W.J. Athey | J.H. Childs | Zaheer Abbas |
|---|---|---|---|---|---|---|---|---|---|
| *v.* Kent (Bristol)<br>28–30 April | 18–1–82–2 | 25–3–84–1 | 22–6–91–2 | 14.1–3–59–1 | 20–3–86–1 | | | | |
| *v.* Hampshire (Southampton)<br>9–11 May | 18–2–58–0<br>17.5–4–68–2 | 14–5–34–0<br>19–5–56–3 | 13–3–27–0<br>10–0–28–0 | | 14–2–40–1<br>12.5–4–20–1 | 18–4–65–0<br>2.1–1–7–1 | 5–1–16–0 | | |
| *v.* Glamorgan (Cardiff)<br>23–25 May | | 19–6–52–0<br>10.3–0–35–0 | 17–2–64–0<br>9–1–19–1 | 16–7–32–0<br>1–1–0–0 | 19–4–54–0 | 10.5–1–44–1 | | | |
| *v.* Somerset (Taunton)<br>26–29 May | 11–3–42–2<br>5–0–20–0 | 15–4–44–1<br>16–3–51–3 | 12–1–31–1<br>16–5–52–3 | 8–1–28–3<br>4–1–26–0 | | | | | |
| *v.* Oxford University<br>(Oxford) 30 May–1 June | 4–3–2–1<br>5–2–14–0 | | 4–1–7–0<br>5–3–4–0 | | 23–14–28–5<br>7–3–15–0 | 10.3–6–10–3<br>2–0–5–0 | | 13–7–23–1<br>9–3–11–0 | |
| *v.* Kent (Canterbury)<br>2–5 June | 18.3–2–54–2<br>4–1–14–0 | 33–14–39–4<br>21.4–6–30–5 | 28–8–57–3<br>18–11–19–5 | 11–7–8–0 | 2–0–10–0 | | | | |
| *v.* Derbyshire (Gloucester)<br>9–12 June | | 13.3–5–22–1<br>4–0–12–0 | 21–3–70–3<br>4–0–20–0 | 2–0–7–0 | 35–11–90–1<br>19–5–57–4 | | | 36–11–127–2<br>17–2–100–3 | <br>2.4–2–0–0 |
| *v.* Worcestershire<br>(Gloucester) 13–15 June | | 14–3–53–1<br>10–5–18–2 | 10–4–19–1<br>8–5–11–3 | | 53–24–73–6<br>17–10–37–3 | | | 55–22–68–1<br>16–11–21–1 | 3–2–1–0 |
| *v.* Nottinghamshire<br>(Trent Bridge) 16–19 June | 28–3–99–1 | 23–7–73–1 | 29–4–98–2 | 25–8–66–3 | 14–4–41–0 | | | | |
| *v.* Hampshire (Bristol)<br>23–26 June | 6–0–31–0<br>7–4–11–0 | 22–7–67–0<br>5–1–12–0 | 27–7–70–1<br>4–0–26–0 | 19–3–64–0 | 24–2–61–3<br>28–6–83–5 | | | 19–4–51–0<br>26–5–80–1 | |
| *v.* Lancashire (Old Trafford)<br>27–29 June | 20.3–4–64–5<br>19–2–59–2 | 20–6–42–2<br>30–10–71–2 | 18–4–43–1<br>26–9–56–2 | 22–5–37–1<br>7–0–28–0 | <br>18–8–38–2 | <br>4–1–12–0 | | | |
| *v.* Warwickshire (Edgbaston)<br>30 June–3 July | 13.1–1–37–2<br>13–1–63–1 | 32–7–116–5<br>14–4–30–0 | 19–4–58–3<br>6–0–25–0 | 9–3–25–0<br>8–0–32–2 | <br>0.1–0–2–0 | | | | |
| *v.* Yorkshire (Bradford)<br>7–10 July | 23–6–76–2<br>2–1–1–0 | 20–8–40–1<br>15–1–74–0 | | 18–4–62–0<br>13.1–0–70–2 | 20–2–70–0<br>8–1–57–0 | 15–1–59–0<br>12–0–72–0 | | | |
| *v.* Middlesex (Uxbridge)<br>11–13 July | | 26–8–79–2<br>17–1–56–1 | | 30–8–76–4<br>2–0–12–0 | 24–10–35–1 | 13.4–1–53–2 | | | |
| *v.* Essex (Bristol)<br>14–17 July | | | 17–3–62–0<br>14–5–51–2 | 21–6–53–0<br>6–1–25–0 | 15–3–43–1 | | 4–0–20–0 | | |
| *v.* Leicestershire (Bristol)<br>25–27 July | 14–2–47–0<br>11–2–46–1 | 31–9–75–4<br>25–2–68–2 | 21–7–45–1<br>18–5–45–1 | 15–2–75–0<br>9–3–26–1 | 19–6–42–2<br>10–5–21–0 | | | | |
| *v.* Northamptonshire<br>(Bristol) 28–31 July | | 18.1–4–64–4<br>22–8–57–0 | 22–4–59–1<br>12–3–29–1 | 11–3–21–1 | 24–6–54–3<br>34–11–64–4 | 9–2–31–0<br>16–3–59–0 | | | |
| *v.* Sri Lankans (Cheltenham)<br>4–7 August | | 17–2–73–0 | 21–5–70–1 | | 12–4–20–0 | | 4–0–18–0 | 24–9–41–0 | |
| *v.* Glamorgan (Cheltenham)<br>8–10 August | 15–4–26–0<br>13–3–41–1 | 27–10–50–3<br>19–7–27–2 | 20–5–53–3<br>4–1–10–0 | | 33.4–6–62–3<br>17–1–71–0 | | | 18–4–42–1<br>22–2–72–3 | |
| *v.* Surrey (Cheltenham)<br>11–14 August | 31·2–4–103–5 | 21–5–64–2 | 6–1–21–0 | | 19–5–42–0 | | | 39–3–100–2 | |
| *v.* Worcestershire (Worcester)<br>18–21 August | 15–1–73–0<br>13.5–1–64–2 | 17–6–55–2<br>10–2–43–0 | 14–4–33–0<br>11–2–43–2 | 1–0–2–0 | 32–13–46–3<br>16–3–52–1 | | | | |
| *v.* Leicestershire (Leicester)<br>22–24 August | 29–4–91–3 | 28–3–99–4 | | 12–0–47–0 | 18–6–39–0 | 12–2–50–0 | | | |
| *v.* Lancashire (Bristol)<br>25–28 August | 8–3–24–0<br>18–6–40–2 | 18–4–52–2<br>14–3–28–1 | 19.2–6–32–5<br>12–4–38–0 | | <br>25–14–31–4 | | | | |
| *v.* Sussex (Hove)<br>29–31 August | 14–0–50–0 | 27–8–91–4 | 11–3–31–0 | 4–1–16–0 | 22–4–49–0 | | | | |
| *v.* Somerset (Bristol)<br>5–7 September | 21–5–58–5 | 20.2–3–70–2 | 18–2–79–0 | 8–3–43–0 | 13–2–55–0 | | | | |
| *v.* Middlesex (Bristol)<br>8–11 September | 13–5–40–0<br>5–0–33–0 | 23–5–67–3<br>24.2–8–52–2 | | <br>7–3–19–0 | | | | | |
| | 455.1–80–<br>1531–41<br>*av.* 37.34 | 800.3–208–<br>2225–72<br>*av.* 30.90 | 566.2–141–<br>1596–48<br>*av.* 33.25 | 303.2–73–<br>959–18<br>*av.* 53.27 | 667.4–202–<br>1588–54<br>*av.* 29.40 | 125.1–22–<br>467–7<br>*av.* 66.71 | 13–1–<br>54–0<br>— | 294–83–<br>736–15<br>*av.* 49.06 | 5.4–4–<br>1–0<br>— |

a R.A. Woolmer retired hurt
b P.W. Romaines 0.3–0–8–0
c E.J. Cunningham 7–0–36–0
d L.H. Rolls 15–1–49–0
e E.J. Cunningham 7–2–11–0
f E.J. Cunningham 1–0–1–0, 6–1–22–0

| C.R. Trembath | D.A. Burrows | C.A. Walsh | Byes | Leg-byes | Wides | No-balls | Total | Wkts |
|---|---|---|---|---|---|---|---|---|
| | | | | 7 | | 3 | 412 | 7 |
| | | | 6 | 2 | | 4 | 252 | 1 |
| | | | | 4 | 1 | 3 | 187 | 7 |
| | | | | 2 | 1 | 2 | 251 | 1 |
| | | | 3 | 4 | | | 61 | 1 |
| | | | 4 | | | 1 | 150 | 7 |
| | | | 1 | 4 | 1 | | 155 | 6 |
| | | | 1 | | | 1 | 72 | 10 |
| | | | | | | 2 | 51 | 0 |
| | | | | 3 | 1 | 3 | 175 | 9a |
| | | | | 5 | 2 | | 70 | 10 |
| | | | 5 | 7 | 1 | 2 | 331 | 9 |
| | | | | 6 | | | 195 | 7 |
| | | | 4 | 2 | 2 | 3 | 225 | 9 |
| | | | 3 | | | 1 | 91 | 9 |
| | | | 1 | 12 | 1 | 7 | 398 | 7 |
| | | | 1 | 5 | | 1 | 351 | 4 |
| | | | | 1 | | 1 | 214 | 7 |
| | | | 4 | 7 | | | 197 | 10 |
| | | | | 6 | | 11 | 281 | 8 |
| | | | 4 | 8 | | 4 | 252 | 10 |
| | | | 5 | 10 | | 2 | 169 | 3 |
| | | | | 11 | 3 | 7 | 328 | 3 |
| | | | | 6 | | 1 | 281 | 2 |
| 7–0–49–1 | | | 4 | 11 | | | 307 | 10 |
| 19–1–106–3 | | | | 1 | | 1 | 176 | 4 |
| 16.5–4–65–1 | 11–0–46–0 | | | 4 | | 7 | 300 | 2 |
| 4–0–5–0 | 4–0–30–0 | | | 1 | | 1 | 121 | 2b |
| | | | 5 | 10 | 2 | | 301 | 7 |
| | | | | 9 | 5 | | 220 | 6 |
| | | | | 9 | | 1 | 239 | 10 |
| | | | 7 | 6 | | | 258 | 6c |
| | | | 2 | 9 | 1 | 3 | 286 | 1d |
| | | | 9 | 12 | 2 | 2 | 258 | 10 |
| | | | 12 | 7 | 1 | 2 | 243 | 6 |
| | | | 11 | 8 | 2 | 5 | 367 | 10e |
| | | 18–9–45–2 | 11 | 19 | 9 | 10 | 303 | 7 |
| | | 10–0–72–0 | 4 | 10 | 1 | | 289 | 5 |
| | | 29–3–106–3 | 1 | 11 | 2 | 10 | 456 | 10 |
| | | 14–3–56–1 | 4 | 3 | 5 | 2 | 178 | 10 |
| | | 19–9–44–1 | 5 | 3 | 1 | 5 | 195 | 9 |
| | | 31.4–13–92–2 | | 7 | 4 | 8 | 348 | 6 |
| | | 21–4–61–2 | 2 | 16 | 5 | 1 | 390 | 10 |
| | | 26.4–6–70–6 | 1 | 2 | 5 | 5 | 191 | 10f |
| | | 16–1–76–1 | | 7 | 3 | 1 | 213 | 3 |
| 46.5–5–225–5 av. 45.00 | 15–0–76–0 — | 185.2–48–622–18 av. 34.55 | | | | | | |

### *at Canterbury*

**Kent** 195 (R.C. Ontong 6 for 52) and 350 for 9 dec (L. Potter 117, D.G. Aslett 87, M.R. Benson 59, C.J. Tavare 55, J.F. Steele 5 for 53)
**Glamorgan** 296 (J.F. Steele 60 not out, J. Derrick 53, H. Morris 50) and 209 for 9 (A.L. Jones 67, G.C. Holmes 57, G.W. Johnson 5 for 97, D.L. Underwood 4 for 61)

*Match drawn*
*Glamorgan 7 pts, Kent 4 pts*

### *at Old Trafford*

**Lancashire** 229 (N.H. Fairbrother 77, G. Fowler 63, D.R. Pringle 4 for 75) and 229 (M. Watkinson 70, J.K. Lever 4 for 81)
**Essex** 446 (K.S. McEwan 132, P.J. Pritchard 100, G.A. Gooch 70, J. Simmons 7 for 176) and 14 for 0.
*Essex won by 10 wickets*
*Essex 24 pts, Lancashire 6 pts*

*Geoff Humpage, Warwickshire. No batsman in the country hit the ball harder. He had his best season ever with the bat and maintained good form behind the stumps. (Ken Kelly)*

**Hampshire C.C.C.**
First-Class Matches – Batting, 1984

| | v. Cambridge Univ. (Cambridge) 25–27 April | | v. Essex (Southampton) 28–30 April | | v. Gloucestershire (Southampton) 9–11 May | | v. Sussex (Hove) 23–25 May | | v. Kent (Canterbury) 26–29 May | | v. Somerset (Southampton) 30 May–1 June | | v. Nottinghamshire (Bournemouth) 2–5 June | |
|---|---|---|---|---|---|---|---|---|---|---|---|---|---|---|
| V.P. Terry | 137 | — | 0 | 26 | 105* | 37 | 75 | — | — | 11 | 68 | 4* | 54 | 0 |
| D.R. Turner | 6 | 76 | | | | | | | — | 9 | 27 | — | 38 | 26 |
| T.E. Jesty | 248 | — | 9 | 7 | — | 4 | 96 | — | — | 0 | 7 | — | 33 | 8 |
| N.E.J. Pocock | 37* | — | 6 | 55 | — | 6 | 1 | — | 1 | 17 | 17 | — | | |
| J.J.E. Hardy | – | 30* | | | | | | | | | | | | |
| N.G. Cowley | — | 11 | 20 | 26 | — | 13 | 37 | — | — | 1 | 51 | — | 24 | 30 |
| R.J. Parks | — | 89 | 1 | 5 | — | 10 | 0 | — | — | 0 | 0 | — | 12 | 11* |
| R.J. Maru | — | — | 20* | 16* | — | 13* | 9 | — | | | | | 30 | 4 |
| T.M. Tremlett | — | 10* | 16 | 0 | — | 8* | 27 | — | — | 4 | — | — | 74 | 8 |
| E.L. Reifer | — | — | 19 | 2 | — | — | 2 | — | — | 1* | 47 | — | 18 | 16 |
| S.J. Malone | — | — | 0 | 4 | — | — | | | | | | | | |
| C.L. Smith | | | 20 | 4 | 125 | 67 | 37 | — | — | 5 | 24 | 0* | 9 | 12 |
| M.C.J. Nicholas | | | 147 | 40 | 10* | 21 | 0 | — | — | 0 | 65 | — | 2 | 0 |
| S.J.W. Andrew | | | | | | | 0* | — | — | 3 | | | | |
| C.A. Connor | | | | | | | | | | | 4* | — | 1* | 0 |
| R.A. Smith | | | | | | | | | | | | | | |
| C.F.E. Goldie | | | | | | | | | | | | | | |
| T.C. Middleton | | | | | | | | | | | | | | |
| Byes | 6 | 1 | | 1 | 6 | | | | | | 1 | | | |
| Leg-byes | 7 | 5 | 4 | 1 | 2 | 4 | 4 | | | 4 | 12 | | 7 | 12 |
| Wides | | | | | | 1 | 2 | | | 1 | 2 | | | |
| No-balls | 7 | 4 | 14 | 2 | 4 | 3 | 8 | | | | 8 | 1 | 1 | |
| Total | 448 | 226 | 276 | 189 | 252 | 187 | 298 | | 0 | 56 | 333 | 5 | 303 | 127 |
| Wickets | 3 | 3 | 10 | 10 | 1 | 7 | 10 | | 0 | 10 | 9 | 0 | 10 | 10 |
| Result | W | | L | | D | | D | | L | | W | | L | |
| Points | — | | 5 | | 7 | | 7 | | 1 | | 24 | | 5 | |

| | v. Worcestershire (Worcester) 9–12 June | | v. Yorkshire (Basingstoke) 13–15 June | | v. Leicestershire (Southampton) 16–19 June | | v. Gloucestershire (Bristol) 23–26 June | | v. Sussex (Bournemouth) 27–29 June | | v. Surrey (The Oval) 30 June–3 July | | v. Somerset (Taunton) 7–10 July | |
|---|---|---|---|---|---|---|---|---|---|---|---|---|---|---|
| V.P. Terry | 63 | 2 | 50 | 8 | 17 | 4 | 175* | 73 | 136 | 22 | 3 | 102 | 9 | 11 |
| D.R. Turner | 70* | 26* | 9 | 0 | | | | | | | 3 | 9 | 0 | 0 |
| T.E. Jesty | 143* | 141 | 10 | 18 | 34 | 1 | 13 | 12 | 16 | 1 | 2 | 4 | 7 | 17 |
| N.E.J. Pocock | — | 15* | 32 | 8 | 6 | 0 | — | 35 | 9 | 15 | 14 | 1 | | |
| J.J.E. Hardy | | | | | | | | | | | | | 94* | 6 |
| N.G. Cowley | — | — | 46 | 26 | 42 | 15 | 33 | 11 | 80 | 0 | 29 | 36 | 34 | 19 |
| R.J. Parks | — | — | 11 | 15 | 31 | 0 | — | 14* | 3* | 0 | 8 | 6* | 1 | 53* |
| R.J. Maru | | | | | 28 | 2 | — | — | 9 | 36 | | | | |
| T.M. Tremlett | — | — | 0 | 0 | 4 | 8 | — | 11* | 32 | 4 | 20 | 11 | 0 | 18 |
| E.L. Reifer | — | — | 21 | 23 | 26* | 6* | 8* | 17 | 6 | 0 | 17* | 20 | 3 | 9* |
| S.J. Malone | | | | | | | | | | | | | | |
| C.L. Smith | 11 | 4 | 10 | 0 | 26 | 75 | 78 | 21 | 29 | 3 | 7 | 4 | 25 | 21 |
| M.C.J. Nicholas | 10 | 100 | 5 | 128 | 2 | 55 | 37 | 18 | 24 | 22 | 31 | 25 | 53 | 6 |
| S.J.W. Andrew | | | | | | | | | | | | | | |
| C.A. Connor | — | — | 6* | 6* | 3 | 3 | — | — | 0 | 1* | 7 | 1 | 6 | — |
| R.A. Smith | | | | | | | | | | | | | | |
| C.F.E. Goldie | | | | | | | | | | | | | | |
| T.C. Middleton | | | | | | | | | | | | | | |
| Byes | 2 | 4 | 4 | | 3 | 7 | 1 | | | | | 9 | 1 | |
| Leg-byes | 10 | 8 | 18 | 10 | 9 | 2 | 5 | 1 | 11 | 6 | 12 | 7 | 11 | 5 |
| Wides | | 1 | | | | | | | | | 1 | | | 1 |
| No-balls | 7 | 3 | 8 | 13 | 13 | 12 | 1 | 1 | 1 | 1 | | 3 | | |
| Total | 316 | 304 | 230 | 255 | 244 | 190 | 351 | 214 | 356 | 111 | 154 | 238 | 244 | 166 |
| Wickets | 3 | 4 | 10 | 10 | 10 | 10 | 4 | 7 | 10 | 10 | 10 | 10 | 10 | 8 |
| Result | L | | D | | L | | D | | W | | L | | D | |
| Points | 5 | | 3 | | 3 | | 5 | | 23 | | 5 | | 3 | |

*Catches*
71 – R.J. Parks (ct 61/st 10)
22 – R.J. Maru
16 – T.E. Jesty
15 – V.P. Terry and M.C.J. Nicholas
13 – C.L. Smith and N.E.J. Pocock
9 – N.G. Cowley and J.J.E. Hardy
7 – C.A. Connor and D.R. Turner
6 – E.L. Reifer
4 – R.A. Smith and T.M. Tremlett

| (Southampton) 11–13 July | | v. Lancashire (Portsmouth) 14–17 July | | v. Warwickshire (Edgbaston) 25–27 July | | v. Middlesex (Lord's) 28–31 July | | v. Warwickshire (Southampton) 4–7 August | | v. Sri Lankans (Southampton) 8–10 August | | v. Glamorgan (Cardiff) 11–14 August | | v. Essex (Colchester) 18–21 August | | v. Middlesex (Bournemouth) 22–24 August | | v. Kent (Bournemouth) 25–28 August | | v. Yorkshire (Scarborough) 5–7 September | | v. Derbyshire (Derby) 8–11 September | | | *M* | *Inns* | *NOs* | *Runs* | *H/S* | *Av* |
|---|---|---|---|---|---|---|---|---|---|---|---|---|---|---|---|---|---|---|---|---|---|---|---|---|---|---|---|---|---|---|
| | | | | | | | | | | | | | | | | | | | | | | | | | 14 | 25 | 3 | 1192 | 175* | 54.18 |
| 6 | 8 | 31 | 76* | 153 | 37 | 117 | 0 | 68 | 42 | 39 | 25 | 89 | — | 2 | 47 | 5 | 21 | 15 | 36 | 0 | 56* | 124 | 69 | | 20 | 37 | 4 | 1365 | 153 | 41.36 |
| 23 | 86* | 131 | 15* | 0 | 22 | 17 | 0 | 10 | 6 | 47 | 1 | 9 | — | 74 | 120 | 86 | 32 | | | 43 | 39* | 4 | 29 | | 25 | 44 | 4 | 1625 | 248 | 40.62 |
| | | 40 | — | | | | | | | | | | | | | | | | | | | | | | 13 | 18 | 2 | 314 | 55 | 19.62 |
| 55 | 64* | 5 | — | 95 | 2 | 10 | 6 | — | 15* | 18 | 29* | 10 | — | 0 | 22 | | | 2 | 4 | 0 | — | — | 46* | | 13 | 20 | 6 | 513 | 95 | 36.64 |
| 5 | — | 12 | — | 58 | 20 | 35 | 57* | — | — | 11* | — | 76 | — | 40 | 13 | 11 | 0 | 6 | 29 | 14* | — | 58* | 13 | | 26 | 38 | 4 | 1042 | 80 | 30.64 |
| 32* | — | 24 | — | 13* | 1 | — | 5 | — | — | | | 31 | — | 1 | 4 | 10 | 10 | 12 | 24* | 4* | — | — | 3 | | 25 | 34 | 9 | 444 | 89 | 17.76 |
| 4 | — | | | — | 0 | — | 29 | | | 11* | — | 5 | — | | | 11 | 9 | 6 | 4 | — | — | — | 0 | | 17 | 20 | 4 | 246 | 36 | 15.37 |
| 13 | — | 6* | — | 14* | 30 | 25* | — | — | — | | | 68* | — | 0 | 0 | 7 | 10 | 5 | 5 | | | | | | 23 | 31 | 7 | 438 | 74 | 18.25 |
| 11 | — | 26* | — | 6 | 11 | 10* | 15 | | | — | — | 17 | — | | | | | | | | | | | | 20 | 26 | 8 | 357 | 47 | 19.83 |
| | | | | | | | | | | | | | | | | | | | | | | | | | 3 | 2 | — | 4 | 4 | 2.00 |
| 4 | 10 | 7 | 15 | 3 | 32 | 15 | 10 | 110* | 13 | 29 | 103* | 10 | — | 4 | 29 | 20 | 6 | 4 | 1 | 47 | 27 | 121 | 7 | | 25 | 47 | 3 | 1244 | 125 | 28.27 |
| 15 | 26 | 0 | 158 | 14 | 16 | 96 | 18 | 6 | 12 | 4 | 25 | 2 | — | 40 | 49 | 9 | 19 | 26 | 18 | 70 | 22 | 0 | 36 | | 25 | 46 | 1 | 1482 | 158 | 32.93 |
| | | | | | | | | — | — | | | | | 3 | 0* | 6* | 0* | | | — | — | — | — | | 7 | 6 | 4 | 12 | 6* | 6.00 |
| 1 | — | — | — | — | 0* | — | 0 | — | — | — | — | 2 | — | 2* | 0 | 2 | 2 | 13* | 0 | — | — | — | 5* | | 21 | 23 | 9 | 65 | 13* | 4.64 |
| | | | | | | | | 4* | 23* | 132 | 97 | | | 15 | 9 | 14 | 15 | 13 | 34 | 62 | — | 41* | 24 | | 7 | 13 | 3 | 483 | 132 | 48.30 |
| | | | | | | | | | | — | — | | | | | | | | | | | | | | 1 | | | | | — |
| | | | | | | | | | | | | | | | | | | 10 | 5 | | | | | | 1 | 2 | | 15 | 10 | 7.50 |
| | 4 | | 1 | 23 | | 2 | 1 | 4 | | | 5 | 2 | | 4 | | 1 | 12 | | 8 | 5 | 5 | | 4 | | †T.M. Tremlett absent | | | | | |
| 9 | | 11 | 11 | 11 | 3 | 9 | 2 | 7 | 14 | 7 | 2 | 4 | | 2 | 10 | | 2 | | 6 | 5 | 5 | 5 | 7 | | | | | | | |
| 1 | | 2 | | | 1 | 1 | 2 | | | 3 | 1 | 1 | | 1 | 1 | | | | | | | | 1 | | | | | | | |
| 15 | 3 | 5 | 3 | 8 | 1 | 13 | 8 | 3 | | 11 | 3 | 2 | | 1 | 8 | 6 | 1 | 2 | 4 | 4 | 1 | | 1 | | | | | | | |
| 94 | 201 | 300 | 279 | 398 | 176 | 350 | 153 | 212 | 125 | 312 | 291 | 328 | | 189 | 312 | 188 | 139 | 114 | 178 | 254 | 155 | 353 | 245 | | | | | | | |
| 10 | 3 | 8 | 2 | 7 | 10 | 6 | 9† | 3 | 4 | 6 | 4 | 10 | | 10 | 10 | 10 | 10 | 10 | 10 | 6 | 2 | 4 | 8 | | | | | | | |
| L | | W | | L | | L | | D | | D | | D | | L | | L | | L | | D | | L | | | | | | | | |
| 2 | | 22 | | 7 | | 8 | | 6 | | — | | 6 | | 4 | | 5 | | 4 | | 3 | | 5 | | | | | | | | |

– C.F.E. Goldie (ct 2/st 1)
– S.J. Malone
– S.J.W. Andrew and sub

| **Hampshire C.C.C.**<br>First-Class Matches –<br>Bowling, 1984 | E.L. Reifer | S.J. Malone | R.J. Maru | T.M. Tremlett | T.E. Jesty | N.G. Cowley | N.E.J. Pocock | C.L. Smith | M.C.J. Nicholas |
|---|---|---|---|---|---|---|---|---|---|
| *v.* Cambridge University (Cambridge) 25–27 April | 12.5–4–43–4<br>22.3–6–65–4 | 11–6–19–2<br>17–5–40–3 | 11–4–15–0<br>31–17–31–0 | 11–8–5–3<br>24–13–36–1 | 6–1–12–1<br>6–3–11–1 | 3–2–1–0<br>17–10–14–1 | <br>1–1–0–0 | | |
| *v.* Essex (Southampton) 28–30 April | 12–0–70–0<br>1 2–0–10–0 | 16–3–70–0<br>2–0–6–0 | 10–0–63–0 | 23–7–55–1 | 3–0–15–0 | 26–5–90–2 | | 14–0–70–2 | |
| *v.* Gloucestershire (Southampton) 9–11 May | 29–6–92–3<br>4–2–6–0 | 6–1–27–0<br>13–2–42–1 | 15.1–4–48–2<br>23–5–81–1 | 30–11–48–5<br>6–1–8–0 | <br>9–2–33–0 | 11–3–27–0<br>15–1–64–1 | | 2–1–1–0<br>2–0–10–0 | 9–3–24–0<br>7–2–33–0 |
| *v.* Sussex (Hove) 23–25 May | 17–3–47–2<br>28–9–77–3 | | <br>20–1–62–0 | 13–4–26–4<br>30–7–65–0 | <br>1.1–1–4–1 | <br>19–1–44–3 | | | <br>19–4–56–2 |
| *v.* Kent (Canterbury) 26–29 May | 17–4–41–2 | | | 20.2–7–43–1 | | | | | 8–0–35–0 |
| *v.* Somerset (Southampton) 30 May–1 June | 21.2–4–65–3<br>24–5–52–4 | | | 13–7–19–2<br>20.2–5–43–4 | | 4–1–6–0<br>10–5–9–0 | | 1–0–2–1<br>3–0–11–0 | <br>4–0–12–0 |
| *v.* Nottinghamshire (Bournemouth) 2–5 June | 15–3–62–0<br>12.5–3–41–1 | | 8–1–21–0 | 13–2–34–0<br>14–6–23–3 | 2–0–7–0 | 22.1–5–65–2<br>6–2–12–0 | | | 9–0–35–1 |
| *v.* Worcestershire (Worcester) 9–12 June | 17–5–34–2<br>15–1–74–2 | | | 17–5–43–1<br>16–2–66–1 | 4–0–20–0 | 13–2–83–0<br>19.4–3–89–2 | | 2–0–9–0<br>1–0–4–1 | |
| *v.* Yorkshire (Basingstoke) 13–15 June | 32–4–107–2<br>2–0–14–0 | | | 38–11–63–5<br>5–0–33–4 | | 18.1–2–36–1 | | 13–1–58–0 | 6–2–15–0 |
| *v.* Leicestershire (Southampton) 16–19 June | 16–1–55–2<br>6–2–9–0 | | 33.2–6–101–2<br>38–13–75–6 | 9–3–20–1<br>13–5–21–1 | | 18–1–54–3<br>21.4–8–43–3 | | | 10–3–25–0 |
| *v.* Gloucestershire (Bristol) 23–26 June | 12–3–29–2<br>1–0–7–0 | | 34–11–85–0<br>15–4–64–4 | 10–5–15–0<br>11.5–2–22–2 | | 19.1–4–67–1<br>16–2–48–0 | <br>1–0–1–0 | 9–3–20–0<br>8–1–39–0 | |
| *v.* Sussex (Bournemouth) 27–29 June | 15–5–34–2<br>7–2–18–0 | | 12.5–1–24–2<br>10.3–4–23–4 | 18–9–36–2<br>18–7–16–2 | | 14–4–36–2<br>11–3–40–2 | | 3–0–20–0 | |
| *v.* Surrey (The Oval) 30 June–3 July | 15–3–63–0<br>9–1–30–0 | | | 30–11–50–1<br>17–8–30–2 | <br>8.4–3–15–3 | 16.1–4–33–4<br>6–2–15–1 | | 1–0–5–0 | 23–5–90–2 |
| *v.* Somerset (Taunton) 7–10 July | 21–2–76–0 | | | 20–3–48–1 | | 22–5–101–0 | | 4–0–11–0 | 21–2–73–1 |
| *v.* Northamptonshire (Southampton) 11–13 July | 12–4–29–0<br>3–0–27–1 | | <br>7–0–39–2 | 10–4–17–0<br>15–1–62–3 | 7–2–21–1 | 4–2–5–3<br>11–0–49–2 | | <br>5–0–38–0 | 3–0–16–0 |
| *v.* Lancashire (Portsmouth) 14–17 July | 25–3–88–1<br>2–0–18–0 | | | 24–7–46–2<br>5–1–25–0 | 10–0–34–1 | 1–0–1–0<br>14–4–39–1 | <br>9–0–60–0 | 1–0–9–0<br>16–1–89–0 | |
| *v.* Warwickshire (Edgbaston) 25–27 July | 28–5–104–3<br>8–1–38–1 | | 8–3–33–2<br>12–1–51–0 | 30–5–105–1<br>9–2–16–1 | 19–3–68–3<br>6–1–15–0 | 4–0–18–0 | | <br>9–0–61–2 | |
| *v.* Middlesex (Lord's) 28–31 July | 15–1–86–2<br>10–1–39–0 | | 23–10–54–1<br>11.3–0–65–0 | | 17–2–55–3<br>5–1–12–0 | 5–0–17–0<br>4–1–28–0 | | <br>3–0–17–0 | |
| *v.* Warwickshire (Southampton) 4–7 August | | | | 29–8–61–4 | 16–5–38–0<br>6–1–11–1 | 9–5–11–1<br>14–4–60–3 | | 6–0–41–2<br>11–2–54–0 | <br>1–0–8–0 |
| *v.* Sri Lankans (Southampton) 8–10 August | 17–3–46–3<br>3–1–3–0 | | 19–3–73–1<br>20–5–51–3 | | 9–2–42–0 | 24.1–4–86–3<br>6–2–11–0 | | 1–0–4–0<br>14–3–33–0 | |
| *v.* Glamorgan (Cardiff) 11–14 August | 10–1–28–0<br>7–2–34–0 | | 1–0–3–0<br>41–6–133–3 | 19–8–20–1<br>10–3–16–0 | 18.2–8–26–3<br>10–1–39–0 | 2–2–0–1<br>30–5–105–1 | | 2–1–3–0<br>17–6–27–0 | <br>4–1–5–1 |
| *v.* Essex (Colchester) 18–21 August | | | | 25–6–75–4<br>11–3–49–0 | 18–4–42–0 | 7–0–29–1<br>2–0–12–1 | | <br>1–0–9–0 | 1–1–0–0 |
| *v.* Middlesex (Bournemouth) 22–24 August | | | 40.3–14–79–7<br>6.4–0–45–1 | <br>3–0–16–1 | 9–2–28–0 | 31–8–70–3<br>2–0–11–0 | | | |
| *v.* Kent (Bournemouth) 25–28 August | | | 19–4–55–0<br>15–2–39–1 | 22–8–39–3<br>17.2–5–29–4 | | 7–2–14–0<br>23–8–45–3 | | <br>2–0–11–0 | |
| *v.* Yorkshire (Scarborough) 5–7 September | | | 11–2–32–0<br>13–4–48–2 | | 6–4–15–0<br>8–2–24–0 | 4–2–8–0<br>14–3–36–3 | | <br>6–0–21–1 | <br>4–0–11–0 |
| *v.* Derbyshire (Derby) 8–11 September | | | 20–3–67–0<br>20.1–1–104–3 | | 12–2–55–2<br>4–0–26–0 | 25–6–79–0<br>17–0–68–2 | | 1–0–10–0 | |
| | 524.5–100–<br>1761–49<br>*av.* 35.93 | 65–17–<br>204–6<br>*av.* 34.00 | 549.4–129–<br>1664–47<br>*av.* 35.40 | 669.5–210–<br>1444–71<br>*av.* 20.33 | 220.1–50–<br>668–19<br>*av.* 35.15 | 588.1–133–<br>1779–56<br>*av.* 31.76 | 11–1–<br>61–0<br>— | 158–19–<br>687–9<br>*av.* 76.33 | 129–23–<br>438–7<br>*av.* 62.57 |

a J.J.E. Hardy 1–0–3–0

| S.J.W. Andrew | C.A. Connor | D.R. Turner | *Byes* | *Leg-byes* | *Wides* | *No-balls* | *Total* | *Wkts* |
|---|---|---|---|---|---|---|---|---|
| | | | 3 | 3 | | 5 | 106 | 10 |
| | | | 4 | 3 | 1 | 2 | 207 | 10 |
| | | | 1 | 7 | 2 | 6 | 449 | 5 |
| | | | 1 | | | 1 | 18 | 0 |
| | | | 6 | 10 | 5 | 2 | 290 | 10 |
| | | | | 9 | | 2 | 288 | 3 |
| 11.2–3–30–4 | | | | 5 | | 1 | 109 | 10 |
| 33–8–115–0 | | | | 20 | 5 | 2 | 450 | 9 |
| 18–3–52–1 | | | | 4 | 2 | 2 | 179 | 4 |
| | 19–7–31–4 | | | 4 | 1 | 8 | 136 | 10 |
| | 25–8–53–2 | | 6 | 7 | 1 | 7 | 201 | 10 |
| | 25–5–72–2 | | | 7 | 4 | 1 | 308 | 5 |
| | 15–3–39–4 | | 2 | 7 | | | 124 | 8 |
| | 26–2–111–2 | | 2 | 7 | 7 | 12 | 328 | 5 |
| | 11–0–49–0 | | | 13 | | 1 | 296 | 6 |
| | 38–10–76–2 | | | 19 | 1 | 26 | 401 | 10 |
| | 5–0–29–1 | | 2 | 4 | 1 | | 83 | 5 |
| | 19–5–50–0 | | 8 | 4 | 3 | 5 | 325 | 8 |
| | 8–4–9–0 | | 6 | 5 | 2 | 2 | 172 | 10 |
| | 15–2–50–2 | | 13 | 13 | 3 | 5 | 300 | 5 |
| | 8–1–25–1 | | 3 | | 2 | 4 | 215 | 8 |
| | 23–8–60–2 | | 10 | 3 | 5 | 4 | 232 | 10 |
| | 13–2–20–1 | | | 7 | | 3 | 127 | 10 |
| | 12–3–32–3 | | 3 | 13 | 3 | 4 | 296 | 10 |
| | | | | | 5 | 5 | 100 | 7 |
| | 22.2–6–66–2 | | | 11 | 6 | 5 | 397 | 4 |
| | 10–2–30–0 | | 4 | 4 | 3 | 6 | 135 | 4 |
| | 8–0–43–0 | | | 4 | | 2 | 264 | 8 |
| | 45–15–95–3 | | 1 | 15 | | 9 | 298 | 7 |
| | 12–4–36–0 | | 1 | 5 | | 4 | 277 | 1 |
| | 22–2–97–2 | | 7 | 30 | 1 | 9 | 472 | 10 |
| | 12–4–40–0 | | | 5 | 1 | | 227 | 4 |
| | 18.4–4–67–4 | | 1 | 2 | | 9 | 291 | 10 |
| | 11–2–41–1 | | 2 | 3 | 1 | 7 | 215 | 1 |
| 16–3–45–1 | 24–6–84–1 | | | 6 | | 9 | 295 | 9 |
| 8–2–25–0 | 7–0–24–1 | | | 8 | | 4 | 194 | 5 |
| | 19–4–54–2 | | 5 | 4 | 1 | 21 | 336 | 9 |
| | 2–1–2–0 | | | | 1 | 1 | 102 | 3 |
| | 15–4–46–3 | | | 9 | | 7 | 142 | 10 |
| | 14–3–44–2 | 5–1–9–0 | | 1 | | 9 | 425 | 7a |
| 23–8–74–2 | 30–8–91–3 | | | 10 | 3 | 5 | 329 | 10 |
| 2–0–31–0 | 12–1–68–1 | | | 1 | | 3 | 173 | 2 |
| 10–3–20–0 | 13–3–34–0 | | 2 | 5 | 1 | 1 | 240 | 10 |
| | 4–2–17–0 | | 1 | 1 | | | 91 | 3 |
| | 21.5–11–37–7 | | 2 | | | | 147 | 10 |
| | 16–4–59–3 | | 1 | 1 | | 4 | 189 | 10 |
| 9–4–14–0 | 7–2–29–1 | | 4 | 2 | | 4 | 108 | 1 |
| 15–2–57–2 | 13–5–44–1 | | 4 | 4 | | 3 | 252 | 9 |
| 14–6–51–1 | 10–0–47–0 | | 2 | 7 | | 4 | 322 | 3 |
| 3–1–16–0 | 12–2–48–0 | | 3 | 9 | | 3 | 277 | 5 |
| 162.2–43–530–11 *av.* 48.18 | 642.5–155–1949–62 *av.* 31.43 | 5–1–9–0 — | | | | | | |

**Kent C.C.C.**
First-Class Matches – Batting, 1984

| Kent C.C.C. | v. Gloucestershire (Bristol) 28–30 April | | v. Essex (Canterbury) 2–4 May | | v. Lancashire (Old Trafford) 9–11 May | | v. Hampshire (Canterbury) 26–29 May | | v. Middlesex (Dartford) 30 May–1 June | | v. Gloucestershire (Canterbury) 2–5 June | | v. Yorkshire (Tunbridge Wells) 9–12 June | |
|---|---|---|---|---|---|---|---|---|---|---|---|---|---|---|
| R.A. Woolmer | 153 | — | 42 | 5 | 1 | 46* | 17 | — | 5 | 86 | 8* | 1 | 58 | 1 |
| N.R. Taylor | 21 | — | 35 | 24 | 10 | 27* | 10 | — | 66 | 7 | 19 | 13 | | |
| C.J. Tavare | 4 | — | 11 | 43 | 28 | — | 69 | — | 1 | 2 | 0 | 11 | 2 | 28 |
| D.G. Aslett | 140 | — | 13 | 14 | 12 | — | 68 | — | 12 | 129* | 23 | 3 | 47 | 0 |
| C.S. Cowdrey | 34 | — | 3 | 0 | | | | | | | | | 32 | 4 |
| R.M. Ellison | 0 | — | 15 | 11 | | | 1* | — | 1 | — | 25 | 0 | 8 | 16* |
| A.P.E. Knott | 43 | — | 4 | 4 | | | — | — | 30 | 23* | 2 | 0 | 37 | 9 |
| G.W. Johnson | 7* | — | 6 | 12* | 50 | — | 6* | — | 0 | — | 49 | 16 | 4 | 37 |
| C. Penn | — | — | 36 | 10* | 115 | — | — | — | 49 | — | 0 | 12 | 9 | 8* |
| D.L. Underwood | — | — | 6* | — | 20 | — | — | — | 0 | — | 36 | 7 | 16 | — |
| K.B.S. Jarvis | — | — | 1 | — | 0* | — | — | — | 0 | — | 1* | 0* | | |
| L. Potter | | | | | 1 | — | | | | | | | 44 | 6 |
| S.N.V. Waterton | | | | | 50 | — | | | | | | | | |
| T.M. Alderman | | | | | 0 | — | — | — | 10* | — | 5 | 0 | 0* | — |
| S.G. Hinks | | | | | | | | | | | | | | |
| M.R. Benson | | | | | | | | | | | | | | |
| S.A. Marsh | | | | | | | | | | | | | | |
| G.R. Cowdrey | | | | | | | | | | | | | | |
| K.D. Masters | | | | | | | | | | | | | | |
| Byes | | | | | | | | | | | | | | 1 |
| Leg-byes | 7 | | 4 | 3 | 5 | | 4 | | 3 | 1 | 3 | 5 | 8 | |
| Wides | | | | | | | 2 | | | 2 | 1 | 2 | 2 | |
| No-balls | 3 | | 7 | 10 | 4 | 2 | 2 | | 11 | 3 | 3 | | 10 | 11 |
| Total | 412 | | 183 | 136 | 296 | 75 | 179 | 0 | 188 | 253 | 175 | 70 | 277 | 121 |
| Wickets | 7 | | 10 | 7 | 10 | 0 | 4 | 0 | 10 | 3 | 9† | 10 | 10 | 7 |
| Result | D | | W | | D | | W | | W | | L | | D | |
| Points | 7 | | 21 | | 3 | | 17 | | 19 | | 5 | | 7 | |

| Kent C.C.C. | v. Sussex (Tunbridge Wells) 13–15 June | | v. Oxford University (Oxford) 16–19 June | | v. Derbyshire (Derby) 23–26 June | | v. Worcestershire (Worcester) 27–29 June | | v. Sussex (Hastings) 30 June–3 July | | v. Lancashire (Maidstone) 7–10 July | | v. Derbyshire (Maidstone) 11–13 July | |
|---|---|---|---|---|---|---|---|---|---|---|---|---|---|---|
| R.A. Woolmer | 4 | 0* | | | | | | | | | | | | |
| N.R. Taylor | | | 28 | — | 9 | 45* | 23 | 21 | 50 | 7 | 17 | 108 | 11 | 6 |
| C.J. Tavare | 34 | 5 | 102 | — | 32 | 8 | 12 | 96 | 2 | 1 | — | 79 | 34 | 18 |
| D.G. Aslett | 9 | 0 | 33 | — | 20 | 2* | 17 | 109 | 12 | 0 | — | 47 | 55 | 36 |
| C.S. Cowdrey | 8 | 63 | 42 | — | 95 | — | 32 | 28* | 8 | 5 | — | — | 54 | 23 |
| R.M. Ellison | | | 108 | — | 35 | — | 10 | — | 0 | 18 | — | 5* | 24 | 5 |
| A.P.E. Knott | 0 | 14 | | | | | | | 0 | 21 | — | 0 | 25 | 8 |
| G.W. Johnson | 0 | 9 | 0 | — | 35 | — | 15 | 17* | 0 | 0 | — | 4 | 0 | 37 |
| C. Penn | | | | | | | | | | | | | | |
| D.L. Underwood | 16 | 2 | | | 4 | — | 12 | — | 6 | 111 | 26* | 0 | 1 | 10 |
| K.B.S. Jarvis | 7 | 1* | 3 | — | 0 | — | 0 | — | 0* | 1 | — | — | 19 | 0* |
| L. Potter | 7 | 13 | 38 | — | 39 | 0 | 22 | 16 | 2 | 14 | | | | |
| S.N.V. Waterton | | | 36* | — | | | | | | | | | | |
| T.M. Alderman | 10* | 1 | | | 1 | — | 9* | — | 3 | 52* | — | 0* | 24* | 2 |
| S.G. Hinks | 14 | 16 | 4 | — | | | | | | | | | | |
| M.R. Benson | | | 20 | — | | | | | | | 25* | 12 | 25 | 3 |
| S.A. Marsh | | | | | 30* | — | 5 | — | | | | | | |
| G.R. Cowdrey | | | | | | | | | | | | | | |
| K.D. Masters | | | | | | | | | | | | | | |
| Byes | | | | | | | 7 | 4 | | 1 | | | 2 | |
| Leg-byes | 2 | 6 | 3 | | 4 | 1 | 10 | 8 | 5 | 3 | 5 | 3 | 2 | |
| Wides | | 10 | 1 | | 1 | 1 | | 2 | | 2 | | | 3 | 1 |
| No-balls | 3 | 2 | 1 | | | 1 | 6 | 2 | 4 | 7 | 1 | 11 | | 3 |
| Total | 114 | 142 | 419 | | 310 | 58 | 180 | 303 | 92 | 243 | 74 | 279 | 279 | 152 |
| Wickets | 10 | 9† | 10 | | 10 | 2 | 10 | 4 | 10 | 10 | 1 | 8 | 10 | 10 |
| Result | L | | W | | W | | D | | Tie | | D | | W | |
| Points | 3 | | — | | 23 | | 2 | | 12 | | 1 | | 21 | |

*Catches* 30–A.P.E. Knott (ct 29/st 1)
29–T.M. Alderman
28–G.W. Johnson
21–C.J. Tavare
18–C.S. Cowdrey
15–D.G. Aslett and S.N.V. Waterton (ct 12/st 3)
11–D.L. Underwood and S.A. Marsh
8–N.R. Taylor and C. Penn
7–R.M. Ellison, M.R. Benson and subs

*Canterbury, Kent. (Adrian Murrell)*

| v. Northamptonshire (Northampton) 14–17 July | v. Surrey (The Oval) 25–27 July | v. Warwickshire (Edgbaston) 28–31 July | v. Leicestershire (Canterbury) 4–7 August | v. Surrey (Canterbury) 8–10 August | v. Sri Lankans (Canterbury) 11–13 August | v. Nottinghamshire (Folkestone) 18–21 August | v. Essex (Colchester) 22–24 August | v. Hampshire (Bournemouth) 25–28 August | v. Somerset (Taunton) 29–31 August | v. Middlesex (Lord's) 5–7 September | v. Glamorgan (Canterbury) 8–11 September | M | Inns | NOs | Runs | H/S | Av |
|---|---|---|---|---|---|---|---|---|---|---|---|---|---|---|---|---|---|
| | | | | | | | | | | | | 8 | 14 | 3 | 427 | 153 | 38·81 |
| 22 86* | 6 5* | 73 6 | 10 48* | 14 1 | 17 14 | 1 67 | | 1 0 | 139 31 | | | 21 | 39 | 5 | 1098 | 139 | 32·29 |
| 45 12 | 6 25 | 62 40 | 117 1 | | | 32 0 | | | 39 19 | 42 — | 2 55 | 22 | 38 | — | 1119 | 117 | 29.44 |
| 10 6 | 29 11 | 8 1 | 33 12 | 0 4 | 6 221* | 5 1 | 1 — | 42 0 | 15 152 | 3 — | 43 87 | 26 | 45 | 3 | 1491 | 221* | 35.50 |
| 6 32 | 59 5 | 33 4 | 6 51* | 102 14 | 16 16 | 28 19 | 125* — | 0 1 | | 26 — | 40 1 | 21 | 36 | 3 | 1025 | 125* | 31.06 |
| 38* 26* | | 79* 0 | 45 — | | | 6 35 | | | 23 10 | 1 — | 0 1 | 19 | 29 | 6 | 546 | 108 | 23.73 |
| 13* — | 0 23 | | 32 — | | | | | 3 4 | | | | 14 | 22 | 2 | 295 | 43 | 14.75 |
| 45 2 | | 42 3 | 37 — | 84 3 | 12 52* | 2 24 | 15 — | 17 47 | 21 0 | 8 — | 8 — | 25 | 39 | 5 | 726 | 84 | 21.35 |
| | 0 0 | | | | 13 — | | 0 — | 0 65 | | 0 — | | 12 | 15 | 2 | 317 | 115 | 24.38 |
| — — | 24* 27* | 12* 26* | 6 — | 6 18* | | 19 0 | 1 — | 14 0 | 14 20 | 0* — | 33* 5 | 24 | 33 | 9 | 498 | 111 | 20.75 |
| — — | — — | — 0 | 0 — | 1* — | | 0* 0* | 0 — | | 4* 0* | 0* — | 0 3* | 23 | 25 | 13 | 41 | 19 | 3.41 |
| | | | | 14 57 | 15 27 | | 10 5* | 46 1 | 0 10 | 61 — | 9 117 | 14 | 25 | 1 | 574 | 117 | 23.91 |
| | | 40 0 | | | 6 — | | 16 — | | 0 20 | | 19 6 | 7 | 10 | 1 | 193 | 50 | 21.44 |
| — — | 1 8* | — 4 | 0* — | 2 1* | | 22 8* | 18 — | 16* 4* | | | 16 3 | 20 | 27 | 13 | 220 | 52* | 15.71 |
| | 27 0 | | 39 8 | 1 4 | 36 4 | | 0 — | 0 9 | | | | 8 | 14 | — | 162 | 39 | 11.57 |
| 45 32 | 1 30 | 2 18 | | 1 120 | 24 65 | 54 115 | 4 5* | 6 52 | 21 48 | 127 — | 0 59 | 14 | 26 | 2 | 914 | 127 | 38.08 |
| | | | | 0 9 | | 48 9 | | | | 5 — | | 5 | 7 | 1 | 106 | 48 | 17.66 |
| | | | | | 7 — | | | | | | | 1 | 1 | | 7 | 7 | 7.00 |
| | | | | | 0* — | | | | 0 0 | | | 2 | 3 | 1 | 0 | 0* | 0.00 |
| 5 4 | 12 5 | 1 2 | | 4 9 | 11 1 | 3 | | 2 1 | 2 | 1 | 8 | | | | | | |
| 8 1 | 3 1 | 9 9 | 1 3 | 4 6 | 7 12 | 6 3 | 3 | 1 | 13 2 | 10 | 7 9 | | | | | | |
| 1 | 2 | 1 | | 1 | 2 | | 1 | | 1 | | 2 | | | | | | |
| 12 3 | 1 3 | 4 12 | 9 3 | 2 | 10 8 | 5 4 | 7 | 4 | | 1 | 8 4 | | | | | | |
| 250 204 | 171 143 | 366 125 | 335 126 | 236 246 | 182 420 | 231 285 | 201 10 | 147 189 | 290 314 | 285 | 195 350 | | | | | | |
| 6 5 | 9 7 | 7 10 | 10 3 | 10 8 | 10 5 | 10 9 | 10 0 | 10 10 | 10 10 | 9 | 10 9 | | | | | | |
| Tie | D | L | D | W | D | D | W | W | D | D | D | | | | | | |
| 15 | 2 | 5 | 8 | 22 | — | 6 | 22 | 20 | 3 | 6 | 4 | | | | | | |

† R.A. Woolmer retired hurt

6 – L. Potter
5 – K.B.S. Jarvis
4 – R.A. Woolmer
3 – S.G. Hinks
2 – G.R. Cowdrey

| **Kent C.C.C.** First-Class Matches – Bowling, 1984 | K.B.S. Jarvis | R.M. Ellison | C. Penn | D.L. Underwood | G.W. Johnson | R.A. Woolmer | N.R. Taylor | D.G. Aslett | C.S. Cowdrey |
|---|---|---|---|---|---|---|---|---|---|
| *v.* Gloucestershire (Bristol) 28–30 April | 23–6–51–3<br>22–4–63–0 | 28–6–52–3<br>25–7–70–0 | 16–2–36–0<br>18–6–50–0 | 27–14–25–2<br>33–7–74–4 | 8–2–17–0<br>14–1–45–0 | 4–0–16–2 | <br>5–0–19–0 | <br>1–0–7–0 | |
| *v.* Essex (Canterbury) 2–4 May | 17–5–45–3<br>15–2–57–3 | 20.5–5–35–4<br>19.4–5–27–5 | 3–1–12–0 | 11–4–28–1 | | 4–2–2–1 | | | 18–3–66–0<br>12–3–26–2 |
| *v.* Lancashire (Old Trafford) 9–11 May | 14–5–28–1<br>17–6–39–2 | | 8–1–22–0<br>6–0–12–0 | 15–10–14–1<br>26–15–33–3 | 5–2–13–0<br>22–14–24–3 | | | | |
| *v.* Hampshire (Canterbury) 26–29 May | 2–1–1–0 | 7–3–9–3 | | 11.2–2–21–7 | | | | | |
| *v.* Middlesex (Dartford) 30 May–1 June | 14–0–66–4<br>9–2–33–2 | 18–6–36–0<br>3–2–2–0 | 6–0–29–0 | 32–14–49–2<br>15–7–41–2 | 13–3–34–1 | 9–1–25–1<br>3–0–8–1 | | | |
| *v.* Gloucestershire (Canterbury) 2–5 June | 17–6–36–1<br>17.2–6–49–3 | 22–10–31–3<br>11–7–14–1 | 6–2–11–2<br>5–1–11–0 | 1–1–0–0<br>3–1–6–0 | | | | | |
| *v.* Yorkshire (Tunbridge Wells) 9–12 June | | 28–4–80–2<br>18–8–22–3 | 4–1–13–0<br>8–0–33–0 | 26–17–27–4<br>20–5–41–1 | 11–0–50–0<br>11–0–64–0 | | | | 10.3–5–21–2<br>6–0–22–0 |
| *v.* Sussex (Tunbridge Wells) 13–15 June | 26.3–6–78–2 | | | 9–4–12–2 | | | | | 29–10–64–3 |
| *v.* Oxford University 16–19 June | 14–4–43–4<br>14–6–30–5 | 5–1–12–0 | | | 26.3–10–65–4<br>42.4–16–52–5 | | 1–0–7–0<br>5–2–12–0 | <br>5–1–14–0 | 7–1–18–0<br>6–1–18–0 |
| *v.* Derbyshire (Derby) 23–26 June | 18–6–46–1<br>16–3–41–4 | 16–8–34–4<br>10.5–3–41–3 | | | | | | | 10–0–40–2<br>6–2–8–1 |
| *v.* Worcestershire (Worcester) 27–29 June | 6–1–20–0 | 21–2–72–1 | | 35–11–95–2 | 22–4–60–0 | | | | 9–0–42–0 |
| *v.* Sussex (Hastings) 30 June–3 July | 16–7–34–4<br>11–2–33–2 | 14.4–4–29–2<br>17–5–29–2 | | 2–0–14–0<br>13–3–43–1 | | | | | 6–1–15–0<br>4–0–21–0 |
| *v.* Lancashire (Maidstone) 7–10 July | 13–2–57–0 | 8–1–37–0 | | 22–8–47–1 | 17.4–4–73–2 | | | | 13–2–50–0 |
| *v.* Derbyshire (Maidstone) 11–13 July | 13–3–40–0<br>10–1–41–2 | 14–1–47–3<br>7–3–12–0 | | 22–9–57–1<br>14.5–7–25–4 | 11.4–3–25–0 | | | | 7–1–31–0 |
| *v.* Northamptonshire (Northampton) 14–17 July | 13–3–43–1<br>9–1–52–2 | 14–6–22–4<br>21–2–77–1 | | <br>13–4–49–0 | <br>10–1–41–0 | | | | 7–1–20–0<br>7–1–21–2 |
| *v.* Surrey (The Oval) 25–27 July | 18–5–46–1<br>19–3–49–5 | | 18–3–48–1<br>9–0–61–1 | 18–3–60–0 | | | | | 9–1–34–0<br>7–0–36–1 |
| *v.* Warwickshire (Edgbaston) 28–31 July | 15–4–50–1<br>5–2–27–0 | 17–4–45–2<br>10–0–41–2 | | 22.5–8–37–0<br>5–1–11–0 | 12–2–42–0<br>7–2–21–0 | | | <br>2.4–0–10–0 | 13–4–25–1<br>7–0–32–0 |
| *v.* Leicestershire (Canterbury) 4–7 August | 16–2–53–1 | 16–4–57–0 | | 13–6–22–4 | | | | | 6–1–32–0 |
| *v.* Surrey (Canterbury) 8–10 August | 18–4–45–2<br>14–3–44–2 | | | 11.3–5–36–3<br>8–4–24–3 | 7–1–18–0 | | | | 7–0–21–0<br>8–1–18–2 |
| *v.* Sri Lankans (Canterbury) 11–13 August | | | 18–4–51–1 | | 19–4–47–1 | | 4–1–16–10 | 4–0–20–0 | |
| *v.* Nottinghamshire 18–21 August | 13–3–32–1<br>19–2–78–2 | 10.5–2–50–2<br>13–2–60–0 | | 7–2–23–0<br>16–2–75–0 | <br>19–3–59–2 | | | | 15–4–53–2 |
| *v.* Essex (Colchester) 22–24 August | 11–2–45–4<br>7–0–41–0 | | 4–1–9–0<br>3–0–8–1 | <br>10–3–20–3 | | | | | 6.4–3–6–2<br>5–0–10–1 |
| *v.* Hampshire (Bournemouth) 25–28 August | | | 5–1–17–0<br>6–0–15–1 | 27–13–34–4<br>42–15–87–8 | 11.5–3–38–5<br>32–12–53–1 | | | | 4–2–7–1 |
| *v.* Somerset (Taunton) 29–31 August | 27–5–91–0<br>5–0–29–2 | 4–1–9–0 | | 40.1–11–145–3<br>5–0–21–3 | 31–4–114–3<br>1–0–5–0 | | | | |
| *v.* Middlesex (Lord's) 5–7 September | 14–1–61–1<br>5–0–11–0 | 10–2–23–0<br>9–2–18–0 | 9–1–42–1<br>5–2–11–0 | 33–10–62–3<br>12–4–35–0 | 36–6–75–4<br>14–6–18–1 | | | <br>6–0–41–0 | |
| *v.* Glamorgan (Canterbury) 8–11 September | 13–2–42–1<br>6–2–18–0 | 18–10–30–3 | | 32–14–57–1<br>23–6–61–4 | 30–9–70–2<br>25–5–97–5 | | | | |
| | 571.5–128–<br>1788–72<br>*av.* 24.83 | 456.3–126–<br>1123–53<br>*av.* 21.19 | 157–26–<br>491–8<br>*av.* 61.37 | 676.4–250–<br>1511–77<br>*av.* 19.62 | 462.2–117–<br>1220–39<br>*av.* 31.28 | 20–3–<br>51–5<br>*av.* 10.20 | 15–3–<br>54–0<br>— | 18.4–1–<br>92–0<br>— | 245.1–47–<br>757–22<br>*av.* 34.40 |

a C.J. Tavare 1–0–1–0

b G.R. Cowdrey 7–0–22–1
K.D. Masters 19.5–1–88–2

c K.D. Masters 22–5–85–2
d C.J. Tavare 1–0–17–0

| T.M. Alderman | L. Potter | S.G. Hinks | Byes | Leg-byes | Wides | No-balls | Total | Wkts |
|---|---|---|---|---|---|---|---|---|
| | | | 1 | 3 | | 3 | 204 | 10 |
| | | | 4 | 1 | | 1 | 334 | 4 |
| | | | | 10 | 1 | 3 | 202 | 10 |
| | | | | | 1 | 2 | 113 | 10 |
| 12–6–12–0 | | | | 4 | | 3 | 96 | 2 |
| 16–6–35–1 | 3–2–4–0 | | 9 | 2 | | 8 | 166 | 9 |
| | | | | | | | — | — |
| 6–0–20–0 | | | | 4 | 1 | | 56 | 10 |
| 17–3–58–2 | | | 4 | 2 | 1 | 6 | 310 | 10 |
| 12–3–36–1 | | | | 2 | | 7 | 129 | 6 |
| 24.5–11–40–4 | | | | 2 | 1 | 9 | 130 | 10 |
| 19–9–32–2 | | | | 1 | | 3 | 116 | 6 |
| 30–8–88–2 | | | | 6 | 3 | 9 | 297 | 10 |
| 12–1–27–0 | 4–1–16–1 | | 3 | 3 | 1 | 2 | 234 | 5 |
| 31–11–72–2 | | 7–2–26–1 | | 3 | 1 | 1 | 257 | 10 |
| | 15–8–31–2 | | | 4 | | 4 | 184 | 10 |
| | 17–4–43–0 | | 4 | 3 | 1 | 1 | 178 | 10 |
| 19.2–3–66–3 | | | | 5 | | 8 | 199 | 10 |
| 20–6–69–2 | | | | | | 2 | 161 | 10 |
| 28–3–129–3 | | | 4 | 9 | 1 | 3 | 436 | 6a |
| 16–7–46–4 | | | | 1 | | 4 | 143 | 10 |
| 23.1–7–60–5 | | | 1 | | 1 | 4 | 192 | 10 |
| 24–2–131–1 | | | 2 | 6 | | 1 | 404 | 4 |
| | | | | | | | 0 | 0 |
| 14–3–46–1 | | | | 2 | 1 | 2 | 251 | 5 |
| 12–3–40–3 | | | | 4 | | 5 | 127 | 10 |
| 15.5–6–34–5 | | | | 3 | 1 | 1 | 124 | 10 |
| 20–4–89–3 | | | | 1 | | | 330 | 10 |
| 21.5–5–51–1 | | | 7 | 3 | 1 | 5 | 255 | 3 |
| 2–0–12–0 | | | 2 | | | 2 | 162 | 8 |
| 16–3–76–1 | | | 4 | 16 | 2 | 4 | 301 | 6 |
| 8–0–49–0 | | | | 2 | | | 193 | 2 |
| 15–7–25–5 | | | 4 | 3 | | 1 | 197 | 10 |
| 18–8–52–5 | | | 8 | 1 | 1 | 1 | 183 | 10 |
| 9.4–2–35–3 | | | | 2 | | 1 | 124 | 10 |
| | 12–2–45–1 | 9–1–27–1 | 2 | 10 | 1 | 11 | 340 | 7b |
| 18–6–44–5 | | | 1 | 6 | | 3 | 212 | 10 |
| 20–2–74–0 | | | | 16 | | 5 | 367 | 4 |
| 9–4–19–4 | | | | 4 | | 7 | 90 | 10 |
| 12–2–27–5 | | | | 4 | 5 | 3 | 118 | 10 |
| 7–2–16–0 | | | | | | 2 | 114 | 10 |
| 1–0–5–0 | | | 8 | 6 | | 4 | 178 | 10 |
| | 4–1–20–1 | | 1 | 10 | | 19 | 494 | 10c |
| | | | | 8 | | | 63 | 5 |
| | | | 6 | 2 | | 1 | 272 | 9 |
| | 8–0–37–0 | | | | | 2 | 190 | 1d |
| 23–4–89–3 | | | | 6 | 1 | 1 | 296 | 10 |
| 7–2–21–0 | | | 5 | 4 | | 3 | 209 | 9 |
| 559.4–149–1725–76 av. 22.69 | 63–18–196–5 av. 39.20 | 16–3–53–2 av. 26.50 | | | | | | |

*Paul Johnson. His brisk and stylish batting did much to bolster Notts' title challenge. (Adrian Murrell)*

### at Taunton

**Somerset** 274 (J.W. Lloyds 94, M.D. Crowe 57, R.J. Hadlee 4 for 59, K.E. Cooper 4 for 57) and 244 for 5 dec (P.M. Roebuck 78, J.W. Lloyds 63 not out, E.E. Hemmings 4 for 123)
**Nottinghamshire** 227 for 7 dec (B.C. Broad 88 not out, D.W. Randall 64) and 293 (C.E.B. Rice 98, V. J. Marks 6 for 111, S.C. Booth 4 for 138)

*Somerset won by 3 runs*
*Somerset 22 pts, Nottinghamshire 6 pts*

### at The Oval

**Worcestershire** 329 for 3 dec (T.S. Curtis 105, D.M. Smith 100 not out, D.N. Patel 81) and 327 for 7 (G. Hick 82 not out, P.A. Neale 76 not out, D.M. Smith 55)
**Surrey** 307 for 7 dec (C.J. Richards 100 not out)

*Match drawn*
*Worcestershire 7 pts, Surrey 5 pts*

### at Hove

**Yorkshire** 250 for 5 dec (M.D. Moxon 84, G. Boycott 77) and 98 for 2 (G. Boycott 50 not out)
**Sussex** 202 for 4 dec (G.D. Mendis 78, P.W.G. Parker 65)

*Match drawn*
*Sussex 4 pts., Yorkshire 4 pts.*

### at Edgbaston

**Warwickshire** 133 (P.B. Clift 8 for 26) and 303 (D.L. Amiss 122, I.R. Carmichael 5 for 84)
**Leicestershire** 174 (D.I. Gower 61, A.M. Ferreira 6 for 70) and 263 for 6 (D.I. Gower 117 not out, I.P. Butcher 77)

*Leicestershire won by 4 wickets*
*Leicestershire 21 pts, Warwickshire 4 pts*

| **Lancashire C.C.C.** First-Class Matches – Batting, 1984 | v. Oxford University (Oxford) 28 April–1 May | | v. Derbyshire (Old Trafford) 2–4 May | | v. Kent (Old Trafford) 9–11 May | | v. Warwickshire (Nuneaton) 23–25 May | | v. Yorkshire (Leeds) 26–28 May | | v. Northamptonshire (Northampton) 30 May–1 June | | v. Surrey (Old Trafford) 2–5 June | | v. Sussex (Old Trafford) 9–12 June | | v. Somerset (Bath) 13–15 June | | v. Glamorgan (Cardiff) 16–19 June | | v. Worcestershire (Old Trafford) 23–26 June | | v. Gloucestershire (Old Trafford) 27–29 June | | v. Middlesex (Liverpool) 30 June–3 July | | v. Kent (Maidstone) 7–10 July | |
|---|---|---|---|---|---|---|---|---|---|---|---|---|---|---|---|---|---|---|---|---|---|---|---|---|---|---|---|---|
| J.A. Ormrod | 50 | — | 35 | 19 | 40* | 0 | | | 60 | — | 31 | — | 67 | 32 | 15 | 2 | 26 | 95* | 62 | — | | | 48 | 29 | 11 | 7 | 73 | — |
| S.J. O'Shaughnessy | 17 | — | 1 | 32* | 0 | 14 | 28 | 8 | 7 | — | | | 46 | 23 | 86 | 28 | 159* | 18 | | | 13 | 0 | 43 | 0 | 30 | 51 | 39 | — |
| F.C. Hayes | 11 | — | | | | | | | | | | | | | | | | | | | | | | | | | | |
| D.P. Hughes | 105 | — | 72 | 43* | — | 6 | 9 | 0 | 14 | — | 12 | — | 38 | 19 | | | 113 | 4 | 30 | 16 | 10 | 12 | | | 0 | 4 | | |
| N.H. Fairbrother | 38 | — | | | | | 0 | 19 | 42* | — | 72 | — | 1 | 62 | 55 | 0 | 10 | 3 | 66 | 68 | 42 | 49 | 8 | 8 | 0 | 2 | — | — |
| J. Abrahams | 123 | — | 26 | — | 31* | 39 | 201* | 45 | 12 | — | 47 | — | 8 | 9 | 12 | 20 | 0 | 5 | 83 | 14 | 1 | 28 | 3 | 81 | 6 | 58* | 22* | — |
| S.T. Jefferies | 65 | — | 25 | — | — | 2 | — | 14 | 0 | — | | | 31 | 14 | 48 | 28* | | | 3 | 55* | 38 | 45 | 23 | 43 | 11 | 6 | 20 | — |
| L.L. McFarlane | — | — | 0* | — | — | 1* | | | — | — | 1 | — | 0* | — | 1* | 0 | | | | | | | | | | | | |
| C. Maynard | — | — | | | — | 23 | — | 50* | 32* | — | 22 | — | 5 | 16 | 1* | — | | | | | | | | | | | | |
| P.J.W. Allott | 50* | — | 30 | — | — | 22 | — | 10 | — | — | 7 | — | | | 22 | 20 | — | 1 | 1 | — | 27 | 5 | 4 | 11* | 20 | 0 | — | — |
| S.M.N. Zaidi | 18* | — | 36 | — | — | 34* | — | — | | | | | | | 6 | 0 | — | 4* | | | | | | | | | | |
| G. Fowler | | | 30 | 70 | 18 | 0 | 6 | 18 | 107 | — | | | | | 0 | 21 | | | | | 17 | 22 | | | | | 226 | — |
| J. Simmons | | | 6 | — | | | 72* | 14 | 4 | — | 54 | — | 13 | 22 | 38 | 26 | 20* | 0 | 16 | 16 | 10 | 9 | 18 | 23 | | | — | — |
| J. Stanworth | | | 6 | — | | | | | | | | | | | | | — | — | — | — | 1 | 0* | 3 | — | 3 | 0* | — | — |
| I. Folley | | | | | — | 6 | | | | | 5 | — | 0 | 7* | | | | | — | 14 | 6* | 2 | 2 | 2* | 13* | 4 | — | — |
| D.W. Varey | | | | | | | 19 | — | | | 20 | — | | | | | | | | | | | | | | | | |
| D.J. Makinson | | | | | | | | | | | 5* | — | | | | | | | | | | | | | | | | |
| M. Watkinson | | | | | | | | | | | | | 0 | 22* | | | — | 41 | 2* | 10* | | | 26* | 24 | 77 | 6 | 15* | — |
| M.R. Chadwick | | | | | | | | | | | | | | | | | 30 | 16 | 52 | 29 | 3 | 7 | 8 | 3 | 19 | 0 | | |
| N.V. Radford | | | | | | | | | | | | | | | | | | | | | | | | | | | | |
| B.P. Patterson | | | | | | | | | | | | | | | | | | | | | | | | | | | | |
| K.A. Hayes | | | | | | | | | | | | | | | | | | | | | | | | | | | | |
| Byes | 14 | | | 15 | | 9 | 4 | 2 | | | 3 | | 5 | 18 | | 1 | | 7 | 4 | 11 | 7 | 6 | 4 | | | | 2 | |
| Leg-byes | 4 | | 2 | 9 | 4 | 2 | 9 | | 6 | | 2 | | 4 | 3 | 6 | 9 | 6 | 4 | 8 | 7 | 3 | 8 | 7 | 6 | 10 | | 6 | |
| Wides | | | | | | | 5 | | 1 | | 1 | | | 1 | 1 | | 1 | 1 | 1 | | 1 | 1 | | | 1 | | | |
| No-balls | | | | 2 | 3 | 8 | 16 | 6 | 3 | | 7 | | 1 | 3 | 5 | 4 | 4 | 2 | 9 | 11 | 4 | 2 | | 11 | 7 | 3 | 1 | |
| Total | 495 | | 269 | 190 | 96 | 166 | 369 | 186 | 288 | | 289 | | 219 | 251 | 296 | 159 | 369 | 201 | 337 | 251 | 183 | 196 | 197 | 281 | 208 | 141 | 404 | 0 |
| Wickets | 7 | | 10 | 1 | 2 | 9 | 5 | 8 | 7 | | 10 | | 10 | 8 | 9† | 9 | 5 | 8 | 8 | 6 | 10 | 10 | 10 | 8 | 10 | 9 | 4 | 0 |
| Result | W | | D | | D | | D | | D | | D | | D | | L | | D | | D | | D | | D | | D | | D | |
| Points | — | | 4 | | 3 | | 4 | | 6 | | 4 | | 6 | | 6 | | 8 | | 8 | | 5 | | 5 | | 5 | | 4 | |

*Catches* 33 – C. Maynard (ct 28/st 5); 19 – J. Abrahams and N.H. Fairbrother; 17 – J. Stanworth (ct 16/st 1); 14 – J. Simmons; 12 – D.P. Hughes; 11 – S.J. O'Shaughnessy; 10 – J.A. Ormrod; 7 – M. Watkinson; 6 – I. Folley, Nasir Zaidi and P.J.W. Allott

Not since Plum Warner's last season, 1920, when Middlesex won the title, has the County Championship had such a magnificent climax. The issue at the start of the last round of matches was simple. If both Essex and Nottinghamshire won, then Notts would take the title; if Essex won and Notts failed to win, the champions would retain the pennant.

Essex accomplished their part of the task in two days. Fletcher viewed the Old Trafford wicket with some suspicion and included two spinners in his side for the first time in the season. He asked Lancashire to bat when he won the toss and watched Fowler begin at a furious and fortuitous rate. Pringle then gnawed away at the middle order, however, and, in spite of a typical Fairbrother flourish, Lancashire were bowled out for 229. Essex attacked the bowling from the start and in dreadful light they reached 153 for the loss of Gooch by the close. It was worth reflecting, however, that if cricketers showed more urgency in June and July, they wouldn't find it necessary to bat in the dark in September. On the Monday, the Essex assault on the Lancashire bowling continued. Paul Prichard, whose praises we have sung fully since he was nine years old, reached a splendid maiden century and Ken McEwan was denied the fastest hundred of the season only because, having reached 95 in 75 minutes, he was denied an adequate share of the bowling. His 132 came off 117 balls and included thirteen fours and four sixes. There was a merry thrash by all and Lancashire were batting again by 2.55, 217 runs behind. Jack Simmons had secured seven wickets as the ball flew in all directions. Lever, far from fit, reduced the home side to 50 for 5, taking 4 of the wickets himself, and although Abrahams, Watkinson and Maynard offered resistance, Essex needed only three overs to win the game by seven o'clock on Monday evening.

Nottinghamshire now knew that they had to win at Taunton, but they were very much at the mercy of Botham, who had elected to bat, and the weather, which had restricted play on the first day and washed out the last day's play at Hove. Somerset, with Lloyds, rumoured to be leaving the county for Gloucestershire, playing a fine innings, were bowled out on Monday morning for 274. Bruce French held a record six catches behind the stumps for Notts, but he missed three chances on the Monday morning which could have had serious repercussions for his side. Rice declared 72 behind in an effort to force a win, but he could capture no Somerset wicket before the close. To Botham's eternal credit, he rid his mind of all external pressures and concentrated solely on trying to win the match for Somerset. He declared in mid-afternoon and asked Notts to make 297 in 52 overs. In effect, with two spinners operating for most of the innings,

| v. Essex (Southend) 11–13 July | | v. Hampshire (Portsmouth) 14–17 July | | v. Derbyshire (Buxton) 25–27 July | | v. Nottinghamshire (Trent Bridge) 28–31 July | | v. Yorkshire (Old Trafford) 4–7 August | | v. Northamptonshire (Southport) 8–10 August | | v. Leicestershire (Leicester) 11–14 August | | v. Warwickshire (Old Trafford) 18–21 August | | v. Nottinghamshire (Blackpool) 22–24 August | | v. Gloucestershire (Bristol) 25–28 August | | v. Essex (Old Trafford) 8–11 September | | M | Inns | NOs | Runs | H/S | Av |
|---|---|---|---|---|---|---|---|---|---|---|---|---|---|---|---|---|---|---|---|---|---|---|---|---|---|---|---|---|---|
| 2 | 10 | 51 | 139* | 9 | 4 | 33 | 41 | 4 | — | 2 | 29 | 44 | 33 | 16 | 0 | 15 | 8 | 33 | 9 | 12 | 3 | 23 | 40 | 3 | 1199 | 139* | 32.40 |
| | | 26 | 103* | 9 | 10 | 19 | 39 | 18 | — | 27* | 75 | 29 | 19 | 129 | 12 | 1 | 0 | 5 | 3 | | | 21 | 38 | 4 | 1167 | 159* | 34.32 |
| | | | | | | | | | | | | | | | | | | | | | | 1 | 1 | — | 11 | 11 | 11.00 |
| 3 | 29 | 8 | — | 3 | 33 | 0 | 5 | 2 | — | | | | | | | 18 | 43 | 8 | 9 | 29 | 0 | 19 | 32 | 1 | 707 | 113 | 22.80 |
| 9 | 61 | 14 | — | 36 | 102 | 32 | 3 | 40 | — | 12 | 65 | 8 | 15 | 15 | 66 | 9 | 10 | 1 | 81 | 77 | 0 | 23 | 39 | 1 | 1201 | 102 | 31.60 |
| 6 | 10 | 67 | — | 11 | 37* | 14 | 11 | 12 | — | 0 | 1 | 36 | 100* | 2 | 3 | | | | | 1 | 31 | 23 | 39 | 6 | 1216 | 201* | 36.84 |
| 12 | 8 | | | | | 12 | 37 | 29 | — | | | 14 | 27* | 23 | 0 | 0 | — | | | | | 18 | 28 | 3 | 633 | 65 | 25.32 |
| | | | | | | | | | | 1 | 15* | 0* | — | | | 3 | 2 | 0 | 9* | 2 | 6 | 12 | 15 | 7 | 41 | 15* | 5.12 |
| | | | | | | 1 | 5 | 6 | — | 5 | 1 | 19 | — | 23 | 17 | 19 | 31* | 47* | 5 | 25 | 49 | 15 | 21 | 5 | 402 | 50* | 25.12 |
| | | | | | | | | 2* | — | | | | | 4* | 23 | | | | | | | 15 | 18 | 4 | 259 | 50* | 18.50 |
| | | | | | | | | | | | | | | | | | | | | | | 6 | 6 | 3 | 98 | 36 | 32.66 |
| | | | | | | | | 1 | — | | | | | 38 | 7 | | | | | 63 | 17 | 10 | 17 | — | 661 | 226 | 38.88 |
| 20 | 42* | 1* | — | 58 | 3 | | | 17 | — | 2 | 17 | 16 | — | 0 | 59 | 72 | 0 | 18 | 2 | 1 | 19* | 21 | 34 | 5 | 748 | 72* | 25.79 |
| 0* | 0 | — | — | 5 | 0 | | | | | | | | | | | | | | | | | 10 | 10 | 3 | 18 | 6 | 2.57 |
| 0 | 5 | | | 22* | 0 | 3 | 22 | | | 1 | 3 | 2 | — | 17* | 18* | 7* | 10 | 3 | 14 | 5* | 1 | 17 | 28 | 9 | 194 | 22* | 10.21 |
| 11 | 1 | 61 | 25 | 3 | 7 | 6 | 24 | | | 8 | 5 | 26 | 19* | | | | | | | | | 8 | 14 | 1 | 235 | 61 | 18.07 |
| 0 | 1 | — | — | | | | | | | | | | | | | | | 9 | 3* | | | 4 | 5 | 2 | 18 | 9 | 6.00 |
| 8 | 21 | 45 | — | 7 | 19 | 26* | 3 | | | 0 | 43 | 9 | 59 | 11 | 0 | 14 | 61 | 2 | 42 | 4 | 70 | 16 | 29 | 6 | 667 | 77 | 29.00 |
| | | | | | | | | | | | | | | | | 61 | 23 | 38 | 4 | | | 7 | 14 | — | 293 | 61 | 20.92 |
| | | — | — | 36 | 1 | 0 | 10* | 6 | — | | | | | | | | | | | | | 4 | 5 | 1 | 53 | 36 | 13.25 |
| | | | | | | | | | | 0 | 10 | | | | | | | | | | | 1 | 2 | | 10 | 10 | 5.00 |
| | | | | | | | | | | | | | | | | | | | | 2 | 13 | 1 | 2 | | 15 | 13 | 7.50 |
| 4 | 5 | 1 | 1 | | 4 | | 1 | | | | | 4 | 4 | 14 | 8 | | 2 | 4 | 5 | | 8 | † C. Maynard, retired hurt | | | | | |
| 1 | 6 | 15 | 5 | 9 | 4 | 5 | 10 | 3 | | | 3 | 9 | 5 | 4 | 5 | 5 | 2 | 3 | 3 | 4 | 2 | absent hurt | | | | | |
| | | | | | 1 | | | 5 | | | | 1 | | | | | | 5 | 1 | | | ‡ S.T. Jefferies absent hurt | | | | | |
| | 1 | 9 | 4 | 3 | 6 | 3 | 2 | 6 | | 12 | 13 | 1 | 4 | 4 | 3 | 11 | 1 | 2 | 5 | 4 | | | | | | | |
| 76 | 200 | 298 | 277 | 211 | 231 | 154 | 213 | 151 | | 70 | 280 | 218 | 285 | 300 | 221 | 235 | 193 | 178 | 195 | 229 | 229 | | | | | | |
| 10 | 10 | 7 | 1 | 10 | 10 | 10 | 10 | 10 | | 10 | 10 | 10 | 4 | 9 | 10 | 10 | 9‡ | 10 | 9 | 10 | 10 | | | | | | |
| L | | L | | L | | L | | D | | L | | W | | L | | L | | D | | L | | | | | | | |
| 4 | | 6 | | 6 | | 4 | | 3 | | 1 | | 22 | | 8 | | 4 | | 5 | | 6 | | | | | | | |

4 – S.T. Jefferies
3 – D.W. Varey and subs
2 – G. Fowler, M.R. Chadwick and L.L. McFarlane

*The Champions. Essex C.C.C. (back row) l to r – D.E. East, A.W. Lilley, K.R. Pont, N.A. Foster, D.R. Pringle, N.A. Phillip, C. Gladwin, B.R. Hardie, K.S. McEwan (front row) l to r – S. Turner, J.K. Lever, K.W.R. Fletcher (capt), G.A. Gooch, D.L. Acfield (P.J. Pritchard and R.E. East are absent). (George Herringshaw)*

| **Lancashire C.C.C.** First-Class Matches – Bowling, 1984 | P.J.W. Allott | S.T. Jefferies | L.L. McFarlane | S.M.N. Zaidi | D.P. Hughes | S.J. O'Shaugnessy | J. Abrahams | J. Simmons | N.V. Radford |
|---|---|---|---|---|---|---|---|---|---|
| *v.* Oxford University (Oxford) 28 April–1 May | 14.2–7–21–4<br>24–8–88–1 | 9–5–18–1<br>12.3–8–13–3 | 16–6–32–3 | 8–3–10–2<br>13–3–34–0 | 29–18–42–3 | 27–6–69–2 | 20–9–25–1 | | |
| *v.* Derbyshire (Old Trafford) 2–4 May | 25–11–47–3 | 14–2–58–0 | 22–5–65–4 | 12–3–39–0 | 29–8–46–1 | 4–3–2–0 | | 47–16–110–2 | |
| *v.* Kent (Old Trafford) 9–11 May | 28–13–56–5<br>1–0–6–0 | 17–3–64–1<br>5–1–18–0 | 17–2–48–2<br>6–0–20–0 | 7–0–25–1 | 7–1–30–0 | 9–1–22–1<br>1–0–2–0 | 12–3–22–0<br>4–0–25–0 | | |
| *v.* Warwickshire (Nuneaton) 23–25 May | 14–4–36–1<br>18–4–54–4 | 10–1–29–0<br>11–1–45–1 | | 8–1–41–0<br>5–0–32–0 | 12.1–0–47–0 | 5–2–13–0<br>10–1–56–0 | 4–1–9–0 | 31–8–66–2<br>12–3–42–1 | |
| *v.* Yorkshire (Leeds) 26–29 May | 15.3–7–31–6<br>5.4–3–5–1 | 17–4–51–2<br>5–2–10–1 | 10–1–53–1 | | | | | 16–3–41–1 | |
| *v.* Northants. (Northampton) 30 May–1 June | 21–4–63–2 | | 17–4–61–0<br>3–2–3–0 | | | | 7–0–26–0 | 28–6–78–2<br>1–1–0–0 | |
| *v.* Surrey (Old Trafford) 2–5 June | | 20–7–34–1<br>13–2–27–0 | 13–2–41–1<br>14–3–46–3 | | 10–3–29–0 | 3–1–15–0 | | 26.5–12–71–5<br>31.4–10–85–5 | |
| *v.* Sussex (Old Trafford 9–12 June | 17–3–57–2<br>13–2–36–1 | 24–6–74–4<br>12–0–38–1 | 7–0–33–0<br>10–2–28–1 | 10–2–30–0<br>4–0–13–0 | | 6–1–24–0 | | 22–2–77–1<br>6–1–21–0 | |
| *v.* Somerset (Bath) 13–15 June | 28–7–72–7<br>16–7–24–2 | | | 4–0–21–0<br>9–0–52–0 | 10–1–43–0<br>4.5–2–21–0 | 15–5–41–0<br>4–0–15–0 | | 24–11–34–1<br>16–6–31–5 | |
| *v.* Glamorgan (Cardiff) 16–19 June | 20–3–56–1<br>6–1–19–1 | 21–4–52–1<br>4–0–15–0 | | | 3–1–3–0 | | 9–1–25–2<br>5–0–15–0 | 25–9–70–0<br>13.5–2–48–2 | |
| *v.* Worcestershire (Old Trafford) 23–26 June | 19–4–53–1<br>4–0–27–2 | 11·4–2–47–1<br>1–0–16–0 | | | | 11–1–40–2 | 5–1–14–1 | 39–9–104–5<br>4–0–30–3 | |
| *v.* Gloucestershire (Old Trafford) 27–29 June | 28.4–8–58–3<br>11–1–31–0 | 21–5–56–5<br>7–1–37–1 | | | | 3–0–17–0 | 1–0–5–0 | 9–5–7–0<br>12–6–22–1 | |
| *v.* Middlesex (Liverpool) 30 June–3 July | 20–6–44–1<br>29–10–46–6 | 17.3–4–61–1<br>25–2–92–2 | | | | 10–3–23–1 | 4–1–14–0<br>1–1–0–0 | | |
| *v.* Kent (Maidstone) 7–10 July | 14.5–6–36–1<br>12–2–44–1 | 12–3–27–0<br>16–3–50–0 | | | | 2–1–2–0<br>4–0–14–0 | 1–1–0–0 | 1–0–1–0<br>25–7–59–5 | |
| *v.* Essex (Southend) 11–13 July | | 17–2–65–0 | | | | | 2–0–6–0 | 28.4–13–51–6 | |
| *v.* Hampshire (Portsmouth) 14–17 July | | | | | | 18–1–75–1<br>7.3–0–53–1 | 4–0–10–0 | 6–0–33–0 | 25.4–4–83–2<br>13–3–67–0 |
| *v.* Derbyshire (Buxton) 25–27 July | | | | | | 6.2–1–18–1 | | 25–6–68–0<br>7–2–30–0 | 26–4–95–5<br>5–2–26–1 |
| *v.* Nottinghamshire (Trent Bridge) 28–31 July | | 32–2–109–4 | | | | 6.4–0–21–2 | | | 32–4–97–2 |
| *v.* Yorkshire (Old Trafford) 4–7 August | 16–5–32–3 | 9–2–27–0 | | | | 8–2–29–2 | | 3–0–8–0 | 5–0–22–0 |
| *v.* Northamptonshire (Southport) 8–10 August | | | 22–4–61–3 | | | 13–3–39–1 | | 26–7–87–0 | |
| *v.* Leicestershire (Leicester) 11–14 August | | 25.2–4–67–6<br>19–2–65–3 | 15–2–33–2<br>7–2–16–1 | | | | | | |
| *v.* Warwickshire (Old Trafford) 18–21 August | 25–9–44–5<br>15–3–37–0 | 19–4–56–2<br>14–3–46–1 | | | | 3–0–10–0<br>4–2–16–0 | 9–1–51–0 | 19.1–4–33–2<br>16–5–34–1 | |
| *v.* Nottinghamshire (Blackpool) 22–24 August | | 9–1–25–1 | 20–2–71–1<br>5–0–12–0 | | | 5–0–29–0 | | 36–9–76–2 | |
| *v.* Gloucestershire (Bristol) 25–28 August | | | 24–3–78–4<br>20.5–3–72–4 | | | 20–4–76–3<br>9–1–32–2 | | 7.3–1–22–2<br>15–8–29–2 | |
| *v.* Essex (Old Trafford) 8–11 September | | | 24–2–102–1 | | | | | 40–5–176–7 | |
| | 461–138–<br>1123–64<br>*av.* 17.54 | 450–86–<br>1392–43<br>*av.* 32.37 | 272.5–45–<br>875–31<br>*av.* 28.22 | 80–12–<br>297–3<br>*av.* 99.00 | 105–34–<br>261–4<br>*av.* 65.25 | 214.3–39–<br>753–19<br>*av.* 39.63 | 88–19–<br>247–4<br>*av.* 61.75 | 619.4–177–<br>1644–63<br>*av.* 26.09 | 106.4–17–<br>390–10<br>*av.* 39.00 |

a G. Fowler 1–0–2–0
b N.H. Fairbrother 3.1–1–11–1
c N.H. Fairbrother 0.1–0–4–0
d B.P. Patterson 21–3–51–0
e N.H. Fairbrother 0.5–0–5–0
f K.A. Hayes 4–0–25–0

| I. Folley | D.J. Makinson | M Watkinson | Byes | Leg-byes | Wides | No-balls | Total | Wkts |
|---|---|---|---|---|---|---|---|---|
| | | | 2 | 5 | 1 | 1 | 90 | 10 |
| | | | 7 | 2 | 5 | 5 | 290 | 10 |
| | | | 12 | 11 | | 4 | 394 | 10 |
| 12-3-20-0 | | | | 5 | | 4 | 296 | 10 |
| | | | | | | 2 | 75 | 0a |
| | | | | 5 | 1 | 6 | 253 | 3 |
| | | | | 6 | 4 | 6 | 245 | 6 |
| | | | | 2 | 5 | 5 | 188 | 10 |
| | | | | 1 | | | 16 | 2 |
| 25-3-81-0 | 10-2-53-1 | | | 12 | | 4 | 378 | 5 |
| | 3-1-8-0 | | | 1 | | 2 | 14 | 0 |
| 3-1-12-0 | | 17-5-43-3 | | 4 | | 1 | 221 | 10 |
| 14-2-40-0 | | 5-1-12-1 | 2 | 3 | | 7 | 251 | 10 |
| | | | | 4 | 1 | 3 | 303 | 7 |
| | | | 5 | | | 1 | 153 | 4b |
| | | 15-1-79-0 | | 7 | | 6 | 303 | 9 |
| | | 4-0-25-0 | 4 | 5 | | 2 | 179 | 8 |
| 19.3-5-65-5 | | 8-0-27-1 | 1 | 4 | 1 | 5 | 306 | 10 |
| 28-5-58-4 | | 2-2-0-1 | 3 | 6 | 1 | 1 | 169 | 8 |
| 16-9-31-0 | | | 1 | 10 | 1 | 2 | 303 | 10 |
| | | | | 1 | | | 74 | 6 |
| 5-2-8-0 | | 17-7-39-2 | | 1 | | 4 | 190 | 10 |
| 14-7-28-3 | | 5-1-22-0 | 4 | 1 | | | 150 | 5 |
| 38-8-101-5 | | 14-1-49-1 | 8 | 7 | | 6 | 313 | 10 |
| 8.3-2-16-2 | | 4-1-11-0 | | 2 | | 2 | 169 | 10 |
| | | 3-1-2-0 | | 5 | | 1 | 74 | 1 |
| 25-5-51-0 | | 12-1-47-1 | | 3 | | 11 | 279 | 8 |
| 12-2-56-0 | 16-3-49-2 | 27-6-68-2 | 2 | 11 | | 14 | 322 | 10 |
| | 20-4-59-1 | 22-7-55-3 | | 11 | 2 | 5 | 300 | 8 |
| | 14-1-55-1 | 11-0-56-0 | 1 | 11 | | 3 | 279 | 2 |
| 21-8-49-2 | | 23-8-71-2 | 6 | 1 | | 5 | 313 | 10 |
| 8.5-2-33-2 | | 7-0-36-0 | | 1 | | 5 | 131 | 3 |
| 22-4-56-1 | | 22-8-56-1 | 1 | 12 | 2 | 10 | 364 | 10 |
| | | | | | | | 4 | 0c |
| | | | | 2 | | 4 | 124 | 5 |
| 18-6-52-2 | | 17-2-59-2 | 4 | 12 | 6 | 9 | 380 | 9d |
| | | 11-3-29-2 | 1 | 2 | 1 | 6 | 139 | 10 |
| | | 12-2-39-6 | 4 | | | | 124 | 10 |
| 18-5-48-1 | | 7-0-39-0 | | 2 | | 12 | 244 | 10 |
| 16.1-1-73-2 | | 13-2-47-0 | 5 | 13 | | 5 | 327 | 4 |
| 28-5-71-3 | | 17-5-75-1 | 5 | 7 | 1 | 5 | 365 | 9 |
| 6-2-8-0 | | 10-1-32-0 | 4 | | 1 | 2 | 64 | 0e |
| | 18-4-58-1 | 16-2-66-0 | | 7 | 2 | 12 | 321 | 10 |
| 1-1-0-0 | 12-2-31-1 | 8-0-39-0 | 1 | 10 | 2 | 4 | 220 | 9 |
| 14-2-58-2 | | 20-4-79-0 | | 3 | | 3 | 446 | 10f |
| | | | | | | | 14 | 0g |
| 373-90-1015-34 av. 29.85 | 93-17-313-7 av. 44.71 | 349-71-1202-29 av. 41.44 | | | | | | |

g C. Maynard 2-0-8-0
G. Fowler 1.1-0-6-0

Somerset bowled 60 overs. Those captains who failed to lead their sides with a positive approach might care to reflect that Botham scorned the idea of batting throughout the final day, which many would have done, and Rice had no hesitation in going for the win, a target far stiffer than many which lesser captains had deemed impossible. Broad batted splendidly and he and Robinson gave the chase a fine start, 70 being scored before Robinson fell to the excitingly promising slow left-arm of Booth and Broad became the first of Gard's five stumpings. At 92 for 3, Notts were losing impetus, but Rice, first with Johnson and then with Hadlee, made victory look probable. Hadlee was spectacularly caught on the mid-wicket boundary by Lloyds and with 39 needed from 4 overs, Rice, after a marvellous innings, hit a full toss from Marks into the hands of substitute Ollis also on the mid-wicket boundary. Cooper and Hemmings went quickly so that 27 were needed from two overs with Bore and French at the wicket and only Pick to come. Bore launched a magnificent attack and hit Marks for six. French was caught on the boundary where all save Gard, the bowler and one other were fielding, and 14 were needed off the last over to be bowled by young Booth who, like Marks, had maintained

*Stephen Booth of Somerset. A left-arm spinner of immense promise who did much to thwart Notts on the final afternoon of the season. (David Munden)*

# LANCASHIRE COUNTY CRICKET CLUB

## OLD TRAFFORD, MANCHESTER

| Leicestershire C.C.C. First-Class Matches – Batting, 1984 | v. Cambridge Univ. (Cambridge) 18–20 April | | v. Derbyshire (Chesterfield) 28 April–1 May | | v. Nottinghamshire (Trent Bridge) 2–4 May | | v. Worcestershire (Leicester) 9–11 May | | v. Somerset (Leicester) 19–22 May | | v. Worcestershire (Worcester) 23–25 May | | v. Northamptonshire (Leicester) 26–29 May | | v. Essex (Hinkley) 2–5 June | | v. Surrey (The Oval) 9–12 June | | v. Warwickshire (Leicester) 13–15 June | | v. Hampshire (Southampton) 16–19 June | | v. Nottinghamshire (Leicester) 23–26 June | | v. Somerset (Taunton) 27–29 June | | v. Glamorgan (Swansea) 30 June–3 July | |
|---|---|---|---|---|---|---|---|---|---|---|---|---|---|---|---|---|---|---|---|---|---|---|---|---|---|---|---|---|
| J.C. Balderstone | 105 | — | 48 | 33 | 17 | 11 | 1 | 50 | 30 | 8 | 3 | 5 | — | 21 | | | | | 44 | 27 | 17 | 18 | | | | | | |
| I.P. Butcher | 22 | 109 | 7 | 130 | 2 | 62 | 26 | 24 | 17 | 1 | 23 | 13 | — | 1 | 29 | — | 0 | 2* | | | | | 54 | — | 44 | 7 | 36 | 16 |
| D.I. Gower | 32 | 2 | 70 | — | | | | | | | 103 | 4 | — | 74 | | | 5 | 13 | | | | | 43 | — | | | | |
| P. Willey | 141* | — | 102 | 19 | 12 | 12 | 47 | — | 0 | 25 | 18 | 9 | — | 104 | 38 | — | 3 | 5 | 159* | 25 | 156 | 5 | 6 | — | 37 | 8 | 9 | 9 |
| N.E. Briers | 0 | 73 | 36 | 27 | 6 | 20 | 1 | 18* | 0 | 18* | 0 | 0 | — | 18 | 8 | — | | | — | 9 | 2 | 5 | | | 20 | 16 | 34 | 9 |
| M.D. Haysman | 1 | 102* | 12 | 20* | 28 | 29 | 34 | 3* | 0 | 1* | | | | | | | | | | | | | | | | | | |
| M.A. Garnham | 2 | 65* | 1 | 11* | 25 | 20* | 57* | — | 13 | — | 10 | 74 | — | 24 | 9 | — | 84 | 0 | — | 13 | 6 | 8 | 6 | — | 9 | 53 | 17 | 5 |
| G.J. Parsons | 36* | — | 10 | — | 38* | 54* | 33 | — | 55 | — | 31* | 4 | — | 11* | 15 | — | 0 | 0 | — | 25 | 0 | 26* | 41 | — | 11 | 0 | 52 | 38 |
| N.G.B. Cook | — | — | 3* | — | 2 | — | 30 | — | 3 | — | 1 | 6 | — | — | 44 | — | 3* | 3* | | | | | 4 | — | 8 | 17 | 6* | 18* |
| J.P. Agnew | — | — | 0 | — | 30 | — | 1 | — | 20 | — | 12 | 2* | — | — | 1 | — | 1 | — | — | 0* | — | 0 | 9* | — | 2 | 22* | 4 | — |
| L.B. Taylor | — | — | 3 | — | 6 | — | | | 16* | — | 11 | 1 | — | — | | | | | | | | | | | | | | |
| T.J. Boon | | | | | 10 | 7 | 2 | 6 | | | | | | | 8 | — | 51 | 8 | 103* | 38 | 75 | 3 | 25 | — | 45 | 41 | 113 | 1 |
| J.J. Whitaker | | | | | | | | | 160 | — | 1 | 61 | — | 68* | 43 | — | 26 | 37 | 36 | 73 | 5 | 20 | 12 | — | 13 | 67 | 14 | 45 |
| P.B. Clift | | | | | | | | | | | | | | | 10 | — | 58 | 9 | — | 3 | 0* | 17 | 25 | — | 49 | 26* | 0 | 27* |
| A.M.E. Roberts | | | | | | | | | | | | | | | 8* | — | 14 | 32* | — | 0 | — | 7 | 18 | — | 10* | 9 | 89 | 0 |
| R.A. Cobb | | | | | | | | | | | | | | | | | | | 4 | 9 | 44 | 48 | | | | | | |
| P.J. Whitticase | | | | | | | | | | | | | | | | | | | | | | | | | | | | |
| G.J.F. Ferris | | | | | | | | | | | | | | | | | | | | | | | | | | | | |
| I.R. Carmichael | | | | | | | | | | | | | | | | | | | | | | | | | | | | |
| Byes | 7 | 2 | | 6 | 10 | | 8 | | | | 1 | | | 3 | 2 | | 1 | 11 | | | 8 | 6 | 5 | | 1 | 1 | 7 | |
| Leg-byes | 1 | 3 | 1 | 2 | 7 | 1 | 9 | 8 | 2 | 4 | 5 | 10 | | 3 | 3 | | 5 | 3 | 21 | 10 | 4 | 5 | 5 | | 5 | 8 | 2 | 4 |
| Wides | | | 1 | | 2 | | | | 1 | | 1 | | | | | | 3 | | | | 3 | 2 | 2 | | | | 1 | 1 |
| No-balls | 6 | 5 | 3 | 1 | 1 | 3 | 7 | 1 | 1 | | 2 | 7 | | 8 | 8 | | 5 | | 15 | 9 | 5 | 2 | 2 | | | 3 | 5 | 2 |
| Total | 353 | 361 | 297 | 249 | 196 | 219 | 256 | 110 | 318 | 57 | 222 | 196 | 0 | 335 | 226 | | 259 | 123 | 382 | 241 | 325 | 172 | 257 | | 254 | 278 | 389 | 175 |
| Wickets | 6 | 3 | 10 | 4 | 10 | 6 | 10 | 3 | 10 | 3 | 10 | 10 | 0 | 6 | 10 | | 10 | 7 | 3 | 10 | 8 | 10 | 10 | | 10 | 9 | 10 | 8 |
| Result | W | | W | | D | | D | | D | | W | | W | | D | | W | | W | | W | | D | | L | | D | |
| Points | — | | 23 | | 4 | | 5 | | 6 | | 22 | | 20 | | 6 | | 23 | | 21 | | 24 | | 5 | | 7 | | 5 | |

*Catches* 48 – M.A. Garnham (ct 45/st 3)
20 – J.J. Whitaker
19 – I.P. Butcher
18 – P.J. Whitticase
16 – P. Willey and N.G.B. Cook
14 – J.C. Balderstone
10 – M.D. Haysman and D.I. Gower
9 – N.E. Briers, T.J. Boon and subs
8 – G.J. Parsons

excellent control in the face of the violent assault. Bore savaged the first two balls of the over for four, then he turned the third for two. Four were needed off three balls. He blocked the first of these three deliveries from Booth and hit the second high to long-off where Ollis, the substitute fielder, took a catch just inside the boundary to give Somerset victory by three runs and Essex the championship. No side has ever lost a title more bravely than did Notts at Taunton.

Against such drama and magnificence, it seems almost blasphemous to talk of other matches, but Gower led his side to a fine win at Edgbaston after Amiss had produced an innings of the highest quality for his ninety-first first-class hundred and Middlesex clinched third place with a win at Bristol which was more comfortable than it had looked at one time. Derbyshire, with the splendid Barnett and the rapidly improving Fowler adding 196 in 45 overs in the first innings, beat Hampshire with five balls to spare. The dependable and attractive David Turner capped an excellent season with 193 runs in the match. There was a tense draw at Canterbury and a boring one at The Oval. Potter hit his first hundred of the season, Hick of Zimbabwe made his debut for Worcestershire and Paddy Clift returned the best bowling figures of the season. At county level, which is what really matters, it had been a year to remember.

**Britannic Assurance Championship Final Table**

| | P | W | L | D | Tie | Bonus pts Bt | Bonus pts Bl | Pts |
|---|---|---|---|---|---|---|---|---|
| Essex (1) | 24 | 13 | 3 | 8 | 0 | 64 | 83 | 355 |
| Notts (14) | 24 | 12 | 3 | 9 | 0 | 68 | 81 | 341 |
| Middx (2) | 24 | 8 | 7 | 9 | 0 | 63 | 78 | 269 |
| Leics (4) | 24 | 8 | 2 | 14 | 0 | 60 | 78 | 266 |
| Kent (7) | 24 | 8 | 3 | 11 | 2 | 45 | 65 | 254 |
| Sussex (11) | 24 | 7 | 6 | 10 | 1 | 54 | 79 | 249 |
| Somerset (10) | 24 | 6 | 7 | 11 | 0 | 60 | 78 | 234 |
| Surrey (8) | 24 | 6 | 6 | 12 | 0 | 62 | 72 | 230 |
| Warwicks (5) | 24 | 6 | 7 | 11 | 0 | 71 | 60 | 227 |
| Worcs (16) | 24 | 5 | 5 | 14 | 0 | 66 | 74 | 220 |
| Derby (9) | 24 | 4 | 6 | 14 | 0 | 72 | 66 | 202 |
| Northants (6) | 24 | 5 | 9 | 9 | 1 | 58 | 56 | 202 |
| Glamorgan (15) | 24 | 4 | 2 | 18 | 0 | 65 | 71 | 200 |
| Yorks (17) | 24 | 5 | 4 | 15 | 0 | 59 | 55 | 194 |
| Hants (3) | 24 | 3 | 13 | 8 | 0 | 58 | 62 | 168 |
| Lancs (13) | 24 | 1 | 9 | 14 | 0 | 49 | 72 | 137 |
| Glos (12) | 24 | 1 | 10 | 13 | 0 | 56 | 61 | 133 |

1983 positions in brackets.
Sussex total includes 12pts for a win in a match reduced to one innings.

| v. West Indians (Leicester) 7–9 July | | v. Sussex (Leicester) 11–13 July | | v. Gloucestershire (Bristol) 25–27 July | | v. Yorkshire (Sheffield) 28–31 July | | v. Kent (Canterbury) 4–7 August | | v. Yorkshire (Leicester) 8–10 August | | v. Lancashire (Leicester) 11–14 August | | v. Middlesex (Leicester) 18–21 August | | v. Gloucestershire (Leicester) 22–24 August | | v. Northamptonshire (Leicester) 25–28 August | | v. Derbyshire (Leicester) 5–7 September | | v. Warwickshire (Edgbaston) 8–11 September | | *M* | *Inns* | *NOs* | *Runs* | *H/S* | *Av* |
|---|---|---|---|---|---|---|---|---|---|---|---|---|---|---|---|---|---|---|---|---|---|---|---|---|---|---|---|---|---|
| | | 8 | 49 | 83 | 76 | 59 | 45 | 6 | — | 1 | 29 | 6 | 12 | 72 | 14 | 181* | — | 1 | 4 | 143* | 24 | 4 | 5 | 20 | 36 | 2 | 1260 | 181* | 37.05 |
| 118 | 14 | 13 | 102 | 28 | 0 | 130 | 34 | 40 | — | 0 | 13 | 12 | 13 | 26 | — | 12 | — | 45 | 2 | 15 | 8 | 22 | 77 | 24 | 42 | 1 | 1349 | 130 | 32.90 |
| 33 | 34 | | | | | | | 48 | — | | | | | 64 | 19 | | | | | — | 39 | 61 | 117* | 11 | 17 | 1 | 761 | 117* | 47.56 |
| 9 | 0* | 15 | 0 | 57 | 2 | 21 | 38 | 18 | — | 85 | 167 | 1 | 14 | 16 | 1 | 0 | — | 21 | 35* | 11 | 2 | 5 | 6 | 26 | 45 | 4 | 1472 | 167 | 35.90 |
| 16 | 27 | 20 | 21 | 0 | — | — | 47 | 4 | — | 1 | 32 | 32 | 32 | 0 | 15* | 21 | — | 28 | 0 | | | | | 22 | 37 | 3 | 616 | 73 | 18.11 |
| | | | | | | | | | | | | | | | | | | | | | | | | 5 | 10 | 4 | 230 | 102* | 38.33 |
| | | 25* | 4 | 49* | 4 | — | 0 | | | | | | | 18 | 54 | | | | | | | | | 18 | 29 | 6 | 666 | 84 | 28.95 |
| 1 | 1 | 3 | 7* | 16* | 27 | 53* | 58 | 21 | — | 63 | — | 8 | 0 | 2 | 9* | 17 | — | 13 | — | — | 29 | 16 | 29 | 26 | 39 | 10 | 853 | 63 | 29.41 |
| 1* | — | | | | | | | 3 | — | 11* | 28 | 13 | 1 | 12* | — | 14 | — | 0 | — | — | 0* | | | 20 | 24 | 9 | 231 | 44 | 15.40 |
| | | 1 | — | — | — | — | 21 | 7 | — | | | | | 6 | — | | | | | — | 0* | 9 | — | 21 | 20 | 5 | 148 | 30 | 9.86 |
| | | | | | | | | | | | | | | | | | | | | | | | | 6 | 5 | 1 | 37 | 16* | 9.25 |
| 9 | 47* | 14 | 17 | 32 | 82* | 4* | — | 11 | — | 22 | 12* | 31 | 4 | 70 | 15 | 144 | — | 2 | 26 | 123* | 9 | 20 | 3 | 21 | 37 | 6 | 1233 | 144 | 39.77 |
| 14 | 6 | 8 | 33 | 8 | 7 | | | | | 8 | 54* | 17 | 5 | | | 23 | — | 99 | 0 | — | 117 | 17 | 0 | 19 | 32 | 2 | 1097 | 160 | 36.56 |
| 54 | — | 0 | 10 | 11 | 8* | — | 11* | 24 | — | 1 | — | 5 | 25 | 4 | — | 20 | — | 18 | 27* | — | 26 | 13 | 2* | 19 | 28 | 7 | 483 | 58 | 23.00 |
| | | 0 | 1* | | | | | | | | | | | | | | | | | | | | | 8 | 12 | 4 | 188 | 89 | 23.50 |
| | | | | | | 37 | — | | | | | | | | | | | | | | | | | 2 | 4 | | 105 | 48 | 26.25 |
| 3 | — | | | | | | | 7* | — | 10 | — | 0 | 14 | | | 0 | — | 0* | — | — | 1 | 0 | — | 8 | 9 | 2 | 35 | 10 | 5.00 |
| 0 | — | | | | | | | | | | | | | | | | | | | | | | | 1 | 1 | | 0 | 0 | 0.00 |
| | | | | — | — | — | — | | | 0 | — | 4* | 0* | | | 0 | — | 2 | — | | | 0* | — | 7 | 6 | 3 | 6 | 4* | 2.00 |
| 5 | 1 | 4 | 2 | 5 | | 7 | | 4 | | | 7 | 1 | 4 | | 4 | 1 | | 1 | | 8 | | 2 | 6 | | | | | | |
| 2 | 4 | 4 | 6 | 10 | 9 | 7 | 8 | 3 | | 2 | 9 | 2 | | 5 | 1 | 11 | | | 11 | 3 | 2 | 4 | 9 | | | | | | |
| 3 | | | | 2 | 5 | | | | | 1 | | 1 | | 11 | | 2 | | 4 | | | | | 3 | | | | | | |
| 15 | 2 | | 6 | | | 9 | 3 | 1 | | 1 | 12 | 6 | | 7 | 2 | 10 | | 13 | 12 | 3 | 2 | 1 | 6 | | | | | | |
| 283 | 136 | 115 | 258 | 301 | 220 | 327 | 265 | 197 | | 206 | 363 | 139 | 124 | 313 | 134 | 456 | | 247 | 117 | 305 | 259 | 174 | 263 | | | | | | |
| 10 | 5 | 10 | 8 | 7 | 6 | 4 | 7 | 10 | | 10 | 5 | 10 | 10 | 10 | 5 | 10 | | 10 | 5 | 2 | 9 | 10 | 6 | | | | | | |
| D | | D | | D | | D | | D | | D | | L | | D | | W | | D | | D | | W | | | | | | | |
| — | | 4 | | 8 | | 7 | | 3 | | 6 | | 4 | | 5 | | 24 | | 6 | | 7 | | 21 | | | | | | | |

6– P.B. Clift
4 – J.P. Agnew
3 – I.R. Carmichael
2 – A.M.E. Roberts and R.A. Cobb

## First-Class Averages

### BATTING

| | M | Inns | NOs | Runs | HS | Av | 100s | 50s |
|---|---|---|---|---|---|---|---|---|
| M.W. Gatting | 24 | 43 | 10 | 2257 | 258 | 68.39 | 8 | 10 |
| P.W. Denning | 5 | 8 | 3 | 338 | 90 | 67.60 | | 3 |
| G.A. Gooch | 26 | 45 | 7 | 2559 | 227 | 67.34 | 8 | 13 |
| Javed Miandad | 8 | 15 | 2 | 832 | 212* | 64.00 | 2 | 3 |
| G. Boycott | 20 | 35 | 10 | 1567 | 153* | 62.68 | 4 | 9 |
| J.G. Wright | 12 | 21 | 1 | 1202 | 177 | 60.05 | 2 | 9 |
| D.L. Amiss | 26 | 50 | 10 | 2239 | 122 | 55.97 | 6 | 14 |
| M.D. Crowe | 25 | 41 | 6 | 1870 | 190 | 53.42 | 6 | 11 |
| V.J. Marks | 24 | 34 | 10 | 1262 | 134 | 52.58 | 3 | 6 |
| A.I. Kallicharran | 26 | 50 | 6 | 2301 | 200* | 52.29 | 9 | 7 |
| R.J. Hadlee | 24 | 31 | 8 | 1179 | 210* | 51.26 | 2 | 7 |
| R.T. Robinson | 27 | 47 | 7 | 2032 | 171 | 50.80 | 5 | 11 |
| P. Johnson | 10 | 14 | 1 | 647 | 133 | 49.76 | 2 | 3 |
| T.A. Lloyd | 8 | 14 | 2 | 590 | 110 | 49.16 | 2 | 4 |
| C.E.B. Rice | 24 | 39 | 7 | 1553 | 152* | 48.35 | 3 | 6 |
| G.W. Humpage | 26 | 47 | 8 | 1891 | 205 | 48.48 | 5 | 9 |
| V.P. Terry | 16 | 28 | 3 | 1208 | 175* | 48.32 | 5 | 6 |
| R.A. Smith | 7 | 13 | 3 | 483 | 132 | 48.30 | 1 | 2 |
| P.A. Neale | 25 | 42 | 6 | 1706 | 143 | 47.38 | 2 | 11 |
| P.M. Roebuck | 24 | 37 | 1 | 1702 | 159 | 47.27 | 7 | 4 |
| P.W.G. Parker | 26 | 40 | 4 | 1692 | 181 | 47.00 | 6 | 6 |
| K.S. McEwan | 27 | 44 | 6 | 1755 | 142* | 46.18 | 4 | 10 |
| K.J. Barnett | 24 | 41 | 3 | 1734 | 144 | 45.63 | 6 | 9 |
| B.C. Broad | 23 | 40 | 5 | 1459 | 108* | 44.25 | 1 | 13 |
| Younis Ahmed | 21 | 35 | 4 | 1369 | 158* | 44.16 | 2 | 9 |
| J. Derrick | 10 | 15 | 7 | 351 | 69* | 43.87 | | 3 |
| D.L. Haynes | 13 | 18 | 1 | 743 | 125 | 43.70 | 2 | 5 |
| C.M. Wells | 26 | 39 | 7 | 1389 | 203 | 43.40 | 5 | 4 |
| G.S. Clinton | 19 | 28 | 6 | 948 | 192 | 43.09 | 2 | 5 |
| W.N. Slack | 25 | 46 | 8 | 1631 | 145 | 42.92 | 4 | 6 |
| R.N. Kapil Dev | 12 | 19 | 4 | 640 | 95 | 42.66 | | 6 |
| T.S. Curtis | 22 | 36 | 3 | 1405 | 129 | 42.57 | 3 | 8 |
| D.M. Smith | 17 | 31 | 5 | 1093 | 189* | 42.03 | 2 | 6 |
| D.R. Turner | 20 | 37 | 4 | 1365 | 153 | 41.36 | 3 | 7 |
| D.W. Randall | 25 | 40 | 3 | 1528 | 136 | 41.29 | 3 | 12 |
| T.E. Jesty | 25 | 44 | 4 | 1625 | 248 | 40.62 | 5 | 4 |
| J.W. Lloyds | 20 | 30 | 10 | 812 | 113* | 40.60 | 1 | 5 |
| A.J. Lamb | 18 | 34 | 4 | 1209 | 133* | 40.30 | 5 | 5 |
| R.O. Butcher | 23 | 40 | 7 | 1326 | 116 | 40.18 | 2 | 10 |
| P.E. Robinson | 15 | 24 | 5 | 746 | 92 | 39.78 | | 6 |
| T.J. Boon | 21 | 37 | 6 | 1233 | 144 | 39.77 | 4 | 4 |
| G. Cook | 22 | 43 | 4 | 1539 | 102 | 39.46 | 2 | 9 |
| R.D.V. Knight | 21 | 35 | 3 | 1254 | 142 | 39.18 | 3 | 7 |
| K. Sharp | 24 | 39 | 2 | 1445 | 173 | 39.05 | 3 | 8 |
| R.A. Woolmer | 8 | 14 | 3 | 427 | 153 | 38.81 | 1 | 2 |
| M.A. Lynch | 25 | 41 | 1 | 1546 | 144 | 38.65 | 4 | 8 |
| M.D. Haysman | 5 | 10 | 4 | 230 | 102* | 38.33 | 1 | |
| A.R. Butcher | 24 | 41 | 4 | 1415 | 135* | 38.24 | 5 | 5 |
| M.R. Benson | 14 | 26 | 2 | 914 | 127 | 38.08 | 3 | 4 |
| R.J. Bailey | 25 | 45 | 8 | 1405 | 114 | 37.97 | 3 | 8 |

| **Leicestershire C.C.C.** First-Class Matches – Bowling, 1984 | L.B. Taylor | J.P. Agnew | N.G.B. Cook | G.J. Parsons | N.E. Briers | P. Willey | J.C. Balderstone | A.M.E. Roberts | P.B. Clift |
|---|---|---|---|---|---|---|---|---|---|
| *v.* Cambridge University | 12–5–18–1 | 20.4–4–47–8 | 2–0–2–0 | 9–3–25–0 | 9–4–18–0 | | | | |
| (Cambridge) 18–20 April | 7–1–13–1 | 8–3–15–0 | 12.2–9–4–2 | 8–3–14–1 | | 9–6–6–3 | 7–4–3–2 | | |
| *v.* Derbyshire (Chesterfield) | 14–6–36–1 | 16–2–70–3 | 16.2–8–35–2 | 12–3–41–3 | | 3–0–6–0 | | | |
| 28 April–1 May | 18–6–43–1 | 27.3–8–100–5 | 20–4–58–1 | 14–3–54–3 | | 12–1–37–0 | 1–0–7–0 | | |
| *v.* Nottinghamshire | 7–4–9–0 | 17–4–57–2 | 11.1–2–32–3 | 21–7–68–1 | 27–9–56–2 | 18–4–45–0 | | | |
| (Trent Bridge) 2–4 May | 12–1–51–2 | 5–1–8–0 | 30–8–57–1 | 5–0–21–0 | 18–3–39–2 | | | | |
| *v.* Worcestershire (Leicester) | 15–6–35–0 | 18–4–70–3 | 24.2–8–50–3 | 5–1–17–0 | | 9–5–20–1 | | | |
| 9–11 May | 3–0–18–0 | 4–0–14–0 | 15–1–45–4 | | | 15–5–48–1 | | | |
| *v.* Somerset (Leicester) | 12–1–34–1 | 22–0–110–1 | 35–11–68–2 | 9–0–31–0 | | 38–11–78–6 | | | |
| 19–22 May | | | | | | | | | |
| *v.* Worcestershire | 13–4–22–2 | 15–2–54–2 | 11–2–42–0 | 11.2–1–42–5 | | 1–0–1–0 | | | |
| (Worcester) 23–25 May | 11–6–20–0 | 18–4–52–3 | 25–10–44–3 | 25.4–4–55–3 | 2–1–2–0 | 2–1–4–0 | 1–0–8–0 | | |
| *v.* Northamptonshire | 9–1–34–0 | 26.5–8–84–2 | 22–7–70–2 | 16–2–46–1 | 5–1–20–2 | 2–2–0–0 | | | |
| (Leicester) 26–29 May | 9–1–36–1 | | | 9–1–29–1 | | | | | |
| *v.* Essex (Hinckley) | | 14–6–23–1 | 14–1–59–0 | 11–3–38–2 | | 2–0–4–2 | | 17–8–23–4 | 14–5–33–1 |
| 2–5 June | | 6–1–34–0 | 7–2–17–0 | 14–4–30–2 | | 11–3–18–0 | | 12–1–41–0 | 11–3–33–0 |
| *v.* Surrey (The Oval) | | 13.5–2–44–5 | | 8–1–25–2 | | | | 14–6–21–1 | 8–2–15–1 |
| 9–12 June | | 18.2–3–76–5 | 13–2–35–0 | 9–4–19–1 | | 3–1–12–0 | | 17–3–62–1 | 16–4–44–2 |
| *v.* Warwickshire (Leicester) | | 17–4–61–1 | | 12–1–44–0 | 1–0–5–0 | 24–7–64–1 | | 20–6–70–0 | 17–3–65–0 |
| 13–15 June | | 11.5–3–61–4 | | 7–1–48–1 | | | | 10–3–30–1 | 9–3–17–4 |
| *v.* Hampshire (Southampton) | | 15–6–31–1 | | 15–3–58–2 | | 16–6–41–2 | 1–0–8–0 | 21.5–7–53–5 | 9–3–28–0 |
| 16–19 June | | 18–4–57–3 | | 4–0–16–0 | | 18–9–35–2 | 3–0–8–0 | 16–6–31–3 | 10.1–4–22–2 |
| *v.* Nottinghamshire (Leicester) | | 31–1–137–3 | 19–7–30–1 | 10–2–38–1 | | | | 29.1–5–104–5 | 23–3–63–0 |
| 23–26 June | | 4–2–7–0 | 16–5–44–0 | 11–1–36–0 | | 7–3–6–0 | | 3–0–12–0 | 10–3–21–0 |
| *v.* Somerset (Taunton) | | 25–4–53–2 | 5–3–11–0 | 8–3–19–0 | | 2–0–3–0 | | 30–8–74–7 | 13–6–23–1 |
| 27–29 June | | 13–4–41–2 | 24.5–6–79–2 | 9–0–45–0 | | 17–2–50–0 | | 14–1–70–0 | 9–0–43–0 |
| *v.* Glamorgan (Swansea) | | 7–0–35–0 | 33–6–130–1 | 24–2–91–0 | | 21–6–66–1 | | 18–4–43–2 | 14–3–46–0 |
| 30 June–3 July | | 8–2–23–1 | 30–10–71–3 | | | 10–4–33–1 | | 7–4–14–2 | 17–10–27–3 |
| *v.* West Indians (Leicester) | | | 27–8–72–0 | 29–5–112–1 | 1–0–3–0 | 23–5–88–0 | | | 33–4–120–4 |
| 7–9 July | | | | | | | | | |
| *v.* Sussex (Leicester) | | 15–2–79–0 | | 20.5–8–46–5 | | 17–7–17–1 | | 16–3–47–1 | 20–6–33–3 |
| 11–13 July | | 10–2–55–1 | | 13–2–59–4 | | 10–0–24–1 | | 20–5–74–1 | 15–2–26–0 |
| *v.* Gloucestershire (Bristol) | | 20–7–52–1 | | 15–4–36–2 | | 11.3–3–29–2 | | | 12–5–27–2 |
| 25–27 July | | 15.3–1–54–1 | | 6–2–10–0 | | 37–7–76–4 | | | 14–3–36–1 |
| *v.* Yorkshire (Sheffield) | | 21.1–4–76–2 | | 14–2–62–2 | | 22–6–50–1 | | | 19–6–33–2 |
| 28–31 July | | 14–3–41–0 | | 15–4–48–3 | | 7–2–15–1 | 5–1–26–0 | | 13–4–38–1 |
| *v.* Kent (Canterbury) | | 22.2–4–71–5 | 22–4–70–0 | 31–10–92–1 | 2–0–3–1 | 6–2–19–0 | | | 28–9–70–3 |
| 4–7 August | | 10–4–14–1 | 5–1–24–0 | 17–5–52–2 | 3–0–12–0 | | | | 13–5–18–0 |
| *v.* Yorkshire (Leicester) | | | 20–5–46–3 | 30–11–74–2 | 9–2–16–1 | 9–1–14–0 | | | 32.4–13–70–4 |
| 8–10 August | | | | | | | | | |
| *v.* Lancashire (Leicester) | | | | 19–7–33–2 | 17–2–48–3 | 6–1–15–0 | | | 24.3–5–67–5 |
| 11–14 August | | | 18–5–50–0 | 17–4–58–0 | 10–2–25–1 | 8–2–40–1 | | | 20–2–58–0 |
| *v.* Middlesex (Leicester) | | 7.1–2–18–0 | 23.5–9–80–0 | 26–4–99–2 | 4–0–16–0 | 25–6–87–3 | | | 24.3–4–76–1 |
| 18–21 August | | 12–1–78–3 | 27–7–64–2 | 7–2–16–0 | | 14–2–31–1 | 1–0–9–0 | | 6–3–15–0 |
| *v.* Gloucestershire | | | 24.5–11–57–2 | 21–3–67–3 | 1–0–1–0 | 17–7–17–1 | | | 25–5–58–3 |
| (Leicester) 22–24 August | | | 31–12–55–1 | 11–2–26–1 | | 33.4–18–40–5 | | | 19–7–37–3 |
| *v.* Northamptonshire | | | 13–1–45–0 | 21–2–62–4 | | 17–7–27–0 | | | 20–2–69–2 |
| (Leicester) 25–28 August | | | 18–9–36–1 | 14–2–50–1 | | 9–1–30–1 | | | 26–8–47–2 |
| *v.* Derbyshire (Leicester) | | 20–1–102–2 | 36–7–95–2 | 20.2–0–93–2 | | 10–3–19–1 | | | 27–2–97–3 |
| 5–7 September | | 11–2–36–0 | 8–2–17–0 | 8–0–42–1 | | 15–5–54–0 | | | 10–2–44–0 |
| *v.* Warwickshire (Edgbaston) | | 10–1–45–1 | | 7–3–12–0 | | | | | 16.1–7–26–8 |
| 8–11 September | | 13–1–54–3 | | 13–0–65–0 | | 7–2–22–0 | | | 25.1–6–63–2 |
| | 142–42–369–10 *av.* 36.90 | 601.1–117–2139–80 *av.* 26.73 | 659.4–193–1694–41 *av.* 41.31 | 662.1–135–2164–67 *av.* 32.29 | 109–24–264–12 *av.* 22.00 | 544.1–163–1291–43 *av.* 30.02 | 19–5–69–2 *av.* 34.50 | 265–70–769–33 *av.* 23.30 | 623.1–162–1608–63 *av.* 25.52 |

a D. G. Price absent hurt
b T. S. Curtis absent hurt
c G. S. Clinton retired hurt, absent hurt

| I.P. Butcher | G.J.F. Ferris | I.R. Carmichael | Byes | Leg-byes | Wides | No-balls | Total | Wkts |
|---|---|---|---|---|---|---|---|---|
| | | | 1 | 11 | 1 | 4 | 127 | 9a |
| | | | 3 | 3 | | 4 | 65 | 9 |
| | | | 4 | 3 | 1 | 18 | 214 | 10 |
| | | | 1 | 5 | | 16 | 321 | 10 |
| | | | 1 | 16 | 1 | 6 | 291 | 9 |
| | | | 3 | 4 | | 5 | 188 | 5 |
| | | | 4 | 6 | 4 | 8 | 214 | 7 |
| | | | 9 | 15 | | 1 | 150 | 5 |
| | | | 1 | 11 | 1 | 4 | 338 | 10 |
| | | | | | | | | |
| | | | 1 | | 3 | 9 | 174 | 9b |
| | | | 8 | 19 | | 9 | 221 | 10 |
| | | | | 4 | | 6 | 264 | 9 |
| | | | | 1 | 1 | | 67 | 2 |
| | | | 1 | 4 | 4 | | 189 | 10 |
| | | | 4 | 5 | 1 | | 183 | 2 |
| | | | 2 | 4 | 1 | 3 | 115 | 9c |
| | | | 8 | 7 | 1 | 2 | 266 | 9 |
| | | | 4 | 3 | 1 | 13 | 330 | 3 |
| | | | 1 | 2 | | 2 | 161 | 10 |
| | | | 3 | 9 | | 13 | 244 | 10 |
| | | | 7 | 2 | | 12 | 190 | 10 |
| | | | 9 | 6 | 8 | 9 | 404 | 10 |
| 1–1–0–0 | | | | 1 | | 1 | 128 | 0 |
| | | | 3 | 1 | | 5 | 192 | 10 |
| | | | 8 | 3 | | 2 | 341 | 4 |
| | | | 4 | 11 | | 1 | 427 | 4 |
| | | | 6 | 3 | | 1 | 178 | 10 |
| | 21–4–83–0 | | 1 | 6 | 5 | 16 | 506 | 5 |
| | | | | | | | | |
| | | | 4 | 3 | 1 | 10 | 240 | 10 |
| | | | 5 | 4 | | 3 | 250 | 7 |
| | | 12–5–33–2 | 4 | 6 | 1 | 12 | 200 | 10 |
| | | 12–1–55–0 | 5 | 5 | 4 | 1 | 246 | 6 |
| | | 18–2–61–1 | | 1 | 2 | 18 | 303 | 8 |
| | | 11–2–24–0 | 4 | 1 | 7 | | 204 | 6 |
| | | | | 1 | | 9 | 335 | 10 |
| | | | | 3 | | 3 | 126 | 3 |
| | | 22–5–76–0 | | 7 | | 3 | 306 | 10 |
| | | | | | | | | |
| | | 21–3–40–0 | 4 | 9 | 1 | 1 | 218 | 10 |
| | | 15–4–41–2 | 4 | 5 | | 4 | 285 | 4 |
| | | | 4 | 5 | 1 | 5 | 391 | 6 |
| | | | | 1 | | 1 | 215 | 6 |
| | | 10–1–43–0 | 5 | 2 | | | 250 | 10 |
| | | 7–1–27–0 | 5 | 2 | | 3 | 195 | 10 |
| | | 18–2–59–4 | | 2 | | 2 | 266 | 10 |
| | | 29–8–83–2 | 3 | 5 | | 1 | 255 | 9 |
| | | | 1 | 9 | | 15 | 431 | 10 |
| 1–0–13–0 | | | | 1 | | 4 | 211 | 2 |
| | | 14–3–35–1 | 3 | 1 | 2 | 9 | 133 | 10 |
| | | 19–3–84–5 | | 8 | 3 | 4 | 303 | 10 |
| 2–1–13–0<br>— | 21–4–83–0<br>— | 208–40–661–17<br>*av.* 38.88 | | | | | | |

| | M | Inns | NOs | Runs | HS | Av | 100s | 50s |
|---|---|---|---|---|---|---|---|---|
| C.W.J.Athey | 26 | 52 | 4 | 1812 | 114* | 37.75 | 4 | 11 |
| D.L. Bairstow | 23 | 26 | 5 | 787 | 94 | 37.47 | | 7 |
| J.C. Balderstone | 20 | 36 | 2 | 1260 | 181* | 37.05 | 2 | 5 |
| A.L. Jones | 27 | 51 | 2 | 1811 | 132 | 36.95 | 5 | 7 |
| J. Abrahams | 23 | 39 | 6 | 1216 | 201* | 36.84 | 3 | 4 |
| J.J.E. Hardy | 13 | 20 | 6 | 513 | 95 | 36.64 | | 4 |
| J.J. Whitaker | 19 | 32 | 2 | 1097 | 160 | 36.56 | 2 | 6 |
| W. Larkins | 25 | 49 | 3 | 1656 | 183* | 36.00 | 3 | 7 |
| P. Willey | 26 | 45 | 4 | 1472 | 167 | 35.90 | 6 | 2 |
| D.I. Gower | 18 | 30 | 2 | 999 | 117* | 35.67 | 2 | 6 |
| R.C. Ontong | 25 | 45 | 8 | 1320 | 204* | 35.67 | 1 | 7 |
| M.D. Moxon | 19 | 32 | 3 | 1034 | 126* | 35.65 | 2 | 6 |
| R.G. Lumb | 10 | 17 | 2 | 534 | 165* | 35.60 | 2 | 1 |
| D.G. Aslett | 26 | 45 | 3 | 1491 | 221* | 35.50 | 5 | 3 |
| P.W. Romaines | 26 | 52 | | 1844 | 141 | 35.46 | 4 | 10 |
| J.E. Morris | 15 | 28 | 1 | 948 | 135 | 35.11 | 3 | 3 |
| R.I.H.B. Dyer | 18 | 36 | 2 | 1187 | 106* | 34.91 | 1 | 9 |
| B.R. Hardie | 27 | 38 | 7 | 1077 | 99 | 34.74 | | 6 |
| G. Fowler | 17 | 29 | | 1007 | 226 | 34.72 | 3 | 4 |
| C.T. Radley | 24 | 38 | 7 | 1072 | 128* | 34.58 | 2 | 7 |
| S.J. O'Shaughnessy | 21 | 38 | 4 | 1167 | 159* | 34.32 | 3 | 3 |
| D.J. Capel | 17 | 28 | 5 | 789 | 81 | 34.30 | | 6 |
| A.G. Davies | 7 | 14 | 5 | 308 | 69 | 34.22 | | 3 |
| D.J. Wild | 15 | 27 | 2 | 855 | 144 | 34.20 | 2 | 2 |
| M.C.J. Nicholas | 26 | 48 | 2 | 1559 | 158 | 33.89 | 4 | 6 |
| H. Morris | 12 | 20 | 4 | 542 | 114* | 33.87 | 1 | 4 |
| D.N. Patel | 25 | 41 | 1 | 1348 | 197 | 33.70 | 2 | 7 |
| G.D. Mendis | 23 | 36 | 2 | 1141 | 209* | 33.55 | 3 | 4 |
| J.D. Carr | 9 | 14 | | 468 | 123 | 33.42 | 2 | 2 |
| J.A. Hopkins | 26 | 50 | 5 | 1500 | 128* | 33.33 | 2 | 9 |
| C. Gladwin | 26 | 45 | 3 | 1396 | 162 | 33.23 | 1 | 9 |
| K.W.R. Fletcher | 25 | 37 | 5 | 1056 | 131 | 33.00 | 3 | 4 |
| A. Hill | 25 | 44 | 3 | 1352 | 125 | 32.97 | 1 | 11 |
| I.P. Butcher | 24 | 42 | 1 | 1349 | 130 | 32.90 | 5 | 3 |
| P.J. Prichard | 20 | 29 | 2 | 888 | 100 | 32.88 | 1 | 6 |
| N.F.M. Popplewell | 22 | 36 | 2 | 1116 | 133 | 32.82 | 1 | 7 |
| A.P. Wells | 25 | 39 | 7 | 1045 | 127 | 32.65 | 2 | 7 |
| R.G. Williams | 20 | 37 | 4 | 1073 | 169 | 32.51 | 1 | 5 |
| J.A. Ormrod | 23 | 40 | 3 | 1199 | 139* | 32.40 | 1 | 7 |
| P. Bainbridge | 22 | 42 | 7 | 1133 | 134* | 32.37 | 2 | 6 |
| J.D. Birch | 22 | 33 | 5 | 905 | 110* | 32.32 | 1 | 5 |
| N.R. Taylor | 21 | 39 | 5 | 1098 | 139 | 32.29 | 2 | 5 |
| G. Miller | 23 | 34 | 5 | 933 | 130 | 32.17 | 1 | 5 |
| A. Sidebottom | 20 | 22 | 6 | 511 | 54* | 31.93 | | 2 |
| I.T. Botham | 17 | 26 | 1 | 797 | 90 | 31.88 | | 7 |
| A.W. Stovold | 25 | 50 | 2 | 1524 | 139* | 31.75 | 2 | 11 |
| A.J. Stewart | 15 | 21 | 3 | 570 | 73 | 31.66 | | 4 |
| N.H. Fairbrother | 23 | 39 | 1 | 1201 | 102 | 31.60 | 1 | 10 |
| W.P. Fowler | 22 | 38 | 8 | 948 | 116 | 31.60 | 2 | 7 |
| P.J. Newport | 10 | 11 | 5 | 187 | 40* | 31.16 | | |
| Zaheer Abbas | 14 | 28 | 4 | 738 | 157* | 30.75 | 1 | 4 |
| N.G. Cowley | 26 | 38 | 4 | 1042 | 80 | 30.64 | | 6 |
| C.S. Cowdrey | 22 | 37 | 3 | 1039 | 125* | 30.55 | 2 | 5 |
| S.P. Henderson | 10 | 17 | 1 | 487 | 108 | 30.43 | 1 | 3 |
| G.J. Toogood | 8 | 15 | 1 | 425 | 109 | 30.35 | 1 | 2 |
| C.J. Richards | 25 | 38 | 8 | 908 | 109 | 30.26 | 2 | 4 |
| R.J. Boyd-Moss | 17 | 32 | 2 | 904 | 105 | 30.13 | 1 | 6 |
| A.M. Ferreira | 26 | 39 | 13 | 77 | 76* | 29.88 | | 4 |
| R.A. Harper | 14 | 13 | 2 | 328 | 58 | 29.81 | | 2 |
| G.C. Holmes | 21 | 37 | 2 | 1039 | 90 | 29.68 | | 6 |
| B.C. Rose | 20 | 33 | 4 | 856 | 123 | 29.51 | 1 | 4 |
| G.J. Parsons | 26 | 39 | 10 | 853 | 63 | 29.41 | | 6 |
| C.J. Tavare | 24 | 41 | | 1198 | 117 | 29.21 | 2 | 5 |
| M. Watkinson | 16 | 29 | 6 | 667 | 77 | 29.00 | | 4 |
| M.A. Garnham | 18 | 29 | 6 | 666 | 84 | 28.95 | | 6 |
| P.G.P. Roebuck | 6 | 12 | 2 | 286 | 62 | 28.60 | | 2 |
| J.H. Hampshire | 21 | 32 | 4 | 792 | 101* | 28.28 | 1 | 4 |
| J.F. Steele | 26 | 41 | 12 | 820 | 60* | 28.27 | | 1 |
| C.L. Smith | 26 | 49 | 3 | 1298 | 125 | 28.21 | 4 | 3 |
| P.A. Smith | 23 | 41 | 4 | 1040 | 89 | 28.10 | | 8 |
| R.M. Edbrooke | 8 | 16 | 1 | 420 | 66 | 28.00 | | 2 |
| D.J. Humphries | 22 | 32 | 9 | 644 | 133* | 28.00 | 2 | 2 |
| M.J. Weston | 24 | 41 | 3 | 1061 | 145* | 27.92 | 1 | 6 |
| S.H. Wootton | 4 | 8 | 1 | 194 | 97 | 27.71 | | 1 |
| J.N. Shepherd | 24 | 39 | 7 | 885 | 87 | 27.65 | | 6 |
| I.A. Greig | 26 | 35 | 5 | 813 | 106* | 27.10 | 1 | 2 |

| **Middlesex C.C.C.** First-Class Matches – Batting, 1984 | v. Glamorgan (Lord's) 28 April–1 May | v. Oxford University (Oxford) 9–11 May | v. Northamptonshire (Lord's) 23–25 May | v. Sussex (Lord's) 26–29 May | v. Kent (Dartford) 30 May–1 June | v. Derbyshire (Derby) 2–5 June | v. Somerset (Bath) 9–12 June | v. Surrey (Lord's) 13–15 June | v. Warwickshire (Lord's) 16–19 June | v. Surrey (The Oval) 23–26 June | v. Glamorgan (Swansea) 27–29 June | v. Lancashire (Liverpool) 30 June–3 July | v. Worcestershire (Uxbridge) 7–10 July | v. Gloucestershire (Uxbridge) 11–13 July |
|---|---|---|---|---|---|---|---|---|---|---|---|---|---|---|
| G.D. Barlow | 10 8* | | 13 8 | 27 — | 24 18 | 1 — | 34 39 | 10 59 | 0 27 | 16 8 | | | | 0 30 |
| W.N. Slack | 37 6* | 145 — | 1 17 | 19 — | 17 0 | 93 44* | 53 39* | 94 46 | | 3 12 | 39 — | 39 4 | 100 28 | 16 22 |
| M.W. Gatting | 55 — | 102* — | 1 71 | 23 — | | | 258 — | 58 24 | 12 2 | 6 10 | | | 104 23 | 55 32 |
| R.O. Butcher | 27 — | 0 12 | 25 16 | | 104 27 | 7 — | 33 4* | 0 0 | 35 11 | 23 6 | | | 64 22* | 2 56* |
| C.T. Radley | 128* — | 7 — | | 8 — | 61 0 | 17 3* | 9 — | 118* 2 | 5 4 | 41 6 | 45 — | 88 7 | 59 57* | 7 33* |
| J.E. Emburey | 10 — | 40 — | 17 19 | 3 — | 46 26 | 3 — | 8 — | 0 0 | 4 3 | 28 8 | 15 — | 0 57 | 1 — | 0 — |
| P.H. Edmonds | 44 — | 2* — | 3 4 | 3 — | 36* 34* | 8 — | 55 1 | 0 0 | 1 8 | 10 4 | 142 — | 21 3 | 2 — | 35 1 |
| P.R. Downton | 52 — | 9 18 | 21 31 | 25* — | 0 2* | 88 — | 13* — | | | 7 6 | | | 3* 19 | |
| N.F. Williams | 1* — | — 13* | | | 0 — | 24 — | — — | 5 0 | 21* 0 | 4 0 | 44 — | 42 5 | | 35 — |
| W.W. Daniel | — — | | 0* 0* | 5* — | 5 — | 2* — | — — | 6 4 | 15 0 | 7* 10* | | 0* 0* | 6 — | 5 — |
| N.G. Cowans | — — | | 0 20 | 2 — | | | — — | 17 66 | 7 3 | 7 8 | | 45 19 | 1 — | |
| K.P. Tomlins | | 10 103* | 47 0 | 44 — | 2 13 | 0 11 | | | 22 13 | | 19 — | 7 24 | | |
| K.D. James | | 28* — | | | 2 — | | | | | | | | | |
| S.P. Hughes | | — — | 3 1 | 5 — | | 13 — | | | | | 12 — | | | 41* — |
| C.P. Metson | | | | | | | | 1* 23* | 9 18* | | 24* — | 1 0 | | 96 — |
| R.G.P. Ellis | | | | | | | | | | | 18 — | 33 3 | | |
| C.R. Cook | | | | | | | | | | | 47 — | 16 43 | | |
| A. Fraser | | | | | | | | | | | — — | | | |
| A.J.T. Miller | | | | | | | | | | | | | 20 — | |
| J.D. Carr | | | | | | | | | | | | | 0 — | |
| K.R. Brown | | | | | | | | | | | | | | |
| Byes | 1 4 | 1 1 | | 1 | 4 | 1 | 2 2 | 4 6 | | 4 | 4 | 8 | 2 5 | 4 |
| Leg-byes | 3 2 | 9 1 | 3 8 | 11 | 2 2 | 9 1 | 3 2 | 6 7 | 4 2 | 3 7 | 10 | 7 2 | 12 2 | 11 1 |
| Wides | 2 | 3 | | | 1 | 4 | 3 | | | | | | 1 | |
| No-balls | 3 | 3 2 | 5 4 | 1 | 6 7 | 4 1 | 2 1 | 1 | 4 3 | 1 | 19 | 6 2 | 2 | 1 |
| Total | 373 20 | 359 150 | 139 199 | 177 | 310 129 | 274 60 | 473 88 | 320 237 | 139 94 | 155 90 | 438 | 313 169 | 377 156 | 307 176 |
| Wickets | 7 0 | 6 2 | 10 10 | 9 | 10 6 | 10 1 | 7 2 | 9† 10 | 10 10 | 10 10 | 9 | 10 10 | 10 3 | 10 4 |
| Result | W | D | D | L | L | D | D | L | L | L | D | D | W | D |
| Points | 24 | — | 4 | 0 | 7 | 7 | 4 | 6 | 4 | 4 | 8 | 7 | 24 | 8 |

*Catches* 32 – P.R. Downton (ct 26/st 6); 30 – C.P. Metson (ct 28/st 2); 23 – W.N. Slack; 21 – C.T. Radley and M.W. Gatting; 20 – P.H. Edmonds; 18 – J.E. Emburey; 16 – R.O. Butcher; 10 – G.D. Barlow; 8 – K.P. Tomlins and N.G. Cowans

| | M | Inns | NOs | Runs | HS | Av | 100s | 50s |
|---|---|---|---|---|---|---|---|---|
| J.D. Love | 15 | 23 | 2 | 568 | 112 | 27.04 | 1 | 3 |
| D.A. Reeve | 21 | 22 | 4 | 486 | 119 | 27.00 | 1 | 3 |
| A.J. Wright | 22 | 39 | 3 | 971 | 139 | 26.97 | 1 | 6 |
| R.M. Ellcock | 9 | 8 | 3 | 134 | 45* | 26.80 | | |
| B.N. French | 26 | 32 | 6 | 697 | 98 | 26.80 | | 3 |
| R.K. Illingworth | 21 | 20 | 7 | 346 | 43* | 26.61 | | |
| G.D. Barlow | 19 | 36 | 2 | 903 | 96 | 26.55 | | 4 |
| A.M. Green | 24 | 40 | 2 | 1006 | 81 | 26.47 | | 4 |
| B. Roberts | 17 | 26 | 5 | 554 | 80 | 26.38 | | 3 |
| J. Simmons | 21 | 34 | 5 | 748 | 72* | 25.79 | | 6 |
| P.R. Downton | 21 | 33 | 9 | 618 | 88 | 25.75 | | 3 |
| S.N. Hartley | 13 | 21 | 4 | 437 | 104* | 25.70 | 1 | 1 |
| D.B. d'Oliveira | 23 | 34 | 3 | 796 | 74 | 25.67 | | 5 |
| S.T. Jefferies | 18 | 28 | 3 | 633 | 65 | 25.32 | | 2 |
| C. Maynard | 15 | 21 | 5 | 402 | 50* | 25.12 | | 1 |
| C.P. Metson | 12 | 17 | 5 | 300 | 96 | 25.00 | | 2 |
| R.M. Ellison | 21 | 32 | 7 | 620 | 108 | 24.80 | 1 | 1 |
| S. Turner | 12 | 13 | 5 | 197 | 59* | 24.62 | | 2 |
| D.S. Steele | 25 | 39 | 13 | 639 | 78* | 24.57 | | 3 |
| G.P. Howarth | 22 | 37 | 3 | 833 | 113 | 24.50 | 2 | 4 |
| D.B. Pauline | 10 | 16 | 1 | 367 | 88 | 24.46 | | 3 |
| M.J. Bamber | 5 | 10 | 1 | 220 | 51 | 24.44 | | 1 |
| R.C. Russell | 21 | 27 | 6 | 513 | 63 | 24.42 | | 1 |
| C. Penn | 12 | 15 | 2 | 317 | 115 | 24.38 | 1 | 1 |
| D.G. Moir | 20 | 28 | 6 | 534 | 107 | 24.27 | 1 | 2 |
| L. Potter | 14 | 25 | 1 | 574 | 117 | 23.91 | 1 | 2 |
| C.R. Andrew | 9 | 18 | 1 | 405 | 101* | 23.82 | 1 | 1 |
| J.R.T. Barclay | 26 | 35 | 3 | 761 | 82 | 23.78 | | 4 |
| J.G. Wyatt | 17 | 28 | | 666 | 103 | 23.78 | 1 | 3 |
| D.A. Thorne | 9 | 16 | 3 | 306 | 69* | 23.53 | | 1 |
| D.R. Pringle | 21 | 35 | 7 | 658 | 96 | 23.50 | | 4 |
| A.M. Roberts | 8 | 12 | 4 | 188 | 89 | 23.50 | | 1 |
| C. Lethbridge | 15 | 17 | 3 | 324 | 46 | 23.14 | | |
| C.M. Old | 18 | 21 | 4 | 393 | 70 | 23.11 | | 2 |
| P.B. Clift | 19 | 28 | 7 | 483 | 58 | 23.00 | | 2 |
| I.J. Gould | 23 | 27 | 4 | 529 | 84 | 23.00 | | 2 |
| W.W. Davis | 21 | 24 | 7 | 390 | 77 | 22.94 | | 2 |
| D.P. Hughes | 19 | 32 | 1 | 707 | 113 | 22.80 | 2 | 1 |
| I.G. Swallow | 11 | 9 | 3 | 136 | 34* | 22.66 | | |
| M.R. Davis | 19 | 14 | 6 | 178 | 60* | 22.25 | | 1 |
| A. Needham | 19 | 30 | 1 | 644 | 70 | 22.20 | | 4 |
| A.E. Lea | 9 | 18 | | 395 | 119 | 21.94 | 1 | |
| D.G. Price | 7 | 11 | | 239 | 49 | 21.72 | | |
| N.A. Felton | 14 | 24 | 1 | 499 | 101 | 21.69 | 1 | 3 |
| S.B. Hassan | 17 | 27 | 4 | 499 | 103* | 21.69 | 1 | 1 |
| S.N.V. Waterton | 7 | 10 | 1 | 193 | 50 | 21.44 | | 1 |
| G.W. Johnson | 25 | 39 | 5 | 726 | 84 | 21.35 | | 3 |
| K.P. Tomlins | 10 | 18 | 1 | 363 | 103* | 21.35 | 1 | |
| R.J. Finney | 24 | 37 | 5 | 679 | 78 | 21.21 | | 4 |
| M.R. Chadwick | 7 | 14 | | 293 | 61 | 20.92 | | 2 |
| W.R. Bristowe | 5 | 8 | 3 | 104 | 30* | 20.80 | | |
| S.J. Dennis | 9 | 9 | 4 | 104 | 53* | 20.80 | | 1 |
| D.L. Underwood | 24 | 33 | 9 | 498 | 111 | 20.75 | 1 | |
| P.H. Edmonds | 25 | 33 | 4 | 600 | 142 | 20.68 | 1 | 2 |
| I.S. Anderson | 14 | 23 | 1 | 454 | 79 | 20.63 | | 1 |
| M.A. Feltham | 12 | 15 | 5 | 206 | 44 | 20.60 | | |
| E.J. Cunningham | 6 | 11 | 3 | 162 | 61* | 20.25 | | 1 |
| R.W. Taylor | 18 | 22 | 7 | 303 | 46 | 20.20 | | |

| v. Yorkshire (Lord's) 14–17 July | | v. Northamptonshire (Northampton) 25–27 July | | v. Hampshire (Lord's) 28–31 July | | v. West Indians (Lord's) 4–6 August | | v. Essex (Lord's) 8–10 August | | v. Nottinghamshire (Lord's) 11–14 August | | v. Leicestershire (Leicester) 18–21 August | | v. Hampshire (Bournemouth) 22–24 August | | v. Sussex (Hove) 25–28 August | | v. Essex (Chelmsford) 29–31 August | | v. Kent (Lord's) 5–7 September | | v. Gloucestershire (Bristol) 8–11 September | | M | Inns | NOs | Runs | H/S | Av |
|---|---|---|---|---|---|---|---|---|---|---|---|---|---|---|---|---|---|---|---|---|---|---|---|---|---|---|---|---|---|
| | | | | | | 19 | 9 | 2 | 12 | 2 | 31 | 96 | 39 | 93 | 45 | 2 | 63* | 58 | 39 | 24 | 17 | 9 | 11 | 19 | 36 | 2 | 903 | 96 | 26.55 |
| 35 | 5* | 4 | 91 | 0 | 52* | 26 | 40* | 24 | 0 | 1 | 0 | 106 | 16 | 22 | — | 24 | 13 | 19 | 122* | 42 | 71* | 36 | 8 | 25 | 46 | 8 | 1631 | 145 | 42.92 |
| 131* | 9* | 146 | 91* | 46 | 128* | 50* | — | 116 | 47 | 25 | 30 | 64 | 27 | 0 | 21 | 76 | 49 | 5 | 35* | 45 | 100* | 1 | 72* | 22 | 39 | 9 | 2150 | 258 | 71.66 |
| 62 | — | 0 | 17* | 116 | — | 41 | 22* | 3 | 78 | 2 | 46 | 62 | 81 | 27 | 5* | 55 | 51* | 30 | — | 28 | — | 61 | 65 | 23 | 40 | 7 | 1326 | 116 | 40.18 |
| 3 | — | 58 | 0 | 4 | — | | | 34 | 11 | 50 | 13 | 30 | 2 | 13 | — | 0 | 1 | 22* | — | 61 | — | 19 | 46* | 24 | 38 | 7 | 1072 | 128* | 34.58 |
| 3 | — | 54 | — | 53 | — | — | — | 2 | 26 | 6 | 0 | 17 | 11* | 25 | 17* | 40 | — | 0 | — | 30 | — | 9 | — | 26 | 35 | 2 | 581 | 57 | 17.60 |
| 20 | — | 14 | — | 6 | — | — | — | 58* | 4 | 21 | 0 | — | — | 4 | — | 15 | — | 26 | — | | | 15 | — | 25 | 33 | 4 | 600 | 142 | 20.68 |
| | | | | | | 15* | — | | | | | 1* | 32 | | | | | 20 | 5 | 8 | — | 18* | — | 14 | 21 | 7 | 393 | 88 | 28.07 |
| — | — | 0 | — | 6 | — | — | — | 3 | 25 | 12 | 19 | | | | | | | 26 | — | | | | | 18 | 21 | 3 | 285 | 44 | 15.83 |
| | | 0* | — | 16* | — | | | — | 4 | 0 | 0* | — | — | 0* | — | 0* | — | | | 2* | — | 0 | — | 21 | 24 | 14 | 87 | 16* | 8.70 |
| 4 | — | | | | | — | — | 0 | 2* | 4 | 0 | — | — | 33 | 1 | 0 | — | 0 | — | 6 | — | 10 | — | 19 | 23 | 1 | 255 | 66 | 11.59 |
| | | | | 14 | 22 | 7 | 5 | | | | | | | | | | | | | | | | | 10 | 18 | 1 | 363 | 103* | 21.35 |
| | | | | | | | | | | | | | | | | | | | | | | | | 2 | 2 | 1 | 30 | 28* | 30.00 |
| 2* | — | 21 | — | 18 | — | — | — | | | | | — | 5* | | | 3 | — | 1 | — | 17* | — | 0 | — | 15 | 14 | 4 | 142 | 41* | 14.20 |
| 4 | — | 4 | — | 0 | — | | | 64 | 19 | 17* | 4 | | | 8 | — | 8 | — | | | | | | | 12 | 17 | 5 | 300 | 96 | 25.00 |
| | | | | | | | | | | | | | | | | | | | | | | | | 2 | 3 | — | 54 | 33 | 18.00 |
| | | | | | | | | | | | | | | | | | | | | | | | | 2 | 3 | — | 106 | 47 | 35.33 |
| | | | | | | | | | | | | | | | | | | | | | | | | 1 | | | | | — |
| 29 | 5 | 3 | 0 | | | | | | | | | | | | | | | | | | | | | 3 | 5 | — | 57 | 29 | 11.40 |
| | | | | | | | | | | | | | | | | | | | | 0 | — | | | 2 | 2 | — | 0 | 0 | 0.00 |
| | | | | | | | | | | | | | | 6 | — | | | | | | | | | 1 | 1 | — | 6 | 6 | 6.00 |
| 1 | | 1 | 4 | 1 | 2 | 2 | 2 | 2 | | 2 | 4 | 4 | | 2 | 1 | | | 9 | 8 | 6 | | 1 | | † C.P. Metson retired hurt | | | | | |
| 8 | | 5 | 1 | 2 | 3 | 4 | 6 | 6 | 5 | 10 | 2 | 5 | 1 | 5 | 1 | 7 | 3 | 2 | 5 | 2 | | 2 | 7 | | | | | | |
| | 3 | 5 | | | 1 | | | | | | | 1 | | 1 | | 1 | | 2 | 1 | | | 5 | 3 | | | | | | |
| 1 | | 9 | 4 | 9 | 7 | 13 | 3 | 15 | 12 | | | 5 | 1 | 1 | | 12 | 6 | 3 | 3 | 1 | 2 | 5 | 1 | | | | | | |
| 303 | 22 | 324 | 208 | 291 | 215 | 177 | 87 | 329 | 245 | 152 | 149 | 391 | 215 | 240 | 91 | 243 | 186 | 223 | 218 | 272 | 190 | 191 | 213 | | | | | | |
| 8 | 1 | 10 | 3 | 10 | 1 | 4 | 2 | 9 | 10 | 10 | 10 | 6 | 6 | 10 | 3 | 10 | 3 | 10 | 2 | 9 | 1 | 10 | 3 | | | | | | |
| W | | W | | W | | D | | L | | L | | D | | W | | W | | D | | D | | W | | | | | | | |
| 24 | | 23 | | 21 | | — | | 7 | | 5 | | 8 | | 22 | | 22 | | 4 | | 5 | | 21 | | | | | | | |

6 – N.F. Williams
4 – S.P. Hughes and W.W. Daniel
2 – subs

1 – C.R. Cook,
K.R. Brown and
A.J.T. Miller

| | M | Inns | NOs | Runs | HS | Av | 100s | 50s |
|---|---|---|---|---|---|---|---|---|
| E.L. Reifer | 20 | 26 | 8 | 357 | 47 | 19.83 | | |
| N.E.J. Pocock | 13 | 18 | 2 | 314 | 55 | 19.62 | | 1 |
| N. Phillip | 13 | 17 | 2 | 293 | 71 | 19.53 | | 1 |
| R.A. Pick | 12 | 10 | 5 | 96 | 27* | 19.20 | | |
| N.A. Foster | 22 | 27 | 8 | 356 | 54* | 18.73 | | 1 |
| R.G.D. Willis | 8 | 8 | 5 | 56 | 33 | 18.66 | | |
| D.J. Thomas | 20 | 28 | 5 | 425 | 48 | 18.47 | | |
| J.D. Inchmore | 23 | 24 | 8 | 295 | 34 | 18.43 | | |
| S.N. Siddiqi | 6 | 12 | | 219 | 52 | 18.25 | | 1 |
| T.M. Tremlett | 23 | 31 | 7 | 438 | 74 | 18.25 | | 2 |
| G. Monkhouse | 18 | 25 | 7 | 328 | 100* | 18.22 | 1 | |
| G.C. Small | 25 | 30 | 8 | 400 | 41* | 18.18 | | |
| N.E. Briers | 22 | 37 | 3 | 616 | 73 | 18.11 | | 1 |
| A.J.T. Miller | 8 | 15 | 1 | 253 | 128* | 18.07 | 1 | |
| D.W. Varey | 8 | 14 | 1 | 235 | 61 | 18.07 | | 1 |
| M.N. Breddy | 10 | 20 | 1 | 339 | 61 | 17.84 | | 1 |
| G.S. le Roux | 24 | 24 | 6 | 321 | 68* | 17.83 | | 2 |
| K. Saxelby | 20 | 19 | 8 | 196 | 27 | 17.81 | | |
| R.J. Parks | 25 | 34 | 9 | 44 | 89 | 17.76 | | 2 |
| K.D. Smith | 21 | 40 | 1 | 692 | 93 | 17.74 | | 3 |
| J.E. Emburey | 26 | 35 | 2 | 581 | 57 | 17.60 | | 3 |
| P. Carrick | 22 | 28 | 5 | 400 | 47* | 17.39 | | |
| C.J.C. Rowe | 6 | 11 | 2 | 155 | 60* | 17.22 | | 1 |
| C. Dale | 8 | 8 | 2 | 100 | 49 | 16.66 | | |
| A.A. Metcalfe | 9 | 13 | | 216 | 60 | 16.61 | | 2 |
| G.V. Palmer | 15 | 20 | 2 | 299 | 73* | 16.61 | | 1 |
| T.A. Cotterell | 10 | 16 | 1 | 247 | 52 | 16.46 | | 1 |
| B.J.M. Maher | 7 | 11 | 2 | 146 | 66 | 16.22 | | 1 |
| D.A. Graveney | 26 | 40 | 13 | 430 | 33 | 15.92 | | |

| | M | Inns | NOs | Runs | HS | Av | 100s | 50s |
|---|---|---|---|---|---|---|---|---|
| N.F. Williams | 19 | 21 | 3 | 285 | 44 | 15.83 | | |
| O.H. Mortensen | 8 | 8 | 4 | 63 | 40* | 15.75 | | |
| T.M. Alderman | 20 | 27 | 13 | 220 | 52* | 15.71 | | 1 |
| P.W. Jarvis | 12 | 14 | 4 | 157 | 37 | 15.70 | | |
| D. Ripley | 14 | 21 | 3 | 281 | 61 | 15.61 | | 1 |
| P.J.W. Allott | 19 | 25 | 4 | 326 | 50* | 15.52 | | 1 |
| J.G. Franks | 8 | 13 | 2 | 170 | 42* | 15.45 | | |
| R.J. Maru | 17 | 20 | 4 | 246 | 36 | 15.37 | | |
| S.T. Clarke | 23 | 25 | 3 | 329 | 35 | 14.95 | | |
| J.G. Thomas | 20 | 26 | 5 | 314 | 36* | 14.95 | | |
| A.P.E. Knott | 14 | 22 | 2 | 295 | 43 | 14.75 | | |
| D.A. Banks | 6 | 9 | | 132 | 43 | 14.66 | | |
| E.E. Hemmings | 24 | 24 | 7 | 248 | 35 | 14.58 | | |
| D.E. East | 27 | 37 | 2 | 510 | 81 | 14.57 | | 3 |
| A.K. Golding | 8 | 13 | | 189 | 44 | 14.53 | | |
| M.S.A. McEvoy | 10 | 13 | | 188 | 46 | 14.46 | | |
| S.C. Booth | 12 | 14 | 7 | 100 | 42 | 14.28 | | |
| T. Davies | 27 | 35 | 7 | 398 | 43 | 14.21 | | |
| S.P. Hughes | 15 | 14 | 4 | 142 | 41* | 14.20 | | |
| P.G. Newman | 16 | 21 | 2 | 269 | 40 | 14.15 | | |
| Asif Din | 6 | 9 | 2 | 99 | 35* | 14.14 | | |
| G. Sharp | 11 | 12 | | 168 | 28 | 14.00 | | |
| K.A. Haynes | 9 | 16 | 1 | 209 | 37 | 13.93 | | |
| A.P. Pridgeon | 24 | 23 | 7 | 211 | 67 | 13.18 | | 1 |
| M.R. Cullinan | 7 | 12 | | 155 | 59 | 12.91 | | 2 |
| N.G.B. Cook | 24 | 30 | 9 | 256 | 44 | 12.19 | | |
| J.K. Lever | 24 | 22 | 7 | 182 | 37 | 12.13 | | |
| G.B. Stevenson | 14 | 16 | 1 | 180 | 27 | 12.00 | | |
| C.H. Dredge | 22 | 26 | 8 | 214 | 25* | 11.88 | | |

| **Middlesex C.C.C.** First-Class Matches – Bowling, 1984 | W.W. Daniel | N.G. Cowans | N.F. Williams | J.E. Emburey | P.H. Edmonds | M.W. Gatting | S.P. Hughes | K.D. James | W.N. Slack |
|---|---|---|---|---|---|---|---|---|---|
| *v.* Glamorgan (Lord's)<br>28 April–1 May | 15–3–36–1<br>17–1–65–2 | 8–3–25–1<br>16–2–48–4 | 14–3–45–2<br>12–3–30–0 | 12–7–17–3<br>15–6–23–1 | 13–5–25–1<br>12–8–19–0 | 1–0–2–0<br>13–6–17–1 | | | |
| *v.* Oxford University<br>(Oxford) 9–11 May | | | 20–8–48–3<br>9–2–19–4 | 40–21–51–2<br>3.4–2–1–0 | | | 20–5–61–1<br>7.2–2–11–0 | 16–2–75–0<br>15–11–9–2 | 4–1–3–0 |
| *v.* Northamptonshire (Lord's)<br>23–25 May | 21–11–21–3<br>6.5–2–18–0 | 21–6–50–2<br>7–2–19–3 | | 22–6–50–2 | 7–0–25–1 | 2–1–3–0 | 9.5–2–36–2<br>3–0–9–1 | | |
| *v.* Sussex (Lord's)<br>26–29 May | 9–1–28–1 | 10–3–29–0 | | 10–1–29–1 | 11.1–1–28–1 | 5–1–20–1 | 5–0–31–0 | | |
| *v.* Kent (Dartford)<br>30 May–1 June | 6–3–10–0<br>5–0–42–0 | | 22–5–55–4<br>12–2–51–0 | 26–7–67–3<br>10.2–0–70–1 | 25–11–39–3<br>14–2–65–0 | | | 1–0–3–0<br>9–3–19–2 | |
| *v.* Derbyshire (Derby)<br>2–5 June | 19–6–40–3 | | 21–4–63–0 | 23–7–75–3 | 18–5–44–1 | | 19–5–51–3 | | 2–0–4–0 |
| *v.* Somerset (Bath)<br>9–12 June | 18–1–61–1 | 13–1–47–0 | 21–2–67–0 | 73–21–156–2 | 64.3–22–111–6 | 5–1–9–0 | | | 7–0–15–0 |
| *v.* Surrey (Lord's)<br>13–15 June | 17–2–53–0<br>6–0–26–1 | 14–4–48–1<br>16–0–68–2 | 14–2–62–1<br>16–5–39–2 | 27–6–68–4<br>16–5–49–0 | 20–1–95–2<br>9–2–26–1 | 12–1–44–0 | | | |
| *v.* Warwickshire (Lord's)<br>16–19 June | 20–4–41–1<br>12.5–2–56–3 | 20–4–64–6<br>13–1–33–1 | 15.3–2–59–1<br>3–2–1–0 | 5–1–14–0<br>2–2–0–0 | 1–0–8–0<br>20–14–12–2 | 10–2–23–1<br>9–4–16–3 | | | |
| *v.* Surrey (The Oval)<br>23–26 June | 18–2–50–3 | 24.5–6–76–3 | 29–6–119–2 | 21–4–57–1 | 17–3–47–1 | | | | 5–1–14–0 |
| *v.* Glamorgan (Swansea)<br>27–29 June | | | 15.2–3–55–1<br>20–5–81–0 | 22–8–37–3<br>22–5–58–0 | 28–3–72–3<br>28–5–83–3 | | 19–4–64–1<br>9–0–24–1 | | <br>5–1–17–0 |
| *v.* Lancashire (Liverpool)<br>30 June–3 July | 5–0–18–1<br>11–2–18–2 | 14–5–39–3<br>7–2–12–2 | 16–6–32–3<br>4–0–20–0 | 18–5–33–1<br>24–11–36–3 | 43–21–68–2<br>23–11–52–2 | | | | |
| *v.* Worcestershire (Uxbridge)<br>7–10 July | 15–2–59–1<br>14–4–47–2 | 9–0–40–1<br>16–2–44–3 | | 27–3–70–2<br>14.4–3–57–3 | 36.1–9–101–4<br>11–2–36–1 | 1–0–4–0<br>6–2–17–1 | | | |
| *v.* Gloucestershire<br>(Uxbridge) 11–13 July | 17–2–76–3<br>5–2–11–0 | | 25–7–72–4<br>6–1–25–0 | 3–1–2–0<br>14–0–55–4 | 5.4–1–20–0<br>14–0–93–1 | | 17–0–60–2<br>6–0–22–1 | | |
| *v.* Yorkshire (Lord's)<br>14–17 July | | 13.4–3–25–4<br>16–4–40–3 | 12–1–58–4<br>20–4–45–2 | <br>17–7–17–1 | <br>6–2–7–0 | <br>6–0–11–0 | 11–3–28–0<br>17–1–58–3 | | |
| *v.* Northamptonshire<br>(Northampton) 25–27 July | 10–0–49–1<br>9.2–0–31–1 | | 6–0–38–0<br>13–4–41–2 | 36–7–89–1<br>15–2–27–2 | 38–13–93–3<br>25–10–42–4 | 1–0–1–0<br>1–0–1–0 | 10.3–0–54–2<br>7–0–28–1 | | |
| *v.* Hampshire (Lord's)<br>28–31 July | 11–3–18–1<br>14–2–46–3 | | 11–1–49–0<br>6–2–31–0 | 39–9–107–1<br>3–0–8–0 | 33–6–104–4<br>11–3–20–1 | | 14–0–47–0<br>9.3–2–27–4 | | <br>2–0–8–0 |
| *v.* West Indians (Lord's)<br>4–6 August | | 15–1–52–4<br>11–1–34–2 | 13–2–69–3<br>15–2–48–0 | <br>15–5–42–3 | <br>21–6–65–0 | 3–0–8–1 | 10.3–0–54–2<br>6–1–30–1 | | |
| *v.* Essex (Lord's)<br>8–10 August | 18–4–74–2<br>8–0–65–0 | 11–3–36–1 | 13–1–73–0<br>8–0–46–1 | 26–8–53–2<br>8–0–46–3 | 29–3–95–2<br>7.5–0–46–1 | | | | |
| *v.* Nottinghamshire (Lord's)<br>11–14 August | 22–3–85–4 | 23.4–1–82–3 | 16–2–64–3 | 5–1–20–0 | 20–4–61–0 | | | | |
| *v.* Leicestershire (Leicester)<br>18–21 August | 12–1–30–1<br>3–1–3–0 | 18–3–54–3<br>3–0–18–0 | | 23–4–59–2<br>29.5–12–52–2 | 36–8–108–3<br>28–11–52–3 | <br>3–1–2–0 | 11–2–35–0 | | 1–0–4–0 |
| *v.* Hampshire (Bournemouth)<br>22–24 August | 5–2–14–1<br>2–0–10–0 | 13–1–46–3<br>3–0–9–0 | | 28–9–54–2<br>30.1–13–52–2 | 29.2–11–67–4<br>32–11–53–8 | | | | |
| *v.* Sussex (Hove)<br>25–28 August | 15–4–49–3<br>12–3–29–2 | 18–4–51–4<br>17–2–46–2 | | 1–0–1–0<br>26–9–43–1 | 9–3–18–2<br>34–6–73–3 | <br>2–1–1–0 | 7–3–25–1<br>28–9–55–2 | | |
| *v.* Essex (Chelmsford)<br>29–31 August | | 17–1–49–1<br>14–1–58–3 | 6–2–16–0<br>14–1–47–0 | 35.5–11–94–5<br>3–0–24–0 | 33–6–98–2 | 4–0–17–0 | 14–5–40–1<br>12–0–68–0 | | <br>2–0–11–0 |
| *v.* Kent (Lord's)<br>5–7 September | 27–6–59–2 | 13–1–53–0 | | 52–18–83–4 | | | 12–2–36–1 | | |
| v. Gloucestershire (Bristol)<br>8–11 September | 18–2–53–4<br>18–2–71–1 | 20–4–63–5<br>10–2–28–1 | | <br>22–8–32–2 | <br>10.5–4–25–2 | 2–0–4–0<br>1–0–5–0 | 11.4–2–48–1<br>23–5–49–4 | | |
| | 462–86–<br>1463–54<br>*av.* 27.09 | 445.1–73–<br>1386–71<br>*av.* 19.52 | 447.5–90–<br>1568–42<br>*av.* 37.33 | 865.3–255–<br>1978–72<br>*av.* 27.47 | 823.3–233–<br>2096–77<br>*av.* 27.22 | 87–20–<br>205–8<br>*av.* 25.62 | 319.2–53–<br>1051–35<br>*av.* 30.02 | 41–16–<br>106–4<br>*av.* 26.50 | 28–3–<br>76–0<br>— |

a D. L. Bairstow, retired hurt, absent hurt
b T. M. Tremlett, absent

| A. Fraser | K.P. Tomlins | J.D. Carr | Byes | Leg-byes | Wides | No-balls | Total | Wkts |
|---|---|---|---|---|---|---|---|---|
| | | | 1 | 7 | 1 | 15 | 174 | 10 |
| | | | 1 | 5 | 2 | 8 | 218 | 10 |
| | | | 1 | 6 | 1 | 11 | 257 | 7 |
| | | | 4 | 3 | 1 | 7 | 55 | 6 |
| | | | 2 | 4 | | 11 | 202 | 10 |
| | | | | 3 | | 5 | 54 | 4 |
| | | | | 8 | | 5 | 178 | 5 |
| | | | | 3 | | 11 | 188 | 10 |
| | | | | 1 | 2 | 3 | 253 | 3 |
| | | | 1 | 7 | 2 | 27 | 314 | 10 |
| | | | 15 | 22 | | 13 | 516 | 9 |
| | | | 11 | 8 | 6 | | 395 | 8 |
| | | | | 9 | | 9 | 226 | 6 |
| | | | 4 | 7 | | 11 | 231 | 10 |
| | | | 2 | 1 | | 1 | 122 | 10 |
| | | | | 15 | 1 | 20 | 399 | 10 |
| 16–2–68–1 | | | 8 | 5 | | 18 | 327 | 10 |
| 18–5–56–0 | 5–1–9–0 | | | 15 | | 16 | 359 | 4 |
| | | | | 10 | 1 | 7 | 208 | 10 |
| | | | | | | 3 | 141 | 9 |
| | | 10–1–31–2 | 4 | 3 | | 9 | 321 | 10 |
| | | | | 2 | 8 | | 211 | 10 |
| | | | 4 | 1 | | 16 | 251 | 9 |
| | | | 5 | 8 | | 3 | 222 | 7 |
| | | | | 1 | 1 | 8 | 121 | 9 |
| | | | 4 | 8 | 3 | 10 | 203 | 9a |
| | | | 4 | 7 | | 3 | 338 | 10 |
| | | | 1 | 4 | 2 | 12 | 190 | 10 |
| | | | 2 | 9 | 1 | 13 | 350 | 6 |
| | | | 1 | 2 | 2 | 8 | 153 | 9b |
| | | | 4 | 5 | 3 | 16 | 211 | 10 |
| | | | | 1 | | 4 | 244 | 6 |
| | | | 3 | 13 | | 17 | 364 | 7 |
| | | | 4 | 7 | | | 214 | 6 |
| | | | 1 | 16 | 1 | 14 | 344 | 10 |
| | | | | 5 | 11 | 7 | 313 | 10 |
| | | | 4 | 1 | | 2 | 134 | 5 |
| | | | 1 | | | 6 | 188 | 10 |
| | | | 12 | 2 | | 1 | 139 | 10 |
| | | | 4 | 5 | 3 | 7 | 163 | 10 |
| | | | 1 | 8 | 1 | 6 | 263 | 10 |
| | | | 1 | 10 | | 4 | 329 | 10 |
| | | | 4 | 14 | | 7 | 233 | 4 |
| | | 20–4–42–2 | 1 | 10 | | 1 | 285 | 9 |
| | | | | 4 | | 2 | 174 | 10 |
| | | | | 7 | | 10 | 227 | 10 |
| 34–7–124–1 av. 124.00 | 5–1–9–0 — | 30–5–73–4 av. 18.25 | | | | | | |

| | M | Inns | NOs | Runs | HS | Av | 100s | 50s |
|---|---|---|---|---|---|---|---|---|
| S.G. Hinks | 8 | 14 | | 162 | 39 | 11.57 | | |
| N.G. Cowans | 21 | 25 | 1 | 269 | 66 | 11.20 | | 1 |
| M.W.W. Selvey | 15 | 18 | 8 | 111 | 20 | 11.10 | | |
| T. Gard | 21 | 24 | 5 | 209 | 26 | 11.00 | | |
| A.J. Pollock | 6 | 9 | | 97 | 32 | 10.77 | | |
| S.R. Barwick | 20 | 19 | 9 | 105 | 25 | 10.50 | | |
| N. Gifford | 25 | 24 | 10 | 146 | 28* | 10.42 | | |
| I. Folley | 17 | 28 | 9 | 194 | 22* | 10.21 | | |
| R.L. Ollis | 6 | 12 | 1 | 112 | 22 | 10.18 | | |
| N.A. Mallender | 20 | 30 | 4 | 261 | 33* | 10.03 | | |

**(Qualification – 8 innings, average 10.00)**

## BOWLING

| | Overs | Mds | Runs | Wkts | Av | Best | 5/in | 10/m |
|---|---|---|---|---|---|---|---|---|
| R.J. Hadlee | 772.2 | 245 | 1645 | 117 | 14.05 | 7/35 | 6 | 1 |
| R.A. Harper | 314.1 | 112 | 676 | 37 | 18.27 | 6/57 | 3 | |
| P.J.W. Allott | 602.5 | 171 | 1496 | 79 | 18.93 | 7/72 | 6 | |
| D.L. Underwood | 676.4 | 250 | 1511 | 77 | 19.62 | 8/87 | 2 | 1 |
| T.M. Tremlett | 669.5 | 210 | 1444 | 71 | 20.33 | 5/48 | 2 | |
| A. Sidebottom | 488.1 | 105 | 1292 | 63 | 20.50 | 6/41 | 3 | |
| G.S. le Roux | 604.2 | 154 | 1647 | 78 | 21.11 | 6/57 | 2 | |
| S.T. Clarke | 651 | 165 | 1687 | 78 | 21.62 | 6/62 | 2 | |
| N.G. Cowans | 493.1 | 76 | 1593 | 73 | 21.82 | 6/64 | 2 | |
| J.K. Lever | 874.5 | 195 | 2550 | 116 | 21.98 | 8/37 | 8 | 3 |
| N.E. Briers | 109 | 24 | 264 | 12 | 22.00 | 3/48 | | |
| P.M. Such | 386.5 | 122 | 937 | 42 | 22.30 | 5/34 | 2 | |
| G.A. Gooch | 321.1 | 74 | 850 | 38 | 22.36 | 4/54 | | |
| R.M. Ellison | 535.5 | 142 | 1323 | 59 | 22.42 | 5/27 | 1 | |
| M.J. Weston | 123.4 | 29 | 315 | 14 | 22.50 | 4/44 | | |
| T.M. Alderman | 559.4 | 149 | 1725 | 76 | 22.69 | 5/25 | 6 | |
| A.M.E. Roberts | 265 | 70 | 769 | 33 | 23.30 | 7/74 | 3 | |
| R.N. Kapil Dev | 296.3 | 75 | 819 | 35 | 23.40 | 5/30 | 2 | |
| E.E. Hemmings | 797.5 | 234 | 2220 | 94 | 23.61 | 7/47 | 7 | 1 |
| C.M. Wells | 497.2 | 146 | 1396 | 59 | 23.66 | 5/25 | 2 | |
| M.R. Davis | 500.4 | 108 | 1569 | 66 | 23.77 | 7/55 | 4 | 1 |
| N.A. Foster | 687.1 | 151 | 2098 | 87 | 24.11 | 6/79 | 4 | |
| R.M. Ellcock | 221.2 | 32 | 714 | 29 | 24.62 | 4/34 | | |
| K.B.S. Jarvis | 571.5 | 128 | 1788 | 72 | 24.83 | 5/30 | 2 | |
| N.S. Taylor | 80 | 21 | 254 | 10 | 25.40 | 3/38 | | |
| A.N. Jones | 208.1 | 44 | 636 | 25 | 25.44 | 5/29 | 1 | |
| C.E. Waller | 618.3 | 221 | 1349 | 53 | 25.45 | 6/75 | 1 | |
| G. Monkhouse | 460.5 | 120 | 1273 | 50 | 25.46 | 4/41 | | |
| P.B. Clift | 623.1 | 162 | 1608 | 63 | 25.52 | 8/26 | 2 | 1 |
| G. Miller | 897.2 | 257 | 2236 | 87 | 25.70 | 6/30 | 6 | |
| P.I. Pocock | 640.1 | 167 | 1621 | 63 | 25.73 | 7/74 | 3 | 1 |
| D.A. Reeve | 572.4 | 175 | 1420 | 55 | 25.81 | 5/22 | 1 | |
| V.J. Marks | 808 | 226 | 2233 | 86 | 25.96 | 8/141 | 5 | 1 |
| J. Simmons | 619.4 | 177 | 1644 | 63 | 26.09 | 7/176 | 7 | 1 |
| S.R. Barwick | 477.4 | 128 | 1314 | 50 | 26.28 | 7/38 | 2 | |
| I.T. Botham | 449.4 | 93 | 1562 | 59 | 26.47 | 8/103 | 4 | |
| K.E. Cooper | 623.2 | 207 | 1364 | 51 | 26.74 | 8/44 | 1 | |
| N. Phillip | 275.2 | 48 | 911 | 34 | 26.79 | 5/48 | 1 | |
| W.W. Daniel | 462 | 86 | 1463 | 54 | 27.09 | 4/53 | | |
| P.H. Edmonds | 823.3 | 233 | 2096 | 77 | 27.22 | 8/53 | 2 | 1 |
| J.F. Steele | 674 | 175 | 1867 | 68 | 27.45 | 5/42 | 4 | |
| J.E. Emburey | 865.3 | 255 | 1978 | 72 | 27.47 | 5/94 | 1 | |
| D.J. Thomas | 505.4 | 114 | 1654 | 60 | 27.56 | 6/36 | 2 | 1 |
| W.W. Davis | 547.5 | 117 | 1725 | 62 | 27.82 | 5/32 | 5 | |
| D.R. Pringle | 580.1 | 127 | 1784 | 64 | 27.87 | 7/53 | 3 | |
| A.M. Ferreira | 772.1 | 156 | 2208 | 79 | 27.94 | 6/70 | 1 | |
| L.L. McFarlane | 272.5 | 45 | 875 | 31 | 28.22 | 4/65 | | |
| J.R.T. Barclay | 417 | 117 | 1023 | 36 | 28.41 | 4/32 | | |
| R.J. Finney | 584 | 125 | 1770 | 62 | 28.54 | 5/55 | 2 | |
| G.C. Small | 643.4 | 127 | 2027 | 71 | 28.54 | 5/41 | 2 | |
| J.P. Agnew | 670.1 | 127 | 2413 | 84 | 28.72 | 8/47 | 4 | 1 |
| C.H. Dredge | 533 | 125 | 1534 | 53 | 28.94 | 4/48 | | |
| C.M. Old | 496 | 134 | 1306 | 45 | 29.02 | 6/46 | 3 | 1 |
| R.C. Ontong | 837.4 | 221 | 2155 | 74 | 29.12 | 7/96 | 4 | |
| S. Turner | 285 | 95 | 617 | 21 | 29.38 | 3/29 | | |
| D.A. Graveney | 667.4 | 202 | 1588 | 54 | 29.40 | 6/73 | 3 | |
| R.E. East | 152.4 | 48 | 324 | 11 | 29.45 | 3/24 | | |
| N. Gifford | 811.4 | 240 | 1919 | 65 | 29.52 | 6/83 | 2 | |
| A.P. Pridgeon | 718.5 | 168 | 1949 | 66 | 29.53 | 5/50 | 2 | |
| C.J.C. Rowe | 135 | 41 | 356 | 12 | 29.66 | 3/20 | | |
| C.S. Cowdrey | 271.1 | 57 | 832 | 28 | 29.71 | 3/28 | | |
| D.L. Acfield | 577.4 | 174 | 1368 | 46 | 29.73 | 6/44 | 2 | |

| **Northamptonshire C.C.C.** First-Class Matches – Batting, 1984 | v. Warwickshire (Edgbaston) 28–30 April | | v. Surrey (The Oval) 2–4 May | | v. Essex (Northampton) 9–11 May | | v. Middlesex (Lord's) 23–25 May | | v. Leicestershire (Leicester) 26–29 May | | v. Lancashire (Northampton) 30 May–1 June | | v. Sussex (Horsham) 2–5 June | | v. West Indians (Milton Keynes) 9–11 June | | v. Essex (Chelmsford) 16–19 June | | v. Yorkshire (Northampton) 23–26 June | | v. Warwickshire (Northampton) 27–29 June | | v. Somerset (Northampton) 30 June–3 July | | v. Surrey (Northampton) 7–10 July | | v. Hampshire (Southampton) 11–13 July | |
|---|---|---|---|---|---|---|---|---|---|---|---|---|---|---|---|---|---|---|---|---|---|---|---|---|---|---|---|---|
| G. Cook | 102 | 16 | 5 | 9* | | | | | | | 56 | 9* | 34 | 32 | 0 | 32 | 28 | 84 | 1 | 39 | 82 | 56 | 23 | 3 | 29* | 16* | 50 | 32 |
| W. Larkins | 45 | 17 | 32 | 46 | 23 | 4 | 46 | 16* | 22 | 19 | 151 | 2* | 2 | 18 | 7 | 48 | 24 | 55 | 0 | 6 | 78 | 63 | 108 | 14 | 30 | 89 | 41 | 82 |
| R.J. Boyd-Moss | 1 | 19 | 20 | 79 | 0* | — | | | | | | | | | | | | | | | 4 | 32 | 10 | 1 | 0 | 86 | 20* | 0 |
| A.J. Lamb | 57 | 67* | 74 | 27 | 37 | 64* | 18 | 4 | 65 | — | | | | | 4 | 19 | | | 34 | 7 | | | | | 11 | 3 | | |
| R.J. Bailey | 100* | 26* | 65 | 35* | 0 | 6 | 1 | 7 | 3 | — | 9 | — | 5 | 17 | 95 | 19* | 75 | 17 | 0 | 1 | 15 | 17* | 0 | 114 | 82 | 6 | — | 14 |
| D.J. Capel | 48 | — | 3 | 29 | 51 | 4 | | | | | 2 | — | 45* | 16 | 63 | — | 12 | 25* | | | | | | | | | | |
| D.S. Steele | 8* | — | 20 | 0* | 3 | 2 | 13 | — | 1 | — | 6* | — | 2 | 0 | 16* | — | 0 | 15* | 1 | 6* | 23 | 18 | 15 | 41* | 66* | 6 | — | 25 |
| G. Sharp | — | — | 27 | — | 18 | 16 | 3 | — | | | — | — | 20 | 24 | | | 21 | — | 28 | 3 | — | — | | | | | | |
| N.A. Mallender | — | — | 27 | — | 5 | 5 | | | | | | | | | | | 6 | 9 | 11 | 0 | 33* | 0 | 14 | 2 | 0 | — | 0 | 1 |
| A. Walker | — | — | 0 | — | | | 5 | — | 7* | — | — | — | 19 | 0 | | | 0 | — | | | 5 | 0 | 7* | 4 | 0 | — | — | 6* |
| R.W. Hanley | — | — | 3* | — | 19 | 9 | 2* | — | 24 | — | — | — | 1 | 11 | 0 | — | | | 1 | 4 | 33* | 0* | 0 | 6 | 0 | — | | |
| R.G. Williams | | | | | 36 | 23 | 23 | 13 | 45 | 8 | 47* | — | 44 | 43 | 14 | 10 | 8 | 65 | 26 | 35 | 2 | 5 | 50 | 65 | 26 | 19 | 7* | 34 |
| B.J. Griffiths | | | | | 8* | 0 | 12 | — | — | — | — | — | 2 | 0* | 0 | — | 0* | — | 0* | 0 | | | | | | | — | — |
| M.J. Bamber | | | | | | | 3 | 4 | 28 | 38* | | | | | | | | | 19 | 51 | 37 | 40 | 0 | 0 | | | | |
| D.J. Wild | | | | | | | 59 | 2* | 39 | — | 91 | — | 18 | 10 | 0 | 36* | 24 | 23 | | | | | | | | | 0 | 44 |
| D. Ripley | | | | | | | | | 20 | — | | | | | 2 | 42 | | | | | | | 17 | 4 | 61 | 6* | — | 20* |
| Byes | | 1 | 3 | 13 | | 4 | 2 | | | | | | 2 | 2 | 2 | 1 | 1 | | 7 | | 4 | | | | 2 | 12 | 4 | |
| Leg-byes | 19 | 10 | 16 | | 7 | 4 | 4 | 3 | 4 | 1 | 12 | 1 | 4 | 2 | 8 | 7 | 5 | 12 | 3 | 5 | 6 | 4 | 9 | 15 | 11 | 5 | 4 | 4 |
| Wides | | | | 1 | | 1 | | | | 1 | | | | 3 | | | | 5 | | | 6 | | 1 | | | 1 | 3 | |
| No-balls | 11 | 1 | 5 | 5 | 3 | 3 | 11 | 5 | 6 | | 4 | 2 | 2 | | 9 | 6 | | 5 | 4 | 3 | 5 | 1 | 1 | 1 | 4 | 1 | 6 | 2 |
| Total | 391 | 157 | 300 | 244 | 210 | 145 | 202 | 54 | 264 | 67 | 378 | 14 | 200 | 178 | 220 | 220 | 204 | 315 | 135 | 160 | 333 | 236 | 255 | 270 | 322 | 250 | 135 | 264 |
| Wickets | 5 | 3 | 10 | 4 | 9† | 9† | 10 | 4 | 9 | 2 | 5 | 0 | 10 | 10 | 10 | 5 | 10 | 6 | 10 | 10 | 8 | 8 | 10 | 10 | 9‡ | 6 | 4 | 8 |
| Result | D | | W | | L | | D | | L | | D | | L | | D | | D | | L | | D | | L | | W | | W | |
| Points | 5 | | 23 | | 5 | | 6 | | 3 | | 6 | | 3 | | — | | 4 | | 2 | | 5 | | 4 | | 22 | | 20 | |

*Catches* 38 – D. Ripley (ct 26/st 12); 29 – D.S. Steele; 17 – G. Sharp (ct 15/st 2); 15 – G. Cook; 14 – R.J. Bailey; 12 – W. Larkins; 11 – R.J. Boyd-Moss; 9 – A.J. Lamb and R.G. Williams; 8 – D.J. Capel; 7 – N.A. Mallender and subs; 5 – D.J. Wild

| v. Kent (Northampton) 14–17 July | | v. Middlesex (Northampton) 25–27 July | | v. Gloucestershire (Bristol) 28–31 July | | v. Derbyshire (Northampton) 4–7 August | | v. Lancashire (Southport) 8–10 August | | v. Worcestershire (Wellingborough) 11–14 August | | v. Glamorgan (Swansea) 18–21 August | | v. Sussex (Northampton) 22–24 August | | v. Leicestershire (Northampton) 25–28 August | | v. Nottinghamshire (Trent Bridge) 29–31 August | | v. Worcestershire (Worcester) 5–7 September | | M | Inns | NOs | Runs | H/S | Av |
|---|---|---|---|---|---|---|---|---|---|---|---|---|---|---|---|---|---|---|---|---|---|---|---|---|---|---|---|
| 40 | 59 | 71 | 8 | 11 | 33 | 80 | 102 | 28 | — | 19 | 91 | 9 | 32 | 47 | 27 | 17 | 35 | 45 | 24 | 9 | 14 | 22 | 43 | 4 | 1539 | 102 | 39.46 |
| 12 | 5 | 31 | 0 | 0 | 6 | 8 | 16 | 20 | — | 24 | 0 | 0 | 86 | 27 | 183* | 65 | 18 | 16 | 26 | 0 | 25 | 25 | 49 | 3 | 1656 | 183* | 36.00 |
| 2 | 39 | 3 | 15 | | | 18 | 87 | 105 | — | 36 | 5 | 73 | 18 | 12 | 46 | 23 | 1 | 1 | 34 | 63 | 51 | 17 | 32 | 2 | 904 | 105 | 30.13 |
| | | | | | | 9 | 13 | | | | | 13 | 19 | | | | | 0 | 38 | 0 | 133* | 12 | 23 | 3 | 716 | 133* | 35.80 |
| 35 | 8 | 95 | 14 | 15 | 48 | 2 | 17* | 0 | — | 64 | 53 | 25 | 13 | 106* | 15* | 24 | 55 | 22 | 30 | 35 | — | 25 | 45 | 8 | 1405 | 114 | 37.97 |
| 2 | 54 | 49 | 70 | 2 | 29 | 0 | 6* | 14 | — | 25 | 12* | | | 37* | — | 81 | 79 | 13 | 6 | 12 | — | 17 | 28 | 5 | 789 | 81 | 34.30 |
| 0 | 3 | 36 | 29* | 70 | 78* | 14 | — | 2 | — | 21* | 10* | 6 | 7 | — | — | 23 | 32 | 5* | 0 | 16 | — | 25 | 39 | 13 | 639 | 78* | 24.57 |
| | | | | | | | | | | | | | | | | | | 7 | 1 | 0 | — | 11 | 12 | — | 168 | 28 | 14.00 |
| 7 | 11 | 8 | 17 | 9 | 15* | 7 | — | 11 | — | 10 | — | 1 | 12 | — | — | 5* | 8 | 13 | 6 | 8* | — | 20 | 30 | 4 | 261 | 33* | 10.03 |
| 0 | 11* | | | 0 | — | | | | | | | | | | | | | | | | | 13 | 15 | 4 | 64 | 19 | 5.81 |
| | | 0 | 2 | 11* | — | 2* | — | 3* | — | 0 | — | | | | | | | | | | | 17 | 21 | 7 | 131 | 33* | 9.35 |
| | | 10 | 13 | 61 | — | | | | | | | 17 | 5 | 39 | 28 | 2 | 2 | 1 | 50* | 169 | 5* | 19 | 36 | 4 | 1050 | 169 | 32.81 |
| 0 | 11 | 0* | 0 | | | | | 3* | — | 1 | — | 0* | 0* | — | — | 5 | 6* | 0 | 0 | — | — | 18 | 21 | 9 | 48 | 12 | 4.00 |
| | | | | | | | | | | | | | | | | | | | | | | 5 | 10 | 1 | 220 | 51 | 24.44 |
| 3 | 128 | | | 36 | 27 | 9 | 17 | 144 | — | 45 | 21 | 6 | 24 | 28 | 1 | 11 | 9 | | | | | 15 | 27 | 2 | 855 | 144 | 34.20 |
| 18* | 0 | 21 | 3 | 14 | 9 | 4 | — | 19 | — | 9 | — | 0 | 5 | — | — | 6 | 1 | | | | | 14 | 21 | 3 | 281 | 61 | 15.61 |
| | | 4 | 1 | | 7 | | 4 | 4 | | | 13 | | 4 | | | | 3 | | 5 | 2 | 1 | | | | | | |
| 3 | 1 | 7 | 4 | 9 | 6 | 1 | 10 | 12 | | 2 | 4 | 2 | 12 | 5 | 4 | 2 | 5 | 6 | 1 | 16 | 4 | | | | | | |
| 1 | | | 2 | | | 1 | | 6 | | | | | | 1 | | | | | | 4 | 1 | | | | | | |
| 1 | | 2 | 12 | 1 | | 3 | | 9 | | 7 | 6 | 9 | 5 | 1 | 2 | 2 | 1 | | 3 | 8 | 6 | | | | | | |
| 24 | 330 | 338 | 190 | 239 | 258 | 158 | 272 | 380 | | 263 | 215 | 161 | 242 | 303 | 306 | 266 | 255 | 129 | 224 | 342 | 240 | | | | | | |
| 10 | 10 | 10 | 10 | 10 | 6 | 10 | 5 | 9 | | 10 | 5 | 10 | 10 | 5 | 4 | 10 | 10 | 10 | 10 | 9 | 3 | | | | | | |
| Tie | | L | | D | | D | | W | | D | | L | | W | | D | | L | | L | | | | | | | |
| 10 | | 7 | | 4 | | 2 | | 23 | | 5 | | 2 | | 23 | | 7 | | 3 | | 8 | | | | | | | |

†R.J. Boyd-Moss retired hurt, absent hurt

‡G. Cook retired hurt

–A. Walker and B.J. Griffiths

–R.W. Hanley

–M.J. Bamber

| Northamptonshire C.C.C. First-Class Matches – Bowling, 1984 | R.W. Hanley | N.A. Mallender | A. Walker | D.S. Steele | D.J. Capel | W. Larkins | R.J. Boyd-Moss | G. Cook | B.J. Griffiths |
|---|---|---|---|---|---|---|---|---|---|
| *v.* Warwickshire (Edgbaston) | 23–4–80–1 | 18–6–47–2 | 19–2–80–0 | 31–7–114–2 | 10–0–59–0 | 5–0–22–0 | | | |
| 28–30 April | 13–3–29–0 | 13–3–33–2 | 6–1–35–1 | 13–4–43–1 | 6–0–46–0 | 4–1–28–0 | 10–2–35–0 | 4–0–38–0 | |
| *v.* Surrey (The Oval) | 25–10–49–3 | 22–4–60–3 | 20–5–85–0 | 13–3–44–0 | 11–2–42–1 | 10–5–17–0 | | | |
| 2–4 May | 14–0–47–1 | 16–5–34–1 | 16–0–48–2 | 9–2–54–0 | 10–3–28–5 | | | | |
| *v.* Essex (Northampton) | 31–4–94–3 | 26–9–69–4 | | | 10–2–46–0 | | | | 23–5–88–0 |
| 9–11 May | | | | | 0.4–0–8–0 | | | | 1–1–0–0 |
| *v.* Middlesex (Lord's) | 19–8–29–1 | | 13.3–3–50–4 | | | | | | 23–8–52–5 |
| 23–25 May | 20.4–2–58–5 | | 14–5–30–1 | 4–2–4–0 | | | | | 25–4–71–4 |
| *v.* Leicestershire (Leicester) | | | | | | | | | |
| 26–29 May | 13–2–65–1 | | 5–1–35–0 | 25–3–113–2 | | | | | 9–4–22–2 |
| *v.* Lancashire (Northampton) | 27–5–77–5 | | 14–2–50–1 | 32–11–62–1 | | | | | 21–4–51–1 |
| 30 May–1 June | | | | | | | | | |
| *v.* Sussex (Horsham) | 19.3–5–64–1 | | 14–5–52–0 | 22–8–40–0 | 11–1–52–1 | | | | 23–4–62–1 |
| 2–5 June | | | | | 2–0–7–0 | | | | |
| *v.* West Indians | 11–3–27–3 | | | 13–2–36–1 | 13–2–49–2 | 5–3–5–1 | | | 18–4–35–1 |
| (Milton Keynes) 9–11 June | 3–1–7–0 | | | 4–0–8–0 | 3–0–15–0 | | | | 4–0–18–0 |
| *v.* Essex (Chelmsford) | | 21–6–67–1 | 23.2–6–85–4 | 26–7–81–3 | 5–1–13–0 | | | | 32–14–70–1 |
| 16–19 June | | | | | | | | | |
| *v.* Yorkshire (Northampton) | 19–4–53–0 | 23–6–41–2 | | 27.5–8–97–4 | | | | | 30–6–71–2 |
| 23–26 June | | | | | | | | | |
| *v.* Warwickshire (Northampton) | 21–4–73–2 | 18–2–72–3 | 24–5–116–3 | 23–11–53–1 | | 6–1–11–0 | | | |
| 27–29 June | 6–1–16–0 | 8–3–15–0 | 6–1–28–0 | 16–3–76–3 | | 4–0–9–0 | | | |
| *v.* Somerset (Northampton) | 24–4–99–0 | 24–2–97–0 | 25–2–96–3 | 17–4–73–0 | | | 4–1–6–0 | 1–0–7–0 | |
| 30 June–3 July | | 2–0–10–0 | 1–0–7–0 | | | | | | |
| *v.* Surrey (Northampton) | 7–1–28–0 | 17–2–77–1 | 18–2–54–1 | 28–10–60–3 | | | | | |
| 7–10 July | | 9–0–45–2 | 18–1–79–1 | 16–0–100–3 | | | | | |
| *v.* Hampshire (Southampton) | | 20–5–48–1 | 13–2–29–0 | | | | | | 24–5–63–5 |
| 11–13 July | | 8–2–15–0 | | 8–6–5–3 | | | 9–0–94–0 | 7–0–46–0 | 6–3–7–0 |
| *v.* Kent (Northampton) | | 20–5–56–1 | 20–3–56–1 | 19–10–33–2 | | | | | 25–8–55–0 |
| 14–17 July | | 11–1–39–0 | 15–2–38–2 | 6–5–1–0 | 3–0–19–0 | | | | 12–3–36–0 |
| *v.* Middlesex (Northampton) | 16–1–58–2 | 13.2–3–34–2 | | 37–9–87–2 | 4–0–21–0 | | | | 5–1–17–0 |
| 25–27 July | 9–2–20–0 | 10–2–32–1 | | 10–1–50–0 | | | | 0.1–0–4–0 | 3–0–19–0 |
| *v.* Gloucestershire (Bristol) | 17–2–48–1 | 23–5–54–3 | 21–3–56–3 | 42–17–70–2 | | | | | |
| 28–31 July | 5–2–18–0 | 8–2–17–2 | 3–1–9–0 | 12–5–28–2 | | | | 3–1–4–0 | |
| *v.* Derbyshire (Northampton) | 7–3–13–0 | 15–3–45–4 | | 7–4–17–0 | 4.2–1–21–0 | | | | |
| 4–7 August | | | | | | | | | |
| *v.* Lancashire (Southport) | 13–5–21–6 | 6–3–12–1 | | 6–3–8–1 | | | | | 4–0–17–1 |
| 8–10 August | 18–5–44–0 | 15–0–61–3 | | 32.3–12–86–5 | | | 3–1–14–0 | | 17–4–53–2 |
| *v.* Worcestershire | 12–6–46–2 | 18–7–51–3 | | 24–5–56–0 | 7–0–20–1 | | 15–3–68–1 | | 20–3–76–2 |
| (Wellingborough) 11–14 August | 3–0–19–0 | 10–2–23–0 | | 29–7–79–3 | 4–0–16–1 | 4–0–11–0 | | | 13–3–30–1 |
| *v.* Glamorgan (Swansea) | | 10–6–36–0 | | 30–10–81–0 | | | | | 18–6–44–2 |
| 18–21 August | | 1–0–3–0 | | 13–3–41–3 | | | | | |
| *v.* Sussex (Northampton) | | 19–5–68–0 | | 16–5–38–2 | 18–5–70–2 | 5–2–13–0 | 1–0–4–0 | | 28–5–89–4 |
| 22–24 August | | 10–2–28–1 | | 9.2–2–43–0 | 7–0–42–2 | | | | 14–5–23–1 |
| *v.* Leicestershire | | 18–2–65–1 | | 20–11–23–1 | 8–1–33–1 | | 1–1–0–0 | | 24–4–67–2 |
| (Northampton) 25–28 August | | 8–3–17–1 | | 17–7–49–1 | | | 6–4–6–0 | | 6–3–5–1 |
| *v.* Nottinghamshire | | 11–1–78–1 | | 35.2–8–122–5 | 5–0–22–0 | | 6–0–41–0 | | 13–1–70–0 |
| (Trent Bridge) 29–31 August | | | | | | | | | |
| *v.* Worcestershire (Worcester) | | 19–5–42–0 | | 18–6–25–2 | 13–2–50–0 | 25–7–59–5 | | | 22–4–67–3 |
| 5–7 September | | 9.4–2–42–1 | | 21–6–100–3 | | | | | 11–2–54–2 |
| | 396.1–87–<br>1182–37<br>*av.* 31.94 | 500–114–<br>1533–47<br>*av.* 32.61 | 308.5–52–<br>1118–27<br>*av.* 41.40 | 732–227–<br>2100–61<br>*av.* 34.42 | 155–20–<br>679–16<br>*av.* 42.43 | 68–19–<br>175–6<br>*av.* 29.16 | 55–12–<br>268–1<br>*av.* 268.00 | 15.1–1<br>99–0<br>— | 474–114–<br>1332–43<br>*av.* 30.97 |

a G. Sharp 1–1–0–0
b M. J. Bamber 2.3–1–3–0
c P. Bainbridge, absent hurt

| R.G. Williams | R.J. Bailey | D.J. Wild | *Byes* | *Leg-byes* | *Wides* | *No-balls* | *Total* | *Wkts* |
|---|---|---|---|---|---|---|---|---|
| | | | 6 | 13 | | 17 | 438 | 5 |
| | | | | 8 | | 6 | 301 | 4 |
| | | | 1 | 12 | | 8 | 318 | 7 |
| | | | 2 | 9 | | 3 | 225 | 9 |
| 12–4–20–0 | | | 9 | 11 | 1 | 11 | 349 | 7 |
| | | | | | | | 8 | 0 |
| | | | | 3 | | 5 | 139 | 10 |
| 10–0–24–0 | | | | 8 | | 4 | 199 | 10 |
| | | | | | | | — | — |
| 24–4–86–1 | | | 3 | 3 | | 8 | 335 | 6 |
| 9–5–12–1 | 10–2–24–1 | | 3 | 2 | 1 | 7 | 289 | 10 |
| 19–2–76–1 | | | | 11 | | 1 | 358 | 4 |
| | | 2.2–0–8–0 | | | 4 | 2 | 21 | 0a |
| 14–1–73–1 | | 10–3–30–1 | | 9 | | 4 | 268 | 10 |
| | | | 2 | | | | 50 | 0 |
| 16–3–52–1 | | 4–0–23–0 | 3 | 1 | 3 | 19 | 417 | 10 |
| 20–4–51–2 | | | | 4 | | 12 | 329 | 10 |
| 15–7–47–0 | | | 2 | 7 | 1 | 18 | 400 | 9 |
| 11–0–56–1 | | | | 1 | | 7 | 208 | 4 |
| 33–8–83–2 | | | 6 | 11 | | 23 | 501 | 5 |
| | 2–2–0–0 | | | 5 | | | 25 | 0b |
| 21.5–3–61–0 | | | 7 | 7 | 2 | 8 | 304 | 5 |
| 4.3–0–28–3 | | | 4 | 2 | 1 | 2 | 261 | 10 |
| 7–2–14–1 | | 6.2–1–15–3 | | 9 | 1 | 15 | 194 | 10 |
| 7–2–19–0 | 2–0–8–0 | | 4 | | | 3 | 201 | 3 |
| | | 11–3–24–2 | 5 | 8 | 1 | 12 | 250 | 6 |
| | | 11–1–63–3 | 4 | 1 | | 3 | 204 | 5 |
| 27–9–83–4 | 1–0–4–0 | | 1 | 5 | 5 | 9 | 324 | 10 |
| 15–1–74–2 | | | 4 | 1 | | 4 | 208 | 3 |
| | | 3–0–16–0 | 5 | 10 | 2 | 16 | 277 | 9c |
| | 2–1–3–0 | | 3 | | | 4 | 86 | 4 |
| | | 12–2–48–0 | 1 | 3 | | 2 | 150 | 4 |
| | | | | | | 12 | 70 | 10 |
| | 4–1–6–0 | | | 3 | | 13 | 280 | 10 |
| | | 5–0–19–0 | 4 | 7 | | 4 | 351 | 9 |
| | | | 3 | 8 | 2 | 2 | 193 | 5 |
| 46–18–115–4 | | 5–1–11–0 | 2 | 9 | 1 | 15 | 314 | 6 |
| 13–1–43–1 | | | 1 | 1 | | 1 | 90 | 4 |
| 27–7–66–1 | | 3–0–18–0 | 4 | 8 | | 13 | 391 | 9 |
| 7–0–37–0 | | 12–4–35–0 | 2 | | 1 | 3 | 214 | 4 |
| 14–4–22–4 | | 7–3–19–1 | 1 | | 4 | 13 | 247 | 10 |
| 15–8–17–2 | | | | 11 | | 12 | 117 | 5 |
| 29–9–91–0 | | | | 8 | 2 | 16 | 450 | 7 |
| 5–1–8–0 | | | 8 | 7 | 4 | 12 | 282 | 10 |
| 21–1–90–0 | | | 3 | 15 | | | 304 | 6 |
| 442.–104–1348–32 *av.* 42.12 | 21–6–45–1 *av.* 45.00 | 91.4–18–329–10 *av.* 32.90 | | | | | | |

| Nottinghamshire C.C.C. First-Class Matches – Batting, 1984 | v. Oxford University (Oxford) 21–24 April | | v. Surrey (Trent Bridge) 28–30 April | | v. Leicestershire (Trent Bridge) 2–4 May | | v. Yorkshire (Leeds) 9–11 May | | v. Essex (Chelmsford) 23–25 May | | v. Derbyshire (Derby) 26–29 May | | v. Warwickshire (Edgbaston) 30 May–1 June | | v. Hampshire (Bournemouth) 2–5 June | | v. Glamorgan (Trent Bridge) 9–12 June | | v. Gloucestershire (Trent Bridge) 16–19 June | | v. Leicestershire (Leicester) 23–26 June | | v. Yorkshire (Trent Bridge) 27–29 June | | v. Cambridge Univ. (Trent Bridge) 30 June–3 July | | v. Sussex (Trent Bridge) 7–10 July | | v. Somerset (Trent Bridge) 11–13 July | |
|---|---|---|---|---|---|---|---|---|---|---|---|---|---|---|---|---|---|---|---|---|---|---|---|---|---|---|---|---|---|---|
| R.T. Robinson | 79 | 100* | 1 | 43 | 36 | 20 | 10* | 10 | 0 | 51* | 33 | 54 | 16 | — | 12 | 15 | 28 | 3* | 78 | — | 171 | 85* | 169 | 45 | | | 59 | 3 | 22 | 7 |
| B.C. Broad | 88 | 108* | 27 | 63 | 43 | 22 | 7 | 62 | 4 | 35* | 46 | 9 | 64 | — | 54 | 0 | 57 | 13* | 71 | — | 39 | 41* | | | | | 18 | 14 | | |
| D.W. Randall | 34 | — | 0 | 9 | 44 | 75* | 2 | 45 | 56 | — | 55* | 31 | | | | | 79 | — | | | 45 | — | 136 | 73 | | | 53 | 110* | 0 | 36 |
| J.D. Birch | 52 | — | 28 | 75 | 10 | 9 | — | 28 | 39 | — | — | 26 | 28* | — | 13 | 7 | 16 | — | 110* | — | 0 | — | 14 | 17* | 69 | 54* | 18 | 28 | 0 | 33 |
| P. Johnson | 29 | — | | | | | | | | | | | | | | | | | | | | | | | 31 | 63 | | | | |
| B.N. French | 30* | — | 21 | — | 29 | — | — | 55 | 39 | — | — | 0 | — | — | 70* | 26* | 10 | — | 33 | — | | | 1 | 2 | | | 8 | 3* | 8 | 9* |
| K. Saxelby | 6 | — | 5 | — | 6* | — | — | 4* | 0 | — | — | 22* | — | — | — | 7 | 24* | — | 0 | — | | | 4* | — | | | 15* | — | 17 | — |
| R.A. Pick | 27* | — | | | | | | | | | | | — | — | | | | | | | 1 | — | | | 15 | — | | | | |
| M.K. Bore | — | — | | | | | | | | | | | | | | | | | | | | | | | | | | | | |
| J.A. Afford | — | — | | | | | | | | | | | | | | | | | | | | | | | — | — | | | | |
| P.M. Such | — | — | 3* | — | — | — | | | | | | | | | | | | | — | — | | | — | — | — | — | 0 | — | 0 | — |
| C.E.B. Rice | | | 48 | 86 | 33 | 16 | 16 | 32 | 31 | — | 77* | 3 | 129 | — | 30 | 8 | 7 | — | 32 | — | 20 | — | 31* | 35 | | | 34 | 6 | 61 | 80 |
| S.B. Hassan | | | 8 | 36* | 36 | 9 | — | 17 | 9 | — | — | 3 | 27 | — | 17 | 0 | 7 | — | 7 | — | 25 | — | 23 | 70 | 6 | 103* | | | 37 | 10* |
| R.J. Hadlee | | | 11 | — | 14 | 25* | — | 1 | 71* | — | — | 10* | — | — | 100* | 37 | 71 | — | 17 | — | 9 | — | — | — | | | 16 | 67 | 41 | 6 |
| K.E. Cooper | | | 6 | — | 16 | — | — | 7 | 4 | — | | | | | — | 5* | — | — | — | — | 12* | — | — | — | | | 0 | — | 0* | — |
| E.E. Hemmings | | | | | | | — | 13 | 1 | — | — | 0* | — | — | — | 10 | 33* | — | 29* | — | 35 | — | — | — | | | 0 | — | 0 | — |
| M. Hendrick | | | | | | | | | | | — | — | — | — | — | — | | | | | | | | | | | | | | |
| C.W. Scott | | | | | | | | | | | | | | | | | | | | | 15 | — | | | 11* | — | | | | |
| M. Newell | | | | | | | | | | | | | | | | | | | | | | | | | 76 | 0 | | | | |
| K. Evans | | | | | | | | | | | | | | | | | | | | | | | | | 42 | 1 | | | | |
| D. Fraser-Darling | | | | | | | | | | | | | | | | | | | | | | | | | — | — | | | | |
| S. Mee | | | | | | | | | | | | | | | | | | | | | | | | | — | — | | | | |
| Byes | 5 | | | 6 | 1 | 3 | | 7 | 8 | | 1 | 2 | 3 | | | 2 | | | 1 | | 9 | | 1 | | | 1 | | 3 | 5 | 7 |
| Leg-byes | 2 | 11 | 5 | 5 | 16 | 4 | | 10 | | 1 | 4 | 3 | 19 | | 7 | 7 | 8 | | 12 | | 6 | 1 | 3 | 13 | 3 | 3 | 11 | 4 | 12 | 10 |
| Wides | 3 | | 1 | | 1 | | | 1 | | | 1 | 1 | | | 4 | | | | 1 | | 8 | | 2 | 2 | 3 | 2 | 1 | 3 | | 3 |
| No-balls | | 1 | 11 | 4 | 6 | 5 | 1 | 2 | 2 | | 1 | 2 | 10 | | 1 | | 9 | | 7 | | 9 | 1 | 6 | 2 | | | | 1 | | 1 |
| Total | 355 | 220 | 175 | 327 | 291 | 188 | 36 | 294 | 264 | 87 | 218 | 166 | 296 | | 308 | 124 | 349 | 16 | 398 | | 404 | 128 | 390 | 259 | 256 | 227 | 233 | 242 | 203 | 202 |
| Wickets | 6 | 0 | 10 | 5 | 9 | 5 | 3 | 10 | 10 | 0 | 2 | 7 | 4 | | 5 | 8 | 8 | 0 | 7 | | 10 | 0 | 5 | 5 | 5 | 3 | 10 | 5 | 10 | 5 |
| Result | W | | W | | D | | L | | W | | D | | D | | W | | W | | W | | D | | D | | W | | W | | D | |
| Points | — | | 21 | | 7 | | 2 | | 23 | | 4 | | 4 | | 23 | | 22 | | 24 | | 7 | | 8 | | — | | 22 | | 5 | |

*Catches* 87 – B.N. French (ct 76/st 11)
25 – D.W. Randall
23 – R.J. Hadlee
22 – S.B. Hassan
21 – C.E.B. Rice
20 – J.D. Birch
16 – R.T. Robinson
14 – B.C. Broad
10 – K.E. Cooper
7 – E.E. Hemmings and P. Johnson (ct 6/st 1)
6 – C.W. Scott, M. Newell, P.M. Such and subs

| | Overs | Mds | Runs | Wkts | Av | Best | 5/in | 10/m |
|---|---|---|---|---|---|---|---|---|
| I. Folley | 373 | 90 | 1015 | 34 | 29.85 | 5/65 | 2 | |
| C.E.B. Rice | 206 | 53 | 569 | 19 | 29.94 | 4/61 | | |
| S.P. Hughes | 319.2 | 53 | 1051 | 35 | 30.02 | 4/49 | | |
| P. Willey | 544.1 | 163 | 1291 | 43 | 30.02 | 6/78 | 2 | |
| M.D. Crowe | 452 | 101 | 1353 | 44 | 30.75 | 5/66 | 1 | |
| S.C. Booth | 409.2 | 117 | 1172 | 38 | 30.84 | 4/50 | | |
| I.A. Greig | 648 | 153 | 1913 | 62 | 30.85 | 4/39 | | |
| J.N. Shepherd | 800.3 | 208 | 2225 | 72 | 30.90 | 5/30 | 2 | |
| R.A. Pick | 243.5 | 52 | 773 | 25 | 30.92 | 5/25 | 2 | 1 |
| B.J. Griffiths | 474 | 114 | 1332 | 43 | 30.97 | 5/52 | 2 | |
| J.D. Inchmore | 497 | 110 | 1364 | 44 | 31.00 | 4/37 | | |
| G.W. Johnson | 462.2 | 117 | 1220 | 39 | 31.28 | 5/38 | 3 | |
| C.A. Connor | 642.5 | 155 | 1949 | 62 | 31.43 | 7/37 | 1 | |
| M.A. Feltham | 291.2 | 53 | 1012 | 32 | 31.62 | 5/62 | 1 | |
| O.H. Mortensen | 212.3 | 55 | 570 | 18 | 31.66 | 3/37 | | |
| M.K. Bore | 151.2 | 40 | 413 | 13 | 31.76 | 5/30 | 1 | |
| N.G. Cowley | 588.1 | 133 | 1779 | 56 | 31.76 | 4/33 | | |
| R.W. Hanley | 396.1 | 87 | 1182 | 37 | 31.94 | 6/21 | 3 | |
| G.J. Parsons | 662.1 | 135 | 2164 | 67 | 32.29 | 5/42 | 2 | |
| S.T. Jefferies | 450 | 86 | 1392 | 43 | 32.37 | 6/67 | 2 | |
| N.A. Mallender | 500 | 114 | 1533 | 47 | 32.61 | 4/45 | | |
| P.J. Newport | 204.4 | 36 | 689 | 21 | 32.80 | 5/51 | 1 | |
| R.K. Illingworth | 744 | 220 | 1872 | 57 | 32.84 | 5/32 | 2 | |
| C. Lethbridge | 279.5 | 42 | 987 | 30 | 32.90 | 4/35 | | |
| D.J. Wild | 91.4 | 18 | 329 | 10 | 32.90 | 3/15 | | |
| G.E. Sainsbury | 566.2 | 141 | 1596 | 48 | 33.25 | 5/19 | 1 | |
| J.G. Thomas | 435.2 | 95 | 1575 | 47 | 33.51 | 5/56 | 2 | 1 |
| S.D. Fletcher | 162 | 35 | 471 | 14 | 33.64 | 4/24 | | |
| N.F. Williams | 474.1 | 95 | 1653 | 49 | 33.73 | 4/19 | | |
| D.N. Patel | 770 | 219 | 2063 | 61 | 33.81 | 5/28 | 2 | |
| K. Saxelby | 516.5 | 140 | 1592 | 47 | 33.87 | 5/43 | 1 | |
| D.B. d'Oliveira | 113 | 24 | 341 | 10 | 34.10 | 2/50 | | |
| R.D.V. Knight | 349.4 | 99 | 925 | 27 | 34.25 | 4/7 | | |
| P.G. Newman | 505.2 | 89 | 1717 | 50 | 34.34 | 7/104 | 1 | |
| D.S. Steele | 732 | 227 | 2100 | 61 | 34.42 | 5/86 | 2 | |
| P.W. Jarvis | 304 | 53 | 1115 | 32 | 34.84 | 6/61 | 2 | |
| T.E. Jesty | 220.1 | 50 | 668 | 19 | 35.15 | 3/15 | | |
| R.J. Maru | 549.4 | 129 | 1664 | 47 | 35.40 | 7/79 | 2 | |
| E.L. Reifer | 524.5 | 100 | 1761 | 49 | 35.93 | 4/43 | | |
| A. Needham | 328.5 | 79 | 1047 | 29 | 36.10 | 5/82 | 1 | |
| P. Carrick | 665.5 | 219 | 1606 | 44 | 36.50 | 6/32 | 3 | 1 |
| C.A. Walsh | 341.3 | 80 | 1179 | 32 | 36.84 | 6/70 | 1 | |
| L.B. Taylor | 142 | 42 | 369 | 10 | 36.90 | 2/22 | | |
| D.G. Moir | 822.5 | 206 | 2419 | 65 | 37.21 | 6/60 | 3 | 1 |
| D.V. Lawrence | 455.1 | 80 | 1531 | 41 | 37.34 | 5/58 | 3 | |
| D.A. Thorne | 203.1 | 42 | 565 | 15 | 37.66 | 5/39 | 1 | |
| S.J. Dennis | 277.2 | 48 | 953 | 25 | 38.12 | 5/124 | 1 | |
| I.R. Carmichael | 208 | 40 | 661 | 17 | 38.88 | 5/84 | 1 | |
| N.V. Radford | 106.4 | 17 | 390 | 10 | 39.00 | 5/95 | 1 | |
| S. Oldham | 244.5 | 57 | 703 | 18 | 39.05 | 4/59 | | |
| W.A. Morton | 189.5 | 45 | 549 | 14 | 39.21 | 4/85 | | |
| S.J. O'Shaughnessy | 214.3 | 39 | 753 | 19 | 39.63 | 3/76 | | |
| M.W.W. Selvey | 311.3 | 69 | 997 | 25 | 39.88 | 6/31 | 1 | |
| J.D. Carr | 343 | 94 | 885 | 22 | 40.22 | 5/57 | 2 | |
| G.V. Palmer | 320.3 | 56 | 1231 | 30 | 41.03 | 4/58 | | |
| I.G. Swallow | 229.1 | 62 | 620 | 15 | 41.33 | 4/52 | | |
| A. Walker | 308.5 | 52 | 1118 | 27 | 41.40 | 4/50 | | |
| N.G.B. Cook | 769.3 | 209 | 2053 | 49 | 41.89 | 4/45 | | |

| v. Worcestershire (Trent Bridge) 14–17 July | v. Sri Lankans (Cleethorpes) 25–27 July | v. Lancashire (Trent Bridge) 28–31 July | v. West Indians (Trent Bridge) 1–3 August | v. Worcestershire (Worcester) 4–7 August | v. Derbyshire (Trent Bridge) 8–10 August | v. Middlesex (Lord's) 11–14 August | v. Kent (Folkestone) 18–21 August | v. Lancashire (Blackpool) 22–24 August | v. Warwickshire (Trent Bridge) 25–28 August | v. Northamptonshire (Trent Bridge) 29–31 August | v. Sussex (Hove) 5–7 September | v. Somerset (Taunton) 8–11 September | M | Inns | NOs | Runs | H/S | Av |
|---|---|---|---|---|---|---|---|---|---|---|---|---|---|---|---|---|---|---|
| 0 21 | 38 115* | 117 — | — — | 3 46 | 54 20 | 0 — | 56 0 | 72 39* | 97 33 | 86 — | 27 33 | 4 21 | 27 | 47 | 7 | 2032 | 171 | 50.80 |
| | | | — — | 13 53 | | | 58 28 | | | 94 — | 1 3 | 88* 45 | 18 | 31 | 5 | 1268 | 108* | 48.76 |
| 39 70 | 52 14 | 8 — | — — | 0 1 | 57 30 | 11 — | 7 23 | 60 — | 113 4 | 4 — | 65 8 | 64 14 | 24 | 38 | 3 | 1527 | 136 | 43.62 |
| 32 1 | 80 9 | 17 — | — — | 12 11 | 16 9 | | | | 16 28* | | | | 22 | 33 | 5 | 905 | 110* | 32.32 |
| | 80 20 | | — — | | | 36 — | 10 133 | 104 — | | 32 — | 53 19* | 16 21 | 10 | 14 | 1 | 647 | 133 | 49.76 |
| 0 12 | 9 31 | 98 — | — — | 6 — | 42 12 | 26 — | 0 — | 29 — | 37* — | 15 — | 2 — | 10 24 | 26 | 32 | 6 | 697 | 98 | 26.80 |
| | | 16 — | | 27 — | 8 8* | 4 — | 12 — | | — — | | 11* — | | 20 | 19 | 8 | 196 | 27 | 17.81 |
| 12 — | 1 10* | | — — | 22* — | | | | 2 — | — — | 2* — | | — 4 | 12 | 10 | 5 | 96 | 27* | 19.20 |
| | | | | | | | | | | — — | 1 — | — 27 | 4 | 2 | — | 28 | 27 | 14.00 |
| | | | | | | | | — — | | | | | 3 | | | | | — |
| 1* — | — — | 2* 4* | — — | | 0* 1 | 16 — | 2 — | | | | | | 15 | 10 | 5 | 29 | 16 | 5.80 |
| 38 37* | | 18 — | | 30 26* | 64 17 | 2 — | 4 152* | 12 — | 20 41* | 103* — | 49 10 | 17 98 | 24 | 39 | 7 | 1553 | 152* | 48.53 |
| 20 12 | 1 3 | 9 0* | | | 0 4 | | | | | | | | 17 | 27 | 4 | 499 | 103* | 21.69 |
| 0 — | | 17 — | | 70 21* | 56 10 | 210* — | 51 10* | 38 — | 39 — | 78 — | 31 14* | 10 28 | 24 | 31 | 8 | 1179 | 210* | 51.26 |
| 0 — | 11* — | 19 — | — — | 0 — | 18 11 | 3 — | 2* — | 3* — | — — | — — | 0 — | — 0 | 24 | 19 | 6 | 117 | 18 | 9.00 |
| 8 4* | 9* — | 18 — | — — | 0 — | 18 7 | 1 — | 0 — | 27 — | 2* — | 10 — | 17* — | 5 1 | 24 | 24 | 7 | 248 | 35 | 14.58 |
| | | | | | | | | | | | | | 3 | | | | | — |
| | | | | | | | | | | | | | 2 | 2 | 1 | 26 | 15 | 26.00 |
| | | | | | | 3 — | | 0 18* | 10 2 | | | | 4 | 7 | 1 | 109 | 76 | 18.16 |
| | 3 2 | | — — | | | | | | | | | | 3 | 4 | — | 48 | 42 | 12.00 |
| | | | | | | | | | | | | | 1 | | | | | — |
| | | | | | | | | | | | | | 1 | | | | | — |
| 4 | 1 | 1 | | 4 4 | | 1 | 1 | 5 4 | 6 | | 17 4 | 1 | | | | | | |
| 3 1 | 4 1 | 12 | | 3 3 | 10 2 | 16 | 6 16 | 7 | 6 3 | 8 | 15 1 | 7 9 | | | | | | |
| | 4 | 2 | | | 5 | 1 | | 1 1 | 1 | 2 | 3 | 1 | | | | | | |
| 2 | 18 5 | 10 | | 12 2 | 13 | 14 | 3 5 | 5 2 | 9 | 16 | 8 1 | | | | | | | |
| 153 164 | 311 210 | 364 4 | | 202 167 | 361 131 | 344 | 212 367 | 365 64 | 350 117 | 450 | 300 93 | 222 293 | | | | | | |
| 10 5 | 8 6 | 10 0 | | 10 4 | 10 10 | 10 | 10 4 | 9 0 | 6 3 | 7 | 9 4 | 7 10 | | | | | | |
| W | D | W | D | D | L | W | D | W | W | W | D | L | | | | | | |
| 21 | — | 23 | — | 4 | 8 | 24 | 6 | 24 | 24 | 24 | 5 | 6 | | | | | | |

4 – R.A. Pick
3 – K.P. Evans
2 – K. Saxelby and M. Hendrick

1 – K.P. Evans, J.A. Afford and D. Fraser-Darling

| | Overs | Mds | Runs | Wkts | Av | Best | 5/in | 10/m |
|---|---|---|---|---|---|---|---|---|
| P.A. Smith | 194.4 | 23 | 839 | 20 | 41.95 | 4/41 | | |
| D.E. Malcolm | 156.2 | 24 | 674 | 16 | 42.12 | 3/78 | | |
| R.G. Williams | 442.2 | 104 | 1348 | 32 | 42.12 | 4/22 | | |
| A.E. Warner | 186 | 33 | 632 | 15 | 42.13 | 5/27 | 1 | |
| M. Watkinson | 359 | 73 | 1229 | 29 | 42.37 | 6/39 | 1 | |
| D.J. Capel | 155 | 20 | 679 | 16 | 42.43 | 5/28 | 1 | |
| P.A. Booth | 347 | 124 | 749 | 17 | 44.05 | 3/22 | | |
| A.J. Pollock | 161.2 | 32 | 620 | 14 | 44.28 | 4/104 | | |
| G.B. Stevenson | 262.3 | 44 | 892 | 19 | 46.94 | 4/35 | | |
| B. Roberts | 277 | 44 | 1044 | 22 | 47.45 | 4/77 | | |
| S.J.W. Andrew | 162.2 | 43 | 530 | 11 | 48.18 | 4/30 | | |
| J.H. Childs | 294 | 83 | 736 | 15 | 49.06 | 3/72 | | |
| J.W. Lloyds | 240.2 | 70 | 697 | 14 | 49.78 | 3/62 | | |
| R.G.D. Willis | 213 | 41 | 747 | 15 | 49.80 | 2/19 | | |
| P. Bainbridge | 303.2 | 73 | 959 | 18 | 53.27 | 4/76 | | |
| M.P. Lawrence | 291.1 | 61 | 869 | 13 | 66.84 | 3/79 | | |
| T.A. Cotterell | 293.4 | 42 | 1074 | 13 | 82.61 | 3/95 | | |
| P. Garlick | 253 | 31 | 1092 | 12 | 91.00 | 2/69 | | |

**(Qualification – 10 wickets)**

**LEADING FIELDERS**

87 – B.N. French (ct 76/st 11)
77 – D.E. East (ct 76/st 1)
71 – R.J. Parks (ct 61/st 10)
67 – I.J. Gould (ct 61/st 6)
66 – G.W. Humpage (ct 56/st 10)
57 – T. Gard (ct 47/st 10)
53 – T. Davies (ct 43/st 10)
52 – C.J. Richards (ct 46/st 6)
48 – P.R. Downton (ct42/st 6) and M.A. Garnham (ct 45/st 3)
44 – D.J. Humphries (ct 37/st 7)
45 – D.L. Bairstow (ct 38/st 7)
38 – D. Ripley (ct 26/st 12)
36 – R.C. Russell (ct 29/st 7)
33 – C. Maynard (ct 28/st 5) and J.F. Steele
32 – M.A. Lynch
31 – R.W. Taylor (ct 26/st 5)
30 – A.P.E. Knott (ct 29/st 1), C.P. Metson (ct 28/st 2) and A.L. Jones
29 – D.S. Steele and T.M. Alderman
28 – M.D. Crowe and G.W. Johnson
27 – N.F.M. Popplewell
26 – D.W. Randall, G.A. Gooch, B.R. Hardie, A.J. Stewart and C.W.J. Athey
25 – G. Miller
23 – C.J. Tavare, W.N. Slack, M.W. Gatting, R.J. Hadlee and P.W.G Parker
22 – K.W.R. Fletcher, C.S. Cowdrey, R.J. Maru, S.T. Clarke, J.W. Lloyds, J.R.T. Barclay and S.B. Hassan
21 – K.J. Barnett, C.T. Radley and C.E.B. Rice
20 – K.S. McEwan, A.W. Stovold (ct 18/st 2), J.J. Whitaker, P.H. Edmonds J.H. Hampshire and J.D. Birch

| **Nottinghamshire C.C.C.** First-Class Matches – Bowling, 1984 | K. Saxelby | M.K. Bore | P.M. Such | R.A. Pick | J.A. Afford | R.J. Hadlee | K.E. Cooper | C.E.B. Rice | B.C. Broad |
|---|---|---|---|---|---|---|---|---|---|
| v. Oxford University | 12–2–49–0 | 7–2–12–0 | 19–9–34–5 | 11.3–2–33–5 | 8–2–25–0 | | | | |
| (Oxford) 21–24 April | 12–6–27–0 | 13–10–12–1 | 19.2–8–50–3 | 14–6–25–5 | 9–1–43–1 | | | | |
| v. Surrey (Trent Bridge) | 8–0–33–0 | | 23–4–52–5 | | | 19.3–13–8–4 | 7–3–10–1 | 5–1–20–0 | |
| 28–30 April | 9–1–41–2 | | 16–5–44–3 | | | 8.1–3–14–4 | 9–5–7–1 | 8–2–29–0 | |
| v. Leicestershire | 16–6–42–2 | | 9–4–9–1 | | | 24–6–68–2 | 13.1–8–10–2 | 17–5–28–3 | 4–1–19–0 |
| (Trent Bridge) 2–4 May | 15–5–41–2 | | 5–1–12–0 | | | 20–7–47–0 | 18–6–43–2 | 15–3–62–2 | 5–2–10–0 |
| v. Yorkshire (Leeds) | 23–7–80–2 | | | | | 18.5–4–62–1 | 26–9–63–0 | 18–3–55–1 | |
| 9–11 May | 7–3–12–0 | | | | | | 7–3–21–1 | | |
| v. Essex (Chelmsford) | 6.1–3–15–4 | | | | | 13–4–32–1 | 18–8–28–1 | 11–7–15–3 | |
| 23–25 May | 26–5–77–3 | | | | | 27–11–52–6 | 20–9–23–0 | 16–4–56–0 | 4–1–10–0 |
| v. Derbyshire | 24–7–79–0 | | | | | 24–9–40–2 | | 25–7–61–4 | 4.2–1–23–2 |
| (Derby) 26–29 May | 11–5–22–2 | | | | | 6–5–3–0 | | 6–1–20–1 | 7–1–36–0 |
| v. Warwickshire (Edgbaston) | 16–3–59–0 | | | 15–1–85–0 | | 17–3–40–0 | | 14–4–39–1 | |
| 30 May–1 June | 7–1–18–1 | | | 5–0–20–0 | | 6–3–7–0 | | | |
| v. Hampshire (Bournemouth) | 22–7–52–2 | | | | | 26–10–51–2 | 23–4–85–2 | 18–5–53–0 | |
| 2–5 June | 12–0–44–0 | | | | | 18–7–35–5 | | 4–0–7–0 | |
| v. Glamorgan (Trent Bridge) | 15–5–42–0 | | | | | 16–5–31–2 | 10–4–15–0 | 11–5–25–1 | |
| 9–12 June | 13–5–20–1 | | | | | 12–5–28–2 | 5–0–26–0 | 9–2–29–1 | |
| v. Gloucestershire | 10–1–37–3 | | | | | 15.3–7–35–7 | 8–3–16–0 | 10–2–17–0 | |
| (Trent Bridge) 16–19 June | 10–3–46–3 | | 9–3–26–0 | | | 18–4–41–4 | 7–4–6–0 | | |
| v. Leicestershire (Leicester) | | | | 20–4–63–1 | | 27–7–60–3 | 29.4–14–51–2 | | |
| 23–26 June | | | | | | | | | |
| v. Yorkshire (Trent Bridge) | 21.5–9–76–1 | | 12–0–32–1 | | | 26–7–75–4 | 26–7–93–4 | | |
| 27–29 June | 6–2–14–0 | | 15–7–29–1 | | | 5–1–13–0 | 6–2–19–0 | | |
| v. Cambridge University | | | 30–11–48–3 | 19.2–6–40–1 | 19–11–18–1 | | | | |
| (Trent Bridge) 30 June–3 July | | | 22–5–75–2 | 9–3–12–0 | 18–4–66–1 | | | | |
| v. Sussex (Trent Bridge) | 12–6–30–0 | | 14.3–6–34–4 | | | 22–9–41–4 | 12–4–22–1 | | |
| 7–10 July | 3.5–1–21–1 | | 10–1–47–2 | | | 10–5–6–4 | 4–3–2–0 | | |
| v. Somerset (Trent Bridge) | 25–5–68–3 | | 17–5–27–1 | | | 22–3–45–4 | 29–6–50–2 | | |
| 11–13 July | 5–0–19–0 | | 19–5–60–0 | | | 12–3–31–2 | 19–7–32–0 | | |
| v. Worcestershire | | | 1–0–8–0 | 15–4–52–4 | | 13–4–22–1 | 19–6–41–2 | | |
| (Trent Bridge) 14–17 July | | | 6–2–12–0 | 14–1–52–2 | | 18–2–61–5 | 11–5–22–2 | | |
| v. Sri Lankans (Cleethorpes) | | | 4–0–19–0 | 14–4–39–0 | | | 14–5–41–3 | | |
| 25–27 July | | | 10–3–25–1 | 11–1–34–1 | | | 6–1–13–0 | | |
| v. Lancashire (Trent Bridge) | 17–8–34–3 | | | | | 19.2–6–49–4 | 11–2–20–1 | | |
| 28–31 July | 11–4–28–2 | | 32–18–37–2 | | | 23–6–48–2 | 3–2–6–0 | | |
| v. West Indians | | | 17–4–46–0 | 23–6–95–2 | | | 25–1–44–1 | | |
| (Trent Bridge) 1–3 August | | | | | | | | | |
| v. Worcestershire (Worcester) | 22–6–71–1 | | | 5–3–4–1 | | 23–11–41–1 | 13–2–43–0 | | |
| 4–7 August | | | | | | | | | |
| v. Derbyshire (Trent Bridge) | 8–2–20–1 | | 11–3–27–1 | | | 13–1–30–4 | 5–1–9–0 | | |
| 8–10 August | 15–3–52–1 | | 33–9–115–1 | | | 25–9–47–3 | 13.4–4–46–3 | | |
| v. Middlesex (Lord's) | 18–6–43–5 | | 1.4–0–2–1 | | | 20–4–55–4 | 28–12–40–0 | | |
| 11–14 August | 12–1–45–0 | | 7.3–1–24–1 | | | 10–3–14–1 | 26–10–44–8 | 7–1–16–0 | |
| v. Kent (Folkestone) | 12–2–51–1 | | 9–3–9–1 | | | 28–9–51–3 | 27–7–67–3 | | |
| 18–21 August | 8–2–35–0 | | 14.5–5–34–3 | | | 20–6–49–2 | 17–5–51–1 | | |
| v. Lancashire (Blackpool) | | | | 13–3–34–0 | 19.3–8–49–2 | 14–2–32–2 | 13–4–26–1 | | |
| 22–24 August | | | | 3–0–9–0 | 15–6–55–2 | 18.4–6–40–5 | 10–3–24–1 | | |
| v. Warwickshire | 23–2–68–1 | | | 13–1–52–2 | | 26.2–9–55–6 | 23–7–63–1 | | |
| (Trent Bridge) 25–28 August | 11–2–41–0 | | | 14–2–44–1 | | 24–7–48–3 | 8–2–14–0 | | |
| v. Northamptonshire | | 20.2–10–30–5 | | 2–0–8–0 | | 13–3–26–3 | | | |
| (Trent Bridge) 29–31 August | | 29–5–94–4 | | 3–0–14–0 | | | 3–0–14–0 | | |
| v. Sussex (Hove) | 12–4–40–0 | 51–9–172–2 | | | | 23–7–40–1 | 20–6–49–1 | | |
| 5–7 September | | 1–0–2–0 | | | | | 3–1–5–0 | 2–0–8–2 | 7–0–33–0 |
| v. Somerset (Taunton) | | 4–1–6–0 | | 15–3–46–0 | | 23–8–59–4 | 22.5–9–57–4 | 10–1–29–0 | |
| 8–11 September | | 26–3–85–1 | | 5–2–12–0 | | 5–1–13–0 | 5–3–3–0 | | |
| | 516.5–140–1592–47 av. 33.87 | 151.2–40–413–13 av. 31.76 | 386.5–122–937–42 av. 22.30 | 243.5–52–773–25 av. 30.92 | 88.3–32–256–7 av. 36.57 | 772.2–245–1645–117 av. 14.05 | 623.2–207–1364–51 av. 26.74 | 206–53–569–19 av. 29.94 | 31.2–6–131–2 av. 65.50 |

a J. D. Birch 3–0–20–0

b D. Fraser-Darling 20–7–41–1, 9–2–14–2; P. Johnson 2–0–9–1; M. Newell 4–0–14–0; S. Mee 16–2–44–2, 7–2–19–0

| E.E. Hemmings | M. Hendrick | K.P. Evans | *Byes* | *Leg-byes* | *Wides* | *No-balls* | *Total* | *Wkts* |
|---|---|---|---|---|---|---|---|---|
| | | | | | | 1 | 154 | 10 |
| | | | 4 | 2 | | | 163 | 10 |
| | | | | 4 | | 2 | 129 | 10 |
| | | | 4 | 6 | | 3 | 148 | 10 |
| | | | 10 | 7 | 2 | 1 | 196 | 10 |
| | | | | 1 | | 3 | 219 | 6 |
| 5–0–22–0 | | | 2 | 6 | 4 | 7 | 301 | 5 |
| | | | 1 | 1 | | | 35 | 1 |
| | | | | 3 | | | 93 | 10 |
| 16–6–35–1 | | | 1 | 2 | | 1 | 257 | 10 |
| 11–1–51–1 | 22–9–22–0 | | 8 | 8 | 2 | | 294 | 9 |
| 18.2–1–73–1 | | | | 2 | 1 | | 177 | 4a |
| 27–6–90–2 | 10–4–14–1 | | | 11 | | | 338 | 4 |
| 3–2–1–0 | 4–3–1–0 | | | 1 | 1 | | 49 | 1 |
| 8.4–2–22–2 | 18–5–32–2 | | | 7 | | 1 | 303 | 10 |
| 6–2–12–0 | 18.1–12–17–5 | | 2 | 7 | | | 124 | 10 |
| 29.3–12–50–6 | | | | 6 | | 1 | 170 | 10 |
| 28.3–10–73–6 | | | 6 | 7 | | 2 | 191 | 10 |
| | | | | 7 | | 1 | 113 | 10 |
| 10.1–3–37–3 | | | | 2 | 1 | 1 | 160 | 10 |
| 35–16–69–4 | | | 5 | 5 | 2 | 2 | 257 | 10 |
| 19–4–51–0 | | | 1 | 10 | | 3 | 341 | 10 |
| 14–3–42–2 | | | | 5 | | | 122 | 3 |
| | | 12–3–31–2 | 1 | 8 | 2 | 4 | 237 | 10b |
| | | 9–3–17–0 | 5 | 9 | 1 | 4 | 245 | 6 |
| 15–4–26–1 | | | | 2 | 4 | 2 | 161 | 10 |
| 15–2–88–3 | | | 7 | 1 | | | 172 | 10 |
| 18–6–44–0 | | | 7 | 5 | 1 | 2 | 249 | 10 |
| 35–3–131–1 | | | 4 | 4 | 1 | | 282 | 3 |
| 4.5–3–4–2 | | | 5 | 4 | | 2 | 138 | 10 |
| 4–0–10–1 | | | 6 | 14 | | 1 | 178 | 10 |
| 16–8–47–7 | | 8–1–35–0 | | 7 | | 11 | 199 | 10 |
| 10–5–13–0 | | 5–0–21–0 | 6 | 7 | | 4 | 123 | 2 |
| 13–2–43–2 | | | | 5 | | 3 | 154 | 10 |
| 29–11–81–4 | | | 1 | 10 | | 2 | 213 | 10 |
| 17–5–80–1 | | 14–1–69–0 | | 20 | 2 | 5 | 361 | 4 |
| 32–9–86–2 | | | 4 | 7 | | 5 | 261 | 5 |
| 22–7–45–4 | | | | 5 | 1 | 2 | 139 | 10 |
| 44–12–98–2 | | | 14 | 5 | | 4 | 381 | 10 |
| | | | 2 | 10 | | | 152 | 10 |
| | | | 4 | 2 | | | 149 | 10 |
| 21–7–39–2 | | | 3 | 6 | | 5 | 231 | 10 |
| 27.1–10–109–3 | | | | 3 | | 4 | 285 | 9 |
| 36–16–78–5 | | | | 5 | | 11 | 235 | 10 |
| 29–14–60–1 | | | 2 | 2 | | 1 | 193 | 9e |
| 2–0–12–0 | | | 2 | 3 | 3 | 3 | 261 | 10 |
| 27.1–11–49–6 | | | | 4 | 1 | 4 | 205 | 10 |
| 18–3–59–2 | | | | 6 | | | 129 | 10 |
| 30–6–93–6 | | | 5 | 1 | | 3 | 224 | 10 |
| 46.3–11–111–5 | | | 7 | 10 | 1 | 6 | 436 | 9 |
| | | | 4 | 9 | | 1 | 141 | 6d |
| 20–5–63–2 | | | 4 | 6 | 1 | 3 | 274 | 10 |
| 35–6–123–4 | | | 4 | 4 | | | 244 | 5 |
| 797.5–234–<br>2220–94<br>*av.* 23.61 | 72.1–33–<br>86–8<br>*av.* 10.75 | 48–8–<br>173–2<br>*av.* 86.50 | | | | | | |

c S. T. Jefferies absent hurt
d D. W. Randall 9.4–0–43–3; P. Johnson 2–0–14–1; B. N. French 1–0–22–0

## REVIEW OF THE SEASON

### By David Lemmon

It was a Jekyll and Hyde year. First, there were the fine achievements of Pakistan and New Zealand in winning the series against England, but the memory of these victories was almost obliterated by the trouncing that England received at the hands of the West Indies, the worst defeat that England has ever suffered in this country.

Much praise was lavished on the West Indies, and much of it was justified, but they were not as good or as well balanced a side as Bradman's Australians of 1948, and it is probable that they are not the best side that the West Indies themselves have ever fielded. They were opposed by a very weak England side, and they were aided by some limp umpiring which allowed intimidatory bowling in violation of Law 42, section 8, to go unchallenged. Dickie Bird, in the first Test, invoked the Law, but received a poor reaction from both the West Indian bowler and the West Indian captain, and one wondered what was said off the field after that incident, for, at The Oval in particular, it seemed that the spirit of the game was totally ignored and consistent short-pitched bowling of an intimidatory nature went uncensured. It is not unfair to suggest that this bowling contributed in some measure to the unpleasant scenes at the end of the match and the abuse to which some of the England players were subjected.

It was totally unnecessary for the West Indies outclassed England in every department of the game and would have won easily enough without such tactics. Their batting was a joy and their fielding a delight, and there are few lovelier sights than Marshall or Holding in full flow. To the pace quartet was added the dimension of Harper's spin and in the field this cricketer emphasised the belief that he will be the West Indies captain within the next few years.

One had some sympathy for the England side in trying to cope with this fine West Indian side, but none at all for them in their shabby display against Sri Lanka, for here, at times, they lacked both discipline and dignity, and without these qualities they can never hope to attain a true international standard, certainly not one that is worthy of an England sweater.

For the Sri Lankans one can have nothing but praise. They were delightful company and cricketers of charm, eager to learn and to succeed. The first two days of the Test at Lord's were arguably the best cricket of the summer, batting of classical dimension, all elegance and off-side beauty.

If consideration of the England side spotlights the Mr Hyde character of the year, then a glance at the four domestic competitions will give a glimpse of Dr Jekyll. The sun shone and there was some sparkling cricket played by those counties who had captains brave enough to realise that you do not deserve to win a match if you not prepared to lose it.

The surprise of the season was Lancashire's victory in the Benson and Hedges Cup. They were a team of limited talents, but they overcame Essex and Notts, the two best sides in the country, and in beating Warwickshire in a disappointing final at Lord's, they showed that the qualities of enthusiasm and fielding of the highest standard can win you a coveted

| **Somerset C.C.C.** First-Class Matches – Batting, 1984 | v. Yorkshire (Taunton) 28–30 April | | v. Oxford University (Oxford) 2–4 May | | v. Leicestershire (Leicester) 19–22 May | | v. West Indians (Taunton) 23–25 May | | v. Gloucestershire (Taunton) 26–29 May | | v. Hampshire (Southampton) 30 May–1 June | | v. Yorkshire (Middlesbrough) 2–5 June | | v. Middlesex (Bath) 9–12 June | | v. Lancashire (Bath) 13–15 June | | v. Warwickshire (Edgbaston) 23–26 June | | v. Leicestershire (Taunton) 27–29 June | | v. Northamptonshire (Northampton) 30 June–3 July | | v. Hampshire (Taunton) 7–10 July | | v. Nottinghamshire (Trent Bridge) 11–13 July | |
|---|---|---|---|---|---|---|---|---|---|---|---|---|---|---|---|---|---|---|---|---|---|---|---|---|---|---|---|---|
| J.G. Wyatt | 87 | 13 | 103 | — | 5 | — | 45 | 69 | 5 | 31 | 3 | 0 | 17 | — | 31 | — | 0 | 61 | 20 | 4 | 47 | 3 | — | — | | | | |
| P.M. Roebuck | 145 | 69 | 152* | — | 64 | — | 7 | 8 | 33 | 3 | 15 | 14 | 49 | — | 30 | — | 24 | 11 | 102 | 21 | 20 | 128 | 159 | — | 101 | — | 45 | — |
| M.D. Crowe | 1 | 10 | 100* | — | 77 | — | 1 | 0 | 3 | 5 | 3 | 53 | 3* | — | 125 | — | 113 | 54 | 12 | 152* | 70* | 190 | 21 | — | 51* | — | 14 | 74 |
| B.C. Rose | 22 | 44 | | | 70 | — | 9 | 0 | 41 | 10 | 0 | 0 | 8 | — | 97 | — | 2 | 13 | 40 | 60 | 3 | 5* | 16 | — | | | 17 | 47* |
| I.T. Botham | 12 | 3 | | | 30 | — | | | 0 | 20 | | | | | — | — | | | 15 | 38 | | | | | 87 | — | | |
| P.W. Denning | 13* | 53* | — | 49 | | | | | | | 33 | 66 | 19 | — | | | | | | | | | 90 | 15* | | | | |
| J.W. Lloyds | — | 21* | — | 18 | 4 | — | 13 | 1 | 26* | 42* | 33 | 13 | 16 | — | | | 73* | 0 | 11 | — | 3 | — | 48* | 3* | 61* | — | 63 | 4 |
| V.J. Marks | — | — | — | 45* | 25 | — | 3 | 17 | 9 | 19* | | | | | 31 | — | 29 | 6 | 40 | — | 16 | 2* | 53* | — | — | — | 55 | 25* |
| T. Gard | — | — | — | 6 | 0 | — | 3 | 8* | — | — | 14 | 23 | 1* | — | 0 | — | 2 | 19* | 5* | — | 1 | — | — | — | | | | |
| C.H. Dredge | — | — | — | 7* | 14 | — | 7* | 6 | 6* | — | 0 | 5* | | | 6 | — | 25* | — | 0* | — | 3 | — | — | — | — | — | 3 | — |
| M.R. Davis | — | — | — | — | 6* | — | 0* | — | — | — | 0* | 2 | — | — | 7 | — | | | — | — | 9 | — | — | — | — | — | 1* | — |
| N.F.M. Popplewell | | | — | 50 | 26 | — | 5 | 5 | | | | | 17 | — | 133 | — | 12 | 2 | 90 | 26 | 9 | 0 | 74 | 2* | 17 | — | 10 | 62* |
| P.H.L. Wilson | | | — | — | | | 0 | 0 | | | | | — | — | | | | | | | | | | | | | | |
| R.L. Ollis | | | | | | | | | 22 | 19 | 0 | 2 | | | | | | | | | | | | | | | | |
| G.V. Palmer | | | | | | | | | | | 22 | 2 | — | — | | | | | | | 2 | — | | | | | 4 | — |
| S.C. Booth | | | | | | | | | | | | | | | 6* | — | 10 | 1* | | | | | | | — | — | | |
| M. Turner | | | | | | | | | | | | | | | | | 0 | 1 | | | | | | | | | | |
| N.A. Felton | | | | | | | | | | | | | | | | | | | | | | | | | 58 | — | 22 | 61 |
| S.J. Turner | | | | | | | | | | | | | | | | | | | | | | | | | — | — | 0 | — |
| Byes | | 5 | 4 | 6 | 1 | | 6 | 2 | 4 | 1 | | 6 | | | 15 | | | 4 | 1 | 1 | 3 | 8 | 6 | | | | 7 | 4 |
| Leg-byes | 7 | 23 | 6 | 5 | 11 | | 5 | 4 | | 4 | 4 | 7 | | | 22 | | 7 | 5 | 9 | 5 | 1 | 3 | 11 | 5 | 11 | | 5 | 4 |
| Wides | | | | | 1 | | 1 | 1 | | 1 | 1 | 1 | 6 | | | | | | 2 | 4 | | | | | 6 | | 1 | 1 |
| No-balls | 11 | 8 | | | 4 | | 11 | 4 | 1 | | 8 | 7 | 5 | | 13 | | 6 | 2 | 7 | 4 | 5 | 2 | 23 | | 5 | | 2 | |
| Total | 298 | 249 | 365 | 186 | 338 | | 116 | 125 | 150 | 155 | 136 | 201 | 141 | | 516 | | 303 | 179 | 354 | 315 | 192 | 341 | 501 | 25 | 397 | | 249 | 282 |
| Wickets | 5 | 5 | 1 | 4 | 10 | | 9† | 9† | 7 | 6 | 10 | 10 | 6 | | 9 | | 9 | 8 | 8 | 5 | 10 | 4 | 5 | 0 | 4 | | 10 | 3 |
| Result | L | | W | | D | | L | | W | | L | | D | | D | | D | | W | | W | | W | | D | | D | |
| Points | 7 | | — | | 8 | | — | | 19 | | 4 | | 4 | | 5 | | 6 | | 22 | | 21 | | 24 | | 8 | | 6 | |

*Catches*
57 – T. Gard (ct 47/st 10)
28 – M.D. Crowe
27 – N.F.M. Popplewell
22 – J.W. Lloyds
16 – V.J. Marks
15 – G.V. Palmer and S.J. Turner (ct 12/st 3)
13 – S.C. Booth
12 – C.H. Dredge
8 – J.G. Wyatt and R.L. Ollis
6 – B.C. Rose and M.R. Davis

trophy.

Middlesex took the NatWest Trophy, but theirs was a strange year. Gatting, so excellent a captain in his first year in the job, revealed depressingly negative tendencies and that his approach did not meet with the full approval of his side became apparent in mid-season, after which the team recovered its composure and played more fully to its potential. Emburey had a poor season by his standards and Edmonds remained the enigma. He was undoubtedly the best left-arm spinner available to England, but he did not face the West Indies and when he was chosen to tour India it was only a week after he had been suspended for one match by Middlesex and his name was being rumoured as the next captain of Hampshire. But no recent season has ended without speculation as to his future and one must just wait and see. He is a very fine cricketer and a man of intelligence and charm.

Nottinghamshire ran Essex close in two competitions and finished second in both because they were the lesser of two good teams. They relied so heavily on Richard Hadlee as a glance at their record in 1983, when he was playing for New Zealand, will show. Nevertheless, they played with a great team spirit and were well led by Clive Rice. Derek Randall gave joy to all everywhere and that he failed for England was a loss to the team and a disappointment to all who cherish the spirit of the game. Robinson and Broad were a solid opening pair and whatever Broad may lack in technical expertise, he compensates for by determination and courage. He battled bravely against the West Indian pace men and, having done enough to justify himself, was passed over when the side to tour India was chosen, some who had not faced the West Indies, nor even Sylvester Clarke on a green wicket at The Oval being preferred. When the Packer and South African rebellions erupted there was much talk of loyalty, but loyalty is of the ruler and the ruled, of the leaders and the led. If another lucrative circus is evolved within the next few years and Broad is tempted to turn his back on England and play for pots of gold, who then has been disloyal?

Essex carried off both the County Championship and the John Player League and they were unquestionably the best side in the country. They did not owe a single victory to the declaration of an opposing captain. Everything that they won, they won on their own merit. In Gooch they had the best batsman in England, and indeed only the West Indies can field his equal, and in Lever the most honest, untiring and enthusiastic bowler ever to don a county sweater. Lever maintained that the two games in Ilford week which produced remarkable victories over Warwickshire, after having been asked to follow-on, and Derbyshire, against all the odds

| v. Glamorgan (Cardiff) 14–17 July | v. Glamorgan (Taunton) 25–27 July | v. Sussex (Hove) 28–31 July | v. Surrey (Weston-s-Mare) 4–7 August | v. Worcestershire (Weston-s-Mare) 8–10 August | v. Essex (Chelmsford) 11–14 August | v. Derbyshire (Taunton) 18–21 August | v. Surrey (The Oval) 22–24 August | v. Worcestershire (Worcester) 25–28 August | v. Kent (Taunton) 29–31 August | v. Gloucestershire (Bristol) 5–7 September | v. Nottinghamshire (Taunton) 8–11 September | *M* | *Inns* | *NOs* | *Runs* | *H/S* | *Av* |
|---|---|---|---|---|---|---|---|---|---|---|---|---|---|---|---|---|---|
| 21 11 | | 31 7 | | | | | 21 2 | 6 0 | | | 5 18 | 17 | 28 | — | 666 | 103 | 23.78 |
| 23 1 | 63 41 | | 0 15 | 0 — | | 40 — | 48 0 | 12 8 | 125 — | 4 — | 44 78 | 24 | 37 | 1 | 1702 | 159 | 47.27 |
| 27 74 | 33 5 | 28 0 | 39 35* | 53 — | 20 23 | 48 — | | 8 50 | 72 13 | 108 — | 57 45 | 25 | 41 | 6 | 1870 | 190 | 53.42 |
| 4 123 | 14 28* | 0 35 | 32 7 | 30 — | 13 59 | 7 — | 0* — | | | | | 20 | 33 | 4 | 856 | 123 | 29.51 |
| | | | 9 15* | | | 90 — | | | 54 2 | 69 — | 0 — | 11 | 15 | 1 | 444 | 90 | 31.71 |
| | | | | | | | | | | | | 5 | 8 | 3 | 338 | 90 | 67.60 |
| 17 17 | 2 18* | 11 0 | 0 — | 113* — | | | | | | 24 — | 94 63* | 20 | 30 | 10 | 812 | 113* | 40.60 |
| 8 1 | 53 — | 59* 0 | 35 — | 134 — | 36* 60 | 116* — | 38 76 | 108 46* | 49 4 | 34 — | 22 8* | 24 | 34 | 10 | 1262 | 134 | 52.58 |
| | | | 24 — | 17* — | 20 6 | 26 — | 7 2 | 7 2 | 2 — | 14 — | 0 — | 21 | 24 | 5 | 209 | 26 | 11.00 |
| 7 5* | — — | 15 2 | | | 0 9 | 20 — | 5 1 | 25* 0 | 22 6 | 15 — | | 22 | 26 | 8 | 214 | 25* | 11.88 |
| 18 23 | 60* — | 18 16 | 13* — | — — | 5 — | | | | | | | 19 | 14 | 6 | 178 | 60* | 22.25 |
| | 0 11 | 46 48 | 11 9 | 88 — | 42 4 | 42 — | 11 27 | 31 7 | 78 19 | 74 — | 19 9 | 22 | 36 | 2 | 1116 | 133 | 32.82 |
| | | | | | | | | | | | | 3 | 2 | — | 0 | 0 | 0.00 |
| | | | | | 4 8 | | 11 21 | 9 2 | 9 5* | | | 6 | 12 | 1 | 112 | 22 | 10.18 |
| 8 2 | 41 — | 14 26 | | 13 — | 14 15 | 8 — | 2 73* | 0 17 | 9* — | 8 — | 19 — | 15 | 20 | 2 | 299 | 73* | 16.61 |
| | | | 1* — | — — | 0 3* | 42 — | 0* 15 | 6 0 | 0 — | 16* — | 0* — | 12 | 14 | 7 | 100 | 42 | 14.28 |
| | | | | | | | | | | | | 1 | 2 | | 1 | 1 | 0.50 |
| 19 15 | 0 1 | 2 22 | 101 22 | 0 — | 2 1 | 52 — | 5 0 | 38 13 | 44 6* | 0 — | 0 15 | 14 | 24 | 1 | 499 | 101 | 21.69 |
| 15* 9 | 27* — | 4 20* | | | | | | | | | | 5 | 6 | 3 | 75 | 27* | 25.00 |
| 2 4 | | | 7 | 8 | 4 | | 6 4 | 4 | 1 | 2 | 4 4 | † M.R. Davis retired hurt, absent injured | | | | | |
| 10 4 | 9 5 | 5 9 | 13 1 | 14 | 14 3 | 11 | 2 2 | 6 5 | 10 8 | 16 | 6 4 | ‡ B.C. Rose retired hurt, absent hurt | | | | | |
| 1 | 4 1 | | 1 | 2 | 4 | 1 | | 5 | | 5 | 1 | | | | | | |
| 7 6 | 2 2 | 2 | 7 | | 6 4 | 5 | 1 3 | 4 2 | 19 | 1 | 3 | | | | | | |
| 187 295 | 308 112 | 235 185 | 293 104 | 472 | 180 199 | 508 | 157 226 | 269 152 | 494 63 | 390 | 274 244 | | | | | | |
| 10 10 | 8 4 | 10 10 | 9 4 | 7 | 10 9† | 10 | 9‡ 9 | 10 10 | 10 5 | 10 | 10 5 | | | | | | |
| L | D | L | D | D | L | D | L | L | D | W | W | | | | | | |
| 5 | 7 | 2 | 7 | 6 | 5 | 6 | 4 | 6 | 6 | 24 | 22 | | | | | | |

5 – N.A. Felton and subs
4 – P.M. Roebuck
2 – I.T. Botham and P.W. Denning
1 – P.H.L. Wilson

on the last afternoon, were the best cricket matches he has ever played in, and his appetite for the game remains undiminished. He takes the field and wickets when others would take to their bed.

Perhaps even greater than the victories at Ilford was the victory over Middlesex at Lord's when, in the gathering gloom, Gooch's hundred brought the points at 7.30 pm on the Friday evening. This win would not have been possible but for the new ruling which stipulates 117 overs must be bowled on the first two days and 110 on the third. This number was arrived at on the assumption that 17 overs an hour should be bowled in a normal day. Sadly, most counties, Essex included, found this totally beyond them and matches dragged on late into the evening. Fines and legislation have failed to produce an over-rate that the public deserves, and one can only reiterate that the well-being of the game, and the spectators, is in the hands of the players themselves and that they must act to save us from tedium and stagnation.

The triumph of Essex, from which we have digressed, was due in no small measure to the leadership of Keith Fletcher. His record in Test and first-class cricket places him among the leading players in cricket history, yet no man has been more severely criticised in a career which has spanned more than two decades. He was sacked from the England captaincy after the briefest of reigns, yet many who advocated his dismissal were clambering for his recall at the end of 1984, a fact that was not lost on him. He is

> A man that fortune's buffets and rewards
> Hast ta'en with equal thanks: and blest are those
> Whose blood and judgement are so well commedled
> That they are not a pipe for fortune's finger
> To sound what stop she please.

He is the shrewdest captain in England and he leads his side with firmness and humour. They are essentially a team and delight in other's achievements and for the zestful, meaningful cricket that Essex give we have Keith Fletcher to thank. It seems that at last the rewards are his and he has come into his kingdom respected and cherished.

So we shall remember the glorious sunshine of 1984 and Fletcher with his cap tilted and shoulders hunched smiling his men into position; and we shall hold the image of the economic and purposeful Richard Hadlee and his attacking cricket; and we shall recall with pleasure the intelligent, committed urgings of Clive Rice; the grace of Wettimuny and the vigour of Mendis; the brilliance of Greenidge, the dependability of Gomes; and much else.

| **Somerset C.C.C.** First-Class Matches – Bowling, 1984 | I.T. Botham | M.R. Davis | M.D. Crowe | C.H. Dredge | V.J. Marks | J.W. Lloyds | P.H.L. Wilson | N.F.M. Popplewell | G.V. Palmer |
|---|---|---|---|---|---|---|---|---|---|
| v. Yorkshire (Taunton) | 13–4–23–2 | 19.2–2–76–4 | 19–4–57–1 | 18–3–74–3 | 3–1–5–0 | | | | |
| 28–30 April | 11.1–1–43–2 | 14–3–51–1 | 30–0–50–0 | 18–8–37–1 | 19–2–97–2 | 1–0–4–0 | | | |
| v. Oxford University | | 20.2–5–82–6 | 18–9–22–2 | 11–5–32–0 | 12–8–5–2 | 6–3–4–0 | 3–1–4–0 | 5–1–6–0 | |
| (Oxford) 2–4 May | | 16–2–55–1 | 8–3–29–2 | 7–0–26–1 | 26.2–9–62–3 | 29–13–62–3 | | 3–2–5–0 | |
| v. Leicestershire (Leicester) | 19–5–58–3 | 19–3–77–1 | 18.3–2–66–5 | 9–1–36–1 | 14–2–51–0 | 8–0–26–0 | | | |
| 19–22 May | 1–0–3–1 | 6–3–11–0 | 10–3–23–1 | 8–5–11–1 | 4–0–5–0 | 1–1–0–0 | | | |
| v. West Indians (Taunton) | | | 10–1–54–1 | 24.2–7–62–3 | 36–13–103–3 | 22–8–59–1 | 17–4–58–1 | 1–1–0–1 | |
| 23–25 May | | | | | | | | | |
| v. Gloucestershire (Taunton) | 2.5–0–23–0 | 10–0–47–3 | | 9–3–29–3 | | | | | |
| 26–29 May | 7.5–2–14–4 | 12–3–25–4 | 3–2–1–0 | 11–2–29–2 | | 5–4–1–0 | | | |
| v. Hampshire (Southampton) | | 27.2–6–86–2 | 11–3–40–0 | 27–9–59–4 | | 13–4–50–2 | | | 16–1–71–0 |
| 30 May–1 June | | | | | | | | | 0.1–0–4–0 |
| v. Yorkshire (Middlesbrough) | | 24–6–70–3 | 17–5–40–2 | | | 12–3–31–0 | 15–2–55–1 | 12.1–5–31–1 | 13–2–59–3 |
| 2–5 June | | | | | | | | | |
| v. Middlesex (Bath) | 16–1–57–1 | 6–0–42–0 | 11–2–42–1 | 8.1–0–35–1 | 29–5–136–2 | | | 7–1–31–1 | |
| 9–12 June | | 8–3–23–0 | | 4–0–23–0 | 10–2–22–2 | | | | |
| v. Lancashire (Bath) | | | 9–1–43–1 | 27–4–66–1 | 14–3–72–0 | | | 16–6–42–0 | |
| 13–15 June | | | | 5–0–16–0 | 34–14–63–6 | 4–0–16–0 | | 3–0–13–0 | |
| v. Warwickshire (Edgbaston) | 11–3–29–0 | 20–2–82–1 | 12–2–23–2 | 22–2–90–1 | 10–0–30–1 | 1.2–1–4–0 | | 6–1–17–0 | |
| 23–26 June | 14.1–2–64–4 | 10–0–55–1 | 10–1–37–3 | 8–0–43–0 | 11–3–37–1 | 2–0–10–0 | | | |
| v. Leicestershire (Taunton) | | 21–3–57–0 | 8–2–22–0 | 20–6–48–4 | 19–5–44–1 | 10–3–41–2 | | | 13–3–36–3 |
| 27–29 June | | 23–3–82–5 | | 12–0–52–1 | 14–5–49–1 | 11–1–24–2 | | | 14–3–59–0 |
| v. Northamptonshire | | 24.2–6–55–7 | 8–3–22–0 | | 6–1–19–0 | 16–7–36–0 | 16–6–36–3 | 8–2–28–0 | 12–2–48–0 |
| (Northampton) 30 June–3 July | | 21.4–5–64–4 | 4–0–18–0 | | 15–2–52–1 | 8–4–16–1 | 5–1–23–0 | 1–0–3–0 | 22–2–78–4 |
| v. Hampshire (Taunton) | 13–3–27–0 | 29.4–8–83–6 | 16–6–29–3 | 20–6–52–1 | 16–8–31–0 | | | 3–1–5–0 | |
| 7–10 July | 17–6–39–2 | 13–2–45–3 | 10–3–22–1 | 17–7–25–2 | 9–2–26–0 | | | | |
| v. Nottinghamshire | | 14–4–34–2 | 16–4–41–2 | 14–4–45–1 | 21.4–12–41–4 | | | | 6–0–25–0 |
| (Trent Bridge) 11–13 July | | 14–4–30–1 | 14–2–40–2 | 10–2–39–1 | 6–2–12–0 | 7–0–36–0 | | | 10–4–24–1 |
| v. Glamorgan (Cardiff) | | 17–7–34–2 | 17–5–37–4 | 19–6–45–1 | 16–8–16–0 | 7–4–9–1 | | | 17–3–44–1 |
| 14–17 July | | | 6–2–15–0 | | 12–2–91–4 | 26–2–102–2 | | | 8–0–41–1 |
| v. Glamorgan (Taunton) | | 28–5–82–2 | 16.3–5–56–2 | 33–8–81–1 | 27–8–63–2 | 2–1–2–0 | | 1–0–2–0 | 9–0–42–0 |
| 25–27 July | | 5–2–13–0 | 5–1–23–0 | 6–2–12–0 | 7–0–40–0 | 16–1–62–0 | | 11–1–50–1 | 5–1–17–0 |
| v. Sussex (Hove) | | 8–3–13–0 | 15–1–53–0 | 6–2–14–0 | 34–7–98–0 | 18–6–57–0 | | 25.2–4–79–3 | 19–1–84–0 |
| 28–31 July | | | | | | | | | |
| v. Surrey (Weston-super- | 8–1–33–2 | 6–2–15–0 | 4–0–8–0 | | 28–4–80–4 | | | | |
| Mare) 4–7 August | | 2–0–6–0 | 4–0–33–0 | | 16–3–55–5 | | | | |
| v. Worcestershire (Weston- | | 16–4–39–3 | 6–1–21–1 | | 19–9–36–1 | | | | 10–4–23–2 |
| super-Mare) 8–10 August | | 18–6–38–2 | 12–9–11–1 | | 34–15–50–0 | 14–4–31–0 | | 2–0–13–0 | 13–2–63–2 |
| v. Essex (Chelmsford) | | 18–5–43–2 | 20–6–40–1 | 19–6–49–3 | 5.5–1–15–3 | | | | 10–4–33–1 |
| 11–14 August | | 10–1–54–0 | 20–0–18–0 | 18–0–51–2 | 15–4–27–1 | | | | 18–5–43–3 |
| v. Derbyshire (Taunton) | 4–3–4–0 | | 17–4–70–2 | 17.3–1–70–4 | 35–12–79–2 | | | | 14–1–72–1 |
| 18–21 August | 3–1–14–0 | | | 3–1–16–0 | 33–12–83–7 | | | | 4–0–30–0 |
| v. Surrey (The Oval) | | | | 32–4–99–2 | 25.1–8–63–3 | | | 14–1–36–1 | 29–2–117–2 |
| 22–24 August | | | | | | | | | |
| v. Worcestershire | | | 17–1–62–2 | 20–6–34–1 | 9–2–18–0 | | | | 17.2–5–58–4 |
| (Worcester) 25–28 August | | | 10–2–36–1 | 11–2–44–2 | 12–6–28–0 | | | 7–4–9–0 | 13–5–39–0 |
| v. Kent (Taunton) | 23.2–7–57–5 | | 15–4–46–0 | 13–4–30–1 | 18–5–59–2 | | | | 14–3–51–1 |
| 29–31 August | 7–1–20–0 | | 4–1–17–0 | 3–0–7–0 | 45–7–141–8 | | | | |
| v. Gloucestershire (Bristol) | 26–3–80–3 | | 5–0–36–0 | 12–5–35–2 | 19–7–46–4 | | | | 4–0–31–0 |
| 5–7 September | 17–5–43–4 | | | 11–4–18–2 | 6–3–8–3 | | | | |
| v. Nottinghamshire | 10–2–42–0 | | 12–1–34–1 | | 22–4–64–2 | 1–0–5–0 | | | 10–3–39–1 |
| (Taunton) 8–11 September | 6–1–18–0 | | 2–0–16–0 | | 27–0–111–6 | | | | |
| | 230.2–51–691–33 *av.* 20.93 | 500.4–108–1569–66 *av.* 23.77 | 452–101–1353–44 *av.* 30.75 | 533–125–1534–53 *av.* 28.94 | 808–226–2233–86 *av.* 25.96 | 240.2–70–697–14 *av.* 49.78 | 56–14–176–5 *av.* 35.20 | 125.3–50–370–8 *av.* 46.25 | 320.3–56–1231–30 *av.* 41.03 |

a C. M. Old retired hurt
b J. G. Wyatt 1–1–0–1; N. A. Felton 0.1–0–4–0
c J. G. Wyatt 2–0–4–0

| P.M. Roebuck | S.C. Booth | M. Turner | *Byes* | *Leg-byes* | *Wides* | *No-balls* | *Total* | *Wkts* |
|---|---|---|---|---|---|---|---|---|
| | | | 4 | 2 | 1 | | 242 | 10 |
| | | | 8 | 18 | | 1 | 309 | 7 |
| | | | 2 | 3 | | 2 | 171 | 10 |
| | | | | 1 | | 1 | 241 | 10 |
| | | | | 2 | 1 | 1 | 318 | 10 |
| | | | | 4 | | | 57 | 3 |
| | | | | 3 | 2 | 1 | 342 | 10 |
| | | | | 4 | | | 103 | 6 |
| | | | 1 | 1 | | | 72 | 10 |
| 1–0–4–0 | | | 1 | 12 | 2 | 8 | 333 | 9 |
| | | | | | | 1 | 5 | 0 |
| | | | | 11 | 4 | 8 | 309 | 10 |
| | 30–5–120–1 | | 2 | 3 | 3 | 2 | 473 | 7 |
| | 7–4–15–0 | | 2 | 2 | | 1 | 88 | 2 |
| | 14–2–61–2 | 22–6–74–0 | | 6 | 1 | 4 | 369 | 5 |
| | 35–15–68–1 | 7–2–11–0 | 7 | 4 | 1 | 2 | 201 | 8 |
| | | | 3 | 21 | | 2 | 301 | 5 |
| | | | 1 | 5 | | | 252 | 9a |
| | | | 1 | 5 | | | 254 | 10 |
| | | | 1 | 8 | | 3 | 278 | 9 |
| | | | | 9 | 1 | 1 | 255 | 10 |
| | | | | 15 | | 1 | 270 | 10 |
| | 3–1–5–0 | | 1 | 11 | | | 244 | 10 |
| | 3–2–3–0 | | | 5 | 1 | | 166 | 8 |
| | | | 5 | 12 | | | 203 | 10 |
| | | | 7 | 10 | 3 | 1 | 202 | 5 |
| | | | 9 | 11 | 2 | 4 | 211 | 10 |
| | | | 10 | 11 | | 2 | 272 | 8 |
| | | | 3 | 11 | 1 | 10 | 353 | 7 |
| | | | 8 | 5 | | 1 | 231 | 1 |
| | | | 3 | 7 | 3 | 6 | 417 | 3 |
| | | | | | | | 4 | 1b |
| | 21.5–3–76–4 | | | 5 | | | 217 | 10 |
| | 13–1–57–4 | | 2 | 3 | 1 | | 157 | 9 |
| | 18.2–8–32–3 | | 3 | 2 | 3 | 1 | 160 | 10 |
| | 33.4–12–83–2 | | 3 | 3 | 2 | 1 | 298 | 7 |
| | | | 4 | 12 | | 4 | 200 | 10 |
| | 21.3–7–50–4 | | 5 | 6 | 5 | 15 | 264 | 10 |
| | 31–10–71–1 | | 1 | 4 | 1 | 1 | 373 | 10 |
| 9–5–10–0 | 21–5–64–0 | | 4 | 1 | 4 | | 226 | 7 |
| | 23–4–71–2 | | 4 | 10 | | 1 | 401 | 10 |
| | 19–8–38–3 | | 1 | 9 | 1 | 1 | 222 | 10 |
| 0.2–0–4–0 | 18–9–30–0 | | | 9 | | | 203 | 3c |
| | 20–10–33–1 | | | 13 | 1 | | 290 | 10 |
| | 40–8–125–2 | | 2 | 2 | | | 314 | 10 |
| | 0.5–0–2–1 | | | 3 | 1 | | 234 | 10 |
| | 0.5–0–0–1 | | 4 | | | | 73 | 10 |
| | 10.3–1–30–2 | | | 7 | 1 | | 222 | 7 |
| | 24.5–2–138–4 | | | | | | | |
| 10.2–5–<br>18–0<br>— | 409.2–117–<br>1172–38<br>*av.* 30.84 | 29–8–<br>85–0<br>— | | | | | | |

*Graham Gooch of Essex. (Adrian Murrell)*

*In their battle against the West Indies, England desperately missed the services of GRAHAM GOOCH who scored more runs than any other batsman in the country and always in an exciting manner. Gooch's three-year ban for playing international cricket in South Africa ends next spring and he will be available for selection for the series against Australia in 1985, which is also his benefit year. He talks to David Lemmon –*

*G.G.* I think winning the county championship on the last afternoon of the season was the most exciting, and nerve-racking, thing that has happened to me in cricket. We went to Old Trafford determined to win and everything went right for us. Lancashire played the game in the proper spirit and we stuck out there in the dark on Saturday evening because we knew we had to use every over that was available to us and get runs quickly. After we had won on Tuesday we stayed the night in Manchester to celebrate a little and drove to Chelmsford next day to be together to hear the result from

**Surrey C.C.C.**
First-Class Matches – Batting, 1984

| | v. Nottinghamshire (Trent Bridge) 28–30 April | | v. Northamptonshire (The Oval) 2–4 May | | v. Warwickshire (Edgbaston) 5–8 May | | v. Sussex (Hove) 9–11 May | | v. Derbyshire (Chesterfield) 23–25 May | | v. Essex (Chelmsford) 26–29 May | | v. Glamorgan (The Oval) 30 May–1 June | |
|---|---|---|---|---|---|---|---|---|---|---|---|---|---|---|
| A.R. Butcher | 13 | 10 | 14 | 23 | 8 | 12 | 2 | 11* | 40 | 7 | 79 | — | 117* | 114 |
| D.B. Pauline | 8 | 3 | 21 | 65 | 57 | 11 | 13 | 3 | 1 | 88 | 13 | — | 47 | — |
| G.P. Howarth | 4 | 5 | 7 | 10 | 32 | 3 | 8 | 108* | | | | | | |
| M.A. Lynch | 0 | 35 | 60 | 66 | 0 | 15 | 33 | 24 | 45 | 14 | 68 | — | 18 | 4* |
| R.D.V. Knight | 8 | 58* | 87 | 0 | 22 | 50* | 9 | 45* | 12 | 59 | 9 | — | 18 | 6 |
| A. Needham | 50 | 0 | 27 | 25 | 25 | 0 | 0 | — | 15 | 42* | 10 | — | 26 | 10 |
| C.J. Richards | 27 | 2 | 56* | 11 | 28 | 18 | 32 | — | 109 | 12* | 33 | — | 4* | — |
| D.J. Thomas | 1 | 13 | 1 | 5 | 10 | 13 | | | 19 | — | 1 | — | — | — |
| P.I. Pocock | 3 | 9 | — | — | 12* | — | | | 29* | — | | | — | — |
| S.T. Clarke | 5 | 0 | — | 0 | 7 | — | 28 | — | 11 | — | 0 | — | — | — |
| G. Monkhouse | 4* | 0 | | | | | 17 | — | | | 8* | — | | |
| M.A. Feltham | | | 24* | 6* | 28 | 2* | 19 | — | 1 | — | 0 | — | — | — |
| I.J. Curtis | | | | | | | 1* | — | | | | | | |
| G.S. Clinton | | | | | | | | | 11 | 10 | 0 | — | 65 | 78* |
| I.R. Payne | | | | | | | | | | | | | | |
| P. Waterman | | | | | | | | | | | | | | |
| A.J. Stewart | | | | | | | | | | | | | | |
| N.J. Falkner | | | | | | | | | | | | | | |
| K. Medlycott | | | | | | | | | | | | | | |
| N.S. Taylor | | | | | | | | | | | | | | |
| Byes | | 4 | 1 | 2 | 2 | 6 | 4 | | 1 | | 5 | | | 1 |
| Leg-byes | 4 | 6 | 12 | 9 | 15 | | 2 | 4 | 8 | 9 | 5 | | 4 | 8 |
| Wides | | | | | | | 1 | 1 | 2 | 1 | | | 1 | 1 |
| No-balls | 2 | 3 | 8 | 3 | 1 | 2 | 10 | 9 | 2 | 4 | 4 | | | |
| Total | 129 | 148 | 318 | 235 | 247 | 132 | 179 | 205 | 306 | 246 | 235 | | 300 | 222 |
| Wickets | 10 | 10 | 7 | 9 | 10 | 7 | 10 | 2 | 10 | 5 | 10 | | 5 | 3 |
| Result | L | | L | | D | | D | | D | | D | | D | |
| Points | 4 | | 8 | | 6 | | 5 | | 7 | | 0 | | 5 | |

| | v. Lancashire (Old Trafford) 2–5 June | | v. Leicestershire (The Oval) 9–12 June | | v. Middlesex (Lord's) 13–15 June | | v. Sussex (Guildford) 16–19 June | | v. Middlesex (The Oval) 23–26 June | | v. Cambridge Univ. (Banstead) 27–29 June | | v. Hampshire (The Oval) 30 June–3 July | |
|---|---|---|---|---|---|---|---|---|---|---|---|---|---|---|
| A.R. Butcher | 52 | 30 | 3 | 0 | 20 | 67 | 2 | 135* | 0 | — | | | 45 | 2 |
| D.B. Pauline | 11 | 5 | | | | | | | | | 13 | — | | |
| G.P. Howarth | 15 | 20 | 4 | 3 | 11 | 38 | 3 | 19 | 13 | — | 0 | — | 0 | 16 |
| M.A. Lynch | 12 | 13 | 12 | 144 | 112 | 43 | 6 | 33 | 118 | — | | | 104 | 3 |
| R.D.V. Knight | 60 | 29 | | | 57 | 7 | 11 | 21 | 44 | — | | | 12 | 19 |
| A. Needham | 2 | 30 | 0 | 29 | 70 | 7 | 25 | 16 | | | 9 | — | | |
| C.J. Richards | 24* | 18 | 6 | 16 | 0 | 10 | 28 | 0 | 64 | — | | | 53 | 5 |
| D.J. Thomas | | | 32* | 4 | | | 46* | 0* | 9 | — | | | 11 | 6* |
| P.I. Pocock | 6 | 0* | 19 | 0 | 17* | — | 1 | — | 3* | — | | | 0 | — |
| S.T. Clarke | 20 | 23 | 1 | 35 | 14 | — | 0 | — | 8 | — | | | 16 | — |
| G. Monkhouse | 0 | 5 | | | 0 | 1* | 4 | — | 51 | — | | | 18* | 8* |
| M.A. Feltham | | | | | | | | | | | 23 | — | | |
| I.J. Curtis | | | | | | | | | | | | | | |
| G.S. Clinton | 14 | 66 | 28* | — | | | | | 33 | — | 37 | — | 0 | 30 |
| I.R. Payne | | | 0 | 17 | | | | | | | 13 | — | | |
| P. Waterman | | | 0 | 0* | — | | | | | | — | — | | |
| A.J. Stewart | | | | | 69* | 35* | 73 | 31 | 20 | — | 26 | — | 14 | 1 |
| N.J. Falkner | | | | | | | | | | | 101* | — | | |
| K. Medlycott | | | | | | | | | | | 117* | — | | |
| N.S. Taylor | | | | | | | | | | | — | — | | |
| Byes | | 2 | 2 | 8 | 11 | | 1 | 2 | | | 4 | | 3 | |
| Leg-byes | 4 | 3 | 4 | 7 | 8 | 9 | 3 | 5 | 15 | | 14 | | 13 | |
| Wides | | | 1 | 1 | 6 | | 1 | | 1 | | 4 | | 3 | 5 |
| No-balls | 1 | 7 | 3 | 2 | | 9 | 4 | | 20 | | | | 4 | 5 |
| Total | 221 | 251 | 115 | 266 | 395 | 226 | 208 | 262 | 399 | | 361 | | 296 | 100 |
| Wickets | 10 | 10 | 9 | † 9 | 8 | 6 | 10 | 6 | 10 | | 7 | | 10 | 7 |
| Result | D | | L | | W | | D | | W | | D | | W | |
| Points | 6 | | 4 | | 23 | | 2 | | 24 | | — | | 23 | |

*Catches* 52 – C.J. Richards (ct 46/st 6); 32 – M.A. Lynch; 26 – A.J. Stewart; 22 – S.T. Clarke; 19 – R.D.V. Knight; 17 – G.P. Howarth; 11 – A.R. Butcher; 10 – D.J. Thomas; 9 – A. Needham; 8 – P.I. Pocock, D.B. Pauline and G. Monkhouse

Taunton. It was worse than playing and we thought the way Mike Bore was batting that he would win the game for Notts, but in the end it went our way. Both's declaration had been just right and made a great game of it and a wonderful end to the season.

I suppose many people felt sorry for Notts and they were a fine side. Richard Hadlee is a great player and had a fabulous season, and they have got some other very good players as well as Clive Rice and Derek Randall, but I think we deserved to win because we were the better side. I know that they beat us at Chelmsford, but we got caught on a bad wicket there, and I feel that throughout the season we were just that bit better.

We have brought some youngsters into the side over the past few years. David East has done a great job behind the stumps and has really worked hard at his game, and Neil Foster is getting better all the time and can hit a few runs when they are needed. Derek Pringle is going to be a really top class all-rounder and Chris Gladwin carried on from where he ended last season and must be one of the best and fastest-scoring opening bats in the country. The lad we brought in this year was Paul Prichard. Fletch said we weren't playing to our full potential and our middle order was very unpredictable. We knew he was a good player from the time he joined us when he was sixteen. He came in to the side at number seven and by the end of the season he was number three. If he goes on developing he could become an England player.

When we won the Benson and Hedges Cup at Lord's in 1979 it was the greatest thing that had ever happened to Essex and some of the lads had been waiting a long time. We've followed that with three championships and two John Player League wins and we feel we have a side that is young enough and strong enough to be successful for some time.

*D.L.* Graham, you have talked at some length about Essex and your obvious pride in their achievements and hopes for the future, but you also mentioned the England side. Many people throughout the country are looking forward to seeing you back for England next season. What is your reaction to that?

*G.G.* There is nothing I want more than to get back in the England side and I only hope that I can play well enough next season and score enough runs to get in the side against Australia. I feel that I have played as well this year as at any time in my career. I was pleased to get a hundred against the West Indies at Chelmsford although their attack was not at its strongest that day, and obviously there is no greater honour than playing for your country. I am sorry I have

| v. Northamptonshire (Northampton) 7–10 July | | v. Derbyshire (The Oval) 14–17 July | | v. Kent (The Oval) 25–27 July | | v. Sri Lankans (The Oval) 28–30 July | | v. Somerset (Weston-s-Mare) 4–7 August | | v. Kent (Canterbury) 8–10 August | | v. Gloucestershire (Cheltenham) 11–14 August | | v. Yorkshire (The Oval) 18–21 August | | v. Somerset (The Oval) 22–24 August | | v. Essex (The Oval) 25–28 August | | v. Glamorgan (Swansea) 29–31 August | | v. Worcestershire (The Oval) 8–11 September | | M | Inns | NOs | Runs | H/S | Av |
|---|---|---|---|---|---|---|---|---|---|---|---|---|---|---|---|---|---|---|---|---|---|---|---|---|---|---|---|---|---|
| 11 | 63 | 8 | 27 | 39* | 13 | 4 | 49 | 85 | 38 | 7 | 8 | 43 | — | 118 | — | 31 | — | 47 | — | | | 18 | — | 24 | 41 | 4 | 1415 | 135* | 38.24 |
| | | | | | | | | | | | | | | | | | | | | 8* | — | | | 10 | 16 | 1 | 367 | 88 | 24.46 |
| 113 | 38 | 6 | 25 | 11 | 22 | 77 | 8* | 50 | 23 | 2 | 9 | 55 | — | 1 | — | 55 | — | — | 0* | | | 19 | — | 22 | 37 | 3 | 833 | 113 | 24.50 |
| 34 | 53 | 8 | 55 | — | 17 | 2 | 33 | 17 | 38 | 80 | 2 | 15 | — | 85 | — | 9 | — | 58 | 17 | — | — | 41 | — | 25 | 41 | 1 | 1546 | 144 | 38.65 |
| 50 | 32 | | | 11 | 34 | 1 | 9 | | | 7 | 9 | 142 | — | 77 | — | 114 | — | 109 | 16 | — | — | | | 21 | 35 | 3 | 1254 | 142 | 39.18 |
| | | | | | | 54 | 5 | | | 16 | 20 | 8 | — | | | 25 | — | 37 | 57 | — | — | 4 | — | 19 | 30 | 1 | 644 | 70 | 22.20 |
| 26* | 9 | 0 | 19* | — | 57* | 31 | 25 | 0 | 4 | 26 | 12 | 17 | — | — | — | 17 | — | 0 | 9 | — | — | 100* | — | 25 | 38 | 8 | 908 | 109 | 30.26 |
| 11* | 13 | 19 | — | | | 45 | 18 | 4 | 1 | 16 | 4 | 30 | — | — | — | 48 | — | 2 | 43 | — | — | | | 20 | 28 | 5 | 425 | 48 | 18.47 |
| — | 1 | 3 | — | | | | | 7 | 0* | | | | | — | — | | | | | — | — | — | — | 17 | 16 | 6 | 110 | 29* | 11.00 |
| — | 19 | 33 | — | — | 7* | | | 24* | 14 | 15 | 8 | 23 | — | 10* | — | | | — | 8 | — | — | — | — | 23 | 25 | 3 | 329 | 35 | 14.95 |
| — | 1 | 0 | — | 100* | 5 | 10 | 26 | 0 | 5* | 2 | 12 | 0 | — | — | — | 31 | — | | | | | 20 | — | 18 | 25 | 7 | 328 | 100* | 18.22 |
| | | 44 | — | — | 1 | | | 0 | 3 | | | | | | | | | 3* | 13 | | | 39* | — | 12 | 15 | 5 | 206 | 44 | 20.60 |
| | | | | | | | | | | | | | | | | | | | | | | | | 1 | 1 | 1 | 1 | 1* | — |
| 2* | 0* | 113* | 67 | 78 | — | | | 5 | 21 | 1 | 37 | 1 | — | 192 | — | 27 | — | 9 | 8 | 7* | — | 8 | — | 19 | 28 | 6 | 948 | 192 | 43.09 |
| | | | | | | | | | | | | | | | | | | | | | | | | 2 | 3 | — | 30 | 17 | 10.00 |
| | | | | | | | | | | | | | | | | | | | | | | | | 2 | 2 | 1 | 0 | 0* | — |
| 33 | 23 | 20 | 60* | — | 0 | 2 | 18 | 20 | 4 | | | | | — | — | 23 | — | 54 | 4 | — | — | 40 | — | 15 | 21 | 3 | 570 | 73 | 31.66 |
| | | | | | | | | | | | | | | | | | | | | | | | | 1 | 1 | 1 | 101 | 101* | — |
| | | | | — | 2 | 2* | — | | | 0* | 0* | 7* | — | | | | | | | — | — | | | 6 | 6 | 5 | 128 | 117* | 128.00 |
| | | | | | | — | — | | | | | | | | | 6* | — | | | | | | | 3 | 1 | 1 | 6 | 6* | — |
| 7 | 4 | | | 7 | 2 | 7 | 4 | | 2 | 8 | | 11 | | 8 | | 4 | | | | | | 2 | | † G.S. Clinton retired hurt, absent hurt | | | | | |
| 7 | 2 | 1 | 2 | 3 | | 4 | 7 | 5 | 3 | 1 | 2 | 8 | | 16 | | 10 | | 5 | 2 | 1 | | 8 | | ‡ A.R. Butcher absent ill | | | | | |
| 2 | 1 | 1 | 4 | 1 | | 1 | | | 1 | 1 | | 2 | | 5 | | | | 2 | 2 | | | 1 | | | | | | | |
| 8 | 2 | 4 | 7 | 5 | 2 | 10 | 6 | | | 1 | 1 | 5 | | 6 | | 1 | | 1 | | 1 | | 7 | | | | | | | |
| 304 | 261 | 260 | 266 | 255 | 162 | 250 | 208 | 217 | 157 | 183 | 124 | 367 | | 518 | | 401 | | 327 | 179 | 17 | | 307 | | | | | | | |
| 5 | 10 | 10 | 4 | 3 | 8 | 9 | 8 | 10 | 9 | 10 | 10 | 10 | | 5 | | 10 | | 8 | 9‡ | 0 | | 7 | | | | | | | |
| L | | W | | D | | W | | D | | L | | D | | W | | W | | L | | D | | D | | | | | | | |
| 8 | | 21 | | 7 | | — | | 6 | | 4 | | 5 | | 24 | | 24 | | 7 | | 2 | | 5 | | | | | | | |

7 – G.S. Clinton
5 – M.A. Feltham
4 – I.R. Payne and subs
2 – P Waterman and N.S. Taylor

missed the last three years, but I still don't feel that I did anything wrong and I think I would do the same thing again. However, all I want to do now is get back in the England side.

The thing that worries me is that people might expect miracles. There were suggestions that if those of us who had been banned had been playing against the West Indies this summer, England would have won. We were all available and playing when West Indies came here in 1980 and we were beaten, and we were beaten when we went to the West Indies. I've only played in one winning side against the West Indies and that was in a one-day international at Lord's. I like to think I might have helped a bit and that we wouldn't have lost five–nil, but England were up against a good side and I don't think if any of us who were banned had been playing, we would have stopped West Indies winning the series. Mind you, we'd have tried.

I think people should look positively at what happened. We had some bad luck with the injuries to Andy Lloyd and Paul Terry, but our batting wasn't too bad. People like Chris Broad played with a lot of guts and Paul Downton showed what could be done as, of course, did Allan Lamb. What we lacked most was bowling of penetration. We have relied a tremendous amount on Bob Willis over the past few years and it was inevitable that he would be missed. He was a great bowler and now he has gone there is a gap.

Hopefully, it is going to be filled by a young man like Neil Foster or even by somebody who has not yet forced his way into a county side. There are lot of good players about and I am sure England will be back on top again before long, and I hope I am in the side when they're back on top.

| **Surrey C.C.C.** First-Class Matches – Bowling, 1984 | S.T. Clarke | D.J. Thomas | G. Monkhouse | R.D.V. Knight | P.I. Pocock | A. Needham | M.A. Feltham | N.S. Taylor | A.R. Butcher |
|---|---|---|---|---|---|---|---|---|---|
| v. Nottinghamshire | 13–5–34–1 | 9–4–19–2 | 14.2–2–41–4 | 7–2–17–0 | 20–5–47–3 | | | | |
| (Trent Bridge) 28–30 April | 18–1–55–1 | 12–1–38–1 | 6–1–26–0 | 14.4–5–49–1 | 33–12–88–2 | 17–2–56–0 | | | |
| v. Northamptonshire (The Oval) | 21–4–65–2 | 22–7–46–3 | | 15–4–51–1 | 18.2–5–43–3 | | 20–5–71–1 | | |
| 2–4 May | 12–1–63–2 | 11–1–37–0 | | 6–0–36–0 | 6–1–26–0 | | 11–0–63–2 | | |
| v. Warwickshire (Edgbaston) | 17–2–54–1 | 16–6–45–2 | | 17.5–2–55–2 | 14–4–31–2 | 21–10–35–0 | 21–8–42–3 | | |
| 5–8 May | 18–3–55–2 | 6.4–1–30–2 | | | 17–7–24–0 | 9–5–6–0 | 22–6–62–5 | | |
| v. Sussex (Hove) | 32–11–105–4 | | 20–6–56–2 | 20–5–36–2 | | | 16–0–79–1 | | |
| 9–11 May | | | | | | | | | |
| v. Derbyshire (Chesterfield) | 22–9–47–3 | 20–2–76–0 | | 8–1–31–1 | 29–3–66–2 | 7.1–1–30–2 | 13–1–39–0 | | |
| 23–25 May | | | | | | | | | |
| v. Essex (Chelmsford) | | | | | | | | | |
| 26–29 May | | | | | | | | | |
| v. Glamorgan (The Oval) | 17–5–39–1 | 16–4–46–0 | | 8–0–18–1 | 19–3–43–1 | 13–1–37–0 | 17–6–48–1 | | 2–0–12–0 |
| 30 May–1 June | 16–1–57–1 | 9–0–59–0 | | 9–1–35–1 | 11–0–37–4 | | 13–0–58–2 | | |
| v. Lancashire (Old Trafford) | 17–6–41–1 | | 13–3–43–0 | 9–3–16–0 | 30–6–74–7 | 10.1–3–34–1 | | | |
| 2–5 June | 13–2–55–1 | | 4–1–11–0 | 9–2–19–2 | 23–4–93–3 | 10–2–48–2 | | | |
| v. Leicestershire (The Oval) | 24.4–4–62–6 | 24–8–74–1 | | | 4–3–2–0 | | | | |
| 9–12 June | 12.3–1–43–0 | 11–0–32–3 | | | 5–1–18–2 | | | | |
| v. Middlesex (Lord's) | 24–7–51–1 | | 18–5–45–2 | 15–1–53–0 | 27–7–61–2 | 15–3–48–4 | | | |
| 13–15 June | 13.1–1–43–1 | | 6–1–35–2 | 7–0–29–1 | 6–2–12–0 | 16–4–82–5 | | | |
| v. Sussex (Guildford) | 24–11–35–2 | 34–4–105–1 | 38–11–96–3 | 19–4–48–3 | 22–5–58–0 | | | | |
| 16–19 June | | | | | | | | | |
| v. Middlesex (The Oval) | 14–4–46–3 | 15–3–66–3 | 15–6–24–0 | 12.1–6–7–4 | 7–1–9–0 | | | | |
| 23–26 June | 10–1–28–4 | 9–2–33–3 | 12.1–5–17–3 | | | | | | |
| v. Cambridge University | | | | | | | 20–7–57–4 | 16–3–38–3 | |
| (Banstead) 27–29 June | | | | | | 10–4–20–0 | 15–4–23–2 | 12–6–25–0 | |
| v. Hampshire (The Oval) | 17–7–28–4 | 12–1–48–1 | 11–3–27–3 | 11–5–26–0 | 5–2–12–2 | | | | |
| 30 June–3 July | 20.4–9–41–5 | 21–5–81–3 | 14–2–49–1 | 8–3–23–0 | 11–3–25–1 | | | | |
| v. Northamptonshire | 17–3–53–1 | 23–8–63–5 | 24–9–74–1 | 10–1–56–0 | 23–4–59–2 | | | | |
| (Northampton) 7–10 July | 13–4–24–1 | | 9–1–49–1 | 5–1–15–0 | 12–1–42–0 | | | | 16–2–65–3 |
| v. Derbyshire (The Oval) | 15–6–30–0 | 14–2–57–0 | 17–1–57–3 | | 20.3–5–53–1 | | 15–4–37–1 | | |
| 14–17 July | 7–3–9–1 | 5–0–38–0 | 9–0–49–1 | | 15–3–43–5 | | 10–0–42–2 | | |
| v. Kent (The Oval) | 15.4–1–50–3 | | 9–3–23–1 | 11–5–21–2 | | | 14–1–53–2 | | |
| 25–27 July | 15–5–31–3 | | 12.4–3–29–2 | 7–5–9–0 | | | 12–1–48–1 | | |
| v. Sri Lankans (The Oval) | | 16.3–3–57–3 | 11–2–39–2 | | | | | 16–4–83–3 | |
| 28–30 July | | 9–2–40–1 | 9–2–29–3 | 4–2–4–0 | | 2.1–0–4–1 | | 9–2–23–2 | |
| v. Somerset (Weston-super- | 17–4–31–1 | 20–5–48–2 | 23–7–49–3 | | 23–1–78–2 | | 17–2–59–1 | | |
| Mare) 4–7 August | | 11–3–25–1 | 15–4–44–3 | | 5–3–3–0 | | 5–1–15–0 | | 3–1–16–0 |
| v. Kent (Canterbury) | 13–6–17–0 | 14–7–33–3 | 23.4–7–50–3 | 22–6–55–2 | | 24–7–55–0 | | | |
| 8–10 August | 18–4–39–3 | 12.3–3–50–1 | 17–5–44–0 | 16–7–32–2 | | 12–0–41–2 | | | |
| v. Gloucestershire | 16.2–4–38–4 | 17–3–56–3 | 15–4–28–1 | 12–6–23–0 | | 21–3–80–1 | | | |
| (Cheltenham) 11–14 August | 17–3–50–3 | 9–3–33–0 | 3–0–15–0 | | | 19–6–74–2 | | | 5–2–12–1 |
| v. Yorkshire (The Oval) | 14–1–44–1 | 14–5–45–1 | 14–2–47–2 | | 18.3–8–30–6 | | | | |
| 18–21 August | 11–4–23–2 | 18.4–3–57–4 | 10–1–33–2 | 4–1–7–1 | 8–3–17–1 | | | | |
| v. Somerset (The Oval) | | 17.2–4–36–6 | 19–11–25–0 | 20–9–23–0 | | 12–5–24–2 | | 14–2–38–1 | 1–0–2–0 |
| 22–24 August | | 18–4–67–4 | 14–5–36–0 | 7–2–11–1 | | 13.3–3–56–3 | | 13–4–47–1 | |
| v. Essex (The Oval) | 19.5–5–43–3 | 12–1–46–1 | | 24–7–66–0 | | 28–7–89–2 | 18–4–59–2 | | |
| 25–28 August | 9–0–37–1 | 7–2–26–0 | | 8–2–39–0 | | 15.5–1–82–0 | 13–1–67–1 | | |
| v. Glamorgan (Swansea) | 21.1–9–28–3 | 20–7–42–0 | | 4–1–15–0 | 39–10–101–2 | 17–2–41–0 | | | |
| 29–31 August | | | | | | | | | |
| v. Worcestershire (The Oval) | 17–5–45–0 | | 26–4–62–2 | | 20–2–69–1 | 19–3–70–0 | 10–1–57–0 | | |
| 8–11 September | 19–3–47–2 | | 9–3–21–0 | | 26–9–59–2 | 17–7–35–2 | 9.2–1–33–1 | | 11–4–27–0 |
| | 651–165–<br>1687–78<br>*av.* 21.62 | 505.4–114–<br>1654–60<br>*av.* 27.56 | 460.5–120–<br>1273–50<br>*av.* 25.46 | 349.4–99–<br>925–27<br>*av.* 34.25 | 517.2–123–<br>1323–56<br>*av.* 23.62 | 328.5–79–<br>1047–29<br>*av.* 36.10 | 291.2–53–<br>1012–32<br>*av.* 31.62 | 80–21–<br>254–10<br>*av.* 25.40 | 38–9–<br>134–4<br>*av.* 33.50 |

a W.A. Morton retired hurt
b I.J. Curtis 11.3–3–36–1
c G.S. Clinton 1–1–0–0
D.B. Pauline 6–4–6–0
G.P. Howarth 0.4–0–2–0
d G. Cook retired hurt
e M.A. Lynch 7.3–0–36–1
f R. G. de Alwis retired hurt
A.L.F. de Mel absent hurt
g M.A. Lynch 2–2–0–0
h B.C. Rose retired hurt absent hurt

| P.A. Waterman | I.R. Payne | K. Medlycott | Byes | Leg-byes | Wides | No-balls | Total | Wkts |
|---|---|---|---|---|---|---|---|---|
| | | | | 5 | 1 | 11 | 175 | 10 |
| | | | 6 | 5 | | 4 | 327 | 5 |
| | | | 3 | 16 | | 5 | 300 | 10 |
| | | | 13 | | 1 | 5 | 244 | 4 |
| | | | 1 | 8 | | 4 | 275 | 10 |
| | | | 8 | 2 | 1 | 1 | 189 | 9a |
| | | | 9 | 7 | | 12 | 340 | 10b |
| | | | 1 | 1 | 1 | 10 | 302 | 8 |
| | | | | | | | — | — |
| | | | | | | | — | — |
| | | | 4 | 3 | 8 | 2 | 260 | 4 |
| | | | 4 | 9 | | 2 | 261 | 9 |
| | | | 5 | 4 | | 1 | 219 | 10 |
| | | | 18 | 3 | 1 | 3 | 251 | 8 |
| 12–1–49–2 | 17–5–58–1 | | 1 | 5 | 3 | 5 | 259 | 10 |
| 5–1–16–2 | | | 11 | 3 | | | 123 | 7 |
| 11–0–51–0 | | | 4 | 6 | | 1 | 320 | 9 |
| 4–0–23–0 | | | 6 | 7 | | | 237 | 10 |
| | | | 5 | 6 | 1 | 1 | 355 | 9 |
| | | | | 3 | | | 155 | 10 |
| | | | 4 | 7 | | 1 | 90 | 10 |
| 15–3–41–1 | 10.5–5–24–2 | 9–4–18–0 | 3 | 9 | 10 | 1 | 201 | 10 |
| 11.2–2–14–0 | 15–8–20–0 | 20–10–19–2 | 10 | 3 | 3 | 17 | 162 | 4c |
| | | | | 12 | 1 | | 154 | 10 |
| | | | 9 | 7 | | 3 | 238 | 10 |
| | | | 2 | 11 | | 4 | 322 | 9d |
| | | | 12 | 5 | 1 | 1 | 250 | 6e |
| | | | | 3 | | 13 | 250 | 5 |
| | | | 6 | 11 | | 3 | 201 | 10 |
| | | 3–1–6–1 | 12 | 3 | 2 | 1 | 171 | 9 |
| | | 8–4–17–1 | 5 | 1 | | 3 | 143 | 7 |
| | | | 1 | 3 | | 11 | 194 | 4f |
| | | | 1 | 1 | 1 | 2 | 105 | 8 |
| | | | 7 | 13 | 1 | 7 | 293 | 9 |
| | | | | 1 | | | 104 | 4 |
| | | 8–2–15–2 | 4 | 4 | 1 | 2 | 236 | 10 |
| | | 5–0–25–0 | 9 | 6 | | | 246 | 8 |
| | | 25–6–42–1 | | 8 | | 5 | 280 | 10 |
| | | 16–7–19–0 | 13 | 7 | | 2 | 225 | 6g |
| | | | 2 | 2 | | 5 | 175 | 10 |
| | | | 8 | 2 | 1 | | 148 | 10 |
| | | | 6 | 2 | | 1 | 157 | 9h |
| | | | 4 | 2 | | 3 | 226 | 9 |
| | | | 5 | 4 | 2 | | 314 | 8 |
| | | | 1 | 7 | | 5 | 274 | 5i |
| | | 4–0–25–0 | 4 | 9 | | 1 | 266 | 5 |
| | | | 6 | 11 | | 2 | 329 | 3j |
| | | | 9 | 7 | 1 | 2 | 327 | 7k |
| 58.2–7–194–5 av. 38.80 | 42.5–18–102–3 av. 34.00 | 98–34–186–7 av. 26.57 | | | | | | |

ABOVE: *Alec Stewart of Surrey. (Dave Cannon)* BELOW: *David Ward, Surrey. A promising young batsman. (Adrian Murrell)*

i M.A. Lynch 3–0–10–3
j M.A. Lynch 1–0–7–0; 9–1–36–0
k G.S. Clinton 5–0–30–0, C.J. Richards 4–0–20–0

| **Sussex C.C.C.** First-Class Matches – Batting, 1984 | v. Worcestershire (Worcester) 28–30 April | | v. Cambridge Univ. (Cambridge) 2–4 May | | v. Surrey (Hove) 9–11 May | | v. Hampshire (Hove) 23–25 May | | v. Middlesex (Lord's) 26–29 May | | v. Yorkshire (Sheffield) 30 May–1 June | | v. Northamptonshire (Horsham) 2–5 June | | v. Lancashire (Old Trafford) 9–12 June | | v. Kent (Tunbridge Wells) 13–15 June | | v. Surrey (Guildford) 16–19 June | | v. Glamorgan (Hove) 23–26 June | | v. Hampshire (Bournemouth) 27–29 June | | v. Kent (Hastings) 30 June–3 July | | v. Nottinghamshire (Trent Bridge) 7–10 July | |
|---|---|---|---|---|---|---|---|---|---|---|---|---|---|---|---|---|---|---|---|---|---|---|---|---|---|---|---|---|
| G.D. Mendis | 3 | 116 | 69 | — | 18 | — | 7 | 32 | 11 | — | 47 | — | 107 | 8* | 80 | 14 | 65 | — | | | | | | | 1 | 16 | 20 | 0 |
| D.K. Standing | 5* | — | | | 7 | — | | | | | | | | | | | | | | | | | | | | | | |
| J.R.T. Barclay | 23 | 0 | 46 | — | 51 | — | 7 | 10 | 73* | — | 28 | — | 23 | — | 0 | 49 | 7 | — | 76 | — | 28 | 16 | 0 | 6 | 0 | 10 | 28 | 1 |
| P.W.G. Parker | 40 | 15 | 100* | — | 39 | — | 5 | 11 | 4 | — | 67* | — | 76 | — | 92 | 43 | 0 | — | 3 | — | 19 | 31 | 14 | 35 | 14 | 16 | 17 | 56* |
| C.M. Wells | 8 | 9 | 2 | 61* | 7 | — | 6 | 203 | 27 | — | 5 | — | 127* | — | 24 | 13* | 31 | — | 38 | — | 138* | 1 | 8 | 14 | 51 | 81 | 0 | 2 |
| A.P. Wells | 19 | 0 | 1 | 53* | 6 | — | 1 | 29 | 9 | — | 56* | — | — | — | 57* | 8* | 93 | — | 6 | — | 24 | 37 | 28 | 12 | 8 | 6 | 19 | 54 |
| I.A. Greig | 19 | 32 | 106* | — | 48 | — | 34 | 19 | 37* | — | — | — | — | — | 4 | — | 2 | — | 5 | — | 5 | 12 | 14 | 2 | 15 | 27 | 29 | 22 |
| I.J. Gould | 33 | 16 | — | 22 | 21 | — | 2 | 25 | — | — | — | — | — | — | 26* | — | 9 | — | 20 | — | 1 | 24 | 32 | 2 | | | 0 | 8 |
| G.S. Le Roux | 8 | 16 | — | — | 50 | — | 0 | 9* | — | — | — | — | — | — | — | — | 17 | — | | | 2* | 7 | 4 | 28 | 18 | 0 | 0 | 0 |
| D.A. Reeve | 28* | 0 | — | — | 61 | — | 27 | 36 | — | — | | | — | — | 11 | — | | | 119 | — | 52 | 1* | 65 | 8 | 0 | 3 | 6 | 0 |
| C.E. Waller | 3 | 4* | | | 4* | — | 0* | 0* | | | — | — | — | — | — | — | 2 | — | 5* | — | — | 0 | 2* | 0* | 0* | 1* | 4* | 8 |
| A.M. Green | | | 22 | 4 | | | 14 | 49 | 4 | — | 47 | — | 13 | 7* | 1 | 20 | 26 | — | 48 | — | 0 | 81 | 31 | 5 | 29 | 25 | 30 | 13 |
| A.N. Jones | | | — | — | | | | | | | | | | | | | 0* | — | 7* | — | — | 0* | | | | | | |
| A.C.S. Pigott | | | | | | | | | — | — | — | — | | | | | | | | | | | | | | | | |
| D.J. Wood | | | | | | | | | | | | | | | | | | | 15 | — | | | 12 | 5 | | | | |
| D.J. Smith | | | | | | | | | | | | | | | | | | | | | | | | | 2 | 1 | | |
| N.J. Lenham | | | | | | | | | | | | | | | | | | | | | | | | | | | | |
| Byes | | 4 | 1 | | 9 | | | | | | 1 | | | | | 5 | | | 5 | | 4 | 3 | 10 | | | 1 | | 7 |
| Leg-byes | 4 | 2 | 3 | 1 | 7 | | 5 | 20 | 8 | | 10 | | 11 | 4 | 4 | | 3 | | 6 | | 7 | 9 | 3 | 7 | 1 | | 2 | 1 |
| Wides | 4 | | | | | | | 5 | | | 2 | | | | 1 | | 1 | | 1 | | 3 | | 5 | | | 1 | 4 | |
| No-balls | 10 | 8 | 9 | | 12 | | 1 | 2 | 5 | | 4 | | 1 | 2 | 3 | 1 | 1 | | 1 | | 17 | 5 | 4 | 3 | 4 | 4 | 2 | |
| Total | 207 | 222 | 359 | 141 | 340 | | 109 | 450 | 178 | | 267 | | 358 | 21 | 303 | 153 | 257 | | 355 | | 300 | 227 | 232 | 127 | 143 | 192 | 161 | 172 |
| Wickets | 9† | 9† | 5 | 2 | 10 | | 10 | 9 | 5 | | 4 | | 4 | 0 | 7 | 4 | 10 | | 9 | | 7 | 9 | 10 | 10 | 10 | 10 | 10 | 10 |
| Result | L | | D | | D | | D | | W | | D | | W | | W | | W | | D | | D | | L | | Tie | | L | |
| Points | 6 | | — | | 8 | | 4 | | 12 | | 6 | | 24 | | 23 | | 23 | | 7 | | 6 | | 4 | | 12 | | 5 | |

*Catches* 67 – I.J. Gould (ct 61/st 6); 23 – P.W.G. Parker; 22 – J.R.T. Barclay; 17 – I.A. Greig; 14 – D.A. Reeve; 13 – C.E. Waller and A.M. Green; 11 – A.P. Wells; 10 – D.J. Smith; 9 – G.D. Mendis; 5 – subs; 4 – G.S. Le Roux and C.M. Wells

*Gehan Mendis, Sussex. (Adrian Murrell)*

*Neil Fairbrother, Lancashire. (A.S.P.)*

| v. Leicestershire (Leicester) 11–13 July | | v. Warwickshire (Edgbaston) 14–17 July | | v. Somerset (Hove) 28–31 July | | v. Essex (Eastbourne) 4–7 August | | v. Warwickshire (Eastbourne) 8–10 August | | v. Derbyshire (Derby) 11–14 August | | v. Sri Lankans (Hove) 18–21 August | | v. Northamptonshire (Northampton) 22–24 August | | v. Middlesex (Hove) 25–28 August | | v. Gloucestershire (Hove) 29–31 August | | v. Nottinghamshire (Hove) 5–7 September | | v. Yorkshire (Hove) 8–11 September | | | *M* | *Inns* | *NOs* | *Runs* | *H/S* | *Av* |
|---|---|---|---|---|---|---|---|---|---|---|---|---|---|---|---|---|---|---|---|---|---|---|---|---|---|---|---|---|---|---|
| 39 | 7 | 24 | 5 | 209* | — | 21 | 8 | 9 | — | 9 | 18 | 16 | — | 16 | 5 | 6 | 19 | 2 | — | 28 | 8 | 78 | — | | 23 | 36 | 2 | 1141 | 209* | 33.55 |
| | | | | | | | | | | | | | | | | | | | | | | | | | 2 | 2 | 1 | 12 | 7 | 12.00 |
| 30 | 22 | 5 | 18* | — | — | 11 | 2 | 40 | — | 3 | 23 | 2* | — | 82 | — | 3 | 0 | — | — | 38 | — | — | — | | 26 | 35 | 3 | 761 | 82 | 23.78 |
| 19 | 44 | 2 | 35* | 69 | — | 114 | 33 | 122 | — | 0 | 1 | 181 | — | 2 | 33 | 11 | 19 | 140 | — | 101 | 4 | 65 | — | | 26 | 40 | 4 | 1692 | 181 | 47.00 |
| 0 | 1 | — | 0 | — | — | 11 | 22* | 132* | — | 0 | 60 | 27 | — | 13 | 25 | 10 | 42 | 121 | — | 14 | 30 | 25* | — | | 26 | 39 | 7 | 1389 | 203 | 43.40 |
| 2 | 105* | 33* | 3 | 41 | — | 0 | 32 | 0 | — | 7 | 0 | | | 127 | 64* | 1 | 11 | 1 | — | 59 | 20 | 13 | — | | 25 | 39 | 7 | 1045 | 127 | 32.65 |
| 40 | 34 | — | — | — | 0 | 20 | 0 | 0 | — | 11 | 2 | 50 | — | 4 | 64* | 31 | 18 | 29 | — | 39 | 27* | 12* | — | | 26 | 35 | 5 | 813 | 106* | 27.10 |
| 43 | 1* | — | — | — | — | 15 | 2 | 17* | — | 58 | 2 | | | 84 | — | 17 | 32 | 6* | — | 11 | — | | | | 23 | 27 | 4 | 529 | 84 | 23.00 |
| 5* | — | — | — | — | — | 2* | 8* | — | — | 6 | 0 | | | 34 | — | 5 | 30 | — | — | 68* | 4 | — | — | | 24 | 24 | 6 | 321 | 68* | 17.83 |
| 25 | 0 | — | — | — | 4* | 2 | 10 | — | — | 26 | 2* | — | — | | | | | — | — | | | — | — | | 21 | 22 | 4 | 486 | 119 | 27.00 |
| 0 | — | — | — | — | — | 2 | — | — | — | 0* | 5 | — | — | 0* | — | 16* | 0* | | | — | — | | | | 22 | 21 | 14 | 56 | 16* | 8.00 |
| 19 | 24 | 46 | 45 | 79 | 0* | 51 | 1 | 44 | — | 1 | 26 | 7 | — | 4 | 17 | 9 | 61 | 30 | — | 38 | 34 | 0 | — | | 24 | 40 | 2 | 1006 | 81 | 26.47 |
| | | | | | | | | | | | | — | — | 0* | — | 35 | 15 | — | — | 16 | — | — | — | | 10 | 7 | 4 | 73 | 35 | 24.33 |
| | | | | | | | | | | | | | | | | | | | | | | | | | 2 | | | | | — |
| | | | | | | | | | | | | | | | | | | | | | | | | | 2 | 3 | — | 32 | 15 | 10.66 |
| | | | | | | | | | | | | — | — | | | | | | | | | — | — | | 3 | 2 | — | 3 | 2 | 1.50 |
| | | | | | | | | | | | | 31 | — | | | | | | | | | | | | 1 | 1 | — | 31 | 31 | 31.00 |
| 4 | 5 | | 5 | 3 | | 1 | 2 | 6 | | 3 | | 1 | | 4 | 2 | 4 | 1 | | | 7 | 4 | 2 | | | | | | | | |
| 3 | 4 | 7 | 7 | 7 | | 6 | 10 | 16 | | 9 | 12 | 10 | | 8 | | 5 | 8 | 7 | | 10 | 9 | 2 | | | | | | | | |
| 1 | | 1 | | 3 | | | 1 | | | 1 | | 2 | | | 1 | 3 | 1 | 4 | | 1 | | 2 | | | | | | | | |
| 10 | 3 | 4 | 5 | 6 | | 2 | 2 | 3 | | 1 | | 18 | | 13 | 3 | 7 | 6 | 8 | | 6 | 1 | 3 | | | | | | | | |
| 240 | 250 | 122 | 123 | 417 | 4 | 259 | 133 | 389 | | 135 | 151 | 345 | | 391 | 214 | 163 | 263 | 348 | | 436 | 141 | 202 | | | | | | | | |
| 10 | 7 | 4 | 4 | 3 | 1 | 10 | 8 | 6 | | 10 | 10 | 6 | | 9 | 4 | 10 | 10 | 6 | | 9 | 6 | 4 | | | | | | | | |
| D | | D | | W | | D | | W | | L | | D | | L | | L | | W | | D | | D | | | | | | | | |
| 6 | | 3 | | 24 | | 7 | | 23 | | 2 | | — | | 6 | | 5 | | 23 | | 6 | | 4 | | | | | | | | |

† D.K. Standing retired hurt, absent hurt

2 – A.N. Jones
1 – N. J. Lenham and D.K. Standing

## Book Reviews

All books that have been received by the editor are reviewed in the following pages.

THE FIGHT FOR THE ASHES, 1982–83. *Chris Harte*: Cathedral End Publications: pp, 246
There is no more indefatigable character in cricket than Chris Harte. A man of unbounded enthusiasm and energy who hovers between his home in Adelaide and England so that he rarely misses a Test match between the two great rivals, his editorship of *Cathedral End*, the journal of the Australian Cricket Society, has made that publication one of the most exciting and interesting of periodicals. This study of the 1982–83 series is equally enthralling. It is the sanest, best balanced book on the tour and is accompanied by full and excellent statistics and some good illustrations. Chris Harte is now working on a history of the Sheffield Shield and I look forward to this as being one of the most important publishing ventures of the decade.

WORCESTERSHIRE COUNTY CRICKET CLUB – A PICTORIAL HISTORY. *M.D. Vockins*: Severn House: 128 pp, £6.95
No apologies are offered for reviewing a book which was first published four years ago, but which has only recently come to our notice. This is a delightful little history, well illustrated and lovingly told, with emphasis, rightly, on people. The Worcestershire secretary is passionately committed to his county, but the passion is tempered by humour and good sense and the double narrative in text and picture is most readable. No Worcestershire supporter should be without this book, nor, indeed, any who love the game. I look forward to a fuller, more detailed history by the same author in the not too distant future.

WORCESTERSHIRE C.C.C. YEAR BOOK, 1984: 136 pp, £1.00
We tend to take the county annuals too much for granted. This one, produced by the Year Book sub-committee led by secretary Mike Vockins, is an excellent publication. The comment on the season is balanced, the score-cards, reports and statistics are clear and the whole conception is ordered, attractive and complete. There is a sprinkling of nostalgia and a lovely piece on old and faithful followers, Annie Rowley and Horace Hopkins. Highly recommended.

TEST MATCH SPECIAL 2: *edited by Peter Baxter*: Queen Anne Press: 175 pp, £9.95
The pleasure that the Test match special team give to their millions of listeners in the course of an English summer is

| **Sussex C.C.C.**<br>First-Class Matches –<br>Bowling, 1984 | G.S. Le Roux | D.A. Reeve | I.A. Greig | C.M. Wells | C.E. Waller | P.W.G. Parker | A.N. Jones | J.R.T. Barclay | A.M. Green |
|---|---|---|---|---|---|---|---|---|---|
| *v.* Worcestershire (Worcester)<br>28–30 April | 16–4–53–2<br>11–2–42–1 | 14–0–61–2<br>11–2–41–1 | 25–5–91–4<br>9–1–32–1 | 7–1–37–1 | 12–5–23–0<br>2–0–10–1 | <br>0.2–0–4–0 | | | |
| *v.* Cambridge University<br>(Cambridge) 2–4 May | 12–4–24–1<br>6–4–11–1 | 21.1–10–22–5<br>14–7–23–0 | 27–13–37–2<br>7–3–17–0 | 8–1–16–1<br>9–5–13–1 | | | 10–1–29–0<br>14–10–11–0 | 15–8–20–1<br>21–11–29–1 | <br>12–2–25–1 |
| *v.* Surrey (Hove)<br>9–11 May | 17–6–41–4<br>13–7–19–0 | 10.2–47–2<br>15–7–37–1 | 21–6–46–3<br>20–7–50–1 | 12–5–20–1<br>10–2–51–0 | 8–4–8–0<br>10–3–27–0 | | | <br>2–0–7–0 | |
| *v.* Hampshire (Hove)<br>23–25 May | 21–4–61–3 | 20–7–63–2 | 24–4–112–3 | 12.2–4–25–1 | 17–3–23–0 | | | | |
| *v.* Middlesex (Lord's)<br>26–29 May | 7–1–23–1 | 11–4–35–2 | 11–1–31–1 | 11–1–37–3 | | | | 4–0–14–1 | |
| *v.* Yorkshire (Sheffield)<br>30 May–1 June | 20–4–49–1<br>9–3–20–0 | | 21–4–61–2<br>9–4–19–0 | 19–7–51–0<br>8–2–16–0 | 17–4–49–1<br>6–3–4–1 | | | 11–0–50–2 | |
| *v.* Northamptonshire (Horsham)<br>2–5 June | 10–4–35–1<br>5–0–22–0 | 9.5–2–23–3<br>26.3–9–54–1 | 16–3–39–1<br>18–3–41–2 | 4–1–8–0 | 25–11–40–2<br>20–11–22–3 | | | 26–5–47–3<br>17–7–32–4 | |
| *v.* Lancashire (Old Trafford)<br>9–12 June | 21–4–62–2<br>21–10–44–4 | 24–8–56–1<br>13–4–35–2 | 13–2–42–1<br>9–2–28–0 | 5–2–9–0<br>5–1–19–1 | 24.2–9–57–2<br>8.2–3–10–2 | | | 17–5–58–2<br>9–6–9–0 | |
| *v.* Kent (Tunbridge Wells)<br>13–15 June | 15–3–39–3<br>14.4–6–19–5 | | 17.2–6–39–4<br>10–2–50–2 | 8–3–21–0<br>9–1–30–0 | 1–1–0–0<br>3–2–5–0 | | 6–0–10–2<br>10–2–20–2 | | |
| *v.* Surrey (Guildford)<br>16–19 June | | 23–3–51–3<br>18–6–39–1 | 21–8–52–1<br>16–3–40–0 | 10–6–14–1<br>2–1–4–0 | 5–3–9–0<br>30–4–70–3 | <br>7–2–21–2 | 14–2–50–2<br>11–1–45–0 | 9–3–23–3<br>17–8–29–0 | <br>4–0–7–0 |
| *v.* Glamorgan (Hove)<br>23–26 June | 24–5–40–3<br>17–5–42–1 | 22–7–59–0<br>5–1–14–0 | 23–5–56–0<br>26–6–68–4 | <br>12–2–42–2 | 18–8–33–0<br>17–4–47–0 | | 14.5–2–55–2<br>11–3–17–1 | 22–4–44–1 | |
| *v.* Hampshire (Bournemouth)<br>27–29 June | 13–3–33–1<br>13–6–22–2 | 25–8–85–2<br>4–0–21–0 | 5–0–29–0<br>3–0–9–0 | 7–3–27–2<br>20–7–42–4 | 44–18–87–1<br>8–5–10–3 | | | 24.3–3–83–3 | |
| *v.* Kent (Hastings)<br>30 June–3 July | 15–5–30–2<br>25–7–69–3 | 10–5–13–0<br>18.5–6–28–2 | 8.3–1–15–2<br>23–4–87–2 | 13–4–25–5<br>16–4–35–3 | <br>3–0–11–0 | | | | |
| *v.* Nottinghamshire<br>(Trent Bridge) 7–10 July | 17–5–40–2<br>15–3–46–1 | 22–8–44–1<br>9–1–35–1 | 19–7–47–1<br>5–0–28–1 | 6–0–24–0 | 21–10–47–2<br>18–1–52–1 | | | 10.3–4–19–3<br>26–6–70–1 | |
| *v.* Leicestershire (Leicester)<br>11–13 July | 13–5–25–1<br>23.5–6–48–1 | 18–5–39–4<br>7–2–17–0 | 9.5–3–15–3<br>4–0–26–0 | <br>13–7–26–0 | 20–9–28–2<br>34–11–75–6 | | | <br>29–11–52–1 | |
| *v.* Warwickshire (Edgbaston)<br>14–17 July | 6–2–16–2 | 17–7–31–0 | 12–2–42–1<br>11–2–35–1 | 12–4–33–0<br>12–2–23–0 | 34–10–72–4<br>17–3–58–3 | | | 14–3–31–0<br>9–0–56–1 | |
| *v.* Somerset (Hove)<br>28–31 July | 17–1–67–2<br>23–6–57–6 | 19–4–41–1<br>21–7–58–2 | 22–6–50–1<br>3–1–18–0 | 17–5–52–4<br>13–5–38–1 | 8–3–18–1 | | | <br>5–3–5–1 | |
| *v.* Essex (Eastbourne)<br>4–7 August | 17–3–42–3<br>7.4–1–13–0 | 19.3–9–35–4<br>3–0–12–0 | 11–1–36–0<br>9–2–30–1 | 17–8–24–2<br>4–0–19–0 | 17–6–52–1 | | | <br>9–1–31–1 | |
| *v.* Warwickshire (Eastbourne)<br>8–10 August | 11–2–48–1<br>5.1–1–11–2 | 19–8–28–4<br>13–6–23–2 | 3–0–3–0<br>5–2–14–0 | 12–2–37–3<br>27–9–59–5 | 23.5–14–26–2<br>20–12–18–1 | | | <br>6–5–1–0 | |
| *v.* Derbyshire (Derby)<br>11–14 August | 14–3–72–0 | 37.3–3–130–4 | 16–3–58–2 | 19–7–46–1 | 33–7–100–3 | | | 16–3–54–0 | |
| *v.* Sri Lankans (Hove)<br>18–20 August | | 13–4–26–1<br>8–4–10–0 | 17–4–53–1<br>15–7–36–3 | 17–3–50–4<br>15–6–36–3 | <br>19–7–52–2 | | 13.4–2–48–3<br>19.4–2–72–2 | <br>8–3–22–0 | |
| *v.* Northamptonshire<br>(Northampton) 22–24 August | 5–0–23–0<br>7–0–45–0 | | 8–3–20–2<br>7–0–42–1 | 15–2–58–0<br>8–1–53–2 | 30–11–74–2<br>16–3–71–0 | <br>1–0–7–0 | 10–2–41–1<br>2–0–22–0 | 27.4–5–80–0<br>18–2–60–1 | |
| *v.* Middlesex (Hove)<br>25–28 August | 17.2–3–67–4<br>8–1–25–1 | | 20–4–63–3<br>7–1–23–0 | 20–4–66–2<br>12–3–35–2 | | <br>2.2–0–8–0 | 7–1–27–1<br>12–2–46–0 | <br>13–2–31–0 | <br>2–0–9–0 |
| *v.* Gloucestershire (Hove)<br>29–31 August | 11–0–40–2<br>16.4–5–24–4 | <br>6–2–13–0 | 15.2–4–50–4<br>12–2–24–1 | 10–2–27–3<br>5–1–22–0 | | | 5–1–15–1<br>15–5–29–5 | | |
| *v.* Nottinghamshire (Hove)<br>5–7 September | 16–1–58–2<br>5–1–23–1 | | 6–1–30–0 | 16–6–49–0<br>5–1–31–1 | 25–10–55–4<br>4–3–6–0 | 0.3–0–0–0 | 10–3–28–1<br>3–1–19–1 | 16–6–37–2<br>2–0–8–1 | |
| *v.* Yorkshire (Hove)<br>8–11 September | 12–4–35–1<br>11–4–22–1 | 15–2–46–1<br>10–5–25–0 | 20–4–56–0<br>8–1–23–0 | 15–5–46–0 | | | 10–0–31–0<br>10–4–21–1 | 10.2–2–18–3<br>3–1–3–0 | |
| | 604.2–154–<br>1647–78<br>*av.* 21.11 | 572.4–175–<br>1420–55<br>*av.* 25.81 | 648–153–<br>1913–62<br>*av.* 30.85 | 497.2–146–<br>1396–59<br>*av.* 23.66 | 618.3–221–<br>1349–53<br>*av.* 25.45 | 11.1–2–<br>40–2<br>*av.* 20.00 | 208.1–44–<br>636–25<br>*av.* 25.44 | 417–117–<br>1023–36<br>*av.* 28.41 | 18–2–<br>41–1<br>*av.* 41.00 |

a C. Maynard retired hurt, absent hurt b R.A. Woolmer, retired hurt

| A.C.S. Pigott | Byes | Leg-byes | Wides | No-balls | Total | Wkts |
|---|---|---|---|---|---|---|
| | 6 | 4 | 2 | 4 | 281 | 10 |
| | 1 | 18 | 2 | 1 | 151 | 4 |
| | 5 | 3 | | | 156 | 10 |
| | | 1 | 1 | 1 | 132 | 4 |
| | 4 | 2 | 1 | 10 | 179 | 10 |
| | | 4 | 1 | 9 | 205 | 2 |
| | | 4 | 2 | 8 | 298 | 10 |
| 11–2–24–1 | 1 | 11 | | 1 | 177 | 9 |
| 18–3–58–1 | 6 | 10 | 1 | 7 | 342 | 8 |
| 3–0–14–0 | | 4 | | 3 | 80 | 1 |
| | 2 | 4 | | 2 | 200 | 10 |
| | 2 | 2 | 3 | | 178 | 10 |
| | | 6 | 1 | 5 | 296 | 9a |
| | 1 | 9 | | 4 | 159 | 9 |
| | | 2 | | 3 | 114 | 10 |
| | | 6 | 10 | 2 | 142 | 9b |
| | 1 | 3 | 1 | 4 | 208 | 10 |
| | 2 | 5 | | | 262 | 6 |
| | | 3 | 3 | 7 | 300 | 7 |
| | | 6 | 1 | 9 | 243 | 8 |
| | | 11 | | 1 | 356 | 10 |
| | | 6 | | 1 | 111 | 10 |
| | | 5 | | 4 | 92 | 10 |
| | 1 | 3 | 2 | 7 | 243 | 10 |
| | | 11 | 1 | | 233 | 10 |
| | 3 | 4 | 3 | 1 | 242 | 5 |
| | 4 | 4 | | | 115 | 10 |
| | 2 | 6 | | 6 | 258 | 8 |
| | | 1 | | 1 | 227 | 8 |
| | | | | 1 | 173 | 5 |
| | | 5 | | 2 | 235 | 10 |
| | | 9 | | | 185 | 10 |
| | | 7 | | 1 | 197 | 10 |
| | 2 | 6 | 1 | 1 | 115 | 2 |
| | | 7 | 1 | | 150 | 10 |
| | 8 | 3 | | | 137 | 10 |
| | 9 | 4 | | 2 | 475 | 10 |
| | | 11 | | 5 | 193 | 10 |
| | | 3 | 3 | 1 | 235 | 10 |
| | | 5 | 1 | 1 | 303 | 5 |
| | | 4 | | 2 | 306 | 4 |
| | | 7 | 1 | 12 | 243 | 10 |
| | | 3 | | 6 | 186 | 3 |
| | | 1 | | 4 | 137 | 10 |
| | 3 | 1 | 6 | 8 | 130 | 10 |
| | 17 | 15 | 3 | 8 | 300 | 9 |
| | 4 | 1 | | 1 | 93 | 4 |
| | 5 | 6 | 1 | 6 | 250 | 5 |
| | 2 | | | 2 | 98 | 2 |
| 32–5–96–2 *av.* 48.00 | | | | | | |

immeasurable, and it was inevitable that their achievements should be recorded in print. The first *Test Match Special* book was a great success as it gave devotees of the broadcasts an opportunity to purchase a souvenir and to feel closer to the commentators. This second publication, however, has less reason for being.

It covers the tour of India by Fletcher's team which now seems long in the past and the tour of Australia and the World Cup and the series against India and Pakistan in 1982, but it must be said that all these series have been covered far better elsewhere and this hardly represents a standard reference work.

The warmth and friendliness that exudes from the broadcasts is essentially in the oral tradition, and, when an attempt is made to transcribe it to print, it takes on a self-indulgent and self-congratulatory tone. Essentially, the book is very uneven, but one should first applaud Peter Baxter, not only for what he achieves on the radio, but what he has done here in organising very limited material.

There are some sections which lift themselves above the others, Peter Baxter's own contributions among them, and John Arlott's *History of Test Match Special* is worth the rest of the book put together.

The publication just about survives, and I am sure it will give some people a lot of pleasure, which is the important thing, but I am equally sure that *two* is enough.

THE COMPLETE WHO'S WHO OF TEST CRICKETERS. *Christopher Martin-Jenkins (with research by Jim Coldham)*: Orbis: 487 pp, £12.50

This book was first published in 1980 and has now been completely revised and brought up to date so that Sri Lanka now finds inclusion as well as all others who have made their Test debut since the book was first published.

There are in any serious cricket library three or four essential books. *The Bibliography of Cricket*, *The Wisden Book of Test Cricket*, *The Wisden Book of Cricket Records* and *The Book of One-Day Internationals* are essential works of reference, but none is more essential nor more readable than *The Complete Who's Who of Test Cricket*. Its strength is that it is so much more than a reference book. You may turn to find some statistical data and you end by reading a brief, but warm and accurate character study. You are left with the feeling that each man whose name appears in this book has been carefully considered so that V.W.C. Jupp is not merely an all-rounder who played eight times for England in the 1920s but 'a short, prematurely bald man ... with broad shoulders, long arms, great strength, and a rough humour'.

It is a rich book, beautifully produced and excellent value. It is a book to be cherished.

A WORD FROM ARLOTT. *edited by David Rayvern Allen*: Pelham Books: 240 pp, £9.95

This is a collection of John Arlott's broadcasts, cricket commentaries and writings which have been selected and edited with great sensitivity and intelligence by David Rayvern Allen, a friend of Arlott's and one who has worked with him at the BBC. Like any collection of this nature, some pieces read better than others. There is the occasional transcript of a radio commentary which does not transfer well to the printed page, but these are far outnumbered by the quality of many others. Some of the passages, like *Packing*

**Warwickshire C.C.C.**
First-Class Matches – Batting, 1984

| | v. Northamptonshire (Edgbaston) 28–30 April | | v. Surrey (Edgbaston) 5–8 May | | v. Cambridge Univ. (Cambridge) 9–11 May | | v. Lancashire (Nuneaton) 23–25 May | | v. Worcestershire (Edgbaston) 26–29 May | | v. Nottinghamshire (Edgbaston) 30 May–1 June | | v. Essex (Ilford) 9–12 June | |
|---|---|---|---|---|---|---|---|---|---|---|---|---|---|---|
| T.A. Lloyd | 110 | 24 | 32 | 50 | 21 | — | 76 | 13 | 2 | 14 | | | 72 | 4 |
| K.D. Smith | 33 | 2 | 33 | 3 | 27 | — | 3 | 1 | | | 41 | 22* | | |
| A.I. Kallicharran | 200* | 117* | 17 | 8 | 180 | — | 101 | 12 | 31 | 11 | 116 | 19* | 100 | 0 |
| D.L. Amiss | 2 | 32 | 19 | 3 | 54 | — | 34* | 80 | 15 | 84* | 100* | — | 7 | 24 |
| G.W. Humpage | 53 | 86* | 12 | 15 | 21 | — | 27* | 67 | 100* | 27 | 42 | — | 21 | 32 |
| G.J. Lord | 1 | — | 55 | 0 | 4 | — | | | | | | | | |
| A.M. Ferreira | 3* | — | 19 | 20 | 0 | — | — | 43* | 0 | — | — | — | 36 | 11 |
| P.A. Smith | — | — | | | | | | | 5 | 81 | 18 | 6 | 22 | 26 |
| C. Lethbridge | — | — | 27 | 32 | 46 | — | | | | | — | — | | |
| G.C. Small | — | 26 | 14 | 27* | 0* | — | — | — | 11 | — | — | — | 12 | 0 |
| N. Gifford | — | — | 28* | 6 | — | — | — | — | 5* | — | — | — | 1 | 0 |
| W.A. Morton | | | 6 | 13* | | | | | | | | | | |
| C.M. Old | | | | | 10 | — | — | 10* | 3 | — | — | — | 43 | 4 |
| Asif Din | | | | | | | — | 3 | 1 | 35* | 10* | — | 0 | 1 |
| R.G.D. Willis | | | | | | | — | — | — | — | | | 4* | 4* |
| S. Wall | | | | | | | | | | | | | | |
| R.I.H.B. Dyer | | | | | | | | | | | | | | |
| D.A. Thorne | | | | | | | | | | | | | | |
| G.A. Tedstone | | | | | | | | | | | | | | |
| Byes | 6 | | 1 | 8 | 4 | | | | 8 | | | | 4 | 2 |
| Leg-byes | 13 | 8 | 8 | 2 | 2 | | 5 | 6 | 11 | 11 | 11 | 1 | 9 | 9 |
| Wides | | | | 1 | 1 | | 1 | 4 | 3 | | | 1 | 1 | |
| No-balls | 17 | 6 | 4 | 1 | | | 6 | 6 | 5 | 1 | | | 2 | 2 |
| Total | 438 | 301 | 275 | 189 | 370 | | 253 | 245 | 200 | 284 | 338 | 49 | 334 | 119 |
| Wickets | 5 | 4 | 10 | 9† | 9 | | 3 | 6 | 8 | 4 | 4 | 1 | 10 | 10 |
| Result | D | | D | | W | | D | | D | | D | | L | |
| Points | 5 | | 7 | | — | | 5 | | 5 | | 5 | | 8 | |

| | v. Leicestershire (Leicester) 13–15 June | | v. Middlesex (Lord's) 16–19 June | | v. Somerset (Edgbaston) 23–26 June | | v. Northamptonshire (Northampton) 27–29 June | | v. Gloucestershire (Edgbaston) 30 June–3 July | | v. Derbyshire (Chesterfield) 7–10 July | | v. Worcestershire (Worcester) 11–13 July | |
|---|---|---|---|---|---|---|---|---|---|---|---|---|---|---|
| T.A. Lloyd | | | | | | | | | | | | | | |
| K.D. Smith | 93 | 17 | 8 | 11 | 77 | 15 | 0 | 32 | 17 | 6 | 17 | 2 | 2 | 8 |
| A.I. Kallicharran | 155 | 0 | 28 | 14 | 6 | 5 | 26 | 65 | 40 | 62 | 14 | 87 | 22 | 25 |
| D.L. Amiss | 26* | 1 | 0 | 1 | 80 | 43 | 121 | 4 | 87 | 25* | 86 | 55* | 14 | 101* |
| G.W. Humpage | 31* | 41 | 8 | 2 | 44 | 24 | 55 | 27* | 16 | 31* | 205 | 1 | 2 | 1 |
| G.J. Lord | | | | | | | | | | | | | | |
| A.M. Ferreira | — | 7 | 21 | 2 | 11* | 61 | 76* | — | 11 | — | 46 | 12* | 39 | — |
| P.A. Smith | 4 | 32 | 80 | 4 | 31* | 38 | 33 | 17* | 2 | — | 12 | 16 | 11 | 8* |
| C. Lethbridge | — | 4 | 24 | 25* | | | 41 | — | 19 | — | | | 27 | — |
| G.C. Small | — | 25 | 18 | 0 | — | 14 | 9 | — | 24 | — | 1* | 40 | 12 | — |
| N. Gifford | — | 17 | 16 | 12 | — | 10* | 6* | — | 8* | — | — | — | 2* | — |
| W.A. Morton | | | | | | | | | | | | | | |
| C.M. Old | | | | | — | 29* | 4 | — | 1 | — | 39 | — | 70 | — |
| Asif Din | — | 0 | | | | | | | | | | | | |
| R.G.D. Willis | | | | | — | 5 | | | | | — | — | | |
| S. Wall | — | 12* | 4* | 0 | | | | | | | | | | |
| R.I.H.B. Dyer | | | 2 | 47 | 26 | 2 | 1 | 55 | 11 | 28 | 6 | 53 | 24 | 64 |
| D.A. Thorne | | | | | | | | | | | | | | |
| G.A. Tedstone | | | | | | | | | | | | | | |
| Byes | 4 | 1 | 4 | 2 | 3 | 1 | 2 | | 4 | 5 | 4 | | 7 | 6 |
| Leg-byes | 3 | 2 | 7 | 1 | 21 | 5 | 7 | 1 | 8 | 10 | 9 | 2 | 4 | 6 |
| Wides | 1 | | | | | | 1 | | | | 1 | 1 | 5 | |
| No-balls | 13 | 2 | 11 | 1 | 2 | | 18 | 7 | 4 | 2 | 4 | 10 | 11 | 4 |
| Total | 330 | 161 | 231 | 122 | 301 | 252 | 400 | 208 | 252 | 169 | 444 | 279 | 252 | 223 |
| Wickets | 3 | 10 | 10 | 10 | 5 | 9‡ | 9 | 4 | 10 | 3 | 8 | 6 | 10 | 4 |
| Result | L | | W | | L | | D | | W | | D | | D | |
| Points | 5 | | 22 | | 6 | | 7 | | 23 | | 6 | | 5 | |

*Catches* 66 – G.W. Humpage (ct 56/st 10); 17 – A.I. Kallicharran; 16 – D.L. Amiss; 12 – A.M. Ferreira; 10 – N. Gifford and P.A. Smith; 8 – C.M. Old; 7 – R.I.H.B. Dyer; 6 – C. Lethbridge and G.C. Small; 3 – G.J. Lord, T.A. Lloyd, K.D. Smith and W.A. Morton

*My Cricket Bag* from *Holidays and Happy Days*, 1949, are essays of great interest, full of warmth, humour and essential humanity, and these are not restricted to the theme of cricket. There is a personal tribute to Ian Mackay, pieces on cheese, wine and the collecting of books, and a delightful short story, *Ain't Half a Bloomin' Game*. There is poetry, conversations with authors like Simenon and a comment on E.M. Forster. In spite of the failure of some of the commentaries to come alive on the printed page, it all adds to a remarkably fine book.

There are none who are close to cricket who are not in debt to John Arlott in some way. His kindness and compassion are the qualities which have throbbed through his voice and given pleasure and understanding to millions. The strength of this collection is that it captures these qualities.

This is an important work. It is finely produced and well illustrated. It is a credit to editor and publisher, and it is a book to treasure for the warmth of the man whom it represents.

IMRAN. THE AUTOBIOGRAPHY OF IMRAN KHAN WITH PAT MURPHY: Pelham Books: 164 pp, £7.95

There is an inevitability that the leading cricketers of our time will produce an autobiography. Indeed, we are lucky if they restrict themselves to one, so that Imran's comes as no surprise. He has lived through some stormy times and the book reveals some of this tempestuousness, but, ultimately, it lacks self-evaluation.

There are some relevant comments on the organisation of cricket in Pakistan and on Imran's championing of Abdul Qadir. There is an assessment of Imran's relationship with the Karachi press which seems a balanced one, but one is less impressed with his blinkered view of Arnold Long who did much for Sussex (and Surrey) and who was also a wicket-keeper of quality. Such criticism as Imran makes of Long stems from a limited appraisal of the professional game in England and one would have hoped that since he became an outstanding captain of Pakistan, his view would have become broader and his assessments more compassionate. Perhaps, after his recent experiences in Australia and the World Cup, he will now have a more appreciative reponse to the efforts of Mushtaq Mohammad who may not have been a very good captain but certainly did not have the easiest of jobs.

It is good to note the debt he feels to Sarfraz and his appreciation of Wasim Bari. Not unexpectedly, he is critical of umpires and of England Test selectors. He fails to understand why there is so much hostility to overseas players

| v. Sussex (Edgbaston) 14–17 July | v. Hampshire (Edgbaston) 25–27 July | v. Kent (Edgbaston) 28–31 July | v. Hampshire (Southampton) 4–7 August | v. Sussex (Eastbourne) 8–10 August | v. Yorkshire (Leeds) 11–14 August | v. Lancashire (Old Trafford) 18–21 August | v. Glamorgan (Edgbaston) 22–24 August | v. Nottinghamshire (Trent Bridge) 25–28 August | v. Sri Lankans (Edgbaston) 29–31 August | v. Glamorgan (Cardiff) 5–7 September | v. Leicestershire (Edgbaston) 8–11 September | M | Inns | NOs | Runs | H/S | Av |
|---|---|---|---|---|---|---|---|---|---|---|---|---|---|---|---|---|---|
| | | | | | | | | | | | | 6 | 11 | — | 418 | 110 | 38.00 |
| 0 34 | | | 39 18 | 1 0 | 9 0 | 1 — | 13 19 | 4 11 | 13 54 | 2 4 | | 21 | 40 | 1 | 692 | 93 | 17.74 |
| 5 83* | 84 — | 20 29 | 9 59* | 17 41 | 0 17 | 1 117 | 0 25 | 22 25 | 79* 30 | 155 6 | 16 0 | 26 | 50 | 6 | 2301 | 200 | 52.29 |
| 94 2 | 23 98* | 68 35* | 69 35 | 19 1 | 32 54 | 118 38 | 26 1 | 70 62 | 29 19 | 11 115* | 0 122 | 26 | 50 | 10 | 2239 | 122 | 55.97 |
| 14 — | 101 5 | 56 — | 4 16 | 0 15 | 112 77 | 4 61* | 22 89 | 89 3 | 10* 47 | 127 — | 8 40 | 26 | 47 | 8 | 1891 | 205 | 48.48 |
| | | | | | | | | | | | 6 17 | 4 | 6 | — | 83 | 55 | 13.83 |
| 10 7* | 54 6* | 62* — | 21* 6* | 16 5 | 2 18 | 6 0* | 16 0 | 12 30 | — 11 | 14* — | 36* 27 | 26 | 39 | 13 | 777 | 76* | 29.88 |
| 57 20 | 69 17 | 0 52 | 54 21 | 8 14* | 4 30 | 89 4 | 13 0 | 1 24 | — 8 | 74 — | 17 18 | 23 | 41 | 4 | 1040 | 89 | 28.10 |
| 14* — | 17 — | 6 — | | | | | 23 4 | 0 11 | — 4* | | | 15 | 17 | 3 | 324 | 46 | 23.14 |
| | 41* — | 14* — | 0 — | 27* 30 | 6* — | 0 — | 2 15 | 4 3 | — — | 9 — | 3 13* | 25 | 30 | 8 | 400 | 41* | 18.18 |
| — — | 4 — | — — | 1* — | 3 2 | 0 — | 1* — | 7* 10 | 3 0* | | — — | 0 4 | 25 | 24 | 10 | 146 | 28* | 10.42 |
| | | — — | 0 — | 1 4 | | 1 — | 10 4* | | | — — | | 7 | 8 | 2 | 39 | 13* | 6.50 |
| 3 14 | 31 — | — — | 22 — | 14 0 | 52 13* | 9 — | | 21* 1 | | | | 18 | 21 | 4 | 393 | 70 | 23.11 |
| | | | | | | | | | | | 25 24 | 6 | 9 | 2 | 99 | 35* | 14.14 |
| | | | | | | | | | | | | 5 | 3 | 2 | 13 | 5 | 13.00 |
| 2* — | 1 19 | | | | | | | | — — | 4* — | 0 5 | 7 | 9 | 4 | 47 | 19 | 9.40 |
| 26 12 | 0 76 | 49 75* | 61 27 | 36 14 | 10 0 | 0 84 | 46 8 | 24 26 | 80 60 | 23 106* | 7 18 | 18 | 36 | 2 | 1187 | 106* | 34.91 |
| | | | | | 49 20* | | | | | | | 1 | 2 | 1 | 69 | 49 | 69.00 |
| | | | | | | | | | — 0* | | | 1 | 1 | 1 | 0 | 0* | — |
| | 7 | 4 | | 8 | | 5 | | 2 | 2 | 3 1 | 3 | †W.A. Morton retired hurt | | | | | |
| 1 | 30 5 | 16 2 | 6 8 | 7 3 | 1 4 | 2 13 | 6 6 | 3 4 | 12 6 | 4 2 | 1 8 | ‡C.M. Old retired hurt | | | | | |
| | 1 1 | 2 | | 1 | | | | 3 1 | 5 | 1 | 2 3 | | | | | | |
| 1 1 | 9 | 4 | 9 4 | | 8 9 | 12 5 | 10 1 | 3 4 | 14 5 | 11 8 | 9 4 | | | | | | |
| 227 173 | 472 227 | 301 193 | 295 194 | 150 137 | 285 242 | 244 327 | 194 182 | 261 205 | 242 246 | 438 242 | 133 303 | | | | | | |
| 8 5 | 10 4 | 6 2 | 9 5 | 10 10 | 10 7 | 10 4 | 10 10 | 10 10 | 3 7 | 7 2 | 10 10 | | | | | | |
| D | W | W | D | L | W | W | L | L | D | D | L | | | | | | |
| 3 | 23 | 22 | 4 | 2 | 23 | 22 | 4 | 5 | — | 6 | 4 | | | | | | |

2 – R.G.D. Willis, Asif Din and G.A. Tedstone (ct 1/st 1)

1 – S. Wall, D. Thorne and sub

and he considers 'English first-class cricket is not sold enough to the public', 'it just doesn't appeal to the right age group'. He may want to alter that opinion in twenty years time.

Obviously, Imran has little idea of the efforts that many people make on behalf of the game in England, and none of them takes as much out of the game as he does. All this I suppose means that the book does demand a reaction, but one senses that this more due to Pat Murphy's admirable clarity and organisation of Imran's material than to the limited views of the subject himself.

IT NEVER RAINS . . . A CRICKETER'S LOT. *Peter Roebuck*: Allen & Unwin: 151 pp, £7.95

This is the third attempt at the diary of a cricket season to be published in the past four years and it is undoubtedly the best of the three. Having said that, Peter Roebuck's second book is far from totally satisfying. There is a certain lack of joy, too much niggling complaint. Those who walk when they know they are out are fools we are told, yet other counties are criticised for appealing too much and evidently some umpires do not give lbw's. In between the rather superior carping there is some shrewd comment and intelligent observation, but there is a lot of tedium. It is a book that stirs a response, however, and that cannot be bad.

DOUGLAS JARDINE, SPARTAN CRICKETER. *Christopher Douglas*: Allen & Unwin: 206 pp, £9.95

This is an excellent biography. It is balanced, broad, well-researched and eminently readable. It traces Jardine's life in full and avoids none of the controversies. We are presented with an introvert who had steely determination. We come close to the man and we feel the worth of an honest human being who did not compromise his integrity. Neither does the book. In the spate of the books that were published to celebrate the fiftieth anniversary of body-line, this was the best and most important. It should be read by serious students of the history of the game.

CHAMPIONS. *edited Peter Edwards*: pub. Essex C.C.C/Access: 60 pp, £1.50

Issued by Essex County Cricket Club as a record of their Schweppes County Championship win in 1983, this is a splendid pictorial record and excellent value at £1.50. It is a fine souvenir for followers of the county.

SLICES OF CRICKET. *Peter Roebuck*: Unwin Paperbacks: 140 pp, £2.50

This is the paperback edition of the book reviewed last year. Entertaining, with some interesting essays.

| **Warwickshire C.C.C.** First-Class Matches – Bowling, 1984 | G.C. Small | A.M. Ferreira | N. Gifford | C. Lethbridge | P.A. Smith | C.M. Old | T.A. Lloyd | A.I. Kallicharran | R.G.D. Willis |
|---|---|---|---|---|---|---|---|---|---|
| *v.* Northamptonshire (Edgbaston) 28–30 April | 20–3–83–0<br>6–1–28–2 | 26–7–54–2<br>11–2–39–0 | 27–7–75–1<br>12–3–12–0 | 21–3–75–2<br>10–0–45–1 | 12–0–74–0<br>4–1–21–0 | | | | |
| *v.* Surrey (Edgbaston) 5–8 May | 25.3–8–52–3<br>16–5–50–4 | 20–4–54–1<br>11–2–26–2 | 33–12–62–4<br>18–6–37–1 | 18–0–61–2<br>3–1–11–0 | | | | | |
| *v.* Cambridge University (Cambridge) 9–11 May | 3–1–4–0<br>11–2–26–1 | 17.1–5–27–1<br>12–7–10–2 | 27–10–52–4<br>27–9–44–3 | 16–3–34–2<br>15.4–3–41–4 | | 16–3–42–2<br>12–6–16–0 | 4–1–6–1<br>1–1–0–0 | 10–5–12–0 | |
| *v.* Lancashire (Nuneaton) 23–25 May | 15–2–53–1<br>7–2–17–0 | 24–9–50–2<br>3–1–7–1 | 28–11–69–1<br>12–4–30–1 | | | 29–7–88–1<br>9–2–21–1 | <br>3–0–35–0 | | 21–5–75–0<br>7–1–19–2 |
| *v.* Worcestershire (Edgbaston) 26–29 May | 11–4–21–1<br>9–1–31–1 | 24–5–59–1 | 2–2–0–0<br>8–2–18–0 | | <br>8–0–41–4 | 27–11–52–5 | | | 13–5–18–0<br>8–2–24–0 |
| *v.* Nottinghamshire (Edgbaston) 30 May–1 June | 18–4–37–1 | 18–0–51–1 | 27–11–44–0 | 10–1–47–0 | 9.4–2–35–2 | 23–4–46–0 | | | |
| *v.* Essex (Ilford) 9–12 June | <br>22–5–49–2 | 13.2–2–44–4<br>24–7–71–2 | 7–3–6–3<br>47–9–144–4 | | <br>9–3–31–1 | 17–10–26–2<br>4–1–20–0 | | | 11–4–29–1<br>14–4–28–1 |
| *v.* Leicestershire (Leicester) 13–15 June | 11–1–46–1<br>16–2–55–1 | 29–6–68–1<br>15–2–44–2 | 13–5–28–0<br>11–5–18–0 | 20–3–66–1<br>16–2–55–3 | 12–0–74–0<br>6–0–30–1 | | | | |
| *v.* Middlesex (Lord's) 16–19 June | 11–2–47–3<br>14.3–1–41–5 | 8.3–2–22–2<br>13–3–26–4 | <br>4–3–2–1 | 10–2–35–4 | 4–1–15–1<br>4–0–20–0 | | | | |
| *v.* Somerset (Edgbaston) 23–26 June | 17–2–44–1<br>10–1–32–1 | 18–3–51–1<br>11.5–0–76–2 | 27–5–74–1<br>27–3–135–2 | | 4–0–17–0<br>4–0–23–0 | 25–6–80–3<br>16–4–27–0 | | | 17–1–69–2<br>7–1–8–0 |
| *v.* Northamptonshire (Northampton) 27–29 June | 22–5–65–1<br>8–0–37–0 | 24–5–87–4<br>11–1–48–3 | 36–8–68–0<br>21–4–79–5 | | 12–2–35–3<br>5–0–34–0 | 15–3–57–0<br>11–1–33–0 | | | |
| *v.* Gloucestershire (Edgbaston) 30 June–3 July | 19–2–85–3<br>15–4–33–2 | 12–5–38–1<br>17.2–4–42–3 | | 6.4–0–22–1 | 8–3–30–1<br>4–0–23–0 | 26–10–58–4<br>25–11–45–4 | | | |
| *v.* Derbyshire (Chesterfield) 7–10 July | 18.5–3–64–1<br>10–1–36–2 | 25–3–80–3<br>5–1–17–0 | 22–8–81–2<br>12–4–27–1 | | 4–0–21–0<br>5–0–9–1 | 18–4–64–0<br>4–2–3–0 | | | 22–2–78–2<br>8–2–32–1 |
| *v.* Worcestershire (Worcester) 11–13 July | 24–6–76–2 | 39–5–137–1 | 25–9–46–1 | 8–1–45–0 | 11–1–40–1 | 22–5–71–2 | | | |
| *v.* Sussex (Edgbaston) 14–17 July | | <br>10–0–32–1 | 11–5–22–1<br>14–5–17–2 | 12.3–2–32–0<br>2–1–4–0 | 5–0–28–1<br>5–1–16–0 | <br>9–3–14–0 | | | |
| *v.* Hampshire (Edgbaston) 25–27 July | 19–3–59–2<br>14.5–6–35–4 | 19–5–52–1<br>11–2–32–2 | 18–3–54–0<br>13–8–24–2 | 17–1–70–2 | | 13–2–56–0<br>16–5–59–2 | | | |
| *v.* Kent (Edgbaston) 28–31 July | 23–6–77–2<br>21–4–56–4 | 30–9–91–1<br>25–9–27–4 | 7–3–15–1<br>2–0–5–0 | 25–6–68–2<br>8–5–14–2 | | 18–4–59–0 | | | |
| *v.* Hampshire (Southampton) 4–7 August | 10–0–45–0<br>9–1–31–0 | 8–1–16–0<br>8–1–28–1 | 26–9–61–2<br>11–4–24–1 | | | 11–2–23–1<br>9–2–16–2 | | | |
| *v.* Sussex (Eastbourne) 8–10 August | 19–3–70–0 | 23–3–78–0 | 48–18–102–4 | | | 16–2–47–1 | | | |
| *v.* Yorkshire (Leeds) 11–14 August | 8–2–37–1<br>16–4–60–2 | 21.3–2–61–4 | <br>23.3–8–54–2 | | | 29–8–53–5<br>20–2–46–6 | | | |
| *v.* Lancashire (Old Trafford) 18–21 August | 18–2–63–3<br>11–2–42–5 | 29–4–98–3<br>12–1–39–1 | 23–6–42–1<br>18–5–47–1 | | | 16–3–55–1<br>3–1–16–1 | | | |
| *v.* Glamorgan (Edgbaston) 22–24 August | 14–3–44–1<br>8–3–18–0 | 19–4–36–2<br>3–1–9–0 | 32–6–83–6<br>24–4–80–1 | 19–2–64–0<br>1–0–1–0 | 9–1–28–0<br>3–0–10–0 | | | | |
| *v.* Nottinghamshire (Trent Bridge) 25–28 August | 23–3–67–1<br>8–2–26–1 | 26–5–65–3<br>12–3–41–1 | 2–0–3–0<br>9–3–15–0 | 11–1–71–1<br>2–0–6–0 | 7–1–35–0 | 29–7–93–1<br>8–3–20–1 | | | |
| *v.* Sri Lankans (Edgbaston) 29–31 August | | 9–1–39–1<br>6–1–22–0 | | 17–4–67–1<br>11–1–53–2 | 11–2–45–1<br>11–2–40–1 | | | | |
| *v.* Glamorgan (Cardiff) 5–7 September | 19–6–48–2<br>13–4–37–1 | 12–4–28–0<br>12–2–43–1 | 19–3–42–2<br>18–2–41–1 | | 11–3–42–1<br>7–0–22–1 | | | | |
| *v.* Leicestershire (Edgbaston) 8–11 September | 19–2–71–3<br>11–3–29–0 | 22.3–3–70–6<br>22–4–73–1 | <br>20.1–3–37–3 | | | | | | |
| | 643.4–127–<br>2027–71<br>*av.* 28.54 | 772.1–156–<br>2208–79<br>*av.* 27.94 | 811.4–240–<br>1919–65<br>*av.* 29.52 | 279.5–42–<br>987–30<br>*av.* 32.90 | 194.4–23–<br>839–20<br>*av.* 41.95 | 496–134–<br>1306–45<br>*av.* 29.02 | 8–2–<br>41–1<br>*av.* 41.00 | 10–5–<br>12–0<br>— | 128–27–<br>380–9<br>*av.* 42.22 |

a A.J. Brussington retired hurt
b D.A. Thorne 3–1–9–0
c G.W. Humpage 6–0–13–0, 8–0–44–2
R.I.H.B. Dyer —, 5–0–39–0

| Asif Din | S. Wall | W.A. Morton | Byes | Leg-byes | Wides | No-balls | Total | Wkts |
|---|---|---|---|---|---|---|---|---|
| | | | | 19 | | 11 | 391 | 5 |
| | | | 1 | 10 | | 1 | 157 | 3 |
| | | | 2 | 15 | | 1 | 247 | 10 |
| | | | 6 | | | 2 | 132 | 7 |
| | | | | 4 | | | 181 | 10 |
| | | | 8 | 6 | | | 151 | 10 |
| | | | 4 | 9 | 5 | 16 | 369 | 5 |
| 8–0–49–3 | | | 2 | | | 6 | 186 | 8 |
| | | | 4 | 11 | | 7 | 172 | 7 |
| 1–0–2–0 | | | | 1 | | 10 | 127 | 5 |
| 1–0–4–0 | | | 3 | 19 | | 10 | 296 | 4 |
| | | | | 8 | | 1 | 114 | 10 |
| | | | 2 | 4 | | 25 | 374 | 10 |
| | 14.4–3–64–0 | | | 21 | | 15 | 382 | 3 |
| 1.3–1–0–2 | 3–2–20–1 | | | 10 | | 9 | 241 | 10 |
| | 2–0–12–0 | | | 4 | | 4 | 139 | 10 |
| | | | | 2 | | 3 | 94 | 10 |
| | | | 1 | 9 | 2 | 7 | 354 | 8 |
| | | | 1 | 5 | 4 | 4 | 315 | 5 |
| | | | 4 | 6 | 6 | 5 | 333 | 8 |
| | | | | 4 | | 1 | 236 | 8 |
| | | | 4 | 10 | 1 | 9 | 257 | 10 |
| | | | 2 | 10 | | 8 | 163 | 9a |
| | | | | 7 | 3 | 34 | 432 | 8 |
| | | | 1 | 6 | | 11 | 142 | 5 |
| | | | 6 | 9 | | 15 | 445 | 7 |
| | 10–3–28–1 | | | 7 | 1 | 4 | 122 | 4 |
| | 7–1–23–1 | | 5 | 7 | | 5 | 123 | 4 |
| | 19–6–65–2 | | 23 | 11 | | 8 | 398 | 7 |
| | 6–1–21–0 | | | 3 | 1 | 1 | 176 | 10 |
| | | 14–4–41–1 | 1 | 9 | 1 | 4 | 366 | 7 |
| | | | 2 | 9 | | 12 | 125 | 10 |
| | | 19–5–53–0 | 4 | 7 | | 3 | 212 | 3 |
| | | 3.3–0–12–0 | | 14 | | | 125 | 4 |
| | | 24–6–67–0 | 6 | 16 | | 3 | 389 | 6 |
| | | | | 2 | | | 153 | 10 |
| | | | | 12 | | 2 | 183 | 10b |
| | | 4.4–0–20–1 | 14 | 4 | | 4 | 300 | 9 |
| | | 9.4–3–61–2 | 8 | 5 | | 3 | 221 | 10 |
| | | 12–1–45–1 | 10 | 3 | 1 | 12 | 326 | 10 |
| | | 26–4–85–4 | 5 | 8 | 1 | 1 | 218 | 5 |
| | | | | 6 | 1 | 9 | 350 | 6 |
| | | | 6 | 3 | | | 117 | 3 |
| | 17–4–55–1 | 32–9–55–3 | | 8 | 1 | 18 | 301 | 7c |
| | 7–2–28–0 | 11–2–32–0 | 2 | 4 | | 12 | 276 | 5 |
| | 15–1–73–1 | 21–5–47–0 | 2 | 17 | 5 | 9 | 313 | 6 |
| | 8–1–30–0 | 13–6–31–2 | 12 | 7 | | 7 | 230 | 6 |
| | 4–0–26–0 | | 2 | 4 | | 1 | 174 | 10 |
| | 22–4–100–2 | | 6 | 9 | 3 | 6 | 263 | 6 |
| 11.3–1 55–5 *av.* 11.00 | 140.4–28– 545–9 *av.* 60.55 | 189.5–45– 549–14 *av.* 39.21 | | | | | | |

WALTER HAMMOND. *Gerald Howat*: Allen & Unwin: 160 pp, £9.95

The only reason for writing a biography of a man who has already been well documented is that the author has discovered new material and is able to make revelations that have not been made before. Sadly, Gerald Howat's biography of Wally Hammond tells us nothing new and the picture he paints is, as a friend of the great player remarked, 'not the Wally Hammond I knew'. There is an avoidance of painful episodes at the close of Hammond's life and as a study of the man the book cannot compare with Ronald Mason's work of a few years back. Gerald Howat has given us some fine books on the game, but this must be the most disappointing serious cricket book of the year.

THE GUIDE TO REAL VILLAGE CRICKET. *Robert Holles*: Unwin Paperbacks: 120 pp, £1.95

This is the paperback edition of the book reviewed last year.

THE BRADMAN ERA. *Bill O'Reilly and Jack Egan*: Collins Willow: 207 pp, £8.95

This is a collection of photographs, not all of top quality, and what text there is, is very superficial. The pictures cover the period of Bradman's Test career from 1928–29 to 1948. The emphasis, naturally, is Australian as this was originally an Australian publication. Some of the pictures have been taken from film and may not have appeared in book form before, but there are no scenic revelations. It all suggests book-making as part of the 'Bradman is 75' market. It has not as much value as *Bradman's First Tour*, published last year, but collectors of pictures may like it.

A FUNNY TURN. *Ray East (with Ralph Dellor)*: Unwin Paperbacks: 126 pp, £1.75

This is the paperback edition of Ray East's memoirs which was reviewed last year. The hardback edition was certainly very popular.

GREAT ONE-DAY CRICKET MATCHES. *David Lemmon*: Unwin Paperbacks: 167 pp, £1.75

First issued last year in hardback and now brought up to date with the addition of three matches from 1983, this paperback edition of a popular book is good value by today's prices.

HAROLD GIMBLETT. *David Foot*: A Star Book (W.H. Allen): 147 pp, £1.95

David Foot's much praised study of Harold Gimblett, first published in 1982, is now published in paperback and it is good to have the opportunity to add to the welcome that was given to this book. It is founded on strength for David Foot knew and admired Gimblett and the book is a work of love, which is all the deeper for being tinged with sadness and regret. The story of Gimblett is one that is unlikely to be repeated in that his romantic, instant rise from working on a farm to scorer of the fastest century of the season would be hard to repeat to-day when county staffs are highly professional and late recruits from local clubs are never needed. It is to be hoped that the second half of the Gimblett story will also never be repeated; shot by melancholy, disturbed by a feeling of rejection, haunted by some demon, the man who gave so much pleasure with his glorious array of strokes took his own life.

Much of David Foot's book is based on tapes which Gimblett had made before his death, and these add to the

**Worcestershire C.C.C.**
First-Class Matches – Batting, 1984

| | v. Sussex (Worcester) 28–30 April | | v. Glamorgan (Worcester) 2–4 May | | v. Leicestershire (Leicester) 9–11 May | | v. West Indians (Worcester) 19–21 May | | v. Leicestershire (Worcester) 23–25 May | | v. Warwickshire (Edgbaston) 26–29 May | | v. Essex (Worcester) 30 May–1 June | |
|---|---|---|---|---|---|---|---|---|---|---|---|---|---|---|
| M.J. Weston | 5 | 14 | 0 | 16 | 25 | 43 | 19 | — | 54 | 9 | 51 | 10 | 24 | — |
| T.S. Curtis | 69 | 5 | 1 | 0 | 6 | 42* | 82* | — | — | 2 | | | | |
| D.M. Smith | 23 | 53* | 14 | 0 | 15 | 9 | | | | | | | | |
| D.N. Patel | 3 | 30 | 6 | 59 | 30 | 0 | — | — | 2 | 4 | 6 | 31 | 21 | — |
| P.A. Neale | 38 | 8 | 73 | 22 | 5 | 4 | 14* | — | 10 | 80 | 1 | 30* | 41 | — |
| D.B. D'Oliveira | 2 | 19* | 10 | 35 | 21 | — | — | — | 29 | 38 | 0 | 13 | 0 | — |
| D.J. Humphries | 88* | — | 37 | 1 | 52 | 7* | — | — | 1 | 28 | 7 | 11* | 0 | — |
| R.K. Illingworth | 33 | — | | | 26* | — | — | — | 0 | 3 | 26* | — | | |
| J.D. Inchmore | 3 | — | 14 | 3* | 12* | 20 | — | — | 28 | 20* | 20* | — | 11 | — |
| R.M. Ellcock | 1 | — | 9* | 7 | | | | | | | — | — | 45* | — |
| A.P. Pridgeon | 0 | — | 3 | 10 | — | — | — | — | 1 | 1 | — | — | 28 | — |
| A.E. Warner | | | 27 | 0 | — | — | — | — | 14* | 0 | | | | |
| M.S.A. McEvoy | | | | | | | — | — | 22 | 0 | 25 | 21 | 34 | — |
| D.A. Banks | | | | | | | | | | | 14 | 0 | 1 | — |
| P.J. Newport | | | | | | | | | | | | | 6 | — |
| R.N. Kapil Dev | | | | | | | | | | | | | | |
| P. Moores | | | | | | | | | | | | | | |
| G. Hick | | | | | | | | | | | | | | |
| Byes | 6 | 1 | 4 | 3 | 4 | 9 | 1 | | 1 | 8 | 4 | | | |
| Leg-byes | 4 | 18 | 8 | 7 | 6 | 15 | 1 | | | 19 | 11 | 1 | 5 | |
| Wides | 2 | 2 | 1 | | 4 | | | | 3 | | | | | |
| No-balls | 4 | 1 | 2 | 5 | 8 | 1 | 7 | | 9 | 9 | 7 | 10 | 6 | |
| Total | 281 | 151 | 209 | 168 | 214 | 150 | 124 | | 174 | 221 | 172 | 127 | 222 | |
| Wickets | 10 | 4 | 10 | 10 | 7 | 5 | 1 | | 9† | 10 | 7 | 5 | 10 | |
| Result | W | | L | | D | | D | | L | | D | | D | |
| Points | 23 | | 5 | | 5 | | — | | 4 | | 4 | | 5 | |

| | v. Glamorgan (Swansea) 2–5 June | | v. Hampshire (Worcester) 9–12 June | | v. Gloucestershire (Gloucester) 13–15 June | | v. Cambridge Univ. (Worcester) 16–19 June | | v. Lancashire (Old Trafford) 23–26 June | | v. Kent (Worcester) 27–29 June | | v. Derbyshire (Worcester) 30 June–3 July | |
|---|---|---|---|---|---|---|---|---|---|---|---|---|---|---|
| M.J. Weston | 60 | — | 2 | 54 | 14 | 11 | — | 14* | 61 | 7 | 13 | — | 67 | 21 |
| T.S. Curtis | | | | | 44 | 6 | 129 | — | 48 | — | 65 | — | 4 | 17 |
| D.M. Smith | 29 | — | 83* | 42* | 42 | 0 | | | 77 | 5 | 189* | — | 52 | 22 |
| D.N. Patel | 153 | — | 52 | 22 | 4 | 7 | 197 | — | 2 | — | | | 35 | 30 |
| P.A. Neale | 14 | — | 11 | 66 | 43* | 17 | | | 46 | 5 | 17 | — | 60 | 69 |
| D.B. D'Oliveira | 51 | — | 34* | 35 | 3 | 4 | 15 | — | 25 | 34 | 60 | — | 6 | 29 |
| D.J. Humphries | 100* | — | — | 26 | 0 | 6 | 1* | — | 4 | 15* | 0 | — | 133* | 15* |
| R.K. Illingworth | 43* | — | — | — | 36 | 8* | — | — | 4 | — | — | — | 34* | 35 |
| J.D. Inchmore | — | — | — | 3* | 6* | 25* | — | — | 5 | 5 | — | — | — | 19* |
| R.M. Ellcock | — | — | | | | | | | | | | | — | — |
| A.P. Pridgeon | — | — | 23 | — | 22 | 2 | | | 2* | — | — | — | — | — |
| A.E. Warner | | | — | — | | | — | — | | | | | | |
| M.S.A. McEvoy | 1 | — | | | | | 27 | — | | | | | | |
| D.A. Banks | | | | | | | 5 | — | | | | | | |
| P.J. Newport | | | | | | | — | 7* | | | 33* | — | | |
| R.N. Kapil Dev | | | 95 | 34 | 0 | 1 | | | 15 | 2 | 42 | — | | |
| P. Moores | | | | | | | | | | | | | | |
| G. Hick | | | | | | | | | | | | | | |
| Byes | 1 | | 2 | | 4 | 3 | 4 | | 1 | | 4 | | 1 | 1 |
| Leg-byes | 11 | | 7 | 13 | 2 | | 8 | | 10 | 1 | 9 | | 6 | 6 |
| Wides | 1 | | 7 | | 2 | | 4 | | 1 | | 1 | | 1 | 1 |
| No-balls | 2 | | 12 | 1 | 3 | 1 | 5 | | 2 | | 3 | | 1 | 5 |
| Total | 466 | | 328 | 296 | 225 | 91 | 395 | 21 | 303 | 74 | 436 | | 400 | 270 |
| Wickets | 6 | | 5 | 6 | 9 | 9 | 5 | 0 | 10 | 6 | 6 | | 6 | 7 |
| Result | D | | W | | D | | W | | D | | D | | D | |
| Points | 8 | | 21 | | 2 | | — | | 8 | | 8 | | 7 | |

*Catches* 44 – D.J. Humphries (ct 37/st 7); 18 – D.B. D'Oliveira; 15 – M.J. Weston; 14 – A.P. Pridgeon; 13 – T.S. Curtis; 12 – D.M. Smith; 11 – D.N. Patel, M.S.A. McEvoy and P. Moores (ct 7/st 4); 10 – J.D. Inchmore, R.K. Illingworth and R.N. Kapil Dev; 9 – P.A. Neale; 5 – A.E. Warner; 4 – D.A. Banks

poignancy of the story. This is an important book and an essential part of any serious cricket library.

WISDEN CRICKETER'S ALMANACK, 1984. *edited by John Woodcock*: Queen Anne Press: 1290 pp, £11.95
What else can one add to what has been said so many times about this indispensable reference book which is now in its 121st year. Again John Woodcock has done a splendid job in the accumulation and organisation of material. The task becomes harder each year with so many Test matches and one-day internationals being played in all parts of the world and to miss one is to miss everything. Inevitably, reports on some of the limited-over tournaments have had to be curtailed, but the record section is as exhaustive as ever and the articles are of the usual high quality – how good it is to see Matthew Engel and Marcus Williams finding a place. In short, another essential addition to the line of yellow covers already in place on so many shelves.

THE GREAT WICKET-KEEPERS. *David Lemmon*: Stanley Paul: 176 pp, £6.95
It is not customary for authors to review their own books. This is a study of wicket-keepers from the earliest times to the present day and contains profiles of many who have graced an under-praised art.

MILESTONES OF HAMPSHIRE CRICKET. *compiled by Alan Edwards*: Hampshire Cricket Society: 20 pp, 80p
What a splendid little publication this is. Neatly set down are the facts from 1647 to 1982 which constitute a potted history of Hampshire. Alan Edwards has done a superb job. The booklet makes fascinating reading and it is a credit to both the author and the Society which had the courage and foresight to publish it. If you are interested in cricket, you should not be without this book.

PLAYFAIR CRICKET ANNUAL. *edited Gordon Ross*: Queen Anne Press: 256 pp, £1.50
A familiar sight at any cricket ground, this mine of statistical information, a descendant of the old *News Chronicle Cricket Annual*, is the best who's who and pocket reference for English county players. The strength of the book lies in its wonderful team of statisticians, Brian Croudy, Brian Heald and Barry McCaully, to whom we all have cause to be grateful.

CRICKET '84. *edited David Lemmon*: T.C.C.B.: 40 pp, £1.00
The Test and County Cricket Board's official annual publication gives a splendid guide to the season and there are

| v. Middlesex (Uxbridge) 7–10 July | | v. Warwickshire (Worcester) 11–13 July | | v. Nottinghamshire (Trent Bridge) 14–17 July | | v. Yorkshire (Scarborough) 25–27 July | | v. Essex (Chelmsford) 28–31 July | | v. Nottinghamshire (Worcester) 4–7 August | | v. Somerset (Weston-s-Mare) 8–10 August | | v. Northamptonshire (Wellingborough) 11–14 August | | v. Gloucestershire (Worcester) 18–21 August | | v. Somerset (Worcester) 25–28 August | | v. Northamptonshire (Worcester) 5–7 September | | v. Surrey (The Oval) 8–11 September | | *M* | *Inns* | *NOs* | *Runs* | *H/S* | *Av* |
|---|---|---|---|---|---|---|---|---|---|---|---|---|---|---|---|---|---|---|---|---|---|---|---|---|---|---|---|---|---|
| 18 | 8 | 4 | — | 10 | 5 | | | | | 27* | — | 3 | 16 | 66 | 30 | 0 | 39 | 13 | 1 | 18 | 145* | 24 | 40 | 24 | 41 | 3 | 1061 | 145* | 27.92 |
| 48 | 8 | 15 | — | 18 | 14 | 22 | — | 52 | 40 | 70 | — | 10 | 76 | 124 | 13 | 32 | 26 | 85 | 87* | 37 | 2 | 105 | 1 | 22 | 36 | 3 | 1405 | 129 | 42.57 |
| 45 | 14 | | | | | | | | | 4 | — | 7 | 46 | 10 | 22 | 27 | 15 | 22 | 0 | 0 | 71 | 100* | 55 | 17 | 31 | 5 | 1093 | 189* | 42.03 |
| 39 | 82 | 35 | — | 7 | 14 | 90 | — | 39 | 7 | 24 | — | 4 | 5 | 30 | 55* | 0 | 39 | 5 | 31 | 54 | 0 | 81 | 13 | 25 | 41 | 1 | 1348 | 197 | 33.70 |
| 77 | 28 | 86* | — | 13 | 83 | 143 | — | 15 | 9 | 5 | — | 42 | 105 | 36 | 38 | 73 | 36 | 39 | 75* | 36 | 17 | — | 76* | 25 | 42 | 6 | 1706 | 143 | 47.38 |
| 21 | 50 | 74 | — | 5 | 1 | 3 | — | | | | | | | 7 | — | 24 | 57* | 10 | — | 30 | 24 | — | 27 | 23 | 34 | 3 | 796 | 74 | 25.67 |
| 6 | 6 | 0 | — | 17 | 6 | 47 | — | 2 | 12 | | | | | | | | | 0 | — | 2 | 10* | — | 4 | 22 | 32 | 9 | 644 | 133* | 28.00 |
| 9 | 4 | — | — | 2 | 5 | 13 | — | 39* | 10 | — | — | 2 | — | | | — | — | 14* | — | | | | | 21 | 20 | 7 | 346 | 43* | 26.61 |
| 0 | 0 | — | — | | | 6 | — | | | — | — | 7 | — | 34 | 17 | | | 8 | — | 12 | 17 | — | — | 23 | 24 | 8 | 295 | 34 | 18.43 |
| 42 | 1 | | | | | | | | | | | | | 6* | — | | | | | 23 | — | | | 9 | 8 | 3 | 134 | 45* | 26.80 |
| 0* | 0* | 67 | — | 2* | 4* | | | 4 | 0* | — | — | 2* | 5 | — | — | 23 | — | 1 | — | 1 | — | — | 10 | 24 | 23 | 7 | 211 | 67 | 13.18 |
| | | | | | | 12* | — | 5 | 4 | | | | | | | | | | | | | | | 8 | 7 | 2 | 62 | 27 | 12.40 |
| | | | | | | 8 | — | 2 | 1* | 46 | — | 1 | 0 | | | | | | | | | | | 10 | 13 | — | 188 | 46 | 14.46 |
| | | | | 43 | 12 | 28 | — | 29 | 0 | | | | | | | | | | | | | | | 6 | 9 | — | 132 | 43 | 14.66 |
| | | 40* | — | 10 | 0 | | | 13 | 8 | | | | | 15 | — | 17* | — | | | 38* | — | — | — | 10 | 11 | 5 | 187 | 40* | 31.16 |
| | | 94 | — | 0 | 13 | 8 | — | 4 | 71 | 69* | — | 28 | 31* | | | 58* | 62* | 13 | — | | | | | 12 | 19 | 4 | 640 | 95 | 42.66 |
| | | | | | | | | | | — | — | 45 | 5* | 8 | 3* | — | — | | | | | | | 4 | 4 | 2 | 61 | 45 | 30.50 |
| | | | | | | | | | | | | | | | | | | | | | | — | 82* | 1 | 1 | 1 | 82 | 82* | — |
| 4 | | 6 | | 5 | 6 | 12 | | 4 | 5 | 4 | | 3 | 3 | 4 | 3 | 11 | 4 | 1 | | 8 | 3 | 6 | 9 | | | | | | |
| 3 | 2 | 9 | | 4 | 14 | 10 | | 7 | 2 | 7 | | 2 | 3 | 7 | 8 | 19 | 10 | 9 | 9 | 7 | 15 | 11 | 7 | | | | | | |
| | 8 | | | | | | | | 3 | | | 3 | 2 | | 2 | 9 | 1 | 1 | | 4 | | | 1 | | | | | | |
| 9 | | 15 | | 2 | 1 | | | 2 | | 5 | | 1 | 1 | 4 | 2 | 10 | | 1 | | 12 | | 2 | 2 | | | | | | |
| 321 | 211 | 445 | | 138 | 178 | 402 | | 217 | 172 | 261 | | 160 | 298 | 351 | 193 | 303 | 289 | 222 | 203 | 282 | 304 | 329 | 327 | | | | | | |
| 10 | 10 | 7 | | 10 | 10 | 10 | | 10 | 10 | 5 | | 10 | 7 | 9 | 5 | 7 | 5 | 10 | 3 | 10 | 6 | 3 | 7 | | | | | | |
| L | | D | | L | | D | | L | | D | | D | | D | | W | | W | | W | | D | | | | | | | |
| 5 | | 8 | | 4 | | 7 | | 6 | | 7 | | 3 | | 8 | | 21 | | 22 | | 22 | | 7 | | | | | | | |

†T.S. Curtis absent hurt

2 – P.J. Newport and subs
1 – R.M. Ellcock and G. Hick

excellent articles from Ted Dexter and Barry Norman among others. It is well designed and, with all receipts going to the counties, it is very good value for money and for the game.

THE INSIDE EDGE. *Rodney Marsh*: Lansdowne-Rigby: 128 pp, £5.95
This is the second book to come out in Rodney Marsh's name in the past two years and it is hard to decide which was the worse. Here is another offering of coarse writing and invective that does no credit to the man who gave so much pleasure with his extrovert wicket-keeping. I shall prefer to remember him for his diving catches rather than for his literary offerings. This second book, well illustrated, covers the seasons in 1982–83.

MIDDLESEX C.C.C. REVIEW 1983–84. *edited by Alvan Seth-Smith*: Middlesex C.C.C.: 128 pp, £3.25
This again is an excellent production from Alvan Seth-Smith. There is a complete statistical review of Middlesex in 1983 and, splendidly, each match score-card is accompanied by a photograph, a remarkable achievement. There is a pleasant piece from Edrich and Compton and, all in all, this is another highly commendable publication from the Middlesex Club. Having reached such eminence in so short a time, perhaps the editor should now consider broadening the literary scope of the publication where there is room for development.

FIFTY YEARS OF CRICKET. *Len Hutton (with Alex Bannister)*: Stanley Paul: 202 pp, £8.95
The only thing that I did not like about this book was a certain unevenness which seemed to insist, at times, that it was not Len Hutton speaking. Having said that, one should say immediately that this is a fascinating, eminently readable book. It does not set out to be chronologically autobiographical but ranges widely over main events and characters of an illustrious career. It is never arrogant, never self-deceptive, always honest and should be compulsory reading for some of the younger players in the game. Hutton talks about Arthur Mitchell, Don Bradman, cricket in the West Indies, 364 at The Oval and much else, and there are personal reflections which give the book value. Perhaps, in view of recent events, the most interesting chapter is that towards the end of the book which deals with Boycott and the decline of Yorkshire. Hutton's sadness, his concern for great men of integrity like Norman Yardley and his fear for the future of his beloved county are feelings that anyone who has the well-being of the game at heart will share.

| **Worcestershire C.C.C.** First-Class Matches – Bowling, 1984 | R.M. Ellcock | A.P. Pridgeon | J.D. Inchmore | D.N. Patel | R.K. Illingworth | A.E. Warner | B.D. D'Oliveira | M.J. Weston | D.A. Banks |
|---|---|---|---|---|---|---|---|---|---|
| *v.* Sussex (Worcester) | 16–1–60–2 | 19–3–78–4 | 14–4–33–2 | 6–1–18–1 | | | | | |
| 28–30 April | 17–2–69–3 | 15–2–47–2 | 16–0–71–4 | 2–1–2–0 | 7–0–19–0 | | | | |
| *v.* Glamorgan (Worcester) | 13–3–35–1 | 24–4–53–2 | 20–6–45–1 | 26–9–57–2 | | 19–3–84–2 | | | |
| 2–4 May | 14.2–3–34–4 | 8–0–37–1 | 3–0–13–0 | | | 11–2–27–5 | | | |
| *v.* Leicestershire (Leicester) | | 20.4–5–53–3 | 20–6–50–2 | 16–8–23–0 | 33–13–57–3 | 18–4–49–1 | | | |
| 9–11 May | | 5–3–2–0 | 6–1–17–0 | 20–10–24–3 | 26–10–46–0 | 6–3–12–0 | | | |
| *v.* West Indians (Worcester) | | 36–8–94–1 | 28–5–91–3 | 8–0–43–2 | 24–6–76–2 | 20–2–87–1 | | | |
| 19–21 May | | | | | | | | | |
| *v.* Leicestershire (Worcester) | | 16.2–7–31–3 | 10–4–27–1 | 38–10–68–3 | 15–4–34–2 | 15–3–38–0 | 12–3–15–1 | | |
| 23–25 May | | 22–5–56–5 | 13.4–4–38–1 | 14–4–34–2 | 13–7–13–1 | 11–2–38–1 | | | |
| *v.* Warwickshire (Edgbaston) | 19–5–45–2 | 30–8–65–3 | 17–6–35–2 | | 13–5–28–1 | | | | |
| 26–29 May | 7–0–27–0 | 9–3–40–1 | 8–1–20–1 | 27–3–97–0 | 15–5–32–1 | | 4–0–22–0 | 2–0–11–0 | 1–0–3–0 |
| *v.* Essex (Worcester) | 25–6–62–4 | 29–14–33–1 | 21–4–65–1 | 23.2–6–40–2 | | | | | |
| 30 May–1 June | 4–0–21–1 | 9–2–12–0 | 5–0–18–1 | | | | | | |
| *v.* Glamorgan (Swansea) | 8–1–23–0 | 16–5–41–2 | 11–2–31–0 | 31–13–58–4 | 31.1–15–60–4 | | | | |
| 2–5 June | 3–0–9–0 | 5–3–11–0 | | 15–9–31–2 | 11.4–5–32–5 | | 4–2–8–1 | | |
| *v.* Hampshire (Worcester) | | 14–3–31–0 | 19–5–58–1 | 17–3–60–1 | 26–4–82–0 | 14–4–30–1 | | | |
| 9–12 June | | 13–4–36–1 | 13–3–31–0 | 23–5–73–1 | 26–4–90–1 | 8–1–26–0 | | | |
| *v.* Gloucestershire | | 15–2–41–0 | 13–2–33–0 | 18–3–53–1 | 36–7–95–1 | | | 22–7–53–0 | |
| (Gloucester) 13–15 June | | 8–1–14–0 | 7–2–5–1 | 25–5–71–0 | 24–3–66–2 | | | | |
| *v.* Cambridge University | | | 11–4–20–0 | 26–8–56–4 | 33–15–55–0 | 12–2–34–2 | 5–3–3–1 | | |
| (Worcester) 16–19 June | | | 3–0–3–0 | 23.3–10–28–5 | 40–21–48–3 | 17–5–29–1 | 15–3–47–1 | | |
| *v.* Lancashire (Old Trafford) | | 23–6–57–3 | 22.5–7–53–3 | 25–10–40–2 | 3–1–9–1 | | | | |
| 23–26 June | | 14–4–36–1 | 3–1–2–0 | | 24.2–10–58–5 | | 20–6–50–2 | | |
| *v.* Kent (Worcester) | | 20.4–4–48–3 | 11–1–34–2 | | 22–13–21–4 | | 1–1–0–0 | | |
| 27–29 June | | 16–3–43–2 | 15–6–34–0 | | 29–13–63–0 | | 11–3–44–0 | 4–0–9–1 | |
| *v.* Derbyshire (Worcester) | 22–3–67–3 | 19–4–56–1 | 8–3–27–0 | | 31–6–104–2 | | 22–2–74–2 | | |
| 30 June–3 July | 11–0–44–2 | 6–1–20–0 | 6–0–22–0 | 23–4–108–2 | 13–2–34–3 | | 1–0–5–0 | | |
| *v.* Middlesex (Uxbridge) | 23–4–69–4 | 24.4–9–50–5 | 3–1–9–0 | 24–4–97–0 | 35–5–121–1 | | 3–0–14–0 | | |
| 7–10 July | 4–0–20–0 | 4–1–18–0 | 5–0–25–2 | 14–2–41–0 | 8–1–29–1 | | 3–0–5–0 | | |
| *v.* Warwickshire (Worcester) | | 23–4–59–2 | 14–2–45–1 | 7–1–20–0 | 1–1–0–0 | | | | |
| 11–13 July | | 13–3–42–1 | 9–1–25–0 | | 13–2–43–1 | | | 14–0–40–1 | |
| *v.* Nottinghamshire (Trent | | 22–5–58–4 | | 2–0–10–1 | | | | | |
| Bridge) 14–17 July | | 13–2–59–0 | | | 7–1–17–1 | | | | |
| *v.* Yorkshire (Scarborough) | | | 18–5–37–4 | 14–3–32–1 | 6.2–2–6–1 | 9–0–50–0 | | | |
| 25–27 July | | | 11–3–26–1 | 19–4–50–1 | 19–5–50–0 | 6–1–20–0 | | | 3–0–14–0 |
| *v.* Essex (Chelmsford) | | 12–2–41–2 | | 29–12–78–2 | 25.3–9–51–4 | 14–0–81–0 | | | |
| 28–31 July | | 10–3–25–0 | | 24.4–4–117–5 | 7–1–23–1 | 6–1–27–1 | | | |
| *v.* Nottinghamshire (Worcester) | | 16–6–39–4 | 14.3–1–51–2 | 13–2–38–1 | 1–0–1–0 | | | | |
| 4–7 August | | 5–0–12–0 | 3–0–20–0 | 17–2–58–2 | 16–3–48–2 | | | | |
| *v.* Somerset (Weston-super- | | 25–3–64–1 | 18–3–59–1 | 51–13–125–2 | 63–12–194–2 | | | 2–0–6–1 | |
| Mare) 8–10 August | | | | | | | | | |
| *v.* Northamptonshire | 9–1–31–0 | 18–5–36–0 | 12–5–23–0 | 22.3–8–56–1 | | | 4–0–17–1 | 16–3–44–4 | |
| (Wellingborough) 11–14 August | | 12–1–45–0 | 11–2–31–2 | 26–8–73–1 | | | | 1–0–4–0 | |
| *v.* Gloucestershire (Worcester) | | 16–4–44–0 | | 24–8–58–0 | 22–5–87–0 | | | 10–4–20–1 | |
| 18–21 August | | 11–1–43–0 | | 9–2–24–0 | 16–4–48–1 | | 3–0–6–1 | 2.4–1–2–2 | |
| *v.* Somerset (Worcester) | | 21.3–5–56–2 | 17–4–40–1 | 21–10–52–2 | 4–0–7–0 | | | 16–7–23–2 | |
| 25–28 August | | 14–4–42–3 | 6–0–22–0 | | 4–0–25–1 | | | 11–2–26–1 | |
| *v.* Northamptonshire | 17–1–66–2 | 21–3–64–1 | 17–4–37–2 | 22–9–54–2 | | | | 16–5–35–1 | |
| (Worcester) 5–7 September | 9–2–32–1 | 8–2–44–0 | 14–2–38–2 | 2–0–17–0 | | | | 3–0–27–0 | |
| *v.* Surrey (The Oval) | | 17–1–73–2 | | 22–5–79–3 | | | 5–1–31–0 | 4–0–15–0 | |
| 8–11 September | | | | | | | | | |
| | 221.2–32–714–29 *av.* 24.62 | 718.5–168–1949–66 *av.* 29.53 | 497–110–1364–44 *av.* 31.00 | 770–219–2063–61 *av.* 33.81 | 744–220–1872–57 *av.* 32.84 | 186–33–632–15 *av.* 42.13 | 113–24–341–10 *av.* 34.10 | 123.4–29–315–14 *av.* 22.50 | 4–0–17–0 — |

a D.K. Standing retired hurt, absent hurt
b T.S. Curtis 3–0–14–0
c P.A. Neale 1.3–0–11–0
d T.S. Curtis 0.3–0–8–0
e G. Hick 6–0–27–0

| P.J. Newport | R.N. Kapil Dev | D.M. Smith | Byes | Leg-byes | Wides | No-balls | Total | Wkts |
|---|---|---|---|---|---|---|---|---|
| | | | | 4 | 4 | 10 | 207 | 9a |
| | | | 4 | 2 | | 8 | 222 | 9 |
| | | | 12 | 8 | | 15 | 309 | 8 |
| | | | 9 | 13 | | 1 | 134 | 10 |
| | | | 8 | 9 | | 7 | 256 | 9 |
| | | | | 8 | | 1 | 110 | 3 |
| | | | | 19 | | 2 | 412 | 9 |
| | | | 1 | 5 | 1 | 2 | 222 | 10 |
| | | | | 10 | | 7 | 196 | 10 |
| | | | 8 | 11 | 3 | 5 | 200 | 8 |
| | | | | 11 | | 1 | 264 | 4 |
| 14-4-45-0 | | | 7 | 10 | 2 | 2 | 266 | 10 |
| | | | | 1 | | 3 | 55 | 2 |
| | | | 9 | 4 | 1 | 3 | 230 | 10 |
| | | | | 2 | | | 93 | 8 |
| | 14-3-34-0 | 1-0-2-0 | 2 | 10 | | 7 | 316 | 3 |
| | 8-1-32-1 | | 4 | 8 | 1 | 3 | 304 | 4 |
| | 7-2-22-0 | 5-0-20-1 | | 8 | 2 | 1 | 328 | 3 |
| | | | | 6 | | | 162 | 3 |
| 11-2-19-3 | | | 7 | 14 | 1 | 8 | 217 | 10 |
| | | | 17 | 5 | 1 | 4 | 196 | 10b |
| | 6-3-9-1 | | 7 | 3 | 1 | 4 | 183 | 10 |
| | 14-5-33-2 | | 6 | 8 | 1 | 2 | 196 | 10 |
| 10-2-18-1 | 11-1-36-0 | | 7 | 10 | | 6 | 180 | 10 |
| 19-4-55-1 | 16-4-39-0 | | 4 | 8 | 2 | 2 | 303 | 4 |
| | | | 1 | 8 | 2 | 8 | 347 | 8 |
| | | | 4 | 6 | 4 | 7 | 254 | 7 |
| | | | 2 | 12 | 1 | 2 | 377 | 10 |
| | | | 5 | 2 | | | 156 | 3c |
| 17-4-51-5 | 21.4-7-50-2 | | 7 | 4 | 5 | 11 | 252 | 10 |
| 8-0-21-0 | 12-4-28-1 | | 6 | 6 | | 4 | 223 | 4d |
| 3-0-25-0 | 17-3-57-5 | | | 3 | | | 153 | 10 |
| 6-0-31-2 | 14.5-2-50-2 | | 4 | 1 | | 2 | 164 | 5 |
| | 17-2-48-3 | | | 14 | 1 | | 188 | 10 |
| | 16-4-46-1 | | 2 | 6 | 4 | 3 | 221 | 3 |
| 6-1-27-0 | 13-3-33-2 | | | 12 | 2 | 4 | 329 | 10 |
| | 14-1-42-1 | | 4 | 3 | 2 | | 243 | 10 |
| | 20-6-54-3 | | 4 | 3 | | 12 | 202 | 10 |
| | 6-1-20-0 | | 4 | 3 | | 2 | 167 | 4 |
| | | | 8 | 14 | 2 | | 472 | 7 |
| 15-4-47-4 | | | | 2 | | 7 | 263 | 10 |
| 16-4-39-2 | | | 13 | 4 | | 6 | 215 | 5 |
| 17-3-76-0 | 17-10-36-3 | | 5 | 12 | 6 | 12 | 356 | 4 |
| 13-1-45-1 | 13-2-48-1 | | 7 | 6 | 1 | 2 | 232 | 6 |
| | 24-6-72-2 | | 4 | 6 | 5 | 4 | 269 | 10 |
| | 15-5-30-5 | | | 5 | | 2 | 152 | 10 |
| 16-3-56-0 | | | 2 | 16 | 4 | 8 | 342 | 9 |
| 13.4-0-70-0 | | | 1 | 4 | 1 | 6 | 240 | 3 |
| 20-4-64-2 | | | 2 | 8 | 1 | 7 | 307 | 7e |
| 204.4-36-689-21 *av.* 32.80 | 296.3-75-819-35 *av.* 23.40 | 6-0-22-1 *av.* 22.00 | | | | | | |

FAST BOWLING WITH BOB WILLIS. Collins Willow: 112 pp, £6.95
Bob Willis was such a natural, unorthodox fast bowler that he is hardly the best person to coach the art, yet this is a straightforward instruction book and it has much of Bob's great enthusiasm. If it leads one boy to follow him and achieve half as much, it will be the book of any season.

AS I SAID AT THE TIME. *E.W. Swanton (ed. George Plumptre)*: Collins Willow: 542 pp, £14.95
A year that produces a collection of the writings of John Arlott and of E.W. Swanton must be a vintage year for cricket books. Certainly the publishers and editor of the volume of Swanton's collected articles are to be congratulated. This is a mighty book, worthy of the man and of his standing in the game and contribution to it. It evokes memories of past players and past matches and it breathes integrity and perception, and the style is so consistently lucid and eloquent as to give the book a literary merit irrespective of its interest to the cricket fanatic. It is certainly one of the publishing events of the year.

THE SLOW MEN. *David Frith*: Allen & Unwin: 198 pp, £8.95
No book by David Frith is without interest and *The Slow Men*, his sequel to his work on the pace bowlers, is a valuable work written in a breezy style and, naturally, well researched and organised. It deals with an important subject and if it has a failing, it is that there is a lack of selectivity. The names of slow bowlers tumble over each other and one wonders whether all of them are worthy of a place in this study.

IDOLS. *Sunil Gavaskar*: Allen & Unwin: 289 pp, £9.95
This is a collection of thirty-one essays on cricketers whom Gavaskar admires. There is a lack of spark in some of the studies and one would have hoped for a deeper breath of personal reminiscence and involvement. Surely, for example, we could have had a richer study of Rajinder Goel whose achievements in the Ranji Trophy have become legendary. Inevitably we have Boycott, Lillee, Botham and the rest of the famous, but the portraits are flat and one senses that the only reason for the publication was Gavaskar's achievement in beating Don Bradman's record number of Test centuries.

SOMERSET COUNTY CRICKET SCRAPBOOK. *Vic Marks*: Souvenir Press: 128 pp, £6.95 (paperback)
Vic Marks joins the line of authors emanating from the Somerset dressing-room with this picture scrapbook which deals almost exclusively with the past few years. It is bright and breezy and pleasing to look at and will, no doubt, give much pleasure in Taunton.

CRICKET CRISIS. *Jack Fingleton*: Pavilion Books: 306 pp, £9.95
To celebrate the fiftieth anniversary of bodyline Pavilion Books, interesting and exciting publishers, reissued Fingleton's study of the series which was first published in 1946. It is, obviously, the least objective account of what happened in Australia in 1932–33, for Fingleton was one of the main sufferers in the series, scarcely putting bat to ball against Larwood and co. He was, however, one of the very best of journalists and anyone who has not read this book should do so immediately. There are some cricketers who, when they take up the pen, have an ability to please which is comparable to the pleasure that they gave as cricketers.

| Yorkshire C.C.C. First-Class Matches – Batting, 1984 | v. Somerset (Taunton) 28–30 April | | v. Nottinghamshire (Leeds) 9–11 May | | v. Lancashire (Leeds) 26–28 May | | v. Sussex (Sheffield) 30 May–1 June | | v. Somerset (Middlesbrough) 2–5 June | | v. Kent (Tunbridge Wells) 9–12 June | | v. Hampshire (Basingstoke) 13–15 June | | v. Derbyshire (Harrogate) 16–19 June | | v. Northamptonshire (Northampton) 23–26 June | | v. Nottinghamshire (Trent Bridge) 27–29 June | | v. Essex (Leeds) 30 June–3 July | | v. Gloucestershire (Bradford) 7–10 July | | v. Glamorgan (Cardiff) 11–13 July | | v. Middlesex (Lord's) 14–17 July | |
|---|---|---|---|---|---|---|---|---|---|---|---|---|---|---|---|---|---|---|---|---|---|---|---|---|---|---|---|---|
| G. Boycott | 6 | 60 | 73 | 16* | | | 38 | 42* | 12 | — | 59 | 104* | 53 | — | 153* | 48 | 8 | — | 33 | 25 | 36 | 19 | 4 | 126* | 10 | 101* | 29 | 40 |
| M.D. Moxon | 61 | 36 | 3 | 5 | 3 | 9* | 49 | 31 | 1 | — | 110 | 7 | 68 | 8 | 5 | 74 | 90 | — | | | | | | | | | | |
| R.G. Lumb | 0 | 22 | 28 | — | 5 | 3 | 38 | 0* | 31 | — | 0 | 0 | 55 | — | | | | | | | | | 165* | 18 | 144 | 11 | 6 | 8 |
| K. Sharp | 30 | 13 | 64 | 12* | 2 | 3 | 54 | — | 0 | — | 4 | 99 | 64 | 24 | 104 | 7 | 39 | — | 4 | 52* | 44 | 24 | 27 | 95 | 132 | 62 | 0 | 7 |
| J.D. Love | 27 | 53 | 49 | — | 0 | 0* | 61 | — | 112 | — | | | | | 1 | 19 | 45 | — | 0 | 19 | 6 | 10 | | | | | | |
| D.L. Bairstow | 5 | 53 | 62* | — | 62 | — | | | | | 25 | — | 7 | 19* | — | 0 | 3 | — | 91 | — | 14 | 9 | — | — | 43 | — | 0* | — |
| P. Carrick | 5 | 2 | 3* | — | 38 | — | 10 | — | 20 | — | 2 | — | 34* | — | — | 12* | 26 | — | 25 | — | 6 | 39 | — | — | 0 | — | 2 | 33 |
| G.B. Stevenson | 27 | 10* | | | 13 | — | 12 | — | 8 | — | 1 | — | 20 | 2 | — | 6 | 13 | — | | | | | | | | | | |
| A. Sidebottom | 54* | 33* | — | — | 1 | — | 42 | — | 33 | — | 13 | — | 2 | 5* | | | 29 | — | 49 | — | | | | | 0 | 16 | | |
| S.J. Dennis | 16 | — | — | — | 0 | — | | | | | | | | | | | | | 53* | — | 0 | 0 | — | — | 22* | — | 13* | 0 |
| S.D. Fletcher | 4 | — | — | — | | | — | — | 0 | — | 28* | 2 | | | — | — | 1 | — | | | | | — | — | | | | |
| I.G. Swallow | | | — | — | 8* | — | 8* | — | 34* | — | 24 | 13 | 14 | — | — | — | | | | | | | — | — | | | | |
| S.N. Hartley | | | | | 44 | — | | | | | 13 | — | 19 | 17 | 6 | — | | | | | | | 104* | 35* | 9 | 1* | 2 | 54 |
| S.J. Rhodes | | | | | | | 6* | — | 35 | — | | | | | | | | | | | | | | | | | | |
| S. Oldham | | | | | | | | | | | | | 19 | — | | | | | 22 | — | 14 | 14* | — | — | — | — | | |
| P.E. Robinson | | | | | | | | | | | | | | | 74* | 32* | | | 45 | 1* | 21 | 50 | 7 | — | 33 | 52 | 28 | 26 |
| A.A. Metcalfe | | | | | | | | | | | | | | | | | 58 | — | 5 | 20 | 20 | 5 | | | | | 8 | 0 |
| P.A. Booth | | | | | | | | | | | | | | | | | 1* | — | | | 0 | 3 | | | 8 | — | | |
| P.W. Jarvis | | | | | | | | | | | | | | | | | | | 0 | — | 13* | 7 | | | | | 12 | 6* |
| C. Shaw | | | | | | | | | | | | | | | | | | | | | | | | | | | 11 | 4 |
| Byes | 4 | 8 | 2 | 1 | | | 6 | | | | | 3 | | 2 | 5 | 1 | | | 1 | | | 5 | | | 4 | 12 | | 4 |
| Leg-byes | 2 | 18 | 6 | 1 | 2 | 1 | 10 | 4 | 11 | | 6 | 3 | 19 | 4 | 2 | 5 | 4 | | 10 | 5 | 5 | 2 | 11 | 6 | 2 | 1 | 1 | 8 |
| Wides | 1 | | 4 | | 5 | | 1 | | 4 | | 3 | 1 | 1 | 1 | | | | | | | 1 | | 3 | | 2 | 2 | 1 | 3 |
| No-balls | | 1 | 7 | | 5 | | 7 | 3 | 8 | | 9 | 2 | 26 | | 2 | | 12 | | 3 | | 3 | 1 | 7 | 1 | 6 | 4 | 8 | 10 |
| Total | 242 | 309 | 301 | 35 | 188 | 16 | 342 | 80 | 309 | | 297 | 234 | 401 | 83 | 352 | 204 | 329 | | 341 | 122 | 183 | 188 | 328 | 281 | 415 | 262 | 121 | 203 |
| Wickets | 10 | 7 | 5 | 1 | 10 | 2 | 8 | 1 | 10 | | 10 | 5 | 10 | 5 | 4 | 6 | 10 | | 10 | 3 | 10 | 10 | 3 | 2 | 9 | 4 | 9† | 9 |
| Result | W | | W | | D | | D | | D | | D | | D | | D | | W | | D | | L | | W | | D | | L | |
| Points | 18 | | 21 | | 4 | | 5 | | 6 | | 6 | | 7 | | 6 | | 23 | | 6 | | 3 | | 21 | | 6 | | 3 | |

*Catches* 45 – D.L. Bairstow (ct 38/st 7); 19 – M.D. Moxon; 16 – K. Sharp; 13 – P. Carrick; 11 – G. Boycott; 9 – I.G. Swallow; 7 – J.D. Love; 6 – P.E. Robinson; 5 – G.B. Stevenson and A.A. Metcalfe

Mailey was one and Fingleton was another. Whether you agree with his views or not, you can never escape the sense of immediacy. He is compulsive reading and if you have not read *Cricket Crisis*, you have a treat in store.

GLOUCESTERSHIRE COUNTY CRICKET CLUB YEAR BOOK 1984. pp 144, £1.00

A neat, compact, mainly statistical record of the county which, for value and presentation, stands second to none in county year books. One of the most fascinating items is a complete statistical record of every player who has appeared for Gloucestershire. This book deserves success and its interest is not limited to the West Country.

ESSEX COUNTY CRICKET CLUB 1984 HANDBOOK. *edited by Peter Edwards*: 220 pp, £3.00

The Essex handbook, under the determined editorship of Peter Edwards, has become renowned for the quality of match reports, statistics and general organisation. There are once more some good articles, Mike Marshall on cricket in Chalkwell Park, Peter Edwards himself with *The Last Laugh, Good Days Remembered* etc., but one would have liked to have seen a more substantial piece on the championship year than the rather flippant offering. If this sounds like carping, it is only because the standard set has been so high.

FROM LARWOOD TO LILLEE. *Trevor Bailey and Fred Trueman*: Queen Anne Press: 207 pp, £8.95

As the title suggests this is a look at pace bowlers over the past fifty years. It is structured so that the contributions of the joint authors are clearly defined. It is friendly, interesting reading rather than deep analysis or well researched history. There are comments on all the leading practitioners and the book is pervaded by a sense of camaraderie.

TALES FROM FAR PAVILIONS. *compiled by Allen Synge and Leo Cooper*: Pavilion Books: 162 pp, £8.95

This is a fascinating anthology of cricket in out of way places. While we range through amusing incidents in Denmark, Argentina, the South Seas, prisoner of war camps and the like, we never lose touch with the spirit of the game. The book is humorous, but it is also quite poignant and the indestructible monument it raises is that cricket is a game to be enjoyed and that place or persons cannot alter that fact. The extracts and articles are well chosen. The book is a delight, all the more so because it covers new ground.

MOST MEMORABLE MATCHES. *Gary Sobers (with Tony Cozier)*: Stanley Paul: 142 pp, £6.95

One of a series of memorable sporting occasions, Gary

| v. Worcestershire (Scarborough) 25–27 July | | v. Leicestershire (Sheffield) 28–31 July | | v. Lancashire (Old Trafford) 4–7 August | | v. Leicestershire (Leicester) 8–10 August | | v. Warwickshire (Leeds) 11–14 August | | v. Surrey (The Oval) 18–21 August | | v. Derbyshire (Chesterfield) 22–24 August | | v. Glamorgan (Bradford) 25–28 August | | v. Hampshire (Scarborough) 5–7 September | | v. Sussex (Hove) 8–11 September | | *M* | *Inns* | *NOs* | *Runs* | *H/S* | *Av* |
|---|---|---|---|---|---|---|---|---|---|---|---|---|---|---|---|---|---|---|---|---|---|---|---|---|---|
| 6 | — | 3 | 74 | | | 17 | — | 24 | 55* | | | | | 65 | 16* | 46* | 39 | 77 | 50* | 20 | 35 | 10 | 1567 | 153* | 62.68 |
| 0 | 126* | 2 | 39 | 37 | — | 67 | — | 13 | 0 | | | 7 | — | 24 | 25* | 9 | 11 | 84 | 12 | 18 | 31 | 3 | 1016 | 126* | 36.28 |
| | | | | | | | | | | | | | | | | | | | | 10 | 17 | 2 | 534 | 165* | 35.60 |
| 4 | 5 | 53 | 17 | 1 | — | 26 | — | 20 | 30 | 45 | 8 | 173 | — | 14 | — | — | 36 | 47 | — | 24 | 39 | 2 | 1445 | 173 | 39.05 |
| | | 84 | — | | | | | | | 6 | 2 | 1 | — | 0 | — | 43* | 0 | 14 | 16 | 15 | 23 | 2 | 568 | 112 | 27.04 |
| 94 | — | 65 | 44* | — | — | 15 | — | 23 | 37 | 25 | 0 | 50 | 0 | 0 | — | — | 37 | 4* | — | 22 | 26 | 5 | 787 | 94 | 37.47 |
| 2 | 4 | 1 | 0 | — | — | 47* | — | 17 | 4 | 28 | 16 | | | | | — | 22 | 1* | — | 22 | 28 | 5 | 400 | 47* | 17.39 |
| | | | | — | — | 10 | — | 3 | 16 | 15 | 13 | | | | | — | 11 | — | — | 14 | 16 | 1 | 180 | 27 | 12.00 |
| | | 26* | 13* | — | — | 30 | — | 9 | 11 | 33 | 5 | 26 | — | 53 | — | — | 28* | — | — | 19 | 22 | 6 | 511 | 54* | 31.93 |
| 0* | — | | | | | | | | | | | | | | | | | | | 9 | 9 | 4 | 104 | 53* | 20.80 |
| | | | | | | | | | | | | | | | | | | | | 7 | 5 | 1 | 35 | 28* | 8.75 |
| | | | | 4 | — | | | | | | | 27 | — | 4 | — | | | | | 11 | 9 | 3 | 136 | 34* | 22.66 |
| 1 | 16 | 17 | 0 | 37* | — | 2 | — | 14 | 3 | 2 | 41 | | | | | | | | | 13 | 21 | 4 | 437 | 104* | 25.70 |
| | | | | | | | | | | | | | | | | | | | | 2 | 2 | 1 | 41 | 35 | 41.00 |
| | | | | | | | | | | | | 0* | — | | | — | 16* | — | — | 8 | 6 | 3 | 85 | 22 | 28.33 |
| 13 | 55* | 11 | 5 | 28 | — | 47 | — | 15 | 5 | | | 54 | — | 92 | — | — | 41 | 5 | 16* | 15 | 24 | 5 | 756 | 92 | 39.78 |
| | | | | 11 | — | | | | | 7 | 15 | 60 | — | 7 | — | — | 0 | | | 9 | 13 | | 216 | 60 | 16.61 |
| 26 | — | 20* | — | | | 4 | — | 11 | 0 | 5 | 0 | 0 | — | 0* | — | | | | | 10 | 13 | 3 | 78 | 26 | 7.80 |
| 10 | — | — | — | 0* | — | 31 | — | 2* | 8 | 0 | 37 | 24 | — | 7 | — | | | — | — | 12 | 14 | 4 | 157 | 37 | 15.70 |
| 17 | — | | | | | | | | | 0* | 0* | | | | | | | | | 3 | 5 | 2 | 32 | 17 | 10.66 |
| | 2 | | 4 | | | | | | | 2 | 8 | 2 | | | | 4 | 4 | 5 | 2 | | | | | | |
| 14 | 6 | 1 | 1 | 2 | | 7 | | 2 | 12 | 2 | 2 | 6 | | 11 | | 2 | 4 | 6 | | | | | | | |
| 1 | 4 | 2 | 7 | | | | | | | | 1 | 1 | | 4 | | | | 1 | | | | | | | |
| | 3 | 18 | | 4 | | 3 | | | 2 | 5 | | 8 | | 2 | | 4 | 3 | 6 | 2 | | | | | | |
| 188 | 221 | 303 | 204 | 124 | | 306 | | 153 | 183 | 175 | 148 | 439 | | 283 | 41 | 108 | 252 | 250 | 98 | | | | | | |
| 10 | 3 | 8 | 6 | 5 | | 10 | | 10 | 10 | 10 | 10 | 10 | | 10 | 0 | 1 | 9 | 5 | 2 | | | | | | |
| D | | D | | D | | D | | L | | L | | W | | D | | D | | D | | | | | | | |
| 2 | | 5 | | 4 | | 6 | | 5 | | 1 | | 24 | | 6 | | 2 | | 4 | | | | | | | |

† D.L. Bairstow retired hurt, absent hurt

3–S.J. Rhodes

2–R.G. Lumb, S.N. Hartley, S. Oldham, P.W. Jarvis, A. Sidebottom and subs

1–S.J. Dennis and P.A. Booth

Sober's offering will evoke happy memories from many and stimulate all of us with accounts of matches we did not witness but will enjoy reading about. There are the six sixes in an over at Swansea and the marvellous 254 at Adelaide, but there are also Radcliffe against Oldham in 1958 and several other small gems. A happy book.

CRICKET AND THE EMPIRE. *Ric Sissons and Brian Stoddart*: Allen & Unwin: 150 pp, £7.95
The fiftieth anniversary of the bodyline tour brought forth a crop of books and *Cricket and the Empire* was one of them. It is an attempt to reanalyse the tour and place it in its social context. There is the claim of new material, and certainly much research has been done, but one cannot feel that we are brought much closer to the truth. Indeed, it is doubtful now if the full facts will ever be known, for any who have spoken to players who were on that tour will know that some truths will remain unpublished if not unuttered. Nevertheless, this book is an interesting and useful addition to the literature of the most documented tour in cricket history.

THE SUN HAS GOT HIS HAT ON. *Derek Randall*: Collins Willow: 144 pp, £7.95
As this is the second 'autobiographical' offering from Derek Randall in the past few years, one had expected some new revelations or deeper character analysis than the previous book with Terry Bowles, but this is not the case. The second book, in spite of its appropriate title, is superficial and one can see no reason for its publication as it is no advance on the previous volume.

ON REFLECTION. *Richie Benaud*: Collins Willow: 248 pp, £8.95
Benaud is an intelligent commentator and perceptive critic so that a new book from him is awaited eagerly. We were not disappointed. This is a stimulating, wide-ranging volume, witty in anecdote, lucid in style. His comments on captaincy are as interesting as they are sound, sound because of the eloquent reasoning for his choices of Ian Chappell as Australia's best captain and Keith Miller as the best he played under. His comments on Packer, sponsorship and the leading all-rounders of to-day are thought-provoking. It is a book of good humour and very good sense, one to read and re-read.

YORKSHIRE'S PRIDE. *John Callaghan*: Pelham Books: 240 pp, £10.95
Handsomely produced and easy to read, this is an excellent addition to the histories of Yorkshire cricket. It is, perhaps, a little sketchy on the earliest years, but there are some fascinating and original sections like those on the record

| **Yorkshire C.C.C.** First-Class Matches – Bowling, 1984 | G.B. Stevenson | S.J. Dennis | A. Sidebottom | S.D. Fletcher | P. Carrick | M.D. Moxon | I.G. Swallow | S.N. Hartley | S. Oldham |
|---|---|---|---|---|---|---|---|---|---|
| *v.* Somerset (Taunton) 28–30 April | 16–1–59–1 | 19–5–57–2<br>25–5–66–1 | 23–5–48–2<br>20–5–45–1 | 22–3–49–0<br>13–4–61–0 | 17–5–30–0<br>20–7–41–3 | 10–0–37–0<br>2–2–0–0 | | | |
| *v.* Nottinghamshire (Leeds) 9–11 May | | 3.1–1–4–1<br>17.4–2–77–4 | 6–2–9–1<br>19–2–51–4 | 8–2–22–1<br>9–1–40–0 | <br>19–4–61–2 | | <br>12–1–45–0 | | |
| *v.* Lancashire (Leeds) 26–28 May | 23–7–62–1 | 23–5–77–2 | 26–7–50–4 | | 21–6–35–0 | 16–6–39–0 | 3–0–15–0 | | |
| *v.* Sussex (Sheffield) 30 May–1 June | 22–2–66–1 | | 12–1–50–0 | 15–3–37–1 | 34–17–63–2 | | 11–1–34–0 | | |
| *v.* Somerset (Middlesbrough) 2–5 June | 13–4–33–0 | | 19–5–44–1 | 16–6–24–4 | | 8–2–19–1 | 5–2–10–0 | | |
| *v.* Kent (Tunbridge Wells) 9–12 June | 14–1–42–2<br>11–3–27–1 | | 18–5–31–1<br>16–5–41–6 | 11.1–0–30–2<br>5–4–3–0 | 23–7–71–1<br>16–12–20–0 | | 18–2–52–4<br>9–4–18–0 | 7–1–31–0 | |
| *v.* Hampshire (Basingstoke) 13–15 June | 15.3–2–35–4<br>19–5–49–0 | | 18–3–51–3<br>24–2–62–3 | | 13–3–33–0<br>36–27–32–3 | 3–0–13–1 | <br>17–6–44–1 | | 20–4–68–2<br>13.1–4–45–3 |
| *v.* Derbyshire (Harrogate) 16–19 June | 12–2–58–0<br>4–1–10–1 | | | 20–3–58–1<br>7–4–17–0 | 53–14–165–6<br>30–6–60–5 | <br>5–1–21–0 | 41.2–12–103–3<br>12–2–32–1 | 9–0–35–0 | |
| *v.* Northamptonshire (Northampton) 23–26 June | 5–1–18–0<br>5–0–17–0 | | 12–3–38–3<br>11–1–44–1 | 11.5–3–42–4<br>7–0–23–1 | 1–0–1–0<br>20–9–32–6 | | | | |
| *v.* Nottinghamshire (Trent Bridge) 27–29 June | | 21–1–76–2<br>25–5–74–1 | 16–4–73–0 | | 19–1–68–0<br>6–1–21–1 | | | | 23–3–68–1<br>19.4–2–74–2 |
| *v.* Essex (Leeds) 30 June–3 July | | 23–4–106–0 | | | 30.5–9–80–1 | | | | 38–9–105–1 |
| *v.* Gloucestershire (Bradford) 7–10 July | | 25–4–96–2<br>12–2–38–2 | | 17–2–65–0 | 38–15–85–1<br>23–6–93–3 | | 14–3–48–2<br>13–3–37–0 | | 23–7–61–0<br>14–2–48–0 |
| *v.* Glamorgan (Cardiff) 11–13 July | | 31–4–124–5<br>5–2–10–0 | 3–0–12–1 | | 10–2–25–0<br>5–3–2–0 | | | 32–4–106–3 | 16–6–35–0<br>4–2–3–0 |
| *v.* Middlesex (Lord's) 14–17 July | | 17–3–50–0<br>3.1–0–7–0 | | | 10–0–43–0 | | | 8–0–47–1 | |
| *v.* Worcestershire (Scarborough) 25–27 July | | 27.2–5–91–3 | | | 25–9–64–0 | | | | |
| *v.* Leicestershire (Sheffield) 28–31 July | | | 22–2–54–1<br>13–3–33–1 | | 32–9–81–2<br>11–3–29–0 | | | 12–2–45–1<br>9–2–40–0 | |
| *v.* Lancashire (Old Trafford) 4–7 August | 8–3–46–2 | | 12.3–3–30–2 | | | | | | |
| *v.* Leicestershire (Leicester) 8–10 August | 13–1–61–2<br>13–0–61–0 | | 19–7–39–5<br>9–3–19–1 | | 8–5–9–0<br>37–12–72–2 | <br>11–3–40–0 | | 10–4–26–0<br>6–0–29–1 | |
| *v.* Warwickshire (Leeds) 11–14 August | 20–3–63–1<br>5–0–12–0 | | 21.4–3–64–6<br>22–3–77–3 | | 11–4–18–0<br>23–4–59–3 | 4–0–15–0<br>4–0–13–0 | | | |
| *v.* Surrey (The Oval) 18–21 August | 14–3–68–0 | | 21–3–72–0 | | 36–6–102–1 | | | | |
| *v.* Derbyshire (Chesterfield) 22–24 August | | | 19–8–43–3<br>8–2–21–1 | | | | 13–4–36–0<br>17.5–9–34–1 | | 21–3–59–4<br>15–5–35–3 |
| *v.* Glamorgan (Bradford) 25–28 August | | | 22–5–50–3<br>15–3–34–4 | | | 9–3–13–0<br>3–0–9–1 | 22–6–58–3<br>21–7–54–0 | | |
| *v.* Hampshire (Scarborough) 5–7 September | 13–2–46–2<br>7–1–26–1 | | 16–4–38–1<br>5–1–14–0 | | 26–12–69–2<br>10–0–38–0 | 12–1–60–1<br>3–0–19–0 | | | 13–4–27–0<br>7–1–24–0 |
| *v.* Sussex (Hove) 8–11 September | 10–2–33–0 | | 11–3–28–1 | | 2–1–4–0 | 8–1–29–0 | | | 18–5–51–2 |
| | 262.3–44–892–19<br>*av.* 46.94 | 277.2–48–953–25<br>*av.* 38.12 | 479.1–103–1265–63<br>*av.* 20.07 | 162–35–471–14<br>*av.* 33.64 | 665.5–219–1606–44<br>*av.* 36.50 | 98–19–327–4<br>*av.* 81.75 | 229.1–62–620–15<br>*av.* 41.33 | 93–13–359–6<br>*av.* 59.83 | 244.5–57–703–18<br>*av.* 39.05 |

a P.E. Robinson 1–0–4–0
b G. Boycott 3–0–4–0, 4–0–11–0
c G.Boycott 3–0–9–0
d D.L.Bairstow 7–0–24–0
R.G. Lumb 1–0–5–0
e C. Shaw 19.4–0–68–4
f C. Shaw 23–5–66–1
g P.E. Robinson 1–0–8–0
h C. Shaw 11–0–43–0
j G. Boycott 1–0–1–0
D.L. Bairstow 4–1–15–0
J.F. Steele retired hurt

| P.A. Booth | P.W. Jarvis | K. Sharp | *Byes* | *Leg-byes* | *Wides* | *No-balls* | *Total* | *Wkts* |
|---|---|---|---|---|---|---|---|---|
| | | | | 7 | | 11 | 298 | 5 |
| | | | 5 | 23 | | 8 | 249 | 5 |
| | | | | | | 1 | 36 | 3 |
| | | | 7 | 10 | 1 | 2 | 294 | 10 |
| | | | | 6 | 1 | 3 | 288 | 7 |
| | | | 1 | 10 | 2 | 4 | 267 | 4 |
| | | | | | 6 | 5 | 141 | 6 |
| | | | | 8 | 2 | 10 | 277 | 10 |
| | | | | 1 | | 11 | 121 | 7 |
| | | | 4 | 18 | | 8 | 230 | 10 |
| | | | | 10 | | 13 | 255 | 10 |
| | | | | 11 | | 9 | 439 | 10 |
| | | 4.2–0–27–0 | | 3 | | 1 | 175 | 7a |
| 21–8–22–3 | | | 7 | 3 | | 4 | 135 | 10 |
| 24–10–36–1 | | | | 5 | | 3 | 160 | 10 |
| | 18–0–89–1 | | 1 | 3 | 2 | 6 | 390 | 5b |
| | 14–1–62–1 | | | 13 | 2 | 2 | 259 | 5 |
| 19–1–90–3 | 25–3–118–1 | | 3 | 17 | 3 | 2 | 524 | 7 |
| | | | 5 | 13 | 1 | 7 | 381 | 5 |
| | | | 4 | 4 | | 2 | 226 | 5 |
| 15–5–23–0 | | | 2 | 7 | 1 | 13 | 357 | 9c |
| 16–5–34–0 | | 5–1–8–0 | 1 | 4 | 1 | | 92 | 0d |
| | 17–2–85–3 | | 1 | 8 | | 1 | 303 | 8e |
| | 3–0–12–1 | | | | 3 | | 22 | 1 |
| 22–7–44–0 | 31–4–115–6 | | 12 | 10 | | | 402 | 10f |
| 15–2–31–0 | 23–5–93–0 | | 7 | 7 | | 9 | 327 | 4 |
| 10–4–48–2 | 21–5–51–2 | 5.5–0–53–2 | | 8 | | 3 | 265 | 7 |
| | 17–3–61–6 | | | 3 | 5 | 6 | 151 | 10 |
| 7–4–13–0 | 20.2–2–54–3 | | | 2 | 1 | 1 | 206 | 10 |
| 28–15–49–0 | 12–5–20–0 | 18–7–37–1 | 7 | 9 | | 12 | 363 | 5g |
| 23–9–51–2 | 14–2–57–0 | 1–0–8–0 | | 1 | | 8 | 285 | 10 |
| 15–4–35–1 | 8–1–33–0 | | | 4 | | 9 | 242 | 7 |
| 21–4–61–0 | 13–0–77–1 | 23–6–60–2 | 8 | 16 | 5 | 6 | 518 | 5h |
| 20–10–49–1 | 9.1–2–39–2 | | 3 | 1 | | 23 | 253 | 10 |
| 20–11–32–2 | 8–2–19–3 | 1–1–0–0 | 2 | 2 | | 11 | 156 | 10 |
| 44–12–101–2 | 25–9–58–1 | | 5 | 6 | | 15 | 306 | 10 |
| 27–13–30–0 | 13–3–24–0 | 7.5–3–13–2 | 2 | 6 | 1 | 12 | 201 | 9i |
| | | | 5 | 5 | | 4 | 254 | 6 |
| | | 5–0–23–0 | 5 | 5 | | 1 | 155 | 2 |
| | 12.3–4–48–1 | | 2 | 2 | 2 | 3 | 202 | 4 |
| 347–124–749–17 *av.* 44.05 | 304–53–1115–32 *av.* 34.84 | 71–18–229–7 *av.* 32.71 | | | | | | |

stands and on the Yorkshire wicket-keepers. There is a certain naivity in John Callaghan's approach to recent history which was apparent in his biography of Boycott, but there is a happiness about this book which justifies the title and it is never pedantic. It is good reading in counties other than Yorkshire even if the deeper story is yet to be told.

THE CAPTAIN'S DIARY, 1983–84. *Bob Willis*: Collins Willow: 160 pp, £8.95

Like Derek Randall, Bob Willis has enlisted the help of Alan Lee in writing his book which, one supposes, will be his last, certainly his last diary of an English tour. This book, for all its annoying lapses into nicknames and in-talk, is likely to remain popular as the testimony of Willis' farewell to the England captaincy and his becoming his country's leading wicket-taker. It is at moments like the one when he is describing his feelings at becoming the record-breaker, feelings which surprise him, that the book is at its best; when carping about official functions it is at its worst. There is a sense of Willis in the pages and when one flips through them one can only have a sense of regret that we cannot put the clock back ten years and see him pounding in to open the England attack.

TWENTY YEARS ON. *Christopher Martin-Jenkins*: Collins Willow: 159 pp, £8.95

Christopher Martin-Jenkins gives a general review of events in cricket over the past twenty years. Really the issues he raises demand a deeper analysis than this all-embracing, brief volume allows, and one is left with an appetite aroused but not satisfied. Nevertheless, Christopher Martin-Jenkins is incapable of writing anything that is without interest and the book is both stimulating and enjoyable, evoking, as it does, discussion of the numerous changes in the game in the past two decades.

TESTING THE WICKET. *Jim Fairbrother and Reginald Moore*: Pelham Books: 144 pp, £8.95

The groundsman has been the most neglected part of the game when it comes to literature, so that this book by Jim Fairbrother, partly autobiographical, partly instructional, is doubly welcome. Preparing a wicket is a vocation and we need young men who are dedicated to the cause. They would do well to read Fairbrother's story and heed his advice. It is the wisdom of experience and, with Reginald Morre's aid, it is excellent reading even to the layman. This is a fitting farewell from one who has served the game well.

VIJAY MERCHANT. *Dr Vijay Naik*: Bandodkar Publishing Co.: 151 pp

(This book is obtainable from the distributors, The Marine Sports, 63-A, Gokhale Road (North), Dadar, Bombay 400 028.)

A study of the great Indian batsman is most welcome and this account by Dr Vijay Naik chronicles the career in a straight-forward and honest manner. It is a story that has been too long neglected and lovers of the game should be grateful that this Indian edition is now available. There is a glimpse of the man as well as the cricketer and a brief statistical appendix. The Indian price is Rs 25.

SOMERSET
COUNTY CRICKET CLUB